THE NATIONAL EXPERIENCE

PART TWO

A HISTORY OF THE UNITED STATES SINCE 1865

THE NATIONAL EXPERIENCE

PART TWO
A HISTORY OF THE UNITED STATES SINCE 1865

EIGHTH EDITION

JOHN M. BLUM Yale University
WILLIAM S. McFEELY University of Georgia
EDMUND S. MORGAN Yale University
ARTHUR M. SCHLESINGER, JR. The City University of New York
KENNETH M. STAMPP University of California, Berkeley
C. VANN WOODWARD Yale University

HARCOURT BRACE COLLEGE PUBLISHERS

Fort Worth Philadelphia San Diego New York Orlando Austin San Antonio
Toronto Montreal London Sydney Tokyo

Cover Photo:
Margaret Bourke-White,
Life Magazine ©1936,
Time Warner Inc.

Editor-in-Chief: Ted Buchholz
Acquisitions Editor: Drake Bush
Developmental Editor: Phoebe Culp
Senior Project Editor: Kay Kaylor
Production Manager: Mandy Van Dusen
Book Designer: Garry Harman
Photo Permissions Editor: Lili Weiner

Copyright © 1993, 1989, 1985, 1981, 1977, 1973, 1968, 1963 by Harcourt Brace & Company
Copyright renewed 1991 by Edmund S. Morgan; Arthur M. Schlesinger, Jr.; William B. Catton; John M. Blum; C. Vann Woodward; and Kenneth M. Stampp.

All rights reserved. No part of this publication may be reproduced or transmitted in any form or by any means, electronic or mechanical, including photocopy, recording, or any information storage and retrieval system, without permission in writing from the publisher.

Requests for permission to make copies of any part of the work should be mailed to: Permissions Department, Harcourt Brace & Company, 8th Floor, Orlando, Florida 32887.

Address for Editorial Correspondence: Harcourt Brace & Company, 301 Commerce Street, Suite 3700, Fort Worth, TX 76102.

Address for Orders: Harcourt Brace & Company, 6277 Sea Harbor Drive, Orlando, FL 32887; 1-800-782-4479 or 1-800-433-0001 (in Florida).

Picture Credits on pages P1 – P6 constitute a continuation of the copyright page.

ISBN: 0-15-500731-9

Library of Congress Catalog Card Number: 92-72977

Printed in the United States of America

345678901 069 98765432

A NOTE ON THE PAPERBOUND EDITION

This volume is part of a variant printing, not a new or revised edition, of *The National Experience,* Eighth Edition. Many of the users of the Sixth Edition found the two-volume paperbound version of that edition useful because it enabled them to fit the text into the particular patterns of their teaching and scheduling. The publishers have continued that format in preparing this printing, which exactly reproduces the text of the one-volume version of *The National Experience,* Eighth Edition. The first of these volumes begins with the discovery of America and continues through Reconstruction. The second volume, repeating the chapter on Reconstruction (Chapter 15), carries the account forward to the present day. The variant printing, then, is intended as a convenience to those instructors and students who have occasion to use either one part or the other of *The National Experience.* Consequently, the pagination and index of the one-volume version, as well as its illustrations, maps, and other related materials, are retained in the new printing. The difference between the one-volume and the two-volume versions of the book is a difference only in form.

PREFACE

Men and women make history. Their ideas and their hopes, their goals and contrivances for reaching those goals, shape all experience, past and present. The Indians, the first Americans, had to decide, by deliberation or by default, how to use the continent and its extraordinary resources. So have the successors of the Indians and the children of those successors—the early European settlers, the English colonists, the men and women of the new United States, and the generations that have followed them. Each generation has committed the nation to a complex of policies, some the product of thought and debate, others of habit or inadvertence, still others of calculated or undiscerning indifference. As the nation has grown, as its population has diversified, its economy matured, and its responsibilities multiplied, questions of national policy have become more difficult to understand but no more troubling. It took long thought and hard debate to settle the issues of independence, of democratic reform, of expansion, of slavery, of union itself, of control of private economic power, of resistance to totalitarianism across two oceans. All those issues and many more have made up the national experience.

This book endeavors to recount and explain that experience. It examines both the aspirations (often contradictory among themselves) and the achievements (often less grand than the best hopes) of the American people. It examines, too, the ideas, the institutions, and the processes that fed hope and affected achievement. It focuses on the decisions, positive and negative, that reflected national goals and directed national purposes, and consequently it focuses continually on the men and women who made those decisions, on those who made history. The book emphasizes public policy, but the history of public policy perforce demands continuing discussion of the whole culture that influenced it.

The authors of this book believe that a history emphasizing public policy, so conceived, reveals the fabric and experience of the past more completely than does any other kind of history. They believe, too, that an emphasis on questions of public policy provides the most useful introduction to the history of the United States. In the light of those convictions, they have agreed on the focus of this book, on its organization, and on the selection and interpretation of the data it contains. The structure of the separate parts and chapters is now chronological, now topical, depending on the form that seemed most suitable for the explanation of the period or the subject under discussion. The increasing complexity of public issues in the recent past, moreover, has persuaded the authors to devote half of this volume to the period since Reconstruction, indeed more than a third to the twentieth century.

The authors have elected, furthermore, to confine their work to one volume so as to permit instructors to make generous supplementary assignments from the abundance of excellent monographs, biographies, and "problems" books now readily available. Just as there are clear interpretations of the past in those books, so are there in this, for the authors without exception find meaning in history and feel obliged to say what they see. The authors also believe that, especially for the beginning student of history, literature is better read than read about. Consequently, in commenting on belles lettres and the other arts, they have consciously stressed those expressions and aspects of the arts relevant to an understanding of public policy. Finally, they have arranged to choose the illustrations and the boxed selections from contemporary and other sources in order to enhance and supplement not only the text but also its particular focus.

This is a collaborative book in which each of the six contributors has ordinarily written about a period in which he is a specialist. Yet each has also executed the general purpose of the whole book. Each section of the book has been read and criticized by several of the contributors. This revision has profited from the assistance of many historians who were kind enough to review portions of the book before it was revised. These include Russell Duncan, John Carroll University; William Freehling, State University of New York, Buffalo; Steven Hahn, University of California, San Diego; and Samuel T. McSeveney, Vanderbilt University.

Not even a collaboration as easy and agreeable as this one has been can erase the individuality of the collaborators. Each section of this book displays the particular intellectual and literary style of its contributor; all the contributors have been permitted, indeed urged, to remain themselves. The ultimate as well as the original responsibility for prose, for historical accuracy, and for interpretation remains that of the author of each section of this book: Edmund S. Morgan, Chapters 1–6; Kenneth M. Stampp, Chapters 7–12; William S. McFeely, Chapters 13–15; C. Vann Woodward, Chapters 16–21; John M. Blum, Chapters 22–26; Arthur M. Schlesinger, Jr., Chapters 27–35, revised by John M. Blum.

JOHN M. BLUM, *Editor*
New Haven, Connecticut

A NOTE ON THE SUGGESTIONS FOR READING

The lists of suggested readings that follow the chapters of this book are obviously and intentionally selective. They are obviously so because a reasonably complete bibliography of American history would fill a volume larger than this one. They are intentionally so because the authors of the various chapters have tried to suggest to students only those stimulating and useful works that they might profitably and enjoyably explore while studying this text. Consequently each list of suggested readings points to a relatively few significant and well-written books, and each list attempts to emphasize, in so far as possible, books available in inexpensive, paperback editions.

Use of the suggested readings, then, permits a student to begin to range through the rich literature of American history, but interested and energetic students will want to go beyond the lists. They will profit from the bibliographies in many of the works listed. They should also consult the card catalogs in the libraries of their colleges and the invaluable bibliography in the *Harvard Guide to American History*, rev. ed. (Belknap). For critical comments about the titles they find, they should go on, when they can, to the reviews in such learned journals as the *American Historical Review*, the *Journal of American History*, the *Journal of Southern History*, and the *William and Mary Quarterly*.

Those students who want to acquire libraries of their own and who want also to economize by purchasing paperback editions will find the availability of titles in paperbacks at best uncertain. Every few months new titles are published and other titles go out of print. For the most recent information about paperbacks, students should consult *Paperbound Books in Print* (Bowker), which appears biannually.

The reading lists refer to very few articles, not because articles are unimportant, but because they are often rather inaccessible to undergraduates. There are, however, many useful collections of important selected articles, often available in inexpensive editions. So, too, students will have no difficulty in finding collections of contemporary historical documents that add depth and excitement to the study of history. A growing number of thoughtful books organize both contemporary and scholarly materials in units designed to facilitate the investigation of historical problems.

The problems books, documents books, and collections of articles will whet the appetite of engaged students for further reading in the fields of their interest. They can serve in their way, then, as can the lists of suggested readings in this volume, as avenues leading to the adventures of the mind and the development of the understanding that American history affords.

CONTENTS

APPENDIX A *A1*

APPENDIX B *A17*

INDEX *I1*

MAPS

FLAG ART

The drawings of U.S. flags used with chapter titles in Chapters 5–35 show the growth of the nation as reflected in its national banner. The U.S. flag is a unique symbol. Its basic design has remained the same since 1777, yet it has changed with the growing nation. By gaining a new star to represent each newly admitted state, the flag has changed from its original 13 stars to 50 stars today.

The Grand Union flag used in Chapter 5, while not the first official standard, was the first flag to be widely recognized as a banner that represented the thirteen united colonies in revolt against Great Britain. It was the flag under which General George Washington proclaimed the organization of the Continental Army at his headquarters in Cambridge, Massachusetts, on January 1, 1776. The first flag legislation that established a national banner was passed by the Continental Congress on June 14, 1777, and gave the flag its design of alternating red and white stripes and a constellation of stars in a canton of blue. This first official flag is used in Chapter 6.

Only 18 of the 27 U.S. flags have been used in these chapters. Each flag corresponds to the period discussed in its chapter. The flags were drawn by Linda Wild.

THE NATIONAL EXPERIENCE

PART TWO

A HISTORY OF THE UNITED STATES SINCE 1865

CHAPTER FIFTEEN

RICHMOND, VIRGINIA: THE RUINS OF WAR

RECONSTRUCTION

The American Revolution brought great and, in some cases, uniquely American political changes with the birth of a new nation. The Second American Revolution, as the Civil War has been called, forced a country aged by battle to confront one of the most ancient themes of world history, slavery and emancipation. Slavery had existed for as long as history had been written, and now, the American republic experienced, as older societies had, the dramatic shift of a portion of its population from a rigidly enforced legal servitude into an as yet undefined condition of freedom. Intense argument and dramatic political action characterized the Era of Reconstruction, the period after the Civil War when some determined Americans struggled to restructure society in order to give meaning to the freedom that the former slaves had achieved.

Proud optimists thought that simply ending slavery was all there was to the job. They did not realize that the freedpeople would have to struggle to find their next meal in a society that often was anything but welcoming. Despite this uncertain beginning, the former slaves made their way into the economy and achieved a remarkable entry into the body politic as well. But initial optimism yielded to pessimism and shame as these ambitious hopes were cruelly rebuffed. The American people's outraged sense of fairness was unmatched by actions sufficient to end the mistreatment of the black former slaves during Reconstruction and long afterwards.

Yet, if the former slaves were slowed in the pursuit of a chance to share equally in the lean rewards of an impoverished South, no one could take away the fact that when the Civil War was over 4,000,000 Americans who had been slaves were slaves no longer. They were a freed people—a free people—and, by their very presence, they said to their country that they had to be taken into account in a new way. The nation would have to reconstruct itself to adjust to their emancipation.

ANDREW JOHNSON AND RECONSTRUCTION

"Malice toward None" In March 1865, as the war was ending, Abraham Lincoln, in his second inaugural address, had committed the nation to a peace in which the victors would bear "malice toward none." This magnificent phrase carried a promise of forgiveness of former slaveholders in the South, but implied reliance on their benevolence to provide for the welfare of their former slaves. A bit uneasily, the president was also mindful of the claims of the freedmen to something more than economic dependence on their former masters. Conferring with highly educated, free-born black leaders from New Orleans, he contemplated the possibility of a suffrage, limited by literacy or property ownership, that would give strength to a leadership group among the black citizens. He was groping towards a Reconstruction policy, and so was the Congress.

On March 3, 1865, the Congress adjourned according to its usual schedule, which meant the legislators were to be out of Washington all through the crucial spring, summer, and fall that followed the war. On their last day in Washington, the lawmakers, with the president's approval, established the Freedman's Savings Bank, an interstate federally sponsored private bank in which the freedmen were urged to put their savings as they sold crops or earned wages. The legislators and the president also created the Bureau of Refugees, Freedmen, and Abandoned Lands—a welfare agency, soon known as the Freedmen's Bureau—which was to provide relief supplies and transportation for Union war refugees, black and white, serve as a labor referral and arbitration service, and provide a local court system. The agents were also directed to divide lands abandoned to the United States Army into 40-acre lots and distribute them to freed families. The drafters of the legislation expected that the land would be farmed after the manner of the Port Royal Experiment of the Sea Islands (see p. 363). Lincoln, having signed the bills, appointed a well-meaning and devout Christian, General O. O. Howard, to head the Freedmen's Bureau.

With Lincoln's assassination, all eyes turned to the new president, Andrew Johnson, to see what his Reconstruction policies would be. Radicals hoped that his stern wartime attitude toward slaveholding planters in his home state of Tennessee would herald a policy favorable to the former slaves. Shrewder friends of the retention of white supremacy in the South guessed, correctly, that the insecure new president would respond well to the flattering proposition that he could come to be thought of as the great president who reunited the Union. They proposed that he should do so by restoring a social structure not unlike the one that had existed before the war.

Born to poverty in North Carolina, Johnson was apprenticed to a tailor and, at 18, moved to Greenville in mountainous eastern Tennessee to practice his skilled trade. His wife, Eliza McCardle, taught him to write and Johnson, a good Jacksonian, joined volunteer associations, including a debating club, and became an active citizen in the small city. He entered politics and, before the war, served not only in the Tennessee legislature and as governor, but also in both houses of Congress. Having risen from indentured servitude, Johnson was an example of the advancement possible in a society that opened opportunities to even its poorest members. At the Civil War's end, he had a unique opportunity to extend at least some of these possibilities to another group of poor Americans, the freed slaves, but, escaping the greatness within his grasp, Johnson could not bring himself to identify his own position with theirs.

Northern advocates of black rights had misunderstood the president's policies as wartime governor of Tennessee. When he had ruled in favor of the former slaves rather than their former masters, he did so not so much to assist the impoverished as to punish rich planters, who had long considered themselves superior to men like him. In a pathetic, but moving, drunken inaugural speech when he was sworn in as vice president in March 1865, Johnson exposed not only his awareness of the realities of social and economic injustice but also his lack of confidence. When he became president, powerful members of the very class he had feared and despised, seized the opportunity. With flattery and, even more, with appeals to his staunch support for the Union and to his determination to be thought to be a responsible president, they encouraged him to follow a policy that would sustain black subordination in the South. Shrewdly aware of how thin the commitment to black equality was in the North, Johnson thought he had a formula for a new political alignment and for reelection to the presidency.

On May 29, 1865, Johnson issued two proclamations. The first granted amnesty to former Confederates who would take an oath of loyalty to the Constitution and the federal laws. Their property was to be restored to them, except for slaves and any lands and goods that were already in the process of being confiscated by federal authorities. Fourteen classes of persons were excepted from the general amnesty, including the highest-ranking civil and military officers of the Confederacy, all those who had deserted judicial posts or seats in Congress to serve the Confederacy, and persons whose taxable property was worth more than $20,000. To regain their rights, men in these categories were required to make individual applications for amnesty directly to the president. The former leaders of the South would be applying to him in order to regain the chance to once again be its leaders. With the pardons granted, Johnson would have the most powerful voices in the South indebted to him politically.

Prisoners from the Front, *1866, by Winslow Homer*

The second proclamation, in which Johnson outlined his requirements for the reconstruction of North Carolina, foreshadowed the policy he would follow in future proclamations to other states. He appointed William W. Holden, an announced Unionist, as provisional governor and directed him to call a convention for the purpose of amending the state constitution "to restore said State to its constitutional relations to the Federal government." He also accepted the governments already established in Arkansas, Louisiana, Tennessee, and Virginia which had been brought back into the Union under Lincoln's plan.

In addition to these formal proclamations and programs of political restoration of the South, Andrew Johnson gave informal instructions that not just political rights but lands abandoned to Union armies were also to be given back to Confederates. A few Freedmen's Bureau agents and a good many black farmers protested this abrogation of the will of Congress expressed in the legislation creating the Freedmen's Bureau. On the Georgia coast, black Bureau agent Tunis Campbell refused to allow lands to be taken from black farmers; only Johnson's federal troops forced him to do so. Such protests were of little avail; by the end of the year almost all of the acreage that the freedmen thought would be distributed to them was returned to Confederate planters.

The easy terms that Johnson set for the restoration of Southern states bothered many Northerners. Governor B. F. Perry of South Carolina forwarded every pardon petition he received and President Johnson responded with almost equal generosity. Soon ardent Confederates turned up as duly elected congressmen and officers of the restored state governments. Others, knowing Johnson would grant their pardons, did not wait for them before being elected to office. A Confederate general, Benjamin G. Humphreys, was governor of Mississippi and the former vice president of the Confederacy, Alexander H. Stephens, was elected senator from Georgia. The persisting loyalty of the Southern voters to their former leaders alarmed the North and the freedpeople of the South.

There were other signs of white Southern obstinacy. Some states refused to repudiate the Confederate war debt, and South Carolina merely "repealed" its ordinance of secession, thus refusing to admit that rebelling had been unconstitutional. Mississippi would not ratify the proposed Thirteenth Amendment, formally ending slavery. Southern Unionists and freedmen complained that they were not safe under the Johnson state governments. In late summer of 1865 Governor Holden warned the president that there was "much of a rebellion spirit" left in North Carolina. He feared that Johnson's "leniency" had "emboldened" the enemies of the government. Privately Johnson counseled Southern leaders to avoid antagonizing Congress, but he was too stubborn to modify his plan or even to alter his pardoning policy.

Only after a public outcry against the leniency of his terms did Johnson require the returning states to disavow their ordinances of secession, repudiate the Southern war debt, and ratify the Thirteenth Amendment. That amendment, which would end slavery forever in the United States, had cleared Congress in January 1865, but had required the approval of at least some of the former Confederate states to reach ratification by three-fourths of the states. The agreement that slavery must end seemed only grudgingly forthcoming.

The Defeated South Agriculture, the South's economic bulwark, had been battered wherever armies had clashed and passed. Houses and outbuildings had been burned, crops destroyed, and livestock killed. Seed to plant new crops was often unavailable, and many farmers could not afford to buy it when they found it. Credit was almost unobtainable. Horses and mules to plow the land were even harder to find. Labor was scarce because a quarter of a million soldiers had lost their lives and many former slaves were reluctant to work for their former masters.

Much of Southern industry had been badly damaged, and assets that would have supported desperately needed loans had been wiped out. At one stroke, emancipation had destroyed a credit base made up of billions of dollars invested in slaves. Land values plummeted. The appearance of cities that had stood in the path of the armies was bleak. Charleston, South Carolina, was "a city of ruins, of desolation, of vacant houses, of widowed women, of rotting wharves." Columbia lay in ashes, as did most of Richmond.

Most white Southerners, accepting defeat with fortitude and resignation, set about working their land. Many felt considerable relief that slavery was over. Some did so out of simple goodwill; others saw that with its demise any formal responsibility for the welfare of their slaves also ended. They, like those freed, were anxious about how the races would now live together. Some white people at first feared that black people would engage in violent vengeance. Others could not adjust to dealing with a free labor force. They continued to think of themselves as members of a superior group and to believe in the old myths about paternalistic masters and contented slaves. Consequently they were shocked and hurt when their former slaves rejoiced in freedom.

For their part, black Southerners felt an urge to test the meaning of freedom, but few interpreted "Jubilee Day" as a license for perpetual celebration. While some seemed psychologically conditioned to expect continued support from their former masters, most freedmen responded by cautiously but firmly throwing off the constraints of slavery as a first step toward building a responsible life. They ventured to move about freely from place to place, which slavery had forbidden, and to reunite members of their families —parents, spouses, children—whom slavery had separated. Thousands of these poignant reunions succeeded; more of them failed as lost children and spouses could not be located. The freedpeople yearned to leave the regimented conditions of plantation life and live instead in family units. They yearned especially for a farm of their own on land they had long worked and thought of as theirs.

Freedmen, Richmond, Virginia

In the spring of 1865, both groups of farmers, the former slaves and their former masters, knew that unless vegetable crops were planted, no one would eat the following winter. Unless cotton or some other cash crop was raised, there would be no money to buy even so much as a replacement for a broken hoe. The point in contention was the conditions under which fields were to be worked, which, in the end, came down to a quarrel over who was to control the land.

Organizing Southern Agriculture During the war, the Union government had turned over some plantations that had been abandoned, as Union armies approached, to slaves living on those lands. Southern freedmen hoped for months that this pattern would be followed and that they would receive a portion of their former master's land and some assistance in working it — the famous 40 acres and a mule — from the government. The desire for a normal family life and for the privacy and independence of a small farm — normal American expectations in the mid-nineteenth century — moved black Southerners to resist signing up to work for their old masters.

The Freedmen's Bureau agents, many of them young Union army officers who thought a great, progressive change in the Southern economy was in the making, sought both to introduce Northern concepts of wage labor and to retain the status quo in sufficient degree to assure survival. The Bureau required both former slaves and former masters to sign contracts, a practice new to both. But the freed people were uncomfortable about signing with an "X" or having their old master sign for them handwritten contracts that called for the planting and harvesting of crops "in the usual way as before the war." Such wording sounded too much like more slavery to them. Not much more reassuring were formally printed contracts in which clauses calling for wages were neatly struck through with a pen stroke. Those wages that were agreed to were paid not weekly, but only when the crops were harvested and sold — and then only if the planter made a profit sufficient to care for his own family as well as the former slaves living on his land.

The Bureau contracts gave the workers a lien on the crops they had raised to protect the wages due them. But the freedpeople, scarcely prepared to go into court to enforce the lien, were dependent on appeals to their former master's good will or the intervention of the Bureau agents if their fair share of the crop's value was to be paid to them. Often the agents, finding the white planters easier to understand and identify with, were

Visit from the Old Mistress, *by Winslow Homer, 1876*

more sympathetic with them than with the workers. There is evidence of their using both threats of force and actual physical coercion to make the former slaves work.

As the Freedmen's Bureau agents, resented by the landlords and distrusted by the freedmen, became less and less active in monitoring Southern labor practices after 1866, the planters and the freedmen began to make their own arrangements. The black workers, hating work in field gangs that had been standard under slavery, found a way to approximate having a farm of their own by striking bargains with their former masters or other landlords. Aware that their labor was in huge demand, they forced landowners to rent them land. The white planters, short of cash and relieved to be free of the obligation to care for the freedmen's children and elderly dependents, agreed to allow their former slaves to have a plot of land to farm on their own, provided they care for their own families. Those planters who would rent land not only got a portion of the cash crop raised by the freed people but gained workers for their own fields in the bargain. Black women workers who had left the fields now came back to help secure the family farm.

These informal but binding tenancy agreements, sometimes similar to those into which impoverished white farmers had begun entering before the war, called for the tenant and the landlord to divide the proceeds from the annual crop into shares that varied according to the condition of the land and the proportion of work, animals, seed, fertilizer, and other necessities each supplied. Merchants put up the money for the goods that had to be bought in return for a lien on the crop. So low was the return on what was raised on sharecroppers' farms that the farmers often found themselves in perpetual debt. The system had many defects. It pushed the poor farmers of the region into a burdensome tenancy, a peonage of a kind, and allowed them only meager return for their labor. At the price of discouraging crop diversification, it did permit the resumption of cotton and tobacco culture, and it allowed the ex-slaves to engage, within the bonds of poverty, in a family life of their own. For all its liabilities, it was better than slavery or gang labor.

Reordering Southern Society The conflicting expectations of white Southerners, embittered by defeat, and black Southerners, emboldened by emancipation, guaranteed that Reconstruction would be controversial. That controversy was symbolized by the presence of outsiders, the Freedmen's Bureau agents in army uniform. Some soldiers, seeking acceptance from fellow white people, often sided with them rather than with the freedmen who counted on their help. Conscientious agents did protect some freedmen from exploitative planters, provide others with help in

Cotton Market in New Orleans, *by Edgar Degas*

School for former slaves

locating and reaching their families, formalize marriages, and provide facilities for Northern teachers to begin the education of illiterate black people. Many of the schools and colleges that have played such a vital part in educating black Southerners were begun with Bureau help. These efforts at restructuring the society did not, however, transform the attitudes of all Southern white people towards black people, and during 1865 reports reached the North about many incidents of whippings, mutilations, and murders of former slaves.

These private acts of vengeance were accompanied, in the public sphere, by the Black Codes passed by the legislatures of the Southern states. These laws looked to many like the old slave codes, but were actually more like the laws governing free African-Americans in antebellum times. They could now own property, witness, sue and be sued in court, and contract legal marriages; in some states they could even serve on juries. But despite these seemingly liberal provisions, the thrust of the new codes revealed a determination to keep black people in an inferior position. Interracial marriage was forbidden and, in Mississippi, black artisans had to buy a special license in order to engage in certain trades. Everywhere special punishments were prescribed for black vagrants and for those who broke labor contracts. In some states black people who could show no means of support could be bound out by the courts to do labor in the fields. The vagrancy

School for Black Children

Most of my children were very small . . . but after some days of positive . . . treatment . . . I found but little difficulty in managing . . . the tiniest and most restless spirits. I never before saw children so eager to learn. . . . Coming to school is a constant delight . . . to them. They come here as other children go to play. The older ones, during the summer, work in the fields from early morning until eleven or twelve o'clock, and then come to school . . . as bright and as anxious to learn as ever. . . .

The majority learn with wonderful rapidity. Many of the grown people are desirous of learning to read. It is wonderful how a people who have been so long crushed to the earth . . . can have so great a desire for knowledge, and such a capability for attaining it. . . . One's indignition increases against those who, North as well as South, taunt the colored race with inferiority while they themselves use every means in their power to crush . . . them.

From a letter by Charlotte Forten, a Northern black woman teaching in South Carolina laws were used not so much to rid the streets of wanderers as to control a labor force without the consent of the laborers.

In many societies and over many centuries, involuntary servitude of a lesser sort than slavery has followed emancipation. This seemed now to be coming about in the United States. The Black Codes severely restricted the activities of the freed people. In Mississippi, which had the most restrictive code, black farmers, some of whom had become successful working on rich delta lands abandoned during the war, were denied the right to lease land outside towns. Blatantly, the mobility open to the freedmen who sought to become prosperous independent farmers was to be blocked. The unstated premise of the codes was that the freed people were to continue to be a dependent and dependable source of farm labor, much as they had been when they were slaves.

Thaddeus Stevens

Congress and Reconstruction Congressmen, returning to Washington in December 1865, were well posted on these alarming events in the South. The Republican majority had come to have grave doubts about Johnson's program. The Radicals, a minority within the party, were genuinely concerned for the safety of the freedmen, whom they considered to be the most trustworthy Unionists in the South. African-Americans had ably supported the Northern cause during the war, and many of them had served in the Union army. The Radicals, therefore, worked for the rapid advancement of the freedmen. They saw to it that the Congress excluded Southerners who had been elected to serve as senators and congressmen. The seating of these representatives was to have marked the completion of President Johnson's program of Reconstruction. Instead, the Radicals in Congress set out to devise their own plan for reordering the South.

Thaddeus Stevens, an able congressman from Pennsylvania, with close personal ties to his black housekeeper's family, led the fight. At this early date he opposed black suffrage, because he feared that the Southern planters would use their economic power to control the freedmen's votes and because he was convinced that an economic base was the primary need of the people. Instead of the vote, he proposed to give the freedmen land. He would confiscate the holdings of former Confederates and divide it into small freeholds. "Forty acres . . . and a hut," he declared, would "be more valuable . . . than the . . . right to vote." Stevens had in mind not only the Sea Islands, but also the whole South Carolina and Georgia coastal area, where freedmen were already farming land under possessory titles that had been assigned them by the government on estates confiscated during the war. Stevens wanted this policy extended throughout the South, but Johnson had already restored to the former owners the lands that Stevens wanted redistributed.

Senator Charles Sumner of Massachusetts, another Radical, pinned his hopes on suffrage. He called first for votes solely for educated black citizens and black veterans but soon advocated general black suffrage. He argued that freedmen required the vote for their own protection. Other Radicals agreed with Sumner and, in New Orleans, African-Americans made their own voice heard on the matter. Turning their backs on a limited suffrage proposal that would have formally divided the community along caste lines, the black citizens of Louisiana demanded "universal suffrage" —for fieldhands as well as free-born literate men —and staged a mock election, complete with a registration system and polls, to prove both the capacity and desire of black citizens to participate in the political process. In New Orleans, to the embarrassment of white supremacists, the candidate of the black activists received more votes in the mock election than did the regularly elected governor in the regular election. Alert now to just how ambitious the freedmen were, chagrined moderates in Congress quickly sought to discover a middle road short of suffrage between Johnson's simple restoration and the Radicals' more sweeping plans. The moderates dominated the Joint Committee on Reconstruction, which was created in December 1865 to formulate a plan for the South.

As the Joint Committee began its work, signs of Southern intransigence multiplied. Republican congressmen received countless letters from Southern Unionists, both black and white, complaining that they were being threatened. Both Radicals and more moderate members of the party, agreeing that the safety of the former slaves had to be secured and that the Black Codes should be circumscribed by federal legislation guaranteeing rights to the freedmen, enacted two bills early in 1866. The first, passed in February, extended the life and expanded the powers of the Freedmen's Bureau. The second was a Civil Rights bill. Unabashedly, moderates, who supported both bills, warned that if the black Southerners were not safeguarded in their own region, they could be expected to leave the South and come North. Congress intended that the Freedmen's Bureau agents would enforce the Civil Rights bill. They were authorized to conduct courts not only to adjudicate labor disputes but to hear other complaints of injustice as well.

President Johnson, contending that such provisions would lead to military rule, considered both bills unconstitutional in time of peace. Accused persons tried in the Bureau courts would be tried and even convicted, he stated, without benefit of jury, rules of evidence, or right of appeal. In the Freedmen's Bureau veto, Johnson rebuked Congress for continuing to exclude the Southern members. Although his observations about the dubious constitutionality of the legislation had some merit, they angered congressmen who knew that former slaves were not getting justice in Southern courts. Four days after the veto, which the Congress narrowly sustained, Johnson harangued a crowd gathered outside the White House to hear him deliver a Washington's Birthday greeting. In a rambling speech he denounced his opponents as traitors, suggested that they wanted to kill him, and compared himself to the crucified Christ. Johnson clearly saw himself as the martyred champion of the Southern states and constitutional liberty.

Furious, Congress passed the Civil Rights bill, which granted the freedmen the protection of federal citizenship and access to federal courts in order to secure for them the same rights and protection as white citizens, regardless of local statutes. Further, it authorized the use of troops to enforce its privileges and penalties. Again the president resorted to a veto. But this time Congress overrode him and in April the strong Civil Rights Act of 1866 became the law of the land. Heartened by this success, congressional leaders put through a mildly amended version of the Freedmen's Bureau bill. Once again Johnson vetoed it, but this time the Congress overrode his veto. Some Republican senators had supported Johnson's veto of the first Freedmen's Bureau bill, but only three of them supported his veto of the amended bill. The broad middle section of the Republican party had joined forces with the Radicals to guarantee civil rights for the freedmen. The president in his obstinacy had consolidated his adopted party into opposition.

The Thirteenth and Fourteenth Amendments The Civil Rights bill was designed to enforce the Thirteenth Amendment to the Constitution, which states in part that "neither slavery nor involuntary servitude, except as a punishment for a crime where of the party shall have been duly convicted, shall exist in the United States." Far from being a mere stamp of approval on the Emancipation Proclamation, the amendment, proposed during the war and ratified in December 1865, was necessary to prevent any involuntary servitude measures that might be devised as a substitute for slavery. In Maryland, since long before the war, slavery had been undergoing a transition from a plantation labor system to that of slave leasing for nonagricultural pursuits. The change had been accompanied by less rigid discipline and the state government had been seeking methods of social control other than that of slavery. One law, which could have set a dangerous precedent, was a nonvoluntary child apprentice system, but, when challenged in a federal court, it was declared unconstitutional under the Thirteenth Amendment. Without the amendment and the Civil Rights Act enforcing it, no legal redress would have been possible for the black people who resisted seeing their children forced into a new bondage and other injustices. In Louisiana, when country people had come into New Orleans to sell chickens, local judges were sometimes ready to find them guilty of vagrancy and sentence them to six months' labor on a sugar plantation that was short of workers. Now when such injustices occurred, there was a Constitutional principle with respect to involuntary servitude that could be appealed to in the courts.

As valuable as the Thirteenth Amendment was, clearly it was not enough to safeguard the freedmen's uncertain position as citizens. In the Dred Scott case Chief Justice Roger B. Taney had given his opinion that no African-American, whether free or slave, could be regarded as a United States citizen or was entitled to the privileges that the Constitution granted citizens. Many Republicans, remembering that decision, were afraid to depend on an act of Congress, which would be subject to Supreme Court review, to secure civil rights for the freedmen. They decided that only an amendment to the Constitution would safeguard the freedmen and secure a new electorate in the South loyal to the Union. The Fourteenth Amendment, proposed in April 1866 by the Joint Committee on Reconstruction, was passed by Congress on June 19 and sent to the states for ratification. First it defined American citizenship: "All persons born or naturalized in the United States, and subject to the jurisdiction thereof, are citizens of the United States and of the State wherein they reside." The amendment then prohibited states from passing laws "which shall abridge the privileges or immunities of citizens of the United States," from depriving "any person of life, liberty, or property, without due process of law," and from denying "to any person within its jurisdiction the equal protection of the laws." The concept of a national citizenship had been introduced into the Constitution, as had the Declaration of Independence's proposition that "all men are created equal."

The second and third sections of the Fourteenth Amendment attempted to bring about a basic change in the Southern electorate. The second section gave the Southern states a choice of either enfranchising all male citizens, including black Americans, or else losing seats in the House of Representatives proportionate to the number they excluded. Some Radicals would have preferred a specific guarantee of universal manhood suffrage, but practical politicians realized that such a guarantee might lead to the defeat of the amendment in the North, for only a few Northern states had enfranchised black people. The third section disqualified from officeholding at the state and federal level all who, before the war, had taken an oath to support the Constitution in order to hold public office and who had subsequently supported the Confederacy. Only Congress could remove this disability.

The Battle Joined The congressional elections of 1866 caught the voters in a widening rift between president and Congress, with the Fourteenth Amendment as the central issue. As had been true with the Thirteenth Amendment, favorable action by some Southern legislatures was needed to secure ratification by the required three-fourths of the states. President Johnson opposed the Fourteenth Amendment and encouraged Southern legislatures to oppose it too. Of all the former Confederate states only Tennessee ratified the amendment. Vainly hoping to prompt other states to follow suit, Congress seated Tennessee's delegates.

Johnson continued not to implement Republican congressional measures, especially the Civil Rights Act and the Freedmen's Bureau Act. He replaced Freedmen's Bureau agents who showed themselves to be genuinely committed to the freedmen's cause, interpreted acts of Congress passed over his veto so narrowly that he almost negated their intent, and, his critics said, violated his constitutional responsibility to execute the laws of the land. Though Johnson claimed to be working for peace and reconciliation, he was actually trying to unite moderate and conservative Republicans with willing Democrats into a new National Union party, the name Lincoln and he had used in 1864. His purpose was to elect his own supporters to Congress in 1866.

Andrew Johnson did his own cause great damage in his personal campaign to win support for conservative congressmen. In a "Swing Around the Circle" throughout the Middle West, he met hecklers on their own terms and sacrificed the dignity of his office at every whistlestop. The President was losing the sympathy of the voters and he had almost entirely lost the confidence of those who had counted on the chief executive to safeguard the lives of the former slaves. In recent outbreaks of racial violence in Memphis and New Orleans scores of black citizens had been killed and hundreds wounded. The president, when warned of impending trouble, had done nothing to prevent those occurrences, even when Union troops were available and could have been used to keep the peace.

Radical Reconstruction When the results of the election were in, Republicans committed to a Reconstruction program far different from President Johnson's had won a commanding victory. Many Democrats and most of Johnson's Republican sup-

Veto of the Radicals' Plan

The power . . . given to the commanding officer over all the people of each district is that of an absolute monarch. His mere will is to take the place of all law. The law of the States is now the only rule applicable to the subjects placed under his control, and that is completely displaced by the clause which declares all interference of State authority to be null and void. . . .

It is plain that the authority here given to the military officer amounts to absolute despotism. But to make it still more unendurable, the bill provides that it may be delegated to as many subordinates as he chooses to appoint, for it declares that he shall "punish or cause to be punished." Such a power has not been wielded by any monarch in England for more than five hundred years. In all that time no people who speak the English language have borne such servitude. It reduces the whole population of the ten States—all persons, of every color, sex, and condition, and every stranger within their limits—to the most abject and degrading slavery.

From Andrew Johnson, Veto of the Reconstruction Act, 1867

porters were swept out of office and the election was seen as a mandate for the ratification of the Fourteenth Amendment as a basis of Reconstruction. Both the Radicals and the moderates knew that securing sufficient support in the South to ensure the adoption of the amendment would require forceful measures, which they were prepared to take.

On March 2, 1867, in its final hours and after long debate, the outgoing Thirty-ninth Congress passed a bill "to provide for more efficient Government of the Rebel States." This Reconstruction Act established military rule throughout the South two years after the war was over. Johnson's veto, not unexpected, condemned the bill as "utterly destructive" to "principles of liberty," but his veto was promptly overridden.

The new law divided the ten Confederate states into five military districts (Tennessee had already been readmitted to Congress), each under the command of an army general, backed by troops, who was granted full authority over judicial and civil functions (see Map 15-1). Each of these military governors had police power in his district. Each had as his immediate assignment the registration of a new, verifiably loyal electorate. Among the voters who were to be registered were adult males who only two years ago had been slaves. This action, remarkable in the history of emancipation, could have achieved the grant of franchise for over a million black men, and it did result in many thousands of freedmen becoming voters. Denied the franchise for the time being were former Confederates already excluded under the provisions of the proposed Fourteenth Amendment.

In each of the ten states, newly registered voters elected delegates to a state constitutional convention at which a new constitution was adopted that granted universal manhood suffrage. Although the conventions interpreted that grant variously, most new state constitutions excluded former Confederate leaders from voting and holding office. The Reconstruction Act further declared that after a state had presented an acceptable constitution to Congress and had ratified the Fourteenth Amendment, Congress would then admit that state's members.

Even with this impressive program of political reform underway, congressional leaders feared that Johnson might use his authority as commander in chief to subvert their intentions and passed two more measures to trim his power. The Army Appropriations

Map 15-1 *Reconstruction*

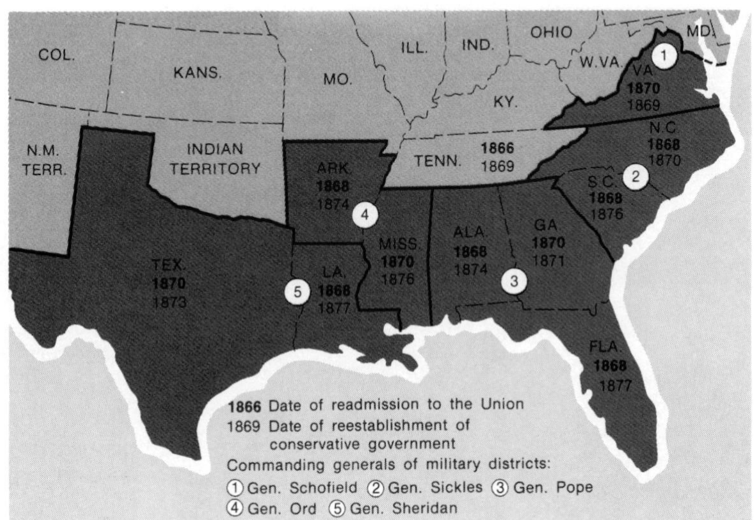

Act directed the president and the secretary of state to issue their orders to the five commanders for the governing of the South through the General of the Army —Ulysses S. Grant's new title—while the Tenure of Office Act provided that any officeholder appointed by the president with the Senate's consent was to serve until the Senate had approved a successor. If the president replaced a Cabinet member while the Senate was out of session, the replacement would serve after the Senate reconvened only with its consent; otherwise, the former incumbent would resume his duties.

The Tenure of Office Act was designed to keep Johnson from using the power of appointment to destroy those who opposed his views on Reconstruction and, in particular, to prevent his replacing Edwin Stanton, secretary of war. It further provided that, unless the Senate approved a change, Cabinet members were to hold office "during the term of the President by whom they may have been appointed, and for one month thereafter." Stanton, appointed by President Lincoln, was the only member left in the Cabinet who was friendly to the Radicals, and many Radicals, including Stanton himself, believed that the safety of the nation depended on his remaining in office. As the Cabinet member in charge of the army, he had great influence over Reconstruction in the South.

A Changed South Freedmen emboldened both by the results of the 1866 election and the initiatives in Congress, began to move forward on both the economic and political fronts. In the Low Country of South Carolina, black workers, unhappy about low or unpaid wages, struck against the planters who had hired them, counting on newly elected black officials to support them in these actions. During the last half of 1867, black and white delegates to the conventions wrote liberal constitutions, elected legislators and governors, and ratified the Fourteenth Amendment. Black delegates and black legislators were in no instance dominant in the deliberations, but the image of servants insolently seizing the seats of their masters has been so firmly implanted in the American historical tradition that it can be forgotten how unprecedented and yet, in the event, how unremarkable their participation was.

All but three states were readmitted to the Union in 1868. There was much foot dragging over the disfranchisement of former Confederates, who were often the most popular leaders in their states. Endless discussions of this bitter point delayed the writing of constitutions in Virginia and Texas; in Mississippi ratification of the new constitution was defeated because of it. Not until 1870 did those three states win congressional approval of their constitutions and reenter Congress. Georgia, admitted in 1868 but cast out again when its new legislature dismissed duly elected black members, was also readmitted in 1870, when the dismissal was rescinded.

The new constitutions of the Southern states were in many respects better than the antebellum constitutions. The states now assumed responsibility for many social services that had formerly been left to local officials and private initiative. States without public school systems now established them, along with hospitals and other institutions for the care of the indigent, homeless, and the physically handicapped. Tax systems were made more equitable, penal codes more humane, and the rights of women more comprehensive. For the first time in its history, South Carolina had a divorce law. In states where planters had enjoyed advantages over upcountry farmers, districting for representation in the legislature was made fairer. The new constitutions also empowered state governments to undertake programs in economic recovery, especially for the rebuilding of the ruined railroads. Some of these constitutions, modern for their time, served the Southern states long after Reconstruction had ended.

Southern racial conservatives denounced the new governments, mainly because they detested the political coalition that had created them and that served in the first legislatures. They called resident Northerners who held office in the new governments "carpetbaggers," a name suggesting that as transients they had no stake in Southern society. They denounced Southern whites who cooperated with the new regimes as "scalawags" — runty, poorly bred cattle — suggesting at once both smallness of means and disloyalty. The spectacle of black Southerners voting and holding public office shocked the conservatives, but pragmatic scalawags found it useful, if awkward, to cooperate with their black colleagues. These latter politicians, using the time-honored "you vote for my bill, I'll vote for yours" procedure, were, in a few instances, able to develop real local political power that workers could appeal to when planters threatened their interests. Robert Smalls, representing the Sea Islands in South Carolina, could intercede when striking freedmen were threatened with violence and succeed in both restoring the peace and protecting his constituents' wages. Similarly, in Georgia Tunis Campbell, as a local justice of the peace and state legislator, could help his own black community gather strength. Although black Southerners never held office in proportion to their numbers, their very presence in government fostered bitter complaints of "nigger rule."

Behind criticism of the "Black Republicans" lay the assumption that none of the groups governing the South were fit to do so. Actually there was little truth in the stereotypes that conservatives fastened on the Republican coalition. Many scalawags were prominent and affluent leaders who found Republican economic policies not unlike the old Whig program. Others were small farmers, who sensed that their interests might be better protected than they had been before the war. Entrepreneurs hoped for tax policies favorable to them rather than to planters. And not all these Republicans were troubled by sharing political rights with black Southerners. The carpetbaggers included all sorts of people who had business in the South after the war: military personnel, planters, as well as adventuring businessmen and speculators. Unlike politicians with outside incomes, many carpetbaggers who held office had to depend on their incomes as officeholders for a living. There were fewer carpetbaggers than there were scalawags and black citizens, but their undoubted loyalty to the Union and their connections with the federal government gave them considerable influence. Working through local groups called Loyal Leagues or Union Leagues, they organized the black Republican vote in the South.

Tunis Campbell: Georgia politician

The great weakness of the Republican coalition was that it had, in part, come to power as a result of policy generated in Washington. Its strength lay in the sense, never fully realized, that a new class of Southern working people was coalescing. Unable to accept this movement, members of the once powerful class of planters, as well as many new landowners, chose to regard the Republican governments as fraudulent and

The Problems of Southern Unionists

. . . Those Union men who really maintained their integrity and devotion to the Federal Union through the war, and embraced the republican view at its close, were . . . mostly of that class who are neither rich nor poor, who were land-owners, but not slave-owners. The few who were of the higher class had been so completely shut out from the intellectual movements of the North during those momentous years, that, as a rule, they were utterly confounded at the result which was before them. They had looked for the nation to come back to them, when its power was re-established, absolutely unchanged and unmodified. It came back, instead, with a new impetus, a new life, born of the stormy years that had intervened, putting under its feet the old issues which had divided parties, scornful of ancient statesmanship, and mocking the gray-beards who had been venerated as sages in "the good old days of the Republic."

But for those Southern men, who, knowing and realizing all these changes, facing all these dangers and discomforts, recognizing the inexorable logic of events, and believing in and desiring to promote the ultimate good which must flow therefrom, in good faith accepted the arbitrament of war, and staked their "lives, fortunes, and sacred honor," in support of this new dispensation of liberty, words enough of praise can not be found! Nor yet words enough of scorn for their associates and affiliates of the North, who not only refused them the meed of due credit for their self-sacrifice and devotion, but also made haste to visit them with coolness, indignity, and discrediting contempt, because they did not perform the impossible task which the Wise men had imposed upon them.

From Albion W. Tourgée, *A Fool's Errand; By One of the Fools,* 1879

alien. Indeed, most white Southerners would not recognize the legitimacy of governments which they saw as having been imposed upon them. Yet idealism and high purpose marked the early stages of the Republican effort to rebuild the South.

The Impeachment of a President Congress had been right in suspecting that Johnson would use his control of the army to weaken programs called for in the Reconstruction acts. His behavior was technically correct, but by instructing district commanders not to question the past behavior of those who took an oath of allegiance, he permitted Southerners of doubtful loyalty to the Union and of undoubted hostility to their black fellow citizens to regain the vote and the power that went with it. To the dismay of the advocates of the new Reconstruction policies, Johnson removed three generals who were sympathetic to Radical policies and, in December 1867 in his message to Congress, he rashly challenged Congress by declaring that he would maintain his rights as president, "regardless of all consequences."

The Radicals in Congress had contemplated impeaching Johnson for some time and held hearings that produced impressive evidence of Johnson's refusal to execute laws designed to safeguard the freedmen and other Unionists, but they could not agree on legal grounds for action. Their opening came when Johnson resolved to test the constitutionality of the Tenure of Office Act. While Congress was in the 1867 summer recess, he dismissed Stanton and appointed Grant as temporary secretary of war. When Congress reconvened, the Senate refused to consent to Stanton's removal. Grant, protesting that he had never agreed to break the law, left the building and Stanton retrieved his office. Grant's critics suggested that he had done so after a hint from the Radicals that he might himself become a presidential candidate. Johnson, angry with Grant, now embarked on an opéra-bouffe search for a more cooperative general. As stand-in, he finally produced General Lorenzo Thomas, but Johnson had no success in installing his protégé in the War Department. Stanton, barricading himself in his office, cooked his own meals and regularly consulted with the Radical leaders. Removing Stanton was bad enough, but trying to replace him with a pliable secretary of war convinced most Republicans that Johnson now intended to have a free hand in his use of the army to undo what the military Reconstruction acts were bringing about in the South, and to do so in face of specific laws passed by the Congress. Even moderate Republicans gave up on the president. Aware that in the 1867 fall elections the voters had given the Radicals signs of displeasure over the measures they had taken, the Republican moderates had in December blocked a vote of impeachment, but by February their patience was gone.

Confident that most citizens believed Johnson had broken the law, the Republican majority in the House of Representatives voted, unanimously, on February 24, 1868, to impeach Johnson for "high crimes and misdemeanors in office." The Radicals then drew up a list of specific charges, centering on his alleged violation of the Tenure of Office Act. The most significant was the charge that Johnson had been "unmindful of the high duties of his office . . . and of the harmony and courtesies which ought to exist . . . between the executive and legislative branches." He had attempted to bring Congress into "contempt and reproach." Essentially the House, by this charge, was accusing Johnson of disagreement with congressional policies. A conviction on that charge might have established a precedent for the removal of any president who could not command a majority in the House of Representatives on an important issue.

To convict the president, two-thirds of the Senate sitting as a court presided over by the Chief Justice would have to agree that Johnson had broken the law (with the implication that he had no right to test the constitutionality of an act of Congress) and that he was unfit to hold his office. Johnson's able legal defense successfully disposed of the contention that he had broken the Tenure of Office Act by arguing that Stanton had been appointed by Lincoln and not by Johnson and had served beyond the term of the president who appointed him. On the issue of fitness, cautious senators were troubled by the magnitude of the possible consequences of the removal of a president on the political charge that he had not worked for "harmony" with Congress. By a margin of only one vote, the Senate acquitted Johnson. Chief Justice Chase, who presided at the trial, was in sympathy with the president's arguments, and additional Republican senators would have voted for acquittal had their votes been needed. Many of those who voted to acquit the president did so because they distrusted the radicalism of Benjamin Wade, acting president of the Senate, who would have become president if Johnson had been convicted. Wade's views on public finance, labor, and women's

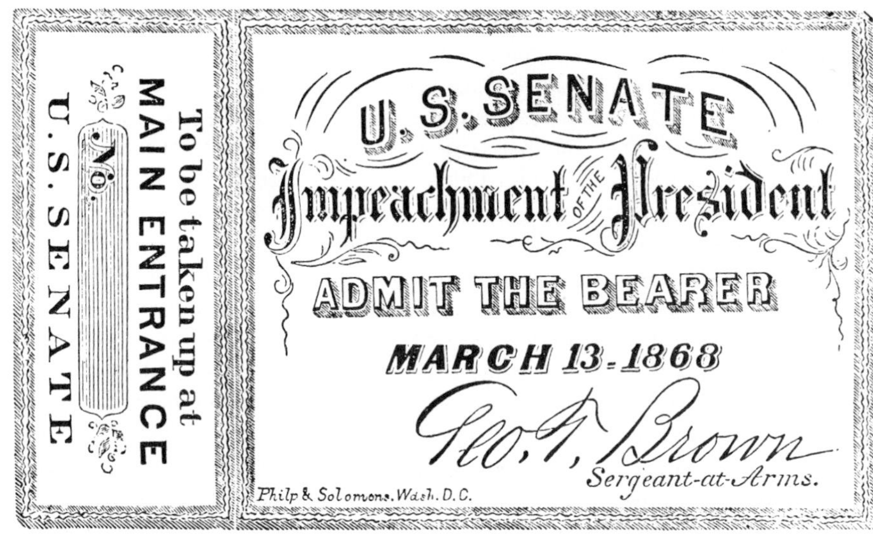

suffrage were fully as radical as his views on civil rights for black citizens, and were far more shocking to the moderate Republicans. After Johnson's narrow escape, Stanton resigned, the Senate adjourned, and President Johnson completed his term in a dignified way. The defeat of the impeachment was an ominous sign for the future of the new Republican governments in the Southern states.

The Supreme Court and Reconstruction The Supreme Court was not entirely silent during the prolonged struggle between the president and the Congress over the direction of Reconstruction. The Court had started off boldly late in 1866. In the case, *ex parte Milligan,* it had ruled unanimously that neither Congress nor the president had the power to create military courts to try civilians in areas remote from war. That noteworthy civil-liberties decision freed several men who had been condemned by such courts for military subversion in the North during the war, but, ironically, it was a threat to the newly established civil rights of the freed people. The *Milligan* decision cast doubt on the legality of the courts the Freedmen's Bureau was then conducting in Southern states.

Congress, by passing the Reconstruction acts in the spring of 1867, delivered an overt challenge to the Court. Unsure of the Court's response, the Radicals began to talk of reducing its size, with some even urging that it be abolished. In 1867, by a five-to-four decision in the twin cases, *Cummings* v. *Missouri* and *ex parte Garland,* the Court invalidated the use of loyalty oaths, pronouncing them ex post facto and bills of attainder. In the same year, however, the Court grew more cautious in its rebukes to Radical Reconstruction policies. In the cases *Georgia* v. *Stanton* and *Mississippi* v. *Johnson,* the Court was challenged to rule on the constitutionality of the Reconstruction acts. In both instances it refused jurisdiction on technical grounds.

The Court had been in low repute since the Dred Scott decision, but when Lincoln replaced pro-Southern justices with staunch Unionists some of its prestige had returned. This change, however, did not ensure that the rights of black citizens would be sustained. In 1873, almost unaware of what the implications of its actions were, the Court robbed the Fourteenth Amendment of its power to protect the freedmen in their precarious postwar position.

In the *Slaughter-House Cases* of 1873, the Court, in a matter unrelated to racial issues, held that the states could define the rules by which its citizens could conduct their lives—in this case, butchers could be required to use a central slaughterhouse—despite an appeal of individual citizens to the new Fourteenth Amendment's guarantee that no person could be deprived of his liberty without due process of law. Shrewd lawyers soon saw that this principle could be used to permit local authorities to establish jurisdiction over the lives of black citizens and make the Fourteenth Amendment impotent as an instrument for their protection. This was precisely what happened once the Radicals were driven from office in the South. Black citizens were deprived of federal protection of many of their basic civil rights for many decades. No longer did the Fourteenth Amendment serve, as Justice Miller in *Slaughter-House* contended that it should, "that race and that emergency."

THE EBULLIENT NORTH

The Gilded Age The Northern economy gained strength in the postwar years. Only briefly did it stumble over reconversion to peace. The demobilization of 800,000 Union veterans within six months, and the abrupt cancellation of war contracts, threw a million people out of work. The economy was further restricted in 1867 when Secretary of the Treasury Hugh McCulluch, who considered gold and silver the only sound basis for currency, began to withdraw from circulation nearly $100 million in greenbacks that had been issued during the war. Within a year, however, railroad expansion and other commercial ventures ended the wartime retardation of the economy and spurred a strong recovery.

The South had seceded from a union of states. It returned to a nation hardened by war and vindicated by victory. The new spirit of nationalism in the North had revealed itself clearly in economic legislation enacted during the war years. The absence of traditional Southern opposition in Congress then had made it easy for Republicans to adopt a protective tariff and reduce foreign competition in industry, to create a national banking system, to put through a homestead act, and to start funding a transcontinental railroad. Those measures signaled a new era of expansion in industry, agriculture, and transportation—all under the favoring hand of the national government.

Prosperity fed a mood of confident materialism and Mark Twain, with sardonic aptness, christened the era "The Gilded Age." Seizing the opportunities of wartime economic expansion and inflation, entrepreneurs amassed new wealth that they now sought to invest. They had not far to look. Technological advances opened thousands of new opportunities to put capital to work. Mills in Bethlehem and Pittsburgh, Pennsylvania, made use of the Bessemer Process in which oxygen was forced through molten iron to produce steel, a metal far more adaptable to manufacturing needs than iron. In the new oil industry, the perfection of refining techniques, the opening of the first pipeline, and John D. Rockefeller's mastery of competitive marketing techniques resulted in similarly strong growth. Industrial production in the country increased dramatically and natural resources, seemingly inexhaustible, were ruthlessly and often wastefully exploited. So, too, were industrial workers.

The iron horse symbolized the new age of energy. The 40,000 miles of railroad track laid in the decade after 1865 stimulated heavy industry and opened the farther West to agriculture. Food for an expanding army of industrial workers rolled eastward. Congress made loans and land grants that sped the construction of the Central Pacific Railroad eastward from California and the Union Pacific westward across the plains. For every mile of track laid, the railway company received 6,400 acres of free land. The government also made generous loans on second-mortgage bonds: $16,000 for each mile of level ground covered, $48,000 in the mountains, and $32,000 in the high plains. As the two roads raced for their share of the federal subsidies, they sacrificed quality to speed. Still, their accomplishment was spectacular. The Union Pacific built 1,089 miles of track; the Central Pacific, 689. They met at Promontory Point, west of Ogden, Utah. At ceremonies there on May 10, 1869, the blows of a silver sledge drove in the golden spikes connecting the rails. Now only a week's journey separated the Atlantic Ocean from the Pacific.

Foreign Affairs under Johnson National confidence also marked the able conduct of foreign relations by Secretary of State William H. Seward. During the war, the French under Napoleon III had affronted the Monroe Doctrine by setting up a puppet government in Mexico under the pliant and ambitious Austrian Archduke Maximilian. Fully occupied with fighting the Confederacy, Lincoln and Seward had denounced the French action but had been unable to challenge Napoleon's bid to restore French imperial power in the Western Hemisphere. Seward lost no time once the war was over. In 1866 President Johnson sent 50,000 veteran troops to the Mexican border, and Seward demanded the withdrawal of French forces. This bold action was of assistance to the Mexicans who, bravely asserting their independence, expelled the French.

A vigorous expansionist, Seward believed that trade with other countries would help convince the world of the superiority of American democracy. In 1868 he signed a treaty of friendship and commerce with China. In 1867 he negotiated a treaty to buy the Virgin Islands from Denmark for $7,500,000. The Senate rejected that treaty but at the same time approved one that Seward had arranged with Russia for the purchase of Alaska for $7,200,000. The tsar's government, with a territory already so vast that Alaska seemed superfluous, was reluctant to commit the naval forces necessary to protect its North American domain, which it did not want to fall into British hands. The Russian minister in Washington, Baron Edoard de Stoeckl, was inordinately fond of intrigue and enjoyed the machinations—including the bribing of some Representatives whose votes for the necessary appropriation were needed—which resulted in the completion of the sale. At the time, many Americans joked about Seward's "ice-box," for it seemed more a frozen wasteland than the immensely valuable state that it has become.

The Election of 1868 Members of Congress had been bold and imaginative in discussing social programs for the former slaves, but much of this constructive discourse had been reflected into strident criticism of President Johnson during the impeachment crisis. Not one of the senators or congressmen emerged as a strong national leader, and the Republicans, determined to win the White House, turned instead to the greatest of the war heroes, Ulysses S. Grant. At the war's end, both Johnsonian conservatives and congressional radicals had sought Grant as an ally. The general, while disclaiming any political ambition, was concerned about slipping back into the obscurity from which he had rescued himself during the Civil War. He wanted the presidency, the only office comparable to his exalted position as Commanding General during the war. Grant and his wife skillfully avoided any talk of the White House in 1864 so that President Lincoln had felt no usurping pressure, but they felt no such loyalty to President Johnson. Grant broke with the president in the Tenure of Office struggle and, thereby, persuaded the Radical

Republicans that he would be amenable to their policies. He was nominated by the Republican convention with Speaker of the House Schuyler Colfax of Indiana as the vice-presidential candidate.

Johnson's hope of creating a new national party had been dashed by his inability to bring Southern representatives loyal to his policies into the Congress, by his disastrous performance on the Swing Around the Circle in the election of 1866, and by his bitter quarrels with Congress that ended in the impeachment trial. The Democratic party looked not to him for a bid to retain the White House, but to Horatio Seymour, who had served as governor of New York during the war. For vice president they chose Francis P. Blair, Jr., a member of the famous Jacksonian political family who had been a Union general and could stoutly maintain that the Democrats were not a party of disloyalty. Determined to defeat "Black Reconstruction," their platform called for amnesty for former Confederates and restoration of their political rights, which would have resulted in the readmission of Mississippi, Virginia, and Texas, the last three states not represented in the Congress. With the intent of ending black officeholding and voting, the Democrats maintained that black suffrage should be left to the states.

The Democrats' only hope for victory was to focus public attention on the question of money and the repayment of the war debt, which was under hot debate. During the war, the government had issued some $450 million in greenbacks. The value of that currency had fluctuated over the years, but it was always below the value of coins and gold-backed currency. Attacking McCulluch's retirement of greenbacks, the Democrats adopted the "Ohio Idea," sponsored by George H. Pendleton, congressman from that state, who demanded that the notes be reissued to redeem outstanding war bonds not explicitly requiring redemption in gold. This demand for cheap money appealed to debtors, especially farmers with long-term mortgages who stood to benefit from inflation. It appealed also to critics of the war profiteers who had speculated in the bonds. The Republicans, on the other hand, pledged themselves to the redemption of the national debt in gold. They knew that conservative financiers would approve this adherence to sound money. Grant and his advisors were listening to these hard-money men and not to the farmers whose debts would be harder to pay if money increased in value or to wage earners who would find jobs harder to get if there was less money in circulation and, therefore, fewer buyers for the goods they might produce. The Republicans were hoping that both the farmers and the workers would remember the passions of war vividly enough to distrust the Democrats' amnesty proposal for the South. With this strategy, the Republican party turned its back on the working-class people whom some of its founders and many of its more radical members during Reconstruction had vowed to protect.

In the campaign of 1868, the Republicans, with extravagant rhetoric, concentrated on the alleged treason of the Democrats and waved the "bloody shirt" of war to demonstrate their own valor. They knew they could count on the support of the Southern states where black voters, as well as federal officeholders, both local and from the North, were loyal to the party of liberation and Union. The Democrats lost whatever appeal they might have enjoyed from the Ohio Idea when Seymour repudiated that plank in the platform. Even with all their advantages, however, including Grant's great popularity, the Republican victory was not a landslide. Grant carried the Electoral College by 214 votes to 80 but received only 53 percent of the popular vote. Using violent intimidation of black voters Seymour carried Louisiana and Georgia and showed strength in all the border states. Mississippi, Virginia, and Texas had not been readmitted to the Congress, and their votes were not counted. The most interesting facet of the election was that black men voted in significant numbers in a national election for the first time. Grant did not owe his victory to them, but without them he would have had only a minority of the popular vote. He owed them a political debt.

THE GRANT ERA

Government under Grant An immensely popular war hero was in the White House, and members of his own party were in the majority in both houses of Congress, while Lincoln appointees made up a majority of members of the Supreme Court. Nothing, it seemed, could stand in the way of a Republican triumph for Reconstruction now that the frustrating battles with President Johnson were over. And yet, black Americans, who had the highest hopes as Grant entered the White House, saw their aspirations severely curtailed by the time he moved out. This trend was foreshadowed as early as 1869 when Secretary of War John A. Rawlins, the only true champion of black rights in the original Grant Cabinet, died of tuberculosis.

Rawlins had been Grant's chief of staff during the war and, more important, he had been a friend who was not afraid to criticize his commander. With his death in September 1869, Grant lost not only his wisest counselor on public issues, but also an intimate friend who might have helped the president achieve a greater sense of purpose. Rawlins was replaced by William W. Belknap, a weak and, it turned out, corrupt man of little intelligence. Unfortunately, Belknap and not Rawlins was typical of the many men who sat in the Grant Cabinet. One exception was Secretary of State Hamilton Fish, an elegant, honest, quiet, and intelligent former Whig from New York. Fish was, however, unsympathetic toward people of a color other than his own and was wary not only of the freedmen in the South but also of insurgents in Cuba who tried vainly to get support from the United States government. He also was only barely tolerant of President Grant's almost obsessive determination to annex the Dominican Republic, a goal that was frustrated by the Senate, led by the chairman of the Foreign Relations Committee, Charles Sumner. Grant thought that black Americans, frustrated in their attempts to establish themselves satisfactorily in the South, might move to the island and establish a black state. Both people who wanted the former slaves to succeed within the Union and those who did not were highly dubious of the proposed segregated state. Although his break with the president over this issue was to cost Sumner his chairmanship of the Foreign Relations Committee, the Senator blocked annexation.

Fish proved himself to be a master of diplomacy when conducting American relations with Europe. The greatest problem facing him in that sphere arose from the wartime claims of the United States that the British government had permitted their shipbuilders to supply the Confederacy with warships that had done great damage to Union cargo ships. The most famous of these Confederate raiders was the *Alabama,* and the complaints to Britain about their raids were called the Alabama Claims. Senator Sumner was, as Massachusetts politicians with Irish-American constituents are apt to be, an outspoken critic of England, and called not only for reparations equal to the lost cargoes, but for "indirect claims"—vast sums to compensate for losses to the Union caused, indirectly, by the raiders.

Fish, skillfully sidestepping the sensitive and difficult Sumner, conducted gentlemanly negotiations with the British minister to Washington. Under the Treaty of Washington of 1871, the claims were referred to an international board of arbitration. Charles Francis Adams was the leading member of the commission that presented the American case to the board which determined that Britain should apologize and pay the United States $15,500,000 to cover the direct claims. Britain did so and not only was a major crisis in Anglo-American relations resolved but also a much-neglected precedent for the peaceful settlement of international disputes was established.

While these negotiations were under way, the nation was treated to a far less edifying spectacle. During the postwar boom in transcontinental railroad building, the press revealed in the fall of 1872 that prominent members of Congress had accepted bribes, in the form of stock, in return for promises not to investigate Crédit Mobilier, a corporation established to build the Union Pacific Railroad. Crédit Mobilier's purpose was not to get the road built, but to divert profits from building contracts to the Union Pacific's promoters. The fraudulent enterprise was conducted blatantly and exposed. Though many members of Congress, including Vice President Schuyler Colfax and future president James A. Garfield, were tainted by the scandal, only Congressman Oakes Ames was censured by the House for his leading role in the unethical business. Save for the involvement of the vice president, (Colfax was replaced by Henry Wilson as the Republican candidate for vice president in 1872) the congressional scandal did not touch the White House, but the Grant administration could take small comfort in that omission. Evidence of greed had already been revealed within the executive mansion itself in a scandal that involved members of the president's own family.

In the fall of 1869, James Fisk, Jr., and Jay Gould, two bold and unscrupulous young speculators, had attempted to corner the gold market on the basis of inside information about the governments' handling of the money supply, which they claimed they were receiving from their partner, Abel R. Corbin, President Grant's brother-in-law. The price of gold was bid up to dizzying heights, but when Grant learned that his sister and very possibly his wife were carrying speculative gold accounts, he moved, effectively, to bring the market under control. He and Secretary of the Treasury George Boutwell, one of the honest and able members of his Cabinet, sold $4 million in gold at a time that the insiders were claiming the government would not do so. That sale caused the market to recede suddenly. When the crash came on "Black Friday," September 24, 1869, many investors were ruined, but Gould and Fisk were not. The gold market, which fluctuated in part because of the variable value of the greenbacks, was steadied and no general economic collapse occurred.

In their management of the money supply, Grant and Boutwell, ignoring their party's espousal of the gold standard, counted on the continued use of the greenbacks issued during the war. In 1870, however, in *Hepburn* v. *Griswold* the Supreme Court decided that the wartime act stipulating that contracts could be discharged by greenbacks—which had a shifting value—as well as by the currency originally stipulated, was unconstitutional. The administration wanted the decision reversed and Grant's first two appointments to the Supreme Court (after Edwin M. Stanton had died before being seated and E. R. Hoar had been rejected by the Senate) were men known to favor continued use of the greenbacks. In 1871, with new Justices William Strong and Joseph P. Bradley voting with the majority, the Supreme Court held, in the second *Legal Tender Case,* that the wartime currency could be used to pay debts currently and was not legal simply during the years of military emergency. Although the Strong and Bradley votes were often pointed to as the product of a corrupt conspiracy, some observers have noted that there is nothing unethical about a president's appointment of justices who agree with administration policy.

Corruption was not confined to Washington and Wall Street. At City Hall in New York, "Boss" William Marcy Tweed relieved the city of an estimated $200 million. That figure included the proceeds from fraudulent bond issues and the sale of franchises as well as graft collected from corrupt contractors and merchants dealing directly with the city government. Since the governor of New York was a Tweed henchman, the "Boss," though a Democrat himself, had little trouble silencing the Republican legislature with bribes. Control of the police, the courts, and the district attorney made Tweed almost invulnerable. At last, when the city was nearly bankrupt, Samuel J. Tilden successfully challenged Tweed for control of the Democratic organization in the city. Tilden gained a national reputation for having "smashed" the ring. Tweed's was only the most notorious of the party machines; others operated in Philadelphia, Chicago, and Washington. In their heyday they had little trouble winning the cooperation of otherwise reputable public figures.

Southern state governments were under particular scrutiny by observers of corruption who hoped to discredit black lawmakers who differed very little from their white colleagues. Although there were more black citizens than white in three states, no black man was elected governor. Only in South Carolina did black people make up a majority in one house of the legislature for one session. Two men, Hiram R. Revels, a dignified clergyman, and Blanche K. Bruce, a skillful politician, were sent to the Senate by Mississippi and 15 black men entered the House of Representatives. These gains were significant, but they did not represent political dominance. Many Southern whites condemned what they called "Black Reconstruction" simply because they objected to any black participation in the political life of the South, and they seized upon any incident of corruption to discredit Republican rule.

In the South, as elsewhere, there were such incidents. Bold efforts to rebuild the South's transportation system foundered in the end on the wholesale theft of railroad stock. In South Carolina the land commission designed to help blacks buy farms ended up as a device for transferring state funds to the private accounts of unscrupulous assessors and their friends in high places. "Damn it," expostulated Henry Clay Warmoth, carpetbag governor of Louisiana and one of the worst spoilers, "everybody is demoralized down here. Corruption is the fashion." He had a point. But it took two to make a deal, and many of those who bribed the legislature for favors were native Southerners and Democrats.

Black people, seldom the beneficiaries of these schemes, were learning to survive in a white world. Nevertheless, the presence of black politicians in the legislatures and their loyalty to the carpetbag Republicans enabled disfranchised white citizens to blame corruption on the experiment in political equality. Even the performance of the honest and efficient Radical government of Mississippi and of remarkable black leaders like South Carolina's Secretary of State Francis Cardozo changed few opinions. Political association with black voters and carpetbaggers became increasingly suspect among Southern white people. Scalawags found themselves ostracized by their neighbors. As one former Whig planter explained when he withdrew from the Republican party, a man with four marriageable daughters could do no less.

If social pressure could block some democratic goals, there were others that were achieved. The Fifteenth Amendment, put forward by the more radical Republicans in February 1869 and supported by President Grant when he was inaugurated, was ratified on March 30, 1870. It forbade the states to deny the right to vote "on account of race, color, or previous condition of servitude." Its sponsors hoped it would prevent unfriendly legislatures from disfranchising freedmen in the future; those hopes were later dashed. The amendment's most immediate effect was to enfranchise Northern black citizens since black Southerners were already voters under the new state constitutions.

Proponents of the amendment hoped it would give a strong signal that the ballot box was designed to provide the freedmen with sufficient access to those chosen to govern them to protect them from violence.

The Ku Klux Klan In Pulaski, Tennessee, just after the passage of the Civil Rights Bill of 1866, white men, determined to intimidate their black neighbors and force them into submission, founded the Ku Klux Klan. General Nathan Bedford Forrest was the grand wizard of the secret terrorist organization that operated outside the law and soon had dens, led by grand cyclops, across the South. The Klan's strength increased in direct proportion to Southern black citizens' assertions of their rights, overlapping memberships made the Klan the military arm of the Democratic party in many areas. As the freedmen responded to the opportunities presented by both federal legislation passed to implement the three constitutional Reconstruction amendments and their own state constitutions, the Klan reacted with rides in the night. A tortured corpse was a grim warning to an aspiring citizen who might be considering starting his own farm or running for office.

Shortly after the ratification of the Fifteenth Amendment, Congress created the Justice Department and gave the attorney general a staff of lawyers with which he could prosecute violators of the new federal civil rights legislation. Grant's first attorney general, E. R. Hoar, had not favored aggressive federal action in the civil rights field, but his successor, Amos T. Akerman, appointed with the backing of Southern Republicans, was a native of New Hampshire who had long lived in the South and had been a colonel in the Confederate army. He knew the Klan at first hand in his home country of north Georgia. Congressmen also learned about the Klan through extensive hearings. In the spring of 1871, with the active support of President Grant, Congress enacted the strong Ku Klux Klan Act designed specifically to bring those who attacked black people into the federal courts.

Akerman, assisted by able United States attorneys located in the South, directed the prosecution of cases that were heard by conscientious federal judges, most notably Hugh L. Bond. In some areas, such as North Carolina, cases against the Klan were so well prepared and promptly heard that the violence was restrained. But in South Carolina no jury would convict a white man, and freed Klansmen took terrible reprisals on people who had appeared as witnesses in their trials. Precisely because he was a general, President Grant was reluctant to use the army to maintain civilian order, but in 1871, under the provisions of the Ku Klux Klan Act, he lifted the writ of habeas corpus in nine counties of South Carolina. Akerman worked closely with carefully chosen army officers who arrested violators and held them for trial. Elsewhere across the South, federal marshals also brought Klansmen to court. These vigorous prosecutions and the resulting convictions continued after Akerman, under pressure both from opponents of his civil rights policy and from railroad men who disliked his stern scrutiny of their activities, was forced to resign. The 600 convictions, and threats of more, did much to break up the Klan as an organized force. Black voters felt free to participate in the election of 1872, but more intimidation lay ahead.

The Liberal Republican Movement As the 1872 election approached, Grant's popularity was still great, but the strongest challenge to his reelection came not from the opposition Democrats, but from dissidents within his own party. Those who led it have been called, in an apt phrase, "the best men"—well-educated gentlemen who deplored disorder and corruption and wanted not so much government by

Amos T. Akerman, attorney general from Georgia

the people as government, good government, they insisted, for the people.

As they looked around, they saw a lack of intellectual force in the government and corruption reaching into city halls, state legislative chambers, the houses of Congress, and even the White House. They also considered the use of military officers to assist in the Ku Klux Klan cases to have been the exercise of military rather than civilian rule. In the increasingly high tariffs that fed the profits of newly rich industrialists and the unrestrained supply of greenbacks, they saw a failure to observe the "laws" of liberal capitalism expounded by Adam Smith and John Stuart Mill.

Liberal Republicans proposed cures for all these problems. In commercial matters, they would follow the principles of free trade, redeem the greenbacks, and establish a stable currency, even though this might be painful in credit-starved agricultural areas of the country. In the South, where their disgust with the Klan was matched by their dislike and distrust of black people, they would restore governing responsibilities to "thinking people," men like themselves who, before the war, had maintained order in the region. In the matter of corruption in government, they put forth their favorite proposal, civil service reform. Only people of merit would be allowed to work for the government; they hoped that both bribery and stupidity would be banished. In the process, the absence of formal education credentials might result in the loss of the toehold that African-American clerks had made in government offices.

Senator Carl Schurz of Missouri, a German immigrant, who was both an intellectual and a war hero, led the revolt. By 1872, Missouri Liberals had been joined by anti-Grant midwestern Republicans, War Democrats (particularly in Ohio), and patricians in the northeast. Two brilliant journalists, E. L. Godkin, the British editor at *The Nation* and Henry Adams, grandson and greatgrandson of presidents, who edited *The North American Review,* added lustre to the cause. Adams's father, Charles Francis Adams, the patriarch of the movement, hoped for the presidential nomination, which it would be beneath his dignity to seek, but the Liberals' convention in Cincinnati in 1872 proved more chaotic than reverential and made the quixotic choice of Horace Greeley for president.

Greeley, editor at the influential *New York Tribune,* was a bright and interesting man, but political consistency was not one of his virtues. His advocacy of high tariffs made a mockery of the Liberals' antiprotectionist doctrine, his long-held antislavery positions made him unattractive to voters who wanted to hear no more of racial problems and, as an editor, he had long excorciated the Democrats, whose support he now needed. What was more, he was almost the antithesis of the charismatic political candidate. In an unprecedented move, the Democratic party fielded no candidate of its own and instead endorsed Greeley.

Grant and his allies were smart enough politicians not to be complacent. The president took a stance above the battle, from which he could keep his eye on every happening in the campaign, while his loyalists again waved "the bloody shirt" of the regular Republicans' patriotism. On posters, Ulysses Grant and Henry Wilson were pictured as "the tanner and the cobbler." Grant had hated working in his father's tannery and his senatorial running mate, who had once been apprenticed to a shoemaker, had not made many shoes lately, but they did make a strong and successful appeal for the working-class vote. They got this support despite evidence that Grant had long depended on and favored some of the richest of the nation's capitalists. In appealing to the working class, the Republicans stole much of the thunder of the nascent National Labor Reform party. The voters, somewhat bemused by Greeley and his erudite supporters and still intensely loyal to General Grant, as most people called their president, gave him a strong reelection victory. Greeley's death a few weeks after the election symbolized the demise of the Liberal Republican movement.

The Collapse On September 18, 1873, Jay Cooke & Company failed. The pious banker, who had successfully sold government bonds to finance the war, overextended his bank in his efforts to sell securities of the Northern Pacific Railway. Once again, such a failure, and the panic that ensued, exposed weakness in the whole of the economy, most notably in railroad speculations and in the European market for agricultural exports. Many of the huge European investments in American western expansions were withdrawn at the time of the Franco-Prussian War of 1870–71. The result was a depression of great severity which, by some reckonings, lasted six years; other economists link it to the nation's economic difficulties that persisted until the end of the century. One of the immediate results in 1873, when many banks failed, was the collapse of the Freedman's Savings Bank. Its investments had been managed by Henry D. Cooke, who sold conservative securities, bought speculative issues, and made high-risk loans. As the bank's troubles grew fatal, Frederick Douglass (brought in, many said, so that a black man could be blamed when failure came) was made head of the bank by the white trustees to restore depositors' confidence. When the bank closed its doors, thousands of poor black people found that their passbooks, recording hard-earned small deposits, were worthless. Efforts to get the Congress to make compensation for the losses in the bank, which it had sponsored, were to no avail.

The nation's economic problems, coupled with the continuing reports of scandals within the ranks of the Grant administration and the Republican party, enabled the Democrats to regain control of the House of Representatives in the election of 1874 for the first time since before the Civil War. As the new majority took its seats in 1875, investigations were launched into each of the Cabinet departments. The most serious allegations were made against George M. Robeson, secretary of the Navy, who had received what amounted to bribes from naval suppliers; Columbus Delano, secretary of the interior, whose son sold surveying contracts; and William W. Belknap, who regularly accepted payments from the holders of lucrative Indian trading posts. Robeson rode out the storm, but Delano was forced to resign, and the House voted a bill of impeachment against Belknap. In the summer of 1876, when other Americans were celebrating at the great Centennial Exposition in Philadelphia, which featured the immense and varied manufacturing capacities of the Republic, Washingtonians were treated to a dramatic impeachment trial in the Senate. The evidence against Belknap was indisputable, and he won acquittal only because President Grant had accepted his hasty resignation just hours before the House voted the indictment that led to the Senate's trial. The senators, therefore, were not trying an incumbent official and to save Belknap enough senators concluded that, despite his guilt, they lacked jurisdiction over the case.

As sorry as these scandals were, another struck closer to Grant personally. His private secretary, Orville Babcock, was shown to have been directly involved in widespread and lucrative schemes to defraud the government of taxes on the production of whiskey. Even when Attorney General Benjamin H. Bristow confronted Grant with damning evidence, Grant refused to fire Babcock. Instead, feeling under siege himself, he came to despise Bristow. Knowing of his secretary's guilt, the president nevertheless gave Chief Justice Waite, whom he had appointed following the death in 1873 of Chief Justice Chase, a deposition which, when read in Babcock's trial in St. Louis, won his acquittal. After the trial, Hamilton Fish was appalled to find Babcock at work as usual in the White House. The secretary of state persuaded Grant to send Babcock off to inspect lighthouses, but his demotion, like Belknap's resignation, was not enough to save the moral reputation of the Grant administration.

The still-popular president, often talked about for a third term, was neither put forward as a strong contender for renomination nor permitted to control the choice of his successor. Grant took only slight comfort in the fact that the Republican convention passed up Bristow and gave the nomination to the pious and innocuous Rutherford B. Hayes. When they left the White House, the Grants, feeling homeless, set off on a two-and-one-half-year trip around the world.

The End of Reconstruction The greatest tragedy of the Grant era was not the corruption on which a frustrated nation fixed its attention, but the failure to complete the basic work of Reconstruction. In the end, the physical safety of the former slaves was bought only at the cost of the deprivation of their economic independence and political equality. White supremacy was reasserted through a combination of political chicanery and outright physical violence.

A handful of neighbors riding to a family's remote cabin to murder or torment a man unwilling to be quiet about his rights as a worker and voter, or an organized band of Ku Klux Klansmen spreading terror across a county—each gave evidence that violence would not be avoided if it were needed to drive black citizens back into a subordinate position in the South. Army officers in the Freedmen's Bureau or under the direction of a military district commander and the Justice Department had been able to prevent some of this violence. More was stopped when black citizens could count on the support of local black sheriffs or other politicians participating in the integrated administrations that were governing the Southern states. The white supremacists concluded that it would take violence, skillfully directed, to break the power of these administrations and reestablish white domination.

Their method, differently, but effectively, applied in several states, came to be called the "Mississippi Plan." In 1875, Mississippi had a carpetbag governor, Adelbert Ames, a Union general from Maine; a scalawag senator, James L. Alcorn, a native planter who had been willing, to a degree, to cooperate with his black constituents; and a black senator, Blanche K. Bruce. One of the state's congressmen, John R. Lynch, was black, as were members of the state legislature, sheriffs, and other local officials. The "white liners"

Adelbert Ames, from Maine to Mississippi

had their work cut out for them. In an off-year election campaign that fall, they proved equal to the task. Instead of refusing to engage in politics as long as black citizens held the vote, the white supremacists now reentered politics determined to dominate the black voters. The Democratic party was frank about its aim: its slogan, printed prominently in the *Yazoo City Democrat,* the *Hinds County Gazette,* and the *Aberdeen Examiner,* was "Carry the election peaceably if we can, forcibly if we must."

In town after town across the state, the Democrats organized in a disciplined way and not only put forward their "white line" candidates forcefully, but demonstrated what their opponents could expect if they continued to resist. In Macon, as investigating Senators were later told, the Republican candidate for county treasurer was "shot down walking on the pavements, shot by the democrats" because he was running for office and "because he made a speech and said he never did expect to vote a democratic ticket, and also advised the colored citizens to do the same." Such murders were carefully reported in order to frighten voters in neighboring towns. The survivors of a bloody assault on a Republican meeting in Clinton fled to Jackson and begged Governor Ames to protect them. When he asked the president for federal troops to provide that protection, still another of Grant's attorneys general, Edwards Pierrepont, replied: "The whole public are tired of these autumnal outbursts in the South." He told the governor to first exhaust all local means of keeping order, all of which had already proved insufficient.

When election day came, there was no violence. There was no need for any; the intimidation had worked. Democrats were elected to a majority in both houses of the state legislature and Governor Ames was impeached and removed from office. Neither Senator Bruce nor Senator Alcorn was reelected. Neither was Congressman Lynch, although he regained his seat for a term in the 1880s and long remained a symbol of the reluctance of black citizens to play a docile role in politics.

Conservatives had already regained control in Georgia, Tennessee, North Carolina, and Virginia when first Texas in 1873, and then Arkansas and Alabama in 1874 were "redeemed" by Democratic exponents of white superiority. With the recapture of Mississippi in 1875, only Louisiana, Florida, and South Carolina remained in Radical hands. They rejoined the other states of the old Confederacy as a result of the election of 1876 (see p. 422). In South Carolina, a gentleman planter and former Confederate general, Wade Hampton, was elected governor with the help of the Red Shirts, a band that had studied the Mississippi Plan well.

The Redeemers had succeeded in ending Reconstruction, but they had had a potent ally. Poverty was less overtly cruel than violence but no less an effective way of limiting the lives of poor but free people. In many cases Southern farmers who had owned many slaves, who had owned none, or who had been slaves were willing to share their corner of the region with each other. But, as each group struggled to scratch out a living, the competition for spare markets led landlords, seeking the cheapest possible labor force, to drive a wedge of hatred between impoverished white and black workers. In the rest of the nation, the white majority gave up trying to define a humane policy favorable to the former slaves and turned its attention to other matters. The promises that Reconstruction had held out to black Americans as well as the aspirations they cherished were not forgotten, but their fulfillment was long deferred.

SUGGESTIONS FOR READING

GENERAL

E. Foner, *Reconstruction: America's Unfinished Revolution, 1863–1877* (1988), tells in rich detail the full story of emancipation and its aftermath, drawing both on the extensive monographic literature on the period and his own archival research. Like Foner, W. L. Rose understands that Reconstruction began early in the war. Her *Rehearsal for Reconstruction: The Port Royal Experiment* (1964), is a brilliant assessment of both the possibilities and limitations which the freed people confronted. An eloquent and radical account of the period is W. E. B. DuBois, *Black Reconstruction in America* (1935), and the opposite point of view is represented by C. G. Bowers, *The Tragic Era* (1929). Essential to an understanding of the former slaves' problems and aspirations is the series I. Berlin, ed. *Freedom* cited at close of Chapter 14.

THE PRESIDENT AND CONGRESS

H. L. Trefousse, *Andrew Johnson: A Biography* (1989), and W. S. McFeely, *Grant: A Biography* (1981) treat the postwar Reconstruction presidents. M. L. Benedict, *A Compromise of Principle: Congressional Republicans, 1863–1869* (1974), *The Impeachment and Trial of Andrew Johnson* (1973) are studies of Congress.

JUDICIAL ISSUES

Constitutional changes of the period are treated in H. M. Hyman, *A More Perfect Union* (1973), and S. I. Kutler, *The Judicial Power and Reconstruction Politics* (1968). The most thorough study of the Supreme Court in this period is C. Fairman, *Reconstruction and Reunion, 1864–88* (1987), and see J. B. James, *The Framing of the Fourteenth Amendment* (1956). A searching, critical examination of the motivation behind the Fifteenth Amendment is W. Gillette, *The Right to Vote* (1969), and see his *Retreat from Reconstruction* (1979). An important study is H. Belz, *Emancipation and Equal Rights: Politics and Constitutionalism in the Civil War Era* (1978).

POSTWAR SOUTH

D. T. Carter, *When the War Was Over* (1985), is a fine starting point. On individual states some of the best works are V. L. Wharton, *The Negro in Mississippi, 1865–1890* (1947); on South Carolina, W. L. Rose, *Rehearsal for Reconstruction: The Port Royal Experiment* (1964); J. Williamson, *After Slavery: The Negro in South Carolina During Reconstruction, 1861–1877* (1965), T. C. Holt, *Black over White: Negro Political Leadership in South Carolina during Reconstruction* (1979), on Georgia, C. L. Mohr, *On the Threshold of Freedom: Masters and Slaves in Civil Georgia* (1986), and R. Duncan, *Freedom's Shore: Tunis Campbell and the Georgia Freedmen* (1986); and, on Louisiana, J. G. Taylor, *Louisiana Reconstructed, 1863–1877* (1974), J. Blassingame, *Black New Orleans, 1860–1880* (1973), P. McCrary, *Abraham Lincoln and Reconstruction: The Louisiana Experiment* (1978), and C. P. Ripley, *Slaves and Freedmen in Civil War Louisiana* (1976). Perceptive essays on emancipation are in E. Foner, *Politics and Ideology in the Age of the Civil War* (1980); see also his brilliant *Nothing but Freedom: Emancipation and its Legacy* (1983). Also see G. Jaynes, *Branches without Roots: Genesis of the Black Workingclass in the American South* (1986).

The Freedmen's Bureau is treated in W. E. B. DuBois, "Of the Dawn of Freedom," *The Souls of Black Folk* (1903); G. R. Bentley, *A History of the Freedmen's Bureau* (1955); and W. S. McFeely, *Yankee Stepfather: General O. O. Howard and the Freedmen* (1968). Northerners in the postwar South are the subject of L. N. Powell, *New Masters: Northern Planters during the Civil War and Reconstruction* (1980); Otto Olsen, *Carpetbagger's Crusade: The Life of Albion Winegar Tourgee* (1965); Richard N. Current, *Those Terrible Carpetbaggers* (1988); and J. Jones, *Soldiers of Light and Love: Northern Teachers and Georgia Blacks, 1865–1873* (1980). Four studies cast much light on the transition from slavery to freedom: J. L. Roark, *Masters Without Slaves: Southern Planters in the Civil War and Reconstruction* (1977); R. Higgs, *Competition and Coercion: Blacks in the American Economy, 1865–1914* (1977); L. F. Litwack, *Been in the Storm So Long: The Aftermath of Slavery* (1980); and V. Harding, *There Is a River: The Black Struggle for Freedom in America* (1981).

Southern resistance to Reconstruction is illuminated in M. Perman, *Reunion Without Compromise: The South and Reconstruction, 1865–1868* (1973), and his *The Road to Redemption: Southern Politics, 1869–1880* (1984), as well as A. W. Trelease, *White Terror: The Ku Klux Klan Conspiracy and Southern Reconstruction* (1971). S. Hahn, *The Roots of Southern Populism* (1983), examines the poverty of Southern white farmers and their attempts to find a constructive voice of protest.

ECONOMY

Essential are G. Wright, *Old South, New South: Revolutions in the Southern Economy Since the Civil War* (1986), and M. Summer *Railroads, Reconstruction, and the Gospel of Prosperity* (1984). D. Montgomery, *Beyond Equality* studies the attempt of working people to make the Reconstruction revolution of the former slaves theirs as well.

END OF RECONSTRUCTION

For the breakdown of Northern support of Reconstruction, see W. S. McFeely, *Grant: A Biography* (1981); the scathing, racist view of black legislators by J. S. Pike, an abolitionist who visited South Carolina and wrote *The Prostrate State* (1874); and V. L. Wharton, *The Negro in Mississippi, 1865–1890* (1965). For black farmers who gave up on the South, see N. I. Painter, *Exodusters: Black Migration to Kansas after Reconstruction* (1986). D. W. Griffith, *Birth of a Nation* (1915), is a film classic that all too successfully imprinted a racist view of Reconstruction on the American conscience.

CHAPTER SIXTEEN

COTTON TO MARKET: THE SOUTH WAS STILL RURAL

THE NEW SOUTH: REUNION AND READJUSTMENT

The first centennial anniversary of American independence made 1876 a time of reckoning as well as a year for celebration. Ceremonies of commemoration, centering at the International Exhibition in Philadelphia, went forward with due pomp and display. But citizens who took thought about just what there was to celebrate in this particular year must have been troubled by their reflections. The safest theme was material progress. Surely the nation was richer, bigger, stronger, and more populous under General U. S. Grant than it had been in the time of General George Washington. Furthermore, it had survived a terrible Civil War and had emerged from that ordeal with the Union restored, with a stronger central government, and with slavery abolished. All these were valid reasons for celebration, and patriots dwelt on them gratefully, to the exclusion of themes that were less safe and more painful. Yet even the "safe" themes of material and political progress exposed their uglier aspects during the centennial year.

On the material side the national economy slumped toward the bottom of the longest and most severe depression up to that time. In national politics the year 1876 was noted for the exposure of scandals and corrupt deals that completed the disgrace of President Grant's administration, the most shameful of the century. The same year witnessed a presidential election with the most doubtful and disputed results on record. As seamy and sordid in their politics as the national and state governments, many of the country's cities were also disgraced by gigantic slums filled with disease and human misery. Those who celebrated the rise of the new industrial establishment—a central theme of the Philadelphia Exhibition—had to admit that a great part of its factories and furnaces and work force stood idle throughout the centennial year.

Both those who looked to the West—traditional avenue of escape—and those concerned about the South—perennial source of conflict—had cause for dismay in 1876. Two violent events a few days apart at the peak of the centennial celebration symbolized these troubles in the West and in the South. On June 25 General George A. Custer and 265 of his troops were wiped out in battle with Sioux Indians in Montana; and on July 4, in Hamburg, South Carolina, a pitched battle between black militia and armed white terrorists, was followed by the murder of four black prisoners. It was a rough time for a national birthday party. In 1876 Herman Melville's poem "Clarel" viewed the present as one "Dead level of rank commonplace" and a future "In the Dark Ages of Democracy."

SECTIONAL COMPROMISE RESTORED

For the South, 1876 proved to be a turning point. For sixteen years, ever since Fort Sumter, North and South had settled their differences by armed force—not only during the four years of war but in some measure during the twelve years that followed. And while a great deal of compromise of principle and conciliation of the white South and Northern racism had gone into Reconstruction, in the last resort military force was still available—and still used. For example, after the bloody outbreak in Hamburg, South Carolina, President Grant reversed his policy of no further military intervention and ordered the army into that state to maintain order. More federal soldiers were in the state than at any period since the war by the time of the presidential election. That election, but more particularly the crisis over inaugurating the disputed winner, unexpectedly provided the opportunity to put an end to the policy of force and adherence to principle, and to reinstate the tradition of compromise in sectional disputes on the classic model of 1850. This would mean the end of Reconstruction and the start of a new era.

The Electoral Crisis of 1876 It looked like a good year for the Democrats. Republican prospects for 1876 had been clouded by economic depression, political scandals, and growing reaction against Grant's Southern policy. The elections of 1874 had returned the Democrats to control of the House of Representatives for the first time since the Civil War. During the next two years the depression that had started in 1873 deepened, and discontent increased. The Republicans themselves were divided into factions over Reconstruction policy. Reformers, later known as "mugwumps" (p. 512), continued to fill newspapers with exposure of scandals in the Grant administration.

The Republicans nominated Rutherford B. Hayes of Ohio. Three times governor of his state, Hayes had a creditable war record, an unblemished reputation, and an association with mild civil service reform. In short, he was the ideal nominee for a party bedeviled by smirched reputations and beset by scandal. Of Whig antecedents and puritanical conscience, Hayes was conservative in his economic and financial views, and conciliatory toward Southern white citizens. To balance the ticket, the Republicans chose Congressman William A. Wheeler of New York for vice president.

Stressing the issue of reform, the Democrats nominated Samuel J. Tilden, governor of New York. Before his election to the governorship in 1874, Tilden had won fame by helping to smash the notorious ring of Boss Tweed, head of Tammany Hall, and by sending Tweed and others to jail; as governor, he had shattered a powerful organization of grafters known as the Canal Ring. Tilden had made a private fortune as a corporation lawyer serving railroads, and his conservative economic views and hard-money doctrines were more pleasing to the business community of the East than they were to the South and the West. Popular enthusiasm for Tilden's candidacy was further limited by his railroad associations, his secretive habits, and his poor health. In order to make up for these drawbacks, the Democrats named for vice president Thomas A. Hendricks of Indiana, who had served his state as senator and governor and held soft-money views.

The campaign of 1876 was a struggle of exceptional bitterness and trickery. When the returns came in, the Democrats seemed to have carried the day, for the majority of popular ballots were cast for Tilden with nearly a quarter of a million to spare. And, while Tilden was conceded 184 electoral votes, only one vote short of the 185 required for election, Hayes was conceded only 165 (see Map 16-1). But 19 of the 20 contested electoral votes lay in the three Southern states that were still under Republican government—South Carolina, Louisiana, and Florida. The 20th vote, from the Republican state of Oregon, was claimed by the Democrats on a technicality. Tilden needed only one of the 20 votes to assure his election, while Hayes had to have them all to win a bare majority of one vote. Republican managers promptly claimed all the votes and announced a Hayes victory. Charging that the Democrats had used intimidation and fraud against black voters, Republican returning boards in the three Southern states threw out enough Democratic popular votes to give those states to Hayes. Both parties had resorted to chicanery in the election, but modern scholars hold that Tilden deserved more than enough of the contested votes to win. On December 6, Republican electors met and cast the votes of the three states for Hayes, but on the same day a rival set of Democratic electors cast the votes of the same states solidly for Tilden.

Congress, with a Democratic House and a Republican Senate, now had to decide which returns were authentic and which candidate had won. The Consti-

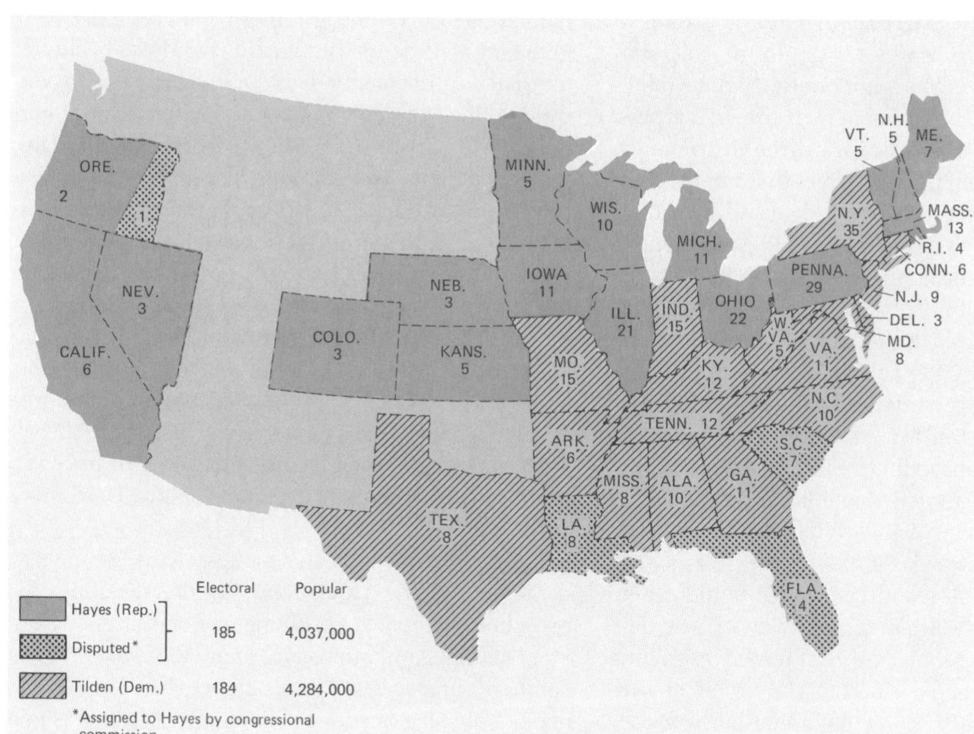

Map 16-1
The election of 1876

tution was not explicit on who should count the electoral votes, and the law was silent. To break the deadlock, a compromise was worked out between the political parties—but not between the sections. That came later.

The solution proposed by moderate congressmen was to refer the disputed returns to an electoral commission created for the purpose, consisting of fifteen members drawn in equal numbers from the Senate, the House, and the Supreme Court. Seven were to be Republicans, seven Democrats, and one was expected to be Justice David Davis, an independent. Counting on Justice Davis to break the tie in their favor, Democrats supported the measure. At the last moment, however, Davis was elected United States senator by the Illinois legislature, and his place on the commission was filled by a Republican justice of the Supreme Court. The commission then decided by strictly partisan votes of 8 to 7 to accept the Republican returns for all 20 contested electoral votes. This in effect removed Tilden from the race and authorized the election of his opponent. But to seat Hayes required formal action of the House, and there it met resistance from the Democratic majority. Enraged by what they denounced as a "conspiracy" to defraud them of their victory, many Democrats refused to abide by the vote of the commission and staged a filibuster that threatened to prevent any election whatever and bring on anarchy. It was during this anxious interval of three weeks before inauguration day that the sectional compromise was worked out.

The Compromise of 1877 There could be no doubt that the majority of Southern white citizens wanted Tilden elected president. That would have guaranteed what they called "home rule" and other favors for the South. When it began to appear that Tilden was destined to be the loser, however, Southern leaders determined to salvage what they could out of defeat. Southern conservatives, some of Whig background, approached like-minded friends of Hayes, himself a former Whig, with offers of help in the electoral crisis and the possibility of future political support in exchange for a firm Republican commitment to "home rule" in the Southern states. In the short run, that meant withdrawal of the federal troops that sustained the Republican governments of South Carolina and

Louisiana in power, governments with as strong a claim to legitimacy as Hayes's claim to the electoral votes of those states. More important, "home rule" meant Republican abandonment of freedmen, carpetbaggers, scalawags, and Radicals, and the virtual nullification of the Fourteenth and Fifteenth Amendments and the Civil Rights Act. In short, it meant forfeiting many of the fruits of the Civil War and Reconstruction and, some thought, the honor of the Republican party. Had such a commitment been made by Tilden, a Democrat, it would have lacked the authority and permanence it gained by Republican endorsement.

Hayes nevertheless readily fell in with this policy. Not only was he looking for help in being inaugurated but he was looking ahead for conservative white allies to support a reconstituted Republican party in the South along old Whig lines. While he knew that "home rule" was always the main objective of the ex-Confederates, Hayes and his friends found other means of attracting Southern Conservatives. The depression had dried up sources of Northern investment, and carpetbaggers had exhausted the credit of the states. The only major source of capital left was the federal Treasury, and Southern congressmen were knocking at its doors with literally hundreds of bills for internal improvements — for building levees and controlling floods along the Mississippi, for clearing harbors, rivers, and canals, for constructing bridges, public buildings, and railroads. The largest appropriation sought was a subsidy of more than $200 million for the construction of the transcontinental Texas & Pacific Railroad with southern terminals. Persuaded by intermediaries that Hayes would be friendly toward his bill, Thomas A. Scott, president of the Pennsylvania Railroad as well as the Texas & Pacific, brought his lobby to the aid of Hayes. Southern seekers of appropriations had already discovered that Republicans were consistently more sympathetic to their internal-improvement bills than were their fellow Democrats of the North.

Meanwhile the filibuster tactics of the Democrats continued in the House, and as the deadline approached without a settlement Republicans grew more alarmed and intensified their efforts to win over Southern Democrats, thus enabling the latter to demand a higher price for their support. Hayes was not

The "strong" government, 1869–1877

The "weak" government, 1877–1881

Rutherford B. Hayes: conciliatory conservative

only committed to withdraw the troops and turn over two states to Conservative control but to appoint a Southern Democrat to his Cabinet and permit him to hand out federal offices to his friends. The Republican candidate and his spokesmen emphasized that the new administration would take a conciliatory policy toward the needs and wishes of Southern white citizens generally and particularly toward bills for internal improvements. All this was very gratifying and essential to the sectional compromise, but without the votes of Northern Democrats the Southerners could not have brought off a peaceful solution to the crisis. Other motives were at work here, and certainly among them was a rational fear of anarchy and a yearning for peace. At last Hayes's cause prevailed, and he was declared elected only two days before he took office.

The Politics of Reconciliation Faithful to his promises of conciliating the Conservative South, President Hayes appointed a Southern Democrat to his Cabinet and ordered the troops out of the capitals of Louisiana and South Carolina, and the last two carpetbagger governments promptly collapsed. All the Southern states and the border states as well were now under Conservative control. Within a year, Louisiana received more federal appropriations for internal improvements than any other state in the Union. The Texas & Pacific did not get its subsidy, but the South got its road to the Pacific by way of Hayes's support of Collis P. Huntington rather than through the support he gave Tom Scott. In his courtship of the South's ex-Whig Democrats, Hayes appointed many of them to federal offices, rejecting Republican applicants to do so. Admirers cheered the president with the rebel yell during his three visits to the South. It was the first of many experiments to come in the alliance of Southern Democrats with conservative Northern Republicans.

Conciliation pleased Southern white citizens and eased somewhat the old tensions between North and South. But results of that policy disappointed the president. Republicans returned to the practice of bloody-shirt oratory and to charges of Southern disloyalty. Only a few Republicans, mainly of the abolitionist tradition, seemed disturbed by their party's desertion of the carpetbaggers and the freedmen and by its repudiation of the goals of Reconstruction policy.

The most durable aspect of conciliation was "home rule," for never between 1877 and the Little Rock crisis of 1957 were federal troops used in the South for purposes precluded by the Compromise of 1877. Eighty years is a long period as sectional compromises go—longer than any previous one lasted, even longer than the sum of them all.

SUBORDINATION OF THE FREEDMEN

The Abandonment of Equality By constitutional amendment and statutes, the United States was presumably committed to the principle of equal civil and political rights for the freedmen and to the use of federal power to guarantee them. Yet after Reconstruction the country quickly broke this commitment and virtually forgot about it for more than two generations. That the North was also remiss was indicated by racial discrimination in employment, the policies of labor unions, and the discriminatory laws of Northern cities and states. Furthermore, the Radical promise of equality was an embarrassment to Hayes's effort to reconcile the estranged South and to put aside bitter war memories.

In short, the white people of the North and South were reconciled at the expense of black people. When Hayes visited Atlanta in the fall of 1877, he told the

A Case for Segregation

We consider the underlying fallacy of the plaintiff's argument to consist in the assumption that the enforced separation of the two races stamps the colored race with a badge of inferiority. If this be so, it is not by reason of anything found in the act, but solely because the colored race chooses to put that construction upon it. . . . The argument also assumes that social prejudices may be overcome by legislation, and that equal rights cannot be secured to the negro except by an enforced commingling of the two races. We cannot accept this proposition. . . . Legislation is powerless to eradicate racial instincts or to abolish distinctions based upon physical differences, and the attempt to do so can only result in accentuating the difficulties of the present situation. If the civil and political rights of both races be equal one cannot be inferior to the other civilly or politically. If one race be inferior to the other socially, the Constitution of the United States cannot put them upon the same plane.

From *Plessy v. Ferguson,* 163 U.S. 537, 1896

former slaves that their "rights and interests would be safer" if Southern whites were "let alone by the general government." This sentiment was greeted with "immense enthusiasm"—by the whites. "Let alone" became the watchword of government policy in race relations as well as in industrial and business affairs. Many of the former champions of the freedmen in the North took up the new slogan and dropped their concern for the rights of the black American. The *Nation* declared that the federal government should have "nothing more to do with him" and doubted that he could ever "be worked into a system of government for which you and I would have much respect."

The plea for reconciliation, the let-alone philosophy, and the prevailing disillusionment with high ideals and promises also had their effect on the Supreme Court. In a long series of decisions the Court favored white supremacy, state rights, and laissez-faire and virtually nullified the Fourteenth and Fifteenth Amendments insofar as they applied to the rights of freedmen. In 1876 Chief Justice Morrison R. Waite, in *United States* v. *Cruikshank,* decided that the Fourteenth Amendment "adds nothing to the rights of one citizen as against another" and does not extend federal protection to other rights except when they are infringed by a state. Applying the same interpretation in the *Civil Rights Cases* of 1883, the Court pronounced the Civil Rights Act of 1875 void. This act had provided that all persons, regardless of race, were entitled to "the full and equal enjoyment" of all public facilities such as inns and railroads, as well as theaters and other places of amusement.

Now, with the official approval of the federal courts, the acquiescence of many Northern liberals and Radicals, and the cooperation of the Republicans, the white South completed the relegation of black citizens. Their legal freedom was not seriously challenged, but their equality most certainly was.

Black Culture and Alienation After the brief involvement of black people in the mainstream of American political, civil, and cultural life encouraged by Reconstruction, the end of that era hastened the disengagement and alienation of black Americans from the white world and diminished contacts between the races. Withdrawal into separate churches, underway already, was soon completed with all-black members and all-black clergy. As states took over black education from missionaries, white teachers disappeared from black schools to be entirely replaced by black teachers. The growing separation of the black world from the white world taking place in religion and education also proceeded at varying rates in politics and civic affairs, in commerce and industry, in professions and public entertainments. As access to

A Case for Equality

The white race deems itself to be the dominant race in this country. And so it is, in prestige, in achievements, in education, in wealth and in power. So, I doubt not, it will continue to be for all time, if it remains true to its great heritage and holds fast to the principles of constitutional liberty. But in view of the Constitution in the eye of the law, there is in this country no superior, dominant, ruling class of citizens. There is no caste here. Our Constitution is color-blind, and neither knows nor tolerates classes among citizens. In respect of civil rights, all citizens are equal before the law. The humblest is the peer of the most powerful. The law regards man as man, and takes no account of his surroundings or of his color when his civil rights as guaranteed by the supreme law of the land are involved. It is, therefore, to be regretted that this high tribunal, the final expositor of the fundamental law of the land, has reached the conclusion that it is competent for a State to regulate the enjoyment by citizens of their civil rights solely upon the basis of race.

From the Dissent of Mr. Justice John Marshall Harlan, *Plessy v. Ferguson,* 163 U.S. 537, 1896

white culture and models diminished, even the language black people used increased in distinctiveness. Black culture was not simply a heritage of race or slavery, but also the product of a kind of freedom that separated and differentiated the black world even more in some ways than had slavery.

Until the end of the century, some 90 percent of American black people lived in the South, the majority of them working land owned by white Southerners. Caught in debt peonage as sharecroppers (p. 433–34), many sought to escape by migration. A few of them, including about 20,000 "Exodusters" who migrated to Kansas in 1879, left the South, but the black exodus to Northern cities did not come until a later generation. Until then, black migration was confined very largely to movement from one part of the South to another, from the old states of the Southeast to newer lands in the southwestern states, and from country to towns and cities within the South. Hundreds of labor-recruiting agents scoured the countryside to round up discontented and largely unskilled workers for the lands and mines to the west.

In Southern towns and cities, skilled black workers entered trades and crafts, such as bricklaying and carpentry, and for some years greatly outnumbered white workers so employed. White employers, however, increasingly discriminated against black craftsmen, often at the demand of white workers. The latter brought pressure to drive black workers out of the betterpaid, more attractive work and confine them to "Negro jobs." Gradually black workers disappeared from skilled trades that they had traditionally monopolized and were excluded almost entirely from the newer industries such as cotton textiles. Generally barred from emerging labor unions, they were occasionally used as strikebreakers, thereby earning additional ill will from the unions.

Disfranchisement and Segregation Part of the Compromise of 1877 had been a public pledge on the part of the Southern Conservatives to protect the rights of the freedmen abandoned to their care. The pledge soon proved to be of little value. The Conservative idea of protection was the old one of paternalistic responsibility for inferiors with few rights to protect. Black men continued to vote in many parts of the South for two decades or more, and Conservatives sought the vote of black citizens, assuring them that Southern whites were their "best friends." They tolerated elected black officials and appointed some to local, state, and federal jobs. Black state legislators and a few black congressmen continued in office until the end of the century. When these tactics failed, they coerced, bribed, and defrauded black voters or resorted to piecemeal disfranchisement. Nevertheless, competition for black votes continued through the 1880s and into the 1890s with a fluidity and freedom unknown after wholesale disfranchisement.

Conservatives left no doubt about their intention to "keep the Negro in his place" and to preserve white dominance in social, economic, and public relations. The enforced intimacy of slavery had left its traces in Southern residential patterns, and the "distant intimacy" of paternalism separated the races so widely by social distance that formal segregation was often unneeded. Status was defined by race. But in public or private institutions such as schools, hospitals, asylums, orphanages, poorhouses, institutions for the blind, deaf, or dumb, and even many prisons, the prevailing practice, often unsupported by law, was segregation of the races—with as little equality for black citizens as later under the law. Even so, this was an advance over the antebellum rule of exclusion, a change initiated by the Radicals, continued by the Conservatives, and often supported by the black citizens themselves. It was an advance in the sense that it was better to get separate and inferior services than none at all. In public accommodations—in trains, streetcars, and public parks, for example—race relations were more fluid and variable than elsewhere. Exclusion and erratic segregation were combined with a degree of racial integration that would later—after the turn of the century—be unthinkable.

In the 1890s, whatever fluidity, moderation, or variety remained in race relations was swept away by a new wave of Southern racism that imposed segregation by law. "Jim Crow law" made the system universal, rigid, and thorough. It was law rather than custom that reached into every corner of society and put the authority of the state and city in the voice of the railway conductor, the theater usher, or the hoodlum of street and playground. The Southern movement was supported by a rising mood of racism in other parts of the nation and met little resistance from Northern opinion or federal courts. In 1896 the Supreme Court in *Plessy v. Ferguson* explicitly sanctioned Jim Crow law by declaring "separate but equal" facilities constitutional.

Another reason for Southern white citizens to replace custom with law to control the black population was the arrival of a new generation of black Americans. Unlike their parents, the younger generation was not born in slavery, was less bound by habit to bow to white demands, and was more prone to resistance. And when the law did not humble black youngsters sufficiently to satisfy the mob, the mob was ready to take the law in its hands and resort to lynching—a crime that reached its peak between 1889 and 1899, when an average of some 187 lynchings a year occurred in the United States. About four-fifths of the lynchings took place in the South, and the great majority of the victims were black Americans.

So long as black men voted in large numbers and cast their votes for an opposition party, as they did into the 1890s, Conservative Democratic control was insecure—especially in the black belt. Failing to coopt the black vote and dissatisfied with chicanery, ballot-box stuffing, and other fraudulent controls, Conservatives turned increasingly to outright disfranchisement by law. Throughout the 1880s they had experimented with restrictive measures of several kinds to reduce the black electorate. This disfranchisement movement, like that for the Jim Crow laws, received encouragement from Northern opinion and the federal courts. Elitist Northern advocates of "good government" had turned against democratic ideals of universal suffrage and blamed recent immigrants and minority races for lowering standards. In 1898 the Supreme Court in *Williams* v. *Mississippi* threw open the legal road to disfranchisement by approving the Mississippi Plan, written into the state constitution, for depriving black citizens of the franchise by means of a literacy test.

The reactionary reforms of Southern politics came in waves, with two high tides eventually sweeping all states of the region, most of them in the last decade of the century. The chief advocates of disfranchisement were upper-class Democrats of the black belt, who had most to gain from it; the main opponents were Republicans, Populists, a radical third party, and black voters, who had most to lose. The main devices of disfranchisement were the poll tax, registration laws, and literacy and property qualifications, some with loopholes to admit desirable poor whites and illiterates. Disfranchisement was a disastrous blow to the democratic process. Both voter participation and party opposition had been rising before the blow and fell sharply thereafter among white as well as black voters. Black voter turnout dropped an average of 62 percent, white 26 percent, and overall turnout 37 percent. While an average of 73 percent of adult males voted in the 1890s before disfranchisement, the Southern turnout in the next decade averaged only 30

Lynch mob, 1893

percent. Opposition parties virtually collapsed, and Southern politics became a one-party system. It had changed from a democracy to a more or less broadly based white oligarchy and was to remain so for nearly a half century.

The Atlanta Compromise By the 1880s a new black middle class, consisting largely of business and professional people, had grown up among the freedmen. Proportionately smaller and much poorer and weaker than the corresponding class of white people, the minority middle class nevertheless shared some of the attitudes and aspirations of its white counterpart. A member of that class, Booker T. Washington, became head of an industrial school for black students at Tuskegee, Alabama, in 1881. There he preached the doctrine of work, thrift, self-help, and sobriety, conformed humbly to segregation in the South, condoned disfranchisement, and said little about lynching. Washington's attitude of humility contrasted strikingly with the influence he came to wield in dispensing Republican patronage and in shaping philanthropic and educational policies. He believed that education for black workers should stress industrial training rather than intellectual development, and his views attracted support from people of wealth and power in the North.

Booker Washington's reputation as a leader also owed much to the favor he won in the eyes of dominant whites of the South. They greeted with enthusiasm a famous speech he gave in Atlanta in 1895 at their invitation, setting forth what later came to be known as the Atlanta Compromise. In it he made sweeping concessions to the white desire for segregation, abandoned the Reconstruction demand for black equality, emphasized economic opportunity rather than political and civil rights, and identified himself and his people with the industrial and social order established by the Conservatives. To his own race he preached patience, conservatism, and the primacy of material progress. To black critics who rejected Washington's Atlanta doctrine, it looked more like a capitulation than a compromise.

POLITICS IN THE NEW SOUTH

The New Regime The new rulers of the South, claiming they had "redeemed" their states from the carpetbaggers, earned the name Redeemers. Predominantly Democrats, they often called their party the

Students at Tuskegee Institute

Conservative or Democratic-Conservative party out of regard for the ex-Whigs they had attracted as members. In the top ranks of the reconstituted party, along with numerous old Whigs, were to be found many businessmen and industrialists or lawyers who served their interests. They shared power and exchanged favors with planters in most states, but the combination did not represent a restoration of the old order.

The new state constitutions framed by the Redeemers embodied a strong reaction against the Reconstruction regimes. They revealed suspicion and distrust of legislatures and placed such hampering restrictions upon government that positive action of any sort became difficult. The new Southern Redeemer governments also reacted against Reconstruction through their policy of "retrenchment," which meant cutting taxes and starving or eliminating tax-supported public services. The chief beneficiaries of the tax policy were the railroads, the utilities, and the factories, whose burdens were lightened. The chief victims were the public schools. The Redeemers also cut appropriations for other public institutions, but none so severely as those for prisons. The state governments actually turned prisoners, largely black, into a source of revenue by leasing them as cheap labor to industrialists with the right political connections. The convict-lease system, often marked by brutal exploitation, became an ugly blot on the reputation of the new regime.

This was not an era free of corrupt government and lax public morals across the country, and it would be unfair to single out the Redeemers for special censure. They invited such censure, however, by the attack they made on graft and corruption in their campaigns to overthrow the carpetbaggers. Faced with no effective party of opposition, protected by long tenure of office, and consequently immune from criticism and exposure, the Redeemers acquired habits of laxity that eventually covered several of the state governments with disgrace. In the 1880s one scandal after another

Booker T. Washington: preacher of patience

came to light. Some were exposed only by the absconding of state treasurers, nine of whom were found guilty of defalcation or embezzlement. The "Solid South" won its name prematurely. Hardly had "home rule" been restored when revolt began to stir against the Redeemer regime.

The most disruptive issue of all was the "readjustment," or repudiation, of state debts. So disruptive was it, in fact, that it unseated the Redeemers in some states and threatened the security of the whole regime. Naturally the states' creditors and bondholders protested bitterly, and in each state a faction of Redeemers fought the debt-readjusters. The advocates of repudiation argued that much of the debt was a heritage from carpetbagger looting, that the states themselves had derived little benefit from the sale of Reconstruction bonds, and that in any event the section was too impoverished and ravaged to carry the burden of Reconstruction debts.

Encouraged by the revolt against the Conservative Democrats, the Republicans began to dream of returning to power in the South through an alliance with local third parties. Even though the Republicans had little in common with these parties save their opposition to Democrats, they threw their support to the reformers and debt-repudiators. The Conservatives responded by reviving the tactics of fraud and intimidation once used against the carpetbaggers. Not for a decade was there to be further talk of insurgency in the South. This period of political torpor was not to be broken until the agrarian revolt of the 1890s.

The Doctrine of the New South There had been antebellum advocates of industrialism in the South, but they had looked on factories as a means of buttressing the old social order. Propagandists of the New South, by contrast, sought to replace the old order with an economy like that of the North, a business civilization of cities, factories, and trade, with new values and new aims. This was what the "New South" meant to its champions in the 1880s.

Propaganda for the New South point of view found full voice during the 1880s and 1890s in such journals as the Atlanta *Constitution,* edited by orator Henry W. Grady. Full of the bustle and salesmanship of business enterprise, Grady exuded optimism and good will. In an address on "The New South" delivered in 1886 to the New England Society of New York he proclaimed: "We have sowed towns and cities in the place of theories and put business above politics. We have challenged your spinners in Massachusetts and your iron-makers in Pennsylvania. . . . We have fallen in love with work." What Grady and his friends were preaching was laissez-faire capitalism freed of restraints, a new industrial way of life, and a businessman's scale of values.

One sign of the popularity of the New South doctrine was the Southerner's eagerness for Northern approval. "Beyond all question," declared a Richmond journal, "we have been on the wrong track and should take a new departure." And Henry Watterson, a Louisville editor and orator, thought that "the ambition of the South is to out-Yankee the Yankee." But the appeal of the New South doctrine would have been less compelling had it not been embellished by sentimental tribute to the past: a heritage "never to be equalled in its chivalric strength and grace," as Grady put it. The invention of a legendary Old South and the cult of the "lost cause" revealed the curiously divided mind and the conflicting impulses of the Southern people in the new era. They marched hopefully in one direction and looked back longingly in the other.

The inner tensions of the Southern mind were reflected in the career of the Georgia writer Joel Chandler Harris, author of *Uncle Remus* (1881). A gentle,

The New South through Rose-Colored Glasses

Who can picture the vast, illimitable future of this glorious sunny South? . . . Here is a land possessing in its matchless resources the combined advantages of almost every other country of the world without their most serious disadvantages. . . . It is beyond the power of the human mind to fully grasp the future that is in store for this country. . . . The more we contemplate these advantages and contrast them with those of other countries, the more deeply we will be impressed with the unquestionable truth that here in this glorious land 'Creation's Garden Spot,' is to be the richest and greatest country upon which the sun ever shone.

From Richard H. Edmonds, in *Manufacturers Record,* 1888

rather wistful man of humble origins, Harris portrayed the old slave in quaint dialect with humor and affection, casting a spell of charm over memories of the antebellum plantation. But while he was writing his nostalgic stories about the Old South, Harris was also chief editorial writer for Grady's Atlanta *Constitution,* doing his daily best to encourage the growth of the New South of business and industry. Both the admirers of the old order and the propagandists of the new advocated sectional "reconciliation," urging that the North abandon its reformist aims and accept the new order in the South. In political terms reconciliation was simply an alliance between conservatives of both regions built on foundations of white supremacy.

Henry W. Grady: spokesman for "the New South"

THE COLONIAL ECONOMY

The Agrarian Pattern The dream and design of the new leaders of the South was to build an urbanized, industrialized society like that of the Yankees. But the habits and economic realities of the Old South were slow to change and hard to shake off. Despite all the factories that were constructed and the proliferation of small agricultural market towns in the interior, 96.1 percent of the North Carolinians and 94.1 percent of the Alabamians were still not classified "urban" by the census of 1890. Only 8.5 percent of the population of the South Atlantic states below Maryland was urban in 1890, as compared with 51.7 percent of the population of the North Atlantic states from Pennsylvania north. By 1900 the South was still the most rural and agrarian section in the settled portions of the country.

On the surface it would seem that deep changes had occurred in the distribution of land ownership in the South. The census of 1880 reported an amazing in-

The New South through a Glass Darkly

Twenty-odd years ago . . . I fondly imagined a great era of prosperity for the South. Guided by history and by a knowledge of our people and our climatic and physical advantages, I saw in anticipation all her tribulations ended . . . and I beheld the South greater, richer and mightier than when she molded the political policy of the whole country. But year by year these hopes, chastened by experience, have waned and faded, until now, instead of beholding the glorious South of my imagination, I see her sons poorer than when war ceased his ravages, weaker than when rehabilitated with her original rights, and with the bitter memories smoldering, if not rankling, in the bosoms of many.

From Lewis H. Blair, *The Prosperity of the South Dependent on the Elevation of the Negro,* 1889

crease in the number of farms since 1860, and the average farm turned out to be less than half its former size. Optimists concluded that the Civil War had broken up the concentration of land in the hands of planters and had brought about "economic democracy." The truth was, however, that the old plantation lands had been parceled out in small plots among sharecroppers, each plot counting as a new "farm," and that large tracts of new land had been brought under cultivation. The sharecropper (white and black)

Sharecroppers: trapped in the system

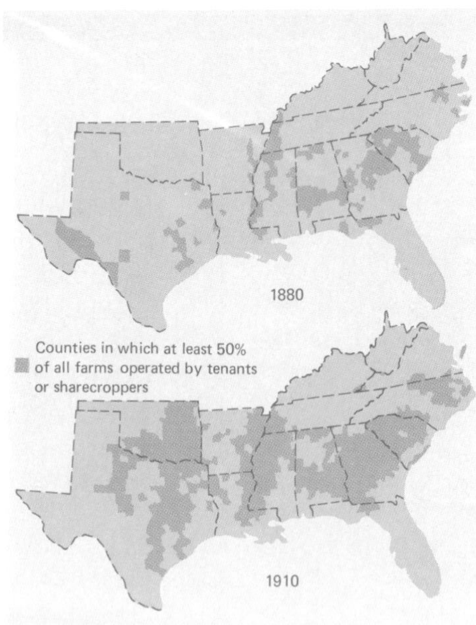

Map 16-2 *The increase of farm tenancy in the South*

had replaced the slave, and his share of the crop depended largely on the tools, work animals, and feed the landlord furnished (see Map 16-2).

Ownership of the land tended to shift into the hands of merchants or other townspeople. Moreover, whatever efficiency and planning, whatever virtues of proprietorship, had resided in the old plantation system were largely missing from the sharecropper system. From a strictly economic point of view, cropping was probably worse for the agriculture of the region than slavery had been (see Map 16-3).

The most desperate need of the Southern farmer after the war was credit. The farmer was at the mercy of the country merchants, who enjoyed a local monopoly over credit and exploited their customers by charging outrageous prices. Merchants advanced supplies for the year with a mortgage, or "lien," on the future crop. The farmer pledged an unplanted crop for a loan of an unstipulated amount at an undesignated but enormous rate of interest averaging about 60 percent a year. Trapped by the system, a farmer might continue year after year as a sort of peon, under debt to the same merchant and under constant oversight. The

Map 16-3
A Georgia plantation in 1861 and 1881

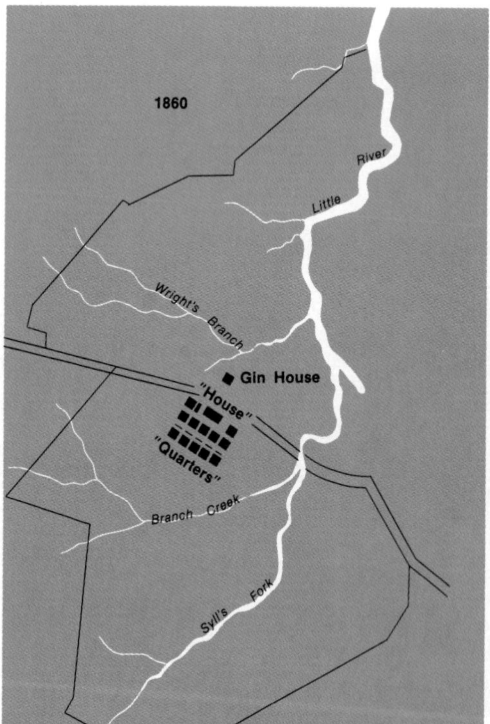

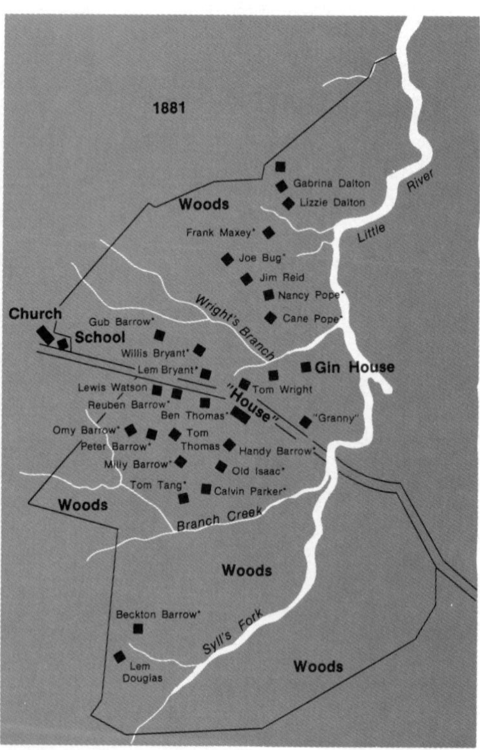

*Blacks who had lived on plantation as slaves

lien system imposed the one-crop system, for the merchant would advance credit only against cash crops such as cotton or tobacco. The system not only impoverished farmers but stifled their hopes and depleted their incentive.

During the last quarter of the nineteenth century, farmers the country over were plagued by low crop prices and depression. Southern farmers shared these ills with farmers elsewhere, but they also suffered from a combination of burdens peculiar to the South. Among these was the heritage of military defeat, pillage, and occupation that had cost the section every third horse or mule. On top of these burdens were heaped the ills of sharecropping peonage and the lien system. By the 1890s, a spirit of grim desperation had settled on the farmers of the South, a spirit that long manifested itself in a suspicion of city folk and their ways and a resentment of wealth and its display.

Industrial Stirrings Toward the end of the 1870s the depression that had settled over the nation in 1873 started to lift. Once again Northern investors began to show interest in opportunities below the Potomac and freed the springs of capital. The propagandists of the New South boasted that the South, like the West, was an empire ripe for exploiting. The Redeemers welcomed investors with open arms, tax exemptions, and promises of cheap and docile labor.

With the willing cooperation of Southern legislatures, speculators rounded up huge grants of public lands and mineral resources. Florida attempted to grant several million more acres than were in its public domain, and Texas surrendered an area larger than the state of Indiana. In 1877 the law reserving federal lands in five Southern states for homesteaders was scrapped, and the rich Southern empire of timber, coal, and iron was thrown open to unrestricted exploitation. In the next decade nearly 6 million acres of federal lands were sold, most of them to Northern speculators, who indulged in a reckless destruction of forests and a rifling of other resources.

Exploitation of this sort, as well as more laudable schemes of industrial development, would have been impossible without dramatic improvements in transportation. Between 1880 and 1890 railroad mileage in the South, starting from a low base, increased from 16,605 miles to 39,108, a growth of 135.5 percent, 50

Industry in the New South: New Orleans sugar refinery

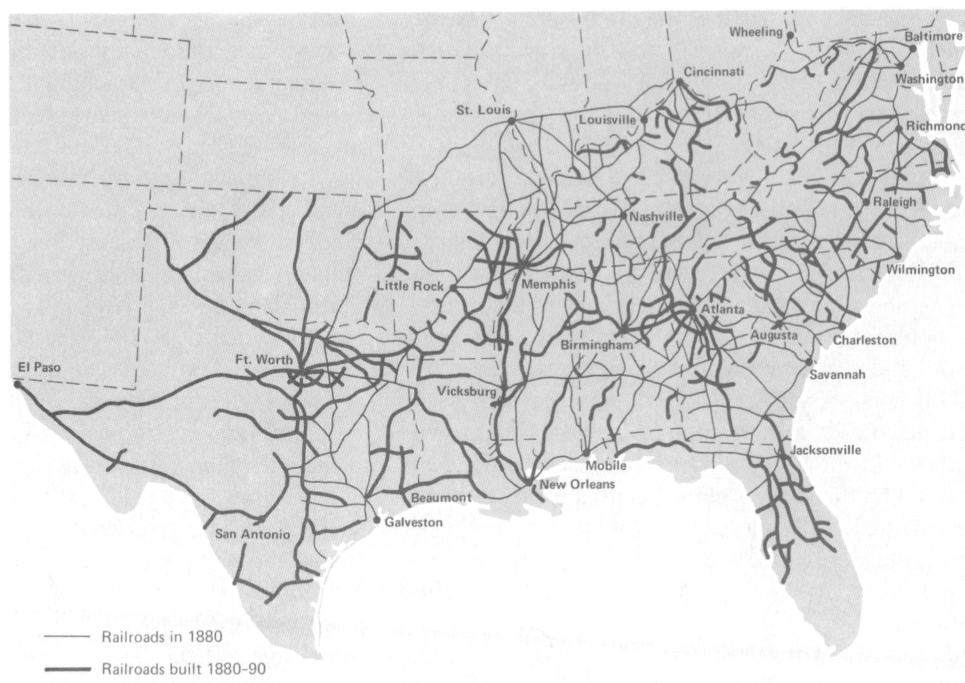

Map 16-4
The growth of the railroad network in the South

percent greater than the national rate of growth in mileage in the same period (see Map 16-4). Railroads opened to development the land-locked mineral resources of the South, particularly the iron mines of Tennessee, Virginia, and Alabama. By 1898 Birmingham was the largest shipping point for pig iron in the country and the third largest in the world.

So long as the Southern economy stuck to its traditional role of supplying raw materials of mine, forest, and farm, it met with encouragement from Northern bankers and investors. Production of lumber and forestry products soared sensationally, as did the output of such fuels as coal and oil, and such ores as iron, sulfur, bauxite, phosphate rock, and manganese. Eastern capital entered each of these enterprises, and Eastern control followed. The same pattern was followed in the modern era of oil production, which opened with an unprecedented gusher at Spindletop, near Beaumont, Texas, in January 1901.

The tobacco industry, the oldest in the region, discovered new markets and developed new techniques of manufacture during the new era. The genius of concentrated control was a tall, rugged, red-headed North Carolinian named James Buchanan Duke, called "Buck," whose rise paralleled that of the industry. He started out in 1865 with two blind mules and a load of tobacco, all the war had left on his father's small farm. "Tobacco is the poor man's luxury," he observed, and on that insight he founded a fortune. By 1889 his industry was producing half the country's cigarettes, and the following year he absorbed his main competitors into the American Tobacco Company.

The true symbol of the New South, however, was the cotton mill, and the zeal of its promoters stirred up a veritable "cotton mill crusade." Actually, the industry was confined largely to the Carolinas, Georgia, and Alabama. Cotton manufacturing began in the Old South and continued to grow through the Civil War and Reconstruction, but between 1880 and 1900 the amount of capital invested in the Southern mills increased sevenfold. The chief textile products of the South were unfinished goods that were sent north for final processing, and in this, as in the use of cheap labor, the cotton mills were typical of the South's new industries.

The Colonial Status For all its boasts of industrial progress, the New South lagged far behind the rest of the country. The region remained poor, its economy undeveloped, technologically backward, and stagnant. By the end of the century the South had a smaller percentage of the nation's factories and a slightly smaller percentage of the nation's capital than it had

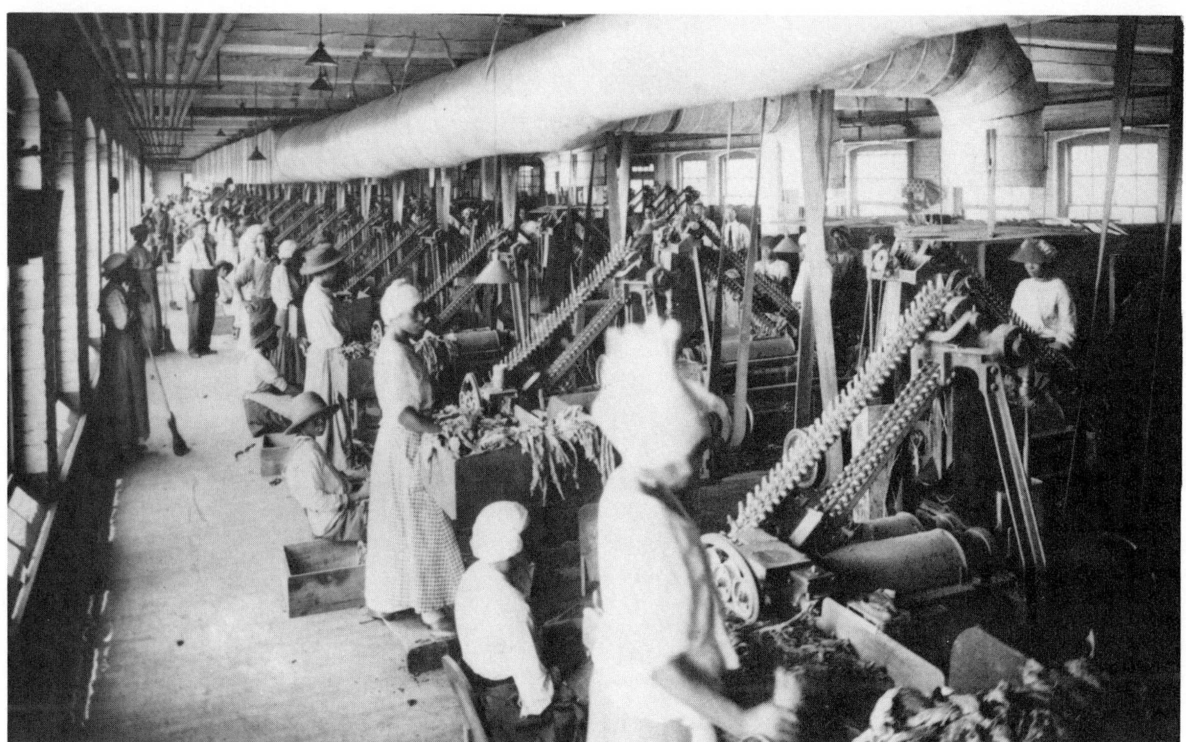

Tobacco: new techniques of manufacture

in 1860. With few exceptions, the industries that did take root in the South were low-wage industries that gave the first rough processing to the agricultural, forestry, and mining products of the region. The final processing of these products was usually done in the North, and from the final processing came the greatest profits.

There was no law relegating the South to a raw-material economy, no plot to exclude Southerners from the better-paying jobs and the more profitable industries. What, then, were the reasons for the persistent economic backwardness of the section? A lost war, a late start, and a lack of capital were some of the reasons. More important was a credit system that entrapped great numbers of black and white Americans in debt peonage, stifled their initiative, bound them to a stagnant one-crop agriculture, and immobilized them as a labor force.

Industrialization was seen as a way out, but the development of manufactures was handicapped by some special barriers. One of these barriers was the system of regional freight rate differentials adopted in the 1870s and 1880s by private railway associations and later given legal sanction by the Interstate Commerce Commission. These differentials meant that shippers of manufactured goods in the South and West were charged far higher rates than shippers in the privileged "Official Territory," north of the Ohio and Potomac and east of the Mississippi. Taken together, these rate differentials discouraged the South from developing manufactures of its own and encouraged it to concentrate on raw materials. A price differential imposed on Birmingham steel by the Pittsburgh steel masters and their allied railroads had a similar effect.

During these years the Northeast assumed something like an imperial power over the other sections, and the national economy fell into a neomercantilism reminiscent of colonial days. The Northeast discouraged the rise of competing manufactures by the combination of regionalized freight rates, steel price differentials, and patent control, and reduced foreign competition in its domestic markets by the protective tariff. It also monopolized the carrying trade and promoted ample supplies of raw material for its factories. In brief, the Northeast became for a long time the workshop of the nation, reserving for its own coffers

Wharf in Virginia: a tributary economy

the profits of processing, transporting, and distributing goods. The South was left to produce the raw materials for the new economic order, to serve as a tributary of industrial power.

Division of labor was, of course, natural in a national economy, and the South derived real benefits from its role in the form of increased job opportunities, payrolls, and taxable assets. On the other hand, this subordinate economic status imposed grave penalties on the South. As late as 1910 some 62 percent of its workers were engaged in the extractive industries. Throughout the country, these industries paid the lowest wages of all, and the wages of Southern workers were even lower than the national average.

In wealth, living standards, and general welfare, the Union was more a "house divided" now than when Lincoln first used the phrase. In 1880 the estimated per capita wealth in the South was $376 as compared with a national average of $870. No Southern state came within $300 of the national average nor within $550 of the average outside the South. In 1900 the national average in per capita wealth stood at $1,165, and in the South the average was $509. Per capita

"Poor whites" in Kentucky

income of the same year in the South Atlantic and East South Central states was less than 50 percent of the national average. Little wonder that the region was noted for its "poor whites" and its "poor blacks" as well. Poverty was a characteristic of the regional economy. Closely related to that poverty was a lag in education, libraries, public health, and living standard.

The New South represented a striking shift in the geography of political power. In the 72 years between Washington and Lincoln, Southerners held the presidency for 50 years and the title of chief justice of the Supreme Court for 60 years. They furnished more than half the justices, nearly half the men of Cabinet rank, and more than half the Speakers of the House of Representatives. During the next half century, by contrast, no Southerner save Andrew Johnson served as president or vice president, and the South furnished only 14 of the 133 Cabinet members, 7 of the 31 justices of the Supreme Court, and 2 of the 12 Speakers of the House. From the power and glory of the eighteenth and early nineteenth centuries, the South had fallen to a lowly state. In the process of reunion it had become the frontier of a new order that was expanding southward as well as westward.

SUGGESTIONS FOR READING

An excellent book by E. L. Ayers, *After Reconstruction: The American South in the Late Nineteenth Century* (1992), updates and reinterprets a period treated in an earlier work by C. V. Woodward, *Origins of the New South, 1877–1913* (1951). See also C. V. Woodward, *The Burden of Southern History* (1968). W. J. Cash, *The Mind of the South* (1941), still evokes controversy. P. M. Gaston, *The New South Creed: A Study in Southern Mythmaking* (1970), is well described by its title.

On the sectional settlement of 1877, C. V. Woodward, *Reunion and Reaction: The Compromise of 1877 and the End of Reconstruction* (1951), is challenged in part by K. J. Polakoff, *The Politics of Inertia: The Election of 1876 and the End of Reconstruction* (1973), and reassessed by T. L. Seip, *The South Returns to Congress: Men, Economic Measures, and Intersectional Relationships, 1868–1879* (1983), and by M. Perman, *The Road to Redemption: Southern Politics, 1869–1879* (1984). President Hayes's Southern policy is treated in K. E. Davidson, *The Presidency of Rutherford B. Hayes* (1972).

On race relations the fullest treatment is Joel Williamson, *The Crucible of Race: Black-White Relations in the American South Since Emancipation* (1984). The plight of black Americans is described by R. L. Ransom and R. Sutch, *One Kind of Freedom: The Economic Consequences of Emancipation* (1977), and from a different view by R. Higgs, *Competition and Coercion: Blacks in the American Economy, 1865–1914* (1977). G. M. Fredrickson, *Black Image on the White Mind* is good on this period. C. V. Woodward, *The Strange Career of Jim Crow* (3d rev. ed., 1974), emphasizes legal segregation, and H. N. Rabinowitz, *Race Relations in the Urban South, 1865–1890* (1978), shows how exclusion preceded segregation. L. R. Harlan, *Booker T. Washington: The Making of a Negro Leader, 1856–1901* (1972), is fine.

Our understanding of political history is deepened by J. M. Kousser, *The Shaping of Southern Politics: Suffrage Restriction and the Establishment of the One-Party South, 1880–1910* (1974). He revises some of V. O. Key, Jr., *Southern Politics in State and Nation* (1949), though it is still helpful. A state study is R. L. Hart, *Redeemers, Bourbons, & Populists: Tennessee, 1870–1896* (1975). New appraisals of the Populist movement are G. Clanton, *Populism: The Humane Preference in America, 1890–1900* (1991), B. Palmer, *"Man Over Money": The Southern Populist Critique of American Capitalism* (1985), and N. Pollack, *The Just Policy: Populism, Law, and Human Welfare* (1987). Also see M. Hyman, *The Anti-Redeemers: Hill Country Political Dissenters in the Lower South from Redemption to Populism* (1990); C. V. Woodward, *Tom Watson: Agrarian Rebel* (1938); B. C. Shaw, *The Wool-Hat Boys: Georgia's Populist Party* (1984); and S. Hahn, *The Roots of Southern Populism: Yeomen Farmers and the Transformation of the Georgia Upcountry, 1850–1890* (1983).

Economic change is the theme of G. Wright, *Old South, New South: Revolutions in the Southern Economy since the Civil War* (1986). J. F. Stover, *The Railroads of the South* (1955), is the best on that subject. The development of industry is covered by J. C. Cobb, *Industrialization and Southern Society, 1877–1984* (1984). On the South's oldest industry, see N. M. Tilley, *The Bright Tobacco Industry, 1860–1929* (1948), and R. Durden, *The Dukes of Durham, 1865–1929* (1975). On cotton mills, P. J. Hearden, *Independence and Empire: The New South's Cotton Mill Campaign, 1865–1901* (1982), is a general account. D. Carlton, *Mill and Town in South Carolina, 1880–1920* (1982), revises older interpretations.

For literary insights on this period of Southern life, see William Faulkner's works, particularly *The Hamlet* (1940) and *Go Down Moses* (1942).

CHAPTER SEVENTEEN

A CHEYENNE INDIAN CAMP

THE NEW WEST: EMPIRE WITHIN A NATION

After the Civil War, the American people embarked on the taming and exploiting of an area greater than all the territory that had been settled since the landing at Jamestown in 1607. Up to this time the settlers of the trans-Mississippi West had occupied only its eastern and western fringes, in one tier of states beyond the Mississippi and in another tier half a continent beyond along the Pacific coast. Between these two frontiers, separated by 1,500 miles, lay 1.2 billion acres inhabited by only 1.5 million souls. A vast and fabulous expanse of oceanlike plains, it was a scene broken by spired and towering mountain ranges, grassy plateaus, painted deserts, and breathtaking canyons. Of all the American wests, this was the one that most completely captured the imagination of the world.

Americans had conquered many frontiers in the past, but the New West was different from all the others. The experience of the pioneers there was less like that of their forebears in settling the forested "wests" of the East and more like the adventures of nineteenth-century Europeans in Africa and Asia. America was a nation with a built-in empire, an empire incorporated in a nation. What the English and the western Europeans had to seek "somewhere east of Suez," their American contemporaries, until the region was tamed and settled, might find somewhere west of the wide Missouri. The impulse behind this late-nineteenth-century quest was more than a desire for private gain. It partook of the strange drive that was sending Western men and women into all the remote corners of the world to impose their will upon people of color and to master exotic environments. If in Rudyard Kipling's Mandalay there were no Ten Commandments and the best was like the worst, so it was too in Deadwood Gulch and in a hundred mining towns, cow towns, and trading posts of the Wild West.

SUBORDINATION OF THE INDIANS

The Great Plains Environment The steady westward advance of the agricultural frontier ground to a halt in Texas and Kansas and then (except for Utah, p. 289) skipped all the way to the Pacific coast. What stopped the pioneer was the forbidding new environment of the Great Plains. Abnormally dry, almost treeless, and mostly level, the plains had their own particular soil, weather, plant life, animal life, and human life. Writing of the Texas plains, Colonel Richard J. Dodge warned: "Every bush had its thorns, every animal, reptile, or insect had its horn, tooth, or sting, every male human his revolver, and each was ready to use his weapon of defense on any unfortunate sojourner, on the smallest, or even without the smallest provocation."

So harsh and uninhabitable did the plains at first appear that the Easterner wrote them off as wasteland and until 1860 labeled much of the vast area on maps "The Great American Desert." Dry winds parched the throats of Easterners, cracked their lips, and made their eyes smart. Everything seemed different. There were chinooks, or warm mountain winds, northers, blizzards, and hailstorms, and all but the chinooks could bring distress or disaster. The rivers dried up unexpectedly, and when they flowed their waters were often unpalatable and sometimes treacherous. The slight rainfall, usually under 15 inches a year, made traditional methods of farming impractical, and the new environment rendered useless many other traditions and familiar methods. The woodcraft and Indian craft that had enabled the frontier people to master the humid, forested East were not adapted to the treeless, arid plains, and neither were ax, plow, canoe, or long rifle. And neither, for that matter, were some laws and institutions.

Once rebellion in the South had been put down, Americans turned anew to the taming of the Great Plains. Here they encountered rebels of a different breed.

The Plains Indians Of some 300,000 Indians left in the United States in 1865, more than two-thirds lived on the Great Plains. The frontier people called them "wild Indians"—and so they were, in comparison with their sedentary cousins of the Eastern forests. The only mounted Indians the white man ever encountered, most of them, were nomadic and nonagricultural. Above all, they were fierce, skillful, and implacable warriors—"the most effectual barrier," according to Walter P. Webb, "ever set up by a native American population against European invaders in a temperate zone." Against all comers—Spanish, French, English, and American—they had held their own as masters of the plains for two and a half centuries.

The Spanish had introduced horses into Mexico in the sixteenth century, and the animals had revolutionized the life of the tribes and brought on the golden era of the plains Indians—an era that had about reached its peak when the Anglo-Americans first encountered them. The horse made the Indians more mobile and hence more nomadic than ever, less agricultural, more warlike, and, most important of all, far more effective buffalo hunters. Estimates of the buffalo population of the Great Plains at the end of the Civil War range up to 12 million and more. The buffalo was even more indispensable to the plains Indians than the horse, for it provided them with food, clothing, shelter, and even fuel. Necessities, luxuries, ornaments, tools, bedding, their very tepees—all were fashioned from the flesh, bone, and hide of the buffalo. The nomadic tribes moved back and forth across the plains with the great herds and organized their life and religion around the hunt. Whatever threatened the buffalo threatened their very existence.

Present knowledge about the great diversity of Indian cultures, languages, tribal alliances, and intertribal wars makes the old concept of a clear white-Indian conflict as outmoded as the old notion of civilization versus savagery. Each tribe had its own pattern of white-Indian relations, and tribes differed in the degree to which they adopted white ways, combined them with tribal ways, or sought to revive and maintain tribal traditions. They entered alliances with Anglos and Hispanics to fight enemy tribes. To picture them as entirely passive or the sole victims is false. And it does not increase understanding to foster white ancestral guilt and romanticize the Indian.

Although their cultures varied, all the plains Indians shared the culture of neolithic primatives, using stone knives, stone scrapers, and bone awls as tools. The warriors carried bows and arrows and fourteen-foot, stone-tipped lances for hunting and warfare. Yet in combat the stoneage warrior asked no quarter of the early industrial settler. With his short three-foot bow and a quiver of two-score arrows or more, the Comanche would ride 300 yards and get off 20 arrows with startling force and accuracy while the Texan was firing one shot and reloading his long and cumbersome rifle. Even the Colt six-shooter did not entirely overcome the Indian's advantage. As armor he carried a loosely slung shield made of buffalo hide so tough that it could deflect a bullet. The arrows he used against an enemy, unlike those he used in the hunt, were fitted with heads that came off in the wound when the shaft was withdrawn. The plains Indians could hang by a heel to one side of the horse and discharge arrows under its neck. They could execute intricate cavalry maneuvers controlled by a secret system of communications and signals that was the envy of white military experts.

Until the white people finally crushed the plains Indians, they were conscious of Indians mainly as warriors, as ruthless and dreaded enemies who sometimes held military supremacy in their own country. The Indian's conception of the conduct of war and the treatment of captives differed from that of the white man. His reputation for cruelty was probably as much deserved as his opponent's reputation for ruthlessness. The military struggle between the two races on the Great Plains was marked on both sides by a peculiar ferocity and savagery.

White Supremacy in the West So long as Americans thought of the plains as the "Great American Desert" and as "one big reservation" for plains Indians, conflict as well as contact between the races was rare. But in the 1850s the situation changed. Mass migrations got under way across the plains to Oregon; miners began to beg for protection; the Kansas and Nebraska territories were organized; and politicians demanded that the Indians be pushed aside to north and south to clear the way for transportation and settlement. In 1851 the federal government adopted a new Indian policy of "concentration," under which the chiefs of the plains tribes were persuaded to restrict their people to areas the white newcomers solemnly promised they would never violate. The plains Indian was soon to learn what the forest Indian had learned long before: trust none of the white man's promises, however solemn. The Indians were further embittered by the behavior of corrupt officials of the Indian Bureau of the Interior Department, who defrauded them of their land and cheated them in trade, and by the treachery of a reckless breed of beaver trappers, gold prospectors, hunters, and outlaws. Then in 1858 and 1859 the Pike's Peak Gold Rush sent thousands hell-bent for Colorado and trouble, soon to be joined by deserters and draft dodgers from the Union and Confederate armies.

Indian war broke out in Colorado about the time the Civil War was starting in the East. The immediate provocation was the effort of government officials to

Westering

force the Arapaho and Cheyenne to abandon all claim to the area that had been granted them forever only ten years before. Many braves rejected the agreement made by their chiefs and took the warpath. After an intermittent warfare of pillaging, home burning, and murdering that went on for more than three years, they sued for peace. Chief Black Kettle of the Cheyenne, after being assured of protection, was surprised and trapped by a force led by Colonel John M. Chivington on the night of November 29, 1864. Ignoring Black Kettle's attempts to surrender, the militia shot, knifed, scalped, clubbed, and mutilated men, women, and children indiscriminately (see Map 17-1). Chief Black Kettle and a few warriors escaped, but before a year had passed the Cheyenne and Arapaho, as well as the Kiowa and Comanche, were compelled to surrender their claims and move on to more restricted area assigned them.

Hardly had peace been restored to the Southwest in the fall of 1865 when war broke out in the Northwest. The bloody Sioux War of 1865–67 was brought on by many forces, but it was triggered by the demands of miners who had invaded the Sioux country. Sioux warriors ambushed a party of soldiers under Captain W. J. Fetterman near Fort Phil Kearny in December 1866 and slaughtered all 82 of its members.

The Chivington and Fetterman massacres, together with scores of minor battles and endless shooting scrapes, prompted the federal government to review its Indian policy in 1867. Easterners clashed with Westerners, humanitarian impulses with fire-and-sword military policies. The Westerner's disgust was

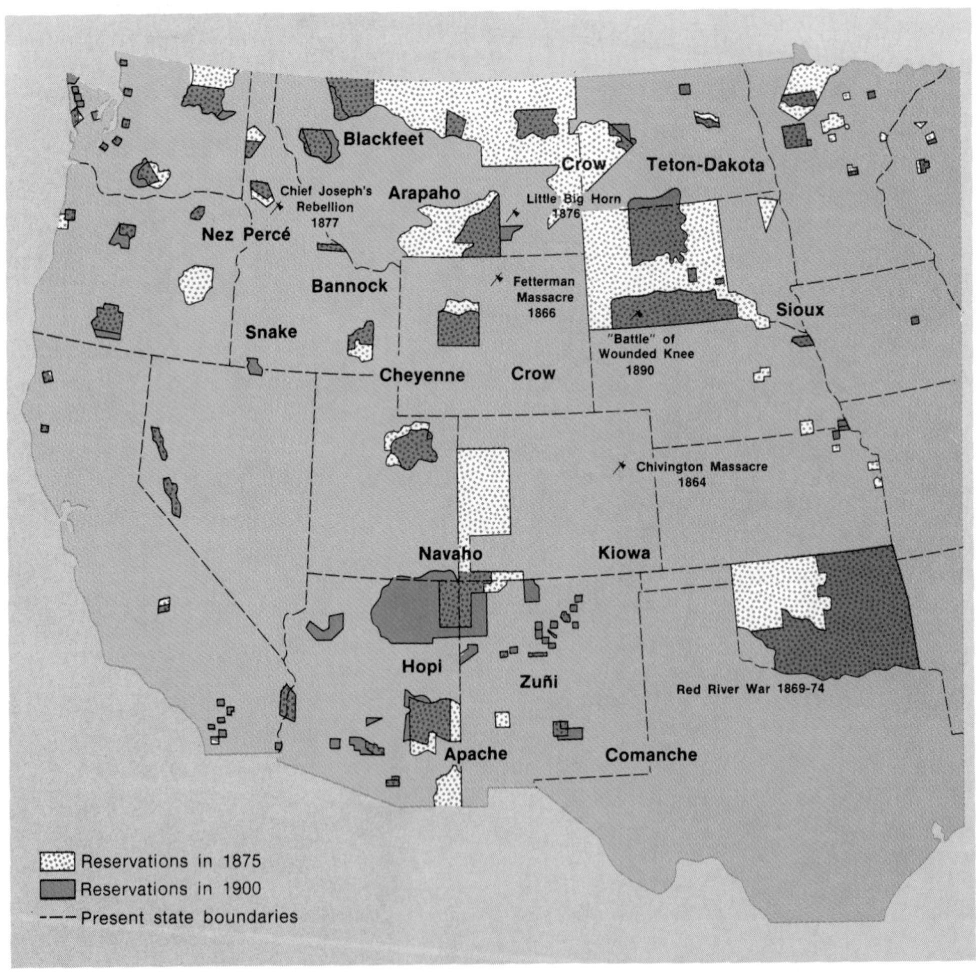

Map 17-1
Indian affairs in the West

General Sherman: negotiating with the Sioux

reflected in a letter signed "Texas" in the Chicago *Tribune:* "Give us Phil Sheridan, and send Philanthropy to the devil." It is hard to say at times whether West or South was in fiercer revolt against the Eastern philanthropists. The East prevailed temporarily against the West as it had against the South, however, and sent out a Peace Commission in 1867 to end the Sioux War and to inaugurate a policy of "small reservations" to replace the old one of "concentration." The new policy meant that the Indians were to abandon their way of life, submit to segregation in small out-of-the-way reservations on land spurned by white Americans, and accept government tutelage in learning "to walk the white man's road."

The government's policy toward red Indians in these years contrasted strangely with professed policy toward black freedmen, though both policies promised uplift by education. The same Congress that devised Reconstruction to bring equality and integration to the former slaves of the South approved strict segregation and inequality for the Indians of the West. General William T. Sherman, the deliverer of the Southern slaves, was now in command in the West to enforce policy toward Indians.

But many Indians refused to renounce their way of life and enter meekly into the reservations. When they took the warpath in the summer of 1868, General Sherman unleashed his troops and launched a decade of remorseless war against them. "I will urge General Sheridan to push his measures for the utter destruction and subjugation of all who are outside [the reservations] in a hostile attitude," Sherman wrote. "I propose that [he] shall prosecute the war with vindictive earnestness against all hostile Indians, till they are obliterated or beg for mercy." It took more than 200 battles from 1869 through 1874 to restore peace. Sometimes called a war of "extermination," this, like other Indian conflicts, was not one-sided. A recent study finds that during the entire nineteenth century no more than 5,000 Indians were killed, while the Indians killed some 7,000 soldiers and civilians in the same period. These figures, however, do not include indirect casualties caused by starvation and disease.

Little Bighorn: a pictographic account

President Grant was persuaded early in his administration to place under a dozen religious denominations the control of Indians living on reservations. Supported by government funds, agents chosen by religious bodies sought to educate, "civilize," and assimilate their charges. These actions became known unofficially as "Grant's Peace Policy." Indians refusing to settle on the reservations, however, were mercilessly subjected to the very unpeaceful policy of the United States Army. Coordination of the two policies served to remove most Indians from the path of white settlers and developers.

By the end of 1874 all seemed calm. Then in 1875, when government authorities permitted tens of thousands of gold prospectors to crowd into the Black Hills, the Sioux and other northern Indians reacted violently. At the Battle of the Little Bighorn on June 25, 1876, the rash young General George A. Custer and 265 men were wiped out in the new Sioux War. In spite of this victory, the Indians were compelled to surrender the following fall. Chief Sitting Bull and a few warriors fled to Canada, but, facing starvation, they were forced to sue for peace in 1881. The Nez Percé Indians of Oregon staged a rebellion that was repressed in 1877, and the survivors of this once-proud tribe were herded into a barren preserve in Indian Territory to be ravaged by disease and hunger. The last incident of the Indian wars was the sickening "Battle" of Wounded Knee in 1890, in which United States troops mowed down 200 Dakota men, women, and children.

Long before the fighting ended, the near extermination of the buffalo herds had hastened the collapse of Indian resistance. When it was discovered that buffalo pelts and leather could be marketed at a profit, the slaughter was organized on a commercial basis. Now professional hunters and skinners working in teams stepped up the butchery. The advance of the railroads hastened the end of the herds as well as the subduing of the Indians. By 1878 the vast southern herd, the larger of the two main herds, had been wiped out. Five years later, when collectors tried to round up a few specimens of what had recently been the most numerous breed of large animals in the world, they found fewer than 200 in all the West.

The slaughter of the buffalo, the expansion of railroads and settlers, and the pressure of the army did much to disintegrate the tribal culture of the Indians, but the humanitarian reformers waged a different kind of attack on that culture. They won their fight against physical extermination of the Indian only to substitute their own policy of relentless attack on Indian society, customs and religion and on tribal unity and authority. This, they sincerely believed, was necessary to "civilize" the Indians and assimilate them into white civilization. It was an article of faith among reformers that work, education, and the ownership of private property were the only way to salvation. They were especially opposed to tribal as against individual ownership of land.

Supported by humanitarian "friends of the Indian" and land grabbers alike, the reform program was partly realized by the Dawes Act of 1887, which struck at tribal authority by authorizing the breakup of reservations and the "allotment in severalty" of small holdings to individuals. The land allotted was often unsuited to farming and the new owners unprepared to be farmers. Allotments were held in trust at first, but when final title was granted, four out of five of the holders were quickly fleeced of their property or lost it in other ways. The surplus of reservation tribal lands after allotments was put up for sale and much the greater part of it lost to the tribes. By the early years of the twentieth century, the only considerable reservations remaining were those in the semiarid country of the Southwest.

Indians receiving allotments were to become citizens of the United States. Thus the oldest residents of the land became its newest citizens. But their government simultaneously deprived them of some of the basic rights of citizens. Those remaining on reservations were virtually imprisoned and pauperized. They were subject to the withholding of rations—those still entitled to them—in an effort to compel them to abandon tribal customs and loyalties. The government carried religious persecution to the point of espionage and force. The real trouble, according to John Collier, a reformer critic of a later generation, was not corrupt agents but "collective corruption, corruption which did not know it was corrupt."

Plains Indians were by no means the only nonwhite people in the West, and not the only Indians. Numerous native tribes of varied cultures, dialects, and ways of life had roots there. In addition to white and some black people from the East and established Hispanic peoples, came many Mexican, Chinese, and Japanese immigrants. The multiple ethnic encounters of the West, as Patricia Limerick suggests, make the confrontation between old-stock Americans of the East and European immigrants of the time "look like a family reunion." Differences brought on conflicts for all these groups in the West. Conflicts in which the Chinese immigrants were victims were especially grievous. Imported as cheap labor for railroad construction originally, and sought by many other employers, the Chinese "coolies" were resented as unfair competition and "tools of monopoly" by white workers. They became a favorite scapegoat in California politics and the target of more extreme violence than was inflicted on any other immigrant minority. As with the Indians, the white citizen's solution for violence was to banish the victims. In 1882, support for a Chinese Exclusion Act in Congress was gained in the East when the Asians were used as strikebreakers there. But the persecution of the Chinese continued even after the Exclusion Act was passed.

THE ERA OF THE BONANZAS

Webb in *The Great Frontier* distinguishes between the "primary windfalls" and the "secondary windfalls" that are gleaned from any frontier. The primary windfalls are the first easy pickings—gold, silver, furs—that are gained with little investment of energy or time. The secondary windfalls require more patience and expense. Anglo-Americans were obliged to concentrate on secondary windfalls. Then late in the nineteenth century, after the frontier had become a prosaic matter of timber, corn, and cotton, they belatedly entered upon a fabulous phase of frontier history that for the rest of the world had faded into the mists of legend with the conquistadors and the Spanish treasure ships. The beaver pelts had been gathered, and we have seen what happened to the buffalo. But there remained the bonanzas of gold and silver and the lush grass left by the bison.

The Miner's Bonanza There had been gold rushes from time to time in the East, but from 1804 to 1866 the five-state Appalachian gold field had yielded less than $20 million. An entirely new scale was set by the California yield of $555 million in a single decade, 1848–58. In the 1860s and 1870s the turbulent gold rush of the forty-niners (see p. 298) was to be repeated with variations time and again in the mountain areas of Nevada, Colorado, Arizona, Idaho, Montana, and Wyoming. Since the Californians usually led the invasion of these areas, the mining frontier advanced eastward instead of westward. The Californians also developed the primitive technology of "placer" mining, by which "pay dirt" was washed in pans, "cradles," or sluice boxes. Armed with nothing more than a pick and shovel and a crude pan, the lucky prospector could gather up loose gold that had washed down through debris to bedrock. The richer deposits of gold, usually in deep-lying veins of quartz, could only be mined with machinery that was beyond the means of the prospector and had to await the corporation. During the 1860s placer mining was more and more superseded by quartz mining.

The lure of the bonanza—even the hope of modest pay dirt—was enough to keep thousands of prospectors feverishly exploring gulches and canyons for three decades. After the discovery came the inevitable leak of the secret and the headlong scramble by other prospectors to stake a claim.

The lure of the bonanza: placer mining

The prospectors' invasion of the interior was started by discoveries in Colorado and Nevada. During the summer of 1858 prospectors made a number of small strikes in the vicinity of what was later to become Denver. Rumors of these finds, wildly and perhaps deliberately exaggerated, spread rapidly through the frontier region and started a rush for the Pike's Peak country that fall. A new discovery in May 1859, followed by several smaller ones, had offered some justification for the excitement, but the great majority of fortune hunters were doomed to disappointment (see Map 17-2).

In the meantime, prospectors had struck it rich on the eastern slope of the Sierras in Nevada opposite the California fields on the western slope: the incredibly rich Comstock Lode, the biggest bonanza of them all! Not until 1873, after heroic tunneling operations and giant engineering feats under the direction of John W. Mackay and his partners, was the greatest lode of silver and gold struck. From 1859 to 1879 the total output of the Comstock mines was $350 million, of which 45 percent was in gold and 55 percent in silver. No deposits of equal richness have ever been recorded in ancient or modern mining history.

Perched on the roof of this subterranean treasure house on the steep side of Mount Davidson, 7,200 feet above sea level, was Virginia City, the most celebrated of the Western mining towns. Mark Twain, who arrived at the diggings in the early days, described the town in *Roughing It:*

> So great was the pack, that buggies frequently had to wait half an hour for an opportunity to cross the principal street. Joy sat on every countenance, and there was a glad, almost fierce, intensity in every eye, that told of the money-getting schemes that were seething in every brain and the high hope that held sway in every heart.

After Comstock one strike followed another in western Nevada. None was so rich as Comstock, but all served to attract an unstable population to the territory and to increase the demand for statehood. Eight days before the election of 1864 Nevada became a state and promptly furnished three electoral votes for Lincoln (see Map 17-3).

In the meantime, the future states of Washington, Idaho, and Montana were the scene of gold rushes and

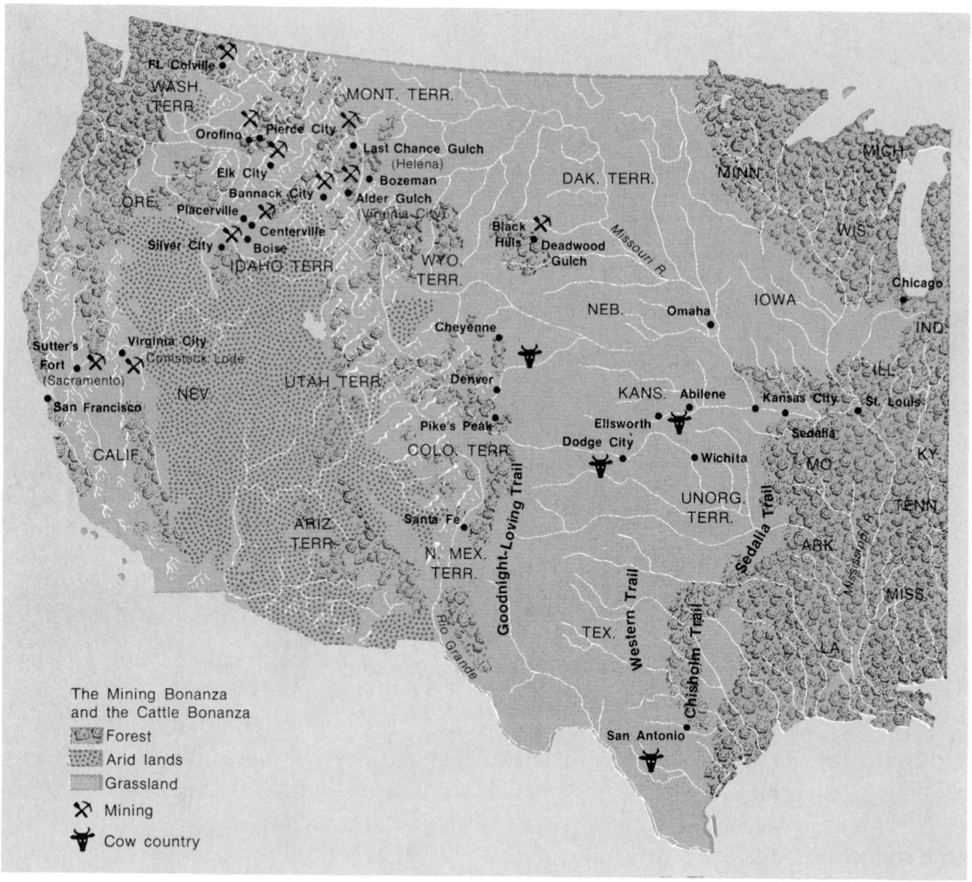

Map 17-2
The Great Plains environment

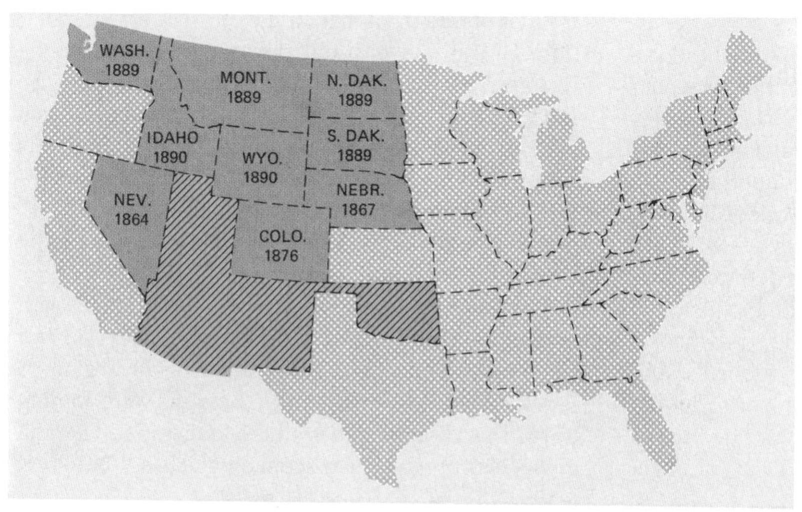

Map 17-3 *New states, 1864–1890*

Last Chance Gulch, 1865

flush times. During the years from Bull Run to Appomattox "yonder-siders" from California joined "pilgrims" from the East and seasoned prospectors from Nevada in stampedes to Orofino, Pierce City, Elk City, Boise, Placerville, Centerville, and Silver City. Many joined the great Montana gold rush around Bannack City, then jumped on to the spectacular diggings in Alder Gulch that produced $30 million of gold in three years, and ended up at Last Chance Gulch, where Helena was first laid out as a mining camp. A few more strikes after the war turned up the last surface gold in Idaho and Montana; then the placer miners passed on, leaving ghost towns behind them.

During the gold rushes a motley assortment of humanity accumulated on the mining frontier. The population of one camp was somewhat unscientifically classified as "Saxon, Celt, Teuton, Gaul, Greaser, Celestial, and Indian." The 206 souls of another camp were more carefully tabulated as 73 American white citizens, 37 Chinese, 35 British subjects, 29 Mexicans and Spaniards, 8 Negroes, and the rest assorted Europeans. Every camp of any size attracted its share of lawless outcasts—jailbirds, gamblers, prostitutes, deserters, desperadoes, stagecoach robbers. And every town had to decide whether or not to let the outcasts take over. As one observer described life in Last Chance Gulch in 1864: "Not a day or night passed which did not yield its full fruition of fights, quarrels, wounds, or murders. The crack of the revolver was often heard above the merry notes of the violin. . . . Pistols flashed, bowie knives flourished, and braggart oaths filled the air." The United States government was far off and preoccupied with other matters, and its arm was not always long enough to reach into Nevada and Idaho. As a result the miners developed their own informal codes of law and their own informal means of enforcement.

In a grand finale at Deadwood Gulch in the Black Hills of what later became South Dakota the miners' frontier outdid itself in a lurid caricature of its reputation. The curtain was rung down in the 1870s on the rowdiest brawls, the wildest desperadoes, and the most vigilant vigilantes of them all. After the Black Hills rush the prospectors and their supporting casts trooped off the scene, leaving mining to heavy investors and engineers. The frontier's "primary windfall" of precious metals had been stripped off, though the serious business of mining had only begun.

Maps of the West in this period are filled with "cities"—Virginia City, Elk City, Silver City, on and on—suggesting rapid urbanization of the region. A few survived, but many of the "cities" were mining towns that disappeared with the lode mined, like the towns less pretentiously named "gulches." But great

Western cities did begin their development in this period, six of them by 1880 rating among the hundred "principal American cities," with San Francisco dwarfing all others. They had distinctive Western traits, but they also shared patterns of urbanization established in the East (see pp. 487–89).

The Cattleman's Bonanza The windfall of the early cattlemen was almost as rich and free as that of the early miners. The cows harvested the free crop of grass, turned it into beef and hides, transported these commodities to market on the hoof, and obligingly dropped calves as replacements.

For a brief interlude between the passing of Indian and the buffalo and the entry of the farmer and the barbed wire fence, the Great Plains witnessed the most picturesque industrial drama ever staged —the drama of the open range and the cattle ranch. If the Southern planter could once claim that cotton was king, the Western cattleman could proclaim with equal fervor that grass was king. For the time being, at least, the plains were one limitless, fenceless, gateless pasture of rich, succulent, and ownerless grass that was there for the taking. Within an incredibly short period the herds of bison had been replaced and outnumbered by the herds of cattle.

The miner's invasion of the mountain and plains country came mainly from the Far West: the cattlemen, their animals, and their ranch culture invaded from the South. Herdsmen had acquired some of the cowboy's arts and lingo on their long trek across the Gulf states and the antebellum Southwest, but it was not until they had reached Texas and had begun to handle Spanish cattle from horseback that the craft took on its Mexican flavor and exotic style. A diamond-shaped area of the tip of Texas, with San Antonio at its apex, was the cradle of the future cowboy and his long-horned charges. The bulk of the cattle, a Spanish stock, grew up wild and were said to be "fifty times more dangerous to footmen than the fiercest buffalo." A tough, stringy, durable breed, wonderfully adapted to the plains, they multiplied so rapidly that they became a pest. Within just one decade the cattle population of Texas increased over 1,000 percent, and by 1860 cattle were estimated at nearly 5 million in that state alone.

Even before the Civil War, Texas cattlemen had made a few inconsequential drives to Northern markets, and after the war inducements multiplied. Texans were not to be daunted by the mere 1,500 miles that separated them from the fabulous meat markets and profits in the North. In 1866 they set forth on long drives north with more than a quarter of a million head during that year (see Map 17-2). Taking the most direct route to the nearest railhead, Sedalia, Missouri, the cattlemen fell into the hands of thieves along the wooded parts of their route. Thereafter they kept to the open plains. The first town founded for the specific purpose of receiving cows for shipment was Abilene, Kansas.

Other cow towns followed—Wichita, Ellsworth, Dodge City—pushing farther and farther westward and southward with the railroad, an indispensable adjunct to the cattle kingdom. The Texas trails themselves pushed in the same direction toward the Texas Panhandle and eastern New Mexico and Colorado. The trails shifted during the years of the long drive, to take advantage of the best grazing and water supplies. Some of them—the Goodnight-Loving Trail, the Western Trail, and the Chisholm Trail—left broad, brown, beaten tracks across hundreds of miles of grasslands. Riders of the long drive drove more than 5 million head of cattle northward over these trails between 1866 and 1888, after which the trails faded out of the industry.

Not all the Texas cattle were sold directly for beef. Many herds were driven to the ranges of New Mexico, Arizona, Colorado, Wyoming, Montana, and the Dakotas to feed mining camps and railroad builders and to supply the ranchers' demand for fresh stock. In the amazingly brief period of 15 years, by 1880, the cattlemen and their ranches had spread over the whole vast grassland from the Rio Grande into Canada as well as up into the recesses of the Rockies.

With the boom of the 1880s, the monarchs of the cattle kingdom became intoxicated with the magnificence of their domain and its immediate prospects. The depression of the 1870s had been rolled aside, the Indians had been driven into reservations, the railroads were coming on, and neither the homesteader nor barbed wire had yet arrived in menacing quantity. Beef prices were soaring and the grass was growing higher by the hour. No wonder the cow king got a wonderful feeling that everything was going his way. His optimism spread abroad, and investors from the four corners of the earth rushed to the plains to seek their fortunes.

As a symbol of this spectacular adventure, the public took to its heart not the cow king but his hired hand,

Cowboy branding a critter

and there the cowboy has remained enshrined, his cult faithfully tended by votaries of screen and television. Known sometimes as "cowpoke" or "cowpuncher," names derived from an early method of prodding lagging critters with long poles, the cowboy is more popularly identified with the lariat and the branding iron. His picturesque accouterments—sombrero, spurs, long-heeled boots, chaps, gloves, and saddle, which he called his "workbench"—were strictly functional, not ornamental, and strictly adapted to life on horseback. There, indeed, much of his life was spent—18 hours or more a day during phases of the long drive. Each cowboy had a "mount" of from eight to fourteen horses, depending on the work he was doing and the class of horses. Normally a hard-working man of Spartan and sober habits, the cowboy has come to share with the sailor a public image derived from his rare escapades of frantic recreation after long ordeals. As for the cowboy's addiction to lethal six-guns, it was exaggerated.

Violence of the shooting-iron sort, however, was unavoidable in the open-range cattle kingdom. With millions of dollars' worth of property wandering at large on public lands, unfenced and poorly marked, rustlers found the temptation overwhelming. Since government was remote and undependable, cattlemen resorted to private associations for protection and self-government in matters of roundup, branding, and breeding. These associations sometimes furnished all the government there was. The sort of justice they dispensed and the methods they used were similar to the rough frontier government produced in the mining camps.

Even with free pasturage and virgin grassland, cattle raising on the open range was extravagant and uneconomical. It exposed the herds to weather hazards, made adequate care of animals impossible and improvement of breeds difficult, encouraged rough and wasteful handling of cattle, and provoked costly and sometimes bloody range disputes. The approaching doom of the free range was further hastened by the expanding railroads and their loads of settlers, who staked claims and ran fences, and by the sheepherders. But the cattlemen contributed to their own downfall. They resorted to land fraud, monopoly, and ruthless violence to protect their interests. They even adopted for their own use before homesteaders arrived that concrete denial of the open range, the barbed wire fence: Charles Goodnight ran one all the way across the Texas Panhandle into New Mexico. Worse still, they overstocked and overgrazed the range.

The day of reckoning dawned in 1885, when beef prices started to tumble. On top of that, during the severe winter of 1885–86 as many as 85 percent of the herds on the southern ranges either starved or froze to death. A bad drought the following summer scorched the grass and left the remaining animals in poor condition. Then the legendary winter of 1886–87 fastened its cruel grip on the plains and brought panic to men as well as animals. When the thaw finally came, emaciated corpses of enormous herds were left stacked up against fences or piled deep in coulees. Loss of cattle in the northern plains was estimated to be 40 to 50 percent.

The disaster spelled the end of the great beef bonanza. It ruined large corporations and many individual ranchers and took the heart out of the open-range enterprise. There was little left of the reckless confidence with which cattlemen had greeted the great risks of the open range in its heyday.

THE FARMER MOVES WEST

Ever since 1607 American farmers had been moving west to break new ground. But in the last three decades of the nineteenth century they occupied and brought under cultivation more land than in all the years before 1870. It might seem natural to attribute this rapid expansion to the free-homestead policy adopted in 1862 (see p. 374). Homesteading did work very well in the upper prairie frontier prior to 1880, but before we jump to the conclusion that free land explained the rapid multiplication of farms, however, it would be well to review that policy as a whole.

American Land Policy The number of farms in the United States increased from some 2,000,000 in 1860 to 5,737,000 in 1900. And yet fewer than 600,000 homesteads were patented in those years, and they accounted for only 80,000,000 acres out of the more than 430,000,000 acres that were added to the total land in farms. Thus even if all the farmers who filed claims had been bona fide homesteaders, they would have accounted for fewer than one-sixth of the new farms and a little more than one-sixth of the added acreage. Actually, a great number of the so-called homesteads fell into the hands of large landholders and did not become farms until they were sold to settlers by speculators.

Nothing could have been further from the intention of the framers of the Homestead Act than the promotion of land monopoly. On the contrary, by distributing the bounty of free land among needy people they had hoped to defeat land monopoly. In practice, however, the great American promise of free land—a promise that was published around the world—turned out to be pretty much a delusion for the majority of new farmers. One trouble was that few prospective homesteaders could afford to take advantage of the opportunity, because they lacked the capital to transport their families and possessions to the public domain, stock up with expensive machinery, and stick it out for years until the farm became self-supporting. Fewer still understood the new type of agriculture required on the arid plains. Two-thirds of all homestead claimants before 1890 failed at the venture. Speculators hired people to stake out homesteads, falsely claim they had fulfilled the required conditions, and then turn over the land to their employer.

But the fundamental weakness of the Homestead Act was that it was not appropriate to much of the region where it applied. The law covered all public lands, of course, but not long after the act was passed the great bulk of public lands available for homesteading lay on the Great Plains and beyond. The Eastern congressmen who framed the law for the plains knew little about the needs of the people who were eventually going to live there. To the farmer back in the humid East a 160-acre tract seemed ideal for a family-sized farm—a good deal larger than the average, in fact. In the arid or semiarid West, however, a 160-acre tract was too small for grazing or dry farming and too large for irrigated farming. If the East persisted in writing laws for the West that did not work, said the Westerners, then the West was justified in ignoring or violating them.

In land policy, as in Indian policy, it proved difficult to reconcile the views of East and West—particularly since the Eastern outcry was against land monopoly and the Western demand was for larger and larger units of land. One attempt to adjust land policy to Western needs was the Timber Culture Act of 1873, which permitted homesteaders to add another 160 acres of relatively treeless land to their holdings provided they would plant trees on one-quarter of it within four years. The law failed to increase rainfall,

Guthrie, Oklahoma, 1889: holding down a claim

however, and nine out of ten claimants are said to have made no serious effort to forest their holdings.

A more absurd law was the Desert Land Act of 1877, which offered 640 acres to anyone who would pay 25 cents an acre down and promise to irrigate the land within three years. The trouble here was that the law required irrigation where no water was to be had and at least 95 percent of the "proofs" of irrigation were estimated to be fraudulent. The Timber and Stone Act of 1878 permitted any citizen, or any alien with first papers, to buy at $2.50 an acre 160 acres of land "unfit for cultivation" and valuable chiefly for timber and stone. This act was as enticing an invitation to the timber barons as the Desert Land Act had been to the cattlemen. When bona fide homesteaders finally arrived on the scene to stake out their claims, they usually had to choose from the less desirable and the poorly located tracts or else pay the speculators' price. In addition to about 100 million acres bought from the federal land office, the entrepreneurs bought up another 100 million acres from shrinking Indian reservations that became available under the government's policy of concentration and 140 million acres from state land holdings. This accounted for some 340 million acres that were beyond the reach of homestead privileges.

Between 1850 and 1871 the federal government and the states had granted railroad corporations more than 200 million acres of land to encourage construction (see p. 411), making the railroads the largest land jobbers of the West. Not all of this land was patented. But the form of the federal grants meant that many millions of acres in addition to the actual land granted were withheld from settlement. The railroad lands lay on both sides of the track, from 20 to 40 square miles for every mile of track laid in the territories and up to 20 for every mile laid in the states (see Map 17-4). This land was not arranged in solid strips, however, but in

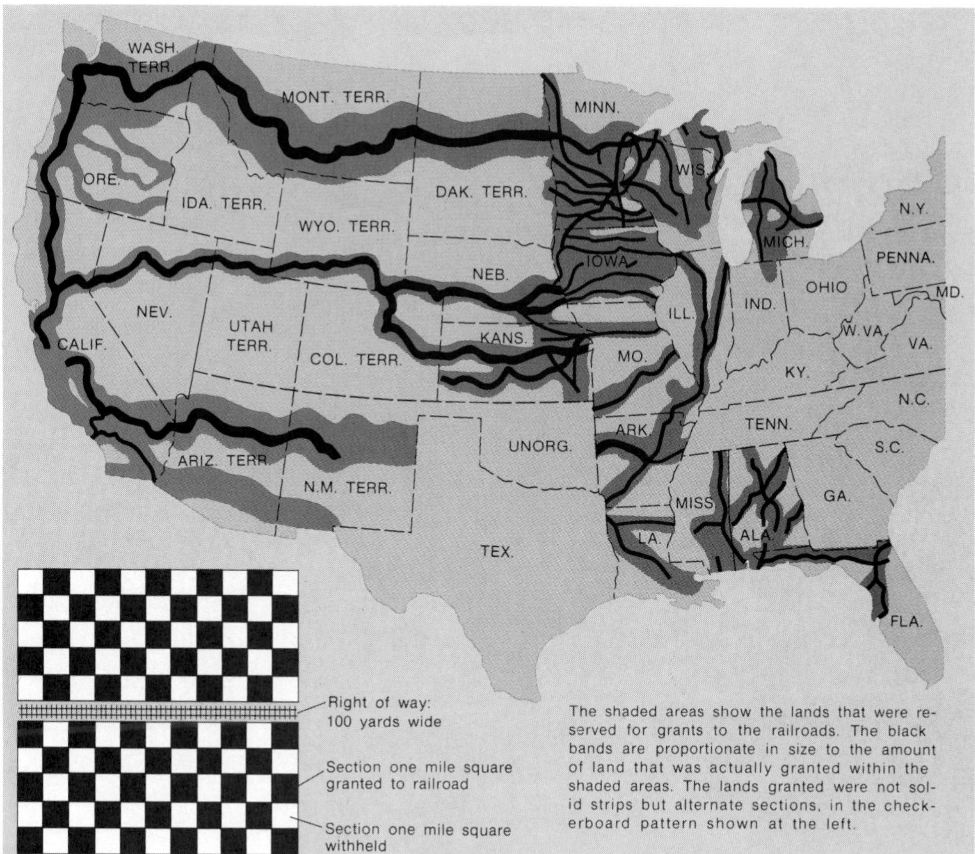

Map 17-4
Federal grants to the railroads

alternate sections, checkerboard fashion. But the whole solid strip was commonly withheld from settlement until the railroad chose its right-of-way and decided which alternate sections to keep. Great belts of land on either side of the tracks were placed beyond the homesteader's reach. At one time or another some three-tenths of the area of the country, and a much greater proportion of the West, was forbidden to use. Homesteaders were obliged either to accept areas remote from the rails or to pay the higher price the railroads asked. In 1887 this evil was alleviated by the Cleveland administration, which threw open to settlement most of the land thus withheld.

The Advance of Settlement The railroads became the principal colonizers as well as the biggest landowners of the New West. Rapid settlement along their lines meant larger revenues from passenger fares and freight charges and more land sales. Railroads and states sold settlers nearly six times as much land as the farmers were able to obtain by homesteading. Each Western road had its land department and its bureau of immigration, and each Western state its agency to advertise and exaggerate opportunities for settlers. Steamship companies with an eye to emigrant passengers joined in the campaign abroad. Working with railroad agents, they plastered Europe with posters and literature in all important languages calculated to attract settlers to the "Garden of the West." The railroads provided what the Homestead Act had neglected — credit terms, special passenger rates, and agricultural guidance and assistance for prospective purchasers and settlers. The success of the railroad colonizers was striking, and their campaigns in Europe infected whole countries with the "American fever." From Norway, Sweden, and Denmark, which were especially susceptible, peasants by the millions

The Frontier as Imitator

To Turner the westerner was a radical in both thought and actions, developing new ideas to meet new conditions. The modern trend of thinking, while far from uniform, tends to move in the opposite direction, with more and more people asserting that the West was essentially conservative. True enough the westerner made some unpleasant innovations such as the sod house, was forced to develop several new techniques as in the arid parts of the West, and supported certain drastic actions for his own advantage—as free land and the elimination of Indian power; and yet the great bulk of his customs, including the building of log cabins, was derivative. More basic, however, he accepted in general the virtues and ideals which he had been taught as a youth and which were common in the United States. He was a God-fearing man along traditional lines. He joined the rest of the United states in judging success as the attainment of wealth. He respected personal property and the sanctity of contracts just as did his eastern contemporary. In fact he had moved to the West not in protest at current ideals but to attain them more quickly. His objective was the same kind of life which he had envied in his eastern neighbors.

From Robert E. Riegel, *Current Ideas of the Significance of the United States Frontier,* 1952

emigrated to the Northwest. By 1890 Minnesota had 400 towns bearing Swedish names, and Irish and German colonies were sprinkled across Minnesota, Nebraska, and Dakota Territory. Whatever the shortcomings, frauds, and injustices of Western land policy, and whatever the delusions spread by promoters about a Land of Promise, all these evils should be viewed in comparison with realities in Europe. There productive land was almost totally unavailable save at prohibitive prices, and land ownership beyond the dreams of most rural people. Of some 14 million Europeans who moved to America in the 1870s and 1880s many of them came with the hope of a farm of their own, most of them to stay in the belief that they had improved their lot.

As in the past, however, the states immediately to the east of the advancing frontier furnished a large proportion of the new settlers. In the 1870s some 190 million acres, an area equal to that of Great Britain and France combined, were added to the cultivated area of the country, mostly just to the west of the Minnesota-Louisiana tier of states. The line of settlement surged westward irregularly, first along the river valleys, rapidly along the growing railroad lines, and out over the rolling plains. A frontier in Kansas that had not budged perceptibly in two decades forged rapidly ahead in the 1870s, and both Kansas and Nebraska had filled out to the edge of the semiarid plains by 1880. To the north the frontier advanced in a succession of three "Dakota Booms" roughly coinciding with three contemporaneous gold rushes. A demonstration of how to make a 100 percent profit in wheat growing, put on by the Northern Pacific Railway after the Panic of 1873, started a rush that covered 300 miles of the Red River Valley with "bonanza farms" ranging up to 100,000 acres in size. Farther north in Dakota Territory was the special province of James J. Hill, inspired colonizer of the Northwest and head of the Great Northern Railway. Hill planned and directed the settlement of thousands of pioneers along the tracks of his road to the Pacific.

Far to the south, in what was to become New Mexico and Arizona, a frontier of Mexican-American settlers moved north and west after the Civil War. Spreading out from their historic settlements along the upper Rio Grande that dated back to the sixteenth

The Frontier as Innovator

To the frontier the American intellect owes its striking characteristics. That coarseness and strength combined with acuteness and inquisitiveness; that practical, inventive turn of mind, quick to find expedients; that masterful grasp of material things, lacking in the artistic but powerful to effect great ends; that restless, nervous energy; that dominant individualism, working for good and for evil, and withal that buoyancy and exuberance which comes with freedom—these are traits of the frontier, or traits called out elsewhere because of the existence of the frontier. Since the days when the fleet of Columbus sailed into the waters of the New World, America has been another name for opportunity, and the people of the United States have taken their tone from the incessant expansion which has not only been open but has even been forced upon them. He would be a rash prophet who should assert that the expansive character of American life has not entirely ceased. Movement has been its dominant fact, and, unless this training has no effect upon a people, the American energy will continually demand a wider field for its exercise. But never again will such gifts of free land offer themselves.

From Frederick Jackson Turner, "The Significance of the Frontier in American History," 1893

century, these Hispano sheepmen ran head-on into expanding Anglo cattlemen. Not until the twentieth century, however, did the wave of Mexican migration crest—a wave that was to make these people one of the largest minority groups in the country.

In the meantime, farms in Texas more than doubled during the 1870s. As both the Texas and the Kansas frontiers approached the semiarid country to the west, avid land seekers began to eye the tempting lands of the Indian Territory between the two states. Egged on by railroad companies with actual or projected lines in the territory, agitators defied the troops guarding the boundaries, repeatedly invaded the territory, and besieged Congress with demands to throw the cowed and defeated Indian tribes out of their last refuge. Congress yielded to their demands and on April 22, 1889, threw open some 2 million acres of the Oklahoma District in the heart of the territory. At the signal, thousands of "Boomers" ("Sooners" had sneaked in earlier) riding on every conceivable vehicle, including 15 trains with passengers jamming the roofs, swarmed into the district, staked it off in claims, and founded two cities—all within a few hours. Congress yielded to pressure again and created the Oklahoma Territory on May 2, 1890. In succeeding years one strip after another was opened—the largest, the 6 million acres of the Cherokee Outlet, in 1893—until the entire area of Oklahoma had been settled.

The superintendent of the census of 1890 discovered after the returns were in that something was missing: the long-familiar frontier. "Up to and including 1880," he reported, "the country had a frontier of settlement, but at present the unsettled area has been so broken into by isolated bodies of settlement that there can hardly be said to be a frontier line." In 1893 Frederick Jackson Turner, a young historian from Wisconsin, undertook to interpret the meaning of this development in a paper entitled "The Significance of the Frontier in American History." A devoted son of the West, Turner maintained that contact with the frontier fostered, among other things, a continuous rebirth and rejuvenation of democracy—a conclusion not always easy to reconcile with the way land was distributed and the frontier advanced.

New Farms and New Methods The tribulations of the new pioneers of prairie and plain rivaled those of the Jamestown settlers in the early seventeenth century. Like the plagues that the God of Moses sent against the Egyptians, new calamities visited Western farmers with each season (see Map 17-5.) Hardly had the winter blizzards ceased when melting snow brought flash floods to menace man and beast. Summer temperatures soared to 118°; drought and hot winds seared corn to crisp blades and whitened settlers' faces with the salt of sweat. Worst of all were the grasshoppers, especially during the terrible plagues of the mid-1870s. Prairie fires, dust storms, marauding Indians, claim jumpers, and rattlesnakes further chastened the spirit of the pioneers and discouraged all but the sturdiest.

Mrs. Abigail Scott Duniway, woman suffrage leader in the Northwest, described her own lot later in a pioneer community of Oregon: "To bear two children in two and a half years from my marriage . . . to sew and cook, and wash and iron; to bake and clean and stew and fry; to be, in short, a general pioneer drudge, with never a penny of my own, was not pleasant business for an erstwhile school teacher."

Gradually inventiveness and industry solved many of the problems of soil and climate and overcame the lack of wood and water. In their first few years the homesteaders lived in miserable sod houses, half buried in the prairie and roofed with slabs of cut turf. But later, when the railroad brought down the cost of lumber, they built frame houses. The problem of how to fence their land in a woodless, railless, stoneless region was solved by the invention of barbed wire. Of the several types devised, the most successful was patented by Joseph F. Glidden, an Illinois farmer, in November 1874.

The problem of water supply was harder to solve. The only reliable sources of supply lay far below the surface, too deep to reach by open, hand-dug wells. And even when a well was drilled, pumping the water up 200 to 800 feet by hand was impractical. The obvious solution was to harness the free power of the winds and by 1880 scores of small firms were installing windmills adapted to this purpose.

To meet the problem of cultivating soil in semiarid country without irrigation, Westerners developed the technique of "dry farming" where rainfall was at least ten inches per year. To break the tough soil of the plains and cultivate larger farms where labor was scarcer than ever, the farmer needed a new type of machinery. A revolution in farm machinery had started before 1860, and most of the basic patents had been granted by that year. But the mass production of machines came only after the Civil War.

The plow that most successfully broke the plains was devised by James Oliver of Indiana, a chilled-iron plow and smooth-surfaced moldboard. Machine harvesting of wheat was improved in 1880 by a mechanical twine binder that tied up the cut bundles. An even speedier device, used in drier parts of the West, was the header, which cut off the heads of the grain and left the stalk for pasturage or plowing under.

The soft winter wheat of the East could not withstand the rigors of the new climate and was replaced by a new variety imported from northern Europe and by Turkey Red from the Crimea. To mill the hard grain of the new varieties, the basic idea of the roller mill was borrowed from Hungary, and chilled-iron rollers were

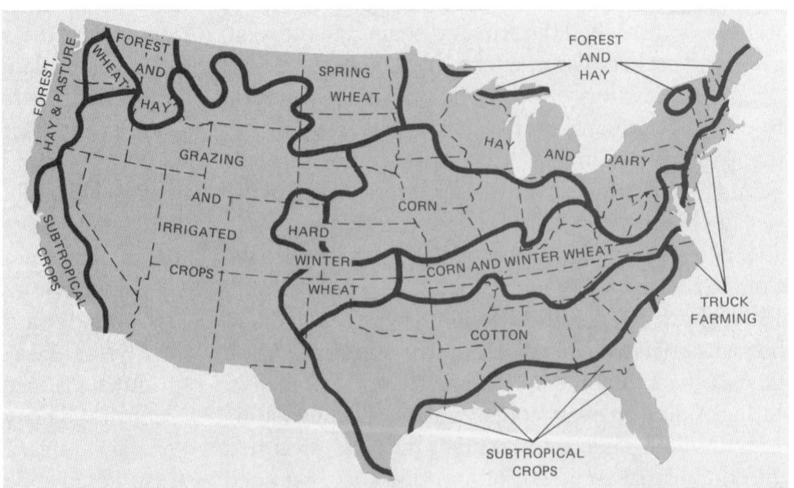

Map 17-5
Agricultural regions of the United States

Sod house: "harsh realities"

added by 1879. By the early 1870s the storing, loading, handling, and transporting of wheat had all been reduced to mechanical processes.

The most striking results of mechanized farming were achieved in wheat production. An acre that had required 61 hours to farm by hand took only 3 hours to farm by machine, and where one man could farm only 7½ acres by old methods he could take on 135 acres in the 1890s. Mechanization released men from drudgery and stupefying toil. On the other hand, in the very

Harvesting in Washington State

states where mechanization was most prevalent there was a remarkable growth of tenancy. The farmers, like the placer miners and the range cattlemen, were destined in the late 1880s for trouble and disenchantment with the Golden West. They fell victims to their own illusions.

The illusions of the farmer were part of a great national illusion dating from the early years of the republic. This was what Henry Nash Smith in *Virgin Land* has called "The Myth of the Garden"—the myth that the West was a realizable utopia, an agrarian Eden where free land and honest toil would produce a virtuous yeomanry and the good life. According to the myth, the West was the true source of national regeneration, the means of realizing the ideals of democracy and equality, and it was celebrated by poets, novelists, and historians alike. "All of the associations called up by the spoken word, the West," wrote the Western novelist Hamlin Garland in 1891, "were fabulous, mythic, hopeful." To the frontier West, Frederick Jackson Turner attributed "that buoyancy and exuberance which comes with freedom." But the stark contrast between the hopes fostered by the myth and the harsh realities of experience could not escape even the dullest farmer. Far from utopian were the sod house, the dust storm, the grasshopper plague. "So this is the reality of the dream!" exclaims a character in a Garland novel. "A shanty on a barren plain, hot and lone as a desert. My God!"

To end on a note of defeat and disenchantment, however, would be to misrepresent the history of the last and most colorful of the nation's many wests. That adventure was too full of the "buoyancy and exuberance" that Turner celebrated to be fully characterized in terms of greed, oppression, and disappointment. The Western experience left a profound and lasting impact on the American mind and culture: in literature as reflected in Mark Twain, Bret Harte, or Willa Cather; in the arts as seen in painting, photography, and film; and in science as represented in the work of Clarence King and John Muir. In folklore, ballad, and story the legends of Billy the Kid, Wild Bill Hickok, Calamity Jane, and Buffalo Bill captured the popular imagination. They also captured the imagination of Europe. Buffalo Bill Cody landed his "Wild West Show" with hundreds of cowboys and Indians in England in 1887, opened with a command performance before Queen Victoria and Prime Minister Gladstone, and went on to tour western Europe, a tour that was repeated annually into the following century. Cody himself was the hero of some 200 novels, and the "Original Buffalo Bill Library" contained more than 700 titles. Karl May, a German novelist who wrote 70 Westerns, was the favorite writer of both Albert Einstein and Adolf Hitler. Italian filmmakers alone released 130 Western movies in 1964 and 1965. The West became and remained an international frontier of the popular imagination.

SUGGESTIONS FOR READING

The best recent survey of the subject is R. W. Paul, *The Far West and the Great Plains in Transition, 1859–1900* (1988). R. A. Billington, *Westward Expansion: A History of the American Frontier* (1967), stresses the Turner thesis. The thesis itself appears in "The Significance of the Frontier in American History," in F. J. Turner, *The Frontier in American History* (1920). W. P. Webb, *The Great Plains* (1931), is a provocative study of environmental determinism. H. R. Lamar, *The Far Southwest, 1846–1912* (1966), is an excellent study of territories. W. Gard, *The Great Buffalo Hunt* (1959), is the best book on this subject, and R. G. Atherton, *Union Pacific Country* (1976), is the best on another. The West as symbol and myth is brilliantly analyzed in H. N. Smith, *Virgin Land* (1950), and in European culture by R. A. Billington, *Land of Savagery, Land of Promise: The European Image of the American Frontier* (1981). Fresh points of view enliven P. N. Limerick, *The Legacy of Conquest: The Unbroken Past of the American West* (1987); Joanne Stratton, *Pioneer Women* (1981); and W. Cronon, *Nature's Metropolis: Chicago and the Great West* (1991).

Four general histories of the Indians are recommended: R. M. Utley, *The Indian Frontier of the American West, 1846–1890* (1984); W. E. Washburn, *The Indian in America* (1975); W. T. Hagan, *American Indians* (1961); and J. R. Swanton, *The Indian Tribes of North America* (1953). On reform, see F. P. Prucha, *American Indian Policy in Crisis: Christian Reformers and the Indians, 1880–1920* (1984), and F. E. Hoxie, *The Final Promise: The Campaign to Assimilate the Indians, 1880–1920* (1984). Insight on military leaders appears in R. G. Atherton, *William Tecumseh Sherman and the Settlement of the West* (1956), and C. C. Rister, *Border Command: General Phil Sheridan in the West* (1944). White stereotypes are studied in R. F. Berkhofer, Jr., *The White Man's Indian: Images of the American Indian from Columbus to the Present* (1978). On Chinese immigrants, see S. H.

Tsai, *China and Overseas Chinese in the United States, 1868–1911* (1983).

On mining, the best reading on this period is R. W. Paul, *Mining Frontiers of the Far West, 1848–1880* (1963); D. A. Smith, *Rocky Mountain Mining Camps* (1967); and W. S. Greever, *The Bonanza West: The Story of the Western Mining Rushes, 1848–1900* (1963). For colorful reminiscences, see Mark Twain, *Roughing It* (1872), and Dan De Quille, *History of the Big Bonanza* (1876, reprinted 1947).

M. Frank, W. T. Jackson, and A. W. Spring, *When Grass Was King* (1957), is a roundup of scholarship. L. Atherton, *The Cattle Kings* (1961), is thoughtful and sympathetic. Also helpful are J. M. Skaggs, *The Cattle Trailing Industry: Between Supply and Demand, 1865–1890* (1973); G. M. Gressley, *Bankers and Cattlemen* (1966); E. C. Abbott and H. H. Smith, *We Pointed Them North* (1955); and R. R. Dykstra, *The Cattle Towns* (1968). Of the vast cowboy literature, A. Adams, *The Log of a Cowboy* (1927), and J. F. Dobie, ed., *A Texas Cowboy* (1950), contain firsthand experiences; J. B. Frantz and J. E. Choate, *The American Cowboy: The Myth and the Reality* (1955), is a realistic analysis.

The plight of the farmers of the West appears grim in F. A. Shannon, *The Farmer's Last Frontier: Agriculture, 1860–1897* (1945), and more hopeful in G. C. Fite, *The Farmer's Frontier, 1865–1900* (1966). On the history of American land policy and its administration, see P. W. Gates, *History of Public Land Development* (1968), and R. M. Robbins, *Our Landed Heritage: The Public Domain, 1776–1936* (1942). The history of the new farm machinery is found in W. Kaempffert, *A Popular History of American Invention* (1924), and R. M. Wik, *Steam Power on the American Farm* (1953). On a neglected minority, see M. S. Meier and F. Rivera, *The Chicanos: A History of Mexican Americans* (1972), and D. W. Meinig, *Southwest* (1971). The pioneer farm on the Western frontier is pictured in E. Dick, *The Sod-House Frontier, 1854–1890* (1937).

Vivid fictional accounts are Willa Cather, *O Pioneers!* (1913) and *My Antonia* (1918); O. E. Rølvaag, *Giants in the Earth* (1927); and M. Sandoz, *Old Jules* (1935).

CHAPTER EIGHTEEN

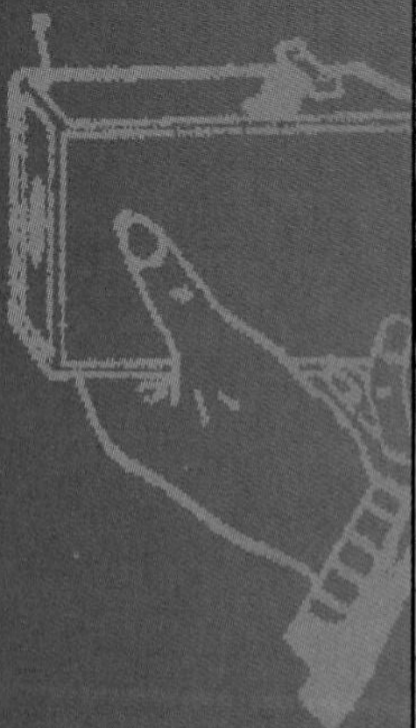

INDUSTRIAL WORKERS

THE ORDEAL OF INDUSTRIALIZATION

The return of peace in 1865 had stimulated magnificent expectations among fortune builders, profit makers, and industrial entrepreneurs. "The truth is," Senator John Sherman wrote his brother General William T. Sherman, "the close of the war with our resources unimpaired gives an elevation, a scope to the ideas of leading capitalists, far higher than anything ever undertaken in this country before. They talk of millions as confidently as formerly of thousands." Their high hopes and expectations seemed justified by all they surveyed: half a continent to be developed; a built-in empire rich in coal, iron, oil, waterpower, lumber — most of the resources essential for great industrial power; a responsive federal government eager to further business interests; the greatest free-trade market in the world surrounded by a high protective tariff barrier; and European immigrants swarming in to provide cheap labor. Surely the stage appeared to be set for the "heroic age" of industrial enterprise that has been glorified in legend.

Americans believed then and have continued to believe that their economy set the pace and outstripped all others in its rapid rate of industrial growth in the late nineteenth century and after. In recent years, however, students of comparative growth have questioned the validity of that faith. They point out that because of rapid population growth in the United States its gross national product increased faster than that in the nations of Europe, but that in growth measured by product per capita the American economy did not take the lead. And production and distribution per capita are more closely related to individual welfare than is gross production. The legend of American economic superiority needs to be revised in some respects.

However unavoidable the Civil War may have been, it was more devastating and exhausting than any European war between 1815 and 1914. On balance it probably did more to retard than to stimulate growth in the national economy. The same may be said of some of the very endowments once thought to have been unique American advantages. The high rate of natural increase in population, for example, produced a larger percentage of nonworkers, higher investment in child rearing and new households, as well as retarded savings and lower per capita income. The millions of immigrants provided cheap labor (and again, low per capita income), but not well-adjusted, educated, or geographically distributed labor — or labor highly endowed with "the Protestant work ethic." The very size of the country, whose vast expanse was the pride of patriots, contrasts unfavorably with the compact location of factories, resources, and markets in Europe and points up American disadvantages. Where a 100-mile railroad was adequate there, it took 1,000 miles of rails to do the job here. Far-flung raw materials and settlements deprived manufacturers of usable capital, slowed the movement of capital, created problems of management, curbed technological innovation, and produced conflict and frustration with local jurisdictions, jealousies, and corrupt governments.

Whether because of these or other deterrents and handicaps, American economic growth in product per capita during the famous age of enterprise lagged behind that of European leaders such as Germany, France, and Sweden, though it remained above that of Great Britain. It is the economic paradox of the period 1880–1914, when Americans were exploiting their fabulous natural resources and developing mass production and were assumed to be leading the world, that their country instead remained at about the average level of growth per capita maintained in northwestern European countries. Of course, it should be remembered that the leading countries had a very high rate and that western Europe was increasing its industrial power enormously in those years. To have kept up with the average in such a race was a remarkable achievement.

Size and numbers and rate of population increase did count heavily in gross national product and sheer value of manufactured goods, and the United States looked better in comparative growth on those terms. In 1860 the United States was a second-rate industrial country, lagging behind the United Kingdom and perhaps France and Germany. But by 1890 the United States had stepped into first place, and the value of its manufactured goods almost equaled the combined production of all the three former leaders. Between the eve of the Civil War and First World War, American manufacturing production multiplied twelve times over. The growth rate of national product in those years was consistently higher than that of any other technologically advanced nation. In sheer size there was surely something "heroic" about the scale, if nothing else.

THE RAILROAD EMPIRE

"The generation between 1865 and 1895 was already mortgaged to the railways," reflected Henry Adams, "and no one knew it better than the generation itself." This was the generation that planned, built, financed, and made the first attempts to control the most extensive railroad network in the world. The headlong haste and heedless ethics of its experience are caught in the national expression "railroaded through." No one, not even the enemies of the railroad, could be found in that age to deny its importance. Everyone believed it was the key to mass production and mass consumption, to the utilization of natural resources and the creation of a national market, and to the binding together and settlement of a continental area. The railroad dominated the imagination, the politics, the economy, and the hopes of a generation, and the outsized cowcatcher and smokestack of the old-fashioned steam locomotive might well be taken as the symbol of the age. The poet William Ellery Leonard, who was born in 1876, entitled an autobiographical work *The Locomotive-God,* and the popular ballad makers lavished a devotion on the iron horse they had formerly reserved for the flesh-and-blood steed and the sailing ship.

Building the Network The laying of rails went forward in fits and starts. Slowed by the Civil War, total mileage of rails increased from 31,000 to 53,000 in

Railroad workers: spanning the continent

the 1860s. In spite of depression, the 1870s added 40,000 miles of new rails. The 1880s, the great decade of railway expansion, opened with some 93,000 miles and ended with 166,000, an increase of more than 73,000 miles in ten years. By the end of the century the United States had a total of nearly 200,000 miles, or more than all Europe including Russia. In the meantime the ungainly little "bullgine" with the disproportionate funnel had evolved into a giant that could master mountain and plain, a giant that dwarfed any foreign make of locomotive.

To build this vast railway network was an undertaking comparable in magnitude to the construction of a navy, and for the United States it was even more costly and was thought to be more essential to the national interest. European governments assumed a large part of the responsibility for building and running their railroad establishments as readily as for their military establishments. In America, apart from a few state-owned roads of antebellum origin, initiative and management were left primarily in the hands of private enterprise. Even by 1880, before half the network was completed, an investment of more than $4,600 million had gone into the nation's railroads. By 1897 their stocks and bonds totaled $10,635 million as compared with a total national debt of less than $1,227 million.

While public enthusiasm for railroad building was at its height, government at all levels thrust credit and resources upon the railroad promoters. Villages, towns, cities, and states came forward with extravagant support in the form of bonds and other commitments. The federal government committed 175,000,000 acres of the public domain, of which the railroads actually received more than 131,000,000 acres. In addition they received 49,000,000 acres from the states. These grants made a substantial contribution toward paying for the railroad investment. Although government subsidies were often obtained through bribery and were responsible for much corruption, the policy of subsidizing the railroads with grants of public land was probably justified in the long run. By attaching conditions to the land grants that obliged the railroads to furnish cheap transportation for mail and military shipments, the government has enjoyed substantial savings over the years. Actually, less than 10 percent of the railroad mileage of the country was built with federal land grants. And most of that mileage was on the roads built across the Great Plains, where investment was slow in yielding returns and where some form of public credit was essential.

The transcontinental lines called for the most heroic efforts and attracted some of the ablest—and some of the most unscrupulous—enterprisers. The completion of the Union Pacific-Central Pacific in 1869 realized the antebellum dream of spanning the continent with rails, and within the next quarter of a century four more lines flanked the original one, two

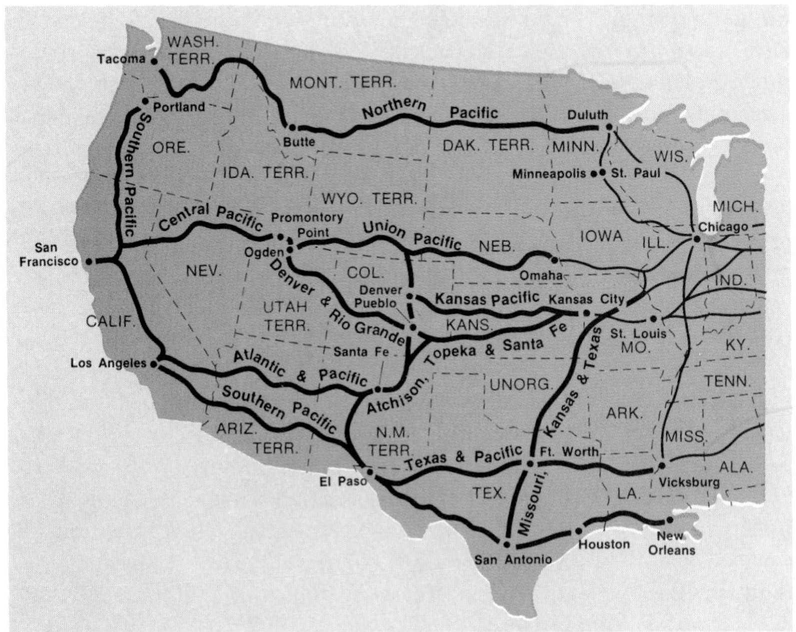

Map 18-1
Early Pacific railroad lines, about 1884

on either side: the Southern Pacific and the Santa Fe to the south and the Northern Pacific and the Great Northern to the north (for some, see Map 18-1). Each line excited intense rivalries and ambitions in the cities they connected and the sections they served, as well as among the railroad builders and promoters.

Railroads east of the Mississippi, with exceptions such as the New York Central, were built mainly to serve local needs and to promote the interests of particular cities. Hundreds of small lines using a variety of gauges were built after the Civil War. The South alone had 400 companies averaging not more than 40 miles apiece. One task of the postwar generation was to fill in the gaps between lines and to weld them into an integrated national network. Through consolidation by lease, purchase, or merger, nearly two-thirds of the country's railroad companies were absorbed by the other third. In 1880 alone, 115 companies lost their identity, and between 1880 and 1888 some 425 companies were brought under control of other roads. The Pennsylvania Railroad by 1890 was an amalgamation of 73 smaller companies and some 5,000 miles of rails. By 1906 two-thirds of the nation's mileage was operated under 7 groups.

In tandem and often in close alliance with the expanding railroads went the development of other communication and transportation services. Besides providing the means of a more modern postal system, the railroads were tied in with the development of the nation's telegraph network, dominated by the Western Union Company, and later with the growth of the telephone network. By the end of the century the railroads operated nearly all the country's domestic steamship lines, and typically the railroad stations were the central points of the new urban transportation systems.

The Managerial Revolution The lives of the entrepreneurs and financiers who built the transcontinentals and welded together the great railroad systems—colorful figures like Collis P. Huntington, Thomas A. Scott, Jay Gould, and James J. Hill—make fascinating reading. Of more profound importance however, was the revolution their operations brought about in the scale, management, and character of business enterprise. Up to their time the traditional business firm normally handled a single economic function in one geographic area and was managed by the owners or members of their families. By the 1890s, however, the great railroad systems were not only the largest business enterprises in America but the largest in the world. A single railroad system out of the 30 largest in that decade managed more workers, handled more funds, and used more capital than the most complex government organizations, including the Postal Department or the combined national military establishments of that time.

Neither the owners and their families nor the investment bankers and financiers had enough qualified members to provide the great corps of managers required by operations of this complexity and scale. To fill this need railroads recruited salaried professional managers selected for skill and experience rather than family or money, and organized them in a hierarchical bureaucracy. Where in traditional firms owners managed and managers owned, in the new system management became separated from ownership. As pioneered by the railroads, this form of modern business enterprise became the most powerful institution in the American economy and its managers the most influential group of decision makers. It also became the model of modern business enterprise at home as well as in all developed countries.

As the managerial revolution developed, the railroads modernized their technology and services. Steel rails replaced iron rails, and safety precautions such as double tracks, block signals, automatic couplers, and air brakes were standardized, as were time zones and track gauges. On November 18, 1883, the American Railway Association divided the continent into four time zones and millions of citizens set their watches accordingly—in spite of outraged advocates of "God's time." And on the last night in May 1886, the Southern roads moved one rail three inches nearer to the other to comply with the national standard gauge of 4 feet 8½ inches. Some results of these changes were tangible improvements, including more reliable, more punctual, and cheaper transportation. In the last half of the century, real passenger charges fell 50 percent and freight rates much more.

Competition and Disorder In spite of all these improvements, the American railroads were in serious difficulties. The construction boom of the 1880s resulted in a network of railroads much greater than was needed at the time. Managers resorted to ruinous competitive wars, offering fantastic "rebates" and secret rates to secure the traffic of big shippers and overcharging outrageously where they had no competition. They employed all manner of rate jugglery and deception and trusted neither customer nor competitor. Under such conditions competition, instead of being "the life of trade" and a benefit to the enterprise as well as to the public, proved a curse to both. In their efforts to curb piratical rate cutting and blackmail, competitors tried treaties, solemn agreements, and traffic "pools," but these proved difficult to enforce and were always breaking down. Demoralization of the industry was a serious threat.

If the railroad industry could not set its own house in order, then order would have to be imposed from outside. The state governments took the initiative and made the first experiments in regulation and control. In 1869 Massachusetts established a commission to supervise railroad activities and investigate grievances. Within the next ten years, a dozen more states established commissions modeled on that of Massachusetts. Several state legislatures in the Middle West adopted more thoroughgoing measures of regulation. The Supreme Court upheld the constitutionality of the legislation in the case of *Munn* v. *Illinois* (1877) and declared that when private property is "affected with a public interest" it "must submit to be controlled by the public for the common good" and that in the absence of federal policy states could lay down regulations. Railroads nevertheless waged relentless war against such legislation, which in some states was carelessly drawn and of limited effectiveness from the start. Then in the Wabash case of 1886 (*Wabash, St. Louis & Pacific Railway Co.* v. *Illinois*) the Supreme Court reversed earlier decisions and held an Illinois statute invalid on the ground that it was the exclusive power of Congress to regulate interstate commerce. With the states thus largely excluded, any effective regulatory action would have to be taken by the federal government.

A second spur to federal action in 1886 was the report of a Senate committee headed by Senator Shelby M. Cullom of Illinois, which denounced railroads sharply for the "reckless strife" of their competition and for "unjust discrimination between persons, places, commodities, or particular descriptions to traffic." Railroad leaders themselves urged federal regulation, for they acknowledged the necessity for measures to end the anarchy in which they struggled. The Republican platform of 1884 had declared that "the principle of the public regulation of railroad corporations is a wise and salutory one." The Interstate Commerce Act, which eventually grew out of demands for regulation, was a milestone in American history, but it was not a triumph of radicals over conservatives or of the people over the corporation.

The Interstate Commerce Act, passed by large majorities in both houses of Congress and signed by President Grover Cleveland on February 4, 1887, forbade railroads to engage in discriminatory practices, required them to publish their rate schedules, prohibited them from entering pooling agreements for the purpose of maintaining high rates, and declared that rates should be "reasonable and just." The act placed enforcement in the hands of an Interstate Commerce Commission of five members, who were to hear complaints and issue orders to the railroads to "cease and desist." Vague and obscure in many sections, the act proved difficult to interpret, administer, and enforce. The commission found it virtually impossible to determine whether or not rates were "reasonable and just," proceeded cautiously, and leaned over backward to accommodate the complaints of the railroads. As an assertion of the federal government's right to regulate private enterprise and as a precedent for more effective measures in the future, the Interstate Commerce Act was important. But it did not provide any immediate answer to the problem of cutthroat competition. It was a conservative measure, based on the belief that competition was beneficial rather than harmful and adopted mainly to alleviate the anxieties of the public.

Morgan and Banker Control Within a year of the passage of the Interstate Commerce Act, the railroads began to return to the discriminatory practices that were now illegal. They were somewhat more secretive about rebates and blackmail competition, but it quickly became evident that the law had no teeth and that there was nothing to fear from the courts. With no effective government control, the industry appeared as anarchic as ever and management as quick to resort to speculative looting and stock watering—issuing stock in excess of paid-in capital. After decades of waste, mismanagement, and folly, many railroads were in a shaky financial plight and in no condition to weather hard times. Railroad speculation and overexpansion had prepared the way for the panics of 1857 and 1873, and the first signal of the Panic of 1893 was the bankruptcy of the Philadelphia and Reading Railroad, on February 20. This panic was less closely connected with railroad overexpansion than the earlier panics. Railroad failures were not the only index of calamity, but by the middle of 1894 there were 192 railroads in the hands of the receivers. About one-third of the total mileage of the country were foreclosed by the middle of 1898. To obtain the funds needed for reorganization, the distressed railroads turned to the bankers. The railroads received not only reorganization but a measure of control that neither they themselves nor the state and federal governments had so far been able to contrive.

Numerous bankers took part in the railway reorganizations of the 1890s, but none took so prominent and conspicuous a part as J. Pierpont Morgan, the dominant investment banker of his time. For the quarter of a century ending with his death in 1913, this tall, massive figure with piercing eyes and fiery nose was the very symbol of American financial power. Morgan began his life near the top of the economic and social ladder, the son of a rich merchant from Hartford, Connecticut, who established a bank in London during the Civil War. He grew up with all the advantages of wealth, including a good education, travel, and residence abroad. He established his firm and his family in New York during the 1870s in princely fashion and began to collect treasures of art and rare books. Aboard his yacht or in the library of his home at 219 Madison Avenue the titans of industry and finance met at his call and submitted to agreements that made history in the world of business and sometimes in the world of politics as well. At such meetings he brought to bear his passion for order and his interest as a seller of securities. It was natural that the managers of the sick railroads of the 1890s should come to him, as to a famous surgeon, for the strong medicine and heroic surgery the bankrupt roads needed for recovery.

J. Pierpont Morgan: a passion for order

Steichen, Edward. J. P. Morgan *(1903). Silver bromide, 16¾ × 13½". Collection, The Museum of Modern Art, New York. Reprinted with the permission of Joanna T. Steichen.*

Other investment banking firms, such as Kuhn, Loeb and Company, employed the same methods as Morgan and charged huge fees for their services. First they ruthlessly pared down the fixed debt of the railroad, then assessed holders of the old stock for working funds, and next issued lavish amounts of new stock, heavily watered. To assure control along lines that suited them and to veto unwise expansion plans, the bankers usually installed a president of their own selection and placed members of their own firms on the boards of railroad directors. Between 1894 and 1898 the House of Morgan reorganized the lion's share of big railroads. Banker control was not the ideal solution or the final answer to the problems of competition and control, but it did curb prevailing anarchy and improved the management and efficiency of railroad service.

INDUSTRIAL EMPIRE

Carnegie and Steel The new industrial order of America was based on steel, and by 1870 the techniques of production, the supply of raw materials, and the home market were sufficiently developed to make the United States the world's greatest steel producer. A cheap and practical process of making steel by forcing a blast of cold air through molten iron to clean it of impurities had been invented in 1857. In 1867 the United States made 1,643 tons of steel ingots; in 1897 it made 7,156,957. In the meantime new discoveries of ore deposits—all within close proximity to Lake Superior and cheap water transportation—were opened up. Together they constituted the greatest iron-ore district in the world.

By 1880 there were 1,005 iron companies in the nation, all of them subject to the competitive struggle under which the railroads labored, with all its uncertainties, anxieties, and ruthlessness. Like railroad operators, the iron- and steelmasters resorted to cutthroat tactics, price slashing, and blackmail. Faced with large fixed costs, they sometimes ran their plants at a loss rather than let them remain idle. They sought rebates and unfair advantages and rushed into pools, combinations, and mergers to hedge against competition. Out of the melee emerged one dominant figure, Andrew Carnegie, the most articulate industrialist America ever had.

Quite untypical of industrial leaders of his day in several respects, Carnegie was of immigrant and working-class origin, a voluble speaker, a facile writer, and a religious skeptic. He came to the United States from Scotland with his family when he was 13 years old and went to work immediately to earn a living. At age 17 he became a telegraph clerk in the office of Thomas A. Scott, then a rising official of the Pennsylvania Railroad, and won his employer's favor and confidence. His service with Scott, which lasted through the Civil War, not only brought valuable acquaintance with the foremost railroad and industrial leaders of the country but guided him in making shrewd and extremely profitable investments. With a salary of only $2,400 a year, he was receiving a millionaire's income from investments when he was 28 years old. He was drawn into the iron business and then in 1872 into a venture for building a huge steel plant on the Monongahela River, twelve miles from Pittsburgh, a site with excellent river transportation and service from both the Pennsylvania and the Baltimore and Ohio railroads. The new plant rolled its first rail in 1875.

Without pretense of engineering or technological skill, Carnegie was first of all a superb salesman with a genius for picking the right subordinates to supervise production. He was personally acquainted with all the railroad barons of the day and, as he said, simply "went out and persuaded them to give us orders." He did not have to remind them that steel rails lasted 20 times as long as iron. Drawing directly on his experience as an executive of one of the best managed railroads of the time, he put together the administrative structure for his steel works on that model. The supreme example of the industrial capitalist, Carnegie refused to permit his company to become a corporation, maintained it as a limited partnership, and retained a majority of the shares himself. Giving no hostages to the bankers, he used the firm's enormous profits to construct new plants, acquire raw materials, buy out competitors, and win fights with organized labor. His independent resources enabled him to go on building and spending, and lead the way in the development of integrated production. After hesitation about entering the ore business, he bought ore deposits in the Mesabi Range and ore ships on the Great Lakes, and he acquired docks, warehouses, and railroad lines to supply his great furnaces and mills with raw materials.

Carnegie had a remarkable gift for finding able lieutenants — men like Henry Clay Frick, Charles M. Schwab, and Alexander R. Peacock. He pitted these men against one another, rewarding the successful with shares and partnerships. At the crest of his power he held the whole steel industry in his grasp except for steel finishing, which he had not entered. His trail to the top was strewn with ruined competitors, crushed partners, and broken labor movements including his bloody victory over labor at Homestead (see p. 481). Carnegie increased his annual production from 322,000 tons in 1890 to 3,000,000 tons in 1900. Over the same decade he and his lieutenants increased the annual profits of the Carnegie Steel Company from $5,400,000 in 1890 to $40,000,000 in 1900. Carnegie's own share of the 1900 profits was approximately $25,000,000.

In the meantime J. Pierpont Morgan turned his attention from railroads to steel, and the bankers challenged the industrialists for the control of heavy industry. The American Steel and Wire Company, the first big combination in steel, was constructed without his help. Then in the summer of 1898 Morgan swung his support to Judge Elbert H. Gary of Chicago and other Midwesterners who merged several big concerns to form the Federal Steel Company, second in size to Carnegie Steel. The next obvious move in the drive for mergers was to consolidate the whole industry into one vast supercorporation, the greatest in the world. Blocking that dream was the mighty Carnegie Steel Company and the known prejudice of its head against banker control. Even Morgan threw up his hands when it was proposed that he buy up Carnegie Steel outright; "I don't believe I could raise the money," he said. The new combinations for making finished steel products then decided in the summer of 1900 to produce their own raw steel, free themselves from dependence on Carnegie, and cancel their contracts with him. Carnegie's response was a cable from Skibo Castle, his summer home in Scotland, declaring

Carnegie steel mill, Braddock, Pennsylvania

open war: "Have no fear as to result. Victory certain." He proposed to go into the production of finished steel, which he had urged on his partners since 1898, and to drive all his competitors to the wall.

Alarmed at the prospect of a war that would place the new steel combinations in deadly peril and demoralize the whole industry. Morgan determined to buy out Carnegie and consolidate the supercorporation. After a night-long conference in the famous Morgan library, Charles M. Schwab agreed to take the matter up with Carnegie. The Scotsman scribbled a few figures on a scrap of paper, and Schwab took it to Morgan. The banker glanced at it and said, "I accept this price." There was no bargaining. The figure was nearly one-half billion dollars. In a few weeks Morgan pushed and pulled the big steel companies into combination and, on March 3, 1901, announced the organization of the United States Steel Corporation. The new concern brought under a single management three-fifths of the steel business of the country.

Although U. S. Steel was never without competition within the industry, the uneasy popular sentiment about the gigantic deal was reflected in the words the humorist Finley Peter Dunne put in the mouth of his Irish saloon-keeper, "Mr. Dooley":

> Pierpont Morgan calls in wan iv his office boys, th' presidint iv a national bank, an' says he, "James," he says, "take some change out iv th' damper an' r-run out an' buy Europe f'r me," he says. "I intind to re-organize it an' put it on a paying basis," he says. "Call up the Czar an' th' Pope an' th' Sultan an' th' Impror Willum, an' tell thim we won't need their savices afther nex' week," he says. "Give thim a year's salary in advance."

Rockefeller and the Trusts An industrial giant of power and influence comparable to that wielded by Carnegie was John D. Rockefeller, who did for oil what the Scotsman did for steel. The two contemporaries were strikingly different in temperament and taste: Carnegie was exuberant and communicative, Rockefeller silent and taciturn; Carnegie was a skeptic and an agnostic, Rockefeller a Bible-class teacher and a devout Baptist. In their business methods and their achievements, however, there were many similarities. Both men showed the same astuteness in selecting lieutenants and putting them in the right jobs, the same abhorrence of waste and gambling, the same ability to transform depressions into opportunities for building, buying, and expanding. The Standard Oil Company, with Rockefeller its head, made ruthless use of railroad-rate discrimination, espionage, bogus companies, and other reprehensible practices. On the other hand, it had positive achievements to its credit, including improved and lower-priced products, the elimination of waste, and efficiency in distribution.

Rockefeller was the outstanding American exponent of consolidation in industry. Of the trend toward consolidation he wrote:

> This movement was the origin of the whole system of modern economic administration. It has revolutionized the way of doing business all over the world. The time was ripe for it. It had to come, though all we saw at the moment was the need to save ourselves from wasteful conditions. . . . The day of combination is here to stay. Individualism has gone, never to return.

By "wasteful conditions" he meant the glutted markets in crude and refined oil and the disorder, uncertainty, and wild fluctuation of prices and profits that attended free competition among thousands of small producers and hundreds of small refiners. Rockefeller hated free competition and believed that monopoly was the way of the future. His early method of dealing with competitors was to gain unfair advantage over them through special rates and rebates arranged with railroads. With the aid of these advantages, Standard became the largest refiner of oil in the country. By the end of the 1870s the Standard Oil Company had created an "alliance," or cartel, of 40 leading refiners of the country and held a majority of the securities of the members. In 1881 the alliance controlled nearly 90 percent of the country's oil refining capacity and could crush any remaining competitors at will.

A change in the technology of transportation — the completion of a long-distance pipeline for crude oil — triggered the decision of the Standard Oil alliance to solidify legal control and centralize management. Their railroad-rate advantages threatened by an independent pipeline that they were unable to stop, the alliance began construction of a huge interregional pipeline network of its own. The next problem was to establish a central authority with power to close down, modernize, or build refineries to take advantage of the new pipeline network. The solution was found in an old legal device put to new use — the trust. On January 2, 1882, the shareholders of the 40 companies exchanged their stock for certificates of the new Standard Oil Trust. The board of nine trustees was given power to "exercise general supervision over the affairs of the several Standard Oil Companies." By the early 1890s Standard Oil completed the process of vertical integration through entering the production of crude oil as well.

The term *trust* was popularly and loosely applied to numerous industrial combinations that were formed after Standard Oil pointed the way, but it appears that in addition to petroleum, only seven were formed to operate in the national market, and two of those were short-lived. Of the successful trusts put together in the 1880s, all were in refining and distilling industries. The sugar and whiskey trusts did not move into national marketing, but cottonseed oil, linseed oil, and lead processing followed the Standard Oil example in this respect and others. In less than a decade after their formation they became fully integrated enterprises, organized according to the managerial revolution, and dominated their industries for decades.

The trust movement encountered popular suspicion and hostility from the start. The American creed, bred of an agrarian heritage, held that business should be organized in small units, that competition should be unfettered, and that opportunity should be open to all. The trusts were an affront to this traditional faith: they were gigantic, powerful, even awe-inspiring. To the public, the trusts were the product of an evil plot born of greed, and that was the way the cartoonists pictured them in the newspapers and journals and the way popular political leaders described them in their speeches in the 1880s. The popular attitude was not without foundation, for the trusts often did use their enormous power to the detriment of both consumers and small businesspeople. Businesspeople adversely affected were among the most influential antitrust advocates. Even the big-business community, increasingly aware that mergers and trusts were not likely to stabilize and control industry, looked to the federal government for the answer.

As in railroad regulation, the state legislatures took the lead against the trusts. The laws they passed were never very effective, however, and the Wabash decision of 1886 limited the states here as it did in the regulation of railroads and left the problem up to the federal government. John Sherman of Ohio submitted an antitrust bill in the Senate, one of many similar bills. Debate in Congress revealed concern for the interests of both the consumer and the small business proprietor. It illustrated both the "folklore" of the old capitalism and apprehension about the new. The so-called Sherman Antitrust Act became law on July 2, 1890.

On the face of it, the new act would seem to have spelled the end of every trust or trustlike combination. The opening sentence of the first section declares, "Every contract, combination in the form of trust or otherwise, or conspiracy, in restraint of trade or commerce among the several States, or with foreign nations, is hereby declared to be illegal." And the second section pronounces guilty of a misdemeanor "every person who shall monopolize, or attempt to monopolize, or combine or conspire with any other person or persons, to monopolize any part of the trade or commerce among the several States, or with foreign nations." The word *person* was specifically defined to include corporations, and the act fixed penalties, as the Interstate Commerce Act had not, for violations.

Efforts to enforce the act during the 1890s were not very vigorous, and clever lawyers found loopholes and various ways of evading its provisions. Some trusts merely reorganized as huge corporations, while others pointed the way to the future by finding refuge in holding companies — that is, giant financial structures that held enough stock in member companies to control their policies. In the first five years after the act was passed, 25 new combinations came into being. The fact is the public wanted the benefits of large-scale enterprise without the evils of big business and monopoly — a dilemma never fully resolved.

The course of Standard Oil from trust to holding company illustrates the trend. The company formally abandoned the trust agreement of 1882 under an Ohio court order in 1892, but in practice the same nine men who had served as trustees continued to conduct the business of the member companies for five years after the trust was formally dissolved. Charged with evading the court order, the trust reorganized as a holding company under the laws of New Jersey, which permitted corporations of that state to own and control corporations of other states. The Standard Oil Company of New Jersey simply increased its stock some tenfold and exchanged it for stock of the member companies. These in turn elected directors of the New Jersey company, who carried on in the place of the old trustees. With concentration of control unimpaired and power enhanced instead of diminished, Standard made money as never before. In the eight years following its reorganization as a holding company, annual dividends on its stock varied between 30 and 48 percent.

In 1895 the court dealt a heavy blow to the Sherman law by its decision in the case of *United States* v. *E. C. Knight Company,* which was charged with furthering monopoly by selling out to the American Sugar Refining Company. Although the sale rounded out one of the most complete monopolies in the country, the court decided that it did not violate the antitrust act. It reasoned that manufacturing was not "commerce" within the meaning of the law, and that monopoly of manufacturing without "direct" effect on commerce was not subject to regulation by the federal government. With this encouragement and economic incentives, consolidation in the dominant industries went forward with a rush in the next five years. The movement reached its peak in 1899, when 1,207 firms disappeared and merger capitalization rose to $2,263 million. Then in 1898 and 1899 the Supreme Court ruled clearly and precisely in two cases that any combination of business firms formed to fix prices or allocate markets violated the Sherman Antitrust Act. After that, lawyers usually advised corporate clients to abandon such efforts. The merger movement declined temporarily after the formation of U. S. Steel in 1901.

The Technology of Centralization The management of a vast railroad network, a continent-wide industry, or an international market required a new technology of control and communication. American inventors outdid themselves to meet these demands. The number of patents issued to inventors jumped from fewer than 2,000 a year in the 1850s to more than 13,000 a year in the 1870s and better than 21,000 a year in the 1880s and 1890s. In those days the typical inventor was not a trained engineer in an industrial or a university laboratory but an individual tinkerer who frequently operated on a shoestring.

Such a man was Christopher L. Sholes, printer and journalist from Pennsylvania and Wisconsin, who invented a typewriter in 1867. He sold his rights to the Remington Arms Company, which put the typewriter on the market in 1875. The year Sholes invented the typewriter, E. A. Callahan of Boston developed a superior stock ticker. In the summer of 1866 Cyrus W. Field employed new techniques to repair and improve his transatlantic cable, broken since 1858, and stock quotations crossed the ocean. Numerous other inventions, including the adding machine (1888), quickened the pace of business transactions.

None of these inventions, however, could rival the importance of the telephone. This was the work of Alexander Graham Bell, a Scotsman who emigrated to Canada in 1870, when he was 23, and then to Boston two years later. His experiments over three years resulted in the magnetoelectric telephone. He transmitted the first intelligible sentence on March 10, 1876, and a year later conducted a conversation between Boston and New York. The inventor and his supporters organized the Bell Telephone Company in 1877 and promptly plunged into law suits to defend their patent. The most formidable challenger was the Western Union Telegraph Company, which had originally spurned an opportunity to buy the patent for the "scientific toy" for a mere $100,000. Western Union settled out of court and left the field to Bell and his company, which continued to win hundreds of suits, improve the telephone, buy out competitors, and expand facilities. In 1885 the directors of Bell, led by Theodore N. Vail, organized the American Telephone

Thomas Alva Edison: hundreds of inventions

Andrew Carnegie: The Duties of Wealth

This, then, is held to be the duty of the man of wealth: To set an example of modest, unostentatious living, shunning display or extravagance; to provide moderately for the legitimate wants of those dependent upon him; and, after doing so to consider all surplus revenues which come to him simply as trust funds, which he is called upon to administer, and strictly bound as a matter of duty to administer in the manner which, in his judgment, is best calculated to produce the most beneficial results for the community—the man of wealth thus becoming the mere trustee and agent for his poorer brethren, bringing to their service his superior wisdom, experience, and ability to administer, doing for them better than they would or could do for themselves.

From Andrew Carnegie, *The Gospel of Wealth and Other Essays,* 1901

and Telegraph Company. By 1900 it had become the holding company for the whole system, with some 35 subsidiaries.

Among the numerous social consequences of the new technology of communications was the emergence of a new social class. This was the white-collar clerical worker, the fastest growing part of the urban labor force in the late nineteenth century. Although a majority of the new workers were male, the clerical services also opened up employment opportunities for female high school graduates and added many women to the labor force.

The use of electricity for light is justly linked with the name of Thomas Alva Edison, who outdid his contemporary Bell as an inventor. The son of a Canadian who settled and prospered in Ohio, Edison grew up without formal schooling. He became a telegraph operator and while still quite young made some very profitable inventions to improve transmission. He then established himself as a businessman-inventor and built his own "invention factory," forerunner of the modern industrial research laboratory, at Menlo Park, New Jersey, in 1876. There in 1877 he invented the phonograph, and in later years his laboratories turned out hundreds of inventions or improvements, including the storage battery, the motion picture projector, an electric dynamo, and an electric locomotive. The incandescent light required a vacuum bulb with a durable filament. Edison made one that burned for 40 hours in 1879 and improved it until it was commercially practicable. With the backing of J. Pierpont Morgan, he organized the Edison Illuminating Company and moved to New York City to install an electric-light plant. On September 4, 1882, in the presence of Morgan, Edison threw a switch and the House of Morgan, the New York Stock Exchange, the New York *Times,* the New York *Herald,* and smaller buildings in lower Manhattan began to glow with incandescent light.

Edison's plant used direct current, but in order to transmit electricity any distance its voltage had to be stepped up and then stepped down again. For this purpose alternating current and transformers were necessary. George Westinghouse of Pittsburgh, who had invented the railroad air brake in 1869, developed a power plant and a transformer in 1886 that could transmit high-voltage alternating current efficiently, safely, and cheaply over long distances.

For this type of current to be converted into mechanical power, an alternating-current motor had to be developed. In 1888 Nikola Tesla, a Hungarian engineer who immigrated to the United States in 1884, invented such a motor. Westinghouse and his associates bought the patent, improved it with the aid of Tesla, and dramatically demonstrated the practicability of alternating current by illuminating the Colum-

Henry George: The Nature of Property

What constitutes the rightful basis of property? What is it that enables a man justly to say of a thing, "It is mine"? From what springs the sentiment which acknowledges his exclusive right as against all the world? Is it not, primarily, the right of a man to himself, to the use of his own powers, to the enjoyment of the fruits of his own exertions? Is it not this individual right, which springs from and is testified to by the natural facts of individual organization—the fact that each particular pair of hands obey a particular brain and are related to a particular stomach; the fact that each man is a definite, coherent, independent whole—which alone justifies individual ownership? As a man belongs to himself, so his labor when put in concrete form belongs to him. . . .

If production give to the producer the right to exclusive possession and enjoyment, there can rightfully be no exclusive possession and enjoyment of anything not the production of labor, and the recognition of private property in land is a wrong.

From Henry George, *Progress and Poverty*, 1879

bian Exposition at Chicago in 1893. The shift to electrical power had begun, and factories no longer had to hover around waterfalls and coal supplies. They were now ready for the electrical revolution that came in the twentieth century.

LAISSEZ-FAIRE CONSERVATISM

The Gospel of Wealth A survey of private fortunes conducted in 1892 revealed that there were 4,047 millionaires in the United States. These were largely new fortunes. Very few of them dated from before the Civil War, when a millionaire was a rarity, though most of the millionaires came from well-to-do backgrounds. Only 84 of the millionaires of 1892 were in agriculture, and most of those were cattle barons. The fortunes of the new plutocracy were based on industry, trade, railroads. The new plutocrats were the masters and directors of the economic revolution that was changing the face of American society.

To say that these men were conservative is to put a strain on customary usage of the word, for conservatives are usually opposed to change and devoted to tradition. Yet these men flouted tradition and preached progress. The new conservatives of wealth took over virtually the whole liberal vocabulary of concepts and slogans, including "democracy," "liberty," "equality," "opportunity," and "individualism," and turned it against the liberals. In short, they gave an economic and material turn to ethical and idealistic concepts. "Man" became "economic man," democracy was identified with capitalism, liberty with property and the use of it, equality with opportunity for gain, and progress with economic change and the accumulation of capital. God and nature were thus in league with the Gospel of Wealth.

The new doctrine was conservative, however, in the sense that it was bent on defending the status quo, conserving the privileges by which vast accumulations of wealth were gained, and preventing government interference with those privileges. The laissez-faire conservatives naturally found comfort in classical economics, and those who had heard of them found special fascination in the biological theories of Charles Darwin and the sociological theory of Herbert Spencer, an English philosopher. Spencer applied biological concepts, especially the concept of natural selection, to social principles and justified the unimpeded struggle for existence on the ground that "survival of the fittest" made for human progress. State interference in behalf of the weak would only impede progress. Spencer was more readily acclaimed and more widely admired in America than in England.

The most articulate and influential American exponent of Herbert Spencer's doctrines was Professor William Graham Sumner, the son of an immigrant artisan from England. In 1872 he accepted a professorship in political and social science at Yale, where he spent the rest of his life. A prodigious scholar, he mastered all the social sciences of his time, several natural sciences, and a dozen or more languages. His numerous writings included not only learned contributions to the founding of the new field of sociology but essays that commanded nationwide attention on virtually every public issue of his time. More consistent than most adherents of laissez-faire, Sumner vigorously opposed protectionism and imperialism. On essentials of the Gospel of Wealth, however, he wrote an essay called "The Concentration of Wealth: Its Economic Justification."

By the time it had become fully elaborated, the Gospel of Wealth and its corollaries of social Darwinism included many propositions widely accepted. Among them were the following: (1) that the American economy was controlled for the benefit of all by a natural aristocracy and that these leaders were brought to the top by a competitive struggle that weeded out the weak, the incompetent, and the unfit and selected the strong, the able, and the wise; (2) that politicians were not subject to rigorous natural selection and therefore could not be trusted to the same degree as businessmen; (3) that the state should confine itself to police activities of protecting property and maintaining order and that if it interfered with economic affairs it would upset the beneficent effect of natural selection; (4) that slums and poverty were the unfortunate but inevitable negative results of the competitive struggle and that state intervention to eliminate them was misguided; (5) that the stewardship of wealth obliged the rich to try to ameliorate social injustice.

In the Supreme Court, the Gospel of Wealth found institutional support of great prestige and incomparable value. Under the persistent tutelage of Justice Stephen J. Field, the Court had been converted by the late 1880s to the view that Herbert Spencer's *Social Statics* coincided remarkably well with the will of the Founding Fathers and the soundest moral precepts of the ages. Interpreting the "due process" clause of the Fourteenth Amendment as a protection of corporate interests, the Court proceeded to declare state regulatory measures unconstitutional on the ground that they deprived corporations of property without due process of law. By the end of the century, the Court's laissez-faire interpretation of the Constitution had gone far toward debarring the states from the exercise of ancient police powers for the protection of the public interest and the welfare of their citizens.

Social Critics and Dissenters The Gospel of Wealth and the Darwinian apology for unrestrained capitalism did not meet with universal acceptance. The dissenters rejected the survival-of-the-fittest concept of social progress and found a place for ethical values in economic theory, as well as a need for governmental intervention to restrain the strong and protect the weak. A strong religious impulse often motivated the nonclerical as well as the clerical critics of social Darwinism.

Lester Frank Ward, one of the founders of sociology in America, was an outspoken critic of Spencer's theories. Ward took a job in a Washington bureau in 1865, after service in the Union army, and remained in government work for some 40 years. Largely self-educated, he compensated for his impoverished background by astonishing feats of learning. He mastered ten languages and several fields of science in addition to sociology. Ward pointed out that there was a difference between animal and human economics. Bears have claws, but humans have intelligence. Darwinian laws governed the former, but the human mind transformed the environment of human economics and substituted rational choice for natural selection. This was as it should be, for nature was terribly wasteful in its crude methods of evolution. For competition to survive, government regulation was necessary. Ward believed in social planning. This, he said, should be done by social engineers, scientific planners, and managers of society.

A second self-taught social philosopher of the age, and one of the most original economists of the time, was Henry George, author of the famous book *Progress and Poverty* (1879). Born in Philadelphia, George traveled in the Orient and in 1868 settled in California, where he had ample opportunity to observe the land speculation, land monopoly, and social distress that played so important a part in his economics. Addressing himself to the problem of unequal distribution of wealth, he inveighed against the "shocking contrast between monstrous wealth and debasing want." Wealth is produced, he concluded, by applying labor to land, and capital is the surplus above the cost of labor. Labor therefore creates all capital. But capitalists, by withholding advantageous land sites until their value has been enhanced by labor, improvements in production, and speculation in adjacent areas, reap a profit out of all proportion to their contribution. This profit George called the "unearned increment." Since land should no more be monopolized than air and sunshine, George's solution was to tax land in such a fashion as to appropriate the unearned increment. This was to be done by a "single tax," which would make other taxes unnecessary. After 1885 he put aside the hope that this would result in common ownership of the land by the people. George's book and his lectures won him a political following at home and abroad and enabled him to make a strong showing as candidate for mayor of New York in 1886.

Another political aspiration born of a book was the Nationalist movement; this time the book was Edward Bellamy's *Looking Backward* (1888). The most successful of several utopian novels published during the same decade, Bellamy's book "looked backward" to the benighted 1880s from the collectivized society of the year A.D. 2000. By that time selfishness has been eliminated by the abolition of corporate property and the nationalization of industry. Competition is seen to have killed nineteenth-century society and its individualism. "Competition," says the protagonist, "which is the instinct of selfishness, is another word for dissipation of energy, while combination is the secret of efficient production." The utopian remedy was one big trust, bloodlessly achieved, and mandatory male service in an industrial army in place of wage competition. Women were promised a better place in this brave new world. Bellamy's attack on the ethic of "survival of the fittest" appealed to a wide variety of people. Nationalist clubs and periodicals advocated municipal ownership of utilities and public ownership of railroads. As agrarian reform mounted in the 1890s, however, the Nationalists tended to join the farmers' parties and abandon their own organization.

From the viewpoint of a later day, the debate over laissez-faire doctrine and social Darwinism appears confused and paradoxical. If free competition was the goal of laissez-faire, the industrialists who hated competition and sought to restrain it would seem to have embraced the wrong doctrine. If social Darwinism taught hands off by the government, those who sought subsidies, protection, and favors from the government again seemed inconsistent. But insofar as these doctrines were useful for the defense of the status quo and the discouragement of efforts to reform or change society by conscious purpose the conservatives were right in embracing them and the radicals in rejecting them.

THE HOUSE OF LABOR

Man and the Machine In the long run, industrialization raises the living standard and increases the opportunities of labor, but around the world labor has discovered that the revolution that establishes industrialization comes at heavy cost and that the workers' adjustment to the machine and the factory way of life is often painful and difficult. In America the labor shortage that had persisted since colonial times had kept the level of wages higher than the level that prevailed abroad; and yet American workers had their full share of troubles in the grim iron age of industry.

Many of the changes in the way of life workers had to make were hard to understand and painful to accept, for these changes meant loss of status and surrender of independence. The skilled artisans who owned the tools they used were likely to be individualists who took pride in the quality of their products and enjoyed a strong bargaining position. The new factory discipline offered a humbler role and a lower status. In the factory, workers surrendered their tools, nearly all the creative pride of their products, most of their independence, and much of their bargaining power. They became the tenders of machines that set the work pace and the employees of owners whom they probably never met and never saw. The artisans were becoming laborers. The craftsmanship that had been the skilled workers' source of pride and security was no longer of any significance, for their places at the machines could be taken by unskilled workers. The growing impersonality of their relations to their work and their employers and the ever increasing size of the industrial organization meant a sacrifice in security, identity, and the satisfactions that bestow meaning and value on work.

Adjustment would have been easier had the change been less swift and the workers better prepared. But the mechanization and expansion of the factory system hit a breathtaking pace during the 1880s. Between 1880 and 1890 the total capital invested in the production of machinery increased two and a half times, and the average investment in machinery increased 200 percent for each establishment and 50 percent for each employee. Manufacturers, with their capital tied up in new machinery, were driven to seek a rapid return on their investment, generally at low prices in a highly competitive market. Real wages actually rose, but hard-pressed employers often made economies at the expense of the factory workers, who suffered from working conditions that impaired their safety, their comfort, and their health. While some states had enacted factory laws, the great body of legislation that now protects factory workers had not yet been written in the 1880s and 1890s. Employers thought nothing of using detectives and armed force to thwart the organization of labor unions. In "company towns," where all houses, stores, and services were company-owned, employers subjected workers to endless harassments and petty tyranny. There was nothing but the urging of conscience and the weak protest of labor to keep employers from cutting costs at the expense of their workers.

After the 1880s, there occurred a large shift into the paid labor force among married women. In 1890 more than 90 percent of women over age 35 were married, and up to that time the vast majority of them remained unemployed outside the home. There they were subjected to what Charlotte Perkins Gilman, in *Women and Economics* (1898) called a type of "slave labor" and "the relic of a patriarchal age." Domestic servants, almost all of whom were women, were in a worse plight. They accounted for well over half the women employed before the 1880s. Then rather suddenly wives began to take jobs in large numbers and go "out to work." The change in employment followed a sharp decline in the birth rate. Between 1860 and 1890 the number of children under age five per thousand women dropped nearly a third, while at the end of the century women were having half the number of children they were bearing at its start. The amount of home labor required of them decreased with the size of the family. In the workplace women accepted wages strikingly lower than those men were paid for comparable work and were often blamed by employers as well as by male employees for lowering the general wage level by taking jobs they did not "need." Organized labor made only weak gestures in behalf of women, often cutting them out of the kind of jobs held by unionized men. Without union help, women had few means of overcoming low pay, exploitation, and terrible work conditions—all of which resulted in a mortality rate more than double that of nonwage earners.

The average weekly wages of common laborers remained less than $9 throughout the 1890s, and farm laborers got less than half that amount. After the depression of the 1870s, however, there was a fairly steady increase in real wages—for those who had jobs. Over all, real wages rose more than 15 percent between 1873 and 1893, though those gains were by no means distributed equally, and many did not share them at all. The rise in real wages helps explain labor's relative indifference to socialism. Among other explanations that have been offered are mobility through the labor force and mobility through the ethnic ghettos. The millions who suffered unemployment during the depressions of the last three decades of the century were not even enumerated, much less assisted, by the government. Unemployment during the years 1893–1896 allowed employers to slash wages and ignore union standards and demands. The United States

Common laborers

commissioner of labor estimated that 75 percent of the workers who went out on strike in 1894 were fired. The most insistent demand of organized labor was for the eight-hour day, but the main result was the adoption of a federal law passed in 1869, and amended in 1892, limiting the work day of federal employees to eight hours. In private industry, however, most workers continued to work a ten-hour day and a six-day week, and in steel and other industries they worked even longer. The accident toll and the damage done by poor ventilation and lighting, dust, and fumes — insofar as the facts were known at all — were charged off as the cost of progress.

A special handicap of American labor was its lack of homogeneity. The working class was fragmented by race and color, as well as by geography, philosophy, concepts of organization, style of protest, and national origin. Some formed exclusive groups to protect their own privilege and to keep underprivileged groups at bay. Between 1882 and 1900 there were 50 strikes waged against the employment of black labor.

Immigrants formed a large segment of the American labor force, except in the South, where few of them settled. There had been immigrant workers from the start in the United States, and while the percentage in the labor force remained about the same after the Civil War, immigrants were coming in greater numbers and from different parts of Europe, mainly the southern and eastern countries. Nineteenth-century immigration reached high tide in the 1880s, when nearly 5¼ million immigrants arrived, 2½ million more than had come in the 1870s and 1½ million more than were to come in the 1890s. Set apart by language and culture, accustomed to lower wages and living standards, the newcomers often concentrated as ethnic groups in certain industries — Irish in building construction, Germans in brewing and furniture, Italians in street and sewer work, Slavs in anthracite, Jews in the garment industry.

Native workers often looked down on them with contempt and spoke of work for which they were suited as "foreign jobs." The foreign newcomers were often regarded as unassimilable, unable to understand or become a part of the American way, and unfit to be "union men." Both the Knights of Labor and the American Federation of Labor (AFL) called for immigrant restriction. The new immigrants crowded into the coal mining and steel industries, with each wave pushing the earlier comers a step up the ladder. The bitterest and most implacable labor opposition to immigrants was directed at the Asians, particularly the Chinese of California. Supported by labor organizations in the East, the Californians persuaded Congress in 1882 to suspend admission of Chinese immigrants for ten years.

Unions and Strikes For a long time, the attitude of American labor toward unions and collective bargaining was typically that of the skilled artisan or the small shopkeeper. Instead of accepting the new industrial order and its conditions, they looked back nostalgically to the past and longed for the good old days. Longings of this sort found expression in such slogans as "every man his own master" or "every man his own employer." Labor unions remained every weak throughout the nineteenth century, embracing not more than 1 or 2 percent of the total labor force and less than 10 percent of the industrial workers.

During and after the Civil War, the typical national trade union was designed primarily to protect the status of skilled workers. In 1866 William H. Sylvis, an iron molder of Pennsylvania, attempted to unite the trade unions into a single organization called the National Labor Union. This organization bore no resemblance to modern labor unions. It was led by visionaries and idealists who did not believe in strikes and who were unconcerned with the immediate needs of working people, apart from the eight-hour day.

Women delegates, Knights of Labor

With many of the same generous impulses and naive assumptions, the Noble and Holy Order of the Knights of Labor was founded in 1869. A secret fraternal order with high-flown titles and elaborate rituals, the Knights sought to unite all labor and welcomed all "toilers" of whatever color, race, nationality, or craft, whether skilled or unskilled. Utopian and nostalgic in many of their views, the Knights frowned on the use of the strike and promoted dreams of restoring the past. Their labor program, however, included demands for a federal bureau of statistics, equal pay for both sexes, the eight-hour day, and the abolition of child and prison labor. In practice they acted like a labor union. Many of their political demands resembled those of contemporary farmers' organizations, for they included paper money, an income tax, abolition of the national banking system, and prohibition.

The Knights grasped one important fact of the new economy—that the consolidation of industry made necessary the consolidation of labor. They founded their General Assembly in 1878 with a view to centralizing control over labor in order to combat the monopolistic power of corporations. In 1879 they elected Terence V. Powderly as their Grand Master Workman. The dominant figure in the Order during the years of its power and influence, Powderly was described at a labor convention in 1886 as elegantly dressed in "double-breasted, black, broadcloth coat, stand-up collar, plain tie, dark trousers and narrow small shoes," surrounded by "horny-fisted sons of toil" and acting "like Queen Victoria at a national Democratic convention." Powderly constantly preached against strikes, and yet it was a result of strikes in 1885–86 that the Order made its most sensational gains in membership, from about 100,000 to more than 700,000. The strength of the Order quickly ebbed after the upheavals of 1886. It lingered through the 1890s but with declining membership and influence.

In the meantime, the American Federation of Labor, founded in 1881, was hammering out a labor philosophy more closely related to the realities of the industrial economy and more in harmony with the future. Rejecting the utopian radicalism of the Knights of Labor, the AFL foreswore political goals for economic objectives. Instead of embracing the brotherhood of all workers, it devoted its attention to gaining concrete benefits for skilled workers organized along craft lines. It was a loose alliance of national trade unions, each of which retained a large amount of autonomy, with jurisdiction over its own affairs and with the power to call its own strikes. By 1900 the AFL did not hesitate to acknowledge the strike and the boycott as legitimate means of collective bargaining. These principles had been formulated by 1881 and reaffirmed when the AFL was reorganized in 1886.

Samuel Gompers: higher wages, lower hours

As its first president the AFL elected Samuel Gompers, who retained the office for nearly 40 years. An immigrant boy, born in London in 1850, Gompers grew up in the trade-union movement. Under the impact of his experience in America, he gradually put aside his earlier leanings to socialism and slowly shaped a more conservative approach to the problems of labor. He felt that labor should accept the economic system and should try to win for itself a respectable place as a "legitimate" group within that system, as legitimate as business or the church. And to do so, he urged, labor would have to struggle day by day for higher wages and fewer hours. Gompers strove to impose order by resolving jurisdictional disputes between unions and by consolidating local unions in state and national federations. The AFL grew as the Knights declined. By 1902 its membership topped the million mark.

Labor's struggle to win acceptance and to improve its lot was marked by an extraordinary number of strikes and lockouts, conflicts that sometimes flared into bloodshed, particularly in time of depression. It is likely that the history of labor relations in the United States included more violence than that of any other industrializing country in the world. In July 1877 a series of wage cuts and abortive strikes provoked an upheaval of insurrectionary violence along the trunk lines of three big railroads. In Pittsburgh the community joined the strikers against the Pennsylvania Railroad and destroyed $5 million worth of property before being dispersed with heavy loss of life. Other disturbances broke out in Philadelphia, Harrisburg, Reading, Scranton, Buffalo, and Toledo, and farther west in St. Louis, Chicago, and San Francisco. Scores of people lost their lives, and property valued at millions of dollars went up in flames. The courts clamped down, the police became more ruthless, and the public began to withdraw its sympathy from the labor movement. Another upsurge of labor militancy occurred during the mid-1880s. During 1886, a climactic year in labor history, 610,000 workers were unemployed because of strikes, lockouts, or shutdowns due to strikes, more than three times the average of the five preceding years. Then on May 4, during an anarchist demonstration against police brutalities at Haymarket Square in Chicago, a bomb was thrown that killed a policeman and fatally wounded six other persons. A jury found eight anarchists guilty, and four were hanged, though the identity of the bomb thrower was never established.

Resort to violence was common in the turbulent 1890s but often labor was merely replying to force with force. In the remote Coeur d'Alene district of Idaho, company guards and miners fought it out in 1892 with rifles and dynamite until at last federal troops came in, crushed the strike, and turned the miners' jobs over to striker-breakers. At Carnegie's Homestead steel plant in Pennsylvania the same year, 3,800 members of the Amalgamated Association of Iron and Steel Workers struck over wage cuts and working conditions. Henry C. Frick, the manager, imported 300 Pinkerton detectives. When they arrived at the plant on barges, the strikers resisted and a gunfight ensued that resulted in the death of seven detectives and nine strikers, the wounding of a much larger number, and the surrender of the detectives. In the end, however, the strike failed miserably, and its failure heralded the end of unionism in the steel industry for many years to come.

The great depression that started in 1893 (see p. 526) brought on a new wave of wage cuts, layoffs, and strikes. More workers were thrown out of work by strikes in 1894, a year of exceptional unemployment and labor violence, than in any previous year. The big railroad strike originated not among railway workers but among factor workers in George M. Pullman's "model" company town just south of Chicago. The Pullman workers had recently joined the new American Railway Union, headed by Eugene V. Debs and frowned on by the older Railway Brotherhoods of the AFL. Although Debs urged caution, his union voted to refuse to handle Pullman cars if the management would not accept arbitration of the strike. Pullman rejected all arbitration, and the General Managers Association came to his aid by dismissing switchmen who boycotted his cars. The union then struck against the railroads, and by the end of June 1894 nearly all railroad workers on roads west of Chicago were on strike.

The General Managers Association then appealed directly to the federal government to intervene with armed force and end the strike. Railroad lawyers had no trouble persuading President Cleveland and Attorney General Richard Olney that intervention could nevertheless be justified on the ground that the strike had obstructed the delivery of United States mail. Actually, the railroads themselves refused, against the union's wishes, to attach mail cars to trains that did not include Pullman cars. Nevertheless, Olney secured an injunction against the union, and on July 4 Cleveland sent some 2,000 troops to Chicago to enforce the injunction and protect the mails. After the troops arrived, the union completely lost control of the situation, and mobs of looters destroyed cars and burned and stole property. Twelve people were killed and many arrested at the scene, but none were strikers. The effect of the troop action was to break the strike, a result that Olney, by his own confession, intended to accomplish. The mood of labor at this time is suggested by the narrow defeat of a socialist demand for the collective ownership of the means of production in the AFL convention of 1894. The vote suggests that there were limits to labor's relative indifference toward collectivism (p. 479).

The failure of the Pullman strike had important consequences for the future of American labor. Debs and other union officials were tried and sentenced to jail for contempt of court in disobeying the injunction against the union. Another unforeseen consequence of the Pullman strike and the Court's decision was to bring into national prominence for the first time the name of Eugene V. Debs. Within a few years he became the foremost leader of the socialist movement in the country, a position he held during the years when that movement enjoyed its greatest strength.

Any realistic account of the ordeal of industrialization in America will tell of heedless waste and ruthless exploitation, of cutthroat competition and consolidation. Whatever economic progress came out of the grim struggle—and undoubtedly much was gained—was purchased at a high cost in brutalized labor, wasted resources, and deterioration in business and public ethics. The costs of industrialization have never been low and when reckoned in human suffering and social turmoil the price has been even more appalling in other countries than in the United States. And in all fairness, the American ordeal should be judged in comparison with that of England, which preceded it, and that of Russia, which came after it. In neither case does the American record, as bad as it was, suffer by comparison.

SUGGESTIONS FOR READING

On this period important insights come from A. D. Chandler, Jr., *The Visible Hand: The Managerial Revolution in American Business* (1977), and his *Scale and Scope: The Dynamics of Industrial Capitalism* (1991). The latter is a comparative study, as is T. C. Cochran, "The Paradox of American Economic Growth," *Journal of American History* 61 (1975): 925–42. Useful surveys include G. Porter, *The Rise of Big Business, 1860–1910* (1973), and E. C. Kirkland, *Industry Comes of Age: Business, Labor, and Public Policy, 1860–1897* (1961). A briefer sketch is S. P. Hays, *The Response to Industrialism: 1885–1914* (1957). L. Galambos, *The Public Image of Big Business in America, 1880–1940: A Quantitative Study of Social Change* (1975), assesses public opinion.

The railroad establishment of the period is described in G. R. Taylor and I. D. Neu, *The American Railroad Network, 1861–1890* (1956). Railroading in the West is treated in R. C. Overton, *Burlington West* (1941) and *Gulf to Rockies* (1953); in New England by E. C. Kirkland, *Men, Cities and Transportation*, 2 vols. (1948); and in the South by J. F. Stover, *The Railroads of the South, 1865–1900* (1955). On consolidation and management, see E. G. Campbell, *The Reorganization of the American Railroad System, 1893–1900* (1938). T. C. Cochran, *Railroad Leaders, 1845–1890* (1953), emphasizes their attitudes and problems. Light on government regulation comes from L. Benson, *Merchants, Farmers, and Railroads* (1955); and G. H. Miller, *Railroads and the Granger Laws* (1971).

On technological developments, L. Mumford, *Technics and Civilization* (1934), is suggestive. H. J. Habakkuk, *American and British Technology in the Nineteenth Century* (1962), is a comparative study. An authoritative work of reference is C. Singer et al., eds., *A History of Technology, Vol. V: The Late Nineteenth Century, c. 1850 to c. 1900* (1958). W. Kaempffert, *A Popular History of American Invention*, 2 vols. (1924), is full of interesting detail. Heavy industry and manufacturing generally are treated in V. S. Clark, *History of Manufactures in the United States from 1607–1928*, 3 vols., Vol. II (1929). H. C. Passer, *The Electrical Manufacturers, 1875–1900* (1953), reveals much about technical change and economic growth.

On the steel industry, Andrew Carnegie, *Autobiography* (1920), and J. F. Wall, *Andrew Carnegie* (1970), are highly informative. Oil and Rockefeller are the subject of an exhaustive study by A. Nevins, *John D. Rockefeller*, 2 vols. (1940). For contrasting points of view on Rockefeller, see E. Latham, *John D. Rockefeller: Robber Baron or Industrial Statesman?* (1949). J. Hughes, *The Vital Few* (1966), is another study of big-business leaders, as is S. Englebourg, *Power and Morality: American Business Ethics* (1980). The trust and early regulatory legislation are most fully treated in H. B. Thorelli, *The Federal Antitrust Policy* (1955). See also A. Paul, *Conservative Crisis and the Rule of Law: Attitudes of Bar and Bench* (1969).

The business philosophy of laissez-faire is perceptively treated in E. C. Kirkland, *Business in the Gilded Age* (1952) and *Dream and Thought in the Business Community, 1860–1900* (1956). R. Hofstadter, *Social Darwinism in American Thought* (1944, rev. ed., 1959), should be compared with R. Bannister, *Social Darwinism* (1979); see also S. Fine, *Laissez Faire and the General Welfare State: A Study of Conflict in American Thought, 1865–1901* (1956). The authority on Henry George is C. A. Barker, *Henry George* (1955). See S. Chugerman, *Lester F. Ward: The American Aristotle* (1939), J. L. Thomas, *Alternative America: Henry George, Edward Bellamy, Henry Demarest Lloyd* (1983), and A. Lipow, *Authoritarian Socialism in America: Edward Bellamy and the Nationalist Movement* (1982), are recommended.

On the social history of labor, D. Montgomery has two important books: *The Fall of the House of Labor* (1988), and *Workers Control in America* (1979); see also H. G. Gutman, *Work Culture & Society in Industrializing America* (1976), and M. Dubofsky, *Industrialism and the American Worker* (1975). Unionism and reformers are treated in L. Fink, *Workingmen's Democracy: The Knights of Labor and American*

Politics (1983), and G. N. Grob, *Workers and Utopia* (1961). On working women, see A. Kessler-Harris, *Out to Work* (1982), and Susan Levine, *Labor's True Woman* (1984). And on labor struggles are B. Laurie, *Artisans into Workers: Labor in Nineteenth Century America* (1989); R. V. Bruce, *1877: Year of Violence* (1959), P. Avrich, *The Haymarket Tragedy* (1984), and S. B. Kaufman, *Samuel Gompers and the Origins of the American Federation of Labor* (1973).

Industrial life and business struggles have been the subjects of such novels as Henry James, *The American* (1877); John Hay, *The Bread-winners* (1883), an antilabor work; W. D. Howells, *The Rise of Silas Lapham* (1885), the study of a businessman; and Theodore Dreiser, *The Financier* (1912) and *The Titan* (1914), portraits of industrial tycoons. Edward Bellamy, *Looking Backward, 2000–1887* (1888), is a utopian novel that started a reform movement.

CHAPTER NINETEEN

THE BOWERY AT NIGHT, BY W. LOUIS SONNTAG, JR., 1895

THE URBAN SOCIETY

For a nation of cities to have been nourished on a long antiurban tradition is one of the paradoxes of America. Antiurbanism ranged from fear and revulsion to deep alienation and revolt from the cities. It was not a product of popular culture, which more often celebrated urban life, but of some of the most talented and influential intellectuals of the eighteenth and nineteenth centuries. Thomas Jefferson spoke of cities as "pestilential" and as "sores," and his friend the distinguished scientist Benjamin Rush compared them to "absesses on the human body," and called them "reservoirs of all the impurities of a community." A favorite metaphor of the next generation was the city as "cancer." The antiurban outcry continued with Emerson, Thoreau, Hawthorne, Melville, and Poe—drowning out the few defenders such as Whitman—and was carried into the twentieth century by Henry Adams, Henry James, and William Dean Howells. Urban America enjoyed no mystique of attachment such as the Greeks professed for their city, the *polis,* or the affection French writers felt for Paris. No simple explanation is possible, but one reason was that the Founding Fathers, their children, and their grandchildren were almost completely rural by birth, by breeding, and in outlook. The grandchildren and great-grandchildren as well as later immigrants had only recently moved to town.

AMERICA MOVES TO TOWN

The Pull of the City In 1790, the year of the first census, only 3.35 percent of the population lived in towns of 8,000 or more. By the end of the nineteenth century, ten times that percentage, a third of the population, was classified "urban" by this definition (see Maps 19-1 and 19-2). The cities grew with the nation, of course, but after about 1820 they grew much faster than the nation. Between 1800 and 1890 the population of the entire country increased twelvefold, but over the same period the urban population multiplied 87-fold. In 1800 there were only 6 cities with more than 8,000 people; by 1890 there were 448, and 26 of them had a population greater than 100,000. More striking still was the rise of the American metropolis, the big city of more than half a million. The ancient world produced only two of that size, Rome and Alexandria, and western Europe had only two by the beginning of the eighteenth century, London and Paris. By 1900 six cities were that large in the United States, and three of them had a population of over a million. Rapid urbanization was not limited to this country, but the pace was faster in the United States than in Europe. The New World metropolis grew at a pace unprecedented in history. Chicago more than tripled its size between 1880 and 1900, when it had more than

Map 19-1
America moves to town, 1870

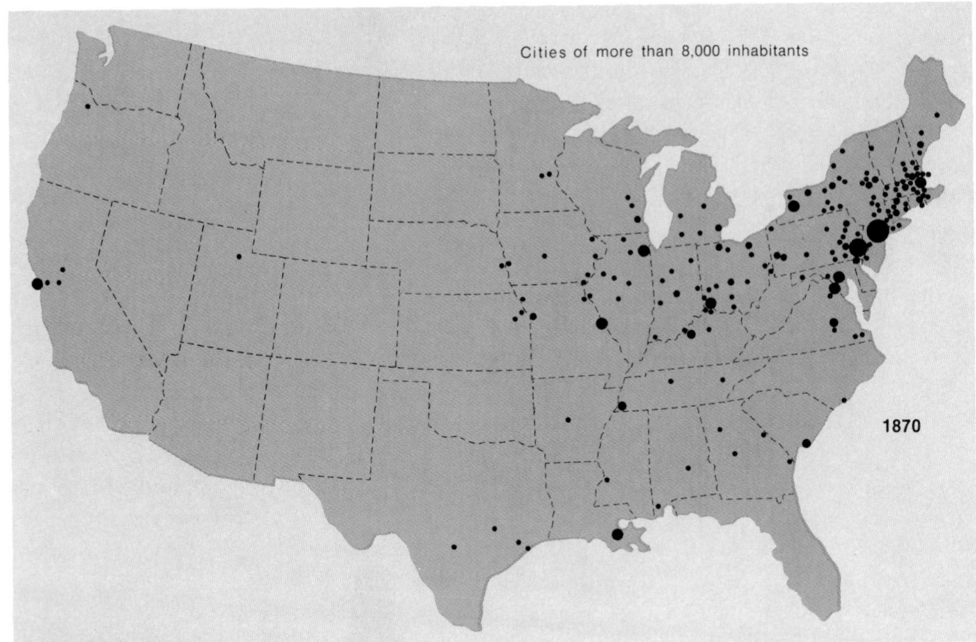

1½ million, and New York grew from not quite 2 million to nearly 3½ million in those two decades. Buffalo, Detroit, and Milwaukee more than doubled, and St. Paul, Minneapolis, and Denver more than quadrupled their size. The surge of people from country to city spoke more eloquently of national preference than did the antiurban tradition of the intellectuals.

Urban growth was very unequally distributed, and some parts of the country did not really participate in the movement significantly until the twentieth century. In fact, half the entire urban population in 1890

Map 19-2
America moves to town, 1900

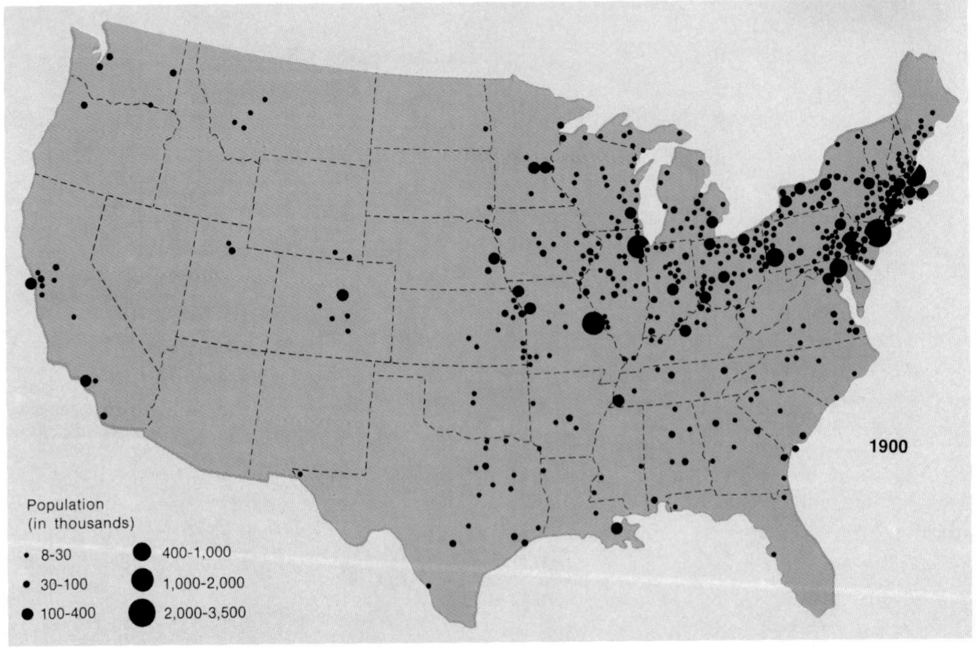

was in the North Atlantic states and only 7.7 percent was in the South Atlantic states. More than half the nation's city dwellers lived in the five states of New York, Pennsylvania, Massachusetts, Illinois, and Ohio. Four-fifths of them lived north of the Ohio and Missouri rivers. Urbanization affected all parts of the country, but in some parts toward the end of the century it was less an immediate experience than a distant and powerful lure.

The drain on the countryside was especially noticeable in the Middle West and the North Atlantic states. Some of it was due, as in the past, to the lure of the West. But the pull of the city was growing stronger and stronger. Between 1880 and 1890 more than half the townships of Iowa and Illinois declined in population, and yet both states gained substantially in total number of inhabitants. Rural decline was even greater in the North Atlantic states, where the flight to the city had long been in progress. In New England 932 out of the total of 1,502 townships declined in population during the 1880s. Thousands of farms were abandoned, houses were left to decay, and scores of villages were completely deserted. Yet in that decade New England actually gained 20 percent in total population.

In the 1880s and 1890s, rural defenses against the lure of the city reached a new low. The 1870s and the 1890s were the worst decades of agricultural depression (see Chapter 20), when everything seemed to go wrong with the farming economy. At the same time, the glamour and attraction of the city were enhanced by the glitter of the new electric lights, as well as by the telephones, the trolley cars, and a thousand other wonders. The city was the only place Americans could enjoy such amenities. The contrast between rural ills and urban attractions made farmers regard their harsh lot and isolation as even more intolerable than ever before, as indeed they were. Many farmers resorted to political rebellion for relief. A great many others simply moved to town.

Cities did not simply increase in number and expand in size. They changed in character, in pattern, and in structure, and all rather suddenly. In antebellum times the downtown business section huddled around a harbor with factories, banks, slaughterhouses, and retail houses side by side. Surrounding them were slum streets as well as streets of wealth and fashion. Beyond them stretched acres that mixed residential, industrial, and commercial neighborhoods. It was the era of "walking cities," when nearness to work was all important. There was no central city of poverty with an outer rim of affluence. Classes, races, and ethnic groups were jumbled together to a degree unknown later, all in proximity to business and industry.

Telephone exchange: urban wonder

The segregated city of modern times, with a core of poverty and rings of rising affluence, developed swiftly after 1870. The changes were brought on by street railways, job locations, housing prices, racial prejudice, and class distinction. The result was a highly fragmented city tightly structured along economic lines. Smaller cities were identified by their economic specializations. There were beer cities, steel cities, textile towns, glass towns, even a candy town—Hershey, Pennsylvania. Albany concentrated on shirts, Troy on collars, Bridgeport on corsets and machine tools; Richmond and Durham made cigarettes, Tampa cigars, Tulsa petroleum, and Dayton was famous for producing cash registers—the very symbol of the urban culture. City people were tied together by the cash nexus, bound into an economic web, and lived under the absolute dictatorship of the clock.

Out West most of the mining towns—the gold, silver, copper, lead, coal, and oil towns—vanished with the depletion of their mineral resources. Hundreds of "paper" towns with thousands of lots laid out for sale by speculators and boomers died aborning without an inhabitant. At least 62 of more than 100 such "cities" in Los Angeles County, one of which sold some 4,000 lots before it was discovered to be "most easily accessible by means of a balloon," vanished without a trace. Those that did flourish in the West, with few exceptions, were founded as commercial enterprises, mainly the work of railroad and real estate promoters.

City Lights and Cesspools The new technology and the factories probably produced more discomforts and inconveniences than comforts and amenities for most of the city dwellers of the late nineteenth century. But to the outsider the advantages and attractions were more readily apparent. First among these were the bright lights that were replacing the dim gas lamps in the streets and the kerosene lamps and gas jets indoors. Cleveland and San Francisco led the way in 1879 by installing brilliant electric arc lamps in their streets, and their example was quickly followed in cities across the country. The noisy, sputtering arc lamp was impractical for indoor use, but for that purpose the incandescent light bulb patented by Edison in 1880 (see p. 474) became available in a few years and spread as swiftly as the growth of power plants permitted. In 1882 there were only 38 central power stations in the whole country, but before the end of the century there were 3,000. Improved lighting not only made cities safer at night but enabled factories to run night shifts, proved a boon to theaters and other amusement houses, and extended the hours of libraries, shops, and schools.

Electrical power provided the answer to a city problem that was even more pressing than that of lighting—the problem of moving vast numbers of people rapidly through the streets and the replacement of the walking city by the "streetcar suburbs." The expansion began in the 1870s with streetcars pulled by horses. Streetcars broke down the self-contained economies of outlying towns and bound the suburbs to the cities. Construction of cheap housing, typically of the three-decker style, and expansion of public utilities and services extended the suburbs until they dwarfed the old central cities and transformed the character of both city and suburb. The transformation and the expansion were greatly increased when electric trolley cars began to replace horse cars in the late 1880s.

Suburbs were extended everywhere the trolley car spread, though whether they were more a result or a cause of trollies is unclear. Among cities of the world, American suburbs are unique in the classes they attracted, the high rate of home ownership, the low density of population, and their distance from the workplace. What relief of congestion they provided

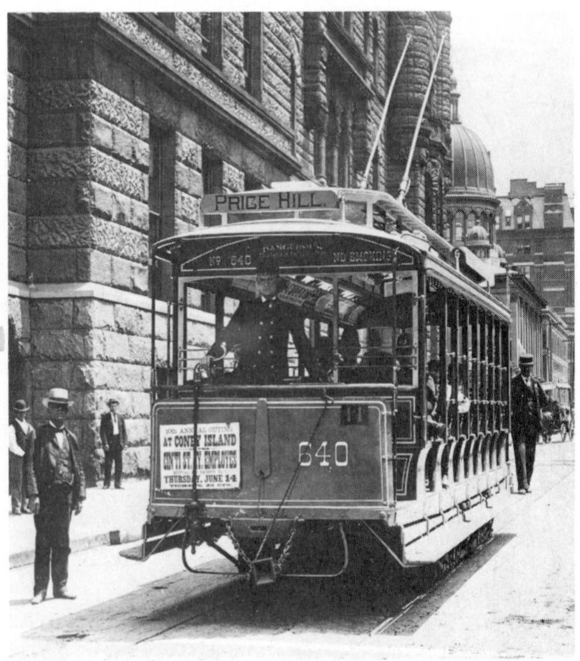

Cincinnati trolley, 1890

came at the cost of increased segregation according to income and class in suburban residential patterns.

Technology and invention were slower to yield solutions to city problems that were traditionally assigned to the public domain, such as street paving, water supply, and sewage disposal. In the 1870s the streets even of the larger cities were poorly paved—usually with cobblestones or granite blocks along the eastern seaboard, with wooden blocks in the Middle West, and with gravel or macadam in the South. The national capital in 1878 set the pace in adapting asphalt to street paving, the method that eventually proved the favorite.

Water supply and sewage disposal lagged behind the demands and needs of mushrooming city populations. The typical urbanite of the 1870s relied on the rural solution of individual well and privy or cesspool. Baltimore in the 1880s smelled "like a billion polecats," according to H. L. Mencken, and a Chicagoan said in his city "the stink is enough to knock you down." Improvement was slow, and large cities of the East and South depended to the end of the century mainly on drainage through open gutters. Pollution of water supplies by sewage as well as by the dumping of industrial waste accounted in large measure for the wretched public health records and staggering mortality rates of the period. The number of public waterworks multiplied more than fivefold in the 1880s but filtering and purification were slow to be adopted. Throughout the 1890s the American city remained poorly prepared to accommodate the hordes that continued to pour in upon it.

The Immigrant and the City The cities grew at the expense of the European as well as the American countryside and village. For the pull of America was felt in Europe more powerfully than ever before, and the great majority of the immigrants crowded into the nation's cities. Like the new native city dwellers, the immigrants were also country people. In spite of the distance they had come, they were usually no more familiar with city ways and city life than Americans fresh from the farm, and for the immigrants the uprooting was even more of a shock and a bewilderment.

The immigrants were often thought of as the primary cause of the urban crisis. Actually, the percentage of foreign born in the total population remained about the same, the immigrants came from much the same social classes as they always had, and they came for the same old reason—to better their lot. A much larger percentage of the new immigrants than previously returned to their native lands, and there were other significant changes. For one thing, they began to come in far greater numbers than ever before. From 1850 to 1880 about 2½ million had arrived per decade, with the rate falling off a bit in the 1860s but picking up again in the 1870s. Big passenger ships, built for the purpose, altered immigration in many ways. In the 1880s the number more than doubled, with nearly 5¼ million arriving during that decade, and with nearly 3¾ million more landing in the next. For another thing, immigrants showed a greater tendency than ever to congregate in the large Eastern cities and less disposition to disperse over the countryside. This concentration naturally made them more conspicuous. And finally there came a shift to what was called "new" immigration—from southern and eastern Europe—as contrasted with the "old" immigrants from northern and western Europe. The old immigrants had come typically from Britain, Ireland, Germany, or one of the Scandinavian countries, and they were usually Protestant. The new immigrants were Italians, Austrians, Hungarians, Poles, Serbs, and Russians (see Map 19-3). They were Catholic or Jewish in religion and had habits and ways that appeared outlandish to older Americans. Immigrants of the new type in the 1890s suddenly climbed to more than 50 percent and in the next decade to more than 70 percent. This increasing proportion of new immigrants coincided with an increasing concern over the ills of urban life and an increasing tendency to stress racial

The pull of America: immigrants at Ellis Island

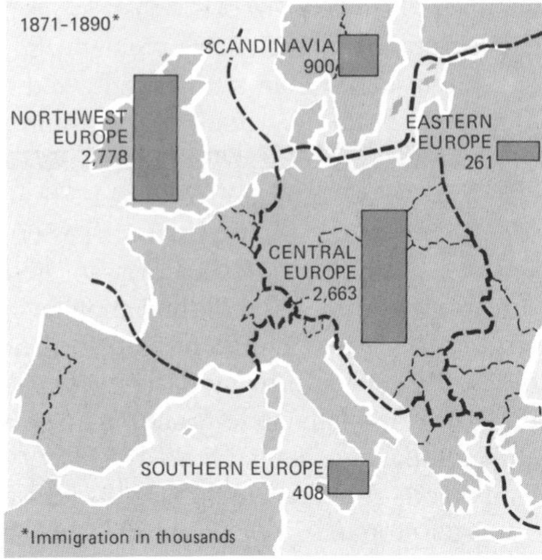

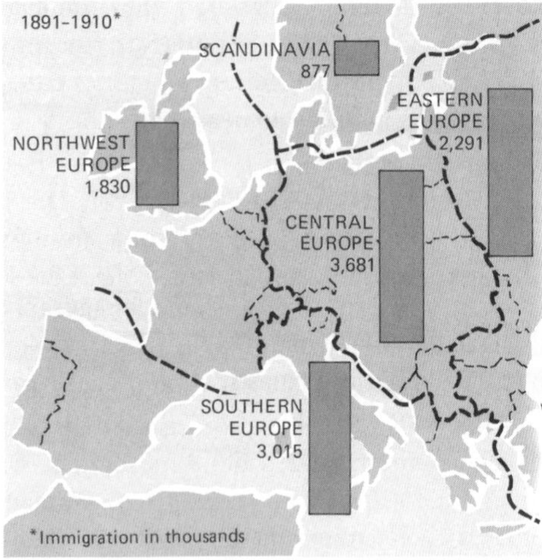

Map 19-3 *Sources of immigration, 1871–1910*

differences. Because of this coincidence, the new immigrants were blamed for many serious city problems that had little to do with racial or national origin.

There could be no doubt, however, that the foreigner had become conspicuous in American life. By 1890 one-fourth of the Philadelphians and one-third of the Bostonians and Chicagoans were of foreign birth, and in Greater New York four out of five residents were of foreign birth or foreign parentage. Of the male population of the 18 largest cities in the country, two and a half times as many were of foreign birth or foreign parentage as were of the older American stock. New York City had half as many Italians as Naples and two and a half times as many Irish as Dublin. The newcomers tended more than the "old" immigrants to huddle together clannishly by nationality.

Slums and Palaces The city of that period grew without plan, with a minimum of control, guided mainly by the dictates of industrial enterprise and private greed. Even with an alert and informed citizenry and an honest and efficient municipal government a city would have faced staggering difficulties, and few cities could boast either asset.

One product of the haphazard growth was the city slum, an old evil that took on new life in 1879 with the invention, in New York City, of the "dumbbell" tenement house, so named for the shape of its floor plan. Designed to get the maximum return for the landlord, the new tenement was no better than a barracks honeycombed with rooms, many of them with no direct access to light or air. Lacking sanitary facilities, privacy, or health precautions, these tenements rapidly degenerated into human pigsties—vile smelling and vermin infested. In 1890 half the city's population lived in them.

William Dean Howells, a novelist, admitted in 1896 that from a distance the tenement might sometimes appear picturesque:

> But to be in it, and not have the distance, is to inhale the stenches of the neglected street, and to catch the yet fouler and dreadfuller poverty-smell which breathes from the open doorways. . . . It is to see the work-worn look of mothers, the squalor of the babes, the haggish ugliness of the old women, the slovenly frowziness of the young girls.

Crime and prostitution flourished, and organized gangs operated securely within their protection. In years when the homicide rate in England and Germany was less than half that in the United States and when the rate in Europe was declining, the rate in the United States was increasing, and lawlessness was growing at an alarming pace. Extremes of human misery and degradation had become common sights.

In the 1880s and 1890s the gulfs between social classes were dramatically emphasized rather than concealed. The economist Thorstein Veblen, in his *Theory of the Leisure Class* (1899), hit on the expression "conspicuous consumption." Displaying habits of consumption that were competitive as well as conspicuous, Chicagoans sported liveried servants and dwelt in lavish palaces built in plain view. The contrast with conspicuous poverty was glaring and unconcealed; squalor and splendor paraded the same streets. The palaces of the wealthy that lined New

Tenement: how the other half lived

York's Fifth Avenue were paralleled a few blocks away by the desolation of Shantytown, inhabited by Irish paupers and goats and stretching along the East Side for 60 blocks or more. In the same year in which Jacob Riis published his shocking study of the slums, *How the Other Half Lives* (1890), Ward McAllister published his *Society As I Have Found It* (1890), lovingly recounting the extravagances of New York's Four Hundred, the self-elected social élite. One exploit of this set was the Bradley Martin costume ball, staged in the Waldorf Hotel at a cost of $368,200. It took place on February 10, 1897, when thousands of unemployed roamed the street, and was attended by guests decked in costumes costing as much as $10,000. Scenes of this sort help to explain the violence in the rhetoric of Populism and other protest movements of the 1890s.

THE AWAKENING OF THE SOCIAL CONSCIENCE

The city was a shock to the American conscience. American country folk or European peasants who emigrated were repelled as well as fascinated by the city. They accepted it and rejected it at the same time. Their feelings were torn and their consciences were bruised by the experience.

City Government: Reputation and Record The knavery and rascality of American city governments and bosses have long been a favorite subject of reformers of the Progressive era and the historians who followed their tradition. The resulting picture of urban corruption and scandal carried a natural appeal for citizens still under the spell of the antiurban tradition and the agrarian myth. The consequence has been a perpetuation of a stereotype of political venality and municiple disarray and failure that stands in need of correction. Granted that valid grounds for complaint existed, that opportunity for graft abounded, and that political bosses often defrauded the public, these abuses should be viewed in relation to the unprecedented problems and staggering difficulties cities then faced. And it is only fair to remember the best their governments produced under the circumstances. Any system of government that could produce, as this one did in the Gilded Age, such wonders as the Brooklyn Bridge, New York's Central Park, San Francisco's Golden Gate Park, and the Boston Public Library could hardly have been as "unspeakable" as often pictured.

The rapid growth of cities had made necessary the large-scale expansion of public utilities of all sorts, as well as the construction of public buildings, sewage systems, docks, street and sidewalk pavement. For this work a multitude of valuable contracts, franchises, monopolies, subsidies, and privileges had to be granted. Such prizes were worth fortunes, and politicians often sold them to the highest bidder. For all that, a recent critical survey of merit has found that in American cities by the end of the nineteenth century, "the supply of water was the most abundant, the street lights were the most brilliant, the parks the grandest, the libraries the largest, and public transportation the fastest of any place in the world."

Never in America had a more colorful set of politicians wielded such power as the great bosses of this period. With a disposition toward large girth, shiny hats, and heavy jewelry, the boss played the role of a freehanded spender, the Robin Hood of the masses. Revenue flowed into their coffers from office seekers, contractors, public utilities, railroads, prostitutes, gamblers — anybody who happened to need protection or favors.

The city boss and his lieutenants in the wards and precincts found their most reliable supporters among

The Immigrant and the Boss

What tells in holdin' your grip on your district is to go right down among the poor families and help them in the different ways they need help. I've got a regular system for this. If there's a fire . . . any hour of the day or night, I'm usually there with some of my election district captains as soon as the fire-engines. If a family is burned out I don't ask whether they are Republicans or Democrats, and I don't refer them to the Charity Organization Society, which would investigate their case in a month or two and decide they were worthy of help about the time they are dead from starvation. I just get quarters for them . . . and fix them up till they get things runnin' again. . . .

Another thing, I can always get a job for a deservin' man. I make it a point to keep on the track of jobs, and it seldom happens that I don't have a few up my sleeve ready for use . . .

And the children—the little roses of the district! Do I forget them? Oh, no! They know me, every one of them, and they know that a sight of Uncle George and candy means the same thing. Some of them are the best kind of vote-getters.

From William L. Riordon *Plunkitt of Tammany Hall,* 1905

the immigrants. These new voters certainly had no monopoly on ignorance and apathy, and many of them were intelligent and useful citizens. But they were usually unaccustomed to the ballot, unpracticed in the ways of democracy, and bewildered by city life in a strange land. Moreover, the great majority of them were unskilled laborers who lived close to the margin of existence and were often in need of a job and a friend. The boss dealt primarily in jobs and votes. He had sometimes sprung from the immigrant community himself, shared its sense of solidarity, knew its leaders by name, and remained one of them. The immigrants responded to him with group loyalty and devotion. They knew him as a man to whom they could always take their troubles. The boss made it his business to know their needs and to give them tangible evidence of his interest in them. His favors took the form of getting them jobs, intervening with the law in their behalf, bailing them out of jail, and handing out Christmas baskets. In short, he performed services for which there was as yet no public agency and which no one else was ready to perform.

Irish politicians were especially adept at these arts, and it was a prevailing conviction that, as one writer put it, "The function of the Irishman is to administer the affairs of the American city." One of them put his political theory in these words: "I think that there's got to be in every ward a guy that any bloke can go to when he's in trouble and get help—not justice and the law, but help, no matter what he's done." Theodore Roosevelt, who studied the matter, concluded that urban reformers would have to create social agencies to fulfill the role the boss played before they could replace him.

As the reformers found out for themselves, after a little experience, many "good" people supported the bosses and machines. Some of these were businessmen who were quite willing to cooperate with the

The Immigrant in the City

I am polish man. I want to be american citizen. . . . But my friends are polish people—I must live with them—I work in the shoe-shop with polish people—I stay all the time with them—at home—in the shop—anywhere. I want live with american people, but I do not know anybody of american. I go 4 times to teacher and must pay $2 weekly. I wanted take board in english house, but I could not, for I earn only $5 or 6 in a week. . . . Better job to get is very hard for me, because I do not speak well english and I cannot understand what they say to me. The teacher teach me—but when I come home—I must speak polish and in the shop also. In this way I can live in your country many years—like my friends—and never speak—write well english—and never be good american citizen. I know here many persons, they live here 10 or more years, and they are not citizens, they don't speak well english, they don't know geography and history of this country, they don't know constitution of America.

From, "Letter of an Anonymous Polish Immigrant . . . ," Report of the Commission on the Problem of Immigration in Massachusetts, 1914

machine to secure the favors, privileges, and exemptions they desired. Other respectable citizens voted regularly, if regretfully, for the machine because of their sincere devotion to the national party, with which the machine was identified. In short, city machine and city boss were buttressed by some of the strongest as well as by some of the weakest elements of the population. Anyone who undertook to change the system would need to be very powerful indeed.

Humanitarians and Reformers The conscience of the middle class was eventually stirred to indignation and action by the misery of the city. But first the middle class had to discover what poverty was. Early humanitarians and reformers did not understand the poor—the "depraved classes," as they called them. Attributing their plight to moral shortcomings, they sent agents to discover which of the poor were "deserving." But it was the young social workers, nearly all of them women, patiently investigating and visiting the sweatshops and tenement firetraps, who began to establish contact between the middle class and the working class.

Jane Addams, the most famous American woman of her time, took up the settlement-house idea and established Hull House on Halsted Street in Chicago in

New York City settlement house

1889. She wished, she said, "to share the lives of the poor" and to make social service "express the spirit of Christ." One such house had already been established in New York in 1886, and in the next ten years some 50 or more were founded in Northern and Eastern cities. They offered a variety of services, maintained playgrounds, nurseries, club rooms, libraries, and kindergartens, and conducted classes in various subjects. But perhaps of more significance was the education they provided for the young middle-class social workers who came to live in the slums to gain firsthand knowledge of the workers' problems. By bringing them together with women of a very different class—poor, uneducated immigrants—the experience proved of importance to American women's history. Within a few years the settlement houses had become the spawning ground of women reformers. Among them were Lillian Wald, founder of the Henry Street Settlement in New York, Florence Kelley, leading spirit in the National Consumers League, and Frances Perkins, with a great future as a Progressive leader.

On the political front the battle for municipal reform began under leaders recruited from the substantial middle class. These included Seth Low and George William Curtis in New York, Richard Henry Dana, Jr., and Nathan Matthews, Jr., in Boston, and Joseph W. Folk in St. Louis. Good-government clubs, committees, commissions, and reform organizations for municipal improvement proliferated rapidly in the 1880s. One of the most prominent was the National Civil Service Reform League, founded in 1881. Cynics called the good-government people the "goo-goos," but they made their influence felt in practical reforms.

The National Municipal League was launched on a wave of public interest in 1894, and within two years more than 200 branch leagues were founded. The League put forward as its program a model city charter that embodied such advanced reforms as the short ballot, greater freedom from state interference, limited franchise for utilities, separate city and state elections, the merit system, government by experts, and, above all, more authority for the mayor. It was slow to endorse two of the most important structural reforms: the commission and later the city manager plan. In 1880 only one of the nation's 23 principal cities was dominated by the mayor, but by 1900 there were 12.

All these were mere structural reforms inspired by the model of business efficiency, however, and their inadequacy was pointed up by the program of social reforms carried out by Mayor Hazen Pingree of Detroit, Mayor Samuel M. "Golden Rule" Jones of Toledo, Mayor Josiah Quincy of Boston, and Mayor Thomas L. Johnson of Cleveland. Their social reforms provided laws protecting working-class interests and included municipal ownership of utilities, unemployment relief, the eight-hour day, and a minimum wage. Reforms of this type, overlooked by the good-government reformers, attracted popular support that structural reforms often lacked. Their proponents were called "reform bosses" when they used machine methods and played politics with jobs and contracts.

Reform leaders and bosses, and the class of people from which they came, were surely motivated in good part by humanitarian impulses. They wished the best for the people they served, but they were not beyond criticism themselves. Too often they manifested impatience with democracy and its institutions, disdain for other cultures and races, and fear of the working class and the new immigrants. Some came to regard themselves as a privileged professional elite with authority and competence to manage public affairs and make decisions for ordinary citizens and untutored voters.

The Rights of Women Women reformers responded to the social problems of the city, as we have seen, but another of their preoccupations was the plight of their own sex in a male-dominated society. Their bill of grievances, well-documented and long-standing, included political disfranchisement, legal discrimination, economic exploitation, cultural and educational deprivation, and domestic drudgery. If black people had their "place," women had their "sphere," and to many women its limitations seemed increasingly oppressive. Woman's sphere was The Home, and beyond its walls she ventured, save on religious missions, only at the risk of breaching "the cult of true womanhood"—piety, purity, submissiveness, and domesticity.

The Victorian family undoubtedly proved an important source of personal security against urban disorder for both the working class and those above them, but it came at a heavy cost to women. It was difficult if not impossible to reconcile women's right to equality with the demands made on women by the institution of the family in nineteenth-century America. The principle of equality denied a difference, while the practice of wifehood and motherhood demanded a difference in the roles of men and women.

The demand was for the subordination of the wife. Personal achievement and self-fulfillment required attitudes of competitiveness and self-assertion and job opportunities usually denied her.

For a growing number of middle-class women, technology—gas lighting, domestic plumbing, manufactured ice, and improved furnaces, stoves, washtubs, and sewing machines—provided some escape from the domestic treadmill. For others, cheap domestic servants from the immigrant ships furnished release. New women's colleges and older men's colleges turned coeducational were graduating larger numbers of women—2,500 a year by 1890. But they were educated to fill places that, save for underpaid teaching, did not yet exist. Like their sisters who were venturing out of the "sphere," they found themselves in a society that had no use for them.

What organizations women then had were chiefly devoted to "self-culture." Founded in 1882, the Association of Collegial Alumnae remained small and exclusive for a long time, limited in 1889 to the graduates of the 14 colleges that met their rigorous standards. At the opposite extreme of inclusiveness was the sprawling General Federation of Women's Clubs. Organized in 1890, it federated hundreds of clubs, had 150,000 members by 1900, and was soon to top a million. Mainly limited to "self-culture" and entertainment, most members were middle-aged, middle-class, conservative women. The General Federation took pains to avoid antagonizing the cautious rank and file, many of them antisuffragists, and did not endorse woman suffrage until the eve of victory. The leaders of the Federation were usually suffragists, however, and their movement furnished the hard core of feminism. Split into two organizations, the militant National and the conservative American associations, since the struggle over black suffrage in the 1860s, the rival groups resolved their differences and merged as the National American Woman Suffrage Association in 1890.

A new generation of women leaders had arrived by this time, though veterans like Susan B. Anthony, Elizabeth Cady Stanton, and Lucy Stone were still on the scene. Like them, Anna Howard Shaw met working women as equals, but she was an exception. "The younger women," as historian Eleanor Flexner writes, "were not, for the most part, distinguished by the breadth of their social views." This was true of Carrie Chapman Catt, May Wright Sewall, Rachel Foster Avery, and Harriet Taylor Upton. They reflected the drift of their times toward conservative views on labor and race relations and were more concerned with decorum in pressing their cause. Rejecting their radical origins, the new feminists also turned away from the disturbing and fundamental questions that their contemporary, Charlotte Perkins Gilman, asked in her book *Woman and Economics* (1898). Instead they narrowed their objectives to suffrage, submerged all women's rights in the political struggle, and as a consequence came to exaggerate the value of the ballot as the sovereign remedy for women's ills.

By 1890, 17 states and territories had given women limited suffrage in school elections, but not until that year did Wyoming enter the Union as the first state with full suffrage for women. Three more underpopulated Western states followed suit, Colorado in 1893 and Utah and Idaho in 1896, but not for 14 years did another state adopt woman suffrage. Congress gave formal hearings to pleas for a federal woman suffrage amendment, but neither house reported the bill favorably after 1893, and the question disappeared from Congress as an issue for 20 years. Women kept up their campaigns for state action, waging hundreds of them, many heroically under adverse conditions. Among their arguments were some that appealed to nativism and racism. The 1893 convention of the Woman Suffrage Association urged suffrage with literacy instead of sex qualifications, since there were "more white women who can read and write than all negro voters; more American women who can read and write than all foreign voters." For all that they continued to be rewarded with defeat until the First World War.

The Conscience of the Church The church community was eventually to respond both in faith and in works to the human needs and social problems of city and industry. But in 1876, as Henry May has observed, "Protestantism presented a massive, almost unbroken front in its defense of the status quo." Religion was a spiritual and individual, not a social, concern, and salvation came through the striving of the individual with sin and conscience, not through social welfare and betterment. The churches, middle-class in outlook, were dedicated to the early social creed of individualism and laissez-faire, and the mightiest preachers of that era expressed these attitudes forcefully and repeatedly. There was no better exponent of laissez-faire and social Darwinism than Henry Ward Beecher in his Brooklyn pulpit.

Revivalism and professional revivalists were usually powerful propagators of the old-time religion—orthodox fundamentalism—and had very little or no social awareness. Throughout the 1880s and 1890s the annual revival was a regular feature of the program of Methodist, Baptist, Presbyterian, Congregational, and smaller churches. The most famous of the professional revivalists was Dwight L. Moody, an impressive figure of 280 pounds who got his start with a successful campaign in Britain during the 1870s. Returning to America in 1875, he set out with Ira D. Sankey, his equally weighty singer, to "evangelize the world in this generation." Moody brought into play all his great executive and publicity talents to attract huge crowds and with forceful and colloquial sermons converted sinners by the thousands in all parts of the United States. His popularity continued unflagging until his death in 1899. Moody and another famous revivalist, T. DeWitt Talmage, along with numerous imitators, set a record for professional revivalism in America. Whether as a result of their work or the growth of population, Protestant churches grew rapidly in the last two decades of the century, increasing their membership from somewhat over 10 million to almost 18 million.

In spite of this growth, clergymen complained constantly that the working people were drifting away from the church. Moved either by the pulpit's lack of sympathy for their plight or by the elegance of the clothing they saw in the pews, working people found the churches of the older Protestant denominations less suited to their tastes than they once had been. Large working-class districts in the cities were without church facilities of any kind. Some found solace in new sects. Many "holiness" people were recruited from the Methodist, Baptist, and other Protestant churches. Usually originating in the country and then moving to the city, a dozen or more pentecostal and millennial sects sprang up in the 1880s and 1890s.

A new sect of a different sort was the Church of Christ, Scientist, usually called Christian Scientist, which was chartered by a small group of the followers of Mary Baker Eddy in 1879. The prophet of the new faith was born in 1821 to a New England family of the pious, humble sort to which Joseph Smith, the Mormon prophet (see p. 263), had been born 15 years earlier. Inspired by the help she received from a faith healer for her own rather complex health problems, she developed the belief that "disease is caused by mind alone." At the end of Eddy's long life in 1910, adherents of her church numbered 100,000, and her estate was appraised at more than 2½ million.

Addressing its appeal to the downtrodden, the Salvation Army invaded America in 1879 under the command of George Railton and seven women officers. Founded the year before in London by William Booth, it was born of his desire to reach the city poor. Using revivalist methods and brass bands to attract crowds, the uniformed army and its lassies preached repentance in the streets and sent "slum brigades" into the tenement districts to bring relief as well as the gospel to the poor. Also of English origins was the Young Mens Christian Association, first imported in the 1850s. After the Civil War the YMCA grew rapidly and built inexpensive residential hotels that were also religious, cultural, and recreational centers in the larger cities.

It would have been impossible for the Catholic Church to ignore the working class and the social problems of the city. Since the "new" immigration was overwhelmingly Catholic, working class, and urban, the American Catholic Church of the late nineteenth century became more than ever the church of the city, the worker, and the immigrant. The number of Catholics in the country increased from over 6 million to more than 10 million in the last two decades of the century. Responsibility for training and adjusting the new Americans to their country compelled the church to adjust its social policy to urban needs and persuaded James Gibbons, then in Rome to be installed as cardinal, to defend the cause of American labor before the Holy See in 1887. The papal encyclical *Rerum Novarum,* of May 1891, enunciated social ideals and responsibilities for Catholics that gave additional sanction to the social views of the Americans.

In the meantime, a small group of Protestant clergymen, at first responding as individuals to the social crises and labor struggles of the 1870s to 1890s, had begun to shape a reinterpretation of their religion that in later years came to be known as the Social Gospel. Turning away from the traditional emphasis on spiritual and moral concerns, the new gospel stressed the social and pragmatic implications of Christian ethics and called for good works in social reform and betterment. The Episcopal Church, the most aristocratic denomination and yet the one most influenced by the mildly socialistic doctrines then gaining attention in the parent Church of England, took most readily to the new gospel, while the Methodist Church tended to cling to rural individualism and resisted the Social

The Salvation Army: reaching the city poor

Gospel at first. With a similar following and the additional restraint of such wealthy benefactors as John D. Rockefeller, the Baptists nevertheless moved earlier toward the Social Gospel under the inspiration of Walter Rauschenbusch. By 1895 the influence of the Social Gospel was being felt throughout American Protestantism and in secular thought as well. Its main impact, however, was not to come until the following century.

THE SPREAD OF LEARNING

Public Schools and Mass Media The national determination to educate everybody was best reflected in the growth of public schools, which increased at an unprecedented speed after 1870. Free education for all became a foremost article in the American faith, and the schools were unfairly expected to solve all of democracy's problems, from poorly cooked meals to poorly adjusted races. Growing cities expected the schools to take over many functions that parents, police, and priests had once performed and along the way to Americanize the children of the new immigrants. By 1900 the average school attendance and the length of the average school year had increased markedly. There were only 160 public high schools in the whole country in 1870, but by the end of the century there were more than 6,000. The cities reaped the greatest benefits from the public school expansion.

Private schools still held on, particularly in the Eastern states, and certain ethnic and religious groups resisted being integrated into a uniform public school system. Unable to win public support for their own educational efforts, the Catholics in 1884 determined upon an elaborate expansion of their parochial schools. The program was mainly designed to educate the immigrants of that faith in the cities, and most of the schools were located in New England and the Middle Atlantic states.

Since support of the schools was left to local communities, improvement and growth varied widely with the distribution of wealth. In general, the rural districts lagged behind the urban areas and the West and South behind the East. But the South had a staggering burden of special disadvantages. In the first place it had about twice as many children per adult as the North, and it had considerably less than half the per capita taxable wealth with which to educate them. At the century's end the schools of the South were still miserably supported, poorly taught, and wholly inadequate, and as poor as the average school was, the schools for black children were far below that. Efforts to bring up the average in the next decade were largely confined to the white schools.

In spite of the physical growth of the educational plant and the millions of dollars poured into public education, the average American adult by the turn of the century had only about five years of schooling. Illiteracy had been reduced, however, from around 17 percent in 1880 to about 11 percent 20 years later. For all the faddism and quackery, in spite of the low-paid teachers and the attempt to saddle them with all the problems of democracy, the public schools continued to increase in number and grow in popular esteem.

In the larger cities, culture was displayed in magnificent palaces with neoclassical fronts and sweeping staircases that opened to the public in the 1870s: the Metropolitan Museum of Art in New York and the Boston Museum of Fine Arts in 1870, the Philadelphia Museum of Art in 1876, the Art Institute of Chicago in 1879. Conceived by their founders as democratic enterprises to diffuse refinement among the people, they also diffused an association of the idea of art and culture with the munificence of private wealth and power. As displayed in the luxurious museums, art and culture was seen as something that filtered downward from a distant past, from overseas, and from elite and wealthy custodians.

These years also brought a dramatic expansion of public libraries. Librarians laid claim to professional standing in 1876, when they organized the American Library Association. State and local tax money was tapped, and private donors began to put large amounts into library building: Andrew Carnegie, the most munificent of them, launched his library benefactions at Pittsburgh in 1881. In the 1890s six library buildings costing more than a million dollars had been either started or completed. The most splendid were the Boston Public Library and the New York Public Library, both opened in 1895, and the Library of Congress, the largest and most costly in the world, opened in 1897. By 1900 there were more than 9,000 public libraries in the country, with a total of more than 45 million volumes.

The repetitive theme of "more and more and more" that drums through all phases of American life in these years was nowhere so striking as in journalism, especially in periodicals. In the last 15 years of the century the number of periodicals published increased by 2,200, most of them devoted to trades and special interests. More striking was the increase in the number and circulation of periodicals for the general reader. There were only four such monthly magazines in the country in 1885 with circulations of 100,000 or more, and they were usually priced at 35 cents a copy. Twenty years later there were 20 such magazines with an aggregate circulation of more than 5½ million, and all but four of them sold at 10 to 15 cents a copy. The new 10-cent competitors, such as *Munsey's*, *McClure's*, and the *Cosmopolitan*, were lighter in tone, with shorter articles and many illustrations.

Growing cities, increasing literacy, and expanding population combined to create greater and greater markets for newspapers and to heighten the temptation to vulgarize the product in order to exploit the potential market. The number of daily papers, largely confined to the cities, more than doubled, and the number of weekly and semiweekly papers increased more than 50 percent between 1880 and 1900, while subscribers increased even more rapidly. The growth of daily newspapers came as follows:

Year	Number of Dailies	Total Daily Circulation
1860	387	1,478,000
1870	574	2,602,000
1880	971	3,566,000
1890	1,610	8,387,000
1900	2,226	15,102,000

By the end of the century the United States had more than half the newspapers in the world. To reach the masses the news columns became more sensational and vulgar. The father of the new school of journalists was Joseph Pulitzer, who bought the New York *World* in 1883 and ran its circulation up from 15,000 in 1883 to over a million by 1898. The assault on privacy and taste was continued and intensified by his imitator, William Randolph Hearst of the New York *Journal*.

The Higher Learning For all the crassness and materialism that earned for it the name of "Gilded Age," the period could boast of substantial advances in higher education and scholarship. There was obviously much room for improvement. American colleges of 1870, even the better ones, were likely to be

City Room, New York World

strongly sectarian, provincial, and undistinguished. The typical college professor of that year was harshly, but not very unfairly, described as "a nondescript, a jack of all trades, equally ready to teach surveying and Latin eloquence." The traditional curriculum, designed for the training of ministers, did not permit specialization or allow time for research. Library and laboratory facilities were inadequate, and the natural sciences were neglected. There were no graduate schools and no professional schools beyond theological seminaries and the engineering and military academies. Collegiate pedagogy, like the Victorian family, was heavily authoritarian, with emphasis upon rules, discipline, rote learning, and recitations.

With Harvard in the vanguard and with Charles W. Eliot at its head, a small group of academicians undertook to reform the old collegiate order. The reforms they made were not universally acknowledged to be improvements in their day, nor are they yet, but they were widely if slowly imitated. One of them was the elective system, which resulted in a proliferation of courses and subjects from which the student chose as fancy dictated. Additional reforms, such as an increase in the number of science courses and in the use of the laboratory method of instruction, were taken up rapidly, as were discussion periods as substitutes for rote recitation. Among other changes slowly adopted were the decline of authoritarian norms and traditional curricula and a decrease in the proportion of clergy on boards of trustees and in presidents' offices.

Accompanying these changes and reflecting the shift to a secular and scientific emphasis was an increase in German influence in academic circles. During the nineteenth century, more than 9,000 Americans studied at German universities, all but about 200 of them after 1850. The Johns Hopkins University, opened in Baltimore in 1876 with an inaugural address by Thomas Huxley, the Darwinian, was an expression of both English and German influence. The new emphasis implied an increase in the scholar's stature, freedom, and prestige. Inspired more or less by the example of Johns Hopkins, 15 major graduate schools or departments had been established by the end of the century.

Nearly 3,000 students registered in American graduate schools in 1890, as compared with a mere handful two decades before. The professional scholars founded scores of learned societies: the Archaeological Institute of America (1879), the Modern Language Association (1883), and in the next ten years the historians, economists, mathematicians, physicists, and psychologists, to mention only a few, followed suit.

Learned journals and books equal to Europe's best began to appear in America, and American-trained scholars began to acquire international reputations.

Medical and legal education was still primitive in the 1870s and 1890s. None of the schools of medicine or law required a college degree for admission, and the typical medical school turned its graduates loose on a helpless public after only a few months of haphazard lectures. Both medical and legal degrees could easily be bought. Between 1876 and 1900, 86 new medical schools were founded, but the Johns Hopkins Medical School, opened in 1894, was the first to require a college degree for admission and the first to have a full-time teaching staff. Comparable improvement in law schools was to come only later.

This was an era prolific in the birth of new institutions of higher learning, both public and private. In the last two decades of the nineteenth century, the total number of colleges and universities in the country increased by nearly 150, though many of them had no valid claim to academic status and were often short lived. Ten new state universities, all of them coeducational from the start, were founded between 1882 and 1895. In the East, where coeducation was slower to win acceptance, several women's colleges were founded: Vassar in 1861, Smith in 1871, and Bryn Mawr in 1885, while several of the older men's colleges opened affiliated women's colleges nearby. Numerous land-grant colleges, taking advantage of the Morrill Act of 1862, sprang up to teach both agricultural and mechanical arts. A fraction of the new industrial and commercial fortunes of the age went into the founding of universities bearing the names of Cornell (1868), Vanderbilt (1873), Hopkins (1876), Tulane (1884), Stanford (1885), and Clark (1887). The University of Chicago (1891) was one of the few that did not take the name of its benefactor, in this case John D. Rockefeller.

The history of higher learning of this period was not, however, purely a story of expansion and improvement. A mistaken conception of democracy led to the assumption of equality among all academic pursuits and justified the teaching of courses in almost any subject, however trivial. Institutions became overexpanded, overcrowded, and absurdly bureaucratized. A misguided deference to the opinions of alumni, sports enthusiasts, and the unlettered public generally led to an anarchical confusion of values and distortions of academic purpose. For the first time in recorded history, institutions of higher learning assumed the function of providing mass entertainment in spectator sports, particularly football, and the comparative distinction of a university came to depend on its success in pursuing these enterprises.

The business leaders who replaced the clergy on the college boards of trustees were slow to acknowledge the status claimed by the new scholar and were sometimes quite unable to distinguish between their relation to faculty members and their relation to "other employees." The trustees of seven well-known universities approved a statement published in the Chicago *Tribune* in 1899 to the effect that college professors "should promptly and gracefully submit to the determination of the trustees" in deciding what should be taught, and that "if the trustees err it is for the patrons and proprietors, not for the employees, to change either the policy or the personnel of the board." During the 1890s, nine prominent faculty members were dismissed for presuming to express their opinions on such subjects as labor, railroads, and currency. Though there was no legitimate excuse for these gaucheries, we must remember that America was trying to spread learning far more widely than had ever been attempted before.

ARTS, LETTERS, AND CRITICS

Artists and Their Work In matters of taste the Gilded Age has acquired and in part deserved a deplorable reputation. Whether it was because the molders of fashion were insecure in their social position or new to their wealth or for some other reason, their taste ran to excesses in all things. They overloaded their rooms with bric-a-brac, their dresses with bustles, and their houses with gingerbread. They had no trouble finding architects, painters, and sculptors of the sort who would cater to their preferences, but the work these people left behind need not detain us.

Beneath the crass surface and behind the clutter of imitative art, however, there were genuinely original and creative spirits at work in the land. Artists, engineers, architects, sculptors, and painters honestly faced the realities of the new urban, industrial society, contrived original and powerful answers to its problems, and contributed much to the urban vitality of the era. It was the new city that gave them both their challenge and their opportunity. The bold spirit with

The Brooklyn Bridge: daring and magnificent

which they met the challenge and seized the opportunity is caught in a statement by a Georgia-bred architect, John Wellborn Root, who did his work in Chicago:

> In America we are free of artistic traditions. Our freedom begets license, it is true. We do shocking things; we produce works of architecture irremediably bad; we try crude experiments that result in disaster. Yet somewhere in this mass of ungoverned energies lies the principle of life. A new spirit of beauty is being developed and perfected, and even now its first achievements are beginning to delight us.

One achievement of the age that was daring and magnificent enough to meet Root's description was the Brooklyn Bridge, a suspension such as had never before been built, with granite towers 276 feet high and with a central span of 1,600 feet. Sketched by John A. Roebling, who died before construction began, the great bridge was completed by his son Washington A. Roebling in 1883. A product of the new industrialism down to the last of the 19 strands of steel cable and the last riveted girder, the bridge soared out of the soot and slums of Manhattan, monumental proof that the new society could produce a thing of beauty out of its materials. In the same city a landscape architect named Frederick L. Olmsted demonstrated that it was not necessary for a city to be the seat of an absolute monarch in order to create spacious, lovely, and exquisitely designed parks, such as Central Park, Olmsted's masterpiece. It was not his only great park, however, for he designed many more and left scarcely a major city in the country untouched by his influence.

The architect whom Root singled out to illustrate the new spirit in American art was Henry Hobson Richardson. Born in New Orleans, educated at Harvard and abroad, Richardson was a man of gargantuan ambitions and appetites, full of zest for any problem and equally ready to design churches, railroad stations, department stores, libraries, office buildings, anything. "The things I want most to design," he said, "are a grain elevator and the interior of a great river steamboat." His massive granite structures created a style and defined an architectural era. Although he died in 1886 at the age of 48, he left his buildings scattered across the country from Trinity Church in Boston to a monument on the Wyoming plains.

The problem of the skyscraper, called into being by the fantastic extravagance of unplanned city growth and overcrowding, could not be solved by masonry. What was required was a steel skeleton for support

Modern Architecture: The Application

It became evident that the very tall masonry office building was in its nature economically unfit as ground values steadily rose. Not only did its thick walls entail loss of space and therefore revenue, but its unavoidably small window openings could not furnish the proper and desirable ratio of glass area to rentable floor area.

Thus arose a crisis, a seeming *impasse.* What was to do? . . . The need was there, the capacity to satisfy was there, but contact was not there. Then came the flash of imagination, which saw the single thing. The trick was turned; and there swiftly came into being something new under the sun. For the true steel-frame structure stands unique in the flowing of man and his works; a brilliant material example of man's capacity to satisfy his needs through the exercise of his natural powers. . . .

The social significance of the tall building is in finality its most important phase. In and by itself, considered *solus* so to speak, the lofty steel frame makes a powerful appeal to the architectural imagination where there is any. Where imagination is absent and its place usurped by timid pedantry the case is hopeless. The appeal and the inspiration lie, of course, in the element of loftiness, in the suggestion of slenderness and aspiration, the soaring quality as of a thing rising from the earth as a unitary utterance.

From Louis H. Sullivan, *The Autobiography of an Idea, 1924*

and walls reduced to mere fireproof curtains instead of supporting buttresses. With contributions from engineers and steelmasters as well as architects, Chicagoans achieved a solution in the Tacoma Building in 1888. With the arrival of the electric elevator, the age of the skyscraper begins, and with that age the name of Louis Sullivan is intimately associated. Ranking with Richardson as one of the giants of the period, Sullivan was a capricious genius who commanded the respect of the ablest critics: Frank Lloyd Wright referred to him as *Der Meister*. Sullivan revealed the inner conflicts of his generation's adjustment to the city when he characterized the skyscraper as "profoundly antisocial."

It is curious that Chicago, which contributed so many new and original architectural techniques, should also have been the host and creator of the White City at the Columbian Exposition of 1893, which represented a return to Renaissance classicism and other traditional styles. The White City was mainly the work of Easterners, particularly the firm of Charles F. McKim, William R. Mead, and Stanford White. The architects were assisted by the most famous American sculptor of the period, Augustus Saint-Gaudens, and by Olmsted, whose landscaping included the lovely lagoon surrounded by gleaming white-plaster buildings. The ephemeral dream city was undoubtedly an impressive spectacle, but Sullivan, who designed the only nonclassical structure in the Exposition, regarded it as "an appalling calamity" whose influence would "last for half a century." What he feared was a reversion to the academic, classical models of architecture. In the "Federal" style sponsored by McKim, Mead, and White in the national

Henry James: America without a Past

. . . one might enumerate the items of high civilization, as it exists in other countries, which are absent from the texture of American life, until it should become a wonder to know what was left. No State, in the European sense of the word, and indeed barely a significant national name. No sovereign, no court, no personal loyalty, no aristocracy, no church, no clergy, no army, no diplomatic service, no country gentlemen, no palaces, no castles . . . nor ivied ruins; no cathedrals, nor abbeys, nor little Normal churches; no great Universities nor public schools—no Oxford, nor Eton, nor Harrow, no literature, no novels, no museums, no pictures, no political society, no sporting class—No Epsom nor Ascot!

From Henry James, *Hawthorne,* 1879.

capital and elsewhere in the ensuing era, Sullivan's fears were justified. On the other hand, the example of a city intelligently planned for comfort and beauty stimulated the "city beautiful" movement.

Some of the fine arts in what Lewis Mumford called the "Brown Decades" were creditably served by American artists. John La Farge, a gifted interior decorator and art critic, executed thousands of stained-glass windows and won the admiration of Richardson, for whom he did the windows of Trinity Church in Boston. Winslow Homer, a serious illustrator, occasionally struck the note of greatness in his paintings of the weather-beaten ruggedness of common life. But to find American painters who deserve to rank with their European contemporaries we must turn to Thomas Eakins and Albert Pinkham Ryder. Eakins worked in relative obscurity outside fashionable currents and left a house full of unsold paintings at his death. A friend of Walt Whitman, whose portrait he painted, he had a salty contempt for pretense and loved to paint boxers, oarsmen, and surgeons at their work. Ryder was a painter of the sea and the night and has been compared with Melville in the symbolic and lyrical qualities of his art. Among his great symbolic paintings are *Death on a Pale Horse, The Flying Dutchman, Jonah,* and *Macbeth and the Witches*—all eerie, mystic, and tragic.

Beginnings of Realism In letters as in arts the post–Civil War decades have had a poor reputation. Their writers have been tagged with the "genteel" label and condemned for complacency and blindness to the glaring faults of their society. Their reputation for shallowness, complacency, and prudery is not wholly unjustified, but the age was often as blind to its literary merits as to its social faults. It sometimes overlooked and sometimes misunderstood its best talent. Contemporaries of Emily Dickinson, the greatest American poet of the age, and one of the subtlest, never even heard of her, for she lived the life of a recluse and published very few poems before her death in 1886. They mistook Mark Twain, their greatest satirist, for a funny man and a writer for boys. They hardly had time to appreciate the pioneer naturalist Stephen Crane, who died in his twenties. They were misled by the surface mildness of William Dean Howells, their leading realist, and they misunderstood (when they did not neglect) Henry James, their greatest artist. But any age that should produce Dickinson, Twain, Howells, and James should command respect and serious attention.

More completely and richly than any other writer, Mark Twain, who was christened Samuel Langhorne Clemens, embodied in his life and writings the sprawling diversity, the epic adventures, the inner tensions, and the cross-purposes of post–Civil War America. A Southerner by birth and heritage, he became a Westerner while the West was wildest and settled in New England to live out his life. He was a child of the frontier and, like his America, a country man who moved to the city, a provincial who was thrust into a strange new world. His literary record of the experience documents a whole epoch. "I am persuaded," the playwright George Bernard Shaw wrote Mark Twain, "that the future historian of America will find your works as indispensable to him as a French historian finds the political tracts of Voltaire."

Mark Twain: American satirist

Mark Twain's American odyssey started in Missouri on the banks of the Mississippi, where the East bordered on the West and the South overlapped the North. He joined the Confederate army when the war broke out, but, after a trivial accident that involved no fighting, he gave up the war and joined his brother in the Far West. He recorded his adventures in the Nevada mining camps in *Roughing It* (1872) and gave the period a name that has stuck in *The Gilded Age* (1873), a broad political and social satire. His boyhood and his later experience as a pilot on the great river found expression in two of his works, *The Adventures of Tom Sawyer* (1876) and *Life on the Mississippi* (1883). But he surpassed all his other work in *The Adventures of Huckleberry Finn* (1884), a masterpiece of American literature. A composite of satire and nostalgia, it dips deeper into irony than was characteristic of the age, for it aligns the sympathies of every decent reader with Huck, the river rat, against civilization itself and fixes the primitive, superstitious Nigger Jim as one of the most memorable figures in American fiction. Mark Twain wrote a great deal more, but like the miners of his Nevada adventure and America itself, he was a spendthrift with his resources and could not always tell the stuff that glittered from real gold.

Howells, the friend of Twain and the generous friend of letters of his time, was even more prolific. He wrote 30 full-length novels and five volumes of short stories, not to mention an endless stream of literary criticism. In his time he was rightfully called the dean of American letters and the foremost exponent of American realism. Rejected by a later generation that unfairly associated him with complacency and materialism, Howells deserves better from the present perspective. In mid-life he reached a turning point marked by his reaction to the Haymarket executions in 1886, against which he conducted virtually a one-man protest among the intellectuals. The experience coincided with his reading of Tolstoy and Henry George, and he began calling himself a socialist and demanding a sterner realism that would confront the injustice and suffering of industrial society under plutocratic control. Though he was inclined to deal in abstractions, his fiction began at once to reflect his views. *Annie Kilburn* (1889) is an indictment of social injustice and the inadequacies of charity in a New England community, and *A Hazard of New Fortunes* (1890), the best expression of Howells's new phase and the climactic work of American realism, centers around a violent strike. *A Traveler from Altruria* (1894)

James Bryce: America with a Past

After this it may seem a paradox to add that Americans are a conservative people. Yet any one who observes the power of habit among them, the tenacity with which old institutions and usages, legal and theological formulas, have been clung to, will admit the fact. A love for what is old and established is in their English blood. Moveover, prosperity helps to make them conservative. They are satisfied with the world they live in, for they have found it a good world, in which they have grown rich. . . . They are proud of their history and of their Constitution, which has come out of the furnace of civil war with scarcely the smell of fire upon it.

From James Bryce, *The American Commonwealth,* 1888.

is a utopian novel that exposes and attacks social injustice.

Henry James continued to develop as a writer after Howells and Twain began to decline. His wonderfully productive life carried over into the twentieth century, though the bulk of his work appeared before 1900. Unlike Howells and Twain, he was not interested in the common people. His typical subjects are Americans and Europeans of cultivated minds, usually in a cosmopolitan setting. *The American* (1877), *The Europeans* (1878), and *Daisy Miller* (1879) are treatments of national attitudes in transatlantic society. This was only the beginning of four decades of writing that included such masterpieces as *The Portrait of a Lady* (1881), *The Ambassadors* (1903), and *The Golden Bowl* (1904). Henry James was the most completely dedicated and probably the most wholly fulfilled American writer and artist of his time.

The age affords posterity one unflattering but fascinating portrait of itself drawn by a philosopher-historian who stands in a class by himself: Henry Adams, descendant of the two presidents whose name he bore. All serious students of the period must make their own acquaintance and their own peace with this querulous and opinionated critic. His main writing dealt with the history of another period, that of Jefferson and Madison. But his novels *Democracy* (1880) and *Esther* (1883) and more particularly his autobiographical *Education of Henry Adams* (1918) and *The Degradation of the Democratic Dogma* (1919) are the keys to his incisive critique. It was characteristic of him that he had the first two books published anonymously and the last two posthumously. Having mastered those, one is then better prepared to find Adams, in *Mont-Saint-Michel and Chartres* (1913), searching the monuments of the Middle Ages for their meaning to modern America, and projecting lines of change from the year 1200 to the year 1900.

After the end of the century and near the end of his life, Henry Adams looked back philosophically over the American experience since the Civil War. He was astonished at how much history had been telescoped into that brief span of years and how frightfully the pace of change had accelerated. At the outset of the period, in his youth, his fellow citizens were still grappling with stone-age tribes on the Great Plains and debating the issue of African slavery in their midst. America had been a land of villages and farms, a provincial outpost of Western civilization. But now, as he steamed into New York Harbor in 1902, remembering his return from Europe in 1868, he searched in vain for landmarks of the earlier era. "The outline of the city became frantic in its effort to explain something that defied meaning," he observed. Titanic, uncontrollable forces "had exploded, and thrown great masses of stone and steam against the sky. . . . A Traveller in the highways of history looked out of the club window on the turmoil of Fifth Avenue, and felt himself in Rome, under Diocletian. . . . The two-thousand-years failure of Christianity roared upward from Broadway, and no Constantine the Great was in sight." Henry Adams's fellow Americans, less troubled by historical perspective and premonitions of things to come, called the spectacle "progress" and greeted the dawn of the terrible twentieth century with a confidence that was apparently unbounded.

SUGGESTIONS FOR READING

American distaste for urban life is explored by T. J. J. Lears, *No Place of Grace: Antimodernism and the Transformation of American Culture, 1880–1920* (1981), and M. White and L. White, *The Intellectual Versus the City* (1962). General works of value include Daniel Boorstin, *The Americans: The Democratic Experience* (1973); A. Tractenberg, *The Incorporation of America* (1982); D. W. Howe, ed., *Victorian America* (1976); and J. B. Jackson, *American Space: The Centennial Years, 1865–1876* (1972). Cities in this period are studied in B. McKelvey, *The Urbanization of America, 1860–1915* (1963). Selected cities are subjects of W. Cronin, *Nature's Metropolis: Chicago and the Great West* (1991); F. C. Jaher, *The Urban Establishment: Upper Strata in Boston, New York, Charleston, Chicago, and Los Angeles* (1982); C. M. Green, *American Cities in the Building of the Nation* (1956). S. B. Warner, *Streetcar Suburbs* (1962), and K. T. Jackson, *The Crabgrass Frontier: The Suburbanization of the United States* (1985), are illuminating. A good history of American attitudes toward poverty is R. H. Bremner, *From the Depths: The Discovery of Poverty in the United States* (1956).

A sensitive analysis of immigration is O. Handlin, *The Uprooted* (1951). On their reception in the United States consult B. Solomon, *Ancestors and Immigrants* (1956), and J. Higham, *Strangers in the Land* (1955) and *Send These to Me: Jews and Other Immigrants in Urban America* (1975). S. Thernstrom, *The Other Bostonians* (1973) is important. See also K. A. Miller, *Emigrants and Exiles: Ireland and the Irish Exodus to North America* (1985), and John Bodnar, *The Transplanted: A History of Immigrants in Urban America* (1985).

On city politics, J. C. Teaford, *The Unheralded Triumph: City Government in America, 1870–1900* (1984), is a revisionist. For reformers of the period, see G. McFarland, *Mugwumps, Morals and Politics, 1894–1920* (1975). A muckraker who deals with this period informatively is Lincoln Steffens, *The Shame of the Cities* (1904). Later studies of value are F. J. Goodnow, *Municipal Problems* (1907); C. W. Patton, *The Battle for Municipal Reform: Mobilization and Attack, 1875–1900* (1940); A. B. Callow, Jr., *The Tweed Ring* (1966); and S. Mandelbaum, *Boss Tweed's New York* (1965). On these and other aspects of the period, J. A. Garraty, *The New Commonwealth, 1877–1890* (1968), is good reading.

On women's rights and the suffrage movement, see W. L. O'Neill, *Everyone Was Brave: The Rise and Fall of Feminism in America* (1969); E. Flexner, *Century of Struggle: The Woman's Rights Movement in the United States* (1959); A. S. Kraditor, *The Ideas of the Woman Suffrage Movement, 1890–1920* (1965); E. Griffith, *In Her Own Right: The Life of Elizabeth Cady Stanton* (1984); and C. N. Degler, *At Odds: Women and the Family in America from the Revolution to the Present* (1980).

A general history is Sidney Ahlstrom, *A Religious History of the American People* (1972). The reaction of the Protestant churches to social problems is discussed in several books, notably H. F. May, *Protestant Churches and Industrial America* (1949); A. I. Abell, *The Urban Impact on American Protestantism, 1865–1900* (1942); and C. H. Hopkins, *The Rise of the Social Gospel in American Protestantism, 1865–1915* (1940). On evangelists, see B. A. Weisberger, *They Gathered at the River: The Story of the Great Revivalists and Their Impact upon Religion in America* (1958), and J. F. Findlay, Jr., *Dwight L. Moody: American Evangelist, 1837–1899* (1969). On the Catholics there is a fine brief account in J. T. Ellis, *American Catholicism* (1956). W. W. Sweet, *Revivalism in America: Its Origins, Growth and Decline* (1944), is a useful survey. Churchmen as social activists are portrayed in P. J. Frederick, *Knights of the Golden Rule: The Intellectual As Christian Social Reformer in the 1890s* (1976). Part I of A. Dawley, *Struggles for Justice: Social Responsibility and the Liberal State* (1991), is on this period.

The history of public education receives vigorous reinterpretation in L. A. Cremin, *The Transformation of the School: Progressivism in American Education, 1876–1957* (1961). A. E. Meyer, *An Educational History of the American People* (1957), is a useful reference work. F. L. Mott, *A History of American Magazines, 1885–1905* (1957), is an exhaustive and excellent history. The newspapers are treated in W. G. Bleyer, *Main Currents in the History of American Journalism* (1927), and B. A. Weisberger, *The American Newspaperman* (1961).

The history of higher learning has been surveyed by F. Rudolph, *The American College and University, A History* (1962), elaborated on by L. R. Veysey, *The Emergence of the American University* (1965), and much illuminated by R. Hofstadter and W. Metzger, *The Development of Academic Freedom in the United States* (1955), and H. Hawkins, *Between Harvard and America: the Educational Leadership of Charles W. Eliot* (1972). For a stiff and amusing indictment see Thorstein Veblen, *Higher Learning in America* (1918).

On the graphic arts there are several studies of value, notably L. Mumford, *The Brown Decades: A Study of the Arts in America, 1865–1895* (1931); J. Kouwenhoven, *Made in America: The Arts in Modern Civilization* (1948); and O. W. Larkin, *Art and Life in America* (1949, rev. ed., 1960). On architecture, see L. Roth, *A Concise History of American Architecture* (1979), and J. M. Fitch, *American Building: The Historical Forces that Shaped It* (1966).

Literary history in this era is treated by H. N. Smith, *Democracy and the Novel* (1978); L. Ziff, *The American 1890s: Life and Times of a Lost Generation* (1966); J. Martin, *Harvests of Change: American Literature, 1865–1914* (1967); E. Carter, *Howells and the Age of Realism* (1954), who discusses Howells's contemporaries as well; and K. Vanderbilt, *The Achievement of William Dean Howells: A Reinterpretation* (1968). E. H. Cady, *The Realist at War* (1958); K. S. Lynn, *William Dean Howells* (1971); and V. W. Brooks, *New England: Indian Summer, 1865–1915* (1940) and *The Confident Years, 1885–1915* (1952), are full of biographical incident. Some good biographies are J. Kaplan, *Mr. Clemens and Mark Twain* (1966); E. Samuels, *Henry Adams: The Middle Years* (1958) and *Henry Adams: The Major Phase* (1964). H. M. Jones, *The Age of Energy: Varieties of American Experience, 1865–1915* (1971), contains essays on the cultural scene.

CHAPTER TWENTY

COXEY'S ARMY

STALEMENT, AGRARIAN REVOLT, AND REPUBLICAN TRIUMPH, 1877–1896

Like other aspects of American life between Reconstruction and the Progressive Movement, politics in the Gilded Age has suffered from harsh criticism. Compared with the Civil War and Reconstruction in their more heroic aspects, the politics of the postwar generation appears evasive, materialistic, tawdry, and cynical. And compared with the politics of the era after 1900—the progressivism with which many of the critics more or less identified—the Gilded Age is pictured as complacent, irresponsible, indifferent to social injustice, and unwilling to use the powers of government to redress grievances and control an unmanaged economy. Caught between the two comparative models, the interlude has been traditionally represented as a period of apostasy from the ideals of the past and failure to anticipate the goals of the future. And for good measure it is freely blamed for the social and economic evils to which the twentieth century is heir.

Granted its numerous shortcomings, the politics of the Gilded Age deserves to be considered in its own right rather than, in Howard Mumford Jones's words, "as an imperfect prophecy of twentieth century America." Or for that matter as the failed fulfillment of Civil War ideals. Emerging from the searing experience of the great war and plunging directly into massive industrialization, urbanization, and immigration, Americans of that confusing era sought stability and equilibrium ahead of social idealism. They had had their fill of headlong ideological crusades and the politics of zealous causes under national leadership. They took refuge in community and organizational loyalties rather than ideological commitments. If the political leaders of the time shunned great issues of social injustice and inequality and avoided civic activism, they were restrained by more than wealthy patrons, for they had to deal with an electorate that, outside the South, was the most completely democratized in the Western world. Moreover, it was an electorate that turned out and voted and participated to a greater extent than in any previous or subsequent period in American history. In view of the constraints and issues, it is not surprising that the political life under these rules attracted leaders of great skill, but none of true greatness.

THE BUSINESS OF POLITICS

The Party Equilibrium Politics in the post-Reconstruction period was more a business than a game, a highly competitive business with the two major parties as the evenly matched competitors. The Democrats managed to elect only one of their candidates president (for two nonconsecutive terms) in the 52 years between 1860 and 1912. And yet this gives a misleading impression of the relative strength of the Democratic and Republican parties. Actually, there was an extraordinarily narrow margin of difference in the popular vote the two parties polled in the two decades following 1876. In none of the presidential elections from 1876 to 1892 did the Republicans carry a majority of the popular votes, and in only one, that of 1880, did they receive a plurality—but even that plurality was less than one-tenth of 1 percent. In three of the five elections, in fact, the difference between the popular votes for the two major-party candidates was less than 1 percent, and in 1876 and 1888, even though the Democrats received a popular majority, they lost the election. In the Electoral College votes, on the other hand, majorities ranged from 1 in 1876 to 132 in 1892. The narrow margin between victory and defeat encouraged the laissez-faire tendency of politicians, the tendency to avoid social issues and take few chances.

The Republican party was a loose alliance of regional and interest groups with different and sometimes conflicting interests. The basic regional alliance was between the Northeast and the Middle West—an alliance that had been consolidated in 1860 and had fought and won the Civil War. It hung together afterward partly because of wartime loyalties and memories of the heroic days of Lincoln, when the party had emancipated the slaves and saved the Union. Two other large groups traced their attachment to the party back to the Civil War: the freedmen and the Union army veterans. The black voters remained loyal to the party of emancipation and continued to send one or two congressmen to Washington from the South, but after the Republicans abandoned them in 1877 the political power of the freedmen diminished rapidly. On the other hand, the political significance of the war veterans increased as the Grand Army of the Republic (GAR) grew as a pressure group and as Congress responded with larger and larger pensions for veterans. Economic conflict and political rivalry opened breaches in party unity. Republican policies such as high tariffs, sound money, and favors for railroads pleased some Eastern business interests, but Western grain growers often resented those policies and threatened revolt. The noisiest quarrel within Republican ranks was the running war between the Half-Breeds, led by James G. Blaine of Maine, and the Stalwarts, led by Roscoe Conkling of New York. These factions reflected personal loyalties and alliances rather than significant differences of opinion or principle, though they differed somewhat in style. Stalwarts clung to old issues of the South, while Half-Breeds sought a new coalition reflecting changed conditions. Conkling's followers more openly pursued the spoils of office, but both factions wanted all the spoils. Empty as were their battles, however, they sometimes determined the choice of American presidents.

The post-Reconstruction Democratic party was even more regional than the Republican. Its most reliable sources of support were the South and the cities of the Northeast. And the disparity of outlook and interest between the provincial, Protestant cotton farmers of the South and the underprivileged, Catholic, immigrant, industrial workers of the big cities was almost as great as that between the impoverished black people of the South and middle-class white people of the North who supported the Republican party. The Democrats also received support from Northeastern merchants and bankers who opposed the protective tariff and favored contraction of the currency—"sound-money" men, they called themselves. Other business interests favored inflation and tariff. The leaders of the party in the South, some of them of Whig background, preferred to be called Conservatives, and were often called Bourbons by their opponents. They had much in common with the dominant Democratic leaders in the Middle West, who were also business-minded conservatives and were also known as Bourbons. Rank-and-file Democrats, farmers, industrial workers, and small businessmen in the West, the South, and the East, were often restive and sometimes rebellious under such leaders.

"The American, like the Englishman," observed James Bryce in 1888, "usually votes with his party, right or wrong, and the fact that there is little distinction of view between the parties makes it easier to stick to your old friends." Party allegiance during these years was in fact remarkably rigid. In Indiana, for example, 32 counties remained unswervingly Republican from 1876 to 1892, and 39 counties stuck as unswervingly with the Democrats, with neither group varying more than 3 percent (see Map 20-1). In spite of much population mobility, only 21 counties shifted parties at all, and with third parties in the picture neither of the major parties could muster a reliable majority in those counties until 1896. The same pattern had prevailed for years: two-thirds of the Democratic counties had been voting Democratic since 1844, and over four-fifths of the Republican counties had gone down the line for the old party since its founding in 1856. These rigid loyalties carried Hoosier

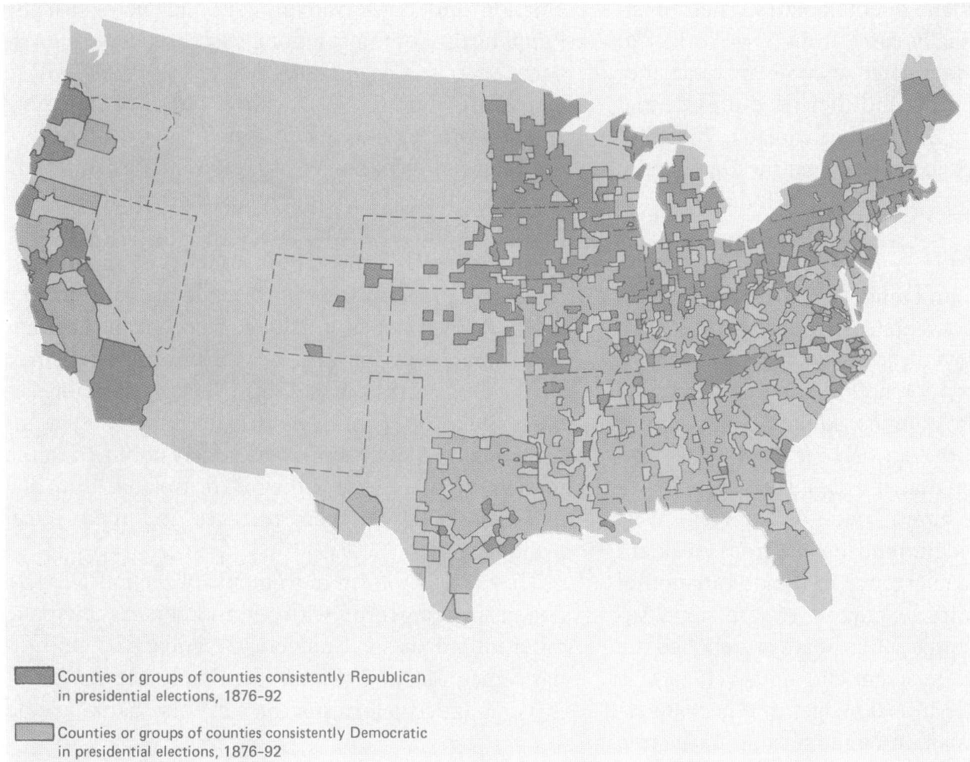

Map 20-1
The consistency of the vote, 1876–1892

voters right through war and peace, through a wide variety of candidates and policies, and through all the economic and social upheavals of the passing years.

Except in periods of hard times, party identifications seemed less determined by economic issues such as tariff and currency, which were handled in Washington, than by cultural, religious, and ethnic issues, which were resolved at the local or state level of politics. Struggles between prohibition and the "saloon power," between Sabbath observance and "desecration," or between public and parochial schools reflected religious and cultural values close to the grass roots. Democrats, calling for "laissez-faire" on cultural issues at the local level as well as on economic issues at the national level, were described as the "Party of Personal Liberty." Their message was "leave us alone." Republicans of this period, on the other hand, being more inclined toward public intervention in private life as well as in the private sector of the economy, were sometimes called the "Party of Piety." Voters took their party identification seriously, because they did not take their religious and cultural values lightly.

Neither party was strong enough, however, to rely for victory on the allegiance of certain states or parts of states that could be counted "in the bag." There were always the "doubtful states"—that is, states with enough shifting voters to turn the tide either way. These states were thought to be Connecticut, New York, New Jersey, Ohio, Indiana, and Illinois, but the key states were New York and Indiana. In the 1880s the Republicans had to carry New York and all three of the doubtful Midwestern states to elect their candidate president. Since the whole contest hinged on a few states, it is no wonder that they commanded great bargaining power, absorbed most of the "slush funds" from the campaign treasuries, and gained desirable offices for their politicians. The strategic importance of the few doubtful Midwestern states also helps to explain why five of the six Republican candidates for president from Grant to McKinley came from those states, including four from Ohio and one from Indiana. And as a running mate for their Midwestern candidate, the Republicans almost invariably chose a man from New York. The Democrats, on the other hand, usually reversed the regional order, though they picked their nominees from the same doubtful states. Their presidential nominees usually came from New York—in four contests they nominated incumbent or former governors of that state—and their vice-presidential nominees from Ohio, Illinois, or Indiana. In 1876, 1880, and 1884 the second place on the Democratic ticket went to the "strategic" state of Indiana.

The Spoilsmen and the Reformers From Grant to McKinley the power and influence of the presidential office remained at low ebb. No president between 1865 and 1897 enjoyed the advantage of having his own party in control of both houses of Congress throughout his tenure of office, so rapidly did control seesaw back and forth between the evenly matched parties. But more than that, the presidency was slow in recovering from the blows struck by Congress in its bitter fight with President Johnson and from President Grant's continual acquiescence in the domination of Congress. For an entire generation, congressional supremacy and presidential subordination remained the rule. Ordinarily the president did not even have a voice in preparing the annual budget, and he was certainly not given the staff or the money to play the role of a real chief executive.

Politics was really controlled by oligarchies of party bosses, many of them United States senators, who headed state machines and commanded armies of henchmen whom they paid off with public offices. The system stressed personal loyalty and the "spoils" of political victory. The spoilsmen sometimes sold offices to the highest bidder, but more regularly they distributed them among faithful workers for service rendered and systematically taxed the holders for "contributions." After the Civil Service Reform Act of 1883 (see p. 516) began to curb patronage as a source of revenue, a new type of boss then began to replace the old flamboyant "stump politician," a quieter, more efficient "desk politician," who worked hand in glove with the lobbyists of public utilities, railroads, industries, and manufacturers. Matthew Quay, who kept a card index of the foibles of Pennsylvania politicians; "Easy Boss" Tom Platt, who eventually succeeded Conkling in New York; Arthur P. Gorman, the friend of business in Maryland; and Marcus Alonzo Hanna, Ohio industrialist turned politician, were bosses of the new type.

A group of liberal reformers called Mugwumps by their deriders kept up a running crusade against patronage and corruption in office for two decades. Earnest and élitist, the Mugwumps held high social position and conservative economic views, usually Republican. Foremost among them was George William Curtis, scholarly editor of *Harper's Weekly,* whose cartoonist Thomas Nast made a career of ridiculing and caricaturing the corrupt. Carl Schurz was a hero of the Mugwumps. Another of the luminaries was E. L. Godkin, editor of the *Nation*. Devoted to laissez-faire principles and unconcerned over the deeper ills of the economy, the reformers of this school confined their economic program to tariff reform and sound money and fixed their hopes on achieving honest and efficient government through civil service reform. Spoilsmen sneered at "snivel service," and Senator Conkling accused them of "canting self-righteousness." The influence of the Mugwumps was largely confined to the literate upper class, for they were isolated from the mass of voters by their attitudes and their social position.

The various reform movements of the period were not on speaking terms with one another, or they spoke different languages. Grangers, Greenbackers, and Alliancemen of the West and the South (see pp. 522–25) demanded reforms in the currency, banking, and

Marcus Alonzo Hanna: industrialist turned politician

credit systems that chilled the blood of Eastern reformers. Agrarian reformers were at the same time divided among themselves: Northerner against Southerner, Republican against Democrat. Both the urban Mugwumps and the rural agrarians had trouble understanding the impulses and strivings of labor reformers. The cause of reform, its forces divided and mutually suspicious, languished and faltered through the 1880s.

THE CONSERVATIVE ASCENDANCY

Hayes in the White House We have already seen how the means used to elect Rutherford B. Hayes cast widespread doubt on his title to the presidency (pp. 422–23). He did not strengthen his position when he announced that he would not run for reelection. Hayes was never an astute politician, but he did not lack courage and determination. From the start of his administration he set out resolutely to redress the balance between the executive and legislative branches and regain for the presidency some of the powers that Congress had preempted.

The nominations for the Cabinet that he sent to the Senate were his first challenge to congressional dominance, for they included names unwelcome to the bosses—notably the name of Carl Schurz for secretary of the interior. The Senate balked and refused confirmation on the whole list at first but later yielded to the president. An old device that the House used to coerce the president was the "rider," a piece of legislation the president had to approve in order to secure the needed appropriation to which it was tied. Hayes vetoed seven such bills, compelled acceptance of his independence, and gained a clear-cut victory over congressional encroachment.

Hayes struck at the spoils system in its most powerful entrenchment, the New York Custom House Ring, the center of Senator Conkling's machine. A commission appointed by the president in 1877 and headed by John Jay of New York investigated the Custom House patronage system and reported that it was "unsound in principle, dangerous in practice, demoralizing in its influence on all connected with the customs service," and ridden with "ignorance, inefficiency, and corruption." Conkling's lieutenants, Collector of the Port Chester A. Arthur and naval officer Alonzo B. Cornell, refused to clean up the corruption and declined to resign. At Conkling's demand the Senate refused to confirm appointment of the successors whom Hayes nominated, but the president stubbornly persisted, dismissed Arthur and Cornell, and eventually filled their places with men of his own choice. Hayes had won a battle, but not a war. His promise of "thorough, radical and complete" civil service reform remained unfulfilled, but a reasonable start had been made.

Economic crises and social protest in the worst years of the depression caught the Hayes administration without a policy and without real comprehension of what was happening. The first great industrial conflict in our history started with a strike on the Baltimore and Ohio Railroad in July 1877. At the request of four state governors, Hayes set the fateful precedent of using federal troops to intervene in a strike and restore order. The president incurred additional ill will from labor, especially on the West Coast, by vetoing a bill passed in 1879 to restrict Chinese "coolie" immigration. The Treaty of 1880 acknowledged the right of restriction, and in 1882 Congress passed a bill putting an end to Chinese immigration for the following decade.

Monetary Policy in Politics The president also took the unpopular side in a series of debates over national currency policies that divided both parties during his administration. Hayes held that the duty of the government was to maintain the value of currency and that the only way to do this was by the demonstrated ability of the Treasury to redeem currency at face value in gold. While tight money appealed to industrial workers, whose real wages were thereby protected from inflation, agrarian spokesmen believed that it was the duty of the government to manage the currency so as to prevent or correct injustice and to relieve distress and suffering. While this was by no means the only explanation for the agricultural distress of the time, the farmer was right that crop prices were falling and that monetary policy was related to this decline.

The first clash between Hayes and the discontented occurred over a movement to repeal the Specie Resumption Act of 1875, which obliged the Treasury to resume the redemption of legal-tender notes in specie at full face value by January 1, 1879, and to reduce the number of greenbacks in circulation. Though offset by increased issuance of national bank notes, the measure contracted the currency and at the same time appreciated its value, the two things most complained of by farmers and debtors. Advocates of repeal, called Greenbackers, argued that fulfillment of the act would further depress prices and increase the burden of private and public debt. They denounced as outrageous the proposal to redeem war bonds that had been bought with greenbacks worth less than 40 cents to the dollar with currency worth 100 cents to the dollar. A National Greenback party gained recruits from labor and additional support from farmers and in February 1878 reorganized as the Greenback Labor party. In the fall elections the new party polled a remarkable total of 1,060,000 votes and elected fourteen representatives to Congress. Resisting all pressure, Hayes clung to the policy of resumption, and greenbacks became worth their face value in gold and no run on the gold reserve developed. Resumption was an accomplished fact.

Inflationist sentiment, by no means dead, found a new outlet in the movement for the free coinage of silver just as the greenback cause was becoming hopeless. Once again Hayes took the more unpopular side. The silver question was to become one of the most hotly debated issues in the history of American politics during the next two decades, but before 1875 it attracted no popular interest. The official government ratio of sixteen to one — sixteen times as much silver in a silver dollar as there was gold in a gold dollar — had undervalued silver ever since the gold rush of 1849 had lowered the price of gold. As a consequence, silver miners sold their product commercially rather than offer it to the Treasury at a loss, and silver dollars virtually disappeared from circulation. Foreseeing a drop in silver prices, a few monetary experts persuaded an ill-informed Congress to abolish the coinage of silver dollars and put the country on the gold standard in 1873. New silver mines in Nevada, Arizona, and Colorado soon flooded the market, and the price of silver began to drop. Miners then discovered that the Treasury rejected their product and that their European market had been reduced by widespread adoption of the gold standard abroad. Denouncing demonetization of silver as the "Crime of 1873," urban publishers in the Midwestern and Middle Atlantic states, not Western miners, started the demand that free coinage at the old ratio be restored. Inflationists eventually took up their cry because they saw in

Republican National Convention, Chicago, 1880

silver a means of halting currency contraction, getting cheaper money, raising crop prices, and securing debtor relief.

So rapidly did the silver movement spread that by the fall of 1877 an overwhelming majority of the lower house of Congress voted for a bill for the "free and unlimited coinage of silver" introduced by Representative Richard "Silver Dick" Bland of Missouri. The Bland bill would have stopped the sale of government bonds for gold and driven that metal out of circulation, since it would have produced silver dollars worth less than 90 cents (and still falling in value) and made them legal tender. Before the Senate acted, however, Senator William B. Allison of Iowa amended and weakened the bill, and in that form it was passed over Hayes's veto in February 1878. The Bland-Allison Act deprived the inflationists of their objective of "unlimited coinage" and substituted the requirement that the Treasury buy not less than $2 million and not more than $4 million worth of silver per month and coin it into dollars. The act did not have the effects that the conservatives feared and the inflationists desired. Silverites were to return to the battle in stronger force, but for more than a decade they made no change in the law.

In spite of the unpopularity of his stand on silver and his quarrels with Congress, Hayes ended his administration on an upswing of confidence and respect. Ordinarily such an upturn would have overcome his announced intention to retire, but no such movement developed. His party virtually ignored him, and he became scarcely more than a spectator during the struggle to nominate his successor.

Chester A. Arthur: wealthy, easygoing, elegant

James A. Garfield: reputation for courage

The Garfield Tragedy The Republicans brought their bitter feuds to the Chicago nominating convention under the banners of rival candidates. The Stalwarts were united under Conkling's leadership to name Grant for a third term. The Half-Breeds were determined to nominate Blaine; and Secretary of the Treasury John Sherman maneuvered to make himself available as a compromise candidate. When it became clear that none of the three could marshal a majority, the Blaine and Sherman forces joined on the 36th ballot and nominated Congressman James A. Garfield of Ohio. Garfield had managed Sherman's campaign and led the anti-Grant forces at the convention. To conciliate the defeated faction, the convention then nominated Conkling's lieutenant, Chester A. Arthur, the deposed spoilsman of the New York Custom House, for vice president.

Prospects for revenging Governor Tilden by nominating him in 1880 looked promising to the Democrats, but at the last moment Tilden declined to run for the presidency again. The party nominated instead General Winfield Scott Hancock, a Pennsylvanian and a Union hero in the Battle of Gettysburg. Hancock had no political experience, but his nomination was an effective answer to the charge of disloyalty that was so often thrown at his party. His running mate was William H. English, from the "doubtful" state of Indiana. Taking charge of his own campaign, Garfield stressed the tariff issue effectively and made protection the basis of a broadened party coalition. The Republican managers did the most decisive work of the campaign in the doubtful states of Ohio, New York, and Indiana, using large amounts of money to carry Indiana by a bare 7,000 votes and New York by 20,000. Garfield won by a plurality of less than 40,000 popular votes in the country at large, though his electoral vote was 214 to 155 for Hancock.

President Garfield's brief tenure in the White House began with embarrassments, continued with party feuds, and ended in tragedy. A handsome, massive figure of a man, with a reputation for courage under fire in the war and for resourcefulness as party leader in the House, Garfield was not without integrity. Under the extraordinary pressures of his new office, he moved cautiously and skillfully in the construction of his Cabinet to consolidate his control. Acknowledging his obligations to Blaine, he made the senator from Maine secretary of state. Then refusing to bow to the dictates of the Stalwart leader Conkling, Garfield moved to assert presidential authority by naming for collector of the port of New York the leading opponent of Conkling in that state. This precipitated a showdown in which Conkling and his friend the newly elected Senator Tom Platt were the losers.

At the very height of the furor over spoils and corruption, on July 2, 1881, Charles J. Guiteau, a crazed and disappointed office seeker, shot the president in the back. With a bullet lodged in his spine, Garfield was incapacitated for eleven weeks before his death on September 19. Then Stalwart Vice President Chester A. Arthur was sworn in as president and assumed control.

The Arthur Interlude The new president was a wealthy, easygoing man with expensive tastes, and 20 years of experience as a spoilsman in the Conkling camp of New York politics. His first year as president did little to dispel the fear that Garfield's martyrdom had been in vain and that the spoils system was there to stay. Arthur did not turn over patronage to his fellow Stalwart Conkling, as many expected, but after Blaine's resignation from the Cabinet, the president did prosecute with vigor those charged with post office frauds, one of whom claimed to have provided the money for carrying Indiana for Garfield and Arthur. The guilty men escaped punishment, and the president's efforts not only failed to win over the reformers but provoked party feuds and gave Democrats ammunition for the off-year campaign. The fall elections of 1882 drove his party from control of the House of Representatives and gave the Democrats a majority of nearly 100 seats.

One cause of the Democratic landslide was the nation's shock over Garfield's assassination and revulsion against the system of patronage and spoils associated with the tragedy. Popular indignation put new power behind the demands of the small band of reformers who, having fought the spoilsmen since the 1860s, had in 1881 organized the National Civil Service Reform League, with George William Curtis as president. It was ironic that "Chet" Arthur, long the very symbol of spoils politics, should be cast in the role of civil service reformer, but he firmly told Congress that "action should no longer be postponed" and promised his full cooperation. In January 1883 large bipartisan majorities in both houses of Congress passed a Democratic bill sponsored by Senator George H. Pendleton of Ohio. The Civil Service Act established a bipartisan Civil Service Commission of three members who were to administer competitive examinations and select appointees on the basis of merit and an apportionment among the states according to population. Arthur demonstrated his good faith by naming as head of the commission an outstanding reformer who drafted the act, and appointing two prominent friends of reform as the other commissioners. The act affected only about one-tenth of the federal employees at first. But it empowered the president to expand the proportion of jobs "classified" or subject to the merit system. By the end of the century 40 percent of the jobs were so classified, the civil service was securely established, and centralized presidential control was reversing the decentralizing pull of the spoils system and Congress.

The Civil Service Commission was not the president's only assertion of independence nor his only praiseworthy effort. Two such efforts, both of them futile as it turned out, were in response to the problem of a surplus accumulated in the United States Treasury by excessive tax revenues. The solution favored by Congress was to spend the surplus in lavish appropriations for river and harbor improvements and pork-barrel handouts. Arthur vetoed one such bill, only to have Congress pass it over his veto. His efforts in tariff reduction amounted to little. As an incidental means of reducing the Treasury surplus, Arthur's naval construction program was more successful. The navy had deteriorated since the Civil War to a collection of wooden antiques with cast-iron guns and rotten hulls. The Arthur administration is properly credited with sweeping away barriers of ignorance and clearing the way for a modern navy. In this as in other ways Arthur proved worthier of the office he held than anyone had reason to believe when he took it.

Changing the Conservative Guard The chances of Arthur's succeeding himself as president in 1884, never very strong in any case, were greatly weakened by the Democratic tidal wave of 1882, in which he lost control of his own state. Blaine remained the dominant figure in the Republican party, and his nomination seemed more and more likely as the convention approached. Ignoring the reformers and overriding the Arthur supporters, the Blaine men nominated their candidate without difficulty and named John A. Logan, favorite son of Illinois, for vice president. The Yankee Mugwumps promptly decided to bolt the party, provided the Democrats nominated the rising hope of the reformers, Grover Cleveland, governor of New York.

Cleveland's rise in New York politics had been recent and rapid. Elected mayor of Buffalo in 1881, he accepted the Democratic nomination for governor in 1882 and won an easy victory because of the split in the Republican party of the state. A burly figure of 240 pounds, he was known for his rugged honesty and his habits of hard work and thrift. As reformer Cleveland was a thoroughgoing conservative. Businessmen, middle-class taxpayers, and reformers of the Mugwump school admired the independence and integrity of Cleveland. The nomination of Blaine and the promise of Mugwump support made Governor Cleveland the logical standard-bearer for the Democrats in 1884. He was nominated with the aid of state bosses and financed in his campaign by corporate wealth. His running mate was Thomas A. Hendricks, yet another available candidate from the shifting counties of Indiana.

The presidential campaign of 1884 was sensational and frenzied. Blaine made some 400 speeches stressing protective tariff as support for high wages. Cleveland said little at all during the campaign. Popular attention and the press focused on the private life and personal morals of the candidates. Democrats and Mugwumps took the initiative by reviving charges that Blaine had been guilty of underhanded deals with railroad promoters. George William Curtis declared that the issue was "moral rather than political." Thereupon the Republicans retaliated with evidence that Cleveland was the father of an illegitimate son. The campaign deteriorated into scandalmongering that became more and more irresponsible.

Cleveland had to carry New York to win the election, and the extreme closeness of the contest in that state concentrated attention on a number of intangible factors, particularly those affecting the Irish electorate, any one of which might conceivably have been decisive. Whatever the explanation, the tide turned narrowly in Cleveland's favor. In addition to all the Southern states, he carried the doubtful states of Indiana, New Jersey, Connecticut, and New York—the last by a plurality of a mere 1,149 votes. His share of the votes in the country as a whole was only slightly greater than Blaine's. Mugwumps and reformers rejoiced at the victory, but it is a mistake to conclude that a moral crusade had defeated Blaine, who came very near winning. Actually, he polled about the same percentage of the total vote as Garfield had in 1880 and a larger percentage than the Republican candidates were to poll in 1888 and 1892. At any rate, the long Republican rule was at an end, and the Democrats were back in power for the first time in 24 years.

Cleveland in Command No one could be sure of the new president's views on any of several leading issues, but everyone could be sure he was a conservative. His inaugural address promising adherence to "business principles" bore this out, and so did his Cabinet appointments, which included representatives of the most conservative and business-minded wing of the party in the East and South. The new administration signified no break with the past on fundamental issues.

If there was any policy to which Cleveland had a clear commitment, it was civil service reform. He came to office with two masters to please: the Mugwump reformer and the hungry spoilsman of his own party with an appetite for office. The president's first moves delighted the reformers. Defying the Democratic bosses and spoilsmen, he retained in office some able Republicans and personally examined applications for office far into the night. The party press

Grover Cleveland: stubborn conservative

thundered against his "ingratitude." Within a few months he yielded to pressure, and Republican heads began to roll. Carl Schurz wrote, "Your attempt to please both reformers and spoilsmen has failed," and Cleveland broke with the Mugwumps. By the end of four years he had removed about two-thirds of the 120,000 federal officers. He did increase the list of classified jobs to 27,380, nearly double the number when he took office, but he filled the Civil Service Commission with weak and incompetent men.

In the role of Treasury watchdog and thrifty steward of public funds, Cleveland showed more consistency than he did as civil service reformer. For one thing, he rebuked a pensions racket run by a powerful lobby for Union veterans of the Civil War. Cleveland called a halt and took to investigating individual claims himself, vetoing many of them, often with sarcastic comment.

Cleveland believed that, except in rare circumstances, the president should confine himself to the execution of the laws. But by his pension vetoes and his stand against congressional patronage powers, and later on tariff reform, he strongly reasserted the integrity and independence of the executive branch and began to curb the long dominance of an imperial Congress. Congress enacted little legislation of lasting significance, and the president's influence on that was largely negative. Cleveland himself deserves no credit for what was probably the most important act passed during his administration, the Interstate Commerce Act of 1887 (see p. 467). He regarded the whole idea with suspicion and signed the bill reluctantly and "with reservations."

The Tariff in Politics In his fight for tariff reform, however, Cleveland took a more forthright stand that may have contributed to his defeat for reelection. The issue was as old as the republic, but since the Civil War it had taken on a new importance and complexity and was treated with caution and evasiveness by politicians of both parties. The tariff acts of the Civil War had been justified on the grounds that high internal war taxes on American industries put them at a competitive disadvantage that had to be offset with protective tariff duties to enable Americans to compete with foreign manufacturers on equal terms. Beginning with modest rates of 18.8 percent on dutiable goods in 1861, a succession of acts raised the average to 40.3 percent in 1866. But, while the American producers were soon relieved of the burden of internal war taxes, the protective tariff remained unrepealed. The protected industries quickly adjusted to the prices, dividends, and profits made possible by a measure of freedom from competition from abroad. Producers who enjoyed or desired these advantages organized to press their desires on Congress. Both major parties, the Republicans explicitly and the Democrats for a time tacitly, accepted the principle of protection—though with dissent in each party, more among Democrats than among Republicans. From time to time a president would make a gesture of reform, but Congress would regularly respond with jugglery that left the situation unchanged or made a mockery of reform.

Cleveland hesitated for three years to take an aggressive stand. Democratic leaders assured him that an all-out fight on the issue would split the party and lose the next election. Finally deciding, however, the president devoted his entire annual message of December 1887 to the tariff question. He made a slashing attack on the injustice, inequity, and absurdity of existing rates, ridiculed the need to protect century-old "infant industries," and denounced high rates as "the vicious, inequitable and illogical source of unnecessary taxation." The House of Representatives, with a Democratic majority, responded by adopting a bill. Far from radical, it did place such raw materials as lumber, wool, and flax on the free list and made moderate reductions in rates for finished goods. The Republican-controlled Senate then rejected the bill, as expected, and adopted a highly protective substitute. The deadlock of tariff reform produced the first clear-cut economic issue between parties since Reconstruction and provided the leading issue of the 1888 election.

For their presidential candidate the Republicans chose Benjamin Harrison of Indiana, whose chief attractions were that he came from a doubtful state and that he was the grandson of former president William Henry Harrison, "Old Tippecanoe," of log-cabin and hard-cider fame. A senator of national reputation, Harrison proved to be an effective campaigner in spite of his chilly personality. His running mate was Levi P. Morton, a wealthy New York banker. The Democrats naturally renominated President Cleveland, and for their vice-presidential candidate they chose the elderly and ailing ex-senator Allen G. Thurman of Ohio.

The campaign for Cleveland's reelection was handicapped by halfhearted and ineffective leadership. By contrast, the Republican campaign had a vigorous leader in Senator Matt Quay, boss of a ruthless machine in Pennsylvania. Quay collected and spent a huge campaign fund. Republican strategists made telling use of this fund to purchase votes and rig elections in Indiana and New York. The winning party proved to have a more effective organization and staged a better campaign.

In spite of much talk about tariff reform, the election did not turn on that issue alone. Cleveland actually carried the manufacturing states of New Jersey and Connecticut, and the Democrats gained ground in Michigan, Ohio, and California, normally protariff states. Cleveland polled a plurality of almost 100,000 popular votes, but Harrison won the electoral vote 233 to 168. It was an extremely narrow victory for the Republicans. As usual, the outcome had hung on a few evenly divided states, in all of which the tariff issue played a part, and Harrison had carried them all, each by a few thousand votes. Prominent factors in what was probably the most corrupt presidential election of national history up to that time appear to have been trickery in Indiana and New York and division within the Democratic party.

Harrison and the Surplus President Harrison's political obligations to Blaine dictated his appointment as secretary of state, and other appointments paid off political debts. John Wanamaker, a wealthy Philadelphia merchant, became postmaster general and turned over the post office patronage to spoilsmen. In spite of his commitment to civil service reform, Harrison watched the process in silence.

For the first time since 1875, the Republicans in 1889–91 held the presidency and a majority in both houses of Congress. Each majority was extremely slight, however, and under existing House rules the Democratic minority could frustrate the majority by simply not answering roll call, thereby depriving the House of a quorum. Speaker Thomas B. Reed of Maine earned the title of "Czar" by sweeping aside the rules over the indignant protest of the minority, strengthening party responsibility, and running House proceedings with an iron will. Under Reed in the House and the protectionist Senator Nelson W. Aldrich of Rhode Island in the Senate, the Republican majority won the name of the "Billion Dollar Congress" for its generosity in spending the Treasury surplus largely created by tariff revenues. The Republican legislative program included a new tariff bill, a federal election law, a silver purchase act, and an antitrust measure, all of which moved through Congress simultaneously, with supporters of one measure bargaining with or frustrating supporters of another.

Among those frustrated were advocates of an election law to protect voters' rights. It was aimed mainly at protecting black Republican voters, and Southern whites denounced it furiously as a "force bill" to restore "Negro rule." City bosses and some Westerners and business interests did not like the bill either. It passed the House but was blocked in the Senate by a filibuster. Republican senators from the silver-mining states joined the Democrats in killing the election reform bill and displacing it with a bill for the free coinage of silver.

With the balance of power in their hands, silver champions stalled the tariff bill further. They had been promised that the Republican party would "do something for silver" in return for support of the tariff. The measure that was finally contrived to fulfill this commitment was the Sherman Silver Purchase Act, named for the senator from Ohio. The Sherman Act fixed the amount of silver to be purchased in ounces rather than dollars: 4½ million ounces per month, approximately the amount of national production of the metal in 1890. The silver was to be paid for in Treasury notes of full legal-tender value, which could be redeemed in either gold or silver at the discretion of the government. As it turned out, the government chose to redeem the notes only in gold, and as the price of silver dropped the Treasury was required to spend fewer and fewer dollars to purchase the specified number of ounces. The product of weak and shifty statesmanship, it pleased neither side and contributed nothing of importance toward solving the currency problems of the nation.

Another reform act passed about the same time, also bearing the name of the Ohio senator, was the Sherman Antitrust Act of June 1890 (see p. 472). Although many congressmen were absent when the vote was taken, the act was adopted with only one vote against it in the Senate and none in the House. Although the law was no sham and had wide support, it had little effect during the following decade, for no administration during those years showed much interest in enforcing it.

The most controversial and, as it turned out, the most politically costly achievement of this productive Republican Congress was the tariff act that took the name of William McKinley of Ohio. The McKinley Act increased selectively an already high tariff scale. Explaining the bill's faults, McKinley freely admitted that they were necessitated by politics rather than economics.

In order to please Union veterans of the Civil War, Harrison appointed as commissioner of pensions James "Corporal" Tanner, a pensions lobbyist who indicated his purpose with the slogan, "God help the surplus!" He favored "an appropriation for every old comrade who needs it" and quickly added millions to the pension budget before the embarrassed president removed him. Congress assisted the veterans' cause, however, with the Dependent Pension Act of 1890, similar to one Cleveland had vetoed in 1887, which recognized claims from virtually everyone connected with the Union war effort with a record of 90 days' service, a disability from any cause, and an honorable discharge. Their widows and children helped swell the pension rolls.

The Billion Dollar Congress did wonders in taking care of the Treasury surplus. The prohibitive tariff rates set by the McKinley Act reduced income, and the combination of excessive pensions and silver purchases increased expenditures. Still in a mood of gen-

erosity and still finding some of the surplus left, Congress hastily devised more handouts in the form of subsidies to steamship lines, lavish pork-barrel bills for river and harbor improvements, enormous premiums for government bondholders, and the return of federal taxes paid during the Civil War by Northern states. These handouts and the onset of depression wiped out the surplus in the Treasury by 1894, and the Treasury-surplus problem has never troubled the United States since.

The first Congress of the Harrison administration promoted the interests of politicians and business leaders — that is, if they belonged to the right party or were engaged in the right business. To other interests, particularly farmers and small businesspeople (with the exception of Northern veterans), Congress appeared a wasteful dispenser of favors to the privileged. In the congressional elections of 1890, Republicans were overwhelmed by a revolt that penetrated traditional strongholds in Ohio, Michigan, Illinois, Wisconsin, Kansas, and even Massachusetts. In these and other states defection among religious and ethnic groups was tied to unpopular Republican positions on local cultural issues regarding prohibition, school regulations, and Sunday blue laws. Republicans were reduced to 88 seats in the House of Representatives, the smallest number in 30 years, while the Democrats took 235 seats. Republicans hung on to a small majority in the Senate. But the election of 1890 ran up danger signals for conservative leaders of both the old parties. A depression was on the way, and a third-party revolt was shaping up.

THE AGRARIAN REVOLT

The Decline of Agriculture The spirit of revolt flamed up most fiercely in the agricultural sections of the South and the West, and it was fed by acute economic distress and a deep sense of grievance. American farmers reached a low point in their history in the 1890s. The past was not the golden age they sometimes dreamed of, but they had certainly been better off before and were to be better off in the future. But ever since the 1860s, agriculture had been slipping backward, and they suspected the government of indifference, if not hostility, to their interests. They searched everywhere for the causes of their plight and the cure for their troubles. Some of their guesses were shrewd and accurate, but they overlooked some of the causes of their troubles.

They were caught up in an international crisis that afflicted agriculture in many parts of the world and provoked rebellion abroad as well as at home. The crisis for producers of export staple crops resulted from a revolution in communication and transportation that created a worldwide market for agricultural products. Ships first steamed through the Suez Canal in 1869, the year locomotives first steamed across the North American continent. The network of railroad and steamship lines was swiftly paralleled by a network of telegraph and telephone lines and transoceanic cables that linked continents and tied the world together.

Forced to compete in a world market without control over output, American farmers watched the prices of their product decline decade after decade. Farmers said they had to buy expensive farm machinery in a protected market and sell their crops in an unprotected market. As the gap between income and expenses widened, farmers were increasingly forced to borrow money to cover the gap. They were therefore chronically in debt, and debtors always suffered most keenly from deflationary monetary policies. Contracting the amount of currency in circulation resulted in lowering the price that crops brought and increasing the difficulty of paying off debts. Farmers in debt had reason for opposing contraction and demanding expansion of currency.

It was no wonder that agrarian discontent was most bitter in the South and the West. The price of cotton and wheat had been falling steadily for two decades. From 1870 to 1873 cotton had averaged about 15.1 cents a pound; from 1894 to 1898 it dropped to an average of 5.8 cents. Over the same period wheat prices dropped from 106.7 to 63.3 cents a bushel, and corn from 43.0 to 29.7 cents. In 1889 corn was actually selling for 10 cents in Kansas, and farmers were burning it for fuel. Georgia farmers were getting 5 cents a pound for their cotton at a time when economists were estimating that it cost about 7 cents a pound to produce. During several of these years the nation's farmers were running a losing business.

The ills of agriculture were reflected in the growing number of mortgages (not always an evil) and tenant farmers. Nearly a third of the country's farms were mortgaged by the end of the 1890s. In Kansas, Nebraska, North Dakota, South Dakota, and Minnesota there were more mortgages than families. In the Southern states mortgages were far fewer, but only because land was such a drug on the market that it could not be mortgaged. The South's substitute was the lien system, the worst credit system of all (see p. 390). Fewer and fewer farmers owned the land they worked, and more and more labored for a landlord, often an absentee landlord.

In the farmer's view, the railroads were the archenemy, and the offenses attributed to them were by no means wholly imaginary, though sometimes exaggerated. The complaint that it took one bushel of wheat or corn to pay the freight on another bushel was no exaggeration. The chief complaints of rate discrimination came from the South and the West, where rates were frequently two or three times what they were between Chicago and New York. Railroads favored large over small shippers and one locality over another, and flagrantly dominated politics and legislatures. The national banks were also a natural target for agrarian abuse, for they refused to lend money on real estate and farm property, and were indifferent to seasonal needs for money for the movement of crops.

The tax laws, like the bank laws, worked to the farmer's disadvantage. And so did the tariff. The injustice was all the harder to bear for those who believed that the tariff bred trusts and the trusts levied tribute on the consumers of all types of goods. Antitrust and antimonopoly feeling ran high in all farmer organizations. While those few who spoke of a "conspiracy" were on the wrong track, the many were right who contended that they had a number of legitimate grievances against a system that worked so consistently to their disadvantage.

In the late 1880s and early 1890s natural calamities came one on top of another with stunning impact. They are not to be confused with the deeper causes of the farmer's revolt, but they added to the feeling of despair—droughts on the plains that not merely damaged the crops but destroyed them; floods in the lower Mississippi Valley that not merely destroyed the crops but left the land unusable; grim, blizzard-bound winters on the high plains that destroyed not merely domestic animals but wild ones as well and threatened even the survival of the human inhabitants. Less spectacular was the loneliness, the drudgery, and the isolation of rural life in America in those years. This was the ancient lot of farmers, but the growing glitter of the city made it less tolerable than ever, especially when coupled with the grinding, ceaseless pressure of economic ills and grievances. To Thomas E. Watson of Georgia, who was to whip agrarian wrath into a frenzied crusade, the farmers of his region seemed to move about "like victims of some horrid nightmare . . . powerless—oppressed—shackled."

Agrarian Protest There was nothing irrational about the farmers' impulse to organize and protest against their lot. The Patrons of Husbandry, organized in local "granges" and better known as the Grangers, served as a model for later and more powerful movements. Founded in 1867, the Grange grew slowly until the pinch of depression quickened interest in the early

Granger meeting in Illinois

1870s. By 1874 the estimated membership was about 1½ million, and growth continued into the next year. Seeking to eliminate the profits of the middleman, Grangers founded cooperatives for buying and selling, for milling and storing grain, even for banking and manufacturing. Membership fell off rapidly after 1875, but the Grangers left their imprint on law and politics.

Of the several farmers' organizations that succeeded the Grange after it subsided in political prominence, by far the most important and powerful was the National Farmers Alliance and Industrial Union, originally known as the Southern Alliance, seedbed of Populism. Originating in 1877 in a frontier county of Texas, the Alliance grew slowly until it launched a crusade of rapid expansion in 1886 under the energetic leadership of Dr. Charles W. Macune. The culmination of the movement was Macune's subtreasury system, a plan for government warehouses where farmers could deposit nonperishable crops and receive greenbacks up to 80 percent of the market value of the crops deposited. The loan was to be secured by the crops and repaid when crops were sold, thus enabling the farmer to hold the produce for a favorable market. It was the most inspiring idea of the movement, but it was never realized.* Other demands of the Alliance's platform of 1890 included the abolition of national banks, a substantial increase in the amount of currency in circulation, free coinage of silver, a federal income tax, reduction of tariff rates, the direct election of senators, "rigid" control of railroad and telegraph companies—and, if that did not work, government ownership of both.

The Farmers Alliance established its own extensive press supported by hundreds of local weekly papers. At its peak in 1891 the Alliance probably had 2 million members. An affiliated but separate Colored Farmers' National Alliance and Cooperative Union probably had about a quarter million members. The expanding Farmers Alliance formed a coalition with the declining Knights of Labor and took firm hold in Kansas and the Dakotas, but it struck a snag in attempts to merge with the Northwestern Alliance with headquarters in Chicago. This was a small, largely paper organization with few members and weak leaders who had little sympathy with Southern radicalism. They had little claim to a place in the agrarian revolt and opposed the Populist party to the end. Yet they and their superficial silver crusade have been mistaken as the essence of Populism.

Though the Alliance, like the Grange, professed to be strictly "nonpolitical," it was clear that its demands could be realized only by political means. Using their demands as a yardstick, the Southern Alliance required all Democratic candidates in the 1890 elections to "stand up and be measured." As a result, the Alliance seemed at the time to have come near taking over the Democratic party in the South, for it elected 4 governors, secured control of 8 legislatures, and elected 44 congressmen and 3 senators who were pledged to support Alliance demands. Instead of working within one of the old parties, Alliance members in the West hastily set up independent third parties, the names of which differed from state to state, and nominated their own candidates. Their most striking successes were in Kansas, where they elected five congressmen and a senator; in Nebraska, where they took control of both houses of the legislature and elected two congressmen; and in South Dakota, where they elected a senator. In other Western states their vote came largely at the expense of the Republicans and accounted in part for the large number of Democratic congressmen elected in 1890. The election served notice of both old parties that the farmers were on the march.

The Populist Crusade Their successes in 1890 inspired Westerners with the ambition to form a national third party to promote Alliance ideas. Southerners hung back, however, in order to try out their plan of working within the Democratic party. They were quickly disillusioned, for all the Southern Democratic congressmen elected on an Alliance platform, with the exception of Tom Watson, entered the Democratic caucus and voted for a conservative anti-Alliance Georgian for Speaker. Thereupon Watson, red-headed and a rebel by temperament, left his party and became the "People's party" candidate for Speaker with the support of eight congressmen from the West. Thus the new party, often called the Populist party, had a congressional delegation before it had a national organization. The National Alliance, however, under the leadership of President Leonidas L. Polk of North Carolina, was moving rapidly in the Populist direction. On February 22, 1892, a huge Confederation of Industrial Organizations met at St. Louis, attended by delegates from the Knights of

* Some components of the subtreasury idea, though not the essential feature of popular control over the currency, were embodied in the New Deal measure of 1933 creating the Commodity Credit Corporation.

Kansas House of Representatives, 1893: a militant pose

Labor, the Nationalists, the Single-Taxers, Greenbackers, Prohibitionists, and other reform groups, but dominated by delegates from the National Alliance. The delegates officially founded the People's party and called for a convention to nominate a ticket for the presidential election of 1892.

Shortly before the convention met in Omaha on July 4, the Populists were deprived of their strongest candidate by the death of Polk. The party nominated the old Greenback campaigner of 1880, General James B. Weaver of Iowa, for president, and, to balance the Union general with a Confederate one, chose General James G. Field of Virginia as his running mate. The platform emphatically reiterated Alliance principles. The fervor and violence of Populist rhetoric is illustrated by the following excerpt from the preamble to the platform, written and delivered by Ignatius Donnelly of Minnesota, Populist writer and orator:

> . . . we meet in the midst of a nation brought to the verge of moral, political, and material ruin. Corruption dominates the ballot-box, the legislatures, the Congress, and touches even the ermine of the bench. The people are demoralized.

Eastern conservatives were frightened by the Populist tone and built up a distorted image of the movement as an insurrection of hayseed anarchists or hick Communists. While it is true that some of the Populist leaders were provincial and ill-informed and tended to oversimplify issues, it is only fair to recall that their conservative opponents, better educated as a rule, entertained absurd monetary and economic theories of their own and talked wildly of conspiracies and subversives themselves. Populism deserves better than it has received at the hands of twentieth-century urban critics. The very word *populist,* with a small *p*, has been converted into a term of opprobrium. Actually, the Populist movement was the first to insist that laissez-faire was not the solution to the industrial problem. It surpassed all previous nineteenth-century movements in exposing the betrayed promises of America and the contrast between what America preached and what it practiced. It moved to restore the humane preference, and in doing so has been called "America's most successful failure."

The first task of the Populists was to bridge the cleavages between parties, sections, races, and classes that kept apart the forces they wished to unite. First, they sought to revive the old agrarian alliance between South and West. Second, they felt that both the Republicans and the Democrats were bent on keeping natural allies divided and sought to replace the old parties with a third party. Third, they tried to unite farmers of the South who were divided by racial

Populist Appeal to Black Voters

Now the People's Party says to these two men, 'You are kept apart that you may be separately fleeced of your earnings. You are made to hate each other because upon that hatred is rested the keystone of the arch of financial despotism which enslaves you both. You are deceived and blinded that you may not see how this race antagonism perpetuates a monetary system which beggars both. . . .'

The conclusion, then, seems to me to be this: the crushing burdens which now oppress both races in the South will cause each to make an effort to cast them off. They will see a similarity of cause and a similarity of remedy. They will recognize that each should help the other in the work of repealing bad laws and enacting good ones. They will become political allies, and neither can injure the other without weakening both. It will be to the interest of both that each should have justice. And on these broad lines of mutual interest, mutual forebearance, and mutual support the present will be made the stepping-stone to future peace and prosperity.

From Thomas E. Watson, *The Arena,* 1892

barriers, and some white and black members worked hard at the effort. Finally, the Populists sought to create an alliance between farmers and labor. In view of all these handicaps, the Populists made a surprisingly good showing in their first appearance at the polls. They cast a little more than a million votes for their presidential candidate and also elected ten representatives, five senators, three governors, and some 1,500 members of state legislatures. But it was obvious that they had a long way to go.

THE DEPRESSION AND THE SILVER ISSUE

Cleveland and the Silverites The Democrats and the Republicans conducted their 1892 campaigns with more sobriety than usual. Cleveland, the choice of conservative Democrats, was nominated by the first ballot of his party's convention, and, in spite of efforts to draft an ailing Blaine, Harrison was the nominee of the Republicans. Adlai E. Stevenson* of Illinois became Cleveland's running mate, and Whitelaw Reid, editor of the New York *Tribune,* was the Republican nominee for vice president. Cleveland improved his poll of 1888, and 1884 as well, winning 5,555,426 votes to 5,182,690 for Harrison, and 277 electoral votes to Harrison's 145. The Democrats carried not only the doubtful states of New York, New Jersey, Connecticut, and Indiana but the normally Republican states of Illinois, Wisconsin, and California. It was not quite a landslide, but it was the most decisive victory either party had won in 20 years.

Populist rally

* Grandfather of the Democratic candidate for president in 1952 and 1956.

President Cleveland moved back into the White House and surrounded himself with a thoroughly conservative Cabinet of Easterners and Southerners who were as out of touch with the radical discontent of the country as he himself. Almost immediately the financial panic of 1893 shattered his peace and ushered in the worst depression the nation had experienced up to that time. The panic had actually started ten days before Harrison left office, when the Philadelphia and Reading Railroad went bankrupt and the New York Stock Exchange was shaken by the greatest selling spree in its history. Two months after Cleveland's inauguration the market collapsed. Banks called in their loans, and credit dried up. Unstable financial conditions abroad had started a drain on the gold reserve that became increasingly severe after 1893. One great railroad after another went down in failure. By the end of the year 500 banks and more than 15,000 business firms had fallen into bankruptcy. Populist Donnelly's apocalyptic picture in 1892 of "a nation brought to the verge of ruin" seemed about to be translated into reality.

The causes of the depression that settled over the country in 1893 were highly complex. But President Cleveland had a simple explanation and a remedy, and never did a dogmatist cling more tenaciously to his theory. His explanation was that the Sherman Silver Purchase Act (see p. 519) had caused the depression, and his remedy was to repeal the act and maintain the gold standard at all costs—that is, continue to redeem all United States Treasury notes in gold. The economic consequences of Cleveland's remedy do not appear to have been decisive one way or the other, but the political consequences were disastrous. No issue since slavery had divided the people more deeply than silver. It disrupted Populism, and caused a revolution in the Democratic party that overthrew conservative control.

Cleveland's theory clashed head on with a theory held with equal dogmatism by the silverites. According to them, the cause of the economic disaster lay in the "Crime of '73" that demonetized silver, and the remedy lay in the free and unlimited coinage of silver at a ratio of sixteen to one of gold. The admission of six new Western states—Montana, North Dakota, South Dakota, and Washington in 1889 and Idaho and Wyoming in 1890—brought reinforcements to the silverites in Congress, especially in the Senate. In the meantime American silver producers suffered additional reductions in their market from the demonetization of silver in Europe and India and become more desperate for relief through free coinage in the United States. At the same time debtor agrarians saw free coinage of silver as one hope of relief from deflation and currency contraction and increased their cry for "free silver," unlimited and free coinage. Cleveland stubbornly insisted, on the other hand, that the Sherman Act was the cause of the trouble and demanded its repeal. Under relentless pressure by the president, Congress finally repealed the Sherman Act. Cleveland got his way by relying on Republican support and splitting his own party.

Repeal of the Sherman Act seemed to have no effect, for the drain on the gold reserve continued unabated, and so did the depression. The president resorted to a series of highly unpopular bond sales to recoup the gold reserves. The third bond sale, in February 1895, caused the greatest indignation of all. This time the president yielded to the demand of J. Pierpont Morgan that the sale be kept private, and the syndicate of bankers that handled the loan drove a hard bargain for their services and were accused of making large profits, though Morgan refused to reveal how much. The bond issue yielded over $65 million to the government, half of it from Europe, and the bankers scotched some of the drain on the gold reserve. Nevertheless, another issue was necessary in January 1896. The four bond sales did save the gold standard, but they did not stop the decline of the gold reserve or restore prosperity. Each one further intensified the silverites' hatred of the president. These bond sales enhanced Cleveland's reputation for courage but not for wisdom. They failed to cure the depression, and they led to political disaster.

The Politics of Depression The blight that had been familiar to farmers for years now began to fall on the factory and the city. Railroad construction fell off drastically, dividends halted, and investment in all business declined sharply. Bankers, businessmen, and employers seemed stricken with a failure of nerve. They laid off workers, cut wages, closed factory doors, and swelled the army of the jobless. Visitors to the "dream city" at the Chicago Exposition in 1893 wondered at the miles of sleeping men who lined the tracks of the elevated railway. "What a spectacle!" exclaimed Ray Stannard Baker, a cub reporter, "What a human downfall after the magnificence and prodigality of the World's Fair."

The year 1894 was the most brutal of the depression. Between 2½ and 3 million, perhaps as many as one out of five workers, were thought to be unemployed, but no one really knew, and the unemployed felt that no one in the government really cared. Some cities provided a little work relief, but this was wholly inadequate, and when hungry men turned to the federal government they were met with cold indifference or angry rejection. Jacob S. Coxey of Massillon, Ohio, a well-to-do businessman who was a Populist and was quite untypical of his class in other ways, proposed a plan of federal work relief on public roads to be financed by an issue of legal-tender Treasury notes. The "good roads" bill was designed to end the depression by providing monetary inflation and internal improvements as well as work relief for the unemployed. When Congress refused to pass it, Coxey declared, "We will send a petition to Washington with boots on." "Coxey's Army" marched peacefully from Massillon picking up sympathizers on the way, including a few visionaries and eccentrics, and paraded into Washington on May Day, about 500 strong. They were cheered by crowds, but Coxey and his lieutenants were arrested by the police, and some 50 people were beaten or trampled. No fewer than 17 "industrial armies" started for Washington in 1894, and some 1,200 men arrived. They were peaceful and sober as a rule, but it was the obvious sympathy they stirred over the country that frightened the government, even President Cleveland.

Not only the government but also private employers resorted to violence in countering labor protest. An extraordinary number of strikes, some 1,400 in all, occurred during 1894, many of them provoked by wage cuts. More than 660,000 people were thrown out of work by strikes or lockouts. Management countered by using violence, employing secret police, or securing injunctions from friendly courts. In the Pullman strike of July, as we have seen (p. 481), the federal government used troops of the regular army to crush the workers. Cleveland earned as much hostility from labor by his use of troops as he had from agrarians by his sale of bonds.

In the meantime, the only serious piece of reform the second Cleveland administration undertook was the reform of the tariff. To fulfill their campaign pledges, the Democrats did put through the House a bill containing modest reductions in the tariff. But in the Senate the protectionists of both parties fell upon it with 600 amendments that restored many of the old rates. The Wilson-Gorman Act, which Cleveland allowed to become law without his signature, did not fulfill the administration's promises of tariff reform. The only sop to reformers was an amendment, slipped in by the agrarians and deplored by the president, that provided for a small income tax of 2 percent on incomes over $4,000. The Supreme Court, which shared Cleveland's unpopularity as an agency of reaction, promptly declared the income tax unconstitutional. For relief of suffering among the unemployed, on the farms, and in the cities, for restoring credit, and for assisting industry afflicted by depression, Cleveland's administration refused to take any responsibility.

In the fall campaigns of 1894, the Republicans capitalized on the spirit of despair over the depression. They identified their party with prosperity and recovery through the Republican program of tariff and sound currency. Governor William McKinley of Ohio proved the hero of the Republican campaign. The elections of 1894 were a triumph for Republicans, who recouped their losses of the previous election and took control of the House with a majority of 140 seats. Many prominent Democrats went down to defeat. In 24 states no Democrat at all won national office and only one each in six others. Populists increased the vote they polled in 1892 by 42 percent but were disappointed in the results and suffered losses in offices held. In all, the elections of 1894 brought about the largest congressional gains and one of the most widespread political realignments in the nation's history. It was this election and not that of 1896 that marked the fall of the Democrats and the beginning of the long Republican ascendancy.

The Democratic party was, in fact, in the midst of a revolution almost as profound as that of 1860, when North and South wings split into two parties. Again it was a sectional split, but this time it was the Northeast Democrats who were isolated instead of the Southern. West and South joined hands in the name of the free coinage of silver, but silver merely served as a symbol for dozens of other sectional issues. And Grover Cleveland became the personification of the Northeastern conservatism against which the two agrarian regions were in revolt. Never since Andrew Johnson had a president been so detested and abused by members of his own party as was Cleveland.

Early in 1895 prominent Democrats in the South and West set to work systematically to use the silver issue as a means of taking over control of their party and unseating Cleveland and the conservatives. They distributed great quantities of silver propaganda, such as Ignatius Donnelly's *The American People's Money* (1895) and the famous booklet by William H. "Coin" Harvey, *Coin's Financial School* (1894). The work of

The Supreme Court and the Income Tax: The Government's Argument

Richard Olney:

The constitutional objection [is] nothing but a call upon the judicial department of the government to supplant the political in the exercise of the taxing power; to substitute its discretion for that of Congress. . . . It is inevitably predestined to failure unless this court shall, for the first time in its history, overlook and overstep the bounds which separate the judicial from the legislative power—bounds, the scrupulous observance of which it has so often declared to be absolutely essential to the integrity of our constitutional system of government.

James C. Carter:

Nothing could be more unwise and dangerous—nothing more foreign to the spirit of the Constitution—than an attempt to baffle and defeat a popular determination by a judgment in a lawsuit. When the opposing forces of sixty millions of people have become arrayed in hostile political ranks upon a question which all men feel is not a question of law, but of legislation, the only path of safety is to accept the voice of the majority as final.

From *Pollock* v. *Farmers' Loan and Trust Co.*, 157 U.S. 429, 1895

the silver Democrats against Cleveland was so effective that after the state conventions in the summer of 1896 no state Democratic organization south of the Potomac and only three west of the Alleghenies remained in the hands of the president's friends. There was no longer any doubt that the silverites would be able to wrest control of the national Democratic convention from Cleveland.

McKinley and Gold versus Bryan and Silver Nor was there any doubt that the Republican convention would nominate William McKinley of Ohio when it met at St. Louis in June. McKinley's nomination had been assured not only by his popularity but by the systematic and patient work of his devoted friend Marcus Alonzo Hanna, who retired from business in 1895 to devote full time to fulfilling his ambition of putting McKinley in the White House. McKinley's nomination rolled forward as planned on the first ballot, and Garret A. Hobart, a relatively unknown corporation lawyer from New Jersey, balanced the ticket. A protectionist platform was obviously called for, since McKinley's name had become synonymous with high tariff. McKinley was for the gold standard, but the only doubt was how explicit the plank on the gold standard should be. Upon the adoption of the gold plank, Senator Henry M. Teller of Colorado led a small group of Western silver Republicans from the hall, and they withdrew from the party.

Eastern Republicans had reason to doubt McKinley's firmness on gold. He had voted for both the Bland-Allison Act and the Sherman Silver Purchase Act, was a moderate on silver, and held out hopes for international bimetalism. In 1896, however, he accepted his party's decision for gold. He was an experienced and skillful politician who had served in Congress from 1876 to 1891, with the exception of one term, and had been governor of Ohio for two terms, completing the second in 1895. A kindly, impressive-looking man, McKinley had won his place of national political prominence on his own and acquired a mass following. The campaign caricature of McKinley as the spineless puppet of the millionaire

The Supreme Court and the Income Tax: The Argument that Prevailed

Joseph H. Choate:

You cannot hereafter exercise any check if you now say that Congress is untrammelled and uncontrollable. My friend says you cannot enforce any limit. He says no matter what Congress does . . . this Court will have nothing to say about it. I agree that it will have nothing to say about it if it now lets go its hold upon this law. . . .

I have thought that one of the fundamental objects of all civilized government was the preservation of the rights of private property. I have thought that it was the very keystone of the arch upon which all civilized government rests, and that this once abandoned, everything was in danger. . . . According to the doctrines that have been propounded here this morning, even that great fundamental principle has been scattered to the winds. . . .

If it be true, as my friend said in closing, that the passions of the people are aroused on this subject, if it be true that a mighty army of sixty million citizens is likely to be incensed by this decision, it is the more vital to the future welfare of this country that this court again resolutely and courageously declare, as Marshall did, that it has the power to set aside an act of Congress violative of the Constitution . . . no matter what the threatened consequences of popular or populistic wrath may be.

From *Pollock* v. *Farmers' Loan and Trust Co.*, 157 U.S. 429, 1895

boss had no foundation in fact, for the evidence is that Hanna constantly deferred to his friend and respected his wishes.

The Democratic convention at Chicago exhibited more disorder and spontaneity. Cleveland supporters, still full of fight, arrived from the East to clash with red-hot silver orators from the South and the West amid a din of hisses, catcalls, and Rebel Yells. But the Easterners had neither the strength to control the convention nor a suitable candidate to put before it, and the agrarian rebels rode over them roughshod. They adopted a platform which denounced virtually everything Cleveland stood for, demanded an income tax, and, most important of all, free coinage of silver at the ratio of sixteen ounces of silver to one of gold.

At a strategic moment of the platform debate a handsome young ex-congressman, William Jennings Bryan of Nebraska, captured the attention and the imagination of the silver forces with a speech that mounted to a thrilling peroration: "You shall not press down upon the brow of labor this crown of thorns, you shall not crucify mankind upon a cross of gold." Bryan was nominated on the fifth ballot, and, to balance the ticket, Arthur Sewall of Maine, a banker and businessman who opposed the gold standard, was nominated for vice president.

While he was only 36 and little known in the East, Bryan was already widely known as a peerless orator in the West and the South, where he had been campaigning for three years to prepare the revolt of the silver forces. Bryan had some naive ideas about money and harbored suspicions of the East, "the enemy's country," as he once called it. He was no radical, and his ties were with the simple agrarian past rather than with the complex future. But conservatives were wrong to dismiss him as a one-idea fanatic. He had an intuitive grasp of the deep mood of protest that stirred the West and South, and he expressed that mood in a moral appeal to the conscience of the country. His real service was to awaken an old faith in social justice and to protest against a generation of plutocratic rule.

In their next maneuver, the silver-leaders of the "revolutionized" Democrats persuaded the Populist party, which held its convention in St. Louis after the Democratic convention had met, to make Bryan its candidate as well. The proposal deeply divided the Populists, who neither wanted to split the reform forces with a separate ticket nor give up their own party identity. Western Populists were eager to nominate Bryan, but Southern members, less devoted to silver, wanted a separate Populist ticket and no compromise. Bryan's nomination was at last secured when Senator William V. Allen of Nebraska, chairman of the convention, told the Southerners that the Democrats had agreed to withdraw Sewall and accept Thomas E. Watson as their vice-presidential nominee if the Populists would nominate Bryan. Southern radicals bitterly resisted fusion with the Democrats, whom they had been fighting for four years. But when their hero Watson agreed to compromise, they reluctantly consented and nominated Bryan and Watson. Only later did they learn that the Democrats refused to withdraw the banker Sewall.

Two more parties were created out of bolters from the old parties. The National Silver Republicans endorsed the Democratic candidates. Later on, the gold Democrats, with encouragement and financial support from Hanna, organized the National Democratic party and nominated a separate ticket that was intended to contribute to Bryan's defeat.

The contest between McKinley and Bryan in 1896 has taken on the legendary character of the combat between Goliath and David—except that it turned out quite differently. Bryan played the David role admirably—the lone youth armed with nothing but shafts of oratory pitted against the armored Gold Giant and all his hosts. Actually, reformers of many schools rallied to Bryan's cause. Bryan's chief reliance, however, was upon his own voice. In a campaign without precedent at that time, he traveled 18,000 miles by train, made more than 600 speeches, and talked to some 3 million people. He spoke not only of silver but of the price of crops, the cost of mortgages, the need for credit, and the regulation of railroads. The powerful popular response to his campaign aroused great hopes for victory.

It also aroused a hysterical wave of fear among conservatives and facilitated Hanna's collection of campaign funds. He exacted tribute from every great trust, railroad, and bank with any stake in the outcome and built up a treasure chest of at least $3.5 million—as against a mere $300,000 at Bryan's disposal. Hanna

William Jennings Bryan: an old faith in social justice

spent the money lavishly but shrewdly, sending out propaganda by the ton and the carload and speakers by the battalion. He also transported trainloads of people, some 750,000 in all, from representative groups, all expenses paid, to hear McKinley read well-prepared speeches from his front porch in Canton, Ohio. From there McKinley set the tone and directed the strategy of his campaign. The press assisted Hanna with blasts of ridicule and charges of socialism and anarchism against Bryan. President Cleveland called Bryan's supporters "madmen" and "criminals," and the New York *Tribune* referred to Bryan as a "wretched, rattle-pated boy."

The combination was too much for the resources of Bryan (see Map 20-2). He polled 6,492,559 votes, more votes than any victorious candidate had ever polled before, nearly a million more than Cleveland polled in 1892, but it was still not enough. McKinley won with 7,102,246 votes, a plurality of 609,687, and an electoral vote of 271 to 176. Bryan did not carry a single state north of the Potomac or east of the Mississippi above its juncture with the Ohio. He did not even carry the farming states of Iowa, Minnesota, and North Dakota. What is more significant, he carried no industrialized, no urbanized state. This may well be the main reason for Bryan's defeat. In spite of widespread unrest among labor, Bryan did not win labor's support, which might have given him victory. He really had little to offer either labor or the cities. He was the

William McKinley, 1896: front porch in Canton

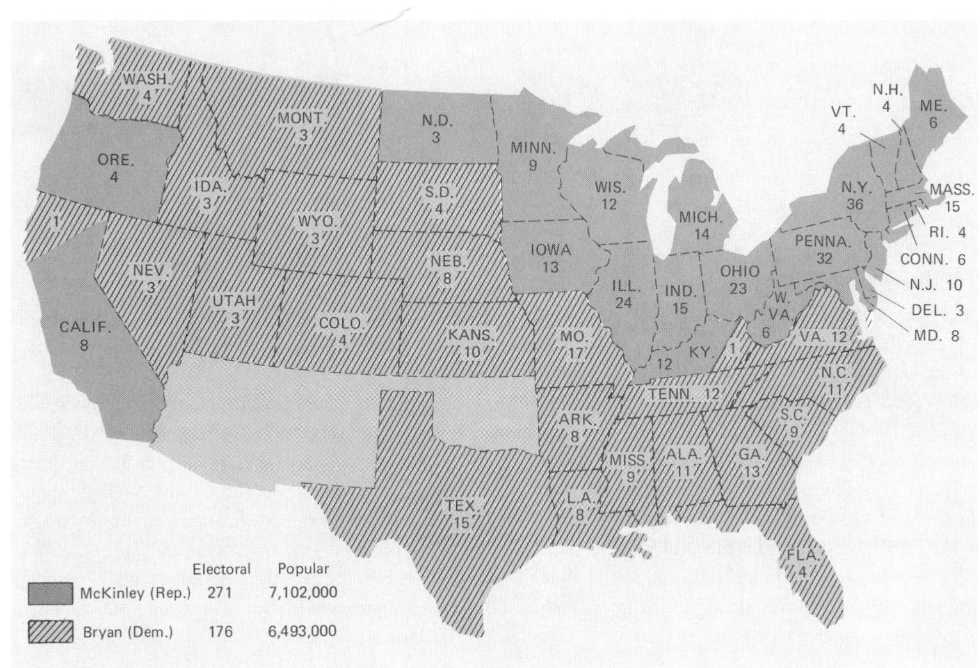

Map 20-2
The election of 1896

first Democratic candidate to lose New York City since 1848, and the largest city to give him a plurality was Troy, New York. Like many other American reformers of his day, he had something of significance for the present, but his true ties were the past. McKinley and Hanna may not have been looking very far into the future, but they clearly had a firmer grip on the present. They also had an appeal for labor, and they evidently won the confidence of the urban middle class. Their victory at the polls meant more conservatism and yet another businessman's regime.

The Aftermath of '96 The election was followed by a brief revival of the economy and three years later by the end of the long depression. The upturn had little if anything to do with the saving of the gold standard or the victory of McKinley. The price of wheat had started to climb before the election, though hardly enough to have influenced the outcome. But in 1897 the European wheat crop fell off 30 percent, and American farmers doubled their exports of the previous year. Prices continued to rise, and the whole economy began to revive. Discoveries of gold in Australia and Alaska revived the flow of gold into the country, and gold production was further increased by discoveries of pay dirt in South Africa and the development of the cyanide process for extracting the metal from ore. The inflation that the agrarians and silverites had demanded came, ironically enough, not through silver but through gold. The influx of gold and capital stimulated industrial expansion, and that in turn touched off a boom in iron and steel.

With a Republican majority in both houses, McKinley called a special session of Congress in the spring of 1897. The Wilson-Gorman Tariff of 1894 was already high enough for most protectionists, but Congress passed a bill framed by Nelson Dingley of Maine, which raised duties to an average of 52 percent and included reciprocal trade provisions. Lacking a Senate majority for a gold standard until after the 1898 election, McKinley avoided action until gold was flowing in and silver sentiment was waning. But in his annual message of 1899 he called for legislation, and Congress adopted by a party vote the Gold Standard Act, which he signed on March 14, 1900, thus writing an end to a generation of controversy, but without producing any significant economic effect, either good or bad.

One significant but often overlooked result of the election of 1896 and the return to prosperity was the demoralization of the Populist movement. Fusion with the enemy party and abandonment of principle for the sake of silver had demoralized the Populists and all but destroyed their party. "The sentiment is still there, the votes are still there, but confidence is gone," thought Tom Watson. The following decade was to see a new upsurge of reform, but it was achieved under urban, not rural, leadership. Nineteenth-century agrarian radicalism made its last significant bid for leadership of a national reform movement in 1896.

SUGGESTIONS FOR READING

The political history of this period is treated by H. W. Morgan, *From Hayes to McKinley: National Party Politics, 1877–1896* (1969), M. Keller, *Affairs of State: Public Life in Late Nineteenth Century America* (1977), and by R. O. Marcus, *Grand Old Party: Political Structure in the Gilded Age, 1880–1896* (1971). A revisionary estimate of politicians is D. J. Rothman, *Politics and Power: The United States Senate, 1869–1901* (1966). On the 1890s, see H. U. Faulkner, *Politics, Reform and Expansion, 1890–1900* (1959), and L. P. Beth, *The Development of the American Constitution, 1877–1901* (1971). R. H. Williams, *Years of Decision: American Politics in the 1890s* (1978), is generous to the Republican party. On cultural factors in party politics, see P. Kleppner, *The Cross of Culture: A Social Analysis of Midwestern Politics, 1850–1900* (1970) and *The Third Electoral System, 1853–1892: Parties, Voters, and Political Cultures* (1979); R. J. Jensen, *The Winning of the Midwest: Social and Political Conflict, 1888–1896* (1971). On popular participation, see M. E. McGerr, *The Decline of Popular Politics: The American North, 1865–1928* (1986); and on regional influences R. F. Bensel, *Sectionalism and American Political Development* (1984).

On the politics and issues of reform, see G. McFarland, *Mugwumps, Morals and Politics, 1884–1920* (1975), and R. Kelley, *The Transatlantic Persuasion: The Liberal-Democratic Mind in the Age of Gladstone* (1969). R. Ginger, *Age of Excess* (1965), is an interpretive study. Civil service reform is the subject of three excellent works: L. D. White, *The Republican Era: 1896–1901* (1958); P. P. Van Riper, *History of the United States Civil Service* (1958); and A. Hogenboom, *Outlawing the Spoils* (1961). Pensions for veterans are treated by M. R. Dearing, *Veterans in Politics: The Story of the G. A. R.* (1952). Monetary controversies of the period are examined in M. Friedman and A. J. Schwartz, *A Monetary History of the United States, 1867–1960* (1963); I. Unger, *The Greenback Era: A Social and Political*

History of American Finance, 1865–1879 (1964); W. T. K. Nugent, *Money and American Society, 1865–1880* (1968).

The background of Populism is treated by S. Hahn, *The Roots of Southern Populism* (1983), and in R. C. McMath, Jr., *Populist Vanguard: a History of the Southern Farmers' Alliance* (1975); and its history in an older work, J. D. Hicks, *The Populist Revolt* (1931), and later in L. Goodwyn, *Democratic Promise: The Populist Movement in America* (1976). R. Hofstadter, *The Age of Reform: From Bryan to F.D.R.* (1955), takes a dim view of Populism. Rejecting that view with new light are N. Pollack, *The Just Polity: Populism, Law, and Human Welfare* (1987) and his *The Humane Economy: Populism, Capitalism, and Democracy* (1990); and also B. Palmer, *"Man Over Money": The Southern Populist Critique of American Capitalism* (1985).

The depression of the 1890s and its political repercussions are intelligently discussed in S. T. McSeveney, *The Politics of Depression: Political Behavior in the Northeast, 1893–1896* (1972); J. E. Wright, *The Politics of Populism: Dissent in Colorado* (1974); and P. H. Argersinger, *Populism and Politics: William Alfred Peffer and the People's Party* (1974). Scholarly studies of protest are A. Lindsey, *The Pullman Strike* (1943); H. Barnard, *"Eagle Forgotten": The Life of John Peter Altgeld* (1938); and R. Ginger, *Altgeld's America — The Lincoln Ideal Versus Changing Realities* (1958).

On the crisis of 1896, many books already mentioned are relevant. In addition, see S. Jones, *The Presidential Election of 1896* (1964); J. R. Hollingsworth, *The Whirligig of Politics: The Democracy of Cleveland and Bryan* (1963); and P. W. Glad, *McKinley, Bryan, and the People* (1964). The best biographies are H. W. Morgan, *William McKinley and His America* (1963); L. Gould, *The Presidency of William McKinley* (1980); and P. E. Coletta, *William Jennings Bryan, Political Evangelist, 1860–1908* (1964) Vol. I of three. Agrarian leaders prominent in 1896 are pictured in C. V. Woodward, *Tom Watson: Agrarian Rebel* (1938), and F. B. Simkins, *Pitchfork Ben Tillman: South Carolinian* (1944).

CHAPTER TWENTY-ONE

ROUGH RIDES AT THE TOP OF SAN JUAN HILL

EMPIRE BEYOND THE SEAS

The United States was not born in isolation, nor with any bias against expansionism. On the contrary, the long colonial experience was lived out in the midst of international rivalries. Independence itself was painfully won and precariously defended by taking shrewd advantage of those rivalries. Expansionism was a fundamental policy in the new nation's negotiations with foreign powers. Louisiana, Florida, Texas, New Mexico, California, Oregon, the Gadsden Purchase, and the Alaska Purchase—in fact the acquisition of all the continental area of the country beyond the original colonies—are dramatic evidence of expansionism, vigorously and steadily pursued.

After about a century, ending in 1867 with the purchase of Alaska, the nation lapsed into what might almost be called isolationism, though a better term would probably be withdrawal, or preoccupation. At any rate, the United States called a halt to territorial expansion for a quarter of a century or more. Then suddenly expansionism reawakened in a new form—overseas expansion—and concern over foreign affairs revived. A war with Spain, though not itself prompted by expansionism, actually brought overseas possessions, colonies, millions of colonial subjects, protectorates—a whole empire. A republic became an empire, a country long preoccupied with internal affairs turned its attention outward. One phase of isolationism ended, and with it one phase of American innocence.

WITHDRAWAL AND RETURN

The Period of Withdrawal The United States' withdrawal from world affairs was not due to any lack of advocates of aggressiveness. William H. Seward, secretary of state under Lincoln and Johnson, proposed, among other things, intervention in Korea, acquisition of the Hawaiian Islands, and adventures in the Caribbean. He could muster no support for these undertakings, however, and only with difficulty persuaded Congress to accept the Alaska bargain offered by Russia. Moved by scheming friends, President Grant devised a treaty for the annexation of Santo Domingo, though the Senate rejected it in 1870. Other expansionists agitated in vain for the annexation of Canada, for intervention in the Cuban rebellion in 1868–78, for securing a naval station in Samoa in the 1870s, and for grabbing naval harbors in Haiti during the 1880s. The standard arguments against such schemes were that it was against American principles to govern without the consent of the governed, that we should abstain from foreign entanglements, avoid large naval commitments and expenditures, and refrain from absorbing peoples of alien race and tradition. One name for this policy was "continentalism"—the idea that the nation should acquire no territory outside its continental limits.

Preoccupation with domestic concerns did not blind Americans entirely to opportunities and temptations abroad. The administrations of Garfield and Arthur sought to advance limited and overlapping goals of prestige, markets, and security, especially in the Caribbean and Central America. Less typical of that period, but suggesting expansionist impulses to come, were the negotiation of a treaty with Korea in 1882 opening up that country to the non-Asian world, and the United States participation in the Berlin Conference of European powers on trade rights in the Congo in 1884–85.

The fact remains, however, that Americans of the 1870s and 1880s were mainly preoccupied with their built-in empire of the West and their economic colonialism in the South, absorbed in political and economic problems of a domestic character, largely content to stay at home. When Cleveland became president in 1885 the State Department had only 60 employees, including clerks. Secretaries of state were usually political appointees with little knowledge of foreign affairs. Until the 1880s the United States Navy was an obsolete and antiquated collection of antiques that provoked foreign ridicule. The American merchant marine had virtually disappeared from the seas, and the army was reduced to a handful of Indian-fighters. America still enjoyed—complacently took for granted—nature's marvelous boon of security, which was not only effective but relatively free. Wide oceans, weak neighbors, and rivalries that kept its potential enemies divided accounted for this blessing of free security. No other great nation enjoyed it. When foreign policy disputes flared up in America during this period, the heat they generated was greatly intensified by the sudden expansion of the tiny circle normally involved to include an uninformed and excitable public in times of crisis. This plus the old habit of relying on free security help explain the tendency of the United States to engage in heated disputes with foreign powers out of all proportion to its military strength.

Some of these disputes were with Great Britain, then the mightiest power in the world, and any such dispute was likely to become a game between the major political parties. The game was to see who could "twist the

British view of Cleveland's policies

lion's tail'' the harder and who could thereby curry the most favor with the Irish and other anti-British elements. One of the disputes during Cleveland's first administration was merely a renewal of the perennial bickering over fishing rights along the coasts of British North America. Off the western shores of the continent the United States and Canada were simultaneously embroiled in another dispute — this one over the fur-seal industry in and out of the Bering Sea. The United States advanced an arrogant claim to exclusive jurisdiction over the Bering Sea with the contention that the seals were domestic animals that had wandered out of bounds. A court of arbitration rejected the American claims and prescribed regulations for the industry that were put into effect by both governments.

The only other embroilment to ruffle the relatively calm waters of foreign affairs during Cleveland's first administration occurred in the Samoan Islands of the remote South Pacific. The splendid harbor of Pago Pago on Tutuila Island had stirred the interest of naval officers of the United States and other countries. In 1878, after rejecting the proposal of annexation or guardianship made by a Samoan chieftain, the Hayes administration negotiated a treaty granting the United States the right to establish a naval station at Pago Pago. Germany and Great Britain secured similar treaties the following year, granting them naval-station rights in the same harbor and elsewhere. Competition precipitated a tropical squall of international temper in the mid-1880s. Conditions grew worse when Germany set up a new regime in the islands, and seven warships anchored at Samoa prepared for hostilities. A sudden storm of hurricane force brought peace unexpectedly by sinking all but one of the warships on March 15, 1889, less than two weeks after Cleveland's term ended. Harrison's administration worked out a tripartite protectorate of the islands with Germany and Great Britain.

In spite of all these flurries and alarms, little had happened down to 1889 to divert Cleveland from his determination to oppose ''acquisition of new and distant territory or the incorporation of remote interests with our own.'' Yet the old tradition of isolation, abstention, and withdrawal was near its end, for America was now about to plunge into world affairs and abandon its tradition of ''continentalism.''

Manifest Destiny, New Style Historians have long had difficulties in agreeing over the nature and causes of this momentous change. Some have seen it as a more or less temporary ''aberration'' induced in large part by chance and coincidence and inspired by humanitarian impulse. The discussion at times recalls the claim that the British Empire was founded in a fit of absentmindedness. The fact remains that by the end of the century the United States found itself with colonial possessions on opposite sides of the globe and new military commitments in Asia. Something of importance had happened to American history that is linked to more than chance and passing moods.

It is best to avoid simplification, for numerous interests were involved and many causes were at work. Among influences probably exaggerated was the idea of social Darwinism propagated by the English sociologist Herbert Spencer and spread by American disciples. Darwinism might best be thought of as a rationalization of the new style of Manifest Destiny rather than its inspiration. The same could be said of various theories of racial superiority and inferiority, some of which had been around a long time. Of growing popularity among the elite was a cult of Anglo-Saxon superiority. Religiously inclined exponents of racial superiority believed it had a divine sanction. One of these was Josiah Strong, who declared in his popular book *Our Country* (1885) that the Anglo-Saxon was ''divinely commissioned to be, in a peculiar sense, his brother's keeper.'' Of more importance than this book in turning America toward expansionist sentiment were Protestant missions established abroad. These increased fivefold in the last 30 years of the century, and in the last decade the number of missionaries in China doubled to more than 1,000. The Protestant missionaries were the first converts to the new definition of the American mission, which was that the republic was destined to spread the national example abroad.

Such a mission could hardly be accomplished with an antiquated navy. Surely one explanation for the decision of Americans to plunge into overseas expansion is that they acquired the physical means to do so in the shape of a modern navy. In 1883 Congress authorized construction of three cruisers and in 1886 two battleships, the *Maine* and the *Texas*. This construction was still guided by the concept of the navy as a defensive force, but the Naval Act of 1890, which authorized the building of three more battleships, the *Indiana*, the *Massachusetts*, and the *Oregon*, all heavier and more powerful ships, announced the government's intention to have a navy that could meet a potential enemy anywhere on the high seas. Before

The Anglo-Saxon Mission

It is not necessary to argue . . . that the two great needs of mankind, that all men may be lifted into the light of the highest Christian civilization, are, first, a pure, spiritual Christianity, and, second, civil liberty. Without controversy, these are the forces, which in the past, have contributed most to the elevation of the human race, and they must continue to be, in the future, the most efficient ministers to its progress. It follows, then, that the Anglo-Saxon, as the great representative of these two ideas, the depositary of these two great blessings, sustains peculiar relations to the world's future, is divinely commissioned to be, in a peculiar sense, his brother's keeper. Add to this the fact of his rapidly increasing strength in modern times, and we have well nigh a demonstration of his destiny. . . . It seems to me that God, with infinite wisdom and skill, is training the Anglo-Saxon race for an hour sure to come in the world's future.

From Josiah Strong, *Our Country,* 1885

the end of the century, the United States had moved from twelfth to third place among naval powers. Thereafter the big-navy advocates began to reap the cumulative benefits of an expanding fleet: new bases and coaling stations, an even larger navy to protect the additional bases, and more bases to accommodate the larger navy.

The foremost exponent of navalism in his time was a historian, Captain Alfred T. Mahan, author of *The Influence of Sea Power upon History* (published in 1890 but delivered as lectures at the new Naval War College in 1886) and *The Interest of America in Sea Power* (1897). "Whether they will or no," wrote Mahan in 1890, "Americans must now begin to look outward." His writings were rather more of a reflection than a cause of events, but his influence was felt in shaping naval policy in Washington and his ideas were seized upon by an elite group earnestly promoting what they called "the large policy" of expansionism. Including Theodore Roosevelt and Henry Cabot Lodge, as well as Captain Mahan, this group has been portrayed as a powerful, influential cabal.

The larger picture, however, would take into account the arrival of a new generation and a new world scene. The central experience of the previous generation had been the Civil War. They had had their fill of war and humanitarian crusades. They were not interested in Grant's efforts to take Santo Domingo, or in Spain's suppression of Cubans in the 1870s. The new men of the 1890s, lacking such experience, looked out on a world teeming with imperialist adventures of other nations. European powers were carving up Africa and Asia, snatching island kingdoms in the Pacific, and looking for opportunities in the Western Hemisphere. The predatory powers moved in on the crumbling dynasty of China from bases already established in Asia: the French from Indochina, the British along the Yangtze Valley, and the Russians from Siberian possessions. Japan felt cheated when, after its victory over China in 1894–95, it received only Formosa (now called Taiwan) as booty. Americans began to wonder if they were not falling behind the times and whether they would ever be able to protect their interests and markets if they did not enter, even belatedly, into the imperialist adventure and "take up the white man's burden," along with the rewards and plunder that went with it. Some, including Theodore Roosevelt, believed that foreign adventures might divert angry farmers and workers as well as a distraught nation from preoccupation with economic ills.

Economic interpretations of American expansionism have provoked the most controversy, and emphasis on them has seesawed up and down. It has long been understood by historians that the depression of

American Interests

Indications are not wanting of an approaching change in the thoughts and policy of Americans as to their relations with the world outside their own borders. . . . The interesting and significant feature of this changing attitude is the turning of the eyes outward, instead of inward only, to seek the welfare of the country. To affirm the importance of distant markets, and the relation to them of our own immense powers of production, implies logically the recognition of the link that joins the products and the markets—that is, the carrying trade; the three together constituting that chain of maritime power to which Great Britain owes her wealth and greatness. Further, is it too much to say that, as two of these links, the shipping and the markets, are exterior to our own borders, the acknowledgment of them carries with it a view of the relations of the United States to the world radically distinct from the simple idea of self-sufficingness? We shall not follow far this line of thought before there will dawn the realization of America's unique position, facing the older worlds of the East and West, her shores washed by the oceans which touch the one or the other, but which are common to her alone.

From Alfred T. Mahan, *The Interest of America in Sea Power,* 1897

the 1890s aroused concern over the need for foreign markets to absorb the surplus products of the American economy as well as the need to acquire new markets to keep the wheels of industry turning or start them up again. Special interest in the China market had increased since 1895. For a generation or more historians gave economic motives primary emphasis. Then in the mid-1930s, Professor Julius Pratt showed that most business leaders opposed intervention in Cuba and war with Spain for fear this would retard economic recovery that was under way in 1897. He did point out that once the war started business sentiment quickly and enthusiastically supported it. Temporary timidity in the business community in 1897 and early 1898 has not eliminated economic motives from a satisfactory explanation of expansionism of the 1890s.

THE NEW DIPLOMACY

American Bellicosity James G. Blaine, secretary of state under Harrison, made the break with the old tradition. Blaine had served briefly in the same office eight years earlier under Garfield and revived the tradition of earlier Republican expansionism under Seward and Grant. Like them he also sought naval bases in Santo Domingo and Haiti, though with no more success. His followers expected him to pursue a "spirited policy" in keeping with his nickname of "Jingo* Jim." Actually, Blaine exerted a moderating influence in several instances.

Closer to Blaine's interests was Latin America, especially the promotion of United States trade with sister republics, the obtaining of naval bases in the Caribbean, and the construction of an isthmian canal. Eight years earlier he had urged calling an international conference of the American republics, and the idea materialized when he became secretary of state for the second time. Delegates arrived in the fall of

* The word was originated in England and popularized in America by a jingle printed in the Detroit *News* during the fisheries dispute with Great Britain and Canada:

We do not want to fight
But, by jingo, if we do
We'll scoop in all the fishing grounds
And the whole Dominion, too.

1889, but all they would accept was the setting up of an information center, which later became the Pan-American Union. More than a half century was to pass before Pan-American conferences would finally accept the sort of agreements Blaine tried to effect in 1889.

In the early 1890s a new martial spirit in America found expression in a succession of chauvinistic outbursts; "jingoism" it was called. Irresponsible talk of war with Italy occurred in American newspapers over the lynching of eleven prisoners of Italian origin, in March 1891, charged with murder in New Orleans. A much more serious outburst almost brought the United States to the point of war with Chile, a republic with not one-twentieth its population, but with a strong navy. In October 1891, when a party from the cruiser *Baltimore* went on shore leave in Valparaiso, a mob of Chileans killed two of the American sailors and injured 17 others. President Harrison invited Congress to declare war at a time when the apologies he had demanded from Chile were hourly expected. Chile fortunately capitulated with apologies and indemnities, and the war scare passed over.

The bellicose mood of the jingo editors and politicians did not pass over, however. Rather, it continued to mount during the 1890s. "The number of men and officials in this country who are now mad to fight somebody is appalling," said the anti-imperialist editor of the *Nation,* E. L. Godkin, in 1894. "Navy officers dream of war and talk and lecture about it incessantly. The Senate debates are filled with predictions of impending war and with talk of preparing for it at once." The irresponsible warmongering of the period was indeed appalling, though it should be remembered that nineteenth-century Americans regarded the Civil War as an exception and still thought of war as a heroic affair filled with splendor and glory. It was an illusion slow to die.

"That's a live wire, gentleman!"

Even the antiexpansionist Cleveland was not immune to the new spirit, as he showed in his handling of relations with Britain in the dispute over the boundary between British Guiana and Venezuela. It was an old dispute that went back into the colonial history of Venezuela, but the discovery of gold in the disputed territory, combined with a bit of Venezuelan propaganda suggesting that British aggression was a challenge to the Monroe Doctrine, stirred up the Anglophobia and pugnacity of the jingo editors of the United States. In 1895 Cleveland had Secretary of State Richard Olney demand that Great Britain conform to the Monroe Doctrine, so broadly interpreted, by submitting the boundary dispute to arbitration. Olney accompanied this demand with the truculent assertion that the United States today "is practically sovereign on this continent, and its fiat is law upon the subjects to which it confines its interposition." The tone of the note, coupled with his request for a quick reply, gave it the favor of an ultimatum.

The British foreign minister, Lord Salisbury, took his time in replying, and when he did reply four months later he repudiated Secretary Olney's interpretation of the Monroe Doctrine and flatly refused to submit the dispute to arbitration. After receiving this rebuff, Cleveland sent a special message to Congress deploring "a supine submission to wrong and injustice and the consequent loss of national self-respect." Defusing the situation by delay, he asked that he be authorized to appoint a commission to determine the boundary and that the commission's decision be enforced at whatever cost. Privately he intended settlement by arbitration. Congress promptly complied, and war sentiment mounted. "Let the fight come if it must," wrote Theodore Roosevelt, who hoped to participate personally. "I rather hope that the fight will come soon. The clamor of the peace faction has convinced me that this country needs a war." Fortunately Britain saw fit to back down. Suddenly finding itself in trouble in South Africa with no ally in Europe on which it could count for support, Great Britain decided to court a friend instead of making an enemy in the New World. It switched to a conciliatory tone and signed a treaty with Venezuela providing for arbitration, which turned out to be mainly in its favor. The upshot of the incident was to enhance American nationalist feeling, but paradoxically it also ushered in an era of Anglo-American understanding.

The Hawaiian Question When it came to expansion overseas, Cleveland clung consistently to traditional views and stood firm against the annexation of Hawaii. American interest in these islands dated back to the China trade in the late eighteenth century. Traders were followed by American missionaries, who converted the native Polynesians to Christianity in the second quarter of the nineteenth century, and the missionaries were followed by American sugar growers. Efforts to annex the islands under President Pierce and again under Secretary Seward failed, but in 1875 a reciprocity treaty was signed opening a free market in the United States to Hawaiian sugar planters. Sugar production in the islands multiplied tenfold in the next 20 years in response to the free American market. So dependent did the industry become on this market, however, that when the McKinley Tariff of 1890 admitted other foreign sugar on the same terms and subsidized domestic producers, the blow precipitated an economic crisis in the island kingdom and contributed to a political crisis.

King Kalakaua, the next to last of the reigning family, had been forced by the white business community in 1887 to accept a new constitution that curbed his power. The dissolute old king was succeeded in 1891 by his sister Liliuokalani, who made it apparent that she was determined to overthrow the constitution her brother had accepted, shake off white control, and restore royal prerogatives. In January 1893 a committee of businessmen-revolutionaries demanded that she abdicate. Thereupon United States Minister John L. Stevens requested that marines be sent ashore from the cruiser *Boston* and raise the American flag. The queen then capitulated, as she said, "to the superior force of the United States of America." A month later, on February 15, Harrison sent to the Senate a treaty annexing the islands. It might have gone through then had it not been for the declared preference of Cleveland, who was to begin his second administration in a few days, that the matter be held over until his inauguration. As soon as he became president again he dispatched a special commissioner to investigate the situation in the islands. The commissioner's report convinced Cleveland that the great majority of the natives supported the queen. Cleveland therefore not only withheld the annexation treaty but insisted that it was his duty to restore "Queen Lil." The revolutionary provisional government refused to step down, however, and continued to rule, biding its time until a more imperialist-minded administration came to power.

Cleveland's firm resistance to annexation, as compared with Harrison's receptive attitude, helped to make the question something of a party issue. The Republican platform of 1896 contained a plank favoring Hawaiian annexation, and McKinley was quickly won over after he became president in March 1897. Comparing him with Cleveland, commissioners from Hawaii reported that there was "the difference between daylight and darkness." On June 16, 1897, Secretary of State John Sherman signed a treaty of annexation and McKinley sent it to the Senate. Congress was strongly interested in Hawaii and alarmed by the interest Japan was manifesting in the islands, but the sentiment against overseas expansion was still too strong to be overcome, and the treaty languished for more than a year without action. Only in July 1898, after the war with Spain had opened the floodgates of expansionism, was Hawaii annexed.

WAR WITH SPAIN

The Cuban Crisis The expansionists and imperialists did not cause the war with Spain. They merely exploited it for their own purposes. The war itself grew out of deplorable conditions in Cuba that seemed intolerable to an aroused popular sentiment in the United States. Spanish misgovernment of the island had given rise to numerous revolts and a Ten Years' War, 1868–78, that brought little relief for Cuban ills. A new civil war broke out in February 1895. As in the case of the Hawaiian revolution, American tariff policy contributed to the uprising, for the tariff law of 1894, by imposing a duty on raw sugar, had added economic suffering to political discontent. Both the Cubans and the Spanish used savage methods. The Cubans systematically destroyed sugar mills, cane fields, and other property. Early in 1896 the Spanish commander, General Valeriano Weyler, resorted to the brutal policy of "reconcentration." This meant driving the entire population of large areas of Cuba—including women, children, and old people—into cities and towns fortified with barbed wire and under armed guard. Left without food or sanitation, the prisoners fell victim to famine and disease. Within two years more than 200,000, or approximately one-eighth of the total population, were commonly believed to have been wiped out.

The American press exaggerated the Spanish atrocities, but the sufferings of the rebels were horrible enough, in any case, to arouse deep sympathies among Americans. The sufferings, moreover, were those of a neighbor, and they were incurred in a fight for independence from a manifestly unjust imperial ruler. Little more was required to whip up popular sympathy for the Cuban patriots and animus against Spain, especially in years when the public mind was as susceptible to jingoism as it had recently proved to be in far less serious disputes with Chile and Great Britain. Indications were abundant that influential Americans were "spoiling for a fight," and the Cuban junta that established itself in New York to dispense propaganda, solicit aid, and arouse sympathy was not without support.

One strong ally of the interventionists was the "yellow press" of New York City. Led by William Randolph Hearst's New York *Journal* and Joseph Pulitzer's New York *World,* which were currently engaged in a war for circulation, the press sent a corps of reporters and artists to cover the Cuban conflict and supply the papers with vivid human-interest stories and pictures. Waves of sympathy for the insurgents swept the country, but three years of sensationalism in the yellow press did not move the public to war with Spain.

American business leaders did not originally share the interventionist sentiment, though important segments of the business community became converts before the intervention. Protestant religious journals and both Republican and Democratic newspapers clamored loudly for intervention and war, though they insisted that they did so on purely humanitarian grounds and disclaimed any desire to annex Cuba or gain territory. Theirs was a moralistic aggression, with imperialism disavowed. Outright imperialists, including Roosevelt, Lodge, and Mahan, were also for war, but for the express purpose of conquest, expansion, and military glory. Two contrasting sets of aggressive impulses, both frustrated in the 1890s, sought outlet in an idealistic crusade for Cuban freedom. One set embraced the impulses of protest and humanitarian reform; the other embraced the impulses of national self-expression, aggressiveness, and expansion. The convergence of these two groups in support of intervention in Cuba goes far toward explaining why Americans worked themselves up into a mood for war with Spain.

American Intervention When Grover Cleveland was president, he had opposed intervention in Cuba on every front. He had resisted pressure from Congress to accord the insurgents belligerent rights, had sought to suppress gunrunning into Cuba from the States, and had tendered his good offices to Spain to settle the colonial war. In the summer of 1896, however, Cleveland underwent a change, and in his last annual message to Congress he came near to laying down a rationalization for America's intervention. McKinley tried to curb the jingoes and halt the drift to war, but a major concern of his was to maintain unity in a Republican party coalition divided over Cuban policy. Six months after he took office, a satisfactory settlement seemed to be in the making. A change of government in Spain brought in a prime minister who recalled General Weyler and offered Cuba a considerable measure of self-government in local affairs. The offer proved unacceptable, however, since the Spanish in Cuba opposed rule by native Cubans and the insurgents refused to settle for anything short of complete independence. Further hopes for a peaceful solution were disrupted by a series of fateful incidents, or accidents, that brought relations between the United States and Spain to the breaking point.

The first incident was the publication on February 9, 1898, of a stolen private letter from the Spanish minister in Washington, Dupuy de Lôme, who indiscreetly described President McKinley as "weak and a bidder for the admiration of the crowd" and said that the Cuban rebels should be suppressed by force. The tone of the letter suggested that Spain was not negotiating seriously. Dupuy de Lôme resigned before his government had time to respond to Washington's inevitable request for his recall. Then, six days later, the battleship *Maine,* recently dispatched to protect American residents in Havana and appease jingoes at home, blew up in Havana harbor with a loss of 260 officers and enlisted men. The Spanish government hastened to offer condolence and propose a joint investigation. An investigation by American naval officers reported that the *Maine's* bottom plates had been thrust inward, indicating an external explosion, but the cause of the tragedy was never discovered. It is highly improbable that the Spanish government would have plotted such an act, but the jingo press held Spain guilty and raised the cry "Remember the Maine!" Before the report of the *Maine* explosion was completed, Congress unanimously voted a defense appropriation of $50 million, and on March 19 Senator Redfield Proctor of Vermont delivered a speech painting the

The USS Maine, *1898*

shocking conditions he had found in Cuba during a recent unofficial visit. His calm tone, his reputation for moderation, and his matter-of-fact manner convinced many who had heretofore been skeptical of the lurid stories in the yellow press that action was indeed necessary.

On March 27, McKinley proposed to Spain a peaceful settlement in which it would abandon its reconcentration policy at once, grant an armistice until October 1, and enter into peace negotiations with the insurgents through his offices. He followed this proposal with a telegram apparently saying that independence would be the only satisfactory outcome of the peace negotiations. The American position was not stated with clarity. Spain was confronted with a cruel dilemma: If it rejected McKinley's demands it faced a disastrous war, and if it complied with them it faced a revolt that might overturn the government and possibly the throne. Spanish appeals for support from European powers won sympathy, but the only tangible response was a visit to President McKinley by the ambassadors of six powers who begged him not to intervene with armed force. Despairing of European aid, Spain replied on March 31 to McKinley's proposals by agreeing to abandon reconcentration and to grant an armistice upon the application of the insurgents. It did not promise Cuban independence but volunteered to submit to arbitration the question of who was responsible for sinking the *Maine*. Spain followed up on April 9 by declaring a suspension of hostilities on its own without waiting for the insurgents to take the initiative. The following day the American minister in Madrid cabled that he believed Cuban independence and a solution satisfactory to all could be worked out during the armistice.

Spain had gone far toward meeting the president's demands, but not so far as conceding independence. The president's insistence on this point made war inevitable. The day after receiving his minister's cable, April 11, McKinley sent a warlike message to Congress. He alluded in passing to Spain's concessions to American demands, but did not stress them. There was, it is true, ground for doubt that the Spanish government could make good its promises and evidence that it was stalling. Congress paused only to debate whether it should recognize the insurgent government as well as the independence of Cuba, decided on the latter only, and adopted the resolution on April 19 by a vote of 42 to 35 in the Senate and 311 to 6 in the House. An amendment to the resolution, which was prepared by Senator Henry M. Teller of Colorado and adopted at the same time without dissent, renounced any intention of annexing or governing Cuba and promised to "leave the government and control of the Island to its people." The Teller Amendment proclaimed American righteousness and abstention with respect to Cuba but, as the author of the resolution carefully pointed out, left the country a free hand "as to some other islands" that also belonged to Spain. Spain responded by declaring war on April 24, and Congress followed suit the next day.

The Little War Within ten weeks of the declaration of war, the fighting was over and the victory assured. For the country at large—and the readers of headlines in particular—it could not have been a more "splendid little war," as John Hay described it, or one conforming more completely with the romantic imagination of the budding imperialists. The whole war seemed to have been fought to the stirring music of "The Stars and Stripes Forever," the battle song of the war, played by a marine band in dress uniform. Even the participants chose to remember it in the manly prose of Richard Harding Davis or in the heroic sketches of Frederic Remington. The Spanish-American War was, in short, the most popular of all American wars. Disillusionment takes a bit of time, especially among noncombatants, and this war was over even before weariness could set in—save among combat troops.

The most hardened skeptics were thrown off balance, less than a week after the war started, by Commodore George Dewey's dazzling naval victory in Manila Bay on the opposite side of the globe (see Map 21-1). In accordance with a navy war plan of 1896, Dewey had been ordered two months earlier to move his squadron to Hong Kong and be prepared for action. On receiving news of the war and his final instructions, Dewey had immediately steamed out of Hong Kong, slipped through the straits of Boca Grande during the night of April 30, and at dawn opened fire on the weak and inferior Spanish squadron at Manila. Before breakfast, and without losing a man, he had sunk the whole fleet to the last of its ten ships. Dewey had crushed Spanish power in the Pacific.

Unfortunately the army was not as well prepared as the navy, but the public did not learn about that until later. The account of the expeditionary force to Cuba that the public read and gloried in was the sort supplied by the debonair reporter Richard Harding Davis:

> It was a most happy-go-lucky expedition, run with real American optimism and readiness to take big chances, and with the spirit of a people who recklessly trust that it will come out all right in the end, and that the barely possible may not happen. . . . As one of the generals on board said, "This is God Almighty's war, and we are only His agents."

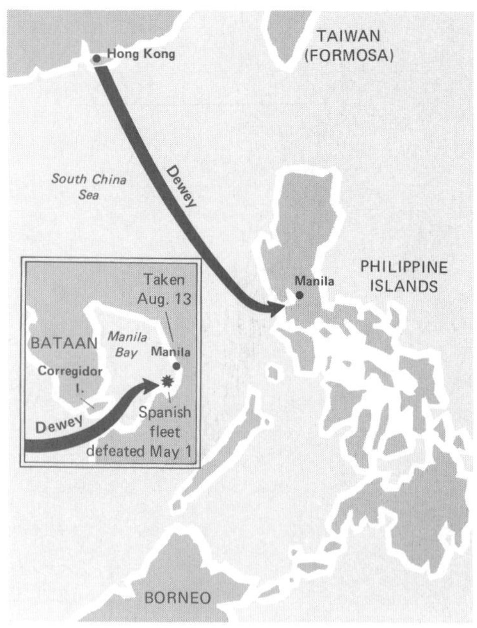

Map 21-1 *Dewey's campaign in the Pacific, 1898*

This was one way of putting it. At least Davis was accurate about the expedition's optimism and recklessness. The army, with only some 26,000 men at the start of the war, had no adequate plans, equipment, or supplies. The War Department was crippled by antiquated methods, incompetent administration, and years of neglect. General William R. Shafter, a 300-pound Civil War hero, presided over the chaos at Tampa preceding the embarkation of the expeditionary force. Transportation broke down and confusion reigned. Thousands of volunteers who rushed to the colors eager for glory could not be supplied with guns, tents, or blankets. With hopeless inefficiency they were clad in woolen uniforms for a summer campaign in the sweltering tropics. Food was inadequate, and sanitation was conspicuously wanting. Over the expeditionary force there spread the stench of dysentery and illness and eventually the horror of plague, the yellow jack. Newspapers exaggerated all this sensationally, and the public found a scapegoat in Secretary of War Russell A. Alger. General Nelson A. Miles broadcast the myth of "embalmed beef" on which his troops were allegedly poisoned. The great losses came *after* the war from malaria, typhoid, and yellow fever.

Fortunately the Spanish blundered even more badly than the Americans. Among other things they obligingly immobilized their Cuban naval power, a small force of four cruisers and three destroyers under the command of Admiral Pascual Cervera, in Santiago

Harbor, where it was immediately blockaded by a vastly superior fleet commanded by Admiral William T. Sampson. The blockade ended the threat to the landing of the expeditionary force, and after much backing and filling and countermanding of orders a force of some 18,000 regulars and volunteers got under way from Tampa, partly equipped and only partially trained. The most publicized unit of volunteers was the Rough Riders, commanded by Colonel Leonard Wood, who was loudly supported by Lieutenant Colonel Theodore Roosevelt, second in command. The landing force blundered slowly ashore on June 20 and established a beachhead at Daiquiri, a few miles east of Santiago (see Map 21-2).

Having some 200,000 troops in Cuba, the Spanish might have destroyed the Americans utterly. But they had only about 13,000 men at Santiago and were so handicapped in transportation that they could not bring their superior forces to bear and so unfortunate in military leadership that they could not employ what power they had at hand to their best advantage. Another handicap, of course, was a hostile population in rebellion. Even so they came near inflicting a disaster upon the invaders. The American objective was to capture the ridges, known as San Juan Hill, that dominated Santiago and then to take the town in whose harbor Admiral Cervera was blockaded. So poorly was the command organized, however, that the American units were largely without coordinated control in their attack. It was in the capture of Kettle Hill, a flanking outpost of San Juan Hill, that Theodore Roosevelt established his reputation for martial zeal and heroism. Later he was to describe the attack volubly and frequently as a "bully fight" that was "great fun," something of a rollicking skylark. Actually the fight, in which his was by no means the only part, was a pretty desperate and bloody affair marked by a great many needless casualties. The capture of the heights proved decisive in the land fighting, for Santiago was now closely invested. But the American troops were believed to be in a dangerous plight. On July 3 Roosevelt wrote Lodge, "We are within measurable distance of a terrible military disaster," in desperate need of reinforcements, food, and ammunition.

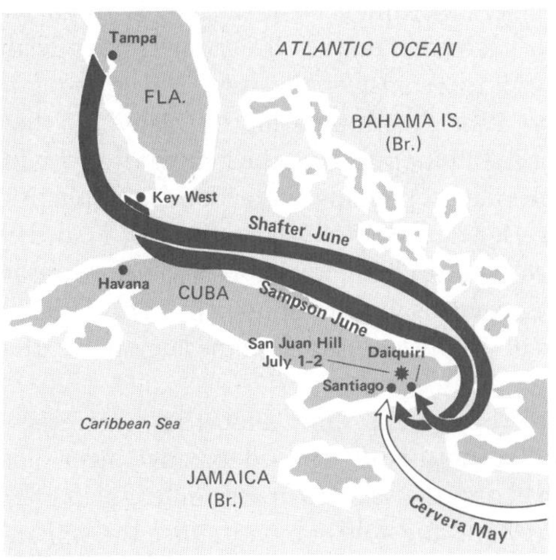

Map 21-2 *The Cuban campaign, 1898*

On that very morning, however, Admiral Cervera hoisted anchor and steamed out of Santiago Harbor to face his doom for the honor of Castile. He knew perfectly well that he was far outclassed and outgunned by the four United States battleships awaiting him just outside the harbor, but he gave battle rather than surrender without a fight. The American battle line opened up with its thirteen-inch guns, and one after another the Spanish ships went down gallantly, guns ablaze. It was all over in a few hours, with 400 enemy killed or wounded and with only one American killed. The next day was the Fourth of July, and orators had not had such an opportunity since the day after Gettysburg and Vicksburg.

Victory at sea left the Americans in command of Caribbean waters and rendered the besieged Spanish ashore in Santiago virtually powerless. General Shafter nevertheless decided to continue the siege rather than attempt assault. Meanwhile he quarrelled with the naval command over aid from the sea, waited for General Miles to bring up army reinforcements, and watched his troops deteriorate from heat, fever, and want of supplies. One very minor and indecisive battle, the last of the campaign, occurred on July 10–11, just before Miles arrived with reinforcements. Faced with inevitable defeat, the Spanish command agreed on July 16 to the terms of surrender, which included turning over nearly 24,000 prisoners to be shipped back to Spain by the Americans. It remained, however, to carry out the planned occupation of Puerto Rico by General Miles, who embarked from Cuba on July 21 on that mission.

The Puerto Rico operation came off far more smoothly and bloodlessly than the Cuban campaign. The island had not suffered the devastation that Cuba had experienced. The inhabitants readily collaborated with the invading forces, and native volunteers, who made up about half the Spanish garrison, deserted en masse. Augmented by a stream of reinforcements from the United States, Miles' army of 17,000 met little opposition. His campaign was well planned and aggressively conducted. By August 12, when an armistice ended the fighting, he had, with the loss of only four dead and some 40 wounded, overrun the island and isolated the only remaining armed resistance of consequence in the fort of San Juan.

While these operations were in progress in the Caribbean, American military forces were in action on the opposite side of the globe. Immediately after the news of Dewey's naval victory in Manila Bay, preparations were under way in Washington to dispatch army expeditionary forces for landing at Manila and reducing Spanish resistance ashore. There was never any question of ordering Dewey to withdraw without completing what he began. While he awaited arrival of the troops, warships of Germany, Britain, France, and Japan dropped anchor in Manila Bay to watch developments with interest. American troops first landed the last day of June and built up strength to take the fortified city. Their commanders avoided recognition of the insurgent Filipino forces under Emilio Aguinaldo, who rightly believed he was to be deprived of fruits of his previous victories over the Spanish. Outgunned on sea and land, the Spanish put up largely token resistance and, after a battle costing Americans 5 dead and 45 wounded, surrendered Manila and 13,000 troops on August 14.

Spain had sued for peace on July 18, but negotiations on the terms of an armistice were not concluded until August 12. The agreement finally dictated by President McKinley called for an immediate ceasefire, word of which did not reach Manila until after the battle. Spain gave up sovereignty over Cuba, leaving its fate to be settled by the Americans and the insurgents.

Filipino insurgents, 1899

The future of the Philippines was to be decided at a peace conference to meet in Paris on October 1, 1898.

THE WHITE MAN'S BURDEN

Mr. McKinley and His Decision The armistice deliberately left open the question of the disposition of the Philippine Islands. They had scarcely figured at all in the war motives of most Americans. To seize those possessions and to rule them by force without consent of their inhabitants would be to violate both the humanitarian motives that prompted the war and the oldest and profoundest American political traditions. Knowing these things in their hearts, whether they admitted them or not, the imperialist-minded minority scarcely dared hope at the onset of the war that their dreams would materialize. As it turned out they were on the eve of sensational success.

Hawaii was the first sign. In the spring before the war, a joint resolution for annexation gained strong support in Congress but was stalled in part by the crisis with Spain. But in the excitement of the Dewey and Sampson victories the traditional arguments were swept aside and the "large policy" of Hay, Lodge, Mahan, and Roosevelt prevailed. The New York *Tribune* maintained that Hawaii was "imperative" as a halfway station to the Philippines, and another expansionist argued later that the Philippines were imperative as an outpost for Hawaii. President McKinley gave strong support to annexation. On June 15 the House of Representatives, and on July 6 the Senate, adopted a joint resolution annexing Hawaii. The large policy was now on the way to further enlargement.

The enlargement was facilitated by the conscience of President McKinley. He advanced his insights in the form of such epigrams as, "Duty determines destiny," but he did not answer the New York *Evening Post's* query, "Who determines duty?" At any rate the destiny of the Philippines was becoming pretty manifest as McKinley's epigrams and actions multiplied. Even before Dewey's victory was confirmed, he ordered a force to capture and hold Manila, and before the end of May, Lodge was writing Roosevelt, "The Administration is now fully committed to the large policy that we both desire."

The commercial and industrial interests now helped swing the tide toward expansionism. Though they had opposed the war at first for fear of its effect on recovery and the gold standard, once the war started and news of the victories poured in and the potentialities of expansion for the advancement of trade became manifest, the business community swung about in support of the policies it had once opposed. Big business saw the Philippines as a key to the China trade and listened appreciatively to Senator Albert Beveridge's declaration that "the trade of the world must and shall be ours." Senator Marcus A. Hanna believed "we can and will take a large slice of the commerce of Asia. That is what we want."

At the same time the religious press, with the support of the missionary movement, stepped up support for the "imperialism of righteousness." Annexation would further the cause of world evangelization, extend the blessings of civilization and sanitation, and "civilize" more of the heathens. A more cynical approach to imperialism was that of editor Henry Watterson, who proposed to "escape the menace and peril of socialism and agrarianism" by means of "a policy of colonization and conquest." One popular way of thinking, however, was to attribute imperialism to a determinism of some sort: the hand of God, the instinct of race, the laws of Darwin, the forces of economics and trade—anything but responsible decision. Though many Americans seemed willing to surrender to imperialist policies, few would admit they did so because they wanted to.

McKinley revealed his intentions pretty clearly by the choice of commissioners he sent to negotiate with Spain at the peace conference held in Paris. Three of the five peace commissioners were open and avowed expansionists. Another indication was his seizure of Spain's island of Guam—whose inhabitants mistook the American bombardment for a salute and apologized for having no ammunition with which to return it. In his instructions to the peace commissioners, the president took the moral position that "without any desire or design on our part" the United States had assumed duties and responsibilities that it must discharge as became a nation of noble destiny. He instructed the commissioners in October with regard to the Philippines that "duty requires we should take the archipelago."

John Hay, who had recently become secretary of state, cabled the delegation in Paris to hold out for the whole of the Philippine Islands. The Spanish commissioners resisted the demand to the point of risking a renewal of hostilities. The talks continued for two months. McKinley stuck to his position that we should "not shirk the moral obligation of our victory" but made one concession, an offer to pay $20 million for the Philippines. The Spanish capitulated, and the treaty was signed December 10, 1898. By its terms Spain was to give up control over Cuba and surrender Guam, Puerto Rico, and the Philippine Islands to the United States.

There is little reason to doubt the sincerity of the reasons for his decision that the president offered a year later, though some critics have questioned his candor. The reasons he gave were that it would be cowardly and dishonorable to give the Philippines back to Spain, "bad business and discreditable" to let France or Germany seize them, impossible to leave them to their own devices since they were unfit for self-rule, and absolutely necessary to follow the humanitarian impulses to "civilize and Christianize" the Filipinos by taking possession of their land. What McKinley had in mind in his reference to the designs of European powers on the Philippines was that in November 1897, Germany landed troops at Kiaochow, and a Russian fleet anchored at Port Arthur. The following March the two European powers forced China to sign agreements giving Germany exclusive rights in Shantung province and Russia exclusive rights in Manchuria. Japan had occupied Korea, and France was established in Kwangchau Bay.

The Debate on the Philippines The treaty with Spain committed the United States to imperialism in the Orient and the Caribbean. But first the treaty had to be ratified by the Senate, and the question of ratification precipitated a debate that spread far beyond the Senate chamber and cast more light on the issues of annexation than had the president's speeches and the expansionists' slogans. After the drums of war were silenced and the people began to think more soberly, it became apparent that opposition to the president's policy was formidable, perhaps enough to defeat it. Far more opposition came from Democrats than from Republicans, and the sentiment was strong enough to unite even such Democratic extremes as Bryan and Cleveland. But prominent members of McKinley's own party broke with the administration over the question. To the very last it was doubtful whether the president could muster the two-thirds of the Senate required for consent to ratify his treaty.

Even before the treaty was signed an Anti-Imperialist league was organized that attracted the support of many distinguished men. For president, the league elected George S. Boutwell, formerly Grant's secretary of the Treasury and later Republican senator from Massachusetts. Among the vice presidents were such contrasting figures as Grover Cleveland and Samuel Gompers, Andrew Carnegie and Carl Schurz, John Sherman and Charles Francis Adams. Intellectuals, novelists, and poets rallied to anti-imperialism in

American Redemption of the World

God has not been preparing the English-speaking and Teutonic peoples for a thousand years for nothing but vain and idle self-admiration. No. He made us master organizers of the world to establish system where chaos reigned. He has given us the spirit of progress to overwhelm the forces of reaction throughout the earth. He has made us adept in government that we may administer government among savage and senile peoples. Were it not for such a force as this the world would relapse into barbarism and night. And of all our race He has marked the American people as His chosen nation to finally lead in the redemption of the world.

From Albert J. Beveridge, Speech in the U.S. Senate, 1900

great numbers, among them President Eliot of Harvard and President David Starr Jordan of Stanford, along with William James, William Dean Howells, William Graham Sumner, Hamlin Garland, William Vaughn Moody, and Mark Twain. In a bitter satire Mark Twain assured his compatriots that the "Blessings-of-Civilization Trust" had the purest of motives. "This world-girdling accumulation of trained morals, high principles, and justice cannot do an unright thing, an unfair thing, an ungenerous thing, an unclean thing," he wrote. "It knows what it is about. Give yourself no uneasiness; it is all right."

While the anti-imperialist movement failed to attract a large popular following, its spokesmen appeared in many parts of the country and appealed to the nation's oldest values and principles. George F. Hoar, a Republican of Massachusetts, led the fight against annexation of the Philippines in the Senate. He held that annexation would be a dangerous break with the past, turn a war of liberation into a war of conquest, and end one imperial rule by imposing another. George Boutwell foresaw a war with Japan as a consequence of American expansion in the western Pacific, and following that, the rise of a warlike China in potential alliance with Russia that would turn against American holdings. A favorite argument was based on the doctrine of the Declaration of Independence: no government without the consent of the governed. Other objections were that the Asiatic people could not be assimilated into our tradition, that imperialism would lead to militarism and racist dogma at home, that overseas expansion was unconstitutional and inconsistent with the Monroe Doctrine. Opponents of empire in the South and West never fully understood those in the Northeast. Southerners viewed the new imperialism as a revival of carpetbaggery and warned of the difficulties of reconciling races of contrasting color and heritage. Racist arguments were used both for and against imperialism, though mainly for it.

The imperialist-minded defenders of the treaty revived with new assurance their old arguments of naval strategy, world power, and commercial interests and incorporated the moralistic line of McKinley on duty, destiny, humanitarianism, and religious mission. In the latter vein Senator Beveridge declared, "It is God's great purpose made manifest in the instincts of our race, whose present phase is our personal profit, but whose far-off end is the redemption of the world and the Christianization of mankind." Senator Lodge dismissed the consent-of-the-governed argument as of no account. He exaggerated the supposed economic advantages of the Philippines — their resources, their trade, and he stressed the political expediency of keeping the islands — they were not ready for self-government, would lapse into anarchy, or would be seized by more ruthless powers.

Before the end of the debate, the anti-imperialists were confused by a strange maneuver and strategic blunder of William Jennings Bryan. Although he was a strong opponent of the acquisition of the Philippines, he decided that the Senate should approve the treaty to assure peace and should leave the future disposition of the islands to be decided at the polls. He undoubtedly believed that this move would provide him with a

American World Empire

The West Indies drift toward us, the Republic of Mexico hardly longer has an independent life, and the city of Mexico is an American town. With the completion of the Panama Canal all Central America will become part of our system. We have expanded into Asia, we have attracted the fragments of the Spanish dominions, and reaching out into China we have checked the advance of Russia and Germany. . . . We are penetrating into Europe, and Great Britain especially is gradually assuming the position of a dependency. . . . The United States will outweigh any single empire, if not all empires combined. The whole world will pay her tribute. Commerce will flow to her from both east and west, and the order which has existed from the dawn of time will be reversed.

From Brooks Adams, *The New Empire,* 1902

winning issue in the presidential election of 1900, but he miscalculated. Approval of the treaty presented the voters with a *fait accompli*. Bryan's advice won some Senate votes over to the side of the administration, though not enough to assure victory. On February 5, 1899, the very day before the final ballot was set, the drama of the decision was complicated and intensified by the arrival of news that the Filipinos had taken up arms in open revolt against the United States. There could be no more doubt of their desire for freedom or that the United States was now in the same position formerly occupied by discredited Spain. The effect of this news is impossible to estimate. The issue remained in doubt until the roll call the next day recorded 57 in favor of the treaty and 27 against—two more than the necessary two-thirds majority.

In the meantime, the American army remained in control of Cuba, and the government refused to withdraw until the Cubans incorporated into their constitution a permanent treaty with the United States, the so-called Platt Amendment, proposed by the United States Senate in 1901. This limited the power of Cuba to make treaties, borrow money, or change certain policies established by the occupation forces and required the sale or lease of lands for a naval base. More important, the United States was granted the right to intervene at will "for the preservation of Cuban independence" and "the protection of life, property, and individual liberty." Having no choice, Cuba submitted.

The motives that prompted America to "take up the white man's burden," as Rudyard Kipling had urged, were even more complex than the motives of the war that prepared the way for the decision. Part of the motivation was fear, the fear of appearing silly and playing the fool in the eyes of the world. Part of it was an uglier impulse of aggression. "The taste of empire is in the mouth of the people even as the taste of blood in the jungle," said the *Washington Post.*

Beyond the Philippines What the other great imperial powers of the world were currently doing to China was a cause more of alarm than of emulation. Even before the Cuban war, John Hay had pressed upon President McKinley the common interest of the United States and Great Britain in forestalling exclusion from the China trade. Now the trade opportunities promised in the Orient by the acquisition of Hawaii and the Philippines were threatened by the impending dissolution of China and its partition among imperial powers.

To meet the problem, Secretary Hay sent his "Open Door" notes to Great Britain, Germany, and Russia in September 1899 and later to Japan, Italy, and France, inviting them to agree to three principles: (1) that no power would interfere with the trading rights of other nations within its sphere of influence, (2) that Chinese tariff duties (which gave America most-favored-nation rights) should be collected on all merchandise by

Chinese officials, and (3) that no power should levy discriminatory harbor dues or railroad charges against other powers within its sphere. Great Britain agreed conditionally, Russia equivocated, and Germany, France, Italy, and Japan agreed on condition of full acceptance by the other powers. It was a chilling response, but Hay saved face by blandly announcing that since all powers agreed on the American proposals, their assent was considered "final and definitive." Since Russia had not agreed, and Britain only with conditions, and since the others made acceptance conditional on full acceptance by all powers, Hay's claims were not very impressive. His proposals at this point did not undertake to preserve the territorial integrity or independence of China.

In May 1900, two months after Hay announced his interpretation of the response to the Open Door notes, the Boxers, an organization of fanatical Chinese patriots, incited an uprising that took the lives of 231 foreigners and many Christian Chinese. In June the Boxers began the seige of the legations in Beijing (Peking) and cut the city off from the outside world for a month. The Western powers and Japan then sent in a military force, to which the United States contributed 5,000 troops. This expeditionary force relieved the besieged legations on August 4.

During the Boxer Rebellion crisis, Secretary Hay labored successfully to prevent the spread of war, limit the extent of intervention, assure the rapid withdrawal of troops, head off the extension of foreign spheres of influence, and keep down punitive demands on China. On July 3, 1900, Hay issued a circular stating it to be the policy of the United States "to seek a solution which may bring about permanent safety and peace to China, preserve Chinese territorial and administrative entity," and protect all trade rights mentioned in the Open Door notes in all parts of the empire. This was an important extension of American policy in the Orient. Although only Great Britain, France, and Germany responded favorably to Hay's circular, its effect was to help soften the punitive terms imposed on China. Unwilling to risk the general war that might be precipitated by a struggle to divide China, the intervening powers were persuaded to accept indemnity in money rather than territory. The United States' share of the reparations was $25 million, more than enough to settle the claims of its nationals. In fact, the United States returned a balance of more than $10 million, and the Chinese government, as a gesture of gratitude, placed the money in trust for the education of Chinese youth in their own country and in the United States.

McKinley's Vindication of 1900 It was Bryan's mistake, in planning to make the election of 1900 a popular referendum on imperialism, to believe that the anti-imperialist sentiment of the great debate of 1898–99 could be sustained or even revived, much less strengthened. Nearly two years were to pass between the ratification of the treaty and the presidential election, and by that time much water had passed under the bridge. Empire was no longer a dangerous menace to tradition and a decision that had to be worried out. It was an accomplished fact to which the people were growing accustomed. They did not like the war that was being waged to suppress Emilio Aguinaldo and his Filipino patriots, even though censorship kept some of its worst aspects from them. Yet American troops on the other side of the globe were, with rifle and bayonet, fully engaged in forcing the most Christian people in all Asia to be "uplifted and Christianized." That war was to drag on for three years, during which the United States was to use more men to deny freedom in the Philippines than it had used to bring freedom to Cuba. And the new American rulers were to repeat in grotesque imitation the tortures and brutalities of their Spanish predecessors. But all that was taking place on the other side of the widest of oceans. When pressed, people admitted, "Peace has to be restored."

At home there were plenty of distractions to divert a burdensome conscience. The most important one was the gradual return to prosperity. The war itself served as an additional stimulus. Business regained its nerve, trade quickened, and the economy bustled into activity.

As the farmers and laborers sloughed off the burden of depression, their radicalism declined. The new imperialism and patriotism also had a dampening effect on radicalism in labor and agrarian movements. "The Spanish War finished us," wrote Tom Watson of the Populist party. "The blare of the bugle drowned the voice of the reformer." The war, coupled with returning prosperity, mounting racism, and the legacy of the Populists' demoralizing fusion with Bryanism in 1896 (see p. 532), did just about finish the party. In the 1900 campaign it split into two feuding factions, neither of which could make a substantial showing. Many of the Populists of the Southwest and Middle West were attracted to the new Social Democratic party, which was founded in 1900 and nominated Eugene V. Debs of Pullman-strike fame as its presidential candidate.

Although McKinley's policies had little to do with the revival of the economy, he was billed as "the advance agent of prosperity," and he prospered politically with the return of good times. With a Cabinet that was even more conservative than he was himself, McKinley's first administration had proved as willing and cooperative as the business community could have hoped. The Dingley Tariff of 1897 raised the rates to a new high, and the gold standard was now safe.

The presidential nominees of the two major parties in 1900 were pretty much a foregone conclusion. The Republicans had no hesitation about McKinley, but only with some difficulty did they settle upon the military hero and New York governor, Theodore Roosevelt for vice president. The Democrats returned to Bryan and picked the silverite Adlai E. Stevenson, who had been vice president during Cleveland's second term, for second place. The Democratic platform stressed imperialism as the "paramount issue" and on Bryan's insistence revived the demand for free silver. His strategy of uniting silverites of West and South with gold men of the Northeast in a coalition against imperialism came to grief. Bryan soon discovered that he had two fairly moribund issues on his hands and therefore shifted his emphasis to monopoly and special privilege.

Bryan, in a poorer showing than he had made in 1896, lost his own state of Nebraska, as well as Kansas, South Dakota, Utah and Wyoming—all silver states he had carried before. The election neither revived the silver issue nor provided a mandate on imperialism. Even if the voters opposed imperialism, they could express their disapproval only by voting against prosperity. Republican leaders acknowledged that Americans had lost their appetite for further colonial expansion. To the majority of voters in 1900, McKinley meant prosperity rather than imperialism or gold, and with him conservatism was triumphant once more.

SUGGESTIONS FOR READING

C. S. Campbell, *The Transformation of American Foreign Relations, 1865–1900* (1976), is a readable and reliable narrative. R. W. Rydell, *All the World's a Fair: Visions of Empire at American International Expositions, 1876–1910* (1985), and J. M. Dobson, *America's Ascent: The United States Becomes a Great Power, 1880–1914* (1978) provide broad perspectives. More briefly, R. L. Beisner, *From the Old Diplomacy to the New, 1865–1900* (1986), assesses conflicting interpretations, and M. B. Young, *American Expansionism: The Critical Issues* (1973), assembles and edits key interpretive essays. Scholarly controversy over expansionism has been shaped by A. K. Weinberg, *Manifest Destiny: A Study in Nationalist Expansionism in American History* (1935), and J. W. Pratt, *Expansionists of 1898: The Aquisition of Hawaii and the Spanish Islands* (1936). Economic influences are debated by W. Le Feber, *The New Empire: An Interpretation of American Expansion, 1860–1898* (1963); W. A. Williams, *The Tragedy of American Diplomacy* (rev. ed., 1972); E. R. May, *American Imperialism: A Speculative Essay* (1968); and D. F. Healy, *U.S. Expansionism: Imperialist Urge in the 1890s* (1970).

More specific aspects of foreign affairs are treated by D. M. Pletcher, *The Awkward Years: American Foreign Relations under Garfield and Arthur* (1962); J. A. S. Grenville and G. B. Young, *Politics, Strategy, and American Diplomacy: Studies in Foreign Policy, 1873–1917* (1966); C. S. Campbell, *Anglo-American Understanding, 1898–1903* (1957); M. Plesur, *America's Outward Thrust: Approaches to Foreign Affairs, 1865–1890* (1971), takes a wider look. Hawaiian relations are treated by W. A. Russ, Jr., *The Hawaiian Republic (1894–98) and the Struggle to Win Annexation* (1961), and T. J. Osborne, *Empire Can Wait: American Opposition to Hawaiian Annexation, 1893–1898* (1981).

On the Spanish-American War, the most complete account is D. R. Trask, *The War with Spain in 1898* (1981), and a shorter account is H. W. Morgan, *America's Road to Empire: The War with Spain and Overseas Expansion* (1965). Contrasting treatments are found in E. R. May, *Imperial Democracy: The Emergence of America as a Great Power* (1961), and P. S. Foner, *The Spanish-Cuban-American War and the Birth of American Imperialism, 1895–1902,* 2 vols. (1972). Military history is enriched by G. A. Cosmas, *An Army for Empire: The United States Army in the Spanish-American War* (1971), and S. C. Miller, *Benevolent Assimilation: American Conquest of the Philippines* (1982). Naval aspects are treated in R. S. West, Jr., *Admirals of the American Empire* (1948). M. Leech, *In the Days of McKinley* (1959), throws light on the war as well as the election of 1900. On the influence of newspapers, see C. H. Brown, *Correspondents' War: Journalists in the Spanish-American War* (1967), and J. E. Wisan, *The Cuban Crisis as Reflected in the New York Press, 1895–1898* (1934).

Oriental affairs are handled in M. B. Young, *Rhetoric of Empire: American China Policy, 1895–1901* (1968), and T. J. McCormick, *China Market: America's Quest for Informal Empire, 1893–1901* (1967). On the opposition to American imperialism, see R. L. Beisner, *Twelve Against Empire: The Anti-Imperialists, 1898–1900* (1968); E. B. Tompkins, *Anti-Imperialism in the United States: The Great Debate, 1890–1920* (1970); and R. E. Welch, Jr., *Response to Imperialism: The United States and the Philippine-American War, 1899–1902* (1982). A look ahead is in W. Cohen, ed., *New Frontiers in American East Asian Relations* (1986).

CHAPTER TWENTY-TWO

HESTER STREET, NEW YORK, 1899

The Progressive Movement and the Square Deal

When the twentieth century began, the prodigious material developments of the preceding several decades (see Chapter 18) had transformed society. Yet almost all of those in positions of authority or influence in government, industry, the professions, even labor and farm organizations had been born during the years before the Civil War when the United States was still primarily a rural country. By 1901 the nation had changed profoundly, as had its problems, which were often perplexing to men and women who had grown up in an earlier age. Some Americans were nostalgic for that past as they remembered it. Others rejoiced in modernity but were eager to control its course and effects. Both of those attitudes pointed, though in different ways, to the desirability, even the exigency, of altering conditions as they had become.

As Americans were increasingly aware, they had yet to accommodate to the social and cultural changes stimulated by industrial and urban growth. They had yet to adjust their laws and their techniques of government to an age of large and complex private organizations. Americans had yet to recognize the international implications of their national wealth. They had yet to fulfill their national promise of individual liberty, opportunity, and dignity for all men and women.

The unprecedented productivity of the economy made comfort potentially available to all Americans. That possibility in turn highlighted the striking contrasts between the few and the many, the white-skinned and the dark, the urban and the rural—the striking contrast between national aspiration and national achievement. Out of an awareness of that contrast, out of the tensions of material development, out of a consciousness of national mission, there emerged the efforts at adjustment and reform that constituted the progressive movement, a striving by men and women of goodwill to understand, improve, and manage the society in which they lived.

National Wealth and the Business Elite

During the first two decades of the twentieth century, the number of people in the United States, their average age, and their average per capita wealth all increased. In that period total national income almost doubled, and average per capita income rose from $450 to $567 a year. Though by the standards of the 1990s about 40 percent of Americans were then poor, growth in and of itself gave confidence to a generation who tended to measure progress in terms of plenty.

There were some 76 million Americans in 1900, some 106 million in 1920 (see Maps 22-1 and 22-2). Advances in medicine and public health, resulting in a declining death rate, accounted for most of the increase. It was accompanied by a continuing movement of people within the United States. In the West the rate of growth was highest—along the Pacific slope, population more than doubled. But growth occurred everywhere, especially in the cities, where it proceeded six and a half times as fast as in rural areas. The cities, in the pattern of the past (see pp. 488–90), absorbed thousands of rural folk as well as almost all of the 14.5 million immigrants who came largely from central and southern Europe in the years 1900–15. Usually swarthy and often unlettered, ordinarily Catholics or Jews, these newcomers differentiated the cities further and further from the patterns of life that rural America remembered and revered. By 1920 more Americans lived in cities and towns of over 2,500 people than in the countryside.

Spurred by the pace of private investment, the nation recovered from the depression of the 1890s. During the first two decades of the century, capital investment rose over 250 percent and the total value of the products of industry rose 222 percent. But not all groups shared equally in national wealth. Though unemployment became negligible, the richest 2 percent of Americans in 1900 owned 60 percent of the nation's wealth, a condition that persisted with little change for two decades.

Those families were at once the agents and the beneficiaries of the process of industrial expansion and consolidation. Corporate mergers and reorganizations had given a dominant influence to a few huge combinations in each of many industries—among others, railroading, iron and steel and copper, meat packing, milling, tobacco, electricals, petroleum, and, by 1920, automobiles. As early as 1909, 1 percent of all the business firms in the nation produced 44 percent of all its manufactured goods. The consolidators had become the richest and in some ways the most powerful men in the United States. They guided the process of investment. They controlled the boards of directors of the great American banks and industries. They interpreted the startling growth of industry as a demonstration of their own wisdom and their optimism about the economic future of the United States. Beyond all that, they were developing, as were the experts whom they hired and consulted, an identification with the entirety of the national economy—the enormous national market, the need for national corporate institutions to reach it, the consequent need for energetic, professional management on a vast scale. Those insights contrasted with the parochialism of smaller

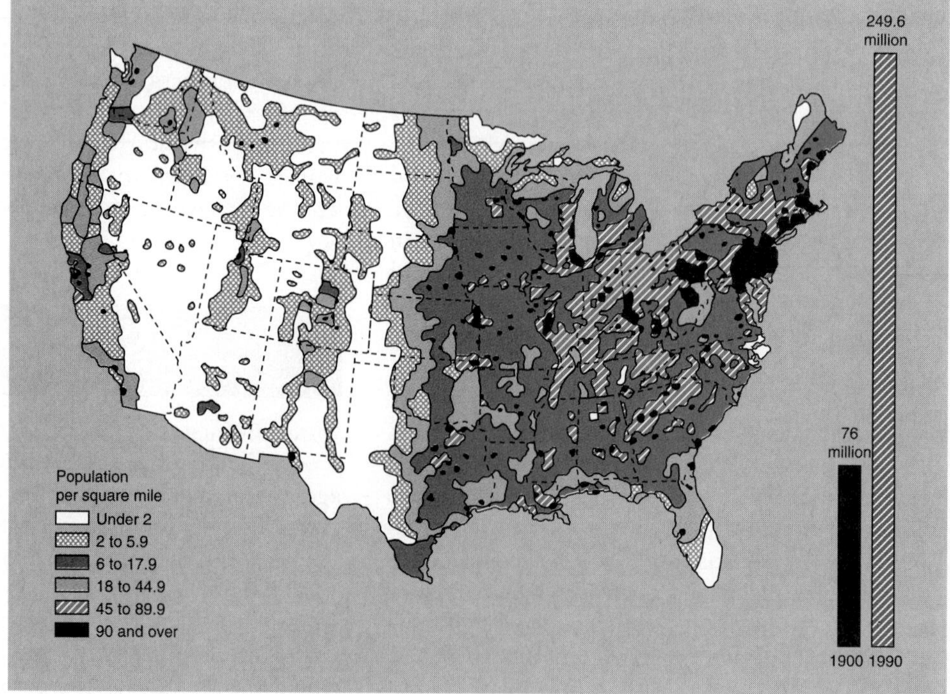

Map 22-1
Population 1900

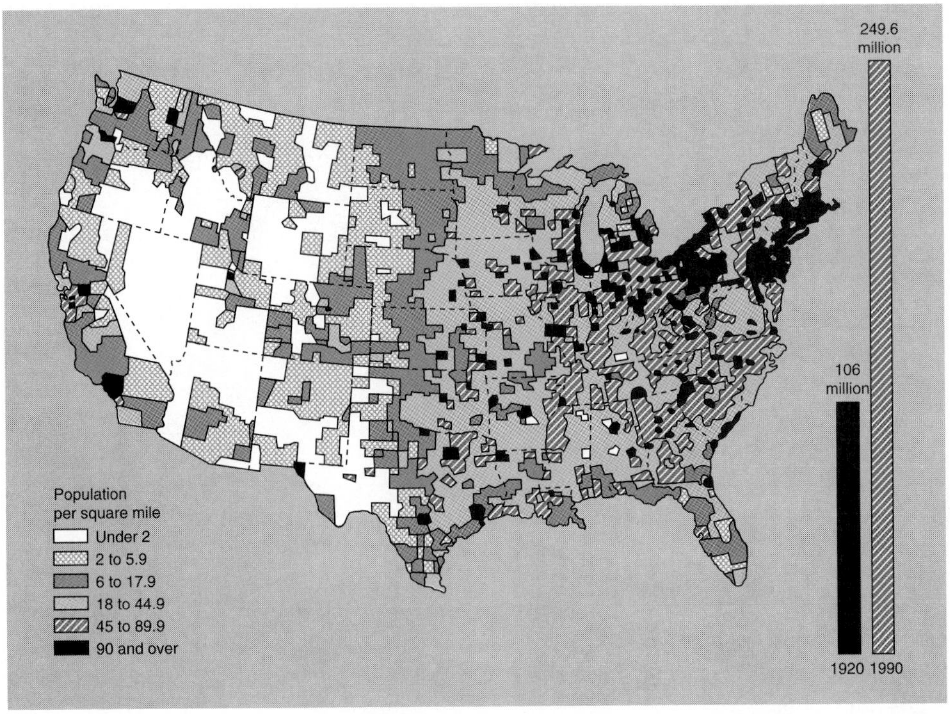

Map 22-2
Population 1920

institutions and of rural America, and with the traditional (and rewarding) faith of the American folk in their own ability to run their affairs and in their own local institutions. The growth of the great corporations raised questions about scale and control as troublesome as were the questions raised by the related problems of poverty and wealth.

The "Leaden-Eyed" The magnificence of American wealth contrasted sharply with the sorry lot of the American poor, whom society, as the poet Vachel Lindsay put it, had made "oxlike, limp, and leaden-eyed." In 1910 the nonagricultural laboring force consisted of more than 30 million men and 8 million women, most of whom worked too long and earned too little. Between one-third and one-half of the industrial population lived in poverty. Their children ordinarily left school to find work—only one-third of the American children enrolled in primary schools completed their courses; less than one-tenth finished high school.

Work for men, women, and children was arduous. Those engaged in manufacturing were on the job between 44 and 55 hours a week—on the average more than 52 hours. Industrial accidents were common and conditions of work unhealthy and sometimes despicable. Usually workers had to suffer their disasters alone. Employer-liability laws, where they existed, were inadequate. There was no social insurance against accident, illness, old age, or unemployment, nor were there child-care centers where women workers could safely leave their children. Indeed child labor remained common throughout the country. And the slums, where most workers lived, were as bad as they had been in the 1890s.

New kinds of mobile slums were developing, the slums of migratory workers—some immigrants, including Asians, some Native Americans, some black workers, and Chicanos. Many were leaving submarginal small farms to follow the wheat harvest north from Texas or to pick fruits and vegetables along the West Coast. So, too, the mining and lumbering camps of the South and West offered to workers only a life of drudgery, brutality, danger, and poverty. Life was equally dreary for the thousands of Chinese, Japanese, Koreans, and Filipinos who worked on the sugar plantations of Hawaii.

Complacency and Dissent The inequities in American society evoked a variety of responses ranging from the complacent to the outraged. Most of the well-to-do—the business élite and the professional men who

Young miners

identified with them and served them—believed as they long had that success was a function of virtue and poverty evidence of sin. As the century turned, they were satisfied with existing conditions, and they remained fixed in their belief in minimal government. Other self-respecting men and women of the comfortable middle class harbored some anxieties about their own futures but few doubts about the merit of American institutions.

But a minority alike of the rich and of the comfortable were receptive to the messages of protest and the efforts at particular social remedy that characterized the early years of the new century. That receptivity reflected in part a dread of drastic change and of the kind of radical agitation that had punctuated the 1890s. Reform, in that view, was preferable to revolution. Further, the center of American consciousness was slowly acquiring a new conscience. It produced a growing understanding of the efforts of some of the less privileged to improve their lot, a sympathy for the protests of the best informed against the inequities of American life, and, though rarely, a tolerance for the outrage of that small minority of Americans who were committed to rapid and radical social improvement.

Organized Labor The craft-union movement, well launched in the 1890s, made significant gains during the early years of the twentieth century. Membership in the affiliates of the American Federation of Labor (AFL) rose from 548,000 in 1900 to 1,676,000 in 1904 and, in the face of strong resistance from employers, to about 2,000,000 by 1914, though even then some 90 percent of industrial workers remained unorganized. The unions and the railroad brotherhoods continued to strive for the bread-and-butter objectives Samuel Gompers and their other leaders had defined earlier. Especially in the building and

Poverty and Death

Poverty and Death are grim companions. Wherever there is much poverty the death-rate is high and rises higher with every rise of the tide of want and misery. . . . In Chicago, the death rate varies from about twelve per thousand in the wards where the well-to-do reside to thirty-seven per thousand in tenement wards. The ill-developed bodies of the poor, underfed and overburdened with toil, have not the powers of resistance to disease possessed by the bodies of the more fortunate. . . . As we ascend the social scale the span of life lengthens and the death-rate gradually diminishes, the death-rate of the poorest class of workers being three and a half times as great as that of the well-to-do. . . . The difference in the death-rate of the various social classes is even more strongly marked in the case of infants.

From John Spargo, *The Bitter Cry of the Children,* 1906

metals trades, they were able to win from management agreements providing for collective bargaining, higher wages, shorter hours, and safer conditions of work.

The craft unions were effective but in some respects selfish agencies of change. Though they excited opposition from business managers not yet prepared to grant labor any voice in industrial decisions, they had little quarrel with the concentration of industrial power. The American Federation of Labor did demand the right to organize workers into national trade unions, consolidations that would parallel the consolidations of capital. In order to organize, labor needed to be unshackled from state and federal prohibitions on the strike and the boycott—and needed, too, state and federal protection from anti-union devices. The unions welcomed legislation setting standards of safety and employer liability, but otherwise they preferred to rely on their own power, rather than on the authority of the state, to reach their goals. They continued to distrust the federal government, for it had so often in the past assisted in breaking strikes, and they were eager to enlarge their own power even at the expense of those they had no intention of organizing. So it was that Gompers and his associates persisted in opposing legislation on wages and hours.

Collective bargaining, even when possible, assisted only union members, and the craft unions were generally unconcerned with the unskilled bulk of the labor force. Indeed, Gompers, along with other labor leaders, looked down on the unskilled, particularly on those who were women or immigrants. Craft leaders feared that management would hire unskilled and unorganized immigrants and black laborers to replace skilled workers (though in fact skilled workers were competing less with the unskilled than with an advancing technology and mechanization). This fear intensified prejudices against Asians, black Americans, and southern and eastern Europeans—prejudices that fed growing sentiments for the restriction of immigration and for racial segregation. Organized labor condoned Jim Crow and sparked the agitation that led in 1902 to the renewed exclusion from the United States of Chinese immigrants and in 1907 to the effective exclusion of the Japanese.

Outsiders Scorned alike by management and by the unions, the immigrants swelling the American labor force had to learn to help themselves. They continued, as in earlier decades, to receive unsystematic assistance in finding employment from urban political machines eager for their votes. Further, each new wave of immigration brought to the United States candidates

Workers

In this community of workers several thousand human beings were struggling fiercely against want. . . . They toiled with marvellous persistency. . . . On cold, rainy mornings, at the dark of dawn, I have been awakened . . . by the monotonous clatter of hobnailed boots on the plank sidewalks, as the procession to the factory passed. . . . Heavy, brooding men, tired, anxious women, thinly dressed, unkempt little girls, and frail, joyless little lads passed along, half awake, not one uttering a word. . . . From all directions thousands were entering the various gates,—children of every nation of Europe. Hundreds of others—obviously a hungrier, poorer lot . . . waited in front of a closed gate until . . . a . . . man came out and selected twenty-three of the strongest. . . . For these the gates were opened, and the others, with down-cast eyes, marched off to seek employment elsewhere. . . . In this community . . . fully fifty thousand men, women and children were all the time either in poverty or on the verge of poverty. It would not be possible to describe how they worked and starved and ached to rise out of it.

From Robert Hunter, *Poverty*, 1904

for the meanest jobs. Their availability permitted their predecessors to climb a notch higher in the hierarchy of the workplace. So it was during the first decade of the century in the needle trades in New York City where men and women from southern Italy took over some of the underpaid and arduous piece work that had fallen in the 1890s to eastern European Jews who moved up to become cutters or other skilled workers with accompanying increases in pay. The experience of those immigrant Jews revealed the need of every immigrant group to organize for its own self-protection and mutual benefit. The Jewish families in New York were able to survive financially only if wives and sometimes children added their earnings to those of husbands and fathers, and to survive emotionally only because of the support they derived from their culture and their community. Their language and religion set them apart, to be sure, but also provided them with a world of their own in which in time they could begin to prosper. Their own unions, especially the International Ladies' Garment Workers Union (ILGWU), fought for their rights. They provided their own theater, their own literature, and gradually their own bourgeoisie. Though they also learned older American ways, they were one part of a pluralistic society in which other cultures also flourished.

In New York City, as elsewhere, that was the aspiration, too, of Italians, Poles, Greeks, Bohemians, Chinese, Japanese, and others, outsiders all, whose labor drove American shops and factories to ever higher levels of production and profit. The large majority of workers needed extraordinary courage and stamina to face the toil, the poverty, and the prejudice of a society eager to use but loath to include them.

Americans of Color Within that majority were Japanese, Chinese, and Korean immigrants who were denied the chance to become citizens by the Naturalization Act of 1790, which limited that right to persons who were "white." Asian immigrants were also targets of race prejudice of particular severity on the West Coast. The children of those immigrants, citizens by virtue of their birth in the United States, suffered along with their parents. Segregated in communities of their own, Asians and Asian-Americans, with few exceptions, could find only marginal employment. That was true also of Hispanic-Americans, most of them agricultural workers in the Southwest.

There were 10 million black Americans, of whom almost 90 percent still lived in the South. In 1910 almost a third of them were still illiterate. All were victimized by the inferior facilities for schooling, housing, traveling, and working that segregation had imposed upon them. Worse still, the incidence of lynchings (over 1,100 between 1900 and 1914) and race riots remained high, dramatized by mass killings in Atlanta in 1906 and by riots in Abraham Lincoln's own Springfield, Illinois, in 1908. As racist concepts spread in the North as well as the South, American blacks experienced their worst season since the Civil War. A few black intellectuals, led by W. E. B. DuBois, a Harvard Ph.D., in 1905 organized the Niagara movement. Abandoning the program of Booker T. Washington, DuBois and his associates demanded immediate action to achieve political and economic equality for black Americans. With some support from informed white sympathizers, the Niagara movement was transformed in 1909 into the National Association for the Advancement of Colored People. But the NAACP, though a hopeful portent for legal redress of black grievances, was some years from becoming an influential instrument of reform.

American Women With varying success women, too, intensified their struggle for political, economic, and social status equal to that of men. Sarah Platt Decker, president of the General Federation of Women's Clubs, converted the energies of that middle-class organization to agitation for improving the conditions of industrial work for women and children (see p. 495). That was also the objective of the Women's Trade Union League and Florence Kelley's National Consumers' League, which sponsored state legislation for minimum wages and maximum hours. In New York City, the International Ladies' Garment Workers Union, financed in part by wealthy matrons, conducted a prolonged strike in 1909 that won limited gains in spite of opposition from employers and police. The Triangle Shirtwaist Company in New York City did not agree to the union's demand for better wages or for safer conditions of work. The company's stubborn parsimony accounted for the tragedy that occurred in 1911 when fire broke out on its premises and resulted in the death of 146 employees, mostly young women, who could not escape from the building. Official investigations following the episode led ultimately to new factory laws and immediately to broader support for the ILGWU, which by 1914 had become the third-largest union in the AFL.

The contributions of women to various movements for social justice demonstrated their creative and organizational abilities, abilities that most Americans—men and women alike—still viewed as inferior to those of men. But women, though exploited by

For the rights of working women

Social Feminism

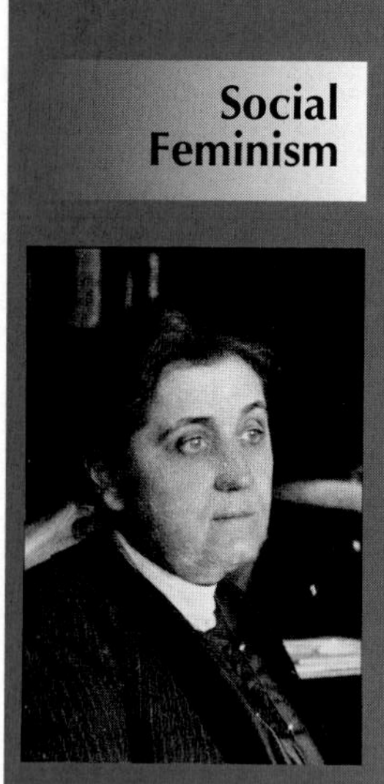

The new demand of women for political enfranchisement comes at a time when unsatisfactory and degraded social conditions are held responsible for so much wretchedness and when the fate of all the unfortunate, the suffering, and the criminal, is daily forced upon woman's attention in painful and intimate ways. At the same moment, governments all over the world are insisting that it is their function, and theirs alone, so to regulate social and industrial conditions that a desirable citizenship may be secured. . . .

Governmental commissions everywhere take woman's testimony as to legislation for better housing, for public health and education, for the care of dependents, and many other remedial measures, because it is obviously a perilous business to turn over delicate social experiments to men who have remained quite untouched by social compunctions and who have been elected to their legislative position solely upon the old political issues. Certainly under this new conception of politics it is much easier to legislate for those human beings of whose condition the electorate are "vividly aware."

From Jane Addams, "The Larger Aspects of the Woman's Movement," 1914

industry, were by no means inferior. To put a stop to the exploitation, social feminists sponsored special factory laws to protect women from hazardous conditions and overlong hours of work. Dr. Alice Hamilton, an advocate of many women's causes, pioneered the study of industrial diseases of men and women alike. Social feminists often contended that women needed special care because they were physically frailer than men. But no man worked as hard or accomplished as much for the settlement house movement in the United States as did Jane Addams at Hull House in Chicago or Lillian Wald at Henry Street in New York. Indeed, those extraordinary women trained a younger generation, both men and women, to understand the problems of poverty and to combat the circumstances that caused them.

Women also served among the officers and troops in the wars against prostitution and whiskey. The Women's Christian Temperance Union, strongest in rural America, was an unequaled force in the growing demand for the prohibition of the manufacture and sale of alcoholic beverages. Prohibition, an issue of continuing political importance during the first three decades of the twentieth century, aligned (with exceptions of course) rural, native-born, fundamentalist Americans against their urban, immigrant, Catholic compatriots. Yet in cities as well as small towns, women expressed a special interest in protecting families against the profligacy of alcoholic breadwinners, and most urban prohibitionists came to view their objective as a scientifically valid effort to improve human life by controlling part of it. If they were naive about the ability of the state to govern private behavior, they were more sophisticated than their critics realized in their recognition of the dangers of addiction to any drug, alcohol included.

It was primarily urban women who absorbed the more unconventional messages of Charlotte Perkins Gilman, Emma Goldman, and Margaret Sanger. Gilman, eager to free women from the burdens and constraints of rearing a family and caring for a house, proposed communal arrangements for child care and domestic chores. She influenced fewer women than did Goldman and Sanger, who had begun to advocate free and open instruction in birth control. Birth control, they argued, by gradually reducing the size of the

The Woman's Movement

The woman's movement rests not alone on her larger personality, with its tingling sense of revolt against injustice, but on the wide, deep sympathy of women for one another. It is a concerted movement, based on the recognition of a common evil and seeking a common good. . . .

In our present stage of social evolution it is increasingly difficult and painful for women to endure their condition of economic dependence, and therefore they are leaving it. This does not mean that at a given day all women will stand forth free together, but that in slowly gathering numbers, now so great that all the world can see, women in the most advanced races are so standing free. . . .

The banner advanced proclaims "equality before the law," woman's share in political freedom, but the main line of progress is and has been toward economic equality and freedom.

From Charlotte Perkins Gilman, *Women and Economics,* 1898

working force, would soon enhance the ability of laborers to bargain with capitalists. Interest in birth control, however, spread largely among women who recognized the physical, social, and psychological advantages of family planning and who were eager to be freed from the demands of the ordinary American home. Under their auspices, the National Birth Control League (NBCL) in 1915 began its attempt through education and lobbying to effect the repeal of state and federal laws that forbade as obscene the dissemination of information about birth control. But like the NAACP, the NBCL was still many years from becoming an effective political force.

The effectiveness of women as individuals—more and more, for example, were attending college and entering the professions of law and medicine—was matched by the effectiveness of the collective demand for women's suffrage. In the second decade of the new century the suffrage movement gained strength under the quiet leadership of Carrie Chapman Catt, president of the American Women's Suffrage Association, and Alice Paul, the more militant head of the new Congressional Union. In 1914 the General Federation of Women's Clubs at last enlisted its significant support for the cause, which was also attracting more and more of those many men who, eager to democratize voting, saw women's suffrage as one part of their program. Indeed, suffrage as an issue came to absorb much of the energy of feminism, to stand out as the central goal of American women. Between 1910 and 1914 they won the ballot in six states and were moving close to the national victory they sought.

PROTEST AND REFORM

Prosperous Farmers The new century brought unparalleled prosperity to American farmers. As domestic and world markets revived, the prices of farm products and the value of farm land just about doubled within a decade. The farmer was still suspicious of bankers, of industry and middlemen, of cities and foreigners. But prosperity tempered farmers' hostilities, softened their rhetoric, turned them from outright attack to flanking maneuvers by which they sought to procure for themselves a larger share both of urban culture and comforts and of the business profits of agriculture.

Suffrage: central goal of American women

Farm organizations continued to press for political reforms designed to give voters a stronger and more direct voice in government. The reforms, they hoped, would help them obtain public policies that would aid agriculture—better roads and marketing facilities, cheaper credit, technical advice on planting and cultivation, more and cheaper electric power, assistance to cooperatives, lower taxes on land, and tariff adjustments that would facilitate sales abroad. Those practical goals, some of which entailed special privileges for farmers, challenged the special privileges and the superior power big business had long enjoyed.

In Washington, farm spokespeople continued to urge the creation of agencies to monitor the growth and the practices of the great consolidations. Reflecting the agrarian bias against monopoly, they also urged the enforcement of the languishing antitrust laws. Some farm leaders believed that federal programs of assistance should extend to labor. Thus the objectives of farm politics sometimes merged with the objectives of urban reformers.

Radical Critics But little remained of the agrarian radicalism of the 1890s and less of anarchism, which had begun to decline as a cult before the assassination of McKinley revived old, middle-class fears for the safety of the Republic. The radicalism of the early century took other forms.

Socialism consistently gained adherents, especially in the cities, though strong groups flourished for a time in the Southwest and in the Rocky Mountain states. Most socialists were not proletarians but middle-class, sometimes even quite comfortable, native Americans, though another influential group consisted of New York Jewish immigrants. Intellectuals like Max Eastman and John Reed gave to the Socialist party a brilliant style but recruited few followers. Moderate party leaders like Morris Hillquit in New York and Victor Berger in Milwaukee stood for peaceful, democratic means to effect reform and gradually acquire for the state private means of production, beginning with natural monopolies in such industries as transportation, communications, and utilities. Their program had only a limited appeal to American workers. Most of them still harbored some faith in the American dream of success, at least for their children, and skilled workers identified their interests not with socialist doctrines but with the strategy of trade unionism.

Eugene V. Debs, the engaging head of the Socialist party and its continual candidate for president, employed a stirring rhetoric that mixed Jeffersonian and Marxist principles. But even he was no revolutionary. Nor were the almost 1 million Americans who supported him in 1912, the year of the party's largest vote. Further, Debs stood with the moderates in 1913 in expelling from the party's national executive committee "Big Bill" Haywood, who at times advocated industrial sabotage and revolution.

In 1905 Haywood and others had founded the Industrial Workers of the World (IWW) the "Wobblies." Determined to organize the most destitute Americans — itinerant farm workers, Western miners (many of whom were immigrants), the primarily immigrant textile workers of the Northeast, and others whom the AFL ignored — the IWW unhesitatingly employed the strike to obtain recognition of industrial unions (unions of all employees in a plant or mine regardless of skills). The industrial union had earlier support from the Knights of Labor and the American Railway Union, and later was advanced by the Congress of Industrial Workers (CIO) of the 1930s. But the AFL preferred trade unions, objected to any dual unionism — that is, to competition between unions for membership — and feared the IWW would give all labor a bad name. IWW rhetoric suggested sympathy for recourse to violence, though the violence of IWW strikes arose largely because of the force with which management resisted. The very appearance of violence disturbed the middle class. Old-stock Americans, moreover, interpreted the combination of the radicalism of the IWW and the union's large immigrant membership as proof of the old stereotype of the immigrant radical. Accordingly, from the time of its founding the IWW knew continued repression from government as well as management. Even occasional victories, as in the Lawrence textile strike of 1912, provided only temporary hopes for the movement's survival.

Eugene V. Debs: Socialist candidate

The growing repression of the Wobblies and the socialists revealed the essential conservatism and ethnocentrism of American culture. The champions of meliorative reform shared those biases with those who opposed any change. But the meliorists, the men and women with a motivating social conscience — that is, the progressives — in contrast to the stand-patters, advocated reform precisely because they believed that the preservation of American institutions depended on altering them sufficiently to remove the most disturbing injustices in American life.

Politics had not created those injustices, but politics did reflect and sustain them, so politics might also help gradually to erase them. The early twentieth century witnessed a flowering of ideas that politics might implement, ideas that in one way or another struck against the thoughtless behavior and special privileges of the wealthy and their allies, against the selfishness that was generating the corrosive discontent of moderate and radical dissenters alike.

Art and Literature of Protest Those ideas took shape as artists, journalists, and social workers exposed the conditions of filth and misery that violated the ideals of middle-class Americans. Realistic literature and art, candid and conscientious journalism, reached the hearts of ladies and gentlemen of goodwill and helped enlist them in the causes of reform.

Theodore Dreiser, an immigrant's son schooled in poverty, used his powerful novels to describe the barren life of the poor "as simply and effectively as the English language will permit." His *Sister Carrie* (1901), *Jennie Gerhardt* (1911), *The Financier* (1912),

IWW and militia, Lawrence, Massachusetts, 1912

and *The Titan* (1914) revealed the human tragedy of inadequate wages, of insecure, hopeless, mechanical existence. Most of Dreiser's characters, driven by greed or sex to bestial violence, tried to fight their way into more splendid circumstances, but Dreiser made it poignantly clear how great were the odds against them, how cruel the cost of success, how sorry the lot of those success left behind. Frank Norris, a lesser talent than Dreiser, made his novel *The Octopus* (1901) a vehicle for condemning the inhumane policies of the Southern Pacific Railroad. In spite of the evils he recounted, he professed a faith that "all things . . . work together for good," but he continued his indictment of wealth in *The Pit* (1903). Jack London, a socialist, was optimistic only about the ultimate triumph of those who had lived, as he had, in "the unending limbo of toil." His fellow socialist and novelist Upton Sinclair, writing *The Jungle* (1906) in a similar vein, showed how those who labored in the poisonous world of the Chicago packinghouses "hated their work . . . the bosses . . . the owners . . . the whole place, the whole neighborhood." The poet Carl Sandburg railed at the stockyards and at "Pittsburgh, Youngstown, Gary—they made their steel with men."

Realistic painters, representatives of the "ash-can school," produced canvases that one of their number, John Sloan, called "unconsciously social conscious." Sloan, Robert Henri, William Glackens, George Luks, and others, experimenting with new brush techniques and new relationships of form, found compelling subject matter in dirty alleys, dank saloons, and squalid tenements—"chapters out of life," which they interpreted with beauty that expressed the sorrow and injustice of an experience previously unrecorded in fashionable galleries.

The art of men like Sloan, Sandburg, and Dreiser, for whom social criticism was often a secondary pur-

Muckraking: Patent Medicine

Peruna . . . is at present the most prominent proprietary nostrum in the country. . . . Peruna is a compound of seven drugs with cologne spirits. . . . None of the seven drugs is of any great potency. Their total is less than one-half of one per cent of the product. . . . There remains in Peruna only water and cologne spirits, roughly in the proportion of three to one. Cologne spirits is the commercial name for alcohol. . . .

What does Peruna cure? . . . A careful study of the literature will suggest its value as a tonic. . . . No matter what you've got . . . Peruna alone will save you. Pneumonia . . . dyspepsia . . . heart disease . . . cancer . . . That alcohol and water, with a little coloring matter and one-half of one per cent of mild drugs, will cure all or any of the ills listed . . . is too ridiculous to need refutation. . . . But it is not a fraud upon the sick alone that Peruna is baleful; but as the maker of drunkards, also.

From Samuel Hopkins Adams, "The Great American Fraud," *Collier's,* October 28, 1905

pose, supplemented and sharpened the message of outraged authors of a deliberate literature of exposure. Social workers, sociologists, and economists, basing their work on hard evidence, recited the facts of poverty in the magazine *Charities and the Commons;* in reports like *The Tenement House Problem* (1903); in books like Robert Hunter's *Poverty* (1904), Father John A. Ryan's *A Living Wage* (1906), John Spargo's *The Bitter Cry of the Children* (1906), Walter Rauschenbusch's *Christianity and the Social Crisis* (1907), and Frances Kellor's *Out of Work* (1915). Those documents demonstrated that between half and two-thirds of all working-class families had incomes too small to buy food, shelter, and clothing—incomes that left nothing for recreation or education, little even for union dues or church contributions. No thoughtful reader of those works could any longer believe that poverty was a function of sloth or moral turpitude. Clearly there was something wrong with a society that permitted so much misery while it pretended to a Christian ethic and a generous standard of living.

But humanitarian striving, effective though it was, influenced fewer Americans than did the hortatory, often sensational, journalism of exposure. *McClure's* set the pace for inexpensive, middle-class magazines. It published Ida M. Tarbell's devastating account of the business methods of the Standard Oil Company, Lincoln Steffens' exposés of the role of respectable citizens as well as ward politicians in the corrupt government of a dozen cities and states, Burton J. Hendrick's disclosures of the fraudulent practices of various insurance companies, and Ray Stannard Baker's indictments of railroad mismanagement, labor-baiting in Colorado, and race discrimination in the South. Though other "muckrakers" (the phrase was Theodore Roosevelt's) sometimes enlivened their work with willful exaggerations, they had no need to distort. The bare facts stirred the awakening conscience of middle-class Americans.

Intellectuals and Experts Meanwhile, American intellectuals were formulating the attitudes and techniques on which reform was to rely. These new attitudes, taken together, suggested the need for skepticism about rigid, formal systems of thought. They suggested also the importance of rigorous, dispassionate inquiry as a foundation for knowledge and of constant testing of hypotheses and modification of them on the basis of experience. These principles, derived

What Pragmatism Means

The pragmatic method is primarily a method of settling metaphysical disputes. . . . Is the world one or many?—fettered or free?—material or spiritual? . . . The pragmatic method in such cases is to try to interpret each notion by tracing its respective consequences. . . .

It is astonishing to see how many philosophical disputes collapse into insignificance the moment you subject them to this simple test of tracing a concrete consequence. . . .

A pragmatist . . . turns away from abstraction . . . from . . . closed systems, and pretended absolutes. He turns towards concreteness . . . towards facts, toward action and power. That means . . . the open air and possibilities of nature, as against dogma, artificiality, and the pretence of finality in truth.

From William James, *Pragmatism,* 1907

from the methods of science, were expected to yield ideas for social action. Indeed for the innovative proponents of the developing philosophy of pragmatism, the value of any idea depended on its utility for the thinker and society.

Among the influential intellectuals of the early century, none better stated the case for enlightened skepticism than did Justice Oliver Wendell Holmes, Jr., who recognized that the prejudices of judges often determined their interpretations of the law. Explaining the divergences between law and ethics, Holmes questioned the propensity of courts to upset the decisions of popularly elected legislatures. Though he understood the fallibility of the majority, he preached judicial restraint, for he understood also the judiciary's fallibility and its tendency to traditionalism and arrogance.

The artificiality and formalism of prevalent theories of social Darwinism invited the attack of William James and John Dewey, the fathers of American pragmatism. A psychologist as well as a philosopher, James emphasized the vagaries and the resilience of the mind, and warned against imprisoning intellectual creativity within arbitrary or mechanistic systems. For him the truth of an idea depended on its consequences. Dewey conceived of philosophy as an instrument for guiding action, an instrument he himself used in advocating experimentation in education and government. Tolerance and freedom of belief and of expression, Dewey noted, were essential if ideas were to enjoy a competitive chance to prove their merit.

Thorstein Veblen continued to strip away the façade of contemporary institutions as he had in the 1890s. His *The Theory of Business Enterprise* (1904) explained the cultural and economic importance of the machine process, and his *The Instinct of Workmanship* (1914) showed that wasteful and destructive monopolistic practices frustrated man's basic drive to create. Veblen's uncompromising analyses contained insights from which reformers, economists, and sociologists —"social engineers"—were then and later to borrow freely and with reward.

Other less angry and less probing students of contemporary economic institutions directed attention to reform. The writings of John R. Commons on labor, Frederick W. Taylor on factory management, Jeremiah W. Jenks on industry, and William Z. Ripley on railroads were characteristic of moderate, but perceptively critical, scholarship. These experts, often counselors to state and federal regulatory or investigatory commissions, understood that business managers were not ordinarily bad but that they were too often timid or unimaginative. With Ripley, the economists Henry C. Adams, Richard T. Ely, and Simon Patten viewed human beings not as the creatures of deterministic forces but as the makers of beneficent change. They urged that the principles of management be applied to government and that the state be empowered to solve the public problems business could not.

Reform in the Cities and the States Democratic government had failed most blatantly in American cities. Now municipal-reform organizations, many of them founded in the 1890s, succeeded gradually in winning home-rule charters and permission to regulate franchises or to provide for public ownership of vital services. The experiments of Galveston, Texas, with a commission form of government, and of Staunton, Virginia, with a city manager, demonstrated how efficient these substitutes for an aldermanic system could be. Over a hundred cities had copied them by 1910. Their concern for efficient government took into account the usefulness for public institutions of the methods of professional private management. It also reflected the desire of the urban middle class to reduce their tax burden by cutting city budgets and to decrease the influence of immigrants by abolishing the election of aldermen from wards that contained large foreign-born constituencies. Those concerns complemented the purpose of reformers animated primarily by a desire to root out corruption and to assist the poor. Such men and women drew inspiration from the examples set by mayors like Hazen Pingree of Detroit and Samuel "Golden Rule" Jones of Toledo.

Those developments impinged continually on state government, partly because urban reform could not proceed without improvements in state laws. A wave of reform in the Middle West began in Wisconsin with the election of Robert M. La Follette as governor in 1900. "Battle Bob," who set precedents for the entire region, had tried for years to overcome the regular Republican machine. A loyal party man, he built his own faction of those who shared his worries about the special advantages the state had given many corporations, about high property taxes, and about rising prices. He attracted both a rural and an urban following that was essentially middle class in its background and aspiration. Before he became United States senator in 1906, La Follette made his administration a model of honesty and efficiency, established a fruitful liaison between the government and the state university, whose distinguished faculty included many valuable advisers on public policy, and overcame the opposition of the Old Guard in the legislature. At the governor's urging, Wisconsin passed laws providing for a direct primary, civil service, restrictions on lobbying, conservation, state control of railroads and banks, higher taxes on all corporations (previously undertaxed), and the first state income tax. Wisconsin had become, as Theodore Roosevelt later said, "the laboratory of democracy."

Progressive government, exemplified by Wisconsin, came also to states as diverse, for example, as Iowa, Minnesota, the Dakotas, Oregon, Arkansas, Mississippi, Georgia, and South Carolina. Progressive administrations in those states moved, with variations in each case, to institute programs like La Follette's, though in the South the democratization of politics followed the disfranchisement of black Americans and many poor white Americans.

Progressivism won similar victories in Northern industrial states, where much of the leadership for reform came from business and professional élites resident in the suburbs as well as the cities. In New Jersey the "New Idea," a local version of progressivism, arose among prosperous suburbanites who were fighting to prevent valuable rapid transit and other franchises from falling into exploitative hands, to empower a state commission to regulate commutation fares, and to extract taxes from corporations (instead of from real estate alone) to defray the costs of public schooling. Objectives like those, along with the characteristic middle-class hostility toward machine politics, brought the New Idea into alliance with the reform mayor of Jersey City, who had built his strength among the workers he befriended. In 1904 the resulting coalition of independent Republicans began to convert New Jersey into a progressive community. In 1910 the state elected a Democratic governor, Woodrow Wilson, and during his administration a bipartisan coalition of progressives completed the program of the New Idea.

New York, Michigan, California, and Ohio, all states with important industrial centers, had political experiences not unlike New Jersey's, though none elected a governor who was so quickly and dramatically successful as Wilson. In the states, as in the nation, progressives looked to a strengthened executive to provide equitable and intelligent solutions for the social and governmental problems of the time. The reformers distrusted legislatures and the interest groups that influenced them. They also distrusted the traditionally conservative courts. But they trusted the people to elect able governors. However transient and frail that faith, reform in the industrial states led to a

"The System": Jersey City

The railroads, the public service companies, and some of the greatest corporations in the world have offices and properties in Jersey City, and their agents there . . . used money so extensively that they ruled absolutely. . . . Bribery at the polls, election fraud, ballot-box stuffing—all sorts of gross political crimes had made this home of "common people" and corporations notorious. "Bob" Davis was the Democratic boss, politically speaking; but Mr. E. F. C. Young, banker, leading citizen, public utility magnate, was the business boss who, backing Davis, was the real power. . . . This was a business nation and . . . the government represented not the people, but business.

From Lincoln Steffens, *Upbuilders*, 1909

salubrious restructuring of government and to major improvements for the working force, which cast some of the crucial votes for progress. Before 1915, 25 states passed employer-liability laws; 5 limited the use of injunctions preventing strikes or boycotts; 9 passed minimum-wage laws for women; 20 granted pensions to indigent widows with children; others restricted hours and conditions of work.

Progressive Attitudes and Ambiguities The strivings of the reformers, in their own word "progressives," revealed a great deal about the reformers themselves—their faith in democratic processes, their hostility to large aggregations of private power, their confidence in public regulatory agencies, their belief in efficiency, their humanitarian and moralistic temper. Yet they were a diverse group, and their movement was a concatenation of similar but independent movements. In rural areas, it retained a Populist flavor modified by time, experience, and prosperity. The traditional middle class of small towns and villages remained skeptical about science, big business, and strong government but often confident about the beneficent possibilities of Prohibition and devices of direct democracy. In the cities, progressivism was visible as a political expression of the attitudes of liberal intellectuals and lawyers, journalists, and business executives who believed in professionalism in public as well as private life. They often distrusted the masses but counted on an elite to govern in behalf of all people. In their view, the state and especially expert agencies created by the state would mediate the tensions between rich and poor, the powerful and the weak.

Many professional and white-collar men and women, many proprietors of small businesses believed that they had to organize to protect themselves and their standing. Mostly native Americans, they resented the immigrant or second-generation political boss. Mostly gentlefolk of modest means and often of old family, they resented the purchased prestige and paraded vulgarity of the newly rich. Though some of them were servants of big business and finance, more of them were the victims of bigness. Where labor unions were strong, as in California, they became targets for the attack on power. More often the attack was pointed toward corporations that dealt directly with many customers—monopolies or near-monopolies selling transportation, utilities, and food—or that were saddled (sometimes unjustly) with especially bad reputations.

Some managers of large corporations realized that reform sentiment might work to their own advantage. Such men, eager to protect the industrial stability they had achieved, worried about the possibility of renewed competition. They recognized that limited and benign federal regulation—for example, of railroading, lumbering, banking, or the manufacture of pharmaceuticals—could restrict the sharp practices of their smaller but aggressive business rivals. Public policy, in that view, instead of being permissive or antimonopoly, had the potentiality of providing positive guidance for industrial behavior, guidance compatible with the interests of big business. Spokesmen of big business who were also reformers — distinctly a minority of their kind — acted either in pursuit of selfish advantage, or out of a sense of social obligation, or in some cases out of both motives.

Whatever their motives, many Americans who considered themselves progressive reasoned from the unstated, paradoxical premises that were characteristic of their thought. They had a sense of their own special status — whether of wealth or social standing or talent — which they felt they deserved. They also believed in representative government and in the agencies it created. They reconciled those beliefs with the comforting assumption that candidates sympathetic to them would win the confidence of the people. Progressives believed at once in breaking up "bad" big business by applying the antitrust laws and in controlling "good" big business. In that way they could reconcile their concern for morality with their concern for efficiency. In that assumption, honest businessmen had little to fear from federal regulation of industry, for the regulators would appreciate the problems of those they regulated. Indeed, urban progressives believed that the growth and prosperity of industry, properly disciplined, was essential to the national interest.

The progressives, men and women of many stripes, included many middle-class people, but not all — or even most — middle-class people were progressives. Those who were, were the most socially conscious, the most anxious to prevent revolution by pursuing reform, and also, by and large, the younger, the better educated, and the more adventurous. They drew much of their inspiration from the most dynamic national exponent of their spirit and purpose, President Theodore Roosevelt. Without Roosevelt, progressivism would doubtless have happened, but it would not have been nearly so exciting.

THE REPUBLICAN ROOSEVELT

In September 1901 McKinley died, the third president to be assassinated in less than 40 years. His successor, Theodore Roosevelt, whom Mark Hanna had called "that damned cowboy," had set his political course for the White House long before McKinley's death. "It is," wrote Roosevelt, "a dreadful thing to come into the Presidency this way; but it would be a far worse thing to be morbid about it." The gift of the gods to Roosevelt — at age 42 the youngest chief executive in American history — was joy in life, and for seven years he brought that joy to his office.

The son of patrician parents, a graduate of Harvard, an accomplished ornithologist and an enthusiastic historian, Roosevelt chose early in life to make politics his career, for he wanted to rule — and he chose to work not as an independent but as a loyal Republican, for he wanted to win. He served successfully, with occasional time out as a rancher in the Dakotas, as an assemblyman in New York, a United States civil service commissioner, a New York City police commissioner, assistant secretary of the navy, colonel of the celebrated Rough Riders, and governor of New York. Senator Thomas C. Platt, the long-time boss of the state Republicans, developed serious apprehensions about Roosevelt's successful ventures in reform and managed in 1900 to get him out of New York by arranging his nomination for vice president, a position Roosevelt accepted with somewhat resigned grace but with characteristic vigor.

Roosevelt and His Office As a campaigner Roosevelt displayed the qualities that were to give him during his presidency an enormous influence with the people. To the Americans who acclaimed him he was many wonderful things — policeman, cowboy, hero in arms, battler for the everlasting right. He was that toothy grin, that restless energy, that high-pitched voice exhorting the worthy to reform. Roosevelt was also a learned man, receptive to the advice of the men of ideas whom he brought to Washington.

A skilled politician, Roosevelt made the presidency a great office and used it boldly. He conceived of the president as "a steward of the people bound actively and affirmatively to do all he could for the people." He set out therefore as president to define the great national problems of his time, to propose for each a practicable solution, to win people and Congress to his proposals, and to infuse the executive department with his own dedication to efficient administration and enforcement of the laws.

Roosevelt summoned to federal service a remarkable group of advisers and subordinates. The president's example and support inspired them; his reorganizations of federal agencies gave scope to their

Theodore Roosevelt: joy in life

talents. They included, among others, Elihu Root, McKinley's secretary of war whom Roosevelt continued in that office and later made secretary of state; William Howard Taft, Root's successor in the War Department; Chief Forester Gifford Pinchot and Secretary of the Interior James R. Garfield, both eminent conservationists.

In filling dozens of lesser federal offices, Roosevelt assured his own control of his party. He manipulated patronage so deftly that Mark Hanna had lost control of Republican affairs months before he died in February 1904. By that time Roosevelt, profiting also because he was the incumbent, could count on the support of every important state delegation to the forthcoming national convention. He could rely, too, on the influential party leaders, for he had satisfied the most urgent demands of the reform wing without offending or frightening the stand-patters.

Attack on the Trusts Roosevelt, always a gradualist, fashioned a circumspect domestic program, which he dressed in a pungent rhetoric. At the outset of his administration he indicated that he would accept the advice of the Old Guard in the Senate on tariff and monetary policies, matters about which they were most sensitive. He was himself much more worried about the problems of industrial consolidation. The "absolutely vital question," Roosevelt believed, "was whether the government had power to control" the trusts. The Supreme Court's decision in the E. C. Knight case (1895) suggested that it did not (see p. 472). Seeking a modification of that interpretation, Roosevelt in 1902 ordered Attorney General Philander C. Knox to bring suit for violation of the Sherman Act against the Northern Securities Company.

The president had chosen his target carefully. The Northern Securities Company was a mammoth holding company for the Northern Pacific, the Great Northern, and the Chicago, Burlington, and Quincy railroads. A battle for the stock of the Northern Pacific, key to control of transportation in the Northwest, had led in 1901 to panic on Wall Street. The antagonists made peace by creating the Northern Securities Company for the immediate purpose of quieting the market and for the ultimate purpose of monopolizing the railroads of a rapidly growing region. The contestants had been the titans of finance: J. P. Morgan and Company, the Rockefeller interests, James J. Hill, and E. H. Harriman. The panic they had brought on, a calamity for many brokers, drew attention to their ruthless speculation. The holding company they formed, in which 30 percent of the stock represented only intangible assets, worried the farmers of the Northwest, who, suspicious as ever of monopolies, expected freight rates to soar.

While several states initiated legal action against the holding company, Roosevelt began his preparations in secret. Announcement of the federal government's suit stunned Wall Street. Morgan, with the arrogance of an independent sovereign, tried in vain to have his lawyer settle things with the attorney general. His failure, like Roosevelt's attack, symbolized a transfer of power from lower New York to Washington. In 1903 a federal court ordered the dissolution of the Northern Securities Company, a decision the Supreme Court sustained the next year.

The government proceeded against 44 more corporations during Roosevelt's term in office. In 1902 action began against the "beef trust," so unpopular with sellers of livestock and buyers of meat. Equally unpopular were four defendants in cases started in 1906 and 1907, the American Tobacco Company, the Du Pont Corporation, the New Haven Railroad, and the Standard Oil Company.

Roosevelt's revival of the Sherman Act won him a reputation as a "trust-buster," but he never believed that the fragmentation of industry could solve the nation's problems. He had, he felt, to establish the authority of the federal executive to use the antitrust law in cases of monopoly or flagrant misbehavior. Trust-busting, however, was in his view inappropriate in the case of most enterprises that had reduced the cost of production and had won for the nation the industrial leadership of the world. The growth of industry was, he argued, natural, unavoidable, and beneficial. Breaking up corporations whose only offense was size would be impossible unless the government also abolished steam, electricity, large cities, indeed all modern conditions. The need was for continuous, informed, and expert regulation, which only the federal government could properly undertake.

The Square Deal In December 1901 Roosevelt made his first modest recommendations to Congress for creating the efficient system of control on which, he believed, the orderly development of industrial life depended. The president, like many of the consolidators, had a national rather than a local view of economic problems, and a confidence in expert management rather than in popular sentiment. Where some consolidators of that mind looked to the federal government to enhance its authority in order to further their needs, Roosevelt favored that enhancement in order to advance what he considered the public interest. Yet his was not primarily an adversary stance. The public interest, as he saw it, did not call for federal punishment of business but for federal regulation to prevent the abuses of predatory business, and thereby to encourage the productive energies of responsible business.

Roosevelt asked first for an act to expedite antitrust prosecutions. The very threat of antitrust action, he knew, would help keep business in line. Congress passed his bill in 1903. Without opposition it then also enacted his proposal for forbidding the granting or receiving of rebates, a practice that powerful shippers had forced upon unwilling railroads. The railroads had wanted the protection they received, as had most shippers. More serious opposition developed to Roosevelt's major objective, the creation of a new Department of Commerce and Labor with a Bureau of Corporations empowered to gather and release information about industry. Such a bureau was essential if the government was to learn what businesses to regulate and how. On that account, conservative Republican senators blocked Roosevelt's bill, though many congressmen preferred it to more stringent measures then under consideration. The president saved his bill by announcing that John D. Rockefeller was secretly organizing the opposition to it. The culprit was actually one of Rockefeller's subordinates, but the purport of Roosevelt's charge was accurate, and the consequent public clamor accelerated the passage of the controversial law.

The new act gave to the Bureau of Corporations authority to investigate significant public issues, as that bureau did, for example, in finding the facts on which Roosevelt later based his hydroelectric policy. For its part, the Bureau of Labor, also primarily a fact-finding agency, demonstrated its usefulness to Roosevelt and to workers by its fair reporting during the strike of anthracite-coal miners that began in May 1902 and lasted until October. The managers of the Eastern coal-carrying railroads that owned most of the mines would not negotiate with the union, the United Mine Workers, which was demanding recognition, an eight-hour day, and a 10 to 20 percent increase in pay. Labor's orderly conduct and willingness to arbitrate won growing public approval, particularly after the intransigent owners, speaking through George F. Baer, the president of the Reading Railroad, insisted that "God in his Infinite Wisdom has given control of the property interests" to the directors of large corporations. This attitude invited public antagonism at a time when fuel was short and the days were growing chilly.

Roosevelt, sympathetic to the workers and worried about the coal shortage, had hesitated to enter the dispute only because his advisers felt that he lacked the legal authority. Early in October he summoned the mine operators and John Mitchell, the union chief, to the White House. Mitchell again offered to submit to arbitration, but the owners remained obdurate. Indeed, they demanded that the president issue an injunction and, if necessary, use the army to end the strike. Their "arrogant stupidity" provoked Roosevelt instead to let them know indirectly that he was prepared to use troops to dispossess them and produce coal. With this kind of intervention in the offing, Mark Hanna, Elihu Root, and other conservative men quickened their efforts for peace, enlisted the help of J. P. Morgan himself, and persuaded the mine owners to accept a compromise settlement. By its terms the miners resumed work, and a commission appointed by the president arbitrated the questions at issue. In March the commission awarded labor a 10 percent raise, a reduction in working hours to nine and in some cases eight per day, but not recognition of the union. The owners in return received a welcome invitation to raise coal prices 10 percent. Roosevelt was the first president to bring both labor and capital to the White House to settle a dispute, the first to get them both to accept the judgment of a commission appointed by the executive, the first to coerce the owners of a crucial industry by threatening to take it over. All this contrasted vividly with the course of the federal government during the Pullman strike (see p. 481).

In other labor episodes, Roosevelt insisted on the open shop for government workers and resisted not only radical unionism but even the principle of the union shop in industry. He believed, as he put it, in "the right of laboring men to join a union . . . without illegal interference." This was less than Gompers advocated, but it was more than most businessmen or conservative politicians were yet willing to concede. It was a position characteristic of Roosevelt — advanced but not radical, cautious but not timorous.

His purpose during the coal strike, Roosevelt explained during the campaign of 1904, had been to give both sides a "square deal." The phrase became a familiar label for his administration, and for his intention to abolish privilege and enlarge individual opportunity. His "natural allies," he said, were "the farmers, small businessmen and upper-class mechanics," middle-class Americans "fundamentally sound, morally, mentally and physically." Like him, they abhorred extremes; like him, they judged in moral terms. They warmed to Roosevelt's fusillades against those he later called the "malefactors of great wealth." They accepted and cheered his image of himself as a champion of fairness.

The Election of 1904 That was the basis of his campaign. It was the basis, too, for his occasional appointment to office of qualified men from minority groups — black Americans, Catholics, Jews, Americans of Hungarian and German and Irish extraction. His appreciation of the inherent dignity in every human being encouraged him to invite to the White House Booker T. Washington, the black educator who doubled as an adviser on patronage. Yet like almost all Americans of his generation, Roosevelt believed that men and women of color, black Americans and Asians particularly, were lesser people than their white neighbors. Washington did not again receive an invitation to the White House. Much worse, in 1906 the president revealed a cruel prejudice by discharging without honor black troops who refused to reveal the names of a few of their fellows who had allegedly shot up the racially prejudiced town of Brownsville, Texas. That hasty and unjust decision reflected the racism of the army, which Roosevelt shared. Black Americans properly resented the ruling, but it was not reversed until 1972.

In 1904, an election year, there was a convenient compatibility between Roosevelt's conscience and the needs of politics. That did not detract from his conscience, though it manifestly strengthened his campaign. He took no chances. A new pension order, making age alone a sufficient qualification for eligibility, held the Grand Army of the Republic to the Grand Old Party. The official platform contained standard Republican platitudes about the tariff and prosperity, sops to the Old Guard, as was the lackluster nominee for vice president, Senator Charles W. Fairbanks of Indiana. Taken together, the platform and the ticket strengthened the basis of the successful Republican coalition of the late 1890s. But the real platform was Roosevelt's record, and the real issue was the man.

That made things difficult for the Democrats. As Bryan complained, Roosevelt had captured his banner. The Republicans now marched as the party of reform. Conservative Democrats returned to the formulas of Grover Cleveland's days, to a platform emphasizing strict construction of the Constitution and a candidate — Judge Alton B. Parker — chosen for his safe views and close ties to New York wealth.

Parker conducted a dull campaign until the vision of impending defeat persuaded him to charge that Roosevelt's campaign manager, George B. Cortelyou, was blackmailing corporations for contributions. Cortelyou, who had been secretary of commerce, had indeed had access to the findings of the Bureau of Corporations, but he neither resorted to blackmail nor needed to. Wealthy Republicans, loyal party men in spite of their reservations about Roosevelt, had responded without stint to the usual appeals for funds. Parker's charges provoked the president to direct his party treasurer to return any contributions that had come from predatory wealth. The treasurer ignored the order, just as the voters by and large ignored Parker's accusations. Roosevelt could have won without much financial support. In a landslide victory, he received 57.4 percent of the popular votes (7,628,461) to Parker's 37.6 percent (5,084,223), and 336 electoral votes to the Democrat's 140.

The Republican triumph remained in the pattern of the elections of 1896 and 1900. Compared to the earlier years of the nineteenth century, the percentage of eligible voters going to the polls was falling. That development arose partly because of the disfranchisement of voters, especially in the Democratic South, partly because the emotional issues of the post–Civil War period had lost most of their force. But those conditions did not in themselves determine the outcome of any particular contest. In 1904 Roosevelt won as he did, not primarily because of long-term characteristics of the American party system, but because he and his program caught the imagination and enthusiasm of the electorate.

ROOSEVELT AND REFORM

Government and Business When Congress convened in December 1904, the progress of reform in Washington and in the states was gathering momentum. President now in his own right, Roosevelt took advantage of the mandate he had helped to create. His prime objective was railroad regulation. Decisions of the Supreme Court had stripped the Interstate Commerce Commission (ICC) of authority over railway rates and rebates, which the roads continued to grant in spite of the government's efforts to enforce the antirebate act of 1903. The only feasible remedy was to give the commission power to set reasonable and nondiscriminatory rates and to prevent inequitable practices. Farmers and small businessmen were demanding that remedy. Some railroad managers saw advantages in dealing with a single federal authority rather than with many state commissions, but even they preferred final decisions to rest with the conservative judiciary rather than with the ICC. Further, most railroads, their privileged customers, and the devotees of conservative economic theory opposed federal ratemaking, which would for the first time in American history give the national government authority to determine prices, the sacrosanct prerogative of private enterprise.

For Roosevelt, laissez-faire theory was not sacred, but moral corporate behavior was. In 1904 and 1905 he urged Congress to endow the ICC with the power to adjust rates against which shippers had complained. Roosevelt advanced his purpose skillfully. Concentrating on the railroad issue, he gave up a tentative plan for a downward revision of the tariff, which agrarian Republicans as well as Democrats favored. At least partly on that account, the House of Representatives passed the president's railroad bill by an overwhelming margin. In 1906 Roosevelt outmaneuvered the Old Guard in the Senate and, after few modifications, the Hepburn Act carried. It gave the ICC the authority upon complaint from a shipper to set aside existing rates and to prescribe substitutes, subject to court review. As it worked out during the next several years, the courts did not overrule the commission. The act was less than the most vocal critics of the roads had wanted but just what Roosevelt was after. It was a keystone in his intended system of continuous, expert federal regulation of American industry.

Congress in 1906 passed several notable laws. One was an employer-liability act for the District of Columbia and all common carriers. Another was a pure-food-and-drug bill, whose chief exponent was Dr. Harvey W. Wiley of the Department of Agriculture. For several years this measure, twice approved by the House, had faltered. Now a series of articles by Samuel Hopkins Adams exposed the dangers of patent medicine, aroused public opinion, and speeded the enactment of the legislation, though appropriations for its enforcement remained inadequate for two decades.

In a similar way, the publication of Upton Sinclair's *The Jungle,* with its description of the scandalous conditions in meatpacking houses, led Roosevelt to order a special investigation. This confirmed Sinclair's findings and precipitated the passage of a federal meat-inspection law. The act revealed the crosscurrents of purpose that characterized the cautious reform of the Roosevelt era. Sinclair had hoped to obtain remedy for the exploited workers, but the statute ignored them. Progressive senators like Beveridge of Indiana had wanted the packers to pay for federal inspection, but the legislation left the cost with the government, and Congress in later years appropriated stingy sums for enforcement. The large packers, in some cases before the act was passed, in all cases thereafter, preferred unitary federal inspection to irregular and uneven inspections by the many states in which they had plants. The packers also expected that federal inspection would discipline small establishments that could not afford sanitary methods. But those small concerns continued to function in intrastate commerce. Further, though the large packers were eager to retain and enlarge their European markets, Roosevelt threatened that goal by publishing reports about conditions in the meat industry. For his part, the president, who turned to the whole issue rather late, used his influence to keep the House of Representatives, where the packers had interested friends, from subjecting meat inspection to broad judicial review. All in all, then, the legislation, like the Hepburn Act and the Pure Food and Drug Act, constituted at best a partial victory for each

The principles of conservation . . . —development, preservation, the common good—have a general application. The development of resources and the prevention of waste and loss, the protection of the public interest, by foresight, prudence, and the ordinary business . . . virtues, all these apply to other things as well as natural resources. . . . The outgrowth of conservation . . . is national efficiency. . . . So from every point of view conservation is a good thing for the American people.

From Gifford Pinchot, *The Fight for Conservation,* 1910

of the various principals involved. The laws improved the structure of federal relationships in the industries affected, but they were at best, as Roosevelt said, not an ultimate reform but a first step which he believed was far better than none at all.

In 1906 Roosevelt also sent Congress a series of recommendations, addressed in large part to social reform, on which it did not act. Labor problems were much on his mind. He proposed the abolition of child labor and an effective workmen's-compensation law. The National Association of Manufacturers (NAM) had won a number of victories in its drive to cripple unions by obtaining injunctions against strikes and boycotts, the unions' most effective weapons. The NAM was also exhorting legislators to oppose all labor legislation. Fighting back, Gompers and his associates submitted to Roosevelt and the Congress a Bill of Grievances voicing their traditional demands, especially for relief from injunctions granted under the Sherman Act. The American Federation of Labor struck politically as well, campaigning in 1906 against congressmen unfriendly to labor, most of whom were Republicans. Caught between his growing sympathy for labor's goals and his partisan loyalties, Roosevelt endorsed all Republican candidates but exhorted them to mend their ways.

New Programs and the Old Guard The gulf between the president and the Old Guard widened in 1907 and 1908. They especially differed over conservation. In 1902 Roosevelt, an ardent conservationist, had spurred the passage of the Newlands Act, which set aside a portion of receipts from the sale of public lands for expenditures on dams and reclamation. Pushing on, largely on the advice of Gifford Pinchot, he had withdrawn from private entry valuable coal and mineral lands, oil reserves, and waterpower sites. He had proceeded vigorously against cattlemen and lumbermen who were poaching on public preserves. These policies offended the Western barons who had become rich by exploiting the nation's natural resources (see p. 451). In 1907 their representatives attached a rider to an appropriation bill for the Department of Agriculture that prevented the creation of new forest reserves in six Western states without the consent of Congress. Roosevelt had to sign the bill, for the department had to have funds, but before signing he added 17 million acres to the national reserves. He later vetoed bills that granted waterpower sites to private interests but that did not provide for federal supervision of waterpower development.

In 1908 Roosevelt called a National Conservation Congress, which governors and hundreds of experts attended. It led to annual meetings of governors and to the creation of state conservation commissions. Congress, more and more hostile, ignored recommendations for river and flood control made by the Inland Waterways Commission, which Roosevelt appointed, and refused to provide funds to publish the report of another of his boards, the Country Life Commission, which advocated federal assistance for rural schools, roads, rural electrification, and farmers' cooperatives. Yet Roosevelt had succeeded in making the conservation of human and natural resources an issue of the first importance to thousands of Americans. He believed in the preservation of threatened species and of areas of great natural beauty. He believed just as strongly in conservation for use. In protecting natural resources from ruthless private exploitation, he intended to assure their use to meet the needs of both his own and later generations. Further, he shared the spirit of progressive reform that stressed the ability of the human mind and will to alter and improve the environment. Conservation provided an obvious laboratory for testing that belief.

Roosevelt's general policies jarred many businessmen who blamed him for the financial panic that occurred in the autumn of 1907 and for the brief depression that preceded and followed it. The basic causes of the slump were beyond his control. Productive facilities had expanded beyond the country's immediate capacity to consume, but the differential would probably have led to no serious trouble if the nation's banking and monetary systems had been stronger and if financiers had not been guilty of speculative excesses. Panic began only after depositors learned that several New York trust companies had failed in an expensive attempt to corner the copper market. As runs began on these and other (sound) banks, some had to close and all had to call in loans from creditors in New York and throughout the country. J. P. Morgan, at his most magnificent in this crisis, supervised a pooling of the funds of the leading Manhattan banks to support the threatened institutions. Undoubtedly this action prevented general disaster.

Morgan and his fellows could not have succeeded without assistance from the Treasury Department, which moved government deposits into threatened New York banks. The complex maneuvers depended in part on the purchase by the United States Steel Corporation of controlling shares of stock in the Tennessee Coal and Iron Company. The transaction, however, was unthinkable if there was any danger that it might lead immediately to an antitrust suit. So informed, Roosevelt, without making "any binding promise," urged Morgan's associates to proceed.

Though the panic quickly subsided, it had demonstrated the urgency of financial reform. It was ridiculous for a great nation in a time of crisis to have to fall back on Morgan or any other private banker. And it was vital to relax the general monetary stringency that intensified the crisis. Both the president and his detractors endorsed the action of Congress authorizing a commission, with Senator Nelson Aldrich as chair, to study and report on monetary and banking policy.

Roosevelt meanwhile had condemned the "speculation, corruption and fraud" that contributed to the panic. His messages to Congress of December 1907 and January 1908 disclosed his zeal for further reform. He had learned more about the problems of society and the capacity of the government. He now favored measures that he would have considered radical a few years earlier — measures that seemed far too sweeping to the conservatives who dominated Congress. The president called for federal incorporation and regulation of all interstate business, federal regulation of the stock market, limitation of injunctions against labor, compulsory investigation of labor disputes, extension of the eight-hour law for federal employees, and imposition of personal income and inheritance taxes He went on to castigate the courts for declaring unconstitutional a worker's-compensation law. He condemned "predatory wealth" for its follies and its unscrupulous opposition to "every measure for honesty in business." Roosevelt in private warned that a revolution would break out if rich men and blind judges made the lot of the worker intolerable. Without reform, capitalism could not survive.

The social reforms to which Roosevelt gave increasing emphasis in his last years in office depended for success on the political reforms he had been pursuing. Power, he knew, was the essence of politics. For him, political reform meant the shift of power from private hands, not accountable to the public, toward government; from states and localities, lacking broad jurisdictions, toward Washington; from the unrepresentative Supreme Court and from an inexpert and inefficient Congress toward the president — who was representative of all the people and positioned to command expert counsel.

He did not invent those goals, but he gave them effective expression, put the dignity of his office at their service, and converted to them the thousands who felt the vitality of his person. All this he did with a faith in the progress that conserves, a conviction that the holder of power has an obligation to promote justice and enforce orderly and moral behavior, and a confidence in his own ability to handle power to those ends. Those beliefs and that confidence also guided his foreign policy.

T. R. on the Peace of Justice

Peace is normally the handmaiden of righteousness; but when peace and righteousness conflict then a great and upright people can never . . . hesitate to follow the path which leads toward righteousness, even though that path leads to war. There are persons who advocate peace at any price. . . . These persons . . . seriously hamper the cause which they advocate by tending to render it absurd in the eyes of sensible and patriotic men. There can be no worse foe of mankind in general . . . than the demagogue of war, the man who . . . seeks to excite his countrymen against foreigners on insufficient pretexts . . . and who may . . . wantonly bring on conflict. . . . It is essential not to be misled by one set of extremists any more than by the other. . . . So long as the world is organized as now the armies and navies of those people who . . . stand for justice, offer not only the best, but the only possible security for a just peace. . . . If the United States . . . disarmed, we might sometimes avoid bloodshed, but we would cease to be of weight in securing the peace of justice.

From Theodore Roosevelt, *Annual Message to Congress,* December 1905

ROOSEVELT AND WORLD POWER

Power, Empire, and Responsibility During the first decade of the twentieth century, more and more Americans, including those who considered themselves progressives, subscribed to a new doctrine of manifest destiny (see p. 537). Along with that concept there grew up other ideas about the international role of the United States. The writings of Alfred T. Mahan, the experience of the Spanish-American War, and awareness of the swelling ambitions and power of Germany and Japan persuaded an influential minority of Americans of the importance of naval preparedness and national defense. Some, like Roosevelt, Root, and Senator Henry Cabot Lodge, also believed that every powerful nation had a stake in world order and an obligation to preserve it, that a great country like the United States could not escape involvement in international affairs.

Roosevelt as president continually reminded Americans of the oneness of the world. Nineteenth-century progress in transportation, communication, and production, he warned, had created situations of potential chaos in which only the availability of power and, when necessary, the application of force could establish a tolerable equilibrium.

He therefore preached preparedness to the frequently reluctant public. For Roosevelt, preparedness was not simply militarism. It entailed, too, the preservation and development of natural and human resources. Sharing the Anglo-Saxon bias of his time, Roosevelt urged Americans of old stock to increase their birth rate. But all Americans, regardless of national origin, could contribute, he maintained, to national well-being if they saw to their physical fitness and cultivated clear minds, clean souls, and brave hearts.

High character and the strenuous life were not in themselves enough, for preparedness ultimately involved the size, equipment, and leadership of the military services. The president heartily supported the reform of the outmoded army organization that Secretary of War Root had begun to plan under McKinley. Root set up an Army War College, demanded rigorous tests for the promotion of officers, and in 1902 asked Congress to authorize the creation of a general staff and the incorporation of the state militia into the regular army. Congress rejected the plan for the militia, but approved a general staff that began to direct the modernization of the army.

Roosevelt also demanded the construction of a modern navy strong enough to protect American interests and to further his "large view" of national obligations. The United States, he realized, could no longer depend on the British fleet for protection. It had to keep pace with the building programs of Japan and Germany and with rapid changes in naval technology. Before Roosevelt left office, Congress acceded to his constant prodding. The navy and army profited, too, from the enthusiastic recognition the president gave to military service and to dedicated and imaginative commanders like General Leonard Wood and Commander William S. Sims.

A strong nation, in Roosevelt's view, had the duty of imposing civilization and justice in the backward territories it ruled. In the Insular cases of 1900 and 1901, the Supreme Court held that inhabitants of the recently acquired American empire were not American citizens and did not have a right to the liberties guaranteed by the Constitution unless Congress expressly conferred them. Except for Hawaii and Alaska, which were destined for statehood, the Court's rulings left the determination of colonial policy to the Roosevelt administration. It adopted a variety of expedients. The navy administered Guam and Tutuila. Puerto Rico elected its own house of delegates, though its decisions had to be confirmed by a council and executed by a governor appointed in Washington. The American protectorate in Cuba ended in May 1902, but the next year a formal treaty between Cuba and the United States provided for American intervention in the event of a foreign threat or domestic disturbance. Insurrection in Cuba in 1906 persuaded Roosevelt to intervene. After three years, the Americans withdrew but retained a major naval base at Guantanamo and continued to exercise a monitory influence over Cuban policy. Earlier, the president had insisted that in return for the rights accorded by the Cuban treaty, the United States had a moral duty to aid the Cuban economy by granting special tariff rates to Cuban sugar, a concession he wrung from protectionist congressmen after a stiff legislative struggle in 1903.

He was unable, in spite of repeated attempts, to obtain tariff concessions for the Philippines. Those islands presented a number of difficult problems. Occasional episodes of cruelty by the American army during the suppression of the independence movement (see p. 549) had whetted native resentment. That resentment began to abate (though for a brief time the revolt continued) when Congress in 1902 passed an organic act for the Philippines, when Roosevelt abolished the office of military governor, and when William Howard Taft, the first civilian governor, proclaimed a general amnesty. Taft got along well with the elected assembly and furthered municipal home rule, improvements in public health, civil affairs, education, and transportation. He was successful, too, in negotiations with the Vatican and with Catholic friars in the islands for the purchase of lands that the Church claimed but the Filipinos held and deserved to keep. Like Roosevelt and Root, Taft believed the Philippines would not be ready for independence for many years. Though native patriots and American anti-imperialists remained impatiently committed to that goal, Taft's benign administration assisted the development of the islanders' economy and helped them prepare for ultimate self-government. Still, the inability of Roosevelt and his associates to understand the urgency of sentiment for self-government among subject peoples made American policy indistinguishable from the imperialism of European powers.

Policing the Caribbean Roosevelt's foreign policies, like his colonial policies, were derived from his assumption that it was "incumbent on all civilized and orderly powers to insist on the proper policing of the world." This was, of course, a highhanded assumption, which Roosevelt defended when he had to by arguing that only with stability could there be justice. An imperious manner characterized his methods as well as his objectives. As president, he believed, he had to conduct foreign policy himself, for in that field the Congress and "the average American" did not "take the trouble to think carefully or deeply."

Stretching his constitutional authority to its limits, Roosevelt intervened to preserve stability and American hegemony in the Caribbean, where, with Mahan, he felt the United States could not afford a rival. Like other small states in that area, Venezuela had borrowed money in Europe, which its prodigal dictator lacked either the means or the will to repay. In December 1902 England, Germany, and Italy, demanding payment for their citizens, blockaded Venezuela and fired on one of its ports. Venezuela asked the United States to arrange arbitration, to which England and Germany agreed. But a German ship again bombarded a port, and later Germany briefly opposed referring the dispute to arbitration. Roosevelt implied to the German ambassador that the United States would insist on that solution. The president did not intend to permit any European power to use the excuse of debt collection for establishing a foothold in the Caribbean.

The best way to keep Europe at home, he believed, was to keep order in the Caribbean. That purpose gave Roosevelt a pretext for incontinent behavior in Panama. In December 1901 the Senate approved the second Hay-Pauncefote Treaty by which England acknowledged the right of the United States alone to build and fortify an isthmian canal, so long an American dream. Such a canal would facilitate intercoastal shipping and would make it easier for the navy to move from ocean to ocean. The preferred route had at one time been through Nicaragua, where a sea-level canal could be built, but the commission of experts that Congress had authorized had come to prefer a lock canal through Panama, which would provide the cheapest and shortest route between the coasts of the United States (see Map 22-3). Accordingly, in June 1902 Congress directed the president to negotiate with Colombia for the acquisition of a strip of land in Panama, provided that the old French canal company, which had begun work decades earlier, agreed to sell the United States its titles and equities in the area on reasonable terms. Members of the American commission had valued the French holdings at not more than $40 million, only half of the company's own official estimate, but the company gratefully accepted the revised figure.

With that matter settled, Roosevelt pressed Colombia to surrender control of the land in return for $10 million and an annual rental of $250,000. A treaty to that effect was rejected by the Colombian government, which wanted more money and greater rights of sovereignty in the zone. Roosevelt, outraged at what he considered "blackmail," though the Colombian request was scarcely that, let it be known privately that he would smile upon insurrection in Panama. Predictably, in November 1903 insurrection occurred (if it had not, the president was prepared to ask Congress for authority to take the zone from Colombia). The United States aided the revolutionists and immediately recognized the new, independent Republic of Panama, which promptly accepted Roosevelt's term for a canal zone.

Roosevelt later boasted that he "took Panama," and most Americans at the time condoned his behavior. But the episode was a national disgrace. There was even suspicion of scandal. Agents of the French company, eager to unload their otherwise worthless assets, had influenced the State Department and members of

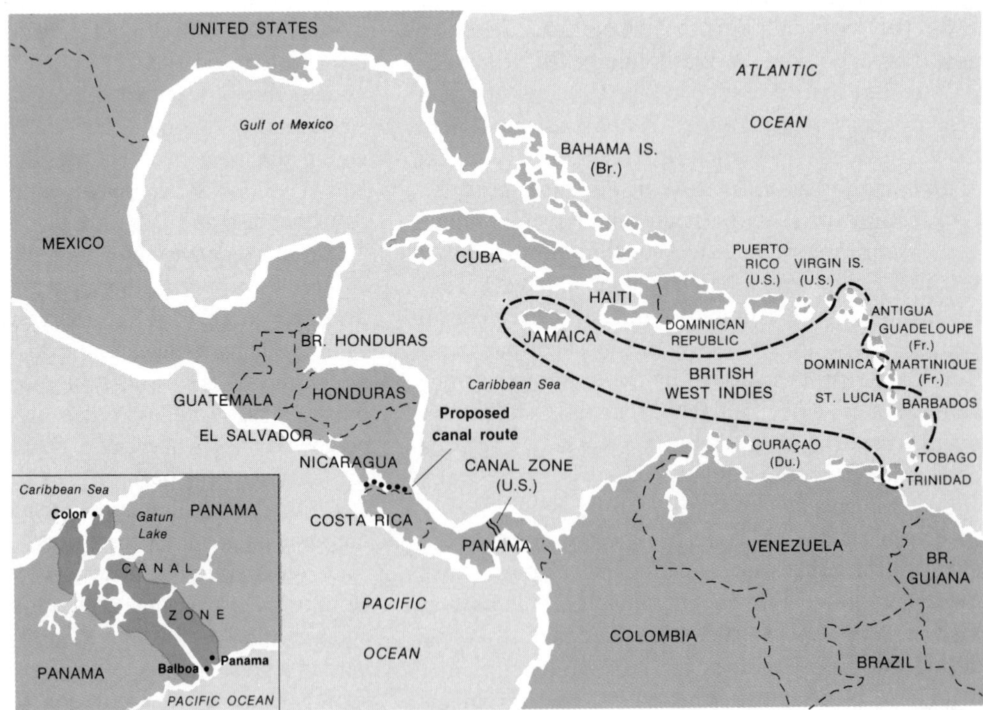

Map 22-3
International interests in the Caribbean

Roosevelt at the Panama Canal

Congress to favor the Panama route and had helped to foment the insurrection. Roosevelt's ruthless pursuit of his own interpretation of national advantage was no more ethical than was their pursuit of profit. Yet he argued that he had stamped out lawlessness in Colombia and disorder in Panama. Thus he used his insistence on stability in the Caribbean as a rationalization for imperialism.

He did have a clear strategic purpose — the control of the Caribbean as one essential part of national defense. That purpose imbued his message to Congress of December 1904, in which he announced that the United States would not interfere with Latin American nations that conducted their affairs with decency, but that "brutal wrongdoing" might require intervention by some civilized power, and that the United States could not "ignore this duty." The Monroe Doctrine told Europe to stay out of the Americas; the Roosevelt Corollary asserted that the United States had a right to move in. In 1905 Roosevelt interceded in Santo Domingo to end the cycle there of debt, revolution, and default. He imposed American supervision of customs collections and finance and established a trust fund to repay the European-held debt. The convention containing those terms was blocked in the United States Senate, which was growing restive under the president's single-handed conduct of foreign affairs, but Roosevelt substituted an executive agreement and protected his policy until the Senate accepted a modified treaty in 1907.

The Balance of Power The international police power that Roosevelt arrogated to the United States he expected other civilized nations to exercise elsewhere —Japan in Korea, England in Egypt and India. Stable and prosperous nations, however, had in his view no right to proceed against one another. World order depended on their restraint and on the shifting balances of their power. British restraint preserved the growing Anglo-American entente during a dispute about the Alaskan boundary. Canada in 1902 claimed Alaskan lands that cut off newly discovered Canadian gold fields from the sea. Roosevelt rightly judged the claim weak, but he wounded Canadian sensibilities by his blustering refusal to arbitrate (for, he said, arbitration usually resulted "in splitting the difference"). To help Canadian officials save face, in 1903 he submitted the issue to negotiation but instructed the commissioners he appointed to concede nothing. He also took pains to inform London of his order. The single English commissioner voted with the three Americans against the two Canadians, thereby straining temporarily the bonds of empire but serving both the merits of the issue and the cause of transatlantic friendship.

As he contemplated the balance of power in Europe, Roosevelt was grateful for England's friendship, dubious about Russia's immediate strength (though he recognized its great potential), and more and more anxious about Germany. Had the Kaiser had the "instinct for the jugular," Roosevelt thought, he would have kept a sharp eye on Russia. As it was, Germany was more jealous of France and England, and the Kaiser entertained "red dreams of glory" that might disrupt Europe and thus the whole world.

Aware of the network of European alliances that would engage every major continental power in a contest between any two, the president worried about the tensions that flared in 1905 over French and German rivalry in Morocco. The Kaiser secretly asked Roosevelt to persuade England not to support France. The president at first hesitated, for, as he said, the United States had "no real interest in Morocco." It did have a major stake in preserving peace, however, and Roosevelt carried on the difficult negotiations that brought all parties, including the United States, to a conference at Algeciras, Spain, in January 1906.

Roosevelt's instructions to the American delegates revealed his concern about German ambitions and his conviction that the entente cordiale between France and England preserved the essential balance of power in Europe. Though American participation had little effect on the outcome of the conference, at which France won a diplomatic victory, Roosevelt's role was nevertheless significant. He had served peace. Furthermore, he had demonstrated to Europe and to the American people, many of whom criticized his departure from the course of isolation, that the president of the United States recognized the nation's legitimate interest in any European crisis.

In Asia, Roosevelt judged, slumbering China was of no account, but to prevent dislocations of power he accepted the prevailing fiction of its territorial integrity, and he gave lip service to the principle of the Open Door. He was little interested in Chinese markets, but to stabilize the Orient politically he counted on a balance between Russia and Japan. He welcomed an Anglo-Japanese defensive alliance of 1902, which committed both signatories to preserve the status quo in Asia. In 1904, when the Russo-Japanese War began, he feared that a Russian triumph would be "a blow to civilization," but the elimination of Russia's "moderative influence" on Japan would be equally unfortunate. That possibility seemed imminent after Japan's initial naval and land victories and the outbreak of revolution in Russia. Though Roosevelt was partial to the Japanese, he intensified his effort through mediation to arrange a peace that would preserve an equilibrium. Proceeding without the knowledge of Congress, he worked secretly through personal friends in the diplomatic corps of Japan, Germany, and Great Britain. By the summer of 1905 Russian distress and Japanese financial infirmity brought both belligerents to accept a peace conference at Portsmouth, New Hampshire.

The president's brilliant diplomacy continued at the conference, which produced a settlement that suited his purpose and earned him a Nobel Prize for Peace. Japan took over the southern half of the island of Sakhalin, Port Arthur, and the South Manchuria Railroad, but Manchuria remained legally a part of China, where the Open Door in theory still permitted all nations to trade and invest. Russia retained effective control over northern Manchuria and all of Siberia, the source of its basic weight in Asian politics. The Japanese failed to get the huge indemnity they had wanted, which made the treaty and Roosevelt the object of considerable public criticism in Japan. But the Japanese government was satisfied, particularly because the United States, like Russia, had recognized Japan's primacy in Korea.

Also in 1905 Taft and Japanese Foreign Minister Taro Katsura reached an agreement by which the United States acknowledged Japan's occupation of Korea and Japan disavowed any ambitions in the Philippines. This, too, was a victory for the president's realistic and essentially cautious diplomacy. Though he sometimes sounded fierce, he never undertook ventures beyond his means to execute them. The United States, he knew, lacked the means to interfere in Korea, and Japan had to be kept friendly or it could easily conquer the Philippines, which Congress would not arm.

Japanese-American relations might have remained excellent had it not been for the problem of immigration. In 1900 Tokyo agreed to deny passports to emigrant laborers bound for the United States. But Japanese workers continued to make their way to the West Coast through Hawaii, Mexico, and Canada. In California anti-Japanese feeling rose. In 1906 San Francisco segregated Asian schoolchildren. The proud Japanese protested officially to Washington. Roosevelt scolded the school board and assured the Japanese that he had no sympathy with the "outrageous agitation" of the Californians. He could not, however, silence the yellow press or the "idiots" in the California legislature. Yet he was unwilling to ask the Japanese to concede any racial inferiority. The State Department resolved the crisis by negotiating the "Gentlemen's Agreement" of 1907, an official but informal understanding that bound both countries to stop direct immigration between them.

This crisis focused attention on the whole immigration question. In large degree Roosevelt shared the common prejudice against the unrestricted entry of southern and eastern Europeans and Asians. Still, he feared that a general debate about immigration in 1906 would complicate relations with Japan and possibly divide the Republicans, some of whom were urging enactment of a literary test for immigrants. He recommended the appointment of a fact-finding commission, a solution that would delay debate, appease the restrictionists, and, he believed, throw light on a complex subject. In 1907 Congress authorized such a commission. Its members, under the chairmanship of Senator Dillingham, approached their task with a formidable bias for the restriction of immigration.

Besides provoking a debate on immigration policy, the Japanese-American crisis stirred up loose talk of war. The president was apparently worried in 1907 about Japan's intentions. His anxiety may have been contrived to stir Congress into pushing ahead with the naval building program. There was no genuine need for alarm, although years later Roosevelt said that he had detected "a very, very slight undertone of veiled truculence" in Japan's communications. "It was essential," he then decided, "that we should have it clearly understood by our own people especially, but also by other peoples, that the Pacific was as much our home waters as the Atlantic." He sent the battle fleet around the world to make his point clear.

Had Japan been belligerent, it could have demolished the American ships that entered Tokyo Bay. Instead it welcomed them heartily. Yet Roosevelt believed their presence curbed any Japanese urge toward aggression and was therefore "the most important service" he ever rendered to peace. It certainly exemplified one of his favorite adages: "Speak softly but carry a big stick." Goodwill rather than fear led the Japanese ambassador to propose a declaration of friendship. In the Root-Takahira Agreement of 1908, the United States acknowledged Japan's special interest in Manchuria, and both nations promised to uphold the status quo in the Pacific and to respect the Open Door and China's territorial integrity.

Prospects for American commerce and investment in China, the objectives of the Open Door, remained important to the Department of State, but the president, according to his own account, was concerned primarily with the balance of power in the Pacific. "A council of war never fights," Roosevelt wrote in his *Autobiography,* "and in a crisis the duty of a leader is to lead." As president he personally conducted the nation's foreign policies, acting with scant regard for the opinion of public or Congress or for the rights or sensitivities of other nations. His magisterial manner and imperialistic ventures set potentially dangerous precedents that his critics deplored. Still, as he asserted, the United States had become part of an interdependent world; the use of force could keep isolated trouble spots from erupting into general war; power was a pervasive element in world affairs and the United States had a vital interest in preserving the balance of power in Europe as well as in Asia. As Roosevelt saw it, the United States had also an obligation to keep its power in a state of readiness and, when necessary, to use it intelligently but with restraint.

The Election of 1908 No harm came from the concentration of power in one man's hands, Roosevelt observed, "provided the holder does not keep it for more than a certain, definite time, and then returns it to the people from whom he sprang." An American president, he believed, should serve only two terms. So he had announced in 1904 that he would not run again, and, though he gloried in his office, he resisted the strong sentiment for his renomination in 1908 and used his power in the party to ensure the nomination of William Howard Taft, whom he had selected as the man most able to continue his policies.

The president's endorsement and Taft's own excellent reputation kept the party united. With the tide of progressivism rising, the Democrats turned again to Bryan, who ran with more prudence but less vigor than before. He had the support of the leaders of organized labor, who applauded the Democratic plank urging the restriction of injunctions, and he made what he could of an attack on the Republican tariff. But Taft polled 52.0 percent of the popular vote and carried the Electoral College 321 to 162.

Taft's identification with Roosevelt accounted for his nomination and assisted his election. In 1901 Roosevelt had inherited a conservative administration. Increasingly he had enlisted with reform. When he bowed out in 1909, off to hunt in the African jungles, a majority of Americans had come to adulate him and to approve, or at least to accept, his policies. It remained to be seen what Taft would do with his inheritance.

SUGGESTIONS FOR READING

GENERAL

John M. Cooper, Jr., *Pivotal Decades* (1990), provides a thorough account of the developments of the first twenty years of the century. An older view is in G. E. Mowry, *The Era of Theodore Roosevelt* (1958). More interpretive and less empirical are S. P. Hays, *The Response to Industrialism* (1957), and R. H. Wiebe, *The Search for Order: 1877–1920* (1966), which together offer the now dominant historical view of the period. There remains much of value in R. Hofstadter, *The Age of Reform* (1955). Other instructive approaches to the progressive era, apart from those listed in the paragraphs that follow, are in C. Lasch, *New Radicalism in America, 1889–1963* (1965); O. L. Graham, Jr., *The Great Campaigns* (1971); J. W. Chambers, *The Tyranny of Change* (1980); W. L. O'Neill, *The Progressive Years* (1975); A. S. Link and R. L. McCormick, *Progressivism* (1983); and M. J. Sklar, *The Corporate Reconstruction of American Capitalism* (1988).

PROGRESSIVISM

Among the best places to begin reading about progressivism are the lucid studies of the underprivileged and their champions in R. H. Bremner, *From the Depths* (1956); J. T. Patterson, *America's Struggle Against Poverty* (1981); and R. Lubove's *The Progressives and the Slums* (1962) and *The Professional Altruist: The Emergence of Social Work as a Career, 1880–1930* (1965). See, too, P. Boyer, *Urban Masses and Moral Order in America* (1978); A. Davis, *Spearheads for Reform: The Social Settlements and the Progressive Movement, 1890–1919* (1967); and J. H. Ehrenreich, *The Altruistic Imagination* (1985). Two of the champions revealed their concerns in J. A. Riis, *How the Other Half Lives* (1890), and Jane Addams, *Forty Years at Hull House* (1935). The contributions of the churches receive analysis in H. F. May, *Protestant Churches and Industrial America* (1949). P. Taft, *The A. F. of L. in the Time of Gompers* (1957), provides an account of the trade unions, as does B. Mandel, *Samuel Gompers, A Biography* (1963). On Jewish immigrants in New York, the best treatment is in I. Howe, *World of Our Fathers* (1976); on Asians, see R. Takaki, *Strangers from a Different Shore* (1989). Accounts of the struggle for women's rights are in A. Kessler-Harris, *Out to Work* (1982); A. Kraditor, *The Ideas of the Women's Suffrage Movement, 1890–1920* (1965); and L. Banner, *Women in America* (1974). On black Americans, see L. Harlan, *Booker T. Washington* (1972); C. F. Kellogg, *NAACP* (1970); E. Rudwick, *W. E. B. DuBois* (1969); B. J. Ross, *J. E. Spingarn and the Rise of the NAACP* (1972); and N. Weiss, *The National Urban League, 1910–1940* (1974). There are good accounts of dissident radicals in P. Renshaw, *The Wobblies* (1967); M. Dobofsky, *We Shall Be All: A History of the Industrial Workers of the World* (1969); D. Shannon, *Socialist Party in America* (1967 ed.); and J. P. Diggins, *The American Left in the Twentieth Century* (1973). Among important interpretations of progressive intellectuals are D. Aaron, *Men of Good Hope* (1951); M. White, *Social Thought in America: The Revolt Against Formalism* (1949); D. W. Noble, *The Paradox of Progressive Thought* (1958); S. Fine, *Laissez Faire and the General-Welfare State* (1956); J. Weinstein, *The Corporate Ideal in the Liberal State, 1900–1918* (1969); S. Haber, *Efficiency and Uplift: Scientific Management in the Progressive Era, 1890–1920* (1964); and H. F. May, *The End of American Innocence* (1959). These should be read in conjunction with the contemporary works mentioned in the text and with such revealing autobiographies as those of Lincoln Steffens and William Allen White. Progressive ferment and achievement in various regions, states, and cities have had excellent treatment in C. V. Woodward, *Origins of the New South, 1877–1913* (1951); D. W. Grantham, *Southern Progressivism* (1983); D. Thelen, *The New Citizenship, 1885–1990* (1972), on the rise of La Follette; G. E. Mowry, *The California Progressives* (1951); J. F. Reynolds, *Testing Democracy* (1988), on New Jersey; R. M. Abrams, *Conservatism in a Progressive Era: Massachusetts Politics, 1900–1912* (1964); S. Hackney, *Populism to Progressivism in Alabama* (1969); R. F. Wesser, *Charles Evans Hughes: Politics and Reform in New York, 1905–10* (1967); and R. L. McCormick, *From Realignment to Reform* (1981).

ROOSEVELT AND HIS ADMINISTRATION

The best introduction to Theodore Roosevelt remains his autobiography, which can be profitably supplemented by reading his voluminous collected works and his published letters, E. E. Morision, ed., *Letters of Theodore Roosevelt,* 8 vols. (1951–54). E. Morris provides a glowing account in *The Rise of Theodore Roosevelt* (1979), as does D. McCullough in *Mornings on Horseback* (1981). Three good biographies are G. W. Chessman, *Theodore Roosevelt and the Politics of Power* (1968); W. H. Harbaugh, *Power and Responsibility* (1961); and L. L. Gould, *The Presidency of Theodore Roosevelt* (1990). J. M. Blum, *The Republican Roosevelt* (1954), focuses on Roosevelt as politician and president; L. L. Gould, *Reform and Regulation: American Politics, 1900–1916* (1978), contains a contrasting interpretation; and H. K. Beale, *Theodore Roosevelt and the Rise of America to World Power* (1956), offers an analysis of Roosevelt's foreign policy, as does F. W. Mark, *Velvet on Iron* (1982). On political style and its importance, see M. E. McGerr, *Decline of Popular Politics* (1986). G. Kolko, *The Triumph of Conservatism* (1963) and *Railroads and Regulation, 1877–1916* (1965), attribute the reforms of the Progressive era largely to conspiratorial big-business leaders; R. H. Wiebe, *Businessmen and Reform* (1962), emphasizes division of opinion about reform issues within the business community; and A. Martin, *Enterprise Denied: Origins of the Decline of American Railroads, 1897–1917* (1971), reveals business resistance to reform. See, too, T. K. McCraw, *Prophets of Regulation* (1984). On the ambiguities of progressive politics, see J. M. Blum, *The Progressive Presidents* (1980). Among other special studies of important public policies, some of the most rewarding are E. L. Peffer, *The Closing of the Public Domain* (1951), which should be supplemented by Gifford Pinchot's autobiography, and S. P. Hays, *Conservation and the Gospel of Efficiency* (1959); O. E. Anderson, Jr., *The Health of a Nation* (1958); R. Esthus, *Theodore Roosevelt and the International Rivalries* (1970); and W. La Feber, *The Panama Canal* (1978). There is a wealth of good autobiography by and biography of the men around Roosevelt. Besides those autobiographies noted earlier, Robert La Follette's is important, and among the most instructive biographies are P. M. Strum, *Louis D. Brandeis* (1984); J. Braeman, *Albert J. Beveridge* (1971); N. W. Stephenson, *Nelson W. Aldrich* (1920); P. C. Jessup, *Elihu Root,* 2 vols. (1938); D. E. Anderson, *William Howard Taft* (1973); R. Lowiett, *George W. Norris: The Making of a Progressive* (1963); and D. P. Thelen, *Robert M. La Follette and the Insurgent Spirit* (1976).

CHAPTER TWENTY-THREE

AGGRESSION AT SEA

PROGRESSIVISM: RETREAT AND RESURGENCE

Republicans celebrating the inauguration of William Howard Taft in March 1909 had no cause for complacency. Their party had won four successive presidential elections, and its national leaders had preserved the alliances on which its majority rested. But the partners in those alliances — the Old Guard, Midwestern townspeople, urban progressives, and Western agrarians — were growing uneasy with one another. The Democrats, secure in the South and in many Northern cities, were gaining strength among labor unions and farmers. In 1906 and 1908 the Republicans had lost seats in the House of Representatives, and in 1908 they had also lost several governorships. If they hoped to remain in power, they would have to satisfy their restive factions and close ranks against their opposition.

INSURGENCY

A Cautious President Taft, the new president and head of the party, had excellent intentions. A kindly, learned man, he saw the need for social-welfare legislation, understood the purposes of the Roosevelt reforms, for which he had worked with skill, and meant to keep his promise to preserve and further his predecessor's program. He was also a loyal Republican who hoped to strengthen his party, which in his opinion was the only fit instrument of government. In a placid time he might have done well.

He was, however, seriously handicapped for the job he had to do. Taft was almost a caricature of the fat man — genial, usually easygoing. He was also both indecisive and untrained in politics. His career had been on the bench and in appointive administrative offices. He had no instinct for manipulation, no nerve for controversy. His reluctance to use the full powers of the presidency grew out of his interpretation of the Constitution, which led him to believe that he should not interfere in the course of legislation. He was uncomfortable in the company of those who did not share his background of old family, personal means, and Eastern education.

The president was by nature and conviction a conservative whose highest confidence was in the law as he and other judges had shaped it. The bench, he believed, was the appropriate arbiter of social issues. He was antagonistic toward labor unions and suspicious of direct democracy, because he did not trust the majority to make laws. He was also cautious about enlarging the power of the executive for fear that it might encroach upon the traditional authorities of the other branches of government.

Taft was not unresilient. He accepted the need for change. But he did not particularly like it, and he did

President Taft

The public image of a jolly fat man offered but one insight into a complex man. . . . Taft was keenly intelligent and proud of it. . . . He was far from lazy. . . . All his life he labored hard. . . . Taft was highly ambitious. . . . Although sociable and hearty, he was seldom careless or impulsive. . . . Though some people agreed with an enemy who called him a "large amiable island surrounded entirely by persons who knew exactly what they wanted." . . . Theodore Roosevelt . . . once said "that Mr. Taft was one of the best haters he had ever known . . . " And the journalist William Allen White . . . noted that behind the twinkle in his eye could be detected "almost the hint of a serpentine glitter." Taft was gregarious and responsive. But he also possessed the cautious, discerning, and well-honed mind of an experienced federal judge.

From James T. Patterson, *Mr. Republican,* 1972

not at all like to be rushed. Yet he came to his office when the progressives were in a hurry. And they expected him, on the basis of his commitment to Roosevelt's programs, to keep pace with them. He preferred an easier pace, an advance in which each forward step was measured carefully against the footprints trailing through the past.

An Old-Guard Tariff Taft began boldly by calling a special session of Congress to revise the tariff. His campaign speeches had suggested that he preferred a moderate downward revision. Republican representatives of manufacturing interests were still wedded to high protectionism, but Midwestern farmers and their party representatives were convinced that the Dingley duties (see p. 532), by protecting the trusts from foreign competition, were sustaining artificial prices for manufactured goods. Furthermore, as proponents of the "Iowa Idea" argued, Europeans had to sell in the American market in order to earn dollars to buy American agricultural surpluses.

The Western progressives counted on the president's support in getting the tariff lowered, but even before the special session got under way they experienced their first disappointment. Taft appointed a Cabinet of conservatives, five of them corporation lawyers. He also turned down young George Norris of Nebraska and other insurgents in the House of Representatives who appealed for his support in their effort to restrict the power of the Speaker, "Uncle Joe" Cannon of Illinois, an arch-Tory and protectionist. And when debate on the tariff began, Taft made no gesture in behalf of the revision he had advocated.

The House of Representatives passed a tariff bill that made modest concessions to reform. It reduced some duties and imposed an inheritance tax graduated from 1 to 5 percent.

In the Senate, however, the Old Guard carried the day. The finance committee struck out the inheritance tax, made more than 800 amendments to the House bill, and even slightly increased the average rates of the Dingley Tariff. On the floor of the Senate, progressives attacked the swollen tariff schedules and joined the Democrats in urging an income tax. Taft's intercession fostered a compromise that set a 2 percent tax on corporate income and assured passage of a constitutional amendment authorizing a personal income tax. But the compromise little affected the tariff itself. A conference committee of the two houses made modest changes in a number of schedules, but most of those revisions benefited manufacturers rather than farmers or consumers.

The Payne-Aldrich Act as it finally passed was a triumph for the protectionists. During the struggle, Taft had alienated the insurgent Midwesterners and their constituents. In September, in a series of implausible speeches he scolded the progressives who had voted against the tariff, which he declared the best the party had ever enacted.

A Divided Party When Congress met again in 1910, the insurgents made common cause with the Democrats and passed a resolution transferring much of Speaker Cannon's authority to the House Rules Committee. The insurgents then joined the Democrats to amend Taft's railway bill, though the president made support of that bill a test of party loyalty. Taft's measure empowered the Interstate Commerce Commission to fix rates on its own initiative. But it established a Court of Commerce with broad powers of review over the commission's decisions, thereby giving the traditionally conservative judiciary a determining veto. The bill also permitted railroads to acquire competing lines. The Democratic-progressive coalition supported the first of those three provisions, attacked the others, and succeeded in eliminating the third. It further amended the bill to bring telephone and telegraph companies under the commission's jurisdiction and to provide for the physical valuation of railway properties as a basis for determining fair rates.

In the Senate, Aldrich eliminated the provision calling for physical valuation and preserved the Commerce Court by making a trade with the Democrats. In return for their help on the railway bill, he agreed to the admission of Arizona and New Mexico, which were sure to elect four Democratic senators in 1912. This was a Pyrrhic victory: it saved the administration's face, but it did not long prevent a physical-valuation law (which Congress passed early in 1913), and it precipitated open warfare within the Republican party. The insurgents had defied the president, who had unwisely raised the question of party regularity. Now he retaliated by denying them partronage and starting a campaign to defeat them in the fall elections of 1910.

Meanwhile Taft had got caught up in a damaging controversy. With his approval, Secretary of the Interior Richard A. Ballinger had reopened to private sale millions of acres of public land and many valuable waterpower sites that Gifford Pinchot, Roosevelt's trusted friend, had previously arranged to have closed. Pinchot, still chief forester of the United States, learned that Ballinger had been instrumental in selling certain government coal lands in Alaska to a wealthy syndicate controlled by J. P. Morgan and David Guggenheim. Pinchot took the case to Taft, who ruled for Ballinger on every count and urged Pinchot to drop the issue.

Pinchot instead supplied material for two magazine articles attacking Ballinger and exciting public indignation about the affair. He also made his case in a letter that was read to the Senate. Taft had no choice but to dismiss him, though he knew that in so doing he would seem to oppose Roosevelt's conservation policies and possibly antagonize the Colonel. His worst fears materialized. A joint congressional committee in 1910 exonerated Ballinger, but Louis D. Brandeis, counsel for the opposition, revealed that Taft and his attorney general had tampered with evidence sent to Congress. Though Taft was an effective conservationist, Brandeis's argument hurt his reputation. The political damage was compounded when Pinchot greeted Roosevelt after he emerged from the African jungles. In the future Roosevelt always saw the matter Pinchot's way.

The Election of 1910 Taft felt that Roosevelt's friends had plotted to cause a rupture between him and their hero. After Roosevelt's triumphant return to New York, the insurgents set out to enlist his help. Roosevelt, who was temperamentally incapable of remaining out of politics and who was sensitive to a coolness on Taft's part, now decided that his principles needed defending. He embarked on a speaking tour during which he endorsed the administration but gave stronger praise to the insurgents. At Osawatomie, Kansas, invoking the spirit of John Brown, Roosevelt announced his New Nationalism, a program of social welfare, federal regulation of business and industry, and direct democracy. In that address he frightened conservatives by attacking the courts for having invalidated progressive labor legislation.

The friction within the Republican party contributed to its losses in the elections of 1910. The Democrats in many states managed to identify themselves with progressivism and to identify the Republican tariff with the rising cost of living, a particularly sensitive issue among city dwellers. The Democrats won several governorships, including those of New York and New Jersey, which had been safely Republican for many years. For the first time since 1892, the Democrats elected a majority to the House of Representatives. The Republicans' loss of New York and the defeat of Senator Beveridge in Indiana saddened Roosevelt. The Democratic victories over Old Guard candidates in the East and the victories of progressive Republicans in the West repudiated Taft. Overall, the returns suggested that only an insurgent could save the Republicans in the presidential election of 1912, but the Old

The New Nationalism

The citizens of the United States must effectively control the mighty commercial forces which they themselves have called into being. . . . We must have complete and effective publicity of corporate affairs, so that people may know . . . whether the corporations obey the law. . . . Laws should be passed to prohibit the use of corporate funds directly or indirectly for political purposes. . . .

We must have government supervision of the capitalization, not only of public service corporations . . . but of all corporations. . . . I do not wish to see the nation forced into the ownership of the railways . . . and the only alternative is . . . effective regulation, which shall be based on a full knowledge of all the facts, including a physical valuation of property. This physical valuation . . . is needed as the basis of honest capitalization.

We have come to recognize that franchises should never be granted except for a limited time, and never without proper provision for compensation to the public. . . . The same kind and degree of control and supervision which should be exercised over public service corporations should be extended also to combinations which control necessities of life, such as meat, oil, and coal, or which deal in them on an important scale.

Theodore Roosevelt, Speech at Osawatomie, 1910

Guard, tense and defensive, prepared to resist the temper of the time.

Taft's political operatives began in 1911 to strengthen their factions in the North and to wrap up the Republican organizations in the South. At the same time, La Follette set out to recruit support for his own candidacy, which many progressives endorsed. Some of them, however, privately hoped to draft Roosevelt, whose personal appeal remained strong even after his announcement that he had retired from politics.

A Divisive Foreign Policy During the year, Taft succeeded in intensifying party discord and stirring the Colonel to action. In January 1911 the president submitted to Congress a reciprocity agreement with Canada. It put on the free list many agricultural products, including important raw materials for industrial use, and some manufactured goods. Western progressives, fearing the competition of Canadian farmers, opposed the measure. So did most high-tariff advocates, who objected to any breach in the wall of protection. Together they rejected the agreement. But Taft called a special session in April during which the Democrats, delighting in the discomfort of the Republicans, helped administration forces put the measure through. The Canadians, however, disturbed by the prospect of economic competition and Americanization, in September repudiated the agreement. Another tariff debate had produced only more wounds. The Democrats kept them open, with help from Republican insurgents, by passing a series of bills reducing specific schedules—"pop-gun" tariffs that the president systematically vetoed.

Taft's foreign policy also aroused opposition. Secretary of State Philander C. Knox intended to use American economic power to promote American influence, a strategy that differed in theory but not much in practice from Roosevelt's balance of power approach. Knox negotiated treaties with Nicaragua and Honduras providing for the assumption of their European-held debt by American investors and for the appointment of Americans to direct their finances and thus assure the collection of those debts. Though the Senate rejected the treaties, Knox pursued his policy throughout the Caribbean with considerable success. He and Taft also emphasized the possibilities for American investments in China. At the instigation of the State Department, American bankers agreed to join in various commercial projects there, including an international railway consortium.

Roosevelt disapproved of that "dollar diplomacy." He had urged Taft to abandon commercial competition with the Japanese in China. It was more important, the Colonel argued, to cultivate Japanese friendship and to arrange a clearer understanding about Japanese immigration.

Roosevelt also opposed arbitration treaties that Taft negotiated with France and England. Taft was confident that international problems could be solved by courts of law. In the summer of 1911 he submitted to the Senate treaties with France and Great Britain that bound the signatories to arbitrate all differences "susceptible of decision by the application of the principles of law or equity." Those treaties raised the hopes of the thousands of Americans who considered them an important step toward avoiding wars. But Roosevelt denounced the arbitration of questions involving "territory" or "national honor," and he cooperated with like-minded senators who succeeded in amending the treaties so drastically that the president scrapped them. Taft was dismayed by the outcome and offended by Roosevelt's scathing language.

The Road to Revolt Roosevelt in turn was offended by Taft's antitrust policies. The Supreme Court in 1911 in the Standard Oil and American Tobacco cases found that the corporations were monopolies guilty of violating the Sherman Act. Yet the decisions also pronounced the "rule of reason," which held that only unreasonable restraints of trade were unlawful. That was a necessary corollary to antitrust law, for an undiscriminating application of the Sherman Act would weaken the structure and impede the functioning of American business. But whereas Taft was content to have the Court define reasonableness, Roosevelt believed that an administrative agency should make that judgment and should base it on considerations of economic efficiency and business behavior.

This difference of opinion was exemplified in the case of the United States Steel Corporation, then the largest of all holding companies, which Taft chose to prosecute. Roosevelt, who considered the company guiltless, concluded that Taft had acted largely to embarrass him, for the prosecution, which resulted ultimately in an acquittal, and the congressional hearings that it provoked, publicized Roosevelt's negotiations of 1907 with J. P. Morgan (see p. 575).

Taft's antitrust and foreign policies gave Roosevelt a chance to rationalize what he would undoubtedly have done anyway. In February 1912 he announced that his hat was in the ring. A furious battle for the Republican presidential nomination was under way.

The struggle was really between Roosevelt and Taft, who denounced each other with unrestrained vehemence. Though La Follette remained in the race, most of his supporters of 1911 deserted him for Roosevelt. Now just as progressive and vastly more sophisticated and popular than La Follette, Roosevelt had in his New Nationalism formulated a program that promised to distribute the abundance of industrialism, while both promoting and controlling the institutions that had made that abundance possible. Roosevelt stood an

Spring 1912

excellent chance of winning the election. Taft had no such chance, but his dander was up, and the Old Guard cared more about nominating him, defeating Roosevelt, and dominating the party than about beating the Democrats.

The Taft forces, moreover, had in their hands the party apparatus through which they could control the convention. In some states Roosevelt's supporters managed to pass legislation establishing preferential primaries for the nomination, but in the end only thirteen states held such elections. They gave 36 delegates to La Follette, 48 to Taft, and 278 to Roosevelt—an overwhelming mandate for the Colonel. Taft, however, controlled the South, New York, and the crucial national committee, which with its affiliates disposed of 254 contested seats at the convention. With a cynical disregard for the merits of the contestants, it allotted 235 of the contested seats to Taft delegates. The rigged convention then renominated the president on the first ballot.

The Bull Moose Before the balloting took place, most of the Roosevelt men bolted, crying fraud. In August they reconvened as delegates of the new Progressive party. To that convention there came social workers, feminists, intellectuals, and industrialists attracted by Roosevelt's personality and program, and Republican politicians disenchanted with their factional rivals—all imbued with a revivalist spirit. Roosevelt, "strong as a Bull Moose," told them they were standing at Armageddon battling for the Lord and accepted the nomination they tendered with thundering unanimity.

"Strong as a Bull Moose"

The Progressive party was hastily and inadequately organized. Roosevelt probably knew in his heart that by splitting the Republican party he was assuring the election of a Democrat. He and Taft, however, had gone too far to turn back toward compromise. The split was much more than just a personal falling out. Taft's adherents by and large stood for the status quo. Some, to be sure, were of a progressive mind but were unwilling to break with their party. Many were genuinely frightened by Roosevelt's advocacy of the recall of state judicial decisions by referendum, a proposal that in their view would substitute the fickle and untutored will of the majority for the presumed majesty of the courts. For the most part they stayed with Taft because they considered him and his sponsors safe, whereas they considered Roosevelt, along with his friends and his platform, downright alarming.

The Bull Moose platform provided a charter of progressive reform for its own time and for years to come. It advocated the familiar devices of popular democracy—presidential primaries, women's suffrage, the initiative and referendum, and popular election of United States senators. It advocated, too, a comprehensive social-welfare program—conservation of natural and human resources, minimum wages for women, the restriction of child labor, workmen's compensation, social insurance, a federal income tax,* and the limitation of injunctions in labor disputes. Finally, in keeping with Roosevelt's ideas about the restructuring of government, it called for expert federal commissions to adjust the tariff and to regulate interstate business and industry. Party and candidate alike stood for social justice and popular rule, and stood, too, for the application of efficiency to the management of public problems, an objective attractive at once to many Progressives and to many men of affairs. As it developed, however, they faced formidable competition as champions of reform from a united and inspired Democratic party.

*The Sixteenth Amendment, which provided for an income tax, was already before the states, as was the Seventeenth, providing for popular election of senators. Both were ratified in 1913.

PROGRESSIVISM AT ZENITH

Woodrow Wilson The Democratic candidate in 1912 had found his way into politics by an unusual route. Woodrow Wilson, the son of a Southern Presbyterian minister, had abandoned a brief and unrewarding career in law for one in education. After earning his doctorate at The Johns Hopkins University, Wilson taught history and political science at Bryn Mawr, Wesleyan of Connecticut, and Princeton, his own alma mater, of which he became president in 1902. He first won national attention for his writings, especially his earliest book, *Congressional Government* (1885), which criticized the weakness of the executive and the inefficiencies of Congress and praised the British parliamentary system. As president of Princeton Wilson initiated a number of celebrated educational reforms, but he lost his battle with faculty members and wealthy alumni over plans for a graduate school. That struggle brought on his resignation but also gave him a reputation as a champion of democracy in education.

Wilson resigned in 1910 to accept the Democratic nomination for governor of New Jersey. He had always had political ambitions. Now he owed his nomination to Democratic machine leaders who were impressed, as were his wealthy New York friends, by his stature and his presumably conservative economic views. But during the campaign Wilson adopted the program of New Jersey progressives. As governor he made a brilliant record that put New Jersey in the van of progressive states (see p. 567) and put Wilson in the lead for the Democratic presidential nomination.

In 1912 the Democrats, like the Republicans, were caught in a momentous struggle over selecting a candidate. Wilson had offended his conservative sponsors, who now helped organize a movement to defeat him. His opponents were particularly successful in the South, where they captured most of the state delegations. In the East, the city machines, alarmed by Wilson's treatment of their counterparts in New Jersey, embarrassed him by publicizing sections of his *History of the American People* (1902), which disparaged the new immigrants. In the farming West, moreover, the favorite candidate was Champ Clark, the folksy "Ol' Hound Dawg" of Missouri. Bryan Democrats there rightly judged that Wilson was not one of them.

During the national convention at Baltimore, Bryan, probably more to further his own ambitions than Wilson's, took the floor to castigate any candidate supported by Tammany. Tammany had just moved New York into the Clark column, thus contributing to his majority. But it took a two-thirds vote to nominate, and Wilson's floor leaders gradually made the deals that turned the convention their way. One of those deals assured the vice-presidential nomination to Thomas R. Marshall of Indiana, a politician best remembered for his fetching assertion that what the country needed was "a good five-cent cigar." On the 43rd ballot Wilson won a majority of the votes; on the 46th, the nomination.

The Election of 1912 The basic contest in 1912 was between the Democrats and the Progressives. Certain of the South, assisted elsewhere by the Republican schism, the Democratic leadership took pains to preserve party unity by placating the factions that had opposed Wilson and by appealing to the urban ethnic groups that had long sustained the party's political machines. But Wilson, though the odds were with him, could not take Roosevelt for granted. He had to meet the challenge for Progressive votes.

In many respects the Bull Moose and Democratic platforms were similar, but there were several significant differences between them. Where the Progressives endorsed a protective tariff, the Democrats called for sharp downward revision. Where the Progressives demanded powerful federal regulatory agencies, the Democrats emphasized state rights. The Democrats did not spell out a broad social-welfare program, but they did advocate limiting the use of injunctions against labor unions. The party's continuing insistence on that issue held the allegiance of Gompers and most of his associates in the American Federation of Labor. Moreover, farmers responded enthusiastically to Democratic promises to make loans for agriculture cheaper and more readily available.

More than the platforms, the attitudes of the candidates marked the differences between the parties. Roosevelt's New Nationalism assumed that the consolidation of the economy was inevitable and healthful. He welcomed big business but demanded big government to supervise it and to promote the welfare of nonbusiness groups. The political theorist Herbert Croly expressed these ideas forcefully in *The Promise of American Life* (1909), an influential book that helped Roosevelt and like-minded people articulate their principles. It demanded positive, comprehensive federal planning for the national interest and for social reform.

The Danger of Bigness

I think we are in a position, after the experience of the last 20 years, to state two things: in the first place, that a corporation may well be too large to be the most efficient instrument of production and distribution, and, in the second place, whether it has exceeded the point of greatest economic efficiency or not, it may be too large to be tolerated among the people who desire to be free. . . . Those propositions should underlie any administration of the law. . . .

It seems to me that there is a distinct peril in the community in having one organization control a very large percentage of the market. . . . Where there is found to be a combination in restraint of trade, if the combination controls 40 percent or more of the market, that creates a presumption of unreasonableness. . . . No corporation ought to control so large a percentage if we desire to maintain competition at all.

From Louis D. Brandies, Testimony Before the Committee on Interstate Commerce, 1911

Wilson had reached dissimilar conclusions. There lingered in his mind a complex of ideas he had cherished since youth. He was a devout Presbyterian who held human beings individually responsible to God for their actions. Guilt in business affairs, he believed, was also personal guilt. Where a corporation misbehaved, his instinct was to punish its officers as the Lord punished sinners. He was more the stern prophet than the vigorous promoter. He was also convinced that laissez-faire principles of economics would work if only the state would protect and encourage competition. It should, he felt, act as a handicapper resolved to make the race equitable at the start and as a policeman determined to keep the runners in their lanes. An enemy of political and business corruption, a believer in popular democracy, a proponent of regulation to prevent industrial abuses, Wilson, a progressive in the tradition of rural America, was uncomfortable with Croly's formulations.

Another able intellectual, Louis D. Brandeis of Massachusetts, helped Wilson organize his developing ideas. The great corporations, Brandeis argued, controlled credit, raw materials, and markets. They prevented competition and guarded their own inefficient methods, excessive profits, and overcapitalized values. They had corrupted government, Brandeis went on, and had to be prosecuted and broken up. He also urged that the rules of competition be defined by law and that federal programs be launched to provide credit for small and new businesses. His ideas and the data with which he supported them confirmed Wilson's own theories, which the candidate set forth in the program he called the New Freedom.

Roosevelt's plans, so Wilson said, would result in "partnership between the government and the trusts." The Democratic alternative would ensure a free economy and preserve free government. "Free men," he asserted, "need no guardians." Indeed, they could not submit to guardians and remain free, for submission would produce "a corruption of the will."

Wilson called for "regulated competition" in preference to "regulated monopoly." He feared that individuals were being "swallowed up" by great organizations, and he condemned what he considered "an extraordinary and very sinister concentration in . . . business." He demanded "a body of laws which will look after the men . . . who are sweating blood to get their foothold in the world of endeavor." Roosevelt called Wilson's program "rural Toryism." In a sense it was. But Wilson affirmed the hopes of the farm, of the small town, of middle-class America. His party, furthermore, retained the allegiance of the South and of urban ethnic groups that had long voted Democratic.

Wilson won a telling victory, though he polled only 41.9 percent of the popular vote. Roosevelt received only 27.4 percent and Taft only 23.2. In the electoral count Wilson led his rivals 435 to 88 and 8, and the Democrats carried both houses of Congress. The Democrats, who ran best in the areas of their traditional strength, had needed the Republican division to win. The returns were just as clearly a triumph for reform. Taft's miserable showing revealed the voters' disdain for standpat government, while the dissatisfaction with existing conditions was evidenced by the nearly 1 million votes for Socialist candidate Eugene V. Debs and by the remarkable support won by the Bull Moose party in its initial test.

It was also remarkable that so lively a contest produced a turnout of voters that, as in other presidential elections of the first decades of the century, fell short of the percentage of eligibles who had voted in the 1880s and 1890s and earlier in the 1840s. Apart from those voters who had been disfranchised in the South, many other Americans were obviously either preoccupied with questions that politics did not address or persuaded that the choices politics offered made little difference. Yet the degree of voter participation never alone measured the significance of elections, for politics had never been wholly rational. In 1912 there was a choice. At the least, the election signaled the resurgence of reform that marked Wilson's first term in office.

A Democratic Tariff Wilson realized that he could work most efficiently through his own party. Though he had come to recognize the power inherent in the presidency, he also considered himself a party leader in the English style, with the right to hold party members in Congress to his programs and, if necessary, to appeal over their heads to the electorate. From the first he set out to unite the Democratic factions, to use his united party to legislate, and to endow it with a record and reputation that would make a majority of Americans prefer it to any rival.

Wilson, however, had neither the temperament nor the experience to get along with professional politicians. A tense and angular man, he was incapable of displaying good fellowship he did not feel. But he knew his limitations and compensated for them by selecting a group of skilled advisers. Among others they included Bryan, the new secretary of state, influential as always with the agrarian liberals; Albert S. Burleson, postmaster general, a veteran Southern congressman popular among the party regulars on the Hill; Secretary of the Treasury William G. McAdoo, a progressive businessman who had the confidence of those who had made Wilson's nomination possible; Joseph P. Tumulty, the president's private secretary, a young Irishman wise in the ways of machine politicians and professional journalists; and Colonel Edward M. House, an urbane Texan who attached himself to Wilson and became his "second personality." Though House had neither title nor office, he quickly acquired important responsibilities as a liaison man between the president and leaders of the party, of American finance, and of the Congress, as well as between the president and foreign heads of state.

Edward M. House: urbane Texan

Informed and assisted by his subordinates, Wilson made his own major decisions and gave a personal stamp to his executive leadership. Right after his inauguration he called a special session of Congress to fulfill the Democratic pledge of tariff revision. He dramatized the session and his intended role by appearing personally, as had no president since Jefferson's time, to address the Congress. He had already begun a fruitful cooperation with the committees responsible for tariff recommendations. In May 1913, only a month after the president's address, the House passed a bill reducing average *ad valorem* rates about

11 percent; adding a number of consumer goods to the free list; and eliminating the protection of iron, steel, and various other products of the trusts. To make up for the attending loss in revenue, the bill levied a modest graduated income tax, which ratification of the Sixteenth Amendment had legalized two months earlier.

The test of Wilson's leadership came in the Senate, where the Democrats had a majority of only three votes. Democratic senators from sugar- and wool-producing states were reluctant to leave those products on the free list where the House had placed them. Wilson urged them to vote with their party, but they wavered, and lobbyists for protection tried to exploit the chance for logrolling. The president then called on public opinion to "check and destroy" the "intolerable burden" of "insidious" lobbyists. His statement helped to initiate an investigation of the private interests of all senators, some of whom, it developed, stood to profit personally from the protection of wool and sugar. With a refreshed sensitivity to public opinion, all but two Democrats voted for the party's bill. It kept sugar and wool on the free list and reduced the general level of rates another 4 percent. It also, thanks to the efforts of progressives in all the parties, doubled the maximum surtax on personal incomes.

The tariff of 1913, the Underwood-Simmons Act, removed an accumulation of privileges and, without abandoning protection, reduced previously swollen schedules. It modified the federal tax structure by shifting some of the burden to those best able to bear it, a significant precedent for the future. It was a convincing demonstration that the Democrats could achieve the goals of the New Freedom, and it was an acknowledged triumph for Wilson's leadership.

Banking Reform Pressing his gains, the president had urged the special session of Congress to correct the nation's anachronistic money and banking system. The Panic of 1907 (see p. 575) had underscored the inflexibility of currency and the inelasticity of credit. The events of the panic also suggested that financial power was concentrated in the hands of a small group of Eastern private bankers. That situation had been the subject of investigation by a House committee chaired by Congressman Arsène P. Pujo. Its findings, later popularized in Louis Brandeis's *Other People's Money* (1914), persuaded many progressives that there existed a "money trust."

Southern and Western farmers had long assumed that there was a bankers' conspiracy against their interests and had long agitated for monetary reform. By 1913 the bankers themselves were in favor of reform, but of their own kind. The experience of the panic and the report of Aldrich's Monetary Commission (see p. 575) led most of them to advocate central control of the banking system and the creation of a currency responsive to, and partly based on, the expansion and contraction of commercial paper—that is, loans that banks made to business.

The bankers, taking as their models the Bank of England and the controversial second United States Bank, wanted a central bank to be authorized by the government but privately controlled. They also wanted it to issue currency on its own liability. The conservative Democrats modified those proposals by replacing a single central bank with a number of regional banks supervised by a federal board that bankers would control. This modification, the plan Wilson at first favored, failed to satisfy the party's progressive and agrarian factions. To meet their minimum demands, the president agreed that the government should appoint the supervising board and that the bank notes issued by the new system should be obligations of the United States.

Those concessions fell short of the program advanced by Southern farmers. They called for a prohibition of interlocking directorates, for public control of the regional banks, for permitting reserve banks to discount agricultural paper, and for preventing the use of commercial paper as a basis for currency. Bryan mediated their differences with Wilson, who met them part way. The president conceded the discounting of agricultural notes and promised later to take care of interlocking directorates. In return, the militants supported the rest of the bill, which the House passed in September 1913.

There was resistance again from conservatives in the Senate. Wilson overcame some of it by another appeal for party responsibility and by a timely use of patronage. Again taking his case to the people, he asserted that bankers were trying to defeat the measure by creating artificial fears of impending panic. Although Senate conservatives managed to increase the percentage of gold reserves required for the issue of bank notes and to reduce the authority of the Federal Reserve Board, the Democrats were sufficiently united to pass the bill without further changes in December 1913.

The Federal Reserve Act was the most important statute of Wilson's administration. The Federal Reserve Board and the regional Reserve Banks gave the United States its first efficient banking system since the time of Andrew Jackson. Their power over currency and credit put into responsible hands the means to provide the flexibility of short-term credit that was so badly needed. Though private banking interests dominated the regional banks with their large powers, the regulatory authority of the board assured a greater degree of public control over banking than ever before. Indeed, the act remedied almost all the deficiencies in American banking and currency that informed observers then recognized. Without the new system the country could not have adjusted to the financial strains of the First World War. There was still need to ease long-term agricultural credit and (though it was not yet understood) to endow public authorities with effective instruments to modulate the business cycle. But the new law was an impressive structural reform. Americans of all points of view and parties applauded it and the president's "great exhibition of leadership" in guiding it through Congress.

The New Freedom and the Trusts When Congress met in regular session in December 1913, Wilson presented his program for regulating industry. He asked Congress for legislation to make it impossible for interrelated groups to control holding companies, to create a commission to help dissolve corporations found in restraint of trade, and to define unfair business practices.

Those recommendations, too strong for conservatives, did not satisfy either labor leaders, who urged the exemption of unions from the Sherman Antitrust Act, or Bull Moosers, who advocated a strong regulatory agency. Louis Brandeis had moved closer to the Bull Moose point of view, and he now drafted a bill that Wilson supported. It created a Federal Trade Commission to prevent the unlawful suppression of competition. The measure passed, but only after Southern conservatives had helped the Republicans amend it to provide for broad court review of the commission's order, a review that soon proved to be debilitating.

A companion measure, the Clayton bill, was also amended before enactment. As the House passed it, it followed the prescriptions of Wilson's message, defined unfair practices, and forbade interlocking directorates. Senate conservatives modified that prohibition by exempting instances that did not tend to decrease competition. That standard failed to assure prosecution of the largest holding companies. It was also in the Senate that friends of labor added to the bill a statement declaring that labor was not to be considered a commodity, a mere article of commerce. The House had earlier included a clause exempting labor unions and farm organizations from antitrust prosecutions, but only when those groups were lawfully pursuing legitimate aims. As the courts were to interpret the Clayton Act, the reservation about legitimate aims canceled the exemption.

The antitrust laws of 1914 failed to prescribe business conduct to the extent Wilson had sought, and they failed to give unions the freedom of activity Gompers had urged. The Federal Trade Commission, moreover, had less power than many progressives had recommended. But the weaknesses of the legislation were not immediately apparent, and the laws seemed to constitute another, though limited, victory for the administration. In less than two years Wilson had reached the major statutory goals of his New Freedom.

The voters responded favorably in the elections of 1914. Superficially the Democrats suffered that year, for the Republicans made sizable gains. But the Democrats retained control of both houses of Congress. The collapse of the Progressive party helped the Republicans in the Northeast, where they made their best showing. Elsewhere the Democrats picked up some progressive support, and in the new Congress that sat in 1915 and 1916 Southern and Western farmers had a larger voice than they had had before. The returns convinced perceptive Democratic strategists that they could carry the nation in 1916 only by winning the Progressives of the West.

In Behalf of Progress As Wilson saw it, the interests of legitimate business did not conflict with the need for social reform. His appointments to the Supreme Court, the Federal Reserve Board, and the Federal Trade Commission had on the whole been conservative. After the election he adjusted to the demands of congressional and national politics. He encouraged reform Democrats, who in 1916 succeeded in passing the Federal Farm Loan Act and the Child Labor Act, which he had earlier opposed. On matters of international trade, the president came to respect the program of the Progressive party for the promotion of American business. He endorsed legislation permitting firms engaged in export trade to combine to meet foreign competition, and he supported an act in 1916 creating a nonpartisan, expert tariff commission designed to prevent the dumping of foreign goods on the American market.

In 1916 Wilson also practically ordered Congress to establish the eight-hour day at ten-hour pay for railway labor. Congress responded with the Adamson Act. In this case the president acted largely to prevent a threatening strike that would have tied up shipping of war materials for France and England, but his intercession won plaudits from organized labor. Labor leaders and reformers had earlier found convincing evidence of Wilson's friendship in his nomination of Louis D. Brandeis, the first Jew to gain the office, as associate justice of the Supreme Court.

The Wilson of 1916 had moved a long way from his position of 1912. His New Freedom had gained larger dimensions as well as a larger constituency. In endeavoring to promote both business and social welfare, the president revealed his faith, a characteristically progressive faith, in a dynamic but humane capitalism, and in the role of government in fostering that end. He had a right to boast that the Democrats had opened their hearts to "the demands of social justice" and had "come very near to carrying out the platform of the Progressive Party" as well as their own.

WILSON AND MORAL DIPLOMACY

The Force of Moral Principle The conditions of world affairs had changed only superficially between 1901, when Theodore Roosevelt took office as president, and 1913, when Wilson and Secretary of State Bryan brought a different perspective to American foreign policy. Wilson and Bryan were guided by attitudes they shared with many progressive Americans, particularly rural reformers, social workers, and Protestant Social Gospelers. "The force of America," the president said during one crisis, "is the force of moral principle." Moral principle, as he interpreted it, involved a duty to work for peace both by example and through diplomacy. Wilson and Bryan also felt that they had a mission to teach semideveloped countries to live according to the kind of legal and constitutional system that existed in the United States. They believed that that system was not only especially efficient but especially ethical. They believed, too, that there was a definable body of international law that moral nations should obey in their relations with one another. And they placed their hope for peace, as well as for American commercial interests, in that law rather than in systems of alliances or in defensive or deterrent military buildups.

Those attitudes led Wilson and Bryan to distrust the career men in the navy, the army, and the State Department, whom they considered conventional and even cynical. The president and the secretary of state were willing to risk offending the experts in order to strike out along new diplomatic paths. Bryan launched his program in 1913 and 1914 by negotiating treaties with Great Britain, France, Italy, and 27 lesser powers. Those treaties provided for submitting all disputes among the signatories to permanent commissions of investigation. For one year, while investigation proceeded, the parties to the treaties promised that they would neither go to war nor increase their armaments. At the end of that year they could either accept or reject the findings of the investigation, but Bryan expected the "cooling-off" period to remove the chance of war.

In a similarly benign spirit Wilson in 1913 withdrew American support from the Chinese railway consortium that Taft had helped to arrange (see

p. 589). The United States, Wilson said, could not be a partner to foreign interference in Chinese affairs. He also recognized the new Republic of China, the first major recognition that government received.

The most imminent threat to China's national integrity was Japan, whose relations with the United States had deteriorated because of the troublesome race issue. Wilson had characteristic Southern prejudices about race. During his administration there was increasing segregation of black Americans within the federal service. Never an enemy of Jim Crow, Wilson made no effort to dissuade California politicians who were determined in 1913 to prohibit Japanese from owning land in that state. On the president's advice, they passed a statute that achieved that end indirectly, and without violating American treaty obligations. But the Japanese were nonetheless humiliated. Their ambassador protested to the State Department; there were anti-American disturbances in Japan; and the Joint Board of the Army and Navy, deeming war probable, advised Wilson to move warships into Chinese and Philippine waters. The president resorted instead to conciliatory diplomacy. The ensuing exchange of notes eased the crisis and ended talk of war, but the issue remained unresolved, and the Japanese remained understandably resentful.

That resentment contributed to a new controversy in 1915. The preoccupation of European powers with the war then raging on their own continent gave Japan a chance to make 21 extraordinary demands of China. Had China agreed to the treaty containing the demands, it would have become a political and economic dependency. American protests, supplemented by pressure from England, persuaded the Japanese temporarily to moderate their terms. The episode revealed how tenuous the balance of power in Asia had become. It also disclosed Bryan's commitment to conventional national policies and to American commercial interests. The United States, Bryan warned Japan in a portentous note, could not recognize any agreement impairing the Open Door policy, the treaty rights of Americans, or the political or territorial integrity of China.

Confusion in Latin America As in Asia, so in Latin America, Wilson intended to abandon "dollar diplomacy" with its attendant intrusions on the sovereignty of weak nations. He also hoped to cultivate the friendship of Latin American peoples and to help them achieve a higher standard of living and a more democratic government. He began convincingly by negotiating a treaty with Colombia providing both apology and indemnity for Roosevelt's Panamanian adventure. But Roosevelt's friends in the Senate prevented approval of that treaty, and the administration's benign purposes soon produced policies that seemed imperialistic to those countries they were designed to assist.

A combination of circumstances made moral diplomacy difficult. The small nations in and around the Caribbean were, as they had long been, impoverished and turbulent. Unwilling to have the United States government assume and service their debts, Wilson relied on private bankers, whose motives he suspected. Like Roosevelt, he would not permit turmoil in the area to breed revolutions or European intercessions that might endanger the approaches to the isthmus. Consequently he turned to American troops and, like Taft, to American dollars to keep order. Since the local forces of order were often also the forces of reaction, Wilson at times resisted reform. Further, he let Bryan send to the Caribbean area "deserving Democrats" lacking any qualifications for diplomacy except faithful party service.

Yet the president tended to attribute qualities of justice and legality to the reactionary government Bryan supported in Nicaragua and to the protectorates the administration established in Santo Domingo and Haiti. Wilson never fully appreciated how closely his policies resembled "dollar diplomacy" or the intensity of the anti-American feeling those policies provoked.

The president also plunged into Mexican affairs. During the late nineteenth century, large landholders, the army, the hierarchy of the Catholic Church, and foreign investors had sustained a dictatorial government in Mexico that had suppressed the landless, uneducated, impoverished peasants and workers. In 1911 a revolution, in this phase instigated by a middle class seeking greater opportunity, overthrew the government, but in 1913 General Victoriano Huerta engineered a coup d'état that restored a reactionary regime under his domination. The revolutionists, who called themselves Constitutionalists, continued to resist under Venustiano Carranza, their able and implacable leader. Though his forces controlled much of the country, the major European powers recognized the Huerta government.

Americans with financial interests in Mexico urged Wilson also to do so, but the president would have no formal dealings with a government of assassins. He therefore refused to appoint an ambassador to Mexico.

Latin America: Wilsonian Doctrine

The dignity, the courage, the self-possession, the self-respect of the Latin American States . . . deserve nothing but the admiration and applause of the world. . . .

We must prove ourselves their friends, and champions upon terms of equality and honor. . . . We must show ourselves friends by comprehending their interests. . . .

Comprehension must be the soil in which shall grow all the fruits of friendship, and there is a reason and a compulsion lying behind all of this which is dearer than anything else to the thoughtful men of America. I mean the development of constitutional liberty in the world. Human rights, national integrity, and opportunity as against material interests—that . . . is the issue which we now have to face.

Woodrow Wilson, Address at Mobile, Alabama, October 27, 1913

He did, however, send a series of special agents, whose reports intensified his dislike for the regime but also led him erroneously to believe that the United States could decree a solution to its neighbor's problems.

Wilson followed a policy of "watchful waiting" until October 1913, when Huerta, supported by British oil interests, proclaimed himself military dictator. The president then demanded that Huerta retire. The United States, he assured the Mexicans, sought no territory but only the advancement of "constitutional liberty."

To cut off the dictator's support, Wilson promised to protect British property if a Constitutionalist victory endangered it. He also, in 1914, drove through Congress a law repealing the exemption from tolls for American coastal shipping using the Panama Canal. That exemption, as the British had argued, violated an Anglo-American treaty that pledged the United States not to discriminate against British shipping using the canal. In full agreement, Wilson timed his action also to serve his Mexican policy. The danger of war in Europe made the British particularly solicitous of American friendship, and in March 1914 they withdrew their recognition of Huerta.

Meanwhile Wilson had told Carranza that the United States would join him in war against Huerta if he would keep the revolution orderly. Opposed to any American interference, Carranza rejected the indiscreet offer. But, since he needed the arms that an American embargo denied all Mexicans, his representatives assured Wilson that he would respect property rights. Somewhat skeptically, the president lifted the embargo in February 1914.

Intervention in Mexico Soon thereafter Wilson seized an excuse for intervention. On April 10, 1914, an Huertista colonel arrested some American sailors who had gone ashore at Tampico. Though the Mexicans immediately apologized, they refused to make a formal salute to the American flag. On that pretext Wilson prepared to occupy Vera Cruz, Mexico's most important port. On April 20 he asked Congress for authority to use military force "to obtain from General Huerta . . . the fullest recognition of the rights and dignity of the United States."

The next day, before Congress could act, Wilson ordered the navy to seize Vera Cruz in order to prevent a German merchant ship from landing arms for Huerta. Both Americans and Mexicans were killed in the action that followed. While American newspapers predicted war and Wilson ordered war plans drawn up, the Constitutionalists as well as the Huertistas denounced the violation of their national sovereignty.

Latin America: Wilsonian Practice

The Government of the United States will . . . aid the Haitian Government in the proper and efficient development of its agricultural, mineral and commercial resources and in the establishment of the finances of Haiti on a firm and solid basis.

The President of Haiti shall appoint, upon nomination by the President of the United States, a General Receiver . . . who shall collect . . . all customs duties on imports and exports [and] . . . a Financial Adviser, who shall . . . devise an adequate system of public accounting, aid in increasing the revenues and adjusting them to the expenses . . . and make such other recommendations . . . as may be deemed necessary for the welfare and prosperity of Haiti. . . .

The Haitian Government obligates itself . . . to create without delay an efficient constabulary . . . composed of native Haitians. This constabulary shall be organized and officered by Americans . . . upon nomination by the President of the United States.

Treaty between the United States and Haiti, 1916

Fortunately both countries accepted an offer of mediation from Argentina, Brazil, and Chile. The resulting proposals were never signed by the Constitutionalists, who had become the dominant faction in Mexico. Huerta abdicated in July, and Carranza marched into Mexico City in August 1914, angry with the United States and disdainful of Wilson.

During 1915 the revolution in Mexico reached high pitch. Violence sometimes accompanied reform. The destruction of private property and attacks on priests and nuns excited American demands for intervention, especially among Catholics, Republicans eager to embarrass Wilson, and jingoes spoiling for a war. The president resisted that pressure, partly because he respected Carranza's objectives, partly because he dared not let embroilments in Mexico tie his hands in the crisis then developing with Germany. In October 1915 he recognized the Constitutionalists as the de facto government.

Within a few months Pancho Villa, a champion of the peasants, created a new crisis. An opponent of Carranza, Villa had earlier won some support from Wilson. In January 1916, however, Villa murdered a

Pancho Villa

group of Americans whom he had removed from a train in Mexico. In March he killed 19 more during a raid on Columbus, New Mexico. Again there were demands in the United States for war, but Wilson tried to contain the situation. He ordered an expedition to cross the border and punish Villa but to avoid engaging the Constitutionalists.

The futile pursuit of Villa aroused Mexican tempers. In April, Carranza insisted the Americans leave his country. Wilson refused. When Villa brazenly raided Texas, the president called up the national guard for service on the border and commissioned plans for a full-scale invasion. Twice serious skirmishes between American and Constitutionalist soldiers occurred. Carranza, however, needed to devote his full energies to his domestic affairs, and Wilson had growing problems in Europe. Both men, moreover, genuinely desired peace. In July 1916 they agreed to appoint a joint commission to resolve their differences. Although Carranza later rejected its decision, the danger of war had passed. In January 1917 Wilson called the troops home, and two months later he granted the Constitutionalists *de jure* recognition.

In the balance Wilson's restraint outweighed his moralism. In attempting to impose American standards upon the Mexicans, the president offended those he wanted to help. But he also succeeded in withstanding the demands for war that he had inadvertently fanned. He succeeded most of all in grasping the need for reform in Mexico. The American people in varying degrees shared his confusions and his distaste for the excesses of revolution. Most of them, however, also shared his reluctance to permit disagreement and discord to grow into war.

PROBLEMS OF NEUTRALITY

War in Europe In August 1914 a crisis within the empire of Austria-Hungary provided the match to light the fire of war in Europe. It had been brewing for more than a decade. Ambitious Germany dominated the alliance of the Central Powers, including Austria-Hungary and the Ottoman Empire. On the other side were the western powers, France and England, their ally, Russia, and soon also Italy, a partner bought by promises of more lands (see Map 23-1).

Though most Americans had known that war was threatening, they were shocked by the outbreak of

Map 23-1
The European powers at war

hostilities and unprepared to face the problems war imposed on them. Relieved that war seemed so far away, they had yet to learn that distance alone could not insulate the United States. Most progressives tended to believe that selfish commercial rivalries had moved the European nations toward disaster. They believed, too, that the United States could serve the world best by concentrating on further reform at home, by setting a noble example of peace and democracy. Even those who were not progressives were slow to recognize the intensity of nationalistic emotions that war bred, slower still in seeing how those emotions blocked a return to peace. Americans, like other peoples, had no experience with the shocks of total war, calculated brutality, and mass hatred.

The administration's initial statements of policy gave official sanction to attitudes that prevailed throughout the nation. Wilson expressed his faith that the United States could play "a part of impartial mediation," and he urged Americans to be "neutral in fact as well as in name." But impartiality of sentiment was impossible. Many Americans of various national origins identified themselves with the loyalties of their forebears. The German- and Irish-Americans particularly supported the Central Powers, as did Czechs, Slovaks, Serbians, and others from Austria-Hungary. British-Americans favored the western Allies. The similarities between British and American speech and institutions, furthermore, fostered widespread sympathy for England. Wilson himself had long been an admirer of England's culture.

Belligerents in both camps tried to enlist American emotions. The Germans circulated stories alleging that the British blockade was causing mass starvation. The British published accounts of atrocities allegedly committed by German soldiers. Both sides exaggerated, but propaganda won few converts. The course of the war itself made a deeper impression. Germany's invasion of Belgium in August 1914, which violated a treaty pledging Germany to respect Belgian neutrality, offended many Americans. Propaganda could not erase that evidence of German ruthlessness, and evidence was to come of German intrigue against the United States. The Allied cause gradually gained adherents, though very few even among them favored American participation in a war across the Atlantic.

Neutral Rights While Wilson remained firm in his purpose to be neutral in fact, he upheld neutral rights to trade and to the use of the ocean. Those traditional objectives of American diplomacy had, the president believed, a clear basis in law and morality. His standards for defining neutral rights were "the existing rules of international law and the treaties of the United States." But those rules were uncertain, especially under the unprecedented conditions created by the tactics of the submarine, the novel weapon on which Germany counted heavily. Particularly with Germany, but also with England, troubles arose over Wilson's interpretations of American neutral rights.

The British, who controlled the seas, were determined that the Allies alone should receive munitions and other essential war materials purchased from the United States. They therefore established a tight blockade of Germany and narrowly limited the kinds of goods that American ships could carry to neutral ports from which they could be sent on to Germany. The British also diverted suspect shipping to their own ports, confiscated many cargoes, interfered with American mail in order to intercept military and economic information, and ultimately forbade British subjects to do any business with American firms "blacklisted" for violating British rules.

Wilson protested often and vigorously against these and other British practices that infringed upon

Neutral in fact

traditional neutral rights. The British, engaged in total war, considered him peevishly legalistic. But, since they had to have American supplies, they made the basic objective of their diplomacy "the maximum blockade that could be enforced without a rupture with the United States."

The success of that policy owed much to the increasing goodwill Americans felt for England. It owed at least as much to the growing importance of war production for the American economy. Allied demands for war materials stimulated American heavy industry and provided a market for American agriculture. Indeed, with a timely solicitude the British even provided funds to help stabilize the price of cotton at a level satisfactory to the Democratic South.

There were no international rules against selling war materials to the Allies. And if Wilson had refused to permit such sales, he would have indirectly aided the Central Powers. Nor were there any rules to prevent American bankers from making loans to finance Allied purchases. Bryan at first maintained that such loans violated "the true spirit of neutrality," but early in 1915, when the Allies were desperate for funds, he partially reversed himself. Before the end of that year the State Department had approved enormous loans, arranged by American financiers, without which England and France could not have continued to buy the materials they had to have. Thereafter the United States had an economic stake in preventing a German triumph.

The Germans, who were unable to transport supplies through the British blockade, protested against American sales of war materials to the Allies and against British interpretations of maritime law. They also sent out submarines to destroy Allied shipping. These U-boats created the issue on which German-American relations ultimately foundered.

The Submarine Issue Submarines could not operate according to the traditional rules governing the conduct of ships bent on destroying commerce. Their effectiveness depended upon surprise. They could not warn their prospective targets before attacking them or remove crews or passengers from stricken ships. Yet Wilson insisted that the Germans observe traditional international law.

The submarine issue arose in February 1915, when Germany proclaimed a war zone around the British Isles (see Map 23-2). Enemy ships, Germany warned, would be sunk on sight, and neutral ships would be in

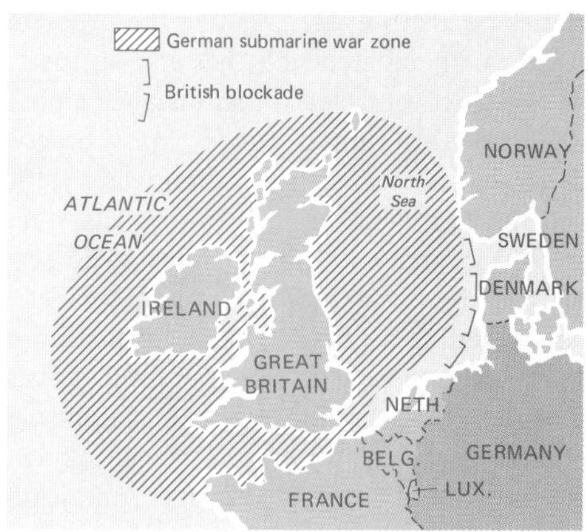

Map 23-2 *The war at sea*

danger of misidentification. In a sharp reply Wilson called the sinking of merchant ships without visit and search "a wanton act." The destruction of an American ship, he declared, or the loss of American lives on belligerent ships, would be regarded as "a flagrant violation of neutral rights." It would be an offensive act for which he would hold Germany to "strict accountability." His note expressed the horror most Americans felt toward the barbarity of modern weapons. It left the Germans with a choice between abandoning their strategic plan or risking American antagonism.

They chose to take the risk. In April 1915 an American went down aboard a British ship. On May 1 an American ship was torpedoed. Six days later the Germans sank the British passenger liner *Lusitania,* and with it died more than 1,200 men, women, and children, 128 of them Americans whom the Germans had warned not to embark. That sinking shocked the nation. A minority wanted to break off relations with Germany, which in their view was guilty of "murder," as Theodore Roosevelt put it. Most Americans of that mind hoped soon to see the United States at war. At the other extreme, those who sympathized with Germany and those who considered war the worst possible calamity were eager to arbitrate the issue, if necessary to prohibit travel on the ships of belligerents. The majority of Americans were angry but anxious to avoid hostilities. Like Wilson, they hoped the problem could be negotiated away.

"There is such a thing," the president told one audience, "as a man being too proud to fight. There is such a thing as a nation being so right that it does not

"All the News That's Fit to Print."

The New York Times.

Weather Today and Sunday, Fair.

VOL. LXIV...NO. 20,923. NEW YORK, SATURDAY, MAY 8, 1915.—TWENTY-FOUR PAGES. ONE CENT In Greater New York, Jersey City and Newark. | Elsewhere TWO CENTS.

LUSITANIA SUNK BY A SUBMARINE, PROBABLY 1,260 DEAD; TWICE TORPEDOED OFF IRISH COAST; SINKS IN 15 MINUTES; CAPT. TURNER SAVED, FROHMAN AND VANDERBILT MISSING; WASHINGTON BELIEVES THAT A GRAVE CRISIS IS AT HAND

SHOCKS THE PRESIDENT

Washington Deeply Stirred by the Loss of American Lives.

BULLETINS AT WHITE HOUSE

Wilson Reads Them Closely, but Is Silent on the Nation's Course.

HINTS OF CONGRESS CALL

Loss of Lusitania Recalls Firm Tone of Our First Warning to Germany.

CAPITAL FULL OF RUMORS

Reports That Liner Was to be Sunk Were Heard Before Actual News Came.

Special to The New York Times.

WASHINGTON, May 7.—Never since that April day, three years ago, when word came that the Titanic had gone down, has Washington been so stirred as it is tonight over the sinking of the Lusitania. The early reports told that there had been no loss of life, but the relief that these advices caused gave way to the greatest concern late this evening when it became known that there had been many

The Lost Cunard Steamship Lusitania
X Where the First Torpedo Struck. XX Where the Second Torpedo Struck.

SOME DEAD TAKEN ASHORE

Several Hundred Survivors at Queenstown and Kinsale.

STEWARD TELLS OF DISASTER

One Torpedo Crashes Into the Doomed Liner's Bow, Another Into the Engine Room.

SHIP LISTS OVER TO PORT

Makes It Impossible to Lower Many Boats, So Hundreds Must Have Gone Down.

ATTACKED IN BROAD DAY

Passengers at Luncheon—Warning Had Been Given by Germans Before the Ship Left New York.

Only 650 Were Saved, Few Cabin Passengers

QUEENSTOWN, Saturday, May 8, 4:28 A. M.—Survivors of the Lusitania who have arrived here estimate that only about 650 of those aboard the steamer

need to convince others by force." In that spirit he began his negotiations. It did not matter, he told Berlin, that the *Lusitania* carried munitions as well as passengers. That was a secondary consideration. The United States was concerned with the "sacred . . . rights of humanity," particularly "the right to life itself." The sinking was an "illegal and inhuman" act, and Wilson demanded an apology and reparations. Since submarines could not be used without violating "principles of justice and humanity," he also by implication demanded that they should not be used at all. And by identifying neutral rights with "sacred" human rights, he charged a difficult issue with needless emotional electricity.

The extremists were dissatisfied. Roosevelt called the president "yellow." Bryan, who had urged Wilson to adopt the principles of the "cooling-off" treaties, considered the notes to Germany too harsh. Sadly he resigned from the Cabinet, to be replaced by Robert Lansing, a New York lawyer with a talent for diplomatic phraseology. As he and the president continued to negotiate, the Germans met them part way. They would not admit the illegality of the sinking, but in February 1916 Germany offered an apology and an indemnity. By and large the American people were relieved. As Lansing put it, they desired only honorable friendship.

Peace with Honor As long as the war continued, however, the submarine issue might involve the United States. The national interest as well as the interests of the besieged people of Europe impelled Wilson to attempt to arrange a peace. He had sent Colonel House to Europe in January 1915 to investigate the possibility of mediation, but House had found the Germans adamant in their decision to hold Belgium and to destroy England's naval power. In October, however, House concocted a plan for peace, which Wilson approved. They intended to force Germany to negotiate by warning that otherwise the United States might enter the war on the Allied side. If the Germans were agreeable to negotiations, House hoped to bring them to reasonable terms at the conference table. Again, failure, according to the plan, would invite American participation in the war. In London in January and February 1916, House made progress toward

On Submarine Warfare

The destruction of the French cross-channel steamer *Sussex* . . . must stand forth, as the sinking of the *Lusitania* did, as so singularly tragical and unjustifiable as to constitute a truly terrible example of the inhumanity of submarine warfare as the commanders of German vessels have . . . been conducting it. . . .

The Imperial German Government has been unable to put any limits or restraints upon its warfare against either freight or passenger ships. It has therefore become painfully evident that the position which this Government took at the very outset is inevitable, namely, that the use of submarines for the destruction of an enemy's commerce is, of necessity, because of the very character of the vessels employed and the very methods of attack . . . incompatible with the principles of humanity, the long established and incontrovertible rights of neutrals, and the sacred immunities of non-combatants.

I have deemed it my duty, therefore, to say to the Imperial Government, that . . . unless [it] . . . should now immediately declare and effect an abandonment of its present methods of warfare . . . this Government can have no choice but to sever diplomatic relations.

Woodrow Wilson, Address to Congress, April 19, 1916

his goal. But the enterprise collapsed when Lansing tried to revise American policy toward the submarines.

Wilson and Lansing had decided to ease the submarine issue by attempting to persuade the Allies not to arm their merchantmen. In that event the U-boats could issue warnings before attacking. The Germans welcomed the idea, for their purpose was not to kill sailors but to destroy cargoes and bottoms. To their advantage, just as House was completing his negotiations in England, Lansing suggested that Allied merchantmen be disarmed. The British of course refused. Lansing had earlier suggested to the Germans that if the Allies declined, Germany might declare unrestricted submarine warfare against all armed ships. In February 1916 the Germans made precisely that declaration. But Lansing then reasserted Wilson's original submarine policy and announced that the United States would not warn Americans against travel on armed ships. "Strict accountability" still applied.

The Roosevelt Republicans prepared to make a major campaign issue during 1916 of the embarrassment the president had caused the Allies. At the opposite pole of opinion, Bryan, La Follette, and other agrarian progressives saw a "sort of moral treason" in letting American citizens create crises by sailing on endangered ships. Resolutions forbidding such travel failed in Congress only because Wilson exerted all his influence to defeat them.

One month later, in March 1916, a German submarine without warning torpedoed an unarmed French steamer, the *Sussex,* which was carrying some American passengers. The president's policy seemed to have failed. But he did not retreat from his principles. After much reflection, in April he sent Germany an ultimatum. Unless it immediately abandoned "its present method of submarine warfare," the United States would "sever diplomatic relations." The Kaiser's advisers decided that since they lacked the submarines to conduct a useful blockade of England, it was more important to keep the United States neutral. In May, Germany acceded to Wilson's demand. Submarines would observe the rules of visit and search, the Germans said, but they might remove that limitation unless the United States compelled England to obey international law.

In spite of the threat that Germany might revert to its earlier tactics, most Americans were again relieved. Unaware of the reasons for the German decision, they felt that the president had avoided war, maintained justice, and conquered the submarines with his pen. They did not realize that Wilson's ultimatum and the German response left an American decision about going to war up to Germany. For if that nation resumed unrestricted submarine warfare, Wilson had committed himself to belligerence. Nevertheless, in 1916 the *Sussex* pledge seemed to promise peace with honor— a happy formula for a campaign year.

Americanism and Preparedness As the war went on, it revealed to Americans as well as to Europeans the terrors of organized brutality and the dangers of organized passions. Intelligence and decency and orderliness gave way before the strains of continual fear. Though the United States was far from the fields of battle, even here the timid sought some symbol that would protect them from the disturbances around them. Others seized the chance to create nationalistic symbols they could use for their own selfish ends. The most avid foes of labor unions underwrote a campaign to equate the open shop with "Americanism." Those who distrusted black citizens or Catholics or Jews now did so in the name of Americanism. It was a word that the opponents of women's suffrage used, a word used also by the advocates of a literacy test for immigrants. The Senate blocked an amendment to enfranchise women, and Congress in 1915 passed a bill establishing a literacy test. Wilson vetoed it, pointing out that it abridged the traditional right of asylum and tested education rather than talent.

The president resisted the spirit of frightened conformity that Roosevelt exalted in the name of Americanism. The name, however, had a political magic no politician could safely ignore, and Wilson himself used it to describe his foreign policy. In 1915, condemning the sabotage of munitions production for the Allies, he attributed it to extremists among the German- and Irish-Americans. Calling on all others to dedicate themselves to the national honor, the president planned to make his version of Americanism the keynote of his campaign for reelection.

The position Wilson and his party took on preparedness also accorded with the middle-of-the-road attitudes of most Americans. Even after the war began, they tended, like the president, to consider arms and munitions the unnecessary tools of evil men. Again like the president, they had an instinctive dislike for widespread military training and a large standing army, neither of which had any place in the American tradition. That tradition persisted, in spite of the nature of modern war, in defining the militia and a citizen-soldiery as proper safeguards for national security. Four months after the sinking of the *Lusitania,* Wilson expressed a popular sentiment when he said he saw no need "to stir the nation up in favor of national defense."

Moved by the possibility of war in Europe and Mexico, a vocal minority began to preach the need to prepare, pointing out that it took time to produce weapons and to train armies and navies for twentieth-century warfare. Theodore Roosevelt led these advocates of preparedness. He was sometimes too strident to be convincing, but more moderate men gradually put their ideas across. Preparedness became a political issue, and Wilson's advisers warned him that he had better do something about it.

In July 1915 the president instructed the armed services to make plans for expansion. In November, asking for much less than they had recommended, he proposed a volunteer army of 400,000 men who were to serve only a few months in each of several successive years. Even this modest proposal met opposition from rural liberals in Congress, most of them Democrats, some of them with great influence. Preparedness also incurred the hostility of a passionate peace party, its membership recruited not least from among women who saw all war as primitive and wantonly destructive. To win support for his program, Wilson went on a speaking trip that took him halfway across the continent. During that tour he came out for a "navy second to none."

Yet in 1916 the president had to make concessions to his opponents. Still close to the middle of the road, he first rejected the War Department's plan for creating a large reserve force under the regular army, and he appointed a new secretary of war, Newton D. Baker, a progressive with a reputation for antimilitarism. Wilson and Baker then worked out a compromise that satisfied the Congress. The resulting statute of May 1916 doubled the regular army but left the national guard still largely independent of the authority of the War Department. The president's influence helped, too, to carry a measure accelerating the building of a strong navy.

The agrarians scored one success. In the face of administration opposition, they fashioned the revenue legislation to pay for the defense program. It increased surtaxes on personal income and put new taxes on

Political Muddle

In addition to the complexity of government, we suffer . . . from the false unity of political parties. It is false because men may agree on foreign politics and disagree on domestic. But they have to vote wholesale though they think retail. . . . We have to choose not between the domestic policies of Woodrow Wilson and Theodore Roosevelt, nor between their foreign policies, but between a muddle of the two. The voter . . . has to make up his mind how the value of Mr. Wilson's diplomacy compares with his views about business and labor. Under these conditions public opinion cannot help being confused and uncertain. . . . The two sets of interests wait upon each other, and there is no such thing as dealing with one and ignoring the other. The whole development of democracy is distorted by the international situation.

From Walter Lippmann, *The Stakes of Diplomacy*, 1915

inheritances. Those best able to pay would have to foot the bill for preparedness.

The Democrats had given the preparedness issue a progressive stamp and had identified their party with national defense. The measures fell short of the demands of the armed services, but they met the most urgent requirements of a nation that still hoped and expected to remain at peace.

The Election of 1916 For the Republicans one major problem in 1916 was how to reassimilate the Progressive party. Roosevelt had kept it alive largely to further his own ambitions, but the Old Guard would not countenance his nomination on the Republican ticket, and the Colonel cared more about defeating Wilson than about nursing old grudges. In order to regain Bull Moose votes, the Republicans selected a candidate with a progressive record, Charles Evans Hughes. He had been a successful reform governor of New York and in 1912, as an associate justice of the Supreme Court, had stayed neutral in the party split. He was an able man and a strong candidate whose cause may have been hurt rather than helped by Roosevelt's obsessive attacks on Democratic foreign policy.

Although Wilson had planned to run on the issues of Americanism and progressivism, foreign policy became a central factor in the campaign. The party managers realized that their most effective slogan would be: "He kept us out of war." Its effectiveness grew as Hughes explained that he would have been tougher on Mexico and Germany than Wilson had been. The president himself told the voters that he was "not expecting this country to get into war," and Democratic propagandists advertised: "Wilson and Peace with Honor? or Hughes with Roosevelt and War?"

There were, of course, other issues. The Irish-American and German-American extremists embarrassed Hughes by supporting him openly. But he failed to repudiate them publicly, while Wilson deliberately attacked them. The Democrats had made a progres-

Election of 1916

sive record that was persuasive with those from the defunct Bull Moose who could not yet tolerate the idea of voting Republican again.

By and large, rural America voted for Wilson, as did labor, the liberals, and most intellectuals. Consequently, he was able to break the pattern of Republican hegemony. His winning coalition, still tenuous, foreshadowed the profile of Democratic dominance that emerged in the 1930s. Wilson carried the South, the states west of those bordering the Mississippi River, and one Eastern state—Ohio. That was the winning combination that had eluded Bryan. The contest in 1916 was so close that it hinged on the ballots in California, which were counted only after Eastern returns had put Hughes ahead. Indeed, Hughes went to bed election night thinking he had won. In California pro-Wilson votes of former Progressives alienated by Hughes made a crucial difference. In all, Wilson received 49.4 percent of the popular vote to 46.2 percent for Hughes and carried the Electoral College 277 to 254. Peace and progressivism had helped to put Wilson across again, but his victory had also depended on traditional Democratic loyalties and the continuing Republican division.

THE ROAD TO WAR

Wilson knew how uncertain was the nation's hold on peace. Before election day the British had tightened their regulations on neutral trade, and the Germans had intensified their submarine campaign against the Allies. Either Wilson had to find ways to end the war or else he would have to sacrifice peace or honor—or both.

The president planned to send a dramatic note to the belligerents. He was ready, his draft said, to pledge the "whole force" of the United States to end the "war of exhaustion and attrition" and to keep the future peace. The draft asked each side for "a concrete definition" of its war objectives. It also demanded an immediate peace conference. Wilson intended to employ every pressure short of war to assist the more reasonable side. While he was still reworking his draft, in December 1916, the German chancellor announced his government's readiness to negotiate.

The offer hid a calculating spirit. The Germans made the gesture out of confidence of impending victory. Masters of the eastern front, where the Russians were collapsing, the Germans expected to smash France and England if their terms were rejected. They had also secretly decided that, if negotiations failed, they would resume unrestricted submarine warfare. And their secret terms were harsh—they would insist on territory along the Baltic, in the Congo, and in Belgium, France, and Luxembourg.

Slowly Wilson discovered the truth. He dispatched the note he had been drafting, but the Germans replied that they wanted no neutral at the peace table. The Allies publicly rejected the president's proposal but privately let him know they would negotiate if the German conditions were reasonable. Wilson made a last effort to define the terms of a "peace without victory" in a memorable address to the Senate on January 22, 1917. Such a peace, he said, would require the substitution of a league of nations for the bankrupt policy of entangling alliances intended to create a balance of power. But that vision drew criticism from both isolationists and bellicose Americans like Roosevelt. On January 31, the Germans revealed their greedy terms for an armistice and announced they would resume unrestricted submarine warfare.

For several weeks Wilson would not admit that he had either to surrender his principles or go to war. He broke off relations with Germany, but he told Congress he wanted no conflict. He remained outwardly temperate even after learning on February 25 that Germany was plotting against the United States. That day the British communicated to Washington secret orders of the German foreign minister, Arthur Zimmermann, which they had intercepted. Those orders told the German minister to Mexico that, in the event of war with the United States, he should invite Mexico and Japan to join the Central Powers and promise Mexico its lost lands in the Southwest as war booty—a shocking prospect to Americans.

Wilson had meanwhile pressed his interpretation of neutral rights. He had asked Congress for authority to arm American merchant vessels and to employ any other means that might be necessary to protect American ships and citizens at sea. To win votes for his proposal, he made the Zimmermann note public on March 1, 1917. A wave of anti-German sentiment swept the country, but the Democratic House of Representatives withheld the broad authority the president wanted, and in the Senate a dozen antiwar progressives talked a stronger bill to death.

That "little group of willful men," as Wilson called them, struggled in vain. The Zimmermann note had dissolved the myth that the war was strictly European. The president on his own ordered the merchantmen armed, and on March 18, two weeks after his second inauguration, U-boats sank three American ships.

The Zimmermann Telegram

We intend to begin unrestricted submarine warfare on the first of February. We shall endeavor in spite of this to keep the United States neutral. In the event of this not succeeding, we make Mexico a proposal of alliance on the following basis: Make war together, make peace together, generous financial support, and an understanding on our part that Mexico is to reconquer the lost territory in Texas, New Mexico, and Arizona. . . .

Inform the President [of Mexico] of the above most secretly as soon as the outbreak of war with the United States is certain and add the suggestion that he should . . . invite Japan to immediate adherence. . . .

Please call the President's attention to the fact that the unrestricted employment of our submarines now offers the prospect of compelling England to make peace within a few months.

Quoted in Barbara W. Tuchman, *The Zimmermann Telegram,* 1959

Moreover, the first Russian revolution established a limited monarchy and a responsible parliament, temporarily destroying the despotism that had made Americans reluctant to associate with the Allied cause. And the Allies could no longer fight without American men, money, and material. The combination of events convinced even the most ardent peace advocates in the Cabinet of the necessity for war.

Wilson was agonized by a conclusion he could not escape. War, he allegedly told one confidant, "would overturn the world we had known," lead to "a dictated peace," require "illiberalism at home." Sadly he predicted that "the spirit of ruthless brutality" would enter the very "fibre of our national life." His pain was shared by most progressives, for progressivism had based its faith on the peaceful, reasonable improvement of the lot of humanity in a world of quiet and intelligence. It was also, however, a moral faith, and in the view of Wilson and other progressive intellectuals, Germany had violated moral principles. It had forced war on France and Belgium. It was bent on conquest. Whatever the definitions of neutral rights, so Wilson had concluded, no one was immune from German aggression, and there could be no real peace while it went unpunished.

With those thoughts in mind, Wilson on April 2 addressed the special session of Congress he had summoned. On April 4 the Senate, by a vote of 82 to 6, and on April 6 the House of Representatives, by a vote of 373 to 50, passed a resolution recognizing the existence of a state of war with Germany.

The decision of the German General Staff to resume unrestricted submarine warfare had rested on the calculation that American belligerency would cost Germany less than continuing shipments of American supplies to the Allies. The decision, as the Germans expected it would, led to the American declaration of war, for Wilson and his supporters had staked the grandeur of the nation and supposedly the rights of humanity on his policies. If Americans had not been allowed to travel upon the ships of belligerents, if American bankers had been forbidden to make loans to England and France, if the United States had surrendered its historic commitment to neutral rights, if Wilson's rhetoric had been more disciplined, the crisis of war would not have developed as it did. But American business interests would not have abandoned their markets without protest. Indeed, Wilson sought a settlement that would serve American interests. With the failure of his efforts at mediation, war provided another path to his goals. As important, the sense of national greatness that had been growing since the 1880s precluded an easy acceptance of limitations on the country imposed by any foreign power. Wilson gave a special cast to American pride and sensitivity, but those sentiments were not his alone. Most

important, though no one of the great powers of Europe was uninvolved in the contest for supremacy that brought on the war, the Germans did precipitate the war and pursue it without the delicate and deliberate care for American sensibilities that the British cultivated. Further, had the Germans prevailed, they intended to impose on Europe and much of the rest of the world a Carthaginian settlement. German intentions, as well as the special conditions of war-making that guided German maritime strategy, created the problems that American policy makers found no way to resolve, in the end, short of war itself.

SUGGESTIONS FOR READING

GENERAL

The best general account of the Taft years and of the breakup of the Republican party is in G. E. Mowry, *The Era of Theodore Roosevelt* (1958). A. S. Link, *Woodrow Wilson and the Progressive Era* (1954), covers the succeeding years to the American entry into the war. Both books are challenged by Gabriel Kolko, *The Triumph of Conservatism* (1963). Also useful are the books on progressivism and on Roosevelt listed in connection with the previous chapter. On the presidential elections of the period, see Paul Kleppner, *Who Voted: The Dynamics of Electoral Turnout, 1870–1980* (1982).

PROGRESSIVES AND REGULARS

A case for Taft is set forth in P. O. Coletta, *The Presidency of William Howard Taft* (1973), and D. E. Anderson, *William Howard Taft* (1973), which should be compared with A. T. Mason, *Bureaucracy Convicts Itself* (1941), and J. L. Holt, *Congressional Insurgents and the Party System, 1909–1916* (1967). For an understanding of progressive social ideas, see the books suggested in the previous chapter and Herbert Croly, *The Promise of American Life* (1909); Walter Weyl, *The New Democracy* (1912); Walter Lippmann, *Drift and Mastery* (1914); and C. B. Forcey, *The Crossroads of Liberalism* (1961). There are no comparable studies of conservative thought, but that subject gets useful treatment in R. W. Leopold, *Elihu Root and the Conservative Tradition* (1954). Useful in the context of its title is W. and M. Scholes, *The Foreign Policies of the Taft Administration* (1970).

WILSON

The outstanding work on Wilson is A. S. Link's multivolume biography. A recent, uncritical interpretation is A. Heckscher, *Woodrow Wilson* (1992). Two brief studies of Wilson are J. M. Blum, *Woodrow Wilson and the Politics of Morality* (1956), and J. A. Garraty, *Woodrow Wilson* (1956). See, too, the comparison of Roosevelt and Wilson in J. M. Cooper, Jr., *The Warrior and the Priest* (1983). Of the special studies of Wilson's diplomacy, the best are A. S. Link, *Wilson the Diplomatist* (1957); N. G. Levin, Jr., *Woodrow Wilson and World Politics* (1968); and P. Devlin, *Too Proud to Fight: Woodrow Wilson's Neutrality* (1974). There are keen analyses of the issues of American foreign policy in R. E. Osgood, *Ideals and Self-Interest in America's Foreign Relations* (1953), and E. R. May, *The World War and American Isolation 1914–1917* (1959). W. A. Williams, *The Tragedy of American Foreign Policy* (1962), presents the most influential interpretation of the dominance of economic considerations. Other important monographs include D. G. Munro, *Intervention and Dollar Diplomacy in the Caribbean, 1900–1921* (1964); R. E. Quirk, *An Affair of Honor: Woodrow Wilson and the Occupation of Vera Cruz* (1962); P. E. Haley, *Revolution and Intervention: The Diplomacy of Taft and Wilson with Mexico, 1910–1917* (1970); R. W. Curry, *Woodrow Wilson and Far Eastern Policy, 1913–1921* (1968); Ross Gregory, *The Origins of American Intervention in the First World War* (1971); D. M. Smith, *The Great Departure: The United States in World War I, 1914–1920* (1965); and J. M. Cooper, Jr., *The Vanity of Power: American Isolationism and the First World War, 1914–1917* (1969). See, too, on the preparedness campaign and its cultural significance, M. Pearlman, *To Make Democracy Safe for America* (1984). Of the various studies of the Wilsonians, one is indispensable: C. Seymour, ed., *The Intimate Papers of Colonel House*, 4 vols. (1921–28), corrected in a new edition of the House Papers by Wilton Fowler. Also useful, particularly on domestic issues, is P. Strum, *Louis D. Brandeis: Justice for the People* (1984). A. Garraty, *Henry Cabot Lodge* (1953), presents an understanding account of one of Wilson's foremost antagonists. The literature on Wilson and his time has been richly expanded with the continuing publication of his letters and papers under the editorship of A. S. Link.

CHAPTER TWENTY-FOUR

SUPPLIES FOR THE FRONT

WAR AND ITS SEQUEL

The American nation was unprepared for the First World War. To begin with, the country had no clear sense of purpose. Many German- and Irish-Americans were unreconciled to fighting on the side of the Allies. Smaller groups of pacifists saw no excuse for any fighting, and some progressives believed that the United States had no business involving itself in what they considered to be a struggle between European imperialists. The majority of Americans were in full accord with the decision to go to war, but they were confused about its origins and objectives. Like the president, they had hoped to remain neutral. Like the president, they regarded the submarine issue as a matter of morality. They had little, if any, understanding of world politics.

Indeed, the moral temper of the times led Americans to seek utopian rather than realistic reasons for the actions to which they were committed. Wilson defined American war aims in idealistic terms. The spirit of his war message and later addresses was noble as well as persuasive. It helped transmute the fervor of progressivism into the selfless bravery of the "great crusade." But it also turned some fervor into frenzy, and it led Americans to expect a paradise that no war could give them. The failure to achieve that expectation tinged the persisting frenzy of the immediate postwar years with bitterness and vindictiveness.

The United States was also unprepared for the total mobilization demanded by modern war and for the special strengths required to fight a war overseas. The nation lacked the necessary army, the plans and facilities to raise it, the guns and tanks and airplanes to equip it, and the ships to transport it. Even the tools and the organization to produce the materials of war were wanting. In every respect — emotional, economic, military — mobilization was urgent but erratic.

THE ARMED FORCES ON LAND AND SEA

Selective Service The president and his military advisers agreed that conscription was the only efficient and democratic way to recruit a large army. Yet the Speaker of the House and the chair of the Military Affairs Committee, both Democrats, led the opposition to the administration's selective-service bill. Many of the bill's opponents considered conscription a threat to democracy. Others had a romantic attachment to the tradition of voluntary military service. But if war had ever been romantic it was no longer so, and selective service, as Wilson argued, spread the obligation to serve among all qualified men without regard to their social position, a desirable contrast to the Union

Attention!

ALL MALES between the ages of 21 and 30 years, both inclusive, must personally appear at the polling place in the Election District in which they reside, on

TUESDAY, JUNE 5th, 1917

between the hours of 7 A.M. and 9 P. M. and

Register

in accordance with the President's Proclamation.

Any male person, between these ages, who fails to register on June 5th, 1917, will be subject to imprisonment in jail or other penal institution for a term of one year.

NO EXCUSE FOR FAILURE TO REGISTER WILL BE ACCEPTED

NON-RESIDENTS must apply personally for registration, at the office of the County Clerk, at Kingston, N. Y., AT ONCE, in order that their registration cards may be in the hands of the Registration Board of their home district before June 5, 1917

Employers of males between these ages are earnestly requested to assits in the enforcement of the President's Proclamation.

Signed,

BOARD OF REGISTRATION
of Ulster County
E. T. SHULTIS, Sheriff
C. K. LOUGHRAN, County Clerk
Dr. FRANK JOHNSTON, Medical Officer

draft during the Civil War. The House passed the bill in May, but only after mollifying American mothers by raising the minimum draft age from 19, which the army recommended, to 21.*

In the Senate the Republicans wasted three weeks in a futile effort to force the administration to accept the volunteer division Theodore Roosevelt was organizing. Roosevelt and his admirers believed that even though his troops were half-trained they would make up the deficiency in dash. Wilson prudently preferred professional to political generals. The Selective Service Act finally passed by the Senate left Wilson free to dispose of volunteer units as he saw fit, and he saw fit to reject Roosevelt's.

Early in June 1917 more than 9 million men registered quietly with the local officials whom the War Department authorized to supervise the draft. Before the war ended, more than 24 million had registered and almost 3 million had been inducted into the army. Some 21,000 men, conscientious objectors to military service, were assigned noncombatant roles. But the 4,000 men who refused to participate in the war at all were imprisoned or otherwise punished. Still, there was relatively little opposition to conscription, and the drafted troops fought as heroically as the 2 million volunteers who enlisted in the various armed services.

The army's top command was strictly professional. Bypassing General Leonard Wood, an intimate of Roosevelt, Wilson made General John J. Pershing head of the American Expeditionary Force and gave his decisions consistent support. "Black Jack" Pershing, a laconic, stern West Pointer, pursued two controversial policies. He refused to send troops into battle until they had completed their training, and he insisted on preserving a separate identity for the American Expeditionary Force, though the French and British were impatient for reinforcements and eager to merge American units with their own.

The War in the West In the fall of 1917 a German offensive routed the Italians. The Russian army disintegrated under the impact of the Bolshevik Revolution of November. That removed Russia from the war and left the western front, manned by war-weary French and British troops, exposed to the full attack Germany was certain to mount the following spring. The

Foch and Pershing

* It was necessary in 1918 to lower the minimum age to 18.

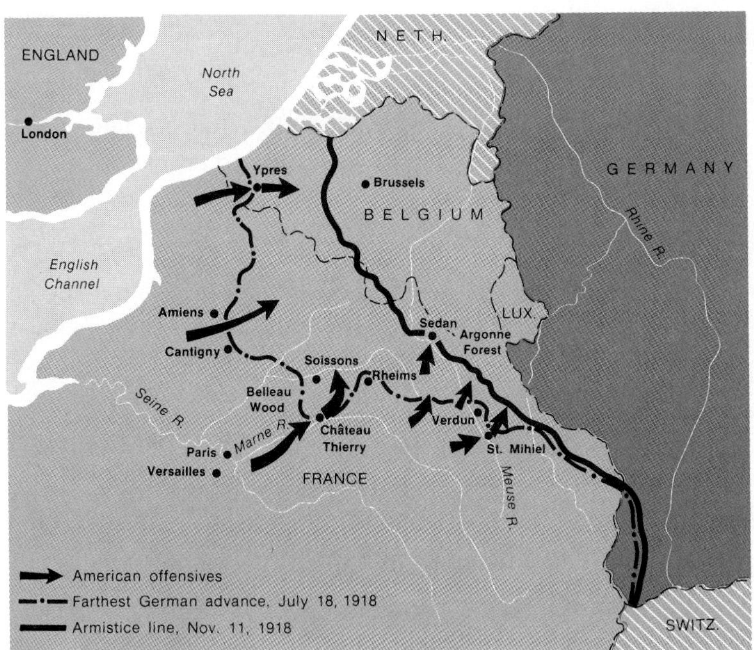

Map 24-1
American operations on the western front, 1918

alarmed Allies created the Supreme War Council to direct their resistance and urged Pershing to supply men, trained or untrained. But Pershing still declined. In the spring of 1918, however, as the Allied lines crumbled before a furious German offensive, Wilson agreed to the appointment of French Marshal Ferdinand Foch as supreme commander, and Pershing put his four available divisions at Foch's disposal.

During May 1918 the Germans pushed the French back to the Marne River, only 50 miles from Paris (see Map 24-1). Foch then called up one American division and a few regiments of marines who met the Germans at Chateau Thierry, carried the intensive battle there, and in June drove the enemy out of Belleau Wood.

Gambling for a quick victory before more American forces could reach France, the Germans in July struck at the sector of the Marne between Rheims and Soissons. Here some 85,000 Americans helped to turn the attack, and eight divisions of Yanks participated in the French counteroffensive that cleared out the sector early in August. The American First Army under Pershing then took over the southern front near St. Mihiel and routed the Germans there in an independent offensive in September. Late that month Pershing attacked the German lines between Verdun and Sedan. This Meuse-Argonne engagement produced a costly but crucial American victory. Along with the success of French and British forces on the northern and central fronts, it defeated the German army and set the stage for an armistice (see p. 621).

Americans "Over There"

On the Ground, in the Air, in the Hospitals

"I got within fifty feet of the German machine-gun nests when a bullet plowed through the top of my skull. . . . As I lay there I could plainly see the German gunners and hear them talking. . . . They reloaded their gun and turned it on me. The first three bullets went through my legs and hip and the rest splashed up dust and dirt. . . . That night . . . one of my comrades . . . who later in the battle was himself killed, crawled out and started to carry me back to the lines. . . . The Germans . . . turned their guns our way. . . . Thinking it impossible for him to get me to the lines alone, he piled up a half-dozen bodies of my poor dead 'buddies' and barricaded my position. There I remained for several hours longer. . . . The boys piled up around me were my own camp-mates whom I knew. . . . Back of the lines the surgeons came out . . . and . . . exclaimed, "What, ain't you dead yet?'" (Joyce Lewis)

"I dove down beside that road . . . and recognized those Boche helmets! In a twinkling I was passed them . . . and came diving down upon them from the rear. I just held both triggers down hard while the fiery bullets flew streaming out of the two guns. . . . I had a vague confused picture of . . . rearing horses, falling men, running men, general mess. . . . I found myself trembling with excitement and overawed at being a cold-blooded murderer, but a sense of keen satisfaction came too. It was only the sort of thing our own poor doughboys have suffered so often." (Hamilton Coolidge)

"Side by side I have Americans, English, Scotch, Irish, and French, and a part in the corners are Boche. They have to watch each other die side by side. I am sent for everywhere—in the . . . operating-room, the dressing room, and back again to the rows of men. . . . Of course, some only stay twenty-four hours, because they send them away just as fast as it is possible, for even this cellar is too dangerous a place to be in. The cannon goes day and night and the shells are breaking over and around us. . . . I have had to write many sad letters to American mothers. I wonder if it will ever end." (Florence Bullard)

From Frank Freidel, *Over There,* 1964

The triumph exacted extraordinary expenditures of nerve and flesh, for in some respects the First World War was the most ghastly in history. Casualties ran high, particularly during offensives, and American troops, along with their allies and foes, suffered a heavy incidence of shell shock, a form of battle fatigue, and of tuberculosis, a companion of the poison gas and the mud, cold, wet, and filth of the trenches. For most soldiers the war was an awful combination of fear, drudgery, and exhaustion.

The signal exceptions were the aviators. Their craft were simple and slow, their tactics rudimentary. Yet the new knights of the air wrote a chapter of military history in their man-to-man combat in the skies, and American aces dramatized for their countrymen the potentialities of aerial warfare.

The Yanks had reached France just in time. The Allies needed the new manpower to stop the Germans' gamble for victory—a gamble that would probably have succeeded had reinforcements failed to appear. Yet the Americans, indispensable during the last months of war, and gallant and effective then, arrived only after the Allies had held the Germans for almost four terrible years. More than 50,000 Americans died in France, but the war took the lives of 3 million English, French, and Russian soldiers. The role of the American army was both relatively small and absolutely vital.

The War at Sea So, too, was the role of the American navy. In all but one respect the war at sea had been won by the success of the British navy in bottling up the German fleet. As the British Admiralty admitted, however, the German submarines also had to be brought under control. During 1917 U-boats sank more than twice the tonnage of shipping that the Allies and Americans built that year. Hard pressed to supply themselves, the British could not guard the American lines of supply to Europe, and the Americans could not afford to risk transporting an army aboard ships unprotected from enemy submarines.

The United States Navy had the ships and the men to take over the patrol of the Western Hemisphere and to assist the English in patrolling the waters around the British Isles. The navy had built enough destroyers and lesser vessels to mount a considerable antisubmarine campaign, but built too few to pursue both of the strategies initially under debate. One faction of the Royal Navy, which had some support in Washington, wanted to concentrate on hunting and attacking German submarines. Another faction argued for using destroyers and other warships primarily to escort convoys of merchantmen across the Atlantic. Though British merchant skippers preferred to sail alone rather than to proceed in formation under naval command, Admiral William S. Sims, the senior American naval officer in Europe, supported the convoy plan. In the summer of 1917, his influence helped to overcome the opposing British camp. By the end of 1917 the use of convoys had cut shipping losses in half.

The escorted convoys were so effective that not one American soldier was lost in transit to Europe. The bridge of ships to France carried the troops and supplies that the Germans had expected to destroy, and the miracle of transportation turned the tide of war. That great American achievement was possible only because the British also provided bottoms for men and equipment, and only because the Yanks at the front could use Allied cannon, tanks, and airplanes.

THE HOME FRONT

Problems of Production By themselves the eventual prodigies of American war production would have been too little and too late for victory. Since there were no precedents for economic mobilization, the administration had to feel its way along in creating agencies to supervise production and distribution and to allocate vital goods and services. When war came, the army did not even have information about the uniforms and shoes it would need. There was no inventory of national resources, no adequate plan for priorities or for stockpiling critical materials. Most of the first nine months of the war were spent in learning about mobilization, and in tooling up for production.

The lost time was especially serious for the aviation program. American planners were so slow in designing and manufacturing aircraft that American aviators had to fly in British and French machines all through the war. The situation was almost as desperate in the production of artillery and tanks. The building program for transports and cargo vessels collapsed completely, and the government had to rely on ships seized from neutrals or purchased from private industry.

These and other difficulties spurred the Senate Military Affairs Committee to investigate the conduct of the war. As 1918 began, the Democratic chair of that committee asserted publicly that the military effort had been impeded by waste and inefficiency. Republican senators, joined by several Democrats, urged that a war cabinet of three distinguished citizens be set up to exercise the powers the Congress had conferred on the president. If that measure had passed, Wilson would have become a figurehead. Even as it was, the Senate committee was close to assuming the role of its predecessor that had harassed Lincoln during the Civil War.

The president, however, had begun to address the problems of mobilization. Neither during 1917 nor later, moreover, did any scandal taint the administration of the war. Aware of the threat from the Senate, Wilson prepared a bill giving him sweeping authority to reorganize and manage all executive agencies. This measure, which Senator Lee S. Overman sponsored, passed Congress in April 1918 and enabled the president to complete his own plans.

Economic Mobilization Those plans were imbued with characteristically progressive hopes that the war would hasten the emergence of a cooperative commonwealth in which industry would substitute productive efficiency for the mere pursuit of profits, and government and business would work together voluntarily in the public interest. In fact, business groups dominated public policy. Eager for efficient management of the economy, Wilson turned to the efficient managers of industry and finance. They had the experience and talents he needed. Able and patriotic men, they nevertheless remained alert to the interests of the firms they had left, which they naturally identified with the public good. Consequently, wartime economic management resulted in continuing boons to business rather than in federal monitoring of private enterprise in the manner that earlier regulatory efforts had contemplated. During the war, in spite of new taxes, corporate profits rose to three times their prewar level.

Agriculture also profited. In the spring of 1917 England, France, and Italy urgently needed food. Stretching the mandate of the Council of National Defense, which Congress had authorized the year before, the president established a food-control program in May under Herbert C. Hoover, who had acquired an international reputation as director of the Belgian Relief Commission. Wilson also asked Congress for emergency authority over agricultural production and distribution. The Lever Act of August 1917 granted him that authority, together with limited power to control the prices of certain scarce commodities. Wilson at once created the Food Administration. With Hoover at its head, that agency controlled prices to stimulate the production of wheat and pork, managed the distribution of those and other foodstuffs, and persuaded the public to observe meatless and breadless days. To that last objective, as to the selling of war bonds, American women contributed impressive energy. The success of Hoover's policies made possible the feeding of the nations fighting Germany and a 25 percent increase in the real income of American farmers.

The mobilization of industry proved less successful. The General Munitions Board, another offshoot of the Council of National Defense, showed itself incapable of coordinating the conflicting demands of the American armed services and the Allied purchasing commissions. Consequently, in July 1917 Wilson appointed a War Industries Board (WIB) with authority to pass on all American and Allied purchasing, to allocate raw materials, to control production, and to supervise labor relations. The WIB, however, failed to elicit the full cooperation either of industry or of the armed services. In March 1918 the president rewrote its charter and named a new chair, the wealthy and influential Democrat Bernard M. Baruch, who utilized the organizational structure of the nation's trade associations, common to many industries by that time. Through that arrangement business executives thereafter dominated WIB policy, including arrangements for price fixing. As one result, big business gained economic power, but the WIB was also able to speed conversion to war production. The agency was helped in its task by a reorganization of the general staff of the army into functional divisions, each under an experienced officer selected without regard to seniority. Nevertheless, both government and business remained hesitant and ambiguous about the proper role of the modern state in wartime.

As in agriculture and industry, so in fuel, transportation, and labor, peacetime practices faltered under the stress of war. To relieve the critical coal shortage, the Lever Act empowered the president to fix the price of coal high enough to encourage operators to work marginal mines. In August 1917 he established the Fuel Administration under Harry A. Garfield, president of Williams College. Though the agency was unpopular with producers, enough coal was mined to meet the nation's needs. Snarls in railway transportation, however, impeded coal deliveries, and for four days in January 1918 Garfield closed all East Coast plants that used coal for any but vital purposes.

That emergency order underlined the crisis in railroading. The roads had tried to handle the extraordinary wartime traffic on the basis of voluntary cooperation, but in the absence of unified authority delays became worse and worse, and the snow and freezing weather of December 1917 precipitated a collapse of internal transportation. With congressional approval, Wilson therefore established the United States Railway Administration under William G. McAdoo. Exercising an even greater authority than Baruch had over industry, McAdoo and his associates, mostly railroad men, improved the railways' equipment, strengthened their finances, and adjusted their operations to the demands of war.

Labor and Inflation In April 1918 the president created the national War Labor Board (WLB) to help resolve labor disputes and prevent attendant losses in production. Under the joint chairmanship of former President Taft and Frank P. Walsh, a labor lawyer, the WLB heard more than 1,200 cases and forestalled many strikes, but it lacked the jurisdiction and the information it needed to set labor policies for the entire country. To remedy that deficiency, Wilson in May 1918 appointed the War Labor Policies Board (WLPB) under Felix Frankfurter, a young law professor who had been the War Department's labor adviser. The WLPB surveyed national labor needs and practices and standardized wages and hours. At its recommendation, the president created the United States Employment Service, an agency that placed almost 4 million workers in essential war jobs.

While keeping the country free from serious strikes during the last months of the war, the government's labor agencies and policies also advanced some peacetime objectives of social reformers. Though the American Federation of Labor continued to resist the recruitment of women for industrial jobs, some 40,000 women replaced men in the workforce by driving busses and trucks and working on assembly lines. Another 20,000 served in the armed forces as nurses or clerks. For its part, the AFL experienced rapid growth, in all more than 50 percent, rising by 1920 to more than 3,200,000 members. The government demanded an eight-hour day for war industry wherever it could and insisted on decent working conditions and living wages. Even though the cost of living rose, booming wages and full employment permitted an increase of 20 percent in the average *real* income of blue-collar labor, considerably less than the increase in corporate and agricultural profits.

The federal agencies that exercised the mediating authority in the wartime economy served the interests primarily of industry but also of agriculture and labor. The agencies did not, however, lessen the conflicts among those major interest groups, nor did they operate according to peculiarly scientific principles. Rather, the various wartime agencies represented their own constituencies whose interests continued to conflict. The superficial reconciliation of those conflicts through administrative rulings bought cooperation at the price of favor, kept the machinery of war going, but charged the costs in the form of accelerated inflation to unrepresented individuals. Between 1916 and 1919 salaried workers suffered a 22 percent loss of purchasing power. Prices rose during 1917 to 31 percent above the level of 1913 and during 1918 to 59 percent above that base.

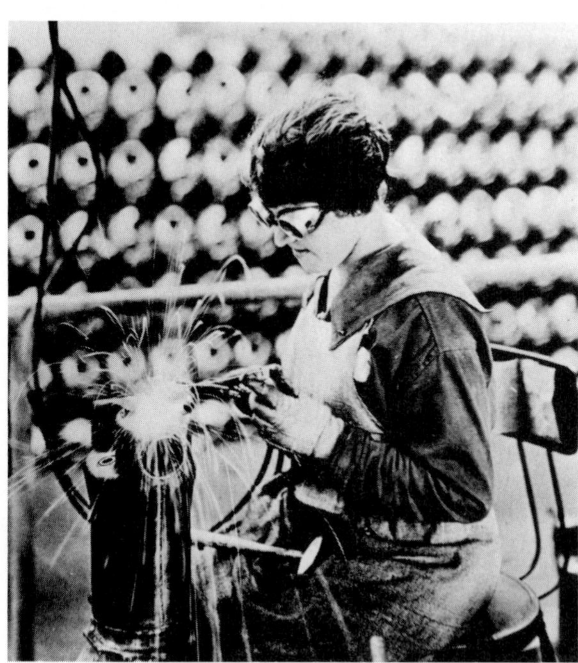

War worker

Propaganda, Public Opinion, and Civil Liberties The growth of federal power gave some of the wartime agencies a dangerous authority over the minds of citizens. A week after war was declared, Wilson created the Committee on Public Information (CPI) to mobilize public opinion. George Creel, chair of the CPI, worked out with newspaper reporters a voluntary censorship that kept the public reasonably well informed while safeguarding sensitive information. He also hired hundreds of artists and writers to mount a propaganda campaign without precedent in American history.

The CPI stressed two major points. One argued, as Wilson did, that the United States was fighting only for freedom and democracy. The other maintained that the Germans were all Huns, diabolic creatures perpetrating atrocities in an effort to conquer the world for their lust and greed. The releases of the Creel committee intensified the unreasoning attitudes of a nation at war. They hinted that German spies had an ear to every wall. Often they carried anti-union overtones, labeling as treason all work stoppages, whatever their real cause. More often they implied that all dissent was unpatriotic and that pacifists and socialists had hidden sympathies for the enemy.

This propaganda helped to sell war bonds, combat absenteeism in the factories, and reconcile some doubters to the war. But the price was high. The attitudes the CPI encouraged were the same as those fostered by private vigilante groups like the National Protective Association, which cultivated a kind of war madness. All dissent became suspect. There were continual spy scares, witch hunts, even kangaroo courts that imposed harsh sentences of tar and feathers. The innocent victims were usually German-Americans or antiwar radicals. The orgy of hatred had its ridiculous as well as its outrageous side. Americans stopped playing German music and stopped teaching or speaking the German language; they called sauerkraut "liberty cabbage"; and in Cincinnati they even removed pretzels from the free-lunch counters of saloons.

It was essential, of course, to protect the country from espionage and sabotage, but wartime legislation and its administration exceeded reasonable bounds. The Espionage Act of 1917, which Wilson requested, provided penalties of up to 20 years in prison and a $10,000 fine for those who helped the enemy, obstructed recruiting, or incited rebellion within the armed services. One section gave the postmaster general authority to deny the use of the mails to any publication that in his opinion advocated treason or forcible resistance to the laws. The Trading-with-the-Enemy Act, which Congress passed in October 1917, added sweeping authority to censor the foreign-language press.

In 1918 Congress went still further. The rising hysteria was stimulated by the demands of the attorney general and by the antipathy toward the Industrial Workers of the World. Copying state statutes, Congress passed the Sabotage Act and the Sedition Act, which empowered the federal government to punish any expression of opinion that, regardless of whether or not it led to action, was "disloyal, profane, scurrilous or abusive" of the American form of government, flag, or uniform. Subsequent systematic persecution effectively destroyed the Wobblies, and in one characteristic case, Eugene V. Debs was sentenced to prison for expressing his revulsion against the war.

The recklessness of Congress in stocking such an arsenal had its source in the frenzy of the people. Timid in the face of public opinion, state and federal officials and judges made a mockery of the right of freedom of speech and belief. Just as those administering the draft subjected conscientious objectors to needless humiliations, often imprisonment, so those administering the espionage, sedition, and other wartime laws made conformity a measure of loyalty. The mails were closed to publications whose only offense was a statement of socialism, a plea for feminism, or anti-British bias. People were haled into court who had done no more than criticize the Red Cross or the financing of the war or who had merely declared that war was contrary to the teachings of Jesus Christ. Of more than 1,500 arrests for sedition, only 10 were alleged to be for actual sabotage. The government's own immoderation and its failure to control private vigilantes shocked men and women of goodwill and good sense, blemished the administration's war record, and exaggerated passions that long outlived the crisis itself.

Politics in Wartime Those exaggerated passions sometimes found expression in partisan, sectional, and factional politics. Though Wilson expressed the wish that politics might be adjourned for the duration, wartime problems raised conflicts of interest and irresistible opportunities to pursue partisan advantages. The Republicans, determined to prevent the Democrats from getting all the credit for American successes, criticized the conduct of the war. But that criticism, much of it valid, hurt the Democrats less than did the behavior of a few Southerners in key congressional posts who consistently voted against war legislation.

Southern agrarians and Western progressives demanded heavy income, inheritance, and excess-profits taxes to prevent war profiteering. Conservatives, in contrast, preferred federal borrowing and excise or sales taxes of various kinds. They argued that future generations should share the cost of a war fought in the national interest and that taxes on consumption would help check wartime inflation. The administration took a middle position. In all, the war cost about $24 billion, with another $11 billion for loans to the Allies. Of that amount, $10.5 billion was raised by taxes, the balance by Treasury borrowing. Secretary of the Treasury McAdoo had intended taxes to carry a larger share, but the soaring cost of the war upset his calculations. As it was, wartime taxes were heavier than they had ever been in the United States. The Revenue Act of October 1917 imposed new and

War and the Disenchanted Liberal

The difficulty with the liberal is that so far he has felt that he could ride two horses at once, he could be a patriot and still frown on greed and violence and predatory militarism; he could desire social reconstruction and yet be most reverent towards the traditional institutions. He feels that the old-fashioned individualist profiteer and old-guard politician is so terribly the enemy that we should all support liberalism in its attack. . . . Somehow in the liberal attack upon the unsocialized beast, liberalism has accepted . . . almost every program that the bigoted unsocialized patriot has demanded. You may accept conscription from motives very different from those of the unregenerate militarist, but . . . war always fortifies military attitudes and autocratic control. . . . The effect is no different from what it would have been if you had willed the worst. . . . It is this that has driven so many of the younger generation back from the liberal camp. . . . The war has run into the sand that fine movement for progressive democracy in which so many of us found hope. . . . We find a liberal war undertaken which could not fail to do far more damage to American democracy at home than it could ever do to the enemy abroad.

From Randolph Bourne, Letter to Van Wyck Brooks, March 1918

larger excise and luxury taxes, a graduated excess-profits tax on business, and increased estate and personal income taxes. It raised the maximum surtax on income to 63 percent, and the Revenue Act of 1918 lifted it and the excess-profits tax still higher.

The revenue measures passed during the war attempted to place a heavy but equitable burden on those best able to carry it. Nevertheless they prospered. During the war years some 42,000 new millionaires emerged, and the number of taxpayers in the \$30,000–\$40,000 bracket tripled. But the newly rich and the middle class complained. Especially in the Northeast, Republican politicians won middle-class support by contending that the agrarian Democrats were deliberately punishing the nation's industrial regions. By 1918 the tax issue was being hotly debated by the affluent who had once supported less expensive progressive policies.

The Republicans also made gains among Midwestern farmers who had defected to the Democrats in 1916. The Lever Act empowered the administration to control the price of wheat but not the price of cotton, and the Western farmers resented the larger profits of their Southern brethren and blamed the Democratic policies that had created the inequity.

The Democratic coalition of 1916 was hurt by other issues as well. Southern votes were crucial in overriding Wilson's veto of an act of 1917 establishing a literacy test for immigrants. The urban laboring force found the Southerners' support of prohibition even more exasperating. Advocates of the prohibition of the manufacture and consumption of alcoholic beverages achieved their goal during the war. First, a section of the Lever Act limited the production of whiskey, and a section of the Selective Service Act limited its sale near army camps. Later, in December 1917, Congress adopted the Eighteenth Amendment—the Prohibition Amendment—and submitted it to the states for ratification (completed in January 1919).

Prohibition offended many Irish-, German-, and Scandinavian-Americans who were also dubious about Wilson's foreign policies. While most of them did not openly oppose the war, they questioned the virtue of the Allied nations and they resented the domestic pressures for conformity that sometimes seemed to denigrate their native lands.

For their part, Northern liberals, disturbed by the administration's threats to civil liberties, were also irritated by Southern resistance to the woman-suffrage amendment, which senators from Dixie blocked to Wilson's disappointment. As he had learned from the suffragists, democratic principles included the right of women to vote. But only in January 1919 did Congress remove the injustice of limiting suffrage on the basis of sex. (Ratification followed in August 1920.)

With the coalition of interests that had elected Wilson in 1916 now weakening, the Republicans effected a powerful reorganization of their party. They approached the elections of 1918 (see p. 621) with more confidence than they had had in a decade, and their campaign threatened not only Democratic control of Congress but the program for a liberal peace on which Wilson pinned his most fervent hopes.

CONSTRUCTING THE PEACE

Wilson's Program During the war, sentiment for a liberal peace developed on both sides of the Atlantic, especially in England and the United States. The plans of various humanitarian groups differed in detail, but they usually advocated four common principles: the substitution of an international organization for the alliance system, the substitution of arbitration for armaments, the institution of self-government among all peoples, and the avoidance of seizures of territories and of demands for reparations.

Wilson embraced those objectives. In 1916 he publicly advocated the idea of a league of nations. In 1917 he had begun to meditate seriously on the components of a generous peace—a "peace without victory." Soon after the United States declared war, he assigned the task of preparing detailed peace plans to Colonel House and a staff of experts. While they were at work, the president in a series of addresses spelled out his own goals, which reflected the principles that had previously characterized his New Freedom and his neutrality policies.

It was necessary, Wilson believed, to remove the military party, including the Kaiser, from authority in Germany, to divest Germany of power over other peoples, to establish democratic self-government in Germany and among each of the national groups rescued from its domination or the domination of its allies. It was necessary then to bring all nations into a world parliament whose collective democratic judgment would guard the peace. "Peace," he said, "should rest upon the rights of peoples, not the rights of governments—the rights of peoples great or small . . . to freedom and security and self-government and to . . . economic opportunities."

This grand vision underestimated the role of power in world affairs and the selfishness of nations torn by war. Indeed, Wilson exacted from the Allies no commitment to a liberal peace. By his own choice the United States had fought not as one of the Allies but as an "associated" belligerent, with the others but not of them. This was the administration's way of paying tribute to the questionable tradition of avoiding "entangling alliances." Wilson chose, too, to avoid facing squarely the punitive intentions of the Allies, intentions that they had recorded in secret treaties. He simply ignored the existence of those treaties, with their clauses providing for the division of German, Austrian, and Turkish territories and for the exaction of huge indemnities. In so doing he surrendered the opportunity to insist that America would help the Allies only if they agreed to give up those plans.

The course of revolution in Russia focused the attention of the world on the problems of peace. After taking over the government in November 1917, the Bolsheviks moved to capitulate to Germany in a separate peace. They also set out, in the midst of ruthless civil war, to solidify their hold at home and to advance the Communist revolution elsewhere. In order to embarrass the Allies, they disclosed the terms of the secret treaties they found in the czar's archives. Both David Lloyd George, the British prime minister, and Wilson countered by reasserting their dedication to a just peace, whereas the Germans imposed humiliating terms on Russia.

In January 1918, while the war was still raging, Wilson announced his celebrated Fourteen Points. They expressed his belief in the inextricable interconnections among free trade, democratic institutions, and human liberty. Five were broad: open diplomacy, by which he meant an end to secret agreements; free use of the seas in peace and war; the reduction of armaments; the removal of barriers to free trade; and an impartial adjustment of colonial claims. Eight points pertained to the principle of national self-determination: German evacuation of Russian territory; the restoration of Belgian independence; the return to France of Alsace-Lorraine (which Germany had conquered in 1870); the establishment of an independent Poland; and the autonomous development of each of the peoples of Austria-Hungary and the Ottoman Empire. The fourteenth and crowning point called for forming "a general assembly of nations" to afford "mutual guarantees of political independence and territorial integrity."

Those objectives conflicted not only with the ambitions of the Allies but with the attitudes of many Americans. Though there was much enthusiasm for the president's ideals, there was also opposition from those who wanted protective tariffs, from those who resisted internationalism of any kind, and particularly from those whose war-born hatreds demanded revenge, a march on Berlin, and gallows for the Kaiser.

The Armistice and the Election of 1918 The president was by no means soft. In October 1918, as the Allies drove through the German lines, the German high command urged the chancellor to propose an armistice to Wilson on the basis of the Fourteen Points. During the ensuing exchange of notes, Wilson took a position charitable enough to lead the Germans on, but firm enough to make them admit defeat. This satisfied all the Allied chiefs of state and military commanders except Pershing, who urged unconditional surrender. The British and French, exhausted by four years of war and frightened by the westward surge of Bolshevism, were eager for an armistice so long as it gave them security.

Aware of those views, Wilson demanded withdrawal of German forces from all invaded territory and immediate cessation of aerial and submarine warfare. When the Germans acceded to those conditions, which were designed to make renewed hostilities impossible, Wilson on October 23 opened negotiations with the Allies and suggested to the Germans that reasonable terms would depend on their establishing a democratic government. This suggestion precipitated the overthrow of the Kaiser, who abdicated on November 9.

The Allied leaders chafed at the Fourteen Points. The British explicitly rejected the point on the freedom of the seas, and the French demanded reparations for civilian damages. They would have insisted on further changes had Colonel House not threatened to make a separate peace if they did not assent to the rest of the Fourteen Points, which were to be the basis for an armistice. The Americans for their part ultimately agreed to add terms forcing the Germans to withdraw well beyond the east bank of the Rhine and to surrender vast quantities of war materials, including their submarines.

Those were tough conditions. But even so the Republicans attacked the president's foreign policy, insisting, as Roosevelt put it, on dictating peace to the hammer of guns instead of to the clicking of typewriters. This demagoguery frightened many Democratic leaders who, with a congressional election coming on, were tempted to seek votes by flag waving. Wilson yielded to his advisers' demand for a blanket endorsement of all Democratic candidates. Angry himself at the onslaughts of men like Roosevelt, Wilson on October 25 urged the people to vote Democratic if they approved of his policies at home and abroad. The return of a Republican majority, he said, would be a repudiation of his leadership.

This appeal made Wilson's foreign policy more than ever a partisan issue. It infuriated the Republicans, and though it helped some Democratic candidates it did not prevent the Republicans from gaining control of both houses of Congress. Republican leaders later claimed that it was foreign policy that had determined the outcome. On November 11, 1918, only a few days after the election, men of all parties rejoiced at the news that an armistice had been arranged. Now, as Wilson turned to negotiating the terms for peace, he had to reckon with a Republican majority in the Senate, where partisanship could delay or even prevent approval of any treaty he submitted.

NEGOTIATING PEACE

The Background of the Paris Conference Wilson failed to appoint any influential Republican to the American delegation to the peace conference at Paris. To advance his liberal program he chose to head the delegation himself, thus becoming the first president to go overseas on a diplomatic mission. Though his critics complained that he would slight his duties at home, his able performance at Paris justified his decision. Wilson named to the delegation Secretary of State Lansing and Colonel House, in his view obvious choices, and two others: General Tasker H. Bliss, a military expert, and Henry White, a career diplomat, ostensibly a Republican but in no sense a politician or a representative of the Senate. The delegation was to be Wilson's instrument, under his domination, but any advantage this control gave him during negotiations was overshadowed by the disadvantages inherent in slighting the Republicans.

Wilson also slighted public opinion. He had little talent for dealing with journalists, many of whom distrusted his official press representative, George Creel. Moreover, at the peace conference he had to yield to the other negotiators' insistence on secret sessions.

Crowds greet Wilson

The American press interpreted this decision as a violation of the principle of open diplomacy, even though there was no secret about the decisions reached at the conference. If Wilson's press relations had been better, American newspapers could have helped explain the president's difficulties to a public that did not fully understand the necessity for give and take.

Wilson had to bargain endlessly with the Allies, for their objectives often conflicted with his. He believed that the Fourteen Points should guide the peace settlement. He did not expect a perfect peace, but he thought that a league of nations could continually improve the terms of a peace treaty, and he counted on enlisting the moral force of the world behind the league. His optimism grew during his tour of Europe before the conference opened. Crowds greeted him as a savior, and he mistook their gratitude for victory as an endorsement of his goals.

Actually, the peoples of Europe and Asia, with unimportant exceptions, supported the demands of their own spokesmen. Four of those men were, with Wilson, the major architects of the peace. There was the self-controlled and resourceful Count Nobuaki Makino of Japan, ambitious for territory that Britain had promised his country in return for Japan's joining the Allies. Equally land-hungry was the cultured and adroit Vittorio Orlando of Italy. There was the perspicacious but shifty British prime minister, David Lloyd George, who had promised his electorate vast reparations. There was the French premier, Georges Clemenceau, cynical, tenacious, weary, aloof, determined to crush Germany forever. These men were bound by treaties to support one another's claims. Their armies, moreover, actually held most of the lands they planned to annex or assign.

Over large parts of the world neither they nor Wilson could exercise much influence. The Bolshevik Revolution had made Russia unwelcome at the conference, and it stood apart brooding, dissatisfied, potentially a mighty and ominous force. Furthermore, war continued within its borders while the peace conference sat. British troops in the northern part of European Russia were trying to assist anti-Bolsheviks there, and in Siberia a Japanese army was pushing west with an eye to conquest. The United States also dispatched forces to both areas. The Bolsheviks resenting the presence of foreigners, believed the British, Japanese, and Americans were agents of counterrevolution, as some authorities in Washington, London, and Tokyo intended them to be.

Revolution and counterrevolution infected all of Russia's European neighbors. The empire of Austria-Hungary had simply ceased to exist in part because Wilson's demand for self-determination had stirred the nationalistic hopes of the various peoples of the area. In the territories it once had ruled, the quarrels of self-conscious ethnic groups, complicated by the conniving of Communists, were forging the new states that were to mark the map of central and eastern Europe whether the men at Paris willed it or not. Within Germany the new republican government faced revolution at the borders, Red plots within, and a populace exasperated by a food shortage imposed by the continuing Allied blockade. In distributing American food supplies, inadequate at best, Herbert Hoover attempted to cut off the Left, particularly in eastern Europe. With the world in turmoil and Europe exhausted by war, the Paris conference had an unpropitious setting. With the Allies opposed to his terms, moreover, the odds against Wilson's program were enormous.

The League of Nations Wilson's plans for a charter for a league of nations included the disposition of former German colonies. In order to bring about an impartial and equitable settlement of colonial claims, as the Fourteen Points promised, Wilson hoped to put the German colonies under the guardianship of small neutrals like Switzerland and Sweden. Those neutrals were to be trustees for the league and were to help the backward colonial peoples to move toward independence.

The British and Japanese, however, would not surrender the territory in Africa and the Pacific that they had seized during hostilities. According to a secret treaty between them, German islands in the Pacific north of the equator were to go to Japan and islands south of the equator were to go to Australia and New Zealand. Wilson prevented the outright transfer of colonies by persuading the Allies to accept instead a system of "mandates," which obliged their holders to render annual accountings and theoretically to help subject peoples to stand alone. The compromise subjected the Allies to little surveillance in their administration of the territory they received. The mandate system was disingenuous, but Wilson felt that the league would gradually better it (though the League never did).

The concept of a league met opposition from the French, who wanted a military alliance of the victors against Germany. Japan further complicated Wilson's negotiations by demanding a statement of racial equality pledging member nations of a league not to discriminate against the nationals of other members. But the president had help from the Italians, who were pleased by his endorsement of the northern boundary they wanted, and from the British, who shared his hopes for the league. The racial pride of the Japanese was assuaged by their new mandates, and the French accepted the idea of a league after they realized that they could obtain their objectives elsewhere in the treaty. Wilson's draft served as the basis for the Covenant of the League of Nations, which the responsible committee approved and reported to the peace conference in February 1919.

It was a simple document. Each signer of the treaty was to have one vote in a Body of Delegates of the League. Larger authority rested with the Executive Council, which was to consist of representatives from the United States, the British Empire, France, Italy, Japan, and four states selected by the Body of Delegates. Decisions of the council required a unanimous vote except when a council member was itself a party to a dispute. The covenant also established a permanent secretariat, an international Bureau of Labor, and the mandate system. It provided for the admission of new members by a two-thirds vote of the delegates and for amendment by a three-fourths vote.

The main purpose of the League was to keep the peace. To that end the covenant obliged signatories, before they resorted to war, to submit disputes either to inquiry by the council or to arbitration by the Permanent Court of International Justice, which the council was to create. Member nations were to punish any breach of this article by severing economic relations with the offending state. The council, moreover, might recommend that members of the League contribute military and naval units to protect its principles. And the council was to advise on means of ensuring that member nations lived up to Article 10, which Wilson considered the heart of the covenant. This article bound signatories "to respect and preserve against external aggression the territorial integrity and . . . political independence of all members of the League."

The League was not a superstate. It could only recommend, but not compel, the recruitment and use of military force. Its deliberations would not bind Germany or Russia until the victorious powers invited

A Critique of the Treaty

The Treaty includes no provision for the economic rehabilitation of Europe, —nothing to make the defeated Central Empires into good neighbors, nothing to stabilize the new States of Europe, nothing to reclaim Russia; nor does it promote in any way a compact of economic solidarity amongst the Allies themselves; no arrangement was reached at Paris for restoring the disordered finances of France and Italy, or to adjust the systems of the Old World and the New.

The Council of Four paid no attention to these issues, being preoccupied with others, —Clemenceau to crush the economic life of his enemy, Lloyd George to do a deal . . . the President to do nothing that was not just and right. It is an extraordinary fact that the fundamental economic problems of a Europe starving and disintegrating before their eyes, was the one question in which it was impossible to arouse the interest of the Four. Reparations was their main excursion into the economic field, and they settled it as a problem of theology, of politics . . . from every point of view except that of the economic future of the States whose destiny they were handling.

From John Maynard Keynes, *The Economic Consequences of the Peace* 1920

them to join. Those powers had sufficient authority, moreover, to use the League to try to perpetuate the status quo. But the covenant did create the first promising international organization in modern history. It also fulfilled Wilson's purpose of recognizing war and the threat of war as everybody's business and of providing a forum for the nations of the world to discuss problems that might lead to conflict. In his view, the covenant organized the moral force of the world.

Consequently the president was distressed by the opposition to the League that he confronted during a brief trip home. The essence of that opposition was Republican partisanship, but it fed on other attitudes as well. Many German-Americans still resented the war and its outcome. Many Irish-Americans believed Wilson should have insisted on Irish independence. The president pointed out that that was a question for England to resolve, but he was pointedly cool toward his Irish critics. He was even less patient with those Americans who viewed the covenant as an "entangling alliance," and hesitated to depart from what to them was a national tradition of isolation from Europe. Those and other sentiments bred susceptibility to the propaganda of Wilson's opponents.

On March 4, 1919, the day before the president returned to Paris, Senator Henry Cabot Lodge produced a round-robin signed by 37 Republican senators and senators-elect, four more than were needed to defeat the treaty. It stated that the covenant was unacceptable and insisted that consideration of the League be deferred until after a treaty had been completed. In a speech that night, Wilson condemned the "careful selfishness" of his critics and their "ignorance of the state of the world." The covenant would be intimately tied to the treaty itself, he said. That interrelationship was essential for working out the problems of the conference, and the president was understandably annoyed. But his strong language intensified the partisanship that provoked it.

The Treaty of Versailles Though Wilson would not separate the League from the treaty, he realized that the covenant would have to be modified to meet the

Architects of the Peace: Orlando, Lloyd George, Clemenceau, Wilson

suggestions of American moderates. The revisions the president sponsored on his return to Paris would certainly have been demanded by the Senate in any event. They defined procedures for withdrawal from the League, stated that the acceptance of mandates was optional, and excluded from the purview of the League domestic issues such as immigration and regional agreements such as the Monroe Doctrine. By reopening the question of the covenant, however, Wilson exposed himself to the bargaining of his associates, who once more pressed their demands for Europe and Asia. The president secured his revisions, but only at an inflated price.

Clemenceau, still determined to assure French security, insisted that Germany be dismembered. He urged that two states, a revivified Poland and a new Czechoslovakia, be set up on Germany's eastern border. He also asked for the creation of a Rhenish buffer state, to be splintered off from Germany's west, and for the cession to France of the Saar Basin, a bountiful source of coal and iron, as well as of Alsace-Lorraine. Wilson balked at those extreme demands. For ten days the conference stalled, but when Wilson threatened to leave, Clemenceau bowed to the proponents of compromise.

The treaty drew generous boundaries for Poland and Czechoslovakia, but it also arranged for the League to conduct a plebiscite to determine the disposition of a part of Silesia coveted by both Germans and Poles. The treaty gave Poland access to the sea through a narrow corridor that put some Germans under Polish rule, just as other German-speaking people became subject to Czechoslovakia. France received Alsace-Lorraine and temporary economic concessions in the Saar, but the League was to administer the Saar and after 15 years was to conduct a plebiscite there. France could also occupy the Rhineland for 15 years. After that time the area was to be demilitarized but left a part of Germany. The German army was limited to a token force.

Furthermore, Wilson and Lloyd George agreed to a special security treaty pledging their nations to assist France if it were attacked. Clemenceau realized that the United States Senate would probably reject the special treaty, but in that case the Rhineland could be occupied indefinitely. All in all, Clemenceau obtained as much safety for France as any treaty could reasonably provide.

The French and the English also pushed Wilson into accepting their demands for reparations in excess of what Germany could pay and in violation of the pre-armistice agreement to limit payments to the cost of civilian damages. The president let the Allies include the cost of pensions, which later permitted the reparations commission to calculate that the Germans owed some $120 billion, the fantastic figure that had

Map 24-2
Europe in 1920

been the British objective. The reparations clause of the treaty, moreover, specifically attributed the cause of war to "the aggression of Germany," a phrase that rankled in German minds for years to come, however accurate it may have been. Along with the economic dislocations that grew out of the exorbitant reparations imposed on Germany, the war-guilt clause proved to be an emotional threat to future peace.

At the time, however, the president's troubles with Italy seemed more ominous. Before the conference Wilson had agreed to a northern frontier for Italy at the line of the Brenner Pass, which put 200,000 Austrians under Italian rule. This left him with nothing else to trade when the Italians also insisted on taking Fiume, an Adriatic port surrounded by Yugoslav land. When the Italians discovered that all the powers were antagonistic to their claim to Fiume, they boldly marched into the city. Wilson appealed to the Italian people in the name of justice, but they, with their leaders, resented the president's miscalculated intrusion. The Italians left Paris in a rage, and, though they returned to sign a treaty that did not give them Fiume, the incident alienated Italian-Americans from Wilson's treaty and almost disrupted the conference.

The Japanese seized on the confusion to advance their own claims. They were seeking endorsement for their economic ambitions in China and for their assumption of the German leasehold at Jiaozhou (Kiaochow*) and of German privileges in the Shandong (Shantung) Peninsula. After the whole conference seemed about to disintegrate, Wilson accepted most of those claims though the Chinese opposed them. Many Americans, including two of the delegates, thought the president conceded too much, but he felt he had obtained a solution "as satisfactory as could be got out of the tangle."

The same could be said of the whole treaty that the victors and the vanquished signed at Versailles in 1919. It was punitive, but Germany had lost the war it had expected to win, and the Allies were less severe than the Germans would have been. The treaty followed the Fourteen Points as closely as world conditions permitted. Europe had a new map that approximated ethnic groupings (see Map 24-2). Ne-

*The spelling of Chinese proper names is given first in the *pinyin* system of romantization then by the Wade-Giles system in parentheses.

gotiations had involved some compromises of the principle of self-determination and created some boundaries that conflicted with the military defense and the economic needs of the new states. But those difficulties and others could be negotiated later in the forum of the League. As Wilson had predicted, the League was inextricably part of the treaty, a "convenient, indeed indispensable" instrument. He had yet, however, to convert two-thirds of the Senate to his way of thinking.

THE STRUGGLE OVER RATIFICATION

The Senate and the Treaty Wilson brought the treaty home to a people initially predisposed in its favor. Though few Americans were familiar with the whole long document, most had learned something about the League, and millions were enthusiastic about it. But the people could not vote on the treaty. The question of its approval, and therefore the portentous question of what direction American foreign policy would take, were for the Senate to decide.

Of the 96 senators 49 were Republican, but only 14—as well as 4 Democrats—were irreconcilably against the League and the treaty. Those irreconcilables, many of them progressives, believed that the mission of the United States was to create a model society for other nations to emulate, not to get involved in international affairs. Indeed, they shared the distrust of foreigners so common among the American people. The other 35 Republicans intended not to reject the treaty but to make its adoption contingent on a number of reservations, of which the most significant had to do with Wilson's League of Nations. While 23 Republicans favored a list of strong reservations drafted and sponsored by Senator Lodge, 12 were willing to settle for milder reservations. A coalition of Democrats and moderate Republicans would have commanded a majority vote. And a majority was all that was needed to settle the kind of reservations that would be demanded. Such a coalition, moreover, could probably have attracted the necessary two-thirds vote for approval. But the crucial coalition was never formed.

The Democratic leaders knew they had to make concessions to their opponents, but they felt that they also had to wait for instructions from the president. They never received those instructions, for Wilson refused to compromise an issue he considered both personal and moral.

It was Lodge who had made the issue personal. Lodge had endorsed the strategy of insisting on reservations. Lodge had packed the important Foreign Relations Committee with irreconcilables and strong reservationists. Lodge, the majority leader of the Senate, was determined to hold his party together and to win in 1920. Further, he honestly believed that the League as Wilson had planned it was a threat to national sovereignty. Lodge was not an isolationist, but he put his faith in armies and navies and the balance of power, the "large view" of his old friend Theodore Roosevelt, who had just died. An arrogant, often exasperating man, Lodge was also moved by mean considerations, including the prejudices of his many Italian- and Irish-American constituents. He was a formidable antagonist who hated Wilson as Wilson hated him.

Lodge's reservations struck the president as unnecessary and immoral. Wilson objected to the very idea of making the approval of the treaty subject to reservations. He also held that reservations would mean that the treaty would have to be renegotiated, though the British, the French, and the State Department did not think so. Two of the reservations would have made Congress the sole judge of whether the United States should accept a mandate and whether it should withdraw from the League. Two others reserved to the United States exclusive authority over tariff policy, immigration, and the Monroe Doctrine. As Wilson argued, the revised covenant already covered those issues. Another reservation exempted the United States from any decision of the League on which any member and its self-governing dominions had cast in the aggregate more than one vote. The American veto in the council, Wilson noted, made superfluous such an ungracious protest against the seats of the British dominions in the Body of Delegates. The president especially opposed the reservation on Article 10, which stated that the United States would assume no obligation to preserve the territorial integrity or political independence of any other country without the approval of Congress. To Wilson this would be a violation of the essential spirit of the League—the moral obligation to protect the peace of the world.

In the abstract Wilson may have been right, but the politics of the Senate made compromise necessary. Lodge's reservations would have damaged the League far less than would outright rejection of treaty and

League alike. Senator Gilbert Hitchcock, the Democratic minority leader, advised Wilson to work out some sort of compromise with Lodge, as did Colonel House, Robert Lansing, Bernard Baruch, and many other friends of the president.

But Wilson would not listen, and as the days passed, the public tended to become bored with the whole question about which most voters were ill-informed. Wilson had advocated a degree of national involvement in foreign affairs greater, in all probability, than most Americans, after reflection, were willing to accept. The idealism of wartime was fading into the problems of the postwar period. Inflation, unemployment, and fears of Bolshevism reduced public enthusiasm for a generous peace and for a genuine internationalism.

The President's Collapse In order to arouse new enthusiasm for the League, Wilson set out in September 1919 on a speaking tour across the country. His train moved through the strongholds of isolationism, over 8,000 miles, stopping 37 times for him to address the voters. As he proceeded through the Middle West to the Pacific Coast, then south, and then east, he was greeted by larger and larger crowds. But their applause did not change one vote in the Senate. Indeed, Wilson's attacks on his opponents stiffened their resolution to resist, and his absence from Washington impeded Democratic efforts to find a basis for compromise. The president's strenuous efforts taxed his limited strength without achieving his political purpose.

On September 25 Wilson spoke at Pueblo, Colorado. That night his head hurt mercilessly. Frightened by the president's exhaustion, his physician canceled the remainder of the trip. Back in Washington Wilson was too tired to work, too tense to rest. On October 2 he fell to the floor unconscious, the victim of a cerebral thrombosis, a blood clot in his brain.

The stroke did not kill the president, but it paralyzed his left side, thickened his speech, totally disabled him for almost two months, and prevented him thereafter from working more than an hour or two at a time. For six months he did not meet with the Cabinet. For six weeks he could not execute the minimum duties of his office. Though his mind was not injured he became petulant, suspicious, and easily moved to tears. He was unable to assess situations with accuracy. His collapse was a tragedy not only for himself but for a nation facing a momentous crisis in foreign policy.

On November 6, while Wilson was still bedridden, Lodge presented his reservations to the Senate. It was obvious that the Republicans had the votes to adopt them but not the two-thirds needed to approve the treaty after the reservations had been attached. The Democratic leaders hesitated to move without the president's consent, and he gave stringent orders on November 18 that they were to reject the treaty so long as it was subject to the Lodge reservations. They were then to move that the treaty be accepted either as it stood or with mild interpretive reservations of which Wilson approved. This order conceded nothing to the Republican moderates, who stood behind Lodge. Though nonpartisan friends of the League preferred accepting Lodge's reservations to rejecting the whole treaty, the Democrats on November 19 voted to reject the treaty with those reservations. Consequently, the resolution to adopt the treaty as Lodge had modified it failed by 39 to 55. Lodge blocked debate of the interpretive reservations that the Democrats then proposed, and minutes later a resolution to approve the unamended treaty also failed, 38 to 53.

The Final Rejection The moderate Republicans and the Democrats were stunned by what they had done and felt they had to try again. Furthermore, organizations representing some 20 million Americans petitioned for compromise and ratification. The same hope was voiced by the British and French press and by the British government. Influential Democrats without exception tried to persuade the president to relieve his party of the hopeless battle to defeat the Lodge reservations.

But Wilson would still not hear of concessions. Instead, on January 8, 1920, he wrote a blistering letter to his fellow Democrats. The majority of the people wanted ratification, he said. Let the Senate accept the treaty without tampering with it or else reject it. If there was any doubt about public opinion, Wilson warned, the issue could be resolved at the next election, which would be "a great and solemn referendum."

This was the counsel of a deluded man, for presidential elections turn on many issues, not just one. The Democratic party had been losing strength for three years, and the treaty, if the Senate rejected it again, would be impossible to resuscitate. Recognizing

A Case for Compromise

My suggestion is this. . . . Send for Senator Hitchcock and tell him that you feel that you have done your duty and have fulfilled your every obligation to your colleagues in Paris by rejecting all offers to alter the document that was formulated there, and you now turn the Treaty over to the Senate for such action as it may deem wise to take. . . .

Advise him to ask the Democratic Senators to vote for the Treaty with such reservations as the majority may formulate, and let the matter then rest with the other signatories of the Treaty. . . . If the Allied and Associated Powers are willing to accept the reservations . . . you will abide by the result being conscious of having done your full duty.

The Allies may not take the Treaty with the Lodge Reservations . . . and this will be your vindication. But even if they should take them . . . your conscience will be clear. After agreement is reached, it can easily be shown that the Covenant in its practical workings in the future will not be seriously hampered and that time will give us a workable machine.

From Colonel Edward M. House to Woodrow Wilson, November 24, 1919, as quoted in Charles Seymour, *The Intimate Papers of Colonel House,* v. 4, 1928

the folly of Wilson's position, Senator Hitchcock and other Democrats tried to work out a satisfactory compromise on the reservations. They failed, partly because the Republican irreconcilables warned Lodge against compromise, partly because Lodge himself probably did not want to rescue the treaty. The president, increasingly peevish, on March 8 again instructed the Democrats to hold the line.

His adherents prevailed. The Lodge reservations, only slightly modified, were adopted, this time with some Democratic help. On March 19, the day of the final test, half the Democrats voted to approve the treaty with the reservations. But 23 Democrats, 20 of them Southerners, did the president's bidding. Together with 12 irreconcilables, they voted against approval and thus prevented by a margin of seven the two-thirds majority needed for adoption.

There was to be no "solemn referendum." The Democratic presidential nominee in 1920, James M. Cox, supported the League, but sometimes with hesitation. The Republican plank on the treaty was deliberately vague, as was the Republican candidate, Warren G. Harding. Though Harding enjoyed the full support of both Republican isolationists and Republican internationalists, he chose to consider his smashing victory a repudiation of the treaty.

The Senate had made the telling decision. In rejecting both treaty and League, the Senate had for the while turned America's back to Europe. The rejection destroyed the best available chance for developing world peace. Perhaps the irreconcilables, the forceful spokesmen of isolation, could have defeated the treaty in any event, but it was not they who did so, though they helped. Wilson's stubbornness and Lodge's partisanship helped even more. Indeed, partisanship was the real culprit, and the outcome of the fight revealed how severely domestic politics could damage foreign policy.

The damage, in the end, affected the whole world, for without the United States the League became an instrument for preserving the status quo. Even if the United States had been a member, the League would probably have acted just about the way it did. But as it was, the League never had a chance to fulfill Wilson's vision. That vision, which rested on the moral intent of the president's peace program, was the most compelling image democracy then offered to the world. With the defeat of the treaty, the United States seemed to have renounced its claims to the imagination of people everywhere. The renunciation came just at the time when Bolshevism was advancing its revolutionary claims more effectively than ever before. The American retreat eased the way for both the advocates of reaction and the advocates of communism. It cost the United States the only available fruits of a gallant victory. It made a travesty of the noble effort to create a world safe for the ideals Wilson cherished.

TRANSITION FROM WAR

Demobilization When the war ended, the government had no plans for demobilization. It simply lifted the controls it had imposed on the economy during the war. In accord with public sentiment, it hastened the discharge of the soldiers, many of whom were unable to find jobs when they returned to civilian life. Though unemployment declined after February 1919, it persisted in troubled areas for another half year, and it soured thousands of veterans who had expected a hero's welcome to include a job.

Immediately after the armistice the War Industries Board began to close up shop, confident that private industry would be able to switch back to a peacetime economy with no help or direction from the federal government. That was a miscalculation. While industry bid for new plants and machinery, consumers dug out their wartime savings to make the purchases they had long postponed. Inflation struck the country. During 1919 the cost of living climbed to 77 percent above pre-war levels; during 1920, another 28 percent.

The government developed only piecemeal and inadequate remedies for unemployment and inflation. There was as yet no body of economic ideas to explain the need for overall federal policies that would ease the process of reconversion. Wilson, moreover, was preoccupied with peacemaking and hampered by an opposition Congress. Yet the Revenue Act of 1919 carried on the policy of progressive taxation, ensured the government the income it needed, and helped check inflation.

Both Congress and the public were anxious to settle the question of what should be done with the railroads, which the government was still running. Private management wanted them back, but labor had found that public administration was more generous and more efficient. An attorney for the railway brotherhoods, Glenn E. Plumb, proposed a plan for nationalizing the roads. The AFL supported the Plumb plan, but elsewhere it evoked little enthusiasm. Congress, in the Transportation Act of 1920, extended the tradition of regulated capitalism by turning the railroads back to their private owners while subjecting them to increased but deliberately benign supervision. In a similar spirit, the Water Power Act of 1920 set up a Federal Power Commission, consisting of the Secretaries of War, Agriculture, and the Interior, to license the building and operation of dams and hydroelectric plants. This clumsy arrangement by its very failure drew attention to the need for genuine public control of waterways.

Labor Strife In the years right after the war, the once-progressive fervor of Americans seemed to have spent itself. The nation's policy makers, like the American people, turned more and more to the past. The administration, which had sympathized with organized labor, now began to favor management. That reversal was prompted by several forces. Wilson's advisers were growing impatient with the strikes that continued to cripple the nation's industries, and management had launched a successful campaign to associate all unions with radicalism, about which the country at large was harboring hysterical fears.

The enforced wartime truce between labor and management ended in 1919. The unions then set out to consolidate their gains and to bring wages into line with the rising cost of living. And the National Association of Manufacturers and other management groups set out to reestablish the open shop, which they liked to call "the American way." Management propaganda extolled the beneficence of business and warned that unions and union demands were inspired by foreign and radical influences. Nevertheless, many of the first strikes after the war were successful, notably those of clothing, textile, telegraph, and telephone workers.

The most celebrated postwar strikes occurred in Seattle and Boston. In February 1919 the Seattle Central Labor Council called a general strike to support shipyard workers who had walked out in quest of higher pay and shorter hours. Those workers and others in Seattle, something of a wartime boom town, were also worried about postwar unemployment. Some of the local labor leaders were unquestionably radical, and a general strike was itself a radical technique, perhaps especially in the view of the residents of a city where the IWW had been active. But Mayor Ole Hanson grossly exaggerated the Red menace and used troops to stamp out the strike.

In Boston the police found that they could not stretch their pre-war wages to cover postwar living costs. Denied a raise and restive because of other grievances, they secured a charter from the AFL and threatened a strike in August 1919. The mayor appointed a citizens' committee, which suggested that most of the policemen's demands, except recognition of their union, be granted. The police commissioner, however, a declared enemy of organized labor, rejected the suggestion and fired 19 of the union's leaders. On September 9 the police went out on strike. Volunteer vigilantes were unable to control the gangs of looters who brought Boston to the point of anarchy. The American middle class was shocked and scared. But just then the governor of Massachusetts, Calvin Coolidge, called out the national guard to restore order. The strike failed, and many of the police were dismissed.

The whole episode was as unnecessary as it was lamentable. Coolidge could have supported the mayor and overruled the police commissioner before the strike began. Instead, he won a national reputation by putting down the strike. The American people knew little about the facts of the case, but they long remembered the governor's characteristic response to Gompers' request that the policemen be reinstated: "There is no right to strike against the public safety by anybody, anywhere, any time."

In November 1919, the bituminous coal miners walked out under the leadership of their new and colorful president, John L. Lewis, who was radical only in his pugnacious manner. A wartime agreement had governed wages in the mines, but the union claimed that the armistice had made that agreement inapplicable. As Lewis observed, there was no ceiling on the rising price of coal. The miners demanded a wage increase, a six-hour day, and a five-day week. When

Boston, 1919: Coolidge called out the guard

the operators refused to negotiate, the miners prepared to strike. With Wilson's approval, Attorney General A. Mitchell Palmer ruled that the wage agreement was still in effect and obtained an injunction against the union. Lewis then capitulated because, as he put it, "we cannot fight the government." Still the miners refused to go back to work until the government ordered an immediate increase in pay. Their other demands were denied.

The AFL faced its crucial test in the steel industry. The secretary of its organizing committee, William Z. Foster, had been radical enough in his beliefs for management to persuade the public that he was a Red. He was also a less than effective organizer. Still, the steelworkers had grave grievances. Most of them put in a twelve-hour workday in return for subsistence wages. After recruiting a substantial minority of workers, the union called a strike in September 1919, for management had rejected its demands for recognition, an eight-hour day, and decent pay. Episodes of violence punctuated the strike. Public opinion, misled by the steel companies' propaganda, condoned the widespread use of state and federal troops to prevent picketing. United States Steel alone used thousands of strikebreakers. In January 1920 the union gave up, thoroughly beaten.

Race Hatred Old prejudices, whetted by new fears, had also provoked a wave of persecution and violence that engulfed black Americans. In response to wartime labor shortages, several hundred thousand black people had moved from the South to Northern industrial centers. Those migrants brought their poverty with them. Segregated in urban slums, they were the continuing objects of the race hatred of their white neighbors, especially of unskilled workers who viewed their black counterparts as competitors for jobs. More and more black citizens, for their part, educated by the experience of military service, by the war's avowedly democratic aims, and by the inequities they met in the North, began to demand rights long denied them, particularly higher wages, equal protection under the law, and the chance to vote and hold political office. Those were key goals of the increasingly militant National Association for the Advancement of Colored People

Militia in Chicago, 1919

Marcus Garvey

(NAACP) and of its foremost leader, W. E. B. DuBois, who had stood for a suspension of agitation during the war. Now white supremacists were determined "to keep the Negro in his place," by force if necessary, and many of them contended that the Reds were inciting a black uprising in the South.

Turning to terrorism, lynch mobs in the South made victims of more than 70 black citizens in 1919, 10 of them veterans in uniform. The new Ku Klux Klan (see p. 635), committed to the intimidation of black Americans, gained some 100,000 members. In 1919 South and North alike saw the worst spate of race riots in American history to that time. Two of the most tragic occurred in Washington, D.C., where a majority of the offenders were white veterans, and in Chicago, where for thirteen days a mob of white people fought black residents of the slums. Before the year ended, 25 race riots had resulted in hundreds of deaths and injuries and millions of dollars of property damage.

Most black people resisted their attackers, as the NAACP advised them to, and liberal white citizens organized to fight intolerance and to lobby for antilynching laws, but by and large black Americans were neither hopeful of remedy nor yet ready to campaign in their own behalf. Instead, by 1923 about half a million of them had joined the Universal Negro Improvement Association of Marcus Garvey, a Jamaican black nationalist who proposed to create a new empire in Africa with himself on the throne. Garvey had a fundamental appeal to black Americans. Touching their traditional sensibilities, he used religious symbols and rituals in his organizational meetings. His attacks on the oppression of his race were based on Christian ethical standards. Though Garvey's financially flimsy scheme for empire collapsed, his movement met the powerful need of black Americans for self-identity, racial pride, and an escape from a society that denied them dignity, opportunity, and even personal safety.

The Red Scare American radicals also felt the sting of old prejudices and new fears. There was, to be sure, genuine cause for concern over the spread of Bolshevism in Europe. In March 1919 Soviet leaders organized the Third International as an agency for world revolution, and during the rest of that year the Communists made striking gains in Germany, Hungary, and along Russia's frontiers. The International fed on the postwar disintegration of eastern Europe—a disintegration the United States did little to check.

Within the United States, however, communism was feeble. In 1919 the Socialist party, its ranks depleted and its morale low, broke into three factions. Some 40,000 moderates retained the old name. One left-wing faction of about 20,000, almost all of them immigrants, formed the Communist Labor party. Another militant group of between 30,000 and 60,000, also largely immigrant, joined the Communist party of America under native-born leaders. But the three groups together constituted less than half of 1 percent of the population.

During the war, public and private propaganda had generated hatred and fear of the Germans, and Americans had already begun to fight the shadows of their anxieties. In the postwar months they transferred much of this hate to the nation's immigrants, whom the suspicious middle class had long stereotyped as radical. Hysteria reached pathological proportions under the influence of business propaganda that branded all labor as radical, under the spur of politicians who exploited the mood of the nation for their own advantage, and under the stimulus of sporadic episodes of violence.

Sacco, Vanzetti, and the "Frameup"

It was a frameup . . . that does not *necessarily* mean that any set of government and employing class detectives deliberately planned to fasten the crime of murder on Sacco and Vanzetti. Though in this case it is almost certain they did. . . . The frameup is an unconscious . . . mechanism . . . a kink in the mind that makes people do something without knowing that they are doing it. It is the sub-rational act of a group, serving in this case, through a series of pointed unintentions, the ends of a governing class. . . . The frameup is a process that you can't help feeling, but like most unconscious processes it's very hard to trace step by step.

From John Dos Passos, *Facing the Chair,* 1927

Scare headlines and legislative investigations of alleged Red activity kept the public edgy. In April the handiwork of a few lunatic radicals created near-panic when bombs were mailed to 38 eminent citizens, including John D. Rockefeller, Justice Holmes, the postmaster general, and the attorney general. The Post Office intercepted all the bombs but one. In June several direct bombings occurred. One weapon exploded in front of the Washington home of Attorney General A. Mitchell Palmer, damaging the building and dismembering his would-be assassin, an Italian anarchist.

The bombings of April and June had been plotted by dangerous criminals. They were not, however, a part of Communist strategy, for the leaders of international communism recognized that simple terror would be an ineffective weapon for overturning a strong capitalist state. But most Americans did not differentiate among radicalisms. They grew more frightened every day, and they saw Red in everything they feared or disliked.

The mood of the nation endorsed the witch hunts conducted by Attorney General Palmer. A Quaker, a progressive Democrat who had worked effectively for women's suffrage and labor reforms, an enthusiast for the League of Nations, Palmer had enjoyed a deserved reputation as a liberal until he took office in March 1919. Then he threw his department, especially the newly created Federal Bureau of Investigation, into a strenuous campaign against aliens and radicals. He may have been hoping to advance his candidacy for the Democratic presidential nomination in 1920. If so, he overreached himself. But he did succeed in violating the Anglo-American heritage of civil liberties.

Congress refused to pass a sedition bill that Palmer had drafted, but the attorney general on his own authority ordered a series of raids, many against the remnants of the IWW, beginning in November 1919. During the first raid his agents arrested 250 members of the Union of Russian Workers and beat many of them up, but the Justice Department could find cause to recommend that only 39 of them be deported. In December Palmer cooperated with the Labor Department in deporting 249 aliens to Russia, most of whom had committed no offense and were not Communists. A nationwide raid on January 1, 1920, led to the arrest of some 6,000 people, many of whom were American citizens and non-Communists. They were herded into prisons and bull pens. Some were seized on suspicion only, taken without warrants from their homes, and held incommunicado. The raids revealed no evidence of a grand plot. Nevertheless, outside of the small membership of the incipient Civil Liberties Union, few Americans spoke out against the high-handed tactics of the attorney general, the chief legal officer of the United States.

Sacco, Vanzetti, and the Red Scare

The citizens of Norfolk county know these men are guilty—On the other hand, in those domains where foreign and un-American principles are in vogue, such as Russia, Harvard, Argentine, Wellesley, China, and Smith, they are sure these men are innocent. . . .

The leader of the movement to set these two murderers free is Felix Frankfurter. . . . As a result of the work of Frankfurter and the rest of the gang . . . emerged the organization known as the American Civil Liberties Union. . . . Radiating out from the organization . . . there are some 500 others, having for their purpose the destruction of our government by force, the weakening of our army, navy and other defenses, the destruction of the home, the Boy Scouts, and all the other institutions that Americans hold dear.

Speech by Frank A. Goodwin, Massachusetts Registrar of Motor Vehicles, quoted in G. L. Joughin and E. M. Morgan, *The Legacy of Sacco and Vanzetti,* 1948

Still worried about preventing a revolution that was not brewing, Palmer continued to warn the nation about Red plots. But the outbreak he predicted for May 1, 1920, failed to materialize, and gradually the public began to tire of his unfounded alarms. The tide of Bolshevism had started to recede in Europe, and Palmer and his imitators had made themselves ridiculous. They could, of course, also be ruthless, as was the New York legislature, which expelled five innocuous Socialists, all properly elected members of the Assembly. This travesty on the American elective system evoked sharp denunciations, the most influential from Charles Evans Hughes. By the summer of 1920, the Red scare was largely over, the hysteria spent. In September Americans were horrified by a bomb explosion at the corner of Broad and Wall streets in New York. But they accepted the episode for what it was, the work of a crazed individual, not the product of a Bolshevik conspiracy as Palmer maintained.

The Red scare left ugly scars. The constitutional rights of thousands of Americans had been violated. Hundreds of innocent people had been deported. Many states had enacted sedition laws even more extreme than those passed during the war. And there lingered a less strident but still pervasive nativism that in the years ahead was to condone the new Ku Klux Klan, an organization dedicated to the hatred of black Americans, Catholics, Jews, and foreigners. Nativism set the stage for a major reversal of immigration policy, which had for so many decades kept the gates of America open to newcomers. In February 1921, Congress passed a bill vetoed by Wilson but later reenacted and signed by his successor. It limited the number of immigrants in any year to 3 percent of the foreign born of each national group who had been living in the United States in 1910. Even this restrictive quota, which just about choked off immigration from Asia and central and southern Europe, was later to be reduced (see p. 653).

Hatred of aliens and radicals made a mockery of justice in the celebrated case of two Italians, confessed anarchists, Nicola Sacco and Bartolomeo Vanzetti. They were arrested, tried, and convicted for murdering two employees of a shoe company in South Braintree, Massachusetts, during a payroll robbery in 1920. Little conclusive evidence was found against them, yet they were condemned, essentially for their language and their beliefs. The judge who conducted the trial referred to them privately as "those anarchist bastards." Many Boston patricians felt the same way, and

Harding: A Contemporary View

If an optimist is a man who makes lemonade out of all the lemons that are handed to him, then Senator Harding is the greatest of all optimists. He has been told by his friends and his critics that he is colorless and without sap, commonplace and dull, weak and servile. Right you are, says the Senator. You have described exactly the kind of man this country needs. It has tried Roosevelt and Wilson, and look!—it can't stand the gaff. I am nothing that they were. I am no superman . . . and no superthinker.— . . . Therefore, I am just the man you are looking for. . . . I am distinguished by the fact that nothing distinguishes me. I am marked for leadership because I have no marks upon me. I am just the man because no one can think of a single reason why I am the man.

From Walter Lippmann, *Men of Destiny,* 1927

most of them, including the presidents of Harvard and Massachusetts Institute of Technology, approved the decision to deny a retrial. Some scholars later held that Sacco was probably guilty; most others disagreed. At the time, Felix Frankfurter, the novelist John Dos Passos, the poet Edna St. Vincent Millay, and other defenders of justice tried for six years to save Sacco and Vanzetti, but they failed. The cause attracted attention throughout the world and engaged the hearts of men and women who were to provide liberal leadership in the years to come. But in 1927, when Sacco and Vanzetti were electrocuted, the wounds of the Red scare festered again. The forces of respectability and conformity and repression seemed to be united against justice and decency and democracy.

The Election of 1920 The Red scare drained away the vestiges of progressive zeal. Americans, weary of public matters great and small, withdrew to a private world of pleasure, entertainment, and sensationalism. The political parties reflected the nation's fatigue and selfishness. The confident Republicans met in Chicago, where the professionals who controlled the party intended to name a candidate they could manage. After six ballots, the bosses arranged for the nomination to go to Senator Warren G. Harding of Ohio. The convention selected Harding on the tenth ballot, and then the delegates, ignoring their orders, named Calvin Coolidge for vice president.

Harding was a handsome, semieducated political hack with a modest talent for golf, a larger taste for liquor and poker, a complaisant disposition, an utterly empty mind, and an enduring loyalty to the Republican creed of 1890. He was one of the least qualified candidates ever nominated by a major party. His platform fitted his creed. It promised lower taxes, a higher tariff, restriction of immigration, and—with opportunistic generosity—aid to farmers. It damned the League of Nations but called vaguely for an "agreement among nations to preserve the peace"—a phrase that made the isolationists happy and that Harding's wordy speeches did nothing to clarify.

The Democrats were at odds with themselves. The failure of President Wilson, in spite of his illness, to disclaim ambition for the nomination impeded the candidacy of his son-in-law, William G. McAdoo, probably the ablest of the hopefuls. Attorney General Palmer had begun to lose support before the convention met. And in any event the Democratic bosses, almost as powerful as their Republican counterparts, wanted no candidate who was identified with the Wilson administration. They preferred Governor James

Newly enfranchised voter

M. Cox of Ohio, a good vote-getter and an opponent of Prohibition. The convention selected as his running mate Assistant Secretary of the Navy Franklin D. Roosevelt. The platform was pro-League (though it allowed for amendments to the covenant), and otherwise undistinguished. So, except in contrast to Harding, was the Democratic candidate.

The movement back to the Republicans, for so long the normal majority party, had begun in 1918 (see p. 621), and it quickened in 1920. Midwestern farmers, alienated by wartime controls, were now troubled by falling prices. Much of the once-progressive middle class had come to resent high taxes, inflation, and labor strife. Urban Democrats of the North were suspicious of Southern "drys," and Irish-Americans were hostile toward Wilson's foreign policy. Many independents could not forgive Palmer his behavior or Wilson his sometimes open endorsement of it.

All these factors combined to produce a Republican "earthquake." Harding received 61 percent of the popular vote, which now included women, carried every state outside the South and also Tennessee, and led Cox by 404 to 127 in the Electoral College. The Republicans also swept the congressional elections, obtaining a majority of 22 in the Senate and 167 in the House of Representatives. Not only had the voters repudiated Wilson and internationalism, they had repudiated progressivism. They restored to power the Republicans who had stuck with the party when Roosevelt bolted in 1912. The party balance of 1896 prevailed again. Harding, for all his limitations, had caught the purpose of his constituency when he called for a return to "not nostrums, but normalcy."

NORMALCY

All the Advantages Harding, Secretary of State Charles Evans Hughes, and the Republican majority in the Senate quickly buried the issue of the Treaty of Versailles. In his first message to Congress the president stated that the United States would have nothing to do with the League of Nations. Since the rejection of the treaty left the United States still technically at war with the Central Powers, the Senate passed again a resolution establishing a separate peace with Germany—a resolution that Wilson had vetoed. Harding signed it in July 1921, and Hughes then negotiated peace treaties with Germany, Austria, and Hungary. Like the resolution, these treaties claimed for the United States all the rights and advantages, but none of the responsibilities, of the Paris settlement.

The pursuit of advantages without responsibility—in Wilson's words "an ineffaceable stain upon . . . the honor of the United States"—also engaged the Harding administration as a diplomatic partner to American oil companies. Harding's advisers, equating national interests with corporate interests, sought to fulfill corporate wishes. Pressure from oil companies persuaded the president to champion a treaty with Colombia, ostensibly designed only to indemnify that republic with $25 million for its loss of land and honor when Roosevelt assisted the Panamanian revolt. The treaty had been under consideration for several years, but Roosevelt's friends had blocked it while he still lived. In 1921, two years after his death, Colombia was preparing to withdraw all private rights to subsurface oil deposits. That possibility helped to move even Lodge to seek the goodwill that would permit Standard Oil to obtain concessions from the Colombian government. In April 1921 the Senate approved the treaty; Colombia ratified it in 1922; and American investments there, largely in oil, grew from about $2 million to $124 million by 1929. The State Department opened even richer prospects for profit by persuading the British to share with American companies the enormous oil fields of the Middle East.

The outstanding diplomatic venture of Harding's term was a 1921 conference on naval disarmament. At the time of Harding's inauguration, the Navy Department was urging the completion of the vast building program that had been launched five years earlier (see p. 605). But businesspeople were impatient to cut federal expenses so taxes could be reduced, and they grumbled about the cost of the program. Continued naval expansion, moreover, was provoking an armament race with two recent associates, Great Britain and Japan. Senator William E. Borah of Idaho suggested a three-power meeting on naval limitation, and large majorities in both houses of Congress endorsed that scheme in a resolution attached to the naval appropriations bill of 1921.

This move was welcomed by the British, who were eager to terminate the defensive alliance made with Japan in 1902, an alliance that the dominions, especially Canada, disliked. The British also felt that the arms race was intimately associated with stability in the Orient. Harding proposed a conference on naval limitations on the same day the British called for a conference on East Asia. They agreed to discuss both matters at a single meeting in Washington.

The double agenda made it necessary to invite all the major naval powers—the United States, Great Britain, Japan, France, and Italy—as well as smaller powers with interests in East Asia—China, Portugal, Belgium, and the Netherlands. Everyone agreed that Bolshevik Russia, though a Pacific power, should be excluded, and its protests were ignored.

The delegates assembled on November 11, 1921, to commemorate the third anniversary of the armistice. The next day they heard an address by Secretary of State Charles Evans Hughes, who had been named presiding officer. He presented the conference with a detailed plan for naval disarmament. The United States was to scrap 30 capital ships—that is, battleships, battle cruisers, and aircraft carriers; the British were to give up 23, Japan, 17. This destruction of more than 1,878,000 aggregate tons afloat, on the ways, or planned, would establish a capital-ship tonnage ratio among the three nations of 5 : 5 : 3. The ratio was to persist for ten years, during which the powers would observe a moratorium on the construction of capital ships. France and Italy were each to have one-third the tonnage allotted the United States and Great Britain.

Hughes's speech stirred the amazed delegates to cheers. The Japanese, however, disliked being on the short end of the ratio. They bargained successfully to keep their newest battleship, and they accepted the Five Power Naval Treaty only after the United States and England had agreed not to fortify their possessions in the western Pacific. Another agreement, the Four Power Treaty, bound the United States, Great Britain, Japan, and France to respect each other's rights affecting insular possessions in the Pacific. It also specifically supplanted the Anglo-Japanese alliance.

Now Hughes pressed on to conclude a Nine Power Treaty that committed all the nations at the conference to observe traditional American policies in the Orient. They agreed to respect the territorial and administrative integrity and the independence of China and to uphold the Open Door.

The Washington treaties, as the British had intended, and as the United States later maintained, were integrally related to each other, and together they reduced tension in East Asia. Japan restored Shandong (Shantung) to China's sovereignty, withdrew from Siberia, and granted the United States cable rights on the former German island of Yap. The naval treaty, moreover, marked the first time in history that major powers had consented to disarm. Hughes had

Equality of Opportunity?

To the average man, it seems not unfair that the taxpayer with an income of over $200,000 a year should pay over half of it to the Government. . . . Taxation, however, is not a means of confiscating wealth but of raising necessary revenues for the Government.

One of the foundations of our American civilization is equality of opportunity, which presupposes the right of each man to enjoy the fruits of his labor after contributing his fair share to the support of the Government, which protects him and his property. But that is a very different matter from confiscating a part of his wealth, not because the country requires it for the prosecution of a war or some other purpose, but because he seems to have more money than he needs. Our civilization, after all, is based on accumulated capital, and that capital is no less vital to our prosperity than is the extraordinary energy which has built up in this country the greatest material civilization the world has ever seen. Any policy that deliberately destroys that accumulated capital under the spur of no necessity is striking directly at the soundness of our financial structure and is full of menace for the future.

From Andrew W. Mellon, *Taxation: The People's Business,* 1924

made a virtue of necessity, for he had really given up nothing he had any reasonable chance of getting from the parsimonious Congress.

Yet the Washington settlement also had shortcomings. It left the powers free to construct smaller naval vessels, such as destroyers, cruisers, and submarines, which were to prove vital weapons in the future. It provided no mechanism for consultations among the four major powers. All in all, it left the western Pacific a Japanese lake. Japan could build up its fleet, fortify its mandate islands, and encroach upon China, unless the United States and the other powers were prepared to defend their stated policies. The test of the settlement lay not in its terms but in whether or not the powers chose to honor them. As Wilson had asserted, peace was a matter of continual negotiation and accommodation. And, as Roosevelt had preached, power was ever a factor in the affairs of nations.

Hughes had done remarkably well, but the spirit with which Americans greeted his accomplishment was ominous. In ratifying the Four Power Treaty, the Senate added a reservation asserting that the United States recognized "no commitment to armed force, no alliance, no obligation to join in any defense." Congress in 1922 and for years thereafter was unwilling to maintain the navy even at treaty strength. In short, the American people accepted words as realities, and the Washington settlement proved to be another case of seeking all the advantages and none of the responsibilities.

The Best Minds Advantages rather than responsibilities were also the goal of the representatives of business and finance who shaped the domestic policies of the Harding administration. The president had promised to recruit for government the "best minds" of the country. Hughes met that standard, as did Secretary of Commerce Herbert C. Hoover and Secretary of Agriculture Henry C. Wallace, who had long devoted himself to the cause of agricultural prosperity. But Wallace's influence was outweighed by that of Hoover, who used his department to promote the interests and enlarge the markets of American business.

Hoover, in Harding's view, had proved his worth by acquiring a magnificent fortune. That was the president's surest criterion for finding the "best minds."

Foremost among Harding's advisers was Secretary of the Treasury Andrew Mellon, a reticent multimillionaire from Pittsburgh whose intricate banking and investment holdings gave him, his family, and his associates control, among many other things, of the aluminum monopoly. A man of slight build, with a cold and weary face, Mellon exuded sober luxury and contemptuous worldliness. "The Government is just a business," he believed, "and can and should be run on business principles."

Great businesses, as Mellon knew, thrive on innovation and expansion. Yet the only business principle he considered relevant to government was economy. With small regard for the services that only government could furnish the nation, Mellon worked unceasingly to reduce federal expenditures. Expenses had to be cut if he was to achieve his corollary purpose — the reduction of taxes, especially taxes on the wealthy. It was better, he argued, to place the burden of taxes on lower-income groups, for taxing the rich inhibited their investments and thus retarded economic growth. A share of the tax-free profits of the rich, Mellon reassured the country, would ultimately trickle down to the middle- and lower-income groups in the form of salaries and wages. Robert La Follette paraphrased that theory succinctly: "Wealth will not and cannot be made to bear its full share of taxation."

The quest for economy in government had some beneficial results. In 1921 Harding signed the Budget and Accounting Act, which improved the budgeting procedures of the federal government. It also served Mellon's purpose, for first Director of the Budget Charles G. Dawes, a Chicago banker, made economy the touchstone of the budget that was presented to Congress in 1922.

Primarily to hold expenditures down, Harding opposed a veterans' bonus bill that Congress debated in 1921, and he vetoed it when it passed the next year. Perhaps veterans did indeed deserve something more than gratitude from their country, but this bonus was little more than a raid on public funds supported by the American Legion, an energetic and increasingly influential veterans' pressure group. The newly created Veterans Administration was already taking care of the disabled. Veterans were not necessarily the neediest candidates for public assistance. Yet the veterans were simply acting in the spirit of the time when they continued to seek special advantages. Congress overrode a second veto in 1924 and granted a bonus in the form of paid-up 20-year insurance policies, against which the veterans could immediately borrow limited funds.

Meanwhile, Mellon had advanced the tax program of the business community. In 1921 he urged Congress to repeal the excess-profits tax and to reduce the surtax on personal income from a maximum of 65 percent to 32 percent for 1921 and 25 percent thereafter. These proposals would have prevailed had it not been for the opposition of a group of Western Republican senators who joined with the Democrats to preserve the progressive principles of wartime revenue legislation. The Revenue Act of 1921 fell short of Mellon's goals. It held the maximum surtax on personal income at 50 percent, and it granted some tax relief to lower- and middle-income groups.

The administration had better luck with its tariff policy. Following the tradition of their party, Republican leaders set out to restore the protective rates that had prevailed before 1913. Two developments eased their way. The spread of industry in the South had dispelled much of the traditional Democratic resistance to tariff protection. More important, farm representatives had concluded that they would profit from protective rates on farm products. This was a delusion, for the farmer really needed larger markets abroad, but there was no spirited debate on the tariff, as there had been in 1909.

Without significant dissent, Congress in 1922 passed the Fordney-McCumber Act, which reestablished prohibitive tariff rates. The act did instruct the Tariff Commission to help the president determine differences in production costs between the United States and other nations. And it did empower the president to raise or lower any rate by 50 percent, on the commission's recommendation. In practice, however, the commission was strongly protectionist, and of the 37 rates that were altered during the life of the act, 32 were actually increased.

The Tariff of 1922 and its administration damaged foreign trade. The war had made the United States a creditor nation. By 1919 American investments abroad, in all $7 billion, were twice the size of foreign investments in the United States. And European governments owed the U.S. Treasury $10 billion. It behooved the United States, therefore, to assume the financial leadership of the world and to help to stimulate international trade and investment. Instead, the

The Supreme Court and Minimum Wages

Legislatures, in limiting freedom of contract between employee and employer by a minimum wage, proceed on the assumption that employees in the class receiving least pay are not upon a full level of equality of choice with their employer, and in their necessitous circumstances are prone to accept pretty much anything that is offered. They are peculiarly subject to the overreaching of the harsh and greedy employer. The evils of the sweating system and of the long hours and low wages which are characteristic of it are well known. . . . It is a disputable question . . . how far a statutory requirement of maximum hours or minimum wages may be a useful remedy for these evils. . . . But it is not the function of this court to hold Congressional acts invalid simply because they are passed to carry out economic views which the court believes to be unwise and unsound.

From Chief Justice William Howard Taft, dissent in *Adkins* v. *Children's Hospital,* 1923

government raised the tariff, a barrier to trade. By preventing Europeans from selling their goods in the United States, it made it impossible for them to buy American products, including agricultural surpluses, except by borrowing dollars and thus increasing the large debts they had incurred during the war. This was an unhealthy situation both for the United States and for Europe.

Nullification by Administration The restoration of tariff protection was only one part of a concerted effort by the administration to restore the conditions of the nineteenth century. Wherever they could, Harding and his associates rolled back the accomplishments of the progressive movement.

The president could not tear down the apparatus that had been constructed for regulating business and industry, but he succeeded in rendering that apparatus useless by turning it over to the very interests it had been designed to regulate. His appointments to federal commissions, as Senator Norris said, "set the country back more than twenty-five years." They achieved "the nullification of federal law by a process of boring from within."

The administration also stood aside while management continued its attack on labor unions and labor legislation. In 1922 Harding interceded to stop the violence that attended a nationwide coal strike. The report of the commission of inquiry he appointed revealed the pitiful, even desperate, state of life in the coal towns. The commission recommended various federal controls over the mining industry, but Congress and the administration ignored the report. In the same year, the national Railway Labor Board approved a 12 percent reduction in the wages of railway shopmen, a decision that precipitated a strike that lasted two months. It ended only when the attorney general got an injunction that forbade the union to picket or in any way to encourage workers to leave their jobs.

In this and other rulings the federal courts, acting in the spirit of the executive establishment, took advantage of the permissiveness of the Clayton Act (see p. 595). Contrary to Gompers's hopes, the injunction was still a handy instrument for breaking strikes. In the same spirit, the courts sustained "yellow-dog" contracts that bound employees not to join unions. The courts' hostility toward labor unions expressed by William Howard Taft, whom Harding appointed chief justice in 1921, not only helped management's campaign for the open shop but destroyed social legislation designed to protect the poorest and weakest workers. The Supreme Court in 1922, in the case of *Bailey* v. *Drexel Furniture Company,* declared unconstitutional a federal statute levying a prohibitive tax on products manufactured by children. The Court had ruled earlier, in *Hammer* v. *Dagenhart* (1918), that federal laws to control child labor were an unconstitutional invasion of the police powers of the states. In the Bailey case, it said that Congress could not use its tax power to accomplish this unconstitutional purpose. The decision protected child labor, a common practice especially in Southern textile mills.

The Supreme Court was just as opposed to regulation of wages, hours, and working conditions. In 1910 it had denied the states the authority to regulate hours of work for women. Now in 1923, in *Adkins* v. *Children's Hospital,* it held unconstitutional—with Taft here dissenting—a District of Columbia statute establishing minimum wages for women. Ignoring the social and economic arguments for the act, the majority of the Court found it a violation of the freedom of women to contract to sell their labor as they pleased. The Adkins decision contravened the spirit of the Clayton Act, which asserted that labor was not a mere commodity. The decision also left labor defenseless, for neither federal nor state governments could insist on minimum standards of health and decency, and the attitudes of the courts denied the unions much of their opportunity to recruit membership or to strike for fair treatment.

The farmers fared better politically, but not economically, under the Harding administration. In 1922 agricultural prices began to recover from their postwar slump, but the farmers were harassed by high interest charges on mortgages and by heavy taxes on land. Agricultural technology raised production and expanded surpluses even though the number of farms and of agricultural workers was steadily declining. And advancing industrialism continually reduced the farmers' share of the national income. Agriculture during the early 1920s was not generally impoverished, though segments of it were. But even the more privileged farmers were anxious about their future and resentful of their diminishing influence on American life. They were jealous, too, of the conveniences, especially electricity, automobiles, and entertainment, that were becoming more and more common in the cities.

In 1921 and 1922 the discontent of farmers generated considerable political force in the South and the Middle West, and the farm bloc in Congress won a series of victories. With few exceptions, however, the leaders of the farm bloc failed to understand the basic difficulties. They made their mark instead where the objectives of the fading progressive movement helped them to define their goals. Legislation in 1921 authorized the secretary of agriculture to compel commission merchants, grain merchants, and stockyard owners to charge reasonable rates. An act of 1922 exempted farm cooperatives from the antitrust laws, and Congress added a representative of agriculture to the Federal Reserve Board. In 1923 the Agricultural Credits Act established twelve Intermediate Credit Banks to make loans to cooperatives and other farm groups for six months to three years. The loans were to help cooperatives to withhold crops from the market when prices were temporarily low. These statutes strengthened the farmer's ability to conduct business, and they created instruments for controlling the middlemen who bought agricultural produce. But they did not ease the farmer's mortgage burden, and they helped the small farmer, sharecropper, and farm laborer not at all.

In the off-year elections of 1922, agrarian dissent carried anti-administration candidates to victory in Republican primaries in most of the West. In November the resurgent Democrats reduced Republican majorities to 8 in the Senate and 18 in the House. And, of the Republicans who were elected, so many were disenchanted that the administration no longer controlled Congress. The elections assured key committee assignments to strong men in both parties who were dubious about the administration's program and methods. Those men, using Congress's power of investigation, soon exposed the Harding regime to publicity it could not afford.

The Harding Scandals The president of the United States sets the tone of his administration. The first two decades of the twentieth century had been marked by McKinley's kindness, Theodore Roosevelt's strenuosity, Taft's decent ineffectuality, and Wilson's idealism. Warren Harding brought to government the qualities of his own weak person. To his credit, he stopped the repression of dissent that marked the late Wilson years, and he pardoned Debs. But he was an ignorant, naive, confused man whose loose standards made him particularly vulnerable to his intellectual deficiencies and to the corrupt character of the hail-fellows with whom he instinctively surrounded himself.

Ruefully aware of some of his limitations, Harding once admitted he did not know whom to trust. Uncomfortable with the "best minds," he preferred the kind of tawdry companionship he had known in his native Marion, Ohio. The "Ohio gang" and their friends met continually with Harding at a house on K Street. There councils of state had an incidental but insinuating part in the rounds of poker and whiskey that made the president feel at home.

For two years the Ohio gang flourished. Early in 1923, however, Harding learned that the head of the Veterans Bureau had pocketed an impressive fraction of the $250 million his agency spent lavishly for hospitals and hospital supplies. Though Harding permitted the culprit to go abroad and resign, he was later exposed, tried, convicted, and sentenced to prison.

It also developed that Attorney General Harry M. Daugherty of Ohio had peddled his power for cash, but two divided juries in 1926 saved Daugherty from prison.

Secretary of the Interior Albert Fall was less fortunate. In 1921 he persuaded Harding to transfer to the Interior Department control over naval oil reserves at Elk Hill, California, and Teapot Dome, Wyoming. The next year Fall secretly leased Elk Hill to the oil company of Edward L. Doheny and Teapot Dome to the company of Harry F. Sinclair. But the leases could not be kept secret very long. In October 1923 a Senate committee under the chairmanship of Thomas J. Walsh, a Montana Democrat, began an investigation, which a special commission completed in 1924. The inquiries disclosed that Doheny had "lent" Fall $100,000 and that Sinclair had given the secretary of the interior more than $300,000. In 1927 the government won a suit for cancellation of the leases and in 1929 Fall was convicted of bribery, fined $100,000, and sentenced to a year in jail. He was the first Cabinet officer ever to go to prison.

Harding knew of only the earliest scandals. In June 1923, before setting out on a speaking tour through the West, the president unburdened himself to William Allen White: "My God, this is a hell of a job. I have no trouble with my enemies. . . . But my damned friends, my Goddamned friends . . . they're the ones that keep me walking the floor nights!" Depressed and tired, Harding grew "nervous and distraught" as he traveled. Late in July, while in Seattle on the way home from Alaska, the president suffered acute pain. His doctor diagnosed it as indigestion, but other physicians in the party believed that Harding had had a heart attack, a diagnosis that was confirmed by a San Francisco specialist. On August 2, Harding died, the victim of a coronary or cerebral thrombosis.

Warren G. Harding: "This is a hell of a job."

Vulgarity and scandal were the sordid fruits of normalcy, of a government that sought all the advantages of power but none of the responsibilities, of organized self-interest that sought special favors in bonuses, bounties, lower taxes, and higher tariffs. Pressure groups had gained advantages for big business even during the progressive years. After the war, those interests dominated the federal government as they had not since the 1890s. The scandals passed, but the equation of national interests with privileged interests did not. That equation satisfied the "best minds" during the decade that followed the great war. It contradicted the best hopes cultivated before that war had begun.

SUGGESTIONS FOR READING

THE WAR

The best study of the United States during the war is D. M. Kennedy, *Over Here: The First World War and American Society* (1980). See, too, R. H. Ferrell, *Woodrow Wilson and World War I, 1917–1921* (1985). There are adequate discussions of economic mobilization in B. M. Baruch, *American Industry in War* (1941) and *The Public Years* (1960), but more important are R. D. Cuff, *The War Industries Board* (1973), and the pertinent parts of O. L. Graham, Jr., *The Great Campaigns* (1971). See, too, the perceptive J. W. Chambers, *To Raise an Army* (1987) and E. M. Coffman, *The War to End Wars* (1968, 1986). On congressional developments, see S. W. Livermore, *Politics Is Adjourned* (1966). On the administration of the War Department, D. R. Braver, *Newton D. Baker and the American War Effort, 1917–1919* (1966), offers considerable information; the Navy Department receives informed treatment in F. Freidel, *Franklin D. Roosevelt: The Apprenticeship* (1952). The most rewarding of the war memoirs is J. J. Pershing, *My Experiences in the World War*, 2 vols. (1931), but there are more useful accounts of military developments in E. E. Morison, *Admiral Sims and the Modern American Navy* (1942), and R. Weigley, *The American Way of War* (1973). There are a number of admirable studies of propaganda, censorship, and civil liberties in wartime, including, J. R. Mock and C. Larson, *Words That Won the War: The Story of the Committee on Public Information, 1917–1919* (1939); H. C. Peterson, *Propaganda for War* (1939); H. C. Peterson and G. C. Fite, *Opponents of War, 1917–1918* (1957); J. M. Jensen, *The Price of Vigilance* (1968); W. Preston, *Aliens and Dissenters: Federal Suppression of Radicals, 1903–1933* (1963); H. N. Scheiber, *The Wilson Administration and Civil Liberties, 1917–1921* (1960); and the classic Z. Chaffee, *Free Speech in the United States* (rev. ed., 1941).

THE PEACE

Students of peacemaking and of the American rejection of the peace treaty have at their disposal a literature that is continually growing. One excellent place to begin reading is in the analysis of H. R. Rudin, *Armistice, 1918* (1944). On the significance of the Bolsheviks in the fashioning of peace terms, see J. M. Thompson, *Russia, Bolshevism, and the Versailles Peace* (1966), and A. J. Mayer, *Political Origins of the New Diplomacy, 1917–1918* (1959) and *Politics and Diplomacy of Peacemaking* (1968). Two detailed accounts of the negotiations at Paris, which applaud Wilson's efforts, are D. F. Fleming, *The United States and the League of Nations, 1918–1920* (1932), and A. Walworth, *Wilson and His Peacemakers* (1986). On the United States and the Soviet Union, there are two superb volumes by G. F. Kennan, *Russia Leaves the War: The Americans in Petrograd and the Bolshevik Revolution* (1956) and *The Decision to Intervene: The Prelude to Allied Intervention in the Bolshevik Revolution* (1958). Also scholarly, and essential on its topic, is R. J. Bartlett, *League to Enforce Peace* (1944). There is a critical analysis in T. A. Bailey, *Woodrow Wilson and the Lost Peace* (1944). The same author, in *Woodrow Wilson and the Great Betrayal* (1945), provides a study of the rejection of the treaty. Also significant on that subject are: R. A. Stone, *The Irreconcilables: The Fight Against the League of Nations* (1970); N. G. Levin, Jr., *Woodrow Wilson and World Politics* (1968); J. A. Garraty, *Henry Cabot Lodge* (1953); W. C. Widenor, *Henry Cabot Lodge** (1980); and R. W. Leopold, *Elihu Root and the Conservative Tradition** (1954). There are conflicting views about the conduct of government during Wilson's illness in E. B. Wilson, *My Memoirs* (1938), and J. M. Blum, *Joe Tumulty and the Wilson Era* (1951). Among the accounts of contemporaries friendly to Wilson, the most valuable is Herbert Hoover, *The Ordeal of Woodrow Wilson* (1958). Two unfriendly statements appear in H. C. Lodge, *The Senate and the League of Nations* (1928), and J. M. Keynes, *Economic Consequences of the Peace* (1919). Several of the books here listed cover the question of the League in the election of 1920, a subject further explored in J. M. Cox, *Journey Through My Years* (1946), and F. Freidel, *Franklin D. Roosevelt: The Ordeal* (1954).

THE RED SCARE

R. K. Murray, *The Red Scare* (1955), contains a comprehensive narrative about the subject. It has to be supplemented by the studies of civil liberties listed earlier, by P. Murphy, *The Constitution in Crisis Times* (1972); and by a biography, S. Coben, *A. Mitchell Palmer: Politician* (1963); the masterful analysis of G. L. Joughin and E. M. Morgan, *The Legacy of Sacco and Vanzetti* (1948); K. Jackson, *The Ku Klux Klan in the City, 1915–1930* (1967); the studies of labor in I. Bernstein, *The Lean Years* (1960), and D. Brody, *Labor in Crisis: The Steel Strike of 1919* (1965); the analysis of black Americans in A. I. Waskow, *From Race to Riot to Sit-In, 1919 and the 1960s* (1966), T. Vincent, *Black Power and the Garvey Movement* (1972), R. Burkett, *Garveyism as a Religious Movement* (1978), A. H. Spear, *Black Chicago* (1967), and N. I. Huggins et al., *Key Issues in Afro-American Experience*, 2 vols. (1971). See, too, the penetrating treatment of nativism in J. Higham, *Strangers in the Land* (1955).

HARDING AND NORMALCY

W. E. Leuchtenburg, *The Perils of Prosperity, 1914–32* (1958), provides a crisp account of the Harding period. Also lively, but less judicious, is F. L. Allen, *Only Yesterday* (1931). There is a short evaluation of the Harding years in A. M. Schlesinger, Jr., *The Crisis of the Old Order* (1957), and a fuller narrative in J. D. Hicks, *Republican Ascendancy, 1921–1933* (1960). The economy and its problems receive able handling in G. Soule, *Prosperity Decade: From War to Depression, 1917–1929* (1947); but for a richer discussion of taxation and agriculture, respectively, the relevant chapters of R. E. Paul, *Taxation in the United States* (1954), and T. Saloutos and J. D. Hicks, *Twentieth Century Populism: Agricultural Discontent in the Middle West, 1900–1939*, (1951), are particularly valuable. The Harding scandals get the treatment they merit in S. H. Adams,

Incredible Era (1939); K. Schriftgiesser, *This Was Normalcy* (1948); and B. L. Noggle, *Teapot Dome* (1962). A. Sinclair, *The Available Man* (1965), tries to redeem Harding's reputation, as does R. K. Murray, *The Harding Era* (1969). Stimulating accounts of the Washington Conference are H. H. and M. T. Sprout, *Toward a New Order of Sea Power* (1946); J. C. Vinson, *The Parchment Peace: The United States Senate and the Washington Conference, 1921–1922* (1950); and T. H. Buckley, ed., *United States and the Washington Conference* (1970). Two biographies have given first-rate attention to the diplomacy of Harding's secretary of state: M. J. Pusey, *Charles Evans Hughes*, 2 vols. (1951), and Dexter Perkins, *Charles Evans Hughes and American Democratic Statesmanship* (1953).

CHAPTER TWENTY-FIVE

ENERGY FOR A NEW ERA

A NEW AGE OF BUSINESS

Calvin Coolidge believed in the kind of luck that Horatio Alger had immortalized. If a man worked hard, saved his pennies, respected the authorities, and kept his mouth shut, an invisible hand would contrive an occasion to make his reputation. Coolidge took no chances while he waited for his breaks. The son of a Vermont storekeeper, he worked his way through Amherst College, studied law in Northampton, Massachusetts, and entered politics there, winning successively those minor state offices on which undistinguished politicians build their careers. His patient course endeared him to the Massachusetts Republicans, who valued his unquestioning acceptance of things as they were, his unwavering preference for inaction, and his obvious personal honesty.

In 1919, 20 years after he first won public office, Coolidge achieved national prominence for his role in stopping the Boston police strike. His delay in dealing with that episode invited anarchy, but his friends used his new reputation to generate the boom that made him the Republican choice for vice president. In that post Coolidge dispatched his ceremonial duties with quiet pleasure, warned Americans against the "Reds in Our Women's Colleges," and awaited his next break. When Harding died, Coolidge's luck had him at home, where his father, a notary public, administered the oath of office. The event was a blessing for the most privileged Republicans, for the accession of Calvin Coolidge gave them a new president who cloaked normalcy with respectability.

A NEW CULT OF ENTERPRISE

Coolidge and the Business Creed Personally neat, even prim, deliberately laconic and undemonstrative in public (though given in private to temper and garrulity), Coolidge scrubbed the White House clean of the filth that Harding had left. Grace Coolidge, the new first lady, erased scandal with her natural dignity, charm, and warmth. The president chose two lawyers of impeccable integrity to prosecute the rascals in government. When the mounting evidence against the attorney general forced his retirement in March 1924, Coolidge named to his place an eminent former dean of the Columbia Law School, Harlan Fiske Stone, whose appointment completed the shift from rascality to virtue.

In other respects Coolidge left the national government unaltered. As much as Harding, Coolidge subscribed to the creed of American business. "The business of America is business," Coolidge believed. "The man who builds a factory," he once said, "builds a temple. . . . The man who works there worships there." The president himself worshiped wealth and those who had it. Worldly possessions were for him evidence of divine election. He stood in awe of Andrew Mellon. He took satisfaction in his own eminence, but as William Allen White put it, Coolidge was "sincerely, genuinely, terribly crazy" about wealth.

This passion coincided exactly with the theories of business leaders. There were, they preached, a superior few and an inferior many. And they were easy to distinguish, for "a man is worth the wages he can earn." Material success marked the élite, and to them the others should leave the important decisions about society. The 1920s witnessed a renaissance of the conservative dogmas of the 1880s, now clothed in new metaphors. Bruce Barton, a magnificently successful advertising man, gave the gospel its most popular phrasing in his best-seller of 1925, *The Man Nobody Knows*. To his infinite satisfaction, Barton, the son of a minister, discovered that Christ was a businessman. "Jesus," he wrote, ". . . picked up twelve men from the bottom ranks of business and forged them into an organization that conquered the world." The parables made incomparable advertisements; the gospel, an incomparable business school.

Coolidge was devoted to the dominant values of his time, to business, materialism, élitism, and their corollaries. If only the rich were worthy, it followed that government should beware the counsels of the majority. Since poverty was the wage of sin, government should not tax the virtuous rich in order to assist the unworthy poor. And since the rich best understood their own interests, government should not interfere with the businesses they ran, though it should help promote them both at home and abroad.

Calvin Coolidge: a smug delight

No devotee of laissez-faire ever abhorred government more than Coolidge did. "If the Federal Government should go out of existence," he said, "the common run of people would not detect the difference . . . for a considerable length of time." Government's grandest service was to minimize itself, its activities, and its expenditures. So persuaded, Coolidge slept more than any other president in this century. He also said and did less when he was awake. "Four-fifths of all our troubles in this life," he told one agitated senator, "would disappear if we would only sit down and keep still." Silence, inactivity, gentility, complacency, and a shrewd political sense—those were the sum and the substance of the Coolidge calculus.

Productivity and Plenty The extraordinary prosperity of the 1920s cast a mantle of credibility over the doctrines of business and its representative president. It was easy for him and others of like mind to interpret prosperity as majestic proof of their beliefs. As the country came out of the short slump of 1921, unemployment became negligible except in sick industries like textiles and coal. By 1923 the average money wages of industrial workers were twice what they had been in 1914, and they continued to advance through 1928. Real wages rose, too, steadily though less dramatically. By 1928 they were about one-third higher than they had been 14 years earlier. Several factors accounted for those increases. Abundant, cheap energy in coal, oil, and waterpower kept down the costs of manufacturing and the goods it supplied. Many employers had begun to realize that higher wages removed one of the incentives that prompted workers to join unions and also provided purchasing power that swelled the market for industrial products. Wages stretched further as prices fell, especially the prices of food and of goods manufactured in industries where mechanization pushed productivity to new peaks.

The profits that came with mechanization invited investment in new plants and new tools. Investment was encouraged also by the growing national market, by the permissive climate of inactive government, and

The Coolidge Genius

Mr. Coolidge's genius for inactivity is developed to a very high point. It is far from being an indolent inactivity. It is a grim, determined, alert inactivity which keeps Mr. Coolidge occupied constantly. Nobody has ever worked harder at inactivity, with such force of character . . . with such conscientious devotion to the task. Inactivity is a political philosophy and a party program with Mr. Coolidge. . . .

Mr. Coolidge . . . has discovered the value of diverting attention from the government, and with an exquisite subtlety that amounts to genius, he has used dullness and boredom as political devises. . . .

He has the country yawning over the outcry against relieving the super-rich of taxes, yawning . . . over the World Court, yawning over the coal strike. . . . This active inactivity suits the mood and certain needs of the country admirably. It suits all business interests which want to be let alone. It suits everybody who is making money. And it suits all those who have become convinced that . . . it is important to reduce and decentralize Federal power.

From Walter Lippmann, *Men of Destiny,* 1927

by Mellon's gradual success in persuading Congress to reduce taxes on large incomes. While investment provided the means for building more and more productivity into American industry, management was mastering new ways to use machinery and to organize production more effectively.

There flowered during the 1920s the profession of industrial engineering, with its concern for continuous process, improved machinery, specialization of jobs, and time-motion studies of performance. Those techniques encouraged a cult of productivity, a rationalization of the glories of making and distributing and consuming ever more bountifully.

The founding father of "scientific management" and the philosopher of the machine process was Frederick W. Taylor, and Henry Ford was commanding general. In 1911 Ford opened his plant at Highland Park, Michigan. There he and his fellow executives arrived at Taylor's principles along their own routes and began to turn out automobiles at prodigious rates. The Ford Motor Company outsped all industry in specializing the tasks of men and machines. After 1913 it also applied the idea of continuous motion, using conveyor belts, gravity slides, and overhead monorails to feed the machinery by which workers stood. The modern assembly line turned out the Model T's that put America on wheels. As his production and market grew, Ford cut prices and increased wages. To be sure, the wages he claimed to pay did not reach all his workers, the speedup at the Ford company was notorious, and the company tolerated no unions. But the $5 day that Ford announced in 1914 seemed to mark the dawn of a new era, and so did Ford's staggering profits. In the mid-1920s Ford had become, in the phrase of Upton Sinclair, the Flivver King.

By that time Ford's production techniques had become standard in the automobile and other industries. The Model T was a very stark car, but America's machines were also producing more comfortable, more sumptuous, and more complex mechanisms. During Coolidge's tenure in office, for the first time in the history of any nation, a mass market developed for cars, for radios, for refrigerators and vacuum cleaners. There was, in a sense, no longer any problem of production. The available stocks of American raw materials, workers, machines, and techniques could saturate the nation, and much of the world, with the necessities and conveniences of modern civilization.

Business executives, however, were interested in more than just the science of production. Their

Texas: the fruits of industry

restrictive labor policies during the 1920s kept the rise in real wages well below the rise in profits. And they guarded their market jealously, trying to produce only as much as the market could absorb without a break in prices. Large firms in heavy industries had long since learned the importance of administered, noncompetitive pricing and had long since contrived the consolidations that made for industrial stability. During the 1920s the tendency toward consolidation proceeded at an accelerating tempo, in old industries as well as new. And, as consolidation advanced, managers became more and more skillful in governing costs, price, and output.

Indeed, professional business management came into its maturity in the 1920s. Before the war, business had integrated vertically, incorporating the stages of industrial activity from extraction through manufacturing, transportation, and marketing under unitary management, as in the steel and food industries. The combination of mass production with mass distribution accounted for the size and much of the efficiency of big business. After the war the growing professionalization of management increased that efficiency. At both senior- and middle-level positions, managers brought a new sophistication to their responsibilities. With increasing diversification of ownership, moreover, no stockholder or group of stockholders could any longer control the policy of most great corporations (the Ford Motor Company, still family-owned, was an exception and began to lose its share of market

Marketing home appliances

On "Sabotage"

"Sabotage" is a derivative of "sabot," which is French for wooden shoes. It means going slow, with a . . . clumsy movement. . . . In American usage, the word is very often taken to mean destructive tactics . . . although that is plainly not its first meaning. . . . Sabotage commonly works within the law. There are many measures of policy and management both in private business and in public administration which are unmistakably of the nature of sabotage. . . . Many such measures are quite the essence of the case under the established system of . . . price and business. . . . The common welfare in any community which is organized on the price system cannot be maintained without a salutary use of sabotage—that is to say, such habitual recourse to delay and obstruction of industry and such restriction of output as will maintain prices at a reasonably profitable level and so guard against business depression. . . . But . . . writers and speakers who dilate on the meritricious exploits of the nation's business men will not commonly allude to this . . . administration of sabotage.

From Thorstein Veblen, *The Engineers and the Price System,* 1921

largely because of the superior management of its major competitors). Consequently, control of policy passed to management, and managers for their part refined corporate strategies in order to appeal to different income and age groups, to enter international markets, and to satisfy the increasing sophistication of consumers about both style and quality. Managers of major enterprises achieved a new independence in planning expansion, diversification, and modernization by reserving portions of current profits for their own future investment, not the least in research and development. That strategy freed those planning it, among others General Motors and Standard Oil of New Jersey, from dependence for new investment on banks or capital markets in Wall Street or elsewhere.

Those developments disturbed Americans for whom the production of wealth for universal use was a more precious objective than the amassing of profits. Thorstein Veblen made the most devastating comparisons between those who made goods and those who made money. In *The Engineers and the Price System* (1921) and *Business Enterprise* (1923), he condemned business managers for artificially curtailing output for the sake of profit—a practice he labeled "sabotage." He called for a revolution of technicians, of men

Thorstein Veblen: perceptive critic

American Individualism

No doubt, individualism run riot, with no tempering principle, would provide a long category of inequalities, of tyrannies . . . and injustices. America, however, has tempered the whole conception of individualism by the injection of a definite principle, and from this principle it follows that attempts at domination, whether in government or in the processes of industry and commerce, are under an insistent curb. If we would have the values of individualism, their stimulation to initiative, to the development of hand and intellect, to the high development of thought and spirituality, they must be tempered with that firm and fixed ideal of American individualism—an equality of opportunity. If we would have these values we must suffer its hardness and stimulate progress through that sense of service that lies in our people.

From Herbert C. Hoover, *American Individualism,* 1922

committed to production, who would free industry of pecuniary restraints and use the machine process to provide plenty for humanity. There was a naiveté in Veblen's attitude toward competition, but while business managers often planned only for profit, Veblen urged public planning for the general welfare. His message helped to bridge the space between the Progressive Era and the next era of reform.

Republican Symbols: 1924 In the Coolidge era, however, the impulse for reform flagged. The spirit of that time saw no conflict between profits and productivity. It found a symbol in the person of Herbert Hoover, who seemed to have walked right out of American mythology. Son of an Iowa farmer, descended of pioneer stock, orphaned at age ten, Hoover went west, worked his way through Stanford University, married a banker's daughter, and as an engineer in Asia earned his first million before he was 40 years old. He was the hero of Belgian relief, the successful Food Administrator of Wilson's war Cabinet, and, in the opinion of one London newspaper, "the biggest man . . . on the Allied side" at Paris. By 1920 Hoover's name stood for personal success, for food for the hungry, and for rigor in administration. His reputation reached its height while he was serving under Harding and Coolidge as secretary of commerce.

To that office Hoover applied, as it were, the principles of scientific shop management. His department studied business trends, fought economic waste through its Office of Simplified Practice, and promoted American commerce and investment abroad. Concurrently it encouraged trade associations to sustain prices and profits and wages by adjusting production to demand. Hoover personally organized the relief of victims of the Mississippi flood of 1927, exercised control over radio and the airwaves, avoided associating with politicians, and harbored an ambition as broad and inconspicuous as his conservative blue suits. He stood at once for "cooperative individualism," humanitarian endeavor, and quiet and humorless efficiency. Coolidge, increasingly jealous of Hoover's reputation, could barely tolerate "the wonder boy."

The president did not suffer any rival kindly. A shrewd political manipulator, he rapidly brought the machinery of the Republican party under his control. As the nominating convention of 1924 approached, he had only one possible opponent—not Hoover, who was biding his time, but Henry Ford. The Flivver King had run as a Democrat, and lost, in the race for senator from Michigan in 1918. His publicity men, who wrote much of what he signed, had begun in 1922 to suggest that he might be available as a Republican candidate for the White House. The prospect was both preposterous and alarming. Away from his machines, Ford was a ludicrous figure who opposed tobacco, liquor, and ballroom dancing, had published and circulated anti-Semitic propaganda, and detested labor unions and Wall Street. Still, a third of those who were polled by *Collier's* in a straw ballot of 1923 named Ford as their first choice for president.

Ford's candidacy may not have been serious, but he was deadly serious in his proposal to take over the government dam, nitrate plant, and other facilities constructed during the war at Muscle Shoals, Alabama, on the Tennessee River. He proposed to purchase the nitrate works for less than 5 percent of what they had cost the government, to lease the waterpower facilities for a hundred years, and to have the government pay him simply by issuing new paper money. In return, he hinted that he would be able to produce fertilizer for American farms at half its current price. As Senator Norris said, this was the "most wonderful real estate speculation since Adam and Eve lost title to the Garden of Eden."

Norris exposed and defeated the scheme, which would have destroyed his cherished plans for the public development of the Tennessee. Yet before the chimera vanished, Coolidge, after talking with Ford, recommended that Congress sell Muscle Shoals to private interests. Ford himself soon put an end to his presidential boomlet by announcing that the nation was "perfectly safe with Coolidge." There may have been no bargain, but the coincidence of events suggested that both men were trading in character.

It was a striking commentary on the times that Ford's nitrate project was even proposed. It was no less striking that Ford's candidacy seemed to be the only barrier to Coolidge's renomination. Robert La Follette and Hiram Johnson, dedicated, doughty old progressives, could muster between them only 44 votes at the Republican convention that gave Coolidge over 1,000 votes on its first and decisive ballot. Only a dozen years earlier almost half the Republicans had cast their lot with Theodore Roosevelt.

ONE NATION DIVISIBLE

For White Protestants Only The temper of the 1920s was marked by narrowness and provincialism as well as by prosperity and complacency. The attitudes on which the Red scare had fed survived the passing of the scare itself. Among many Americans there lingered an intolerance of all "isms," a distrust of foreign nations, and a dislike, often bordering on hatred, of people of foreign origin. Much of the farm community had long been susceptible to those feelings, and organized labor had endorsed the racial as well as the economic arguments of those who advocated the restriction of immigration.

In 1924 Congress adopted the recommendations of the Dillingham commission (p. 581) and passed the National Origins Act. The act provided, in its initial stage, for quotas based on 2 percent of the foreign-born of each nationality as measured in the census of 1890. Then in a second stage—which took effect in 1929—quotas were to be based on "national origin." Each affected nationality was to be assigned a quota bearing the same ratio to 150,000—the annual limit set for immigration from outside of the Western Hemisphere—as the number of inhabitants of that nationality bore to the total population of the United States in 1920. Those provisions ended all but a trickle of immigration from southern and eastern Europe. The act, furthermore, included a provision that West Coast racists had been urging for years. It forbade the immigration of Asians, thus terminating the Gentlemen's Agreement (see p. 581) and insulting the Japanese. "It has undone the work of the Washington Conference," Charles Evans Hughes wrote, "and implanted seeds of . . . antagonism."

Asians, African-Americans, Hispanics, Catholics, and Jews were all victims of the prejudice based on the ethnic self-consciousness of white, Protestant Americans of older stock. Even many educated and comfortable people, who should have known better, attributed to race, religion, or national origin varying qualities of character and intelligence, always with the assumption that Americans of old stock were a superior breed. That kind of bigotry underlay restrictive quotas on admissions to elite colleges and also appealed to the poorer and semieducated who lived or had grown up in rural or small-town America. Rural folk felt threatened. More and more they tended, as they had for at least half a century, to blame their personal disappointments on the growth of industry and to express their anxieties in hostility toward those who peopled the cities.

Those prejudices were the stock in trade of the Ku Klux Klan, an organization founded in Georgia in 1915 on the model of its Reconstruction predecessor. It recruited only "native born, white, gentile Americans," and it gave them a sense of importance by admitting them to membership in a group dedicated to persecuting an alleged enemy within the country. It also gave them a uniform, a hierarchy, and a ritual.

In 1920 two professional fund raisers organized a membership drive and arranged to share with local officers the profits from increased initiation fees and

The new Klan: politics of prejudice

from the sale of uniforms and insignia. By 1925 membership approached 5 million. The Klan grew rapidly in cities like Portland, Oregon; Indianapolis; and Denver, where much of the inflowing population consisted of displaced rural folk who were still suspicious of urban ways of life. They were attracted not the least by the Klan's attacks on wickedness, on saloons and pimps and "deviants" of all kinds.

The Klan used floggings, kidnapings, cross burnings, arson, even murder to terrorize whole communities. It was especially vicious in its treatment of Catholics. An Alabama jury acquitted a Klansman who had murdered a priest. A Klan mob burned a Roman Catholic church in Illinois. The Klan and its sympathizers attempted to crush parochial schools in Oregon. And in Oklahoma they inspired the impeachment of a governor who had declared martial law in a brave effort to rout the organization. Increasingly influential in politics, the Klan held the balance of power in several states.

At its zenith in 1923 and 1924, the Klan by its very excesses attracted increasing opposition. In 1924 William Allen White, its implacable enemy, lost the Kansas governorship to one of the Klan's friends, but White's campaign set a sensible example. In some states the Klan began to fade, especially after "Dragon" David Stephenson of Indiana kidnaped and assaulted his secretary and connived to keep her from medical attention after she took poison. Convicted in 1925 of second-degree murder and sentenced to life imprisonment, Stephenson demanded a pardon from his fellow Klansman, Governor Ed Jackson. When Jackson refused, the vindictive "Dragon" opened a "little black box" whose contents provided evidence that sent one congressman, the mayor of Indianapolis, and various lesser officers to jail. Most important, the Klan, which had pretended to guard civic purity and feminine virtue, now stood exposed for what it was— corrupt, sordid, and licentious.

Prohibition The Prohibitionists, who were always strongest in rural areas and particularly among fundamentalist sects, considered liquor an instrument of the devil. Unaware of the complex personal and social problems that provoke excessive drinking, they insisted that alcoholism was created by alcohol itself and by the saloon-keepers who sold it. Whiskey and beer seemed to them, moreover, the potions of immigrants and political bosses, the poison of the corrupt city.

The Prohibition Amendment of 1919 also drew strength from the belief of many Americans that legislation could somehow control personal behavior of all kinds. They were understandably eager to reduce drunkenness and the diseases and poverty it spawned. But before long only the most rabid or stubborn "drys" failed to recognize the difficulties of enforcement. The Prohibition commissioner, in his quest to prevent the manufacture, transportation, and sale of alcoholic beverages (defined by the Volstead Act of 1919 as one-half of 1 percent by volume), had to depend on a small force of agents who were often third-rate political appointees with neither the background nor the intelligence to resist bribes or needless violence. They simply could not police the millions of Americans who wanted to drink and who either made their brews at home or, more often, bought their beer or whiskey from the hundreds of "bootleggers" who earned an illegal, sometimes dangerous, but remunerative living supplying it.

Smugglers brought whiskey in across the Canadian border, or on fast boats from the Caribbean. To supplement the supplies of these "rum-runners," there were countless domestic distillers of illicit whiskey, much of it bad and some of it poisonous. It was easy to buy whiskey by the case, the bottle, or the drink. Indeed, "speakeasies," illegal saloons, did business in every major city, and obliging policemen and cab-drivers were glad to tell strangers where they were.

The traffic in bootlegging provided a new and rich source of income and influence for organized crime. In 1920 the most notorious gangland chief, "Scarface" Al Capone, moved to Chicago, where within seven years he had established a $60 million enterprise in whiskey, drugs, gambling, and prostitution. Capone applied the techniques of business management to crime, but with a difference. His private army of about a thousand gangsters, who were charged with protecting his domain, accounted for most of the 130 murders in the Chicago area in 1926–27. Such was Capone's influence that not a single murderer was convicted. In New York, Philadelphia, Kansas City, and elsewhere, gangsters put high public officers on their payroll and transformed machine politics into agencies for crime.

Prohibition, manifestly unenforceable, had not created organized crime, but it had given gangland a vast privilege to exploit—a privilege that repeal of Prohibition would at least remove. Urban "wets," who had opposed Prohibition from the first, led the movement for repeal, supported by more and more former "drys." The most adamant foes of repeal were the moralists of the countryside who had failed to distinguish between liquor and crime and who identified both with immigration and the city.

Last-Ditch Fundamentalism Rural hostility to urban culture also showed itself in matters of the mind. The unsophisticated fell prey to antiscientism, partly because they did not understand the methods of science, partly because they resented many of the changes that science and technology brought about. Though most Americans admired the technological advances of the 1920s and recognized them as the products of earlier scientific strivings, some were distressed by the complexities and uncertainties of a machine civilization, by its speed, its capacity for destructive as well as constructive power, its overwhelming challenge to the ways of the "good old days." To those Americans science seemed threatening and mysterious. In the rural areas that modern culture had just begun to reach, Protestant fundamentalism seized on science as an archenemy.

Ben Shahn, gouache mural for the Public Works Administration: New York speakeasy

The fundamentalists insisted that the Bible must be accepted as literal truth. More than 60 years after the publication of Darwin's *Origin of Species,* they still rejected the concept of biological evolution and attacked those who taught it. In the postwar years, William Jennings Bryan, a "dry," a fundamentalist, a folk hero of a kind, and now an old and frustrated man, enlisted in the anti-evolutionist crusade. Strengthened by his leadership, the anti-evolutionists scored partial victories in several Southern states. Bryan himself in 1925 assisted the lobby that pressured the Tennessee legislature into passing a statute making it illegal to teach in public schools any theory that denied the account of creation recorded in Genesis.

The American Civil Liberties Union, responding to this challenge to the freedom of inquiry, offered counsel to any Tennessee teacher who would test the law. More in amusement than in anger, John T. Scopes of the mountain town of Dayton lectured from a Darwinian text and was arrested. Among the lawyers who defended him were Clarence Darrow, the most famous pleader of the time, and Arthur Garfield Hays, a celebrated advocate of civil liberties. Assisting the prosecution was Bryan, who had been retained by the World's Christian Fundamental Association. The all-star cast in the Dayton "monkey trial" engaged the interest of the entire nation.

The prosecution contended that the only issue was Scopes's violation of the law, but the defense raised the question of the validity of the law itself. The case reached its climax when Bryan took the stand as an expert on the Bible. Joshua had made the sun stand still, the commoner said; the whale had swallowed Jonah; if it was in the Bible, it was so. As Darrow pressed the cross-examination, Bryan revealed an invincible ignorance of modern learning.

Scopes was convicted for violating the law, but the state supreme court reversed the decision on a technicality, and the constitutionality of the statute could not be tested. (It was not repealed until the 1970s.) There was no longer any reason to test it. Bryan had admitted in his testimony that creation took centuries; a "day" in Genesis might be an eon. That admission cost the fundamentalists their argument, and the ridicule of Bryan's performance had lost them their cause.

But by 1925 the blind innocence of fundamentalism, together with the pernicious zeal of the Klan, had estranged the ordinary citizen from the intellectual and had divided the underprivileged of the farms from the underprivileged of the cities. Protestant laborers had been set against Jewish and Catholic laborers, white workers against black workers. Americans whom prosperity either did not reach or did not beguile had been sealed off into separate and often hostile groups.

Darrow and Bryan at Dayton: creation took centuries

The Election of 1924 This estrangement made it difficult for the Democratic party to select a national candidate to oppose Coolidge in 1924. One of the two leading contenders was William G. McAdoo, who had won the acclaim of liberals for his administration of the railroads during the war (p. 616), but who had lost their favor by taking a job as counsel to Edward L. Doheny, one of the scoundrels of Teapot Dome. Yet McAdoo, ardently "dry" and equivocal about the Klan, held the support of the South and the West. His major rival, Alfred E. Smith, the governor of New York, was a "wet," a Catholic, and a Tammany man. The darling of the Eastern cities, Smith was anathema to the rural delegates in spite of his progressive record.

The convention met in New York's Madison Square Garden during an early summer heat wave. To the party's shame, a motion not to include a plank in the platform condemning the Klan by name passed by a margin of one vote. There followed a nine-day deadlock over the nomination. Through 95 ballots the hoarse voice of the aged Bryan now and then punctuated the raucous noise of the Tammany gallery, and the contest was relayed by radio to millions of American homes. The split in the party had become irremediable; the sweltering delegates had become exhausted. At last Smith and McAdoo withdrew by mutual agreement. On the 103rd ballot the convention nominated John W. Davis for president and Charles Bryan as his running mate. They were an unlikely brace. Davis, who had served as solicitor general and briefly as ambassador to Great Britain during the Wilson administration was a cultivated gentleman and an eminent corporation lawyer identified with the House of Morgan. The liberals who disdained him could find small solace in Bryan's younger brother Charley. Wall Street and Nebraska could not be squeezed onto a single ticket, but the prolonged bitterness of the convention had made a saner choice impossible.

A third nomination stirred wider interest. The resurgence of reform candidates in the congressional election of 1922 had owed much to the Conference for Progressive Political Action, an organization of farm leaders, social workers, former Bull Moosers, and Socialists. Now the leaders of the conference began to talk about running a separate ticket in 1924. The Communists forced their hand by taking over the Farmer-Labor party and offering its nomination to "Battle Bob" La Follette. Then almost 70, iron-gray, still the indomitable Daniel in the lion's den of "the interests," La Follette scorned the offer. That response prompted his supporters to form a new Progressive party, which named La Follette and the liberal Montana Democrat Burton K. Wheeler as its national candidates.

La Follette's candidacy attracted a host of tireless battlers for reform, among them Felix Frankfurter, John R. Commons, and Jane Addams. It was endorsed by the American Federation of Labor and, curiously, by the Socialists. La Follette stood for conservation, public ownership of waterpower, increased taxes on wealth, curbing the authority of the Supreme Court, limiting the use of injunctions in labor disputes, the popular election of judges, the direct election of presidents, the end of child labor, and a national referendum on declarations of war. But he emphasized the evil of monopoly, ringing again the changes of his early campaigns in Wisconsin. The *Wall Street Journal* called his platform "Wisconsin Bolshevism"; the head of the Communist party in the United States called it "the most reactionary document of the year." Both statements were nonsense. The platform and the campaign were simply refurbished Grangerism, still appealing to many farmers, and the only haven for those who could stomach neither Coolidge nor Davis.

Robert La Follette, 1924: "Wisconsin Bolshevism"

The Republicans ignored Davis and harped on La Follette's radicalism. They need not have worked so hard as they did nor have spent the millions they poured into the campaign, for the nation voted overwhelmingly to "keep cool with Coolidge." The president carried 35 states to Davis's 12 and La Follette's 1, Wisconsin. Coolidge won 382 electoral votes to his opponents' 149. And his popular vote, over 15,000,000, exceeded the combined total of Davis, who polled fewer than 8,500,000, and La Follette, who had slightly more than 4,800,000. Prosperity and "Silent Cal" had enjoyed a major triumph.

Yet the new Progressive party had made a point, though it died in 1925 with La Follette. The point was simply that there was room in politics for dissent from the business creed. The lesson was not lost on the Democrats, who realized that they had to build a coalition that welcomed men and women of all parentages and all sections. If the Democrats were to win in the future they would have to be "unequivocally the party of progress and liberal thought." That phrase was Franklin Roosevelt's, who saw small chance for a victory before 1932. When it came, as its core would be the combination of Davis and La Follette voters.

GRANDIOSE ILLUSIONS

The Good Life Americans were optimistic during Coolidge's second term. The middle class in particular, more comfortable than ever before, experienced a sense of well-being. They admitted no limit to a personal success symbolized by material possessions. They neither liked nor trusted the "knockers," but preferred the "boosters," those with their eyes and hearts set on the rosy future.

Some of the boosters channeled their optimism into the expanding advertising profession. National advertising flourished in the 1920s. It offered an attractive substitute for more painful forms of competition, like price cutting, which, in any event, were being curtailed by trade agreements and informal arrangements among manufacturers. Advertising also helped identify brands for consumers, who were buying more and more of their goods in stores and producing fewer and fewer at home. Advertising men believed they were "inspiring citizens to live a more abundant life." They were creating new wants and encouraging discontent with possessions outmoded but not necessarily outworn. Advertisers sold the ingredients of the good life—health in orange juice, cleanliness in soap, popularity in deodorants, romantic love in voguish clothes.

As one General Motors executive put it, advertising had to make people "healthily dissatisfied with what they have. . . . The old factors of wear and tear . . . are too slow." Built-in obsolescence paved the road to business success. Manufacturing prettier, more comfortable cars than Ford did, changing models annually (while also meeting competitive standards in engineering), General Motors won primacy in the automobile industry largely by catering to luxury and fashion.

Advertising also created and sold reputations, both corporate and personal. Public relations experts, taking over the new game of ballyhoo as their own, fabricated heroes on demand. Some of the celebrated athletes of the 1920s, for example, owed part of their fame to sheer ballyhoo. To be sure, Bobby Jones in golf, Bill Tilden in tennis, Jack Dempsey in boxing, and Babe Ruth in baseball were athletes of genuinely heroic proportions. But their proportions were overdrawn, and cynical public relations men learned to conceal the boorish behavior of Ruth, among others, by planting stories of fictitious noble deeds.

Babe Ruth

The prospering tabloid newspapers catered to a mass audience that delighted in sensationalism and hero worship. The art of sham was especially effective when it could exploit symbols of sex. It publicized the new heroes and heroines of the booming motion picture industry — Rudolph Valentino, the Casanova of the silent films, whose untimely death broke thousands of adolescent hearts; Clara Bow, the "It" girl, whose curves and curls entranced a male multitude; Mary Pickford, the sweet charmer whom a plucky lad could more properly admire; and Charlie Chaplin, the incomparable clown.

In Hollywood's films and in magazines and popular fiction standard success stories followed classic forms — farm boys conquered the city while remaining pure, poor boys struggled and saved their way to wealth, nice boys met and married beautiful rich girls. The protagonist's gleaming teeth, curly hair, lithe muscles, humility, and hard work assured a happy ending. And ordinary Americans could do just as well through diligent use of the right toothpaste, hair lotion, and correspondence course. But the plot was used too often to boost sales and circulation, and it was beginning to wear thin. Just then a real hero revived the faith.

Clara Bow: "It" girl

In the spring of 1927, there was startling news of a young man flying solo, eastward across the Atlantic, in a small monoplane. No one before had made that flight alone. The prayers of the nation followed Charles A. Lindbergh, Jr., to France. His safe landing set off a jubilee; Coolidge sent a cruiser to bring him home; New York extended ecstatic greetings. Briefly, sham and commercialism hid from authentic daring and clean-cut youth. Lindbergh took it calmly. After writing another stanza to his saga by marrying Anne Morrow, the daughter of a Morgan partner, he tried to escape the tabloids and the confetti. Myths need a foundation in truth, and the Lindbergh story had been as genuine as it was refreshing. When it faded from the headlines, myth fed once again on the exploits of hired muscle men who drew crowds to mammoth stadiums.

Advertising and public relations and ballyhoo, like the newspapers and magazines and radio that carried them, exported urban ways to rural people. They were in a sense creating a national culture by disseminating a common set of symbols to diverse groups. They told farmers and laborers and suburbanites to admire the same success stories and buy the same cars and cosmetics. They told them all to spend their money to increase their comfort, to prove their mettle, to live "the good life." They encouraged installment buying to ensure the sale of an expanding national product. They helped Americans with rising wages to forget about the frustrations of their dull and routine jobs. The spurious self-esteem that sprang from possession and fashion would endure only so long as Americans could count on steady income and easy credit. But so long as prosperity lasted, advertisers gilded the promises of a commercial culture, the only brand of Americanism they really understood. This crass and transient boom was rooted in illusion, in calling things by the wrong names and then accepting the names as true. The illusions of public life were similarly deceiving.

The Image of America Abroad The Coolidge administration became involved in Latin-American affairs even though the president, like Harding before him, meant to avoid intervention and allow private interests to carry the burden of policy. Nevertheless, the administration often succeeded only in obscuring national purpose and generating ill will among Latin Americans. Secretary of State Hughes, moved by a concern for peace and order, had helped bring about the peaceful settlement of several Latin American

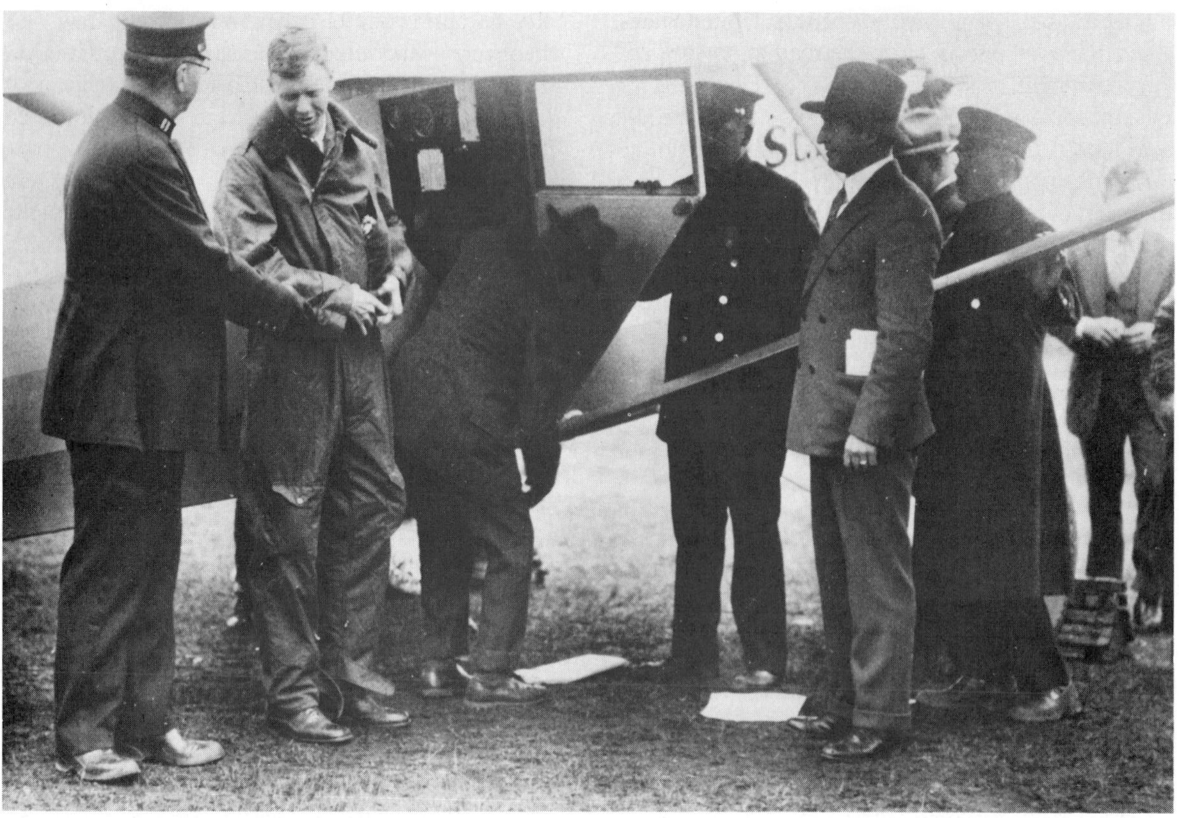

Lindbergh: eastward across the Atlantic

boundary disputes. During Hughes's tenure, the United States also sponsored a conference of Central American powers, which agreed to withhold recognition from any government established by a coup d'état. But this genuflection to stability ignored the realities of Central American politics, for where the government in power had complete control over elections, a coup d'état or revolution was the only means of ousting it.

In Nicaragua Coolidge acted unilaterally. First, in 1925, he withdrew a token force of marines from that nation, which then seemed capable of servicing its foreign debt and preserving its internal stability. But almost at once revolution broke out, and Coolidge again landed the marines, in time some 5,000. In its quest for order and for commercial opportunity the United States chose to support the reactionary faction, whose identification with large landowners and American investors had helped provoke the revolution in the first place.

The marines contained the fighting, but they could not bring it to an end. American bankers were lending money to the conservative faction for the purchase of munitions in the United States, and the rebels were receiving some arms from sympathetic Mexico. Increasingly uncomfortable, Coolidge in 1927 named Henry L. Stimson as his personal emissary to negotiate a peace. Stimson succeeded in arranging an effective truce and an honest election, in which the rebel general triumphed. The marines, however, remained until 1933. They also remained in Haiti but in 1924 left the Dominican Republic, where President Wilson had sent them.

Latin American liberals identified the United States with the forces of reaction. Developments in Mexico contributed to that view. In 1925 Plutarco Elias Calles, the new president of Mexico, revived the spirit of the revolution of 1910. He sponsored laws that permitted foreigners to acquire land only if they renounced the protection of their own government, and laws that defined all subsoil deposits as the inalienable property of the Mexican nation. Oil companies, American and other, were required to apply for a renewal of their concessions before 1927. Four large American companies refused. Their supporters in the United States, asserting that Mexico was on the road to Bolshevism, called for military intervention, but in January 1927 the United States Senate by unanimous vote passed a resolution demanding the peaceful settlement of all contested issues—by arbitration, if necessary.

Several months later Coolidge appointed a new ambassador, Dwight W. Morrow, with the overriding commission "to keep us out of war with Mexico." Morrow's patient negotiations led to a temporary relaxation of the Mexican land laws and restored friendly relations. Yet Morrow's admirable performance could not erase the hostility created by earlier American diplomacy. To reformers south of the border American amity was colored by oil.

At the Pan-American Conference of 1928 the Argentine delegation sponsored a proposal that "no American country have the right to intervene in any other American country." The United States succeeded in defeating the proposal but in doing so incurred resentment. Late in 1928 the State Department concluded that intervention was not justified by the Monroe Doctrine or by the interests of American investors. But it was still not ready to announce that conclusion.

Europeans resented a different kind of diplomacy of the dollar. During the First World War the United States had lent the Allies $7 billion and after the war another $3.3 billion. The recipients had spent their loans almost entirely on American military products and relief supplies. With the return of peace, they regarded the loans merely as one part of the total Allied resistance to Germany, an American contribution toward a victory to which Europeans had given a larger share of flesh and blood. So they were reluctant to repay either the loans or the interest on them. And even those who wanted to square accounts found it difficult to pay. The European nations had depleted their own reserves before borrowing from the United States, and now they found it impossible to replenish those reserves in an American market sealed off by the tariff.

The only way they could meet their obligations to the United States was to draw on the huge reparations that had been imposed on Germany at Versailles. But Germany lacked both the means to pay and the will to scrimp in order to exonerate a war guilt it did not really accept. In 1923 it defaulted, and French and Belgian troops occupied the Ruhr Valley. The Germans there cut down coal production, while the German government inflated its currency recklessly, and the resulting economic distress in both France and Germany seemed to forebode economic collapse and possibly even armed conflict.

The crisis commanded American as well as European attention. An international commission of experts recommended what was called the Dawes Plan, in recognition of the participation of Charles Gates Dawes, who was soon to become Coolidge's running mate. That plan, which went into effect in 1924, arranged for an international loan to stabilize German currency and for a flexible scale of reparations payments. Five years later another American, Owen D. Young, headed a second committee, which substantially reduced the payments. The Allies, satisfied by these terms and concurrent European political agreements, withdrew their forces from the Ruhr and the Rhineland.

American money, however, played a more significant role in the European crisis than did either Dawes or Young. Between 1924 and 1931 Germany managed to meet its payments only because its government, its municipalities, and its banks and business executives were able to borrow $2.6 billion in the United States. Those funds, loaned by private American bankers, were indispensable for the postwar reconstruction of the European economy, especially in Germany. The American investors who lent the money were performing a function, with expectations of profits of course, that was indispensable for the postwar social and political stabilization of Europe. But the network of private debt among the western nations that the loans constructed depended for its stability on the American prosperity that made possible the availability of money for investment overseas, in Latin America as well as in Europe. Indeed, in the course of the decade there grew up a complex of private international debt, potentially unstable, that paralleled the structure of intergovernmental debts spawned by the Great War.

Only the reparations collected from Germany by the Allies enabled them to keep up their payments on their war debts to the United States government. The interdependence of debts and reparations payments was obvious, but the United States refused to acknowledge it. Most Americans, moreover, most of their congressmen, and certainly their president rejected the notion that the debts had in any sense been offset by the Allied losses in battle. For Coolidge the debts were business obligations pure and simple. When the French proposed that the burden of governmental debt be eased, the president unhesitatingly turned them down. "They hired the money," he said. The spirit behind that phrase overshadowed all the efforts of Dawes and Young.

Deluded Diplomacy The administration resisted the facts of international politics as strongly as it resisted the facts of international economics. Like most Americans, Coolidge believed in disarmament, not only because he knew that it would reduce federal expense, but because he presumed that it would assure peace. But he did not understand, or at least would not admit, the continuing importance of power in international affairs.

Further, the conventional men in control of the army and the navy husbanded their meager appropriations and resisted spending anything on airplanes and submarines, even though those weapons had clearly made traditional military tactics and strategy obsolete. The failure to develop aircraft infuriated General William ("Billy") Mitchell of the Army Air Service, whose bombers had sunk a battleship in 1921. In an oracular report two years later, he warned the authorities of the vulnerability of battleships. In 1925, after the navy's sheer incompetence had resulted in the destruction of a dirigible, Mitchell attacked his superiors in public and urged the creation of a separate air command. A court-martial suspended him from duty for five years. The flurry over the episode persuaded Coolidge to appoint a civilian board of inquiry under Dwight Morrow, but it shrugged off Mitchell's arguments. The administration denied public funds to promote commercial aviation as well. By 1929 the productive capacity of the American aircraft industry had fallen to 7,500 planes a year, little more than a third of the capacity available at the war's end. In the absence of responsible public policy, the United States alone of the major powers slept smugly through the morning of the air age.

Coolidge was less complacent about international naval competition. The Five Power Treaty had applied only to capital ships, and the signatories had continued to build smaller vessels. Late in 1924 Congress authorized the construction of eight cruisers. Hoping to avoid the expense of further construction and to end the naval rivalry, the president invited the powers to a conference in 1927. Italy, already infected by Mussolini's fantasies of military glory, refused to attend. So did France, reluctant in the face of Italian resurgence to commit itself to further self-restraint. Coolidge, dedicated to a policy of isolation from European affairs, had failed to assess these obstacles to disarmament, always a difficult international objective. He failed also to negotiate a preliminary understanding with the British. As a consequence, the English-speaking delegates at the 1927 conference wrangled to no purpose, while the Japanese stood contentedly aside.

Coolidge had already retreated from an earlier, cautious gesture toward internationalism. The Permanent Court of International Justice called for by the League of Nations Covenant had been established in 1921. The purpose of this World Court was to adjudicate certain types of case, to render advice whenever the League requested it, and to arbitrate cases brought before it. Americans had long hoped for the development of a body of law that could be applied to international affairs, and in 1923 Harding, influenced by Hughes, recommended conditional American adherence to the court. Coolidge made the same recommendation in his first annual message. But, even though Hughes had drafted four reservations to the court's protocol to protect the United States from contact with the League itself, the isolationists in the Senate balked. After a long delay the Senate adopted a fifth reservation that would limit the court's right even to render advisory opinions to the League. Further, the court could give no opinion, without American consent, on any question in which the United States claimed an interest. In 1926 the Senate finally voted adherence to the court on those conditions. When the members of the court then tried to clarify the meaning of the reservations, Coolidge declared that clarification constituted rejection and that there was no prospect of American adherence to the court.* That denouement, followed by the failure of the naval-armaments conference, left the administration's diplomatic record singularly barren.

During his last months in office, however, Coolidge's diplomacy won wide acclaim. Salmon O. Levinson, a Chicago lawyer, had been recommending that the great powers sign an agreement condemning war. Professor James T. Shotwell, who had been advancing the same suggestion independently, also proposed sanctions to enforce such an agreement. The idea of outlawing war caught the attention of many Americans, including William E. Borah, chair of the Senate Committee on Foreign Relations. Shotwell urged it on Aristide Briand, the French foreign minis-

*Both Hoover and Franklin Roosevelt later recommended adherence to the court on terms like those contemplated by Hughes. But the Senate declined.

ter, who promptly used it for his own purposes. In April 1927, in a gesture of goodwill to compensate for Franco-American friction over disarmament and war debts, Briand wrote an address to the American people in which he proposed a pact outlawing war. Popular enthusiasm for the proposal forced the president's hand.

Secretary of State Frank B. Kellogg, intent on avoiding a bilateral agreement that would imply some sort of alliance between the United States and France, recommended instead "an effort to obtain the adherence of all the principal powers of the world to a declaration renouncing war as an instrument of national policy." While Briand stalled, the secretary of state also let it be known that the United States would consent to sign a pact in Paris. Briand then accepted the American scheme, and in August 1928, 15 nations meeting in Paris endorsed a treaty by which they renounced war and promised to settle all disputes, whatever their nature, by "pacific means."

Americans were jubilant over the banishment of war—so jubilant that they tended to ignore qualifications made in diplomatic notes exchanged by the signatories. These set down reservations safeguarding France's interpretations of its own self-defense and Great Britain's obligations to its empire. In recommending ratification of the pact, the Senate Foreign Relations Committee reported that ratification would not, in its view, curtail the right of the United States to self-defense and to its own interpretations of the Monroe Doctrine, nor would ratification oblige the United States to take any action against a violator of the Kellogg-Briand pact. So interpreted, the pact won approval by a vote of 85 to 1. But so interpreted, it was, in the words of Senator Carter Glass of Virginia, "worthless, but perfectly harmless."

For most Americans the Paris pact constituted a triumph. To declare perpetual peace without assuming the responsibility for preserving it suited the nation's mood. Now the nation could cut its expenditures, disarm, collect its debts, and trust to reassuring words for sunny safety. Yet the hocus-pocus that sold peace in multilingual print was not unlike the hocus-pocus that sold beauty in a bottle.

Get Rich Quick Of all the grandiose illusions of the 1920s, none was more beguiling than the prospect of easy riches. It rested partly on the reality of economic growth and increasing prosperity. But it also rested on the simple faith that the value of property would constantly increase, and that the investor who bought today could sell tomorrow at a handsome profit. Those who had property to sell nourished this faith, and they were helped by the ready credit that enabled speculators to borrow what they needed. The hucksters and the boomers, moreover, made the allure of speculation a favorite fantasy of the time.

For a while in the mid-1920s the quest for a bonanza drew thousands of Americans to ventures in Florida real estate. The population of Miami more than doubled between 1920 and 1925, and other Florida cities and resorts along the Atlantic and Gulf coasts also mushroomed. Florida's boomers pointed to the warm winter climate, the ready accessibility of their region to vacationers from the North, the prospect of an American Riviera. Imagination covered swamps and barren sands with towns and building lots. As the greedy rushed to buy the dream, a few who invested early and sold at the peak of the boom made fortunes. Their success lured others. Most of the transactions took the form of binders—agreements to buy property, which could be had for a fraction of the value of the property itself. The binders could be sold and sold again, each time for more money.

For every sale, of course, there had to be a buyer. The trade in binders was profitable only so long as someone came along to bid them up, and once people began to compare the dream with the reality the buyers were bound to disappear. The balloon began to deflate in the spring and summer of 1926. That fall it burst when a hurricane swept through the Miami area, destroying developments that had emerged from the dream stage, and wrecking the railroad to Key West. The grand plans of the boomers were laid away, the millions of dollars in speculative profits were wiped out, and the Florida craze was over.

But a much larger boom was already under way. During the prosperous 1920s most of the gains from increased productivity and from the growing market for manufactured goods were funneled into corporate profits. And as profits rose, enhanced by Mellon's tax favors to business, so did the value of corporate shares. Initially that rise reflected a genuine increase in the worth of corporate properties and in the earning potential of the corporations themselves. In the mid-1920s, however, the price of stocks began to soar at a dizzying pace. Investors who were looking for securities that would give them a reasonably safe return now had to compete with speculators who were after overnight fortunes. To meet the demand for stocks, promoters organized investment trusts and multitiered holding companies whose only assets were hope and goodwill. They offered their new issues to eager buyers deluded by greed and by a naive confidence in the surging market. In 1923 new capital issues totaled $3.2 billion; in 1927, $10 billion, much of it purely speculative. The volume of sales on the New York Stock Exchange leaped from 236 million shares in 1923 to 577 million in 1927 and to 1,125 million a year later.

Corporations themselves speculated. As the market rose, corporations found that they earned less by investing their reserves in new facilities than by putting them into brokers' loans—that is, loans that brokers made to their customers to enable them to gamble far beyond their cash resources. In "buying on margin," as this practice was called, customers relied on brokers' loans to cover most of the cost of their stock purchases. Brokers and customers alike expected that the growing value of the stocks would make it easy enough to repay the loans. Meeting the pressing demand for brokers' loans, or "call money," corporations emptied their surpluses into the money market, where they received staggering returns.

Instead of tempering the boom, public officials encouraged it. The Federal Reserve System had means to tighten credit—that is, to make loans more expensive. But it chose to use its power to keep interest rates low. It did so in order to discourage the import of gold from Europe, and thus to protect the value of European currency and also to facilitate American loans to Europe, then still in need of investment funds for economic rehabilitation and development. (If interest rates had gone way up, Europeans and Americans would both have tended to invest more of their money within the United States.) Even if the Federal Reserve had tightened credit, however, it could not have controlled the call-money market that the corporations were feeding, for speculators were willing to borrow at usurious rates to finance their march to riches.

In the absence of federal authority over either credit or the chicanery of promoters, the best weapon available to the government was simple candor. There was, however, none of that. Secretary of the Treasury Mellon knew exactly what was going on; indeed, he was himself deep in speculation. Yet whenever sober business leaders questioned the state of the market, he or his colleagues in the administration invariably responded with soothing reassurances. And Coolidge went along. Early in 1927 William Z. Ripley, a Harvard economist, lectured the president on the prevalent "double-shuffling, honey-fuggling, hornswoggling and skulduggery." Coolidge, feet on desk and cigar in teeth, asked gloomily: "Is there anything we can do down here?" Ripley answered that the regulation of securities was the responsibility of the states, not of the federal government. Relieved, the president relaxed and put the incident out of his mind.

By the end of the year, brokers' loans had reached nearly $4 billion. In January 1928 Coolidge reassured the dubious few by announcing that this volume of loans was perfectly natural. Shortly thereafter Roy Young of the Federal Reserve Board, a close friend of Herbert Hoover, told a congressional committee that the loans were "safely and conservatively made." Those sanctions hastened the tempo of the boom and gave a Midas touch to 1928, an election year.

To Coolidge the ascending figures on the ticker tape were evidence of the nation's prosperity and of his own sagacity. He was as much honey-fuggled as hornswoggling. Like the brokers and speculators, he was at once the prisoner and the propagator of the grandiose myths that bemused the nation.

NONCONFORMITY AND DISSENT

The Jazz Age Some Americans, however, were repelled by materialism and its delusions. Disappointed by a progressive faith that seemed to have failed, they were alienated by the emptiness of business civilization. Some few thousands sought a solution in communism, but all kinds of radicalism recovered only slowly from the postwar repression, and the American Communists during the 1920s spent their zeal in factionalism and debate. Most of the disenchanted were equally cynical about serving society and about striving for worldly success. Finding only futility in the past and the future, they chose to seek out the pleasures of the present, to live for their private selves and for immediate self-expression.

Those men and women, many of them young, were no more immoral or promiscuous than men and women had been before. But they dropped pretense. They revealed their impatience with traditional standards of conduct openly and often, as did many of the movies they saw and much of the literature they read. One symbol of their protest was jazz, a serious idiom that owed its development to American musicians—particularly black musicians. Other American artists, notably Martha Graham, contributed to the formative period of modern dance.

Jazz and the Black Artist

Jazz to me is one of the inherent expressions of Negro life in America. the eternal tom-tom beating in the Negro soul—the tom-tom of revolt against weariness in a white world, a world of subway trains, and work, work, work; the tom-tom of joy and laughter, and pain swallowed in a smile. Yet the Philadelphia clubwoman . . . turns up her nose at jazz and all its manifestations—likewise almost anything else distinctly radical. . . . She wants the artist to flatter her, to make the white world believe that all Negroes are as smug and as near white in soul as she wants to be. But, to my mind, it is the duty of the younger Negro artist . . . to change through the force of his art that old whispering "I want to be white," hidden in the aspirations of his people, to "Why should I want to be white? I am Negro—and beautiful."

From Langston Hughes, "The Negro Artist and the Racial Mountain," *The Nation,* 1926

Jazz had other connotations, too—with its sensuality, its spontaneity, its atavistic rhythms, and with the sinuous and intimate dancing it inspired. Jazz was ungenteel, even un-Caucasian, above all uninhibited. It expressed not only protest and art of a kind but a controversial change in sexual mores.

Martha Graham

That change sprang largely from the ways in which city living altered family life. The nuclear family of the city and suburb (man, wife, children) existed in a private world quite different from that of the kinship family of the country or of the immigrant community, where grandparents, aunts, uncles, and cousins provided support and where community was more common than aloneness. The very impersonality of middle-class life in the city obliged its inhabitants to meet and resolve the problems of their lives with neither help nor impediment. Not every marriage was equal to the challenge.

Increasingly, women demanded easier and more equitable divorces, and they struggled for equal rights to jobs, to income, to their own apartments, to cigarettes, to whiskey, and to sexual satisfaction in matrimony or sometimes outside it. Much of the energy of feminism concentrated on the birth control movement. That movement, so Margaret Sanger claimed, freed the mind from "sexual prejudice and taboo." Not the least of its functions was to increase the quantity and quality of sexual relationships. The incidence of premarital and extramarital sexual experience also rose, as it had been rising for two decades. To some extent, especially for young people, adventures in sex released part of a rebellion against the reigning culture and its neopuritanical code.

The modern woman

During the 1920s, moreover, even the unrebellious were learning to understand the significance of sex in human nature. The most important contributions to that understanding were made by Sigmund Freud, whose doctrines had first reached America in the years before the war. After the war Freudian psychology rapidly became a national fad, ordinarily in vastly simplified and distorted forms. Freud himself, while demonstrating that neurotic symptoms and behavior could usually be attributed to sexual origins, did not advocate promiscuity. His first concern was with creating a system of analysis that would enable doctors to help patients find the emotional sources of their disorders, behavioral or somatic. On the basis of that discovery sick people could then reconstruct their lives. His popularizers, however, often interpreted his works as a rationale for "liberation" from sexual "repression." The average American met Freudian ideas only in that sense.

A Literature of Alienation "Society was something alien," Malcolm Cowley wrote about himself and his literary contemporaries of the 1920s. "It was a sort of parlor car in which we rode, over smooth tracks, toward a destination we should never have chosen for ourselves." Gertrude Stein called the young writers of the time "a lost generation." Those she referred to turned their backs on progress, on economics, on Main Street, and on Wall Street. "It was characteristic of the Jazz Age," said novelist F. Scott Fitzgerald, one of its high priests, "that it had no interest in politics at all." And the editor of *The Smart Set,* H. L. Mencken, wrote: "If I am convinced of anything, it is that Doing Good is in bad taste."

Men and women of that mind detested the business culture. Many of them fled, some to Paris, others to Greenwich Village, still others to an impenetrable privacy of creativity. And they attacked the civilization

F. Scott Fitzgerald and family: at home in the Jazz Age

The Lost Generation

It was lost . . . because it was uprooted, schooled away and almost wrenched away from its attachment to any region or tradition. It was lost because its training had prepared it for another world than existed after the war (and because the war prepared it only for travel and excitement). It was lost because it tried to live in exile. It was lost because it accepted no older guides to conduct and because it had formed a false picture of society and the writer's place in it. The generation belonged to a period of transition from values already fixed to values that had to be created. Its members . . . were seceding from the old and yet could adhere to nothing new; they groped their way toward another scheme of life, as yet undefined; in the midst of their doubts and uneasy gestures of defiance they felt homesick for the certainties of childhood.

From Malcolm Cowley, *Exile's Return,* 1951 ed.

they had left. Sinclair Lewis peopled the Middle West with confused men and women, trapped by their own futile materialism and unthinking gentility, narrow, unhappy, stifled. Lewis's *Main Street* (1920) and *Babbit* (1922) created satirical symbols of American life that persisted for a quarter of a century, not in the United States alone, but in Europe as well.

Sherwood Anderson exercised a large influence on his literary compatriots. A compassionate critic of small-town America, Anderson abandoned a business career, after a nervous breakdown in 1912 to devote himself to writing. His *Winesburg, Ohio* (1919) was a moving, autobiographical novel of alienation. Perhaps more important, he exemplified the religion of art, for he had escaped Babylon and had succeeded in his career of the spirit.

Seeking in art a distillation of experience, the young masters experimenting with literary form gave a new beauty and vitality to American letters. Encouraged particularly by Ezra Pound and Gertrude Stein and inspired by their pre-war poetry, the novelists Ernest Hemingway and William Faulkner and the poet T. S. Eliot raised the national literary reputation to its all-time zenith. Hemingway's *The Sun Also Rises* (1926) and *A Farewell to Arms* (1929) expressed a deep revulsion against nineteenth-century standards of conduct and idealizations of war. In *The Sound and the Fury* (1929) Faulkner used Freudian insights and adventurous prose to expose the awful tensions between self and society and the exacerbation of those tensions in the culture of the Deep South. Eliot's "The Love Song of J. Alfred Prufrock" (written in 1911, published six years later) made impotence the weary symbol of modern man. His *The Waste Land* (1922), probably the most emulated poem of the decade, provided a text in fragmentation and despair.

All these works revealed alienation and spoke of protest, but their authors were first, and most self-consciously, artists. So, too, were the other Americans who shared in the extraordinary literary renaissance of the period. They included an impressive number of talented black artists and authors, among them James Weldon Johnson, Countee Cullen, and Langston Hughes. Much of the prose and poetry of the "Harlem Renaissance" borrowed self-consciously from black culture, and the best of it, like the poetry of Hughes, ranked with the best work of white Americans.

The great outburst of artistic creativity had begun before 1920, continued beyond 1929, but came to a crescendo during the Coolidge era. In that time, the arts made a far more enduring mark on the nation than did politics. But the religion of art, then so prevalent, could be as futile as materialism itself. Alienation ordinarily denied social responsibility. The artists who rejected their national culture also accepted most of its claims. They turned away from the Coolidge era not because of its inequities but because of its superficial accomplishments. In contrast to the progressive intellectuals who had preceded them, they sought private escapes and private satisfactions, and they surrendered society to its shortsighted masters. This escapism deprived the nation of the assistance of many of its most imaginative minds.

Worse still, some Americans cast off democracy along with materialism. They agreed with the Mellons and the Fords and the Coolidges who believed that the business cult was the democratic ideal. They concluded that democracy necessarily generated a vulgar, selfish, pecuniary civilization. The critic Van Wyck Brooks, in his *The Ordeal of Mark Twain* (1920), wrote about the Gilded Age, with the 1920s much in mind, as "a horde-life, a herd-life, an epoch without sun and stars," which condemned the artist, and the soul, to frustration. Eliot also scorned democracy and remained rootless until he found salvation in the church, as Brooks did in sentimentality. H. L. Mencken was more acid. He ridiculed not only Prohibition, the Ku Klux Klan, and censorship, but the whole American people, whom he considered a sodden, brutish, ignorant mob. Democracy, for him, was government by orgy. As for democracy as a theory, "all the known facts lie flatly against it." Irving Babbitt, who formulated an aristocratic doctrine of the "inner check," had no patience with the "sickly sentimentalizing of the lot of the underdog," no confidence in social reform, no hope except in pseudo-Platonic comforts, and thus no real hope. The price of complacent materialism was alienation; and the bill of despair that went with alienation was ominously high.

Progressive Hopes and Failures Yet disenchantment did not lead all critics to alienation. Some drew on the legacy of progressivism and on their own undaunted spirit to point out anew the paths toward a good society. John Dewey (see p. 566) continued to examine the practical consequences of social policies in *Human Nature and Conduct* (1922) and *Individualism Old and New* (1929). These books urged experimentation in education for selfless citizenship, and public rather than private planning for social rather than pecuniary goals. Charles Beard in his *The Rise of American Civilization* (1927) stressed optimistically the historical significance of economic change. A year later he called for social engineering, national planning, to organize advancing science and technology for the general good. John R. Commons (see p. 566) worked out theories and techniques for social insurance, and among his fellow economists Irving Fisher showed that the government had to manage the nation's money supply if it was to achieve desirable social and economic ends. William T. Foster and Waddill Catchings advanced even more novel ideas. They attacked the beliefs that savings flowed automatically into investment and that business cycles righted themselves. If the nation was to avoid depressions, they insisted, government would have to resort to public spending when private investment faltered.

In public life, too, the progressive faith persevered, though it suffered major setbacks. Militant feminists, by no means satisfied with suffrage, now worked through the Women's party for the goal of total equality with men, a goal to be achieved through the proposed equal rights amendment to which Congress had yet to give serious consideration. Indeed, the militants lost influence during the decade after 1919. The League of Women Voters, however, a growing organization almost wholly of middle-class membership, reached a broader constituency in its efforts to educate the electorate about reform issues familiar to pre-war progressives, including the protection of working women. But the League won no important legislative victories, partly because women, who did not vote in a bloc, shared the indifference to politics or the conservative bias of most men of the time.

So it was that in 1926, when Mellon again advocated tax relief for the rich, his dwindling opponents could find no telling argument against cutting taxes. Federal revenues were then more than ample for the costs of government, and no one had yet developed a cogent program for spending to improve the nation's housing, roads, and natural resources. Without difficulty, the administration put through Congress a revenue act that cut in half the estate tax and the maximum surtax on individual incomes. Two years later Congress eased the tax on corporations. Mellon had carried the field.

Private utility companies were almost as successful. Sales of electric power doubled during the 1920s, and ingenious promoters with very little cash managed to monopolize the industry by setting up complex holding companies. By the end of the decade ten utility systems controlled approximately three-fourths of the nation's light and power business. The promoters kept the cost of electricity unreasonably high and through financial sleight of hand manipulated securities at the expense of bewildered stockholders. They also carried on a massive propaganda campaign and financed a powerful lobby to beat back demands for public supervision and for public distribution of electrical power.

The reformers, led by George Norris, included Governor Smith of New York and his successor, Franklin Roosevelt, who advocated state ownership and operation of public power. Gifford Pinchot, governor of Pennsylvania, organized a survey in 1923 that paved the way to public rural electrification. Many municipalities built or acquired their own power plants, and Nebraska, Norris's home state, established a public power system.

Farm politics particularly exercised Washington during Coolidge's second term, when farmers stepped up their demands for a government marketing plan. Such a plan had first been suggested in the lean years right after the war. Now it became the basis for legislation sponsored by Senator Charles L. McNary of Oregon and Congressman Gilbert N. Haugen of Iowa. At the heart of the proposal was a two-price scheme — a high domestic price and a low foreign price for staple crops. By purchasing farm surpluses, the government was to sustain a balance of supply and demand that would keep commodity prices at "parity" (see p. 698). In that manner the government would be underwriting the prosperity of the American farmers. The government would sell farm surpluses abroad for whatever price it could get, and any loss would be offset by an equalization tax levied on farmers or on those who processed and transported farm products.

Congress rejected the McNary-Haugen bill in 1924. But it passed a revised measure in 1927 and another one in 1928. Coolidge vetoed both versions. The bill, he said, would create a vast and clumsy bureaucracy, would improperly delegate taxing power from Congress to the administrators of the program, and would involve the government in trying to fix prices. Such prices, he argued, would be artificial and would encourage farmers to overproduce. Moreover, if the American government began to dump farm surpluses abroad, foreign governments would be bound to retaliate. The last two objections were undoubtedly sound, but Coolidge's concern for minimized government and a laissez-faire economy was unconvincing. After all, the government used the tariff, which was simply one kind of taxation, to aid industry. And the tariff, combined with the marketing practices of big business, led to artificial prices for manufactured goods. Those very prices kept farmers' costs high while their incomes lagged. Coolidge's vetoes, as the economist Rexford G. Tugwell put it, revealed "a stubborn determination to do nothing."

The debate over farm policy, like the debate over public power and taxation, highlighted the political issue that dominated the late 1920s: Was the federal government to be the handmaiden of business, the servant of the wealthy? Or was the government to build an equitable society in which all could obtain a fair share of the nation's wealth? Intellectuals like Dewey and politicians like Norris insisted on the second alternative. They were insisting that Americans, both in their private lives and in their conduct of public affairs, accept a responsibility that the spirit of the times rejected.

The Election of 1928 Calvin Coolidge announced that he "did not choose to run" in 1928. He might have been persuaded to accept a draft, but the Republican convention nominated Herbert Hoover on its first ballot. Professional politicians had little liking for Hoover, who was never one of them, and Midwestern farmers had little enthusiasm for a man who had opposed the McNary-Haugen bill precisely as Coolidge had. But business leaders trusted Hoover. His reputation for efficiency and humaneness was at its peak. And his personal success more than compensated for his lack of public glamour.

Hoover stood stolidly on a platform that attributed good times to Republican rule, praised the protective tariff, endorsed Prohibition, offered only platitudes to labor, and warned farmers of the evil of "putting the government into business." In his campaign speeches Hoover emphasized the virtues of individualism and "the American system" of free enterprise. There lay the source of prosperity. "We in America," Hoover said, "are nearer to the final triumph over poverty than ever before in the history of any land. . . . Given a chance to go forward with the policies of the last eight years, we shall soon with the help of God be in the sight of the day when poverty will be banished from this nation."

The Democrats nominated Al Smith. Those who had kept the nomination from him in 1924 had lost much of their credibility as the nation became more urbane. Further, as governor of New York Smith had made a record for efficiency as compelling as Hoover's. He had reordered the state's finances and reorganized its administration. He had promoted public health and public recreation, workmen's compensation, and civil liberties. As a national candidate, Smith stood for public ownership of the principal power sites and generating plants, and he endorsed the McNary-Haugen Plan.

"Socialism," Hoover retorted. But Smith was no radical. Indeed, he, too, deferred to the temper of the time. He accepted the need for protective tariffs. He

A Catholic for President

I am unable to understand how anything I was taught to believe as a Catholic could possibly be in conflict with what is good citizenship. The essence of my faith is built upon the Commandments of God. The law of the land is built upon the Commandments of God. There can be no conflict between them. . . .

What is this conflict about which you talk? It may exist in some lands which do not guarantee religious freedom. But in the wildest dreams of your imagination you cannot conjure up a possible conflict between religious principle and political duty in the United States except on the unthinkable hypothesis that some law were to be passed which violated the common morality of all God-fearing men. And if you can conjure up such a conflict, how would a Protestant resolve it? Obviously by the dictates of his conscience. That is exactly what a Catholic would do. There is no ecclesiastical tribunal which would have the slightest claim upon the obedience of Catholic communicants in the resolution of such a conflict.

From Alfred E. Smith, Article in the *Atlantic Monthly*, May 1927

chose as his campaign manager John J. Raskob, a Republican industrialist, identified with Du Pont and General Motors. The Democratic campaign may have reassured the conservatives, but it converted almost none of them, and it disappointed the liberals.

Raskob's appointment, furthermore, reopened the party wounds of 1924, for, like Smith, Raskob was a Catholic and a "wet." Rural America dug out its old suspicions of the city, booze, Tammany, and the pope. Particularly in the South, fundamentalist preachers associated Smith with all the old fears and hatreds. Smith explained that his religion had not and would not affect his policies, and his record confirmed his words. But the suspicious took their cue instead from his East Side accent, his brown derby, his open advocacy of repeal, his unabashed cityness. Hoover, for his part, made no convincing effort to dispel the religious issue.

As much as bigotry, prosperity defeated Smith, who could not counter Republican claims to credit for "the new era." He received only 87 electoral votes to Hoover's 444; some 41 percent of the popular vote to Hoover's 58. Five Southern states and all the border states went Republican. The Grand Old Party had won another landslide.

The returns, however, were not that unambiguous. Smith won a majority of the total vote cast in the county's twelve largest cities, which the Republicans had won handily four years before. The Democrats also cut into the traditionally Republican agricultural vote in the West. The farmers had doubts about prosperity, and in the cities the ethnic issue helped the Democrats in the urban North as much as it hurt them in the rural South. In 1928, as in 1924, the vote suggested the emergence of a new party balance and dramatized the need for Democratic unity and for a positive commitment to social reconstruction. But the prospects seemed poor, for the Coolidge era ended much as it had begun. Ethnic, religious, and cultural issues had divided Americans who had yet to achieve middle-class incomes, and prosperity had obscured public irresponsibility. Most Americans, as they had shown at the polls, were remarkably content. And confident, too. The stock market boomed as it awaited Hoover's inauguration and the nation's final triumph over poverty.

SUGGESTIONS FOR READING

GENERAL

The outstanding general accounts of the Coolidge years and their implications are in A. M. Schlesinger, Jr., *The Crisis of the Old Order* (1957); W. E. Leuchtenburg, *The Perils of Prosperity, 1914–32* (1958); and John Braeman, ed., *Change and Continuity in 20th Century America: The 1920's* (1968). See, too, E. Hawley, *The Great War and the Search for a Modern Order* (1979). The most entertaining biography of Coolidge is W. A. White, *A Puritan in Babylon* (1938); but see also Donald McCoy, *Calvin Coolidge* (1967). Coolidge speaks often but rarely well in H. H. Quint and R. H. Ferrell, eds., *The Talkative President* (1964). Still important is R. and H. L. Lynd, *Middletown* (1929).

BUSINESS ENTERPRISE

The economics of prosperity are described in George Soule, *Prosperity Decade: From War to Depression, 1917–1929* (1947); the institutions of business, in A. D. Chandler, Jr., *The Visible Hand* (1977); laborers and their unions, in D. Brody, *Workers in Industrial America* (1980); the business creed, in J. W. Prothro, *The Dollar Decade: Business Ideas in the 1920's* (1954); and the techniques of advertising, in Otis Pease, *The Responsibilities of American Advertising* (1958). On advertising and the culture, see R. W. Fox, and T. J. Lears, eds., *The Culture of Consumption* (1983). On the Ford Motor Company, its master, and the automobile industry in general, the preeminent works are A. Nevins and F. E. Hill, *Ford: The Times, the Man and the Company* (1954) and *Ford: Expansion and Challenge* (1957). There is also an acid analysis in Keith Sward, *The Legend of Henry Ford* (1948). See, too, John Rae, *The Road and Car in American Life* (1971). The best introduction to F. W. Taylor is his own *The Principles of Scientific Management* (1907). Siegfried Giedion, *Mechanization Takes Command: A Contribution to Anonymous History* (1948), offers brilliant observations about technology, which is handled on a more elementary level in Stuart Chase, *Men and Machines* (1929). By far the fullest and best account of labor during the 1920s is in Irving Bernstein, *The Lean Years* (1960). See also Robert Zieger, *Republicans and Labor, 1915–1929* (1969). Two studies of the first rank on corporate concentration and on the business cycle, respectively, are A. A. Berle, Jr., and G. F. Means, *The Modern Corporation and Private Property* (1932, rev. ed., 1969), and Thomas Wilson, *Fluctuations in Income and Employment* (1948). E. A. Goldenweiser, *American Monetary Policy* (1951), deals expertly with its subject, as does J. Potter, *The American Economy Between the Wars* (1974).

IDEALS AND IDEOLOGIES

The works mentioned in the text, and other works of the authors noted there, provide a good point of departure for studying the artists and intellectuals of the 1920s. For that purpose, Malcolm Cowley, *Exile's Return* (1934), is rewarding; and so are Alfred Kazin, *On Native Grounds* (1942), and Edmund Wilson, *The Shores of Light* (1952) and *The American Earthquake* (1958). The outstanding anthology of the social and cultural expressions of the time is L. Baritz, *The Culture of the Twenties* (1969). There are useful interpretations in R. Nash, *The Nervous Generation* (1969); P. A. Carter, *Another Part of the Twenties* (1977); and R. Crunden, *From Self to Society* (1972). On black artists, see N. Huggins, *Harlem Renaissance* (1971); and D. L. Lewis, *When Harlem Was in Vogue* (1981). American anti-intellectuals and bigots receive their just rewards in N. F. Furniss, *The Fundamentalist Controversy 1918–1931* (1954); Don Kirschner, *City and Country: Rural Responses to Urbanization in the 1920's* (1970); and D. M. Chalmers, *Hooded Americanism* (1965). More sympathetic is W. B. Gatewood, Jr., ed., *Controversy in the Twenties* (1969). Among the engaging works on the ideology and politics of Prohibition, and on the crime it helped to spawn, are Andrew Sinclair, *Prohibition: The Era of Excess* (1962) and Herbert Asbury, *The Great Illusion* (1950). The case for Prohibition emerges in N. H. Clark, *Deliver Us From Evil* (1976). On women during the 1920s, see William Chafe, *The American Woman: Her Changing Social, Economic, and Political Roles, 1920–1960* (1972); J. S. Lemons, *The Woman Citizen: Social Feminism in the 1920's* (1973); and Lois Banner, *Women in Modern America* (1974).

PUBLIC ISSUES AND PUBLIC MEN

Two important accounts of major federal public policies in the period 1923–29 are in the pertinent parts of R. E. Paul, *Taxation in the United States* (1954), and Theodore Saloutos and J. D. Hicks, *Twentieth Century Populism: Agricultural Discontent in the Middle West, 1900–1939* (1951). On the campaigns of 1924 and 1928, there are telling studies in K. C. MacKay, *The Progressive Movement of 1924* (1947); E. A. Moore, *A Catholic Runs for President* (1956); and A. J. Lichtman, *Prejudice and the Old Politics* (1979). O. Handlin, *Al Smith and His America** (1958), is short and thoughtful, while P. Eldot, *Alfred E. Smith* (1983), is detailed. For electoral trends, see D. Burner, *The Politics of Provincialism* (1968). And also, for the 1920s and later, C. W. Eagles, *Democracy Delayed* (1990); J. Allswang, *A Home for All Peoples* (1971); and G. B. Tindall, *The Emergence of the New South* (1967). Among the autobiographies and biographies of other public men of the time, some of the more rewarding are B. C. and F. La Follette, *Robert M. La Follette*, 2 vols. (1953); F. Freidel, *Franklin D. Roosevelt: The Ordeal* (1954); L. Levine's sympathetic study of Bryan, *Defender of the Faith* (1968); R. Lowitt, *George W. Norris: The Persistence of a Progressive* (1971); W. Harbaugh, *Lawyer's Lawyer: The Life of John W. Davis* (1973); D. Burner, *Herbert Hoover* (1978); E. E. Morison, *Turmoil and Tradition: A Study of the Life and Times of Henry L. Stimson* (1960); and H. L. Stimson and M. Bundy, *On Active Service in Peace and War* (1948). The last two shed significant light on the foreign policy of the Coolidge years. On that subject, also useful are R. H. Ferrell, *Peace in Their Time* (1952), J. H. Wilson, *American Business and Foreign Policy, 1920–1933* (1971); M. P. Leffler, *The Elusive Quest: The U.S. and French Security* (1979); and C. S. Maier, *Recasting Bourgeoise Europe* (1975) are also useful.

CHAPTER TWENTY-SIX

BREAD LINE, NEW YORK CITY

THE END OF AN ERA

The United States met the new year of 1929 with a smile and a swagger. The national habit of confidence had grown during three decades in which both the reformers of the early century and the managers of the new age of business believed they were fashioning a national Eden. A college graduate of the class of 1901, 50 years old in 1929, could believe with them that they had succeeded. As evidence of success, he might point to the statutes left over from progressivism, the great war won, the apparent unlikelihood of future war, the excitement of new inventions, and the largess of good times. Not since the mid-1890s, not for a generation, had the nation suffered a serious depression.

PRESIDENT HOOVER

Business Plans "I have no fears for the future of our country," the new president announced at his inauguration. "It is bright with hope." There was no nonsense about Hoover, none of T. R.'s boyishness or Wilson's dreaminess, none of Harding's incontinence or Coolidge's folksiness. The president was a serious man who kept in shape by playing medicine ball in the early morning. He would, most people thought, keep the nation in shape and lead it to ever higher plateaus of prosperity.

Hoover approached his office with his characteristic efficiency. He reorganized the presidential staff by creating a secretariat in which each member was assigned a specific place and duty. Government was also to be respectable. Hoover appointed a Cabinet of men who stood for what the business community admired. Mellon continued as secretary of the Treasury. The others, with one exception, were undistinguished. The exception was Secretary of State Henry L. Stimson, a conservative whose superior perceptions soon made him as uncomfortable as he was valuable.

Always active in pursuit of his own beliefs, Hoover, according to the solicitor of the Federal Power Commission, interceded to prevent private companies from being regulated rigorously. The president also proposed that the federal government withdraw its control from all public lands and from all new reclamation and irrigation projects. The states, he said, were "more competent to manage . . . these affairs." That was a debatable assertion, but it suited Hoover's purpose. In conservation, as in most other matters, he preferred to keep federal government small in both size and power.

Nevertheless, he recognized the need for some aid to agriculture, and he summoned a special session of Congress to provide it. The president suggested that the best way to help American farmers would be to raise the tariff and to give them federal assistance in marketing their produce—policies that would not, he said, undermine the farmers' initiative. In the Agricultural Marketing Act of 1929, Congress acted on Hoover's suggestions. It created a Federal Farm Board that was to be advised by committees representing the cooperative associations that marketed each of the major commodities. It also provided a revolving fund of $500 million from which the board could make loans to cooperatives to help them market their crops more effectively. Another provision, inserted by the farm bloc, permitted loans to be made to stabilization corporations "for the purpose of controlling any surplus." In other words, these corporations could influence prices so long as the Farm Board lent them enough money. But the Farm Board had no control over production. Consequently, not even generous loans for stabilization could long sustain prices if they should begin a major decline in the face either of gross overproduction or of adverse general economic circumstances. From the first, farmers were dissatisfied with the legislation of 1929.

They gained nothing from Hoover's proposal to give them more tariff protection. The president lacked the political skill to guide a tariff bill through Congress. In 1929 Congress put the matter aside. In 1930, with depression afflicting the country, industrial lobbyists and their friends in the Republican majority carried protection to its all-time high. The Hawley-Smoot Tariff of that year raised average *ad valorem* rates from about 32 percent to about 40 percent. It increased rates on some 70 farm products and over 900 manufactured goods. More than 1,000 economists urged Hoover to veto the bill. It would, they pointed out, raise the cost of living, encourage inefficient production, hamper American export trade, including trade in agricultural surpluses, and provoke foreign bitterness and retaliation. Though those arguments were entirely correct, Hoover signed the measure. It reflected the continuing influence of business interests in Washington and their continuing shortsightedness.

The Crash Dramatic evidence of that shortsightedness had already appeared in the stock market, the barometer of prosperity. It soared during the early months of 1929, but unbridled speculation began to worry conservative financiers and the president, too. He privately urged the New York Stock Exchange to curb the manipulation of securities, but with no success. Hoover would not ask Congress to interfere, for he "had no desire to stretch the powers of the Federal Government" that far. Instead he supported the Federal Reserve Board when it warned banks against making loans for speculative purposes, and he approved the board's 1 percent increase in the interest rate first in June and again in August 1929. But the higher cost of funds for speculation did not check the speculative fever.

Gamblers in stocks paid no heed to other warnings. The first signs of danger began to appear during the summer of 1929. Residential construction, important for the many industries that supplied its needs throughout the nation, fell off more than $1 billion. Business inventories trebled. The rate of advance in consumer spending dropped some 400 percent. From June onward, industrial production, employment, and commodity prices declined steadily. Indeed, the August increase in the interest rate came at a time when legitimate enterprise could ill afford it.

Yet the stock market boomed on. Ignoring the evidence of industrial decline, undeterred by the advancing costs of brokers' loans, speculators bid shares to new peaks. The morning after Labor Day the New York *Times* average of selected industrial stocks stood at 452, up more than 200 points since early 1928. The market seemed strong, but it was sustained only by deluded confidence. In one week brokers' loans had risen $137 million, and New York banks had borrowed $64 million to carry the weight of speculation.

During September and most of October the market wavered, moving gently downward. Some days were worrisome, but none of the captains of finance in New York or their lieutenants in Washington voiced alarm. Then on October 24 security prices crumbled in a wave of frenzied selling. Panic was temporarily averted when a group of New York bankers met next morning at J. P. Morgan and Company and agreed to pool their resources to hold the market up. The senior Morgan partner assured reporters that the heavy selling had been "due to a technical condition," not to any basic cause. The following day President Hoover announced that "the fundamental business of the country . . . is on a sound and prosperous basis."

They were wrong. During the next fortnight the market shuddered to collapse. As values fell, all the bets made on a rising market were paid off in panic. An uncontrollable decline swept past the support the bankers had organized. By mid-November the New York *Times* average had fallen to a shattering 224. In

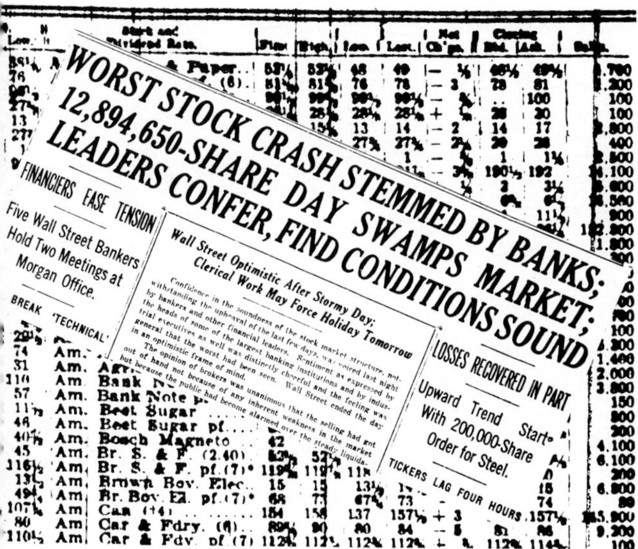

WORST STOCK CRASH STEMMED BY BANKS; 12,894,650-SHARE DAY SWAMPS MARKET; LEADERS CONFER, FIND CONDITIONS SOUND

FINANCIERS EASE TENSION

Five Wall Street Bankers Hold Two Meetings at Morgan Office.

BREAK 'TECHNICAL'

Wall Street Optimistic After Stormy Day; Clerical Work May Force Holiday Tomorrow

LOSSES RECOVERED IN PART

Upward Trend Starts With 200,000-Share Order for Steel.

TICKERS LAG FOUR HOURS

The New York Times: *October 25, 1929*

less than a month, the securities listed on the New York Stock Exchange lost $26 billion—more than 40 percent—of their face value. Nor was the descent over. In July 1932 the *Times* average hit bottom at a mere 58.

Contrary to Hoover's assertion, the fundamental business of the country was unsound. Excessive industrial profits, along with skimpy industrial wages, were distributing one-third of all personal income to 5 percent of the population. Some two years before the crash, the annual rate of increase of national investment (as contrasted to speculation) had started downward, not the least because corporations and their executives had diminished expectations for profits from an economy in which purchasing power could no longer keep pace with productivity. That rate of increase of investment, as economists came to understand a decade later, had to continue to rise if economic growth was to be sustained. Since 1927 the shortage of purchasing power among consumers had had a particularly bad effect on the important automobile and construction industries. The falling market for homes and cars, expensive items, reflected the uneven distribution of American income and wealth that left even the middle class without sufficient cash or credit to continue the buying splurge of the earlier years of the decade. But in the 1920s the level of economic intelligence, like the level of both private and public economic policy, was still relatively low. The surfeit of disposable income among the rich, together with the swollen profits of corporations, had encouraged speculation. When trouble came, the jerry-built corporate structures of many businesses, especially the utilities, toppled. Nor could the American banking system meet the strain, for bankers, though they had been aware of the loose practices of their profession, had long refused to discipline themselves.

Business had failed to keep its house in order. Even worse, it had persuaded the government to follow the unwise economic policies of the decade preceding the crash. The crash itself was the predictable end of a period of intense speculation, and the crash in turn brought the sagging economy down. It wiped out savings and confidence alike. Money lost in the market could not be spent for new consumer goods nor invested in new enterprise. The mood of despair that settled over the nation also stifled renewal of private investment that might have encouraged recovery. It dispelled the confidence of Americans in the business élite. The dominance of business managers and industrialists, in government and out, had brought, not a new Eden, but a panic that marked the onset of the most baleful depression in all history.

THE ONSET OF DEPRESSION

The Hoover Policies: First Phase Few of the leaders of American business and politics, either Republican or Democrat, had expected the crash. And when it came, very few of them understood what had caused it or foresaw the severity of the depression it was to bring. Most of them agreed with the head of Bethlehem Steel, who announced in December 1929 that "never before has American business been as firmly entrenched for prosperity as it is today." Most of them agreed also with Andrew Mellon, who recommended letting the economy run down to the depths, from which it would presumably recover automatically, as it had in the 1870s and 1890s. That policy would entail great suffering, but those who believed that the economy operated according to mechanical laws believed too in the inexorability of business cycles and in the wisdom of leaving them alone, suffering or no. "Liquidate labor," Mellon advised, "liquidate stock, liquidate the farmers."

Hoover knew better. Though he remained convinced that the economy was basically sound and that government should not interfere with business, he

After the Crash: A Contemporary Statement

The Big Bull Market was dead. . . . Coolidge-Hoover prosperity was not yet dead, but it was dying. Under the impact of the shock of panic, a multitude of ills which had passed unnoticed . . . began to beset the body economic . . . : overproduction of capital; overambitious expansion of business concerns; overproduction of commodities under the stimulus of installment buying and buying with stock-market profits; the maintenance of an artificial price level for many commodities; the depressed condition of European trade. No matter how many soothsayers of high finance proclaimed that all was well, no matter how earnestly the President set out to work to repair the damage with soft words and White House conferences, a major depression was . . . under way.

From Frederick L. Allen, *Only Yesterday,* 1931

took steps to prevent the spread of depression. In a series of conferences he tried to persuade business leaders to keep wages and prices up voluntarily. He called on the Federal Reserve to make it easy for business to borrow. He encouraged the Farm Board to provide funds to help the stabilization corporations in their efforts to sustain commodity prices. Above all, he hoped, by offering private advice and by making public pronouncements, to restore the nation's confidence in business.

Hoover welcomed the Tariff Act of 1930 (see p. 674), for he was convinced that business would be encouraged by a continuation of protection. To hearten business leaders further, he recommended, and Congress in 1930 provided, cuts in personal and corporate income taxes. The reductions gave the wealthy more disposable income to use for investment, but they gave lower-income groups, who paid little taxes anyway, no additional money to spend on consumption. In the absence of confidence in business, the investments were not forthcoming. Following Hoover's advice, Congress did make modest appropriations for public works. These gave some boost to the sick construction industry and to the heavy industries that supplied it, and indirectly to the workers who were employed in those industries.

But those efforts were too meager to check the contraction in private spending, investment, and employment that followed the crash. Both Hoover and the Federal Reserve Board opposed a rapid, deliberately inflationary expansion of currency and bank deposits, which the board might have attempted with some possible healthy effect. The president would not countenance any more spending, because he was determined to keep the federal budget as close to balanced as possible. This, he believed, as did most Americans, was sound finance, and it was also an unshakable article of business faith. Large federal deficits, like inflation, would have frightened the business community, which the president wanted to soothe. To that purpose, during 1930 the president continually applied the balm of official optimism. True, official gloom would have caused further alarm; but Hoover, while privately dubious, acted as if his conferences with business leaders had succeeded, whereas wages and prices actually continued to decline.

The Blight of Depression "We have now passed the worst," Hoover announced wishfully in May 1930, "and . . . shall rapidly recover." The statistics told a different story. In 1929 new capital issues in the United States, a rough yardstick of investment, had totaled $10 billion; in 1930 they dropped to $7 billion. As the depression deepened, the figure reached $3 billion in 1931 and $1 billion in 1932. Investment was discouraged by the decline in corporate profits, which fell off steadily from $8.4 billion in 1929 to $3.4 billion in 1932. At the same time, the rate of business failures rose—over 100,000 businesses went under in the period 1929–32. And banks were failing too. In 1929, 659 banks with total deposits of

No rent, no joy, no hope

about $200 million closed their doors; in 1930, 1,352 banks with deposits of $853 million; in 1931, 2,294 banks with deposits of almost $1,700 million, at the rate of almost 200 a month. Each collapse erased the cash and savings of depositors, most of whom had no other resources.

By the last quarter of 1930, industrial production had fallen 26 percent below the 1929 level. By mid-1932 it was off 51 percent from that level. Unemployment mounted, with women losing proportionately more jobs than men: 4 million in October 1930; nearly 7 million a year later; almost 11 million by the fall of 1932. Even those who kept their jobs were earning less and less. Between 1929 and 1933 the total annual income of labor dropped from $53 to $31.5 billion. Average manufacturing wages came down 60 percent, average salaries 40 percent. Farmers fared even worse: their income declined from $11.9 to $5.3 billion. In 1929 national income touched $81 billion; by 1932 it had shrunk to $49 billion.

Liquidation carried a frightful burden of human suffering. Thousands of middle-class families, their incomes dwindling, sometimes entirely gone, lost next their savings, then their insurance, then, unable to pay their mortgages, their very homes. The optimism of the 1920s gave way to gloom and fear. The times were even harder on laboring men and their families. The lost job, the fruitless search for work, the shoes worn

Reginald Marsh, Bread Line—No One Has Starved, *1932.* Katherine Schmidt Schubert Bequest, Collection of the Whitney Museum of American Art, New York.

"Brother can you spare a dime?"

through and the clothes worn thin, the furniture and trinkets pawned, the menu stripped of meat and then of adequate nutrition, no rent, no joy, no hope. And finally the despair of bread lines — these visited every city, leaving in their path sullen men, weeping women, and hungry children. So, too, on the farm — vanished incomes, foreclosures, tenancy, migrancy, and with them, as in the cities, the death of self-respect.

Hoover had predicted the abolition of poverty in America. Instead, within two years there mushroomed around America's cities settlements of shacks built of empty packing boxes, where homeless men squatted, reduced to desultory begging. A new Eden? "Brother, can you spare a dime?"

The Hoover Policies: Second Phase In the congressional elections of 1930 the Democrats conducted a rousing campaign against Hoover, though they offered no clear alternatives to his policies. The intensification of depression hurt the Republicans, as depression had always hurt the party in power. Though Hoover had been by no means unenlightened, he was, by virtue of his office, the most exposed target for abuse. The Democrats made his name a synonym for hardship. A "Hoover blanket" was yesterday's newspaper. A "Hoover flag" was an empty pocket turned inside out. Rough tactics and national discontent produced a slim Democratic victory, the first since 1916. The Republican majority in the Senate was reduced to a single vote, leaving that body dominated by a coalition of Democrats and Western agrarians. The Democrats held a bare majority in the House when the new Congress met.

In December 1930 the Democratic minority of the old Congress used the rump session to develop a program for unemployment relief. Hoover, irritated by the Democratic campaign and appalled by its success, reasserted his own policies.

The president felt that relief was essentially a local problem. The cities, with help from private charity, should and could take care of the needy. That was a fallacious assumption, for nowhere in the nation was there an adequate system of relief. Local public funds in 1929 paid three-fourths of the cost of relief (by 1932, four-fifths), but the localities had neither the means to raise revenue nor the capacity to borrow to defray their mounting obligations. Their relief agencies and programs, moreover, had concentrated on helping unemployables, people unable to work. Local administrators had neither the experience nor the facilities to cope with mass unemployment, and private charity was incapable of meeting the nation's huge need for immediate relief.

As the winter of 1930–31 came on, cold and hunger moved into the homes of the unemployed. Relief payments were only $2.39 a week for a family in New York and even less in most other cities. Two Texas cities barred relief for black citizens. Detroit, unable to tax or borrow, dropped a third of the needy families from its relief rolls. St. Louis cut off half, and children there combed the dumps for rotting food.

In October 1930, the president appointed an Emergency Committee for Employment under Colonel Arthur Woods. Though Hoover told the committee that relief was a local responsibility, Woods recommended a federal public-works program. The president rejected it, and in April 1931 Woods resigned.

Meanwhile Senator Robert Wagner, a New York Democrat, had introduced bills providing for federal public works and a federal employment service. Along with Wagner, Senator Robert M. La Follette, Jr., "Battle Bob's" son and successor, and Republican Senator Bronson Cutting of New Mexico urged federal spend-

Employment: Men versus Women

Even during the "good" decade of the 1920s . . . there was . . . increased competition . . . with women workers for jobs. Women managed almost to hold their own in the total share of . . . jobs . . . but . . . only at the cost of diminishing their hold upon the types of jobs in which male competition is most acute, and concentrating more within a narrowed group of "women's jobs."

It is unlikely . . . that women will regain the ground they have lost. . . . In certain niches—nursing, teaching, clerical work, household servants, hair-dressers and manicurists . . . they occupy a fairly secure position. But elsewhere . . . the pressure of men for women's jobs . . . is likely to increase, particularly if business continues . . . chronically "down" from the 1929 level. . . . Married women workers are doing monotonous . . . jobs in factories that can be done more cheaply by piece-workers who do not have to support themselves. . . . Unmarried women in business and the professions are doing either extremely poorly paid work as retail clerks and teachers, or manifestly "women's work" like stenography . . . or helping professional men as assistants; while those under twenty years of age are accepting prolonged schooling as an alternative to enforced idleness.

From Robert S. Lynd and Helen Merrell Lynd, *Middletown in Transition,* 1937

ing for public works and relief. All this Hoover opposed on the ground that federal action was unnecessary.

Instead, in February 1931 Hoover expressed his continuing dedication to individualism, local responsibility, and mutual self-help. But in the face of depression, the virtues of economic individualism and private charity were outweighed by the needs of the helpless. The sheer shock of the depression and the pervasive ignorance about the causes of the business cycle impeded the search for remedies. Like others in government, the president was a captive of those circumstances as well as an honest man whose convictions nailed him.

Hoover's interpretation of the economic ups and downs of 1931 strengthened his convictions. Between February and June of that year the economic indexes rallied slightly, partly because of a normal seasonal upturn. The gains, though tiny, persuaded the president, and others bent on optimism, that recovery was under way. Then in the spring and summer of 1931 financial panic swept over Europe. The American crash had precipitated the collapse abroad by drying up the loan funds on which the European economy and the interrelated reparations and war-debt payments had come to depend. And the European collapse in turn drove foreigners to dump American securities in their scramble for dollars, thereby driving American stock prices down even further. Moreover, shortages in exchange forced one European nation after another to devalue its currency. This action disrupted international trade, and the prices of American agricultural commodities plummeted. Before the end of the summer, the indexes had resumed their decline. Again the depression deepened.

The depression, worldwide in scope, was provoking individual nations to pursue their separate advantages. The resulting scramble hurt them all, but none of the

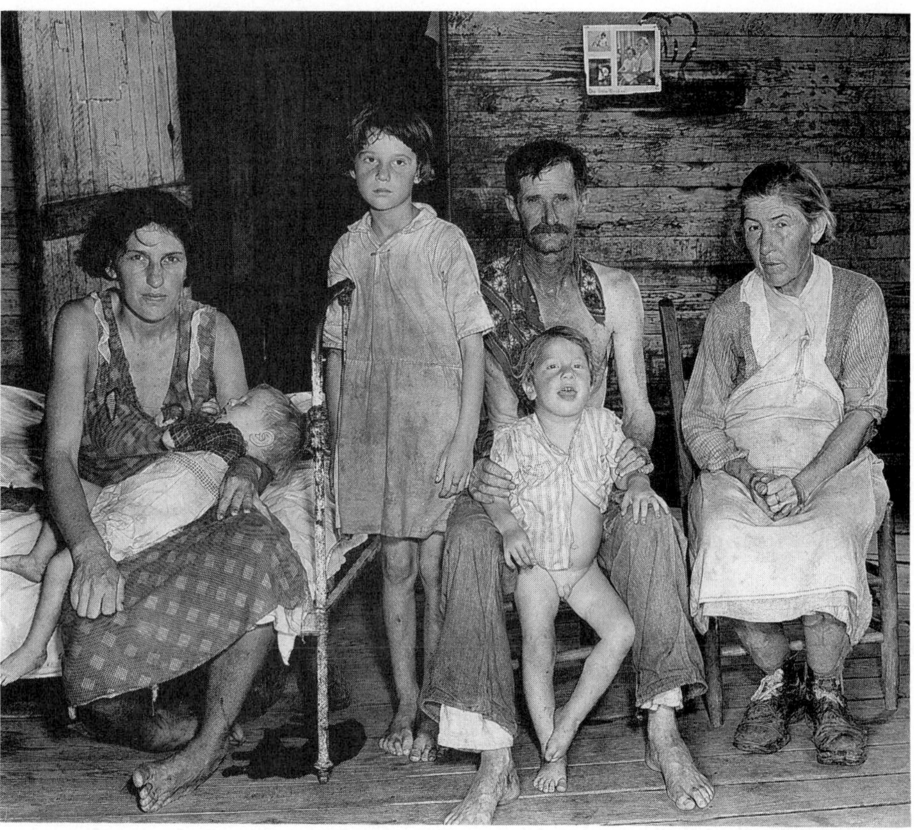

Cold and hunger moved into their homes.

great powers, either in 1931 or for another decade, assumed and sustained the leadership that was required to bring about needed measures of cooperation. The United States was no exception.

The fault, Hoover concluded, lay in Europe. All the calamities since 1929, he came to believe, had originated in the Old World. The war had taxed the world economy beyond repair. The United States had regrettably become involved not only in war but in a morass of bad loans as well. European bankers had collaborated with their New York associates to create the easy-money conditions on which speculation had fed (see p. 664), and from that collusion was born the Panic of 1929. Then, just as recovery beckoned, European disaster in 1931 had reversed the gains so arduously won. This view of the causes of the depression reasserted the persistent myth of American innocence—even wounded innocence—for as Hoover saw the situation American business shared little of the blame; he himself shared none. Hoover's theory, moreover, excused him from embracing the domestic policies he had rejected, for if the basic cause of depression lay outside the United States the most appropriate action would be to ease the strains abroad and to protect the American economy from them.

DIPLOMACY IN DEPRESSION

A Set of Good Intentions The foreign policies on which the Hoover administration embarked in 1929 were marked by goodwill and peaceful purpose. The president and able Secretary of State Stimson believed, as had their immediate predecessors, that the world had fought its last major war a decade earlier. Europe, they expected, could take care of itself, as could Asia and Latin America, with occasional advice from the United States. The aroused morality embodied in the Kellogg-Briand pact would prevent aggression and discourage militarism. Indeed, Hoover expected the powers to put an end to their arms race in the very near future.

Initially Hoover and Stimson made some progress toward their benign goals. While still president-elect, Hoover, a Quaker, had carried friendship to Latin America during a ten-week tour that publicized the "good neighbor" policy.* In Argentina he promised to abstain from intervention in the internal affairs of the nations south of the border. He kept his word. In 1930 Stimson announced that the United States henceforth would grant diplomatic recognition to de facto governments. Moreover, Hoover set about withdrawing the marines from Nicaragua, a task that was completed in 1933, and he arranged to remove them from Haiti.

In 1930 the president formally repudiated the Roosevelt Corollary to the Monroe Doctrine (see p. 579). A memorandum written by former Assistant Secretary of State J. Reuben Clark, which Hoover ordered published, denied that the doctrine justified American intervention in Latin America. Nor did Hoover regard the doctrine as a mandate for collecting the private debts of Americans. Some 50 revolutions or attempts at revolution shook the "good neighbors" of the hemisphere during his administration. But he kept hands off, even though those disturbances often resulted in the repudiation of debts owed to American citizens and in the nationalization of their properties. By abandoning protective imperialism, Hoover created an improved atmosphere in hemispheric relations.

That success contrasted with the administration's diplomatic disappointments in Europe and its agonies in Asia. Intent on naval disarmament, Hoover welcomed the cooperation of Ramsay MacDonald, the head of the new Labour Cabinet in England. Their preliminary negotiations prepared the way for the multipower conference that met in London in 1930. There the Americans, the British, and the Japanese extended the "holiday" on the construction of capital ships, and American and British representatives evolved a formula for limiting the construction of cruisers, destroyers, and submarines. Naval experts of the English-speaking nations, however, deplored a compromise that increased Japan's ratio for cruisers and destroyers and gave it equality in submarines. In effect, this arrangement recognized Japan's primacy in the western Pacific. Japan would have accepted nothing less, and neither the Hoover nor the MacDonald government wanted to engage in an expensive naval race. Neither, moreover, considered Japan unfriendly. They confirmed, therefore, only what they had already conceded.

Even so, they failed to close the door on a naval race. The French, frightened by the militarism of fascist Italy, refused to limit their naval program unless the United States promised to help France in the event of aggression. Such a pledge was unthinkable to Hoover, the Senate, or the American people. When France and Italy would not subscribe to significant parts of the London treaty, the British insisted on adding a clause permitting England, the United States, or Japan to expand their fleets if their national security was threatened by the building program of some other power. This "escalator" clause made naval limitation conditional upon the self-restraint of a resurgent Italy and an alarmed France.

Monetary Diplomacy When the panic struck European banks and security markets in 1931 (see p. 679), the focus of Hoover's diplomacy shifted to money. American investors, hard hit by the depression, cut off the loans to Germany that had so far enabled it to pay reparations for its part in the First World War. Without this source of income, the former Allies were unable to keep up payments on their debts to the United States. Even before the distressed German president appealed for help in the spring of 1930, Hoover had begun to think about a one-year moratorium on all intergovernmental debts and reparations payments. When he announced his proposal late in June, England and Germany endorsed it, but France held back, still hopeful of collecting reparations. The French also suspected that the American plan was partly designed to enable Germany to pay back private debts it owed in the United States. During the two weeks before France endorsed the moratorium, the accelerated flight of funds from Germany forced widespread bank failures.

To his shock, the president discovered that Europe's distress directly embarrassed American banks. They had lent some $1.7 billion, on a short-term basis, without collateral, to central European banks. Bank runs in Europe made those loans impossible to collect, and the solvency of the American banks that had made them was threatened. The loans were part of a complex network of obligations among banks in many countries. In order to stop demands for payments back and forth among them, Secretary Stimson in July 1930 negotiated an emergency "standstill" agreement. It was later extended to September 1931, and again to March 1933. The standstill agreements froze private debts just as the moratorium had frozen public debts. This gave financiers time to try to protect the banks of the Western world from bankruptcy, and

*A phrase later used by and ordinarily associated with Franklin Roosevelt.

On the Hoover Moratorium

The Hoover moratorium made me gloomy . . . as soon as I saw that it was limited to one year. . . . I discounted the ability of the French and Germans to reach an accord for a permanent decent settlement within the year and equally thought it hopeless to expect Germany's recovery for the resumption of reparation payments. . . . To expect the French and Germans to work things out and to have the most powerful and most disinterested nation retire, seemed to me pitiable abdication of responsibility. I know the essential basis that moved the President . . . namely, that we had our domestic troubles and they needed attention. But this of course is the essential fallacy of his whole recent outlook—that we have a "war" on a domestic front rather than an interdependent world maladjustment.

From Felix Frankfurter to Walter Lippmann, April 12, 1932

time to delay putting pressure on borrowers for loans due.

But the freezing came too late to stop panic. Depositors, their confidence in banks shaken, demanded their money, which they intended to hoard. A run on the Bank of England, for decades the world's foremost symbol of financial stability, drained its gold and forced Great Britain off the gold standard in September 1931. That nation devalued the pound—that is, increased the cost of gold in terms of British currency—and established a special government fund to manage the value of the pound in terms of other currencies. By the end of 1931 every major power except Italy, France, and the United States was also forced off the gold standard, and each depreciated its currency and attempted to control its value in international exchange. These efforts at control were often designed to produce selfish advantages in trade, as were the prohibitive tariffs that invariably accompanied devaluation. Exchange controls and high tariffs actually impeded world trade and, worse still, gave rise to international suspicion and distrust.

Hoover had shown commendable initiative in arranging the moratorium and the standstills, but he never saw to the bottom of the problem. He failed to recognize that America's high protective tariffs impeded international commerce and invited foreign retaliation. And he would not support the cancellation of war debts. At the Lausanne Conference of 1932, England and France finally admitted Germany's bankruptcy and agreed to scale reparations down to an insignificant sum provided that the United States would scale war debts down equivalently. Most American bankers favored that plan, as did Stimson, who urged cancellation of "these damn debts." But Congress, reflecting public opinion, would not even consider a new debt commission, and Hoover, equivocal himself, demanded that the European nations resume payments on their debts after the moratorium expired. The debtor nations—except for Finland, whose obligation was tiny—had no choice but to default.

The defaults, like the demand that forced them and the long stalemate over debts and reparations that preceded them, engendered ill feeling on both sides of the Atlantic. The resulting distrust weakened the will of the democracies to cooperate in order to resist the black forces gathering around them.

Fire Bells in the Orient Japan broke the peace of the world. Since its victory over Russia in 1905, it had dominated the economy of southern Manchuria, the northeastern section of China. Tokyo was willing to acknowledge China's political claim to the area so long as that claim did not collide with Japanese military interests and economic privileges. During the late 1920s such a collision grew increasingly likely. In China, Chiang Kai-shek took over the central government and broke with the Communists who had been his allies. Chinese nationalists hoped soon to have the whole country under their control. But the Russians still managed the Chinese Eastern Railway and were developing its Pacific terminus, the Siberian city of Vladivostok. Alarmed by the construction there, Japan resolved to reinforce southern Manchuria. Here it confronted Chiang Kai-shek, who was determined to yield nothing further to any foreign power.

In the fall of 1931 the Japanese army in effect took over the Tokyo government. In September Japanese troops occupied Shenyang (Mukden) and other Manchurian cities and moved rapidly to establish political control over the province. This violation of the Nine Power Treaty and the Kellogg-Briand pact was perfectly timed. China turned to the League of Nations for help, but the West was paralyzed by depression. Hoover, anxious to avoid war, rejected Stimson's suggestion that the United States might have to cooperate with the League in imposing economic sanctions on Japan.

At Hoover's insistence, Stimson proceeded cautiously. He hoped at first to strengthen the civilian moderates in the Japanese cabinet. But in January 1932 the Japanese army drove on. Now Stimson resorted to moral condemnation, the only weapon Hoover would countenance. In identical notes to China and Japan, he revived the doctrine Bryan had enunciated in 1915. The United States, Stimson warned, would not recognize any change brought about by force that impaired American treaty rights or Chinese territorial integrity. Japan scoffed politely.

Before the end of January, the Japanese invaded Shanghai, bombarded the city, and killed thousands of civilians — all on the pretext that they were retaliating against a Chinese boycott. America's warning had proved no deterrent. Yet Stimson could turn only to sterner words. In February he published a letter to Senator Borah, in which he reiterated his nonrecognition doctrine and lamented the failure of other nations to endorse it. He also recalled the interdependence of the various Washington treaties of 1922. "The willingness of the American government to surrender its commanding lead in battleship construction and to leave its positions at Guam and in the Philippines without further fortification," Stimson wrote, "was predicated upon, among other things, the self-denying covenants contained in the Nine Power Treaty."

He hoped that his letter would encourage China, inform the American public, exhort the League and Great Britain, and warn Japan. But sentiment did

The West was paralyzed

China no good. Americans, like the League and its members, shared Hoover's determination to confine deterrence to words, and Japan was confident that neither the president nor his constituents were prepared to heed Stimson's counsel.

The Assembly of the League, with Japan abstaining, unanimously adopted a resolution incorporating the nonrecognition doctrine. A year later a League commission of inquiry named Japan the aggressor in Manchuria and called on the Japanese to return the province to China. They simply withdrew from the League, though they left Shanghai temporarily.

For its part, Congress early in 1933 passed a bill granting independence to the Philippine Islands, largely in response to pressure from American sugar interests eager to raise the tariff barrier between themselves and their Filipino competitors. The measure, enacted over Hoover's veto, demonstrated that Congress was willing to throw the islands to the mercy of

Japan, and it canceled the veiled warning in Stimson's letter to Borah.

The story was much the same in Europe, where the German Nazis were marching to power. At a World Disarmament Conference in Geneva in 1932, the French proposed that an international army be established and that all powers submit to the compulsory arbitration of disputes. Hoover countered with a plan for the immediate abolition of all offensive weapons and the reduction by one-third of existing armies and navies. But with the United States still unwilling to guarantee their security, the French were unimpressed by the arithmetic of arms reduction, and the conference adjourned in July with nothing accomplished. In 1933 Germany was Hitler's.

Good will and high moral purpose had no meaning in the Germany of the Nazis or the Japan of the Imperial Army. For those who hoped for disarmament and peace and the rule of law, the hour of peril was close. Neither the American people nor their leaders had brought the world to the edge of disaster, nor could they alone have prevented the collapse of order. But the foreign policies of the United States lacked the force to check depression or aggression.

THE DEPTHS OF DEPRESSION

The Hoover Policies: Third Phase Hoover, William Allen White once said, was "constitutionally gloomy, a congenital pessimist who always saw the doleful side of any situation." As Hoover put it himself, "I can't be a Theodore Roosevelt." Grim and aloof, he was nonetheless resolute. Just as he tried to halt the panic in Europe in 1931, so did he try to buttress the United States against the effects of that panic. By the fall of that year he had reached certain conclusions that were to shape his policies during the coming months. He intended to do everything he could to keep the nation on the gold standard, in his view an indispensable condition of economic health. The business and financial community shared that belief passionately, as it long had. The president also intended, again with ardor and with the blessing of men of means, to strive for economy, though privately he admitted the budget could not be balanced. Indeed, he was prepared to use federal funds and federal authority on an unprecedented scale to rescue the banks and industry from their troubles. The effects of their recovery, he thought, would reach down to the farmers and laborers, who were to receive little direct aid from the federal government.

The new Congress convened in December 1931. At Hoover's suggestion it appropriated $125 million to expand the lending powers of the Federal Land Banks. Also at his urging, but not until July 1932, it established a system of home-loan banks with a capital of $125 million for discounting home mortgages. The purpose of this scheme was to enable savings banks, insurance companies, and building-and-loan associations to obtain cash for the mortgages they held instead of having to foreclose them. The act not only helped to keep the assets of the lending institutions liquid but also, as Hoover said, spared hundreds of Americans the "heartbreaking . . . loss of their homes." And it set a significant precedent for more extensive legislation later on.

In February 1932 Congress passed the Glass-Steagall Act, as requested by the president. It freed about a billion dollars' worth of gold to meet the demands of Europeans who were converting their dollars to gold. This enabled the United States for the time being to retain enough gold to remain on the gold standard without putting controls on gold movements or on transactions in foreign exchange. Yet the continuing outflow of gold even further reduced bank reserves and thus the availability of bank loans to business. That situation further depressed prices and added to the burden of debts contracted when prices were high. To hold to the gold standard was in keeping with the theories of classical economics, with their emphasis on the automatic workings of domestic and international trade and of the business cycle. Yet now that mechanism spun the business cycle downward and helped depression feed upon itself.

In spite of the Glass-Steagall Act, moreover, many banks remained weak. To supplement their resources, Hoover in the fall of 1931 persuaded New York bankers to create a National Credit Association with a $500 million pool. But the halfhearted use of this fund doomed the effort to failure. The president then gave in to the urgings of Eugene Meyer, governor of the Federal Reserve Board and formerly head of the War Finance Corporation established in 1918. Meyer proposed reviving that agency in order to rescue American finance. Hoover, hoping that the psychological lift provided by this scheme would justify the cost of financing it, made it the keystone of his recovery policy in 1932.

In January Congress created the Reconstruction Finance Corporation (RFC) with a capital stock of $500

The Hoover Presidency: A Positive Assessment

Although the President himself, his chief advisers, and the majority of industrialists who conferred with him . . . celebrated the virtues of laissez-faire and of individualism, in practice, faced with a real emergency, they turned as a matter of course to collective action. They did not merely reject the classic doctrine of liquidation . . . after a boom; they acted as if they had never heard of it. . . . Mr. Hoover regarded it as his obvious duty to take charge and to direct.

He . . . spent billions in protecting banks, insurance companies and railroads against bankruptcy. He . . . spent great sums to maintain the prices of wheat and cotton. He . . . spent great sums on public works. He had striven to maintain wage rates. He had attempted to inflate credit. . . . He pointed with pride to the collective measures he had taken to save individuals from making individual readjustments. . . .

On the point which concerns us here, which is that . . . the modern state has become responsible for the modern economy as a whole, Mr. Hoover is the best of all witnesses. For he acted on a doctrine which he professed to reject. There would be no better evidence of the degree to which the new doctrine is established.

From Walter Lippmann, *The Method of Freedom,* 1934

million and the power to borrow three times that sum in guaranteed, tax-free bonds. It was authorized, as Meyer and Hoover had recommended, to lend money to banks and insurance companies and, with the approval of the Interstate Commerce Commission, to railroads. Most of the $1.5 billion the RFC disbursed before March 1933 went to banks and trust companies. The RFC, however, could lend funds only against adequate collateral, and it could not buy bank stock. Its loans increased bank indebtedness, but it could not satisfy the banks' basic need for new capital.

The RFC kept its transactions secret for five months, largely because Hoover feared that publicity would incite runs on the weak banks that were receiving the loans. More than half of the $126 million that the RFC disbursed during those months went to three large banks. One of them was the bank of Charles G. Dawes, who resigned as president of the RFC only a month before the loan went through. In July 1932 the Democrats in Congress, to Hoover's dismay, put through an amendment compelling the RFC to report its transactions. Thereafter the number of loans made to large institutions fell off. Nevertheless, the establishment and use of the RFC constituted the most vigorous peacetime federal intervention in the economy since the nation's founding.

The Muddle of Relief Late in 1931 Hoover appointed a new committee on unemployment with Walter S. Gifford as its head. Gifford, the president of the American Telephone and Telegraph Company, agreed with Hoover that relief was the responsibility of local government and private charity. Yet Gifford could not convincingly defend this view. In January 1932 he confessed to a Senate committee that he did not know how many people were out of work. He did not know how many needed help, how much help they needed, or how much money localities were raising or could raise. But of one thing he seemed certain: the "grave danger" of taking "the determination of these things into the Federal Government."

Unemployed Alumni

Organization of the Association of Unemployed College Graduates was announced yesterday after a meeting of graduates of nine Eastern colleges. . . . Estimating the number of unemployed alumni in this city alone at more than 10,000, the association made public a plan of action designed to enlist members throughout the country. . . . The group pointed out that since June, 1929, it had become increasingly difficult for university graduates to obtain positions. Distress consequent upon unemployment was more acute among college-trained men and women . . . because of their relatively high standards of living and education. (The *New York Times,* July 27, 1932)

Thousands of college graduates . . . are among the ranks of the unemployed. . . . Many professions are represented, the teaching profession leading . . . engineers next. . . . Business graduates also suffer greatly. . . . Over 100 different occupations are [affected]. . . . Some of the frequent groups include architects . . . bankers, chemists . . . dieticians, journalists, librarians, social workers, salesmen . . . advertising men . . . artists and biologists. (*School and Society,* March 10, 1934)

From David A. Shannon, *The Great Depression,* 1960

The gravest danger, in the view of most congressmen of both parties, was that the budget might be thrown further out of balance. Yet throughout 1932 the need for federal spending increased. In the words of Senator Edward P. Costigan, Colorado's progressive Democrat, "nothing short of federal assistance . . . can possibly satisfy the conscience and heart and safeguard the good name of America." With La Follette, Costigan introduced a bill granting a modest $375 million for relief, but the administration blocked it. Sensing the political importance of the issue, the Democratic leadership now began to press for direct federal aid to the unemployed and for deficit spending for public works.

Hoover insisted on limiting any relief program to RFC loans to localities and on limiting public works to self-liquidating projects, like bridges and housing, which could return enough income from tolls or rentals to pay back the initial cost of construction. But many states had nearly exhausted their legal authority to borrow from any source, and few projects had emerged from the drawing board. Consequently the president's restrictions put a low ceiling on spending.

Even so, Hoover endorsed a federal program without precedent in American history. After a partisan wrangle, on July 21, 1932, he signed a bill that authorized the RFC to lend $1.5 billion for local self-liquidating public works and $300 million at 3 percent interest to supplement local relief funds. He also approved a large increase in taxes on the incomes of wealthy individuals and profitable corporations.

The relief loans, the president said, were to be based on "absolute need and evidence of financial exhaustion." That limitation kept them small. The governor of Pennsylvania asked for a loan of $45 million (three-fourths of the sum, he noted, that would allow the jobless in the state a mere 13 cents apiece a day for food for a year). The RFC let him have only $11 million (enough for little more than 3 cents a person a day). By the end of 1932 the RFC had allotted only $30 million for relief loans and even less for public works.

Urban Distress

I want to tell you about an experience we had in Philadelphia when our private funds were exhausted and before public funds became available. . . .

One woman said she borrowed 50 cents from a friend and bought stale bread for 3½ cents per loaf, and that is all they had for eleven days except for one or two meals.

With the last food order another woman received she bought dried vegetables and canned goods. With this she made a soup and whenever the members of the family felt hungry they just ate some of the soup. . . .

One woman went along the docks and picked up vegetables that fell from the wagons. Sometimes the fish vendors gave her fish at the end of the day. On two different occasions this family was without food for a day and a half. . . .

Another family did not have food for two days. Then the husband went out and gathered dandelions and the family lived on them.

From Hearings Before a Subcommittee of the Senate Committee on Manufactures, 1932

The outlook of the nation's farmers seemed as hopeless as that of the unemployed workers in the cities. Even before the depression destroyed the European market for farm commodities, the Federal Farm Board had recognized that it could never stabilize farm prices without some control over farm production. When in 1932 American prices followed world prices down to bewildering lows, the stabilization corporations made a brief but futile effort to brake the decline. They lost $354 million in market operations, accumulated huge stocks of unsalable commodities, and finally in the summer simply gave up. Wheat, which had brought $2.16 a bushel in 1919 and $1.03 in 1929, sank to 38 cents. Cotton, corn, and other prices suffered comparably. Farmers found themselves without enough income to meet their mortgage payments or even to buy food for their families. And certainly they lacked the money to buy manufactured goods, which still sold at prices sustained by industry.

The members of the Federal Farm Board urged Congress to do something about regulating acreage and production as a first step in setting up some sort of program for boosting farm prices. The only alternative was agricultural bankruptcy. Yet Hoover and Secretary of Agriculture Hyde rejected the idea of imposing federal controls on agriculture. Before the year ended, farmers were burning corn in Nebraska to keep warm, forming angry posses in Minnesota to prevent foreclosures, and joining Milo Reno's militant Farmers' Holiday Association in Iowa to block the shipment of produce until prices rose.

Moods of Despair Father John Ryan, the Catholic social reformer, despaired for the state of the nation. "I wish," he said, "we might double the number of Communists in this country, to put the fear, if not of God, then . . . of something else, into the hearts of our leaders." Communism had a particular appeal for the intellectuals who had been alienated by the culture of the Coolidge era, men like Malcolm Cowley and Sherwood Anderson. But the theories of Karl Marx had

The Problem of Relief

Unemployment has steadily increased in the U.S. since the beginning of the depression. . . . The number of persons totally unemployed is now at least 10,000,000. . . . The number . . . next winter will . . . be 11,000,000 . . . one man of every four employable workers. . . .

This percentage is higher than the percentage of unemployed British workers . . . and higher than the French, the Italians, and the Canadian percentages, but lower than the German. . . .

Eleven million unemployed means 27,500,000 whose regular source of livelihood has been cut off. . . . Taking account of the number of workers on part time, the total of those without adequate income becomes 34,000,000 or better than a quarter of the entire population. . . . It is conservative to estimate that the problem of next winter's relief is a problem of caring for approximately 25,000,000 souls. . . .

And it is not necessary to appeal . . . to class fear in order to point out that there is a limit beyond which hunger and misery become violent.

From *Fortune,* September 1932

little appeal for the general public, which retained the traditional American aspirations for middle-class status. The Communists organized "hunger marches" in Washington and Detroit and preached revolution elsewhere, but Communist party membership was little more than 100,000.

Though desperate Americans spurned communism, they gave way to hatred and violence. Farmers, brandishing shotguns to prevent foreclosures, defied the law to defend their homes. The president of the Farmers' Union damned the rich as "cannibals . . . who live on the labor of the workers." Some of the prosperous took out "riot and civil commotion insurance" and began to suggest that the United States needed a Fascist dictator like Mussolini.

In the spring of 1932 some 15,000 unemployed veterans converged on Washington from every region of the country. They announced that they planned to stay in the capital until Congress voted full and immediate payment of the bonus. The year before, over Hoover's veto, Congress had authorized loans up to 50 percent of the value of each adjusted service certificate (see p. 640). But those funds had been spent, and the unemployed veterans, like all other unemployed Americans, were in dire need of help. When the Senate voted down the bonus bill, half the veterans went home. But the rest had no place to go and no way of getting there, so they camped in a muddy shantytown on Anacostia Flats and in vacant government buildings.

Their plight evoked the sympathy of the chief of the District of Columbia police, who treated them generously and intelligently. But their presence worried the administration. Hoover, anxious to get rid of them, had Congress pass a bill that permitted them to borrow against their bonus certificates in order to get funds for transportation home. Still most veterans waited around after Congress adjourned. They hoped at least for a conference with the president.

Late in July the administration ordered the eviction of all squatters from government buildings. In the ensuing melee, brought about largely by the small corps

Anacostia Flats, 1932

of Communists among the veterans, two men were killed and several policemen wounded. Secretary of War Patrick Hurley had been looking for just such an incident. At his request, the White House now called in the army—four troops of cavalry and four infantry companies, with six tanks, tear gas, and machine guns. Under the personal command of General Douglas MacArthur (whose junior officers included Dwight D. Eisenhower and George Patton), the troops rode into Anacostia Flats, drove out the veterans and their families, and burned their shacks. Crowing over his triumph, MacArthur called the veterans "a mob . . . animated by the essence of revolution." The administration published reports claiming that most of them had been Communists and criminals.

Neither a grand jury nor the Veterans Administration could find evidence to support those charges. The bonus marchers were destitute men. Whether or not they merited special treatment, they deserved, as did unemployed Americans everywhere, compassion and assistance. They received first indifference and veiled hostility, then vicious armed attack. That treatment appalled the nation.

With government seemingly callous and blundering, with the business élite defensive about the disrepute it had brought on itself, with depression still spreading, Americans began to fear that the whole political and economic system might collapse. Yet they waited patiently, as they had so often before in times of trouble, to see whether the presidential campaign would give them a vote for a brighter future.

The Changing of the Guard In the summer of 1932 the Republicans renominated Hoover and Vice President Charles Curtis. A minority of the delegates to the convention were dissatisfied with the administration's policies but were unwilling to repudiate the president. The convention was listless, for the delegates realized that the electorate, rightly or wrongly, blamed the party for the depression and regarded Hoover as the symbol of the party.

The Democrats, in contrast, sensed victory ahead. A majority of the delegates came to Chicago pledged to Franklin D. Roosevelt, who had been the front runner

F. D. R. on Federal Relief

We have two problems: first, to meet the immediate distress; second, to build up on a basis of permanent employment.

As to "immediate relief," the first principle is that this nation, this national Government, if you like, owes a positive duty that no citizen shall be permitted to starve. . . .

In addition to providing emergency relief, the Federal Government should and must provide temporary work wherever that is possible. You and I know that in the national forests, on flood prevention, and on the development of waterway projects that have already been authorized and planned but not yet executed, tens of thousands, and even hundreds of thousands of our unemployed citizens can be given at least temporary employment. . . .

Third, the Federal Government should expedite the actual construction of public works already authorized. . . .

Finally, in that larger field that looks ahead, we call for a coordinated system of employment exchanges, the advance planning of public works, and unemployment reserves.

From Franklin D. Roosevelt, Campaign Address in Boston, October 1932

for the nomination since his easy reelection as governor of New York in 1930. He had the nerve for politics, the sense of fun, and the zest with people that had once made his distant cousin, Theodore Roosevelt, the most popular man in America. Franklin Roosevelt, moreover, had worked effectively with Tammany Hall, had made friends with the masters of other Northern machines, and yet had preserved close relations with the Southern wing of the party. He closed the gap that had divided the party in 1924. Further, though conservative in his economic thinking, Roosevelt believed in positive, active, humane government.

Roosevelt stood to the left of his serious opponents. Their one hope was to organize a coalition to keep him from getting the two-thirds vote necessary for nomination. Al Smith, still a favorite of the machines, hoped to be nominated once again. Ambition had soured Smith's best instincts. When Roosevelt before the convention called for help for "the forgotten man at the bottom of the economic pyramid," Smith remarked testily, "This is no time for demagogues." But Smith lacked allies. The McAdoo faction still opposed him and now backed Speaker of the House John N. Garner. After Roosevelt had failed to win the necessary vote in three ballots, McAdoo, evening up the old scores of 1924 (see p. 657), switched California's delegation to the New York governor. This put Roosevelt across, and in return his lieutenants arranged second place on the ticket for Garner.

In a characteristically dramatic gesture, Roosevelt broke precedent by flying to Chicago to accept the nomination before the convention adjourned. "Let it . . . be symbolic that . . . I broke traditions," he told the cheering delegates. "Republican leaders not only have failed in material things, they have failed in

Roosevelt in 1932: a real choice

national vision, because in disaster they have held out no hope. . . . I pledge you, I pledge myself to a new deal for the American people."

Roosevelt began to define that New Deal during his campaign. He was often deliberately vague and took pains to avoid offending any large bloc of voters. He hedged on the tariff. He made much of his party's demand for the repeal of the Eighteenth Amendment. Prohibition was still an important political issue in 1932, but it had no immediate bearing on the depression, which was the overriding concern of Americans. But he also set forth strong lines of attack on the nation's economic ills. At the Commonwealth Club in San Francisco, Roosevelt said that "government . . . owes to everyone an avenue to possess himself of a portion of that plenty sufficient for his needs, through his own work." In its dealings with business, government was to "assist the development of . . . an economic constitutional order." And such an order, he pointed out, demanded national planning.

Roosevelt's plans drew on the ideas reformers had nurtured throughout the 1920s and promised assistance to the victims of depression. He called for strict public regulation of the utilities and federal development of public power. He advocated federal controls on agricultural production as a part of a program to support commodity prices and federal loans to refinance farm mortgages. He expressed interest in the schemes for currency inflation that agriculture leaders were urging as a means to raise prices and reduce the weight of debt. He appealed to the business community by demanding cuts in government spending in order to balance the budget, but in the same speech he also promised to incur a deficit whenever human suffering made it necessary.

Roosevelt's oratorical flair and personal ebullience contrasted with Hoover's heavy speech and grim manner. The president emphasized his dedication to budget-balancing and the gold standard, defended his record, and charged his opponent with recklessness. The policies Roosevelt advocated, Hoover said, "would destroy the very foundations of our American system." If they were adopted, "grass will grow in the streets of a hundred cities, a thousand towns."

That rhetoric obscured his own expansion of federal control, and it exaggerated Roosevelt's intentions. Actually the Democrat's campaign disappointed many intellectuals who felt, as Walter Lippmann earlier had, that Franklin Roosevelt was "a highly impressionable person . . . without strong convictions . . . a pleasant man, who, without any important qualifications for the office, would very much like to be President."

But there were significant differences between the two candidates and their ideas, between Hoover's pessimism and Roosevelt's effervescence, between Hoover's belief that the origins of the depression lay outside the United States and Roosevelt's belief that they were internal, between Hoover's impulse toward caution and Roosevelt's impulse toward experiment, between Hoover's identification with industry and finance and Roosevelt's identification with the forgotten and with the intellectuals and social workers who championed them. Hoover in his last campaign speech was right in associating Roosevelt with Norris and La Follette, right in asserting that the contest was between two philosophies of government. Both philosophies were fundamentally American, but Hoover's looked backward, while Roosevelt's looked hopefully ahead.

The people had a real choice when they went to the polls in November. Dismissing radicalism (the Socialists—rent by factionalism—polled 881,951 votes, the Communists, only 102,785), they swept the Democrats into office. Roosevelt won over 57 percent of the popular vote and carried the Electoral College 472 to 59. The Democrats also gained a large majority in both houses of Congress. The vote, a protest against the administration, gave Roosevelt a clear mandate for change, though the nature of that change was clear neither to the voters nor the victor. Roosevelt lost only six states, all in the Northeast. He carried the agricultural West as well as the South. He carried the great cities by majorities larger than Smith's in 1928.

Depression had driven a majority of Americans of all backgrounds into the Roosevelt column. Among them, farmers and workers after twelve lean years could again expect to have some voice in Washington. The total vote repudiated business, its policies and its servants; threw out the Old Guard; and placed the direction of government in a new president who saw himself as a tribune of the people.

SUGGESTIONS FOR READING

HOOVER AND HIS POLICIES

A. M. Schlesinger, Jr., *The Crisis of the Old Order* (1957), provides a critical and detailed analysis of the Hoover administration and its problems as does the more generous account in D. Burner, *Herbert Hoover* (1978). Also critical, though the authors intend to be sympathetic, are H. G. Warren, *Herbert Hoover and the Great Depression* (1956), and J. A. Schwarz, *The Interregnum of Despair* (1970). The relevant chapters in J. D. Hicks, *Republican Ascendancy: 1921–1933* (1960), and J. H. Wilson, *Herbert Hoover* (1975), are unsympathetic and those in W. E. Leuchtenburg, *The Perils of Prosperity: 1914–32* (1958), lucid but brief. Two incisive works are A. Romasco, *The Poverty of Abundance: Hoover, the Nation, the Depression* (1965), and E. Rosen, *Hoover, Roosevelt and the Brain Trust* (1977). The most ardent defense of the administration appears in Herbert Hoover, *Memoirs: The Great Depression, 1929–1941* (1952). On Hoover's foreign policies, there is significant material in the biographies of Stimson mentioned in connection with the preceding chapter, and in R. H. Ferrell, *American Diplomacy in the Great Depression: Hoover-Stimson Foreign Policy, 1929–1933* (1957).

DEPRESSION

All the volumes noted above of course deal with the Great Depression. Its impact is also poignantly revealed in the pertinent parts of S. Terkel, *Hard Times* (1970); I. Bernstein, *The Lean Years* (1960); C. Bird, *The Invisible Scar* (1965); B. Sternsher, ed., *Hitting Home* (1970); J. Shover, *Cornbelt Rebellion* (1965); and D. A. Shannon, ed., *The Great Depression* (1960). There are excellent descriptions of the stock market crash in F. L. Allen, *Only Yesterday* (1931), and J. K. Galbraith, *The Great Crash, 1929* (1955). The skillful analysis of the latter should be compared with the also able view in T. Wilson,

Fluctuations in Income and Employment (1948), with the important chapters on Hoover in H. Stein, *The Fiscal Revolution in America* (1969), and in C. P. Kindleberger, *The World in Depression, 1929–1939* (1973); and with the special view of central banking policy in M. Friedman and A. J. Schwartz, *The Great Contraction, 1929–1933* (1965) and in P. Temin, *Did Monetary Forces Cause the Great Depression?* (1976). Within his excellent general study of American radical intellectuals, *Writers on the Left* (1961), D. Aaron discusses the influence of the depression on the spread of radicalism, as does R. H. Pells in his *Radical Visions and American Dreams* (1973).

FDR AND 1932

Franklin D. Roosevelt's governorship and first presidential campaign receive important treatment in A. M. Schlesinger's work, mentioned above, which is brilliant and panoramic on those subjects, and in F. Freidel, *Franklin D. Roosevelt: The Triumph* (1956), a work of outstanding scholarship. Less comprehensive are parts of J. M. Burns, *Roosevelt: The Lion and the Fox* (1956); R. G. Tugwell, *The Democratic Roosevelt* (1957); and K. S. Davis, *FDR: The New York Years* (1985).

CHAPTER TWENTY-SEVEN

WPA: PUTTING PEOPLE TO WORK

THE NEW DEAL

During the winter of 1932–33, the despair born of depression gripped the United States ever more tightly. The four-month interval between the November election and the inauguration of March 1933 found Hoover without influence and Roosevelt without power. Hoover impeded any chance of collaboration with his successor by insisting on policies Roosevelt had condemned. In February, when the president called on Roosevelt to make a series of conservative declarations, he privately wrote a Republican senator, "I realize that if these declarations be made by the President-Elect, he will have ratified the whole major program of the Republican Administration." The incoming president, interpreting Hoover's invitation as a request for capitulation rather than cooperation, naturally rejected it, as he was, in any event, inclined to.

Without making public commitments to any program, Roosevelt awaited his day to take charge. Americans, worried and gloomy, also awaited the change of command, their anxieties deepened by an attempt upon Roosevelt's life by a madman in Miami, Florida, in February. The electorate had no sure sense of what a new deal might bring them, but they had clinching evidence that the old deal was ending in disaster.

The spreading panic was engulfing the banking system. As the economy continued downward, more and more people played it safe by converting their savings to cash. The mounting pressure on financial institutions, the lines of depositors waiting to draw out their savings, the threat of further runs on the banks, led the governor of Michigan in mid-February to proclaim a bank holiday—that is, to order the temporary closing of the banks in his state. That act set off a chain reaction in other states. On the last day of Hoover's administration, with banks shutting their doors across the land, the retiring president said, "We are at the end of our rope. There is nothing more we can do."

FRANKLIN D. ROOSEVELT

His Background The new president was 51 years old. Like his distant cousin Theodore, he had come from a patrician background that gave him both a high sense of civic responsibility and a certain disdain for those whose chief achievement was making money. Like Theodore, Franklin Roosevelt was a man of charm, vivacity, and energy. He had been much influenced by Theodore, and their careers offered curious parallels. Both had made their political debuts in the New York legislature; both had served as assistant secretary of the navy in Washington; both had been governor of New York; both had been candidates for the vice presidency.

Lines of depression, 1933: "The end of our rope"

Unlike Theodore, Franklin was a member of the Democratic branch of the Roosevelt family. He was less of an intellectual than Theodore, but also less moralistic and evangelical. His urbane and conciliatory manner, indeed, led some observers to suppose him too compliant for hard responsibilities and decisions. But as second in command in the Navy Department during the First World War, he had been a resourceful executive. As candidate for vice president in 1920, he had been a vigorous campaigner. In 1921 he had been stricken by poliomyelitis. That illness deprived him of the use of his legs. Many thought it would end his public career. The determination of his comeback revealed an inner spirit that was not only gallant but tough. He had been an imaginative governor of New York. No state had taken so many positive measures to meliorate the effects of depression. His capture of the Democratic nomination in 1932 was the work of a seasoned politician.

The superficial affability of Roosevelt's manner concealed a complex personality—at once lighthearted and somber, candid and disingenuous, open and impenetrable, bold and cautious, decisive and evasive. Throughout his life he pursued certain public ends—especially the improvement of welfare and opportunity for the great masses of people—with steadiness of purpose. But the means he employed to achieve those ends were often inconsistent and occasionally unworthy. Yet his capacity to project the grand moral issues of his day—and his readiness to use the resources of presidential leadership to prepare the country for necessary action—enabled him to command the confidence of a great majority of Americans during his terms in office, despite the persistent opposition of a powerful minority.

His Ideas Roosevelt was a child of the Progressive Era. Theodore Roosevelt and Woodrow Wilson had been his early inspirations. Government seemed to him a necessary instrument of the general welfare, and he had no inhibitions about calling on the state. The problems of 1933 were novel. Progressivism had been a gospel of social improvement rather than a program for economic growth, and progressives were no less baffled than conservatives by economic collapse. But, where faith in laissez-faire constrained conservatives from taking positive government action, progressives like Roosevelt, with an adventurous attitude toward social policy, were ready to invoke affirmative government to bring about economic recovery.

In economics, Roosevelt had leanings rather than theories. In his campaign for the presidency, he had identified himself with two main ideas—action and planning. As to what should be tried, his views were sometimes incompatible.

Certain of his advisers had more clear-cut ideas. A group of college professors, mostly recruited from Columbia University, had served as his campaign brain trust. A book of 1932, *The Modern Corporation and Private Property,* by Adolf A. Berle, Jr., and Gardiner C. Means, provided one foundation for their analysis. The trend toward economic concentration, they contended, was irreversible. Already it had transformed great parts of the old free market of classical economics into "administered" markets, in which basic economic decisions were made, not by equations of supply and demand, but by the policies of those who ran the great corporations. That change in the structure of the market rendered classical laissez-faire theory obsolete.

So persuaded, another Columbia economist, Rexford G. Tugwell, urged the president-elect to bold conclusions. If concentration was inevitable, Tugwell argued, then control over the nation's economic life could not be safely left in private hands. Such private control had brought about the depression. In the 1920s the gains of economic productivity had gone into profits, savings, and speculation when they should have gone into a buildup of purchasing power through the payment of higher wages to workers and higher prices to farmers. The only way to operate the modern integrated economy at capacity, in Tugwell's view, was organized public planning.

Men like Berle, Tugwell, Means, and Raymond Moley, who acted as nominal head of the brain trust, were in a sense heirs of Theodore Roosevelt's New Nationalism. Their predisposition toward new institutions for central planning was reinforced by the views of those who, recalling America's last national emergency, the First World War, reverted to wartime economic agencies in the battle against depression. Now men who had once been associated with the War Industries Board, men like Bernard Baruch, Hugh S. Johnson, and George N. Peek, began to sponsor schemes of industrial and agricultural planning, though with little of Tugwell's zeal for accompanying social reform.

Not all those around Roosevelt accepted the virtues of national planning. Others close to him—especially Associate Justice Louis D. Brandeis of the Supreme Court and Professor Felix Frankfurter of Harvard—rejected the thesis of inevitable economic concentration. They distrusted the idea of central planning and advocated policies designed to encourage more competition. Still others, though these were more powerful in the Democratic party in Congress than in the president's immediate circle, were inflationists in the tradition of William Jennings Bryan. And others, like Lewis W. Douglas, whom Roosevelt was about to appoint Director of the Budget, were sound-money, laissez-faire Democrats deeply committed, like the Republicans, to the gold standard and the annually balanced budget. As now one, now another, of these groups exerted a telling influence, the resulting policies on occasion clashed.

Roosevelt presided benignly over the clash of debate and policy alike. Disagreement stimulated him, enabled him to compare the merits of competing arguments and reassured him that crucial questions would come to him for decision. His choice of Cabinet members reflected his confidence that he could control advisers of divergent opinion. To the State Department he named Cordell Hull, a Tennessee Democrat who had sponsored the income tax amendment in 1913 but who was now cautious in his views except as a passionate foe of international trade barriers. Two vigorous progressive Republicans—Henry A. Wallace of Iowa and Harold L. Ickes of Illinois—were appointed to Agriculture and Interior; the first woman in history to go into the Cabinet, Frances Perkins of New York, a veteran social worker, became secretary of labor; and the other posts were filled largely by Democratic politicians.

THE HUNDRED DAYS

The Inauguration On March 4, 1933, millions of Americans clustered around their radios to hear the new president deliver his inaugural address. "Let me assert my firm belief," Roosevelt began, "that the only thing we have to fear is fear itself." Then he assailed the business leaders whose incompetence and misconduct, he said, had been largely responsible for the economic disaster. "This Nation asks for action, and action now," he concluded, adding that he would seek from Congress "broad Executive powers to wage a war against the emergency, as great as the power that would be given to me if we were in fact invaded by a foreign foe."

Action itself was quick to follow. Immediately after the inauguration, Roosevelt declared a national bank holiday and called Congress into special session. When Congress convened on March 8, it received at once a special message on the banking crisis and a draft of emergency banking legislation. In less than eight hours the House and Senate shouted through the bill. The new legislation made it possible for banks to convert assets into cash. That liquidity permitted almost all banks to reopen, reassuring depositors who no longer withdrew their money in panic. The few insolvent banks were put under control of federal "conservators" who reorganized their affairs. The unprecedented combination of decision and speed in the passage of the act electrified the country.

Quick to seize advantage of the national mood, the president put forward a bill calling for the reduction of government expenses, including veterans' pensions. He followed his economy message with a call for the amendment of the Volstead Act to legalize light wines and beers. The prompt enactment of both the economy and the beer bills increased the national sense of exhilaration. "In one week," wrote Walter Lippmann, "the nation, which had lost confidence in everything and everybody, has regained confidence in the government and in itself."

Planning for Agriculture So far the Roosevelt program had been dashing in style but orthodox in content. Now, focusing on the problem of recovery, the president followed the path of the planners who advocated using the power of the federal government to "rationalize" and to help to manage agriculture and industry. On March 16, Roosevelt sent to Capitol Hill a message calling for a bold national policy in agriculture. "An unprecedented condition," he said, "calls for the trial of new means."

The condition was indeed unprecedented. The per capita cash net income of the American farmer had declined from $162 to $48 between 1929 and 1932. Because farm prices had fallen faster than industrial prices, the farmer's purchasing power was only about 60 percent of what it had been in 1929. The farmer's fixed charges—especially the burden of mortgage debt assumed at higher price levels—weighed more heavily than ever. Since the individual farmer saw no way to fight falling prices except to increase production, more produce was sent to market and prices were driven down further. Some farmers, instead, destroyed their crops.

The central idea in the administration proposal was "agricultural adjustment." This plan aimed to increase farm income by controlling production. It aimed to control production by offering benefit payments to farmers who agreed to regulate their plantings according to a national plan. The adjustment programs were to be financed by processing taxes collected at the flour mill or textile mill or packinghouse. No program would go into effect until a majority of farmers indicated they wanted it by voting in a referendum. The local administration of the plan was to be as much as possible in the hands of the farmers themselves. The ultimate object was to restore to farmers substantially the purchasing power they had had in 1909–14. That concept was known as "parity."

The agricultural-adjustment bill incorporated a number of other approaches to the farm problem. It gave the government authority to maintain prices through loans on nonperishable crops, which would then go into government storage. It also conferred authority to withdraw land from cultivation through leasing and to regulate the release of commodities for sale through marketing agreements. Through the use of those powers the government could not only prevent gluts on the market but could build up reserves against lean years. The inflationists in Congress added an important amendment giving the president power to issue greenbacks, to remonetize silver, and to alter the gold content of the dollar. In the meantime, the newly created Farm Credit Administration provided effective mortgage relief.

While Washington laid its plans, trouble was mounting in the countryside. In late April a mob

Plowing up the cotton

marched on a judge in Le Mars, Iowa, who had refused to suspend foreclosure proceedings, and nearly lynched him. The Farmer's Holiday Association renewed its threat of a farm strike. The governor of Iowa called out the national guard and placed half a dozen counties under martial law.

Those developments speeded passage of the Agricultural Adjustment Act on May 12. It established the Agricultural Adjustment Administration (AAA), which had at once to cut down production in areas already overwhelmed by surpluses. Thus a carryover from previous years of 8 million bales of cotton had driven cotton prices down to 5 cents a pound. Yet, by the time the act had passed, some 40 million acres had already been planted in new cotton. The only way to save the cotton growers was to persuade them to plow under the planted crop in return for benefit payments. This the AAA proceeded to do, as it also relieved the market glut in corn and hogs by buying and slaughtering some 5 million little pigs.

No one perceived more sharply the irony of destroying plenty in the midst of want than the men who ordered the job to be done. "To destroy a standing crop goes against the soundest instincts of human nature," said Henry Wallace. Yet industry, he pointed out, had in effect plowed under much of its potential output after 1929 by cutting down on production; how could agriculture be denied the same right of self-protection?

The terrible logic of scarcity worked. As production declined—aided, in the cases of wheat and corn, by the searing droughts of 1933–34—prices rose. Between 1932 and 1936 gross farm income increased by 50 percent, and cash receipts from marketing (including government benefit payments) nearly doubled. The parity ratio rose from 55 in 1932 to 90 in 1936. The chief beneficiaries were commercial farmers, owners of large holdings and recipients of a disproportionate share of benefit payments. Many owners of family-sized farms also benefited, though tenant farmers and sharecroppers suffered (see p. 708).

Planning for Industry Agricultural planning covered only the lesser part of the American economy. By 1933 American industry was employing some 5 million fewer workers than in 1929 and producing less than half the value of goods. Businesses, striving to maintain a margin of profits, had lowered wages and laid off employees. But the more wages and employment were reduced, the more mass purchasing power declined.

There was increasing agreement that the only way to stop the industrial decline was through joint planning by government and business. This view was backed not just by some of Roosevelt's advisers but by powerful voices in business, especially the United States Chamber of Commerce, which now urged that private trade associations be given authority to fix prices, divide markets, and "stabilize" industrial production. Recovery, they argued, depended on limiting the play of "savage and wolfish individualism."

In the spring, the administration worked out its national industrial-recovery bill, divided into two parts. The first part was designed "to promote the organization of industry for the purpose of cooperative action among trade groups" through codes of fair competition that granted exemption from the antitrust laws. An important provision—the celebrated Section 7a—sought to win labor support by offering federal guarantees of the right of trade unions to organize and bargain collectively. The second part of the bill provided for the establishment of a Public Works Administration with an appropriation of $3.3 billion. Roosevelt signed the bill on June 16, calling it "a challenge to industry, which has long insisted that, given the right to act in unison, it could do much for the general good which has hitherto been unlawful. From today it has that right."

Two agencies were set up under the National Industrial Recovery Act—the National Recovery Administration (NRA), with General Johnson as head, and the Public Works Administration (PWA), under Harold L. Ickes. Slow to develop projects that met his high standards of efficiency and honesty, Ickes spent his funds too sparingly to boost the economy. But Johnson saw the NRA as a national crusade designed to restore employment and regenerate industry in an excitement of torchlight processions and giant rallies. Finding the negotiation of codes with specific industries disappointingly slow, Johnson came up in July with the idea of a "blanket code" in which cooperating employers would pledge themselves to observe NRA standards on minimum wages and maximum hours. The Blue Eagle, modeled on the American Indian thunderbird, became the symbol of compliance. Briefly, in the revivalist atmosphere conjured up by Johnson, the Blue Eagle soared. Two million employers accepted the blanket code, and the great industries of the country began to accept special codes.

Protected from competition by those codes, managers were able to stop cutting prices and with them wages. But the codes also protected marginal firms

that might best have been allowed to fail, as well as strong firms that could have produced at a profit at prices lower than those that tended to obtain. Further the codes decreased the probability of investment in new, improved facilities. Yet new capital investment would have helped to stimulate the overall economy.

Those liabilities were balanced in part by the attempts of the NRA to pursue some of the long-term objectives of American reformers. In the economic field, it hoped to bring about permanent reemployment by raising wages and shortening working hours. In the social field, it sought the abolition of child labor, an improvement of working conditions, an encouragement of labor organization, an extension of fair trade practices.

Soon the NRA began to overextend its efforts. Instead of concentrating on codification in the major industries, it often set codes for local and service trades. There was good humanitarian reason for this effort, for these were the trades where the sweatshop was most deeply entrenched. But it involved the NRA in a host of petty enforcement problems, which distracted its energies and dissipated its credit. Johnson

National Planning and the NRA

If we could have perfect balance among all producing segments—agriculture, capital, industry, workers in industry . . . there would be almost no limit to our consuming capacity. . . . All law, all administration . . . should be directed toward that goal. . . . *The essence of the New Deal is to point toward that balance. . . .*

That is the reason for NRA, AAA, PWA and all the loan and fiscal acts. . . . The most obvious, immediate way to erase the effect of the depression on wages and hours was the NRA project to decrease hours . . . and to increase wages to maintain purchasing power. . . .

We relied . . . on PWA to activate the heavy industries . . . and thus increase the *total number of available purchasers.* We relied on AAA to increase farm purchasing power . . . and thus still further add to the *number of purchasers.* These added to NRA additions would so far increase *volume* that we thought . . . the increased labor cost could be absorbed without much increase in price. . . . We also relied on the principle . . . that many men with a little each is a far better market than one man with much, and all the rest with nothing.

From Hugh Johnson, *The Blue Eagle from Egg to Earth,* 1935

was reluctant to use the NRA's coercive powers, since he wanted to avoid a court test of the NRA's constitutionality. Consequently his chief reliance was on public opinion. So long as the nation felt itself in acute crisis, this compulsion worked. But as soon as economic conditions began to grow better, more and more employers tried to beat the codes.

Within the NRA, moreover, there was constant pressure from trade associations to use the code mechanism as a means of raising prices. Many business executives felt that price fixing would be an appropriate quid pro quo for their concessions on wages, hours, and collective bargaining. But many inside the NRA and out argued that excessive price increases would defeat the policy of expanding purchasing power and turn the codes into a vehicle for the sort of monopoly Congress had tried to outlaw in the Sherman Act. An investigation by a special committee in 1934 under the chair of Clarence Darrow, the criminal lawyer, seemed to substantiate that charge.

In the meantime the labor provisions in Section 7a had given a great stimulus to trade-union organization, and this embittered many employers. Hugh Johnson's unstable personality and increasingly erratic course further complicated the NRA's existence. Roosevelt forced him out in the fall of 1934 and replaced him by a five-man board. By now the NRA had lost its allure. By 1935 most people — except for the trade associations and the trade unions — were against NRA. When the Supreme Court then declared the National Industrial Recovery Act unconstitutional, the administration accepted the verdict with relief. From the outset it had been seeking other roads to recovery and reform.

The End of the Hundred Days The AAA and the NRA set the pattern of national planning and were, in this sense, crucial measures of the early New Deal. But they by no means exhausted the achievement of the special session of 1933. During the Hundred Days after March 4, 1933, Roosevelt sent 15 messages to Congress and saw 15 major bills through to enactment.

Advocates of inflation, strongest in Congress but vocal also within the executive branch, were eager to relieve the burden of debt contracted when the price level was much higher. Since the closing of the banks and the Economy Act had a deflationary impact, the administration looked, too, for means to induce a general price increase. Conservative officials opposed anything that savored of inflation. In contrast, many Southern and Western congressmen demanded either a massive printing of greenbacks or an extensive monetization of silver. Those prospects had broad support among farmers and even some members of the business community. Roosevelt himself had no desire for currency inflation, but he was determined to bring about a rise of prices — not so fast as to absorb the increases in wages and farm income but fast enough to reduce the drag of debt on the economy. It seemed evident to him that the United States had to choose between the old gold standard and the price-raising policy. On April 18, 1933, the president abandoned the gold standard officially by executive orders authorizing the control of the flow of gold from the United States. In a few weeks Congress confirmed the departure from gold by passing a resolution providing for the abrogation of the gold clause in public and private contracts.

In the meantime, the inflationist amendment to the Agricultural Adjustment Act (see p. 698) had bestowed a variety of monetary powers on the president. He protected the independence of American monetary policy by refusing at the London Economic Conference in July to peg the dollar at a fixed value in international exchange. In so doing, he shocked the British and Europeans, but he kept his own options open. When farm prices sagged in November, Roosevelt embarked on a program designed to raise the level of prices, especially commodity prices, by Treasury purchases of gold. The program, though lacking economic validity, permitted Roosevelt to retain control of monetary policy at a time when both inflationists and bankers were demanding that he take action that he deemed positively harmful. By January 1934 the experiment had obviously failed to raise prices, but the pressure for inflation had abated. The administration then stabilized the dollar at $35 for an ounce of gold, 59.06 percent of the pre-1933 gold value. Roosevelt also guided through Congress the Gold Act of 1934, which gave the Treasury large new authority in managing the value of the dollar abroad and the conditions of credit at home.

The gold policy, along with the banking and securities legislation of 1933–34, shifted the financial capital of the nation from Wall Street to Washington. The adventure in inflation and the Treasury's use of its new powers established a continuing policy of "cheap money" — that is, low interest rates. Those low rates made private borrowing more attractive and the financing of government borrowing less expensive. But the inducement to private or public investment proved inadequate, for the private sector still envisaged small opportunities for profit and the administration still hesitated deliberately to incur heavy deficits. Like planning for industry, inflation and cheap money did not produce recovery. They did establish public authority over an area of economic activity that private power had previously dominated. That authority was expanded by a landmark act of 1935 that amended the Federal Reserve Act of 1913. The earlier statute had left most of the authority over the banking system with the regional Federal Reserve Banks, which were dominated by private bankers. The new law concentrated authority in the Board of Governors of the Federal Reserve System, the public agency in Washington, which now had direct control over the volume of money and credit.

The Securities Act of 1933, a first step toward disciplining the practices of Wall Street, required full disclosure of relevant information in the issuance of new securities, and the Glass-Steagall Act, also of 1933, provided for the separation of commercial and investment banking in order to limit speculation by banks. Legislation in 1934 strengthened the Securities Act and established the Securities and Exchange Commission to prevent and punish misrepresentation and fraud in the securities business.

Other actions of the Hundred Days were designed at once to help the banks and to reduce the human cost of depression. The Home Owners' Loan Act saved countless homes by providing means for the refinancing of mortgages. That refinancing, along with the similar operations of the Farm Credit Administration for agricultural mortgages, protected homes and farms from foreclosure and assisted banks and insurance companies as well. In return for mortgages that were not being paid, those lending institutions received government bonds that they could always convert to cash and on which regular interest payments were assured. Still another New Deal measure, the Federal Deposit Insurance Corporation, set up a system for the insurance of savings and demand deposits and thereby helped restore confidence in the banks. That restoration revealed the New Deal's commitment to saving capitalism while reforming it.

More precedent-breaking was the Federal Emergency Relief Act, which established for the first time a

Civilian Conservation Corps: a useful role

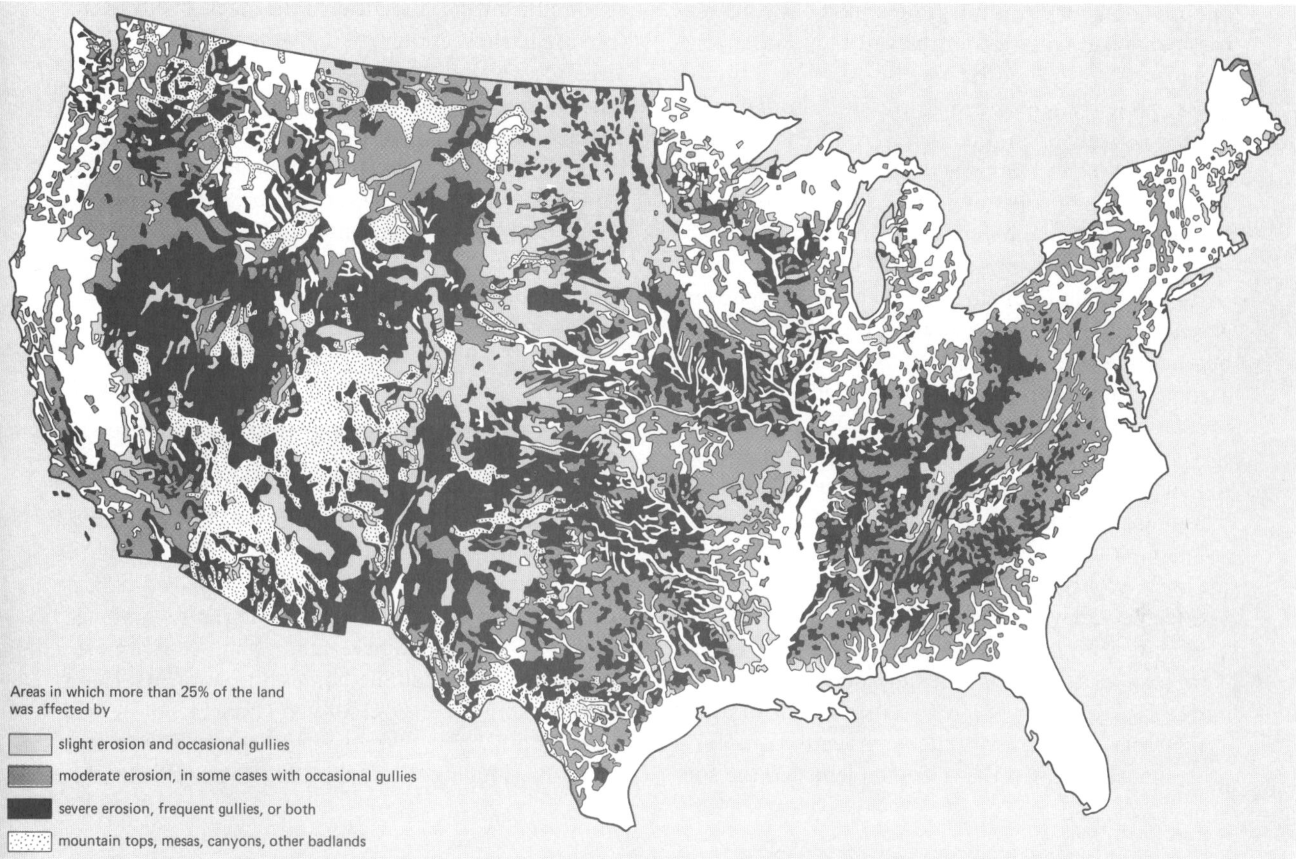

Map 27-1 *The extent of erosion, 1935*

system of federal relief. Under the resourceful direction of Harry L. Hopkins, a New York social worker, the new relief agency rapidly supplied the states with cash for immediate assistance to the indigent unemployed. Hopkins the next winter began to experiment with "work relief"—jobs rather than handouts—a program that pointed toward the policies Congress endorsed in 1935.

Another measure of the Hundred Days linked work relief to the conservation of natural resources. This was the Civilian Conservation Corps (CCC), an organization that recruited young men between the ages of 18 and 25 to work in the countryside. CCC camps, set up in all parts of the country, played a useful role in protecting and developing reservoirs, watersheds, forests, and parks. The dust storms of the early 1930s, whirling up from the parched and eroded land of the Great Plains, emphasized the need for a revitalized national conservation policy (see Map 27-1). A "shelter-belt" of trees was planted along the 100th meridian from Canada to Texas. Other measures were undertaken to promote reforestation, to control overgrazing, and to encourage farmers to adopt soil-conservation practices.

In some respects the most striking innovation of the Hundred Days was an effort to rescue an entire region. The Tennessee Valley was a conspicuous example of what later generations would know as an "underdeveloped" territory. Recurrent floods washed away the topsoil, the forests were thin and overcut, income was less than half the national average, and in the highland counties more than half the families were on relief. Only two out of every 100 farms had electricity. Yet the Valley also contained one of the most valuable power sites in the country, at Muscle Shoals, Alabama. And some people, especially Senator George W. Norris of Nebraska, saw in cheap electric power the means of transforming life in the Valley. But Norris's bill providing for government operation of hydroelectric plants had fallen under the vetoes of Republican presidents.

Many factors—some opportunities, some problems—converged in the Valley: not only electric power and conservation but fertilizer production, flood control, inland waterways, and, above all, the hopeless cycle of human poverty. In a bold change of perspective, Roosevelt now saw all these elements as parts of a single problem. The solution, he believed, was not a collection of separate and unrelated reforms but multipurpose development under the direction of a single authority. In April 1933 he called on Congress to establish "a corporation clothed with the power of Government but possessed of the flexibility and initiative of a private enterprise" charged with "national planning for a complete river watershed."

Despite the opposition of the power companies of the area, Congress passed the bill establishing the Tennessee Valley Authority (TVA) in May 1933. The TVA proved to be one of the most successful of all New Deal undertakings. Seeking local collaboration under TVA director David E. Lilienthal's slogan of "grassroots democracy," the TVA built dams and powerhouses, cleared the rivers, replenished the soil, rebuilt the forests, and brought the magic of electricity into the farthest corners of the Valley (see Map 27-2). Grassroots democracy in the Valley proved to be for whites only. Without protest from Washington, local agencies working with TVA systematically excluded black Americans from participation and benefits. Yet for white Americans, at least, the region vibrated with a new life. Soon visitors came from all over the world to inspect the result. No other New Deal agency had such an international impact.

THE STRUGGLE FOR RECOVERY

The Conquest of Fear The Hundred Days induced a tremendous revival of confidence. In this revival the personality of the president himself played a basic role. His speeches, his radio "fireside chats," his twice-a-week press conferences made him seem almost a constant presence in the homes of Americans. He radiated energy, decision, and good cheer. Along with the administrative inventiveness and political audacity in Washington, he convinced the people that they

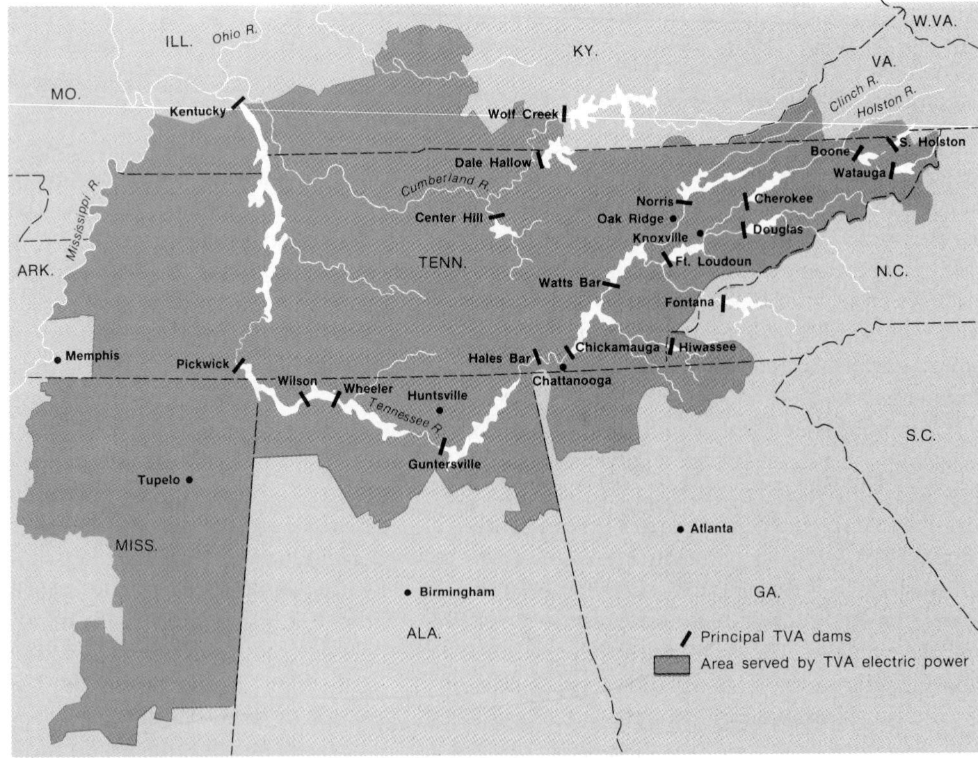

Map 27-2
The Tennessee Valley Authority

had a chance to recover control of their economic destiny.

During 1933 Roosevelt enjoyed almost universal support. As the crisis receded, however, opposition began to emerge—first from the business community on Roosevelt's right, then in a clamor of discordant voices on his left. At the start his critics made little dent in his popularity. The congressional election of 1934 provided an almost unprecedented national endorsement of the president's program. The administration actually increased its strength in both the House and the Senate, and the Republicans were left with the governorship of only seven states. Many of the new Democrats came to Congress from urban districts and were especially responsive to labor and welfare concerns.

Critics, Right and Left Roosevelt confronted the congressional session of 1935 with top-heavy majorities in both houses, but the policy momentum of 1933 had begun to slacken. Full economic recovery still seemed distant, and the voices of criticism were now speaking out with new confidence. The American Liberty League, an organization formed in 1934 by a group of conservative business leaders and politicians, called for minimalist government and offered the most active opposition on the right. On the left the most powerful of the new leaders was Huey Long of Louisiana.

As governor of Louisiana, Long had brought new roads and schools and textbooks to the state, but the price of his impressive program of social improvement was spreading corruption and repression. By 1935 he ruled his native state almost as a dictator. In national politics, Long's role was more that of a demagogue. His "Share Our Wealth" movement, which stressed heavy taxation of the rich and large handouts to the poor, reminded Americans of the need for social justice. But Long used his program primarily as a means of stirring existing resentments in the hope that the Kingfish, as Long fondly called himself, could be propelled into the presidency.

Another rising leader was a California physician, Dr. Francis E. Townsend, who proposed a $200 monthly pension for all those over age 60. They were to spend the money in the month they received it, in order, so the theory went, to boost the economy. The aged had suffered deeply from the depression, and the Townsend Plan seemed for a while in 1935 to be developing genuine mass support. Both Long and Townsend were openly hostile to the New Deal. A third leader, Father Charles E. Coughlin, the famous "radio priest" of Royal Oak, Michigan, had originally endorsed Roosevelt but by 1935 was drifting into opposition. He established in that year the National Union for Social Justice, an organization that appealed especially to the nativist and inflationist traditions of the Middle West and to Irish Catholics of the great cities. Coughlin's particular nostrum was the nationalization of the banks.

Huey Long: "share the wealth"

Long, Townsend, and Coughlin were hawking competing patent medicines for the nation's economic ills. But they drew their following from much the same audience—baffled and disoriented members of the lower-middle class who were seeking attention and protection. They drew, too, from rural Americans, many of them now removed to the cities, who resented the impersonality and unfamiliarity of industrialism and urbanism, and who neither understood nor accepted the nature of the modern industrial state. The emergence of the new movements signified a discontent that the president could not ignore.

The Scope of Congressional Power: A Limiting View

In determining how far the federal government may go in controlling intrastate transactions upon the ground that they "affect" interstate commerce, there is a necessary and well-established distinction between direct and indirect effects. . . .

If the commerce clause were construed to reach all enterprises and transactions which could be said to have an indirect effect upon interstate commerce, the federal authority would embrace practically all the activities of the people and the authority of the state over its domestic concerns would exist only by suffrance of the federal government. . . .

There would be virtually no limit to the federal power, and for all practical purposes we should have a completely centralized government. We must consider the provisions here in question in the light of this distinction.

The question of chief importance relates to the provisions of the [NRA] code as to the hours and wages of those employed. . . . It is plain that these requirements are imposed in order to govern the details of defendants' management of their local business. The persons employed . . . are not employed in interstate commerce. Their wages have no direct relation to interstate commerce. . . .

The authority of the federal government may not be pushed to such an extreme.

From the Majority Opinion of the United States Supreme Court by Chief Justice Charles E. Hughes, *Schechter* v. *United States,* 295 U.S. 495, 1935

Stalemate in 1935 Though the policies of the Hundred Days had ended despair, they had not produced recovery. The gross national product, though nearly $20 billion larger than in 1933, was still $30 billion less than in 1929. Four million more workers were employed in 1935 than in 1933, but 9 million were still unemployed. Roosevelt was still in economic trouble and, as the clamor of the demagogues and the fractiousness of the new Congress made clear, might fall into political trouble. He needed a new forward thrust of policy to maintain his control.

The Supreme Court further increased the pressure against the policies of 1933. For two years the administration had delayed tests of the constitutionality of New Deal legislation, but now the dam was breaking. In 1935 the gold resolution of 1933, one of the foundations of the nation's monetary policy, barely escaped judicial veto in a bitter and ambiguous five-to-four decision. Then the Court, in another five-to-four decision, declared against the whole idea of a federal pension act for railroad employees. And on May 27, 1935, "Black Monday," the Court in three sweeping decisions killed a farm-mortgage-relief act, rebuked the president for what it declared to be an illegal exercise of his removal power, and condemned the National Industrial Recovery Act as unconstitutional.

In the NRA case, the Court pronounced unanimously against the Recovery Act because it delegated excessive powers to the executive. A majority of the Court also ruled that the act ascribed to Congress

The Scope of Congressional Power: A Broader View

The statute goes no further than to safeguard the right of employees to self-organization and to select representatives of their own choosing for collective bargaining. . . .

Respondent says that whatever may be said of employees engaged in interstate commerce, the industrial relations and activities in the manufacturing department of respondent's enterprise are not subject to federal regulation. . . .

The congressional authority to protect interstate commerce from burdens and obstructions is not limited to transactions which can be deemed to be an essential part of a "flow" of interstate or foreign commerce. Burdens and obstructions may be due to injurious action springing from other sources. The fundamental principle is that the power to regulate commerce is the power to enact "all appropriate legislation" for its "protection and advancement." . . . That power is plenary and may be exerted to protect interstate commerce "no matter what the source of the dangers which threaten it." . . . Although activities may be intrastate in character when separately considered, if they have such a close and substantial relation to interstate commerce that their control is essential or appropriate to protect that commerce from burdens and obstructions, Congress cannot be denied the power to exercise that control. . . .

The close and intimate effect which brings the subject within the reach of federal power may be due to activities in relation to productive industry although the industry when separately viewed is local.

From the Majority Opinion of the United States Supreme Court by Chief Justice Charles E. Hughes, *National Labor Relations Board* v. *Jones and Laughlin Steel Corporation,* 301 U.S. 1, 1937

powers of economic regulation that could not be justified under the commerce clause. This second objection was particularly devastating. The language used in the decision seemed to say that the Court regarded mining, manufacturing, and construction as "essentially local" activities. In a press conference a few days later Roosevelt concluded, "We have been relegated to the horse-and-buggy definition of interstate commerce."

New Directions in Policy The Court's action came at a time when Roosevelt himself was losing faith in the efficacy of national planning. Now he turned to a convincing new program of action he had anticipated in his annual message to Congress in 1935. That address called for weeding out the overprivileged and lifting up the underprivileged. To that end, Roosevelt intended to propose progressive revenue legislation and programs to assure "the security of . . . livelihood . . . security against the major . . . vicissitudes of life . . . the security of decent homes."

Spurred by the revival of Roosevelt's leadership, the 1935 congressional session enacted a stunning program. A $4.8 billion relief bill had already passed in April. It gave Harry Hopkins the authority and some of the appropriations he had been seeking to establish the Works Progress Administration (WPA) and thus to

New Directions, 1935

We find our population suffering from old inequalities. . . . We have not weeded out the over-privileged. . . . We have not effectively lifted up the under-privileged. . . . We have, however, a clear mandate from the people, that Americans must forswear that conception of the acquisition of wealth which . . . creates undue private power over private affairs and, to our misfortune, over public affairs as well. . . . We . . . assert that the ambition of the individual to obtain for him and his a proper security . . . and a decent living . . . is an ambition to be preferred to the appetite for great wealth and great power. . . .

We are ready to begin to meet this problem—the intelligent care of population throughout our nation, in accordance with an intelligent distribution of the means of livelihood for that population. . . . Closely related . . . is . . . security against the major hazards of life.

From Franklin D. Roosevelt, Annual Message to Congress, January 4, 1935

pursue his belief that the solution for aid to the unemployed lay in work relief. Though his new program led to a small amount of made work, known invidiously as "boondoggling," it also built roads, airports, and schools, improved parks and waterways, produced plays and concerts, maps and guidebooks, and sustained the morale and preserved the skills of millions of Americans unable through no fault of their own to find private employment. Where Hopkins's WPA specialized in light public works, Ickes's Public Works Administration (PWA) which shared the $4.8 billion, concentrated on heavy and durable projects, ranging from dams and bridges to aircraft carriers. The activities of the PWA not only gave some stimulation, albeit inadequate, to the national economy but permanently improved the national estate.

Meanwhile the Court's elimination of the NRA had created an urgent need for a new labor law. Unions had experienced severe difficulties in attempting to organize industrial workers under Section 7a, but that section of the National Industrial Recovery Act had strengthened the principle of collective bargaining between management and unions of the workers' own choice. To replace Section 7a and to facilitate unionization, Congress, now with Roosevelt's support, in 1935 passed the Wagner Labor Relations Act. It outlawed unfair labor practices, including the firing or blacklisting of employees for union activities. It also established the National Labor Relations Board to enforce its provisions, which provided more reliable guarantees for collective bargaining. The Public Contracts Act applied NRA wage and hour standards to firms doing business with the federal government. The Guffey Coal Act tried to put the NRA Coal Code into constitutional form. No one could be sure whether these laws would survive the Supreme Court, though they had been drawn up to avoid the more obvious defects of the National Industrial Recovery Act.

The defects of the Agricultural Adjustment Act (AAA) also needed remedy, even before the Supreme Court found it unconstitutional in 1936. The crop limitation and support programs of the AAA operated to the disadvantage of tenant farmers and sharecroppers, especially in the South. Owners of the land they tilled took much of that land out of cultivation in order to qualify for federal subsidies. The displaced tenants and croppers either drifted to the cities, where they had difficulty finding employment, or became migrant agricultural workers who followed the harvest from place to place. The dust storms of the Great Plains were forcing small farmers there to join the migration, primarily toward California. The poverty both of the migrants and of the croppers, who remained near starvation on the land where they had grown up, contrasted with the growing prosperity of the large landowners, the chief beneficiaries of the AAA. In 1935

Heading West: displaced farmers

Roosevelt first addressed the problem by establishing the Resettlement Administration (RA), financed by part of the $4.8 billion relief appropriation. The RA was to rehabilitate tenants and small farmers, establish cooperative farm communities, and resettle farm families existing on submarginal land. The program never received adequate funds from Congress, as the President's Committee on Farm Tenancy reported in 1937. That report, an encyclopedia of agricultural distress, provoked Congress to reorganize the RA as the Farm Security Administration to provide financial help for tenants hoping to become landowners, to

Oklahoma dust storm

refinance small farmers, and to assist migratory workers. The new program assured many of the neediest farmers of federal aid, though never on the scale that the largest landowners enjoyed.

Most important for the future, the Congress passed in August 1935 the Social Security Act, setting up the Social Security Board to operate both a national plan of contributory old-age and survivors insurance and a federal-state plan of unemployment compensation. Both programs, though at first limited in their coverage, provided the men and women they affected with a measure of protection against vicissitudes beyond their control. They started the government toward a permanent and inclusive system of social welfare. In addition, the Social Security Act, along with other measures of the session, helped further to consolidate a political alliance between the New Deal and organized labor.

Other acts of the 1935 session reflected the influence on Roosevelt of the Brandeis-Frankfurter group (see p. 697). During the Hundred Days, that group had played a subordinate role except in their work on banking and securities legislation. In 1935 their ideas marked the president's message to Congress of June 19, in which he said that "without . . . small enterprises our competitive economic society would cease. Size begets monopoly." Congress responded with the Public Utilities Holding Company Act limiting each holding company after 1938 to a single integrated public-utility system unless it could made a convincing economic case for holding more than one system. The tax law of 1935, with its increased surtaxes and estate taxes and its substitution of a graduated for a uniform corporation income tax, sought to discriminate in favor of small business and the small taxpayer. The tax act of 1936, deeply resented by business, made an attempt to force management to distribute most corporate profits to shareholders. Once distributed, those profits would be subject to the high personal surtax rates. Most important, the forced distribution of profits would reduce the power of management and enhance the options of shareholders who might spend their larger incomes or seek alternative investments. Still another tax act in 1937 aimed to close the loopholes through which rich Americans had been escaping taxes.

The New Deal's revenue acts fell short of their purpose. With the economy still lagging, the increased tax rates did not yield their potential revenue, nor did they effect their social objectives. Further, the states continued to rely upon sales taxes and the tax to finance Social Security fell disproportionately on industrial and clerical workers. Yet with the return of full employment after 1940, the revenue measures at last had considerable, progressive impact.

The Philosophy of the New Deal Alike in its earlier and later emphases, the New Deal strove continuously for both economic recovery and social reform. The focus of policy shifted partly as a consequence of the change in national mood between 1933 and 1935. The desperation of 1933 seemed to demand sweeping economic measures. At the same time, it produced a large measure of political unity. The partial recovery of 1935 increased political disunity and decreased the desire for centralized economic control. By 1935 the New Deal had abandoned its early adventures in inflation. More important, while the New Deal had at first accepted the logic of the administered market and tried to devise new institutions to do what competition had once done to keep the economy in balance, the New Deal by 1935 was stressing a more competitive market and a more egalitarian distribution of income, wealth, and private power. It was politically more radical. Earlier the New Deal had sought government-business cooperation to achieve national objectives. Now the New Deal, persuaded that equitable competition required government enforcement of the rules of the competitive game, was antibusiness in rhetoric.

The fight against economic concentration constituted only part of the changing emphasis of the New Deal. A new theory of recovery through the use of the federal budget was beginning to emerge within the administration. The chief spokesman for this new view was Marriner Eccles of the Federal Reserve Board, who contended that, when the decline of private spending brought about a depression, it was the obligation of government to offset the decline by increasing public spending. Eccles felt that the deliberate creation of compensatory government deficits would stimulate capital formation and purchasing power until the consequent rise in national income produced enough revenue to bring the budget once again into balance. In 1935 these ideas were still tentative and unorthodox, even among New Dealers. The New Deal was spending large sums and was running budgetary deficits (the largest in the pre-war years was $4.5 billion, in 1936), but it was doing these things in response to conditions, not to theories. Further, the deficits were too small to spur recovery effectively. In 1936 the English economist John Maynard (later

Lord) Keynes gave Eccles's approach its first extended theoretical justification in his influential book *The General Theory of Employment, Interest, and Money.* Many of the younger New Dealers found Keynesian ideas increasingly congenial, and their alliance with the compensatory spenders was decisive in the final evolution of New Deal policies.

THE 1936 ELECTION

The Estrangement of Business The emergence of big government and big labor in the mid-1930s ended the unchallenged primacy of the business community in American society. Resentment over loss of status, resentment over government regulation and taxation, resentment over uncertainty and strain—all these emotions joined in many cases to a sincere conviction that the New Deal was a first step toward a totalitarian state, gradually produced among many business leaders a state of bitter opposition to Roosevelt's administration. In alienating those business managers, the New Deal also discouraged them from new investment, but they had not invested while Hoover cultivated their interests and solicited their confidence. Further, had the New Deal ignored social problems, and had it provided favors for business, the administration would have surrendered the social interests of the whole people to the possibility, by no means certain, of a recovery beneficial primarily to the wealthy. Even if recovery had occurred under those conditions, it would have left unaltered the many injustices of American society in the 1920s. New Deal social reforms may have involved some short-run economic and political liabilities, but, for the long run, Roosevelt's emphasis was indispensable for preserving democratic possibilities in the United States.

Still the attitude of the Supreme Court seemed to validate the notion of business executives that the New Deal was using unconstitutional means to achieve unconstitutional objectives. When the Court returned in 1936 to its assault on the New Deal—vetoing the Agricultural Adjustment Act in January, the Guffey Coal Act and the Municipal Bankruptcy Act in May, and a New York minimum-wage law in June—its actions deepened convictions on both sides that an impassable gulf existed between the America of individualism and the America of reform. Hoover denounced the New Deal as an attack on "the whole philosophy of individual liberty." Some conservatives began to trace the New Deal to subversive foreign ideas—to fascism or, more generally and fashionably, to communism. Rumors were even put into circulation that Roosevelt was a madman given to bursts of maniacal laughter.

The 1936 Campaign The "hate-Roosevelt" feeling, the conviction that the New Deal represented the end of the American way of life, permeated the conservative wing of the Republican party. Other Republicans, recognizing Roosevelt's popularity and, in many cases, agreeing with his policies, opposed making the 1936 campaign an all-out fight against the New Deal. This view prevailed in the Republican convention of 1936. The Republicans nominated Governor Alfred M. Landon of Kansas, a former Bull Moose Progressive, who, while conservative on matters of public finance, had shown himself tolerant of many aspects of the New Deal. Frank Knox, a newspaper publisher from Chicago, was chosen as Landon's running mate. The Democrats meanwhile renominated Roosevelt and Garner. The forces of Coughlin, Townsend, and Long (Long himself had been assassinated in September 1935) coalesced in the Union party and nominated Congressman William Lemke of North Dakota for the presidency.

At the start Landon took a moderate line, accepting New Deal objectives but arguing that only the Republican party could achieve them thriftily and constitutionally. In the later stages of the campaign, however, his line became almost indistinguishable from Hoover's. In a moment of last-minute desperation the Republican high command even decided to make an issue of the social security program, which was due to go into effect on January 1, 1937. The Social Security Act, declared Frank Knox, "puts half the working people of America under federal control."

Such efforts were unavailing. Roosevelt conducted his campaign in a mood of buoyant confidence. He was aware, however, of the bitterness of feeling against him, and he gave vent to bitterness of his own. "Never before in all our history have these forces [of selfishness and greed] been so united against one candidate as they stand today," he said. "They are unanimous in their hate for me—and I welcome their hatred."

The election revealed that the attacks on Roosevelt had made little impression on the voters. In a victory without previous precedent in American politics, Roosevelt carried every state except Maine and Vermont. Turnout increased substantially in 1936, with

Roosevelt receiving overwhelming support from first-time voters—both from young Americans just coming of age and from older men and women previously apathetic about politics but now mobilized by their stake in the New Deal. The Republicans were routed, and the Union party sank without a trace. In 1936, the celebrated Roosevelt coalition had emerged in its full strength. The coalition of 1936 included the farmers, West and South, who had supported the party in 1916. It included also the city machines and workers of all ethnic origins, most of whom had rallied to Al Smith in 1928. In 1936 increasing numbers of black Americans in Northern cities were also voting Democratic, as they had never before. So were reform-minded intellectuals, as they had not consistently since 1916, and so was much of the middle class, its confidence revived since 1932, its debt to the New Deal considerable, and its previous Republicanism in eclipse. Though with continuing shifts of influence and support within it, that coalition was to dominate national elections, especially presidential elections, for a generation.

THE SUPREME COURT FIGHT

The Court versus the New Deal Roosevelt opened his second administration by issuing a vigorous call for an extension of the New Deal. "I see one-third of a nation ill-housed, ill-clad, ill-nourished," he said in his inaugural address. But he faced a formidable roadblock in his determination to push ahead. That roadblock was the Supreme Court. By the end of its 1936 term, the Court had heard nine cases involving New Deal legislation. In seven of those cases a majority of the Court had found the legislation unconstitutional, though three verdicts of unconstitutionality were by the narrow margin of 5 to 4 and two more by 6 to 3. In addition, the Court, having denied the federal government power to set minimum wages, had now denied that power to the state of New York, thereby apparently saying that no power existed in the United States to outlaw the sweatshop.

So sustained and devastating a use of the judicial veto to kill social and economic legislation had never before occurred. Moreover, the minority, which in several cases had affirmed its belief in the constitutionality of the disputed laws, comprised by far the more distinguished members of the Court—Louis D. Brandeis, Benjamin N. Cardozo, Harlan F. Stone, and, on occasion, Chief Justice Charles Evans Hughes. "Courts are not the only agency of government that must be assumed to have a capacity to govern," Stone had warned his conservative brethren.

The whole future of the New Deal appeared uncertain. Such laws as the Social Security Act, the Wagner Act, and the Holding Company Act seemed the next candidates for execution by the Court. And, so long as the majority's narrow reading of the Constitution prevailed, there was little chance that the New Deal could take further steps to meet the problems of the forgotten third of a nation. During 1936 Roosevelt and Attorney General Homer Cummings came to feel that something had to be done about the Court. They dismissed the idea of a constitutional amendment, partly because of the difficulties of the ratification process, partly because the amendment itself would be at the mercy of judicial interpretation. In any case, the trouble seemed to lie, not with the Constitution, which they regarded as a spacious charter of government, but with the Court majority. They concluded that the best solution would be to do something directly about the personnel of the Court.

"Packing" the Supreme Court In February 1937 Roosevelt sent a message to Congress calling for the reorganization of the federal judiciary. He contended that the Supreme Court could not keep up with its work burden, and that the interests of efficient administration required the appointment of an additional justice for each justice age 70 or over. The argument about overcrowded dockets was disingenuous and damaged the Court plan. Chief Justice Hughes was soon able to demonstrate that the Court had, in fact, been keeping abreast of its responsibilities. In March Roosevelt tried to wrench the debate back to the real issue. His object, he said, was "to save the Constitution from the Court and the Court from itself." But protest against the measure was now too great to be diverted.

Those who disliked the New Deal found in the Court plan verification of their claim that Roosevelt was trying to destroy the American system. Many who had supported the New Deal were genuinely shocked both by the idea of "packing" the Court and by Roosevelt's circuitous approach to his objective. The proposal set in motion a bitter national debate. In Congress the Republicans held back and allowed dissident Democrats to lead the fight against the president. The measure might have carried with some modifications had

"Furnishing the Supreme Court some practical assistance"

not the Court itself suddenly changed its attitude toward New Deal legislation. On March 29, 1937, the Court in effect reversed its decision of 1936 and affirmed the constitutionality of a Washington minimum-wage law. Two weeks later it sustained the Wagner Act. Plainly the Court majority had abandoned the narrow ground of 1935–36. In Robert H. Jackson's phrase, it had retreated to the Constitution. The way had apparently been cleared for the New Deal without the appointment of a single new justice. And the resignation of one of the conservative justices in June, giving the president his first Supreme Court appointment, made his plan of enlarging the Court seem less necessary than ever. The bill was defeated, though Roosevelt could later claim with some justice that if he had lost the battle he had won the war. But the New Deal had lost momentum in Congress, where the Court fight both revealed and widened the rift between reform Democrats and the conservatives in the party.

SOCIAL AND ECONOMIC CRISES

The Rise of the CIO The Court battle had struck a blow at Roosevelt's prestige as well as at the unity of the Democratic party. And the surging militance of organized labor was creating new problems. The NRA had given the trade-union movement its first impetus to mass organization since the First World War. Under the leadership of John L. Lewis and the United Mine Workers, a great campaign had begun in 1933 to organize the unorganized in the mass-production industries. This campaign soon led to a major conflict within the labor movement itself. The American Federation of Labor (AFL) was dominated by craft unions. Under the craft theory, the automobile industry, for example, was to be organized, not by a single union, but by as many different unions as there were different crafts involved in making a car. But Lewis, as head of one of the few industrial unions in the AFL, thought instinctively in terms of organization, not by craft, but by industry. Moreover, craft unionism had failed to organize the basic industries, to which industrial unionism seemed peculiarly adapted. A fight within the AFL between craft unionism and industrial unionism culminated in the expulsion of Lewis and his associates in 1936 and their formation of a rival labor federation, the Congress of Industrial Organizations (CIO).

The CIO came into existence at a time when workers throughout the country, especially in the mass-production industries, were hungering for organization in unions of their own choosing. Further, the CIO, unlike the AFL, appealed to women and black and Hispanic Americans in its drive for unionization. The spontaneous character of the labor uprising was shown in 1936 and 1937 by the development of a new strike technique, frowned upon by national labor

Militant Labor

The Committee for Industrial Organization . . . is carrying its plans forward. Extensive unions have been promoted . . . in the steel, automotive, glass, shipbuilding, electrical manufacturing, oil and . . . coke industries. Tremendous enrollment of the workers is under way. Unabashed by employer opposition, they are joining the unions . . . by the thousands.

The year 1936 has witnessed the beginning of this great movement in the mass production industries. The year 1937 will witness an unparalleled growth in the numerical strength of labor . . . and the definite achievement of modern collective bargaining on a wide front. . . .

Some of the largest and most powerful corporations in this country . . . deny the entirely reasonable and just demands of their employees for legitimate collective bargaining, decent incomes, shorter hours, and for protection against a destructive speed-up. . . .

It is the refusal of employers to grant such reasonable conditions and to deal with their employees through collective bargaining that leads to wide-spread labor unrest. The strikes which have broken out . . . especially in the automobile industry, are due to such "employee trouble". . . . Huge corporations, such as United States Steel and General Motors, . . . have no right to transgress the law which gives to the workers the right of self-organization and collective bargaining.

The people of our nation have just participated in a national referendum. By an overwhelming majority they voted for industrial democracy and elected its champion, Franklin D. Roosevelt. . . . Labor . . . now demands a new deal in America's great industries.

From John L. Lewis, speech broadcast by the National Broadcasting Company, December 13, 1936

leadership—the "sit-down strike," in which workers sat down by their machines in factories and refused to work until employers would concede them the right of collective bargaining. To many employers, the sit-down strike threatened property rights and smacked of revolution. Its vogue led them to fight all the more savagely against any recognition of industrial unions as bargaining agents.

But the CIO pushed its organizing campaigns ahead vigorously, especially in automobiles and steel. There were shocking moments of violence. In May 1937 police shot and killed ten pickets outside the Republic Steel plant in Chicago. In Detroit, leaders of the United Automobile Workers (UAW) were brutally beaten by company guards at Henry Ford's River Rouge plant. But the decision of General Motors to negotiate with the UAW in February 1937 and of United States Steel to negotiate with the Steel Workers Organizing Committee in March marked the start of a new era. The battle for collective bargaining was not yet wholly won. But the courage and spirit of working men and women in their determination to gain their rights gave a romance to the labor movement of the time that appealed to many Americans who were not themselves directly involved. Union membership, which had been less than 3 million in 1933 and barely

Steel strike: shocking moments of violence

over 4 million at the start of 1937, grew to 7.2 million by the end of the year and to 9 million by 1939.

The Recession of 1937–1938 The years 1935 and 1936 had been years of slow but steady economic improvement. Some leading bankers began to worry about inflation, though resources and labor were still widely underemployed. Under pressure from the bankers, the Federal Reserve Board tried to put on the brakes by raising interest rates in 1936 and 1937. This action was less significant in arresting the upward swing than the decline between 1936 and 1937 in the federal government's net contribution to the economy. In 1936 the payment of the veterans' bonus of $1.7 billion on top of relief and public-works expenditures and the normal costs of government resulted in a net federal government contribution of $4.1 billion. In 1937 several factors — the collection of taxes under the Social Security Act as well as the attempt to reduce public spending and to move toward a balanced budget — resulted in a decrease of the net government contribution to $800 million, a drop of $3.3 billion in a single year. Private business investment did not fill the gap created by the contraction of public spending.

The collapse in the months after September 1937 was actually more severe than it had been in the first nine months after the crash. National income fell 13 percent, payrolls 35 percent, durable-goods production 50 percent, profits 78 percent. The increase in unemployment reproduced scenes of the early depression and imposed new burdens on the relief agencies.

The recession brought to a head a policy debate within the administration. One group, led by Henry Morgenthau, Jr., the secretary of the Treasury, had supported the policy of government retrenchment and favored balancing the budget as soon as practicable. Those steps, they believed, though historical evidence contradicted them, would restore business confidence and lift private investment. Another group, led by Hopkins of the WPA and Eccles of the Federal Reserve Board, urged the immediate resumption of public spending. Economists advising them and like-minded New Dealers could now buttress their case by reference to the theories of J. M. Keynes, which were gradually winning converts in Washington (see p. 710). Roosevelt himself favored for a while the first group. But, as the downward slide speeded up, he reluctantly accepted the necessity for spending. In March 1938 he announced a new spending program. Again too small to achieve its intended results, this program, which included as much as Congress would tolerate, did begin to reverse the decline. It sopped up some unemployment and by 1939 effected a gross national product larger than in 1937. The recession, however, killed Roosevelt's hope of attaining full economic recovery before the end of his second term.

The recession also persuaded Roosevelt to resume his antimonopoly drive and to urge a redistribution of income in order to increase the purchasing power of wage earners. Congress balked at the latter objective, but the president appointed Thurman Arnold as head of the Antitrust Division of the Department of Justice, and, while Arnold began a series of antitrust suits, Congress created the Temporary National Economic Committee to survey the concentration of economic power. But the survey resulted in no new legislation.

1938 and the Purge The antitrust campaign, the Court fight, the new aggressiveness of organized labor, and the resumption of the spending policy all tended to widen the gap between the liberal and the conservative wings of the Democratic party. The liberals were mostly Northerners, the conservatives mostly Southerners, and other events of 1938 hastened the alienation of the Bourbon Democrats from the New Deal. Southern employers were bitterly opposed to the administration's Fair Labor Standards (or Wages and Hours) Act, which was passed in June 1938. They objected that its policy of setting minimum wages and maximum hours and outlawing child labor would increase labor costs. Southern planters were equally bitter against the Farm Security Administration and its activities on behalf of tenant farmers and sharecroppers. Conservative Democrats in Congress prepared to resist. And the alliance between Southern Democrats and Northern Republicans, tentatively initiated in 1937 during the Supreme Court fight, began to harden in 1938 into a major obstacle to further New Deal legislation. The House Committee on Un-American Activities, dedicated under the chair of Martin Dies of Texas to the harrying of radicals in and out of government, became an instrument of conservative retaliation against the New Deal.

The defection of the Southern conservatives raised difficult problems for the administration. Roosevelt felt that many conservative Democrats had taken a free ride on the popularity of the New Deal. Their refusal to support liberal policies, in his judgment, served to blur essential distinctions in American politics. "An election cannot give a country a firm sense of direction," he said in June 1938, "if it has two or more

1938: the New Deal was the issue

national parties which merely have different names but are as alike in their principles and aims as peas in the same pod." Accordingly he made the New Deal itself an issue by intervening personally in state primaries in the hope of replacing conservative senators and representatives with liberals. Such intervention was a striking departure from precedent, which his opponents denounced as a "purge." The largely unsuccessful result of Roosevelt's efforts was a prelude to administration setbacks in the general election: the Republicans gained 7 seats in the Senate and 80 in the House.

The year 1938 marked the end of the forward thrust of the New Deal. The public demand for reform seemed to be slackening. Congress, now controlled by a conservative coalition, rejected the administration's Lending Bill of 1939, a measure based on Keynesian principles. By that time the drift toward war in Europe was leading both the president and the people to shift their attention to foreign policy. In his State of the Union message in January 1939 Roosevelt had spoken significantly of the need "to invigorate the processes of recovery in order to *preserve* our reforms."

THE AMERICAN PEOPLE IN THE DEPRESSION

The Trauma of Depression The Great Depression had been a severe shock to the American people — to their expectations, their values, and their confidence in themselves and their future. Mute evidence of a declining faith in their prospects was the sudden slowdown of the marriage and birth rates. Immigration also fell off. Population grew at a rate of less than a million a year. The total population increase (to 131.7 million in 1940) was hardly more than half that of the preceding decade. In 1938 there were 1.6 million fewer children under ten than there had been five years before. With the increase in life expectancy (from 56 in 1920 to 64 in 1940), the proportion of people over 65 increased from 5.4 percent in 1930 to 6.9 percent in 1940. In the perspective of depression, America began to look like an aging country. The demographic trend led economic theorists to argue that the nation had reached "economic maturity" and could not hope to resume growth without aggressive government intervention.

Americans brought up in the tradition of the bright future and the happy ending found it hard to adjust to bread lines and mass unemployment. Some fell into listlessness. Others flocked behind one or another of the social demagogues with their promises of miraculous deliverance. A few believed that depression was an ineradicable evil of the capitalist system and concluded that the only way out was to abolish capitalism.

Some of these, excited by the success of fascism in Italy and Germany, formed Fascist groups, bearing such names as the Silver Shirts. In a vivid novel, *It Can't Happen Here* (1935), Sinclair Lewis showed how a 100 percent American Fascist movement might take over the United States. But, though the American Fascists diligently imitated many of the Nazi techniques and appeals (including anti-Semitism), they had little impact on American life.

More of those who despaired of capitalism turned toward Marxism. In 1932 just under a million Americans voted against the capitalist system. Most of the votes went to the Socialist party, a reformist group under the appealing leadership of Norman Thomas. But over 100,000 voted for the Communist party ticket. The Communist movement, the more serious of the two, was controlled by a hard core of disciplined devotees, faithfully conforming to the turns and twists of the party line laid down in Moscow. Not all those who joined the party, however, were aware of its whole nature. At one time or another during the decade, a large number of people passed rather quickly through the movement, attracted primarily by the apparent idealism of Communist promises but soon bored by the sectarian inflexibility of Communist analysis or repelled by the ruthless dishonesty of Communist performance, especially in Europe. Secret Communists had some success in penetrating certain labor unions and even a few government offices, though without significantly influencing American policy.

The Social Revolution If depression induced despair, it also discredited the structure of status and prestige that had ruled the United States in the 1920s. Business leaders had been the culture heroes of the prosperity decade. In 1929 this New Era had exploded. In the 1930s their pretensions to wisdom were derided, their leadership rejected, and they were often dismissed as fools.

People from outside the business community — especially politicians and intellectuals — were now in power, and in their wake came a rush for status of the forgotten men and women of America — those who had been denied opportunities in the past because of their class or ethnic origin. The New Deal, by revising the structure of status, brought about profound social changes, including visible gains for previously disadvantaged ethnic groups, that diminished the attractiveness to Americans of radical ideologies.

Organized labor's rise to respectability typified the tendencies of the decade. The social revolution enhanced the quality of life, particularly in rural America. Though the Supreme Court knocked out the original AAA in 1936, the principle of national responsibility for the agricultural economy was established and reaffirmed in legislation of 1938. No other federal agency had such an impact on the quality of country life as did the Rural Electrification Administration (REA). When it was founded in 1935, only about one farm in ten had power-line electric service. Through low-interest loans to cooperatives, the REA enabled farmers to build their own power lines and generate their own electricity. The spread of electricity, bringing with it the radio and power for labor-saving machinery, transformed the countryside.

The Ethnic Revolution Immigration substantially stopped in the 1930s (except for refugees from fascism toward the end of the decade). The last wave of immigrants, mostly from southern and eastern Europe in the earlier part of the century, had not yet achieved full acceptance in American society. The upheaval of depression gave many Italians, Poles, Slavs, and Jews their first opportunities. Where craft unions, for example, had often discriminated against them, as against black Americans, the industrial unions of the CIO opened their doors to them. Similarly the New Deal gave them their first chance in politics and public service, as did many of the states.

Roosevelt himself had no patience with the old American attitude of superiority toward more recent immigrants. "Remember, remember always," he once told the Daughters of the American Revolution, "that all of us, and you and I especially, are descended from immigrants and revolutionists." Of the 214 federal judges appointed by Harding, Coolidge, and Hoover, only 8 were Catholics; of the 196 appointed by Roosevelt, 51 were Catholics. Political figures in the great cities, like Fiorello La Guardia, the independent Republican mayor of New York, acted as brokers in gaining recognition for ethnic minorities previously shut out from political preferment. Concurrently there was a notable decline in the foreign-language press and a more effective acculturation of ethnic minorities into American life.

Most striking of all, perhaps, was the rise in expectations of black Americans, for many years the victims of economic and political neglect. During the depression, the black American was, in the phrase of the day, "the first man fired and the last man hired." And, though they had voted Republican since the Civil War, the Republican administrations had shown little concern for their welfare. Black leaders had denounced Hoover as "the man in the lily-White House." Roosevelt brought to Washington a larger sympathy for black problems. New Deal agencies generally conformed to local folkways that perpetuated segregation and discrimination within the CCC and in the distribution of work relief in the South, for two of many examples. But the New Dealers appointed many able black citizens to administrative positions which symbolized new opportunities for their race. Eleanor Roosevelt and Harold Ickes actively promoted civil rights. Roosevelt himself repeatedly denounced lynching, though he would not provide direct support to the Northern Democrats in the Senate who took the initiative in sponsoring bills to make lynching a federal crime. The New Deal did far less for black Americans than their circumstances warranted, but it did far more than had any administration since Reconstruction. By 1936 black voters had begun to shift to the Democratic party.

Hispanic-Americans also benefited from the New Deal. Rexford G. Tugwell brought New Deal principles to Puerto Rico while he served as governor there. The WPA provided jobs, though never enough, for many Mexican-Americans in western and southwestern states. Luisa Moreno, one of their leaders, helped to organize the militant United Cannery, Agricultural, Packing, and Allied Workers Union (CIO) and the Spanish-Speaking Congress, which joined liberals with radicals in a commitment to cultural pluralism and feminism.

The American Indians also had a new champion in Washington, John Collier, the administration's Commissioner of Indian Affairs. Collier, an experienced social worker, had long believed in the importance of preserving the cultural heritage of immigrant groups and of solving the social problems of poverty by community cooperation. Those concepts underlay his work as founder and guiding spirit of the American Indian Defense Association. In 1933, with the support

For Pluralism and Feminism

Whereas: The Mexican woman, who for centuries has suffered oppression, has the responsibility of raising her children and of caring for the home, and even that of earning a livelihood for herself and her family, and since in this country she suffers double discrimination, as a woman and as a Mexican.

Be It Resolved: That the Congress carry out a program of organization and education of Mexican women, concerning home problems . . . that it support and work for women's equality, so that she may receive equal wages, enjoy the same rights as men in social, economic, and civil liberties, and use her vote in defense of Mexican and Spanish American people, and American democracy.

Resolution of the Second Spanish-Speaking Congress, 1939. Quoted in Mario T. Garciá, *Mexican Americans,* (1989)

John Collier: new champion of the American Indians

of Secretary of the Interior Ickes, Collier began directly to influence federal policy. During his years in office, he forbade discrimination against Indian religious ceremonies, introduced instruction in Indian languages and culture in schools on reservations, doubled the proportion of Native Americans employed by his agency, and moved millions of dollars of New Deal funds into improving the Indian landed estate. The Indian Reorganization Act of 1934 explicitly recognized the right of Indians to organize "for the purpose of local self-government and economic enterprise," committed the federal government to promoting "the study of Indian civilization," created a special Court of Indian Affairs to remove Indians from the jurisdiction of the states, and perhaps most important, abandoned the division of Indian lands into individual parcels—the discredited policy of the Dawes Severalty Act of 1887 (see p. 447)—and pledged the government to a constructive program of Indian land use. Collier's sympathetic and creative management of Indian affairs did not outlast the New Deal, but he started the nation toward a belated rectification of centuries of injustice.

New Deal policies also mitigated, though they did not eliminate, discrimination against women. As they had during the 1920s, so during the 1930s educated women confronted formidable obstacles to entering the professions. A much larger number of women than ever before needed industrial or clerical employment in order to support themselves or to help support their families. Yet with the onset of depression, employers tended to discharge women before they discharged men, and during the 1930s women found it harder than did men to secure new jobs. Consequently many women dropped out of the working force. Those who remained ordinarily earned less than did men in similar positions and normally received no consideration for promotion to supervisory posts. New Deal policies provided partial remedies for those conditions. First the NRA codes and later the Fair Labor Standards Act at least set minimum wages for women as well as men. The WPA created some jobs for women clerical workers, teachers, and lawyers. And the CIO, flourishing under the New Deal, set out, as the AFL had not, vigorously to recruit women into industrial unions and thus to assure them of the gains obtained through collective bargaining.

The New Deal did succeed in recruiting women voters. The president and particularly his wife encouraged women to work for the Democratic party, as did their friend Molly Dewson, a leader of the National Consumers League. Dewson enlisted thousands of women in the precincts and helped to persuade the Democratic national committee to appoint eight women as vice-chairs. In 1936 the Democratic convention required each delegate to the platform committee to have an alternate of the opposite sex, a reversal of earlier policy. Dewson also solicited federal patronage for women, who received more postmasterships than ever before and more recognition in major offices. Eleanor Roosevelt, the most visible and influential woman New Dealer, became a national symbol for advocates of social justice. Though feminism as a social movement remained subdued, her spirit heartened all women, workers and intellectuals alike.

The release of energy brought about by the New Deal, the invigorating sense that the "forgotten" man and woman could still make a place for themselves in American life — all this gradually began to heal the trauma of depression. The sense of America as an exhausted nation gave way to the image of a purposeful society capable of meeting its problems with energy and conviction.

In the 1920s, the intellectuals who scorned the American present had turned to "debunking" the American past. In the 1930s, when the American present was acquiring purpose and dignity, they began to read this purpose and dignity back into American history. The title of John Dos Passos's book *The Ground We Stand On* (1941) summed up the new attitude. "In times of change and danger," Dos Passos wrote, "when there is a quicksand of fear under men's reasoning, a sense of continuity with generations gone before can stretch like a lifeline across the scary present." Other skeptics of the 1920s joined Dos Passos in taking a more affirmative view of American traditions. Van Wyck Brooks, who had once seen American culture as pinched and sterile, now portrayed it, in *The Flowering of New England* (1936) and succeeding volumes, as rich and abundant. The publication of a number of important biographies helped meet the new national desire to repossess the past in all its solidity. This impulse came into happy conjunction with the New Deal in the valuable series of state guidebooks produced by the WPA.

As never before in American history, the federal government, through the WPA especially, sponsored the arts — not literature only but architecture, the fine

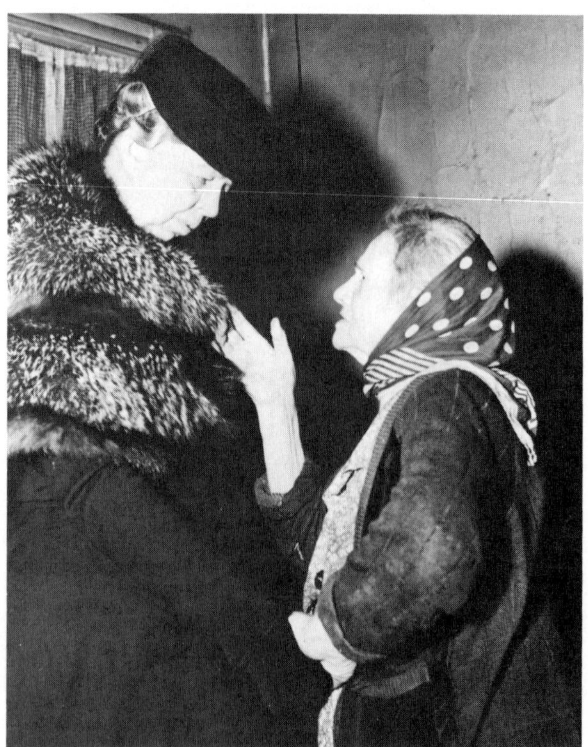

Eleanor Roosevelt, symbol of social justice

WPA: making music available

arts, music, dance and drama. Hallie Flanagan of Vassar presided over the strikingly successful Federal Theater Project. The plays she and her associates produced reached thousands of Americans who had never before attended theater. Sponsored or not, much of the art of the time included a strong and self-conscious strain of social criticism. With a critical but constructive urgency artists rejected the mood of inwardness of the 1920s, attacked those like Thornton Wilder and T. S. Eliot who still worked in creative privacy, and often devoted themselves to political causes. Among others, the novelist Mike Gold and the playwright Clifford Odets wrote from the perspective of the far left. Edmund Wilson and James Agee, both less doctrinaire, moved a larger audience toward their causes. Ernest Hemingway moved still more readers with his socially conscious fiction.

The New Pattern of American Society The recovery of American faith in the 1930s both derived from and contributed to the capacity of the American people to reassert a measure of control over their social and economic destiny. In so doing, American society was countering the prevailing ideologies of the day. Both laissez-faire and Marxism were philosophies of economic determinism with narrow views of social possibility. The New Deal, with all its improvisations, contradictions, sentimentalisms, and errors, did have the signal advantage of rejecting economic fatalism and of affirming a faith in intelligent experiment.

By Roosevelt's second term the essential pattern of the new society was complete for his generation. The American nation had renounced laissez-faire without embracing socialism. Government had acquired the obligation to underwrite the economic and social health of the nation. The budget provided the means by which the government through the use of fiscal policy could compensate for a decline in private economic activity. The state had abandoned efforts aimed at the direct control of industrial production, but industry had to accept ground rules covering minimum standards of life and labor. And the state continued to intervene to maintain, in modified form, the free play of competition. Special areas of economic activity required more comprehensive government control—banking, transportation, public utilities, agriculture, oil. Human welfare was to be protected through various forms of public insurance. A collection of "built-in stabilizers"—minimum wages, unemployment compensation, farm-price supports, social security payments—were to help secure the economy against a future crash as devastating as that of 1929.

Was the Roosevelt Way Possible? These measures involved more government intervention in the economy than some had thought the economy could stand and still remain free. This was the critical question raised by the New Deal—whether a policy of limited and piecemeal government intervention in economic life was feasible; whether a mixed system was possible that gave the state power enough to assure economic and social security but still not so much as to create an all-powerful dictatorship; whether active government could remain uncorrupted by the large influence of powerful industrial, labor, and agricultural groups.

The New Deal especially assisted the American middle class. It protected their savings, homes, and farms. It opened the way to middle-class comforts and status for previously stigmatized ethnic groups and many clerical and blue-collar workers. But the New Deal also knew many failures. It did not achieve recovery. It did not sufficiently redistribute income and wealth, though it proposed more effectual policies than Congress would accept. It did not bring black Americans or women an equitable share in the country's social and economic life. It could not overcome the conservative social and regressive economic policies of most American states. It could not permanently insulate its new regulatory agencies from the tendency of regulators to develop excessive sympathy for those they were supposed to control.

Those failures, clearer in retrospect than at the time, suggested that the particular middle way of the Roosevelt years would later need modifications. But to the question of the viability of any middle way, doctrinaires returned a categorical *no* through the decade.

"The Roosevelt Way"

There is nothing mysterious about the foundations of a healthy and strong democracy. The basic things expected by our people of the political and economic systems are simple. They are: equality of opportunity for youth and others; jobs for those who can work; security for those who need it; the ending of special privilege for the few; the preservation of civil liberties for all; the enjoyment of the fruits of scientific progress in a wider and constantly rising standard of living.

Democracy in order to live must become a positive force in the daily lives of its people. It must make men and women . . . feel that it cares for the security of every individual; that it is tolerant enough to inspire an essential unity among its citizens; and that it is militant enough to maintain liberty against social oppression at home and against military aggression abroad.

Franklin D. Roosevelt, Addresses of January 6, 1941, and November 4, 1938, as quoted in H. S. Commager, *Living Ideas in America,* 1951

Rebuilding Harlem: the New Deal at work

Ogden Mills stated the issue with precision for the conservatives: "We can have a free country or a socialistic one. We cannot have both. . . . There is no middle ground . . . between tyranny and freedom."

In such sentiments, at least, the critics of capitalism agreed with the conservatives. "Either the nation must put up with the confusions and miseries of an essentially unregulated capitalism," said a radical weekly in 1935, "or it must prepare to supersede capitalism with socialism. There is no longer a feasible middle course." The proponents of individualism and the proponents of collectivism agreed on this if on nothing else: no regulated capitalism was possible, no mixed economy, no middle way between laissez-faire and socialism.

But the New Dealers cheerfully rejected the conclusion. They believed that there was more on heaven and earth than could be found in any ideology. Roosevelt himself was blithe and humane in his undeviating rejection of any all-encompassing doctrine. He might have undertaken social experiments either more or less bold than those he chose. But his aim was consistent—to steer "slightly to the left of center," avoiding alike "the revolution of radicalism and the revolution of conservatism," combining personal freedom and economic growth. For the generation that lived through it, the decade of the New Deal, with all its confusion and recrimination, rekindled confidence in free society, not in America alone, but throughout the Western world.

SUGGESTIONS FOR READING

GENERAL

The most comprehensive account of domestic developments in 1933–36, is in A. M. Schlesinger, Jr., *The Coming of the New Deal* (1959) and *The Politics of Upheaval* (1960). W. E. Leuchtenburg, *Franklin D. Roosevelt and the New Deal, 1932–40* (1963), provides the best short account. There are valuable insights in J. M. Burns,

Roosevelt: The Lion and the Fox (1956) and E. W. Hawley, *The New Deal and the Problem of Monopoly* (1966). P. Conkin, *The New Deal* (1967), criticizes Roosevelt and his policies from the point of view of the revisionists of the 1960s and 1970s. Compare with J. M. Blum, *The Progressive Presidents* (1980), which is sympathetic. Caroline Bird, *The Invisible Scar* (1965), recounts the social impact of continuing depression. For recent reinterpretation of the period, see M. Parrish, *Anxious Decades* (1992); A. W. Romasco, *The Politics of Recovery: Roosevelt's New Deal* (1983); and especially S. Fraser and G. Gerstle, eds., *The Rise and Fall of the New Deal Order* (1989). On voting patterns, see K. Andersen, *The Creation of a Democratic Majority* (1979); and G. H. Gamm, *The Making of New Deal Democrats* (1989).

MEMOIRS AND BIOGRAPHIES

Memoirs of the New Dealers and biographies based on their papers throw important light on Roosevelt and his problems. R. E. Sherwood, *Roosevelt and Hopkins: An Intimate History* (1948, rev. ed., 1950), provides a view of an important friendship and a favorable account of relief policies. Frances Perkins, *The Roosevelt I Knew* (1946), is significant for its compassion but must be compared with George Martin, *Madame Secretary: Frances Perkins* (1976); see R. G. Tugwell, *The Democratic Roosevelt* (1957) and *The Brain Trust* (1968), for retrospective reflections; *The Secret Diary of Harold L. Ickes*, 3 vols. (1953–54), for its gossip and atmosphere. On politics, two illuminating memoirs are J. A. Farley, *Behind the Ballots* (1938), and Edward Flynn, *You're the Boss* (1947). J. M. Blum, *Roosevelt and Morgenthau* (1970), recounts the activities of one of the president's influential advisers. H. S. Johnson, *The Blue Eagle* (1935), presents a contemporary view of the National Recovery Administration. There is a contemporary critique of the early New Deal in Raymond Moley, *After Seven Years* (1939); this may be supplemented by his retrospective *The First New Deal* (1966). In *Beckoning Frontiers* (1935), M. S. Eccles describes the evolution of economic policy. Samuel Rosenman writes as a counselor to the president in *Working with Roosevelt* (1952). J. J. Huthmacher, *Senator Robert Wagner and the Rise of American Liberalism* (1968), is a telling study of a leading liberal senator. On a colorful mayor, see T. Kessner, *Fiorello La Guardia and the Making of Modern New York* (1989). There is indispensable personal material in Eleanor Roosevelt, *This I Remember* (1949), and in J. P. Lash, *Eleanor and Franklin* (1971). F. Freidel has completed five volumes of his long biography of Roosevelt, and K. S. Davis has completed three of his parallel work. Though there is no useful edition of Roosevelt's private papers, one source for study of the man and his times is Samuel Rosenman, ed., *The Public Papers and Addresses of Franklin D. Roosevelt,* 13 vols. (1930–50). Also important is M. Dubofsky and W. Van Tine, *John L. Lewis* (1977).

NEW DEAL POLITICAL THOUGHT

Students wishing to study New Deal political thought in the important works of the time should consult, as the text suggests, at least the following influential sources: A. A. Berle, Jr., and G. C. Means, *The Modern Corporation and Private Property* (1932, rev. ed., 1969), significant on economic concentration as is J. Burnham, *Managerial Revolution* (1941); M. S. Eccles, *Economic Balance and a Balanced Budget* (1940), significant on countercyclical spending; R. G. Tugwell, *The Battle for Democracy* (1935), and H. L. Ickes, *The New Democracy* (1934), both important on social goals and public planning, as is H. A. Wallace, *New Frontiers* (1934); and D. E. Lilienthal, *TVA* (rev. ed., 1953), on regional development. Two incisive books by Thurman Arnold—*The Symbols of Government* (1935) and *The Folklore of Capitalism* (1937)—well express the iconoclastic side of the New Deal. For a revisionistic view, see Howard Zinn, ed., *New Deal Thought* (1966).

SPECIAL STUDIES

Outstanding studies of economic problems in the 1930s include the analytical T. Wilson, *Fluctuations in Income and Employment* (1948); R. E. Paul, *Taxation in the United States* (1954); and M. H. Leff, *The Limits of Economic Reform: The New Deal and Reaction, 1933–1939* (1984). Some of the most useful among recent works are Irving Bernstein, *Turbulent Years* (1970), which describes the labor movement, as, in one major case, does S. Fine, *Sit-Down: The General Motors Strike of 1936–37* (1969). See, too, D. Brody, *Workers in Industrial America* (1980). R. Lekachman, *The Age of Keynes* (1966), discusses the acceptance of the ideas of the new economics, as does H. Stein, *The Fiscal Revolution in America* (1969). See also D. L. May, *From New Deal to New Economics* (1981). Significant, too, are R. Kirkendall, *Social Scientists and Farm Politics in the Age of Roosevelt* (1966); J. T. Patterson, *The New Deal and the States* (1969); R. Lubove, *The Struggle for Social Security, 1900–1935* (1968); T. McCraw, *TVA and the Power Fight, 1933–1939* (1970); and M. Parrish, *Securities Regulation and the New Deal* (1970).

Among the stimulating works about social and intellectual currents are R. A. Lawson, *The Failure of Independent Liberalism, 1930–1941* (1971); R. Pells, *Radical Visions and American Dreams* (1973); C. Alexander, *Nationalism in American Thought, 1930–1945* (1969); E. Purcell, Jr., *The Crisis of Democratic Theory* (1972) D. Meyer, *The Protestant Search for Social Realism, 1919–1941* (1960); and D. O'Brien, *American Catholics and Social Reform* (1965). For a thoughtful account of the appeal of communism and other radical ideas, see D. Aaron, *Writers on the Left* (1961); R. Crossman, ed., *The God That Failed* (1949); F. A. Warren, *Liberals and Communism: The "Red" Decade Revisited* (1966); H. Klehr, *Heyday of American Communism* (1984); and B. Johnpoll, *Pacifist's Progress* (1970), on Norman Thomas. R. G. Swing, *Forerunners of American Fascism* (1935), offers a contemporary account of the lunatic right, which is modified in A. P. Sindler, *Huey Long's Louisiana* (1956), and D. H. Bennett, *Demagogues in the Depression* (1969), and challenged by T. H. Williams, *Huey Long* (1969) and A. Brinkley, *Voices of Protest* (1982). On the problems of black Americans during the 1930s, see B. Sternsher, ed., *The Negro in Depression and War* (1969); R. Wolters, *Negroes and the Great Depression* (1970); H. Sitkoff, *A New Deal for Blacks* (1978); D. T. Carter, *Scottsboro: A Tragedy of the American South* (1969); J. M. Jones, *Bad Blood* (1981); and N. J. Weiss, *Farewell to the Party of Lincoln: Black Politics in the Age of FDR* (1983). On women, see William Chafe, cited after Chapter 26, and Susan Ware, *Beyond Suffrage: Women and the New Deal* (1981).

Samuel Lubell, *The Future of American Politics* (1952), identifies important political changes in the period; also revealing about politics are T. Lowi, *The End of Liberalism* (1969); G. McConnell, *Private Power and American Democracy* (1969); and B. Stave, *The New Deal and the Last Hurrah* (1970). G. Wolfskill, *The Revolt of the Conservatives* (1962), displays the reaction on the right, as does his volume with J. Hudson, *All But the People* (1969). The career of the ablest Republican senator of the era receives admirable treatment in J. T. Patterson, *Mr. Republican: A Biography of Robert A. Taft* (1972). On the Supreme Court fight, especially rewarding studies are R. H. Jackson, *The Struggle for Judiciary Supremacy* (1941); A. T. Mason, *Harlan Fiske Stone* (1956); and M. J. Pusey, *Charles Evans Hughes,* 2 vols. (1951). The same subject is treated by one of the masters of constitutional history, E. S. Corwin, in his *Twilight of the Supreme Court* (1934), *Court over Constitution* (1938), and *Constitutional Revolution, Ltd.* (rev. ed., 1946).

CHAPTER TWENTY-EIGHT

HITLER IN NUREMBERG, 1938

THE DECAY OF PEACE

The Great Depression intensified nationalism all over the world. The American people, like others in the industrialized nations, were absorbed in gloomy domestic problems. By 1933, isolationism, both political and economic, dominated the American mood. That condition enhanced the opportunity for the Japanese to proceed with their expansionist plans in Asia with little concern about American interference. Similarly, the domestic preoccupations of the British and the French, as well as the Americans, and their grim memories of the losses they had suffered during the First World War, eased the path to power in Europe of Adolf Hitler. The Nazi leader became chancellor of Germany on January 30, 1933, and in March received from the Reichstag dictatorial authority to carry forward his program of rearmament, anti-Semitism, and messianic nationalism.

Franklin D. Roosevelt realized, as he said, that "Hitler meant war," but, as he had to, Roosevelt yielded to the temper of the American people. Influenced by the strategic ideas of Theodore Roosevelt and Admiral Alfred T. Mahan, the president understood the importance of power in international affairs. He believed also that the United States had erred in failing to join the League of Nations in 1919, though by 1932 he recognized that Americans were opposed to participation in the League or in the risks of balance-of-power politics. Accordingly at the outset of his administration, he confined his foreign policy in Europe and Asia largely to gestures. He named as Secretary of State Cordell Hull, an unregenerate Wilsonian and low-tariff man, but he continually bypassed Hull and the State Department's professional foreign service officers, whom he disdained. Roosevelt preferred personal diplomacy. He brought to it an amateur's imagination and flair but also at times a deficiency of steadiness.

EARLY VENTURES

The Good Neighbor In his inaugural address, Roosevelt dedicated the United States "to the policy of the good neighbor—the neighbor who resolutely respects himself, and because he does so, respects the rights of others." A sensitivity to the independent sovereignties and the national aspirations of the Latin American nations recommended that objective. Further, the security of the Western Hemisphere depended on improvements in the relations of the United States with the Latin countries. But Roosevelt started awkwardly by interceding in the political affairs of Cuba. The resulting anxieties about Yankee imperialism were diminished by the stance of the

United States at the Seventh International Conference of American States at Montevideo in December 1933. There the United States at last accepted a proposal declaring that "no state has the right to intervene in the internal or external affairs of another." In the spirit of that declaration, Roosevelt withdrew the marines from Haiti; in 1934 abrogated the Platt Amendment, thus abandoning the treaty right to interfere in Cuba; in the case of El Salvador, abandoned also the policy of nonrecognition of revolutionary regimes; renounced in 1936 the right of intervention in Panama and recognized Panama's joint responsibility for operating and protecting the canal; and in 1940 ended American financial controls in the Dominican Republic.

The chief test of the Good Neighbor policy arose in Mexico. The renewed radicalism of the government there, a government openly hostile to the Roman Catholic Church, led to the expropriation of the properties of foreign-owned petroleum companies. In spite of resulting pressures for intervention, Washington merely urged Mexico to provide American companies with due compensation. "Our national interests as a whole," as a State Department memorandum of 1939 maintained, "far outweigh those of the petroleum companies." Those national interests benefited from efforts by the State Department and the Export-Import Bank to promote trade and investment in Latin America. More important, Roosevelt, for whom political considerations were primary, succeeded by 1940 in inspiring confidence throughout the region in the reality of American friendship.

Europe: Money and Trade The Hoover administration had raised tariff levels to historic highs in order to protect the American market from foreign competition. Roosevelt rejected that form of economic nationalism but pursued instead economic nationalism in monetary policy. European nations had retaliated against American protectionism, with Great Britain doing so by devaluing the pound in order to enhance its share of world trade, for a devalued pound made British goods less expensive than the goods of countries that remained on the gold standard. Hoover had agreed to participation in a world economic conference in London in 1933, but Roosevelt had no intention of permitting that conference to tie his hands. He wanted both to stimulate world trade and to manage the value of the dollar for the benefit of the United States. His economic nationalism, in other words, took a different direction from Hoover's but was no more or less self-serving.

In the summer of 1933, the American delegation to the London conference consequently opposed the effort of the British and the Europeans to stabilize the price of gold. Roosevelt himself broke up the conference by sending it an abrupt message refusing to endorse currency stabilization even in principle. The message revealed the rift in Anglo-American relations that the economic rivalry of the two nations had provoked. It also left Roosevelt free to pursue his preferred objectives at home, to lift prices, especially commodity prices, without regard to the fixed price of gold or to the international flow of gold, which had deflated the American economy during the Hoover years. The president then moved, in the fall of 1933, to devalue the dollar by purchasing gold (see p. 701).

In March 1934, with devaluation accomplished, Roosevelt asked Congress for authority to enter into commercial agreements with foreign nations and to revise tariffs in accordance with such agreements up to 50 percent either way. That request for executive negotiation of reciprocal trade agreements met opposition in Congress, especially from protectionists. Only two Republicans in the House and three in the Senate supported the enabling legislation. But with Secretary Hull's devoted backing, the bill became law. By the end of 1935, reciprocal trade agreements were in effect with 14 countries; by 1945, with 29. The program reflected Hull's hopes for economic internationalism, but it did little to advance his related hopes for peace, or to relieve the balance-of-payments problems between the United States and foreign nations (indeed, debts owed the United States grew steadily during the 1930s).

In its reliance on both protectionism and currency manipulation, Hitler's Germany brought economic nationalism to its competitive peak. In the face of that development, and moved also by his hope for closer political relations among the democracies, in 1936 Roosevelt permitted the negotiation with Great Britain and France of a stabilization agreement that called for cooperation among the treasuries of the signatories to manage the value of their currencies in their common interest. That pact took a small first step toward the monetary cooperation that had been needed so long.

Disarmament Political cooperation had been foundering. Though Roosevelt recognized the dangers in the Nazi program and the "insane rush to further armaments," he remained aloof from engagement in Europe. The United States was geographically remote. The president had to defer to isolationist strength in

Congress; the depression claimed his first attention. If, moreover, war were to come, he was resolved to keep America out of it. Yet international disarmament, which might have reduced the chance of war, required American cooperation, which the president could not arrange. Under those conditions, American foreign policy stumbled.

Since its beginning in 1932, the Geneva conference on disarmament had been stalled over German demands for equal strength and French insistence on reliable protection against the possibility of German aggression. The rise to power of the Nazis in 1933 gave the German demand an ominous cast. In May 1933 Roosevelt authorized the American representative at Geneva to say that, if international agreement effected a substantial reduction in arms, the United States was prepared to consult with the other states in case of a threat to peace. If the others identified an aggressor and the United States agreed, the United States would cooperate by foregoing its traditional insistence on neutral rights, including freedom of the seas. But when the administration asked Congress for a resolution authorizing the executive to embargo arms shipments to aggressors, the Senate Foreign Relations Committee responded with a resolution banning shipments to all belligerents. Since that change would have defeated the president's purpose, and since he could not budge the committee, the episode confirmed European skepticism about American intentions.

The Geneva conference failed, as Hitler's aims would in any case have assured. In 1934 Japan terminated the Washington Naval Treaty. The hope of averting war through disarmament was gone. Since the American government was not prepared to cooperate to keep the peace at the risk of war, its only remaining alternative was neutrality.

Relations with Great Britain and the Soviet Union

The collapse of disarmament was accompanied by continuing difficulties in American relations with the leading anti-Hitler powers. Roosevelt's message to the London Economic Conference had exasperated the British Cabinet, whose policies exasperated him. An important faction of that Cabinet, led by Neville Chamberlain, the chancellor of the exchequer, so deeply distrusted the United States that in 1934 it seriously considered whether Britain should base its strategy on cooperation with Japan instead of with the United States. In that event, Roosevelt warned the British, the United States would endeavor to link its security with that of Canada, Australia, and New Zealand. The Japanese themselves soon took care of the problem by presenting the British with rearmament

Hitler meant war

demands so extreme that even the pro-Tokyo Cabinet members had to abandon their policy.

Roosevelt's efforts to establish friendly relations with the Soviet Union were hardly more successful. Support for the recognition of the Communist regime had been growing for some time before 1933. Business leaders saw in Russia a market for American surplus production. The renewal of Japanese aggression argued for a normalization of Soviet-American relations as a means of restraining the Japanese. In October 1933 Maxim Litvinov, the Soviet commissar for foreign affairs, came to Washington to work out a set of agreements. In one document Litvinov pledged to refrain from any intervention in American internal affairs—a pledge that covered not only the Soviet government itself but any organizations "under its direct or indirect control." Another memorandum provided what seemed to be a formula for the settlement of Russian debts to the United States. The discussions concluded in the establishment of formal relations between the two governments.

Despite this beginning, relations soon returned to a state of mistrust. The attempt to make the Soviet government live up to its promises on propaganda and debts led to frustration. American representatives in Moscow encountered harassment and hostility. When American Communists went to Moscow in July 1935 for the seventh congress of the Comintern, their presence seemed, in the view of the American ambassador, to constitute "a flagrant violation of Litvinov's pledge" and a justification for the severance of diplomatic ties. Though the government did not go that far, relations with Soviet Russia remained cool.

Maxim Litvinov and Cordell Hull

ISOLATIONISM AT FLOOD TIDE

The Rout of the Internationalists Failure to strengthen relations with Britain and the Soviet Union coincided with a crystallization of isolationist sentiment in the United States. By the early 1930s, few Americans were prepared to make an all-out defense of Wilson's decision of 1917. "Revisionist" historians had reconsidered American entry into the war. Their scholarship seemed to reveal the war as a sordid scramble among imperialist powers. Who had drawn the United States in and why? The new disillusion was clinched in 1934 and 1935 by the work of a Senate committee set up under the chairmanship of Gerald P. Nye of North Dakota to investigate the munitions industry. The Nye Committee purported to show that the United States had been shoved into war when international bankers saw no other way to guarantee repayment of the vast credits they had granted to the western Allies. Nye also charged Wilson with duplicity in pretending to be ignorant of the secret treaties.

The Nye Committee consolidated the isolationists' argument. They could conceive of no world war that would present a moral issue between the antagonists or a strategic threat to American security. They were also convinced that American freedom could not survive participation in another holocaust. America's best contribution to peace and democracy, in their judgment, lay in absolute rejection of the power struggles of Europe and Asia.

Roosevelt quickly learned the new power of isolationism. In January 1935, a short time after the stunning Democratic victory in the 1934 elections, he sent the Senate a recommendation that the United States join the World Court. Joining the World Court could hardly have been a more innocuous act, but the isolationist bloc staged an extraordinary appeal to public opinion, and an outpouring of protest defeated the resolution.

The Design of Neutrality The next problem, as the Nye Committee saw it, was to make sure the forces that had brought about American participation in the First World War would never have their way again.

If the United States had been drawn into that war to ensure the repayment of debts owed to American bankers and munitions makers, then to keep out of war it would be necessary to forbid loans and the export of arms to belligerents. The Johnson Act of 1934 prohibited loans to governments that were in default. If the United States had been drawn into that war because American ships carried supplies to belligerent nations or because American citizens insisted on traveling on belligerent ships, then to keep out of war such actions should also be prohibited. If the United States had been drawn into war by the unneutral decisions of a president with too much discretion in the conduct of foreign policy, then the president should be denied that discretion.

The administration, yielding to isolationist pressure, agreed that the president should have authority to prohibit American ships from carrying arms and munitions, to withdraw the protection of the government from Americans traveling on belligerent vessels, and to impose an embargo on arms and loans. But the administration wanted the president to be able to use these powers at his discretion. The senators, with the image of the perfidious Wilson in mind, wanted to make it mandatory that he use them against *all* belligerents—which would nullify American influence in the case of conflict. The resulting compromise of 1935 contained a mandatory arms embargo but made it effective only until March 1, 1936. In other respects the bill gave the president discretion. The administration accepted the measure rather than risk exacerbation of isolationist sentiment.

NEUTRALITY ON TEST

Italy Invades Ethiopia In October 1935 Italian troops invaded Ethiopia from Eritrea and Italian Somaliland. In his message to Congress in January 1936, Roosevelt indicted nations that had the "fantastic conception that they, and they alone, are chosen to fulfill a mission and that all the others . . . in the world must . . . be subject to them." At the same time, he issued a proclamation of neutrality and invoked the mandatory arms embargo.

The supposition in Washington was that the embargo would hurt Italy more than Ethiopia, since Ethiopia lacked dollars to buy arms. Actually the arms embargo did Italy little harm, since it had its own munitions industry. Where the restriction of American exports really could hurt the Italian war-making capacity was in oil. But the Neutrality Act covered only implements of war. Roosevelt accordingly called for a voluntary restriction, a "moral embargo." That embargo aroused the protests of the Italian government and met with general defiance by American oil companies. Still, the American policy preceded by many weeks economic sanctions by the League, which did not include oil.

When Congress convened in 1936, one of its first tasks was to replace the neutrality resolution of 1935, but in the end it extended the existing act until May 1, 1937, with amendments banning credits to belligerents and leaving it up to the president to decide that a state of war existed before the act could be invoked.

The outbreak of civil war in Spain in 1936 deepened Roosevelt's sense of a general European disintegration. In a revealing speech, he set forth his hatred of war, his commitment to neutrality, and his determination to keep the United States out of another world conflict. His correspondence reflected a hope that a conference among heads of state might avert the drift to Armageddon, but he found no formula that promised success and thus took no action.

The attempt of Spanish Fascists, joined by monarchists and clericals, under General Francisco Franco to overthrow the democratic government of Spain created new problems. The mandatory embargo applied to wars between nations, not to civil wars. In January 1937, Congress, with Roosevelt's support and with but one negative vote in both houses, enacted a resolution aligning the United States with Britain and France in a program of nonintervention and in banning shipments of implements of war to either side in Spain. Neutral in intention, the resolution in fact helped Franco, for he received far more military assistance from Italy and Germany than his opponents received from the Soviet Union.

Then Congress faced again the question of rewriting the existing neutrality legislation. The main innovation in 1937 was the cash-and-carry proposal, which provided that, once the president had proclaimed the existence of a state of war, no nonmilitary goods could be shipped to a belligerent until the purchaser acquired full title and took them away itself. The administration supported this idea in order to head off an automatic embargo on all goods. Ironically, the amendment clearly had the unneutral effect of favoring the maritime powers, notably Britain and Japan, and in that way denying American goods to nations like Germany and China. Nevertheless, Congress adopted the provision by sweeping majorities.

AGGRESSION IN ASIA

The Problem of China For many Americans the problems of Europe had come to seem more remote than the problems of Asia. Since the announcement of the Open Door doctrine, the United States had conceived of itself as playing a direct role in the affairs of East Asia. By 1915 Washington had concluded that the threat to the Open Door would come from Japan. Both the Washington Naval Conference and the Stimson Doctrine were designed to restrain Tokyo.

In addition, years of missionary endeavor had given many Americans sympathy with China in its struggle for nationhood. Roosevelt, who shared this sympathy, himself endorsed the Stimson Doctrine. But in April 1934, Eiji Amau, spokesman for the Japanese foreign office, demanded for Japan a free hand in China. Soon Japan denounced the Five Power Treaty.

Those developments confronted the United States with perplexing problems. Some historians have argued that the American motive was to secure markets and investment outlets in China for American capitalism. But American trade with China was negligible, and American investment there far below British. Japan was the most profitable American market in Asia. What concerned Roosevelt was the Japanese challenge to international order—the fear that, if aggression ran on with impunity, the peace system would collapse and war might engulf the United States. The preservation of that system seemed a vital American interest. In addition, an expanding Japan could deny the United States strategic materials, like natural rubber, that were essential to national security.

To the State Department, the cornerstone in a containment policy had to be the buildup of the United States Navy. So long as America remained weak in Asian waters, Cordell Hull reasoned, any attempt to oppose the Japanese or to help the Chinese would serve only to provoke Tokyo unnecessarily. Naval superiority became not only the indispensable condition for a future American policy in East Asia but a powerful argument against present action. Thus the State Department generally opposed proposals to condemn Japan or aid China.

The Renewal of Japanese Aggression In the meantime, the Chinese, under the leadership of Chiang Kai-shek, were making progress toward the unification of their nation. Perhaps wishing to halt that process, the Japanese used troop clashes at the Marco Polo Bridge in July 1937 as an excuse for an invasion of China. By the end of the month, Japanese soldiers had seized Beijing (Peking) and Tianjin (Tientsin). The subsequent bombing of Shanghai by Japanese planes and the sack of Nanjing (Nanking) in December horrified Americans. The Chinese retreated to the interior, established their capital at Chongqing (Chungking), and prepared to keep up their resistance.

Popular sympathy in the United States was wholly with the Chinese, but official reaction was cautious. Britain and America warded off Chinese pressure for invocation of the Nine Power Treaty (see p. 638) and instead allowed the matter to go to the League for perfunctory condemnation. The president, however, displayed his solicitude for the Chinese by refusing to proclaim the existence of a state of war between China and Japan. Without such a proclamation, the arms embargo and the cash-and-carry provision for nonmilitary commodities would not go into effect. Those provisions would hurt China, which had to import implements of war, whereas Japan had ample stockpiles and a productive capacity of its own. Moreover, an arms embargo could not cut off what Japan needed most—oil and scrap metal. And cash-and-carry would favor Japan as a solvent customer and naval power.

AWAKENING THE NATION

The Quarantine Speech The disintegration of the peace system promised to loose war upon the world. Moreover, as peace collapsed, Nazi Germany might seize control of the power and resources of Europe. Roosevelt regarded that prospect as a mortal threat to the United States. He even proposed a personal meeting with Neville Chamberlain, now British prime minister. But Chamberlain had no confidence in the United States and dedicated himself instead to the hope of making Hitler reasonable through a program of appeasement.

The renewal of warfare in China heightened the sense of international urgency. It also turned Roose-

Japanese in Tianjin (Tientsin), China

velt's attention to an idea that had been in the back of his mind for many years—the deterrence of aggression by holding over potential aggressors the threat of the severance of all trade or financial relations. In a speech at Chicago in October 1937, the president declared that "the present reign of terror and international lawlessness" had reached a stage "where the very foundations of civilization are seriously threatened." If aggression continued, he said, "let no one imagine America will escape." In a cryptic passage, he compared "the epidemic of world lawlessness" to an epidemic of physical disease and advocated a "quarantine" to protect the community against the contagion.

Aftermath of the Quarantine Speech Roosevelt's main purpose was to awaken the nation to the dangers of world war. A secondary purpose was very likely to explore the readiness of the American people to support some form of boycott of aggressors—moral or perhaps economic.

In the international sphere, the quarantine speech encouraged the British to call the signatories of the Nine Power Treaty to a conference at Brussels to deal with the new Sino-Japanese conflict. But first the British sent word to Washington that they could do nothing about imposing sanctions against Japan unless they received "assurance of military support" in the event of Japanese retaliation. Roosevelt declined to give such guarantees; the British declined to act without them; and the Brussels Conference came to nothing.

In the meantime, Under Secretary of State Sumner Welles suggested that Roosevelt convene a conference of neutral nations to set forth a peace program based on nonaggressive standards of international behavior. But Chamberlain rejected the American initiative, thus—in Winston Churchill's later words—losing "the last frail chance to save the world from tyranny otherwise than by war."

Within the United States opinion about the quarantine speech was mixed, but the organized reaction

Democracy or Autocracy

The President read us [the Cabinet] excerpts from the speech that he was to make on . . . the hundred and fiftieth anniversary of the signing of the Constitution. . . . In the first part of this speech he made a plea for democracy, as opposed to autocracies, either of the right or the left. . . . He . . . insisted that democracy was the better way of life. [Secretary of State] Hull thought this language ought to be toned down a little, although it didn't seem to me to be anything that anyone could object to. Hull has become so timid that he tries to walk without casting a shadow. After some discussion I could contain myself no longer, so I blurted out that at the Nazi gathering at Nuremberg recently speakers had not pulled their punches when they talked about democracy. They had gone all the way in saying that democracies were a failure and in extolling the virtues of Nazism. The President remarked: "That is right," and it seemed to me that in his mind he decided to disregard Hull's objections. As the President gave his speech [on September 17] . . . he said substantially what he had read us from his draft.

From Harold L. Ickes, *The Secret Diary of Harold L. Ickes*, v. 11 (1–954), on a Cabinet meeting of September 14, 1937

was so unfavorable that the president at a press conference seemed to retreat from what he had said. Further, most Americans, while sharing Roosevelt's detestation of dictators, detested war even more. When Japanese planes sank the American gunboat *Panay* in the Yangtze River in December 1937, the nation accepted Japanese apologies and indemnification with relief. The quarantine idea, vague enough at best, perished between American reluctance and British indifference.

THE ROAD TO WAR

The End of Appeasement In 1936 German troops moved into the Rhineland. In March 1938 Germany invaded and annexed Austria. Roosevelt invited 32 countries to set up a joint committee to facilitate the emigration of persecuted Jews from Germany and Austria, but neither the United States nor any other nation was willing to provide an adequate asylum. The president did arrange for some 15,000 refugees on visitors permits to remain in the United States, but he did not combat congressional and public opinion that opposed any relaxation of the immigration quotas. Among the Jews who reached America were eminent scholars in every field of learning who made striking contributions not only to scientific endeavor but also to national culture.

In the months after he swallowed Austria, Hitler began to use the plight of the German minority in the Sudetenland as a pretext for demands on the government of Czechoslovakia. As the Czech crisis deepened in September 1938, Chamberlain requested a personal conference with Hitler. There followed a series of meetings attended by Hitler and Chamberlain, and ultimately Prime Minister Daladier of France and Mussolini. No representatives of Czechoslovakia or of the Soviet Union were present. At the Munich meeting on September 29, the democratic powers swallowed Hitler's terms. Czechoslovakia had no choice other than to acquiesce bitterly in the German annexation of the Sudetenland (see Map 28-1).

The first reaction in the United States was one of relief. The appeasement policy seemed to have averted war. But soon people began to compute the price of appeasement: not just the establishment of

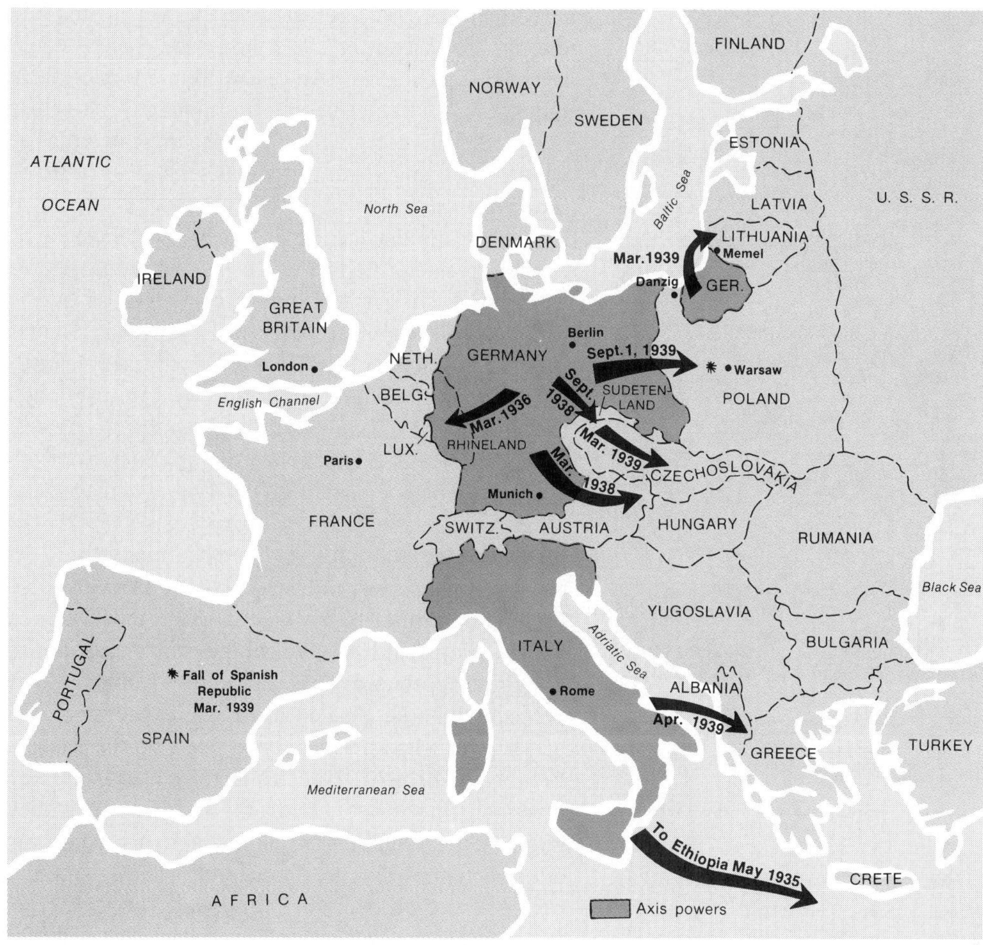

Map 28-1 *Aggressions leading to the Second World War in Europe*

German hegemony in Central Europe, but the incentive offered everywhere to intimidation and aggression.

Rearmament During the 1920s the regular army had fallen well below the size authorized by the National Defense Act of 1920 and the navy below the levels permitted by the various international agreements. Roosevelt tried to rebuild American military and naval power. The Public Works Administration constructed cruisers and aircraft carriers. In 1935 Congress authorized the army to increase its enlisted strength. In 1938 Roosevelt called for larger defense appropriations and Congress passed the Naval Expansion Act. In the months after Munich, Roosevelt requested further increases in the defense budget and encouraged British and French purchasing missions to place defense orders in the United States.

In other respects Roosevelt began to tighten his ship in preparation for storms ahead. Following the failure of his "purge" in 1938 (see p. 717), he moved toward a tacit political truce, moderating his liberal objectives in the hope of gaining support for his foreign and defense policies. He also gathered support in the American hemisphere. In December 1938 in the Declaration of Lima, the American republics announced their collective determination to resist fascist threats to peace.

The Neutrality Act remained the greatest obstacle to a positive policy. Hitler's invasion of Czechoslovakia on March 15, 1939, persuaded even Neville Chamberlain of the bankruptcy of appeasement. The State Department denounced Germany's "wanton lawlessness," and the administration stepped up its campaign for the modification of the arms embargo. But isolationist senators, confident there would be no war

Rushing toward climax: Hitler in Czechoslovakia, 1939

in 1939, insisted that the matter be laid over to the next session of Congress.

In Europe events rushed toward climax. The invasion of Czechoslovakia was followed by the German occupation of Memel (March 23), the collapse of the Spanish Republic (March 28), and the Italian invasion of Albania (April 7)—see Map 28-1. Through the summer Hitler carried on a war of nerves against Poland, using a German minority in Danzig as his tool. In the meantime his emissaries were secretly negotiating a nonaggression pact with the Soviet Union. On August 23 the German-Russian pact was signed in Moscow. The next day Britain and Poland signed a pact of mutual assistance. On September 1 Germany attacked Poland. Two days later Britain and France declared war on Germany. The Second World War was under way.

AMERICA AND THE WAR

First Reactions "When peace has been broken anywhere," Roosevelt said in a fireside chat on the evening of September 3, 1939, "the peace of all countries everywhere is in danger." He reaffirmed his determination to keep war out of America. But, in marked contrast to Wilson in 1914, he added that he could not ask that "every American remain neutral in thought. . . . Even a neutral cannot be asked to close his mind or his conscience." He also indicated that he would call Congress into special session in order to repeal the arms embargo.

The isolationist leaders in the Senate, backed by former President Hoover and by such national figures as Colonel Charles A. Lindbergh, as well as by the American Communist party (following the Soviet-Nazi pact), declared that Roosevelt's course was leading straight to war. The opposition was strong enough to compel the administration to accept restrictive compromises in exchange for the elimination of the embargo. The law signed on November 4 placed the arms trade on a cash-and-carry basis. Where the previous legislation had favored Germany, with its well-established war industries, the new law enabled Britain and France to buy war materials in the United States so long as they were willing to pay cash and to carry their purchases away in their own ships.

Meanwhile the Nazi air force and Panzer divisions had subdued Poland in a three-week campaign. The French and British had been able to do little to create a diversion on the western front, and the war settled into an aspect of apparent quiescence that won it the derisive name of "the phony war." While opinion polls showed an overwhelming public preference in America for the western Allies against Germany (in October 1939, 62 percent of the population favored all possible aid to the Allies short of war), less than 30 percent favored American entry into the war even if Britain and France were in danger of defeat.

American emotions were perhaps more engaged when the Soviet Union, having advanced into eastern Poland in September, moved into the small Baltic republics of Latvia, Estonia, and Lithuania in October and invaded Finland in late November. The American people and their president were indignant over the onslaught on the "gallant little Finns." Isolationists, however, were alert not to let emotion over Finland drag the nation closer toward war. The administration's cautious program of aid to Finland encountered strong opposition in Congress and had hardly gone into effect when the Winter War came to an end in March 1940.

Blitzkrieg Hitler was already preparing the blow that he hoped would break the will of his western

Isolationism: A Confession of Faith

What was pushing behind Communism? What behind Fascism in Italy? What behind Naziism? Is it nothing but a "return to barbarism," to be crushed at all costs by a "crusade"? Or is some new, and perhaps even ultimately good, conception of humanity trying to come to birth, often through evil and horrible forms and abortive attempts? . . . I cannot see this war, then simply and purely as a struggle between the "Forces of Good" and the "Forces of Evil." If I could simplify it into a phrase at all, it would seem truer to say that the "Forces of the Past" are fighting against the "Forces of the Future." . . .

Somehow the leaders in Germany, Italy and Russia have discovered how to use new social and economic forces. . . . They have felt the wave of the future and they have leapt upon it. The evils we deplore in these systems are not in themselves the future; they are scum on the wave of the future. . . . There is no fighting the wave of the future, any more than as a child you could fight against the gigantic roller that loomed up ahead of you.

From Anne Morrow Lindbergh, *The Wave of the Future,* 1940

antagonists. On April 9, 1940, Germany attacked Denmark and Norway, where resistance collapsed by the end of the month. Popular discontent in Britain forced Chamberlain to resign, and Winston Churchill, who had long criticized the appeasement policy and, after the outbreak of war, had served as first lord of the admiralty, became prime minister.

Chamberlain was in the course of resigning on May 10 when Nazi mechanized divisions invaded the Netherlands, Belgium, and Luxembourg. In a week they were thrusting deep into northern France. The British and French were unable to cope with the speed of the German attack. The main part of the British forces retreated to Dunkirk, where they were evacuated, along with some French forces, across the English Channel by small warships of the British navy, assisted by a heroic flotilla of small boats conjured up from British ports. In a few days Italy, joining the war, invaded France from the south. "The hand that held the dagger," Roosevelt said grimly, "has struck it into the back of its neighbor." Soon Paris fell, Marshal Pétain became head of the French government, and on June 22 France and Germany signed an armistice at Compiègne. The next day, from London, General Charles de Gaulle, then an obscure and lonely figure, pledged continued French resistance.

The success of the Nazi blitzkrieg had a stunning effect on American opinion. Citing "the almost incredible events of the past two weeks," Roosevelt asked Congress for more than a billion dollars in additional defense appropriations. He called in particular for the annual production of 50,000 warplanes. He also set up a National Defense Advisory Commission to plan defense production. And he began to consider how he could aid Britain, now standing alone against the Berlin-Rome Axis. Churchill's rise to power ended the glumness that had marked Anglo-American relations during the Chamberlain period. Roosevelt, who had for some months exchanged letters with the new prime minister, recognized him as a man of congenial temperament and stature. When Churchill offered his own people nothing but "blood, toil, tears and sweat," when he promised to "wage war by sea, land and air, with all our might and with all the strength that God can give us," he made a profound appeal to the American imagination.

But Britain needed more than sympathy. On May 15 Churchill sent Roosevelt a long list of specific requirements, including old destroyers, new aircraft, and materials of war. For the moment Washington could do little, partly because of America's own defense needs, partly (as in the case of the destroyers) because Roosevelt feared that congressional assent would not be forthcoming. After Dunkirk the American government did scrape together small arms and ammunition for the British to use in the desperate eventuality of a German invasion. But the problems of American policy were now further complicated by the approach of the 1940 presidential campaign.

Wendell Willkie: magnetic qualities

THE ELECTION OF 1940

The Third Term The struggle between isolationists and interventionists cut across party lines. Roosevelt found some of the most effective supporters of his foreign policy in the ranks of internationalist Republicans—a fact he acknowledged in June 1940, when he appointed Henry L. Stimson of New York as secretary of war and Frank Knox of Illinois as secretary of the navy. But when the Republicans gathered in Philadelphia to select a presidential candidate, they read Stimson and Knox out of the party and prepared to choose between two candidates, Senator Robert A. Taft of Ohio and Thomas E. Dewey of New York, both identified with isolationism though neither held the rigid views of Senator Nye.

The Republican regulars did not allow for the enthusiasm with which a group of internationalists rallied support for a dark-horse candidate, Wendell L. Willkie of Indiana, an affable and articulate businessman with magnetic qualities of personality. Willkie had won attention as an antagonist of the New Deal during the fight over the Tennessee Valley Authority. Actually he had been a Democrat himself most of his life, his personal views were on the liberal side, and he sympathized with the Roosevelt policy of aid to Great Britain. To general astonishment, the Willkie forces staged a blitzkrieg of their own at Philadelphia, and the former Democrat emerged as the Republican candidate.

As for the Democrats, Roosevelt had failed to develop an heir apparent. For many months ardent New Dealers had demanded that he stand himself for a third term. Conservative Democrats, led by Vice President Garner and Postmaster General Farley, sought to organize opposition on the ground that a third term would violate a sacred American tradition. But the international urgencies made Roosevelt seem to most Democrats the indispensable candidate. The Democratic convention accordingly renominated him at Chicago in July, though it swallowed hard at his insistence on Henry A. Wallace, the secretary of agriculture, for vice president.

Foreign Policy and the Campaign While Americans concerned themselves with presidential politics, the German Luftwaffe launched a savage air war against England. If Britain hoped to repulse an anticipated German invasion—as well as maintain its own lines of supply—it needed immediate reinforcement of its battered destroyer fleet, as Churchill cabled Roosevelt on July 31. Roosevelt feared the political repercussions in a campaign in which he was already under attack for unneutral acts, but he was persuaded that he could legally release overage destroyers. And he received assurances that Willkie, the Republican candidate, would not oppose the transaction. Accordingly, on September 2 the United States by executive agreement transferred 50 destroyers to Britain in exchange for 99-year leases of bases in Newfoundland and the Caribbean (see Map 28-2).

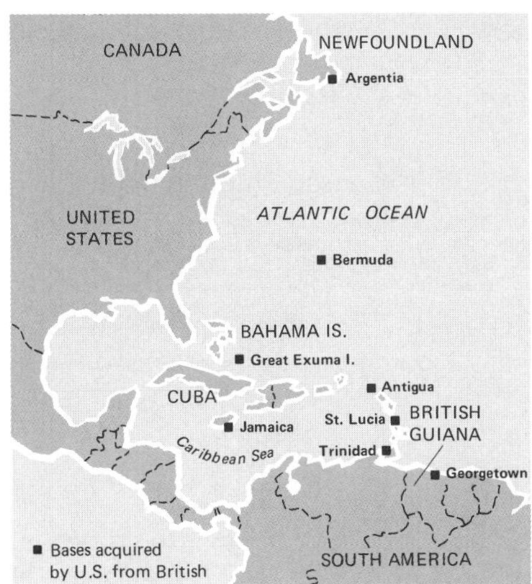

Map 28-2 *The U.S.-British destroyer-bases agreement, 1940*

Willkie's support of conscription also enabled the administration to obtain a Selective Service Act in August. Still, though Willkie's internationalism minimized the role of foreign policy in the campaign, it did not altogether eliminate it. Indeed, as the campaign wore on, the Republican candidate assailed Roosevelt's foreign policy and predicted that Roosevelt, if elected, would have the nation in war by April 1941. Roosevelt was himself assuring American parents: "I have said this before, but I shall say it again and again and again: Your boys are not going to be sent into any foreign wars."

Roosevelt still retained the national confidence. He received 27 million popular votes against 22 million for Willkie; the Electoral College margin was 449 to 82 (see Map 28-3). But he received only 54.8 percent of the vote as against 60.8 percent in 1936, and more than ever before he needed his pluralities in the cities. Because of the equivocal way in which both candidates had presented the foreign policy issues — had, indeed, somewhat misrepresented their own convictions — the election did not serve either to clarify public thinking or to produce a setting for future action.

AID SHORT OF WAR

The Lend-Lease Act Through 1940 Britain had been able to get the goods it needed under the system of cash-and-carry. But, as Churchill urged on Roosevelt in December, both features of the system were in peril — "cash" because Britain's supply of American dollars was nearing exhaustion, "carry" because of the effectiveness of the German submarine campaign against British shipping.

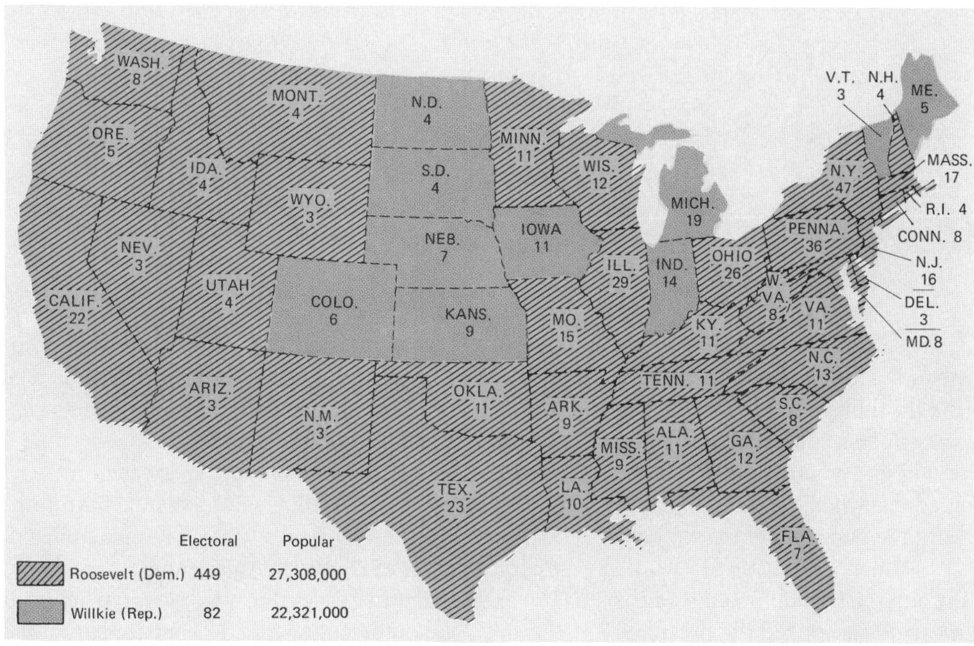

Map 28-3
The election of 1940

Threat and Promise, 1941.

Every realist knows that the democratic way of life is . . . being directly assailed in every part of the world. . . . This assault has blotted out the whole pattern of democratic life in an appalling number of independent nations, great and small. The assailants are still on the march. . . .

The future and safety of our country and our democracy are overwhelmingly involved in events far beyond our borders. . . . No realistic American can expect from a dictator's peace international generosity, or return to true independence, or world disarmament, or freedom . . . or even good business. . . .

The need of the moment is that our action and our policy should be devoted primarily—almost exclusively—to meeting this foreign peril. For all our domestic problems are now a part of the great emergency. . . .

In the future days, which we seek to make secure, we look forward to a world founded upon four essential human freedoms.

The first is freedom of speech and expression—everywhere in the world.

The second is freedom of every person to worship God in his own way—everywhere in the world.

The third is freedom from want—which . . . means economic understandings which will secure to every nation a healthy peacetime life for its inhabitants—everywhere in the world.

The fourth is freedom from fear—which . . . means a world-wide reduction of armaments to such a point and in such a thorough fashion that no nation will be in a position to commit an act of physical aggression against any neighbor—everywhere in the world.

Franklin D. Roosevelt, State of the Union Message to Congress, January 1941

"The thing to do," Roosevelt now told Secretary of the Treasury Morgenthau, "is to get away from a dollar sign. I don't want to put the thing in terms of dollars or loans." As he put it to his press conference, why not say to England, "We will give you the guns and the ships you need, provided that when the war is over you will return to us in kind the guns and ships we have loaned to you"?

In January 1941 the administration introduced the lend-lease bill. The measure authorized the president to sell, transfer, exchange, lend, or lease war equipment and other commodities to the "government of any country whose defense the President deems vital to the defense of the United States." So sweeping a proposal aroused bitter isolationist opposition. "The lend-lease-give program," said Senator Burton K. Wheeler, "is the New Deal's triple A foreign policy; it will plow under every fourth American boy." Senators Taft and Vandenberg feared that Congress, if it passed the bill, would surrender much of its constitutional authority over foreign policy. Among those who testified against the bill were Charles A. Lindbergh, Charles A. Beard, the historian, and Joseph P. Kennedy, the former ambassador to England. Wendell Willkie led a parade of witnesses in its favor. But public sentiment strongly supported the proposal. Assured of biannual review of lend-lease appropriations, Congress passed the bill in March. "Through this legislation," Roosevelt said, "our country has determined to do its full part in creating an adequate arsenal of democracy."

The Battle of the Atlantic The Lend-Lease Act committed the economic power of the United States to the support of Britain. It also implied, as its opponents had predicted, at least a partial commitment of American naval power. For, if the United States deemed aid to Britain vital to American security, then the United States had better make sure that goods intended for Britain actually arrived there. Shortly after the passage of lend-lease, the Germans joined the challenge by extending the North Atlantic war zone westward to the coast of Greenland. As German submarines and destroyers sank increasing numbers of British ships, Roosevelt sought means for protecting the Atlantic lifeline and strengthening the defenses of the Western Hemisphere. In April 1941 he concluded an executive agreement with the Danish government-in-exile to send American troops to Greenland, a part of the Western Hemisphere, and he extended to that area American naval and air patrols. Those moves lessened but did not resolve the problem of the Atlantic lifeline.

Unlimited National Emergency Roosevelt's policy of aid to Great Britain was not limited only by the fear of an adverse public reaction. The president himself apparently cherished the hope, which many around him had abandoned by the spring of 1941, that Hitler might be defeated without direct American military involvement.

Yet Britain's situation was growing worse. German victories in Yugoslavia and Greece drove the British off the continent of Europe. In the United States the attitude of business as usual impeded full mobilization of the economy. The Office of Production Management had succeeded the National Defense Advisory Commission in January 1941, but the new agency lacked adequate authority over allocations and priorities. Many business leaders were disinclined to convert their facilities to defense needs. Strikes, some of them instigated by Communists, troubled defense industries. Some step seemed necessary to galvanize America and to reassure Britain. On May 27, 1941, the president in a speech to the nation proclaimed "that an unlimited national emergency exists and requires the strengthening of our defense to the extreme limit of our national power."

McDonnell Douglas factory: one arsenal of democracy

Roosevelt's proclamation called for preparing American defenses to repel any attack on the Western Hemisphere. To that end, in July by executive agreement he dispatched American troops to Iceland, outside the hemisphere. Had the Nazis reached Iceland first, he argued, they would have threatened the flow of munitions to England, a matter of policy Congress had approved in the Lend-Lease Act. Senator Robert Taft disagreed. The president, he said, had no constitutional right to send troops to Iceland without congressional approval, for there had been no attack upon the United States, nor was there a threat of an attack. Though only one senator supported Taft's protest, the president was stretching his authority to its limits and in so doing moving American forces to the edge of the war.

The Great Debate The slow unfolding of American policy had been accompanied by an intensification of public debate. In 1940 the Committee to Defend America by Aiding the Allies was established under the chair of the Kansas editor William Allen White to argue the moderate interventionist position. In 1941 the Fight for Freedom Committee contended for American entry into the war. On the other side, the America First Committee argued that Hitler's victory would not menace American security.

The resulting debate became more bitter even than the arguments over the New Deal. It cut across political, economic, and geographical lines. Isolationists were to be found in all parts of the country, in all social classes, and in all political parties. Still, to a considerable degree, isolationism as a political force represented the conservative Republican wing of the business community, with special strength in the Middle West. Progressives like Burton K. Wheeler, Socialists like Norman Thomas, and the Communists also criticized Roosevelt's policies. The German-American Bund and the fringe of pro-Nazi groups in America endorsed the isolationist position.

The Isolationist Dilemma Most Americans remained uncertain—against participation in the war but also against totalitarian nations. Votes in Congress revealed not a rigid isolationist-interventionist division, but a large middle bloc trying to steer a course between the two extremes. Most members of Congress, like most Americans, wished that all-out support of Britain short of war would in itself bring British victory, but in providing Britain such support, they edged steadily toward involvement. Yet involvement was the last resort they earnestly hoped to avoid. Activists like Henry L. Stimson, Harold L. Ickes, and the members of the Fight for Freedom Committee felt that Roosevelt himself, by refusing to call for an American declaration of war, was engaged in self-delusion. Still, the president's policy expressed the predominant sense of the electorate in 1941. Had he been more forthright about the risks he took, he might have appeared less duplicitous to his opponents. He might also in so doing have heightened the fears of Americans, lost their support, and thus constrained his ability to combat the terror that was threatening the world.

Hitler Widens the War After the Soviet Union attacked Finland, Roosevelt had condemned Stalin's regime as "a dictatorship as absolute as any other dictatorship in the world." Nonetheless, American diplomats, noting growing evidence of tension between Germany and Russia, told a skeptical Kremlin in the winter of 1940–41 that a German attack might be in the making. Stalin remained impervious to warnings. Hitler hoped that by conquering the Soviet Union he could deprive Britain of its last potential ally for war on the continent. He could then, he believed, persuade the British to sue for peace. He also intended to eliminate the potential threat of Russia by a sudden blow. The Soviet regime was taken by surprise. The Nazi invasion of the USSR on June 22, 1941, brought the European war into a new phase.

Winston Churchill had long since decided that, in such an eventuality, he would offer Russia full British support. Roosevelt was ready to accept that policy. Despite warnings that Russia could not be expected to hold out, he sent Harry Hopkins to Moscow in July. Hopkins's relatively optimistic report confirmed Churchill and Roosevelt in their decision to do what they could to stiffen Soviet resistance.

Most Americans supported this decision. The American Communists, of course, became passionate proponents of national defense. From an isolationist viewpoint, however, Hitler's new embroilment strengthened the case against American participation.

War from the air: Churchill in Parliament, 1941

The Atlantic Charter In August, Roosevelt and Churchill met on warships off Argentia on the coast of Newfoundland. While Roosevelt avoided military commitments, he did agree with Churchill on "certain common principles in the national policies of their respective countries on which they base their hopes for a better future for the world." In the Atlantic Charter, Britain and the United States disclaimed territorial aggrandizement, affirmed the right of all peoples to choose their own form of government and to express freely their wishes concerning territorial changes (though Churchill excepted the peoples within the British Empire), assured all states equal access to trade and raw materials ("with due respect to their existing obligations"), proposed collaboration among all nations in the economic field, and promised "after the final destruction of the Nazi tyranny" the disarmament of all aggressor nations "pending the establishment of a wider and permanent system of general security."

By the time of the Newfoundland conference American destroyers were escorting convoys as far as Iceland, leaving the British navy to conduct them the rest of the way. The question of what American ships should do if they encountered a German raider was left unanswered until a U-boat fired on the destroyer *Greer* early in September. Though the president did not so inform the American people, the *Greer* had provoked the attack. Saying the time had come for "active defense," Roosevelt instructed the navy to "shoot on sight" any Axis ships in the American neutrality zone. In October the Germans badly damaged one American destroyer and sank another with considerable loss of life. In November Congress revised the Neutrality Act to allow merchantmen to carry arms and to proceed to British ports. Roosevelt had consulted Congress about that measure, but he had not told the whole truth. To have done so, he feared, would have risked too much, for the House of Representatives had renewed the Selective Service Act by a margin of only one vote. Accordingly, the president had been disingenuous, as he knew, but in what he believed was a commanding cause.

Both the Argentia meeting and the new Atlantic policy goaded the isolationists into ever more impassioned attacks on the administration. In an angry speech, Charles A. Lindbergh declared that "the three most important groups who have been pressing this

The first summit, Argentia, 1941

country toward war are the British, the Jewish and the Roosevelt administration." Most isolationists disowned Lindbergh's anti-Semitism, but the course of the war and of the American role in it was rapidly diminishing the range of maneuver between the Nazis and their enemies.

THUNDER IN THE EAST

The Japanese Dilemma Despite the Japanese occupation of coastal China in 1937, the Chiang Kai-shek government and the Chinese Communists under Mao Zedong (Mao Tse-tung) had kept up their resistance. Their plight increasingly enlisted sympathy in the United States and Britain. Though neither government had full confidence in Chiang Kai-shek, both governments worried about Japanese expansion and were eager to sustain Chinese resistance. Chiang Kai-shek solicited their aid, which in 1938 they began to seek ways to provide.

Japan and the United States were then on a collision course, for the Japanese military in 1938 began to push their campaign in China southward with the purpose of gaining control over the Dutch East Indies and Singapore. That control would assure Japan of the raw materials—oil, tin, rubber—it needed and would create a huge East Asian fortress under Japanese hegemony. While pursuing that end, the Japanese hoped to maintain amicable relations with the United States. Consequently, they tolerated American financial aid to China. Indeed, Japan still depended on American exports. In 1938, for example, the United States supplied Japan with 90 percent of its metal scrap, 91 percent of its copper, and 66 percent of its oil. This trade was sanctioned by the Japanese-American commercial treaty of 1911, and the commodities involved were beyond the reach of existing neutrality legislation. The United States was left in the position of fueling a war machine of which it disapproved. In an effort to regain freedom of action, Washington informed Tokyo in July 1939 of its intention to terminate the commercial treaty, though, it added in January 1940, it would not for the time being disturb the existing trade.

Then the Nazi successes in Europe transformed the situation. The expansionists in Tokyo felt their opportunity had come to seize the colonial empires of France and the Netherlands, even perhaps of Britain. The relatively moderate government was overthrown. In its place came a tough government, dominated by the military and dedicated openly to the achievement of a "new order in Greater East Asia." In September Japan joined Germany and Italy in the Tripartite Pact. The Axis now extended to Asia, where Japan occupied northern French Indochina.

The American Response The American response was an embargo on essential materials, especially aviation gasoline and scrap metal. Since this action could be justified in terms of America's own defense needs, it did not have the flavor of an open affront to Japan. Behind the scenes, American representatives took part in staff discussions with British and Dutch officials to consider plans for the defense of the western Pacific.

Roosevelt, however, primarily concerned with the crisis in Europe, wished to stave off a showdown with Japan. Accordingly 1941 was marked by intricate and repetitious discussions between the two countries. In June the German invasion of the Soviet Union relieved Japan of its anxieties about a possible attack from Siberia. In mid-July 1941 Japanese troops invaded French Indochina and occupied Saigon. Roosevelt told the Japanese ambassador that if Japan withdrew from Indochina he would secure its neutralization and assure Japan access to its raw materials. If Japan persisted in its course, and especially if it moved into the Dutch East Indies, the United States would help the Dutch and probably cut off oil exports to Japan. When Japan did not reply, Roosevelt on July 26 froze Japanese assets in the United States and a few days later embargoed oil shipments. But the president did not accept Churchill's suggestion at Argentia for warning Japan that continued expansion would provoke hostilities.

The freezing order and embargo brought about a reappraisal in Tokyo. Prime Minister Fumimaro Konoye, a moderate, in August proposed a meeting with Roosevelt. Japan, Konoye's foreign minister promised, would withdraw its troops from Indochina as soon as the "China incident" was settled, would not expand southward or make war on the Soviet Union unless attacked, and would not feel bound by the Tripartite Pact to go to war if the United States became engaged in a defensive war with Germany. Though Roosevelt considered those terms favorable as a basis for peace in the Pacific, he felt that the United States had a responsibility to protect British and Dutch interest in East Asia. Further, Hull insisted on an agreement about China before any conference took place. The secretary of state and his advisers made the territorial integrity of China the crux of their diplomacy partly out of long habit and conviction, and partly in the false belief that Japan would in no event attack the United States. Persuaded by their belief, Roosevelt in his reply to Konoye on September 3 made China the key to negotiations. That was unacceptable to the Japanese war party. Late in September Konoye tried again, only to be rebuffed as before by Hull's demand for a prior agreement on China. Had Hull made a deal with Japan, it would have damaged Chinese morale and probably led to Chinese collapse. That would have freed the Japanese army from the Chinese campaign and facilitated its employment against British and Dutch possessions, which were supplying England with oil and rubber.

There was to be no turning back from that breakdown of diplomacy. As Roosevelt had long recognized, the first interest of the United States lay in preventing Nazi domination of Europe and Great Britain. Pursuit of that interest entailed avoiding, or at the least postponing, war with Japan. On that account the question of China might have been left until after the end of the European war. There was, however, no assurance that Konoye could have continued to restrain the Japanese army, which any concessions might have emboldened. Japan, moreover, had no right to dominion in China, and the Chinese resistance did evoke a natural American sympathy. But the timing of Hull's advice to Roosevelt, the irreconcilable objectives of Japan and the United States in Southeast Asia, and the adamancy of both the American and Japanese positions on China, eliminated the last chance for a Pacific armistice, however transitory.

The Rising Sun over the Pacific In mid-October the militants in the Japanese cabinet forced Konoye's resignation. Though his successor, General Hideki Tojo, was a leader of the war party, debate continued until November 5. The army then agreed to a last effort at accommodation with the United States provided that the emperor approve plans for an immediate attack if

Pearl Harbor, December 7, 1941

negotiations failed. Earlier the Japanese leaders had defined their minimum demands to include the abandonment of China by the United States and the restoration of normal commercial relations, with renewed delivery of oil and scrap metal. Now Tojo told Admiral Kichisabura Nomura, Japanese ambassador, that other matters would be negotiable but that Japan could never yield on the question of China.

By decoding secret Japanese messages, the Americans had been able to follow some of the Japanese moves. Officials in Washington realized that a decisive moment was approaching. Late in November American forces in the Pacific, including those in Hawaii, were sent the first of a number of alerts ordering them onto a war footing. Everyone expected attack, but with the conviction that the Japanese would move toward the south. In Washington, Cordell Hull continued to meet with Japanese representatives. On December 6 Roosevelt sent a final appeal to the emperor.

In the meantime, a striking force of Japanese aircraft carriers was making its way toward Pearl Harbor. On December 7, 1941, while discussions continued in Washington, the Japanese launched a devastating attack on the fleet and air force in Hawaii. An epoch in American history had come to an end.

"In the past few years—and, most violently, in the past few days—we have learned a terrible lesson," said Franklin Roosevelt two days later. He asked Congress to recognize that a state of war existed with Japan. "We must begin," he said, "the great task that is before us by abandoning once and for all the illusion that we can ever again isolate ourselves from the rest of humanity." He added, "We are going to win the war, and we are going to win the peace that follows."

SUGGESTIONS FOR READING

THE MAKING OF AMERICAN FOREIGN POLICY

R. Dallek, *Franklin D. Roosevelt and American Foreign Policy, 1932–1945* (1979), provides a judicious account of its subject. S. Adler, *The Uncertain Giant: American Foreign Policy Between the Wars* (1966), and R. A. Divine, *The Reluctant Belligerent: American Entry into World War II* (1965), cover the main events of the period. For a cogent transatlantic view, see Jean-Baptiste Duroselle, *From Wilson to Roosevelt: Foreign Policy of the United States, 1913–1945* (1963). J. E. Wiltz, *From Isolation to War, 1931–1941* (1968), provides an incisive discussion of leading issues. R. E. Osgood, *Ideals and Self-Interest in America's Foreign Relations* (1953), offers a stimulating analytical framework from which to view American foreign policy. See also G. F. Kennan, *American Diplomacy, 1900–1950* (1951), and W. Lippmann, *U.S. Foreign Policy: Shield of the Republic* (1943).

For Roosevelt's first term, the raw material of foreign affairs can be conveniently found in E. B. Nixon, ed., *Franklin D. Roosevelt and Foreign Affairs*, 3 vols. (1969). F. Freidel, *Franklin D. Roosevelt: Launching the New Deal* (1973), covers the London Economic Conference. M. Tate, *The United States and Armaments* (1948), describes the frustrations of disarmament in the years between the wars. The story from 1937 to Pearl Harbor is recorded in two magisterial volumes by W. L. Langer and S. E. Gleason, *The Challenge to Isolation* (1952) and *The Undeclared War* (1953). The year 1941 is well covered in J. M. Burns, *Roosevelt: The Soldier of Freedom* (1970), and W. E. Kimball, *The Juggler: Franklin Roosevelt as Wartime President* (1991). For military aspects, see M. S. Watson, *Chief of Staff: Prewar Plans and Preparations* (1950). On intelligence problems, the outstanding work is R. Wohlstetter, *Pearl Harbor* (1962).

Cordell Hull, *Memoirs*, 2 vols. (1948), supplies the view from the office of the secretary of state. It may be supplemented by J. W. Pratt, *Cordell Hull*, 2 vols. (1964). S. Welles, *A Time for Decision* (1964), and H. Feis, *Seen From E. A.: Three International Episodes* (1947), amplify the State Department view. For H. L. Stimson, there are three works: his own book with M. Bundy, *On Active Service in Peace and War* (1948), a perceptive biography by E. E. Morison, *Turmoil and Tradition* (1960), and a prosecutor's brief by R. N. Current, *Secretary Stimson* (1954). R. E. Sherwood, *Roosevelt and Hopkins* (1948, rev. ed. 1950), is vivid and penetrating, and the second volume of J. M. Blum, *From the Morgenthau Diaries: Years of Urgency* (1965), is valuable for the years before Pearl Harbor.

Two waves of revisionism have washed over these years. The old isolationist school can be consulted in two books by C. A. Beard—*American Foreign Policy in the Making, 1932–1940* (1946) and *President Roosevelt and the Coming of War, 1941* (1948). C. C. Tansill sums up the isolationist case in *Back Door to War* (1952). A restatement of isolationist ideas is in B. Russett, *No Clear and Present Danger* (1972). In *Roosevelt: From Munich to Pearl Harbor* (1950), B. Rauch provides a careful rebuttal. The contemporary school of revisionism, committed to the thesis that American foreign policy has always been the expression of the imperialist necessities of American capitalism, is represented in L. C. Gardner, *Economic Aspects of New Deal Diplomacy* (1964), and in W. A. Williams, *The Tragedy of American Diplomacy* (1959; rev. ed., 1962).

THE POLITICS OF FOREIGN POLICY

S. Adler, *The Isolationist Impulse* (1957); M. Jonas, *Isolationism in America, 1935–1941* (1966); and S. Lubell, *The Future of American*

Politics (1952), consider the sources of isolationism. F. Waldrop, *McCormick of Chicago* (1966), is an illuminating essay on the isolationist mood. J. K. Nelson, *The Peace Prophets: American Pacifist Thought, 1919–1941* (1967), discusses the peace movement. Congressional reactions to foreign affairs can be traced in F. L. Israel, *Nevada's Key Pittman* (1963); M. C. McKenna, *Borah* (1961); B. K. Wheeler, *Yankee from the West* (1962); and W. S. Cole, *Senator Gerald P. Nye and American Foreign Relations* (1967). See also J. E. Wiltz, *In Search of Peace: The Senate Munitions Inquiry, 1934–1936* (1963), for the neutrality debate; R. A. Divine, *The Illusion of Neutrality* (1962); and for Willkie, D. B. Johnson, *The Republican Party and Wendell Willkie* (1960).

The angry controversy of 1939–41 is well covered in W. Johnson, *The Battle Against Isolationism* (1944); M. L. Chadwin, *The Hawks of World War II* (1968; in paperback as *The Warhawks: American Interventionists before Pearl Harbor*); and W. S. Cole, *America First: The Battle Against Intervention* (1953). The musings of a leading isolationist are in C. A. Lindbergh, *Wartime Journals* (1970).

EUROPE

J. W. Gantenbein, *Documentary Background of World War II* (1948), lives up to its title. For interpretations, K. Eubank, *The Origins of World War II* (1969), sums up the accepted view; and A. J. P. Taylor, *The Origins of the Second World War* (1962), is a stimulating essay in heterodoxy. W. S. Churchill's volumes, *The Gathering Storm* (1948) and *Their Finest Hour* (1949), are majestic. Two important recent works are P. M. H. Bell, *Origins of the Second World War in Europe* (1986), and D. C. Watt, *And the War Came* (1989).

A. Bullock, *Hitler: A Study in Tyranny* (1952), is the best biography. Six useful works discuss Nazi Germany and America: H. L. Trefousse, *Germany and American Neutrality* (1951); J. V. Compton, *The Swastika and the Eagle* (1967); A. Frye, *Nazi Germany and the Western Hemisphere, 1933–1941* (1967); A. A. Offner, *American Appeasement: United States Foreign Policy and Germany, 1933–1938* (1969); R. Dallek, *Democrat and Diplomat: The Life of William E. Dodd* (1968); and H. W. Gatzke, *Germany and the United States* (1981). For American relations with the Soviet Union, see R. P. Browder, *The Origins of Soviet-American Diplomacy* (1953); B. Farnsworth, *William C. Bullitt and the Soviet Union* (1967); and E. M. Bennett, *Recognition of Russia: An American Foreign Policy Dilemma* (1970). B. Harris, *The United States and the Italo-Ethiopian Crisis* (1964), displays the American response to the events of 1935; and F. J. Taylor, *The United States and the Spanish Civil War* (1956), and A. Guttmann, *The Wound in the Heart: America and the Spanish Civil War* (1962), consider the problems of 1936–39. Six books throw light on Anglo-American relations: H. Feis, *1933: Characters in Crisis* (1966); W. F. Kimball, *'The Most Unsordid Act': Lend-Lease, 1939–1941* (1969); T. A. Wilson, *The First Summit: Roosevelt and Churchill at Placentia Bay, 1941* (1969); H. D. Hall, *North American Supply* (1955); J. P. Lash, *Roosevelt and Churchill* (1976); and D. Dingleby and D. Reynolds, *An Ocean Apart* (1988). Indispensable for this and the next chapter is W. F. Kimball, ed., *Churchill and Roosevelt: The Complete Correspondence,* 3 vols. (1984).

ASIA

D. Borg, *The United States and the Far Eastern Crisis of 1933–1938* (1964), is a basic work. The Japanese problem is assessed in H. Feis, *The Road to Pearl Harbor* (1950); D. J. Lu, *From the Marco Polo Bridge to Pearl Harbor: Japan's Entry into World War II* (1961); P. W. Schroeder, *The Axis Alliance and Japanese-American Relations* (1958); C. E. Neu, *The Troubled Encounter: The U.S. and Japan* (1975); R. Butow, *Tojo and the Coming of the War* (1961); and A. Iriye, *Power and Culture: The Japanese-American War* (1981) and *Across the Pacific* (1967). For American diplomatic reactions, see W. Johnson's rendering of the papers of J. C. Grew, *Turbulent Era: A Diplomatic Record of Forty Years,* 2 vols. (1952), and W. H. Heinrichs, *American Ambassador: Joseph C. Grew and the Development of the United States Diplomatic Tradition* (1967).

LATIN AMERICA

B. Wood, *The Making of the Good Neighbor Policy* (1961), is the best historical account; L. Duggan, *The American Search for Hemispheric Security* (1949), is the testimony of a participant. D. Green, *The Containment of Latin America* (1971), is a revisionist critique of the Good Neighbor policy.

CHAPTER TWENTY-NINE

BEACH AT TARAWA, 1943

THE WORLD IN FLAMES

The bitter wreckage of ships and planes at Pearl Harbor ended the illusion that the United States could be a world power and remain safe from world conflict. In the shocking strike from the placid Hawaiian skies, the Japanese crippled the Pacific fleet, destroyed nearly 200 planes, and killed nearly 2,500 men. The navy lost three times as many men in this single attack as it had lost in the Spanish-American and First World wars combined. Four days after Pearl Harbor, on December 11, 1941, Germany and Italy declared war on the United States and Congress declared war on them, as it had on Japan. America was now committed to global war (see Map 29-1).

AMERICA ORGANIZES FOR WAR

Arms for Global War War brought profound changes to American society. The first problem was to produce the machines and weapons for global warfare. In 1941 military spending had reached a monthly rate of about $2 billion. But only 15 percent of industrial output had gone for military purposes, and business managers had resisted pressure to shift to war production. Roosevelt now laid down unprecedented objectives for 1942—60,000 planes, 45,000 tanks, 20,000 antiaircraft guns, 8 million tons of shipping—and set up the War Production Board (WPB) under Donald Nelson to convert the economy to a war basis.

In the first six months of 1942, the government placed over $100 billion in war contracts—more goods on order than the economy had ever produced in a single year. The structure of central control buckled under the strain. An effective priority system was essential, but sometimes more priorities were issued than there were goods to satisfy them. In the confusion the military, who had already gained authority over procurement, demanded control over production. Nelson, backed by the president and Congress, fended off this proposal. In 1943 the WPB's Controlled Materials Plan introduced order into the allocation of critical materials, about which the military continued to have considerable voice.

Roosevelt, in his characteristic style, assigned important areas of authority to other civilian agencies. In December 1942 the War Food Administration assumed direction of the nation's food program. Shortages in oil and rubber brought about the appointment, also outside the WPB, of "czars" with exceptional powers to expedite production. The War Manpower Commission supervised the mobilization of men and women for both civilian and military purposes. And the Office of Scientific Research and Development, under the direction of Dr. Vannevar Bush, conducted scientific and technical mobilization. Its scientists and

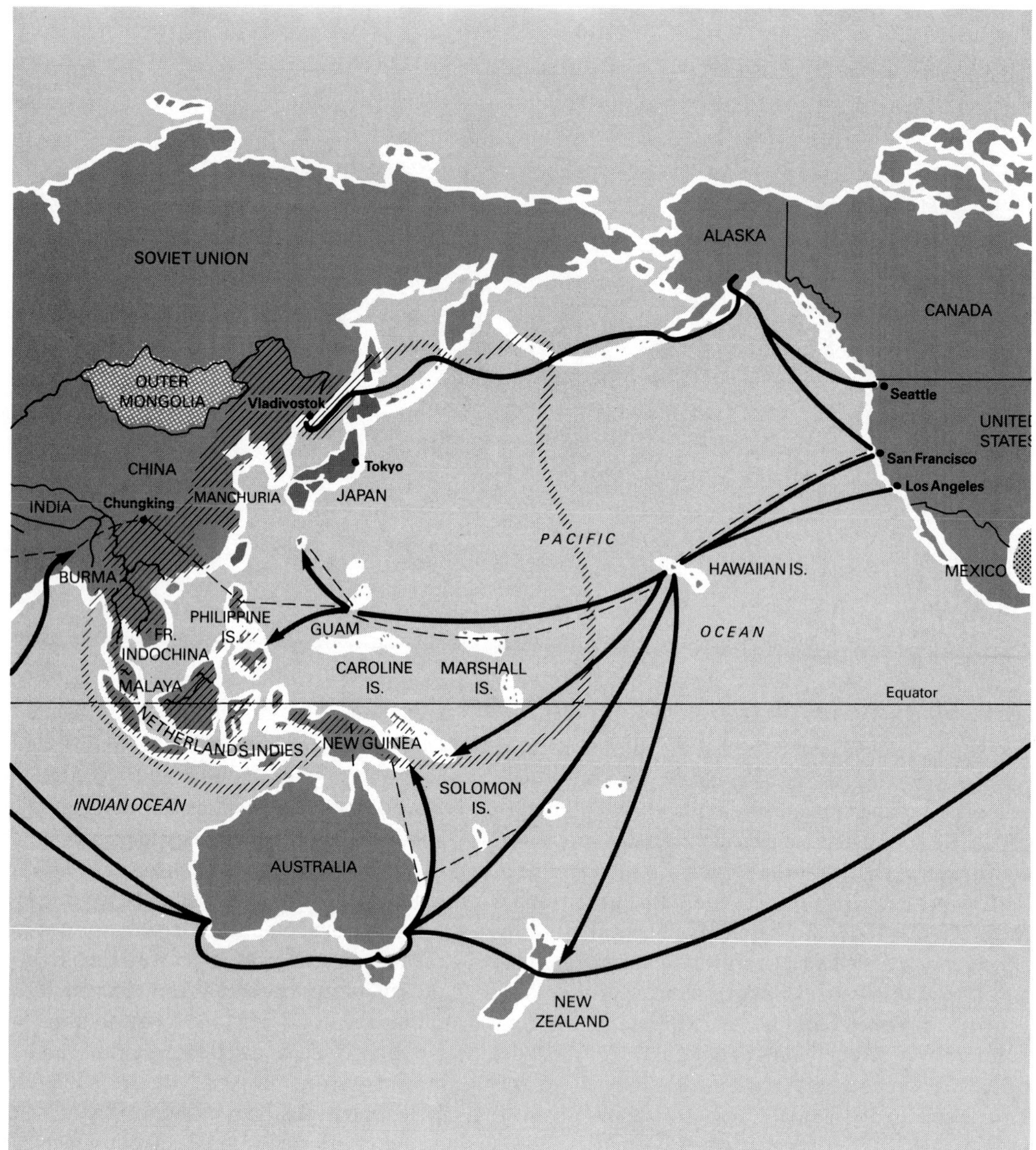

Map 29-1 *The Second World War*

engineers were responsible for short-range rockets (especially the "bazooka"), the development of radar, and the proximity fuse (both British inventions), and other remarkable gains in military technology.

In 1942 the proportion of the economy committed to war production grew from 15 to 33 percent. By the end of 1943 federal expenditures for goods and services constituted a sum larger than the total output of the economy when Roosevelt took office a decade earlier. The gross national product grew from $99.7 billion in 1940 to $211.9 billion in 1945. The WPB continued to be shaken by feuds, both internal and external. In the interest of efficiency in procurement, the army and navy relied increasingly on big business in the awarding of war contracts. Nelson tried without success to divert a substantial proportion of those contracts to smaller concerns, for which he also attempted to get reconversion privileges in 1944.

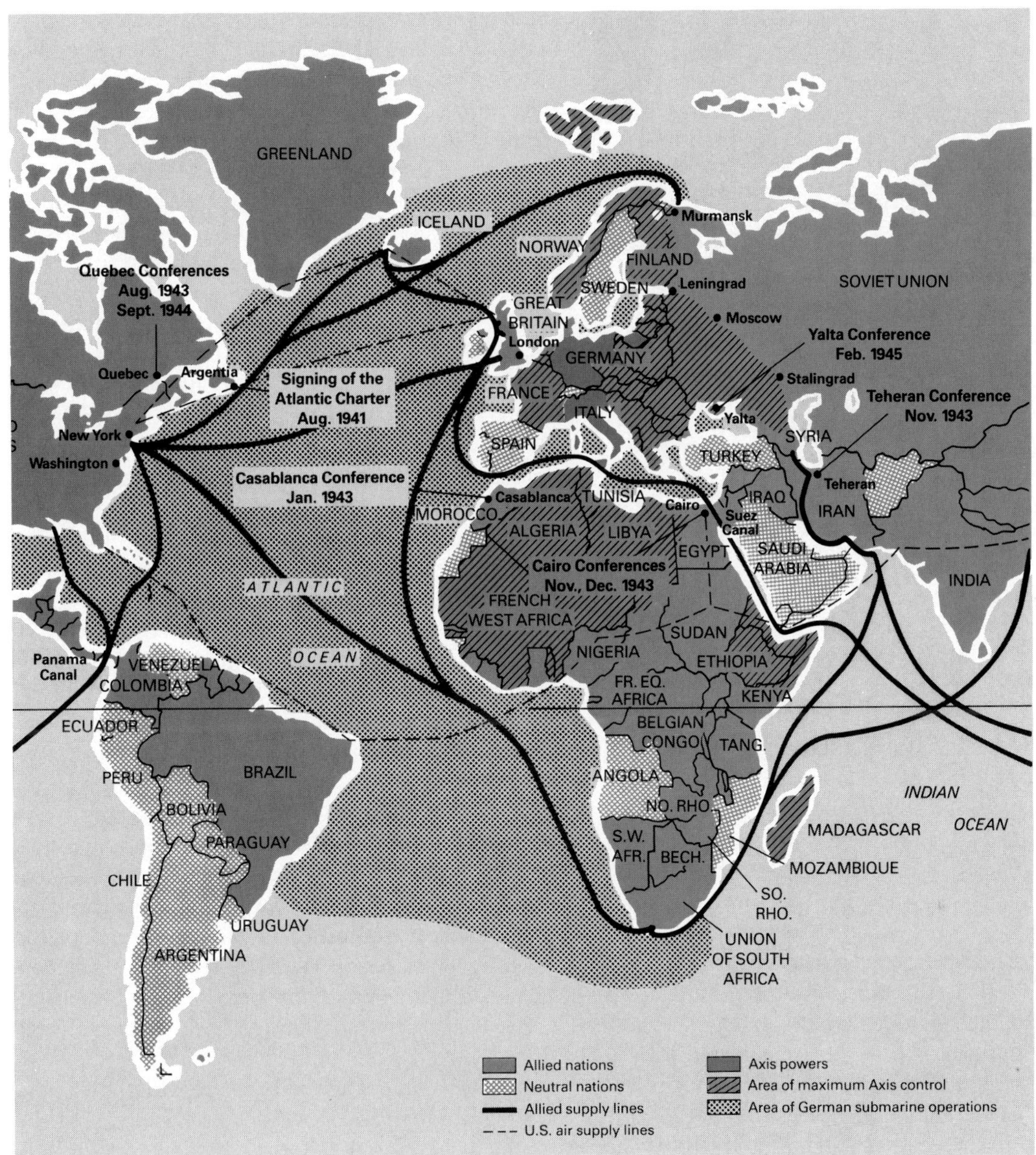

Convinced that any move toward reconversion was premature, the army and navy persuaded Roosevelt to force Nelson to resign. Still, in one way or another, the WPB had succeeded in guiding the productive energies of the economy to enable America in a surprisingly short time to outproduce all other nations in the world.

The Fight for Stabilization This extraordinary feat was a result of the stimulus provided by government spending to the productive talents of American managers and workers. Federal purchases of goods and services rose from $6 billion in 1940 to $89 billion in 1944. Total federal spending during the war years came to over $320 billion—an amount twice as great as the total of all previous federal spending in the history of the republic.

How was this prodigious expenditure to be paid for? The first resort was to a broadening and deepening of the tax structure. By 1944 surtaxes had risen to 94

Waiting for rationing coupons

percent of net income in the highest brackets, and people at every level were paying taxes that would have seemed inconceivable a short time before. Total tax revenues in the war years came to about $130 billion. This was far less than Roosevelt had requested, however, and, as a result, the government was able to meet only about 41 percent of the cost of the war on a pay-as-you-go basis—not enough, though a much larger proportion than during the First World War.

The rest of the defense bill was made up by borrowing. In 1944 alone the excess of expenditures over receipts amounted to more than $50 billion—a figure over twice the total size of the accumulated debt in 1941. By the end of the war the national debt had grown to about $280 billion, nearly six times as large as it had been when bombs fell on Pearl Harbor. The budgetary deficits so loudly bewailed in New Deal days now seemed negligible compared with the deficit spending of war. An incidental effect was to support the Keynesian argument that public spending would end the depression: unemployment rapidly vanished in 1941 and 1942, and Congress abolished old New Deal agencies like the Works Progress Administration. The problem became, not to find jobs for people, but to find people for jobs.

The tremendous increase in public spending released strong inflationary pressures. The shift from civilian to war production reduced the quantity of goods available for purchase just as the quantity of money jingling in people's pockets was increasing. By 1944, for example, the production of civilian automobiles, of washing machines and other consumer durables, of nondefense housing and the like had virtually come to an end. Unless prices were to soar out of sight, means had to be found to hold the volume of spendable money down to the volume of available goods.

One recourse was to fiscal policy. Taxation was an obvious means of reducing the supply of spendable money in people's hands. The war-bond drive was another way by which the government sought to persuade people to put their money away instead of using it to bid up prices. Nearly $100 billion worth of the various series of war bonds were sold in these years. But it was evident from an early point that indirect measures would not be enough to eliminate the "inflationary gap"—the gap, that is, between too few goods and too much money. As early as August 1941 Roosevelt had accordingly established the Office of Price Administration (OPA) under the direction of Leon Henderson, a hard-driving New Deal economist.

Price control presented one of the toughest problems of war administration. Every economic interest wanted rigid policing of the other fellows' prices but tended to regard attempts to police its own prices as subversive of the free-enterprise system. In April 1942 the OPA imposed a general price freeze, joining to this a system by which necessities of life in short supply—meat, gasoline, tires—were rationed to the consumers through an allotment of coupons. The farm bloc, however, succeeded in gaining exceptions for agricultural prices, and the increase in the cost of food brought about demands for wage increases. The War Labor Board, set up in January 1942, sought to meet this problem by the Little Steel formula of July, permitting wage increases to keep pace with the 15 percent rise in the cost of living since January 1941. In September Roosevelt requested new authority to stabilize the cost of living, including farm prices and wages. The Stabilization Act of 1942 established the Office of Economic Stabilization under the direction of former Supreme Court Justice James F. Byrnes.

Special interests nevertheless continued unabashed guerrilla warfare against price control in their own sectors. The farm bloc was unrelenting in its demand that exceptions be made for itself. John L. Lewis led the United Mine Workers in a fight against the Little Steel formula. For a time in 1943 the government was forced to seize and operate the coal mines. Henderson, who had affronted Congress by the unquenchable zeal of his war against inflation, had been forced to resign in December 1942. But a "hold-the-line" order in April 1943, followed by a campaign in May to "roll back" food prices, helped bring the price level to a plateau by mid-1943. For the rest of the war the OPA, under the able direction of Chester Bowles, was able to maintain substantial price stability in spite of the development of some "black markets" in which rationed goods were sold expensively and illegally. From October 1942 to the end of the Pacific war, consumers' prices rose only 8.7 percent. For all its unpopularity, especially among business executives, politicians, and farm leaders, the OPA was one of the war's successes.

The problem remained of concerting the efforts of various agencies dealing with production and stabilization. In May 1943 Roosevelt set up the Office of War Mobilization and put Byrnes in charge. Employing his judicial and political skill to intervene when operating agencies disagreed, Byrnes did an effective job in pulling together the infinitely ramified strands of America's domestic war effort.

The People behind the Lines The attack on Pearl Harbor produced a surge of national unity. Though various groups of Americans remained suspicious of Great Britain or of the Soviet Union, and others were reluctant to contemplate postwar involvements in world affairs, the isolationist-interventionist debate receded. Throughout the war popular confidence in the government remained high. Nevertheless, like any period of war, this was a time of upheaval and anxiety.

To combat the threat of enemy activity within the United States, Roosevelt gave new authority to the Federal Bureau of Investigation, including the power to tap wires in national security cases. That new mandate encouraged the agency to widen its investigations into the beliefs as well as the deeds of Americans. But the years 1941–45 were not marred by the widespread assaults on civil freedom that had characterized the years 1917–20 (see pp. 618, 633). Perhaps because they were seldom perceived to constitute a real threat to the nation, German-Americans and Italian-Americans were not subjected to jingoistic harassment. All enemy aliens, however, were evacuated from sensitive defense areas on the West Coast, and some Italians were interned briefly. For a year the government restricted the movement of unnaturalized Italian immigrants. In contrast, the tragic exception to this general tolerance was the fate of the more than 100,000 Japanese-Americans, immigrants and native-born citizens alike, who were brutally removed from their homes along the Pacific Coast and relocated in internment camps in the interior—an act of national hysteria wholly unjustified.

Roundup of Japanese-Americans

It was also cruel of Congress and the president to fail to open the way for the immigration of European Jews who were desperate to escape Nazi genocide. Indeed, neither Roosevelt nor the State Department made any obvious effort to assist the Jewish population of Europe until the president established the War Refugee Board in 1944. That was too late to keep the Nazis from the Holocaust—their systematic murder of 6 million European Jews.

Of native Americans suspected of sympathy for fascism, some had their publications—for example, Father Coughlin's *Social Justice*—denied the mails. Toward the end of the war, an effort to convict a number of American Fascists in a mass sedition trial miscarried. In the meantime, the Department of Justice had taken effective steps against Nazi agents and organizations. No acts of enemy sabotage were committed in the United States during the war. In the main, Attorney General Francis Biddle strove with success to maintain an atmosphere of moderation.

The war uprooted people from familiar settings, exposed them to new experience, changed the direction of their lives. The rise in output and employment was accompanied by a tremendous increase in real income, partly from the prevalence of overtime pay for workers. Wartime tax policies strengthened the tendency toward income redistribution that had begun under the New Deal. The wealthiest 5 percent of Americans had received 30 percent of national income in 1929 and 24 percent in 1941; by 1944 their share was down to 20.7 percent.

After the long years of depression, both workers and the middle class savored the prosperity of the war years. They spent freely for available consumer goods and saved with the expectation of buying refrigerators and radios, and especially automobiles and houses, after the war. Facilities for housing, transportation, schooling, and recreation were critically short in communities impacted by war industries, particularly in the rapidly growing cities of the South, the Southwest, and the West Coast. Those shortages intensified yearnings for a comfortable tomorrow, yearnings shared by men and women in the armed services. For the duration, most civilians, though irritated by rationing, lived better lives than they had for more than a decade.

War workers

Black Power: 1942

We know that our fate is tied up with the fate of the democratic way of life. And so, out of the depths of our hearts, a cry goes up for the triumph of the United Nations. But we would not be honest with ourselves were we to stop with a call for a victory of arms alone. . . . Unless this war sounds the death knell to the old Anglo-American empire systems, the hapless story of which is one of exploitation for the profit and power of a monopoly capitalist economy, it will have been fought in vain. Our aim then must not only be to defeat nazism, fascism, and militarism on the battlefield but to win the peace, for democracy, for freedom and the Brotherhood of Man without regard to his pigmentation, land of his birth or the God of his fathers. . . .

While the March on Washington Movement may find it advisable to form a citizens committee of friendly white citizens to give moral support . . . it does not imply that these white citizens . . . should be taken into the March on Washington Movement as members. The essential value of an all-Negro movement such as the March on Washington is that it helps to create faith by Negroes in Negroes. It develops a sense of self-reliance with Negroes depending on Negroes in vital matters. It helps to break down the slave psychology and inferiority-complex in Negroes which comes and is nourished with Negroes relying on white people for direction and support. This inevitably happens in mixed organizations that are supposed to be in the interest of the Negro.

From A. Philip Randolph, Keynote Address to the Policy Conference of the March on Washington Movement, September 1942

Between 1941 and 1945 shortages of labor brought some 6.5 million women, most of them middle-aged and married, into the working force. Others escaped from menial or servile jobs to blue-collar positions in industry. Still others contributed to the war effort as uniformed members of the women's auxiliaries or nurses corps of the army and navy. Some 2 million became office workers. The federal government employed 1 million more in civilian posts. When the war ended, almost 20 million women were in the labor force, 35 percent of all workers, up from 25 percent in 1940.

While the fighting lasted, much of the conventional discrimination against women receded. Even the medical and legal professions accepted more women. But the biases underlying discrimination against women persisted, to surge again after the war. Even in the war years, women did not achieve equality with men in opportunity or compensation. Yet, except for the rare feminists, they did not much question conventional attitudes toward women's roles or protest against the disparity between men's and women's wages or the lack of day-care centers for the children of working mothers. Some women war workers did not intend to remain on the job after the war, though many of them either did not leave or soon returned. Most took satisfaction in their contributions to wartime tasks, a point the federal government stressed. They were also pleased by their new income. Supplementing their husband's earnings, that income gave their families, often for the first time, access to the necessities and some of the comforts of a middle-class standard of living.

Ultimately the demand for labor also provided new opportunities for black Americans, though throughout the war they received much less than equal treatment.

Their resulting resentments fostered an unprecedented and often effective militancy. During the defense boom before Pearl Harbor, they were, as ever, the last hired. Many remained unemployed. Those who found jobs ordinarily received low wages, small chance for promotion, and often no chance to join self-consciously segregated labor unions. Worse, the army and navy persisted in the segregation of the armed forces, consigned most black soldiers to menial tasks, and with few exceptions denied them training for commissions or for élite service like that of the air corps. "A Jim Crow army," as one critic said, "cannot fight for a free world." So persuaded, the head of the Brotherhood of Sleeping Car Porters, A. Philip Randolph, one of the great black leaders of the century, organized the Negro March on Washington Committee, which planned to recruit thousands of black citizens for a rally at the Lincoln Memorial in the spring of 1941 to demand equal rights to work and the desegregation of the armed forces. Roosevelt persuaded Randolph to call off the march in return for Executive Order 8802 of June 1941, which made it national policy to forbid discrimination in employment in defense industries. Roosevelt also appointed the Fair Employment Practices Committee (FEPC) to enforce that policy by investigating complaints and taking steps to redress grievances.

Detroit, 1943: two days of guerrilla fighting

The FEPC, detested though it was in the South, lacked the authority to fulfill its mission. Though war industries did hire black, Mexican-American, and other minority workers, discrimination in wages and seniority remained the rule. The War and Navy Departments took only token steps toward desegregation in the services. Consequently Randolph kept alive his March on Washington Movement with its black membership and its commitment to mass, nonviolent protest. Gandhian nonviolent techniques became the tactics of newer organizations, most notably the Congress on Racial Equality (CORE), which included whites among its members and successfully employed sit-ins during the war to desegregate various Northern restaurants, theaters, and skating rinks. By 1945 CORE was planning freedom rides to desegregate public transportation in the South.

The movement of thousands of black workers to industrial centers, south and north, provoked the hostility of many white citizens, who objected to black neighbors and even more to their competition for jobs, housing, and schooling. Episodes of racial violence visited a dozen cities and culminated in 1943 in riots involving attacks on Mexican-Americans in Los Angeles and on black Americans in New York and most grimly in Detroit. There in June over 30 people, white and black, died during two days of guerrilla fighting that ceased only with the intervention of the National Guard. Continuing evidence of white racism, official and private, discouraged black citizens and dampened but did not dispel the new militancy. The achievements of the FEPC, inadequate though they were, raised hopes for the future, as still more did the occasional victories of nonviolent protest. Even the head of the moderate NAACP foresaw that only continuing protest—"a rising wind," as he put it—would fasten public policy to the cause of civil rights.

Early Politics of the War Political developments after Pearl Harbor quickly refuted the isolationist prediction that war must doom democracy and free discussion. In Congress the dominating conservative coalition of Republicans and Southern Democrats seized the opportunity to liquidate New Deal agencies that appeared to have lost their function. On the other hand, Congress also provided responsible counsel on many aspects of the war effort—most notably in the Senate Committee to Investigate the National Defense Program, which, under the able chair of Harry S Truman of Missouri, exposed waste and confusion in the defense effort and made many valuable recommendations to the executive.

Relations with Congress presented Roosevelt with difficult problems. The 1942 congressional election took place in a time when military defeats had yet to be offset by any striking victories, and in an atmosphere suffused with wartime irritations, especially over the OPA's efforts to hold prices and rents down. It resulted in striking Republican gains—10 seats in the Senate, 47 in the House. This outcome confirmed the conservative complexion of the Congress, increased Roosevelt's difficulties in dealing with that body, and filled the Republicans with high hopes for the presidential election of 1944.

THE WAR IN EUROPE

Beat Hitler First The manifold activities at home, however, provided only the backdrop for the essential problem of war—victory over the enemy. For the United States there were two enemies—the Japanese, advancing rapidly into Southeast Asia in the months after Pearl Harbor, and the European Axis, now engaged in savage warfare on the Russian front and presumably preparing an eventual invasion of England (see Map 29-1). The immediate problem for the United States was whether to throw its military might against Germany or against Japan.

American military planners had already concluded by March 1941 that, if the United States entered the war, American strategy must be to beat Hitler first. There were several reasons for this decision. For one thing, Germany, with its command of most of the western coast of Europe and its access to the Atlantic, presented a direct threat to the Western Hemisphere. There was particular concern over Axis penetration of Latin America. For another, Germany seemed far more likely than Japan to achieve some revolutionary breakthrough in military technology. In addition, Great Britain was fully engaged in fighting the Axis, while in East Asia, China was both less active in its resistance to Japan and less accessible to outside support.

The Nazi attack on the Soviet Union in June 1941, far from reversing the Europe-first argument, was considered to reinforce it, for the Russo-German war increased both the chance of defeating Germany and the urgency of doing so before Germany conquered Russia. Nor did the Japanese attack on Pearl Harbor shake the American decision. When Winston Churchill came to Washington in December 1941, he found complete agreement on his proposition that "the defeat of Germany, entailing a collapse, will leave Japan exposed to overwhelming force, whereas the defeat of Japan would not by any means bring the World War to an end."

Diverging Strategies in Europe The agreement between the United States and Britain on beating Germany first was not matched, however, by agreement on the best way of doing it. The British strategy—reflecting the memory of the bitter trench warfare of the First World War, with which Americans had limited experience—was to postpone direct assault on Germany until a combination of naval blockade, aerial bombing, psychological warfare, and military attack on the Axis periphery had sufficiently weakened Germany's capacity to resist.

Where the British strategy was to attack the enemy where he was weakest, the American was to attack the enemy where he was strongest. From the American viewpoint, the Churchill plan of "pecking at the periphery" would waste resources without winning victory. As Roosevelt used to observe when Churchill advocated a landing at one or another European point remote from Germany, "All right, but where do we go from there?" The American Joint Chiefs of Staff, ably led by General George C. Marshall, felt that only a massive thrust across the English Channel and France into the heart of Germany would achieve victory. In their view—a view generally shared by Roosevelt—all Anglo-American efforts should be concentrated on establishing a second front in France.

Detour to North Africa The Soviet Union, in desperate need of relief from the hammer blows of the German army and air force, brought strong pressure for a second front in 1942. Though the British accepted a cross-Channel invasion in principle, they continued to object in practice. They felt that the Americans underestimated the difficulties of amphibious landings on fortified coasts, they regarded American troops as untried, and they doubted whether the

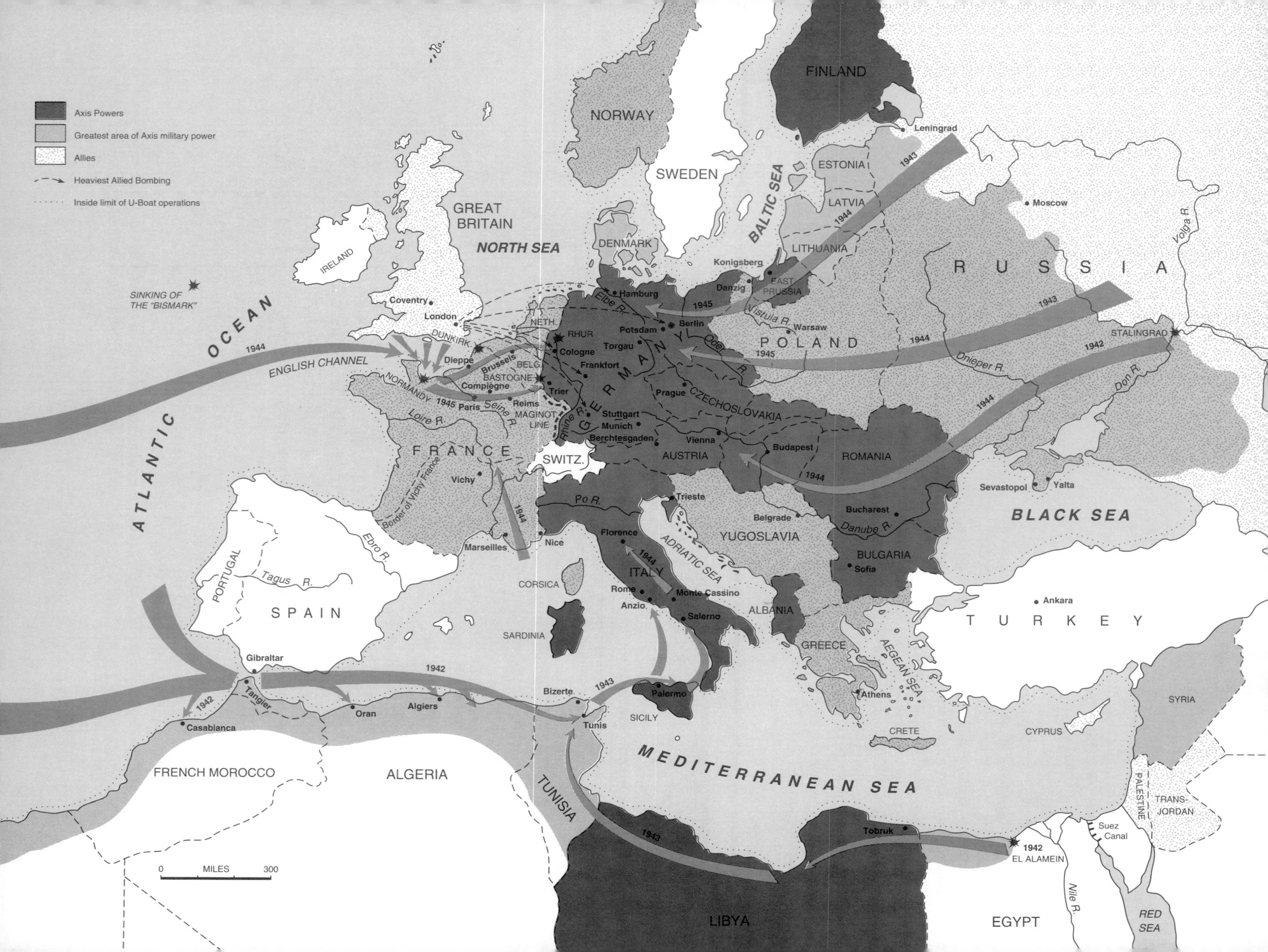
Axis Powers
Greatest area of Axis military power
Allies
Heaviest Allied Bombing
Inside limit of U-Boat operations
SINKING OF THE "BISMARK"
ATLANTIC OCEAN
ENGLISH CHANNEL
NORTH SEA
BALTIC SEA
BLACK SEA
MEDITERRANEAN SEA
ADRIATIC SEA
AEGEAN SEA
RED SEA
GREAT BRITAIN
IRELAND
NORWAY
SWEDEN
FINLAND
DENMARK
ESTONIA
LATVIA
LITHUANIA
EAST PRUSSIA
POLAND
RUSSIA
GERMANY
NETH.
BELG.
FRANCE
SWITZ.
AUSTRIA
CZECHOSLOVAKIA
ROMANIA
BULGARIA
YUGOSLAVIA
ALBANIA
GREECE
ITALY
SPAIN
PORTUGAL
TURKEY
SYRIA
PALESTINE
TRANS-JORDAN
CYPRUS
CRETE
CORSICA
SARDINIA
SICILY
FRENCH MOROCCO
ALGERIA
TUNISIA
LIBYA
EGYPT
Coventry
London
DUNKIRK
Dieppe
NORMANDY
Paris
Compiègne
Brussels
BASTOGNE
Reims
MAGINOT LINE
Trier
RHUR
Cologne
Frankfort
Hamburg
Potsdam
Berlin
Torgau
Prague
Stuttgart
Munich
Berchtesgaden
Vienna
Budapest
Konigsberg
Danzig
Warsaw
Leningrad
Moscow
STALINGRAD
Sevastopol
Yalta
Bucharest
Sofia
Belgrade
Trieste
Florence
Rome
Anzio
Monte Cassino
Salerno
Palermo
Athens
Ankara
Vichy
Marseilles
Nice
Border of Vichy France
Gibraltar
Tangier
Casablanca
Oran
Algiers
Bizerte
Tunis
Tobruk
EL ALAMEIN
Suez Canal
Elbe R.
Vistula R.
Oder R.
Dnieper R.
Don R.
Volga R.
Danube R.
Rhine R.
Seine R.
Loire R.
Po R.
Ebro R.
Tagus R.
Nile R.
1942
1943
1944
1945
0 MILES 300

THE DEFEAT OF GERMANY

WESTERN FRONT			EASTERN FRONT
		Jan. 20, 1942	Russian counteroffensive begins, reaches Kharkov May 12
		June 28, 1942	German summer offensive begins. Reaches Stalingrad Aug. 22
British stop German African drive at El Alamein	June 29, 1942		
British offensive begins with victory at El Alamein; Tobruk falls Nov. 13, Bengasi Nov. 20	Nov. 4, 1942		
U.S. and British landings in North Africa. French sign armistice Nov. 11	Nov. 8, 1942		
		Nov. 19, 1942	Russian counteroffensive begins at Stalingrad
		Jan. 18, 1943	Russians raise siege at Leningrad
British take Tripoli	Jan. 24, 1943		
		Feb. 2, 1943	Germans surrender at Stalingrad
		Feb. 14, 1943	Russians take Rostov, followed by Kharkov Feb. 16, Rzhev Mar. 9
U.S. and British lines meet in North Africa	Apr. 7, 1943		
British take Tunis, Americans take Bizerte	May 7, 1943		
Surrender of Axis in North Africa	May 13, 1943		
Invasion of Sicily, completed Aug. 17	July 10, 1943		
Resignation of Mussolini	July 25, 1943		
		Aug. 4, 1943	Russians reverse German offensive and take Orel and Belgurod
British troops invade Italy	Sept. 3, 1943		
Unconditional surrender of Italy	Sept. 8, 1943		
Americans invade Salerno, Allied advance begins, crosses Volturno River Oct. 14, reaches Sangro River Dec. 25	Sept. 9, 1943		
		Sept. 25, 1943	Russian advance takes Smolensk, moves on to Kiev Nov. 7, enters Poland Jan. 3, 1944
Landing at Anzio	Jan. 22, 1944		
		Jan. 29, 1944	Moscow-Leningrad area clear of German forces
		Apr. 10, 1944	Russians take Odessa
		May 9, 1944	Russians take Sevastopol
Cassino falls after two-month battle	May 18, 1944		
Liberation of Rome	June 4, 1944		
Allied invasion of Normandy	June 6, 1944		
		June 23, 1944	Russians begin summer offensive south of Leningrad
Cherbourg captured	June 27, 1944		
Caen falls	July 9, 1944		
American "Break Out" at St. Lo	July 25, 1944		
British take Florence, Italy	Aug. 12, 1944		
Allies invade southern France	Aug. 15, 1944		
Liberation of Paris	Aug. 25, 1944		
Liberation of Brussels and Antwerp	Sept. 4, 1944		
		Sept. 8, 1944	Surrender of Bulgaria
Liberation of Luxembourg	Sept. 11, 1944		
American forces enter Germany	Sept. 12, 1944		
		Sept. 22, 1944	Russians take Tallinn
		Oct. 20, 1944	Russians enter East Prussia; seize Belgrade, Yugoslavia
Americans take Aachen, followed by Metz, Nov. 22, Strasbourg, Nov. 23	Oct. 21, 1944		
German counteroffensive and Battle of the Bulge until Dec. 26	Dec. 16, 1944		
		Dec. 29, 1944	Russians take Budapest, Hungary
		Jan. 12, 1945	Russians advance in Poland, Warsaw falls Jan. 17, Lodz Jan. 19. Russians at Oder River Jan. 23
British offensive in Holland	Feb. 8, 1945		
Americans cross Saar River	Feb. 22, 1945		
Fall of Cologne and Düsseldorf. Americans capture Remagen Bridge across Rhine	May 7, 1945		
Americans reach Elbe River	Apr. 11, 1945		
		Apr. 13, 1945	Russians begin drive to Berlin, enter Apr. 24
Americans take Nuremberg	Apr. 21, 1945		
Americans meet Russians at Torgau	Apr. 25, 1945	Apr. 25, 1945	Russians meet Americans at Torgau
		May 2, 1945	Berlin falls
Unconditional surrender of Germany. May 8 end of war in Europe	May 7, 1945		

Map 29-2 (*left*) *The defeat of the Axis, 1942–1945*

GIs: Nostalgia in North Africa

Some of the fellows had old hometown papers with them . . . which they had been carrying around since leaving the United States. In the early evening, these papers would be carefully unfolded and passed from one to the other. We had all read them before, but it made no difference. They were from America, and we couldn't get enough of them. I remember reading one paper from a small town in Tennessee over and over. It sounded so small and safe, some place a million miles away, where the fact that some little girl had a birthday party was reported carefully and in full. . . . It was strange, exotic stuff to be reading out there in the desert, waiting for the . . . raid to start.

Veterans in Italy

Where were the slick, unspotted "fighting men" of the ads back home? Not here. Straggle-bearded, haggard-eyed, black-faced men—these weren't . . . garrison soldiers. . . . Unmatched clothing and equipment—everyone wore and carried what he best liked. Dried brown mud from Anzoi's creeks and mudholes clung to them and their weapons. These guys looked tough. . . .

I noticed their eyes. They were tired, bloodshot. . . . Some eyes were continually blinking, some were continually shooting right and left as though something would creep up on them. . . . Most of the fellows couldn't realize that they were away from the front for a while at least.

Quoted in Ralph G. Martin, *The GI War,* 1967

American economy could quickly achieve the production levels necessary to sustain a great invasion. There were particularly ominous shortages in landing craft and in modern tanks. Accordingly, when the American Joint Chiefs submitted in the spring of 1942 a plan for the invasion of France later that year, the British turned it down.

Still, something had to be done in 1942, if only to reassure the hard-pressed and bitterly disappointed Russians. Churchill consequently proposed an invasion of North Africa. The American Joint Chiefs felt that a North African diversion, by committing Anglo-American forces to a Mediterranean campaign as well as by preempting necessary men and material, would delay the invasion of France, perhaps until 1944. But Roosevelt accepted Churchill's argument that an invasion of North Africa in 1942 could be a preliminary to a cross-Channel attack in 1943. The British campaign in North Africa, moving westward from Egypt, made the proposed invasion feasible. It would also divert some German resources from the Russian front, where Soviet troops were carrying the largest burden of the Allies' war. In July the decision was made to invade North Africa in the autumn. The operation was placed under the command of General Dwight D. Eisenhower.

On November 8, 1942, Anglo-American forces disembarked at Casablanca in Morocco and at Oran and Algiers in Algeria (see Map 29-2). The landings achieved tactical surprise. Within short order, local resistance came to an end. But military success raised political problems. The collaborationist regime of Marshal Pétain, established at Vichy and in control of unoccupied southern France, exercised nominal authority in North Africa. The United States, which had maintained diplomatic relations with the Vichy government, had some hope of winning the support of pro-Vichy officials and military leaders in Algeria and Morocco. Roosevelt and Churchill supposed that General Charles de Gaulle, commander of the Free

French in London, would be unacceptable to the North African French, who had sworn oaths of loyalty to Pétain.

The situation was further complicated by the presence in Algiers of Admiral Jean Francois Darlan, a prominent French collaborationist and Pétain's successor-designate. Darlan proved as ready to collaborate with the Americans in 1942 as he had been with the Germans in 1940. On November 11 he signed an armistice agreement and Eisenhower recognized him as de facto political chief in North Africa—an action that provoked a storm of criticism in England and the United States from those who feared that it inaugurated a policy of making deals with Fascists. Roosevelt defended Eisenhower's action as "a temporary expedient, justified solely by the stress of battle." The Darlan deal accelerated the Anglo-American military success in Algeria and Morocco, and Darlan's assassination on December 24 spared Roosevelt and Churchill political embarrassment. But they offended de Gaulle again by denying him Darlan's authority.

In the meantime, Hitler, after ordering the occupation of Vichy France, rushed German troops by sea and air to Tunisia. Eisenhower promptly advanced into Tunisia from the west, while the British Eighth Army, under the command of General Bernard Montgomery, entered from Libya to the east. The Anglo-American forces encountered the brilliant generalship of Field Marshal Erwin Rommel, the "Desert Fox." Nonetheless, the Anglo-American vise closed inexorably. On May 12, 1943, the Axis troops surrendered. The British and Americans captured or destroyed 15 Axis divisions, regained the Mediterranean for their shipping, and laid open to attack what Churchill called the "soft underbelly" of the Axis.

The Mediterranean or France? As the Joint Chiefs of Staff had feared, the British advocated moving on into Sicily and Italy in order to maintain the initiative in the Mediterranean. The Americans reluctantly accepted this logic. The result was the invasion of Sicily in July and of Italy in September (see Map 29-2). When Mussolini fell from his dictatorial seat in July, Eisenhower, with the approval of Roosevelt and Churchill, reorganized a new Italian government under Field Marshal Pietro Badoglio and the reigning king, neither of them democratic in practice or inclination. As part of that deal, Badoglio surrendered in September, though by that time German troops controlled southern Italy, where they put up dogged resistance. The Italian front soon was marked by bitter fighting. When Allied progress up the spine of Italy was stopped at Monte Cassino early in 1944, an attempt was made to circumvent the enemy by amphibious landings at Anzio near Rome late in January. But for many weeks Allied troops could not break out of the Anzio beachhead, and Rome itself did not fall for another four months. The Italian campaign—especially beyond Rome—cost more and achieved less than its proponents had expected.

In the meantime, argument continued over the invasion of France. The British service chiefs still wanted to delay Overlord (the code name for the cross-Channel operation) for the sake of new adventures in the Mediterranean. But the American Joint Chiefs, with Soviet backing, insisted on a firm commitment to a second front in France. Postponement had already soured the Soviet temper, for the Russians were bearing the brunt of the fighting against the Nazis and counted on Roosevelt's promise of a cross-Channel invasion in 1943. At the end of November 1943, Churchill finally consented to May 1944 as a target date.

The actual invasion did not take place until June 6. The Germans, deceived by elaborate stratagems, did not expect a sole attack in Normandy. The Allied forces were thus able to consolidate their position and

St. Malo, France, August 1944

Map 29-3
The Second World War in the Pacific

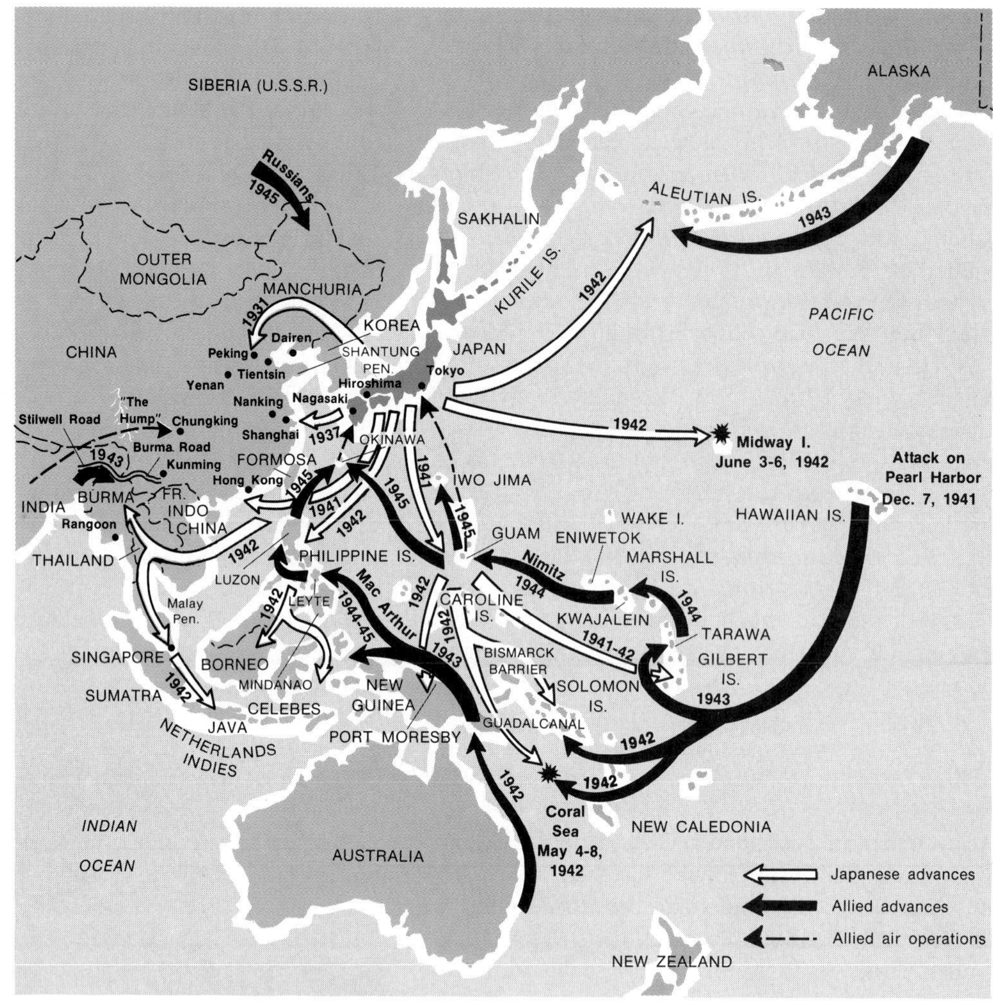

fan out for movement along a larger front. On July 25 General George Patton's Third Army broke through into Brittany. The war in France now developed extraordinary mobility. American and British divisions raced toward Paris, which was liberated on August 25. By September 13 Allied forces had penetrated deep into Belgium and crossed the German frontier at Aachen (see Map 29-2).

These developments, on top of the long-sustained Anglo-American air offensive against Germany, made Hitler's situation more desperate every day. From 1942, when the British and American air forces took substantial command of the air, Germany had been subjected to a series of devastating air raids. Though they were less effective than their advocates claimed at the time, by the autumn of 1944, Allied air attacks—which by the end of the war amounted to 1.5 million bomber sorties and 2.7 million tons of bombs dropped—were exerting a heavy toll on German production (most essentially, of fighter aircraft), and rail and road transportation. The raids also destroyed German cities with inevitable cruelty and ultimately damaged German civilian morale.

In addition, a Soviet offensive, timed to coincide with the Anglo-American landings in France, was driving the Germans back in the east. Indeed, on D-day there were 199 German divisions on the eastern front as against 86 in the west and south. The Russians, who suffered enormous losses throughout the war, seemed to most Germans to be their most fearful enemies. As morale dropped even among high-ranking German officers, an attempt on Hitler's life on July 20, 1944, provided heartening evidence of resistance within the *Reich*.

General Montgomery, the top British commander in the west, now urged Eisenhower to concentrate all

THE DEFEAT OF JAPAN

ISLAND WARFARE The South Pacific: MacArthur			ISLAND WARFARE The Central Pacific: Nimitz
Marines land on Guadalcanal, campaign to control Solomon Islands begins. Feb. 9, 1943, Japanese abandon Guadalcanal	Aug. 7, 1942		
Counteroffensive at Papua begins reconquest of New Guinea, completed Sept. 16, 1943	Jan. 23, 1943		
Landings at Rendova, New Georgia	June 30, 1943		
Landings at Bougainville, Northern Solomons. Solomons secure by end of year	Nov. 1, 1943		
		Nov. 21, 1943	Landings at Tarawa and Makin Islands begin battle for the Gilbert Islands and campaign for the Central Pacific. Tarawa secure Nov. 24
		Jan. 31, 1944	Invasion of Marshall Islands. Roi and Namur fall Feb. 3, Kwajalein Feb. 6, Eniwetok Feb. 22
Invasion of Admiralty Islands. Secure Mar. 25	Mar. 1, 1944		
Conquests of air base, Hollandia, Dutch New Guinea	Apr. 22, 1944		
		June 15, 1944	Invasion of Saipan, Marianas Islands. Secure July 9. Air raids of superfortresses against Japan from Saipan begin Nov. 24
		July 21, 1944	Invasion of Guam, Marianas Islands. Secure Aug. 9
Invasion of Morotai	Sept. 15, 1944	Sept. 15, 1944	Invasion of Peleliu, Palaus Islands. Islands secure Nov. 25
Invasion of Leyte, Philippine Islands	Oct. 29, 1944		
Invasion of Mindoro, Philippine Islands	Dec. 15, 1944		
Invasion of Luzon, Philippine Islands. Fall of Manila Feb. 25	Jan. 9, 1945		
		Feb. 17, 1945	Invasion of Iwo Jima. Secure Mar. 17
		Apr. 1, 1945	Invasion of Okinawa. Secure June 21
		Aug. 6, 1945	Hiroshima. Soviet Union enters war Aug. 8. Nagasaki Aug. 9
		Aug. 10, 1945	Japanese offer of surrender

Allied resources on ending the war by a single decisive thrust into Germany. Eisenhower, looking at Allied port and trucking facilities, concluded that logistic support was lacking for the Montgomery plan. Accordingly, in a controversial decision, he settled instead for a "broad-front" strategy of building up strength along the entire western front in preparation for a general advance into Germany.

Southern France or the Ljublana Gap? A final argument over strategy remained. The Americans had long wished to follow up the invasion of Normandy with troop landings in southern France. Eisenhower regarded this as essential to the invasion of Germany. The British wanted to switch the whole operation to the east and mount instead an invasion through Trieste and the Ljublana Gap of Yugoslavia toward Vienna, but that was never a practical proposition. So the invasion of southern France took place according to schedule on August 15, 1944. With the fresh Allied advance up the Rhone Valley, the iron ring around Germany was drawing tight.

THE WAR IN THE PACIFIC

Holding the Line Though the European theater of war had priority, the United States and Great Britain did not neglect East Asia. Pearl Harbor had marked only the beginning of a period of exultant Japanese aggression. "For three months after the Pearl Harbor attack," Admiral Samuel Eliot Morison wrote, "the Pacific was practically a Japanese lake." One after another the bastions of western empire fell to the Japanese: Guam, Wake Island, and Hong Kong in December 1941; Singapore in February 1942; Java in March; and, after the terrible holding action on Bataan, the Philippines in May. Japanese forces were moving into Burma and threatening advances as far to the west as India and to the south as Australia (see Map 29-3). Japanese politicians were looking forward to the formation of the Greater East Asia Co-Prosperity Sphere, where Japan would mobilize the power of East Asia behind a wall of air and naval defense.

The Allied forces in the Pacific felt themselves the step-children of the war, but their situation was never hopeless. The Japanese had failed to destroy a single aircraft carrier at Pearl Harbor, and the American carrier striking force was not only able to secure the South Pacific supply line between Hawaii and Australia but could conduct sporadic harassments of the enemy (including an air raid on Tokyo in April 1942).

The Japanese themselves, instead of pausing for consolidation, struck out on ambitious new programs of conquest in the spring of 1942. Japanese political leaders hoped to extend the sway of the emperor by isolating and perhaps invading Australia. And Admiral Yamamoto, the chief Japanese sea lord, wished to force the American Pacific Fleet into a final engagement before it had a chance to recoup the losses of Pearl Harbor. In May 1942, therefore, the Japanese occupied Tulagi in the Solomon Islands and launched a naval expedition across the Coral Sea toward Port Moresby in Papua, New Guinea. But an American carrier task force intercepted the Japanese ships, and, in an extraordinary battle of carrier-based aircraft, the Americans turned back the enemy. This was the first sea battle in history in which the ships involved exchanged no shots—indeed, did not even come within sight of one another.

The Battle of the Coral Sea marked the high point of Japanese advances in the south. Yamamoto now shifted his operations to the north-central Pacific. A month later, the bulk of the Japanese navy—some 200 ships—headed toward Midway Island and the western Aleutians. But the Americans, having broken the Japanese code, could anticipate enemy intentions. There followed the decisive naval battle of the war, in which the American fleets, brilliantly led by Admirals Raymond A. Spruance and Frank J. Fletcher, destroyed four Japanese aircraft carriers and a heavy cruiser and forced the enemy into disorderly retreat. The Japanese never again had sufficient naval air strength to take the long-range offensive.

The Road to Tokyo The threat to communications from Hawaii to Australia remained, however, so long as the Japanese held bases in the Solomons and the Bismarcks. The Bismarck Barrier, a chain of small islands, gave the Japanese a powerful defense block athwart the road to Tokyo. Intelligence reports that the Japanese were building an airstrip on the island of Guadalcanal in the Solomons precipitated American action in August 1942. There followed six months of grueling combat in the steaming jungles of Guadalcanal and in the serene waters around the island. By February 1943 the Japanese abandoned Guadalcanal.

In January 1943 the Joint Chiefs, noting that only 15 percent of Allied resources was applied to the Pacific, argued for enough additional strength to permit the launching of an offensive. The British acquiesced, stipulating only that Pacific operations should be kept within such limits as would not handicap the war against Germany. The American planners—for the Pacific war was accepted as essentially an American responsibility—now considered the question of the best route to Tokyo.

If European strategy was a compromise between diverging American and British views, Pacific strategy was a compromise between the diverging view of the American army and navy. General Douglas MacArthur, who had been American commander in the Philippines and had been evacuated to Australia early in 1942 to take command of the army in the south Pacific, argued forcefully for an advance from the southwestern Pacific through New Guinea to the Philippines and then to Japan. Admiral Chester Nimitz, on behalf of the navy, contended for an advance through the central Pacific to Formosa, the Chinese coast, and thence to Japan. MacArthur protested that this would be a gravely mistaken diversion of limited resources. But the navy responded persuasively that a single axis of advance would allow the Japanese to concentrate their defensive action. In the end the Joint Chiefs in Washington decided on parallel offensives along both routes (see Map 29-3, p. 762).

The invention of new tactical techniques facilitated the American offensive. In March 1943, in the Battle of the Bismarck Sea, General George Kenney's bombers destroyed a Japanese troop convoy headed for New

Yanks in New Guinea

Guinea—an action that dissuaded the Japanese thereafter from attempting to move large bodies of troops within range of Allied air power. Knowing that the Japanese would not risk large-scale reinforcement, American forces could simply bypass the stronger Japanese bases. This "leapfrogging" technique became the basic pattern of the American counteroffensive.

By March 1944 Nimitz's forces had leapfrogged at Tarawa and Kwajalein, and MacArthur's forces had broken the Bismarck Barrier. Nimitz was now moving into Guam and Saipan in the Marianas. In June the Pacific Fleet under Admiral Spruance smashed the Japanese navy again in the Battle of the Philippine Sea. MacArthur continued to press along the northwest coast of New Guinea toward the Philippines (see Map 29-3). The time was approaching for a final decision about the road to Tokyo.

Luzon or Formosa? MacArthur insisted on the recapture of the Philippines, and especially of Luzon, as the indispensable preliminary. He invoked not only strategic arguments—that Luzon would be a safer staging area for invasion that Formosa (Taiwan)—but political and emotional arguments. Was the president willing, the general asked, "to accept responsibility for breaking a solemn promise to 18 million Christian Filipinos that the Americans would return?" (The promise had been MacArthur's.) Admirals King and Nimitz advocated leapfrogging part or all of the Philippines in the interest of an immediate attack on Formosa. Roosevelt settled the question in MacArthur's favor in early October 1944.

MacArthur lost no time. On October 20 he disembarked on the beach at Leyte, saying, "People of the

General Douglas MacArthur at Leyte Gulf

Philippines: I have returned." A few days later, in the Battle of Leyte Gulf, the American navy in the Philippines completed the destruction of Japanese naval striking power. In number of ships engaged, this was the greatest naval battle of all history. MacArthur's troops meanwhile pressed on toward Manila, while Nimitz's forces were making their way toward Japan from the central Pacific. Japan itself was now under naval blockade and ever more devastating air attacks.

The Riddle of China Washington had hope that China could play a leading role in the war against Japan. Indeed, through the war, Roosevelt, despite Churchill's skepticism, persisted in treating China as if it were a major power. However, the Nationalist regime of Chiang Kai-shek—driven into the interior, cut off from sources of supply, exhausted by four years of war, and demoralized by inflation, intrigue, and graft—was increasingly incapable of serious action.

Keeping China in the war nevertheless remained a major American objective. In 1941 and 1942 the Chinese government, now established in Chongqing (Chungking), received a trickle of supplies flown over the "hump" of the Himalayas from India. Then in 1943 an assortment of Chinese, Indian, and American troops, under the command of General Joseph W. Stilwell, began to construct a road and pipeline across northern Burma to Kunming. Soon Stilwell was sent to Chongqing (Chungking) as commander of the American forces in China, with orders to maximize the Chinese contribution to the war against Japan. But, where Stilwell saw only one enemy, he discovered that Chiang Kai-shek saw a second—the increasingly powerful Chinese Communists, spreading out from their base in Yenan.

Seeking particularly to mobilize the poverty-stricken and land-hungry peasants, the Communists won respect, even among Westerners, as an embodiment of reform, austerity, and discipline. War sharpened the contrast between the self-indulgence of Chongqing (Chungking) and the dedication of Yenan. Chiang himself seemed to be paying less and less attention to Japan in his preoccupation with the threat of Mao Zedong (Mao Tse-tung) and his Eighth Route Army. By 1944, 400,000 Nationalist troops had been diverted to check the spread of Communist influence. Stilwell, eager to get as many Chinese divisions as possible—whatever their politics—into action against the Japanese, soon came to consider Chiang Kai-shek a main obstacle to the fulfillment of his mission.

In June 1944 the Fourteenth Air Force began to attack Japan from Chinese airstrips. This action provoked the Japanese into counterattacking the bomber bases and renewing their offensive against Chongqing (Chungking). Now the difficulties between Stilwell and Chiang came to a head. A brave, narrow, intense man, Stilwell was devoid of diplomatic skill and baffled by the intricacies of Chinese politics. When the Joint Chiefs recommended that the Chinese army be placed under Stilwell's command, Chiang Kai-shek instead demanded his dismissal. Roosevelt complied. The military potential of China was disappearing in the swirl of Chinese civil discord.

THE FOURTH TERM

Politics As Usual The congressional elections of 1942 brought into office the most conservative Congress Washington had known for a decade. Congressional refusal in the spring of 1943 to continue the National Resources Planning Board was a symbolic rejection of the whole idea of New Deal planning. Passage in June of the Smith-Connally Act over Roosevelt's veto bestowed on a reluctant government new powers to crack down on trade unions in labor disputes. Congress liquidated the National Youth Administration, harassed the Farm Security Administration, and sought in a variety of ways to curtail social programs and expenditures.

Roosevelt himself gave ground before the conservative attack. In a press conference in December 1943 he explained that the New Deal had come into existence because the United States was suffering from a grave internal disorder. But in December 1941 the patient had been in a bad external smashup. He praised the ministrations of the New Deal but added, "At the present time, obviously, the principal emphasis, the overwhelming first emphasis should be on winning the war."

That emphasis had engendered a certain disenchantment in the American liberal community. Though Roosevelt retained the essential confidence of liberals, he was no longer articulating their day-to-day hopes. Many of them had been upset by his wartime suspension of antitrust proceedings, by his relationships with Darlan and Badoglio, by his tepid policies toward civil rights, and by his hesitation in locating areas of asylum for the Jewish population of Europe that the Nazis were systematically murdering. In their frustration, the president's liberal critics listened to other voices. They found consolation in particular in Vice President Henry Wallace, with his celebration of "the century of the common man," and, more surprisingly, in Wendell Willkie, the Republican presidential candidate of 1940 (see p. 738). In the years after his defeat, Willkie had shown himself a political leader generous in disposition and courageous in utterance. Increasingly he was a champion of civil rights and a critic of big business. His book *One World,* published in 1943 after his trip as a presidential emissary to Britain, the Soviet Union, the Middle East, and China seemed to sum up the best aspirations of American liberal internationalism.

The Campaign of 1944 As the titular leader of the Republican party, Willkie retained hopes of a second presidential nomination in 1944. But his liberal and internationalist tendencies, on top of a chronic political maladroitness, had estranged most of the leaders of his party. After suffering a bad defeat in the Wisconsin presidential primary in April, he withdrew from the race. Thomas E. Dewey, who had been elected governor of New York in 1942, was now emerging as the favored Republican contender. A young man—he was just 42—he had already gained a reputation for executive efficiency and vigor. The Republican convention, meeting in Chicago at the end of June, promptly nominated Dewey on the first ballot. To balance Dewey's growing inclinations toward liberalism and internationalism, Governor John W. Bricker of Ohio, a conservative isolationist, was named for second place.

The Democrats renominated Roosevelt without suffering the trauma of 1940. "For myself, I do not want to run," he wrote the chairman of the Democratic National Committee in July. "But as a good soldier . . . I will accept and serve." The struggle was over the vice-presidential nomination. Wallace had the support of the labor-liberal wing of the party, but the Democratic South and the urban bosses opposed him, and, though Roosevelt said he "personally" would vote for Wallace if a delegate, he did not insist on Wallace's renomination. For a time Roosevelt leaned toward James F. Byrnes. When Ed Flynn of New York and Sidney Hillman of the Amalgamated Clothing Workers vetoed Byrnes, Roosevelt said he would be "very glad to run" with either Senator Harry S Truman of Missouri or Justice William O. Douglas of the Supreme Court. Truman, with Roosevelt's private support, won on the third ballot.

Renomination, 1944

The campaign was overshadowed by the war. The initial restraint of Dewey's speeches failed to stir the electorate. He stepped up the harshness of his attack, implying a connection between Roosevelt and communism, but his main achievement was to force Roosevelt himself into the arena. An uproariously successful speech by Roosevelt before the Teamsters Union in Washington on September 23 showed that the old campaigner had lost none of his magic. In October he sought to meet well-founded doubts about his health by riding around New York City all day in an open car through pouring rain. In the meantime, he spoke with eloquence about the need for internationalism in the postwar world and for a postwar economic bill of rights with federal guarantees to education, employment, and expanded social security. On November 7, Roosevelt received 25.6 million popular and 432 electoral votes as against 22 million and 99 for Dewey. The Democrats lost one seat in the Senate, gained 20 in the House, and captured five governorships. The election, though the closest of his triumphs, was a categorical confirmation of Roosevelt as America's chosen leader for the peace.

THE DIPLOMACY OF COALITION

The Question of War Aims Even before Pearl Harbor Roosevelt had outlined his broad ideas on the postwar settlement. In his message to Congress on January 6, 1941, he said that the United States looked forward to a world founded on "four essential human freedoms—freedom of speech and expression, freedom of worship, freedom from want, freedom from fear." In August of the same year, the Atlantic Charter (see p. 743) further particularized the American conception of the postwar world, laying stress on national self-determination, equal access to trade and raw materials, and a lasting peace to be achieved through a permanent system of general security. On January 1, 1942, 26 nations (led by the United States, Britain, the Soviet Union, and China) signed a joint declaration subscribing to the Atlantic Charter, pledging their full resources to victory, promising not to make a separate peace, and dedicating themselves to "defend life, liberty, independence, and religious freedom, and to preserve human rights and justice in their own lands as well as in other lands." Roosevelt called this a "declaration by United Nations," and his phrase was employed thereafter to describe the grand alliance.

In practice, three of the United Nations—the United States, Britain, and the Soviet Union—were more important than the rest. The United States and Britain, with common traditions and interests, had little difficulty in establishing partnership. Roosevelt and Churchill regarded each other with mutual respect and delight and were almost immediately on intimate terms. The formation of the Anglo-American Combined Chiefs of Staff in December 1941 guaranteed close military coordination, while combined boards were subsequently set up in other fields. Friction, of course, was not entirely eliminated. There were persistent differences over European strategy, and Churchill quickly made it clear that he had no intention of applying the Atlantic Charter to British possessions, but disagreements were held within a framework of reciprocal confidence.

With regard to the postwar world, Churchill, though by instinct a balance-of-power man, was prepared to go a considerable distance with Roosevelt's version of the United Nations as one basis of a peace system. In Wilsonian rhetoric, Roosevelt declared that peace must "spell the end of the system of unilateral action, the exclusive alliances, the spheres of influence, the balances of power, and all the other expedients that have been tried for centuries—and have always failed." A reversion to those principles, he held, would create the conditions for future wars: it would also mean the repudiation of the Atlantic Charter, the Four Freedoms, and the values for which the war had presumably been fought. Roosevelt expected the four great powers—the United States, the United Kingdom, the Soviet Union, and China—to work in concert to keep the peace. He also viewed the United States as the dominant influence in the Americas. Indeed whatever his rhetoric, he continued to understand the importance of power in international politics. Still, he recognized that all nations had an interest in all the affairs of the globe, and all would therefore deserve representation in a postwar international organization. As he saw it, moreover, international prosperity was to be assured by the reduction of barriers to an expanding world trade.

The Russians viewed the world primarily in terms of spheres of influence and balances of power. They placed little confidence in the United Nations. Their physical safety, as they read their bitter historical experience, demanded the absolute guarantee that all states along the Russian border in eastern Europe should have "friendly governments," by which they meant governments reliably subservient to Moscow and based upon socialist principles. They had no intention of allowing other states a role in eastern Europe. In 1939 the Soviet-Nazi pact had enabled Russia to begin to fulfill part of what it considered its security requirements through the acquisition of the Baltic states, Karelian Finland, and eastern Poland. In November 1940 Moscow had pressed further demands on Hitler—a free hand in Finland, predominance in Romania and Bulgaria, bases in the Dardanelles. After the German attack, Stalin hoped to gain from the West what Hitler had not dared yield him.

These were traditional Russian objectives not dependent on ideology. But ideology intensified the possibilities of discord. The Soviet view, grounded in the Marxist-Leninist analysis of history, excluded the idea of long-term peace between Communist and capitalist states. The existence of the United States as the citadel of capitalism was, by that definition, a threat to the security of the Soviet Union. But Stalin was not necessarily the helpless prisoner of this ideology. He saw himself less as the disciple of Marx and Lenin than as their fellow prophet. Sensing that Stalin was the only force capable of overcoming Stalinism, Roosevelt placed great emphasis on his personal relations with the Soviet leader.

So long, however, as Russian survival depended on the establishment of a second front, Moscow's purposes, whether strategic or ideological, were muted. Thus the Soviet government adhered to the Atlantic Charter (though with a reservation about adapting its principles to "the circumstances, needs, and historic peculiarities of particular countries") and acquiesced in the British refusal, under American pressure, to recognize the Soviet conquest of the Baltic republics. But Stalin's basic hope, as expressed in a proposal to Britain at the end of 1941, was for a straight sphere-of-influence deal.

The Early Wartime Conferences It soon became evident that the diplomacy of coalition required not only constant communication among the nations but periodic face-to-face meetings among their leaders. Thus Churchill followed his Washington visit in December 1941–January 1942 with a visit to Moscow in August, where he explained to an angry Stalin the reasons for the postponement of the second front.

The successes in North Africa at the end of 1942 opened a new phase of the war and emphasized the need for a conference among all three leaders. Stalin, however, felt that he could not leave the Soviet Union;

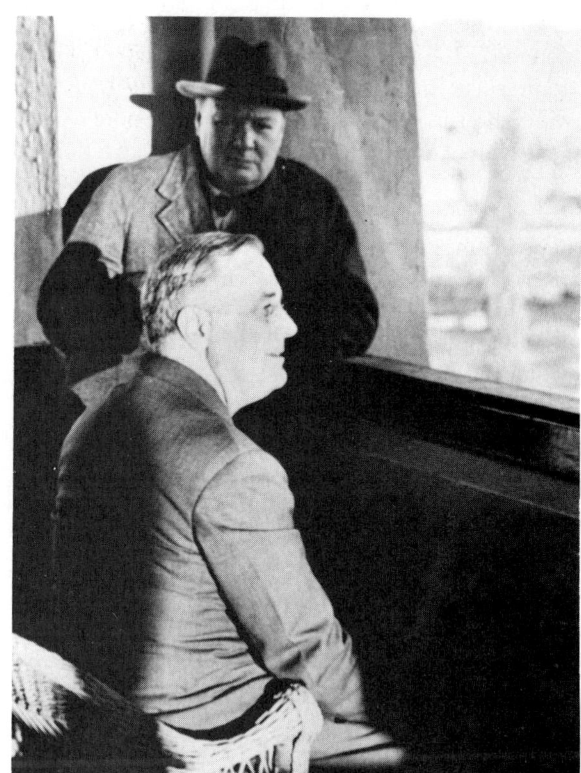

Roosevelt and Churchill, North Africa, 1943

so Roosevelt and Churchill met with their staffs at Casablanca on the Atlantic coast of Morocco in January 1943. The Casablanca Conference laid plans for future military action in the Mediterranean. Roosevelt and Churchill also sought, with little success, to unite the anti-Vichy French by bringing about a reconciliation with General de Gaulle. The main contribution of Casablanca, however, was the doctrine of "unconditional surrender."

By unconditional surrender Roosevelt meant no more than the surrender by Axis governments without conditions—that is, without assurance of the survival of the political leadership that had brought on the war. "It does not mean," he explained at Casablanca, "the destruction of the population of Germany, Italy, or Japan, but it does mean the destruction of the philosophies in those countries which are based on conquest and the subjugation of other people." Unconditional surrender was not a last-minute improvisation. It had been discussed in the State Department since the preceding spring and had been raised with Churchill (who, in turn, raised it with the British War Cabinet) before the press conference at which it was announced. The doctrine was designed partly to overcome misgivings generated by the Anglo-American willingness to deal with Darlan but even more to prevent Hitler from breaking up the Allied coalition by playing off one side against the other. The fear that the Soviet Union might seek a separate peace with Germany haunted British and American policy makers in 1942–43, and unconditional surrender seemed the best insurance against such an eventuality.

The doctrine of unconditional surrender did not prolong the war. It had little effect in delaying the Italian surrender. In the case of Germany, no one seems to have been deterred from surrendering who would have surrendered otherwise, and up to the last moment several Nazi leaders were sure they could work out their own deals with the Allies. Nor did unconditional surrender play into the hands of the Communists. Indeed, Stalin tried hard in 1944 to get Roosevelt and Churchill to modify the doctrine.

From Big Two to Big Three Roosevelt and Churchill met again in Washington in May 1943, and in Quebec in August. Both meetings dealt mainly with Anglo-American military questions. The Soviet Union remained outside the conference circuit until October, when Cordell Hull and Anthony Eden journeyed to Moscow to pave the way for a meeting of the Big Three.

Relations between the Soviet Union and its western allies were now somewhat ambivalent. On the one hand, a temporary recession of ideology was evident when Stalin, in order to rally his people against the invader, replaced the appeal of Marxism with that of nationalism. "We are under no illusions that they are fighting for us," he once observed to Averell Harriman, the American ambassador. "They are fighting for Mother Russia." In May 1943 the Comintern, the instrumentality of Communist revolution, was dissolved.

On the other hand, shadows of future problems were casting themselves ahead, especially in the liberated nations. The Soviet Union protested its exclusion from the Allied Control Commission for Italy. It had made clear its disinclination to relinquish the part of Poland it had seized in 1939, and in April 1943 it broke off relations with the Polish government-in-exile in London because the Poles asked the International Red Cross to investigate German charges, since proven accurate, that the Russians had massacred several thousand Polish officers at Katyn. In Yugoslavia, the Communist partisans, led by Marshal Tito, were already in conflict with a monarchist resistance movement of Chetniks led by General Mihailovich. A similar feud between Communist and non-Communist guerrillas divided the resistance movement in Greece. Further, Roosevelt, at Churchill's instigation, had decided to keep secret Anglo-American development of certain weapons, of which the most important was the atomic bomb, then still far from completion though as the president knew, Stalin had obtained some general information about it. That secrecy reflected an uncertainty about Soviet intentions, a reservation about postwar cooperation, of which Stalin was aware. He harbored similar reservations himself, as well as persistent resentment about the postponement of the second front in France.

But such events remained in the background when the foreign secretaries met in October. Molotov, the Soviet foreign secretary, went agreeably along with a statement of pieties advocated by Hull and soon issued as the Declaration of Moscow. This included affirmation of "the necessity of establishing at the earliest practicable date a general international organization . . . for the maintenance of international peace." The Moscow Conference also established the European Advisory Commission (EAC) to plan for German collapse.

The next step was the long-delayed meeting of the three leaders, arranged for Teheran in late November. This was preceded by a separate conference in Cairo where Roosevelt and Churchill met with Chiang Kai-shek. Stalin did not take part because Russia was not in the Japanese war. The Cairo Declaration promised to strip Japan of its conquests, to free Korea, and to return Manchuria and Taiwan to China. The Teheran meeting concentrated on military problems, including an Anglo-American commitment to a cross-Channel invasion within six months. The meeting also considered the future of Germany, problems in eastern Europe and East Asia, and the shape of the postwar peace system. "We came here with hope and determination," the three leaders wrote in the Declaration of Teheran. "We leave here, friends in fact, in spirit and in purpose."

Postwar Planning More progress was made in defining the structure of the future international organization when the Allies held a series of meetings at Dumbarton Oaks in Washington in August–September 1944. But the creation of broad frameworks for postwar collaboration did not solve the concrete problems of the postwar settlement. The fate

The Polish Question: Stalin

We must now be interested in supporting the National [Lublin] Committee and all who are . . . cooperating with it. . . . For the Soviet Union, which is bearing the whole burden of the struggle for freeing Poland from Germany, the problem of relations with Poland is . . . a matter of . . . close and friendly relations with an authority . . . which has already grown strong and has armed forces of its own. . . .

In the event of the Polish [Lublin] Committee of National Liberation becoming a Provisional Police Government, the Soviet Government will . . . have no serious reasons for postponing its recognition. . . . The Soviet Union, more than any other Power, has a stake in strengthening a pro-Ally and democratic Poland . . . because Poland borders on the Soviet Union and because the Polish problem is inseparable from that of the security of the Soviet Union. . . .

In the conditions now prevailing in Poland there are no grounds for continuing to support the émigré [London] Government, which has completely forfeited the trust of the population inside the country. . . .

From a message of Joseph Stalin to Franklin D. Roosevelt, December 27, 1944

of Germany posed especially perplexing questions. All members of the Big Three had played at one time or another with notions of German dismemberment; this approach seemed to prevail as late as Teheran. But when the European Advisory Commission took over, dismemberment receded into the background. The EAC concentrated instead on determining the zones of Allied occupation. In the end, Britain took the northwestern zone, America the southwestern, and Russia the eastern. Berlin, though situated in the Soviet zone, was to be jointly held. The question of access to Berlin was left, on military advice, to the commanders in the field.

As for the German economy, the most drastic proposals came from the United States Treasury Department in August 1944. Secretary Morgenthau urged both territorial transfers and partition. In addition, he recommended the dismantling of German heavy industry and the transformation of Germany into an agricultural state. For a moment Roosevelt fell in with the Morgenthau plan though it would have crippled the European economy. Even Churchill accepted it briefly during the second Quebec Conference in September, partly in the hope of securing postwar economic aid in exchange. But in a few weeks this scheme dropped by the wayside, though its emphasis on a Spartan treatment of occupied Germany remained American doctrine.

Growing doubts about Soviet policy compounded the uncertainty over the future. The Polish question was more acute than ever. Churchill, in an effort to restore the position of the Polish government-in-exile in London, had been urging that government to accept Soviet territorial demands, including the Curzon line to the east and (in compensation) the Oder-Neisse line to the west (see Map 30-1). In November 1944 the British government pledged support for the Oder-Neisse line even if the United States refused to go along. But Stalin, who saw Poland as "the corridor for attack on Russia," considered the Polish question as "one of life and death" and refused to accept the London regime. In August the Polish Home Army, whose affiliations were with London, set off a revolt against the Germans in Warsaw. The Red Army, a few miles outside the city, declined to aid the uprising; the Soviet Union would not even permit planes carrying

The Polish Question: FDR

I am disturbed and deeply disappointed by your message . . . regarding Poland. . . . I would have thought that no serious inconvenience would have been caused your Government or your Armies if you were to delay the purely juridical act of recognition for the . . . month remaining until our meeting. . . . I had urged this delay upon you because of my feeling that you would realize how extremely unfortunate . . . it would be in its effect on world opinion and enemy morale . . . if your Government should formally recognize one Government of Poland while the majority of the other United Nations including Great Britain and the United States continue to recognize the Polish Government in London. . . .

With frankness equal to your own I must tell you that I see no prospect of this Government's following suit. . . . Neither the Government nor the people of the United States have seen any evidence . . . to justify the conclusion that the Lublin Committee . . . represents the people of Poland. . . . No opportunity to express themselves in regard to the Lublin Committee has yet been afforded the people of Poland.

If there is established . . . following the liberation of Poland a Provisional Government . . . with popular support, the attitude of this Government would of course be governed by the Polish people's decision. . . .

From a reply from Franklin D. Roosevelt to Joseph Stalin, December 31, 1944

supplies to Warsaw from the west to land on Russian soil. This seemed a calculated attempt to destroy non-Communist Poles. In addition, the Soviet Union was setting up a group of pro-Communists in Lublin as the nucleus of a postwar Polish government. And, citing the Anglo-American example in Italy, the Russians, after the surrender of Bulgaria, denied the western Allies any role in the Bulgarian Control Commission.

In October Churchill paid another visit to Moscow. His effort to bring about a reconciliation between the London and Lublin Poles failed. But he and Stalin agreed on a scheme for southeastern Europe, according to which in the period after liberation Britain would recognize Russia's predominant interest in Romania, Bulgaria, and Hungary, and Russia would recognize Britain's predominant interest in Greece, with Yugoslavia split fifty-fifty. Roosevelt went along with this only as a temporary wartime arrangement, but Stalin and perhaps Churchill, too, probably expected it to register postwar realities.

TRIUMPH AND TRAGEDY

The Big Three at Yalta Roosevelt's reelection in November 1944 found the Allied forces pressing hard down the last mile to victory. But bloodshed was far from over. With Eisenhower's forces deployed along the length of the Siegfried line and north and west from there, the Germans saw an opportunity in December 1944 to launch an attack in the Ardennes Forest. The desperate German offensive resulted in some early breakthroughs, but the Americans held at Bastogne, and, after weeks of severe fighting, the Battle of the Bulge came to an end in January. On the other side of the world, the Japanese continued their resistance. Manila was not liberated until February 1945. And the forces of Admiral Nimitz, coming in from the central Pacific, had to fight every step of the way before they could gain such islands to the south of Japan as Iwo Jima (in February) and Okinawa (in April).

Yanks on the Champs-Élysées, 1944

The approach of victory did not simplify the political problems of the triumphant coalition. The Polish tangle showed no signs of unraveling. The fate of Germany remained undecided. The future of eastern Europe and East Asia was still obscure. The persistence of these problems argued for another meeting of the Big Three. They met in a conference at Yalta in the Crimea in February 1945.

Some of the decisions taken at Yalta pertained to Europe. The most critical of these had to do with the liberated nations of eastern Europe. Roosevelt and Churchill rejected Stalin's proposal that they accept the Lublin government in Poland. Instead, the three leaders agreed on a reorganization of the Polish government to include leaders from abroad—this provisional government to be "pledged to the holding of free and unfettered elections as soon as possible." For liberated Europe in general, the conference promised "interim governmental authorities broadly representative of all democratic elements in the population and pledged to the earliest possible establishment through free elections of governments responsive to the will of the people." With regard to Germany, the conference postponed decisions on dismemberment and on future frontiers, endorsed the EAC provisions for zonal occupation (adding a zone for France) and for an Allied Control Council, and evaded a Soviet demand of $20 billion for German reparations while conceding the figure as a "basis for discussion."

The Yalta discussions also dealt with East Asia, where the American Joint Chiefs were eager to secure from Stalin a precise commitment about entering the war. Some feared that Russia would let the United States undertake a costly invasion of Japan and then move into Manchuria and China at the last minute to reap the benefits of victory. Moreover, the military estimated that the invasion of Japan, scheduled for the spring of 1946, might cost over a million casualties to American forces alone—another reason for desiring early Soviet participation. In secret discussions with

Yalta, 1945: hopeful assumptions soon to be falsified

Roosevelt, Stalin agreed to declare war on Japan within two or three months after the surrender of Germany on condition that the Kurile Islands and southern Sakhalin be restored to Russia and that the commercial interest of the Soviet Union in Dairen (Lüda) and its rail communications be recognized. When Roosevelt obtained the assent of Chiang Kai-shek to these measures, the Soviet Union would agree "that China shall retain full sovereignty in Manchuria" and would conclude a treaty of friendship and alliance with the Chiang Kai-shek government.

A third topic at Yalta was the organization of the United Nations. Here the Soviet Union accepted American proposals on voting procedure that it had opposed at Dumbarton Oaks and agreed that a United Nations conference should be called at San Francisco in April to prepare the charter for a permanent organization. With British support, the Russians also secured votes in the General Assembly for Byelorussia and the Ukraine. Roosevelt attached great importance to the apparent Soviet willingness to collaborate in a structure of international order. He doubtless also supposed that the deliberations of the United Nations, especially among the great powers, would provide the means of remedying the omissions or errors or ambiguities of the various summit conferences.

Roosevelt and Churchill returned from Yalta well satisfied. They expected Stalin, as Churchill put it, "to live in honourable friendship and equality with the Western democracies." During the war, the Soviet government had discharged its military commitments with commendable promptitude. The Yalta agreements, however, represented the first experiment in postwar political collaboration. Here, as Churchill himself later wrote, "Our hopeful assumptions were soon to be falsified. Still, they were the only ones possible at the time."

Right-wing critics later held that Roosevelt and Churchill had perpetrated a "betrayal" at Yalta, selling eastern Europe and China "down the river" in a vain

Holocaust: Concentration Camps

To those soldiers who had never thought about it much, the war's meaning was beginning to sink in deep. . . . "You mean they took all these people and worked them like slaves?". . . Soon to come were more of the same. . . Soon to come were the concentration camps, the huge piles of naked, stinking, beaten bodies . . . piled up like cordwood, the living dead with skin so tight over their gaping bodies that you expected it to crack when they bent over . . . the walls of torture chambers covered with the imprint of feet which had kicked and kicked before death finally came . . . the incredible stories which you didn't believe until they took off their clothes and showed you. . . . People whipped like dogs. . . . People buried alive. . . . How many millions of people? . . . Soldiers who never knew what fascism really was knew it now.

From Ralph G. Martin, *The GI War,* 1967

effort to "appease" Stalin. The Yalta text belied such charges. Had the agreements been kept, eastern Europe would have had freely elected democratic governments and Chiang Kai-shek would have been confirmed in control of China and Manchuria. Stalin later abandoned his Yalta pledges in order to achieve his purposes. The Soviet Union, moreover, gained no territory as a result of Yalta (except the Kurile Islands) that was not already, or about to be, under Soviet domination as a result of military operations—and such operations could have been checked only by countervailing force from the West.

Left-wing critics made opposite charges: that Stalin conceded more at Yalta than did Roosevelt and Churchill, and that behind American policy was an aggressive determination to dominate the world, promote counterrevolution and, in particular, make eastern Europe and East Asia safe for American capitalism. Again the Yalta documents fail to sustain such charges. Roosevelt remarked at Yalta that "two years would be the limit" for keeping American troops in Europe. The Western Allies would have been wholly satisfied with an eastern Europe composed of nations friendly to Russia and (in the words of a State Department analysis) "in favor of far-reaching economic and social reforms, but not, however, in favor of a left-wing totalitarian regime to achieve these reforms."

All in all, military realities at the time set the terms of the agreements at Yalta. Roosevelt let those realities take precedence over political considerations. Short of preparing for a war against the Soviet Union, he had no other choice. And as he saw it, American interests then lay essentially in speeding victory in Europe and Asia. Like Churchill, he could depend only on hopeful assumptions about the future of eastern Europe.

Victory in Europe Within a few weeks of Yalta, American and British armies were crossing the Rhine at many points. To their horror, they discovered the concentration camps at Buchenwald, Belsen, and elsewhere where the Nazis had been confining millions of Jews. The "barbarous treatment," Eisenhower said, was "almost unbelievable." Conditions in the camps were dismal: "massive starvation, untreated disease, terrible crowding, thousands of unburied corpses." At Auschwitz and other extermination centers, the Nazis had murdered their victims—gypsies, homosexuals, and other proscribed groups, as well as the millions of Jews. With few exceptions, Americans became aware of the Holocaust and its ghastly crimes only when the GIs and the newspaper reporters accompanying them began to describe the awful scenes they were encountering.

For the Soviet Union, cooperation with non-Communists had been a response to the rise of Nazism. The Yalta Conference, taking place in the shadow of the Ardennes counteroffensive, reflected the still dangerous Nazi military threat. But with the end of the war in sight, the Soviet need for wartime cooperation was disappearing. Within a few weeks the Soviet Union took swift action in Romania and Poland to frustrate the Yalta pledges of political freedom. Stalin himself opened up a political offensive charging that the United States and Britain were engaged in separate peace negotiations with Germany, as indeed some of their agents secretly were in Switzerland. Roosevelt replied with indignation that he deeply resented these "vile misrepresentations."

At the end of March 1945, Roosevelt cabled Churchill that he was "watching with anxiety and concern the development of the Soviet attitude." This attitude portended danger for "future world cooperation." The president sent stern warnings to the Soviet leader and on April 6 told Churchill, "We must not permit anybody to entertain a false impression that we are afraid. Our Armies will in a very few days be in a position that will permit us to become 'tougher' than has heretofore appeared advantageous to the war effort." But Roosevelt, worn out by long years of terrible responsibility, was reaching the end. On April 12 he died of a massive cerebral hemorrhage, as truly a casualty of war as any man who died in battle.

These ominous political developments put military problems in a new context. As the Anglo-American armies plunged ahead into Germany, Churchill argued in March and April that they should race the Russians to Berlin. "From a political standpoint," he said, "we should march as far east into Germany as possible." But General Eisenhower regarded it "as militarily unsound . . . to make Berlin a major objective," and he was eager to sustain good relations with the Russians. The imperative consideration, in the view of the American Joint Chiefs, was the destruction of the German armed forces, and this, Eisenhower believed (incorrectly, as it turned out), required the pursuit of the remaining German troops to a supposed last stand in the south.

A month later, Churchill renewed his pleading, this time in connection with Prague, at least until Soviet Russia clarified its intentions with regard to Poland and Germany. Harry S Truman, who had succeeded to the American presidency, hesitated at deeper American involvement in central Europe, partly because of a

Americans and Russians, Torgau, Germany, April 1945

fear of prejudicing future Soviet cooperation with the United Nations, partly because of the need for redeploying American troops to the Pacific. He accordingly treated the problem as a tactical one to be decided by the commander in the field. Eisenhower, for his part, declined to abandon strictly military criteria in the absence of orders from above. Though he could have put American troops into Prague far in advance of the Red Army, he refused to do so. It is by no means clear that Churchill's plan would have changed the postwar balance in Europe, but American generals, as General Omar Bradley later wrote, "looked naïvely on this British inclination to complicate the war with political foresight and non-military objectives."

By now events in Europe were rushing to climax. Hitler's thousand-year *Reich,* overrun by Allied armies, was falling to pieces. The German dictator himself took refuge in his bunker in Berlin and on April 30 committed suicide. On May 3 the process of piecemeal German surrender began, with a ceremony of unconditional surrender at Eisenhower's headquarters in Rheims on May 7, and a surrender to the Russians in Berlin the next day. As Churchill later wrote, the end of hostilities was "the signal for the greatest outburst of joy in the history of mankind," but he moved amid cheering crowds "with an aching heart and a mind oppressed by forebodings."

Victory in East Asia While the European war was coming to its troubled end, American forces continued to make steady progress in the Pacific. But Japanese resistance grew every day more fanatical. The use of kamikaze suicide planes and the last-ditch fighting in Iwo Jima and Okinawa seemed to confirm the horrendous American estimates of casualties to be expected in an invasion of the homeland. Within civilian Japan, though, sensible people recognized that the war was irretrievably lost.

In the meantime, an extraordinary new factor entered into American calculations. In 1939 the scientist Albert Einstein had called Roosevelt's attention to the possibility of using atomic energy for military purposes. In the next years the government sponsored a secret $2 billion operation known as the Manhattan Project to attempt the building of an atomic bomb. A brilliant group of physicists, working under the direction of J. Robert Oppenheimer in Los Alamos, New Mexico, steadily broke down the incredibly complex scientific and technological problems involved in the production of the weapon. On April 25, 1945, Secretary of War Stimson could tell President Truman, "Within four months we shall in all probability have completed the most terrible weapon ever known in human history, one bomb of which could destroy a whole city."

The next question was how and when this frightful weapon should be employed. Roosevelt seems never to have doubted that, once available, the bomb would be dropped. The momentum of wartime atomic policy militated to that conclusion. On June 1 a special committee recommended to Truman that the bomb be used against Japan as soon as possible. Many Manhattan Project scientists, aware of the ghastly character of the weapon, opposed this recommendation, favoring a preliminary demonstration to the world in a desert or on a barren island. But this course was rejected, partly because of the fear that the bomb might not go off, partly because only two bombs would be available by August and it seemed essential to reserve them for direct military use.

Within Japan, where American bombers from Guam and Saipan had been destroying the cities, a new government was looking for a way out. In July it requested Soviet mediation to bring the war to an end, though it added, "So long as the enemy demands unconditional surrender, we will fight as one man." Moscow was cold to this request while Stalin departed for a new Big Three meeting at Potsdam, near Berlin. At the same time, the American government, following the Japanese peace explorations through decoded cable intercepts, came to the conclusion that the best way to hasten the end of the war would be to issue a solemn plea to the Japanese to surrender before it was too late. This warning was embodied somewhat cryptically in a declaration issued at Potsdam by Truman and Clement Attlee, who had succeeded Churchill as British prime minister, urging the Japanese to give up or face "the utter devastation of the Japanese homeland." The Japanese government was inclined to accept this ultimatum, but the military leaders angrily disagreed. On July 28 the Japanese prime minister, in a statement designed for domestic consumption, pronounced the Potsdam Declaration "unworthy of public notice."

Truman had already been informed while at Potsdam that the first bomb test in New Mexico on July 16 had been a triumphant success. The rejection of the Potsdam Declaration now convinced him that the militarists were in control of Tokyo and that there was

The Atomic Bomb: A Plea for Restraint

The development of nuclear power not only constitutes an important addition to the technological and military power of the United States, but creates grave political and economic problems for the future of this country.

Nuclear bombs cannot possibly remain a "secret weapon" at the exclusive disposal of this country for more than a few years. The scientific facts on which their construction is based are well known to scientists of other countries. Unless an effective international control of nuclear explosives is instituted, a race for nuclear armaments is certain to ensue following the first revelation of our possession of nuclear weapons to the world. Within ten years other countries may have nuclear bombs. . . . In the war to which such an armaments race is likely to lead, the United States, with its agglomeration of population and industry in comparatively few metropolitan districts, will be at a disadvantage compared to nations whose population and industry are scattered over large areas.

We believe that these considerations make the use of nuclear bombs for an early unannounced attack against Japan inadvisable. If the United States were to be the first to release this new means of indiscriminate destruction upon mankind, we would sacrifice public support throughout the world, precipitate the race for armaments, and prejudice the possibility of reaching international agreement on the future control of such weapons.

From the Committee on Social and Political Implications, Report to the Secretary of War, June 1945

no point in delaying the use of the bomb against Japan. Some of the president's advisers, Secretary of State Byrnes particularly, believed that the use of the bomb would enhance the American position in negotiations with the Soviet Union. For Truman, that possibility was at most a secondary consideration, though he did decide neither to consult Stalin about the bomb nor to offer him, any more than Roosevelt had, any broad scientific information about the nature of the weapon. Primarily Truman was moved by his interpretation of Japanese political and military conditions. On his orders, on August 6, in a blinding flash of heat and horror, the first atomic bomb fell on Hiroshima, killing nearly 100,000 people, fatally injuring another 100,000 through blast or radiation, and reducing the city to rubble.

Even after this appalling blow the Japanese military vetoed the civilian desire to accept the Potsdam Declaration. Two days after Hiroshima, the Red Army invaded Manchuria and, on the third day, with no word from Tokyo, the American air command, operating on earlier orders, dropped a second bomb on Nagasaki. In Tokyo the military still objected to unconditional surrender. It required the personal intervention of the emperor to overcome their opposition. With Japanese acceptance of Potsdam conditioned on the preservation of the imperial prerogatives, the act of surrender took place on September 2, 1945.

The Atomic Bomb: The President's View

I realize the tragic significance of the atomic bomb.

Its production and its use were not lightly undertaken by this Government. But we knew that our enemies were on the search for it. We know now how close they were to finding it. And we know the disaster which would come to this nation, and to all peaceful nations, to all civilizations, if they had found it first.

That is why we felt compelled to undertake the long and uncertain and costly labor of discovery and production.

We won the race of discovery against the Germans.

Having found the bomb we have used it. We have used it against those who attacked us without warning at Pearl Harbor, against those who have starved and beaten and executed American prisoners of war, against those who have abandoned the pretense of obeying international laws of warfare. We have used it in order to shorten the agony of war, in order to save the lives of thousands and thousands of young Americans.

We shall continue to use it until we completely destroy Japan's power to make war. Only a Japanese surrender will stop us.

From Harry S Truman, Radio Address, August 1945

The decision to drop the atomic bomb was the most tragic in the long course of American history. Perhaps only so drastic a step would have achieved unconditional surrender so rapidly. Still, thoughtful observers have wondered whether the American government, with Japan on the verge of capitulation, had exhausted all possible alternatives before at last having recourse to the bomb—whether there were not resources of negotiation or demonstration that, even at the cost of prolonging the war, should have been first attempted, with the bomb held in reserve as a weapon of last resort. Here perhaps prior atomic policy and, still more, the doctrine of unconditional surrender had terrible consequences. Certainly, though the bomb terminated the war, it also placed the United States for many years in an ambiguous position before the world as the only nation to have employed so horrible a weapon.

Victory thus came—but in a way that converted triumph into tragedy. The Second World War ended. More than 25 million persons, soldiers and civilians, had died during the five years. Sixteen million Americans—more than 10 percent of the population—had been under arms. Total casualties amounted to more than 1 million, with nearly 300,000 deaths in battle. Now, in the autumn of 1945, the world stood on the threshold of a new epoch in history—an epoch incalculably rich in hazards and potentialities. With apprehensive steps, humanity was entering the atomic age.

SUGGESTIONS FOR READING

THE SECOND WORLD WAR: THE HOME FRONT

R. E. Sherwood, *Roosevelt and Hopkins* (1948, rev. ed., 1950), remains the most vivid account of Roosevelt as a war leader; it should be supplemented by J. M. Burns's valuable study, *Roosevelt: The Soldier of Freedom* (1970). For war mobilization, see the Bureau of the Budget, *The United States at War* (1946); E. Janeway, *The Struggle for Survival* (1951); and H. M. Somers, *Presidential Agency: OWMR* (1950); on price control, L. V. Chandler, *Inflation in the United States, 1940–1948* (1951); C. Bowles, *Promises to Keep* (1971); and, for the penetrating reflections of a leading controller, J. K. Galbraith, *Theory of Price Control* (1952). The mobilization of science and technology is incisively depicted in J. P. Baxter, III, *Scientists Against Time* (1946); on mobilization of manpower, see G. Flynn, *The Mess in Washington* (1979); R. G. Hewlett and O. E. Anderson, Jr., *The New World* (1962), is authoritative on the development of the atomic bomb. Volume III of J. M. Blum, *From the Morgenthau Diaries: Years of War, 1941–1945* (1967), throws light on a variety of issues that concerned the Treasury.

For American society in wartime, see Studs Terkel, *The Good War* (1984); J. M. Blum, *V Was For Victory* (1976), which also deals with politics; R. Polenberg, *War and Society: The United States, 1941–1945* (1971); R. Polenberg, ed., *America at War: The Home Front, 1941–1945* (1968); R. Lingeman, *Don't You Know There's a War On* (1970); and Paul Fussell, *Wartime: Understanding and Behavior in the Second World War* (1989). Also illuminating is A. W. Winkler, *The Politics of Propaganda: The Office of War Information, 1942–1945* (1978). Francis Biddle provides thoughtful discussion of the civil-liberties problems he faced as attorney general in *Democratic Thinking and the War* (1944) and in his memoir *In Brief Authority* (1962). On labor, see N. Lichtenstein, *Labor's War at Home* (1982). On the Japanese-Americans, there are several good studies of which a trenchant one is R. Daniels, *Concentration Camps* (1971). L. S. Wittner, *Rebels Against War: The American Peace Movement, 1946–1960* (1969), is excellent on its subject. For black Americans, see H. Garfinkel, *When Negroes March* (1959); L. Ruchames, *Race, Jobs and Politics: The Story of FEPC* (1953); R. M. Dalfiume, *Desegregation of the United States Armed Forces* (1969); A. Meier and E. Rudwick, *CORE* (1973); and the magisterial study by G. Myrdal, *An American Dilemma* (1944; rev. ed., 1962). On wartime politics, besides various studies cited above, see E. Barnard, *Wendell Willkie: Fighter for Freedom* (1966), and J. M. Blum, ed., *The Price of Vision: The Diary of Henry A. Wallace, 1942–1946* (1973). On women during the war, four instructive books are D'Ann Campbell, *Women at War with America* (1984); S. M. Hartmann, *The Home Front and Beyond* (1982); Ruth Milkman, *Gender and Work* (1987); and K. T. Anderson, *Wartime Women* (1981).

THE SECOND WORLD WAR: MILITARY OPERATIONS

A. R. Buchanan, *The United States and World War II*, 2 vols. (1964), is a survey. For able analyses of American strategy, see S. E. Morison, *Strategy and Compromise* (1958); L. Morton, *Strategy and Command* (1962); K. R. Greenfield, ed., *Command Decisions* (1959); K. R. Greenfield, *American Strategy in World War II: A Reconsideration* (1963); R. F. Weigley, *Eisenhower's Lieutenants* (1981); and especially E. Larrabee, *Commander-in-Chief* (1987), and M. Sherry, *The Rise of American Air Power* (1987). The role of the American services is intensively portrayed in three multivolume series: Office of the Chief of Military History, *The United States Army in World War II;* S. E. Morison, *History of United States Naval Operations in World War II* (summarized in *The Two-Ocean* War, 1963); and W. F. Craven and J. L. Cate, *The Army Air Forces in World War II*, 7 vols. (1949–58). See also H. P. Willmott, *The Great Crusade: A New Complete History of the Second World War* (1989). There is indispensable background in the six volumes of W. S. Churchill, *The Second World War* (1948–53); in two volumes on the secretary of war, H. L. Stimson and McGeorge Bundy, *On Active Service in Peace and War* (1948), and E. E. Morison, *Turmoil and Tradition* (1960); and in the biography of the Chief of Staff, F. C. Pogue, *George C. Marshall*, 4 vols. (1963–87), and D. Eisenhower, *Eisenhower at War* (1986). Among the formidable number of American war memoirs, the most useful on the European theater are those of Dwight D. Eisenhower, Omar Bradley, H. H. Arnold, W. Bedell Smith, and Mark Clark; on the Pacific Theater, those of Douglas MacArthur, Joseph Stilwell, Claire Chennault, Albert Wedemeyer, Courtney Whitney, Robert Eichelberger, W. F. Halsey, George C. Kenney, Walter Kreuger, and, as recounted by Walter Whitehill, Ernest J. King.

For the American military role in Europe, C. B. MacDonald, *The Mighty Endeavor: American Armed Forces in the European Theater in World War II* (1969), offers a comprehensive account. For strategic debates in Europe, see C. Wilmot, *The Struggle for Europe* (1952); S. E. Ambrose, *The Supreme Commander: The War Years of General Dwight D. Eisenhower* (1970); M. Howard, *The Mediterranean Strategy in the Second World War* (1968); and two volumes by T. Higgins: *Winston Churchill and the Second Front, 1940–1943* (1957) and *Soft Underbelly: The Anglo-American Controversy Over the Italian Campaign, 1939–1945* (1968). J. Toland, *The Last Hundred Days* (1966), and C. Ryan, *The Last Battle* (1966), cover the fall of Germany. For the Pacific war, see R. Spector, *Eagle Against the Sun* (1985); J. Toland, *The Rising Sun: The Decline and Fall of the Japanese Empire* (1970); B. Tuchman, *Stilwell and the American Experience in China, 1911–1945* (1971); T. H. White and A. Jacoby, *Thunder Out of China* (1946); J. Hersey, *Hiroshima* (1946); W. S. Schoenberger, *Decisions of Destiny* (1970); W. Manchester, *MacArthur* (1979); and various volumes in the army history, especially those by Louis Morton, C. F. Romanus, and Riley Sunderland.

The GI's view of the war is candidly portrayed in the gritty newspaper reporting of Ernie Pyle, *Here Is Your War* (1943) and *Brave Men* (1944); and the sardonic cartoons of Bill Mauldin, *Up Front* (1945). See also L. Kennett, *G.I.: The American Soldier in World War II* (1987); the *New Yorker Book of War Pieces* (1947); and such novels as Norman Mailer, *The Naked and the Dead* (1948); James Jones, *From*

Here to Eternity (1951); William Styron, *The Long March* (1952); and Joseph Heller, *Catch-22* (1961). S. A. Stouffer et al., *The American Soldier,* 2 vols. (1949), contains important sociological data.

THE SECOND WORLD WAR: DIPLOMACY

J. L. Snell, *Illusion and Necessity: The Diplomacy of Global War* (1963); G. Smith, *American Diplomacy During the Second World War* (1965); and especially R. Dallek, *Franklin D. Roosevelt and American Foreign Policy, 1932–1945* (1979), are useful surveys. The volumes of H. Feis—*The China Tangle* (1953), *Churchill, Roosevelt, Stalin* (1957, 2d ed., 1967), *The Atomic Bomb and the End of World War II* (rev. ed., 1966)—provide brilliant coverage of diplomatic questions. Two books by R. A. Divine, *Roosevelt and World War II* (1969) and *Second Chance: The Triumph of Internationalism in America* (1967), deal with war and postwar issues. For revisionist views of American policy, see S. Ambrose, *Rise to Globalism* (1971), and G. Kolko, *The Politics of War: The World and United States Foreign Policy, 1943–1945* (1969). On the question of the Anglo-American invasion of Europe, see M. Stoler, *The Politics of the Second Front* (1977). On Yalta, E. R. Stettinius, *Roosevelt and the Russians—The Yalta Conference* (1949), defends administration policy, W. H. Chamberlin, *America's Second Crusade* (1950), attacks it from the right, and D. S. Clemens, *Yalta* (1970), questions it from the left. On relations with Russia, see W. H. McNeill, *America, Britain and Russia* (1953); J. L. Gaddis, *The United States and the Origins of the Cold War* (1972); A. Ulam, *Expansion and Coexistence* (1968); J. R. Deane, *The Strange Alliance* (1953); P. E. Mosely, *The Kremlin and World Politics* (1960); M. Herz, *Beginnings of the Cold War* (1966); G. C. Herring, *Aid to Russia, 1941–1946* (1973); W. A. Harriman, *America and Russia in a Changing World* (1971); and D. Yergin, *Shattered Peace* (1977). On relations with France, see W. L. Langer, *Our Vichy Gamble* (1947), and M. Viorst, *Hostile Allies* (1965). On China, see Tang Tsou, *America's Failure in China, 1941–1950* (1963). On atomic diplomacy, see R. G. Hewlett and O. E. Anderson, *The New World* (1962), and M. J. Sherwin, *A World Destroyed: The Atomic Bomb and the Grand Alliance* (1975). One of the nation's great failures receives able analysis in D. S. Wyman, *The Abandonment of the Jews: America and the Holocaust, 1941–1945* (1984).

Particularly useful memoirs are Cordell Hull, *Memoirs,* 2 vols. (1948); W. D. Leahy, *I Was There* (1950); J. F. Byrnes, *Speaking Frankly* (1974) and *All in One Lifetime* (1958); Sumner Welles, *The Time for Decision* (1944) and *Seven Decisions That Shaped History* (1951); R. D. Murphy, *Diplomat Among Warriors* (1964); J. C. Grew, *Turbulent Era: A Diplomatic Record of Forty Years,* 2 vols. (1952); G. F. Kennan, *Memoirs 1925–1950* (1967); and A. Harriman and E. Abel, *Special Envoy to Churchill and Stalin* (1975). Indispensable glimpses of American policy from foreign perspectives can be found in the memoirs or diaries of Winston Churchill, Charles de Gaulle, Joseph Goebbels, Albert Speer, Galeazzo Ciano, Milovan Djilas, Ivan Maisky, Lord Avon (Anthony Eden), Lord Halifax, Lord Montgomery, Harold Macmillan, Lord Alexander, Lord Tedder, Sir Frederick Morgan, Sir John Slessor, Sir Alexander Cadogan, Harold Nicolson, Lord Casey, and Sir Robert Menzies.

CHAPTER THIRTY

SOUTH KOREA: TO THE FRONT FOR LIMITED OBJECTIVES

THE COLD WAR

The United States emerged from the Second World War a relatively unified, powerful, and confident nation. Victory gave Americans a guileless pride in the prowess of their armed forces, in the productivity of their economy, in the rectitude of their motives, and in the strength of their ideals.

American cities, intact when the war ended, stood in stark contrast to the devastated cities of Europe and Japan. The American economy, richer than ever before, contrasted just as vividly with the disrupted economies of every other major power. "America," Winston Churchill said a week after the atomic bomb fell on Nagasaki, "stands at this moment at the summit of the world." The United States entered the postwar world a great creditor nation, producing nearly half the world's manufactures, with every indication of continuing technological and financial supremacy. The Americans of 1945 did not suppose, as their parents had in 1918, that victory licensed retreat from international responsibility. But they had differing conceptions of America's world role. Some aimed to use American power to build a lasting structure of peace. Some sought new outlets for an ebullient American capitalism. Some, like the former Vice President Henry Wallace, called for "the century of the common man." Some, like the magazine publisher Henry Luce, dreamed imperially of "the American century."

TRUMAN TAKES OVER

The New President "I feel as though the moon and all the stars and all the planets have fallen on me," Harry S Truman told newspaper reporters on the April day in 1945 when he heard the report of Roosevelt's death. "Please, boys, give me your prayers. I need them very much." A back-bencher from Missouri who had barely retained his own seat in the Senate four and a half years before, he had to fill the mighty place of the man who had dominated the affairs of the United States and the world for a dozen years.

On the record Truman seemed a courthouse politician, a beneficiary of the notorious Pendergast machine in Kansas City, a party man whose chief attribute was loyalty to his organization and his president. But those who knew him valued the spontaneous decency that had led him to fight the Ku Klux Klan at the height of its power in Missouri, the courage in adversity that had enabled him to hold his Senate seat in 1940, and the concern for popular welfare he had displayed throughout his public career. As wartime chair of what had come to be known as the Truman

Committee, he had discharged with intelligence and responsibility the delicate job of monitoring the defense program. No one could tell what the chemistry of the presidency would do to him.

Initial impressions were not encouraging. In his fourth week as president, Truman casually signed an order that abruptly stopped the delivery of goods under the lend-lease program. The sudden termination of lend-lease deliveries caused resentment and misunderstanding abroad. "This experience brought home to me," Truman subsequently wrote, "not only that I had to know exactly where I was going but also that I had to know that my basic policies were being carried out. If I had read that order, as I should have, the incident would not have occurred. But the best time to learn that lesson was right at the beginning of my duties as President."

The candor, the humility, and the cockiness were all characteristic. Though he never totally divested himself of a tendency to shoot from the hip, Truman gradually developed authority in his new role. His wide knowledge of history gave him a vigorous sense of the dignity of the presidency. He worked hard. He accepted responsibility: he used to say of the presidential desk, "The buck stops here." He reconstructed the Cabinet, gradually transforming a Roosevelt administration into a Truman administration. Winston Churchill, meeting him at Potsdam in July 1945, was impressed by "his gay, precise, sparkling manner and obvious power of decision."

EXPERIMENT IN WORLD ORDER

The Postwar Atmosphere This power of decision was almost immediately put to the test. For war had left the international order in a condition of acute derangement. With the Axis states vanquished, the European Allies battered and exhausted, the colonial empires in dissolution, and the underdeveloped world in tumult, great gaping holes appeared in the structure of world power. War had also left only two states—the United States and the Soviet Union—with the political dynamism, ideological confidence, and military force to flow into these vacuums of power. The war had accustomed both states, moreover, to thinking and acting on a grand scale.

The United States had greater range. Soviet wartime losses had been appalling: 7.5 million dead in the armed forces, between 6 and 8 million civilians killed, another 20–25 million prematurely dead from privation and exhaustion. Destruction of the Soviet economy was just as awful, for example, in the loss of 65,000 kilometers of railway track, as well as almost half of all urban housing and thousands of villages. But the Soviet army remained the largest in the world, capable of controlling neighboring areas of Europe and Asia that the Russians had long considered crucial to their defense. Yet the Soviet Union, though by far the most formidable military presence in Europe, could not compete with the United States in global strength. American naval forces controlled the oceans and American strategic air forces dominated the skies. The United States had acquired overseas bases that ringed the globe and, in the Soviet view, constituted a threatening encirclement.

The war's end thus saw a geopolitical rivalry between America and Russia as well as a difference in emphasis over the principles on which the peace should be organized—whether in terms of great-power spheres of influence or United Nations universalism (see p. 768). The factor that transformed this structural conflict into something akin to a religious war was the apparently irreconcilable ideological disagreement between the two superpowers. With the pre-war world in pieces, America and Russia appeared in 1945 as the only powers capable of exerting their influence beyond their borders, encountering no serious opposition except from each other—each, as Tocqueville had prophesied in *Democracy in America* a century earlier, seemingly "marked out by the will of Heaven to sway the destinies of half the globe."

Launching the United Nations Nevertheless, war had bound the victors together in coalition, and the Dumbarton Oaks Conference of 1944 had laid down the main lines for a postwar structure. On April 29, 1945, representatives of 50 nations met at San Francisco to create a permanent United Nations organization.

The UN Charter, essentially an American product, was in the direct line of descent from the Covenant of the League of Nations. Of the UN organs, the General Assembly and the Security Council had the widest authority. The Assembly was the legislative body, though its powers were limited to discussion and recommendation. The Security Council was the action agency assigned, in the language of the charter, "the primary responsibility for the maintenance of international peace and security."

Signing the UN Charter

The Security Council consisted of five permanent members—the United States, Britain, Russia, France, and China—with six further members (after 1966, ten) elected by the General Assembly. The charter gave the Council authority to settle international disputes by peaceful means—through investigation or mediation or whatever method seemed suitable. If such methods failed, Chapter 7 of the charter authorized the Council to take appropriate measures against any state that broke the peace. If necessary, it might use armed force supplied by the member states. However, the charter also limited the Security Council's authority to invoke these powers—especially by giving each permanent member a veto. Neither the United States nor the Soviet Union would have joined the UN without this means of protecting its interests.

Multilateral Effort Surrounding the UN was a constellation of subsidiary agencies, among which the United Nations Relief and Rehabilitation Administration (UNRRA) had particularly urgent responsibilities. Established in 1943 to bring food, clothing, medicine, and other supplies to liberated countries, UNRRA disbursed $2.7 billion over the next five years. Its director and many of its workers were American, and the United States contributed nearly three-quarters of its financial support.

While UNRRA tackled the immediate crisis, the western Allies, meeting in July 1944 at Bretton Woods, New Hampshire, planned a long-term international economic framework. Bretton Woods led to the establishment of two institutions: the International Monetary Fund, designed to create a world monetary system, and the International Bank for Reconstruction and Development (better known as the World Bank), designed to supply capital for investment and trade in underdeveloped areas. As the wealthiest nation in the world, the United States dominated both institutions. The Soviet Union, though represented at Bretton Woods, referred to the Fund and Bank as the instruments of international capitalism and declined to participate.

It did, however, join other specialized UN agencies—the Food and Agricultural Organization, the International Trade Organization, the World Health Organization, and the International Labor Organization (taken over from the League). In addition, the United Nations Educational, Scientific, and Cultural Organization (UNESCO) fostered international efforts to raise cultural standards and promote intellectual exchange.

THE COLD WAR BEGINS

The Coalition in Trouble The United Nations could not abolish profound disagreements in interest and ideology. These disagreements, held in check during the war by common opposition to Hitler, emerged in the aftermath of victory. Each of the three wartime allies entered the postwar period with its own objectives.

For Stalin the overriding concern remained the security of the Soviet Union. Determined to safeguard Soviet frontiers by placing eastern Europe under Soviet control, he may well have construed the Yalta agreement in terms of his sphere-of-influence deal with Churchill in Moscow four months before (see p. 772). In addition, he doubtless expected that east European countries would hail the Red Army as liberators and that the free elections promised at Yalta would produce pro-Soviet regimes. But events soon made it clear that he had overestimated Soviet popularity in eastern Europe and underestimated Western anxieties about the threat Soviet power posed to central Europe.

For Churchill the increasing concern was the expansion of Soviet power. With Britain exhausted by the war, he had diminished influence even in bargaining with the United States. After Roosevelt's death

Churchill vainly urged Truman to order American armies to reach Berlin and Prague in advance of the Russians. The Yalta agreements, he later wrote, were "broken or brushed aside by the triumphant Kremlin. New perils, perhaps as terrible as those we had surmounted, loomed and glared upon the torn and harassed world." Churchill's defeat in the British general election in July brought a Labour government under Clement Attlee to power; but Attlee and his formidable foreign minister Ernest Bevin, were democratic socialists, as intent as Churchill to stop the spread of Soviet totalitarianism.

Truman's initial concern was to carry forward, as best he understood it, Roosevelt's policy of preserving the wartime alliance. At the same time, he was impressed by warnings from Ambassador Averell Harriman in Moscow that the Russians were on the march. "The Soviet Union," Harriman predicted, "once it had control of bordering areas would attempt to penetrate the next adjacent countries." Accordingly, when Stalin in April gave his Communists firm control of the Polish government, the new American president expressed his disapproval in salty language to Molotov, the Soviet foreign minister.

But this was more a passing irritation than a shift in policy. In May Truman sent Harry Hopkins to Moscow to signify the American interest in postwar collaboration. Truman soon accepted the Soviet-dominated Polish regime that Roosevelt had rejected at Yalta, turned down Churchill's military proposals and sought—at least as the British saw it—to make the United States the mediator between Britain and the Soviet Union.

At the end of July 1945 Stalin, Churchill (superseded in midconference by Attlee) and Truman met at Potsdam outside Berlin. It was here that Truman told Stalin that the United States had developed a highly destructive new weapon. Stalin showed little interest, no doubt because Soviet espionage had already informed him about the atomic bomb, and said only that he hoped it would be used against Japan.

After consideration of policy toward Japan, the Potsdam Conference concentrated on Germany. The Western powers acquiesced in a temporary Polish occupation of Germany up to the Oder-Neisse line, with the final territorial settlement reserved for a future peace conference. Concerned by Soviet "looting" of German industry, the West refused the Soviet demand for reparations at the level Moscow believed had been promised at Yalta. The Russians resentfully accepted a compromise. Each of the four occupying nations—America, Britain, the Soviet Union, and France—received control of its own zone. An International Military Tribunal, established at American instigation, tried 22 top Nazis in Nuremberg from November 1945 to October 1946; 19 were convicted of war crimes, and 12 were sentenced to death. Though condemned by some as "victors' justice," the Nuremberg and later trials compiled a mass of evidence documenting the viciousness of Nazi rule.

Potsdam: new perils

Truman Vacillates "Stalin was an SOB," Truman said genially on his way home from Potsdam, "but of course he thinks I'm one, too." "I like Stalin," he said later. "Stalin is as near like Tom Pendergast [the old political boss in Missouri] as any man I know."

Aware that under the Succession Act of 1886 the secretary of state stood next in line for the presidency and doubtful of the qualifications for the office of Edward Stettinius, the secretary he had inherited from Roosevelt, Truman replaced Stettinius by James F. Byrnes, an experienced politician who had served with ability in the executive and legislative branches as well as on the Supreme Court.* Byrnes was an indefat-

* But Truman rejected as undemocratic the whole idea that a president could nominate his immediate successor. In 1947 he secured enactment of a new law transferring the succession, in case of vacancies in the presidency and vice presidency, to the Speaker of the House, thereby reverting to the principle of the Succession Act of 1792. The Twenty-fifth Amendment, adopted in 1967, in turn rejected Truman's scruples and empowered a president, when the vice presidency was vacant, to nominate a new vice president. This amendment produced in 1974 a singular situation in which, contrary to the original constitutional provision that the president and vice president were to "be elected," both President Ford and Vice President Rockefeller had received their positions through appointment.

Map 30-1 *The partition of Germany and Austria*

igable negotiator. Dealing with the Russians, he supposed, was "just like the U.S. Senate. You build a post office in their state and they'll build a post office in our state." Byrnes readily acknowledged Soviet security needs and accepted the Soviet desire for "friendly governments" on Russia's western frontiers. Working through the Council of Foreign Ministers set up at Potsdam, Byrnes carried forward the task of drawing up peace treaties with Axis satellites. In December 1946, treaties were concluded with Italy, Bulgaria, Hungary, Romania, and Finland. These treaties confirmed Soviet ascendancy in eastern Europe. In tacit exchange, the Soviet Union accepted American control of occupied Japan (see Map 30-1).

The Curtain Falls In the meantime, unexpected difficulties in eastern Europe had hardened the Soviet line. When the Communist party won only 17 percent of the vote in the Hungarian election of November 1945, Stalin moved to eradicate opposition and to consolidate the Soviet position. In an important speech on February 9, 1946, he declared that the capitalist system rendered war inevitable. On March 5, Churchill, speaking at Fulton, Missouri, with Truman beside him on the platform, responded by warning against the "expansive tendencies" of Soviet Russia. "From Stettin in the Baltic to Trieste in the Adriatic," he said, "an iron curtain has descended across the Continent." How should the West meet the Soviet challenge? "I am convinced that there is nothing they admire so much as strength, and there is nothing for which they have less respect than weakness, especially military weakness."

Contention over Iran in the winter of 1945–46 deepened American mistrust of the Soviet Union. At the wartime Teheran Conference, the Big Three had agreed to respect the territorial integrity of Iran, a country rich in oil to which they had sent troops as a protection against a German invasion. After the war, Britain and America withdrew their forces; the Russians did not. A brief crisis ended when American pressure forced Soviet withdrawal in May 1946.

The British government still feared that the Truman administration was too soft on the Russians. But the American outlook was changing.

A "long telegram" in February 1946 from the American diplomat-scholar George F. Kennan in Moscow crystallized mounting apprehensions in Washington. Kennan described Soviet communism as "a political force committed fanatically to the belief that with [the] U.S. there can be no permanent *modus vivendi.*" Still, Stalin, unlike Hitler, was "neither schematic nor adventuristic" in his policies and would withdraw "when strong resistance is encountered." Much depended on the health and vigor of Western societies. "The greatest danger that can befall us in coping with this problem of Soviet communism," Kennan concluded, "is that we shall allow ourselves to become like those with whom we are coping."

In March 1946, the British charge in Moscow, Frank Roberts, cabled a similar message to London. In September the Soviet ambassador to the United States, Nikolai Novikov, sent Moscow an assessment of American intentions as full of mistrust as were the Kennan and Roberts views of Russia. "The foreign policy of the United States," Novikov began, "which reflects the imperial tendencies of American monopolistic capital, is characterized in the postwar period by a striving for world supremacy." The reciprocal suspicions expressed in those messages colored the conflicting interpretations of developing events by both sides in the emerging rivalry between the English-speaking countries and the Soviet Union. The attendant misunderstandings complicated the problems of the Cold War.

Such was the case with Soviet-American disagreement about controlling the power of the atom. The unleashed power of the atom intensified mutual distrust. In June 1946 Bernard Baruch, an American delegate to the UN Atomic Energy Commission, proposed that all nuclear technology, civil and military,

Soviet-American Relations: A Dissenting View

We are reckoning with a force which cannot be handled successfully by a 'Get tough with Russia' policy. 'Getting tough' never bought anything real and lasting—whether for schoolyard bullies or businessmen or world powers. The tougher we get, the tougher the Russians get. . . . I believe that we can get cooperation once Russia understands that our primary objective is neither saving the British Empire nor purchasing oil in the Near East with the lives of American soldiers. . . .

On our part, we should recognize that we have no more business in the political affairs of Eastern Europe than Russia has in the political affairs of Latin America, Western Europe and the United States. We may not like what Russia does in Eastern Europe. Her type of land reform, industrial expropriation, and suppression of basic liberties offends the great majority of the people of the United States. But whether we like it or not the Russians will try to socialize their sphere of influence just as we try to democratize our sphere of influence. . . . We cannot permit the door to be closed against our trade in Eastern Europe any more than we can in China. But at the same time we have to recognize that the Balkans are closer to Russia than to us—and that Russia cannot permit either England or the United States to dominate the politics of that area. . . . Under friendly peaceful competition the Russian world and the American world will gradually become more alike. The Russians will be forced to grant more and more of the personal freedoms; and we shall become more and more absorbed with the problems of social-economic justice.

From Henry A. Wallace, Speech at Madison Square Garden, September 12, 1946

be placed under control of an UN agency exempt from the great-power veto and equipped with powers of inspection. While ostensibly evenhanded in its approach, the Baruch plan, as the Russians quickly noted, placed authority in an international agency under American domination. They were unwilling to surrender their veto or to accept inspection within the Soviet Union. The future of nuclear weapons remained in national hands.

Hope for a peace treaty settling the future of Germany vanished. The occupation zones now evolved into de facto partition. Each side softened its German policy and sponsored revival in its own zone. In 1949 the German Federal Republic was established in the west, the German Democratic Republic in the east (see Map 30-1).

Truman now, as he told Byrnes, had become "tired of babying the Soviets." Republicans attacked the policy of accommodation as appeasement. Within the administration, Secretary of Commerce Henry A. Wallace argued that the Russians should be given the benefit of the doubt, but, when he publicly attacked American policy in September 1946, Truman fired him.

The Truman Doctrine Early in 1947, Byrnes, who had lost Truman's confidence, resigned, and Truman appointed General George C. Marshall in his place. Marshall's unique national eminence helped remove the discussion of foreign policy from a partisan context. So, too, did the collaboration in a "bipartisan" foreign policy of Arthur H. Vandenberg, a Republican senator from Michigan, whose pre-war record as an isolationist gave his views special weight among conservatives.

The Soviet Challenge

The possibilities for American policy are by no means limited to holding the line and hoping for the best. . . . It is rather a question of the degree to which the United States can create among the peoples of the world generally the impression of a country which knows what it wants, which is coping successfully with the problems of its internal life and with the responsibilities of a World Power, and which has a spiritual vitality capable of holding its own among the major ideological currents of the time. To the extent that such an impression can be created and maintained, the aims of Russian Communism must appear sterile and quixotic, the hopes and enthusiasms of Moscow's supporters must wane. . . .

Thus the decision will really fall in large measure in this country itself. The issue of Soviet-American relations is in essence a test of the over-all worth of the United States as a nation among nations. To avoid destruction the United States need only measure up to its own best traditions and prove itself worthy of preservation as a great nation.

From George F. Kennan, "The Sources of Soviet Conduct," *Foreign Affairs,* July 1947

In the meantime, Communist pressure was mounting against Greece and Turkey. Early in 1947, Great Britain, in acute economic straits itself, notified Washington that in five weeks it must end financial support to a Greek government besieged by Communist guerrillas receiving support from Marshal Tito, the Communist leader of Yugoslavia. Though Stalin had not instigated the Greek uprising and regarded it with dubiety, these facts were not known in the West, which supposed that the collapse of Greece would embolden Moscow to move against Italy and France. The United States, like Great Britain, was also determined to sustain Turkish resistance to Soviet territorial demands.

Truman accordingly decided that America must take up the burden. Recalling the hard fight for a loan to Britain itself a year before, Truman feared that a conventional request for aid to Greece and Turkey would not pass the Congress. Accepting Vandenberg's judgment that he had to scare the hell out of the country, he went to Capitol Hill in person to urge what soon became known as the Truman Doctrine. "I believe," Truman said, "that it must be the policy of the United States to support free peoples who are resisting attempted subjugation by armed minorities or outside pressures." Some, within the administration and without, flinched at open-ended language going far beyond the immediate problem. But Congress responded to presidential evangelism and in May 1947 passed a bill granting $400 million in aid to Greece and Turkey over the next 15 months. Though the subsequent collapse of the Greek insurgency was due as much to Tito's break with Stalin in 1948 as to American assistance, the apparent efficacy of the Truman Doctrine in its initial application strengthened belief in both America's ability and its obligation to serve as guardian of freedom throughout the world.

The Containment Policy As the Russians hardened their grip on Eastern Europe, the fear arose that they could use their zone, not just to secure their own frontiers, but as a springboard from which to dominate central and western Europe, now lying economically prostrate and politically vulnerable before them. Stalin's instrumentality, it was supposed, would be not the Red Army but the obedient Communist parties of France, Italy, and Germany through which he might, without military action, promote the Stalinization of the continent.

The American return to Europe under the Truman Doctrine was the first application of an evolving philosophy. Writing anonymously in *Foreign Affairs* in July 1947, George F. Kennan argued that Soviet communism was like "a fluid stream which moves constantly, wherever it is permitted to move, toward a given goal." American policy, Kennan proposed, must be that of "the firm and vigilant containment of Russian expansive tendencies." The purpose of containment was not to enter the Russian sphere or overthrow the Soviet regime but rather to block the Soviet effort to flow into "every nook and cranny available to it in the basin of the world." In time this would force a measure of circumspection on the Kremlin and "promote tendencies which must eventually find their outlet in either the break-up or the gradual mellowing of Soviet power."

The Soviet threat was seen as political, not military. Truman cut back the armed forces from 12.1 million at the end of the war to 1.4 million by 1948. He held down the defense budget to $13 billion annually and made no effort to promote the production of atomic bombs, a weapon he regarded with deep distaste. In the spring of 1947, the United States had no more than a dozen, none ready for immediate use. Truman did, however, reorganize the defense establishment. In 1947 the National Security Act created a Department of Defense, a National Security Council, and a Central Intelligence Agency (CIA).

The containment policy provoked heated debate in the United States. On the right, traditional isolationists, led by Senator Robert A. Taft of Ohio, doubted America's financial or moral capacity to sustain an activist international policy. In the center, commentators like Walter Lippmann feared that the containment psychology would lead people to see the Soviet Union as primarily a military threat to be met by military means and involve the United States beyond its sphere of direct and vital interest. (Kennan, who basically agreed with Lippmann, later regretted the ambiguity of his initial formulation of the containment policy.) On the left, Americans unwilling to surrender the idea of the innocence or moderation of Stalin denounced the policy as aggressive and provocative. This group found a spokesman in Henry Wallace.

The Marshall Plan The Truman Doctrine was an emergency effort to shore up crumbling positions in Greece and Turkey. It had been made necessary by the hard-pressed economic condition of Britain. Britain's plight was symptomatic of the plight of all Western Europe. European city dwellers were living on less than 2,000 calories a day. The cradle of Western civilization seemed to Winston Churchill in 1947 "a rubble heap, a charnel house, a breeding ground for pestilence and hate." "The patient is sinking," said Secretary Marshall, "while the doctors deliberate."

In an address at the Harvard commencement on June 5, 1947, Marshall called on the European countries themselves to draw up a plan for European recovery. "The role of this country should consist of friendly aid in the drafting of a European program and of later support. . . . The program should be a joint one, agreed to by a number, if not all, of European nations." Marshall added, significantly, "Our policy is directed not against any country or doctrine but against hunger, poverty, desperation, and chaos."

This was the proposal that, as British Foreign Secretary Ernest Bevin later told Parliament, he "grabbed . . . with both hands." Within three weeks, representatives of European states, west and east, assembled in Paris. The prospect of east European participation faded, however, when the Russians denounced the plan as American economic imperialism and pulled out of the meeting, taking their satellites with them. A pro-Soviet coup in Czechoslovakia in February 1948—itself conceivably an overreaction to the Marshall Plan—completed the division of Eu-

The Marshall Plan: food for Greece

rope. It also smoothed the way for the passage of the plan by the American Congress in March.

The 16 remaining states (including Turkey) now began integrated economic planning through the Organization of European Economic Cooperation (OEEC). With generous contributions by the United States — $13 billion in four years, 6 to 9 percent of the federal budget (equivalent to more than $90 billion in 1992) — the Marshall Plan countries by 1951 raised their industrial output 40 percent over 1938. The stimulus provided by the Marshall Plan and the OEEC led to further experiments in European integration — especially the European Coal and Steel Community (1952) and the European Economic Community, better known as the Common Market, established by the Rome Treaties in 1957. The dramatic economic recovery reduced the political threat of communism and set Western Europe on the road to independence in world affairs.

The Division of Europe In response to the Truman Doctrine and Marshall Plan, the Soviet Union completed the consolidation of control in Eastern Europe. In 1947 Moscow set up the Cominform to replace the pre-war Comintern as the mechanism by which the Soviet Union managed foreign Communist parties. In 1949 it organized the Council for Mutual Economic Assistance (COMECON) to assure Soviet economic domination of the satellites.

Berlin airlift: it broke the blockade

In addition, Stalin systematically extinguished political dissent in Eastern Europe through staged trials, forced confessions, and executions. At first the Soviet purge concentrated on socialist and peasant politicians, but by 1949 it swept through the Communist parties themselves, liquidating leaders suspected of inadequate loyalty to Moscow. Yugoslavia, which owed its liberation to its own efforts rather than to the Red Army, was relatively inaccessible to Soviet power. Here Tito's independent course led in 1948 to his excommunication by Moscow.

In the spring of 1948, the Soviet Union confronted the West with a new challenge when it cut off West Berlin by blockading all highway, river, and rail traffic into the former German capital. The evident purpose was to force the Western powers out of Berlin. Their answer was to supply West Berlin through an airlift. When it became apparent that even winter could not halt the airlift and that a Western counterblockade was hurting East Germany, Moscow developed second thoughts. On May 12, 1949 — 321 days after the start of the airlift — the Russians ended the blockade.

The Berlin crisis, following so closely on the Communist coup in Czechoslovakia, convinced many Western Europeans of the need for a regional defense arrangement. Truman agreed that only "an inclusive security system" could dispel the fear that the Soviet Union might overrun Western Europe. On April 4, 1949, the North Atlantic nations established an alliance in which (in the language of Article 5 of the final pact) "an armed attack against one or more of them in Europe or North America shall be considered an attack against them all." Article 11, however, provided that the treaty was to be carried out by the signatories "in accordance with their respective constitutional processes," which presumably meant, in the American case, that Congress would have to authorize an American response. The original members of the North Atlantic Treaty Organization (NATO) were the United States, Britain, France, Italy, Belgium, the Netherlands, Denmark, Norway, Portugal, Luxembourg, Iceland, and Canada. Later they were joined by Greece, Turkey, West Germany, and Spain. In 1955, after the admission of West Germany to NATO, Moscow established a counterpart military organization under the Warsaw Pact.

The Occupation of Japan In Japan, where the United States had a free hand in occupation policy, General Douglas MacArthur, the supreme allied

NATO

American international peace and security require a firm belief by the peoples of the world that they will not be subjected to unprovoked attack, to coercion and intimidation, to interference in their own affairs. . . .

The North Atlantic community of nations . . . is based on the affinity and natural interests of the North Atlantic powers. The . . . treaty which will formally unite them is the product of at least 350 years of history. . . . There developed on our Atlantic Coast a community, which has spread across the continent, connected with Western Europe by similar institutions and moral and ethical beliefs. Similarities of this kind . . . are the strongest kind of ties. . . .

The very basis of Western civilization, which we share with the other nations bordering on the North Atlantic, and which all of us share with many other nations, is the ingrained spirit of restraint and tolerance. This is the opposite of the Communist belief that coercion by force is a proper method of hastening the inevitable. Western civilization has lived by mutual restraint and tolerance. This civilization . . . creates the environment of freedom. . . .

Now successful resistance to aggression . . . requires modern arms and trained military forces. As a result of the recent war, the European countries joining in the pact are generally deficient in both requirements. The treaty does not bind the United States to any arms program. But . . . the United States is now the only democratic nation with the resources and productive capacity to help the free nations of Europe to recover their military strength.

Therefore, we expect to ask Congress to supply our European partners some of the weapons they . . . need to be able to resist aggression. . . . We must make it clear that armed attack will be met by collective defense, prompt and effective.

From Dean Acheson, address of March 18, 1949

commander, had ordered a series of political and economic purges, culminating in the trial and punishment of Japanese wartime officials under standards more stringent than at Nuremberg. At the same time he sought to transform the vanquished country into a model western democracy. A new constitution, adopted under American direction in 1946, renounced war as a sovereign right, adding that "land, sea and air forces, as well as other war potential, will never be maintained." The *zaibatsu,* the great family trusts, were threatened with dissolution, trade unions were encouraged, women were given the vote, land was redistributed among the peasants, the educational system was reorganized, and Shinto was abolished as the state religion.

But increasing apprehension about the Soviet Union soon raised the question whether a disarmed Japan would not leave a dangerous power vacuum in East

General Douglas MacArthur and Emperor Hirohito, 1945

Asia. A peace treaty, finally negotiated in 1951, registered the altered American attitude. The treaty terminated the occupation, conceded to Japan "the inherent right of individual or collective self-defense," and opened the way for American troops and installations to remain through bilateral agreement, and for the *zaibatsu* to flourish again.

MacArthur's democratization of Japan was an apparent success. But one dubious result was to increase the confidence of Americans in their capacity to build and rebuild nations around the world.

WHY THE COLD WAR?

The Historical Controversy The postwar antagonism, known by 1947 as the Cold War, was, according to the official Anglo-American thesis, the necessary western response to an unprovoked course of expansion by Soviet communism.

To American eyes, the Russian course portended a new phase in the world struggle between democracy and totalitarianism, with communism inheriting the mantle just relinquished by fascism. For most Americans, communism meant Stalinism, the system that ruled Soviet Russia, a system correctly seen as not only extraordinarily cruel and repressive at home but in secure command of most Communist parties throughout the world. Stalinism was also seen, perhaps less correctly, as inherently aggressive and insatiable.

In later years the official thesis fell under attack, especially in the United States. The "revisionist" critique, echoing Soviet doctrine in 1946–47, took many forms, but predominant arguments were that America was more the postwar aggressor than Russia, that the American government systematically whipped up anti-Communist emotions in order to cloak its real intentions, which were to establish economic hegemony throughout the world, and that Washington had no choice but to seek an "open door" for American trade and investment because American capitalism had to expand in order to survive.

One part of the revisionist critique had lasting influence—that is, its insistence on looking at the postwar situation from the Soviet as well as the Western viewpoint. For the Soviet Union had suffered greater losses in the war than any other nation. The Western interest in Eastern Europe could have been honestly perceived in Moscow as a threat to Soviet security. In retrospect, it seems probable that Moscow was not intent on military aggression or dedicated, as a practical goal, to "world conquest." In many respects, the Soviet Union sought the traditional goals of the tzars. Stalin, cautious and opportunistic, carefully refrained from committing the Red Army outside his own sphere of vital interest. While not forgoing the pleasures and benefits of intrigue and subversion in other parts of the world, he was prepared, in exchange for a free hand in the Soviet sphere, to concede American and Britain free hands in their spheres, including the freedom to suppress Communist movements. He was even perhaps prepared to place China and Greece within the Western sphere.

The "open door" interpretation of American policy has not stood up against the evidence. To be sure, the United States considered vital the economic recovery and political stability of Europe, as George Marshall said. But exports amounted to less than 5 percent of the gross national product, and business leaders regarded the home market as the key to American prosperity. While Washington certainly worked for a freely trading world—against, among other things, the high-tariff predilections of much of American business—it was not this desire that prompted objections to Soviet policy in Eastern Europe, where the American economic stake was negligible. Moreover, some of the most ardent proponents of foreign markets argued that accommodation with Russia, not confrontation, was the surest way to find outlets for American goods. So Henry Wallace both championed the "open door" policy and opposed the policy of "containment."

The postwar American military posture was hardly that of a nation bent on world empire. No government in modern history had conducted so swift a demobilization. Though revisionist historians subsequently argued that American policy makers had seen the atomic bomb as the means of controlling the postwar world, Truman made no serious attempt to practice nuclear diplomacy against the Soviet Union, ignoring those, like the British philosopher Bertrand Russell, who urged the threat of the bomb to compel the Russians to good behavior. The bomb turned out to make little diplomatic difference. The American monopoly did not deter the Communists from taking over eastern Europe and China or from blockading Berlin.

Despite the revisionists, American leaders in the 1940s were hardly obsessively anti-Communist. In China, for example, Truman worked for a coalition between Chiang Kai-shek and Mao Zedong (Mao Tse-tung), and communism in Yugoslavia was not an obstacle to American aid after Tito's break with Stalin. Nor did Washington reject the Soviet point about "friendly" regimes along the Russian border. The Western powers would have been satisfied had the Russians settled for the Finnish pattern throughout Eastern Europe—that is, permitting internal freedoms so long as foreign policy was acceptable to Moscow.

The campaign to get domestic support to contain communism abroad did, however, generate excessive fear of communism at home. Unquestionably there was Communist penetration of the American government, the labor movement, and the intellectual community. Disclosures of Communist espionage in Canada and Britain, especially the theft of atomic secrets by the Soviet spies Klaus Fuchs and Allan Nunn May, increased public apprehension.

Recognizing the reality of the problem and at the same time hoping to keep public reaction under control (and to deny a political issue to the Republicans), Truman in 1947 set up a federal loyalty program. "Disloyal and subversive elements must be removed from the employ of government," Truman said. "We must not, however, permit employees of the Federal government to be labelled as disloyal . . . when no valid basis exists for arriving at such a conclusion." Despite pious injunctions, the loyalty program—as a consequence of overzealous investigators, malicious informers, frightened loyalty boards, and panicky public opinion—assumed a drastic and promiscuous character. Government workers charged with disloyalty were not permitted to confront their accusers. Careers were wrecked. No cases of espionage, however, were uncovered.

"It was not realized at first," Dean Acheson, Truman's last secretary of state, recalled, "how dangerous was the practice of secret evidence and secret informers, how alien to all our conceptions of justice and the rights of the citizen. . . . Experience proved again how soon good men become callous in the use of bad practices." It confirmed, too, Kennan's warning that Americans, in coping with Soviet communism, must not allow themselves to become like those with whom they were coping.

For the fundamental issue, as the Truman administration saw it, lay not between capitalism and revolution but between democracy and Stalinism. In Western Europe democratic socialist leaders—Attlee and Bevin in England, Leon Blum in France, Ernst Reuter and Willy Brandt in West Germany—were in the forefront of opposition to the spread of Stalinism. These men had no interest in an open door for American capitalism. They had a profound interest in the future of democratic socialism. Observing the dismal fate of democratic socialists in Eastern Europe, they concluded that they would meet the same fate if postwar chaos brought communism to power in their own countries. For a time, indeed, they regarded Washington's response to the Stalinist threat as naively slow.

The Cold War soon became an intricate, interlocking, reciprocal process, involving authentic differences in principle, real and supposed clashes of interest, and a wide range of misunderstanding and misperception. Each superpower believed with passion that its own safety as well as world peace depended on the success of its peculiar conception of world order. Each superpower, in pursuing its own clearly expressed and ardently cherished principles, only confirmed the fear of the other that it was bent on aggression. Soviet behavior in Eastern Europe, Iran, and Berlin and the activity of Communist parties elsewhere seemed to confirm the Western notion of an expansive Soviet Union. American postwar policy, especially in its expressions of concern about Eastern Europe, assumed a threatening aspect for the Russians. Each superpower persevered in corroborating the fears of the other. Together they proceeded to deepen the Cold War.

Could the Cold War Have Been Avoided? In retrospect it seems probable that each superpower was acting more on defensive grounds and on local considerations than the other realized. Neither nation had a master plan for world dominion. Yet who could be certain that Soviet aims would have remained local and limited had the West not developed counterpolicies? Dean Acheson wrote 20 years after, "A school of academic criticism has concluded that we overreacted to Stalin, which in turn caused him to overreact to policies of the United States. This may be true. Fortunately, perhaps, these authors were not called upon to analyze a situation in which the United States had not taken the action which it did take."

The Marxist-Leninist analysis asserted that the mere existence of a capitalist superpower was by definition a threat to Soviet survival. Could the democracies really have relied on the self-restraint of a dictator portrayed by his closest associates as increasingly paranoid if there had been no Western resistance—no Truman Doctrine, no Marshall Plan, no NATO, no rearmament, no response to the Berlin blockade? Had the democracies not rallied, would not Moscow have had a powerful temptation to keep moving, always in the name of Soviet security? Even in retrospect the Cold War seemed predictable. Given the international power disequilibrium, the ideological antagonism, and the mutual misperceptions, no one should be surprised at what ensued. The real surprise would have been if there had been no Cold War.

CONFUSION ON THE HOME FRONT

The Process of Reconversion In domestic policy Truman was a down-the-line New Dealer. His message to Congress on September 6, 1945, was his answer to the question (as he later wrote) of whether "the progress of the New Deal [was] to be halted in the aftermath of war as decisively as the progress of Woodrow Wilson's New Freedom had been halted after the first World War." Truman saw himself as both the continuator and the consolidator of Roosevelt's brilliant improvisations.

He faced the problem of reconverting the nation's economy from war to peace. Predictions of 8 or 10 million unemployed were common in 1945. But the economy showed far more resilience than anyone expected. Between 1945 and 1946 government purchases of goods and services declined by a sum equal to almost one-quarter of the gross national product. This decline, according to theorists, should have brought in its wake a disastrous fall in the national output and a rise in unemployment. But the gross national product declined only slightly in the same period, and employment actually increased by 3 million.

This achievement was due in great part to the pent-up demand for consumer goods after the deprivations of the war years. It was also due to sensible government policy. The Servicemen's Readjustment Act of 1944, better known as the G.I. Bill of Rights, was a remarkably creative law by which the federal government offered veterans inexpensive loans for housing, unemployment coverage, and four years of college education as well as vocational training and medical care. The Employment Act of 1946 established the Council of Economic Advisers and charged the federal government with responsibility for maintaining a high level of economic activity.

Inflation rather than depression was the greater threat. With the war over, the nation was chafing more than ever under price and wage controls. Business managers evaded the system through black markets. Labor, seeking wage increases after years of wartime denial, went out on strike. When a railroad strike paralyzed the economy in the spring of 1946, Truman asked Congress for power to draft strikers into the army—a request that even conservatives deemed intemperate and that the Senate rejected. Congress subsequently extended the Office of Price Administration but so weakened its authority that Truman vetoed the bill. There followed an interval in July 1946 with no controls at all, during which time prices shot up almost 25 percent. When Congress passed another bill a few weeks later, it was too late to put back the lid. Supply soon caught up with demand, however, and the average annual inflation rate for the five years after the removal of controls was 6 percent.

The Election of 1946 As the midterm congressional election approached, Truman seemed to have lost control of the economic and political situation. Republicans asked, "Had enough?" "To err is Truman"

Postwar Struggle for Racial Justice

To strengthen the right to equality of opportunity, the President's Committee recommends:

1. In general:
The elimination of segregation, based on race, color, creed, or national origin, from American life.

The separate but equal doctrine has failed in three important respects. First, it is inconsistent with the fundamental equalitarianism of the American way of life in that it marks groups with the brand of inferior status. Secondly, where it has been followed, the results have been separate and unequal facilities for minority peoples. Finally, it has kept people apart despite incontrovertible evidence that an environment favorable to civil rights is fostered whenever groups are permitted to live and work together. There is no adequate defense of segregation. . . . We believe that federal funds, supplied by taxpayers all over the nation, must not be used to support or perpetuate the pattern of segregation in education, public housing, public health services, or other public services and facilities. . . . A federal Fair Employment Practice Act prohibiting discrimination in private employment should provide both educational machinery and legal sanctions for enforcement purposes.

From the President's Committee on Civil Rights, *To Secure These Rights,* 1947

became a popular joke. To no one's surprise, the Republicans carried both houses of Congress for the first time since 1928. The new Eightieth Congress proved a bulwark of conservatism. Its dominant figure was Robert A. Taft of Ohio, son of the former president and a senator of inexhaustible energy, knowledge, and self-confidence. His admirers regarded him as the epitome of old-fashioned American wisdom. His critics said he had the best mind in Washington until he made it up.

Taft had long been concerned with ending what he regarded as the privileged position created for organized labor by the Wagner Act of 1935. The Taft-Hartley bill as amended outlawed the closed shop but permitted a measure of union security through the "union shop" (that is, a contract requiring workers to join the union after being hired—as distinct from the closed shop, which demands that they join before being hired). However, its Section 14B legalized so-called right-to-work laws by which states could forbid the requirement of union membership as a condition of employment. It also provided for a cooling-off period before resort to strikes. Labor leaders denounced the law extravagantly as a "slave labor" measure, and Truman vetoed it. But in early 1947 Congress passed the Taft-Hartley bill over his veto.

The conservatives also passed in 1947 a constitutional amendment forbidding presidential third terms—a belated act of vengeance against Franklin D. Roosevelt. The Twenty-second Amendment was ratified by the required 36 states in February 1951.

Truman Fights Back As the 1948 presidential election approached, Truman concluded that his only hope for reelection lay in the militant advocacy of a liberal program. In early 1948 he bombarded Congress with a series of reform proposals. Much of this was a reaffirmation of New Deal objectives, but in the field of racial justice he broke new ground.

Though reared according to the Southern customs of a border state, Truman was a man of humane instinct. He was also aware of the considerable change in the mood of black America wrought by the New Deal and the war. In 1946 he appointed a President's Committee on Civil Rights. A year later the committee recommended a permanent civil rights commission, a mandatory Fair Employment Practices Commission, antilynching and anti–poll-tax laws, and a strengthening of civil rights statutes and enforcement machinery. In an eloquent message on February 2, 1948, Truman made these proposals part of his program. This attempt to realize the promises of the Declaration of Independence for all Americans, regardless of race or color, was Truman's boldest initiative in the domestic field.

The civil rights proposals alienated the conservative Democrats of the South. Liberals were dismayed by the elimination of New Deal personalities, like Harold Ickes and Henry Morgenthau, from the administration. Old-line Democratic bosses thought the president was sure to be beaten. As the Democratic convention drew near, a "dump-Truman" movement gained momentum. The anti-Truman forces were unable to agree on an alternative, however, and in the end Truman won renomination with little difficulty.

The 1948 Campaign The Republicans had once again nominated Governor Thomas E. Dewey of New York. Dewey campaigned with the complacent confidence of a man who could not lose. Republican optimism swelled even further when a Communist-manipulated Progressive party nominated Henry A. Wallace for the presidency and when diehard Southern Democrats formed the States Rights Democratic party (better known as the Dixiecrats) and nominated Strom Thurmond of South Carolina.

Only Truman thought he could win. He began a "give 'em hell" campaign across the country, telling audiences at every whistlestop that the record of the "do-nothing, good-for-nothing" Republican Eightieth Congress proved the worthlessness of Republican campaign promises. A fall in the price of corn and hogs alarmed the farmers. The Dixiecrat revolt confirmed liberals and black Americans in their Democratic allegiance, while the Wallace movement kept anti-Communist Catholics in the Democratic camp. Neither Dewey's personality nor his campaign roused enthusiasm. Truman, on the other hand, emerged as a pungent orator, an indomitable fighter, and—in contrast to his opponent—an intensely *human* being. Shouting crowds greeted Truman's appearances with the joyful cry, "Pour it on, Harry." By election day he had traveled 31,700 miles and had delivered 356 speeches.

Public opinion polls forecast a sure Republican victory. But Truman received 24.1 million popular votes against 22 million for Dewey, and 303 electoral votes against 189 (see Map 30-2). Thurmond carried four

Truman in 1948: 356 speeches

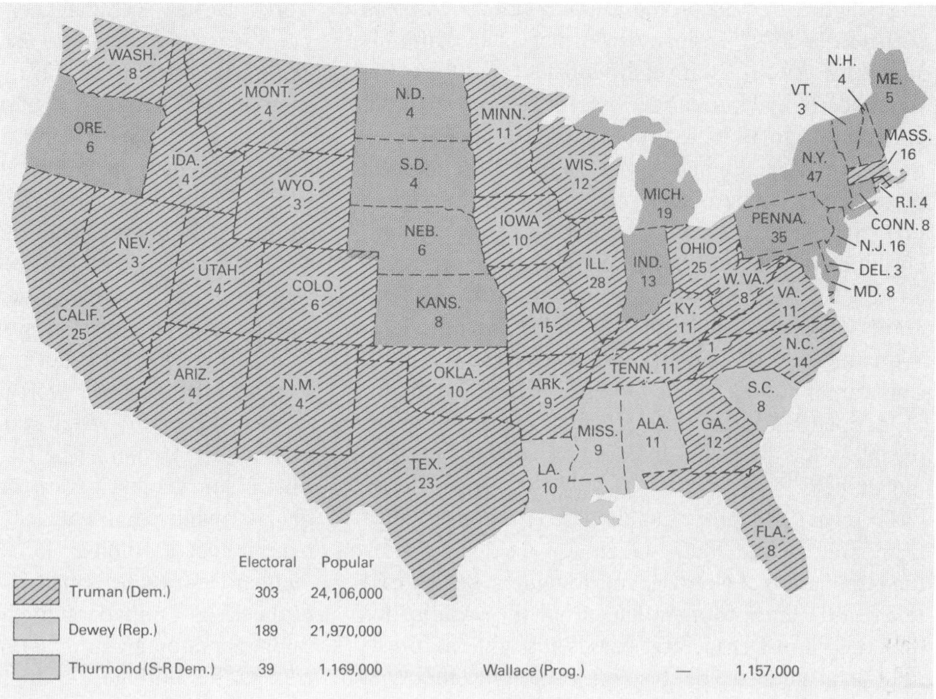

Map 30-2
The election of 1948

states (South Carolina, Mississippi, Alabama, and Louisiana) and polled 1.2 million votes. Wallace also polled 1.2 million votes but carried no states. In addition, the Democrats captured both houses of Congress. Truman, who ran behind the Democratic ticket, owed his victory to the vitality of the Roosevelt coalition as well as to his own efforts.

SECOND TERM

Return to Frustration "We have rejected the discredited theory that the fortunes of the nation should be in the hands of a privileged few," Truman said in January 1949. "Instead, we believe that our economic system should rest on a democratic foundation and that wealth should be created for the benefit of all. The recent election shows that the American people are in favor of this kind of society." His State of the Union message was a ringing summons to a new era of social reform. "Every segment of our population and every individual," he concluded, "has a right to expect from his government a fair deal."

But his Fair Deal roused strong opposition. Secretary of Agriculture Charles F. Brannan's plan to support farm income rather than prices and Federal Security Administrator Oscar Ewing's proposal for national health insurance were condemned as "socialistic." Congress refused to repeal the Taft-Hartley Act and rejected Truman's requests for federal aid to education and for middle-income housing. A Senate filibuster killed the FEPC. On the other hand, though thwarted in his legislative program for civil rights, Truman through executive action ended segregation within the government and the armed services.

The Developing World A "revolution of rising expectations" had been sweeping through the Third World ever since the war. Underdeveloped countries, stridently nationalist in mood, were shaking off the political and economic bonds of western empire and demanding independence, growth, and modernization.

In listing points in his inaugural address in 1949, Truman placed particular emphasis on Point Four—"a bold new program" to offer technical assistance to developing countries. The war against world poverty, Truman said, "is the only war we seek." The Point Four program received limited funding, however, and had only modest impact. Foreign policy under the masterful direction of the new secretary of state, the urbane and imperious Dean Acheson, remained resolutely oriented toward Europe. Though the United States welcomed independence in India (1946) and in Indonesia (1949), elsewhere, as in the case of French Indochina, it subordinated theoretical anticolonial sentiments to the imperial nostalgia of NATO allies.

The Truman administration showed little concern for Latin America and Africa. Economic interests (oil) and domestic political pressures led to a more active role in the Near East. Historically the Americans most involved there had been missionaries, educators, and archaeologists. Strategically and economically the United States had regarded the Middle East, as the region began to be called during the Second World War, as an Anglo-French preserve. But war weakened Anglo-French control, opening the area to American and Soviet penetration as well as to the gathering force of Arab nationalism.

American interest centered especially in Palestine, long known to pilgrims as the Holy Land and ruled since 1922 by Britain under a League of Nations mandate. Jews in America and elsewhere had not forgotten the Balfour Declaration of 1917 pledging British sympathy for "the establishment in Palestine of a National Home for the Jewish people." Nazi anti-Semitism had meanwhile won Zionism wide support among non-Jews in America and Europe.

The birth of Israel, 1948: celebration in Washington

The Balfour Declaration, however, had its ambiguities. Arabs stressed the proviso that "nothing shall be done which may prejudice the civil and religious rights of existing non-Jewish communities in Palestine." While the Arab League, formed in 1945, vowed undying opposition to a Jewish national state, Jewish underground bands, led by Menachem Begin and Yitzhak Shamir, waged a campaign of terror against the British. Efforts to resolve the problem through partition failed. In May 1948 Britain terminated its mandate. Jews proclaimed the republic of Israel with the veteran Zionist Chaim Weizmann as president.

In Washington the defense establishment, seeking access to the vast Middle Eastern oil reserves, favored a pro-Arab policy. So did American oil companies. But Truman, moved by humanitarian and also by political considerations, promptly recognized the new state over the vehement opposition of his national security advisers. The Arab League's invasion of Israel was successfully repelled in 1948–49. Israel now began a robust but perennially hazardous existence, heavily dependent on American support.

The China Conundrum The most conspicuous Communist gain in the Third World was not the result of premeditated Soviet design. Stalin seems to have believed nearly as firmly as the United States in the capacity of the Nationalist regime of Chiang Kai-shek to organize China. Both superpowers underestimated the revolutionary drives in China—the ancient resentments against foreign domination, the pent-up demand for agrarian reform, the growing revulsion against the corruption and autocracy of the Guomindang (Kuomintang), and the skill and tenacity with which the Chinese Communists under Mao Zedong (Mao Tse-tung) exploited these discontents.

After the war Washington began by favoring a coalition between the Nationalists and the Communists. The new American ambassador to China, General Patrick J. Hurley, took enthusiastic personal charge of this effort. When a disenchanted Hurley resigned in November 1945, Truman appointed General George C. Marshall to continue his work. But the Nationalists believed that they could win a civil war. The Communists were committed by ideology to domination. In January 1947 Marshall abandoned his mission, blaming its failure on both the reactionaries in the Guomindang (Kuomintang) and the Communists.

The Nationalists soon overextended themselves. The Communists, welded by messianic conviction and helped by the increasing popular hatred of the Nationalist government, started to win victories. With each victory they captured more arms and attracted more deserters. In 1947 Truman send General Albert Wedemeyer to China on a fact-finding tour. "The only basis on which national Chinese resistance to Soviet aims can be revitalized," Wedemeyer reported, "is through the presently corrupt, reactionary and inefficient Chinese National government." But "until drastic political and economic reforms are undertaken United States aid cannot accomplish its purpose." Chiang made no serious attempt at reform. Washington resolutely opposed proposals that would have entangled the United States in the fighting. By January 1949 the Nationalist armies had abandoned Beijing (Peking). By the end of the year, the Nationalist regime had fled to the island of Taiwan (Formosa).

The collapse of Chiang provoked a bitter political debate in the United States. Some contended that anti-Nationalist prejudice—if not outright treason—in the State Department caused the "loss of China." But, as Wedemeyer explained the Nationalist defeat, it was "lack of spirit, primarily lack of spirit. It was not lack of equipment. In my judgment they could have defended the Yangtze (Chang) with broomsticks if they had the will to do it."

Chinese Communists entering Shanghai, 1949

Truman and Acheson prepared to recognize the Communist regime in the hope of encouraging Titoism in East Asia. "The Russians will turn out to be the 'foreign devils' in China," Truman wrote Vandenberg in 1949, "and that situation will help establish a Chinese Government that we can recognize and support." The American government put out a white paper placing the blame on Chiang, pronounced Taiwan part of mainland China, and declared American neutrality. Recognition was delayed in the hope of getting the communist regime to accept specified international obligations. But the Chinese proved difficult, and in the United States congressional and public opinion stirred up by the well-financed, pro-Chiang "China Lobby," and soon by the Korean War, made recognition of Red China an unmentionable issue.

LIMITED WAR

The End of Nuclear Monopoly If the rhetoric of the Truman Doctrine seemed to call for global containment of communism, Truman himself did not construe the doctrine in any such crusading way. He applied it neither to China nor to eastern Europe. Even with regard to Russia, he made amiable public reference to Stalin in 1948 as "Uncle Joe." In 1949 he seemed to view the contest with the Soviet Union without alarm. The forward drive of communism in Europe had been stopped, in Berlin as well as in western Europe. In China the policy was to "let the dust settle."

All this encouraged the president to continue to clamp down on the defense budget. By 1949 the army was down to ten active divisions. The capacity to fight small wars had dwindled. Deterrence rested on the idea of a retaliatory air-atomic strike against the Soviet Union. If war broke out, it seemed that Washington faced the choice either of doing nothing or of blowing up the world. Observers feared that this situation might invite Communist aggression in some marginal area where the United States would not wish to respond by atomic war and lacked the means to respond otherwise.

Then in September 1949 evidence reached Washington that an atomic explosion had occurred in the Soviet Union. With one stroke the Russians had not only broken the atomic monopoly but had proved to the world their own technological capacity. The era of American invincibility had come to an end.

In response, Truman concluded a bitter argument among his scientific advisers by directing the Atomic Energy Commission to proceed with the construction of a hydrogen bomb, a weapon even more fearful than the atomic bomb. At the same time, he instructed the National Security Council to undertake a basic reappraisal of America's strategic position. The result, a document known as NSC 68 (April 1950), accelerated a shift from a political to a military definition of the Cold War. Postulating a Soviet "design for world domination," NSC 68 called both for a rapid buildup in nuclear weapons and for enlarged capacity to fight conventional wars whenever the Russians threatened "piecemeal aggression." Then a new development reinforced the thesis that air-atomic power would not by itself assure American security and helped NSC 68 gain presidential approval in September.

War in Korea When American and Soviet troops entered Korea after the collapse of Japan in 1945, they had accepted the 38th parallel as a military dividing line. Time and the Cold War converted the military demarcation into a political frontier. In 1948 the Russians set up a People's Democratic Republic in North Korea, while the Americans recognized the Republic of South Korea. In June 1949 Soviet and American forces withdrew from Korea. The position of South Korea in the American security system was not altogether clear. Both General Douglas MacArthur and Secretary of State Acheson declared that it lay outside the American defense perimeter in the Pacific. Should an attack occur, Acheson said, "The initial reliance must be on the people attacked to resist it and then upon the commitments of the entire civilized world under the Charter of the United Nations."

At just this time Kim Il-sung, the Communist dictator of North Korea, came to Moscow to seek Stalin's support for a North Korean invasion of South Korea. Misled perhaps by the MacArthur and Acheson statements, misled too perhaps by Kim's confidence that the South Koreans would welcome the North Koreans as liberators, Stalin gave Kim a green light. On June 25, 1950, North Korean troops crossed the 38th parallel in a surprise invasion.

In retrospect it appears that Stalin acquiesced in a project that Kim designed for internal Korean reasons and that seemed to involve minimal risks for the Soviet Union. But Truman wrongly saw the invasion as a Soviet effort to test the American will. If the United States did not react in Korea, he believed, the Russians would sponsor similar thrusts elsewhere, and the result might be a third world war. And indeed, even if Stalin had not instigated the invasion, no one can tell how he would have interpreted an American failure to respond. Truman saw no alternative but to react.

Without hesitation, Truman committed American forces under General MacArthur to the defense of South Korea. At the same time he brought the matter before the United Nations Security Council. The absence of the Soviet delegate, who was boycotting the Security Council in pique over its refusal to seat Communist China, enabled the UN to endorse the American initiative. Truman rejected proposals that he ask Congress for a joint resolution authorizing the commitment of the American troops to combat. His reliance instead on dubious theories of inherent presidential power enlarged the freedom of future presidents to take the nation into war.

The original UN intention in South Korea was simply to repel the North Korean invasion. At first the Communists drove the UN troops—made up of Republic of Korea forces and American troops, soon to be reinforced by a smattering of units from other nations, especially Great Britain and Turkey—back to the southeastern corner of the peninsula. But on September 15, in a daring move, MacArthur landed an

American artillery in Korea

MacArthur at Inchon

amphibious force at Inchon behind the enemy lines. By September 27 the UN forces were in Seoul, and by October 1 they had recovered almost all of Korea below the 38th parallel (see Map 30-3).

Crossing the Thirty-Eighth Parallel MacArthur's brilliant generalship now raised the question whether the UN forces should pursue the enemy into North Korea. Despite warnings from Beijing (Peking) that crossing the 38th parallel might provoke Chinese intervention, the UN General Assembly at Washington's prompting reaffirmed that the goal was "the establishment of a unified, independent, and democratic Korea," and authorized UN forces on October 7 to move north.

On October 15, 1950, Truman and MacArthur met at Wake Island. When the president asked the general about the chances of Chinese or Soviet intervention in Korea, MacArthur replied, "Very little. . . . If the Chinese tried to get down to Pyongyang there would be the greatest slaughter." Superbly confident, MacArthur deployed his forces in a thin line across North Korea. On November 24 he declared that his final drive to end the war was "now approaching its decisive effort." Two days later, a Chinese Communist army drove a wedge through the central sector. The UN forces retreated in disarray two-thirds of the way down the peninsula.

Relations between MacArthur and Washington, not easy in victory, became prickly in defeat. Years of proconsulship had charged a naturally proud and flamboyant personality with a conviction of independent authority. In a barrage of public statements after his November defeat MacArthur suggested that the blame lay, not in his own faulty intelligence or tactics, but in the Washington decision to limit the war to Korea and to forbid attack on Chinese bases in Manchuria. This "privileged sanctuary," he said in one message, was "an enormous handicap, without precedent in military history." On December 6 Truman ordered MacArthur to clear all subsequent statements with Washington.

No Substitute for Victory? The tension between MacArthur and Truman reflected fundamental disagreement over the purpose of the war. MacArthur believed that the United States must pursue the Korean conflict to a victorious conclusion. If this required an escalation of the war—the bombing of Manchurian bases, the blockade and nuclear bombing of China,

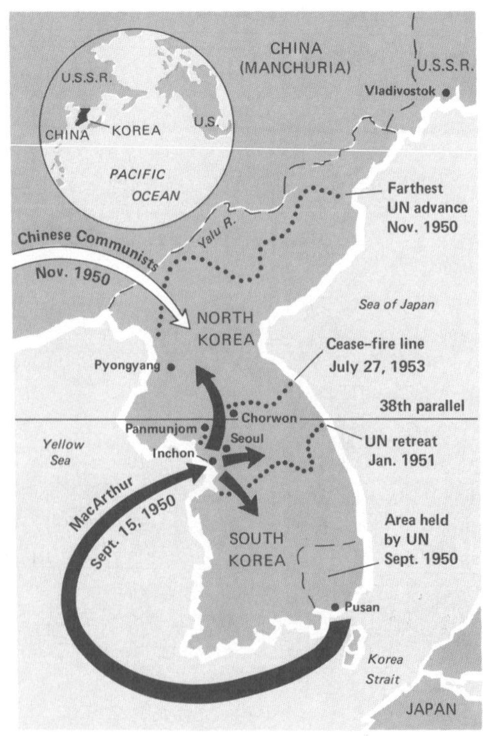

Map 30-3 *The shifting front in Korea*

the entry of Nationalist Chinese—then so be it. "In war there is no substitute for victory."

The administration, on the other hand, saw the conflict as a limited war for limited objectives. If Manchuria was a privileged sanctuary, so were Okinawa and Japan. To commit American military strength to the mainland of Asia might abandon Europe to Soviet aggression. To transform a limited war into a general war against Communist China would be, in General Omar Bradley's phrase, to fight "the wrong war, at the wrong place, at the wrong time, and with the wrong enemy."

The administration was now ready to settle for the original objective of its intervention—the integrity of South Korea. A reversal of military fortunes now gave hope that this limited goal could be won. General Matthew B. Ridgway, who had taken command of the Eighth Army in December, began to recover the initiative. By March most of South Korea was once again free of Communists, and Ridgway's troops were pressing on the 38th parallel. The administration called for a diplomatic settlement. But a defiant MacArthur statement demanding enemy surrender killed the president's move toward negotiation. "By this act," Truman later said, "MacArthur left me no choice—I could no longer tolerate his insubordination." In April, when Congressman Joseph Martin of Massachusetts, the Republican leader in the House, produced a new and provocative MacArthur letter, Truman relieved MacArthur of his command.

Truman's decision caused an outburst of public indignation that reached its pitch on April 19 when MacArthur, returning to the United States for the first time in 14 years, addressed a joint session of Congress. There followed an extraordinary inquiry by the Senate Foreign Relations and Armed Services committees into the circumstances of MacArthur's dismissal. Beginning on May 3, MacArthur, Acheson, Marshall, Bradley, and other military and civilian leaders underwent a congressional interrogation that, in time, canvassed the most basic problems of global strategy. The administration persuaded most of the country that the president and the Joint Chiefs, having the global interests of the country in view, were justified in overruling MacArthur's recommendations.

Though Truman won this battle, he was not an effective war president. He had misjudged the causes of the war, tolerated MacArthur's insubordination too long, backed the disastrous decision to cross the 38th parallel, failed to develop strong public support for a more and more frustrating war, and by 1951 seemed unable to find the way to an acceptable peace. The increasingly unpopular war sullenly continued.

THE KOREAN WAR: REPERCUSSIONS

The Globalization of Containment Though the limitations imposed on the Korean War showed that the defense of Western Europe remained the American priority, the fact that the war was fought at all expressed the growing American belief that Soviet expansion, if blocked in the main theater, would break out in secondary theaters. Interpreting the North Korean invasion as part of a worldwide Communist offensive, Truman proceeded to batten down hatches all around the world. In his response to Korea, he transformed containment from a selective European policy into a general global policy.

The image of an aggressive Russia commanding a highly centralized world Communist movement—an image neither new, nor, in the age of Stalin, altogether false—now fastened itself dogmatically on the American mind. The new China, for example, began to be perceived simply as an extension of Soviet power. Three days after the North Korean attack, Truman canceled the policy of neutrality in the Chinese civil war, declared that the seizure of Taiwan by "communist forces" would threaten American security in the Pacific, and ordered the Seventh Fleet to prevent a mainland attack on the island (and also to prevent a Nationalist attack on the mainland). By 1951 Assistant Secretary of State Dean Rusk could speak of the Mao regime as a "colonial Russian government—a Slavic Manchukuo."

The nationalist uprising against French control in Indochina was incorporated into the larger pattern. Roosevelt had opposed the restoration of Indochina to French rule, favoring instead an international trusteeship to prepare Indochina for independence. This wise suggestion was forgotten after his death, and the return of the French colonial government produced dogged resistance on the part of Ho Chi Minh and the so-called Viet Minh. Ho was a nationalist as well as a Communist, and the Viet Minh were seen by most Indochinese as a movement for national independence. Washington had paid little attention to the fighting in Indochina until the fall of mainland China. After Korea the State Department, condemning Ho as "an agent of world communism," pronounced the

The policy of neutrality canceled: the Seventh Fleet in Taiwan

French role in Indochina "an integral part of the worldwide resistance by the Free Nations to Communist attempts at conquest."

In the United States, the Korean War brought about a quick reversal of the policy of military retrenchment. National defense expenditures rapidly increased from 4 percent of the gross national product in 1948, to above 13 percent by 1953. Two years after the attack on South Korea, the nation had 3.6 million men under arms—an increase of nearly 2.2 million. The Soviet problem was seen more and more in military terms. With American financial backing, Britain and France launched rearmament programs, and in September 1950 Acheson persuaded his European allies to go along with a measure of rearmament in Germany. In 1951 NATO forces were integrated under the command of General Eisenhower. Truman's decision to send four additional American divisions to Europe set off an impassioned but inconclusive "Great Debate" in which conservative legislators, led by Taft, challenged Truman's claim that as president he had the power to send troops abroad without congressional authorization.

Domestic Repercussions The Korean War had widespread domestic impact. Defense spending revived inflationary impulses in the economy until the imposition of controls in January 1951 stabilized prices. Unlike Roosevelt, who had sought when possible to act on the basis of congressional statute, Truman embraced an enlarged view of inherent presidential prerogative. Fearing in April 1952 that a nationwide steel strike would stop the flow of arms to the troops in Korea, he directed the government to seize and operate the steel mills. He defended this action as an exercise of the emergency powers of the president. But the Supreme Court, in the notable case of *Youngstown Steel & Tube Co.* v. *Sawyer,* rejected the presidential thesis, at least in its immediate application.

It was easier to contain the economic than the psychological consequences of Korea. With the intensification of the Cold War, many Americans demanded to know why the nation they deemed so powerful and so safe in 1945 should now, five years later, appear in deadly peril. Some, resenting the complexity of history, found a satisfactory answer by tracing all troubles to the workings of the Communist conspiracy—unsleeping, omnipresent, and diabolically cunning. The denunciation in 1948 by Whittaker Chambers, an ex-Communist, of Alger Hiss, a former State Department official, as a fellow Communist spy and Hiss's conviction for perjury in 1950 seemed to substantiate his hypothesis. If Hiss, a man of apparently unimpeachable respectability, was a Soviet agent, who might not be? The administration compounded its troubles when Truman called the Hiss affair a "red herring" and Acheson, after Hiss's conviction, said, "I do not intend to turn my back on Alger Hiss." In 1951, Julius and Ethel Rosenberg were charged as atomic spies and later executed on the ground of conspiracy to commit espionage in wartime.

The government also initiated prosecutions against top Communist leaders under the Smith Act of 1940, which prohibited groups from conspiring to advocate the violent overthrow of the government. Throughout the country, citizens anxious to protect their communities against the dread infection sometimes, in ardor or panic, failed to distinguish between disloyalty and traditional American radicalism or mere dissent. Then in February 1950 a little-known senator from Wisconsin, Joseph R. McCarthy, gave a speech in Wheeling, West Virginia. "I have here in my hand a list," he said—a list of Communists in the State Department; whether he said there were 205 or 81 or 57 or "a lot" of Communists (and this was a question around which much controversy would revolve) was in the end less important than his insistence that these Communists were "known to the Secretary of State" and were "still working and making policy." With this speech, a remarkable figure began a brief but lurid career on the national stage.

The Rise of McCarthyism McCarthy's charges prompted an astonished Senate to appoint a subcommittee under Senator Millard Tydings of Maryland to look into his allegations. After weeks of hearings, the Tydings Committee declared that McCarthy had worked a "fraud and a hoax." Yet, for all the apparent failure of McCarthy's charges, the hearings also revealed the facility, agility, and lack of scruple with which he operated. His characteristic weapon was what the journalist Richard Rovere called the "multiple untruth"—a statement so complicated, flexible, and grandiose in its mendacity as almost to defy rational refutation. To this McCarthy added unlimited impudence, an instinct for demagoguery, and an unmatched skill in alley fighting. If the Tydings Committee thought it had disciplined McCarthy, it was wrong. In the election of 1950, McCarthy's intervention in Maryland, marked by a broad hint that Tydings, a conservative Democrat whom Roosevelt had tried in vain to purge in 1938, was pro-Communist, brought about Tydings's defeat. From that moment, the Wisconsin senator became a formidable figure in the Senate.

The Korean War meanwhile wrought a significant change in the public atmosphere. It created a climate that transformed McCarthy's crusade from an eccentric sideshow into a popular movement. If Communists were killing American boys in Korea, why should Communists be given the benefit of the doubt in the United States? Though Truman's loyalty program had overridden traditional safeguards of civil freedom, it did not go nearly far enough for McCarthy and his followers. In September 1950, Congress passed over Truman's veto the McCarran Internal Security Act, establishing a Subversive Activities Control Board to follow Communist activities in the United States. A second McCarran Act, also passed over Truman's veto, was the Immigration and Nationality Act of 1952. While this law abolished the Asian-exclusion provisions of 1924, it retained the national-origins quota system and made ideology a ground for excluding foreigners from the United States.

The spectacle of McCarthyism infuriated the president. He told the American Legion:

> Slander, lies, character assassination—these things are a threat to every single citizen everywhere in this country. When even one American—who has done nothing wrong—is forced by fear to shut his mind and close his mouth, then all Americans are in peril.

THE 1952 ELECTION

Truman in Retreat But the backwash of the Korean War gave McCarthy an eager audience. The administration and its leading officials—especially Secretary of State Acheson—fell under unsparing attack as Communist sympathizers. The Republicans scored impressive gains in the congressional elections of 1950 and looked forward with increasing confidence to 1952.

Their confidence grew with revelations of corruption in the Reconstruction Finance Corporation and the Bureau of Internal Revenue. The disclosures of 1951–52 called attention to the decline that had taken place in the governmental service from the relatively incorruptible 1930s—a decline brought about in part because Truman's scorn for the "professional liberal" had driven many of the old New Dealers from government to be replaced by party hacks. When the facts got out, moreover, Truman constrained by loyalty to old political associates, seemed grudging in his response. All this strengthened the idea of a "mess in Washington" and a growing national conviction that the Democratic party had been in power too long.

The Campaign of 1952 Robert A. Taft's triumphant reelection to the Senate in 1950 made him the leading contender for the Republican nomination. But the powerful Eastern wing of the party, regarding the Ohio senator as too isolationist, turned to General Dwight D. Eisenhower. At the convention in July the Eisenhower supporters outmaneuvered their opposition in a battle over contested delegates. Eisenhower was nominated on the first ballot. Senator Richard M. Nixon of California, who had played an important part in the exposure of Alger Hiss, became his running mate.

After Truman withdrew from the Democratic contest, the convention drafted Governor Adlai Stevenson of Illinois. Though Stevenson had served in the Navy Department during the war and thereafter at the UN, he was little known to voters outside his home state. In

The nominees: Chicago, 1952

Adlai Stevenson: brilliant, literate, eloquent

the next three months, carrying out his pledge to "talk sense to the American people," he established himself as a brilliant, literate, and eloquent candidate.

In fact, Eisenhower and Stevenson were not dissimilar in their internationalism in foreign policy. They differed, however, on their attitude toward government and toward McCarthyism, and the Republican campaign, based on the themes of "Korea, communism, and corruption," magnified the differences. Nixon, a more experienced campaigner than Eisenhower, referred to the Democratic candidate as "Adlai the appeaser . . . who got a Ph.D. from Dean Acheson's College of Cowardly Communist Containment." "I further charge," Nixon added, "that Mr. Truman, Dean Acheson and other administration officials for political reasons covered up this Communist Conspiracy and attempted to halt its exposure." Intellectual supporters of Stevenson were derided as "eggheads."

The campaign was interrupted by a revelation that Nixon had been a beneficiary of a fund collected on his behalf by California business leaders. For a moment, Eisenhower considered asking Nixon to retire from the ticket. But a histrionic speech in an autobiographical vein on the potent new medium of television saved the vice-presidential candidate. When Eisenhower, late in the campaign, declared his intention to go to Korea if elected, he clinched his victory. The popular vote showed 33.9 million for Eisenhower, 27.3 million for Stevenson. The margin in the Electoral College was 442 to 89 (see Map 30-4). Though Eisenhower's election was more a personal than a party triumph, the Republicans also captured Congress. Twenty years of Democratic rule had come to an end.

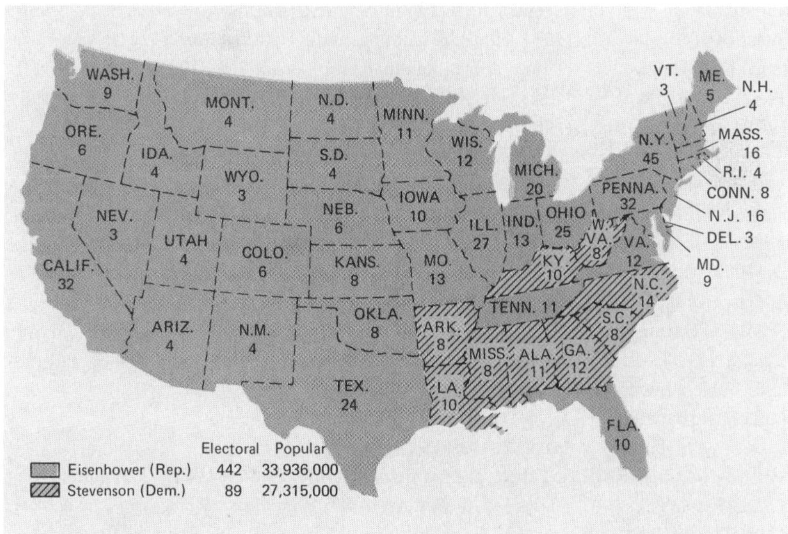

Map 30-4 *The election of 1952*

The presidential reputation of Harry S Truman has improved over the years. "There are two Trumans," the mordant commentator Elmer Davis said at the time, "the White House Truman and the courthouse Truman. He does the big things right, and the little things wrong." In 1952 the little things were on the minds of voters. In retrospect the big things seem more important. Even some of the big things, like the abuse of the loyalty program, the sweeping language of the Truman Doctrine, and the claims to inherent presidential war-making power, remain questionable. The use of the atomic bomb, though arguably justified in the circumstances, was a tragic decision. Still Truman did many very big things right—the defense of western Europe against Stalinism, the Marshall Plan, NATO, the relief of General MacArthur, civil rights. He kept alive the spirit of liberal democracy at home and responsible internationalism abroad. Against the pretentious presidency of later years, the memory of this unpretentious, brave, doughty, forever candid man has grown in popular affection.

SUGGESTIONS FOR READING

TRUMAN AND HIS POLICIES

Truman's *Memoirs*, 2 vols. (1955–56), are pungent and controversial. Two readable volumes by R. J. Donovan—*Conflict and Crisis* (1977) and *Tumultuous Years* (1982)—provide a narrative account of the Truman presidency. A. L. Hamby, *Beyond the New Deal: Harry S. Truman and American Liberalism* (1973), is an analytical study. R. H. Ferrell, *Harry S. Truman and the Modern American Presidency* (1983), pays particular attention to foreign policy. D. McCullough, *Truman* (1992), provides a sympathetic portrait of its subject. On defense policy, see T. Hoopes, *Forrestal* (1992).

FOREIGN AFFAIRS

For the Cold War, W. H. McNeill, *America, Britain and Russia* (1951), and H. Feis, *Churchill, Roosevelt, Stalin* (1957), remain fundamental works. J. L. Gaddis's books—*The United States and the Origins of the Cold War* (1972), *Strategies of Containment* (1981), *The Long Peace* (1987)—are intelligent and dispassionate; Gaddis with T. H. Etzold, eds., *Containment: Documents on American Policy and Strategy* (1978), is a useful compilation. W. Isaacson and E. Thomas, *The Wise Men* (1986), and D. Yergin, *Shattered Peace: The Origins of the Cold War and the National Security State* (1977), are engaging accounts of the formation of policy. The revisionist argument is conveniently summarized in W. Le Feber, *America, Russia, and the Cold War* (rev. ed. 1985); H. Thomas, *The Beginnings of the Cold War* (1986); and T. G. Paterson, *On Every Front: The Making of the Cold War* (1979). R. L. Messer, *The End of an Alliance* (1982), discusses the Truman-Byrnes relationship. Dean Acheson, *Present at the Creation* (1969), is a formidable and stylish memoir. W. A. Harriman (and E. Abel), *Special Envoy to Churchill and Stalin, 1941–1946* (1975), is indispensable. James P. Byrnes, Charles E. Bohlen, Lucius Clay, James Forrestal, G. F. Kennan, and A. H. Vandenberg have left important memoirs and diaries; for dissenting views, see J. M. Blum, ed., *The Price of Victory: The Diary of Henry A. Wallace, 1942–1946* (1973), and N. D. Markowitz, *The Rise and Fall of the People's Century* (1973). M. J. Hogan, *The Marshall Plan* (1987), and R. A. Pollard, *Economic Security and the Origins of the Cold War* (1986), consider economic ramifications. T. H. Anderson, *The United States, Great Britain and the Cold War, 1944–1947* (1981), discloses British pressures on Washington. For Soviet policy, see W. Taubman, *Stalin's American Policy* (1982), and Vojtech Mastny, *Russia's Road to the Cold War* (1979). S. Talbott, ed., *Khrushchev Remembers*, 2 vols. (1970–74), is fascinating.

For the Cold War in other areas, see B. R. Kuniholm, *The Origins of the Cold War in the Near East* (1980); R. Buhite, *Soviet-American Relations in Asia, 1945–1954* (1982); and J. Blum, *Drawing the Line: The Origin of the American Containment Policy in East Asia* (1982). E. J. Kahn, Jr., *The China Hands* (1975), tells the shaming story of the State Department's East Asian experts. C. M. Dobbs, *The Unwanted Symbol: American Foreign Policy, The Cold War, and Korea, 1945–1950* (1981), argues that Washington misperceived an essentially local conflict. On the Korean War, there are instructive accounts in B. Cumings, *The Origins of the Korean War*, 2 vols. (1981, 1990); B. Cumings and J. Halliday, *Korea: The Unknown War* (1988); and B. Kaufman, *The Korean War* (1986). See, too, D. C. James, *The Years of MacArthur: Triumph and Disaster, 1945–1964* (1985).

For the atomic bomb, L. Freedman, *The Evolution of Nuclear Strategy* (1981), is incisive and sophisticated. G. Herken, *The Winning Weapon: The Atomic Bomb in the Cold War, 1945–50* (1980), describes the impact of the bomb on the wartime alliance; P. Boyer, *By the Bomb's Early Light* (1985), the impact on American thought and culture. On nuclear strategy, McG. Bundy, *Danger and Survival: Choices About the Bomb in the First Fifty Years* (1988), is indispensable.

DOMESTIC ISSUES

S. Lubell, *The Future of American Politics* (1951), is an illuminating analysis. J. T. Patterson, *Mr. Republican: A Biography of Robert A. Taft* (1972), and R. N. Smith, *Thomas E. Dewey and His Times* (1982), portray influential Republican leaders. For Truman and civil rights, see D. R. McCoy and R. T. Ruetten, *Quest and Response* (1973). E. Latham, *The Communist Controversy in Washington* (1966), is a sober guide. R. H. Rovere, *Senator Joe McCarthy* (1959), is a brilliant essay; there are scholarly biographies by T. C. Reeves and by D. M. Oshinsky. Larger repercussions are covered analytically in J. P. Diggins, *Up from Communism* (1975), and more tendentiously in D. Caute, *The Great Fear* (1978). Also useful are A. Weinstein, *Perjury: The Hiss Chambers Case* (1978); R. Radosh and J. Milton, *The Rosenberg File* (1983); and A. Theoharis, ed., *Beyond the Hiss Case: The FBI, Congress, and the Cold War* (1982).

CHAPTER THIRTY-ONE

AN AMBITIOUS ROAD PROGRAM

CONSOLIDATION AND CONFLICT

In the years since 1929, the American people had experienced the worst depression in their history, the worst hot war, the worst Cold War, the worst limited war. Since 1933 they had followed presidents who believed strongly in affirmative government and vigorous action. But the high-tension 1930s and 1940s left most people worn out. Tired of crisis and challenge, Americans of the 1950s renewed the 1920s' quest for "normalcy" and turned away from positive government to private action and private interests. The 1950s were to be years of relative prosperity, family togetherness and consumerism—years when social reform, as in the 1920s, struck most Americans as dull and irrelevant.

THE EISENHOWER MOOD

The New President President Dwight D. Eisenhower embodied the changing mood. Sixty-two years old on his inauguration, he was already a national hero, beloved by his people. Eisenhower had been one of that group of remarkable military men who emerged during the Second World War. His service as supreme commander of the Allied forces in Europe was followed by a postwar tour of duty as Chief of Staff. President of Columbia University in 1948, he returned to Europe as supreme commander of NATO in 1951. He resigned this post to seek the Republican nomination in 1952.

People weary of the "mess in Washington" and wanting an end to the controversies of the New Deal era saw him as the man to heal the nation's wounds. His appointed role, wrote the influential columnist Walter Lippmann, was "that of the restorer of order and peace after an age of violence and faction." His experience, his famous geniality, and his expressed dislike of politics recommended him as national conciliator.

Actually his surface affability concealed a concern with large issues, cold and shrewd judgment, a hot temper, much craftiness, and a dazzling instinct for self-preservation. His nonpolitical pose was his major political weapon. Coolly recognizing that he was far more popular than the Republican party, he did not propose to risk national influence by coming on as a partisan leader.

He cultivated the impression that he was a warm-hearted man above the battle who did not always know what his own administration was doing. He posed as an opponent of strong presidential leadership, affirming his wish to redress the balance between executive and legislative branches after the excesses of the Roosevelt years. He encouraged the idea that, within the executive branch, he deferred to Secretary of State John Foster Dulles in foreign affairs and to White House chief of staff Governor Sherman Adams in domestic affairs. He was not, he assured everyone, the desk-pounding sort of president. He exploited his reputation for rambling imprecision in press conferences. Anticipating a question on a tough issue, he once told his press secretary, "Don't worry, Jim, if that question comes, I'll just confuse them."

Eisenhower wanted the press and the Democrats to underestimate him. In fact, he deployed his subordinates to draw opposition fire and was firmly in charge whenever he wished to be, which was a good deal more often than many supposed at the time. Political scientists, belatedly recognizing his executive skills, wrote in later years of his as the "hidden-hand Presidency." "He was a far more complex and devious man than most people realized," Vice President Richard Nixon later said of him, characteristically adding, "and in the best sense of those words."

Ending the Korean War In foreign affairs the general in the White House hoped to be a man of peace. Fulfilling his 1952 campaign pledge, he visited Korea between his election and the inauguration. Cease-fire negotiations, initiated in July 1951, continued to drag on, however, as did hostilities, some of the heaviest fighting of the war taking place around Porkchop Hill in the Chorwon area in July 1953.

The sticking point was whether, and how, prisoners of war should be repatriated. Many of the North Koreans and Chinese in United Nations hands had made clear that they did not want to return to their homelands. United Nations negotiators accordingly rejected Communist insistence on compulsory repatriation. In the spring of 1953, exasperated by the deadlock, Eisenhower decided to let the Chinese know that he "would not feel constrained about crossing the Yalu, or using nuclear weapons." Whether because of this threat of nuclear war, or because the death of Stalin in March 1953 had given new flexibility to Soviet policy, the North Koreans now accepted voluntary repatriation. An armistice was concluded at Panmunjom on July 27, 1953.

The armistice provided for a demilitarized zone and called for a conference to settle the future of Korea. But the conference was never held, and in subsequent years each side repeatedly charged the other with violations of the armistice. The United States signed a mutual-defense treaty with South Korea in 1954 and kept an uncertain hand in South Korean affairs. The increasingly capricious actions of President Syngman Rhee caused widespread protest both in South Korea and in Washington, culminating in his overthrow in April 1960 and the establishment in 1961 of a new—and eventually, more dictatorial—government under General Park Chung Hee.

The Korean War lasted three years and one month. In that time 1.3 million Americans served in Korea, and 33,629 died there, along with about 3,000 from other UN countries and about 50,000 South Koreans. Total Communist battle casualties were estimated at 1.5 million. For all the frustration the war produced at home, it stopped aggression in Korea and showed the Communist world that the democratic nations were prepared to meet military challenge. It also stimulated American rearmament and accustomed the nation to the idea of war on presidential initiative and to the belief that American military force was effective on the Asian mainland.

Eisenhower and Dulles Ending the Korean War marked a first success for Eisenhower as a man of peace. His pacific instincts and pragmatic temper, however, were somewhat at odds with the ideological militancy of his party and his secretary of state. The grandson of one secretary of state (John Foster) and nephew of another (Robert Lansing), John Foster Dulles had emerged by 1944 as the leading Republican authority on foreign affairs. By profession a lawyer and by avocation a Presbyterian layman, Dulles united a talent for close legal argument with a penchant for righteous moralism. Critics found him tricky and sanctimonious. Though identified with many aspects of the Truman-Acheson foreign policy, he had turned against that policy as the 1952 election drew near. Dismissing containment as "negative, futile and immoral," he called for a new policy of "liberation." The mere statement by the United States "that it wants and expects liberation to occur would change, in an electrifying way, the mood of the captive peoples."

In this mood Eisenhower cancelled Truman's 1950 order to neutralize the Straits of Formosa, thereby "unleashing" Chiang Kai-shek for presumed reconquest of the mainland. However, Nationalist forces were in effect releashed by a mutual-security pact in 1955. American inaction in face of anti-Soviet upheavals in East Germany in 1953 and Hungary in 1956 ended talk of "liberation" and "rollback." The administration continued to insist it was reversing the Truman-Acheson policies, but observers were more

John Foster Dulles: a penchant for moralism

impressed by continuities than reversals. Dulles's tone was more moralistic and ideological than Acheson's and his proposals were more belligerent, but his militancy was offset by Eisenhower's caution and optimism. Underneath the rhetoric, containment was quietly reinstated as American policy.

The president and his secretary of state differed in their attitudes toward negotiation. Where Dulles thought a gain for one side must be a loss for the other, Eisenhower sought opportunities for mutual gain. Eisenhower fully accepted the premises of the Cold War and saw value in the tough-cop, nice-cop routine. Dulles's truculent preachments had their uses both in intimidating the Russians and in reserving for the president himself the benign role of guardian of the peace. Even Dulles, for all his public talk about monolithic communism, privately sought to exploit cracks in the monolith.

Massive Retaliation If containment was reinstated, it was containment with a difference. After the Soviet Union developed the atomic bomb, the Truman administration had concluded that American nuclear supremacy could not last and therefore supplied no basis for long-term strategy. Containment, so NSC 68 argued, required an increase in conventional forces, as well as development of the hydrogen bomb. An administration used to the idea of public spending thought the economy could bear the added cost. But Eisenhower considered fiscal conservatism essential to economic health and therefore wanted a course that would simultaneously restrain Soviet aggression and the defense budget. He found the answer in making nuclear weapons the center of American strategy, thereby producing a "bigger bang for a buck."

Although Truman had dropped the atomic bomb and approved the hydrogen bomb, he regarded the nuclear weapon with dismay: "This isn't a military weapon. . . . We have to treat this differently from rifles and cannon." Eisenhower, on the other hand, saw "no distinction between conventional weapons and atomic weapons" (as he told Winston Churchill, again British prime minister, in 1953). He told the National Security Council that "somehow or other the tabu which surrounds the use of atomic weapons would have to be destroyed." And he readily employed the threat of nuclear war (termed "nuclear blackmail" when employed by the Russians) in Korea and elsewhere.

Reliance on conventional means for containment not only cost more but enabled the Soviet Union to take initiatives at times and places of its choosing. In 1954 Dulles proclaimed the "new look" in American strategy based "primarily upon a great capacity to retaliate, instantly, by means and at places of our choosing." "Rather than let the Communists nibble us to death all over the world in little wars," said Vice President Nixon, "we would rely in the future primarily on our massive mobile retaliatory power."

Eisenhower thus moved from Truman's defensive interpretation of containment to the offensive concept of "massive retaliation" and from Truman's balanced forces to major reliance on nuclear weapons. The "new look" expected to deter aggression by instilling uncertainty in the mind of the enemy as to what the United States might do when provoked, with nuclear attack on the Soviet Union now a possible response. The "necessary art," Dulles said, was "the ability to get to the verge without getting into war. . . . If you are scared to go to the brink, you are lost." Success depended on Moscow's believing that Washington would actually drop the bomb—a premise bound to become more problematic as Soviet nuclear strength continued to grow.

American missiles in Germany

Eisenhower and Russia Eisenhower, nevertheless, had a genuine desire for peace. The death of Stalin gave new opportunity to Western diplomacy as well as new outlets both to energies of normalization stirring within the Soviet Union and to energies of nationalism spreading elsewhere in the Communist empire. Anticipating a less rigid Soviet leadership, Churchill argued for a summit meeting. But Dulles, forever fearful that a reduction in Soviet-American tension would relax the Western guard, opposed the idea. In 1953–54 the West may well have lost a chance to test significant new Soviet proposals, especially regarding the neutralization of Germany.

By early 1955 Churchill finally persuaded Dulles to drop his opposition. When the Soviet Union, after a decade's stalemate, agreed to sign an Austrian peace treaty in May, omens for the Big Four meeting at Geneva seemed auspicious. As the Soviet Union increased its nuclear arsenal, Eisenhower abandoned his nonchalance about nuclear weapons and began to affirm the horror of nuclear war. The outlook was ever closer, he wrote the next year, "to destruction of the enemy and suicide for ourselves." At Geneva in July he set forth a creative "Open Skies" plan, proposing that the two superpowers exchange blueprints of military establishments and permit mutual aerial photographic overflights. The Russians rejected this promising idea.

Supplementing Massive Retaliation The problem of small local wars remained. Here Dulles proposed to replace American conventional forces by a network of allies recruited through bilateral military assistance programs and in some parts of the world through collective military pacts. So in 1954 the Americans set up the Southeast Asia Treaty Organization (SEATO), bringing three Asian states (Thailand, Pakistan, and the Philippines) together with the United States, Britain, France, Australia, and New Zealand. SEATO's provisions were less stringent than those of NATO and called only for consultation among the signatories in case of Communist subversion and for action by each state "in accordance with its constitutional processes" in case of armed attack. In the Middle East Dulles induced the British to create a regional defense organization under the Baghdad Pact of 1955 (CENTO—the Central Treaty Organization) (see Map 31-1). But he had undue faith in the capacity of military pacts to

Map 31-1
Europe, North Africa, and the Middle East

stabilize underdeveloped areas, and he was disappointed in his efforts to force neutral nations to choose sides in the Cold War.

For direct American intervention abroad, the Eisenhower administration turned from conventional armed force to the Central Intelligence Agency (CIA). Established in 1947, the CIA under Truman had concentrated on helping democratic (including socialist) parties, trade unions, and newspapers in Western Europe and on espionage in Eastern Europe and the Soviet Union. In the 1950s CIA "covert action"—that is, the attempt by clandestine means to alter policies and governments in other countries—grew ambitious and aggressive.

Because CIA director Allen W. Dulles was the secretary of state's brother, the agency had unusual freedom of initiative. The CIA began not just to support friends but to subvert foes—helping to overthrow governments regarded as pro-Communist in Iran (1953) and Guatemala (1954), failing to do so in Indonesia (1958), helping to install supposedly pro-Western governments in Egypt (1954) and Laos (1959), and plotting the assassination of the pro-Communist Congolese leader Patrice Lumumba (1960). By 1957 the CIA devoted more than 50 percent of its personnel and more than 80 percent of its budget to "covert action."

Eisenhower's own Board of Consultants on Foreign Intelligence Activities repeatedly warned him against CIA meddling in the internal affairs of other countries. As early as 1956 Robert Lovett, a former secretary of defense, and David Bruce, a distinguished diplomat, pleaded for reconsideration of "the long-range wisdom of activities that have entailed our virtual abandonment of the international 'golden rule,' and which, if successful to the degree claimed for them, are responsible in a great measure for stirring up the turmoil and raising the doubts about us that exist in many countries of the world." But Eisenhower consistently ignored his board's recommendations. CIA activity fed the American government's conviction both of its ability and its right to decide the destiny of other nations.

Institutionalizing the Cold War Seeing the godless Communist conspiracy as both evil in itself and the source of all the world's troubles, Dulles absolutized the philosophy of the Cold War. His rigid views took root in a group of government agencies—the State Department (which he purged of active dissenters), the Defense Department, the National Security Council, the CIA—all of which developed vested institutional interests in the idea of a militarily expansionist Soviet Union. The Cold War conferred power, appropriations, and public influence on these agencies. And, by the natural law of bureaucracies, their stake in the conflict steadily increased.

The CIA on Its Own

In August 1960, the CIA took steps to enlist members of the criminal underworld with gambling syndicate contacts to aid in assassinating Castro. . . . [Richard] Bissell and [Sheffield] Edwards testified that they were certain that both [Allen W.] Dulles and his Deputy General [C. P.] Cabell were aware of and authorized the initial phase of the assassination plot involving underworld figures. They acknowledged, however, that Dulles and Cabell were not told about the plot until after the underworld figures had been contacted. . . . [John] McCone testified that he did not know about or authorize the plots. [Richard] Helms, Bissell and [William] Harvey all testified that they did not tell McCone of the assassination effort either when McCone assumed the position of DCI [Director of Central Intelligence] in November 1961 or at any time thereafter until August 1963 when Helms gave McCone a memorandum from which McCone concluded that the operation with underworld figures prior to the Bay of Pigs had involved assassination. The Inspector General's Report states that Harvey received Helms' approval not to brief McCone when the assassination efforts were resumed in 1962. . . . On May 7, 1962, Edwards and the CIA's General Counsel, Lawrence Houston, briefed Attorney General Robert Kennedy on the operation involving underworld figures, describing it as terminated. . . . Two plans to assassinate Castro were explored by Task Force W, the CIA section then concerned with covert Cuban operations, in early 1963.

From *Alleged Assassination Plots Involving Foreign Leaders, an interim report of the Senate Select Committee on Intelligence Activities* (94th Congress, 1st Session), November 20, 1975

The Cold War had long since been institutionalized in the Soviet Union, where the Russians were already equipped with a dogma of inevitable conflict and, through its network of Communist parties, with the means of local intervention. Stalin's death, after harsh and obscure feuds among Soviet leaders, concluded in the victory of N. S. Khrushchev by 1957–58. Khrushchev, an impulsive man with a plunger's instinct, replaced Stalin's Cold War of position by a Cold War of movement.

On both sides there now arose a propensity to perceive local conflicts in global terms, political conflicts in moral terms, and relative differences in absolute terms. Each side saw humanity as divided between forces of light and forces of darkness. Each assumed that the opposing bloc was under the organized and unified control of the other. Washington supposed that what was then called the free world should reshape itself on the American model, Moscow that the Communist world should reshape itself on the Russian model.

NATIONALISM AND THE SUPERPOWERS

Nationalism versus the Cold War Containment had begun in Europe, where it was a rational response to the struggle between democracy and Stalinism. In its extended form after Korea, it now presupposed a world consumed, as Europe had been, by this struggle. And indeed, for a decade after 1945, the United States and the Soviet Union managed to bestride the globe as superpowers, working to consolidate their positions around the planet—America through its pacts, Russia through its parties.

But European concepts of the Cold War did not apply to regions increasingly convulsed by demands for political and economic independence against colonial or neocolonial control. In most cases Third World states had no great interest in the conflict between America and Russia except as they could exploit it for their own purposes. As the superpowers tried to enlist developing countries on one side or the other in their Cold War, the new states tended to respond by playing off one superpower against the other and using the Cold War as a means of getting aid for themselves. Despite pretenses and alliances, the new states—even, it worked out, those that pronounced themselves Communist—responded in the end to their own national interests.

French troops at Dienbienphu

Crisis in East Asia By the early 1950s, the United States was paying 80 percent of the cost of the French war against Ho Chi Minh and the Viet Minh. The French position, however, had grown desperate. In March 1954, with substantial French forces under siege in the valley of Dienbienphu in western Vietnam, Paris asked Washington for armed intervention.

Ho Chi Minh

Eisenhower told a press conference that Indochina was of "transcendent" concern; "you have a row of dominoes set up, you knock over the first one. . . . You could have the beginning of a disintegration that would have the most profound influences." Dulles advocated the use of nuclear weapons to raise the siege of Dienbienphu. Vice President Nixon suggested the possibility of "putting American boys in." But leading senators, among them Lyndon B. Johnson and John F. Kennedy, were skeptical. General Matthew B. Ridgway, now Army Chief of Staff, was vigorously opposed, as was Winston Churchill. Eisenhower decided against military intervention.

Dienbienphu fell on May 7. Four days later Eisenhower informed Paris that he would seek authority from Congress to send troops to Indochina if the French would make political concessions to anti-Communist nationalists. But a new French government preferred negotiations at Geneva. The Geneva Accords provided for the temporary partition of Vietnam at the 17th parallel—this to be a "military demarcation line" and "not in any way [to] be interpreted as constituting a political or territorial boundary"—with reunification to come through elections scheduled for July 1956. The accords also limited the size of foreign military missions in Vietnam.

Washington had watched the negotiations with grim disapproval, and the National Security Council pronounced the result a "disaster . . . a major forward stride of Communism which may lead to the loss of Southeast Asia." After setting up SEATO, the administration now backed South Vietnam's new premier, Ngo Dinh Diem, a devout Catholic and stubborn nationalist whose strength of purpose had impressed many Americans, liberal and conservative, during his American stay in 1950–53. In 1955 Diem rejected the elections provided for in the Geneva Accords. Soon he deposed Emperor Bao Dai, the French puppet, and, as president of the new Republic of Vietnam, moved to revive the economy, suppress political opposition, and confirm his personal control. The discontent aroused by Diem's increasingly arbitrary regime gave South Vietnamese Communists a new chance to seize power. In 1958 a Communist-nationalist movement called the National Liberation Front or, more popularly, the Viet Cong, began guerrilla warfare against Diem. This development alarmed Washington. "The loss of South Vietnam," said Eisenhower on April 4, 1959, "would set in motion a crumbling process that could, as it progressed, have grave consequences for us."

In neighboring Laos, the military crisis was more acute and American intervention more active. The Pathet Lao, a Communist-led guerrilla movement, was roaming the countryside. The United States in 1958 vetoed the effort of Prince Souvanna Phouma to establish a neutral Laos under a coalition government with Pathet Lao participation. In 1959 the CIA installed a pro-Western government in Vientiane.

Eisenhower discerned (incorrectly) Chinese Communist intervention in Indochina. After his unleashing, Chiang Kai-shek had put troops on the offshore islands of Jinman (Quemoy) and Mazu (Matsu) in the Straits of Formosa. When the Chinese Communists started shelling the islands in late 1954, Eisenhower persuaded Congress in January 1955 to pass the Formosa Resolution, authorizing the president to use armed force "as he deems necessary" to defend Taiwan (Formosa) and the neighboring Pescadores islands. This blank-check resolution increased popular acceptance of presidential authority to commit troops to combat, thereby accelerating the development of the "Imperial Presidency."

The shelling subsided, and in the next years Chiang sent 100,000 Nationalist troops to the off-shore islands. Communist bombardment resumed in August 1958. Though Eisenhower was irritated by the reinforcement of the islands, he saw no alternative but to convince Beijing (Peking) that the United States would intervene, "perhaps using nuclear weapons," if the Communists attempted an invasion. After three months the shelling tapered off. Under American pressure Chiang eventually reduced the size of his forces on the islands.

Nationalism in the Middle East Conflicting concerns—about Soviet expansion, about Arab oil, and about the survival of Israel—had thrust the United States into the Middle Eastern cauldron. The first two factors shaped American policy in 1951 when Mohammed Mossadegh, the prime minister of Iran, nationalized British oil holdings and drove the shah, Mohammed Reza Pahlavi, out of the country. Truman, regarding Mossadegh as an honest if exasperating nationalist, attempted mediation lest Iran's quarrel with the British encourage Soviet intervention. The quarrel dragged on, and in 1953 Eisenhower, who regarded Mossadegh as a Communist tool, decided to overthrow him and restore the shah—a program carried through in August 1953 in a coup organized by a CIA agent (who happened to be a grandson of Theodore Roosevelt). Thereafter America succeeded Britain as Iran's Western patron.

The center of Arab nationalism was the new regime in Egypt under the purposeful leadership of Colonel Gamal Abdel Nasser. Moscow established relations with Nasser, sent Egypt arms, and proposed to subsidize the construction of a great dam at Aswan on the Nile. Washington at first offered Western financing for the dam. Then in July 1956 Dulles, annoyed by Nasser's dalliance with the Russians, withdrew the American offer just as Egypt was about to accept it. Nasser retaliated by nationalizing the Suez Canal.

Britain and France regarded Nasser's seizure of the canal as a threat to Western Europe's vital supplies of oil. Moreover, Sir Anthony Eden, now British prime minister, saw Nasser in the image of Hitler and believed on the often misleading analogy of Munich that appeasement would only inflame his ambitions. Israel feared that Egyptian rearmament would permanently alter the balance of power in the Middle East. In October, British and French officials met secretly with Israeli leaders in France. On October 29, Israel attacked Egypt. Two days later Britain and France entered the war against Egypt on the spurious excuse of

Gamal Abdel Nasser, Arab nationalist

localizing the conflict. One result of the Anglo-French intervention was to save Egyptian forces from probable defeat by the Israelis.

Washington, which had not been consulted by the plotters, roundly disowned the Suez expedition and threatened to deny financial support to the faltering British pound. It also initiated action in the United Nations—ironically backed by the Soviet Union and opposed by Britain and France—to condemn Israel as the aggressor. On November 6 Eden ordered a cease-fire. The Anglo-French adventure was ill-conceived and ill-prepared, and Dulles, though his maladroit diplomacy had provoked the crisis, was right in supposing that gunboat imperialism was obsolescent.

Still, despite the power of Arab nationalism, Dulles persisted in regarding Soviet penetration as the essential problem. "The existing vacuum in the Middle East," Eisenhower told Congress in January 1957, "must be filled by the United States before it is filled by Russia. . . . Considering Russia's announced purpose of dominating the world, it is easy to understand its hope of dominating the Middle East." Eisenhower asked Congress to authorize the commitment of American forces to aid Middle Eastern nations "requesting such aid, against overt armed aggression from any nation controlled by International Communism." Congress passed the so-called Eisenhower Doctrine in March 1957. In July 1958 Eisenhower landed 14,000 troops to protect a pro-Western government in Lebanon.

Nationalism in Latin America Latin America, too, was swept by nationalist ferment after the Second World War. The resulting revolutions sometimes (as in Argentina) took authoritarian, sometimes (as in Venezuela) democratic, forms. Then toward the end of the 1940s a counterrevolutionary reaction set in. By 1954 thirteen Latin American presidents were military men. Now a new surge of protest arose against dictatorships, bringing the overthrow of, among others, Perón of Argentina in 1955, Pérez Jiménez of Venezuela in 1958, Batista of Cuba in 1959, and Trujillo of the Dominican Republic in 1961.

Through this ebb and flow, Washington, insofar as it thought about the hemisphere at all, tried to fit it into the framework of the Cold War. Franklin D. Roosevelt's Good Neighbor ideals were neglected. The Truman administration concentrated on military aid to Latin American armies. In 1954 Eisenhower's CIA overthrew the democratic Arbenz government in Guatemala, which the administration regarded as hostile to the United Fruit Company and vulnerable to Marxism. The result for Guatemala was a long series of oppressive military regimes. Throughout the hemisphere, the administration showed a weakness for authoritarian governments. Nixon, visiting Cuba, praised the "competence and stability" of the Batista dictatorship. When in 1958 Nixon visited Peru and Venezuela after dictators personally decorated by Eisenhower had been thrown out, he was stoned and spat on.

Batista fled Cuba in 1959, defeated by the revolutionary forces under the bearded, cigar-smoking leader, the flamboyant and audacious Fidel Castro. Castro initiated a long-needed program of social and agrarian reform. But he combined this program with terror equal to that of his predecessor. A romantic Marxist nationalist rather than a disciplined Communist, Castro needed the United States as his enemy and therefore rebuffed conciliatory American gestures. For its part, Washington grew obsessed with the expropriation of American property in Cuba. Despite his excesses, Castro became for a moment a hero through much of the hemisphere.

Fidel Castro: romantic Marxist

The Cuban revolution altered Washington's indifference to Latin American demands for economic development. When President Kubitschek of Brazil proposed "Operation Pan America" and an Inter-American Development Bank in 1957, Washington had shown no interest, but by 1960 the administration was ready to offer "a broad new social development program for Latin America" based on the Inter-American Development Bank—a program endorsed by the Organization of American States in the Act of Bogotá in September 1960.

In time, surrounded increasingly by Communists and lashed by the intensities of his own turbulent personality, Castro led Cuba into the Soviet camp. Fearful of a Soviet satellite in the Western Hemisphere, Eisenhower in March 1960 agreed to a CIA proposal to arm and train a force of Cuban exiles for use against the Cuban regime. On its own the CIA began planning to assassinate Castro. When Castro ordered the United States to cut its embassy to eleven persons, the Eisenhower administration broke relations in January 1961.

THE UNITED STATES AND THE SOVIET UNION

Khrushchev the Adventurer The Soviet Union, seeing in anticolonialism a potent means of reducing Western power, met the challenge of Third World nationalism with relish. Communism, Moscow assured underdeveloped countries, offered the best road to modernization. This claim acquired plausibility from unexpected Soviet technological breakthroughs—the hydrogen bomb in 1953; *Sputnik,* the first earth satellite, and the first intercontinental ballistic missile (ICBM) in 1957; the first moon satellite in 1959; and the first man in space in 1961.

The ebullient Khrushchev, now securely in command, was boastful and belligerent, and the launching of *Sputnik* seemed to verify his horrendous claims about Soviet ICBM superiority. He liked to tell small countries how many "rockets" would be required to destroy them, and he did not hesitate (as in 1956 against Britain and France over Suez and later against the United States over Cuba) to threaten war. He greatly increased Soviet activity in the Middle East, Southeast Asia, Latin America, and Africa and appeared eager to exploit every Western vulnerability. In November 1958, he reopened the Berlin question threatening a termination of allied rights in West Berlin.

The launching of *Sputnik* caused great alarm in the United States. The Gaither Report to the National Security Council in 1957 predicted that the Soviet Union would soon possess more missiles than the United States. "There is no dispute about the missile gap," Henry Kissinger wrote as late as 1961. Democrats assailed the administration for letting the nation fall behind in nuclear striking power. Educators demanded increased national investment in the sciences. Though the Pentagon welcomed the "missile gap" as an argument for more military spending, Eisenhower himself dismissed the gap with richly justified skepticism. Photographic reconnaissance of Soviet territory by a high-altitude CIA aircraft, the U-2, while limited in its coverage, failed to confirm the fearsome predictions.

Khrushchev the Coexister Khrushchev was more complicated than he first appeared. With his famous "secret speech" denouncing the crimes of Stalin at the Twentieth Party Congress in 1956, he launched the "de-Stalinization" process and started a movement toward normalization in Soviet society. In world affairs he proclaimed the gospel of "peaceful coexistence," amending the Leninist doctrine of the inevitability of war. In the nuclear age, he said, the conflict between capitalism and communism would be decided by peaceful competition.

Soviet as well as Western leaders were increasingly impressed by the incalculable perils presented by nuclear weapons—by the fact, for example, that a single plane could deliver more destructive power than all the planes in all the air forces delivered during the Second World War. Also the problem of radioactive fallout had come sharply to the world's attention in 1954, when both the United States and the Soviet Union tested large-yield nuclear weapons in the atmosphere. As scientists analyzed the effects of radioactive contamination on the bones, blood, and germ plasm of humans, concern mounted over nuclear testing. In March 1958 the Soviet Union suspended testing, and the United States and Britain followed suit in October.

Khrushchev's very truculence may have been an attempt to force the West to accept the Soviet Union and détente. It was also an attempt to head off Communist China, which regarded "peaceful coexistence" as a betrayal of world revolution and which might soon challenge Russia for leadership of the international Communist movement. Sino-Soviet relations began to deteriorate in 1958—a development unrecognized by the State Department, which persisted for another half-dozen years in talking about the "Sino-Soviet bloc."

Exasperated by Khrushchev's inflammatory language and worldwide meddling, Western statesmen doubted his more pacific purposes. Moreover, if Khrushchev could secure "peaceful coexistence" (from which he always rigorously excluded ideological coexistence), he confidently predicted the withering away of capitalism and the triumph of communism by peaceful means. That is what he meant when he told the Western democracies, "We will bury you"—not that the Communists would kill their adversaries but that they would outlive them.

In March 1959, with Khrushchev behaving in his conciliatory manner, the West accepted a summit meeting in principle. Even Secretary of State Dulles, now ravaged by cancer, acquiesced in the drift toward negotiation. In April Dulles resigned, to be replaced by Christian A. Herter; five weeks later Dulles was dead. Though a foreign ministers' meeting in May resulted in a deadlock over Berlin, the movement toward the summit continued. In the summer of 1959 Nixon visited Russia, and in September Khrushchev visited the United States. The Khrushchev tour reached its climax in private talks between Khrushchev and Eisenhower at Camp David, in Maryland. The United States agreed to a summit meeting, and Khrushchev agreed to drop his deadline on Berlin.

Camp David, 1959: Eisenhower and Khrushchev

The Dark Year The summit meeting was scheduled for Paris on May 16, 1960. Then on May 5 Khrushchev announced the shooting down of an American plane over the Soviet Union. Washington promptly said that the plane had innocently strayed from course on a meteorological flight. On May 7 Khrushchev gleefully sprang his trap. The pilot was alive, he said, and had confessed that he was engaged in espionage. Khrushchev added, "I am quite willing to grant that the president knew nothing about the plane."

At this point the administration owned up to the act of espionage. Secretary Herter argued that the United States was morally entitled to conduct U-2 flights in order to protect the "free world" from surprise attack. Herter, and soon Nixon, implied that the flights would continue. Eisenhower, rejecting Khrushchev's proffered escape clause, accepted full responsibility. Khrushchev now came to Paris demanding that Eisenhower apologize for the flights and punish those responsible. Eisenhower rejected these demands, and the summit collapsed. The last year of his administration left Eisenhower's foreign policy in disarray.

REPUBLICAN DOMESTIC POLICY

Eisenhower Economics In domestic policy Eisenhower offered the nation what he called "modern Republicanism." This meant in practice an acceptance of the New Deal tempered by a determination to reduce public spending and the role of the federal government. Actually Eisenhower had little interest in domestic matters and, though he had no wish to dismantle the New Deal, was in some respects more conservative than Robert A. Taft, the most powerful Republican in the Senate until his death in July 1953.

His Cabinet was dominated by Secretary of the Treasury George M. Humphrey, an Ohio businessman with deeply conservative views. When the new secretary of defense, Charles E. Wilson of General Motors, was asked whether he foresaw a conflict between his business and official commitments, he replied, "I cannot conceive of one because for years I thought what was good for our country was good for General Motors, and vice versa." Secretary of the Interior Douglas McKay of Oregon summed up the general attitude when he said, "We're here in the saddle as an Administration representing business and industry."

The administration stalled on social questions. It concentrated instead, without great success, on fiscal conservatism. No administration was more responsive to the business community, but "business confidence" turned out, as so often, to be irrelevant to economic health. Preferring recession to the supposed inflationary risks of public spending, the administration did little to combat downturns in 1953–54, 1957–58, and 1960–61. The average annual rate of economic growth slowed from 4.3 percent in the last six Truman years to 2.5 percent in the Eisenhower years. For all his concern with balancing the budget, Eisenhower achieved a surplus less than half the time and produced in 1959 the largest peacetime deficit to that point in American history.

His most influential domestic initiative was the Interstate Highway Act of 1956, which he proudly described as the "most ambitious road program by any nation in all history." The law authorized the federal government to pay 90 percent of the construction costs of interstate highways. Great freeways now carried the middle class and their shops and services into the suburbs, leaving the city to the poor and the minorities. Pollution, environmental damage, and petroleum consumption increased, while public mass transport, especially the railroads, deteriorated. The automobile continued to remold American life much as railroads had done a century earlier.

The interstate highway program was the great exception to Eisenhower's general dislike of federal intervention. He feared "statism" and proposed to transfer federal functions either to state and local governments or to private enterprise. But in 1960 the size and structure of the federal government were much what they had been in 1952.

McCarthy: Zenith In 1951 Joe McCarthy had denounced General Marshall as part of "a conspiracy so immense and an infamy so black as to dwarf any previous venture in the history of man." During the 1952 campaign, to avoid offending McCarthy, Eisenhower deleted a paragraph of praise for Marshall from a speech delivered in Wisconsin. This action foreshadowed the president's reluctance to engage himself personally in the McCarthy issue. As he later put it, "I will not get in the gutter with *that* guy." The Wisconsin senator, agile and unscrupulous as ever, took full advantage of the administration's indulgence. Before 1953 only the bully of the Senate, he now began, as chair of the Senate Committee on Government Operations, to swagger without challenge through the executive branch in pursuit of alleged Communists and fellow travelers.

A main target was the State Department. Determined to propitiate the right wing, Secretary of State Dulles was ready to collaborate with McCarthy and even to anticipate his demands. Veteran diplomats whose political reporting aroused McCarthy's ire were drummed from the service. A McCarthy disciple was appointed chief of State Department personnel. The secretary ordered State Department libraries abroad to remove books by "authors who obviously follow the Communist line or participate in Communist front organizations." The thrillers of Dashiell Hammett, *The Selected Works of Tom Paine,* and even Whittaker

Senator McCarthy: agile and unscrupulous

Chambers' *Witness* were banned. A number of proscribed books were actually burned. By June 1953 the panic had spread so widely that the president himself cried, "Don't join the book burners."

The panic did not abate. Many Americans looked to the FBI as the bastion of national freedom and turned J. Edgar Hoover, the bureau's able but increasingly grandiose director, into a national hero. Posses of road-company McCarthys sprang up across the land. Eisenhower had stiffened Truman's loyalty program, and the effort to guard the national security became a heresy hunt employing guilt by association, loyalty oaths, secret informers, blacklists, and intimidation by legislative committees. In the 1954 campaign Vice President Nixon boasted of the number of "security risks" who had been driven from government. One notable victim was the great physicist Dr. J. Robert Oppenheimer, the father of the atomic bomb but subsequently an opponent of the hydrogen bomb. Oppenheimer's security clearance was withdrawn in 1953 because of ancient left-wing associations well known to security officers a decade before, when Oppenheimer was heading the Manhattan Project. A review board declared that the Oppenheimer case "demonstrated that the Government can search . . . the soul of an individual whose relationship to his Government is in question." It added that national security "in times of peril must be absolute."

Thoughtful people began to wonder whether such ideas as these might not be the most subversive of all. George Kennan said that "absolute security" was an unattainable and self-devouring end—that its frenzied pursuit would lead only to absolute tyranny. Judge Learned Hand summed up the feelings of many Americans:

> I believe that that community is already in process of dissolution where each man begins to eye his neighbor as a possible enemy, where nonconformity with the accepted creed, political as well as religious, is a mark of disaffection; where denunciation, without specification or backing, takes the place of evidence.

McCarthy: Decline The Korean War had given McCarthy his opportunity for influence, and the end of that war in July 1953 brought about his decline. As war frustrations receded, McCarthyism began to lose its emotional base. By now, in his increasingly erratic course, McCarthy had become embroiled with the army, launching a sensational, if unproductive, search for Communists and spies at Fort Monmouth, New Jersey. Goaded beyond endurance, the army finally fought back. The denouement took place in a series of televised hearings from April 22 to June 17, 1954.

The Army-McCarthy hearings were a compelling spectacle, marked by vivid personalities and passages of passion and conflict. They commanded a fascinated audience, amounting at times to 20 million people. Viewers trained through long exposure to TV Westerns to distinguish between good and bad guys had little trouble deciding to which category McCarthy belonged. After 35 days of the grating voice, the sarcastic condescension, the irrelevant interruption ("point of order, Mr. Chairman, point of order"), and the unsupported accusation, McCarthy effectively achieved his own destruction. The spell was at last broken. On December 2, 1954, the Senate censured McCarthy by a 67 to 22 vote. The Wisconsin senator was finished. His death in 1957 merely ratified his political demise.

Eisenhower welcomed McCarthy's downfall, and admirers later discerned his "hidden hand" in the result. But the president's refusal to make the public case against McCarthyism wasted an opportunity to reaffirm the great traditions of civil freedom and due process that the Wisconsin senator had so effectively damaged. The impact of McCarthyism should not be exaggerated. Many Americans denounced the senator and his works with courage and impunity. He left, however, a heritage — not only in the broken lives of those he attacked but, paradoxically, in a greatly enhanced conception of presidential prerogative. When McCarthy demanded access to Department of Defense files, Eisenhower in May 1954 claimed "an uncontrolled discretion" to refuse information anywhere in the executive branch. This was the most absolute assertion of the presidential right to withhold information from Congress ever uttered to that point. Because of the detestation of McCarthy, right-minded people generally applauded the Eisenhower theory. But this theory, which acquired in 1957 the name of "executive privilege," ushered in an extraordinary time of executive denial. In its remaining years, the Eisenhower administration rejected more congressional requests, often entirely reasonable, for information than presidents had done in the first century of American history.

The Battle of Desegregation The gravest domestic issue lay in the field of race relations. The struggle to assure black Americans their full rights as citizens had gathered momentum during the Second World War. Though most of Truman's civil rights program was rejected by Congress, his fight for that program established civil rights as a national issue.

Thwarted in Congress, the champions of racial justice turned to the courts. The Supreme Court, once chary of taking on cases involving rights of black Americans, started doing so after the war. The early decisions reflected the Fabian tactics of the Court under Chief Justice Fred M. Vinson of Kentucky (1946–53). The Vinson Court sought to work toward equal rights within the inherited legal framework — that is, by accepting the *Plessy* v. *Ferguson* doctrine (see p. 428) of "separate but equal," and rejecting separate facilities when they were not in full and exact fact equal.

Beginning in 1952, attorneys for the National Association for the Advancement of Colored People (NAACP) argued before the Supreme Court against state laws requiring the segregation of children in public education. On May 17, 1954, in the case of *Brown* v. *Board of Education of Topeka,* the Court, speaking through Chief Justice Earl Warren, responded with a unanimous decision reversing *Plessy* v. *Ferguson* and interpreting the Fourteenth Amendment as outlawing racial discrimination in public schools. "We conclude," the Court said, "that in the field of public education, the doctrine of 'separate but equal' has no place. Separate educational facilities are inherently unequal." A year later, the Court called on school authorities to submit plans for desegregation and gave local federal courts the responsibility of deciding whether the plans constituted "good faith compliance." The Court concluded by ordering action "with all deliberate speed," thereby both affirming a constitutional right and deferring its exercise.

The border states moved toward compliance. But in South Carolina, Georgia, Alabama, and Mississippi, resistance began to harden, especially after the spread in 1955–56 of the militantly segregationist White Citizens' Councils and a 1956 manifesto by Southern members of Congress, condemning the decision. Some Southern states passed laws to frustrate the Supreme Court ruling. A favorite device was to divert state funds to what might be passed off technically as a private school system. Extreme segregationists revived the pre–Civil War doctrine of nullification under the more mellifluous name of "interposition."

Crisis in Little Rock Eisenhower declined to endorse the *Brown* decision and remained skeptical about government efforts to promote civil rights: "It is difficult through law and through force to change a man's heart." Southern resistance reached a climax in 1957 in Little Rock, Arkansas, when Governor Orval Faubus tried to deny nine black students enrollment in the Central High School. Faubus's open challenge compelled the president to defend the Supreme Court. When the black boys and girls sought to enter Central High School, they were mobbed by angry whites. On September 24, 1957, Eisenhower sent federal troops into Little Rock. Order was restored, and black children entered the school.

In the meantime, Congress was finally taking action on behalf of racial justice. The Civil Rights Act of 1957, the first of its kind since Reconstruction, authorized the Department of Justice to seek injunctions on behalf of black voters' rights. A second act, in 1960, provided for the appointment of federal referees to safeguard voting rights. For its part, the Warren Court extended the principle of the *Brown* case to new fields,

A Decision of Enormous Significance

Today, education is perhaps the most important function of state and local governments. Compulsory school attendance laws and the great expenditures for education both demonstrate our recognition of the importance of education to our democratic society. It is required in the performance of our most basic public responsibilities, even service in the armed forces. It is the very foundation of good citizenship. Today it is a principal instrument in awakening the child to cultural values . . . and helping him to adjust normally to his environment. . . .

Does segregation of children in public schools solely on the basis of race . . . deprive the children of the minority group of equal educational opportunities? We believe that it does. . . .

We conclude that in the field of public education the doctrine of "separate but equal" has no place. Separate facilities are inherently unequal. . . . Therefore, we hold that the plaintiffs and others similarly situated . . . are, by reason of the segregation complained of, deprived of the equal protection of the laws guaranteed by the Fourteenth Amendment.

From the Unanimous Decision of the United States Supreme Court by Chief Justice Earl Warren in *Brown* v. *Board of Education of Topeka,* 347 U.S. 483, 1954.

striking down segregation over the next years in interstate commerce, in public buildings, in airports and interstate bus terminals, in parks and other public recreational facilities. Both Congress and the Court, by concentrating on segregation as embodied in law, left untouched the wide and bitter realm of de facto discrimination. Consequently the decisions on desegregation affected the South but rarely the North. At the same time, by declaring the moral necessity of equality, the Court was changing the values of American society.

Little Rock, 1957: separate but equal had no place

Black Americans themselves were increasingly in the forefront of the struggle. Lawyers like Thurgood Marshall of the NAACP argued the constitutional cases. In December 1955, the black citizens of Montgomery, Alabama, under the inspiration of an eloquent young minister, Dr. Martin Luther King, Jr., boycotted the city's segregated bus system. King, who was strongly influenced by Thoreau and Gandhi, counseled his followers to avoid violence and to confront "physical force with an even stronger force, namely, soul force." The boycott, reinforced by suits in the federal courts, achieved the desegregation of the bus system in a year. Nonviolent resistance was widely used in the winter of 1959–60 to challenge the refusal to serve black patrons at Southern lunch counters. The

Rosa Parks in desegregated bus, Montgomery, Alabama

rapid spread of "sit-in" demonstrations through the South and the support they evoked in the North and among moderate Southern white citizens testified to the rising moral force of the protest against segregation. Though only limited progress was made in school desegregation and in assuring the right to vote, vast progress was made in gaining acceptance for the moral case against discrimination. During the rather pallid Southern filibuster against a civil rights bill in 1960, with one or two exceptions, no senator tried any longer even to argue the philosophy of white supremacy.

The Warren Court Eisenhower later told his biographer that his biggest mistake was "the appointment of that dumb son of a bitch Earl Warren." The former Republican governor of California turned out to have a spacious view of the Constitution, and his humane approach received support and elaboration from three other distinguished Eisenhower appointees—John M. Harlan, Potter Stewart, and, most consistently, William J. Brennan—as well as from holdovers from the Roosevelt Court, Hugo Black, Felix Frankfurter, and William O. Douglas.

In addition to its initiatives in the field of racial justice, the Warren Court, especially in the 1956–57 term, sought to mend the holes McCarthyism had made in the fabric of civil freedom. The *Watkins* and *Sweezy* cases, with their condemnation of exposure "for the sake of exposure," restricted legislative investigations to questions deemed pertinent to a legislative objective. The *Yates* case construed the Smith Act of 1940 as distinguishing between "the statement of an idea which may prompt its hearers to take unlawful action, and advocacy that such action be taken." The *Jencks* case required that Federal Bureau of Investigation reports, if used by the prosecution in a criminal trial, be made available to the defense. These decisions stirred up passing furor and led to right-wing rage at the Court. In the longer run their impact was less drastic than civil libertarians hoped or than the heirs of McCarthy feared.

Thoughtful critics felt at times that the activism of the Warren Court was carrying the judiciary into questions of policy that properly belonged to legislative or executive processes. Defenders replied that legislative and executive inertia had created a vacuum of power, which, if not filled by the Supreme Court, would have severely strained the bonds of social order.

The Second Term As a national hero, above politics, Eisenhower enjoyed a popularity far exceeding that of his party. In 1954, the Democrats took control of both the House and the Senate. In spite of a coronary thrombosis in 1955 and ileitis in 1956, Eisenhower decided to run for reelection. Most voters accepted with sympathy his need for a more carefully regulated life, made affectionate jokes about his long hours on the golf course, and accorded him undiminished confidence. Though Eisenhower several times suggested to Nixon that he might prefer a Cabinet post, the vice president ignored the hint and secured renomination.

The Democrats, over the brief opposition of Harry Truman, renominated Adlai Stevenson, whose penetrating comment on national issues had kept him in the forefront among the party leaders. Estes Kefauver of Tennessee, who had been Stevenson's chief rival till shortly before the convention, received the vice-presidential nomination over John F. Kennedy of Massachusetts. Eisenhower won decisively, carrying the popular vote by 35.6 to 26 million and the Electoral College by 457 to 73. The Democrats slightly increased their majorities in both houses.

If Eisenhower's first term had seen the end of both the Korean War and McCarthyism — if, indeed, only a Republican could perhaps have presided so tranquilly over the liquidation of those angry issues — his second term proved less successful. The administration's reluctance to move swiftly against 7.5 percent unemployment in 1958 damaged confidence, and its claim to moral rectitude was tarnished in a series of scandals. These scandals forced the resignation of the secretary of the air force, the chair of the Republican National Committee, the chair of the Interstate Commerce Commission, the General Services administrator, the Public Buildings administrator, a number of lesser officials, and, finally, in September 1958, Sherman Adams, the assistant to the president.

The 1958 elections brought a Democratic landslide. The Democratic majority in the House — 282 to 153 — was the largest since 1936. In addition, the Democrats gained a 62 to 34 majority in the Senate. But the Democratic sweep had little effect on the president's conservative policies. The departure of the moderate Adams, ironically, gave Eisenhower's more conservative inclinations free play. His posture in domestic affairs remained to the end one of dogged defense of the budget.

THE AMERICAN PEOPLE IN THE 1950s

A Homogenized Society? During Truman's second term, fighting in Korea had retarded but not diverted the post–Second World War developments that were remaking American society and culture. The momentum of the wartime economy, assisted by the GI bill, carried forward as the gross national product rose 250 percent between 1945 and 1960, with per capita income in that period increasing 35 percent. During Eisenhower's presidency, 60 percent of the American people came to live in families that had incomes between $3,000 and $10,000 a year — incomes then defined as middle class. Technological advances led to higher productivity, with automation now achieving labor-savings with a rapidity greater even than that in the 1920s. New devices like computers and television revolutionized at once the ways Americans worked and the ways they used their leisure. As one consequence of new technologies, the economy of 1956 employed more white-collar than blue-collar laborers, a change that weakened the union movement and drew more and more women into the working force. But women were virtually excluded from the pools of talent from which the great corporations — General Electric, American Telephone and Telegraph, International Business Machines, and the like — recruited their expanding managerial elite.

By the 1950s, worn out by 20 years of crisis, Americans sought respite from public issues. They wanted security rather than adventure, comfort rather than challenge. They believed they found those qualities in the family life that characterized the decade. The rates of marriages and of child birth, up during the war years, continued to increase. New and growing families stimulated the consumerism that helped spur the economy. The demand of new families for housing prompted the growth of suburbs — between 1956 and 1960, 11 million of 13 million new homes were built in suburbs. New homes created related demands for stoves, refrigerators, and other household conveniences. Suburban living required, too, the ownership of a car, sometimes two cars. And the children of the baby boom needed food and clothes, and soon needed new schools.

At home or at work, American society preferred those who lacked rough edges, eschewed eccentricity, and played the company game. In a training film circulated by a leading chemical firm, the sound track said, as the camera panned over men in white coats at a Monsanto laboratory, "No geniuses here; just a bunch of average Americans working together." More and more people were spending their lives in organizations — their days in great corporations, their nights in great suburban enclaves. By 1960 the suburban population had increased nearly 50 percent in a decade and almost equaled that the central cities. Both corporation and suburb appeared to foster a pervasive, and benign conformity. America had become, it was said, a case of the bland leading the bland.

It was especially so for American women who were supposed, according to the prevailing assumptions of the time, to stay home, care for the children, join community organizations, and see to their husbands' needs. Those activities, so the theory held, would provide a full and satisfying life. That "feminine mystique"—in the later phrase of Betty Freidan—ignored the millions of married and unmarried women who were in the labor market and the millions of other women who found housekeeping routines suffocating.

The compelling medium of television advanced the homogenization of American culture. Originally developed in the 1930s, television went on the market in the late 1940s. In 1950, 3.2 million Americans owned sets; in 1960, 50 million. By 1960 more households had television than had running water or indoor toilets. Programming was dominated by three large networks and a collection of advertising agencies. The result dismayed thoughtful viewers. Edward R. Murrow, a news commentator who himself did much to elevate the medium, wrote, "Television in the main is being used to distract, delude, amuse and insulate."

Most striking of all was the hold the mood of quiescence seemed to have on the young. Older generations, recalling their springtimes of revolt—cultural in the 1920s, political in the 1930s—looked with incredulity on this "uncommitted generation" composed of prudent young men and women who shunned risk and subordinated everything to a steady job, a house in the suburbs, and a company retirement plan—a generation apparently fearful of politics, mistrustful of ideas, incurious about society, desperate about personal security.

Even the church threatened to become an instrument of the new acquiescence. Though religious statistics are notoriously unreliable, it appears that in the second quarter of the century church membership grew twice as fast as population. This religiosity was conspicuously indifferent, however, to historical religion. Eighty percent of those responding to one public opinion poll claimed they regarded the Bible as the revealed word of God, but only 35 percent could name the four Gospels and over half could not name one. Belief was deemed good in general. As Eisenhower said, "Our government makes no sense unless it is founded in a deeply felt religious faith—and I don't care what it is." Religion became a part of "belonging," a convenient way to establish social identity.

In place of the austere intellectual structure of the traditional faiths, the best-selling religious books of the period purveyed a "cult of reassurance"—Rabbi Joshua Loth Liebmann's *Peace of Mind* (1946), Bishop

The compelling medium: to distract and amuse

Fulton J. Sheen's *Peace of Soul* (1949), the Reverend Norman Vincent Peale's *The Power of Positive Thinking* (1952). Such books portrayed God as the man upstairs, someone up there watching over us, the everlasting source of protection and comfort. The nondoctrinal faith seemed designed to guarantee success for the individual in his career and victory for the nation in its struggle against atheistic communism.

Stirrings under the Surface Yet under the complacent surface of the 1950s, other tendencies were at work. The religious community, for example, did not watch the outburst of popular religiosity with unqualified enthusiasm. The "neo-orthodoxy" of Reinhold Niebuhr, especially as formulated in *The Nature and Destiny of Man* (1941, 1943), had profound influence among believers and nonbelievers alike as a majestic restatement of traditional Christian insights. Where the cult of reassurance identified faith with middle-class values, the Niebuhrians insisted on the independence of Christian faith from the official culture. Where one used faith to sanction the status quo, the other urged the church to reestablish transcendent norms. Niebuhr himself sharply criticized the notion that public avowals demonstrated authentic belief. "The greatest corruption of all," he wrote, "is a corrupt religion." He agreed that religion could produce peace of soul, but not the peace of positive thoughts or of self-congratulation. True religion aimed rather at the "peace of God which passeth all understanding." "That peace passes understanding," added Niebuhr, "precisely because it is a peace with pain in it." The object of faith was to induce not contentment but contrition, not complacency but repentance.

The intellectual community weighed the decade and found it smug and torpid. Novelists and social critics portrayed American conformism in such books as David Reisman's *The Lonely Crowd* (1952), Sloan Wilson's *The Man in the Gray Flannel Suit* (1955), and W. H. Whyte, Jr.'s, *The Organization Man* (1956). In *The Affluent Society* (1958), J. K. Galbraith pointed out that economic growth had produced a combination of private opulence and public squalor and had notably failed to eradicate poverty.

As the rise of the "lost generation" had expressed a rejection of Babbittry by the youth of the 1920s, so the rise of the "beat generation" expressed a dissent by the youth of the 1950s from the ethos of affluence. These rebels were more chaotic and pitiful than their lighthearted and talented predecessors. Hipsters and beatniks admired "cool cats" like the actors James Dean and Marlon Brando and lost no opportunity to exhibit their contempt for the "squares" of the world. These young rebels rejected the suffocating embrace of a conformist society. Most Americans dismissed them as "rebels without a cause," dedicated to an aimless flight from responsibility. As the beat novelist Jack Kerouac put it in an exchange between two characters in *On The Road* (1957), "We gotta go and never stop going till we get there." "Where we going, man?" "I don't know, but we gotta go."

James Dean: one cool cat

END OF THE EISENHOWER ERA

The Election of 1960 Voters faced the election of 1960 in a troubled state of mind. After the shooting down of the U-2 over Soviet Russia, the request of the Japanese government that, in view of anti-American riots in Tokyo, Eisenhower cancel a scheduled presidential visit provided further evidence of a decline in American influence. Within the United States, the rise of unemployment to over 6 percent caused new problems for the Republicans.

Vice President Nixon won the Republican nomination with Henry Cabot Lodge of Massachusetts as his running mate. The Democrats turned to Senator John F. Kennedy of Massachusetts, who had eliminated

Senator Hubert Humphrey of Minnesota in crucial primaries. The Democratic Senate leader, Lyndon B. Johnson, who ran second to Kennedy in the convention, accepted the vice-presidential nomination.

The 1960 campaign was marked by an innovation in American politics—a series of television debates in which the two candidates responded to questions put by newspaper reporters. Kennedy's poise and command in these confrontations countered the Republican argument that he was too young and inexperienced for the presidency. The campaign itself revolved around the question of America's condition as a nation. The United States, Kennedy contended, was falling behind both in the world competition with communism and in meeting its own goals of economic growth and social progress. The process of decline could be reversed only by a "supreme national effort" under strong presidential leadership to "get the country moving again"—a "New Frontier."

The popular vote was the closest since 1888. With the admission of Alaska (January 3, 1959) and Hawaii (August 21, 1959), there were now 50 states in the Union. Kennedy's popular margin was only 119,057 out of 68.3 million votes (see Map 31-2). Taking into account the votes for splinter-party candidates, he was a minority victor. The margin in the Electoral College was more decisive—303 for Kennedy to 219 for Nixon (with 15 Southern votes for Senator Harry F. Byrd of Virginia).

The Eisenhower Record Like Washington and Jackson, Eisenhower left behind a testament for the American people in the form of a farewell address. Speaking with unaccustomed directness, he said that public policy could become "the captive of a scientific-technological élite" and warned against "the acquisition of unwarranted influence, whether sought or unsought, by the military-industrial complex." Though these had not been themes of his own administration, they identified salient problems of the future.

In domestic policy, Eisenhower's Supreme Court appointments perhaps represented his most distinguished achievement, though ironically the decisions of the Warren Court often dismayed him. His other

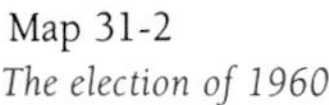

Map 31-2
The election of 1960

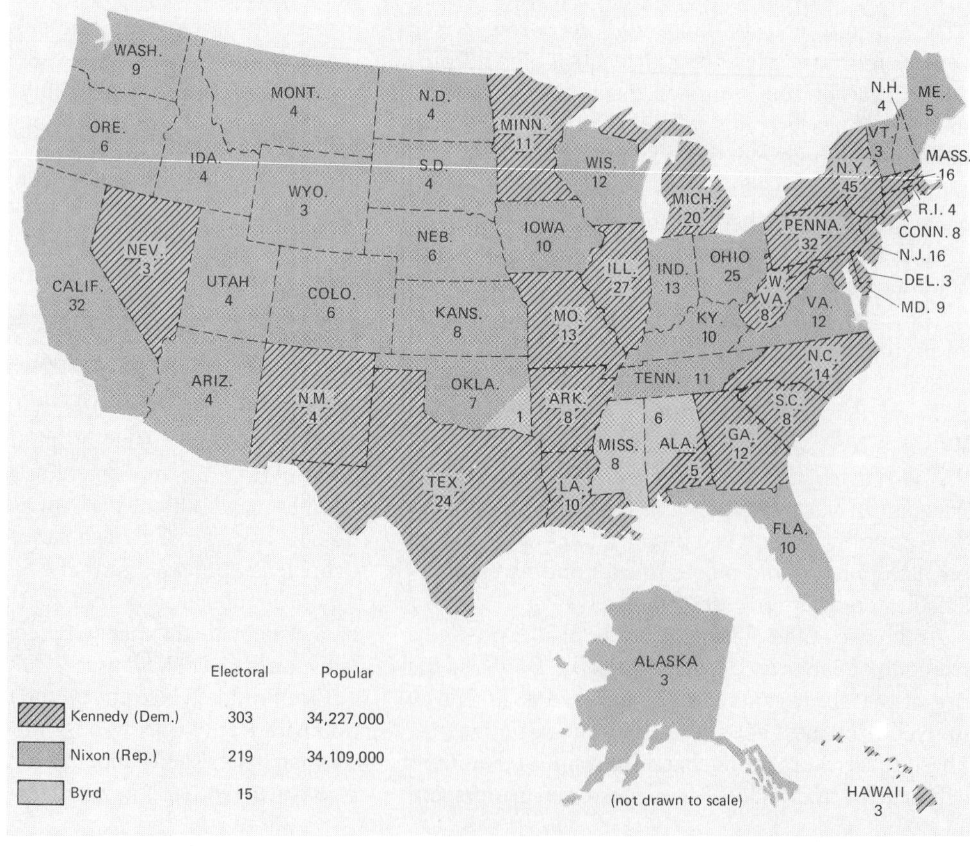

Nixon and Kennedy, 1960: TV, a political innovation

Eisenhower's Farewell Address

The conjunction of an immense military establishment and a large arms industry is new in the American experience. The total influence—economic, political, even spiritual—is felt in every city, every State house, every office of the Federal government. We recognize the imperative need for this development. Yet we must not fail to comprehend its grave implications. Our toil, resources and livelihood are all involved; so is the very structure of our society.

In the councils of government, we must guard against the acquisition of unwarranted influence, whether sought or unsought, by the military-industrial complex. The potential for the disastrous rise of misplaced power exists and will persist. We must never let the weight of this combination endanger our liberties or democratic processes. We should take nothing for granted. . . . Akin to, and largely responsible for the sweeping changes in our industrial-military posture, has been the technological revolution during recent decades. . . . The prospect of domination of the nation's scholars by Federal employment, project allocations, and the power of money is ever present—and is gravely to be regarded. Yet, in holding scientific research and discovery in respect, as we should, we must also be alert to the equal and opposite danger that public policy could itself become the captive of a scientific-technological élite.

From Dwight D. Eisenhower, Farewell Address, January 17, 1961

Eisenhower: president of ability

domestic achievement was to acquiesce in—and thereby legitimize—the changes Franklin Roosevelt had wrought in American society. In domestic affairs, he did little to tackle emerging problems of racial justice, of urban decay, of the environment, of resources and energy—at a time when these problems were still relatively manageable.

In foreign policy, he bequeathed a runaway CIA and a dubious American commitment to undemocratic governments in Southeast Asia. On the day before inauguration, he told Kennedy that the United States should be ready "to intervene unilaterally" in Laos, which he described as the key to that area. As for the Cuban exiles under CIA training, he recommended that "this effort be continued and accelerated."

Yet, for all the bellicosity of this valedictory counsel, his own administration had been a rare interlude of peace in an age of continuous war. Whether through good luck or good management or a combination of both, the American government concluded one war and began no others during the Eisenhower presidency. The people would remember the man of war as a man of peace, and historians eventually discovered that the apparently passive general had been, behind the mask, a president of force and ability.

SUGGESTIONS FOR READING

EISENHOWER AND HIS POLICIES

Eisenhower's memoirs—*The White House Years,* vol. 2, *Mandate for Change* (1963), and vol. 3, *Waging Peace* (1965)—are instructive but formal. The more authentic voice is to be found in R. H. Ferrell, ed., *The Eisenhower Diaries* (1961). The standard biography is S. E. Ambrose, *Eisenhower,* 2 vols. (1983–84); see also H. Parmet, *Eisenhower and the American Crusades* (1972), and C. C. Alexander, *Holding the Line: The Eisenhower Era* (1975). F. I. Greenstein, *The Hidden-Hand Presidency* (1982), makes the case for Eisenhower's covert leadership skills. S. Adams, W. B. Ewald, Jr., E. Hughes, and A. Larson have written revealing memoirs of the Eisenhower presidency; see also R. M. Nixon, *Six Crises* (1962).

FOREIGN AFFAIRS

R. A. Divine, *Eisenhower and the Cold War* (1981), is useful but uncritical and omits Eisenhower's use of the CIA; for which, see J. Prados, *Presidents' Secret Wars* (1986); B. W. Cook, *The Declassified Eisenhower* (1981); and, for the Guatemala case, S. C. Schlesinger and Stephen Kinzer, *Bitter Fruit: The Untold Story of the American Coup in Guatemala* (1982). Townsend Hoopes, *The Devil and John Foster Dulles* (1973), is an able critical biography; R. W. Pruessen, *John Foster Dulles: The Road to Power* (1982), is more sympathetic. B. I. Kaufman, *Trade and Aid: Eisenhower's Foreign Policy, 1953–1961* (1982), is an excellent treatment of economic aspects, as is D. B. Kunz, *The Economic Diplomacy of the Suez Crisis* (1991). R. H. Fifield, *Americans in Southeast Asia: The Roots of Commitment* (1973), sets the Vietnam scene. D. A. Mayers, *Cracking the Monolith* (1986), describes attempts to sever the Sino-Soviet alliance. Peter Grose, *Israel and the Mind of America* (1984), surveys American attitudes and policies. M. Eisenhower, *The Wine is Bitter* (1963), discusses Latin American problems; and P. W. Bonsal, *Cuba, Castro and the United States* (1971), is an authoritative account by the American ambassador to Cuba in 1959–60. For the U-2 affair, see M. R. Beschloss, *Mayday* (1986).

DOMESTIC ISSUES

P. A. Carter, *Another Part of the Fifties* (1983), is a lively and opinionated survey of politics and culture. J. L. Sundquist, *Politics and Policy: The Eisenhower, Kennedy, and Johnson Years* (1968), provides a cogent review of public policy. S. Lubell, *The Revolt of the Moderates* (1956), is a searching contemporaneous diagnosis of the electorate. J. B. Martin, *Adlai Stevenson,* 2 vols. (1976–77), and P. McKeever,

Adlai Stevenson (1989), are first-rate biographies. T. H. White offers a memorable picture of the 1960 election in *The Making of the President, 1960* (1961).

On McCarthyism at high noon and at twilight, see, in addition to works mentioned in Chapter 30, J. A. Wechsler, *The Age of Suspicion* (1953); P. M. Stern, *The Oppenheimer Case* (1969); and Stanley Kutler, *The American Inquisition* (1982). W. L. O'Neill, *A Better World: The Great Schism: Stalinism and the American Intellectuals* (1982), and M. S. McAuliffe, *Crisis on the Left: Cold War Politics and American Liberals* (1978), give diverging pictures of liberal opinion.

H. Sitkoff, *The Struggle for Black Equality, 1954–1980* (1981), and R. Weisbrot, *Freedom Bound* (1990), are able surveys. R. Kluger, *Simple Justice* (1975), is a rich account of the school desegregation decision of 1954. A. Lewis, *Portrait of a Decade* (1964), and J. H. Wilkinson, III, *From Brown to Bakke: The Supreme Court and School Integration, 1954–1978* (1979), describe the aftermath. M. L. King, Jr., *Stride Toward Freedom* (1958), is a central document in the black revolution, as are D. J. Garrow, *Bearing the Cross: Martin Luther King and the Southern Christian Leadership Conference* (1986), and T. Branch, *Parting the Waters: America in the King Years* (1988). B. Schwartz, *Super Chief: Earl Warren and His Supreme Court* (1983), is the standard biography; and R. H. Saylor, B. B. Boyer, and R. E. Goodling, Jr., eds., *The Warren Court: A Critical Analysis* (1969), is informed and sympathetic, as is P. Murphy, *The Constitution in Crisis Times* (1972). A. M. Bickel, *The Supreme Court and Idea of Progress* (1970), enters a thoughtful dissent.

For appraisals of American society, E. Larrabee, *The Self-Conscious Society* (1960), is a useful review. The more enduring works include J. K. Galbraith, *American Capitalism: The Concept of Countervailing Power* (1952); W. H. Whyte, Jr., *The Organization Man* (1956); and for an eclectic view, M. Lerner, *America As a Civilization* (1957). The values of the business community are discussed in F. X. Sutton et al., *The American Business Creed* (1956). C. W. Mills offers a radical analysis in *White Collar* (1951) and *The Power Elite* (1956). For the mass media, see D. J. Boorstin, *The Image* (1962). On the religious boom, see W. Herberg, *Protestant-Catholic-Jew* (2d ed., 1960), and W. L. Miller, *Piety Along the Potomac: Notes on Politics and Morals in the Fifties* (1964). B. Cook, *The Beat Generation* (1971), is an effective account. On women and on the family, some of the most important works are B. Friedan, *The Feminine Mystique* (1963); W. H. Chafe, *The American Woman* (rev. ed., 1988); E. T. May, *Homeward Bound: American Families in the Cold War Era* (1988); A. Kessler-Harris, *Out to Work: A History of White Working-class Women in the United States* (1982), and D. Miller and M. Nowack, *The Fifties: The Way We Really Were* (1977). See, too, R. Acuna, *Occupied America: A History of Chicanos* (rev. ed., 1988).

CHAPTER THIRTY-TWO

MARCH ON WASHINGTON, 1963

REFORM AND REVOLT

John F. Kennedy, 43 years old on his inauguration, was the youngest man and the first Roman Catholic elected to the American presidency as well as the first president born in the twentieth century. Scion of a numerous, spirited, and wealthy Irish-American family, a Harvard graduate and war hero, he was elected after the war to the House of Representatives and in 1952 to the Senate. His book *Profiles in Courage* received the Pulitzer Prize for biography in 1957. Handsome in appearance and graceful in manner, cool, lucid, and ironic in play of mind — he once described himself as an "idealist without illusions"— activist in temperament and purpose, he had an affirmative view of the presidency and a high sense of America's national and world responsibilities. He was proficient in the game of politics, but he also hoped, in the manner of Wilson and Roosevelt, to tap resources of idealism he felt had been too long repressed in American society. "Ask not," he said in his inaugural address, "what your country can do for you; ask what you can do for your country." He attracted and appointed men and women of ideas, making Washington a center of intellectual excitement as it had not been since the New Deal 30 years before. "He was the last president," one of his admirers said, "for whom it was fun to work."

THE THOUSAND DAYS

Kennedy and the Cold War Though a child of the Cold War, the new president saw it not as a religious but as a geopolitical conflict. Still, in those terms, the Cold War seemed active enough, especially after a militant speech delivered by Khrushchev on January 6, 1961, two weeks before Kennedy's inauguration. The Soviet leader exultantly predicted the irresistible triumph of communism, especially — in passages that alarmed Washington — through Soviet support for "national liberation wars" in the Third World.

Khrushchev's bellicosity was probably intended less as a provocation to the United States than as part of a complex maneuver involving China. For he also took occasion to reaffirm his rejection of nuclear war and his belief in "peaceful coexistence"— views that Communist China continued to oppose. By insisting on them in an otherwise truculent context, Khrushchev may have been trying to show the Communist movement that nuclear coexistence was not incompatible with revolution in the Third World. Perhaps he thought militancy would bemuse the Chinese, while softer words would gratify the West. But Beijing (Peking) and Washington read only the passages written for the other.

Kennedy responded grandiloquently in his inaugural address: "Let every nation know, whether it wishes us well or ill, that we shall pay any price, bear any burden, meet any hardship, support any friend, oppose any foe, in order to assure the survival and the success of liberty." The irony was that both leaders wanted to escape from the arms race. While Khrushchev hoped to decrease the risk of nuclear catastrophe without losing ground to China, Kennedy believed that a third world war would mean the end of civilization. His inaugural address went on to condemn the arms race, asked to "bring the absolute power to destroy other nations under the absolute control of all nations," and declared: "Let us never negotiate out of fear. But let us never fear to negotiate."

The World of Diversity Dean Rusk, the new secretary of state, held tenacious Cold War views. Adlai Stevenson, now ambassador to the United Nations, was moving beyond his Cold War positions of the 1950s. Kennedy himself, despite his inaugural extravagance, had an acute sense of the limitations of American power. Later in 1961 he called on the American people to "face the fact that the United States is neither omnipotent nor omniscient—that we are only 6 percent of the world's population—that we cannot impose our will upon the other 94 percent of mankind—that we cannot right every wrong or reverse each adversity—and that therefore there cannot be an American solution to every world problem."

Kennedy thus had no illusions about the feasibility of a *pax Americana.* But he did not intend to leave the world to the Russians. His broad idea, which he set forth to Khrushchev in a meeting in Vienna in June 1961, was that each superpower should abstain from initiatives that, by upsetting the rough balance into which the postwar world had settled, might invite miscalculation and compel reaction by the other. In the longer run, Kennedy envisioned a "world of diversity"—a world of nations various in institutions and creeds, where "every country can solve its own problems according to its own traditions and ideals." Communism could be one element in this pluralistic world, but diversity, he argued, was ultimately incompatible with the Communist belief that all societies went through the same stages and all roads had a single destination. In a speech at American University in June 1963 he summed up his policy in a conscious revision of Wilson's famous line: "If we cannot now end our differences, at least we can help make the world safe for diversity."

Struggle for the Third World Given the nuclear stalemate, Kennedy agreed with Khrushchev that the Third World had become the main battleground between democracy and communism. But he accepted

Khrushchev and Kennedy, Vienna, 1961: "a world of diversity"

neutralism as a legitimate choice for states struggling for nationhood outside the framework of the Cold War. Kennedy's purpose was to encourage the developing countries of Africa, Asia, and Latin America to use democratic methods in their quest for independence and growth. An increasing share of American foreign aid now went to modernize economies rather than to build armies. The Peace Corps — an undertaking especially close to Kennedy's heart — channeled the idealism of individual Americans into face-to-face cooperation in the developing countries. Kennedy himself sought to improve relations with nationalist leaders, a course pursued with some success in black Africa.

There remained the problem of protecting the fragile democratization process against Communist disruption — the problem spotlighted by Khrushchev's fervent espousal of national liberation wars. The American view was that with the nuclear standoff reducing the threat of general war, the great danger to world peace would come if local crises in the Third World led to Soviet-American confrontation. To prevent this, it seemed necessary to persuade Moscow to abandon the strategy of national liberation wars. The search for ways of frustrating Soviet attempts to exploit insurgencies in the Third World became a Washington obsession.

The initial answer was thought to lie in teaching countries under attack to combat Communist guerrillas through techniques of "counterinsurgency." On Kennedy's personal insistence, counterinsurgency schools were established, and elite counterinsurgency units, like the Green Berets, were organized. The theory was that counterinsurgency would operate within a context of social reform. But the political component did not take root, and the counterinsurgency mystique primarily nourished the American belief in the capacity and right to intervene in foreign lands. It brought out the worst in the overconfident activism of the New Frontier: the faith that American energy and technology could solve everything; the officious pragmatism that could quickly degenerate into cynical manipulation.

Latin America: Crisis and Hope It also provided a new outlet for the energies of the CIA. The potential conflict between the constructive and aggressive sides of Kennedy's Third World policy became manifest early in the new administration. Kennedy had inherited from Eisenhower the force of anti-Castro Cubans trained and equipped by the CIA for an invasion of their homeland. Though his advisers were divided about that project, Kennedy gave the expedition the go ahead.

On April 17, 1961, about 1,200 Cubans landed at the Bahia de Cochinas (Bay of Pigs), on the southern coast of Cuba. The American hand could not be concealed. After three days the invasion collapsed. To the world, and to many Americans, the Bay of Pigs was an indefensible exercise in intervention. Refusing escalation, Kennedy spurned proposals that he send in the

Anti-Castro Cubans in Miami, 1961

marines and took full responsibility for the fiasco, remarking wryly that victory had a hundred fathers but defeat was an orphan.

In the longer run, he pursued a policy directed toward Cuba's economic and diplomatic isolation. The CIA developed "Operation Mongoose," a program of covert action designed to encourage resistance and sabotage in Cuba. It even continued to plot the assassination of Castro, though with the usual nonsuccess. Those in charge of this project did not disclose it to John McCone, who became CIA director after the Bay of Pigs, nor, so far as is known, to Kennedy himself. The CIA pinpricks had little effect, except to irritate Castro, who continued to incite guerrilla action against democratic regimes in Latin America.

Kennedy's main reliance, however, was on the Alliance for Progress, a program designed to use United States aid to advance economic development and democratic reform through the hemisphere. "Those who make peaceful revolution impossible," Kennedy told the Latin American diplomatic corps, "will make violent revolution inevitable"; and the Alliance insisted, to the dismay of both North American business and Latin American oligarchies, on economic planning and structural change within a democratic framework. At a conference at Punta del Este, Uruguay, in August 1961 the Latin American states, except for Cuba, subscribed to the goals of the Alliance. Castro himself called the Alliance "a politically wise concept put forth to hold back the time of revolution . . . a very intelligent strategy."

The Alliance was accompanied by a determined effort to reinforce progressive democracy in Latin America. When an army coup nullified the results of a presidential election in Peru in 1962, Kennedy suspended relations until the military junta pledged new elections. His dramatically successful visits to Venezuela, Colombia, Mexico, and Central America enabled the United States for a moment to recover its popularity of Good Neighbor days. No president since Roosevelt had shown such interest in the hemisphere.

Trouble in Southeast Asia Another troubling inheritance was the crisis in Laos. Kennedy, who felt in general that the United States was "overcommitted" in Southeast Asia, felt in particular that neither superpower had enough at stake in Laos to justify armed confrontation. He consequently rejected Eisenhower's counsel of unilateral American military intervention. Instead he sought neutralization under the leadership of Prince Souvanna Phouma.

Khrushchev concurred at Vienna, and in 1962 the superpowers agreed on a neutralist coalition including representatives of the prowestern faction and of the Communist Pathet Lao. True neutrality was not, however, achieved. North Vietnam continued to send supplies to the Viet Cong in South Vietnam via the Ho Chi Minh trails in southeastern Laos and maintained a military presence in Laos to protect the infiltration effort. In response, a CIA mission aided the Souvanna Phouma government. When Pathet Lao ministers withdrew from the coalition in 1963, the Pathet Lao insurgency resumed in the northeast. The result was de facto partition.

In South Vietnam, the situation appeared militarily more manageable. In the spring of 1961 Vice President Johnson, on a visit to Saigon, pronounced Diem the Churchill of South Asia, and said on his return, "We must decide whether to help these countries to the best of our ability or throw in the towel in the area and pull back our defenses to San Francisco." Kennedy sent a small force of Green Berets to instruct the South Vietnamese army in the black arts of counterinsurgency, thereby breaching the Geneva Accords of 1955 (see p. 817). Despite the great numerical superiority of the South Vietnamese forces—250,000 in November 1961 against 15,000 Viet Cong—the situation of the Saigon government grew worse. A presidential mission, headed by General Maxwell Taylor, recommended the dispatch of an American combat force—perhaps 10,000 men—and urged air strikes against the "ultimate source of aggression" in North Vietnam.

Kennedy rejected these recommendations. Nevertheless, he feared that the "loss" of Vietnam would have adverse political consequences at home and abroad and accepted the theory that the assignment of American military "advisers" to the South Vietnamese army would stiffen resistance. By 1962 American helicopters and personnel were taking a limited part in the fighting. At the same time, Kennedy urged the Diem regime to enlarge its base by political and economic reform. Diem disdained that advice.

Deeper into the Quagmire The Viet Cong continued to gain, and Buddhist protests against the Saigon government in the spring of 1963 demonstrated Diem's failure to unite his people. Diem's brother Ngo Dinh Nhu urged him on to further repression. Kennedy intensified pressure on Diem to get rid of his brother and reform his regime.

Henry Cabot Lodge, sent to Saigon in August as American ambassador to carry out this policy, was confronted by new outrages against the Buddhists. Washington was angrily divided about whether to support or abandon Diem, and one cable to Saigon, not fully cleared with Kennedy, assured dissident Vietnamese generals that, if there was a coup, a new regime would receive American support. In October, with Lodge's knowledge, the generals prepared for a coup. On November 1 they overthrew and murdered Diem and Nhu—whom Lodge had arranged to fly out of the country—and South Vietnam moved into a new phase of turmoil.

Kennedy never clarified his views on Vietnam. On the one hand, he accepted the domino theory; "for us to withdraw," he said in July 1963, ". . . would mean a collapse not only of South Vietnam but of Southeast Asia." While regarding the United States as overcommitted in Southeast Asia, Kennedy felt that, the commitment having been made, America could not let South Vietnam fall cheaply to the Communists. He increased the number of American advisers to 16,732 by the end of 1963, though only 73 died in combat in these years.

On the other hand, his memory of the French failure a decade before convinced him that a "white man's war" would only rally Vietnamese nationalism against the alien presence. He rigorously opposed the dispatch of American combat units, American bombers, and any total commitment to the salvation of South Vietnam. "In the final analysis," he said of the people of South Vietnam in September 1963, "it is their war. They are the ones who have to win it or lose it."

In July 1962 he had ordered the Pentagon to prepare a plan for American disengagement within several years. In October 1963 he announced the first troop withdrawal, enjoining his secretary of defense that this meant "all the helicopter pilots too." He confided to Mike Mansfield, the Senate majority leader, that his goal was total withdrawal; "but I can't do it until 1965—after I'm reelected." Still by failing to proclaim this intention, lest the prospect of an American pullout undermine the Saigon government, and by enlarging the American role, Kennedy complicated the problems of subsequent disengagement. The overthrow of Diem drew the United States further into the quagmire.

From "Massive Retaliation" to "Flexible Response"

Confronted by Khrushchev's Cold War of movement, Kennedy felt that the "massive retaliation" strategy of relying on nuclear weapons to deter local as well as general war increased the risk of nuclear holocaust. Secretary of Defense Robert S. McNamara, a professor turned industrial manager, therefore began the diversification of American military force so that the level of reaction could be graduated to meet the level of threat—a shift in strategic doctrine to "flexible response." This shift required an increase in the American capability for conventional war. It was designed primarily to enable the West to respond to Soviet aggression in Europe without immediate resort to nuclear weapons. The fateful side effect was to create forces that could be used in limited "brushfire" wars elsewhere in the world.

Moreover, Kennedy was imprisoned by the "missile gap" illusion he had himself expounded during his campaign. He therefore yielded to Pentagon pressure and in the spring of 1961 requested not only more conventional force but more long-range nuclear missiles. When new reconnaissance satellites disproved the "missile gap," the American buildup was already under way.

The buildup had baleful consequences. It was more than American security demanded, it ended any hope of freezing the rival missile forces at lower levels, and it sent the wrong message to Moscow, compelling Khrushchev to worry about his own missile gap. In September 1961 the Soviet Union began an extensive series of tests in the atmosphere, exploding in October a device nearly 3,000 times more powerful than the bomb dropped on Hiroshima.

The Kennedy-McNamara hope was to achieve a "stable balance of terror" by moving toward a situation in which both superpowers would have sufficient deterrent strength to absorb a surprise first strike and retain the ability to retaliate. Rejecting proposals that the United States aim for a first-strike capability, McNamara argued that overwhelming superiority on one side might tempt the other to launch a preemptive strike in a time of crisis. The best way to avoid nuclear war, he contended, was for each superpower to have a "secure second-strike capability"—an idea he hoped to persuade the Russians to accept, thereby introducing rationality into the arms race. This was the doctrine of "mutual assured destruction" (whose acronym MAD gave great pleasure to its opponents). McNamara recommended to Kennedy and later to Lyndon Johnson that "they never initiate, under any circumstances, the use of nuclear weapons. I believe they accepted my recommendations." Unlike Eisenhower, neither Kennedy nor Johnson ever threatened nonretaliatory nuclear strikes.

For the longer run, Kennedy wanted to stop the arms race altogether. Speaking before the United Nations in 1961, he presented a plan for general and complete disarmament. "Mankind," he said, "must put an end to war—or war will put an end to mankind." The appeal fell on deaf ears. With reluctance, Kennedy himself resumed atmospheric testing in April 1962. So the two superpowers, still in the lockstep of the Cold War, proceeded to intensify the arms race.

Kennedy and Khrushchev The Vienna meeting in June 1961 had not been a success. Doubtless misled by the Bay of Pigs into seeing Kennedy as irresolute, Khrushchev brusquely rejected Kennedy's proposal of a global standstill and adopted an intransigent, even bullying, attitude on most questions.

For Moscow, Germany remained a critical issue, the more so because of the rising flow of refugees—now 30,000 a month—from East Germany into West Berlin. Khrushchev told Kennedy that he planned to conclude with East Germany a peace treaty that would extinguish Western rights in West Berlin. Kennedy replied that so drastic an alteration in the world balance of power was unacceptable. Khrushchev said, if America wanted war over Berlin, there was nothing the Soviet Union could do about it; he would sign the treaty by December 31. Kennedy commented, "It will be a cold winter."

Returning to the United States, Kennedy requested a further increase in the defense budget, called out 150,000 reservists, and announced a program, which set off an ugly outburst of near panic and which he soon regretted, of fallout shelters for protection against nuclear attack. Though these measures soon came to seem an overreaction, they may have persuaded Khrushchev that he could not gain his Berlin objective by intimidation. In addition, Kennedy, acknowledging Russia's security interests in Eastern Europe, declared his readiness to work out arrangements "to meet these concerns." On August 13 the East Germans erected the Berlin Wall, thereby stopping the refugee flow. Khrushchev postponed his treaty deadline in October, and the Berlin crisis subsided.

In Western Europe, Kennedy hoped for steady movement toward unification, particularly through the admission of Great Britain to the European Economic Community (see p. 791). To this end, he secured the passage in September 1962 of the Trade Expansion Act, creating authority to negotiate tariff reductions up to 50 percent for the purpose of bargaining with an enlarged Common Market. But Kennedy's so-called grand design for Europe was frustrated by French president Charles de Gaulle's veto of British membership—an action that deferred British entry until 1972. In the meantime, the "Kennedy Round" of tariff negotiations led to significant reductions of barriers to world trade.

The Missile Crisis In the summer of 1962, in an audacious gamble Khrushchev decided, over Castro's initial objection, to establish nuclear missile bases in Cuba. The Russians had never before placed their missiles in any other country. If successful, the operations would not only protect Cuba from American invasion—the objective later alleged by Khrushchev (though this could have been more simply achieved by stationing Soviet troops on the island)—but would give Russia a potent bargaining counter when it chose to reopen the Berlin question. Moreover, by making shorter-range missiles effective against American targets, it would increase Soviet nuclear first-strike capacity against American targets by half. And it would deal America a shattering political blow by showing the Soviet capacity to penetrate the American sphere of influence. "Our missiles," Khrushchev later declared in his memoirs, "would have equalized . . . 'the balance of power.' "

Washington had not objected to Russian supply of defensive weapons to Cuba. But Kennedy warned in September 1962 that, if there was evidence of "significant offensive capability either in Cuban hands or under Soviet direction . . . the gravest issues would arise." Khrushchev repeatedly denied publicly and privately that he had any such intention. Nor did Washington consider such recklessness likely. Then, on October 14, a U-2 overflight found conclusive evidence that Khrushchev had lied.

Kennedy's decision was that, one way or another, the Soviet nuclear missiles had to be removed from Cuba. Critics have suggested that he should have accepted them without protest. After all the Americans had their Jupiter missiles in Turkey. Moreover, the United States would still retain nuclear superiority even after the Cuban buildup. But Kennedy regarded Soviet missile bases in Cuba as "a deliberately provocative and unjustified change in the status quo." If the United States were to accept so gross an intrusion into what the Russians, themselves so particularly sensitive to spheres of interest, had previously respected as the American zone, this, he feared, might embolden Khrushchev to acts that would make the third world war inescapable.

Soviet missiles in Cuba

For six days Kennedy and a small group of advisers debated behind locked doors how best to get the missiles out. One faction, led by Dean Acheson and all but one of the Joint Chiefs of Staff, advocated the destruction of the bases by surprise air attack. The other, led by Attorney General Robert F. Kennedy, the president's brother, and Secretary of Defense McNamara, sharply opposed this course on moral grounds—as a Pearl Harbor in reverse against a small country—and on practical grounds—because it might kill Russians at the missile sites and force the Soviet Union into drastic retaliation. Naval blockade, this group argued, would both show the American determination to get the missiles out and allow Moscow time to pull back. Kennedy announced his course in the first public disclosure of the crisis on October 22—to establish a naval quarantine against further shipments, to demand the dismantling of the bases and the removal of the missiles, and to warn that any nuclear attack launched from Cuba would be regarded "as an attack by the Soviet Union on the United States, requiring a full retaliatory response upon the Soviet Union."

The days that followed were more tense than any since the Second World War. Moscow continued to deny the presence of nuclear weapons until, in a dramatic moment before the United Nations, Ambassador Adlai Stevenson confronted the Soviet delegate with blown-up aerial photographs of the nuclear installations. Meanwhile work was continuing day and night to make the bases operational. An American invasion force was massing in Florida. Soviet ships, presumably carrying more missiles, were drawing near the island. Kennedy kept the interception line close to Cuba to give Khrushchev maximum time for reflection. Finally, after indescribable suspense, Soviet ships began to turn back, "We're eyeball to eyeball," said Dean Rusk, "and I think the other fellow just blinked."

It remained for negotiation to complete the resolution of the crisis. On October 26 Kennedy received a long, passionate letter from Khrushchev dilating on the horror of nuclear war and offering to remove the missiles and send no more if the United States would end the quarantine and agree not to invade Cuba. But on the following morning there arrived a second letter from Khrushchev, harder in tone and proposing an entirely different trade: the Soviet missiles in Cuba for the American missiles in Turkey. Robert Kennedy now recommended that his brother ignore the second letter and respond to the first. The president followed this advice. Robert Kennedy took the American restatement of the first Khrushchev proposal to the Soviet ambassador, who then asked about the Turkish missiles. The attorney general replied that, while this could be no quid pro quo, "it was our judgment that, within a short time after this crisis was over, those missiles would be gone." The next day, October 28, a favorable reply came from Khrushchev.

American University Speech

What kind of peace do we seek? Not a Pax Americana enforced on the world by American weapons of war. Not the peace of the grave or the security of the slave. I am talking about genuine peace. . . . Some say that it is useless to speak of world peace or world law or world disarmament—and that it will be useless until the leaders of the Soviet Union adopt a more enlightened attitude. I hope they do. I believe we can help them do it. But I also believe that we must reexamine our own attitude—as individuals and as a Nation—for our attitude is as essential as theirs. . . . World peace, like community peace, does not require that each man love his neighbor—it requires only that they live together in mutual tolerance, submitting their disputes to a just and peaceful settlement. And history teaches us that enmities between nations, as between individuals, do not last forever. However fixed our likes and dislikes may seem, the tide of time and events will often bring surprising changes in the relations between nations and neighbors. . . .

It is sad to read these Soviet statements—to realize the extent of the gulf between us. But it is also a warning—a warning to the American people not to fall into the same trap as the Soviets, not to see only a distorted and desperate view of the other side, not to see conflict as inevitable, accommodation as impossible, and communication as nothing more than an exchange of threats. No government or social system is so evil that its people must be considered as lacking in virtue. . . . We are both caught up in a vicious and dangerous cycle in which suspicion on one side breeds suspicion on the other, and new weapons beget counterweapons. . . . If we cannot now end our differences, at least we can help make the world safe for diversity. For, in the final analysis, our most basic common link is that we all inhabit this small planet. We all breathe the same air. We all cherish our children's future. And we are all mortal.

From John F. Kennedy, Speech at American University, Washington, D.C., June 10, 1963

The crisis was over. In short order the bases were dismantled and the missiles on their way home. Castro's resistance made it impossible to establish the UN inspection to which Khrushchev had agreed, and the United States never formally completed the reciprocal pledge not to invade Cuba. But in substance the deal went into effect anyway. U-2 overflights took the place of UN inspection; the Jupiter missiles left Turkey; and the United States, which had no intention of invading Cuba in any case, ended hit-and-run raids by Cuban refugees from American territory. In the autumn of 1963 Kennedy initiated secret explorations looking toward a normalization of relations with Cuba.

Détente: 1963 The American success—Kennedy forbade gloating and refused to claim a triumph—was the result of Kennedy's combination of toughness and restraint and of his careful deployment of power. He hoped he had made to Khrushchev the point he had tried to make in Vienna—that neither side dare tamper carelessly with the complex and explosive international equilibrium. Khrushchev, too, had known better than to push on toward nuclear war.

The missile crisis, by forcing both Kennedy and Khrushchev to stare down the nuclear abyss, now brought them into de facto alliance against their own national security bureaucracies. Kennedy renewed his quest for a test-ban treaty, but negotiations bogged down during the spring. In an effort to break the deadlock, Kennedy, in his notable speech at American University in June 1963, called on Americans as well as Russians to rethink the Cold War: "We must reexamine our own attitude—as individuals and as a Nation—for our attitude is as essential as theirs." He rejected the "holy war" ideology: "No government or social system is so evil that its people must be considered as lacking in virtue." Both sides, he said, were "caught up in a viscious and dangerous cycle in which suspicion on one side breeds suspicion on the other, and new weapons beget counterweapons."

The establishment in June 1963 of the "Hot Line," a direct teletype link between the White House and the Kremlin, was a significant attempt to break the cycle by reducing the risk of conflict through misunderstanding or miscalculation. Kennedy's next hope was for a ban on all nuclear testing. But the Joint Chiefs of Staff claimed that a ban on underground tests could not be verified without at least seven annual on-site inspections of earth shocks. The Russians would not accept more than three. Kennedy settled for a limited ban, to which the United States, the Soviet Union, and Britain agreed in Moscow. It outlawed tests in self-policing environments—in the atmosphere, in outer space, and under water. "Yesterday a shaft of light," Kennedy said, "cut into the darkness." The Joint Chiefs conditioned support for the treaty on continuation of underground testing. With this proviso, the Senate ratified the treaty in September by a vote of 80 to 19. The failure to achieve a comprehensive test ban lost a great opportunity to stop the development of ever more appalling weapons. Still the partial test ban, though France and China declined to sign, represented the most significant formal step toward arms control since the onset of the Cold War.

Space The competition between the superpowers produced at least one benign by-product. In April 1961 the Russians put the first man, Yuri Gagarin, into space orbit. On May 25, 1961, Kennedy declared that the United States "should commit itself to achieving the goal, before this decade is out, of landing a man on the moon and returning him safely to earth." The idea was greeted with disapproval by those who thought the money should be spent in meeting human needs on earth and with skepticism by those who doubted whether the project was feasible.

Nonetheless, Kennedy pushed ahead. In February 1962 John Glenn became the first American to enter space orbit; and National Aeronautic and Space Administration (NASA) scientists in the Apollo program were already hard at work breaking down the technical problems of a moonshot. Six months before the deadline, on July 16, 1969, the moonship *Apollo 11* was launched from Cape Kennedy, Florida. On July 20 Captain Neil A. Armstrong became the first man to walk on the moon.

Beating Russia to the moon was not Kennedy's main interest. Indeed, he suggested at Vienna in 1961 and again at the UN in 1963 that the Americans and the Russians go to the moon together. He also recognized the usefulness of the space program for developing new technologies of military importance. Beyond that, he was responding to the newest frontier, to the ultimate challenge and mystery of space itself. When all

Apollo 11: man on the moon

else about the twentieth century is forgotten, as he realized, it may still be remembered as the century when the human race first burst its terrestrial bonds and began the endless voyage, beyond planet and galaxy, into the illimitable dark.

The New Frontier Kennedy's campaign appeal in 1960 had been to get the country moving again. He meant this in a large sense, hoping to lead an intellectual breakaway from the complacency of the Eisenhower years. He meant it too in an immediate economic sense. Inheriting 7 percent unemployment from his predecessor, he responded with a set of expansionist policies: an investment tax credit, liberalization of tax depreciation allowances, worker training programs, and finally general tax reduction, enacted in 1964. During the Kennedy years economic growth averaged 5.6 percent, and unemployment was brought down to 5.7 percent.

Inflation was meanwhile held at 1.2 percent, in part because of "wage-price guideposts" designed to keep wage increases within the limits of advances in productivity. This early form of what came later to be known as "incomes policy" rested on the perception that increased productivity was the only way to increase wages without increasing prices. United States Steel's cavalier rejection of the guideposts led to the steel battle of 1962. When U.S. Steel raised its prices after the administration had persuaded the union to accept a noninflationary wage contract, Kennedy exploded in cold anger—"My father always told me that all businessmen were sons-of-bitches, but I never believed it till now"—and forced the corporation to retract its action.

While general fiscal stimulus increased aggregate output and employment, it did not reach into pockets of localized and "structural" poverty. Income tax reduction, for example, was of little help for people too poor to pay income taxes. In 1960 one out of every five Americans was living in poverty (as officially defined). Kennedy recognized that the poor of the 1960s, unlike the ambitious immigrants of the 1890s or the angry unemployed of the 1930s, were largely a demoralized and inarticulate minority who in many cases had inherited their poverty and accepted it as a permanent condition. He attacked the problem through the Area Redevelopment Act of 1961 and through programs directed at Appalachia, an eleven-state region stretching from Pennsylvania to Alabama and centering in eastern Kentucky and West Virginia. In 1963 he decided that, if the forgotten Americans were to be helped, tax reduction required a counterpart in the form of a comprehensive war on poverty.

Kennedy was more successful in economic management than in social reform. Elected by an exceptionally narrow popular margin, he was confronted in Congress by the powerful coalition of Republicans and Southern Democrats that had dominated domestic policy since 1938. He could do some things, like government support of the arts, through executive orders. But major proposals—federal aid to education, medical care for the aged (Medicare), a Department of Urban Affairs—required statutes and were blocked by the conservative coalition. Kennedy instead dramatized his proposals through presidential messages and speeches, hoping thereby to build public support for their enactment in his second term.

The Black Revolution Kennedy's most signal domestic achievement lay in the field of racial justice. Congressional opposition compelled him to concentrate at first on executive rather than legislative action. Even there, he began by balancing the demands of restive black Americans against the expectations of white Southerners, for both groups had contributed to his victory in 1960. He delayed issuing an order banning discrimination in housing and appointed segregationist judges to federal courts in the South. But pressure grew. Challenged by "freedom riders" defying Jim Crow in interstate bus terminals, Attorney General Robert Kennedy found ways to end segregation in interstate transportation. In October 1962 the president sent federal troops into Oxford, Mississippi, in order to protect James Meredith, a black student, in the right, assured him by the courts, to attend the University of Mississippi. The administration concentrated on the right to vote as the key to the attainment of other rights. It also appointed an unprecedented number of black citizens to higher office.

But Kennedy still underestimated the moral dynamism of the civil rights cause. To the left of Martin Luther King, Jr.'s Southern Christian Leadership Conference rose more militant organizations—the Congress of Racial Equality (CORE) and the Student Nonviolent Coordinating Committee (SNCC). As black discontent grew, so too did Southern resistance. In April 1963, when King began a campaign to end discrimination in shops, restaurants, and employment in Birmingham, Alabama, Police Commissioner Eugene "Bull" Connor harassed King's marchers with

Washington, D.C., 1963: "I have a dream"

firehoses, electric cattle prods, and growling police dogs.

The Birmingham episode, broadcast on network television, caused a surge of indignation throughout the nation. Then, in June, Governor George Wallace of Alabama personally tried to block the admission of two black students to the state university, but he folded under federal pressure. That night Kennedy went on television to pronounce the civil rights question "a moral issue" and to commit the nation to the proposition "that race has no place in American life or law." With this speech he joined the fight for new and more sweeping civil rights legislation.

In August Dr. King led a quarter of a million people, black and white, on a great march in front of the Lincoln Memorial in Washington, where they listened to King's moving eloquence ("I have a dream") and sang the old Baptist hymn the civil rights movement had made its own, "We Shall Overcome." "In the process of gaining our rightful place," King said at the Lincoln Memorial, "we must not be guilty of wrongful deeds. Let us not seek to satisfy our thirst for freedom by drinking from the cup of bitterness and hatred."

But in the same year one black novelist, James Baldwin, in his bitter tract *The Fire Next Time* wrote that the black American "no longer believes in the good faith of white Americans."

Kennedy and America On November 22, 1963, while riding with his wife in an open car through Dallas, Texas, Kennedy was shot and killed. His murder sent a wave of incredulity, shame, and grief across the United States and around the planet.

In the next decades his place in history became a subject of contention. Revisionists portrayed him as a rigid and embattled Cold Warrior. Khrushchev disagreed, writing that Kennedy "understood better than Eisenhower that an improvement in relations was the only rational course." Some dismissed his leadership in domestic affairs as too much style and too little substance. Others, noting his narrow margins in Congress, valued the educational impact of his dramatization of major issues.

On balance it may be said that Kennedy inherited tough problems at home and abroad and had little enough time and parliamentary leverage to do as much about them as he wished. His brief days in the White

Kennedy's funeral: a wave of grief and shame

House were days of steady growth. He made mistakes but candidly acknowledged them and always learned from them. The Kennedy of 1963 was a very different president from the Kennedy of 1961.

Kennedy was neither a saint nor a crusader. His womanizing offended the sensibilities of later generations. His pragmatic approach to national problems contrasted to the passionate commitments of civil rights activists. But Kennedy left a legacy of cautious optimism that the nation could meet its responsibilities. His openness of mind, his faith in reasoned discussion, his ironic, often self-mocking, wit, his generous vision of American possibility, and his irreverence toward conventional ideas provoked a renewal of social idealism and a discharge of energy reminiscent of the Progressive period and the New Deal. He came to be admired in the black community and was the first president since Roosevelt with anything to say to the young. In other lands he was seen as a carrier of American idealism. The nation had good reason to mourn his untimely death.

THE JOHNSON YEARS

The Great Society The presidency now descended to an older political leader, Lyndon Baines Johnson. A Texan, 55 years old, Johnson had come to the vice presidency from 23 years in Congress, ending as Democratic leader of the Senate. No president since Polk had had such impressive legislative experience. He was also the first president from a Southern state since Andrew Johnson a century before. A New Dealer who had become more conservative in his middle years, he retained an authentic concern for the poor and, though a Southerner, for Hispanic and black Americas. His admirers rejoiced in the power of his formidable personality, the sincerity of his social concern, and the resourcefulness with which he pursued his purposes. Others found him egotistical, secretive, devious, and vindictive.

In the national shock after Dallas, the new president took over his responsibilities with firmness. He appointed a commission under Chief Justice Warren to investigate the assassination. The commission reported in 1964 that the murderer was a rootless and embittered former Communist named Lee Harvey Oswald. Critics later challenged both the commission's procedures and its conclusions.

Johnson made clear his determination to continue his predecessor's policies and (unlike Truman in 1945) his predecessor's Cabinet. His experience and inclination led him toward the field of domestic affairs. Both tax-reduction and civil rights bills were on their way to enactment at the time of Kennedy's death, and the rush of national remorse assured them quick passage. The tax cut, injecting $12 billion into the economy, speeded economic growth. The Civil Rights Act of 1964 prohibited discrimination in the use of federal funds and in places of public accommodation and established an Equal Employment Opportunity Commission.

Seeking a distinctive name for his domestic program, Johnson in May 1964 called for a Great Society —"a place where the city of man serves not only the needs of the body and the demands of commerce but the desire for beauty and the hunger for community." The Great Society incorporated and soon extended Kennedy's New Frontier.

The Great Society provided the central issue of the 1964 presidential campaign. Johnson selected the veteran liberal Senator Hubert Humphrey of Minnesota as his running mate. The Republicans nominated Senator Barry Goldwater of Arizona, a likable businessman with inflexibly conservative views. Convinced that the danger to freedom came from government, Goldwater had proposed in *The Conscience of a Conservative* (1960) that the graduated income tax be abolished. He also urged the sale of the

Victory, 1964: HHH and LBJ

TVA, questioned the social security system, and advocated the bombing of North Vietnam. Though Goldwater evoked passionate enthusiasm among his followers, his program and his manager's brusque treatment of his more liberal party opponents alienated many Republicans.

The Johnson-Humphrey ticket won 61.1 percent of the popular vote and carried all but six states—the most decisive presidential triumph since 1936 (see Map 32-1). Victory added 37 Northern Democrats to the House of Representatives—enough to assure, for the first time since 1938, a working progressive majority. This, along with Johnson's commitment to his programs and his skills in handling Congress, produced the most impressive record of domestic legislation in a single session for 30 years.

Long-sought bills for federal aid to education and for medical care to the old (Medicare) and to the poor (Medicaid) were at last enacted. Responding belatedly to the crisis of the cities, Congress passed low-income housing laws, a rent-supplement program, and the Model Cities Act, under which federal block grants encouraged cities to plan their own future. The Voting Rights Act of 1965 outlawed remaining barriers to the right to vote and empowered the national government to register those whom the states refused to put on the voting list. In an executive order of September 24, 1965, Johnson instituted the "affirmative action" policy, requiring federal contractors and institutions receiving federal assistance to make special efforts to employ women and nonwhite citizens. Congress also liberalized the immigration laws, abolishing the national origins quota of 1924; institutionalized federal support for the arts in the National Foundation on the Arts and Humanities Act; established public broadcasting; gave the government authority to set safety standards for automobiles and highways; set standards for clean air and water; and created two new federal departments—Housing and Urban Development (to which Johnson appointed Robert C. Weaver, the first black American to serve in the Cabinet) and Transportation.

Among Great Society programs the most original was the war on poverty, conducted by the Office of Economic Opportunity (OEO). Headed by Sargent Shriver, Kennedy's brother-in-law and former head of the Peace Corps, OEO included a Job Corps for dropouts from the educational system; a Neighborhood

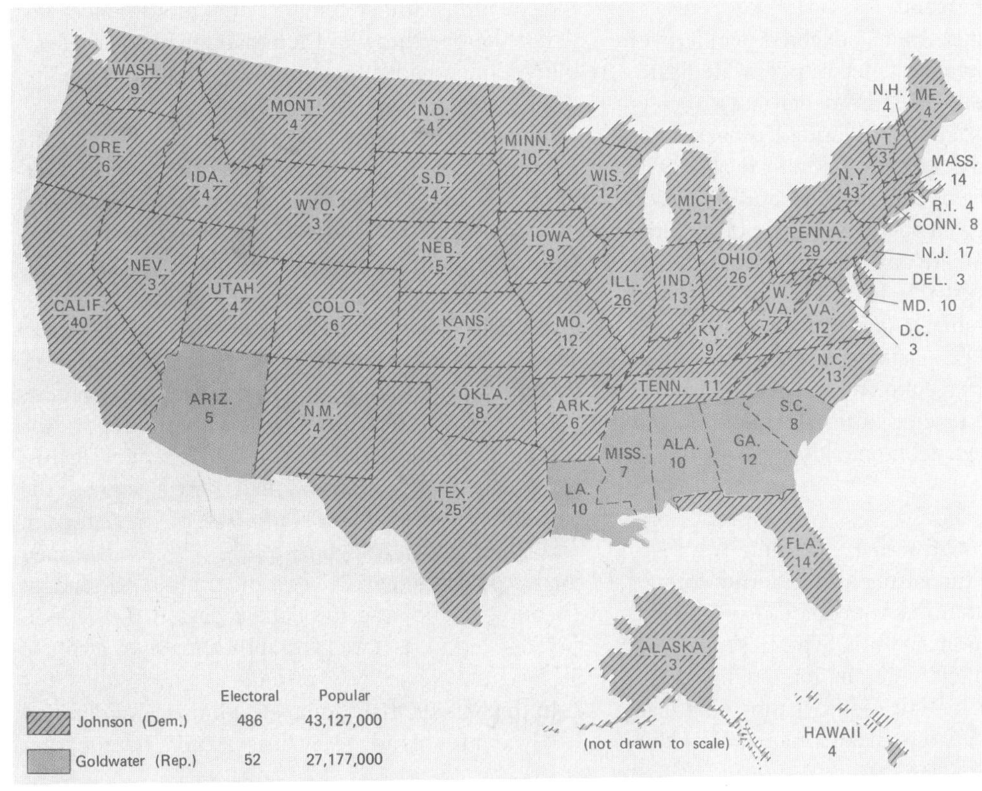

Map 32-1
The election of 1964

Youth Corps for unemployed teenagers; the Volunteers in Service to America (VISTA), in effect a domestic Peace Corps; a Head Start program for young children; an Upward Bound program to send bright children to college; and, in its most controversial feature, a Community Action program designed to secure the "maximum feasible participation" of the poor in planning and running the antipoverty effort. A venture so unprecedented could not avoid experiment and confusion. Local politicians particularly saw Community Action as a threat to their own prerogatives, and other critics felt that OEO gave professionals in the social-welfare field undue opportunity to impose their own ideas on the helpless poor.

Between 1964 and 1970 federal spending for health, education, welfare services, and income maintenance tripled. One significant result was to alter the composition of the federal budget. The "defense shift" of 1948–53 had created a pattern by which government spending held at about 28 to 29 percent of the gross national product, nondefense spending at about 15 percent, and defense spending at about 9 to 10 percent. With the "welfare shift" of the 1960s total government spending rose to about 33 percent of the gross national product, with nondefense spending rising to about 25 percent and defense spending declining to about 6 to 7 percent.

Much of the "welfare shift" benefited people over 65, especially through social security and Medicare. Only a small share went to experimental Great Society programs that, oversold and underfunded, were later too readily dismissed as failures. The reform effort was not directed against endemic poverty and produced no significant change in the distribution of income. But the number of Americans below the poverty line declined by nearly half in the ten years after 1959, and the poor, the old, and black Americans were better off. Though much criticized in later years, Johnson's Great Society represented the culmination of New Deal liberalism in its effort to reverse patterns of privation and inequality in American economic life.

Foreign Policy: Latin America As time went on, however, Johnson's increasing absorption in foreign affairs diverted his attention from domestic problems. Abroad as at home Johnson initially promised to continue Kennedy's policies. But in foreign policy he quickly introduced modifications. Latin American policy was soon reshaped to make it more acceptable both to North American business and to right-wing governments south of the border. While continuing economic assistance, Johnson liquidated the two distinctive goals of the Alliance for Progress—structural reform and political democratization. Thus Washington welcomed the military coup that established military dictatorship in Brazil in 1964.

The reversion to older ways received spectacular expression in Johnson's response to civil war in the Dominican Republic in 1965. Claiming that a popular revolution against a conservative regime had been taken over by "a band of communist conspirators," Johnson, without consulting the Organization of American States, sent more than 20,000 marines to the Dominican Republic. The size, the unilateral character, and the impetuosity of American intervention revived in Latin America the mistrust that Kennedy had striven to dispel.

Vietnam: The War Americanized The most intractable item in Johnson's inheritance was the war in Indochina. For the public, Vietnam was still a marginal issue. Johnson barely mentioned it in his January 1964 State of the Union address and gave it little more than a hundred words a year later. This lack of public emphasis, however, arose from his desire to manage the situation without congressional interference.

For the overthrow of Diem had failed to bring stability. Concerned over the growing strength of the Viet Cong, now presumed to number nearly 100,000, Johnson in 1964 turned to a program of clandestine hit-and-run military operations against North Vietnam. When South Vietnamese commandoes raided two islands in the Gulf of Tonkin at the end of July, North Vietnamese PT boats, pursuing the raiders, encountered the destroyer *Maddox* on electronic intelligence patrol and fired on it on August 2. Two days later another American destroyer was reported under attack in the gulf. Though subsequent investigations raised the greatest doubt about the second report, the administration ordered retaliatory air strikes against North Vietnamese targets, and sent Congress the Southeast Asia resolution authorizing the president to "take all necessary steps, including the use of armed force" to assist South Vietnam and prevent aggression. To popular applause the Senate passed the Tonkin Gulf resolution, as it was promptly known, by a vote of 88 to 2, the House by 416 to 0.

In the presidential campaign, Johnson condemned Goldwater for his advocacy of escalation, but the Joint

Chiefs, as Johnson knew, were already making plans for increasing the American role in Vietnam. Early in 1965 Washington was persuaded that South Vietnam was on the verge of collapse. Something, it was felt, had to be done to save the situation, and a Viet Cong mortar attack killing American advisers at Pleiku in February provided a pretext. Johnson ordered reprisal bombing against northern targets. This in March swelled into the Rolling Thunder campaign of systematic air war against North Vietnam. In April he threw American combat units, for the first time, into offensive action.

Hanoi had meantime sent men into South Vietnam —4,400 to 7,400 in 1964, according to American estimates, and mostly native southerners. Now, in response to American escalation, units of North Vietnamese regular army began for the first time to appear in South Vietnam. In June Johnson satisfied most of the requests of General William C. Westmoreland, the American commander in Saigon for 200,000 American troops. With the sending of American bombers into North Vietnam and American combat units into South Vietnam, the Indochina War entered a new and fatal phase. By the end of 1965 184,300 American troops were in Vietnam.

The Johnson Rationale The immediate reason for the Americanization of the war was to restore morale in Saigon by displaying American determination to stay the course. A second reason was the hope that bombing would break the will of the North Vietnamese and induce them to order the National Liberation Front (NLF) to call off the war. Though the experience of the Second World War and of Korea had demonstrated the limitations of strategic bombing, Johnson simply could not conceive that, if pounded long enough, North Vietnam would not have a breaking point.

He further believed that bombing, if it could not altogether stop infiltration into South Vietnam, would at least make the cost prohibitive. Since most infiltration took place along the Ho Chi Minh trail network, American planes began in 1964 to carry out bombing missions against North Vietnamese units in Laos, where the CIA had already organized an army of Meo tribesmen to resist the Pathet Lao and the North Vietnamese. A secret war in Laos thus developed alongside the open war in Vietnam.

The larger reason for the Americanization of the war lay in the assumption, inherited from the Eisenhower and Kennedy administrations and not reexamined

Vietnam: American technology was not enough

now, that the defense of South Vietnam from Communist takeover was vital to the security of the United States. Johnson felt that concessions to communism in Indochina would encourage Communist aggression first in South Asia and eventually all along the frontiers of freedom. Keeping American commitments in Vietnam thus became a test of American will and credibility everywhere. "We learned from Hitler at Munich," said Johnson, "that success only feeds the appetite of aggression."

Since it was hard to see in Ho Chi Minh and North Vietnam a threat comparable to that presented by Hitler at Munich, the administration contended that the "free world" was confronted by a premeditated plan of Chinese expansion, of which the NLF and North Vietnam were only the spearhead. China and the Soviet Union were indeed supplying North Vietnam with critical military and other equipment, but the North Vietnamese were never their pawns. They were Communists, but also fervid nationalists, intent on uniting their divided nation.

The American effort also had a positive goal. The experience of military occupation after the Second World War had given Americans undue faith in their talent for "nation-building." Johnson, the old New Dealer, talked about constructing TVAs on the Mekong River. Social evangelism thus provided further justification for the American adventure.

Nor did Johnson see the war as reason for hostility toward the Soviet Union. Rather, he believed that, if the problem of national-liberation wars could be solved in Vietnam, relations with the Soviet Union would be stabilized. In October 1964 Khrushchev had been replaced by the collective leadership of L. I. Brezhnev (who in time became the dominant partner) and A. N. Kosygin. Johnson, seeking to thaw the Cold War, in 1966 joined with the Soviet Union in supporting a UN treaty providing for the peaceful uses of outer space. In 1967 he secured the ratification of a consular convention with Russia and met with Kosygin in Glassboro, New Jersey. In 1968 he concluded with Russia and 50 other nations a treaty on the nonproliferation of nuclear weapons.

"Hawks" and "Doves" Despite endless optimistic assurances from General Westmoreland, the Americanization of the war did not produce the expected results. The number of American troops steadily grew —385,300 by the end of 1966; 485,600 by the end of 1967; 538,300 by the end of 1968—but Westmoreland's "meatgrinder" strategy of victory through "attrition" made no progress against the capacity of the NLF and the North Vietnamese to replenish their losses and match every escalation. In the meantime, American casualties also grew: deaths in combat rose from 1,369 in 1965 to 5,008 in 1966, 9,378 in 1967, and 14,592 in 1968.

The bombing increased too. By the end of 1968 American planes had dropped 3.2 million tons of explosives on this hapless land (as against a total of 2 million tons on all fronts in the Second World War and 635,000 tons in the Korean War). The result was a country gutted and devastated by bombs, burned by napalm, turned into a wasteland by chemical defoliation, a land of ruin and wreck. "It became necessary to destroy the town to save it," said an American major standing in the rubble of Ben Tre. For more and more Americans this summed up the ghastly logic of the American intervention. The technological war was too gross to cope with guerrilla warfare: it was like trying to weed a garden with a bulldozer. Bombing failed to stop the movement of troops and supplies. Instead of breaking the spirit of the enemy, it succeeded, if anything, in hardening Hanoi's will. In August 1967, McNamara, who had developed grave doubts about the war and had become the main proponent of negotiation within the administration, told the Senate Armed Services Committee that air power had failed.

Johnson nevertheless escalated the bombing, though never enough to suit the Joint Chiefs of Staff. Fearing that too drastic action might bring China into the war, Johnson also imposed political restrictions on military tactics. Negotiating efforts punctuated the process of escalation, most notably during the 37-day bombing pause of December 1964–January 1965. American proposals always included the preservation of the Saigon regime and the withdrawal of North Vietnamese forces prior to American withdrawal. From the viewpoint of Hanoi and the National Liberation Front, such terms meant defeat.

Within the United States escalation received enthusiastic support from "hawks" in Congress and the country. But, as the national debate intensified, "doves" spoke out with increasing passion. In the Senate, J. William Fulbright, chair of the Foreign Relations Committee, became a caustic and increasingly influential critic of the war. As did Robert Kennedy, now senator from New York. In February 1966 Kennedy proposed that the NLF be admitted "to a share of power and responsibility" in a coalition government as the only way to end the war. Vice President

Humphrey replied that this would be like putting "a fox in the chicken coop." As dove senators, joined by foreign-policy experts like Walter Lippmann, George F. Kennan, and Hans Morgenthau, enlarged the attack on the war, Johnson denounced the opposition as "nervous Nellies" ready to "turn on their own leaders, and their country, and on our fighting men."

In the spring of 1967, Lippmann wrote that the Indochina War had become "the most unpopular war in American history." Antiwar protests exploded in major cities, culminating on October 21, 1967, when 200,000 people including noted literary figures like Norman Mailer and Robert Lowell, marched on the Pentagon. Johnson himself could no longer appear safely in public, except on military installations. Though the campuses had generally supported escalation, the restriction of educational deferments early in 1968 confronted college students with the reality of the war. "L B J, L B J," students chanted, "How Many Kids Did You Kill Today?" Never before in American history were so many young men declaring conscientious objection, burning draft cards, or fleeing abroad to avoid military service. "Hell No, We Won't Go." Many more, accepting what they saw as their democratic obligation, brought antiwar convictions with them into the army. Middle-class parents, oblivious as long as the draft swept up only poor white and black men, began to wonder whether Vietnam was worth the sacrifice of their own sons.

Hawks and Doves, Washington, 1967

Johnson's domestic hopes were a casualty of his increasing absorption in Vietnam. The mounting cost of the war argued against expansion of domestic programs. His refusal until 1967 to ask for a tax increase to pay for the war moved the economy beyond expansion to inflation. The very phrase Great Society disappeared from the president's lexicon.

A DECADE OF UPHEAVAL

Women in Revolt The antiwar agitation was only one expression of a volatile and passionate time. The social criticism of the Kennedy years and the example of the civil rights movement had stimulated a mood of rebellion. Students protested not just the war in Vietnam but also their lack of influence on the curricula and parietal rules of their colleges. They were as "powerless," they complained, as the disfranchised Southern black Americans whom they had joined in voter registration drives in Mississippi. Convicts protested against the miserable conditions of their prisons. Gay Americans began openly to demand social acceptance and equality of treatment. Inspired by the example of black activists, other Americans of color also agitated for equal rights—Asians on the West Coast; Puerto Ricans in eastern cities; Mexican-Americans in the West and Southwest, with Caesar Chavez successful in his heroic efforts to organize agricultural workers in California; Native Americans, most of them destitute, on and off their reservations in every section of the country.

Most striking of all was the revolt of the only "minority" that, in fact, constituted a majority of Americans—women, who, outnumbered by men as late as 1945, exceeded the male population by 5.5 million in 1970.

Earlier feminist pressure had improved the legal position of women and given them the vote. To the American male the notion that women still saw themselves in a state of subjection came as a shock. Philip Wylie's popular polemic *Generation of Vipers* (1942) had portrayed the American man as systematically castrated by his women, from mother to teacher to wife to daughter, and pronounced "momism" the curse of American life. In comic strips Maggie forever chased Jiggs with her rolling pin.

Yet all indexes showed women mired in social and economic inferiority. The "feminine mystique" defined a woman as husband's wife, children's mother,

The new feminism

family's faithful servant—never as a person in her own right. When women struck out on their own, most professions (except for elementary school teaching, nursing, library work, and prostitution) resisted them. Shirley Chisholm, the first black congresswoman, said she endured more discrimination as a woman than as a black.

In some respects the position of women had been getting worse. The early feminist movement had stimulated able women to seek careers. The example of Eleanor Roosevelt and Frances Perkins in the 1930s, the participation of women in the Second World War as WACs and WAVEs and as workers in munitions plants—all this had strengthened the image of the self-reliant woman. But in the 1940s and 1950s the tide had turned, as the tide had turned against black citizens after Reconstruction. The proportion of women undergraduates declined from 47 percent in 1920 to 31 percent in 1950; women's median earnings relative to similarly employed men were declining, and in 1971 the percentage of women in managerial and proprietorial jobs was lower than in 1960. Women constituted more than 51 percent of the population in 1970 but only 9 percent of the full professors on university faculties, 7.6 percent of the doctors, and 2.8 percent of the lawyers. The average earnings of a woman college graduate were less than those of a man with four years of high school.

It was against this background that Betty Friedan in her influential book *The Feminine Mystique* (1963) called on women to recognize what society was doing to them and to demand equal rights and opportunities. Finding even the civil rights groups and the New Left dominated by "male chauvinism"—"the only position for women in SNCC," said the black militant Stokely Carmichael in 1964, "is prone"—Friedan and others established the National Organization for Women (NOW) in 1966. The recruiting instrument for women's liberation was the "consciousness-raising" group, where women met in "rap sessions" to reflect on their lives. Courses in women's studies, widely instituted in these years, provided historical background. Such activity raised the consciousness of many men, too, startled to discover the manifold ways male condescension and female subordination were built into the structure and language of society.

The Black Revolution Turns Left In the black community the center of agitation was shifting from the South to the North. In 1910 only 9 percent of black Americans lived outside the South and only 27 percent

The Emergence of Women

The American always ostentatiously ignored sex, and American history mentioned hardly the name of a woman. . . . American art, like the American language and American education, was as far as possible sexless. . . . [Yet] in every city, town, and farm-house were myriads of new types—or type-writers—telephone and telegraph-girls, shop-clerks, factory-hands, running into millions on millions, and, as classes, unknown to themselves as to historians. . . . All these new women had been created since 1840; all were to show their meaning before 1940.

From *The Education of Henry Adams,* 1918

We, men, and women who hereby constitute ourselves as the National Organization for Women, believe that the time has come for a new movement toward true equality for all women in America, and toward a fully equal partnership of the sexes, as part of the world-wide revolution of human rights now taking place within and beyond our national borders. . . .

WE REJECT the current assumption that a man must carry the sole burden of supporting himself, his wife, and family, and that a woman is automatically entitled to lifelong support by a man upon her marriage, or that marriage, home and family are primarily woman's world and responsibility—hers, to dominate—his to support. We believe that a true partnership between the sexes demands a different concept of marriage, an equitable sharing of the responsibilities of home and children and of the economic burdens of their support. . . .

IN THE INTERESTS OF THE HUMAN DIGNITY OF WOMEN, we will protest, and endeavor to change, the false image of women now prevalent in the mass media, and in the texts, ceremonies, laws, and practices of the major social institutions. Such images perpetuate contempt for women by society and by women for themselves. . . . WE BELIEVE THAT women will do most to create a new image of women by acting now, and by speaking out in behalf of their own equality, freedom, and human dignity—not in pleas for special privilege, nor in enmity toward men, who are also victims of the current, half-equality between the sexes—but in active, self-respective partnership with men.

From the National Organization for Women,
Statement of Purpose, 1966

The Case for Violence

There has always existed in the Black colony of Afro-America a fundamental difference over which tactics from the broad spectrum of alternatives Black people should employ in their struggle for national liberation. One side of this difference contends that Black people . . . must employ no tactic that will anger the oppressor whites. This view holds that Black people constitute a hopeless minority and that salvation for Black people lies in developing brotherly relations. . . .

On the other side of the difference, we find that the point of departure is the principle that the oppressor has no rights that the oppressed is bound to respect. Kill the slavemaster, destroy him utterly, move against him with implacable fortitude. Break his oppressive power by any means necessary. . . . The heirs of Malcolm have picked up the gun and, taking first things first, are moving to expose the endorsed leaders for the Black masses to see them for what they are and always have been. The choice offered by the heirs of Malcolm is to repudiate the oppressor . . . or face a merciless, speedy and most timely execution for treason.

From Huey P. Newton, "In Defense of Self Defense," *The Black Panther,* July 3, 1967

in urban areas. By 1970, 47 percent lived outside the South and 70 percent in urban areas.

Where Southern black citizens sought the removal of legal and political barriers, Northern black Americans, who nominally possessed the freedoms provided by the new civil rights legislation, wanted equal social and economic opportunity. Where Southern black citizens were responsive to religious traditions and accustomed to daily relations with white Americans, Northern black Americans were less involved in the old-time religion and, shut off in ghettos, were more hostile toward white Americans. Though Martin Luther King, Jr., remained the preeminent black leader, he proved less effective in Chicago than in Birmingham.

Despair in the ghettos produced challenges to King's ideals of nonviolence and an integrated society. A movement known as the Black Muslims gathered strength. Its leader was Elijah Muhammad, its most eloquent voice Malcolm X, and its program one of black separatism, self-discipline, and self-defense. Breaking with the Muslims in 1964, Malcolm X called for "a working unity among all peoples, black as well as white." He had hardly embarked in new directions, however, before he was murdered in February 1965, apparently as an aftermath of the feud with the Muslims. His powerful *Autobiography* (1965) became a central document of black nationalism.

Events strengthened the nationalist mood. In August 1965, riots in Watts, California, eventually suppressed by the National Guard, resulted in 34 deaths. In 1966 the National Guard put down riots in Chicago. In 1967 riots swept through the black sections of Tampa; Cincinnati; Atlanta; and New Brunswick, New Jersey, and broke out with desperate force in Detroit and Newark. These developments both encouraged and expressed a growing radicalization of urban black people—a radicalization symbolized in the summer of 1966 when Stokely Carmichael of SNCC raised the standard of "black power."

Black Power Black power implied for some black Americans regrouping and self-reliance as part of the transition to integration on an equal basis. Integration on any other basis, it was contended, would mean surrender to white values. In this sense black power was an affirmation of racial and cultural pride. Black

The Case against Violence

Probably the most destructive feature of Black Power is its unconscious and often conscious call for retaliatory violence. . . .The problem with hatred and violence is that they intensify the fears of the white majority, and leave them less ashamed of their prejudices toward Negroes. In the guilt and confusion confronting our society, violence only adds to the chaos. It deepens the brutality of the oppressor and increases the bitterness of the oppressed. Violence is the antithesis of creativity and wholeness. It destroys community and makes brotherhood impossible. . . .

The ultimate weakness of violence is that it is a descending spiral, begetting the very thing it seeks to destroy. Instead of diminishing evil, it multiplies it. Through violence you may murder the liar, but you cannot murder the lie, nor establish the truth. Through violence you may murder the hater, but you do not murder hate. In fact, violence merely increases hate. So it goes. Returning violence for violence multiplies violence, adding deeper darkness to a night already devoid of stars. Darkness cannot drive out darkness; only light can do that. Hate cannot drive out hate; only love can do that.

From Martin Luther King, Jr., *Where Do We Go from Here: Chaos or Community?,* 1967

became beautiful, black men and women threw away hair straighteners and rejoiced in the Afro, soul music and soul food became badges not of shame but of identity, and black studies programs became common in universities. Black power, said Dr. King, was a "call to manhood."

Detroit, 1967

But, as expounded by black nationalists, black power meant permanent racial separation, even retaliatory vengeance against the "honky." Black Americans, Carmichael said in 1968, must become "the executioners of our executioners." In this more drastic mood, slogans of the King period—"We Shall Overcome"—gave way to more bitter phrases—"Burn, Baby, Burn."

The older black leaders condemned separatism and violence as self-defeating. As King wrote of the new militancy, "In advocating violence it is imitating the worst, the most brutal, and the most uncivilized value of American life." He added, "There is no salvation for the Negro through isolation. . . . The black man needs the white man and the white man needs the black man."

The emergence of black power constituted an unmistakable warning to white America. Lyndon Johnson, appropriating for himself the slogan "We Shall

Malcolm X: an eloquent voice

Overcome," pressed the fight for civil rights legislation, securing the passage of an open-housing law in 1968. He appointed Thurgood Marshall as the first black justice to the Supreme Court. A Presidential Commission on Civil Disorders, set up during the riots of 1967 under the chair of Governor Otto Kerner of Illinois, concluded somberly: "Our nation is moving toward two societies, one black, one white — separate but unequal." But Johnson turned his back to that report.

A few weeks later Martin Luther King, Jr., was assassinated in Memphis. Riots exploded in ghetto after ghetto across the land, resulting in 43 deaths, 3,500 injuries, and 27,000 arrests. The subsequent murder of Robert Kennedy, the one white leader in whom black Americans believed, intensified hopelessness. But this mood was still more a warning than a broad reality. Polls in 1969 showed that the majority of black Americans continued to feel that they could win equality without violence and to accept the ideal of a multiracial society.

Revolt on the Campus The campuses, silent during the 1950s, were stirred into purposeful activity by the New Frontier. The Peace Corps, VISTA, and civil rights projects like "Freedom Summer" in Mississippi in 1964 were only the most dramatic form of the new commitment. But after John Kennedy's murder in 1963 and the Americanization of the Indochina War in 1965, youthful idealism took a new turn.

Generational revolt was hardly novel, but it now assumed unprecedentedly doctrinaire forms, as in the slogan: "You can't trust anyone over 30." The militant young saw the older generation as the instrumentality of a corrupt society controlled by great bureaucracies of government and business. In its influential Port Huron statement (1962), Students for a Democratic Society (SDS) denounced élitism and centralization and raised the standard of "participatory democracy." Against dehumanizing bureaucracy the young cried: "Don't bend, fold, spindle or mutilate!" Against Vietnam: "Make love, not war."

The university, as the first large organization the young encountered, became a prime target in their revolt against the world of structures. More young men and women were going to college than ever before. Total enrollment rose from 3.8 million in 1960 to 8.5 million in 1970. What university presidents hailed as the "multiversity," many students saw as a callously impersonal assembly line of higher education. As the war continued to escalate, radical students, with mounting rage, assailed academic collaboration with the military — the Reserve Officers Training Corps, recruiting on campuses by CIA or by companies manufacturing tools of war like napalm, research financed by the Pentagon or CIA. As undergraduate defiance and provocation increased, university authorities began to call in the local police. In 1968–69 4,000 students were arrested. Where police violence went out of control — as at Columbia University and the Democratic convention in 1968 and at Harvard in 1969 — student radicalization intensified.

The New Left Violence begot violence. In 1967, the SDS national secretary announced, "We are working to build a guerrilla force in an urban environment." Characteristic of the new mood was the SDS's Weatherman faction (so-called because of the Bob Dylan lyric, "You don't need a weatherman to know which way the wind blows"). Seeing American (or, as they

Funeral of Martin Luther King, Jr.

preferred to put it, "Amerikan") society as irretrievably corrupt, they concluded that the only way to deal with an inherently destructive apparatus was to destroy it.

The radical sociologist C. Wright Mills had given the New Left intellectual underpinnings in his book *The Power Elite* (1956), with its portrait of a diabolically clever ruling class, and the philosopher Herbert Marcuse now provided an ideology to justify violence. If "oppressed and overpowered minorities . . . use violence," he wrote in *One Dimensional Man* (1965), "they do not start a new chain of violence but try to break an established one. . . . No third person, and least of all the educator and intellectual, has the right to preach them abstention."

One function of violence in New Left ideology was to "unmask" the "Establishment" by provoking it into acts of violent retaliation. Some of the time, however, the Establishment, whether because of bad conscience or Machiavellian ingenuity, employed a subtler tactic denounced by the militants as "cooptation"—the tactic of disarming dissent by absorbing it. Thus revolutionaries appeared on television talk shows and commanded large lecture fees. But government also showed itself capable of more drastic action. Police officers beat up long-haired demonstrators. The FBI sent agents, who also sometimes turned out to be *provocateurs,* into New Left groups. And the Department of Justice made recurrent efforts to indict and imprison New Left leaders. This produced a series of celebrated trials: in 1968, the trial of Dr. Benjamin Spock and three others for conspiring to encourage draft resistants to violate the Selective Service Act; in 1969–70, the prolonged and raucous trial of seven New Left leaders for crossing state lines with the intent to incite violence at the 1968 Democratic convention; and a number of trials of black militants.

Rise of the Counterculture Not all the disaffected young took the path of political activism. Some responded instead by dropping out of society. These

The Kennedy Legacy

First is the danger of futility, the belief there is nothing one man or one woman can do against the enormous array of the world's ills—against misery and ignorance, injustice and violence. . . . Few will have the greatness to bend history itself; but each of us can work to change a small portion of events, and in the total of all those acts will be written the history of this generation.

It is from numberless diverse acts of courage and belief that human history is shaped. Each time a man stands up for an ideal, or acts to improve the lot of others, or strikes out against injustice, he sends a tiny ripple of hope, and crossing each other from a million different centers of energy and daring those ripples build a current which can sweep down the mightiest walls of oppression and resistance.

From Robert F. Kennedy, speech, Cape Town, South Africa, June 6, 1966

defectors followed trails marked out by the beatniks of the 1950s.

Disdaining ties, jackets, and socks, affecting long hair, beards, and beads, spurning the adult world as "uptight" and "plastic," the "hippies" congregated in the Haight-Ashbury district of San Francisco or the Sunset Strip of Los Angeles or New York's East Village. Some called themselves "flower children," in part because of their custom of offering flowers to cops and other persecutors, and celebrated their rites, not in the teach-ins or sit-ins of the activists, but in "be-ins" or "love-ins." Some joined together in "communes" weirdly reminiscent of the communitarian enthusiasm in nineteenth-century America. By 1970 over 200 communes involved perhaps 40,000 people, mostly under the age of 30.

Haight-Ashbury

Do your own thing, drop out, turn on—these were the principles of the hippie ethos. Above all, the hippie mystique relied on drugs. During the nineteenth century in America, narcotics had been sold freely, and, before the Pure Food and Drug Act of 1906 (see p. 573), popular patent medicines often had a narcotic base. In 1914 the Federal Narcotics Bureau estimated that 1 in every 400 Americans was an addict. The Harrison Act of that year was the first of a series of federal attempts to regulate narcotics, one result of which was to give the underworld control of the drug traffic.

For those trying to blow their minds and open wide what Aldous Huxley called in an influential book *The Doors of Perception* (1954), marijuana ("pot" or

Woodstock, 1969: youth counterculture

"grass") was the most common drug. Others turned to stronger hallucinogens, notably lysergic acid diethylamide (LSD or "acid") and mescaline; others to amphetamines, especially methedrine ("pep pills" or "speed"). LSD "highs" sometimes produced "good trips," with extraordinary heightening of perceptions of sound, color, and motion; they also produced "bad trips" and chemical changes leading to panic, prolonged depression, psychosis, and suicide.

Out of the New Left activism, the hippie movement, the communes, the drug trips, the rock music, emerged what was known from within as "the Movement" and from without as the "counterculture."

Music played a vital role in the formation of the counterculture. English groups, especially the Beatles and later the Rolling Stones, registered the trajectory of the young—from the communal "We All Live in a Yellow Submarine" through the psychedelic "Lucy in the Sky with Diamonds" to Mick Jagger's sinister "Sympathy for the Devil." Bob Dylan was the generation's American bard, singing his poignant and evocative songs—first social conscience and then folk rock—about drugs, race, sex, life, and memory.

After an astonishingly short period, the millennial hope of young Americans in the late 1960s and early 1970s simply evaporated. It came to seem, even to veterans of the Movement, an exotic memory. Sociologists and historians were hard put to account for this short and sharp season of unrest. Some placed emphasis on the extraordinary population increase in the 1960s of persons between the ages of 14 and 24, the children of the postwar baby boom. In the years between 1890 and 1960 that age group had increased by only 12.5 million. In the single decade of the 1960s, it grew by a fantastic 13.8 million. So unprecedented an enlargement in the youth population created for a giddy moment a vivid youth consciousness, a separate youth culture, even perhaps, as the young felt themselves increasingly oppressed, a youth class. The demographic explosion coincided, moreover, with authentic social conflicts, especially over war and race.

Still only a minority of the young entered the counterculture. Most went about the business of growing up without notable alienation or protest. The end of the Indochina War and the rise of unemployment in the early 1970s hastened the decline of the rebel young. Moreover, as the rate of population growth slowed after the mid-1950s, the 14-to-24 age group became a smaller and more manageable injection into society.

Nonetheless, the revolt left its mark. It compelled many people over age 30 to acknowledge the gap between their professed ideals and the lives they actually lived. It helped force issues to the top of the national agenda—not only war and race but the role of women, the protection of the environment, the functions of education, the implications of a runaway technology, the significance of community and selfhood. For all its transience and excess, the youth rebellion of the 1960s contributed to a fundamental reappraisal of American values.

The Social Fabric Unravels As the decade came to an end, the idyl—the Age of Aquarius—was turning sour. In the cities the flower people gave way to a new, tough breed, the "street people," priding themselves on "ripping off" (stealing), "trashing" (vandalism), "gang bangs" (mass rape), and promiscuous violence. Even worse were roving motorcycle gangs, like the sadistic Hell's Angels in California. In August 1969 the atrocious murder of the actress Sharon Tate and six others at the order of Charles Manson by three women members of Manson's hippie "family," though it was briefly glorified by the Weathermen and by some in the drug culture, forced many in the new generation to confront, as one put it, "the pig in ourselves, the childish, egotistical, selfish irresponsibility."

The decade that had begun in exhilaration and hope was dissolving into bitterness and hate. "Before my term is ended," Kennedy had said in 1961, "we shall have to test anew whether a nation organized and governed such as ours can endure. The outcome is by no means certain." Convinced that the inequalities in American society were a source of danger to American life, Kennedy tried to get America moving toward his New Frontier, carrying the poor and nonwhite citizens with him. He was murdered. After his death his brother Robert made himself the champion of the outcasts and victims of American life. He was murdered. Martin Luther King, Jr., was the eloquent advocate of nonviolence. He was murdered. Some Americans regarded these murders as aberrations. Others began to lose faith in a society that destroyed the three leaders of the decade who seemed most to embody American idealism.

Still others, shocked by the panorama of epithets, marches, burnings, riots, shootings, and bombings, became incensed over the new "permissive society" with its liberated women, militant black radicals, and angry youth. The counterculture in its turn provoked a moralistic counterrevolution dedicated to the reinstatement of social discipline. Phyllis Schlafly celebrated the values of old-fashioned femininity against the heresies of women's liberation. George Wallace, now moving onto the national scene, denounced "pointy-head intellectuals" and affirmed local sovereignty against federally enforced equal rights.

The Warren Court became a particular target. In *Gideon* v. *Wainwright* (1963), the Court, overruling its own previous decisions, freed a defendant on the ground that he had been denied counsel in a state court. Even more infuriating to the radical right were decisions in *Escobedo* v. *Illinois* and *Miranda* v. *Arizona* (1964) reversing state criminal convictions on the ground that the defendants had been denied counsel during police interrogations and had not been advised by the police of their constitutional rights. Conserva-

In Defense of Vietnam

Despite the long years of support and vast expenditure of lives and funds, the United States in the end abandoned South Vietnam. There is no other way to put it. . . . After introduction of American combat troops into South Vietnam in 1965, the war still might have been ended within a few years, except for the ill-considered policy of graduated response against North Vietnam. Bomb a little, stop it a while to give the enemy a chance to cry uncle, then bomb a little bit more but never enough to really hurt. That was no way to win. Yet even with the handicap of graduated response, the war still could have been brought to a favorable end following defeat of the enemy's Tet offensive in 1968. The United States had in South Vietnam at that time the finest military force—though not the largest—ever assembled. Had President Johnson provided reinforcements, and had he authorized the operations I had planned in Laos and Cambodia and north of the DMZ, along with intensified bombing and the mining of Haiphong Harbor, the North Vietnamese would have broken. But that was not to be. Press and television had created an aura not of victory but of defeat, and timid officials in Washington listened more to the media than to their own representatives on the scene.

From General William C. Westmoreland, *A Soldier Reports,* 1976

McNamara on Bombing

There may be a limit beyond which many Americans and much of the world will not permit the United States to go. The picture of the world's greatest superpower killing or seriously injuring 1,000 noncombatants a week, while trying to pound a tiny backward nation into submission on an issue whose merits are hotly disputed, is not a pretty one. It could conceivably produce a costly distortion in the American national consciousness and in the world image of the United States—especially if the damage to North Vietnam is complete enough to be 'successful.'

From Secretary of Defense Robert S. McNamara, Memorandum to President Johnson, May 19, 1967

tives assailed these judicial affirmations of the rights of the accused as the "coddling" of criminals.

The 1968 Election The emotions behind the conservative counterrevolution gathered force as the presidential election approached. In the meantime, war continued in Vietnam, and the administration persisted in discerning light at the end of the tunnel.

"I see progress as I travel all over Vietnam," said General Westmoreland in November 1967." . . . The enemy's hopes are bankrupt." In February 1968, during the Tet holiday, the lunar New Year, a massive enemy offensive took American and South Vietnamese forces by surprise, convulsed 30 provincial capitals, and even penetrated the American embassy in Saigon. While the North Vietnamese failed to achieve their objectives and suffered grievous losses, the Tet offensive destroyed what remained of the Johnson administration's credibility on Vietnam.

Westmoreland's reaction was to escalate further, and the Joint Chiefs' February request for 206,000 additional troops produced a showdown within the administration. Johnson, exasperated by McNamara's opposition to escalation, had shifted him to the World Bank. But new Secretary of Defense Clark Clifford, once a hawk, had begun to question the war when a 1967 mission disclosed to him that pro-American Asian states saw much less at stake in Indochina than Washington did. Now in the Pentagon, Clifford concluded that further escalation was futile.

The Tet offensive intensified domestic criticism of the war. "Are we like the God of the Old Testament," Robert Kennedy asked, "that can decide, in Washington, D.C., what cities, what towns, what hamlets in Vietnam are going to be destroyed?" Antiwar activists, having failed to persuade Kennedy to oppose Johnson, turned to another senatorial dove, Eugene McCarthy of Minnesota. A man of enigmatic and mischievous intelligence, McCarthy, followed by a virtual "children's crusade," campaigned masterfully against Johnson and the war in the New Hampshire primary in March. The Tet offensive, McCarthy's strength in New Hampshire, and Kennedy's entry into the contest for Democratic nomination increased the pressure on Johnson. Faced by defeat in the impending Wisconsin primary, Johnson on March 31 withdrew from the presidential contest.

Humphrey became the administration candidate. Once a liberal leader, Humphrey was now identified with Johnson and the war and did nothing to diminish this identification. Kennedy and McCarthy, on the other hand, generated crusading enthusiasm among their followers—Kennedy among the poor, black Americans, Hispanic-Americans; McCarthy among suburbanites and independent voters; both among the young and the intellectuals. Their combined vote in a succession of primaries, none of which Humphrey entered, expressed a widespread repudiation of the Johnson administration within his own party. However, on June 6, the night of his victory in the California primary, Kennedy was murdered by a Palestinian Arab who resented the senator's sympathy for Israel. The nation, appalled at the assassination of a second Kennedy within five years, mourned the death of a man many believed the most brilliant and creative among the national leaders.

After Kennedy's death, Humphrey had no serious opposition. Protest against the war policy erupted, however, in shocking scenes during the Democratic convention in Chicago in August, when local police in a frenzy of violence clubbed hundreds of antiwar agitators in the city's streets. Television carried the carnage into the homes of the American people, of whom only 19 percent felt the police had used too much violence. That response revealed the magnitude of national disaffection with dissenting student and black activists alike. Television also displayed the antagonism between hawks and doves within the Democratic party. "Chicago," Humphrey later wrote, "was a catastrophe." It was for his candidacy. Neither he nor his running mate, Senator Edmund Muskie of Maine, ever fully blotted out the images of the Chicago debacle.

Richard M. Nixon, 1968: an astonishing comeback

Robert F. Kennedy: arousing enthusiasm

Richard M. Nixon, completing an astonishing political comeback, won the Republican nomination and picked Governor Spiro T. Agnew of Maryland, the first suburban politician to rise to national prominence, as his running mate. Nixon, who in past years had been more hawkish than the administration, pledged that "new leadership will end the war." In domestic policy he presented himself as a champion of "law and order." That was part of his calculated appeal to "Middle America"—clerical and blue-collar workers and the suburban middle class—who were fed up alike with protest and with the counterculture. The most picturesque candidate, running on the American Independent party ticket, was George Wallace, who threatened for a time to do well not only in the South

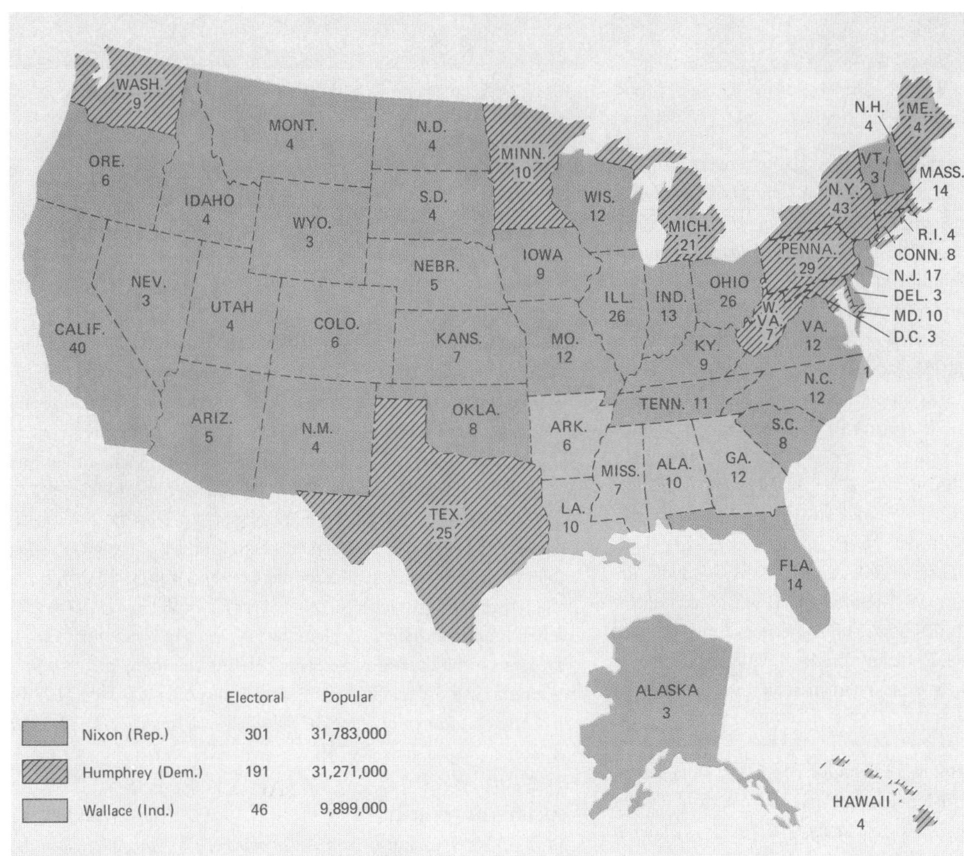

Map 32-2
The election of 1968

but among blue-collar workers in the North. In October, however, when organized labor threw itself into the contest, the working-class vote moved back to the Democrats. But Humphrey came out from under the shadow of the unpopular Johnson presidency too slowly to rouse the enthusiasm of the Kennedy-McCarthy wing of the party.

The vote cast—73.2 million—was the largest in American history, but it included only 60.6 percent of the eligible electorate (as against 61.7 percent in 1964 and 64 in 1960). Nixon received 31.8 million votes compared to 31.3 million for Humphrey and 9.9 million for Wallace (see Map 32-2). With only 43.4 percent of the total, he became a minority president. The margins were greater in the Electoral College: 301 for Nixon, 191 for Humphrey, and 46, all in the Deep South, for Wallace. The Democrats carried both houses of Congress, which made Nixon the first president since Zachary Taylor whose party on his election did not control at least one chamber. But as journalist Theodore White observed: "The election of 1968 was . . . a negative landslide." Between them, Nixon and Wallace polled just under 57 percent of the popular vote, "undeniably a swing to the right." Humphrey lost most of the South to Nixon or Wallace and carried only one-third of the white vote in the North. The conservative tide in the South, West, and mountain states, and in the suburbs, lifted Republican prospects for the future. After 36 years of Democratic primacy, the Republicans, if they could attract the Wallace vote, could become the dominant party in presidential elections.

Lyndon Johnson left the White House an unlamented president. Yet history may judge his Great Society a serious effort to overcome the tensions and inequities produced by social and technological change. The irony of his presidency was that he sacrificed domestic policy, a field in which his knowledge was great and his instinct sure, to foreign policy, where his knowledge was scant and his instinct simplistic.

SUGGESTIONS FOR READING

KENNEDY AND JOHNSON

Three general accounts of the period this chapter covers are J. M. Blum, *Years of Discord* (1991); W. Chafe, *The Unfinished Journey* (2d ed., 1991); and A. Matusow, *The Unraveling of America* (1984). H. Parmet's two volumes—*Jack: The Struggles of John F. Kennedy* (1980) and *JFK: The Presidency of John F. Kennedy* (1983)—are documented and evenhandedly critical. Two comprehensive accounts by participants written shortly after Kennedy's death are T. C. Sorensen, *Kennedy* (1965), and A. M. Schlesinger, Jr., *A Thousand Days* (1965); the latter is supplemented in Schlesinger, *Robert Kennedy and His Times* (1978). Henry Fairlie, *The Kennedy Promise* (1972), is an intelligent critique. Memoirs from the Kennedy administration include P. Salinger, *With Kennedy* (1966); K. P. O'Donnell and D. F. Powers with J. W. McCarthy, *"Johnny, We Hardly Knew Ye"* (1972); L. F. O'Brien, *No Final Victories* (1974); J. K. Galbraith, *A Life in Our Times* (1981); and Richard Goodwin, *Remembering America* (1988). W. Manchester, *Death of a President* (1967), provides a sometimes powerful, sometimes lurid, account of the assassination, and G. R. Blakey and R. N. Billings, *The Plot to Kill the President* (1981), is a reasoned dissent from the Warren Commission report.

For Johnson, his own memoir, *The Vantage Point* (1971), is formal but useful. D. Kearns, *Lyndon Johnson and the American Dream* (1976), is an absorbing psychological analysis; G. Reedy, *Lyndon B. Johnson, A Memoir* (1982), is a brilliant portrait by a close associate; E. F. Goldman, *The Tragedy of Lyndon Johnson* (1969), is the assessment by an historian who served briefly in Johnson's White House; and R. Caro, *The Years of Lyndon Johnson: The Path to Power* (1982), is the first volume of an exhaustive and prosecutorial biography. Compare with P. K. Conkin, *Big Daddy from Pedernales* (1986). H. McPherson, *A Political Education* (1972), and J. Valenti, *A Very Human President* (1975), are sympathetic accounts by Johnson associates, as are the memoirs of Clark Clifford and Dean Rusk. More critical is L. Kalman, *Abe Fortas* (1990). Hubert Humphrey, *The Education of a Public Man* (1976), is an autobiography.

FOREIGN AFFAIRS

For Kennedy's foreign policy, in addition to Sorensen and Schlesinger above, there is wide-ranging coverage in W. W. Rostow, *The Diffusion of Power* (1972), and useful observations in Roger Hilsman, *To Move a Nation* (1967); C. Bowles, *Promises to Keep* (1971); W. W. Attwood, *The Reds and the Blacks* (1967); and G. Ball, *The Past Has Another Pattern* (1982). W. I. Cohen, *Dean Rusk* (1980), is sympathetic. On the missile crisis, R. F. Kennedy, *Thirteen Days* (1969), is indispensable testimony; G. T. Allison, *Essence of Decision* (1971), is an astute analysis. N. Cousins, *The Improbable Triumvirate* (1972), is a fascinating account by a Kennedy emissary of the quest for détente in 1963. G. T. Seaborg, *Kennedy, Khrushchev, and the Test Ban* (1981), describes the test-ban negotiations. For a broader view of nuclear policy, see M. Bundy, *Danger and Survival* (1988), which is equally instructive on earlier and later administrations. D. S. Blaufarb, *The Counterinsurgency Era* (1977), is a good history of a bad idea.

On Vietnam, G. M. Kahin, *Intervention: How America Became Involved in Vietnam* (1986), and G. C. Herring, *America's Longest War* (2d ed., 1986), are scholarly studies. F. FitzGerald, *Fire in the Lake* (1972), illuminates the clash of cultures. D. Halberstam, *The Best and the Brightest* (1972), is a lively indictment; see also N. Sheehan, *A Bright Shining Lie: John Paul Vann and America in Vietnam* (1988). S. Karnow, *Vietnam: A History* (1983), provides a clear and useful narrative about the whole war, from Eisenhower's involvement to the end; see also W. J. Rust, *Kennedy in Vietnam* (1985), and on the Johnson years, L. H. Galb and R. F. Betts, *The Irony of Vietnam: The System Worked* (1979); L. Berman, *Planning a Tragedy: The Americanization of the War in Vietnam* (1982), and L. Berman, *Lyndon Johnson's War* (1989). G. Kolko, *Anatomy of a War* (1985), presents the left-revisionist view; G. Lewy, *America in Vietnam* (1978), defends American policy. E. Hammer, *A Death in November* (1987), focuses on the overthrow of Diem. Among the many novels about Vietnam, see especially T. O'Brien, *Going After Cacciato* (1978); P. Caputo, *A Rumor of War* (1977); M. Herr, *Dispatches* (1977); and R. Stone, *Dog Soldiers* (1974).

SOCIETY IN FERMENT

W. L. O'Neill, *Coming Apart: An Informal History of America in the 1960's* (1971), is perceptive but uneven. M. Harrington, *The Other America* (1963), helped set off the war on poverty, and J. T. Patterson, *America's Struggle Against Poverty, 1900–1980* (1981), puts that war in historical perspective. J. E. Schwarz, *America's Hidden Success* (1983), is a scholar's positive assessment of the Kennedy-Johnson social policy; C. Murray, *Losing Ground* (1984), is sharply critical.

On civil rights, C. Bauer, *John F. Kennedy and the Second Reconstruction* (1977), is sympathetic to the Kennedys; compare with the books by Sitkoff and Weisbrot and the biographies of King by Branch and by Garrow, all cited in the previous chapter. On policy, see also H. D. Graham and N. V. Bartley, *Southern Politics and the Second Reconstruction* (1975), and H. D. Graham, *The Civil Rights Era: Origins and Development of National Policy* (1990). The legislative history of the 1964 act is detailed in C. Whalen and B. Whalen, *The Longest Debate* (1983). The course of the black revolution can be traced in J. Baldwin, *The Fire Next Time* (1963); Malcom X, *Autobiography* (1965); E. Cleaver, *Soul on Ice* (1967); S. Carmichael and C. V. Hamilton, Jr., *Black Power* (1967); and M. L. King, Jr., *Where Do We Go From Here: Chaos or Community?* (1967).

For women's liberation, see W. H. Chafe, *The American Woman, Her Changing Social Economic and Political Roles, 1920–1970* (1974); and G. G. Yates, *What Women Want: The Ideas of the Movement* (1975). B. Friedan, *The Feminine Mystique* (1963), is a basic document. For an antifeminist statement, see P. Schlafly, *The Power of the Positive Woman* (1977).

R. Berman, *America in the Sixties* (1968), provides a survey of intellectual developments from a conservative viewpoint; M. Dickstein, *Gates of Eden: American Culture in the Sixties* (1977), is acute and more sympathetic. G. O. Larson, *The Reluctant Patron: The United States Government and the Arts, 1943–1965* (1983), describes the evolution of a national arts policy. On the counterculture, C. Reich, *The Greening of America* (1971), evokes the dreams of the counterculture; T. Gitlin, *The Sixties: Years of Hope, Days of Rage* (1987), is informative, as are J. Miller, *"Democracy Is in the Streets"* (1987), and D. Caute, *The Year of the Barricades* (1988). See also C. Lasch, *The Agony of the American Left* (1969), and I. Unger, *The Movement* (1974). Mike Nichol's film *The Graduate* (1967), portrays the more amiable side of the youth rebellion; and two later films—John Sayles's *The Return of the Secaucus Seven* (1980) and Lawrence Kasdan's *The Big Chill* (1984)—provide bittersweet retrospectives. D. Musto, *The American Disease* (1973), tells the history of drugs in America.

For the 1968 election, see T. H. White, *The Making of a President 1968* (1969); L. Chester et al., *An American Melodrama* (1969); E. McCarthy, *The Year of the People* (1968); and J. Larner, *Nobody Knows: Reflections on the McCarthy Campaign of 1968* (1970). There are important analyses in J. McGinniss, *The Selling of the President 1968* (1969), and K. P. Phillips, *The Emerging Republican Majority* (1970).

CHAPTER THIRTY-THREE

THE WHITE HOUSE

THE PRESIDENCY REBUKED AND RESTORED

The man who became president in January 1969 was the antithesis of the rebel mood of the 1960s. Fifty-six years old on his inauguration, Richard Milhous Nixon came from a lower-middle-class Quaker family in California, where a frugal upbringing had instilled traditional virtues of work, discipline, and ambition. Receiving a law degree in 1937, he served in the navy during the Second World War and entered politics thereafter, gaining election to the House of Representatives in 1946 and to the Senate in 1950. His diligence as a member of a House investigating committee helped break the case of Alger Hiss, and anticommunism was the issue with which he was most identified in his early career. His alacrity in dispensing accusations of disloyalty outraged his political opponents, who called him Tricky Dick, but Republicans admired him as an intelligent lawyer and a good party man.

Elected vice president in 1952, Nixon did not enjoy easy relations with Eisenhower but served him faithfully. After his defeat by Kennedy in 1960, Nixon was defeated again in 1962 for the governorship of California, and his career was supposed over. "You won't have Nixon to kick around any more," he told the press. But, with dogged perseverance, he rebuilt his position. Lonely and solemn as a young man, he appeared fluent and experienced in middle age. Sympathizers saw him as the embodiment of middle-class values in a degenerate time. Critics found him defensive, righteous, and shifty.

FROM CONFRONTATION TO NEGOTIATION

Once More into the Quagmire Foreign affairs were Nixon's consuming interest and, in his view of himself, his main field of expertise. His first secretary of state, William P. Rogers, had been attorney general during the Eisenhower administration; but the dominating influence was Henry A. Kissinger, Nixon's national security adviser and a Harvard intellectual who had come to the United States from Germany as a boy in 1938. Kissinger was an accomplished diplomatic historian as well as an astute analyst of strategic problems. Nixon and Kissinger shared the view that, as the new president said in 1970, "The postwar period in international relations has ended." The era of overwhelming American military and economic superiority was over. The problem now was to adjust commitments to the emerging limits of power.

The Indochina War remained the nation's most anguishing international concern (see Map 33-1). Nixon and Kissinger hoped for American disengagement but

Map 33-1 *The Indochina War*

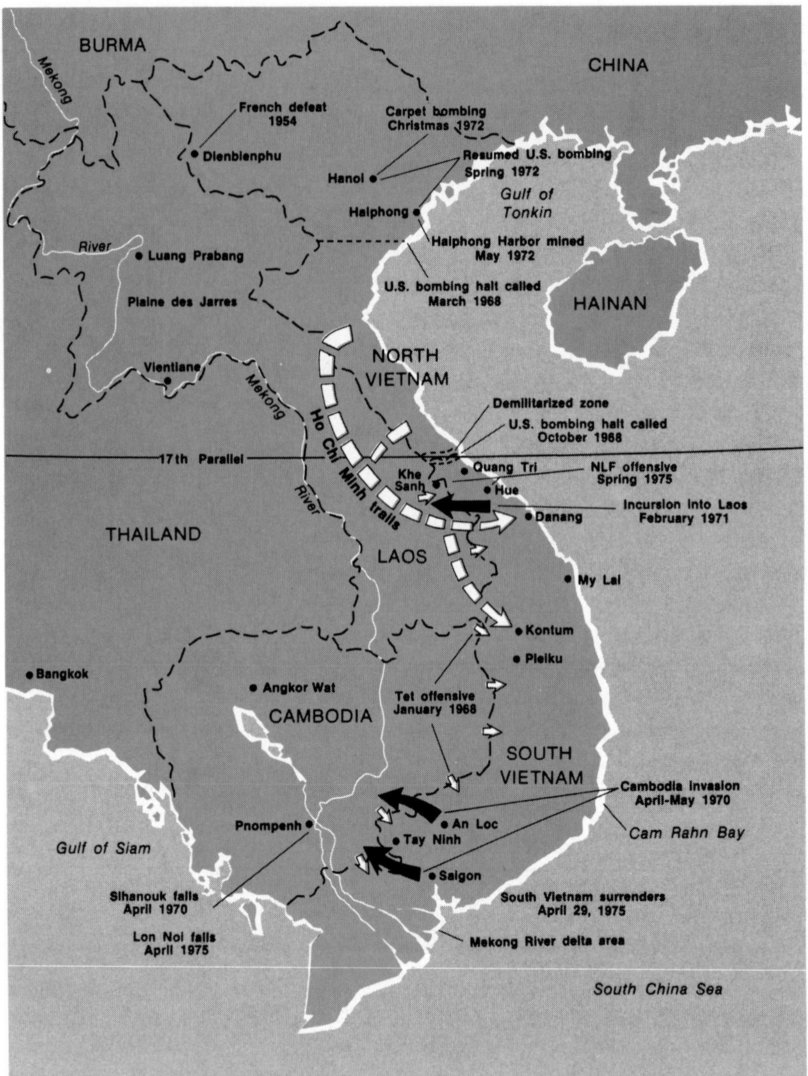

believed that this had to be achieved "honorably." "Our defeat and humiliation in South Vietnam," Nixon said in November 1969, "without question would promote recklessness in the councils of those great powers who have not abandoned their goals of world conquest." The point, said Kissinger, was "to withdraw as an expression of policy and not as a collapse."

Nixon began by "winding down" American participation through a steady policy of "Vietnamization"—the replacement of American by South Vietnamese troops. In April 1969 543,000 American soldiers were in Vietnam; by the summer of 1972, there were 50,000. While troop withdrawals proceeded, Kissinger made thirteen secret trips to France for peace talks with the North Vietnamese. Ho Chi Minh died in September 1969, but neither his successors in Hanoi nor the National Liberation Front in South Vietnam were prepared to abandon the objective of 30 years: the control of South Vietnam. The American proposals, varying in detail, all called for the concurrent withdrawal of American and North Vietnamese forces from South Vietnam, and all involved a favored position for the regime in Saigon, now headed by General Nguyen Van Thieu. The objectives remained irreconcilable.

Widening the War Vietnamization also required measures to reinforce Saigon. Nixon hailed Thieu as

Nixon and Kissinger: central control of foreign policy

one of the four or five greatest political leaders of the world. Further strengthening of Thieu's regime soon demanded, in Nixon's judgment, extraordinary military measures — measures long urged by the Joint Chiefs of Staff, rejected by Johnson, and designed to destroy the North Vietnamese buildup in Cambodia and Laos.

For nearly 20 years the wily Prince Sihanouk had managed through artful dodging to preserve the neutrality of Cambodia. In the middle 1960s, Hanoi had begun to set up staging areas in Cambodia for attacks on South Vietnam. Early in 1969 Nixon initiated secret B-52 raids over Cambodia — 3,500 in the next 14 months, concealed from Congress by a system of false bombing reports. In March 1970 Sihanouk was overthrown by a pro-Western coup headed by General Lon Nol. On April 30 Nixon announced an American incursion into Cambodia to "clean out major enemy sanctuaries." If, said Nixon, "the world's most powerful nation . . . acts like a pitiful, helpless giant . . . all other nations will be on notice that despite its overwhelming power the United States when a real crisis comes will be found wanting."

The invasion of Cambodia set off the most widespread and intense college protests in American history, involving 1.5 million students and half of America's 2,500 campuses. On May 4, 1970, four students were killed and ten wounded by National Guardsmen at Kent State University in Ohio. Nixon, who a few days before had described student agitators as "bums," observed sententiously, "When dissent turns to violence, it invites tragedy." On May 14 police killed two black youths and wounded twelve at Jackson State College in Mississippi.

The Cambodian episode also produced strong reactions on Capitol Hill. For some time legislators had been restive over the loss to the executive of the constitutional power to declare war. The dispatch of American troops into Cambodia now raised the constitutional issue in acute form. Congress, hoping to reclaim lost powers, repealed the Tonkin Gulf resolution (see p. 848) and debated a variety of proposals to cut off funds for the further prosecution of the war. The publication by the New York *Times* and other journals in June 1971 of the so-called Pentagon Papers, made available by a former Pentagon official named Daniel Ellsberg, strengthened the antiwar mood by documenting concealments and deceptions that had accompanied earlier stages of the war.

At the same time, television was bringing the savagery of the "living-room war" into millions of American homes every night. People watched with growing discomfort as the tiny screen showed Vietnamese children horribly burned by American napalm or Americans systematically setting fire to Vietnamese villages. Both sides in the Vietnam War were guilty of wanton violence, but the disclosure that American soldiers had massacred more than 100 unarmed Vietnamese civilians at My Lai in March 1968 made war atrocities a national issue. My Lai forced Americans suddenly to wonder whether the United States had not brutalized itself in Vietnam. Many concluded that the means employed and the destruction wrought had grown out of all proportion to the interests involved and the goals sought. In 1971 public opinion polls reported that 65 percent of respondents believed it "morally wrong" for Americans to be fighting in Vietnam, though 1972 polls showed that a majority still supported Nixon's position that South Vietnam should not fall under Communist control.

Though many American soldiers remained as brave as their predecessors in other wars, disgust with the war in Vietnam was seeping into the army itself. By 1970 some soldiers were wearing peace symbols and refusing to go into combat. The use of marijuana was general, and, according to estimates, 10 to 15 percent

Kent State University, May 4, 1970

of the troops were addicted to heroin. "Fragging"—the use of fragmentation grenades to kill unpopular officers—was not unknown. In the United States, underground newspapers and antiwar coffee houses ventilated G.I. discontent. Amnesty for draft dodgers and deserters became an increasingly popular issue. Military morale and discipline were probably worse than at any point in American history. The incipient demoralization of the army strengthened the spreading determination to get out of the war.

Indochina Dénouement But the war went on. As American ground strength declined, Nixon relied increasingly on air and naval power to persuade Hanoi to lower its price for peace. By the end of 1971 his administration had dropped 3.3 million tons of bombs on South Vietnam, Laos, Cambodia, and, toward the end, North Vietnam—more in three years than the Johnson administration had dropped in five (and the bombing rate mounted in Nixon's fourth year). Yet aerial terror accomplished no more than it had in the past. When a strong North Vietnamese offensive in the spring of 1972 set back South Vietnamese forces, Nixon, fearing loss of "respect for the office of the President of the United States" on the eve of a scheduled trip to Moscow, retaliated by ordering the air force to widen the bombing of North Vietnam and the navy to mine North Vietnamese harbors. This would be, he said, the "decisive military action to end the war" and it was required because "an American defeat in Vietnam would encourage this kind of aggression all over the world . . . in the Mid-East, in Europe, and other areas." Some supposed that intensification of the war would cause the Russians to cancel the summit, but Moscow, fearing that cancellation might throw Washington into the embrace of Beijing (Peking), swallowed hard and digested the new escalation. The war went on.

As the 1972 election approached, the Nixon administration, determined to neutralize the war as a campaign issue, made a change of decisive significance in the American negotiating position. It finally abandoned its longtime insistence that the withdrawal of American troops from South Vietnam be accompanied by the simultaneous withdrawal of North Vietnamese troops. Had this concession been made in 1969, American disengagement might have taken place then, and more than 15,000 Americans (and many more Vietnamese), killed from 1969 to 1972, would have lived.

In August the withdrawal of American ground combat troops was completed. Nixon also soon offered reconstruction assistance to North Vietnam. For its part, Hanoi dropped its demands for a political settlement in advance of a cease-fire and for the immediate elimination of Thieu. "Peace is at hand," Kissinger announced on October 26. But Thieu declined to come aboard. He thought, not unreasonably, that an agreement that removed American troops while leaving 145,000 North Vietnamese in place in South Vietnam did not bode well for his own future.

After the election, Kissinger tried to reshape the agreement to meet some of Thieu's objections. Hanoi resisted the proposed changes. In December the talks broke down. Over Christmas, in one of the most savage acts of a savage war, Nixon ordered the bombing of Hanoi and Haiphong, with B-52s smashing the North Vietnamese cities for twelve days. The ostensible reason was to force concessions from Hanoi. Another purpose was to persuade Thieu to accept the agreement by improving his relative military position and by reminding him of the damage American air power had the capacity to inflict. On January 5, 1973, Nixon secretly promised Thieu that "we will respond with full force should the settlement be violated by North Vietnam." A billion dollars' worth of planes, tanks, and other weapons was rushed to South Vietnam. Thieu remained dubious. But continued American pressure obliged him to accede. The agreement, as signed on Paris on January 23, differed little from the one originally reached in October.

The Paris Accords established a cease-fire and proposed complicated machinery to bring about a political settlement. Given the irreconcilable differences between the two regimes, the machinery was plainly unworkable. Skeptics discerned a cynical policy designed to provide a "decent interval" between American withdrawal and Thieu's collapse. The last American troops, along with American prisoners of war, went at the end of March 1973. Both Vietnamese governments violated the Paris Accords from the start. The "cease-fire war" began. More South Vietnamese soldiers died in 1974 than in 1967. In March 1975 Hanoi launched a major offensive. The American government, asking Congress for emergency military assistance, claimed that failure to go the last mile with Thieu would cause the world to look on the United States as a feeble and perfidious nation. Congress had heard such talk before and was unmoved. At the end of April 1975 Thieu fell in South Vietnam and Lon Nol in Cambodia.

Vietnam: evacuation

The Indochina War was at last at an end. The aftermath refuted the domino theory that had led the United States into the war. Hanoi's victory, while it established a cruelly repressive Communist regime in Vietnam, failed to produce the long-feared coordinated Communist control of East Asia. With the American presence removed, the Communist states fell to fighting among themselves. In Cambodia, now called Kampuchea, a vicious Marxist regime under Pol Pot brutalized, starved, and murdered millions of Cambodians. In 1978–79 Communist Vietnam invaded Communist Kampuchea and overthrew Pol Pot. Communist China thereupon invaded Communist Vietnam. Communist China (and to some degree the United States) supported Pol Pot. Communist Russia supported Vietnam. Conflicting national interests once again proved more potent than ideological affinities. The dominoes, instead of falling against the West, crashed into one another.

Indochina Inquest The war had killed at least 1.5 million Indochinese and turned a third of the population into refugees. The 6.7 million tons of bombs dropped by American planes left the landscape scarred with craters. Defoliation, undertaken to deprive the Viet Cong of forest cover, affected one-third of the forest area of South Vietnam. President Marcos of the Philippines spoke for many Asians when he said in 1971, "Heaven forbid that the U.S. should duplicate what it has done in South Vietnam if the war should come to our country."

For the United States the Indochina War had lasted longer than any war in its history. It left more Americans dead—57,000—than any war except the Civil War and the two World Wars, and cost more money than any war except the Second World War.

The war devastated an American generation. There were no parades for returning veterans. The country that had carelessly sent soldiers to Vietnam treated them with cruel indifference when they came home. Many of the 2.8 million who served in Vietnam suffered from emotional dislocation. One study reported that nearly 60 percent returned with nightmares, diseases, nervous conditions, and alcohol and drug abuse. On the other extreme were the young men who had acted early on the conviction that so many came to in the end: the war was immoral. The debate whether 570,000 "draft offenders," of whom 30,000 went underground or fled the country, mostly to Canada, should receive amnesty carried the divisions of war into the aftermath. As for the 15 million men of military age who neither fought nor fled, the war had gravely weakened their faith in the judgment and the word of their government.

America's myth of itself as benevolent, wise, and invincible drained away in the jungles of Indochina. The bitter experience corroded the spirit of self-confidence that had characterized America in 1945. By the early 1970s the American people were divided, the economy was in trouble, the armed forces were in discredit, national motives were in doubt, and liberal ideals themselves seemed implicated in the disaster. Paradoxically, the war had stimulated what it was supposed to prevent—a resurgence of isolationism.

Most Americans believed that the United States had extended its power around the planet in order to protect free nations from Communist aggression. But the shock of Vietnam put the situation in a chilling new light. In the course of 25 years, it now seemed, America had established a sort of empire of its own. It had military commitments to 47 nations, 375 major bases and 3,000 minor facilities in foreign lands, 1 million troops stationed abroad, and 2.5 million more troops under arms at home.

Anatomy of Empire How had this quasi-empire arisen? On the left, Vietnam confirmed the tendency to ascribe everything—not only the Indochina War but the Cold War and even American participation in the Second World War—to the supposed quest of American capitalism for world hegemony. It was true that American overseas investments had grown strikingly in the postwar period—from $8.4 billion in 1945 to more than $100 billion by 1973. Though it was hard to argue that America went into Vietnam to gain markets or protect investments, sophisticated exponents of the Open Door thesis contended that, because defeat in Vietnam would jeopardize American markets and investments throughout the Third World, economic interest compelled Washington to a course of ruthless counterrevolution.

Close analysis of the figures showed, however, that the dependence of American capitalism on the underdeveloped world was limited. Two-thirds of American exports went to industrialized rather than to developing countries, and sales to the Third World amounted to about 3 percent of the annual national output. Investment in the Third World represented a declining fraction of total foreign investment—35 percent in 1960 and only 26 percent in 1973. Of Third World investment, 40 percent was in petroleum. With that excluded, only about one-sixth of American overseas investment was in the developing nations. In so far as American capitalism depended on the world outside, it depended on markets and investments in developed and not in underdeveloped countries. Nor had American business been, for example, notably eager for escalation in Vietnam.

If not American capitalism, what? No single explanation of the imperial impulse seemed satisfactory. A number of factors converged to lead Americans to appoint themselves custodians of freedom, entitled to intervene freely and righteously around the planet. The American empire, such as it was, resulted from the perversion of initially honorable beliefs: the belief in the necessity of creating an international structure of peace; the belief in America's mission to uplift and save suffering humanity; the belief in America's capacity to rebuild and instruct other nations. The misapplication of these beliefs was brought about initially by the real threat of Stalinist communism—American presence in other lands was mostly at the invitation of governments fearful of the Russians — and then by the rigid form taken by the counterideology of anticommunism.

A special pressure encouraging interventionist policies, above all in Vietnam, was the military establishment. The armed forces had emerged from the Second World War with unprecedented power and status. When the wartime military leaders, most of whom were sober and responsible men, departed the scene, a new group took over, more in the school of MacArthur than of Marshall, professionally persuaded that political problems had military solutions, professionally committed to multiplying threats, appropriations, and weapons, professionally adept at playing upon national desires to appear virile and patriotic. This was not quite Eisenhower's "military-industrial complex." The military establishment was an independent force in its own right, operating according to its institutional aspirations.

A look at other nations corroborated the proposition that the imperial impulse was not rooted in a specific system of ownership. Every great power, whatever its ideology, had its military machine. Every military machine supposed that national security required the domination of "strategic" weaker states, if only to prevent their domination by some rival power. If, for example, the invasion by the Red Army to overthrow a national Communist regime in Czechoslovakia in 1968 was not imperialism, then the term had no meaning. If it was imperialism, then imperialism was not uniquely rooted in capitalism, nor would the abolition of capitalism end it. It seemed likely that no change in systems of ideology or ownership would reduce the power of the professional military in a time of chronic international crisis.

The Pentagon: an independent force

The Decline of the Superpowers After the Second World War, the United States and the Soviet Union had entered the vacuums of power left in the wake of war. Each superpower had sought to extend its reach in order to protect itself from the other. But the reign of the superpowers was drawing to a close. Where American and Soviet power had flowed into the vacuums from without, the resurgence of nationalism — in Europe, within the Communist world, and in the Third World — was now replenishing these vacuums from within. The reinvigoration of nationalism meant growing opposition to the United States in the Western bloc, growing opposition to the Soviet Union in the Communist bloc, and growing opposition to both in the Third World. The consequence was to place limits on the power of the two countries. Tocqueville's celebrated forecast — America and Russia, each "marked out by the will of Heaven to sway the destinies of half the globe" — had in the end an exceedingly short run.

In addition, the fragmentation of the Communist world by nationalism altered the nature of the problem that communism presented to the United States. The intensifying quarrel between Russia and China meant the end of any single center of authority in the Communist movement and hence the end of a unified Communist ideology and discipline. In the age of Stalin, Communist parties everywhere had responded to the directives of Moscow. Now the rise of "polycentrism" set Communist states free to pursue national policies. It could no longer be assumed that the extension of communism meant the automatic extension of Soviet, or Chinese, power.

As the threat of monolithic communism thus receded, Vietnam emphasized the limits of American power. For a season Americans began to conclude that not everything that happened in the world was of equal concern to the United States, that in an age of local upheaval and savagery many terrible things would take place that the United States lacked the power to prevent or the wisdom to cure, and that Washington could not be the permanent guarantor of stability on a turbulent planet.

Responding to the new mood, Nixon in July 1969 promulgated what he thereafter termed the Nixon Doctrine. The "central thesis," Nixon said in 1970, was that "the United States will participate in the defense and development of allies and friends, but cannot—and will not—conceive *all* the plans, design *all* the programs, execute *all* the decisions and undertake *all* the defense of the free nations of the world. We will help where it will make a real difference and is considered in our interest." Even in such cases, he added, the nations directly threatened had the "primary responsibility" of providing the manpower for their own defense.

An era of negotiation: Nixon and Mao

Rapprochement with Communist Powers Though Nixon himself had been a zealous Cold Warrior who had condemned Kennedy and Johnson as inadequately militant in their Cuba and Vietnam policies, he was also a realist. Kissinger, the student of Metternich and Bismarck, reinforced a geopolitical view. Security, as Nixon saw it, demanded no longer the rollback of communism but rather the reestablishment of the classical balance of power. "It will be a safer world and a better world," he said in 1971, "if we have a strong, healthy United States, Europe, Soviet Union, China, Japan—each balancing the other, not playing one against the other, an even balance."

His boldest step in the pursuit of the balance-of-power design was his reversal of American policy toward the Chinese People's Republic. After the Korean War, domestic political pressures had frozen successive administrations into a posture of grim nonrecognition of the Beijing (Peking) regime. The excesses of the Cultural Revolution of 1966–68 seemed to verify the theory that Maoism represented the ultimate in Communist fanaticism. However, China and the Soviet Union had each come to fear the rival Communist state more than the common capitalist adversary. When Russia stationed nearly 50 divisions along its Chinese frontier, Mao Zedong (Mao Tse-tung) and Zhou Enlai (Chou En-lai) evidently decided they must take steps to block a Soviet-American alliance against China. Nixon was eager for an opening to China, and a mission by Kissinger to Beijing (Peking) in July 1971 was followed by an extraordinary presidential trip to China in early 1972. Nixon stayed in China for nearly a week—a longer state visit than any president had ever made to a foreign nation. On February 27, he signed a declaration saying that Taiwan, where Chiang Kai-shek still ruled, was legally part of mainland China, that American forces would eventually withdraw from Taiwan, and that the island's future was to be settled by the Chinese themselves.

Nixon's "China card" pushed the Soviet Union toward an improved relationship with the United States. That relationship, as Nixon said, was moving "from an era of confrontation to an era of negotiation." On May 12, 1972, Nixon and Brezhnev signed a twelve-point agreement on "Basic Principles" of détente. A European Security Conference, long proposed by the Soviet Union and finally held in Helsinki in August 1975, ratified Europe's postwar borders. "Basket Three" of the Helsinki Agreement gave new international status to human rights. At the same time, responding to Russia's need for modern technology, the administration encouraged Soviet-American trade and even undertook to seek most-favored-nation tariff status (that is, the extension of tariff concessions made to other countries) for the Soviet Union.

Through this network of relationships—diplomatic, economic, and commercial—joined together and made mutually dependent by the concept of "linkage," Kissinger hoped to "give the Soviets a stake in international equilibrium." Détente, combined with the Chinese connection, would continue containment in a new form and make up for the relative decline in American military power.

The 1972 Moscow Summit

The context as well as the content of the summit made it a major success for American policy. The fact that we had faced down Hanoi and yet completed major negotiations with Moscow three months after the spectacular in Peking evoked the prospect of a more hopeful future and thus put Vietnam into perspective. The summit helped us complete the isolation of Hanoi by giving Moscow and Peking a stake in their ties with us. What was even more novel, we were freed for the better part of the year from the domestic turmoil on which . . . Hanoi had always been able to count. . . .

But the fundamental achievement was to sketch the outline on which coexistence between the democracies and the Soviet system must be based. SALT embodied our conviction that a wildly spiraling nuclear arms race was in no country's interest and enhanced no one's security; the "Basic Principles" gave at least verbal expression to the necessity of responsible political conduct. The two elements reinforced each other; they symbolized our conviction that a relaxation of tensions could not be based exclusively on arms control; the ultimate test would be restrained international behavior.

From Henry Kissinger, *White House Years,* 1979

The Arms Race In the 1960s the Soviet Union had drastically expanded its production of land-based intercontinental ballistic missiles (ICBMs). By 1972, it had 50 percent more missile launchers than the United States. But the United States retained a more than two-to-one superiority in warheads, and American security rested not only on ICBMs but on submarine-based missiles (the Polaris-Poseidon system) and on the strategic bombing force—three independent systems, each capable of inflicting deadly damage even after a Soviet first strike, and one at least, the sea-based deterrent, invulnerable to Soviet attack. With the Soviet Union now in a comparable state of assured retaliatory capacity, it seemed absurd for the two powers, each with the ability to incinerate the other, to continue piling overkill on overkill.

A first series of Strategic Arms Limitation Talks (SALT-I) began in 1969 and concluded with Nixon and Brezhnev meeting in Moscow in 1972. The resulting antiballistic missile (ABM) treaty prohibited the development, testing, and deployment of future antiballistic missile systems. An interim agreement on offensive systems in effect balanced Soviet quantitative superiority against American qualitative superiority, permitting a Soviet numerical lead in ICBMs in exchange for an American lead in technology and bombers.

SALT-I was based on the MAD conception of nuclear standoff (or what the Nixon administration called nuclear "sufficiency"). "What in the name of God is strategic superiority?" cried Henry Kissinger, who became secretary of state in 1973 (in an outburst he later retracted). "What is the significance of it, politically, militarily, operationally, at these levels of numbers? What can you do with it?" While SALT-I produced no reductions, it set in motion a process that offered hope for reduction in the future.

However, discontent was rising within the administration over MAD. Some critics wanted to reestablish American strategic superiority. Others argued that the threat of reciprocal mass slaughter was barbarous and that it lacked credibility as a deterrent. Technological

Kissinger, Brezhnev, Nixon: Moscow, 1972

improvements gave missiles new accuracy and precision, and James Schlesinger, who became secretary of defense in 1973, favored a widening of nuclear "options" with special attention both to "counterforce" —attacks on military installations and missile sites —and to tactical weapons. Critics questioned Schlesinger's idea of controlled and limited nuclear war and detected in counterforce the potentiality for a first-strike capability. MAD may have been mad, but to many the alternative seemed even madder.

In the meantime, both superpowers continued to develop weapons systems not covered in SALT-I. In 1969 Nixon, over congressional opposition, had made the fateful decision to introduce the multiple independently targeted reentry vehicle (MIRV), which, because it packed several missiles in a single warhead, immensely complicated problems of verification and ushered in a new and more uncontrollable phase of the arms race. (In 1974 Kissinger said, "I wish I had thought through the implications of a MIRVed world.") For its part, the Soviet Union MIRVed its ICBMs, built the Backfire supersonic bomber, and strove in other ways to enlarge its already formidable counterforce power and to add qualitative improvement to quantitative superiority. Technology was the perpetual enemy of stability, and the qualitative arms race was subverting the quantitative limits imposed by SALT-I. Improvement in the delivery and accuracy of smaller warheads made possible the abandonment of huge megatonnage hydrogen weapons and the slight reduction of the nuclear stockpile from a high point of about 32,000 in 1967.

SALT talks continued. An agreement reached at Vladivostok in December 1974 set ICBM and MIRV ceilings at levels so high they became goals, not limitations. The nuclear arms race rushed on.

Beyond the Superpowers Kissinger's theory was that détente could work only if the Soviet Union and the United States respected each other's spheres of influence. He saw the Soviet Union as a status quo power for which revolution beyond the Soviet zone was a temptation, not a necessity—a temptation from which the Kremlin would quickly recede when the United States showed the "will" to defend what Russia would accept as legitimate American interests. He therefore saw no incompatibility between seeking an accommodation with Moscow and reacting vigorously against Communist activities elsewhere. In so doing, the Nixon administration displayed what critics regarded as a fondness for regimes of the authoritarian right.

In Europe Nixon sedulously identified Washington with right-wing dictatorships in Greece and Portugal. In the case of Portugal, when a democratic regime came to power in 1974, Kissinger threatened the provisional government with diplomatic and economic isolation for its inclusion of Communists. He also overreacted to the transient phenomenon of Eurocommunism, seeing democratic professions by Western Communist parties as evidence not of political weakness, but of tactical cunning.

In Asia the Nixon administration ignored Pakistan's brutal repression of the Bangladesh independence movement and, despite public avowals of neutrality, gave secret instructions to "tilt" American power toward Pakistan during its war with India in 1971. In Africa the administration tilted toward white regimes —not only South Africa and Rhodesia but Portuguese colonial regimes in Angola and Mozambique. Portugal's departure from Angola in 1975 left the newly independent state torn between rival guerrilla forces, one side backed by the Soviet Union, the other by South Africa, China, and the United States. Kissinger approved large-scale covert intervention by the CIA, overriding warnings from the State Department that the result would be even larger counterescalation by the Russians. The introduction of 10,000 Cuban troops assisted the side favored by Moscow. In 1976 Congress prohibited further CIA covert action in Angola without express congressional approval. Belatedly recognizing that a successful African policy required a measure of support in black Africa, Kissinger now reversed course and endorsed black majority rule.

In Latin America Nixon commended the military dictatorship in Brazil. The election of a Marxist regime headed by Salvador Allende in Chile in 1970 produced special excitement in Washington. Before the election Kissinger had directed the CIA to take covert action against Allende's candidacy. After the election he authorized the CIA to spend $8 million to "destabilize" the new government. Allende had received only 36 percent of the vote, and his economic policy was neither well-managed nor perhaps acceptable to the Chilean majority. In the end his regime might have fallen anyway. But Washington, reinforcing the CIA by a credit squeeze and other economic measures, contributed to Allende's downfall and probable murder in a military coup in 1973.

The succeeding military regime under General Augusto Pinochet shocked the world by its policies of repression and torture. Yet it remained a favorite of Washington, receiving more than twice as much bilateral economic assistance in 1975 as the next-largest Latin American recipient of United States aid. In Kissinger's view, a Pinochet regime, because it did not upset the existing balance of force, would be better for détente than a regime inclined to the other side. This was the Soviet theory of détente too, as Moscow had shown in Czechoslovakia and elsewhere.

The idea that every Marxist victory in the Third World was an addition to Soviet power denied the reality of polycentrism and made Washington an arsenal of counterrevolution. In a deeper sense, Washington's support of authoritarian regimes for short-run diplomatic purposes ignored the human values involved. Such a policy damaged what had been historically America's most precious international asset—the bond that was felt to run between the United States and ordinary people around the planet.

Middle Eastern Cockpit The Middle East continued to present perplexing questions. The Soviet Union was increasing its influence among the Arab states in pursuit of historic Russian ambitions in the area. The United States had a deep moral interest in Israel and a strong—if conflicting—economic interest in Arab oil. Both Russian and American concerns were superimposed on a region torn by indigenous hatreds with a life and potency of their own.

Visiting Teheran in May 1972, Nixon asked the shah of Iran to become the "protector" of American interests in the Persian Gulf area. In exchange the shah received the unrestricted right to buy the most advanced American weapons. United States arms sales to Iran, which had totaled $1.2 billion over the 22 years since 1950, increased almost 16-fold to a total of $19.5 billion from 1972 to 1979. Though the shah was in his way a modernizer, he was increasingly possessed by delusions of grandeur, he was surrounded by sycophants and thieves, and his secret police systematically tortured and killed his opponents. Nixon's Iranian policy, moreover, was taken by Moscow as the exploitation of détente to forward military encirclement of the Soviet Union.

In the Middle East, the Arab states remained unreconciled to the existence of Israel. In June 1967 Israel, responding to the Egyptian blockade of the port of Elath on the Gulf of Aqaba, launched a surprise attack on Egypt and won a smashing victory in the Six Days War. After the war, Israel retained possession of territories deemed essential to defense against future Arab attack—the Sinai Peninsula against Egypt and the Golan Heights against Syria as well as the Gaza Strip and the West Bank of the Jordan River. In November 1967 the UN Security Council passed Resolution 242 calling for "withdrawal of Israeli forces from territories occupied in the recent conflict" (though not necessarily, it was noted, from *all* such territories) and for the "acknowledgment" of the sovereignty and independence of all states in the area.

The package deal thus outlined was not achieved, the Arab states refusing to recognize Israel, Israel refusing to abandon the territory won in 1967. The bitterness of the Palestinian refugees—Arabs who fled or were expelled from Israel—added another explosive element, especially after the formation of the Palestine Liberation Organization (PLO) and more extreme terrorist groups, mostly operating out of the small kingdom of Jordan. In 1970 King Hussein of Jordan attacked the Palestinian guerrillas, whereupon Syria, with presumed Soviet support, invaded Jordan. The threat of Israeli and U.S. counterintervention forced Syria to withdraw.

The death of Nasser in September 1970 brought Anwar as-Sadat into power in Cairo. A precarious peace, punctuated by Arab raids and Israeli reprisals, prevailed until October 5, 1973. Then, on Yom Kippur, the Jewish holy day of atonement, Egypt and Syria struck at Israel. Caught by surprise, Israeli forces reeled under the blow. The Soviet Union airlifted supplies to Egypt, and the United States similarly supplied Israel, while both superpowers also called for a UN resolution for a cease-fire. On October 22 the UN security council passed that resolution, but the Israelis, now counterattacking, marched on in the Sinai. The Soviet Union warned them to stop or face the possibility of Soviet intervention. Warning for his part against unilateral Soviet action, Nixon on October 24 put American nuclear forces on a worldwide alert, an extraordinary step that may have been intended primarily to buttress his domestic standing at the time of the national uproar over the "Saturday night massacre" (see p. 887). But the Soviets quickly accepted Nixon's suggestion for sending a UN supervisory force to the Middle East, and on October 26 the United States cancelled the nuclear alert. Meanwhile, the Israelis continued to delay falling back to the proposed cease-fire line. Neither superpower had been able to control its client. Nevertheless, the United States succeeded in establishing the position it wanted as mediator in the Middle East. The Soviet Union, its relationship with Egypt now fractured, turned instead to supporting the PLO and other radical Arab groups.

More threatening to the United States was a new development. In 1960 Venezuela had persuaded the oil-producing states of the Middle East to join in forming the Organization of Petroleum Exporting Countries (OPEC). The original point of OPEC was to concert policies in order to defend national economies against the manipulation of the world market by western oil companies. On October 19, 1973, OPEC, now controlled by an Arab majority, imposed a ban on oil exports to the United States and Western Europe in retaliation for American support of Israel. It also quadrupled the price of Middle Eastern oil. These actions represented a historic reversal in the balance of power between the industrialized nations and the Third World. For centuries access to vital raw materials has been a particular motive for Western imperialism. OPEC showed that possession of raw materials, which once placed underdeveloped countries at the mercy of the West, could now place the West at their mercy.

The October War altered the situation in the Middle East in two salient respects: it shattered the belief in Israel's military invincibility, and it demonstrated western vulnerability in face of Arab use of oil as a political weapon. Both American interests—Israel and oil—called more urgently than ever for a political settlement. This became Kissinger's major objective in 1974–75. Relying on his new personal relationship with Sadat as well as on the traditional American influence in Israel, he visited the Middle East on an average of one out of every six weeks. His "shuttle diplomacy" sought to bring Israel and Egypt step by step toward a resolution of outstanding issues. At the same time, he tried to reduce Soviet influence by systematically excluding Moscow from his Middle Eastern negotiations. In September 1975 an interim agreement on the Sinai provided for partial Israeli troop withdrawal in exchange for an American commitment to supply Israel with advanced arms and aircraft and not to negotiate with the Palestine Liberation Organization so long as the PLO refused to recognize Israel's right to exist. The Middle East demonstrated Kissinger's virtuoso qualities as a negotiator—his intelligence, resourcefulness, perseverance, and stamina.

Debate over Détente At first the Nixon-Kissinger policy of rapprochement with China and Russia encountered little resistance at home. Nixon's anti-Communist credentials facilitated the process. Observers wryly noted the irony of the old Red-hunter exchanging unctuous toasts with Zhou Enlai (Chou En-lai) and Brezhnev. Even conservatives confined themselves to stoical warnings.

"Détente," as Kissinger wrote, "was a relationship between adversaries; it did not pretend friendship." It did respond to concrete interests of both superpowers—the prevention of nuclear war, the containment of military budgets, the Soviet apprehension about China and need for Western technology, the American acknowledgment of the disappearance of a monolithic Communist threat, the intensifying claims in both countries of internal problems. But the administration oversold détente as an international cure-all.

Where détente had reality, it was as the expression of stability in the equilibrium of power. It was the recognition of situations that had already come into existence. It was, in short, the consequence rather than the cause of stabilization. It therefore applied primarily to Europe. In parts of the world where power relationships were in flux, détente was a wistful hope. In the Middle East, Africa, East Asia, instability had deep historic roots and was far beyond the joint capacity of the Soviet Union and the United States to control even if they should agree on policy.

In Soviet eyes détente meant only a series of specific and limited agreements. It did not imply a broad guarantee of the status quo nor exclude Soviet support of national-liberation movements. For its part, the administration was unable to make good on all its assurances to Moscow. Thus Soviet restrictions on the migration of Jews led in 1973–74 to the denial by the American Congress of most-favored-nation status and the passage of the Jackson Amendment, an attempt to condition commercial concessions on changes in Soviet emigration policy. American interference in what Moscow regarded as an internal question drove the Kremlin to cancel the Soviet-American trade agreement of 1972.

When détente failed to live up to unrealistic expectations, disenchantment set in. Conservatives were especially disturbed by what they regarded as a decay in American military power. By 1975 defense expenditures were less in constant dollars than they had been at any time since before the Korean War. Defense spending dropped dramatically from 49 percent of federal outlays in Eisenhower's last year to 29 percent in Nixon's last year. The budget for strategic forces was about one-third in real terms what it had been at the end of the Eisenhower administration. If Russia achieved a war-winning capability, conservatives believed, this would demoralize the West and allow Soviet power to expand through nuclear blackmail.

On the issue of human rights, critics were joined by liberals who favored arms control but were outraged by the treatment accorded such Soviet dissenters as the physicist Andrei Sakharov and the novelist Aleksandr Solzhenitsyn. Nor did the Soviet Union comply with Basket Three of the Helsinki Agreement and its pledges to increase the flow of people, information, and ideas across the Iron Curtain.

By 1976 both détente and Henry Kissinger had lost their allure. Many Americans agreed when the French journalist André Fontaine defined détente as simply "the Cold War pursued by other means—and sometimes by the same." As for Kissinger, his wit, insouciance, and proficiency had seized the national imagination for some years. But by the mid-1970s opinion had grown more skeptical. His addiction to ambiguity and secrecy had become self-defeating. His policy alarmed conservatives by its pursuit of détente and liberals by its intervention in countries outside the realm of direct American interest.

Yet together Nixon and Kissinger, an odd couple indeed, had relieved American foreign policy of burdening taboos, shifted national attention from ideology to geopolitics, and adapted American policy to far-reaching changes in the structure of international relationships.

DECLINE AND FALL

Nixon and the Economy For Nixon, domestic policy was secondary to foreign policy. On economics, he had prejudices rather than principles—prejudices against an unbalanced budget and against government controls. But he was also aware of the political dangers of adverse economic conditions. His most urgent economic problem was the inflation generated by the Indochina War. In 1970 the consumer price index was 16 percent higher than in 1967 and prices were still rising. In the tradition of economic orthodoxy, Nixon at first supposed that restrictive monetary policy would bring inflation under control. He denounced "jawboning" (official admonitions against price or wage increases) and price-wage guidelines, as developed in the Kennedy years. Instead he called for tight money and high interest rates.

The immediate effect of what he termed his "game plan" was to produce the first recession in a decade. But inflation did not stop. From January 1969 to August 1971, while unemployment rose from 3.5 to 6 percent, the cost of living increased by an astonishing 14.5 percent. Furthermore, inflation was overpricing American exports and weakening the dollar abroad. In 1971 the balance-of-payments deficit reached the record figure of $29.6 billion.

As "stagflation"—the combination of stagnation and inflation—persisted, Nixon changed his approach. Fortified by the appointment of a Texas Democrat, John B. Connally, as secretary of the Treasury, Nixon declared himself a Keynesian in the summer of 1971 and on August 15 announced a startling reversal of economic course: a 90-day price-wage freeze (Phase 1) to be followed in November by Phase 2, a system of wage and price controls. Inflation promptly subsided for 1971 and 1972. In his August announcement Nixon also suspended the convertibility of dollars into gold, thereby making American goods more competitive in world markets. This was followed in December by the formal devaluation of the dollar. These measures ended the international monetary system set up at Bretton Woods (see p. 785) based on the convertibility of the dollar into gold and resulted in a new system of floating exchange rates.

Social Policy The liberal tide of the Kennedy-Johnson years, still running strong, shaped Nixon's early domestic legislation. Health maintenance organizations, student loan programs, low-income housing, the arts and humanities—all received increased federal support. In 1969–70 Congress strengthened national environmental policy, particularly with the Environmental Protection Agency (EPA) to combat the pollution of air and water. The Occupational Safety and Health Act of 1970 required employers engaged in interstate commerce to furnish working conditions free of hazards to life and health and gave the Occupational Safety and Health Administration (OSHA) authority to enforce industrial safety standards. The business community criticized both EPA and OSHA for meddlesome regulation and increased production costs. But the two new agencies materially improved the nation's air and water and the safety of the workplace.

The welfare system, partly federal and partly local in character, posed difficult problems, stemming in part from the increased awareness of the poor about their rights, in part from the remarkable population growth in the postwar years. The war boom had reversed the decline in the birth rate that had occurred during the Great Depression, while medical advances—penicillin and other antibiotics, antipolio vaccines, new surgical techniques—reduced the death rate. Population, which had grown by only 9 million in the 1930s, grew by 18 million in the 1940s and by 27 million in the 1950s—an increase in this last decade almost equal to the country's total population a century earlier. The result by the late 1960s was a flood of workers swamping an already overcrowded labor market. From 1947 to 1970 the labor force increased by 25 million, more than 40 percent.

One consequence was an enormous expansion of relief rolls, especially in the category of Aid to Families with Dependent Children (AFDC). The number of persons on welfare doubled from 1961 to 1972. Unemployment swelled the rolls by nearly 30 percent in 1970 alone. Of those receiving welfare in 1971, more than half were children, one-sixth were old people, one-tenth were blind or otherwise disabled. AFDC benefits went mostly to households headed by females. Less than 1 percent of the recipients were employable males. Widely condemned for fraud and waste, the system also was believed to drive employed fathers from the household so that their families could qualify for public assistance.

Nixon's initial answer was a bold proposal to replace AFDC by a Family Assistance Program (FAP). It was a path-breaking concept, but its provision for a guaranteed minimum income antagonized conservatives, while a "work requirement" alienated liberals. After passing the House in 1970, the FAP failed in the Senate. The administration now approached the welfare problem in other ways. In 1972 Congress raised social security payments by 20 percent and added cost-of-living "indexing" to compensate for inflation. It also liberalized eligibility and benefits in the food-stamp program, a New Deal innovation revived in the Kennedy years. By 1975 food-stamp enrollment approached 20 million, and the program cost $5 billion a year. In 1973 Congress passed the Comprehensive Employment and Training Act. The nationwide CETA system made government a provider of public service jobs as well as job training for the unemployed.

With exceptions like CETA, the Nixon social policy represented a shift from a "service strategy"—the

The Nixon Purpose

My fears about the American leadership classes had been confirmed and deepened by what I had seen and experienced during my first four years as President. In politics, academics, and the arts, and even in the business community and the churches, there was a successful and fashionable negativism which, in my judgment, reflected an underlying loss of will. . . .

At the beginning of my second term, Congress, the bureaucracy, and the media were still working in concert to maintain the ideas and ideology of the traditional Eastern liberal establishment that had come down to 1973 through the New Deal, the New Frontier, and the Great Society. Now I planned to give expression to the more conservative values and beliefs of the New Majority throughout the country and use my power to put some teeth into my New American Revolution.

As I noted in my diary, "This is going to be quite a shock to the establishment, but it is the only way, and probably the last time, that we can get government under control before it gets so big that it submerges the individual completely and destroys the dynamism which makes the American system what it is."

From Richard M. Nixon, *The Memoirs of Richard Nixon,* 1978

attempt to help the poor through specialized service programs—to an "income strategy"—helping the poor by giving them cash or some cash equivalent, such as food stamps. The services strategy was considered to imply that government and the welfare professional knew best what was good for the poor. The income strategy supposedly gave the poor greater freedom to make their own choices. Though critics felt that cash transfers to poor families would not alleviate such structural problems as education, job training, housing, and transportation, the underlying purpose of FAP was to combat the endemic poverty that would not yield to categorical programs. By 1975 income-support programs claimed nearly one-third of the federal budget.

Nixon's social policy extended the New Frontier and the Great Society. His last budget proposed spending nearly 60 percent more on social programs than Lyndon Johnson had done in 1968. As in foreign policy and in his 1971 advocacy of an incomes policy, he proved pragmatic rather than ideological.

The New Federalism Still, Nixon retained conservative instincts. In the longer run, his hope was to reduce the role of the national government. During the 1968 campaign he talked of the need to "re-establish the sense of community" that he felt had been undermined by the centralizing approach of the New Frontier and the Great Society. "After a third of a century of power flowing from the people and the States to Washington," he said in August 1969, "it is time for a New Federalism in which power, funds, and responsibility will flow from Washington to the States and to the people."

In order to equip local government to assume federal functions, Nixon promoted an idea that had originated in the Jackson administration (see p. 237) and received modern form in the Johnson administration —the distribution of federal revenues to the states. "Revenue-sharing" meant federal aid to state and local authorities through "no-strings" money grants rather than through grants to special categories, like the elderly or the disabled. The State and Local Fiscal Assistance Act of 1972 provided for the distribution of $30 billion in unrestricted funds to states and localities over the next five years.

Critics doubted that state and local units were more honest and efficient than the national government. They also contended that "no-strings" revenue-sharing discriminated against the cities, the poor, and the minorities—all beneficiaries of the now-diminished categorical grant-in-aid programs. Still, revenue-sharing won support, especially from financially hard-pressed local governments, because of its flexibility, and it was applauded by citizens who considered the national government too remote and unmanageable. In the end, revenue-sharing was the notable achievement of Nixon's New Federalism.

Concentration of Presidential Power In pushing his policies, Nixon faced Democratic control in both houses of Congress. The congressional majority had priorities of its own and the capacity to forward them by legislation. Confronted by statutes that conflicted with his own priorities, Nixon increasingly responded by refusing to spend funds voted by Congress.

Impoundment, as this practice was called, had a minor status in law and custom. Previous presidents had used it to effect savings or to stretch out the spending of funds, not to set aside the expressed will of Congress. Nixon not only impounded far more money than any of his predecessors—by 1973, his impoundments affected more than 100 federal programs and reached the level of $15 billion—but used impoundment to nullify laws passed by the legislative branch and even claimed this power as a constitutional right. The courts later rejected this claim and ordered the release of impounded funds.

Nixon also expanded the unconditional theory of executive privilege set forth in the Eisenhower administration. Kennedy and Johnson had returned to the traditional and restricted view of the president's power to withhold information from Congress. But Nixon claimed presidential denial as an inherent and unreviewable constitutional right. His attorneys general asserted on his behalf that Congress had no power to compel testimony over presidential objection from any one of the 2.5 million employees in the executive branch.

In addition to concentrating power in the executive branch, Nixon sought to concentrate power in the White House at the expense of the executive departments. By 1972 he had the largest White House staff up to that point in history. Nixon and his White House aides, especially H. R. Haldeman and John Ehrlichman, had not only a general determination, with which other presidents could have sympathized, to make the executive bureaucracy responsive to presidential purpose but a specific mistrust of the civil service as Democratic and hostile. In the conduct of foreign affairs, Nixon and Kissinger kept crucial initiatives secret from the State Department. Cabinet members found it increasingly difficult to gain access to Nixon. In time the more independent-minded among them departed.

The "Great Silent Majority" "I felt," Nixon wrote in his memoirs, "that the Silent Majority of Americans, with its roots mainly in the Midwest, the West, and the South, had simply never been encouraged to give the Eastern liberal elite a run for its money for control of the nation's key institutions." In Nixon's view, the solid average American, harassed by government, crime, inflation, taxes, riots, drugs, pornography, welfare chiselers, and uppity black Americans, represented the foundation of a future conservative majority based on the combined Nixon and Wallace votes of 1968 (see p. 863).

Nixon stressed the "social issues" in order to attract the bulk of the electorate, which was unyoung, unpoor, and unblack. In particular, there seemed an unprecedented chance to make the South into a Republican stronghold. Those objectives led to a slowdown on civil rights, attacks on the busing of pupils as a means of achieving school integration; a rhetorical barrage against welfare, crime, the media of opinion, and the intellectual community. That strategy had the further advantage of prying away from the Democrats white blue-collar families in the North who felt threatened by racial adjustments demanded of them at a distance by upper-class liberals.

The antiwar demonstrations of 1969–70, and especially the outbursts following the Kent State shootings, encouraged Nixon to persist in emphasizing law and order in the 1970 midterm elections, though with indifferent results, and to continue that tactic for 1972. The reconstitution of the Supreme Court was an

Spiro Agnew: alliteration and tax evasion

important element in the strategy. Nixon, who during his campaign had blamed the Warren Court for encouraging crime, now took advantage of vacancies to appoint justices more to his liking. The retirement of Warren in 1968 enabled him to designate Warren Burger, a conservative, as the new Chief Justice. Nixon's next two nominees, both federal judges from the South, were rejected by the Senate, the first because of conflict of interests, the second because of intellectual mediocrity. Subsequently three wholly qualified nominees were approved.

The Burger Court was markedly more conservative than the Warren Court, especially in its tendency to restrict news media in the gathering of information and to decide criminal law cases in favor of the police and prosecution rather than the defendant. But Burger lacked Warren's skill in massing the Court, and the intellectual leader of the conservatives, William Rehnquist, for the time being stood alone on the Court's far right. For a time, the Burger Court left the Warren inheritance more intact than conservatives had hoped or liberals feared. While qualifying the *Miranda* rule, which Nixon had particularly denounced, it refused opportunities to reverse it. It sustained the cause of school desegregation, approving mandatory busing in *Swann* v. *Charlotte-Mecklenburg* (1971). Some decisions dismayed conservatives — the Pentagon Papers case (*New York Times* v. *United States,* 1971), in which the Court ruled against prior restraint of the rights of publication; *Furman* v. *Georgia* (1972), in which it outlawed mandatory capital punishment statutes; and, most striking of all *Roe* v. *Wade* (1973), in which it upset state laws prohibiting abortion. This last decision brought into being an emotional "right to life" movement. Supporters of abortion counterorganized under the banner of "freedom of choice."

The 1972 Election As 1972 approached, the front-runner for the Democratic nomination was Senator Edmund Muskie of Maine. But Senator George McGovern of South Dakota, a Second World War hero and former professor of history, ardently liberal in his outlook and an early opponent of the Indochina War, succeeded in uniting the Robert Kennedy and Eugene McCarthy forces of 1968. Benefiting by reforms in the delegate-selection process brought about by a Democratic party commission he himself had chaired, McGovern won first-ballot nomination at the Democratic convention in July. Senator Thomas Eagleton of Missouri, his choice as running mate, retired from the ticket after failing to disclose to McGovern a history of psychiatric treatment. His replacement was Sargent

McGovern and Shriver: off stride

Shriver of Maryland, former head of Kennedy's Peace Corps and Johnson's war on poverty. The Republicans renominated Nixon and Agnew.

Thrown off stride by the Eagleton affair, McGovern never recovered momentum. From first to last, his campaign was disorganized. The Republicans, determined to win over those who had voted for Wallace in 1968, played astutely upon racial and cultural nerves. They denounced McGovern as the champion of "acid, abortion, and amnesty." The success of the "Southern strategy" was guaranteed when Wallace, disabled in an assassination attempt in May, decided not to field a party of his own. McGovern was obviously beaten by the time, twelve days before the election, that Kissinger claimed peace was at hand in Vietnam. Nor did the Twenty-sixth Amendment, ratified in 1971 and lowering the voting age to 18, help the Democrats as much as they had expected.

Nixon sailed to an impressive victory, losing only Massachusetts and the District of Columbia. While the turnout of eligible voters continued to decline, falling to 55.4 percent, he polled 46 million votes against 28.5 million for McGovern, winning the largest proportion (60.8 percent) of the popular vote since 1964 and the largest margin in the Electoral College (520 to 17) since 1936. The Democrats added two to their Senate majority and retained control of the House.

But in 1972 the once-majority Democratic presidential coalition crumbled, as the vote in 1968 had portended. Race, the Vietnam War, the women's movement, related questions about amnesty for draft evasion, drug use, and abortion had disquieted the electorate. The "silent majority," as Nixon believed, had come to oppose civil rights, the peace movement, and feminism. While Nixon appealed to those middle Americans, in the McGovern campaign, the Democratic party became identified with the very issues alienating most voters, including many traditional Democrats. The resulting realignment, obvious in 1972, was to shape presidential politics for the rest of the century.

Watergate On the night of June 17, 1972, five men, equipped with cameras and electronic bugging devices, had been arrested in the offices of the Democratic National Committee in the Watergate building in Washington. The burglars gave false names, but one was identified as chief of security for the Committee to Re-elect the President. The committee's chair, John Mitchell, a Nixon intimate who had resigned as attorney general to run his campaign, promptly denied any involvement on the part of the organization (soon known popularly as CREEP). The incident had little

Nixon and staff: one of the most corrupt in American history

impact on the election. McGovern called the Nixon administration "the most corrupt" in American history. Few voters listened.

The object of the break-in was possibly to ascertain whether the Democrats knew about shady dealings involving Nixon, his friend Bebe Rebozo, and the eccentric millionaire Howard Hughes. It is not clear whether Nixon knew in advance about the break-in. He later admitted, however, that the atmosphere he created in the White House stimulated those around him to lawless action. Underneath his conventional exterior Nixon was a man of agitated and compulsive emotion. He saw life as a battlefield and believed that the nation was swarming with personal enemies bent on his destruction. The campus riots after Cambodia in 1970, along with the Weathermen and the Black Panthers, fed his fears. When John Dean became White House counsel in July 1970, he found, he later said, "a climate of excessive concern over the political impact of demonstrators, excessive concern over leaks, an insatiable appetite for political intelligence, all coupled with a do-it-yourself White House staff, regardless of the law."

That spirit generated Nixon's Enemies List, circulated with the injunction to "use the available Federal machinery to screw our political enemies." In 1970 T. C. Huston, a White House aide, drew up a plan approved by Nixon, in the name of national security. The plan authorized burglary, electronic surveillance, mail interception, and other practices forbidden by law. J. Edgar Hoover's protest compelled Nixon to back down, but in 1971 Nixon, unsettled by Daniel Ellsberg's release of the Pentagon Papers, set up a secret White House unit known as "the plumbers" to effectuate the Huston plan. The plumbers soon burgled the office of Ellsberg's psychiatrist, forged official cables in an effort to implicate John F. Kennedy in the assassination of Ngo Dinh Diem, wiretapped foreign embassies, and engaged in other edifying activities. This was again done in the name of "national security."

In the winter of 1971–72, polls showed Nixon trailing Muskie and roused concern in the White House about the forthcoming election. The plumbers now organized a campaign of "dirty tricks" designed to bring Muskie into disrepute. Early in 1972 G. Gordon Liddy, a plumber who became general counsel of CREEP, outlined larger plans of espionage and sabotage to Mitchell. In May the Democratic headquarters were entered for the first time. Bugs were planted on telephones, and documents were copied. All was going well until the night of June 17.

The Cover-up Whether or not Nixon knew of the Watergate entry in advance, he knew about it immediately afterward. In February 1971 he had installed microphones in the White House to record all presidential conversations, and the tapes subsequently provided evidence of Nixon's response to Watergate. By June 23 Haldeman had told him how many of the arrows leading to Watergate pointed back to the White House. "We're back in the problem area because the FBI is out of control," Haldeman said. Nixon told him to tell the FBI, "Don't go any further into this case, period!" The reasons, he made clear, were political; the pretext would be national security.

The cover-up had begun. Incriminating documents were systematically destroyed. But there were problems. Neither the FBI—though Hoover, who died in May, was replaced by a complaisant political appointee—nor the CIA proved as pliable as the White House hoped. The cover-up strategy relied increasingly on two main elements—bribes and lies. Several hundred thousand dollars were raised to buy the silence of the Watergate defendants. Everyone who knew the truth, from Nixon down, denied publicly and privately that Watergate was anything more than a personal adventure by those caught in the act. "Under my direction," Nixon told a press conference in August, "counsel to the President, Mr. Dean, has conducted an investigation. . . . I can say categorically that his investigation indicates that no one in the White House staff, no one in this Administration . . . was involved in this very bizarre incident." Dean had made no such investigation or report.

In September a grand jury indicted the five Watergate burglars and two of the plumbers. Nixon congratulated Dean on the fact that the indictments had gone no further. He added, "I want the most comprehensive notes on all of those that had tried to do us in. . . . They are asking for it and they are going to get it. . . . We have not used the power in the first four years, as you know. We have never used it. We haven't used the Bureau and we haven't used the Justice Department, but things are going to change now."

Things indeed were going to change. In January 1973 the Watergate trial began before Judge John J. Sirica. On February 2 Sirica said he was "not satisfied" that the full story had been disclosed and called for further investigation. On February 7 the Senate voted to establish a select committee to inquire into charges of corruption in the 1972 election. The chair was Senator Sam Ervin of North Carolina. Robert Woodward and Carl Bernstein, two young reporters on the Washington *Post,* were meanwhile beginning to uncover

The Nixon White House

P—We are all in it together. This is a war. We take a few shots and it will be over. We will give them a few shots and it will be over. Don't worry. I wouldn't want to be on the other side right now. . . . I want the most comprehensive notes on all those who tried to do us in. They didn't have to do it. If we had had a very close election, and they were playing the other side I would understand this. No—they were doing this quite deliberately and they are asking for it and they are going to get it. We have not used the power in this first four years as you know. We have never used it. We have not used the Bureau and we have not used the Justice Department but things are going to change now. And they are either going to do it right or go.

D—What an exciting prospect.

P—Thanks. It has to be done. We have been (adjective deleted) fools for us to come into this election campaign and not do anything with regard to the Democratic Senators who are running, et cetera. And who the hell are they after? They are after us. It is absolutely ridiculous. It is not going to be that way any more.

From a conversation in the White House between Richard Nixon and John Dean, September 15, 1972

sources in the executive branch, especially a mysterious and knowledgeable figure whom they identified only as Deep Throat.

Impeachment "We have a cancer—within—close to the presidency, that's growing," John Dean told Nixon on March 21. "It's growing daily. It's compounding." The conspiracy was unraveling. The problem now, as Nixon, Haldeman, and Ehrlichman saw it, was who to throw to the wolves. One candidate, so Dean came to believe, was Dean himself. Another was John Mitchell; "he's the big enchilada," said Ehrlichman. In April Dean and Jeb Magruder, deputy director of CREEP, fearing that they were being set up as fall guys, turned state's evidence. On April 30 Nixon forced Haldeman and Ehrlichman to resign. As for Nixon, his resolve was still, in the language of the tapes, to "tough it out."

On May 17 the Ervin Committee began public hearings, carried by television to an enraptured nation. At the same time, Elliot Richardson, up for confirmation as attorney general, agreed under senatorial pressure to appoint an independent special prosecutor. He named Professor Archibald Cox of the Harvard Law School, Kennedy's solicitor general. Both Ervin and Cox now pressed their somewhat competitive inquiries. Dean's testimony before the Ervin Committee in June was especially precise and effective. Then in July the committee learned for the first time of the existence of the tapes. There began a struggle—Nixon, on the one hand, Ervin and Cox, on the other—for access to the tapes. Nixon, in his own words, stonewalled, claiming executive privilege first for his staff, later for the tapes and himself. Privately he denied to Elliot Richardson and other Republican leaders, any knowledge or complicity, while publicly he put out a succession of statements, each admitting a little more than the one before.

In the meantime, investigations by the federal attorney in Maryland concluded that Spiro T. Agnew

Ervin Committee: they reached an enraptured nation

had received bribes as governor of Maryland and subsequently as vice president. Though Nixon said in August, "My confidence in his integrity has not been shaken," the evidence was compelling. In October, Agnew resigned his position and confessed to falsifying his income tax returns. He was fined $10,000 and put on probation for three years. In exchange, the other charges were dropped. Acting under the Twenty-fifth Amendment, which had been ratified in 1967, Nixon appointed a new vice president, Gerald Ford, the minority leader of the House. After Agnew resigned, Nixon said to Richardson, "Now that that's over, we can get rid of Cox."

Cox, in his pursuit of the tapes, was pressing too close. When the Court of Appeals required that Nixon turn over nine tapes to Judge Sirica, Nixon refused to comply. Nixon then ordered Richardson to fire Cox. Richardson declined to do so and resigned, as did his deputy attorney general. Solicitor General Robert Bork, the ranking official left in the Justice Department, carried out Nixon's order. The "Saturday night massacre" produced a "fire-storm" of national protest, with nearly a half million telegrams inundating the White House in the next week. Newspapers and magazines called for Nixon's resignation. Impeachment resolutions were introduced in the House of Representatives. Under the explosion of public indignation, Nixon yielded the nine tapes.

It was the beginning of the end. More and more of the lesser Watergate actors were indicted. New issues emerged. Nixon, it developed, had paid only $792 in federal income tax in 1970, $878 in 1971. His claim for tax deductions on his vice-presidential papers had been illegally backdated to escape the provisions of a new tax law, and he owed the government nearly half a million dollars. Millions of federal dollars had been dubiously spent on the improvement of his houses in San Clemente, California, and Key Biscayne, Florida. It was another Nixon first. No previous chief executive had ever tried to make himself rich out of the presidency.

In December the House Judiciary Committee began an inquiry to determine whether there were grounds for impeachment. The committee immediately confronted a constitutional question. The Founding Fathers had regarded impeachment, in Madison's words, as a means of defending the community against "the incapacity, negligence or perfidy of the chief Magistrate." Hamilton had written in *The Federalist* No. 65 that it applied to "those offenses which proceed from the misconduct of public men, or, in other words, from the abuse or violation of some public trust. They are of a nature which may with peculiar propriety be denominated POLITICAL." Impeachment in the original view did not require the breaking of any particular law. However, officials confronted by

Impeachment

Article I

In his conduct of the office of President of the United States, Richard M. Nixon, in violation of his constitutional oath faithfully to execute the office of President of the United States . . . and in violation of his constitutional duty to take care that the laws be faithfully executed, has prevented, obstructed, and impeded the administration of justice. . . . Richard M. Nixon, using the powers of his high office, engaged personally and through his subordinates and agents in a course of conduct or plan designed to delay, impede, and obstruct the investigation of such unlawful entry; to cover up, conceal and protect those responsible; and to conceal the existence and scope of other unlawful covert activities. . . . In all of this, Richard M. Nixon has acted in a manner contrary to his trust as President and subversive of constitutional government, to the great prejudice of the cause of law and justice and to the manifest injury of the people of the United States.

Wherefore Richard M. Nixon, by such conduct, warrants impeachment and trial, and removal from office.

Article II

Using the powers of the office of President of the United States, Richard M. Nixon . . . has repeatedly engaged in conduct violating the constitutional rights of citizens, impairing the due and proper administration of justice in the conduct of lawful inquiries, or contravening the laws governing agencies of the executive branch. . . .

Wherefore, Richard M. Nixon, by such conduct, warrants impeachment and trial, and removal from office.

the threat of impeachment had always argued that impeachment applied only to violations of specific criminal statutes.

Nixon, hopeful that no statutory crime could be proved against him, continued to stonewall. There was more talk of executive privilege and of defending the institution of the presidency. In March 1974 a federal grand jury indicted Mitchell, Haldeman, Ehrlichman and four others. Nixon was named as a "co-conspirator," unindicted because of prosecutorial doubts whether a president could be brought to trial. As Leon Jaworski, the new special prosecutor, subpoenaed more tapes, Nixon decided to anticipate the inevitable and release the tapes himself. It was a fatal miscalculation. The reaction was worse than to the Saturday night massacre. The tapes displayed Nixon as bigoted, amoral, and—even with a multitude of "expletives deleted" from the transcript—foul-mouthed. The demand for resignation, even among Republicans, rose to a new crescendo.

In mid-July, after weeks of hearings, the House Judiciary Committee voted three articles of impeachment, charging Nixon with obstruction of justice in the Watergate case, with abuse of presidential power in a

Article III

In his conduct of the office of President of the United States, Richard M. Nixon . . . has failed without lawful cause or excuse to produce papers and things, as directed by duly authorized subpoenas . . . and willfully disobeyed such subpoenas . . . thereby assuming for himself functions and judgments necessary to the exercise of the sole power of impeachment vested by the Constitution in the House of Representatives. . . .

Wherefore, Richard M. Nixon, by such conduct, warrants impeachment and trial, and removal from office.

From the House of Representatives Committee on the Judiciary, August 4, 1974

The House Judiciary Committee: three articles of impeachment

number of specified respects, and with unconstitutionally defying its subpoenas. Six Republicans joined with the Democratic majority in passing the first article, seven on the second, two on the third.

In the meantime, the Supreme Court had ruled in *U.S.* v. *Nixon* (1974) that Nixon must turn over tapes that might contain evidence of crime. Transcripts of his meetings with Haldeman six days after the break-in left no doubt that he had planned the cover-up. This was at last the "smoking pistol" required to still all doubts. Four Republicans on the Judiciary Committee who had voted against impeachment reversed their positions. Senator Goldwater said that Nixon could count on no more than 15 votes in the Senate. Four days later, on August 9, Nixon resigned—the first president to do so in the history of the republic.

The Imperial Presidency Resignation left the exact degree of Nixon's guilt undetermined. But the Watergate inquiries did prove that Nixon's administration was indeed the most corrupt in American history. More than 40 members of the administration underwent criminal prosecution, led by those particular champions of law and order, Agnew and Mitchell. A vice president, two Cabinet members, a dozen members of the White House staff, and nearly 15 others scattered through the executive branch pleaded guilty or were convicted after trial.

"When the President does it," Nixon later asserted in defense of his actions, "that means that it is not illegal." But, while the notion that the sovereign can do no wrong has been the premise of many legal systems, the framers of the United States Constitution had rejected any idea of the divine right of presidents. Watergate confirmed the principle that even the president was not above the law and the Constitution. Most Americans welcomed Nixon's resignation not alone with relief but with a measure of self-congratulation. In the end, it was said, the system had worked. Others took less satisfaction in the result. If Nixon had kept no tapes, or if he had burned them, or if there had not been in the right place at the right time a senator like Ervin, a judge like Sirica, a newspaper like the Washington *Post,* Nixon and his associates might well have survived.

Yet, as Ervin subsequently reflected, "One of the great advantages of the three separate branches of government is that it's difficult to corrupt all three at the same time." A new interest developed in the problem of presidential power and accountability. The separation of powers had worked well enough through American history to restrain presidential aggrandizement in domestic affairs. But foreign affairs, as Vietnam had already demonstrated, constituted the grave weakness in the original system of accountability. Confronted by presidential initiatives abroad, Congress had come to lack confidence in its information and judgment and was happy to abdicate responsibility to the executive. This was especially the case after the Second World War, because the last period of sustained congressional intervention in foreign policy, from the rejection of the Treaty of Versailles to the rigid neutrality legislation of the 1930s, had given Congress itself a severe institutional inferiority complex. International crisis had thus opened the great breach in the system of accountability. Nixon's particular innovation was to take the powers that had flowed to the presidency to meet foreign threats, real or imagined, and try to project them for his own purposes at home.

Since the growth of presidential power had been in the longer run as much a consequence of congressional abdication as of presidential usurpation, Congress had a major role to play in containing the Imperial Presidency, as it came to be known, and restoring the balance of the Constitution. The Vietnam experience had drawn attention to the acquisition by the presidency of the war-making power confided by the Constitution to Congress. In 1973 Congress passed a War Powers Act that, on the one hand, gave the president for the first time explicit authority to go to war in certain specified circumstances but on the other required the termination of hostilities within 90 days unless Congress explicitly authorized their continuation.

Departure of an Imperial President

In the long run, the efforts at reform provoked by Watergate did not succeed. During the next two decades, the ambiguity of the War Powers Act allowed presidents to proceed much as they had since 1945.

In domestic affairs, Congress passed in 1974 the Congressional Budget and Impoundment Control Act. This law instituted procedures to prevent the unlimited impoundment policies of the Nixon era. It also established a legislative budget process comparable to the one Congress had given the president in the Budget and Accounting Act of 1921 (see p. 640). In the same year Congress passed the Federal Election Campaign Act providing for partial federal financing of presidential campaigns and seeking to limit the role of private money in elections. In *Buckley* v. *Valeo* (1976), the Supreme Court sustained the public financing provisions but, by equating money with speech under the First Amendment, removed limits on personal spending. In ensuing presidential elections, and in elections generally, money became an increasingly important factor, especially for the financing of television advertising.

Watergate further stimulated a determination to open up the workings of government. States passed "sunshine laws" designed to increase citizen access to governmental decisions. Political candidates were called on to disclose the sources of their income. A national Freedom of Information Act, passed by Congress in 1966, acquired new vitality. The spotlight even penetrated into the most secretive agencies of government—the CIA and the FBI. Congressional investigations in 1975–76 revealed extraordinary abuses of power by both agencies—not only the CIA assassination and covert action projects but the FBI's use of *agents provocateurs,* burglaries, wiretapping, mail intercepts, and even J. Edgar Hoover's incredible effort to drive Martin Luther King, Jr., to suicide. The public reaction to these revelations dethroned Hoover posthumously from his long reign as a national hero and produced a measure of congressional oversight over the intelligence community. But the efficacy of that oversight depended on the vigilance of Congress and the cooperation of the intelligence agencies, conditions that could not be assured.

As for Nixon, he would be forever remembered as the only president forced to resign his office. But he would be remembered, too, for the geopolitical instincts that led him to seek new directions in world affairs. In subsequent years, with his usual dogged perseverance, he sought to emerge from disgrace and to win rehabilitation and esteem as an elder statesman.

THE PRESIDENCY RESTORED

A Ford, Not a Lincoln Gerald R. Ford, the new president, was 61 years old. A Republican wheelhorse, he had served a quarter-century in the House without ever achieving consideration in any Republican convention as a candidate for president or even for vice president. Democrats underrated him. But even Democrats liked him as an honest, open, even-tempered politician unaccustomed to converting political disagreements into personal enmities.

Gerald R. Ford and Nelson Rockefeller, February 1974

"I am a Ford, not a Lincoln," he had said disarmingly after being sworn in as vice president; and, after being sworn in as president, "I am acutely aware that you have not elected me as your president by your ballots." Complying with the Twenty-fifth Amendment, he named Governor Nelson Rockefeller of New York as his vice president. This meant that for the first time in American history both the president and the vice president had come to office and power not, like all their predecessors, through election but through appointment—a result unintended by the drafters of the Twenty-fifth Amendment seven years before and disconcerting to those who valued the provision in the Constitution (Article II, Section 1) stipulating that the president and vice president were to "be elected."

A people whose nerves had been worn ragged by Nixon's deceit and mystification found the new president's candor and accessibility initially reassuring. Then, 30 days after he took office, Ford stunned the nation by granting Nixon a "full, free, and absolute pardon" for all crimes he committed against the

United States during his presidency. Ford's concern was that a public trial of the disgraced former president would have a divisive effect. His purpose, he explained, was "to heal the wounds throughout the United States."

The effect was the opposite. Most Americans were outraged by the double standard that punished those who had executed Nixon's wishes but spared Nixon himself. Even many who did not wish to put the ex-president behind bars felt that pardon would have been more appropriate after the evidence of Nixon's misdeeds had been clearly established in court and recorded for history. In one stroke Ford inflicted a wound on his administration from which it never recovered.

Lines for gasoline

The Energy Shock OPEC's price increases and oil embargo of October 1973 had extensive domestic repercussions. American economic growth had been based in large part on cheap energy. But significant changes had taken place in the pattern of energy production. In the 1870s, 90 percent of American energy came from sustainable sources, like water power. A century later more than 90 percent came from nonrenewable mineral sources—44 percent from petroleum, 32 percent from natural gas, 18 percent from coal. Moreover, domestic coal production had begun to decline after 1947, domestic oil extraction after 1970, domestic natural gas production after 1974. Estimates of untapped domestic reserves of mineral fuels began to decline too.

In the meantime, demand continued to grow. By the 1970s the United States, with 6 percent of the world's population, was consuming one-third of the world's energy. The increased reliance on oil was accompanied by an increased reliance on imports. Though the United States remained for many years the world's top oil producer, oil imports rose from 8 percent of demand in 1950 to 39 percent in 1976. A steadily increasing proportion of imported oil came from the Middle East—about 30 percent by the early 1970s.

As early as 1952, the Materials Policy Commission had warned the Truman administration of the "extraordinarily rapid rate at which we are utilizing our materials and energy resources." Such warnings, repeated from time to time over a generation, had been ignored in the enthusiasm for economic growth. The oil embargo at last dramatized the resources issue. For a few months, pumps went empty at filling stations, cars queued up for gasoline, speed limits were reduced, conservation measures encouraged.

With energy now squarely on the national agenda, the nation needed to lower domestic demand through measures of energy conservation, and to develop alternative sources of energy. The Energy Policy and Conservation Act of 1975 affirmed these objectives.

The increase in oil prices, along with the abandonment of price and wage controls after the 1972 election, led to a rapid renewal of inflation—from 3.4 percent in 1971–72 to nearly 9 percent in 1973 and over 12 percent in 1974. The value of the dollar continued to fall—from $1 in 1940 to 40 cents when Nixon came to office and 25 cents in 1976. The Ford administration, ideologically opposed to controls, resorted to the orthodox panacea and tried to combat inflation by slowing down the economy. The result in 1974–75 was the worst recession in nearly 40 years. National output had its sharpest decline since the end of war production in 1945–46. Unemployment rose to nearly 9 percent of the labor force—8.25 million people—by mid-1975. By 1976 recession brought the inflation rate down to 4.8 percent, though at painful human cost.

The Presidency Survives During the Watergate crisis some had feared that the exposure of Nixon

Recession, 1975: the worst in nearly 40 years

would damage the presidency as an institution. The aftermath showed the presidency to be relatively indestructible. Despite his stigma of illegitimacy as an unelected president, despite his lack of appetite for power, Ford drew strength from the continuing authority of the office. When the Democrats increased their congressional majorities in 1974, Ford responded by using the veto power with almost unprecedented freedom, vetoing more public bills in his first months than any president had vetoed in so short a period. Few of his vetoes were overridden.

Presidential authority remained real, if temporarily diminished, in foreign affairs. While Ford reconstructed his Cabinet with some promptitude, he retained Kissinger as secretary of state, thereby ensuring continuity in foreign policy. When Cambodian Communists seized an unarmed American ship, the *Mayagüez,* in May 1975, Ford retaliated by ordering air strikes and sending in the marines. Congress joined in the general applause, though Ford had merely informed legislators of his action, rather than consulting them in the spirit of the War Powers Act. Skeptics noted that more marines were killed in the affair than sailors rescued.

The 1976 Election Ford beat back a strong challenge from Ronald Reagan, a former Hollywood actor, a popular governor of California and now the hero of the Republican right, to take his party's nomination. The president's desire to propitiate conservative Republicans had led him to abandon Nelson Rockefeller, and his vice-presidential candidate, selected to cheer the Reaganites, was Senator Robert Dole of Kansas. For the Democrats, James Earl Carter, Jr., who preferred to style himself Jimmy, a former governor of Georgia almost unknown to the nation, emerged as candidate from a series of arduous primaries. He chose the liberal Senator Walter F. Mondale of Minnesota as his running mate.

The campaign was unenlightening. Neither candidate distinguished himself in a series of three debates. Carter, a man of sharp intelligence but enigmatic views, rested his case more on moralistic reassurance —"I'll never lie to you," he promised his audiences —than on clarity in policy. Condemning Washington's "horrible, bloated bureaucracy," pledging "a government that is as good and honest and decent . . . and as filled with love as are the American people," Carter sought support as a political outsider who

Jimmy Carter, 1976: victorious outsider

would restore integrity to government. In that way Carter struck a note that his immediate successors would sound even more frequently: The federal government was a target even as its attackers sought and held the office of president.

Each candidate, in accepting $22 million of federal money for the fall campaign, renounced private fund raising. Ford cut down Carter's early lead, but Carter won the popular vote by 40.3 million to 38.5 million and the Electoral College by 297 to 241. Voter turnout continued to decline—from 55.4 percent in 1972 to 53.3 percent in 1976. Except for Lyndon Johnson, Carter was the only Democrat since 1944 to win a majority of the popular vote. He combined enough Northern states with ten Southern states to gain victory in the Electoral College. But his success in the South differed from that of Democrats during the years before 1948, for it now rested on overwhelming support among black voters, supplemented by enough white votes to carry the Southern states. Those white votes went to Carter largely because he was himself a Southerner, and because of the continuing disgust with Watergate. In its revulsion against the abuse of government power by "insiders," the electorate turned to a classic "outsider," rejecting an honest and likable but pedestrian president.

SUGGESTIONS FOR READING

NIXON AND FORD

RN: The Memoirs of Richard Nixon (1978) is a good deal more revealing, sometimes inadvertently so, than *A Time to Heal: The Autobiography of Gerald Ford* (1979). S. E. Ambrose, *Nixon*, 2 vols. (1987–89), promises to be the standard biography. G. Wills, *Nixon Agonistes* (1970), is arresting portraiture. White House associates offer testimony in H. R. Haldeman, *The Ends of Power* (1978); John Dean, *Blind Ambition: The White House Years* (1976); W. Safire, *Before the Fall* (1975); John Ehrlichman, *Witness to Power: The Nixon Years* (1982), as well as in his novel *The Company* (1976); and R. Price, *With Nixon* (1977). Spiro T. Agnew justifies himself in *Go Quietly . . . or Else* (1980). R. T. Hartmann, *Palace Politics: An Inside Account of the Ford Years* (1980), is lively and candid.

On public policy, A. J. Reichley, *Conservatives in an Age of Change: The Nixon and Ford Administrations* (1981), is discerning and readable. Nixon's domestic efforts are considered in D. P. Moynihan, *The Politics of a Guaranteed Income* (1973) and *Coping* (1973); R. P. Nathan, *The Plot That Failed* (1975); and V. J. and V. Burke, *Nixon's Good Deed: Welfare Reform* (1976). P. R. Dommel, *The Politics of Revenue Sharing* (1974), discusses Nixon's New Federalism. D. E. Kash and R. W. Rycroft, *U. S. Energy Policy: Crisis and Complacency* (1984), recounts the evolution of energy policy since 1973; see also R. Reeves, *A Ford, Not a Lincoln* (1975) and J. T. Patterson, *America's Struggle Against Poverty* (1986 ed).

As for the politics of the Nixon-Ford years, S. Lubell, *The Hidden Crisis in American Politics* (1970), and D. Broder, *The Party's Over* (1972), are useful contemporaneous diagnoses. T. H. White, *The Making of a President 1972* (1973), covers the 1972 election. George McGovern, in his memoir *Grassroots* (1977), and G. Hart, McGovern's campaign manager, in *Right from the Start: A Chronicle of the McGovern Campaign* (1973), present the Democratic view. See also K. P. Phillips, *The Emerging Republican Majority* (1970), and J. M. Blum, *Years of Discord* (1991).

FOREIGN AFFAIRS

The memoirs of Henry Kissinger—*White House Years* (1979) and *Years of Upheaval* (1982)—are formidable, fascinating, flawed, and fundamental. R. L. Garthoff, *Detente and Confrontation* (1985), is an able discussion by a diplomat-scholar of American-Soviet relations from Nixon to Reagan. A. E. Goodman, *The Lost Peace: America's Search for a Negotiated Settlement of the Vietnam War* (1978), and A. R. Isaacs, *Without Honor: Defeat in Vietnam and Cambodia* (1983), describe the last days of the Indochina War. For the South Vietnamese viewpoint, see Nguyen Tien Hung and J. L. Schecter, *The Palace File* (1986), and Bui Diem with D. Chanoff, *In the Jaws of History* (1987). On the Middle East, see W. B. Quandt, *Decade of Decision: American Foreign Policy Toward the Arab-Israeli Conflict, 1967–1976* (1978).

CRISIS OF THE PRESIDENCY

A. M. Schlesinger, Jr., *The Imperial Presidency* (1973), portrays the growth of presidential power. T. E. Cronin, *The State of the Presidency* (2d ed., 1980), and R. M. Pious, *The American Presidency* (1979), ably set forth recent thought about the presidency. T. H. White, *Breach of Faith* (1975), and A. Lukas, *Nightmare* (1976), are vivid surveys of Watergate and its aftermath; see also S. I. Kutler, *The*

Wars of Watergate (1990). Carl Bernstein and Robert Woodward pursue the Watergate story in *All the President's Men* (1974), and Nixon's last days in the White House in *The Final Days* (1975). Leon Jaworski, *The Right and the Power* (1976), John J. Sirica, *To Set the Record Straight* (1979), and Samuel Ervin, *The Whole Truth: The Watergate Conspiracy* (1980), sum up the case against Nixon. The growth of secrecy and deception in government is portrayed in D. Wise, *The Politics of Lying* (1973), and F. Donner, *The Age of Surveillance* (1980). For the Nixon Supreme Court, see V. Blasi, *The Burger Court: The Counterrevolution That Wasn't* (1983).

CHAPTER THIRTY-FOUR

TRIUMPHANT REPUBLICANS, 1981

TIDES OF CONSERVATISM

Jimmy Carter, the 39th president, was 52 years old, a native of Georgia, a graduate of Annapolis, a nuclear engineer who had shifted to the peanut business, and a "born again" Baptist of ostentatious piety. His political career had been limited to service in the Georgia legislature and a single term as governor. He was the first president elected from the Deep South since Zachary Taylor, the first fundamentalist to run for the presidency since William Jennings Bryan, the first ex-governor to win since Franklin Roosevelt, and the first successful businessman (unless Herbert Hoover be so regarded) to occupy the White House in American history. His lack of Washington experience was initially seen, in light of Watergate, as a recommendation, and his election was taken to mark the liquidation of vexing issues—not only Watergate but, in view of his pledge to pardon draft resisters, the Indochina War and, in view of his accent and origin, the Civil War.

FROM NEGOTIATION TO CONFRONTATION

Carter and Foreign Affairs Carter, with little background in world affairs, picked Cyrus Vance, a New York lawyer with long government experience, as secretary of state and Zbigniew Brzezinski, a political scientist and Soviet expert, as special assistant for national security. Vance and Brzezinski differed, however, in their approach to the Soviet Union. Vance was moderate and conciliatory by temperament, while Brzezinski, a native of Poland, wished to confront the Russians at every turn. Carter himself, inclining at times toward Vance and at times toward Brzezinski, left an impression of irresolution.

In his inaugural address Carter struck what became his administration's distinctive note in foreign policy. "We can never be indifferent to the fate of freedom elsewhere," he said. ". . . Our commitment to human rights must be absolute." For 40 years "human rights" had been emerging as an international purpose—implied in Roosevelt's Four Freedoms (1941), proclaimed in the United Nations Charter (1945) and the Universal Declaration of Human Rights (1948), most recently embodied in Basket Three of the Helsinki Accords (1975). It had also won increasing support in the United States. In the early 1970s Congress, rebelling against Kissinger's *Realpolitik,* began to force human-rights standards on the executive, forbidding American aid to countries that engaged "in a consistent pattern of gross violations of internationally recognized human rights." Carter now seized on the issue both out of personal conviction and

Presidents and Human Rights

America . . . has abstained from interference in the concerns of others, even when conflict has been for principles in which she clings, as to the last vital drop that visits the heart. . . . Wherever the standard of freedom and Independence has been or shall be unfurled, there will her heart, her benedictions and her prayers be. But she goes not abroad, in search of monsters to destroy. She is the well-wisher to the freedom and independence of all. She is the champion and vindicator only of her own.

From John Quincy Adams, July 4, 1821

Ordinarily it is very much wiser and more useful for us to concern ourselves with striving for our own moral and material betterment here at home than to concern ourselves with trying to better the condition of things in other nations. We have plenty of sins of our own to war against, and under ordinary circumstances we can do more for the general uplifting of humanity by striving with heart and soul to put a stop to civic corruption, to brutal lawlessness and violent race prejudices here at home than by passing resolutions about wrongdoing elsewhere.

From Theodore Roosevelt, December 6, 1904

Because we are free we can never be indifferent to the fate of freedom elsewhere. Our moral sense dictates a clearcut preference for those societies which share with us an abiding respect for individual human rights. . . . Our commitment to human rights must be absolute. . . . Ours was the first society openly to define itself in terms of both spirituality and of human liberty. It is that unique self-definition which . . . imposes on us a special obligation—to take on those moral duties which, when assumed, seem invariably to be in our own best interests.

From Jimmy Carter, January 20, 1977

in order to give American foreign policy a moral content it had lacked in the Nixon-Ford years. As a unifying principle, it gratified both Cold Warriors, who wanted to indict the Communist world, and idealists, who saw human rights as the only basis for lasting peace.

The human-rights campaign proved easier to announce than to execute. Advocates of détente argued that human-rights pressure jeopardized relations with the Soviet Union. Cold Warriors alleged that it undermined stalwart anti-Communist allies, like Iran and Nicaragua. Carter himself was soon found visiting authoritarian nations, selling them arms, and saluting their leaders. This led to charges of hypocrisy and double standards.

Yet inconsistency was inherent in the situation. In the nature of foreign affairs, human rights could be only one of several contending interests, competing against strategic, political, and economic claims on national policy. By establishing a Bureau of Human Rights in the State Department, Carter institutionalized the human-rights role in American foreign policy. For all its contradictions, the human-rights campaign helped restore the broken link between America and ordinary people around the world. It placed human rights on the world's agenda—and on the world's conscience.

Vicissitudes of Détente The Soviet relationship was still the primary issue. Carter began with high hopes. America, he said in May 1977, was at last free of "inordinate fear of communism." His goal was to reduce the chances of nuclear war by completing a SALT-II treaty with the Soviet Union. His policy, however, wobbled between Vance's hopes—and those of Edmund Muskie, who succeeded him as secretary of state in 1980—and Brzezinski's fears.

SALT-II negotiations had progressed in the last Ford years. But in March 1977, soon after assuming office, Carter shocked the Russians by submitting new proposals that departed from the Vladivostok Accord (see p. 876) and that were, in the Soviet view, excessively one-sided. This action, accompanied by Carter's public support of Soviet dissidents, excited Soviet mistrust and set back negotiations for a year or more. Carter's decision in December 1978 to establish full diplomatic relations with China increased Soviet displeasure. But the SALT negotiators persevered, and in June 1979 agreement was finally reached in Vienna, Carter and Brezhnev kissing each other in celebration at the Hofburg Palace.

Celebration in Vienna, 1979: Carter and Brezhnev

SALT-II, while proposing equal limits on Soviet and American strategic forces, provided no reductions. And the continuing Soviet missile buildup raised fears that Moscow was bent on attaining the nuclear lead. When SALT-II went to the Senate in June 1979, opponents claimed that the treaty would confirm Soviet superiority. Strategic theologians revived the "missile gap" thesis of 20 years before in the form of a "window of vulnerability" through which, it was asserted, Soviet missiles could wipe out American land-based ICBMs. The window of vulnerability turned out to be as mythical as the missile gap, but, as in the case of the missile gap, damage was done. Moscow's deployment of mobile SS-20 missiles in eastern Europe, however, was not a myth. It led in December 1979 to the "two-track" decision by NATO, according to which the United States would deploy 572 Pershing II and cruise missiles in Western Europe to offset the SS-20s and also pursue arms limitation talks with Moscow.

In the same December, the Red Army entered Afghanistan. The Russians had dominated Afghanistan since a pro-Moscow coup in April 1978. But the failure of the Marxist regime to control the country prompted Moscow to install a new regime and send in Russian troops. "This action of the Soviets," Carter said, "has made a more drastic change in my own opinion of what the Soviets' ultimate goals are than anything they've done in the previous time I've been in office." He called the Russian occupation of Afghanistan "a stepping stone to their possible control over much of the world's oil supplies" and the gravest threat to world peace since 1945.

Carter thereupon withdrew the SALT-II treaty from the Senate, imposed an embargo on grain sales to Russia, announced the American boycott of the Olympic games in Moscow and initiated a policy of covert assistance to Afghan guerrillas resisting the Red Army. He also superseded the "Nixon Doctrine" of 1969 (see p. 874) with a "Carter Doctrine." Defining the Persian Gulf region as within the zone of American vital interest, he declared that the United States would repel an assault on that area "by any means necessary—including military force." Critics doubted whether the Soviet invasion of Afghanistan was, as Carter suggested, the first step in the unfolding of a Kremlin

Soviet troops in Afghanistan

master plan, seeing it rather as an ad hoc attempt to forestall the establishment of a hostile regime on the Russian frontier.

The once pacific Carter had already become the first president since the Second World War to raise defense spending for three straight years in peacetime. Now Brzezinski and Secretary of Defense Harold Brown persuaded him to move away from the mutual assured destruction doctrine toward a counterforce strategy. In September 1979 Carter approved the MX, a vulnerable multiple-warhead missile regarded by some as a "use it or lose it" (first-strike) weapon. On July 25, 1980, he signed Presidential Directive 59, which called for the capacity to wage limited and protracted nuclear war. Critics feared that this codification of the "countervailing strategy," with its first-strike potentialities, would only give new and horrible stimulus to the nuclear arms race.

Beginning as a champion of morality and world order, Carter ended as a Cold Warrior. His enlargement of American global commitments came, moreover, at a time when strains in the domestic economy weakened the nation's capacity to discharge those commitments.

The Middle East The Arab-Israeli conflict seemed as far as ever from solution. Fearing outside pressure for an international conference that might have included the Soviet Union and the Palestine Liberation Organization, Anwar as-Sadat of Egypt and Menachem Begin, the former terrorist who became Israel's prime minister in 1977, acted on their own. In November 1977 Sadat undertook a spectacular personal mission to Israel, offering diplomatic recognition in exchange for the return of Arab territories occupied by Israel in 1967. Begin, determined to reestablish the borders of biblical Israel, was ready to yield the Sinai peninsula but neither the Gaza Strip directly to the north nor the West Bank of the River Jordan. Nor would he give ground on the question of political status for the Palestinians.

In venturing his peace initiative, Sadat had risked his own life as well as Egypt's position in the Arab world. He became for a season a popular favorite in the United States, while Begin's rigidity lost Israel a measure of American sympathy. When peace talks stalled, Carter called the two leaders to Camp David in Maryland in September 1978.

After a fortnight of intense negotiation, Carter persuaded Begin and Sadat to sign a "Framework for Peace in the Middle East." The Camp David Accords, which Carter nailed down during a trip to the Middle East the following March, resulted in Egypt's agreement to a peace treaty with Israel ending 30 years of

Camp David Accords: Sadat, Carter, Begin

war in exchange for Israel's return of the Sinai to Egypt. The provisions for the West Bank and the Gaza Strip were ambiguous, envisaging a five-year transitional period during which the Palestinians would receive self-rule and "autonomy" while Israel retained basic control. Israel, Egypt, Jordan, and "representatives of the Palestinian people" would meanwhile settle the final status of the areas. Ambiguity was inescapable because Sadat needed Palestinian self-determination to justify his deal with Israel in the Arab world while Begin regarded a Palestinian state as a mortal threat.

The agreements represented a triumph of personal diplomacy for Carter, but only postponed the problem. By 1988, Palestinian riots against Israeli occupation of the West Bank and Gaza led to brutal reprisals by the Israeli government, now headed by Yitzhak Shamir, an associate of Begin 40 years before in the guerrilla war against the British. The reprisal caused an erosion of traditional support for Israel in America.

American dependence on Middle Eastern oil argued powerfully for the continuing effort to resolve the quarrel between Israel and the Arab world. In the meantime, Washington cultivated its relations with Saudi Arabia, and Carter continued the Nixon policy of regarding the shah of Iran as the American protector in the Persian Gulf region. But the shah's megalomania, the corruption of his entourage, the savagery of his secret police had turned his country against him from the Islamic right to the Marxist left. Vance and Brzezinski, who for once had agreed on Arab-Israeli issues, disagreed over Iran, Brzezinski arguing for a military coup in support of the shah, Vance urging that the United States divorce itself from the shah and arrange a transition government. As Carter dithered in Washington, spreading disaffection forced the shah to flee Iran in January 1979. A theocratic regime, sharply opposed to materialism and modernization, took over under the leadership of an aged Muslim fanatic, the Ayatollah Ruholla Khomeini.

Carter had declined to abandon the shah until the very end. Warned thereafter by the American embassy in Teheran that admitting the shah to the United States would provoke retaliation against American diplomats, Carter nevertheless admitted him for medical treatment in October 1979. A few days later armed students seized the embassy and held 50 Americans hostage, creating a deep and prolonged crisis between the two countries. A rescue attempt by American commandos in 1980 proved a dismal failure and precipitated the resignation in protest of Secretary of State Vance.

The Third World Carter brought to the White House a strong desire to improve American relations with the Third World. The first Spanish-speaking president, he secured in 1978, after a close and bitter fight, Senate ratification of treaties providing for the transfer of the Panama Canal to Panama by the year 2000. In the wake of the retreat from Vietnam, the relinquishment

Anti-Americanism in Iran

of the canal pricked chauvinistic sensitivities. One senator said irritably, "We stole it fair and square." The treaties eased a grievance that had generated much ill feeling in Latin America toward the colossus of the north.

Elsewhere in Central America, for generations greedy oligarchies supported by the military, by North American corporations, and by Washington, had oppressed and exploited landless laborers. Nevertheless, after the Second World War, economic development brought into existence through much of the area a new middle class aspiring to democratic liberties. That hope, encouraged by Kennedy's Alliance for Progress, could not be suppressed. But population growth and persistent poverty also made Central America a ripe field for Communist recruitment.

In July 1979 a popular insurrection in Nicaragua threw out the dictatorship of the Somoza family, which had looted the country for 40 years (see Map 34-1). The revolution, led by radical Sandinistas, soon showed Marxist leanings and received arms from Castro and from the Soviet bloc. The Sandinista victory encouraged revolutionaries in El Salvador and Guatemala. The situation was particularly tense in El Salvador, where a military coup in October 1979 brought in young officers pledged to free the country from domination by the "14 families." Right-wing officers, however, joined the oligarchy to block land reform, and by 1980 civil war had broken out.

In Nicaragua, the Carter administration, after failing to moderate and rescue the Somoza regime, tried in 1980 to come to terms with the Sandinistas. In El Salvador Carter gave conditional support to the October coup. When the new regime moved to the right and began to murder its opponents, Carter suspended aid in the hope of strengthening moderates remaining in the regime. Then, persuaded that Communist countries were sending arms via Nicaragua to the rebels in El Salvador, he resumed military aid at the end of his term.

Carter named as his first ambassador to the United Nations Andrew Young, a black minister and congressman who had been a lieutenant of Martin Luther King. Young's intelligence and fluency so bemused the developing countries that the United States slipped away from its position in the Nixon years as the favorite Third World target—a notable accomplishment when more than two-thirds of UN members were new or underdeveloped states. In 1979, however, the Israeli lobby forced Young's resignation for failing to report secret talks with a PLO representative.

Poverty continued to bedevil the Third World despite brave UN talk of a "new international economic order." The gap between poor and rich nations widened. After 30 years of effort and experiment, no one knew a sure answer to Third World stagnation. Skeptics believed that foreign aid, so long the liberal panacea, tended to enrich native oligarchies and to

Map 34-1
Central and South America, 1952–1984

undercut the disciplines essential for economic development. Nor were the mild ideals of the American Revolution easily exportable to peoples brutalized by the miseries of history. But communism provided no better answer, having failed after half a century even to assure basic food supply in the Soviet Union itself. The World Bank, directed by Robert McNamara, became the last citadel of the old crusade against world poverty. The "North-South dialogue" went on but to growing and mutual exasperation.

DILEMMAS OF THE ECONOMIC ORDER

Carter and Domestic Policy Though Carter had run as a quasi-populist candidate, his attacks on "big government" portended significant departures from New Deal orthodoxy. As his first budget director, Bert Lance, put it, "He campaigns liberal, but he governs conservative."

To a degree, Carter also appointed liberal. He named three women to his Cabinet. More women, black Americans, and Hispanic-Americans received federal jobs and judgeships than ever before. His appointments gave regulatory commissions new zeal in protecting the environment, the workplace, the consumer, and highway safety. He instituted the first comprehensive civil service reform in many years and used Vice President Walter F. Mondale more successfully than any previous president as a partner in his administration. In 1977 he persuaded Congress to create a Department of Energy and in 1979 to divide the Department of Health, Education and Welfare into two new departments—the Department of Education and the Department of Health and Human Services.

But on central economic issues, he was the most conservative Democratic president since Grover Cleveland. "One of my major goals," Carter said in 1977, "is to free the American people from the burden of over-regulation." Deregulation—of the airlines, trucking, railroads, banks, and oil industries—became a major Carter cause. Federal spending on social programs reached its height in 1976 and declined thereafter, as a percentage both of the federal budget and of the gross national product (GNP). In his 1978 State of the Union message, he expressly repudiated the philosophy of affirmative government.

Revolt against Government In his dismissal of affirmative government, Carter reflected the country's swing toward conservatism. The liberalism of the 1960s had exhausted itself in the post-Watergate reforms. But it left in its wake a mass of government social programs and of health, safety, environmental, and equal-opportunity regulations. In addition, there had been a relentless increase in "entitlements," as federal payments to individuals were now known. Social Security and Medicare accounted for almost half the entitlements bill.

Because entitlement payments were determined, not by statutory dollar ceilings, but by the number meeting eligibility standards, costs were hard to control. With the number of people over 65 growing 50 percent from 16.5 million in 1960 to 24.2 million in 1980, and with social security and other benefits now indexed to keep pace with inflation, entitlement payments exploded. By 1980 they had more than doubled as a percentage of GNP since 1960 and now consumed 46 percent of the federal budget. A spreading antigovernment mood found expression in a national drive for a constitutional amendment requiring a balanced budget.

The enforcement of civil rights through busing and affirmative action also excited resentment. The Supreme Court in the *Bakke* case (1978) ruled that affirmative action in university admissions was not unconstitutional in principle, but that the use of numerical quotas in the particular case was. The feeling spread that government was arbitrary, intrusive, and remote; that government intervention was making problems worse rather than better; that regulation, spending, taxes, and deficits had become an intolerable drain on the economy; and that the inexorable growth of government had to be stopped in its tracks.

In fact, the idea of an inexorable growth was something of an illusion. In 1960 the federal work force consisted of 2.4 million. By 1980, while the nation had grown by 50 million, the federal force had grown by only 500,000. The proportion of the total labor force employed by the federal government actually declined from 3.7 to 3 percent. Moreover, defense and the postal service accounted in 1980 for almost three-fifths of federal workers. Where expansion had taken place, it was in state and local government. There the work force more than doubled between 1960 and 1980, accounting in 1980 for over 80 percent of all government employment. Nor had the tax burden increased dramatically. During these years, effective corporate income tax rates fell, property taxes as a percent of personal income stayed about the same, and combined federal and state income taxes rose only from 11 to 13 percent of personal income. Yet acute problems remained, and the national government became a convenient scapegoat.

Inflation Discontent arose especially over the failure of conventional remedies to contain inflation. Prices more than doubled during the 1970s. Inflation, reduced by the 1974–75 recession to 5.8 percent, resumed in 1977. Carter, when exhortation failed, resorted, like Ford, to slowing down the economy, rather than, like Nixon, to controls. In 1979 he appointed Paul Volcker, an advocate of monetary restriction, as chair of the Federal Reserve Board. The highest interest rates within living memory—20 percent—produced recession and 7.8 percent unemployment in 1980. This time inflation persisted—13.5 percent in 1980, which meant nearly 40 percent in the four Carter years.

Controversy mounted about the cause and cure of inflation. Where inflation during the Second World War and the Korean and Indochina wars was clearly associated with an excess of domestic demand over supply, inflation in the 1970s grew out of unprecedented worldwide demand for commodities—oil and grain among them. Population growth was outstripping production of foodstuffs and fuels. Nevertheless, monetarists in the United States saw remedy in controlling the growth of the American money stock, and fiscal conservatives continued to advocate balancing the federal budget. But monetary and fiscal stringency served largely to reduce domestic demand by pushing the economy into recession, with spreading unemployment as the unfortunate result.

Further, economic concentration permitted strong sellers (big unions as well as big business) to collaborate in raising prices and wages. And inflationary tendencies had recently been reinforced by a disturbing decline in American productivity. Yet increased productivity remained the only way higher wages could be absorbed without forcing up prices. Productivity—average output per one hour of work—had risen about 3 percent annually in the first 20 postwar years. In the 1970s it fell below 1 percent a year.

Whatever set off inflation at particular times, it appeared beyond question the malady to which the postwar economic organism most readily succumbed. By this view, just as depression had expressed a structural crisis in the economic order half a century earlier, so inflation expressed a structural crisis in the contemporary order—and the conventional wisdom seemed as bankrupt before inflation as it had once been before depression.

The inflation of the 1970s was a shock to a country that had come to believe that it had solved the riddle of economic growth. Since the late 1940s, there had been a steady increase in family income and in living standards. At the end of the Second World War a substantial proportion of American homes had lacked running water, flush toilets, and central heating, but by the late 1960s such amenities were widespread. Regional poverty had declined; the South was no longer "the nation's No. 1 economic problem." Economic progress had been accepted as automatic and inevitable. Now it seemed in doubt.

Energy The inflation shock was compounded by new energy shocks. Despite presidential exhortations and congressional statutes, Americans continued through the 1970s to increase both their consumption and their importation of oil. By 1979 the United States was importing 43 percent of its annual supply—nearly four times as much as in 1970.

In April 1977 Carter submitted a comprehensive energy plan that he described as the "moral equivalent of war." Presidential follow-up, however, was feeble; the complex proposals bogged down in Congress; and the program faded away. Two years later the cutoff of Iranian oil after the fall of the shah produced a temporary gasoline shortage reminiscent of 1974, with angry lines at filling stations. Congress deregulated the price of domestic crude oil and imposed a "windfall" profits tax.

Analysts concluded that prospects for major increases in domestic energy supplies from the four conventional sources—oil, natural gas, coal, and nuclear energy—were bleak. In the case of oil, which supplied about 50 percent of the energy used each year, and natural gas, which supplied about 25 percent, there were geological limits on expansion. Coal, with its indefinite reserves, supplied about 19 percent, but its exploitation raised difficult health, safety, and environmental problems.

Seventy-two nuclear plants in operation in 1979 accounted for about 13 percent of electricity production and about 4 percent of total energy consumption. But a frightening accident that year at the Three Mile Island nuclear plant near Harrisburg, Pennsylvania—an accident coincidentally portrayed in the contemporaneous film *The China Syndrome*—led to anxious debate about future reliance on nuclear energy. Antinuclear demonstrators shouted "Hell No, We Won't Glow," and legislators called for circumspection in subsequent nuclear energy policy.

In the short run, the best hope lay in conservation policies reducing the flow of energy into heating, air conditioning, industry, and transportation. But conservation had little appeal to a people whose lives were organized around the automobile. Americans owned two-fifths of all the cars in use in the world; in 1980 156 million cars were registered in the United States. But the "gas-guzzling" automobile of the past was on its way out, and engineers hoped to increase gasoline mileage to 50 miles per gallon by the 1990s. That hope was exaggerated, as were expectations for a revival of mass transport. Eventually Americans would probably have to curtail their use of energy substantially, but most of them still resisted significant changes in their habits.

National Malaise? "Why have we not been able to get together as a nation to resolve our serious energy problem?" Carter asked the American people in a televised speech in July 1979. To answer that question Carter invited 130 Americans—some famous, some

Protest at Three Mile Island

not—to Camp David over a ten-day period to tell him what he was doing wrong. His conclusion was that the trouble lay in a "crisis of the American spirit." The people, he believed, had lost "confidence in the future."

Against Carter's theory that a national malaise was the cause of the ineffectuality of his presidency others believed that the ineffectuality of his presidency was the cause of the national malaise. Americans, critics said, had lost confidence, not in their country, but in its leadership. Carter's approval rating sank to 26 percent in the polls. Though a man of high intelligence, his was the intelligence of an engineer rather than that of a political leader; and, like the earlier engineer in the White House, Herbert Hoover, Carter failed at the tasks of education and persuasion essential to the political process. He conveyed no broad sense of the direction in which he wanted to take the country. "Carter believes fifty things," the author of his early presidential messages later recalled, "but no one thing. He holds explicit, thorough positions on every issue under the sun, but he has no large view of relations between them."

Republican nominees, 1980

The 1980 Election Senator Edward Kennedy of Massachusetts, the surviving Kennedy brother, had been leading Carter in the polls. Once he became a candidate for the nomination himself, however, Kennedy, too, dropped in the polls. His behavior during and after an accident at Chappaquiddick in Massachusetts in 1969, resulting in the death of a young woman, troubled many voters. Others regarded Kennedy as too liberal; and, most important, the crises in Iran and Afghanistan led people to rally behind the president at a time of national emergency.

Citing the American hostages in Iran, Carter refused to leave Washington for the primaries but nevertheless won a series of victories. Though Kennedy carried several large states toward the end, the Carter-Mondale ticket was renominated by a comfortable margin. The Republicans turned to Ronald Reagan, movie actor, two-term governor of California, and for a dozen years the favorite of the party's right wing. Reagan selected as his running mate his main challenger in the primaries, George Bush of Texas, a former congressman, party chairman, diplomat, and CIA director, who represented more moderate Republicans.

The campaign was long, angry, and unenlightening. Displaying a nasty streak, Carter portrayed Reagan as a warmonger, racist, and extremist. This portrait was effectively undercut in their single television debate by Reagan's effective counterpunching—and his serene geniality. For his part, Reagan claimed that Carter had placed the country in a state of military weakness that invited Soviet aggression and humiliation at the hands of Khomeini. He condemned the SALT-II treaty as "fatally flawed." He blamed Carter's human-rights campaign for the overthrow of America's "friends" the shah and Somoza. Some voters, dismayed by the choice, found an alternative in John Anderson, a liberal Republican congressman from Illinois running on an independent ticket.

Carter's unpopularity and the state of the economy—runaway inflation and high interest rates—had more impact than foreign policy on the outcome. Reagan also profited from the support of the "Moral Majority," evangelical Protestants who were traditionalists in their values and consequently disturbed by changing American mores. They advocated restoring prayer in public schools and outlawing abortion. In politics they turned to candidates like Reagan who played to their biases. That tactic won over many of the white Southerners so important to Carter four years earlier.

The Reagan campaign drew strength, too, from the continued imprisonment of the American hostages in Iran, a condition mortifying for Carter and the nation. Years later, in 1991, Gary Sick, who had been a member of Carter's National Security Council staff in 1980, charged that William Casey, then Reagan's campaign manager, arranged a deal with Iranian representatives. In return for Casey's promise that Israel would ship arms to Iran — so Sick charged — the Iranians agreed to delay release of the hostages until after the American election. Casey had died before Sick made his accusation, about which Reagan denied any knowledge.

Even in the absence of any deal with Iran, Reagan was heading for victory in 1980. He won easily, carrying 44 states and accumulating 489 electoral votes to Carter's 49. The popular vote was less decisive, the 43.9 million cast for Reagan constituting but 50.8 percent of the total. Carter took 41 percent (35.5 million) and Anderson 7 percent (5.7 million). Since only 52.6 percent of those eligible actually voted, continuing the steady decline in turnout since 1960, Reagan was in fact elected by 28 percent of the voting-age population. The Republicans also captured the Senate for the first time since 1952, defeating several liberal Democrats, including the 1972 presidential candidate George McGovern.

Return of the hostages

The voters decided emphatically against continuing Carter in the White House. Yet in increasing military spending and in moving toward deregulation he had anticipated the policies of his successor. His emphasis on human rights was a salutary reaffirmation of the American heritage. On his final day in office, he at last succeeded in negotiating the release of the hostages in Iran.

THE REAGAN COUNTERREVOLUTION

Reagan in the White House The new president was the oldest man (70 shortly after his inauguration), the first actor, the first labor leader (he had been president of the Screen Actors Guild), and the first divorced man to be elected president. As a young man, he cast his first four presidential votes for Franklin Roosevelt, but later he moved far to the right. Years in Hollywood had not divested him of an image of America as the small-town idyl imagined from his childhood in Illinois. He preached old-time values of individualism, self-help, and upward mobility. Entering politics in the 1960s, he proved a relatively successful governor of California. An accomplished speaker, he radiated affability, optimism, and, despite his age, boyish charm.

Reagan worked much less hard than Carter and had far less command of information and analysis. But, where Carter had the mind of an engineer, Reagan had the outlook of an ideologue. His presidency had the unifying themes that Carter's lacked, and he left no doubt about the direction in which he wished to move the country. His mind was anecdotal rather than analytical, and his ideological bent was tempered by a capacity for practical accommodation. He understood, as his predecessor had not, that politics is ultimately an educational process. With his charm, eloquence, and genius for simplification, he was dubbed "the Great Communicator." Though no student of public affairs, Reagan set the course of his administration, created a new national agenda, and restored faith in the presidency.

President Reagan radiating charm

Reaganomics "Government is not the solution to our problem," Reagan said in his inaugural address. "Government is the problem," Reaganism at home rested on two propositions: that government was the root of evil, and that, once government was "off the people's backs," national problems would solve themselves.

As a candidate, Reagan promised an economic policy that would simultaneously dismantle government regulation, reduce social spending, rebuild American defenses, end inflation, and balance the budget—a mix derided by George Bush during the primaries (in a phrase later repented) as "voodoo economics." In pursuing these objectives, the new administration drew on economic ideas developed during the 1970s in right-wing "think-tanks," in conservative intellectual journals, and among younger Republicans in Congress.

Reaganomics had three divergent theoretical components. Reaganites agreed in regarding the unregulated market place as the means of salvation but disagreed on the tactics of economic policy. "Supply-side" economics argued that a cut in top tax rates would give the rich increased incentive to work, save, and invest. This would stimulate the economy as a whole, and the tax cuts would pay for themselves through increased revenues. "Supply side," as David Stockman, Reagan's first budget director, said, "is 'trickle-down' theory"—the theory of the Coolidge era that, if you help the few at the top, benefits will trickle down to the rest.

"Monetarism," with the Nobel Prize economist Milton Friedman as high priest, saw the control of the monetary stock as the key particularly for wringing inflation out of the economy. Like supply-siders, monetarists did not worry unduly about deficits. Many Republicans, however, especially in Congress, remained faithful to the party's budget-balancing orthodoxy.

In 1981 the administration called for a massive tax cut to stimulate the economy. Congressional Democrats joined with Republicans in decorating the revenue act of that year with tax favors for the rich and for special-interest groups whose lobbyists helped to shape the final provisions. Concurrently, the administration looked to high interest rates to restrain inflation. In the tug-of-war between a soft fiscal policy and a hard monetary policy, monetary policy scored the first victory, throwing the economy in the next year into the worst collapse since the 1930s, unemployment rising to nearly 11 percent.

In the meantime, Reagan, in the vain hope of keeping his pledge of a balanced budget by 1984, cut back on government domestic spending (except Social Security and Medicare) by nearly 10 percent. But these cutbacks were more than offset by the tax reduction of

A Reaganite Assessment of Reaganomics

The White House . . . was holding the American economy hostage to a reckless, unstable fiscal policy based on the politics of high spending and the doctrine of low taxes. Yet rather than acknowledge that the resulting massive buildup of public debt would eventually generate serious economic troubles, the White House proclaimed a roaring economic success. . . .

What economic success there was had almost nothing to do with . . . supply-side doctrine. Instead . . . the business cycle had brought . . . economic activity surging back. But there was nothing new . . . or sustainable about this favorable turn of events. . . . The fundamental reality . . . was not the advent of a new day, but a lapse into fiscal indiscipline on a scale never before experienced in peacetime. . . .

Indeed, just below the surface the American economy was already being twisted and weakened by Washington's free lunch joy ride. . . . Our national savings has been squandered to pay for a tax cut we could not afford. We have consequently borrowed enormous amounts of foreign capital to make up for the shortfall between our national production and our national spending. . . . Borrowing the hundreds of billions of dollars has also distorted the . . . U.S. economy. The high dollar exchange rate . . . required to attract so much foreign capital has devastated our industries. . . . Jobs, capital, and production have been permanently lost. . . .

In eight years of direction by the most conservative administration in modern times, the federal government's spending will have exceeded its income by the staggering sum of $1.5 trillion. . . . In the final analysis, only one conclusion is possible. The American economy and government have literally been taken hostage by the awewome stubbornness of the nation's fortieth President.

From David Stockman, *The Triumph of Politics*, 1986

$131 billion and the $92 billion increase in military spending by 1985. Moreover, with excessively high interest rates, the increase in interest payments on the national debt exceeded the cuts in health, education, welfare, and social programs. At the same time, recession reduced tax revenues and increased entitlement claims (as for unemployment compensation). The results were deficits of $111 billion in 1982 and $195 billion in 1983—more in the second year than all the Carter deficits combined and the largest peacetime deficit in American history. And the deficit rose in ensuing years.

The unprecedented deficit had one ironic consequence. It pulled the economy out of the recession of

1982–83—an old-fashioned, Keynesian, demand-side recovery. A further irony was to hear Democrats righteously denounce deficits while Reaganites casually dismissed them.

Shrinking Government Reagan used the deficit to force further reductions in social programs. "We can lecture our children about extravagance until we run out of voice and breath," he said. "Or we can cut their extravagance by simply reducing their allowance." But the most costly entitlement programs—Social Security, Medicare, civil-service and veterans' pensions—had middle-class constituencies and were deemed politically untouchable.

The available target for budget-cutting, in the administration's view, lay in programs requiring a "means test"—proof of need. Though means-tested entitlements—welfare, food stamps, child nutrition, and the like—consumed only 18 percent of the total expenditures for income security, they had the weakest lobbies behind them and suffered almost $125 billion, nearly 60 percent, of the 1981 cuts. Reductions in benefit payments were greatest for households with incomes under $10,000.

Reagan proposed to keep a "safety net" for the "truly needy"—those who, because of age, disability, or illness, were unemployable. But he disliked income supplements for workers. His reductions therefore fell with particular force on the "working poor," now in many cases deprived of food stamps, employment training, welfare benefits, Medicaid, and reduced-price school lunches for their children. "In order to succeed," wrote George Gilder, a prominent Reaganite theoretician, "the poor need most of all the spur of their poverty." Critics, reflecting on the simultaneous tax reductions for the rich, concluded that, in the Reaganite view, the poor needed the spur of poverty and the rich the spur of wealth.

Reagan's 1982 "New Federalism" proposals for the transfer to the states of more than 40 federal programs, including welfare and food stamps, got nowhere. But his cutbacks in social spending and the elimination in 1986 of general revenue-sharing forced states to assume a number of federal functions, leading to increases in state budgets, taxes, and social innovation. Some state governments rose to the challenge, experimenting in health insurance, industrial and high-technology development, work requirements for welfare recipients ("workfare") and other social and economic policies. But higher state taxes soon met resistance from the electorate that threatened innovative programs, and the loss of a share of federal revenues pushed many states toward severe budgetary crises.

Reagan proposed the transfer of still other federal programs to the private sector. Under this "privatization" policy, the administration sold private investors at advantageous terms CONRAIL, the government-owned freight railroad, and nearly $10 billion of government loans. Reagan also recommended the sale of AMTRAK, the government-owned passenger railroad, the Naval Petroleum Reserve, the Railroad Retirement Board, and other federal undertakings.

Deregulation The campaign to roll back the national government, which Carter had begun, included the systematic reduction of public regulation of the economy. The administration pursued this goal in a variety of ways—by cutting regulatory budgets, by diluting or abolishing regulations, by relaxing enforcement, by staffing regulatory agencies with representatives of the industries to be regulated. One result was the weakening of safeguards in food and drugs, highway safety, nursing homes, and banking and the stock market.

Deregulation had special impact on the environment and resources. Reagan's first secretary of the interior, James Watt, had emerged from the Sagebrush Rebellion, a movement of mine owners and ranchers seeking to rid the West of federal supervision of public lands. The transfer of public property and resources to private control, Watt argued, was essential to promote economic development. Reversing the policies of Theodore Roosevelt, he tried to sell up to 35 million acres of public land, opened the continental shelf to offshore oil and gas drilling, encouraged timber cutting in the national forests, offered public land to coal companies, accelerated the spread of strip-mining, and reduced safety inspection of coal mines. Though he enjoyed Reagan's support, Watt's tasteless cracks about environmentalists, liberals, Indians, Jews and cripples finally led to his resignation in 1983.

Supporters claimed that deregulation was revitalizing industries like transportation, telecommunications, banking, oil drilling, and coal mining. Critics contended that deregulation had begun a dangerous unraveling of the network of health, safety, and environmental protections built up over decades. Consumers were exasperated by the abandonment of unprofitable but convenient air routes and by the complications following the breakup of the American Telephone and Telegraph Company monopoly. Polls showed decisive majorities in favor of stringent standards for air and water, for safety on the highways and in the workplace.

The 1984 Election Reagan's personal popularity, enhanced by the grace with which he had survived an assassination attempt in 1981, remained unabated. His vision of the Republican party as the party of optimism, patriotism, national confidence, and individual opportunity reached across traditional political lines. "America is back and standing tall," he said in announcing for reelection. Moreover, 1984 was a time of economic recovery, with unemployment declining and prices stable. As the election approached, Reagan headed a coalition that portended a long period of conservative ascendancy. Reaganism appealed beyond mainstream Republicans to voters moved by the social issues Nixon had earlier exploited — to blue-collar workers, to Catholics, to a fervent evangelical constituency, to the suburbs, to the Sunbelt — the fastest growing part of the country — and to the young. Those young voters of the future, less anchored to a political party than were their elders, were politically shaped by the contrasting presidencies of Carter and Reagan.

Walter F. Mondale of Minnesota, a veteran liberal of the Hubert Humphrey school and Carter's vice president, won the Democratic nomination after beating back a rough challenge from Senator Gary Hart of Colorado. The Reverend Jesse Jackson, who united the eloquence of a preacher with the resourcefulness of a politician, emerged as the first formidable black contender for a presidential nomination. Mondale chose as his running mate Congresswoman Geraldine Ferraro of New York, the first woman to make the national ticket of a major party. But her failure to disclose promptly her family's financial interests, and Mondale's sensible but unpopular emphasis on the need for new taxes, hurt the Democrats.

On seas of economic well-being, Reagan sailed to a tremendous victory, carrying everything except Minnesota and the District of Columbia and piling up 525 electoral votes to Mondale's 13. His 54 million popular votes constituted over 59 percent of the total cast. The voter turnout — 53.1 percent — represented a slight increase over 1980. Unlike Franklin Roosevelt in 1936, however, Reagan failed to consolidate his

Mondale and Ferraro, 1984

victory by sweeping both houses of Congress, the Democrats retaining control of the House of Representatives.

Still, Reagan, aglow with confidence, announced that it was "morning in America." But historians noted that every president in the twentieth century elected by 60 percent of the popular vote had acquired delusions of immunity that soon led him into bad trouble. Further, much of the success of Reagan's first term had been due to his judicious and politically astute Chief of Staff James Baker. Baker's exchange of jobs with the arrogant secretary of the Treasury Donald Regan in 1985 greatly weakened both policy and political judgment in the White House.

REAGAN AND THE WORLD

Reagan, the Nationalist In foreign affairs, Reagan was an unabashed American nationalist. No president since Wilson had expressed so ardently the idea of "American exceptionalism"—the idea that the United States was exempt from the historic laws and interests that conditioned other countries. Seeing America as a chosen nation, Reagan had no doubt about its inherent moral superiority over lesser countries.

Animated by this faith, he saw world affairs less in geopolitical terms, as a contest shaped by national interest and the balance of power, than in moralistic terms, as a contest between good and evil. The Soviet Union, Reagan said in 1982, is an "evil empire . . . the focus of evil in the modern world." "Let us not delude ourselves," he said. "The Soviet Union underlies all the unrest that is going on. If they weren't engaged in this game of dominos, there wouldn't be any hot spots in the world." Reagan's secretary of state, the highstrung General Alexander Haig, who had served as Nixon's chief of staff and later as NATO commander, agreed that the Soviet Union was carrying out a master plan of world conquest, as did Secretary of Defense Caspar Weinberger, who had been Reagan's budget director in California and later Nixon's secretary of health, education and welfare.

Convinced that the American people were fed up with weakness and humiliation, the Reagan administration proposed to reverse the supposed decay in America's world position by a crusade of military, economic, and psychological renewal. Building on Carter's beginning, it mounted the largest peacetime military increase in American history, the national defense bill for the Reagan years coming to $2 trillion.

The Soviet Union The administration justified the buildup by claiming that the United States had fallen behind the Soviet Union in military power. This claim was much disputed, critics contending that, while Russia led in some categories, America led in others, and that the result was a fragile balance—the Soviet advantage in ICBMs balanced by the American advantage in submarine-based forces and in strategic aircraft.

The administration sought especially to enlarge American nuclear striking power, particularly with the MX missile. Reagan's decision to place the MX in vulnerable Minuteman silos represented, as critics saw it, a further move toward "counterforce" and a first-strike strategy. In 1983–84 the Pershing II missiles began to be deployed in West Germany, a five minute lob to the Soviet Union. In the meantime, National Security Decision Directive 13 set forth plans to enable the United States to "prevail" in a "protracted" nuclear war. The Federal Emergency Management Agency even made straight-faced plans for the evacuation of cities—6.5 million people to be transported out of New York by automobile in 3.3 days to "host areas" in the hinterland.

Those fatuous preparations roused the fear that the administration regarded nuclear weapons as usable and nuclear wars as winnable. Some in the administration believed that an unlimited arms race offered a good way of doing the Soviet Union in. Either the Russians would try to keep up, which would wreck their economy, or they would fail to keep up, which would leave America the decisive military advantage. Others saw the modernization of American strategic forces as a precondition for arms control negotiations.

In the meantime, the administration decided initially to comply with the "fatally flawed" SALT-I agreement (a decision vacated in 1986). In November 1981 Reagan offered to cancel the proposed deployment of Pershing II and ground-launched missiles in Europe if the Soviet Union would dismantle its SS-20 and other intermediate-range missiles. This "zero option" proposal was rejected by Moscow, as indeed its American advocates expected and intended.

In the next years Soviet-American relations grew steadily worse. In 1983, when the Russians shot down

Nuclear War

SCHEER: To dramatize it for the reader, the bomb has dropped [in Los Angeles]. Now, if he's within that two-mile area, he's finished, right? If he's not in the two-mile area, what has happened?

JONES: You've got to be in a hole. . . . The dirt really is the thing that protects. . . . For a high-density area like Los Angeles, shelter stay time should be about a week. . . . With protection of people only, your recovery time to pre-war GNP levels would probably be six or eight years. If we used the Russian methods for protecting both the people and the industrial means of production, recovery times could be two to four years.

From T. K. Jones, Deputy Under Secretary of Defense for Research and Engineering, interviewed by Robert Scheer in *With Enough Shovels: Reagan, Bush and Nuclear War,* 1982

In the first moments of a ten-thousand-megaton attack on the United States . . . flashes of white light would suddenly illumine large areas of the country as thousands of suns, each one brighter than the sun itself, blossomed over cities, suburbs, and towns. In those same moments, when the first wave of missiles arrived, the vast majority of the people in the regions first targeted would be irradiated, crushed, or burned to death. . . . As the attack proceeded, as much as three-quarters of the country could be subjected to incendiary levels of heat, and so, wherever there was inflammable material, could be set ablaze. In the ten seconds or so after each bomb hit, as blast waves swept outward from thousands of ground zeros, the physical plant of the United States would be swept away like leaves in a gust of wind . . . vaporized, blasted, or otherwise pulverized out of existence. Then, as clouds of dust rose from the earth, and mushroom clouds spread overhead, often linking to form vast canopies, day would turn to night. . . . If, in a nuclear holocaust, anyone hid himself deep enough under the earth and stayed there long enough to survive, he would emerge into a dying natural environment.

From Jonathan Schell, *The Fate of the Earth,* 1983

a Korean civilian airliner in Soviet airspace, killing 269 people, Reagan claimed it was done deliberately, though his own CIA had concluded that the Russians had not known it was a civilian plane.

Yet the Reagan foreign policy was often circumspect in action. Without altering his views of communism, Reagan showed a capacity to forsake ideology if confronted by domestic political objection (as when he abandoned Carter's embargo on grain sales to Russia), or by the resistance of allies (as when he abandoned opposition to a pipeline supplying Western Europe with natural gas from the Soviet Union), or by geopolitical necessity (as when he abandoned anti-Communist Taiwan in favor of closer relations with Communist China).

The hard line remained the dominant note. Its advocates said that it had redressed the picture of American weakness, restored the nuclear balance in Europe, dissipated doubts about American readiness to use military force, and increased international respect for the United States. Its critics charged that Reagan's course had frightened America's allies, increased international distrust in American leadership and given new impetus to the nuclear arms race.

Arms Control By 1985 the United States and the Soviet Union already had well over 50,000 nuclear warheads between them. The problem of controlling the arms race fell into three categories: intermediate-range nuclear forces (INF), strategic arms reduction talks (START), and mutual and balanced force reduction (MBFR).

In March 1983 Reagan had introduced a startling new element by calling for a missile defense system in space designed, he said, to "render nuclear weapons impotent and obsolete." The Strategic Defense Initiative (SDI), as the administration called it, was soon known, in tribute to the popular space movie, as Star Wars. As presented by Reagan, SDI seemed to envisage an impenetrable defense shield to be erected over the United States like an astrodome. Scientists doubted whether total defense was technologically attainable and pointed out that anything less would let enough missiles through to kill millions of people. Later models reduced Star Wars from a defense of the nation to a defense of missile silos, in which case its function would be to reinforce, not to replace, deterrence.

The space shield would not in any case stop low-altitude delivery systems. The Soviet Union could respond by building more ICBMs to overwhelm the shield and more cruise missiles, bombers, and other low-flying weapons to rush in under the shield. Since countermeasures were technically far simpler than the construction of the shield and cost far less, they would be relatively easy to sustain. Star Wars, critics said, was not only a fantasy but a fraud.

Nevertheless, to prepare the way for Star Wars, the administration adopted a unilateral reinterpretation of the ABM treaty of 1972—a broad construction rejected both by officials who negotiated the treaty and by senators who ratified it. Since Reagan regarded Star Wars as nonnegotiable and the Soviet Union regarded it as unacceptable, SDI became a further block to arms control agreements.

Enter Gorbachev In the meantime, changes began to take place in the Soviet Union. Brezhnev, who had presided over a time of stagnation, died in November 1982. His successor Yuri Z. Andropov had reform impulses, but he died too and was succeeded in 1984 by a Brezhnev protege Konstantin U. Chernenko. Chernenko then died in his turn, and a new general secretary, Mikhail Gorbachev, coming to power in 1985, initiated a program of radical economic and civil reform under the banners of *glasnost* (openness) and *perestroika* (restructuring).

Gorbachev proved not only a bold reformer at home but a suave and effective operator on the world scene. His top priority was the modernization of the Soviet system. To achieve this he needed to transfer resources, scientists, and engineers from the arms race to the civilian economy. His quest for an international respite, combined with an urbane personality and moderate views, opened new possibilities for arms-control agreements. In November 1985 Reagan and Gorbachev held a genial summit meeting in Geneva where they discussed the possibility of a reduction in strategic forces and an "interim" agreement on INF.

In June 1982 General Haig had resigned as secretary of state. His successor, George Shultz, an economist who had been Nixon's secretary of labor and then of the Treasury, was more equable in temperament and relaxed in outlook. He now served as a cautious counterweight to Weinberger and the Pentagon on arms-control issues. Reagan himself faced the prospect of being the first president in 25 years not to reach an arms-control agreement. Concerned about his place in history and encouraged by his wife and by

Geneva Summit, 1985

Secretary Shultz, and also rather impressed by Gorbachev, Reagan looked on negotiations with new favor. With his arms buildup now well under way, he could claim that his preconditions for agreement had now been fulfilled.

In October 1986 Reagan and Gorbachev met again in Reykjavik, Iceland. The Americans, expecting another preliminary discussion, were suddenly confronted by a wide-ranging series of Soviet proposals, including a 50 percent cut in strategic weapons, the "zero option" for INF and a confirmation of the ABM treaty limitations. The ill-prepared American delegation found itself plunged into major substantive negotiations. Agreement in principle on INF was readily reached, but deep reductions in strategic weapons foundered on the SDI stumbling block. A final meeting between the two leaders degenerated into a confused discussion of the elimination of all nuclear weapons. The summit collapsed, though both leaders were constrained by domestic political needs to proclaim a measure of success.

After an arduous year of negotiation, Gorbachev came to Washington in December 1987, and the two leaders signed a treaty providing for the elimination of medium- and shorter-range nuclear arms. The Soviet Union would destroy 1,752 missiles, the United States 867: enough nuclear power to obliterate 32,000 Hiroshimas. Elaborate verification measures included provisions for short-notice on-site inspection. While the INF treaty covered less than 4 percent of nuclear warheads, its proponents believed that it opened the way to more far-reaching agreement on strategic weapons.

The Washington summit was conducted in an affable spirit. Gorbachev made a strong impression on the American public and on the president himself. Reagan subsequently remarked that the Soviet Union had given up its quest for world domination—a thought that outraged his right-wing supporters. Reagan held that such people accepted the inevitability of war, thereby enraging them further. Other critics argued that the treaty would leave Western Europe naked before Soviet conventional forces and that it would weaken American ties with NATO allies. Such doubts were not, however, widely shared in Western Europe. But the death of William J. Casey, the CIA director, and the departure from the administration of Secretary of Defense Weinberger and other hardliners reduced resistance to Reagan's new direction of policy. In June 1988, Reagan himself, in a startling—and internationally applauded—reversal of the mood in which he began his presidency, went to Moscow, paying a visit to the very heart of the "evil empire." He had responded constructively to the new spirit that Mikhail Gorbachev had initiated in Soviet-American relations, as well as in the internal affairs of the Soviet Union. For good reason, *Time* magazine was to name Gorbachev "man of the decade."

Regional Conflicts: Nicaragua Progress in arms control left unresolved the problem of "regional conflicts"—conflicts that, according to the Reaganite world view, were instigated by the Soviet Union.

Though the population of Nicaragua was less than 3 million and the country was desperately poor, the Sandinista regime Reagan called "an unusual and extraordinary threat to the national security" of the United States. In December 1981 Reagan directed the CIA to arm and organize Nicaraguan exiles, soon known as "Contras," to wage war against the Sandinistas. The aim was ostensibly to stop arms shipments from Nicaragua to the antigovernment rebels in the civil war in El Salvador. But Congress suspected otherwise and in 1982 forbade the use of covert funds to overthrow the Nicaraguan government.

As American intervention increased, the Nicaraguan regime moved to the left, accepting increasing aid from the Soviet Union, and the El Salvador regime moved to the right. By 1983 in El Salvador right-wing "death squads," tolerated if not encouraged by the regime, tortured and assassinated oppositionists. The election in 1984 of a centrist president Jose Napoleon Duarte brought temporary stability, but Duarte proved a weak if well-intentioned leader and the bloody civil war continued.

The CIA meanwhile pressed its not-so-secret war against the Sandinistas. If the Marxists succeeded in Central America, Reagan maintained, "Our credibility would collapse, our alliances would crumble, and the safety of our homeland would be in jeopardy." He called repeatedly for aid to the Contras, describing them as the "moral equivalents" of the Founding Fathers. But the disclosure in 1984 that the CIA had mined Nicaraguan harbors provoked disapproval in Congress, already suspicious of the Contras as dominated by supporters of the Somoza tyranny. That disapproval was expressed in 1984–86 through a series of amendments to appropriation acts sponsored by Congressman Edward P. Boland of Massachusetts.

Nicaraguan Contras

Those amendments denied all government agencies funds to support "directly or indirectly military or paramilitary operations" in Nicaragua. "If we can't move the Contra package," Reagan told his national security adviser in 1986, ". . . I want to figure out a way to take action unilaterally to provide assistance."

Reagan's undeclared war against Nicaragua raised questions of international law. Critics charged that he was pursuing his policy in violation not only of congressional prohibitions but also of nonintervention pledges repeatedly made to the Organization of American States (OAS) since the Montevideo Conference of 1933 when the United States first subscribed to the declaration that "no state has the right to intervene in the internal or external affairs of another" (see p. 728). When Nicaragua brought the harbor-mining episode to the World Court, the Reagan administration walked out of the courtroom.

Most Latin American governments disagreed with Reagan's quest for a military solution, believing that violence in Central America would promote rather than impede the spread of Marxism. In 1983 Venezuela, Mexico, Colombia, and Panama launched the Contadora peace process, and in 1987 President Oscar Arias of Costa Rica, with support from other Central American governments, proposed a detailed peace plan. After Congress rejected Reagan's request for continued military aid to the Contras, the Sandinistas and Contras began discussions in 1988 on a cease-fire, amnesty, and free elections.

Frustrated at the stalemate in Central America, Reagan in October 1983 had ordered an invasion of the former British colony of Grenada in the Caribbean. He did so on the flimsy excuse that he was acting to protect the lives of American medical students there who, so he alleged, were threatened by a Marxist dictatorship. In fact, he was acting to remove Cuban influence from the island. The surprise assault on an island of 110,000 people with no army, navy, or air force was, not surprisingly, successful in spite of poor coordination of the American forces involved in the attack. The intervention was greeted with applause by the Grenadans, by neighboring Caribbean islands, and by most people in the United States. Critics at home and especially abroad questioned the example of unilateral military intervention Washington was setting to the world. "If you are going to pronounce a new law that, wherever communism reigns against the will of the people, . . . the United States shall enter," said Reagan's loyal friend Prime Minister Margaret Thatcher of Britain, "then we are going to have really terrible wars in the world."

The United States and Latin America

Our situation invites and our interests prompt us to aim at an ascendant in the system of American affairs.

From Alexander Hamilton, *Federalist,* No. 11

I candidly confess, that I have ever looked on Cuba as the most interesting addition which could ever be made to our system of States.

From Thomas Jefferson to James Monroe, October 24, 1823

To-day the United States is practically sovereign on this continent, and its fiat is law upon the subjects to which it confines its interposition. . . . Its infinite resources combined with its isolated position render it master of the situation.

From Secretary of State Richard Olney to T. F. Bayard, July 20, 1895

We, the citizens of all the American republics, are, I think, at the threshold of a new era. . . . We are entering a new era in accepting the plan that no one of our nations must hereafter exploit a neighbor nation at the expense of that neighbor.

From Franklin D. Roosevelt in Cartagena, Colombia, July 10, 1934

Social reforms are at the heart of the Alliance for Progress. They are the preconditions to economic modernization. And they are the instrument by which we assure the poor and hungry—the worker and the campesino—his full participation in the benefits of our development and in the human dignity which is the purpose of all free societies. . . . Those who make peaceful revolution impossible will make violent revolution inevitable.

From John F. Kennedy, March 13, 1962

The goal of the professional guerrilla movements in Central America is as simple as it is sinister—to destabilize the entire region from the Panama Canal to Mexico. . . . I do not believe that a majority of the Congress or the country is prepared to stand by passively while the people of Central America are delivered to totalitarianism and we ourselves are left vulnerable to new dangers.

From Ronald Reagan, April 27, 1983

American troops in Grenada

The Reagan administration's preoccupation with supposed Soviet machinations diverted attention, many believed, from more critical hemisphere problems, such as the abiding poverty in Latin American countries and their external debt, rising toward $400 billion in the late 1980s.

The Reagan Doctrine The actions in Nicaragua and Grenada were part of a larger pattern of policy known popularly as the Reagan Doctrine. "We must not break faith," Reagan said in 1985, "with those who are risking their lives on every continent, from Afghanistan to Nicaragua, to defy Soviet-supported aggression." Where previous presidential doctrines had envisaged defensive containment of Soviet expansionism, the Reagan Doctrine, reviving the John Foster Dulles dream of "liberation," proposed to go over to the offensive. The goal was to bring about a "global democratic revolution" defined by respect for human rights and for "market-oriented" economies.

In this spirit, the Reagan administration continued the Carter policy of aid to the *mujahedeen* resistance in Afghanistan and initiated covert support for "freedom fighters" in Angola and Cambodia, as well as Nicaragua. The Reagan Doctrine was supplemented on occasion by American military action. After the dispatch of marines into the midst of a civil war in Lebanon resulted in the death of 241 American servicemen in 1983, the administration became cautious in long-term commitments of armed force. Thereafter it concentrated on quick surprise attacks, as in Grenada and in 1986 against Libya, whose erratic strong man Muammar Qadaffi was held responsible, along with Khomeini of Iran, for anti-Western terrorism. Terrorism became a particular Reagan preoccupation, with categorical declarations to Congress and to foreign governments against any deals with terrorists.

An unexpected by-product of the Reagan Doctrine was the restoration of human rights to a central place in foreign policy. In 1986 Reagan, adding a corollary to his Doctrine, pledged opposition to "tyranny in whatever form, whether of the left or the right." In abandoning the Ferdinand Marcos dictatorship in the Philippines, the Jean-Claude Duvalier dictatorship in Haiti, and the Manuel Antonio Noriega dictatorship in Panama, Reagan unabashedly adopted the policies for which in 1980 he had denounced Carter in the cases of the shah in Iran and the Somozas in Nicaragua.

In practice, the Reagan Doctrine turned out to be more exhortation than action. The administration declined to aid anti-Communist insurgencies in Ethiopia and Mozambique or to subvert right-wing tyrannies in Chile and Paraguay. Congress tended to distinguish between assistance to people who, on their own, were already resisting a foreign invasion, as in Afghanistan, and the manufacture of an insurgency from scratch in order to overthrow a legal government, as in Nicaragua.

Critics questioned the legality of operations taken under the Reagan Doctrine. "Support for freedom fighters," Reagan argued, "is self-defense, and totally consistent with the OAS and UN Charters." International lawyers found this a perilously elastic interpretation of self-defense, reminiscent of Khrushchev's claim of a Soviet entitlement to global intervention in support of "wars of national liberation." Like the Soviet Union, the United States now appeared to be asserting a right to act as a law unto itself on the world scene.

The Iran-Contra Affairs The Reagan Doctrine rested in large part on "covert action," the effort through clandestine means to change policies and regimes in other countries. Covert action, conducted outside the regular channels of government, was in its nature hard to control and immune to normal procedures of accountability. Though realists agreed that great powers had to use unorthodox methods in a cruel world, covert action—founded as it was on law-breaking, deception, and lies—imported dangerous habits into a democratic polity.

On November 3, 1986, a weekly paper in Lebanon reported that the United States had secretly sold arms to Iran. Americans were incredulous. But it soon became clear that the Reagan administration had indeed sold arms to Iran in the hope of obtaining the release of American hostages in Lebanon and had done so in face of its repeated declarations that it would never make deals with terrorists or sell arms to the Ayatollah Khomeini. Further revelations were to come. On November 25, the nation learned that some proceeds from the Iran arms sales had been "diverted" to the Nicaraguan Contras at a time when Congress had prohibited government agencies from providing such aid.

Confronted by these disclosures, the administration, from the president down, at first sought refuge in a bluster of incomplete, misleading and, very often, false accounts of what its members had wrought. The United States had approached moderates in Iran, Reagan said, because of Iran's supreme geopolitical importance to the United States. He denied as "utterly false" the charge that the effort had been to trade arms for hostages—a denial he was later forced to retract. In fact, Reagan had endorsed the sales of arms to Iran and secretly signed authorizations for them that, with his assent, were hidden from congressional oversight committees. Further, determined as he was to circumvent the Boland amendments, Reagan had secretly approved the efforts of his National Security Council (NSC) agents to raise funds for the Contras from nations eager for American favors, Saudia Arabia and Taiwan among others. He had also welcomed at the White House conservative Americans of wealth who had been persuaded by NSC staff to make private contributions to the Contras. Those operations, too, had been concealed from Congress. The initial secrecy and subsequent cover-up reminded observers of Watergate, though the Reagan administration was more forthcoming than the Nixon administration had been, and Reagan had dealt in none of the dirty political tricks that Nixon had conspired to hide.

A special review board, appointed by Reagan and chaired by John Tower, a former Republican senator from Texas, was sharply critical both of the Iran and Contra policies and of the process by which they were made. The majority report of the inquiry conducted by a joint congressional committee in 1987 was even sharper in its judgment of the "pervasive dishonesty and inordinate secrecy" that characterized the affairs. In the meantime, an independent counsel investigated the need for criminal indictments. In its inquiry, however, the congressional committee had granted key witnesses immunity from prosecution for crimes to which they admitted in their testimony. Those grants made it possible for the committee to elicit information that might otherwise not have become public, but the immunity provided these witnesses spared those most guilty of defying the law from prosecution or, in some cases, from conviction.

Those who ultimately escaped included Robert McFarlane and Admiral John Poindexter, Reagan's national security advisers, and their venturesome subordinate, Lieutenant Colonel Oliver North of the NSC staff. They had worked with William Casey and several of his CIA underlings to effect the president's wishes. In order to avoid the CIA's nominal obligation to report its covert activities to congressional oversight committees, Reagan had converted the National Security Council, theretofore a policy-coordination body, into an operating agency. The language of the

The Boland Amendments

No appropriations or funds made available pursuant to this joint resolution to the Central Intelligence Agency, the Department of Defense, or any other agency or entity of the United States involved in intelligence activities may be obligated or expended for the purpose of which would have the effect of supporting, directly or indirectly, military or paramilitary operations in Nicaragua by any nation, group, organization, movement or individual.

Quoted in Theodore Draper, *A Very Thin Line: The Iran-Contra Affairs,* 1991

Boland Amendments did not exempt the NSC from the prohibitions against aiding the Contras, but NSC personnel acted as if it did. First McFarlane and then Poindexter, both using North, had carried forward the Iran and Contra policies of the president—despite the vehement opposition of both Secretary of State Shultz and Secretary of Defense Weinberger, whose views Reagan had also rejected. McFarlane, Poindexter, and North, who often also proceeded on his own, had lied to Congress about their actions, as had several senior officers of the CIA who had assisted them. Poindexter and North admitted they believed they had the power to create a special government, beyond the reach of Congress, to carry out the president's wishes. Poindexter even declared that he knew what the president wanted without being told, and that that was enough to allow his undertakings.

Lieutenant Colonel Oliver North: fund-raiser for the Contras

Both Reagan and Poindexter denied that the president knew about the diversion of Iranian funds to the Contras. But Reagan knew about other aspects of the arms sales, as well as about other efforts to assist the Contras and to deceive the Congress.

The Iran-Contra scandal revealed incompetence, incoherence, recklessness, and duplicity in Reagan's conduct of foreign affairs and weakened the administration gravely before both Congress and the world. The need to regain prestige was no doubt an additional reason for Reagan's interest in an arms-control agreement. It also led, in an effort to recover the confidence of Arab states, to new American commitments in the bitter war between Iran and Iraq.

Since Iraq began the war in 1980, the Reagan administration had pursued a variety of policies: first neutrality; then a pro-Iraq policy, culminating in the restoration of diplomatic relations in 1984; then the arms sales to Iran because of Iran's alleged strategic importance; then in 1987, despite an Iraqi attack on an American naval ship killing 37 sailors, a pro-Iraq policy intended to please the Arab states along the

Reagan and the Iran-Contra Affair

The speculation, the commenting and all, on a story that came out of the Middle East . . . has no foundation.

From Ronald Reagan, November 6, 1986

The charge has been made that the United States has shipped weapons to Iran as ransom payment for the release of American hostages in Lebanon, that the United States undercut its allies and secretly violated American policy against trafficking with terrorists. Those charges are utterly false. . . . We did not—repeat, did not—trade weapons or anything else for hostages, nor will we.

From Ronald Reagan, November 13, 1986

I don't think a mistake was made.

From Ronald Reagan, November 19, 1986

I think we took the only action we could have in Iran. . . . I do not think it was a mistake. . . . I don't see anything I would have done differently. . . . Lieutenant Colonel North . . . is a national hero.

From Ronald Reagan, November 26, 1986

I do not believe it was wrong to establish contacts with a country of strategic importance. . . . We did not achieve what we wished, and serious mistakes were made in trying to do so. We will get to the bottom of this.

From Ronald Reagan, January 27, 1987

A few months ago I told the American people I did not trade arms for hostages. My heart and my best intentions still tell me that's true, but the facts and the evidence tell me it is not. . . . It was a mistake.

From Ronald Reagan, March 4, 1987

It sort of settled down to just trading arms for hostages.

From Ronald Reagan, March 26, 1987

Never at any time did we view this as trading weapons for hostages.

From Ronald Reagan, December 3, 1987

Persian Gulf, including the dispatch of American naval ships to the Gulf, arms sales to Iraq, and the placement of American flags on Kuwaiti tankers. Reagan's decision to raise the military stakes in the Gulf was taken, as so often, without consultation with America's allies and with only sketchy notification to Congress.

ECONOMIC CONSEQUENCES OF REAGANOMICS

America: World Debtor While military deployments continued, observers wondered whether the future international vulnerability of the United States would not be economic rather than military and whether indeed American overseas objectives would not have to be reduced to fit diminishing means. Reaganomics had had one notable success: tight money (along with the collapse of OPEC's high oil prices) had brought down inflation from 10.4 percent in 1981 to 3.7 percent in 1987. The tax cut of 1981 also provided economic stimulus, reducing unemployment from 8.5 to 5.8 percent in these years. But the tax cut, joined with the defense budget and high interest rates, ushered in a period of unprecedented peacetime budget deficits. The supply-side notion that tax cuts would pay for themselves turned out to be an illusion. The gross federal debt, as accumulated in the two centuries since the start of the republic, tripled in the eight Reagan years, rising from $935 billion in January 1981 to $2.7 trillion in 1988. By 1991 the annual deficit exceeded $3 trillion. The increasing national debt and high interest rates together made annual interest payments on the debt a larger and larger federal outlay, one that bought neither guns nor butter.

The United States in the 1980s lived considerably beyond its means—an indulgence made possible by the influx of a trillion dollars of foreign money into the American economy. When Reagan was elected in 1980, the United States was the world's largest creditor, other countries owing America $150 billion. By 1988 the United States had become the world's largest debtor, owing other countries $400 billion—more than a half-trillion-dollar deterioration in the Reagan years and a precipitous decline in America's international position. Foreign trade, which amounted to only 10 percent of the gross national product in 1965, represented nearly 25 percent 20 years later. But the overvalued dollar of 1982–85, a direct result of Reaganomics, both priced American exports out of world markets and drew imports into the United States, thereby contributing to the decline of important manufacturing sectors, with adverse consequences for the working class.

The new dependence on foreign capital meant that never before in its history had the American economy been more at the mercy of decisions taken by foreigners. Japan, the vanquished enemy in the Second World War, was now the world's largest creditor. The center of economic activity was moving toward the Pacific basin. American trade in that area, only half as great as trade with Europe in 1960, was a quarter larger by the 1980s. The Japanese helped finance the American deficit by buying U.S. Treasury bonds and then buying up American corporations, banks, and real estate. Japanese capital flowing to the United States grew from $20 billion in 1982 to $60 billion in 1987. The Japanese, one scholar noted, were "the principal underwriters of President Reagan's policies." If this flow were to stop, the impact on the American economy would be devastating. Nor could the United States "fight another war on the same scale as the Korean or Vietnamese conflicts without Japanese permission and financial support of the dollar." Two centuries after the declaration of independence, said the liberal banker Felix Rohatyn, "the United States has lost its position as an independent power."

Japan had its own reasons for sustaining the United States, however. It needed markets for its exports and outlets for its surplus capital. Japan was reluctant, moreover, to assume the global stabilizing responsibilities exercised by Britain in the nineteenth century and by America in the mid-twentieth century. Without a nation to serve as international buyer and lender of last resort, the global economic equilibrium seemed precarious. Geoeconomics, it was said, was replacing geopolitics as the crucial dimension of foreign affairs.

Reaganomics: Domestic Consequences Meanwhile at home, the Gramm-Rudman Act of 1985 asserted the intention of Congress to balance the budget annually, an intention wholly cosmetic, for deficits continued to rise. In 1986, the Tax Reform Act, championed by both the Treasury and leading Democrats on Capitol Hill, attempted to simplify tax rules on a revenue-neutral basis. But the resulting modifications, while eliminating many tax loopholes previously convenient for the rich, cut the maximum surtax rate for individuals from 50 to 28 percent—a boon for the wealthy. The middle class and working poor received much less generous treatment. Federal revenues now came to depend more and more on the rising rate of the regressive Social Security tax, which applied a flat rate to all earnings up to $52,000 a year. Earned income above that figure and all unearned income were untouched by the Social Security tax, so again the wealthy and the well-paid were favored by Reaganite revenue policy.

The revenue legislation of the Reagan years nevertheless failed to rekindle genuine economic growth, though it did overstimulate commercial construction. Savings and investment, along with productivity and output, grew at a slower rate in the 1980s than in the disdained 1970s. Encouraged by the deregulation of the financial markets, capital flowed rather into speculation, takeovers, arbitrage, and leveraged buy-outs. The 1980s gave the pursuit of self-interest moral priority and systematically weakened and discredited the machinery of regulation in the public interest. "Greed is all right," said the speculator Ivan Boesky in a commencement address at the University of California School of Business Administration. "Greed is healthy. You can be greedy and still feel good about yourself."

The ethos of greed produced a series of scandals in both public and private sectors. *Time* magazine spoke of "an Administration whose clarion call is 'Enrich thyself.'" Reagan, though he had expressed the hope that the lasting imprint of his presidency would be "one of high morality," greeted each new scandal with silence. Edwin Meese, his close personal friend and second attorney general, had filed a false tax return. Other Reagan intimates were also guilty of ethical misconduct. One of them, Michael Deaver, received a suspended jail sentence for lying to Congress about his lobbying. Another, Lyn Nofzinger, violated the 1978 Ethics in Government Act. In the Department of Housing and Urban Development, Reagan's appointees, including Secretary Samuel R. Pierce, Jr., connived in awarding contracts for housing for the poor to Republican stalwarts, among them John Mitchell of Watergate notoriety. Several of the department's senior officers, rejoicing in their opportunities for "privatizing," had their own hands in the till. The

Panic on Wall Street, October 19, 1987

contagion of influence-peddling spread to members of Congress who, zealous to raise funds for their increasingly costly campaigns, doled out favors to generous corporate donors. That practice received little scrutiny from the permissive regulators whom the administration appointed to agencies supervising the savings and loan industry, commercial banking, and stock market transactions.

The lack of proper supervision over savings and loan institutions allowed them to make enormous loans to highly speculative real estate ventures. As those loans went into default in the last years of Reagan's tenure, pressure from members of congress in both parties to protect their donors and indifference on the part of the regulators delayed the closing of saving and loan institutions that were now bankrupt. Reagan's successor inherited the mess. To rescue innocent depositors, whose accounts the federal government had insured, the government assumed more than $150 billion in debt. The taxpayers would have to pay that debt, along with the interest accumulating on it, before holdings of the failed institutions could be liquidated—in all, according to reliable estimates, more than $400–$500 billion. A similar and devastating lack of oversight led to a parallel condition in commercial banking, with bank failures rising dangerously during Reagan's last year in office and then continuing for the ensuing five years. All in all, the scandals of the Reagan years matched those of the corrupt administrations of Grant and Harding.

The permissiveness of the Reagan appointees to the Securities and Exchange Commission nurtured the greed that infested Wall Street. Insider trading became so flagrant that the worst operators, including Ivan Boesky, were finally detected and sent to prison. Then a stock market collapse on October 19, 1987, when prices fell 22.6 percent and cost investors more than $1 trillion, brought disconcerting reminders of the crash of October 1929. Morning in America, a wit observed, had given way to the morning after.

Reaganomics made the rich richer and the poor poorer. The poorest tenth of Americans paid 20 percent more of their earnings in federal taxes in 1988 and in the next several years than they did in 1977, and the richest tenth, almost 20 percent less. The poorest fifth received a smaller share of family income than in the 1970s, while the top fifth increased its share. Federal spending for the poor fell off. Though unemployment declined, the new jobs created were mostly in the service sector, providing lower wages and fewer benefits than the 2 million manufacturing jobs lost in the 1980s. In 1986, 32.4 million Americans—13.6 percent of the population—lived below the poverty line as officially defined. By 1990 a fifth of American children were growing up in poverty. "The United States has become the first society in history," observed the scholar-politician Senator Daniel Patrick Moynihan, "in which a person is more likely to be poor if young rather than old."

Most alarming was the spread of the "underclass"—an estimated 10 million people living in enclaves of deep and chronic poverty characterized by unemployment, female-headed families, school dropouts, illegitimate births, homelessness, drug addiction, crime, and isolation from the larger community. William Julius Wilson in an influential analysis of the

Deep in chronic poverty

"truly disadvantaged" attributed the rise in the underclass especially to the decline of employment opportunities for young black and Hispanic workers. The growth of the urban ghetto promoted racial fears and tensions. The deregulation of civil rights by the Reagan administration meanwhile increased the vulnerability of black Americans. But Wilson, while supporting affirmative action, contended that such programs, by helping middle class black Americans, had the effect of heightening class schisms within black America. The long-run answer, many thought, lay in national policies for educating children, including minority children, in the language and mathematical skills necessary for remunerative employment in an electronic age, and also in national policies for retraining older workers and for sustaining full employment.

The Reagan Legacy Reagan, with his eloquent opposition to big government and defense of free markets, altered the terms of political debate. His patriotic oratory increased national pride and self-esteem. He also had an abiding impact on the federal judiciary, where he appointed about twice as many judges in eight years as Franklin Roosevelt had in twelve. His appointments, predominantly wealthy white Protestant males, amounted to almost half of all federal judges. He did name Sandra Day O'Connor to the Supreme Court, the first woman to serve on that body. She was a conservative, though less doctrinaire than Reagan's other two appointees, Antonin Scalia and Anthony M. Kennedy. Reagan turned to Kennedy after Robert Bork, his preferred choice, was rejected in 1987 by the Senate because of his outspoken advocacy of conservative judicial doctrines and his personal arrogance during the hearings on his confirmation. But with three Reagan appointees on the Supreme Court, and with William H. Rehnquist as the new chief justice following the resignation in 1986 of Warren Burger, conservatives were within one vote of commanding a majority that could modify or overturn controversial earlier decisions about civil rights, the rights of the accused, and abortion.

Reagan failed to shrink the national government. The number of federal employees grew by 7 percent (to nearly 3 million) during his terms. Federal spending also actually increased as a proportion of national output, and the Democrats held a majority in both houses of Congress after 1982. As one consequence, Reagan's social agenda—prayer in public schools and banning abortion—remained unfulfilled. But those issues continued to rankle the Moral Majority, which stayed glued to the Republican party with its calculated appeal to traditional Protestant religion, patriotism, and the conventional family.

Small towns and rural communities, and the evangelicals there and elsewhere, constituted only one part of the Reagan coalition. It also included economic conservatives. That constituency wanted to reduce government regulation and taxes. They had little interest in prosecuting abortion or homosexuality or legalizing prayer in public schools, and they enjoyed the permissive society. The evangelical moralists wanted to ban liberated women, abortion, adultery, "secular humanism," homosexuality, pot, sexual candor, and Darwin. Where libertarian conservatives asked government to leave people alone, the moralists asked government to police private behavior. "They want to get government off our backs," observed a critic, "and put it in our beds."

Fundamentalist preachers used television to acquire mass following and large treasuries, but an explosion of financial and sexual scandal in the late 1980s discredited televangelists among the larger public. Nevertheless the Reverend Pat Robertson had a loyal following in his pursuit of the Republican presidential nomination in 1988. Reagan handled the divergence in the conservative ranks with skill, making ideological speeches to the zealots while investing his political capital in economic rather than in social issues. But it seemed unlikely that his successors could keep the coalition together.

The last year of his presidency saw a decline in Reagan's political reputation though not in his personal popularity. Books by close associates—especially by Donald Regan and other former White House aides—portrayed a passive president, incurious about public affairs, dependent on surreptitious glances at three-by-five cards, dominated by a charming but forceful wife who herself consulted astrologers at times of major decision. Charges of incompetence and corruption dogged his administration.

Still, Reagan had achieved most of his original domestic goals. He had reduced the impact of government on American life; reduced taxes, especially on the wealthy; eviscerated federal regulatory agencies; diminished welfare; and allowed deficits so vast that they would make it difficult to restore social spending. The apparent winding down of the Cold War at the end of his term along with lightening of tensions elsewhere in the world gave an impression that peace was breaking out all over. The economy continued buoyant at home, and Reagan rode into the sunset in a glow of popular affection as a friendly president whose boundless optimism and patriotism had renewed the confidence of Americans in themselves.

Jesse Jackson: arresting presidential contender

The 1988 Election His chosen successor, Vice President George Bush, readily defeated Bob Dole of Kansas, the Republican leader in the Senate, in the contest for the Republican nomination. Bush selected J. Danforth (Dan) Quayle of Indiana, a hitherto inconspicuous second-term senator, as his running mate.

In the meantime, the Democrats, after an exhausting series of primaries, more than twice as many as in 1984, ended with Governor Michael Dukakis of Massachusetts as their candidate. Jesse Jackson, making his second run for the nomination, was the most arresting of the Democratic contenders, but his eloquence and wit could not overcome a widespread conviction that the country was not ready for a black candidate with radical views. Senator Lloyd Bentsen of Texas, an able moderate, received the vice-presidential nomination.

The campaign marked a new stage in the replacement of the political party by television (and its cynical new breed of electronic "handlers") as the chief agency for voter mobilization. It also witnessed large-scale evasion of the policy supposedly established by the Federal Election Campaign Act of 1974 (see p. 891) of banning private money in presidential elections. Each candidate in 1988 received $46 million in public financing. But, when the Federal Election Commission legitimized the use of "soft money"—that is, of private money given not directly to the presidential campaigns but to state parties and ad hoc committees—the way was opened for the return of big-money politics with the attendant corruption and purchased influence.

Dan Quayle and George Bush

Both on television and at the hustings the campaign was singularly unedifying. Bush seemed to be copying the successful techniques of both Nixon and Reagan. He alternated low-blow attacks on Dukakis as soft on crime and deficient in patriotism with lyrical evocations of a "kinder, gentler" America to come. He blamed Dukakis for the pollution in Boston harbor, which was there because of the absence of federal financing to remove it. Bush's television ads also linked crime to black Americans and linked both by innuendo to Dukakis, a tactic designed to woo blue-collar Democrats. Dukakis, who lacked experience in national politics, failed to counter Bush's assaults. He failed, too, to provide a unifying alternative vision of America. There was little discussion of the serious issues facing the country.

With the advantages of peace, prosperity, incumbency, money and organization, and with the issue of race powerfully in the background, Bush polled 48.9 million votes—53.4 percent of the total cast—as against 41.8 million for Dukakis. Carrying 40 states, including the Solid South, Bush took the Electoral College by 426 to 112.

The negative tone of the campaign repelled many voters. Polls showed that two-thirds would have preferred other candidates. Fewer voted in 1988 than in 1984. The turnout of eligible voters barely exceeded 50 percent, the lowest since 1924, and compared badly indeed with the 1888 election, a century earlier, when turnout (under more restricted rules of eligibility) had been 79.3 percent. Bush was elected by less than 27 percent of the voting-age population. In their indifference to politics, Americans seemed to have accepted the Reagan legacy. In five of the last six presidential elections, Republicans had won. And in all six, conservative candidates had prevailed.

SUGGESTIONS FOR READING

CARTER

For Carter, his pre-presidential memoir *Why Not the Best* (1975) is followed by his record of his presidency, *Keeping Faith* (1982); see also Rosalynn Carter, *First Lady from Plains* (1984). G. Glad, *Jimmy Carter, In Search of the Great White House* (1980), is useful through 1976.

For Carter's foreign policy, see G. Smith, *Morality, Reason and Power: American Diplomacy in the Carter Years* (1986). Cyrus Vance's gentlemanly *Hard Choices: Critical Years in American Foreign Policy* (1983) and Zbigniew Brzezinski's pugnacious *Power and Principle: Memoirs of a National Security Adviser* (1983) present diverging views. Jimmy Carter, *The Blood of Abraham* (1985), discusses his role in the Middle East; W. Quandt, *Camp David* (1986), is an expert analysis. For Iran, see J. A. Bill, *The Eagle and the Lion* (1988); Hamilton Jordan, *Crisis* (1982); and G. Sick, *All Fall Down: America's Tragic Encounter with Iran* (1985). S. Turner, *Secrecy and Democracy* (1985), is a memoir by Carter's CIA director. W. LaFeber, *Inevitable Revolutions: The United States in Central America* (1983), provides historical background. R. A. Pastor, *Condemned to Repetition* (1987), is an insider's account of Carter's Central American policy.

On domestic policy, J. Califano, *Governing America* (1981), is an analytical memoir by Carter's secretary of health, education and welfare. W. Greider, *Secrets of the Temple* (1987), discusses the role of the Federal Reserve.

REAGAN

Reagan's pre-presidential memoir is *Where's the Rest of Me?* (1965), with R. G. Hubler. Reagan's presidential memoir is bland; his wife's is defensive. R. Dugger, *On Reagan: The Man and his Presidency* (1983), has valuable material on Reagan's ideological development; see also A. Edwards, *Early Reagan: the Rise to Power* (1987). Reports by Reagan intimates include Donald Regan, *For the Record* (1988), Larry Speakes, *Speaking Out* (1988), and Michael Deaver, *Behind the Scenes* (1987). G. Wills, *Reagan's America: Innocents at Home* (1987), is an often brilliant meditation on the Reagan phenomenon. See also L. Cannon, *President Reagan: The Role of a Lifetime* (1991), and H. Johnson, *Sleepwalking Through History* (1991).

On foreign policy, R. L. Garthoff, *Detente and Confrontation: American-Soviet Relations from Nixon to Reagan* (1985), is a cogent introduction. Alexander Haig defends his record as secretary of state in *Caveat: Realism, Reagan and Foreign Policy* (1984). D. P. Calleo, *The Imperious Economy* (1982) and his *Beyond American Hegemony* (1987), and R. Gilpin, *The Political Economy of International Relations* (1987), are illuminating discussions of economic and security questions. G. F. Treverton, *Covert Action* (1987), considers problems raised by secret intelligence operations; B. Woodward, *Veil: The Secret Wars of the CIA, 1981–1987* (1987), is an informed journalist's account. On nuclear issues, S. Zuckerman, *Nuclear Illusion and Reality* (1982), is an authoritative summation by a leading British defense scientist. R. S. McNamara, *Blundering into Disaster* (1986), is a powerful analysis by a former secretary of defense. S. Talbott, *Deadly Gambit* (1984), is behind-the-scenes account of arms-control negotiations. R. Bonner, *Waltzing with a Dictator* (1987), discusses American policy in the Philippines. T. Draper, *A Very Thin Line: The Iran-Contra Affair* (1991), is authoritative on its topic; but see, too, O. North, *Under Fire: An American Story* (1991).

On domestic policy, David Stockman, *The Triumph of Politics: Why the Reagan Revolution Failed* (1986), is a revealing memoir by Reagan's first budget director. Martin Anderson, *Revolution* (1988), is a sober account by a former White House aide. Milton and Rose

Friedman, *Free to Choose* (1979), and G. Gilder, *Wealth and Poverty* (1981), present the economic rationale of Reaganism. S. J. and M. Tolchin, *Dismantling America* (1983), describes the deregulation movement. W. J. Wilson, *The Truly Disadvantaged: The Inner City, the Underclass, and Public Policy* (1987), analyzes the growth of the underclass. P. Levy, *Dollars and Dreams: the Changing American Income Distribution* (1987), is a careful and objective reading of the evidence. Also useful are B. M. Friedman, *Day of Reckoning: The Consequences of American Economic Policy under Reagan* (1988); K. Phillips, *The Politics of Rich and Poor* (1990); A. Crawford, *Thunder on the Right: The 'New Right' and the Politics of Resentment* (1980); and S. Fraser and P. Gerstle, eds., *The Rise and Fall of the New Deal Order, 1930–1980* (1989). S. Blumenthal, *Pledging Allegiance* (1990), covers the Bush campaign.

P. Steinfels, *The Neoconservatives* (1979), and S. Blumenthal, *The Rise of the Counter-Establishment* (1986), analyze the conservative revival. The future of American politics is considered in A. Schlesinger, Jr., *The Cycles of American History* (1986), W. D. Burnham, *The Current Crisis in American Politics* (1982), and K. Phillips, *Post-Conservative America* (1984).

CHAPTER THIRTY-FIVE

SPACE SHUTTLE LAUNCH

TOWARD THE TWENTY-FIRST CENTURY

In 1945, at the end of the Second World War, the United States of America was top of the heap. No major victor had suffered so little in the war. The United States was the sole owner of the atomic bomb, the decisive weapon of the future. It produced more than 40 percent of all the world's manufactures and was the world's largest producer of oil, natural gas, coal, copper, steel, automobiles. It led the world in technological innovation, in industrial and agricultural productivity, in per capita income. It had over one-fifth of the world's trade. It was the world's leading creditor. Its dollar was the world's strongest currency. Its primacy among the world's democracies was unchallenged. Its self-confidence was unbounded. It looked forward with modest aplomb to the "American century."

DECLINE OR READJUSTMENT

Limitations In the next half century the United States lost its nuclear monopoly; lost its economic, commercial, and financial dominance; lost its lead in high technology, in industrial productivity, and even in per capita income; lost its strong dollar and its low-cost energy; lost the once universal confidence of other democracies in its leadership; lost much of its confidence in itself. Some presidents in these years, like Eisenhower, Kennedy, and Nixon, recognized limitations on America's power to decide the destiny of humankind and sought to shape American foreign policy accordingly. In the 1980s when Ronald Reagan made a convulsive effort through rhetoric and rearmament to reclaim American global primacy, he led the country into an economic quagmire that appeared to substantiate the contention of historian Paul Kennedy that the American republic, like other imperial powers before it, had succumbed to "imperial overstretch" — that is, the assumption of military and political commitments beyond its economic power to fulfill.

As the 1990s began, the United States remained the foremost military power in the world, but deployment of its forces for major operations required large subsidies from its allies. At home America was drowning in debt, public and private. The republic's very "infrastructure" — its framework of highways, waterways, bridges, dams, harbors, irrigation, sanitation, and sewage systems — was in decay, wearing out faster than it was being replaced; public capital spending on infrastructure fell from 2.3 percent of gross national product in the later 1960s to 0.4 percent in the 1980s. Federal investment in human capital — education and research — also declined. And, though the proportion of adults with college degrees quadrupled from 1940 to 1985, the United States had become a nation where Johnny not only

The United States in Decline?

Although the United States is at present still in a class of its own economically and . . . militarily, it cannot avoid confronting the two great tests which challenge the *longevity* of every major power that occupies the "number one" position in world affairs: whether, in the military/strategical realm, it can preserve a reasonable balance between the nation's perceived defense requirements and the means it possesses to maintain those commitments; and whether . . . it can preserve the technological and economic bases of its power from relative erosion in the face of the ever-shifting patterns of global production. This test of American abilities will be the greater because it, like . . . the British Empire around 1900, is the inheritor of a vast array of strategical commitments. . . . In consequence, the United States now runs the risk . . . of . . . "imperial overstretch": that is to say, decision-makers in Washington must face the awkward and enduring fact that the sum total of the United States' global interests and obligations is . . . far larger than the country's power to defend them all simultaneously. . . .

Given the worldwide array of military liabilities which the United States has assumed since 1945, its capacity to carry those burdens is . . . less than it was several decades ago, when its share of global manufacturing and GNP was much larger . . . its balance of payments was far healthier, the government's budget was . . . in balance, and it was not so heavily in debt to the rest of the world. In that larger sense, there is something in the analogy which is made . . . between the United States' position today and that of previous "declining hegemons."

From Paul Kennedy, *The Rise and Fall of the Great Powers,* 1987

could not read but did not know when the Civil War took place, or who Churchill and Stalin were, and where an alarming number of adults were functionally illiterate.

The decline of America, if decline it was, was relative. America's postwar peak was in part a historical accident, as political scientist Joseph Nye argued. The comeback of vanquished foes, exhausted allies and liberated colonies was bound to reduce the American world role. America's main rival, the Soviet Union, had fallen much farther behind in the global competition. The United States still retained the ideological, scientific, and technological dynamism, the political and economic resilience, the diverse and resourceful population, the robust national ideals, which, if joined with creative statecraft, could make it a world leader for years to come.

SOCIETY MOVES INTO THE 1990S

A Changing Population The population of the United States continued to grow, if at a slower rate, exceeding 250 million by 1990. The total had nearly quadrupled in a century and more than doubled since the first election of Franklin Roosevelt. Then in the 1980s the fertility rate — the number of children born to each woman over her lifetime — reached a record low. The "baby boom" of 1946–64 gave way to a "baby bust."

The United States Preponderant?

According to theories of hegemonic transition and imperial overstretch, a great power becomes exhausted through the protection of its far-flung interests. International commitments sap its strength at home, while rising challengers profit from the public order, global economic growth, and diffusion of the hegemon's technology. Eventually, the hegemon is replaced by a rising challenger. . . . However, such theories, and the general historical analogies that accompany them, do not provide an accurate picture of the situation the United States faces at the end of the twentieth century.

The influence derived from American preponderance in the early postwar years tends to be overrated by the theorists of power transition. . . . American power is clearly not what it was in the 1950s, but the decline is exaggerated. . . . The United States never enjoyed a general hegemony after the war, so hegemony can be neither lost nor regained. . . .

The United States remains preponderant in traditional power resources at the end of the 1980s. . . . In terms of military power, the world of the 1990s remains highly bipolar. . . . The distribution of economic power resources . . . involves two major states, the United States and Japan, and Europe. . . . Only one country ranks above the others on all . . . dimensions—the United States. . . .

The United States benefits from the use of the English language, its prominence in science and the arts, and its relative openness to foreigners. . . . International institutions and norms are another potential source of power. . . . The United Nations Security Council . . . frequently serves American purposes, and the veto provides protection when it does not. Alliances are yet another critical . . . resource.

From Joseph S. Nye, Jr., *Bound to Lead,* 1990

At the same time, medical advances brought life expectancy to a record high—79 years for white women, 72 years for white men. One consequence was the "graying of America." People over age 65 were 4 percent of the population in 1900, over 12 percent in the early 1990s. The baby boomers were aging. Having supplied the basis for the youth revolt of the 1960s, the baby boomers promised to have a different political impact as they became middle-aged, suburban and settled, even more different after 2010 when they would become a vociferous claimant lobby of old folks. Already in the early 1990s, older Americans had, thanks to Social Security and expanded pensions, a poverty rate lower than the average for all Americans. Younger Americans, concerned with "generational equity," feared the financial burden of an aging America. Some thought that a disproportionate amount of medical spending went to keeping the old alive at a time when the United States had one of the highest infant mortality rates among democracies, and 20 percent of American children lived in poverty.

The dramatic geographical shift of population was to the "Sunbelt," the states below the 37th parallel from Virginia to southern California—a shift greatly

A vociferous lobby

encouraged by the invention of air conditioning. In 1964 California surpassed New York to become the most populous state. In the 1980s the South and West accounted for over 90 percent of the nation's population growth.

The shift had political consequences. Between the Civil War and the Second World War, only two men born outside the Northeast (including Ohio) made the White House. Of the eight presidents after 1945, only one came from the Northeast. Each new census gave the South and West more weight in the Electoral College as well as in the House of Representatives.

Over a fifth of the population growth during the 1980s was due to immigration. The annual immigration rate had increased from 85,000 in the 1940s to 600,000 in the 1980s. The Immigration and Naturalization Act of 1965 dramatically changed the composition of the new arrivals. That act abolished the discriminatory national-origins quota system (see p. 653), establishing needed skills and the reuniting of families as criteria for admission. Subsequently, in 1987, Congress, over Reagan's objections, repealed the provision of the McCarran Act of 1952 permitting exclusion on ideological grounds (see p. 805).

In the years immediately before the 1965 act, Canada, Mexico, and Great Britain had been the leading sources of immigrants. Soon thereafter Mexico, Vietnam, and the Philippines headed the list. By the 1990s about 40 percent of immigrants were coming from Asia, another 40 percent from Latin America and the Caribbean. Several million Latin Americans entered the country illegally during the 1980s. Though it was charged that these "undocumented" aliens were taking jobs away from American citizens, evidence suggested that they performed menial tasks rejected by native workers and thereby filled a vacuum in the labor market. Their illegal status, however, exposed them to cruel exploitation in city sweatshops and rural peonage. To remedy this situation, Congress in 1986 passed the Simpson-Rodino Act granting amnesty to illegals who had entered before 1982 and imposing sanctions on employers who knowingly hired illegals after 1986.

A Nation of Nations The revisions in immigration policy portended striking changes in the nation's eth-

Suburban America

Mexican-American workers

nic makeup. The nation's Hispanics grew in the 1980s five times as fast as the rest of the population. Spanish-speaking enclaves had survived in New Mexico for five centuries, and for many decades Mexicans had crossed the border to satisfy the demand for cheap agricultural labor. In the 1980s and 1990s, political upheaval and economic misery in their homelands increased the Hispanic flow. Of the more than 20 million Hispanics—the illegals made statistical precision difficult—about 63 percent were Mexican, 12 percent Puerto Rican (and therefore already American citizens), 11 percent Central and South American, 5 percent Cuban. The Mexicans lived in the main in the Southwest, the Puerto Ricans in the Northeast, the Cubans in Florida.

By the 1990s Hispanics were emerging as a political force, electing members of Congress, a governor in New Mexico, and mayors in Denver, San Antonio, Miami, Tampa, and Sante Fe. Mexicans and Puerto Ricans tended to be Democrats. Cubans tended to be Republicans. Income levels for Hispanics averaged slightly higher than for black Americans, while educational levels, with the linguistic handicap, were somewhat lower. In contrast to European and Asian immigrants, Hispanics were less eager to learn English, raising instead the standard of "bilingualism." Some observers feared that bilingualism handicapped the newcomers by reducing their capacity to cope with an English-speaking society and that it threatened to fragment the country into linguistic ghettos. A common language, many believed, was an essential bond of cohesion in an increasingly disparate society.

Asian immigrants, excluded from the United States till 1952, made an especially impressive contribution to the changing society. Though the 5 million Asians constituted only 2 percent of the population, they

Educational achievers, Queens, New York

exceeded national averages in educational achievement and in income. Over a third of Asian-Americans graduated from college, twice the percentage among white Americans, and they won academic honors out of all proportion to their numbers. Tests suggested that the Asians were more intelligent than other Americans. Certainly they worked harder.

Black Americans, almost 30 million in the 1990s, constituted about 12 percent of the population. Their position had improved radically with the civil rights revolution. Talk of "white supremacy" almost vanished. Mandatory legal segregation was abolished, and access to public accommodations assured. The racial wage gap narrowed. In 1940 a black male worker earned only 43 percent as much as his white counterpart; by 1990, 73 percent. The black middle class now outnumbered the black poor. The year 1983 saw the first black astronaut in space and the first black Miss America. The most popular television show in the late 1980s starred the black actor Bill Cosby.

The most striking gain of all—because it accelerated every other form of racial progress—came in politics. The Voting Rights Act of 1965 produced a massive enfranchisement of Southern black citizens and a corresponding change in the attitudes of Southern white politicians. A one-time militant segregationist like Governor George Wallace now crowned a black homecoming queen at the very university that, a

Guion Bluford: astronaut

decade earlier, he had sworn to deny to black students. Washington, Chicago, Los Angeles, New York, Philadelphia, Detroit, Atlanta, New Orleans, Birmingham, Richmond, and Newark elected black mayors. Urban politics was doing for black Americans what it had done for immigrants: providing a means of incorporation into a previously alien political system. In 1990, Virginia, once a Confederate state, elected a black governor. Jesse Jackson meanwhile emerged in the 1980s as the first formidable black contender for the presidency.

Despite the gains, many black citizens remained at the lower end of the economic scale. Life expectancy for them was five years less than for whites. The National Urban League, a black organization, reported that 40 percent of black children were raised in fatherless homes, that 25 percent of all black households were affected by crime, that youth unemployment, teenage pregnancy, drug use, and violence were far greater among black than white Americans. Some analysts argued that the black underclass was the victim, not of prejudice, but of poverty. Others insisted that black Americans were still imprisoned in a legacy of institutionalized racism.

The oldest and truest Americans, the Indians, were no longer the vanishing Americans. As a result of public health improvements, Indian population grew from 343,000 in 1950 to more than 1.4 million in the 1990s. More than half lived on reservations (there were more than 300 federally recognized tribes); most of the rest lived in cities. Wherever they lived, they were the poorest of the poor, at the end of the line in employment, income, education, health, and life expectancy.

White Americans, belatedly developing a bad conscience over their ancestors' treatment of the Indians, regarded the Native Americans with new sympathy but proved unable to find an effective way to help them to help themselves. Indians agitated through their own organizations. The National Congress of American Indians, founded during the Second World War (in which 25,000 Indians had served), became more aggressive; and the American Indian Movement, formed by militant urban Indians in 1968 under the banner of "red power," turned to violent methods. Some Indian nations sued in court for the restoration of land, water, mineral, and fishing rights bestowed on them by treaty and often won compensation.

Until the 1930s the United States had been dominated politically, economically, and culturally by white Anglo-Saxon Protestant males, known in later

Red Power

We, the first Americans, come to the Congress of the United States that you give us the chance to try to solve what you call the Indian problem. You have had two hundred years and you have not succeeded by your standards. It is clear that you have not succeeded in ours. . . . We ask you, as the representatives of the people of the United States, to serve as our representatives too—to help us see that assurances do not become empty promises. And, if necessary, to enact legislation which will create such a process where Indians can really shape government policy and control their own lives and destinies. . . .

The present [congressional] committees have pushed for termination, and have fostered on Congress seemingly neutral and technical legislation, under the guise of Indian expertise, which has taken away our land, our water rights, our mineral resources and handed them over to the white man. You have been duped—as we have been duped. These committees have created a monstrous bureaucracy insensitive to Indians which trembles and cringes before them. . . . We know you are highly conscious of your national obligations when you deliberate on such problems as the war in Viet Nam. We know that you have even taken those obligations seriously enough to go to Viet Nam in order to personally inform yourself on how the Executive carries out the commitments of the United States. We ask that you do no less at home—for the United States has made older and more sacred commitments to the people who have occupied these shores for twenty-five thousand years. . . . In essence, we ask the restoration of what you claimed at the founding of your nation—the inalienable right to pursue happiness.

From the American Indian Task Force, Statement to Congress, November 12, 1969

times as WASPs. The Great Depression and the New Deal had given new opportunities for Catholics and Jews, as had the Fair Employment Practices Commission during the Second World War and the G.I. Bill of Rights, both of which also aided black Americans. The civil rights revolution of the 1960s opened the door further to black citizens. The changes in immigration policy brought in Hispanics and Asians. It was no longer uncommon to hear Korean spoken in the streets of New York, Arabic in Detroit, Hindi in Los Angeles, and Spanish everywhere. In 1950, 87 percent of Californians had been white. By the first decade of the twenty-first century, demographers predicted, California would become a Third World state. By 2080, according to another projection, the non-Hispanic white population for the entire country would fall under 50 percent. Most European immigrants had come to the United States expecting to become Americans. Their goal was assimilation. But many new immigrants from Latin America and Asia, like some of the descendants of immigrants from Africa, subscribed to a cult of ethnicity, as did several groups of European origin. That cult emphasized the preservation of old differences. Pressed too far, as it sometimes was, pluralism challenged the concept of a national American identity. "Instead of a nation composed of individuals making their own free choices," historian Arthur Schlesinger, Jr., warned in 1991,

"America increasingly sees itself as composed of groups more or less indelible in their national character."

"Here is not merely a nation," Walt Whitman had written, "but a teeming Nation of nations." This would never be more true than in the twenty-first century. In the future, as in the past, the newcomers could be expected to infuse American society with variety, vitality, and hope.

West Point graduate

The Role of Women A spectacular change in American life was the new role for women. There were 7 million more females than males by 1990. Women were more than 51 percent of the population as a whole and about 60 percent of those 65 and older. And barriers to women continued to fall. In 1950 a third of the female population had been in the labor force; by 1990, more than a half. The female bridgehead in the professions steadily enlarged. In 1970, 5 percent of law school graduates were women; in 1990 over 40 percent were.

Men were increasingly prepared to taking a larger share in child rearing and in household tasks. Many, noting that "Mr." as a title did not betray marital status, accepted "Ms" as a substitute for both "Miss" and "Mrs." Women were nominated for vice president and elected as governors and senators. Fifteen percent of state legislators were women. San Francisco, Chicago, and Houston elected women mayors. Women sat on the Supreme Court and sailed in outer space. Few male sanctuaries were left. Even West Point and Annapolis surrendered.

Still, frustrations remained. Women earned lower wages than men and climbed the career ladder more slowly. Many women would not escape low-paying traditional women's jobs. The number of female-headed households more than doubled between 1960 and 1990, and some 40 percent lived below the poverty line. Sociologists wrote about the "feminization of poverty."

The women's movement suffered particular disappointment over the failure of the Equal Rights Amendment. This amendment, first submitted by Alice Paul's National Women's party in 1923, proposed to write into the Constitution the rule that "equality of rights under the law shall not be denied or abridged . . . on account of sex." In earlier years, many women leaders, including Eleanor Roosevelt and Frances Perkins, had opposed ERA on the ground that it would deny women protective social legislation. But when the Civil Rights Act of 1964 outlawed discrimination based on gender, previous opponents endorsed ERA. Though polls showed two-thirds of the population in support, women traditionalists, as well as many men, felt threatened by equal rights. A powerful and ultimately successful anti-ERA campaign conjured up such fears as that women would be sent into combat and that separate toilet facilities would be abolished.

The ideological reconsideration of woman's role continued. Women's liberation had generated forms of revolutionary feminism ascribing racism, imperialism, and other evils to male supremacy. Militants saw marriage as a hell where the husband was a rapist, the wife a prostitute, the baby a trap, and the family a prison. Some advocated lesbianism as the only true feminist commitment. The militants provided ammunition for antifeminists like Phyllis Schlafly who wished to reaffirm woman's subordinate role.

The militants also provoked feminist leaders to reformulate their goals. In *The Second Stage* (1981), Betty Friedan worried about "feminist denial of the impor-

ERA: controversial amendment

tance of the family, of women's own needs to give and get love and nurture." Equality, she said, "never meant destruction of the family, repudiation of marriage and motherhood, or implacable sexual war against men." Many women now saw their challenge as that of attaining career fulfillment without neglecting their children.

In 30 years the women's movement had wrought deep changes in women's lives—and men's. The movement had indeed raised the American consciousness, had increased male sensitivity to female frustrations and humiliations, and had bred in women new convictions of self-reliance and entitlement.

Tribulations of the Permissive Society The countercultural revolution of the 1960s had challenged traditional social patterns in the name of the gospel of personal self-fulfillment. This gospel continued in slightly different form in the 1970s. However much the hippie-Weatherman culture of the 1960s and the consumer-*Playboy* culture of the 1970s differed in political attitudes, they agreed in regarding what one writer termed the "quest for the ideal self" as the supreme aim of life. "Getting in touch with your emotions" and "finding yourself" were key phrases. Hedonism became so preoccupying in the 1970s as to produce the description "the Me decade" and learned books about *The Culture of Narcissism.*

But things changed in the 1980s. The baby-boom generation, at last over the fatal age of 30, dropped back into the bourgeois routine. Prosperity gave way to economic uncertainty and stern competition in the job market. It became a time to reappraise values. In this process of sorting out, the new society absorbed some of the changes wrought by the permissive society and repudiated others in the name of a new gospel of social discipline.

The counterculture survived in "laid-back" attitudes toward dress, language, and sexual freedom. Men, once the sober species, continued after the 1960s to sport beards, blue jeans, and cowboy boots. Slacks became the casual dress of women from dowagers to hookers. Old inhibitions and reticences disappeared. Four-letter Anglo-Saxon monosyllables became common not only in movies but in living rooms. "Soft-core" pornography flourished in the cinemas and the magazine racks, and "hard-core" stuff became a staple of the VCR business.

The new tolerance extended to what had been historically the most sensitive of all problems for Americans—sex. The objective study of sexuality had gained impetus from two works by the biologist Alfred Kinsey: *Sexual Behavior in the Human Male* (1948) and *Sexual Behavior in the Human Female* (1953). The sexual act itself received unrelenting scrutiny from William Masters and Virginia Johnson in *Human Sexual Response* (1968). While sociologists doubted that changes in sexual practices had been all that great, there was plainly a vast change in public attitudes. "Cohabitation" no longer raised eyebrows. Ninety-five percent of males and over 80 percent of females between 18 and 24 acknowledged premarital intercourse. Married couples sometimes indulged in "swinging"—group intercourse with other couples. Oral sex and other less conventional forms of sexual expression became common. Homosexuals, male and female, came "out of the closet." Appropriating the word *gay,* they organized in defense of their civil rights, persuading the American Psychiatric Association in 1973 to stop listing homosexuality as a psychiatric disorder. Members of Congress confessed to homosexuality, and in some states "gay rights" groups became forces in politics.

Drugs were another inheritance from the counterculture. Though LSD fell out of fashion, marijuana smoking remained routine in many circles. "Crack," a cheap and powerful cocaine derivative, displaced heroin as the lower-class addiction; cocaine remained the favorite of the affluent professional. Drugs were a big

The New Left Grows Older

When in doubt, burn. Fire is the revolutionary's god. Fire is instant theater. No words can match fire. / Politicians only notice poverty when the ghettos burn. / The burning of the first draft card caused earth tremors under the Pentagon. / Burn the flag. Burn churches. / Burn, burn, burn. . . . / Amerika is falling apart: the alternative is revolution or catastrophy. / *The revolution has replaced the church as the country's moral authority.*

From Jerry Rubin, *Do It!,* 1970

I saw us move out of youth-oriented yippie consciousness to think of ourselves as parents, adults, mature men. I had always feared aging. . . . But I actually enjoy getting older. I have become happier. At 37 I feel better than I have at any other time in my life. I want to be politically active again—but not at the expense of my happiness and health. I do not want to be in a crazy movement that psychologically drains its people.

From Jerry Rubin, *Growing (Up) at 37,* 1976

Politics and rebellion distinguished the 60s. The search for the self characterized the spirit of the 70s. Money and financial interest will capture the passion of the 80s. . . . If I am going to have any effect on my society in the next 40 years, I must develop the power that only control of money can bring. . . . Welcome, Wall Street, here I come!

From Jerry Rubin, "Guess Who's Coming to Wall Street," *New York Times,* July 30, 1980

business for organized crime—the estimated $30 billion annual revenues for cocaine would place it seventh among America's top 500 corporations. Efforts to stop the flow of drugs from Colombia, Pakistan, and other nations were of small avail.

While the commitment to freedom of individual choice remained strong, the reaction against permissiveness also gathered force. Evangelical groups, encouraged by the election of a "born-again" president in 1976 and of a president in 1980 responsive to the Moral Majority, intensified their condemnation of sinful society. They succeeded in censoring textbooks, libraries, and school reading assignments. Dismay over crime, drugs, and drink was widespread among the larger public. States raised the drinking age and cracked down on drunken drivers. The revolt against cigarette smoking led many states and communities to ban smoking in public places as part of the nation's fight against cancer.

The campaign against sexual promiscuity received unexpected support when a new and terrible disease threatened the country and the world. AIDS (Acquired Immune Deficiency Syndrome) attacked the immune system of the infected person. It originated in Africa, was first diagnosed in America in 1981, and thereafter spread with disquieting rapidity among homosexuals, bisexuals, and drug addicts. Infected mothers passed the virus to babies. Infected blood passed the virus in transfusions. Soon AIDS made inroads into the heterosexual community. By 1992 more than 200,000 active cases and more than 30,000 deaths had been reported in the United States. Some 1.7 million Americans carried the virus.

Scientists isolated the virus but made small progress in the search for a remedy. Medical experts predicted that, in the absence of an effective vaccine, AIDS would spread like a plague. In 1991 a national commission, critical of the president's lack of leadership,

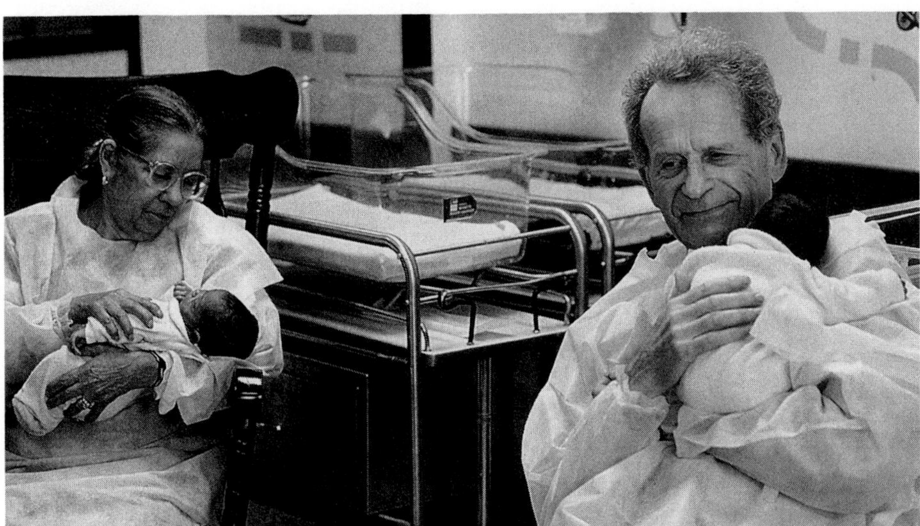

Nursery for victims of AIDS

warned that AIDS had reached epidemic proportions and called for a federal program to finance prevention and treatment of the disease on a universal basis. Fear of AIDS provoked strong reactions, some rational, such as distribution of condoms and mandatory testing, some hysterical, such as the removal from school of innocently infected children and even the segregation of AIDS victims. The threat of AIDS became a powerful force for restraint in sexual relations.

Art and Change Art, as always, reflected changing values and mores. Serious writers in the years after the Second World War, moving away from the social art of the Great Depression, tended to be private, somewhat withdrawn from the problems of society, deeply involved in individual quests for personal identity and meaning. These quests often took place in strongly rendered regional or ethnic contexts. Thus the tradition of Southern writing, intensified and elaborated by Faulkner in the 1920s and 1930s, was continued in the postwar years by Robert Penn Warren, notably in *All the King's Men* (1946), his novel about Huey Long's Louisiana, and by writers of the next generation—William Styron, whose *Confessions of Nat Turner* (1967) was the attempt of a Southern white to come to a reckoning with the historical fact of slavery; and the exquisite women writers Eudora Welty and Flannery O'Connor.

In the North the WASP novel of manners, perfected by Henry James and William Dean Howells, exemplified in the pre-war generation by the astute satire of J. P. Marquand and the sardonic realism of James Gould Cozzens, was still alive, but the age of Anglo-Saxon dominance was receding. Brilliant younger writers like John Cheever and John Updike now portrayed the suburban WASP at bay in an increasingly heterogeneous and bewildering society. Gore Vidal's series of historic novels—*Burr* (1973), *1876* (1976), *Lincoln* (1984)—cast a cold eye on the nineteenth-century past, while the non-WASP E. L. Doctorow drew a radical bead on more recent history in his vivid novels *The Book of Daniel* (1971) and *Ragtime* (1975).

Ethnicity became a potent theme. Following the path broken by James T. Farrell in the 1930s, Edwin O'Connor (*The Last Hurrah*, 1956) and J. F. Powers recorded further phases in the assimilation of the Irish into American life. Mario Puzo dealt with the Italian-Americans in *The Dark Arena* (1955) and in his best seller *The Godfather* (1969). Richard Wright's *Native Son* (1940) was a powerful portrayal of the fate of the black American; and Ralph Ellison's *Invisible Man* (1952), one of the distinguished novels of the period, displayed in forceful terms the struggle of its black protagonist for visibility in American society. Alice Walker and Toni Morrison gave poignant insights into the ordeal of black women. James Baldwin in a series of books played upon the agony of two minorities—black and homosexual Americans.

A gifted generation of Jewish novelists, afflicted by historical and contemporary woes, not only offered vivid annotations of Jewish-American life but spoke in some sense for all minorities in the quest for self-understanding. Philip Roth in *Goodbye, Columbus* (1959), *Portnoy's Complaint* (1969), and his Nathan Zuckerman trilogy combined a merciless novelist's

Novelist Saul Bellow, Nobel laureate

eye with sharp comic and mimetic instincts. J. D. Salinger's tales about the Glass family, especially in *Franny and Zooey* (1961), explored the possibilities of mysticism and sainthood in an affluent society. In *The Catcher in the Rye* (1951), Salinger also portrayed an adolescent crisis of identity in terms that spoke arrestingly to a whole generation. And two other Jewish writers, Saul Bellow and Norman Mailer, transcended their cultural base to deal in large terms with the incoherence and anguish of contemporary life.

No American novelist dealt more searchingly with contemporary humanity than Bellow in such novels as *The Adventures of Augie March* (1953), *Seize the Day* (1954), *Herzog* (1964), and *Humboldt's Gift* (1975). He was the artist of the dialectic between inner consciousness and external society. Where Bellow looked on the ravages of modernity with increasing distaste, his younger and less finished contemporary Mailer plunged truculently into the swirl around him. War veteran, novelist, journalist, film director, political aspirant, pugilist, male chauvinist, the spoiled and symptomatic talent of his time, Mailer saw art as, above all, the precipitate of minority experience. Though some critics believed Mailer more comfortable in his nonfiction, like *The Armies of the Night* (1968) and *Of a Fire on the Moon* (1970), his highly charged reporting was of a piece with the vision of the American experience conveyed brilliantly in his novel *Why Are We in Vietnam?* (1967). The tension between rationality and irrationality, between the public act and the underground emotion, fascinated him, and no writer took on more cheerfully the existential risks of American art.

For many writers, exploration of chaos required the abandonment of realism, a literary mode that could not survive, they believed, the collapse of a coherent world view. Such writers resorted to forms of fabulation, in which mental constructs replaced the workaday world. This writing was antirational, mythological, often magical, sometimes apocalyptic, always hostile to the technological cosmology. The satiric fantasies of Kurt Vonnegut, Jr.; the cabalistic hallucinations of Donald Barthelme; the exuberant, savage anarchism of Joseph Heller's *Catch-22* (1961); the wild, quasiscientific despair of Thomas Pynchon's *Gravity's Rainbow* (1973); the lurid allegory of John Irving's *The World According to Garp* (1978)—all paid tribute through dislocation, parody, and mysticism to an increasingly incomprehensible universe.

The cultural vibrations ran through poetry, where Robert Lowell in *Life Studies* (1959) and *For the Union Dead* (1964) registered the impact of an incoherent age on the Puritan sensibility, and where Sylvia Plath expressed the terror of women in a world of treacherous men. Arthur Miller revived the social drama in strong and somber plays like *Death of a Salesman* (1949); and such dramas as Tennessee Williams's *A Streetcar Named Desire* (1947) and Edward Albee's *Who's Afraid of Virginia Woolf?* (1962) concentrated with brilliant if cold effect on the pathology of modern life.

Other arts were affected by the tendencies toward anarchy and nihilism. In painting, abstract expressionism superseded for a season the representational art of an earlier time. Jackson Pollock, who had died little known in 1956, was now taken up as the forerunner of an attempt to give the tensions of contemporary culture their objective correlative in color and design. In the 1960s, "pop art" sought to discover artistic significance in the commercial artifacts of the consumer culture.

The development of a public arts policy represented a significant change in the position of the arts in American society. The WPA arts projects under the New Deal had given writers (like Bellow, Cheever, and Ellison) and painters (like Pollock, Philip Guston, and

Andy Warhol

Campbell's Soup (1965). Oil silkscreened on canvas, 36⅛ × 24⅛. Collection, the Museum of Modern Art, New York. Elizabeth Bliss Parkinson Fund.

Willem de Kooning) employment as part of the relief program. The National Endowments for the Arts and Humanities established in 1965 acquired sufficient congressional and popular support by the 1980s to survive the Reagan administration's attempts to cut their budgets. After the opening of New York's Lincoln Center in 1962, cultural and performing arts centers, headed by the Kennedy Center in Washington, spread across the land. By the 1990s, several thousand such centers housed arts organizations, decentralized cultural life, and made the arts accessible to millions of people.

More Americans, however, sought solace in the moving image than in the printed word or the painting. The movies remained America's most distinctive art. Where the American contribution to the world's literature, painting, music, and sculpture had been marginal, film without the American contribution would be unimaginable. And the motion picture was in a special sense the people's art—a collective creation delivered by an intricate assembly line to a vast and anonymous audience.

The introduction of television in the 1950s set back Hollywood for a season. But in the 1970s the movies, relinquishing the mass audience to the interloper, found new life in specialized audiences, small theaters, and pictures shot on location. Directors like Robert Altman (*M*A*S*H*, 1970; *Nashville,* 1975), Stanley Kubrick (*2001: A Space Odyssey,* 1969; *A Clockwork Orange,* 1971), Sidney Lumet (*Dog Day Afternoon,* 1975; *Network* 1976), Woody Allen (*Annie Hall,* 1977; *Hannah and Her Sisters,* 1987), Barry Levinson (*Tin Men,* 1986; *Good Morning, Vietnam,* 1987) explored with fresh and curious eye areas of the contemporary scene and the contemporary psyche.

Television, the high-pressure offspring of film and radio, superseded movies as the people's main leisure-time diversion and newspapers as the main source of the people's news. By 1980 more Americans had television sets than had modern plumbing. Many kept their sets on for more than four hours a day. Television copied its programming from radio, expending most of its time on soap opera, sports, "sitcoms" (situation comedies), quiz shows and advertising. A smaller share of time went to news programs and investigative reports, often of high quality, to discussions and documentaries, and to the dramatization, often more boldly than movies, of social questions like racial bigotry (as in Norman Lear's popular show "All in the Family"), adultery, divorce, homosexuality, incest, and child abuse. The introduction of cable television on a large scale in the 1980s reduced the control of the networks and multiplied the number of channels but did little to shake television's unswerving commitment to the mass audience. Only public television, established in 1967 with more than 300 stations 20 years later, made a systematic effort to raise standards.

Defenders of the new medium argued that television extended people's horizons, told them more than their local newspapers about current affairs, and prepared them for a world of danger and violence. Educators and parents demurred, pointing out that the average child spent, between the ages of 6 and 18, 13,000 hours in school and 16,000 hours in front of the tube. Critics contended that television shortened children's attention span, turned them against reading, diluted their sense of reality, and encouraged the idea that problems were readily resolvable by violence.

Child responding to television

ENGINES OF CHANGE

The Velocity of History The salient fact of the modern age was the increasing instability generated by the onward rush of science and technology. Henry Adams had been the first American historian to note the ever-quickening acceleration in the velocity of history. "The world did not [just] double or treble its movement between 1800 and 1900," he wrote in "The Rule of Phase Applied to History" (1909), "but, measured by any standard known to science—by horsepower, calories, volts, mass in any shape—the tension and vibration and volume and so-called progression of society were fully a thousand times greater in 1900 than in 1800." And the pace of change, urged ever onward by the self-generating processes of scientific inquiry, exploded in the twentieth century when, it was noted, of all the scientists who had ever lived in the history of the planet, 90 percent were alive and active.

The acceleration of change was a major factor in the energy crisis with industrial expansion devouring increasing quantities of oil, coal, and natural gas. Nuclear energy, once seen as the key to the world's energy dilemma, was regarded with mounting dubiety. Nuclear plants turned out to be more expensive and less safe than anticipated. Radioactive explosions in 1986 at Chernobyl in Soviet Russia reinforced the lesson of Three Mile Island. The disposal of radioactive wastes also raised difficult problems. While an emotional lobby of environmentalists and others campaigned against nuclear energy, by 1990 more than 100 nuclear reactors produced about 18 percent of the nation's electricity. Nuclear energy, under proper safeguards, was bound to have a role in the future.

The law of acceleration also contributed to the ecological crisis. Unbridled expansion had produced pollution of water and air, erosion of the soil, and disruption of the self-replenishing cycle that for eons had sustained life on earth. America the beautiful was marked by black oil slicks smearing the beaches; by rivers and lakes filled with sewage, detergents and industrial waste; by towns enveloped in smog; by the destruction through the use of pesticides of the balance of nature among plants, animals, and the natural environment.

Impact of Exxon "Valdez"

The accumulation in the atmosphere of carbon dioxide from automobile exhausts, of chlorofluorocarbons (CFCs) from aerosol sprays and of other gaseous pollutants traps heat from the sun, turning the earth into a sort of overheated greenhouse. This "greenhouse effect," scientists predicted, would lead in the short run to drought and eventually to the melting of polar ice and the flooding of coastal cities. CFCs, in addition, erode the shield of ozone that protects humanity from ultraviolet radiation. In 1987, 49 nations endorsed an international agreement to restrict the use of CFCs. But in the United States, industrial lobbyists succeeded in defeating proposals for a stringent federal program for clean air. The United States, to the dismay of environmentalists, in 1991 also opposed European efforts to develop an international policy to retard global warming and in 1992 signed a treaty on that problem only after the Europeans agreed to vague standards.

The Electronic Society Henry Adams had predicted in particular that his law of acceleration would carry the world from what he called the Mechanical Phase into the Electric Phase, "the sharpest change of direction, taken at the highest rate of speed, ever effected by the human mind."

The dream of a machine that would instantaneously solve intricate mathematical problems had a long history, but it was not till 1946 at the University of Pennsylvania that the first electronic digital computer was built. It weighed 30 tons, occupied the space of a two-car garage, and cost nearly $10 million. In 1948 Bell Laboratories developed the transistor, a small, solid-state device that made possible the use of integrated circuits. The computer grew still smaller, swifter, and cheaper with the development in 1959 of semiconductor packages imprinting transistor devices on a piece of silicon. The process of "miniaturization" eventually made it possible to imprint 100,000 transistors on a thin silicon wafer. "In three decades," someone observed, "a whole roomful of vacuum tubes and other components has been reduced to the size of a cornflake." The "microchip" became the pivot of the electronic revolution.

No invention since the steam engine promised so many drastic changes. By incorporating intelligence and memory in machines, the computer brought about a revolution in "data processing"—the storage, retrieval, and analysis of information. People now spoke of the "information society," in which national strength depended less on the goods manufactured than on the information produced and processed. The microchip was inexpensive, easy to produce, low in its energy needs, and capable of an infinite variety of application.

The microchip revolution was predominantly an American creation, though by 1990 Japan had mounted a serious challenge in supercomputers and was far ahead in robotics. Microelectronics were already transforming basic aspects of American life. The home computer and the word processor were in constant use; offices and factories were automated; telecommunications, employing optical fibers and satellites, flashed information across the country and the world; engineers, doctors, bankers, economists, teachers, and students relied increasingly on computers; children congregated in video-game arcades; the invasion of privacy by two-way cable systems and electronic information banks seemed a growing threat.

The microchip brought problems as well as benefits. For the first time in modern history, technological innovation threatened to destroy more jobs than it created. Moreover, high technology created two kinds of jobs: well-paid jobs for skilled engineers and programmers; poorly paid, tedious jobs for unskilled and semiskilled operatives and clerks. This development, along with the rise in dead-end jobs in fast-food and other service industries, led alarmists to foresee the decline of the middle class.

At the same time, the electronic revolution was eroding the traditional structure of American politics. For a century a cluster of agencies—the political party, the farm organization, the trade union, the chamber of commerce, the ethnic federation—had mediated between the politician and the voter, interceding for each on behalf of the other and providing the links that held the party system together. Electronic innovations were now severing those links and bypassing the traditional political structure. Television presented the politicians directly to the voter, computerized public opinion polls presented the voter directly to the politician, and the mediating agencies were withering away.

As voters increasingly made their own judgments on the basis of what they themselves saw on the tiny screen, party loyalties, once as sacred as religious affiliations, lost their grip. Beginning in the 1950s, voters began to use both parties for their own purposes, thus balancing off a Republican president with a Democratic Congress. Not only ticket-splitting but also nonvoting increased. The proportion of voters describing themselves as "independent" grew strikingly. Whether or not the two-party system was in dissolution, no one could deny that it was in crisis. The rhythm of American politics seemed to have changed. As historian Arthur Schlesinger had observed, in the past the cycle of American politics had turned to liberal reformers about every 30 years. But in the early 1990s, that movement was overdue, perhaps because parties no longer exerted the influence they previously had, perhaps because social rather than economic issues were dominating voting behavior.

High technology held out the possibility either of the extreme centralization or decentralization of society. Some feared that the new electronic instruments signalled the rise of an intrusive and authoritarian "computer state." Others predicted that work, education, religion, even shopping would be increasingly concentrated in the home, now become the "electronic cottage," and feared that the family computer terminal would intensify the isolation and alienation of mass society.

Nor could anyone predict the ultimate impact on the human consciousness. The computer, as a machine committed to logic, might strengthen rational and analytic tendencies. On the other hand, the computer's qualities of instantaneity, and collectivity, everything descending on us from everywhere all at once, might carry the contemporary sensibility itself into a stage of profound dissociation. The Canadian Marshall McLuhan saw incalculable consequences in the shift from a typographical to an electronic culture. The sensibility created by the print media, he argued, had given experience a frame and viewed it in sequence and from a distance. The print culture's qualities were logic, precision, specialization, individualism. But in the electronic age, "The contained, the distinct, the separate—our western legacy—are being replaced by the flowing, the unified, the fused." The multiform ways of seeing and experiencing opened by the new modes of communication promised to alter the very reflexes of psychological reaction and expectation. Where the print culture had programmed the mind in a one-at-a-time, step-by-step way, the electronic culture undermined linear processes of thought, replacing one-at-a-time by all-at-once. Though the terms of McLuhan's argument were extravagant, there remained the possibility that he was onto a significant and fertile truth.

Genetic Engineering The winds of acceleration blew through all the sciences. Molecular biology in particular now thrust forward into the very bases of human life. The discovery in 1953 of the double-helix structure of deoxyribonucleic acid (DNA), for which the American James D. Watson and two Englishmen received the Nobel Prize in 1962, showed scientists how the genetic code of life was organized, how it might be deciphered, how it could even be manipulated.

With surprising speed, scientists learned how to sever and splice genes, how to induce cellular organisms to manufacture complex proteins, how to manufacture artificial genes in the test tube. "Recombinant DNA"—the combining of genes into new substances—promised not only the cure of genetic diseases but genetic transplantation, test-tube babies, and "cloning"—that is, the production of genetically identical copies of individual human beings. The Patent Office ruled in 1987 that genetic engineers could patent higher life forms, even mammals—a ruling that both aroused ethical protest and invited commercial application. Biotechnology was on its way to becoming a major industry. Within a generation science had begun to devise the means not only to blow up the world but to transform reproduction, consciousness, intellect, behavior, and the very genetic nature of human beings. Scientists themselves worried about the consequences of their discoveries. Responding to pressure, the Reagan administration in 1986 sufficiently overcame its aversion to government regulation to establish standards governing the testing, use, and sale of products of biotechnology.

The Endless Frontier The most spectacular expression of the onward thrust of science and technology came with the human escape from gravity and wondrous leap into space. The manned landing on the moon (1969) was followed by the dispatch of unmanned spacecraft to far reaches of the solar system. In 1976 *Viking 1* and *2* transmitted photographs and scientific data from Mars back to earth. In 1979 *Voyagers 1* and *2* flew past Jupiter, photographed its great moons, and streaked on to Saturn. In 1983 *Pioneer 10* became the first manufactured object to leave the solar system and sail on forever in the great void of interstellar space. In the 1990s *Galileo* will orbit in space around Jupiter. Such missions greatly enlarged scientific knowledge about the formation of planets and the geology of the solar system.

Under Nixon, emphasis had shifted from exploration and science to the military and commercial exploitation of space. The National Aeronautic and Space Administration (NASA) decided to concentrate its resources on the space shuttle, a reusable manned rocket, a decision favored by private industry and the Reagan administration but opposed by many scientists as a misguided diversion of money and expertise. The explosion in 1986 of the space shuttle *Challenger,* killing its crew of seven, led to the grounding of the shuttle fleet and to widespread criticism of NASA's management and objectives. Reagan nonetheless pressed on with the privatization of space, declaring in 1988 that his goal, in addition to SDI, was "a strong commercial presence in space." Though hampered by a lack of funds and by congressional resistance, Bush continued to espouse Reagan's space policies.

In the meantime, the Soviet Union, though behind in electronic sophistication, forged ahead in almost all aspects of space exploration. In 1987, it established the orbiting *Mir* space station and launched 95 space vehicles, both manned and unmanned, while the United States launched 8. Soviet astronauts had spent more than twice as much time in space as their American counterparts, of whom some were women. Moscow prepared robotic probes to Mars, the only other possibly habitable planet in the solar system, and proposed to the United States a joint manned Mars mission thereafter.

The adventure of space continued to seize the popular imagination. Science fiction was never more popular, and films like Stanley Kubrick's haunting *2001: A Space Odyssey,* George Lucas's *Star Wars* trilogy, and Steven Spielberg's *Close Encounters of the Third Kind* (1977) and *E.T.* (1982) broke box-office records. Credulous people believed that UFOs (unidentified flying objects) were conducting an alien surveillance of the troubled earth.

As the space probes went forward, the question grew ever more insistent whether earthlings were alone in the universe. *Pioneer 10,* in case it might be intercepted by sentient beings in distant galaxies, carried a plaque displaying images of a nude man and woman and a diagram of the solar system. Scientists devised more systematic means to communicate with other intelligences in the cosmos. With every passing year, scientists around the world watched and listened ever more urgently for signals from the sky.

Into the Twenty-first Century As Henry Adams's law of acceleration had predicted, the onward surge of science and technology was drastically speeding the rate of historical change. The first rockets were launched in the 1920s; 40 years later men rocketed to the moon. The first electronic computer was built in 1946; 35 years later scientists were working on fifth-generation computers. The double helix was unveiled in 1953; 30 years later, biotechnology threatened to remake humankind. The first atomic bomb was dropped in 1945; ever after the world lived under the menace of nuclear obliteration.

Humanity was subjected in the last half of the twentieth century to a series of incredible shocks, each of which by itself would have taken decades to digest and control. All the shocks accelerated the velocity of history. The twenty-first century confronted the people of the world with an array of dangers: not only nuclear war, but AIDS, drugs, the greenhouse effect, the depletion of the protective ozone layer, the pollution of land and sea, ecological disaster, moral collapse. But the new century also held out exciting possibilities of liberation and achievement—if humanity would use the energies released by the computer revolution and the electronic era not to destroy but to create. Facing the adventure of the twenty-first century, America was still a nation of hope, fortified by the standards, the purposes and the inspiration nobly embodied two centuries before in the Declaration of Independence and the Constitution of the United States.

TOWARD A NEW WORLD ORDER

The Collapse of Communism Men and women living in countries under Communist regimes aspired for many years to the freedoms guaranteed to Americans by the Bill of Rights, the freedoms Franklin D. Roosevelt had restated in 1941 as freedom of belief and expression, freedom of worship, and freedom from fear and from want. The oppression, universal in Communist nations, and the failure of Communist economies to produce and distribute the material goods essential for a decent standard of living provoked growing disenchantment during the 1980s. So it was in China, where in the spring of 1989 tens of thousands of university students and their sympathizers, mostly young adults, filled Tiananmen Square in Beijing (Peking), as well as public places in other cities, with their rallies for freedom. After tolerating the demonstrations for several weeks, the Chinese Communist leaders imposed martial law, ordered in troops to put down the protests, and then arrested, convicted, and incarcerated the youthful leaders. In Beijing (Peking) the Peoples Army killed thousands of the allegedly disloyal protesters. The hard-liners in the Chinese Communist party then removed their more lenient colleagues from the Central Committee. Communism in China retained its iron rule.

Tiananmen Square: rally for freedom

The harsh Chinese response to dissent contrasted with the restraint with which Mikhail Gorbachev accepted the push for freedom in Eastern Europe and the Soviet Union. Indeed, without Gorbachev's policy of openness, the transformation of communism in those areas could not have occurred as it did. During 1988 and 1989, economic grievances and long-simmering aspirations for freedom combined to cause a peaceful revolution as Gorbachev released the police and military controls that his predecessors had imposed. With only occasional resistance, he allowed the long-latent nationalistic yearnings of the various peoples in the region to burst into the open. As in earlier periods of history, the urge for freedom and the urge for ethnic self-determination, feeding on each other, reached high fever. That fever burned in the Communist world in 1989 and the succeeding several years. It brought the contours of European political geography back toward the boundaries that had marked the continent before the Second World War, and it brought an end to Communist party control in every country of Europe where communism had prevailed. Consequently, it ended the Cold War as the world had known it since 1945.

The rapidity of the movement toward those ends stunned even the participants in the process. In Poland, where the Solidarity labor movement had been active for a decade, its adherents and their anti-Soviet allies put a non-Communist government in power in mid-1989. That new government, turning at once toward a market economy, lifted price controls and set a schedule for privatizing state enterprises. In 1991, free elections for parliament, the first such since 1947, produced a democratic majority, though the unexpected strength of the Communist party reflected rising discontent with high prices for food and fuel, as well as the bitterness of the many Polish poor in agriculture and industry whose sufferings contrasted with the affluence of a small, newly rich minority of successful entrepreneurs. Democracy and capitalism were coming to Poland but not without pains that the rest of Eastern Europe also experienced, and not without the consent of Moscow, which in earlier years would have sent in troops to stamp out the changes.

So it was elsewhere. In Hungary in 1989 Communist leaders surrendered to popular demand, and democratic parties won national elections held in 1990. In Bulgaria the Communist dictator resigned in 1989 to be succeeded in 1990 by an ex-Communist who had earlier been expelled from the party for criticizing Lenin. Romania remained under Communist rule until 1990, when rioting crowds captured and executed the Communist dictator Nicolae Ceausescu, but only after further violence did some stability return in 1991 under a largely democratic government beset by economic problems. Also in 1991 Albania threw over its Communist yoke.

The smoothest transitions from communism occurred, though not without stress, in Czechoslovakia and East Germany. In Czechoslovakia Vaclav Havel, a dissident playwright whom the Communists had imprisoned, organized the democratic opposition that triumphed with little violence late in 1989 and in 1990 elected Havel president. Before 1945 the Czechs had had a more telling experience with freedom and capitalism than had other Eastern European countries, and Havel, an eloquent democrat, called for political forgiveness for former Communists. He moved only cautiously toward a free market. Even so, the Czechs could not avoid the shortages from which their neighbors also suffered, nor could they prevent the movement toward semi-independent status of the Slovak people within the country. Ethnic tensions, rampant in Eastern Europe, peaked in Yugoslavia in 1991 and 1992 in open warfare between the Serbs and the Croatians, accompanied by separate drives toward independence by the other peoples of Yugoslavia.

Meanwhile in East Germany, vociferous popular discontent forced Erich Honecker, the Communist dictator, to resign in 1989. Within months the new government opened the borders to Czechoslovakia and allowed its citizens to enter that newly democratic state. On November 9, 1989, young Germans from both the East and the West climbed the Berlin Wall to celebrate. Thousands of East Germans crossed into West Berlin, all of them exuberant in their unaccustomed freedom, and many of them embarked on a joyful shopping spree. With free elections pending in East Germany, West German Chancellor Helmut Kohl proposed reunification of the two Germanys. Reunification received the endorsement it required from the victorious nations of the Second World War—the United States, Great Britain, France and the Soviet Union—which had divided Germany in 1945. To compensate for Gorbachev's anxieties about the new Germany's geopolitical power, Kohl agreed to the continued presence of Soviet troops in East Germany for four years, signed a treaty of friendship, and promised $10 billion of economic aid for the Soviet Union. In July 1990, the Germans and the four allied powers further agreed to guarantee the border between Poland and Germany. That left the Poles with the land they had acquired after the Second World War. The

The breach in the Berlin Wall, November 1989

two Germanys started unification with the West German mark as their common monetary unit. Formal unification was celebrated in October 1990, but there lay ahead a difficult time of adjustment until West German investment could spur economic growth in the East sufficiently to take up the slack of employment that followed the closing of the inefficient industrial plants of the former Communist region. Unemployment in Germany and the flood into the country of people fleeing the poverty of Eastern Europe generated a rising German nativism, with neo-Nazi organizations in 1991 and 1992 vilifying and attacking foreigners. As elsewhere in Europe, democracy and capitalism could not instantly or completely or peaceably replace the Communist system of the previous half-century.

Nowhere was that limitation as apparent as in the Soviet Union. Gorbachev's efforts to restructure the centralized economy, efforts tentative and unsystematic at best, failed to improve the crumbling infrastructure or to reverse the declining productivity of agriculture, mining, and heavy industry. Most of the bureaucracy, privileged members of the Communist party, resisted economic reform, while most intellectuals, free at last to speak openly, criticized Gorbachev's vacillating programs as inadequate. Gorbachev did succeed in 1990 in ending the Communist party's monopoly of political power. In March of that year anti-Communists won control in several municipal elections. In May Boris Yeltsin, a maverick and charismatic former Communist whom Gorbachev had attacked, won election as president of Russia, the most powerful of the Soviet republics. Pushed by events, Gorbachev then reformed the politburo, reduced the military budget, and completed his retreat from Soviet imperialistic ventures, most notably in Afghanistan. Those policies alienated senior Communist officials whose status and perquisites depended on the institutions Gorbachev was altering and the autocracy he was abandoning. But the old guard had lost its muscle and much of its following, even though the economy continued to decline.

For his part, Gorbachev could no longer contain the centripetal forces that were tearing the Soviet Union apart. In 1990 he tried to prevent the secession of the Baltic states — Latvia, Estonia, and Lithuania — which Stalin had seized in 1939. In 1991 he had to let them go. In August 1991 an attempted coup by the old guard enlisted insignificant popular support, though it provoked little democratic opposition in most of the nation. In Moscow, however, Boris Yeltsin led thousands of protestors into the streets, crowds demonstrated also in Leningrad (soon to be renamed St. Petersburg), and the coup, successfully challenged by Yeltsin's actions, lasted only a week. But Gorbachev had lost most of his stature before his return to the presidency. Increasing assertiveness by the many ethnic constituencies of the nation destroyed the state as Lenin and Stalin had constructed it. Before the end of 1991, Belorus and Ukraine joined Russia and eight other republics in a loose confederation, the Commonwealth of Independent States; the Soviet parliament adjourned forever; and Gorbachev resigned.

By 1992 it was the potential instability of the former Soviet Union, not the power of that collapsed country, that worried the West. Yeltsin seized personal control of the foreign office, the military, and the police in Russia, the strongest of the republics, and controlled, too, most but not all of the commonwealth's nuclear arsenal, although Ukraine challenged Russia's claim to the former Soviet navy. He began 1992 by lifting price controls on many foodstuffs and some other consumer goods in the expectation that higher prices would persuade producers to send their goods to market. But higher prices would be tolerable only with higher wages, and in the absence of increased productivity, that prospect assured inflation that would affect the whole new commonwealth. Inflation accompanied by widespread poverty and complicated by ethnic rivalries boded disorder. Still, the world was free at last of the Cold War, and Western pledges of economic aid promised to ease the transition of the economies of the new states. Even though Yeltsin met severe criticism from Russians who thought he was moving too quickly toward a market-type economy, he seemed agile in 1992 in making political adjustments designed to reinforce his rule. As the advocates of containment had predicted, the Soviet government and economy had imploded. The collapse of communism now presented extraordinary opportunities for creative reconstruction if the heralds of freedom could make palpable the grand promises of their beliefs.

Bush and Gorbachev During the presidential campaign of 1988, neither George Bush nor Michael Dukakis seemed to understand that the Cold War had already receded. Neither addressed the implications of that development for American policy. Indeed, through much of 1989 the new president appeared skeptical about Gorbachev's intentions. As in all matters, Bush believed, so he said, in prudence, which some of his critics interpreted as timidity. George Herbert Walker Bush was 64 when he entered the White House. A son of Prescott Bush, an eastern financier turned senator, he was reared in exurban Connecticut and graduated from Phillips Academy, Andover, and Yale University, in his day thoroughly conventional and conservative institutions. A navy flier and hero in the Pacific during the Second World War, Bush entered the oil business in Texas in the 1950s and was elected to the House of Representatives in 1966. During the Nixon and Ford administrations, he served loyally in a variety of positions—ambassador to the United Nations, chair of the Republican National Committee, envoy to China, director of the CIA. Though he failed to make a deep impression in any of those posts, they exposed him continually to questions of foreign policy, the subject that caught his major interest. Nevertheless, as Reagan's vice president, Bush supported without dissent even the bizarre overseas adventures of his chief, and he learned to be amiable with the right wing of his party. Eager to be one of the boys, he poured his private energy into fishing, golf, jogging, and motorboating, and he dismissed idealism at home or abroad as the "vision thing."

Fortunately for the prudent Bush, his initial ventures in foreign policy benefited from the continuing restraint of the Soviet Union in world affairs. At the United Nations in December 1988, Gorbachev pledged a 10 percent reduction in Soviet armed forces. "You'll see soon enough," the Soviet leader then told Bush privately, "that I'm not doing this for show and I'm not doing this to undermine you . . . or to take advantage of you. I'm playing real politics. . . . I'm doing this because there's a revolution taking place in my country. I started it . . . in 1986. . . . Now they don't like it so much, but it's going to be a revolution, nonetheless." Gorbachev's actions fit those words. In April 1989, he forced the resignations of hard-line members of the Central Committee of the Communist party. In May he announced cutbacks in Soviet nuclear weapons in Eastern Europe and proposed that NATO and the Warsaw Pact agree on reciprocal reductions in conventional arms. In June he and West German Chancellor Kohl signed a statement declaring that every state had the right to choose its own political and social system, a principle Gorbachev was to honor as one after another of the Soviet satellites moved toward independence. In September he shook up the Politburo to create a majority in favor of his reforms. During those months, moreover, Bush's good friend, Secretary of State James Baker, was forging close personal ties with his Soviet counterpart, the liberal Foreign Minister Edward Shevardnadze.

All but the most adamant Cold Warriors now recognized that genuine opportunities lay ahead for further relaxation of Soviet-American rivalries. Accordingly, Bush agreed to a first summit meeting with Gorbachev at Malta in December 1989. There Bush proposed the negotiation during 1990 of bilateral treaties on both strategic and conventional weapons in Europe. The two men stood, they said, on the "threshhold of a brand new era of United States-Soviet relations." With communism fading in Eastern Europe, they met again in late May 1990 when Gorbachev came to Washington. Bush then accepted a trade treaty that Gorbachev considered vital for the Soviet economy. They also discussed the question of a unified Germany joining NATO, a prospect Bush supported but Gorbachev at that time temporarily opposed. Speaking a few days later at Stanford University, Gorbachev said: "The Cold War is now behind us. Let us not wrangle over who won it."

A Free Hand in Central America With the Soviet Union withdrawing from its previous commitments in Central America, and with Castro neutralized by the termination of Soviet aid to Cuba, Bush was able gradually to advance toward American objectives in that region. In doing so he responded favorably to local initiatives that weaned the United States from the domineering goals of the Reagan years. Early in 1989 the five Central American presidents agreed to the disarming and repatriation of the Nicaraguan Contras camped in Honduras, with free elections in Nicaragua to follow. Though Bush said he was "wary," Nicaraguan president Daniel Ortega permitted the election in February 1990. The Sandinistas lost the presidency to a moderate, Violeta Barrios de Chamorro. Recognizing the continuing popularity of the Sandinistas among many of the people, she appointed Ortega's brother chief of the armed forces and worked with him toward the rehabilitation of the country. In Salvador, American influence contributed to the successful presidential campaign of Alfredo Christiani, the candidate of the ARENA party, previously a bastion of the right wing but now more flexible. Christiani called for a cease-fire and negotiation with the rebels still resisting his regime. Though both sides were slow to abandon the brutality they had long practiced, they agreed early in 1992 to a UN proposal for a cease-fire, land reform, and the conversion of military to political resistance.

Manuel Noriega, 1988

It was not the fading Cold War but the tempestuous drug war that drove President Bush's policy toward Panama. In 1983, while he was vice president, Bush had met with the Panamanian strong man, General Manuel A. Noriega, a notoriously corrupt and ruthless autocrat. The Reagan administration was then seeking Noriega's cooperation in its efforts to aid the Nicaraguan Contras, a purpose Bush's mission was intended to serve. Noriega did cooperate and in return received substantial secret payments from Washington. But Noriega was also associated with the infamous Medelline Cartel, the Colombian drug organization, which shipped cocaine through Panama for transshipment to the United States and used Panamanian banks to launder its huge profits. Noriega gained millions of dollars from his drug connections, about which many American officials in the Drug Enforcement Agency, the CIA, and the army were well informed. Accused in 1988 of condoning Noriega's role in the cocaine trade, Bush denied knowing anything about it at the time of his meeting in 1983 with the Panamanian. Yet the Reagan administration by 1988 was offering to drop a federal indictment of Noriega for drug trafficking and racketeering if Noriega would for his part relinquish his authority in Panama. Politically vulnerable because of those negotiations, Bush announced that he would never bargain with a drug lord.

That statement removed the Noriega issue from the 1988 campaign but left the problem unsolved for the new administration, with the new president sensitive about the matter and personally vindictive toward Noriega. In May 1989 Noriega allowed a presidential election in Panama. The United States, Bush said, would not recognize the results of a fraudulent contest. Former president Jimmy Carter was among the international observers who reported that the anti-Noriega candidate won an overwhelming victory. Nevertheless, Noriega had the election annulled. Bush then called on the Panamanian people to overthrow Noriega, whom the Organization of American States (OAS) also denounced. Bush went on to send 2,000 additional American troops to American bases in Panama, to relieve the American commanding general there who had not been tough enough to suit the president, and to replace him with General Maxwell Thurman, "Mad Max" to his army admirers. Thurman, however, in October misread the intentions of the leader of an attempted coup the CIA was financing. Though authorized to use troops, the general held back while Washington hesitated and Noriega captured and murdered his leading opponents.

Again embarrassed by events in Panama, Bush defended his inaction by expressing his concern for protecting the lives of American troops. "I wouldn't mind using force," he said, ". . . if it could be done in a prudent manner." Both he and General Thurman were ready to conduct a personal war against Noriega under favorable conditions and with a plausible excuse. The Justice Department ruled, with no regard for international law, that United States law enforcement officers could make an arrest in a foreign country even if the foreign government had not granted permission for it. But Noriega could not believe the United States would attempt a military kidnapping. Aware the CIA was again plotting against him, he had the Panamanian National Assembly in December adopt a resolution declaring that a state of war existed between the two countries. Moving on recklessly, his Panamanian police the next day detained and tortured an American naval officer and his wife. They also skirmished with some American servicemen, of whom one was killed. That terrorism gave Bush the occasion he had been awaiting to launch a large-scale invasion of Panama that the Joint Chiefs of Staff had been planning. On December 20 American air, sea, and land forces, armed with the most modern weapons, hit Panama. Noriega's guards, though not surprised, were overwhelmed. Sharp fighting lasted only a day, but Noriega hid from the Americans and found temporary asylum in the diplomatic mission of the Vatican, where he remained until he surrendered on January 3, 1990. He was then removed to Florida to be tried late in 1991 and convicted in 1992 of racketeering and drug-trafficking.

Bush and the Joint Chiefs of Staff prevented the media from reporting during the Panamanian invasion. Only that censorship could hide the irony of the venture's official name: "Operation Just Cause." For the Americans had caused extensive damage and casualties in their assault, especially in the area where the poorest Panamanians resided. There 15,000 were left homeless. Those innocent people received the heaviest punishment for Noriega's crimes. Bush promised Panama a billion dollars in relief. It never materialized. Panamanian civilian casualties were estimated between 200 and 1,000, but both the United States and the Panamanian governments prevented a careful count so as to minimize the number of combat-related claims. Between 50 and 300 Panamanian guards were killed, and more than 250 Americans were killed or wounded. Two years later drugs were still moving freely in and out of Panama, and Panamanian banks were still laundering drug money. "Of Bush's objectives," said the head of the Panama Bar Association, "only one was really achieved—getting rid of Manuel Noriega. . . . They could've captured him without an invasion, without destroying the country." The American people, poorly informed, seemed not to care. But the OAS and the United Nations deplored the invasion and American disregard for Panamanian sovereignty and for international law. Panama recovered only slowly and incompletely from the most destructive episode in its entire history. "Every human life is precious," Bush had asserted, "and yet . . . it has been worth it."

The Middle East, As Ever The decline of Soviet power and prestige in the Middle East left the United States with increased influence there, but the problems of the region remained intractable. The Bush administration, committed like its predecessors to preserving Israel's independence, was eager also to serve peace by persuading Israel to return the Arab lands it had seized in 1967. Led by the Palestine Liberation Organization (PLO), an Arab uprising in 1989 and thereafter in territories Israel occupied engendered brutal retaliation that cost Israel much sympathy in the United States. By 1990 the loosening of restrictions on Soviet emigration led tens of thousands of Soviet Jews to enter Israel, strained the resources of the Israeli government that fed and housed them, and pushed Israel toward more rapid and extensive settlements in the occupied territories. Those settlements forced the removal of Palestinians living there, a development that the United States opposed fruitlessly.

During that time, the Bush administration, with small interest in shaping a national policy to conserve exhaustible supplies of energy, was also committed to sustaining the flow of inexpensive oil from the Persian Gulf. In that area the fundamentalist Shiite and the moderate Sunnite Muslims remained hostile to each other, with their antagonism complicating relationships among the Arab states and within many of them. The failed efforts of the Reagan administration to free the hostages held by Shiite terrorists in Lebanon fed American distrust of Syria and Iran. Eager to avoid his predecessor's mistakes, Bush hoped to arrange a settlement of Arab-Israeli differences that would lead to the release of the hostages and please Saudi Arabia and other major oil producers.

In 1988 with the end of the eight-year war between Iran and Iraq, those two countries counted on increasing their oil exports in order to obtain hard currencies to pay their debts and finance their reconstruction. But rising production in Saudi Arabia, Kuwait, and the United Arab Emirates, and the flow of oil from elsewhere in the world, kept oil prices and profits low. Consequently Saddam Hussein, the Iraqi dictator who was attempting to make his nation the dominant power in the gulf, threatened neighboring Kuwait with reprisals if it did not curtail its output of oil. Iraq had long been eager to obtain a port on the Persian Gulf to facilitate its oil shipments. To that end in 1961 Iraq had claimed that Kuwait, which had a desirable port, was historically part of Iraq. Of shaky foundation, that claim served as a convenient excuse for Saddam's territorial and political ambitions. An implacable foe of Israel, Saddam in July 1990 charged the United States with inspiring the overproduction of oil and charged Kuwait and the United Arab Emirates with joining that "imperialist-Zionist" plot to depress oil prices.

The Bush administration at first interpreted those statements as bluster. For some years the United States had been soliciting Iraq's friendship. Though Iraq had been the aggressor in its war with Iran, the Reagan and Bush administrations had permitted extensive sales of military equipment to the Iraqis. Indeed, from 1985 through 1990 the Commerce Department, in spite of objections from the Defense Department, approved the shipment to Iraq of American high-technology components for use in the production of advanced aircraft, rockets, and nuclear weapons. American agricultural credits to Iraq permitted the Iraqis to use other funds to buy military gear from the Soviet Union, Eastern Europe, and China. So Saddam Hussein had the most modern army in the Arab world to back up his threat to Kuwait. But the State Department, as one of its officials said, was "reluctant to draw a line in the sand," particularly after President Hosni Mubarek of Egypt and King ibu Abdul Aziz Fahd of Saudi Arabia assured Washington that Saddam Hussein would not invade Kuwait.

Signals from Washington to Baghdad were confusing. On July 25, 1990, Ambassador April Glaspie, newly appointed to her post in Iraq, told Saddam, so she later said, that the United States would "defend our vital interests . . . support our friends in the Gulf . . . defend their sovereignty and integrity." She added, however, that "we have no opinion on the Arab-Arab conflicts, like your border disagreement with Kuwait." In her view, she was issuing a warning. Uncomprehending or undeterred, Saddam Hussein broke off talks with Kuwait on August 1. He had by that date some 100,000 troops on the border, whereas the Kuwaiti army consisted of only about 20,000. At dawn on August 2, Iraqi forces invaded and quickly gained control of Kuwait, though the emir and his court escaped by air.

Desert Shield Surprised though he was, Bush immediately called the invasion "naked aggression," banned trade with Iraq, froze all Iraqi assets within the United States (a step soon also taken by the Western European nations and Japan), and dispatched an aircraft-carrier group to the Persian Gulf. At the initiation of the United States, the UN Security Council voted unanimously to condemn the invasion and demand the withdrawal of Iraqi forces from Kuwait. On August 6 the council asked all UN members to end all trade and financial dealings with Iraq and its puppet government in Kuwait. The Soviet Union, long the major supplier of arms to Iraq, had already stopped sales of military equipment, and Soviet Foreign Minister Shevardnadze joined Secretary Baker in deploring the invasion.

At the outset of the crisis, Bush began to consult a small circle of advisers who remained his chief counselors for months to come. They included the suave and articulate Secretary of State James Baker; the tough-minded Secretary of Defense Dick Cheney; the experienced National Security Adviser Brent Scowcroft; General Colin L. Powell, the impressive chair of the Joint Chiefs of Staff; and the colorful and intelligent General Norman ("Stormin' Norman") Schwarzkopf, senior Pentagon planner for the Persian Gulf area and soon American commander there. The president kept to a minimum consultation beyond that tight circle. It consisted entirely of men predisposed to use military means to push Iraq out of Kuwait. Bush, so inclined himself, did not discuss his options with Congress or reveal his intentions to the public. He did tell the American people on August 6, 1990, that "this aggression . . . will not stand." And he did set out skillfully to build by transoceanic telephone a global coalition for that purpose.

That diplomatic objective was eased from the first by the vulnerability of Saudi Arabia. If Iraq overran Saudi Arabia, almost defenseless against Saddam, it would control about half of the known oil resources of the world, a prospect intolerable for all industrial nations. So while Bush and Baker were recruiting support from the Soviet Union and Western Europe and among the Arab states, including promises of essential financial assistance from Germany, Saudi Arabia, and later Japan, Schwarzkopf was briefing the president about force levels necessary to hold back Iraq and then to invade it, and Cheney was persuading King Fahd to permit American troops to be stationed in his country. On August 15, with the first American soldiers on their way to the Persian Gulf, Bush told the American people that his Operation Desert Shield was under way to protect "access to energy resources" and thus "our jobs, our way of life." With few exceptions, Americans supported both Desert Shield and the UN sanctions against Iraq, to be enforced primarily by the United States Navy. During September and October the coalition against Iraq took shape, with pledges of military participation from Great Britain, France, and Egypt, among others, and with assurances of billions of dollars of financial backing. Turkey cut off Saddam's access to the pipeline that carried Iraqi oil, the United States brought Israel to promise to remain neutral so as not to roil Arab feelings, and the buildup in Saudi Arabia reached toward 100,000 Americans armed with tanks, cannon, and aircraft.

For his part, Saddam Hussein neither attacked Saudi Arabia nor withdrew from Kuwait. He did continue to rant, to threaten to place American, British, and French citizens in Iraq at military and industrial sites where they would be injured in the event of war, and to call for a "holy war" against the "corrupt" Arab states, including Egypt, Syria, and Morocco, that had joined the alliance against him. He also assured the neutrality of Iran by returning the territory he had taken during their recent war. But among the Muslim countries he retained the support only of Jordan, Libya, and Yemen, as well as the PLO. United Nations' criticism of his intended use of foreigners at military sites persuaded him to release the hostages he had taken for that purpose, but he made no other concessions to diplomacy or to the sanctions that cut Iraq off almost entirely from the rest of the world economy.

In the resulting stalemate, public enthusiasm for Bush's policy flagged. A clash in Jerusalem between Israelis and Palestinians served as a reminder of the stubbornness of Middle Eastern rivalries. A fight between the president and Congress over the budget diverted attention from Kuwait. Reports of Iraqi atrocities in Kuwait, many of them based only on Kuwaiti propaganda, provoked Bush to denounce Saddam Hussein, but the president meant his rhetoric to build support for the military offensive he was pressing the Pentagon to finish planning. Before the end of October, Schwarzkopf did present a plan for a flanking attack around the Iraqis' front lines along the Saudi border. Because the Iraqi force, about 100,000 in August, had grown to 400,000, the United States now needed at the least to match that figure. The Pentagon could reach that level, Schwarzkopf told the president, in time for a major aerial campaign against Iraq in mid-January, to be followed by a ground campaign late in February. Within his private circle Bush endorsed that plan. He also sent Baker on a world tour to gather support for a UN Security Council resolution authorizing the use of force to expel Iraq from Kuwait. And he ordered the recommended increase of American strength in the Persian Gulf to begin. He delayed announcing that order until November 8, 1990, two days after the off-year elections.

The announcement disturbed many Americans who questioned the apparent rush toward war before the sanctions had had adequate time to work, and who questioned, too, the exclusion of Congress from policy making for the gulf. To mollify his critics, Bush said he would send Baker to Baghdad and invite Iraq's Foreign Minister Aziz to Washington. He would go "the extra mile to avert a war" while he continued to prepare for one. On November 29 the Security Council, again at the initiation of the United States and with Soviet concurrence, authorized the use of "all necessary means" to expel Iraqi troops if they had not left Kuwait by January 15, 1991. Still Saddam Hussein did not budge. The prospect of war drew increasing criticism from the media and from Democrats in Congress. Bush maintained that as commander in chief he had the authority to go to war. He also likened Saddam Hussein to Hitler and used the tired analogy to Munich to warn against the perils of appeasement. But the Constitution specifically gave Congress the power to declare war, and members of Congress were justifiably angry that the president had gone on his own to the Security Council for authorization to use force. Further, as Zbigniew Brzezinski commented, to compare Saddam Hussein to Hitler was to trivialize Hitler, and Iraq, a country about the size of the state of Kentucky, constituted a puny threat compared to Germany in 1938.

Prominent journalists and Democrats attacked Bush on several other counts: for sending 400,000 troops to the Persian Gulf without consulting Congress, for making war seem unavoidable without consideration of its probable consequences, for creating a crisis in order to draw attention from the faltering economy. Sam Nunn, the respected Democratic chair of the Senate Military Affairs Committee, ordinarily a hawk, withdrew his support from the administration's gulf policy. The Senate Foreign Relations Committee began hearings about that policy, during which Secretary of State Baker, usually subjected only to praise, was upbraided for giving sanctions too little time and for obtaining too few troops from allies. Admiral William Crowe, a former chair of the Joint Chiefs of Staff, testified that many Arabs would resent any military campaign in which large numbers of Muslims were killed. And the House of Representatives overwhelmingly adopted — 177 to 37 — a nonbinding resolution that the president should order no attack without the consent of Congress.

Against the advice of some of his closest counselors, Bush decided to request that consent. There ensued a congressional debate notable for its solemnity. The members of the House, said Democratic Speaker Thomas Foley, owed the president their "informed and reasoned judgment." If they believed "that Saddam Hussein is growing weaker every day," if they believed that "the coalition will hold," they should vote to continue to rely on sanctions. Stephen Solarz, also a Democrat and once a vocal opponent of the Vietnam War, maintained that circumstances had changed. Echoing Bush, he said: "If we prevail, we will have prevented a brutal dictator from getting his hands on the economic jugular of the world." Republican leaders argued that delay in a recourse to arms would strain the alliance and cost the troops in the field their readiness and morale. In the Senate, George Mitchell, the majority leader, defined the greatest risk as the loss of human life. Robert Dole, the minority leader, urged support for the president. In the end, on January 12, 1991, in a largely partisan vote, both chambers — the House 250 to 183, the Senate 53 to 46 — authorized the president "to use United States armed forces" pursuant to the UN Security Council resolution.

That outcome gave Bush the mandate he wanted. In December he had assured Israeli Prime Minister Yitzhak Shamir that in the event of war, the United States would destroy Iraqi Scud missile launching sites. In return Shamir promised to avoid both preemptive strikes and retaliation against Iraqi attacks. On January 9, 1991, Foreign Minister Aziz, meeting in Geneva with Secretary Baker, delivered a bitter complaint against the United States and the Soviet Union. The Arab allies, he predicted, would leave the coalition if war began, and Iraq would win. Saddam Hussein would not back down, and Bush, fortified by the vote in Congress, would not cease pressing him to meet the UN deadline. Now Bush had drawn a line in the sand. On January 15, after the failure of last-minute efforts by Gorbachev to find a peaceful solution, the president signed a national security directive for war against Iraq. Operation Desert Shield ended; on January 17, 1991, Operation Desert Storm began.

Saddam Hussein, January 17, 1991

Operation Desert Storm The United States and its 27 partners in the coalition against Iraq overwhelmed their enemy. By mid-January 1991 the American land, sea, and air forces in the Persian Gulf contained 527,000 men and women, more than 100 naval vessels, 2,000 tanks, 1,800 airplanes, and 1,700 helicopters. American allies included, among others, 118,000 Saudi troops, and 40,000 Egyptian, 20,000 Syrian, 43,000 British, and 16,000 French troops. Equipped with the most modern weapons, the combined forces outnumbered and outgunned the Iraqi army, still fatigued from its long war with Iran.

Perhaps most important, from the hour the war began the coalition had total command of the air. Within a few days, land-based and carrier-based

American bombers—supplemented by Stealth aircraft, cruise missiles, and combat helicopters—devastated Iraqi communication systems, air bases, and antiaircraft defenses. By day three, American bombers were attacking strategic targets—power plants, bridges, and facilities for producing chemical, biological, and nuclear weapons. By day six, Iraq had no remaining air force or air defenses capable of resisting attack, and the intact Iraqi aircraft fled to neutral bases in Iran, where Iran seized and kept them. From day eight, coalition planes hit the Iraqi army in the field in Kuwait and the élite Republican Guards in Iraq, as well as Iraqi artillery and tank units. By late February more than 40,000 sorties had dropped 85,000 tons of ordnance on Iraqi ground troops and industrial plants. "Smart" precision weapons accounted for less than 10 percent of that tonnage. Most of the air bombardment consisted of the kind of heavy strikes that the United States had used in Vietnam, but in the desert targets were more visible and vulnerable than they had been in the jungle. Iraqi resistance evaporated under the impact of the bombing, which demoralized Iraqi troops, who surrendered by the thousands without fighting.

Saddam Hussein struck back recklessly but ineffectually. On the second day of the war, he began to attack Israel and Saudi Arabia with Scud missiles. None inflicted major damage, and most were intercepted in the air by American Patriot antimissile missiles. Israel accepted the civilian losses without retaliation in return for the positioning of Patriot launchers and their American crews in Jerusalem and other cities, as well as for American efforts to take out Scud launchers in Iraq. Unable to provoke Israel to arms, Saddam Hussein turned his troops loose to pillage and murder Kuwaitis. He also had them set fire to some 600 Kuwaiti oil wells, of which many burned on for more than a year. The smoke from the fires polluted the air for hundreds of miles. In late January the Iraqi release of thousands of gallons of Kuwaiti oil into the Persian Gulf polluted the waters of that area, with devastating effects on marine life and Arab equipment used to convert salt to fresh water. "Environmental terrorism," Bush called it. More accurately it was the last, desperate, and feeble weapon available to Saddam.

The devastation wrought by the air war did not drive Saddam from Kuwait. While permitting the Soviet Union again to try to negotiate a withdrawal, Bush warned Saddam Hussein that the coalition would force him out if he had not begun to leave by February 24. On that day Bush ordered coalition forces to attack. With General Schwarzkopf in command, they executed the plan he had developed the previous autumn. In January he had begun to reposition his forces to undertake two flanking movements west of the central Iraqi line (Map 35-1). In February the American 7th Corps, accompanied by the French, began the outer of the two encirclements, while the 17th Corps and the British advanced in the inner flank. Concurrently, the United States Marines, along with Saudi, Syrian, and Egyptian troops, drove directly toward Kuwait City. Before the Iraqis were aware of it, Schwarzkopf had two armored corps on top of them. That "hail Mary play," as he called it, put the Iraqis in a squeeze they could not escape. With the coalition controlling the air, they did not really try. After 100 hours of ground warfare, Kuwait had been liberated, and the Baghdad area was besieged. Though Saddam Hussein still ruled Iraq, Bush declared a cease-fire.

The dimensions of the victory were extraordinary. The coalition had destroyed some 4,000 Iraqi tanks, more than 1,000 armored vehicles, about 3,000 artillery pieces. In comparison, the coalition had lost only 4 tanks, 9 other vehicles, and 1 cannon. In nearly 110,000 sorties, the coalition lost only 38 aircraft. About 100,000 Iraqi troops were killed. Apart from casualties from misdirected friendly fire, the coalition had suffered less than 200 deaths—148 of them American, 11 of those women. Another 120 American noncombatants were also killed.

Victory at a minimal cost of American lives carried with it major political and emotional gains. Temporarily it removed Iraq's military threat to the Middle East, especially to Israel. It restored the prestige American armed services had lost in Vietnam and confirmed American status as the only remaining military superpower. Though conventional weapons did most of the damage to Iraq, the military's "high-tech gadgets," as *Newsweek* wrote, "seemed to work with surgical lethality," and the war for Americans watching on television "seemed effortless, antiseptic." Victory freed Kuwait, as Bush had promised, and satisfied his other stated purpose, because oil prices, which rose while war threatened, receded as Saudi Arabia began to pump more than enough oil to meet demand. Quick victory also restored a patriotic pride among Americans that grew into a self-satisfied jingoism as the troops returned. Postwar polls showed 89 percent of respondents—an unprecedented figure—approving of Bush's conduct of his office. His forceful leadership was paying political dividends. National pride enveloped the men and women who fought in the Gulf War and imbued their enthusiastic welcome home. Valor in battle had drawn no lines of race or gender. Proportionate to their number in the population, black Americans carried a heavier burden of the fighting than did their white fellow citizens. General Powell, the first black American to be chair of the Joint Chiefs of Staff, became a national hero. Women in combat fought as bravely as men. One among many courageous women, Major Marie Rossi won national acclaim after her death when her helicopter crashed. As a feminist journalist wryly observed, in the Gulf War, women proved their right to equal access to body bags.

But within six months, the euphoria of victory began to fade. Victory had not lessened Saddam Hussein's control over Iraq. Soon after the cease-fire, his army put down a Shiite rebellion and forced the Kurds in Iraq, whom Bush had urged to overthrow Saddam, to flee to Iran and Turkey. They were able to return only with belated American assistance and protection. In the summer of 1991, United Nations inspections, which Saddam impeded, disclosed the continued existence of Iraqi nuclear facilities and stocks of chemical and biological weapons. Though the UN acted to remove those dangers, American bombing had obviously been less effective than it had seemed. A year after the war began, Iraq was well along in rebuilding the infrastructure the coalition had destroyed. The emir of Kuwait and his family returned to their homeland but made no effort to democratize the country, which remained an oligarchy governed for the benefit of its rulers, much as Saudi Arabia also was. Instability still characterized the Persian Gulf area, as Arab members of the coalition drifted apart and neglected their common defense, and as Iran, still hostile to the United States, undertook a crash program of rearmament that forbode new dangers. Successful resistance to any renewed aggression in the region would require another major intervention.

Though the American, British, and French hostages held in Lebanon were released late in 1991, terrorism continued between Jews and Muslims in Palestine. After indefatigable negotiations, Secretary Baker succeeded in bringing together for a peace conference representatives of Israel, its Arab neighbors, and the

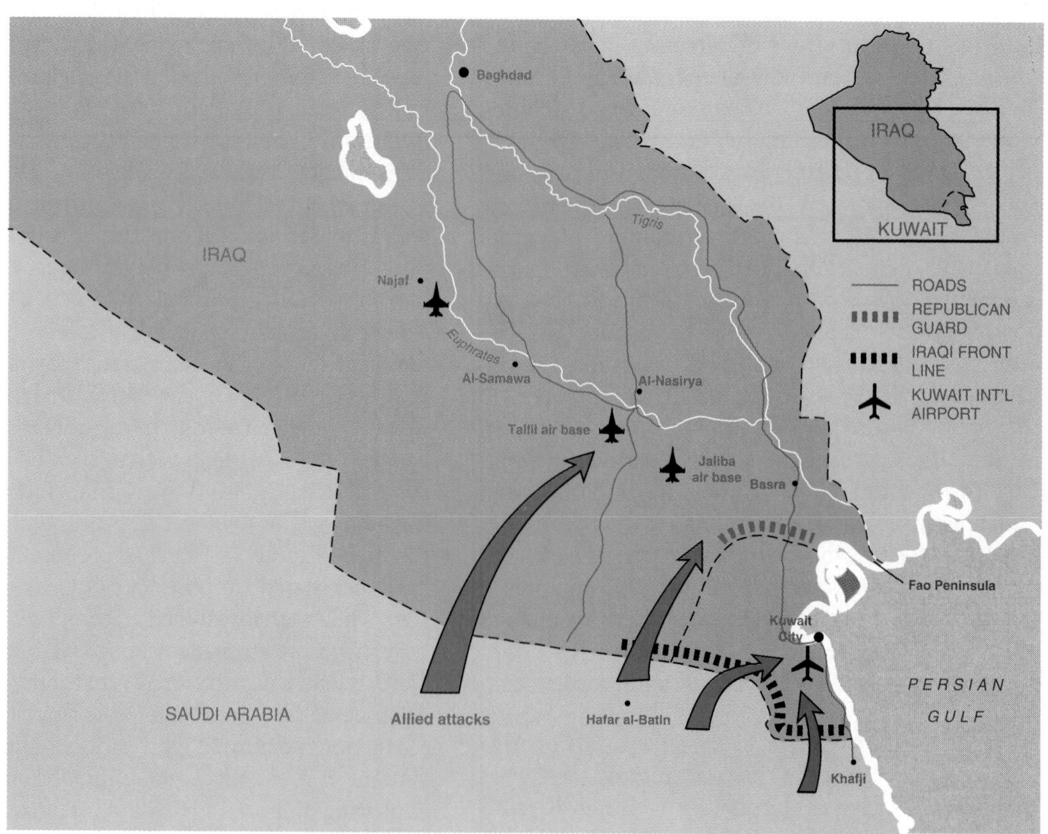

Map 35-1 *Operation Desert Storm*

Devastation in Iraq

PLO. First in Madrid and then early in 1992 in Washington, they began talking to each other, but the talks were surly and inconclusive. With Russian Jews reaching Israel steadily and Israel settling new villages in Palestine, prospects for a genuine peace were remote.

During the war President Bush welcomed a new world order. A year after the war had begun, no new order had emerged. The nations of western Europe were drawing together in the European Economic Community (EEC), but their political differences retarded unification, and Great Britain and France were openly anxious about renascent Germany. The British rejected a proposed common currency; the Germans for their part set monetary policy with little regard for the needs of the other nations in the EEC; and the United States and Japan feared that the protectionist Europeans would lock them out of the continent's huge market. Eastern European countries wanted to join that market but were not yet welcome. Like the former Soviet Union, the former Warsaw Pact nations were torn by internal conflict and handicapped by lagging economies neither wholly controlled nor wholly free. Communism still prevailed in China, and China, Israel, and probably Pakistan and India had nuclear weapons over which the UN lacked effective control. The Bush administration had no clear policies for addressing those formidable conditions. It did not even attempt to pay American dues, so long arrear, to the United Nations. The United States, its national debt multiplied during the Reagan and Bush years and its own economy in disarray, could not afford to police the world even if that had been Bush's intention. The national will for such a task seemed to have spent itself in the Persian Gulf.

A growing recognition of the limits of victory contributed to a decline in the president's popularity. Some of that popularity had been attributable to the administration's success in managing the news from the gulf. As Anthony Lewis wrote in the *New York Times:* "Most of the press was not a detached observer of the war, much less a critical one. It was a claque

The Pentagon's New World Order, 1992

The first objective is to prevent the re-emergence of a new rival, either on the territory of the former Soviet Union or elsewhere, that poses a threat on the order of that posed formerly by the Soviet Union. This . . . requires that we endeavor to prevent any hostile power from dominating a region whose resources would . . . be sufficient to generate global power. . . .

The U.S. must show the leadership necessary to establish and protect a new order that holds the promise of convincing potential competitors that they need not aspire to a greater role. . . . In the non-defense areas, we must account sufficiently for the interests of the advanced industrial nations to discourage them from challenging our leadership or seeking to overturn the established political and economic order. Finally, we must maintain the mechanisms for detering potential competitors from even aspiring to a larger regional or global role.

Quoted in the *New York Times,* March 8, 1992

applauding the American generals and politicians in charge." The television networks, with the occasional exception of CNN, transmitted largely official images of painless battles. The media did not much inform Americans about the destruction of the Iraqi infrastructure, the foundation of a modernizing society, or about the millions of people left without electricity, running water, or sewage. Rarely did the press mention Iraqi deaths. By and large the media had failed to question the necessity or the wisdom of the war. Most journalists accepted uncritically Bush's glib identification of Saddam Hussein with Hitler and accepted, too, dubious and exaggerated Kuwaiti versions of Iraqi atrocities. Much of the blame for those shortcomings belonged to the military, which, as with the Panamanian invasion, limited the reporting of the war by confining it to small, controlled pools of journalists and by censoring their reports. But as Lewis observed, journalists were themselves to blame for "forsaking the independence and skepticism that justify freedom of the press." When the whole story of the war began to enter the news after the fighting was over, the contrived glamor of the conflict started to fade. The resulting disenchantment fed a resurgent isolationism that marked the politics of 1992.

POLITICS AS USUAL

Questions of Ethics That impulse to turn inward arose primarily from public irritation about domestic problems, especially the languishing economy. From the time of his inauguration, Bush faltered in his approach to domestic issues. His advisers lacked the experience, sophistication, and concord of the small group who counseled him on foreign policy. Former New Hampshire governor John Sununu, for three years the president's arrogant and contentious chief of staff, interfered with initiatives that did not emanate from the Republican right wing. Vice President Quayle assisted Sununu's cause. They made it difficult for kinder, gentler policies to emerge. Bush himself, at his congenial and informed best in personal relationships with other world leaders, had trouble defining domestic goals. Ordinarily he let his sense of political expediency set his social and economic priorities. Perhaps on those accounts, he seemed petulant in the face of criticism, sly in his search for partisan advantage.

In the fractious political temper that followed Bush's election, Democrats in the Senate pounced on their former Republican colleague, John Tower of Texas, whom Bush had nominated as secretary of defense. After hearings that focused on Tower's drinking and womanizing, the Senate rejected him, the first Cabinet nominee in 30 years not to be confirmed. The score was evened when the House Ethics Committee reported that Speaker Jim Wright, a Texas Democrat, had violated House rules by accepting gifts and outside income that the rules forbade. Wright resigned in May 1989, as did Tony Coelho, the Democratic Whip, also accused of unethical behavior. Tom Foley of Washington, elected to succeed Wright as Speaker, urged an end to partisan controversy over ethics. Foley had a sure sense of decorum, but the sniping continued as did errant behavior by some members of the House of both parties. Neither party, moreover, made a genuine effort to prevent ethical abuses by regulating the use of money in political campaigns, the source of most questionable conduct.

Questions of Law In keeping with the tone of his presidential campaign, Bush hewed closely to Ronald Reagan's policies on social issues. As a candidate, Bush had made the pledge of allegiance his emblem of patriotism. As president he still wrapped himself in the flag. In June 1989 the Supreme Court ruled 5 to 4 that burning the American flag was a form of political protest protected by the First Amendment. Condemning that decision, Bush supported an amendment to the Constitution banning desecration of the flag. Congress passed a bill for that purpose but not the proposed amendment. Bush's critics noted the irony of the president's eagerness to limit political protest at the very time that much of the rest of the world yearned for the freedoms the Constitution guaranteed.

Bush also continued to oppose abortion. In *Webster* v. *Reproduction Health Services* (1989), the Supreme Court modified its decision in *Roe* v. *Wade* (p. 883). By a 5 to 4 majority it now upheld a Missouri law prohibiting abortions unless the mother's life was in danger and requiring medical tests on any fetus more than 20 weeks old to determine whether it could live outside the womb. Right-to-life advocates, applauding that ruling, organized to bring other states to restrict abortions, a tactic Bush encouraged. As Planned Parenthood and other pro-choice groups organized on the opposite side of the question, frequent confrontations between the contestants kept abortion a divisive political issue through which the president expected to gain and hold conservative support.

To the same end, Bush endorsed Supreme Court decisions weakening affirmative action in hiring and promotion. In six related interpretations of statutory law, the Court shifted much of the burden of proof toward the employee alleging discrimination, and it limited the amount of damages for which affected employees could sue. In 1990 Bush vetoed a Democratic bill to mitigate the impact of those decisions. The measure, he said, would "have the effect of coercing business to adopt quotas" or face expensive litigation. That veto conformed to the mood of many white middle-class and blue-collar men who felt that women and minority groups, especially black Americans, were receiving unjust favoritism through affirmative action. The Democrats, denying that their bill established quotas, introduced a similar measure in 1991. Initially the president opposed it, too, but before the end of the year, developments partly of his own making forced him to reconsider.

Bush consistently made appointments to federal courts of judges who appeared to share his own views about the First Amendment, abortion, and affirmative action. In 1990, with the retirement of Associate Justice William Brennan, a sturdy liberal, Bush nominated to the Supreme Court Judge David Souter, a New Hampshire Republican whose few and insignificant rulings from the bench had disclosed no clear picture of his legal convictions. A laconic nonentity, Souter brought to the hearings on his confirmation a taciturnity that did not obscure his basic conservatism. Nevertheless, he easily won confirmation. In 1991 he joined the 5–4 majority in *Rust* v. *Sullivan,* a decision holding that the government could forbid doctors in federally funded clinics from discussing abortion with their patients. That restriction on the First Amendment freedom of speech fit the right-wing jurisprudence of Chief Justice William Rehnquist.

Upon the retirement in 1991 of Associate Justice Thurgood Marshall, another liberal, Bush acted to give Rehnquist an additional vote. In so doing he tried to exploit the question of race to his own advantage but inadvertently stirred up a major brouhaha. To replace Marshall, Bush named Judge Clarence Thomas, like Marshall a black American. An outspoken foe of affirmative action, Thomas had had little judicial experience. The American Bar Association gave him a competence rating of C. But the nomination of Thomas presented the Democrats in the Senate with the discomforting choice between accepting another second-rate conservative or rejecting a black American. After hearings in September 1991, during which Thomas evaded questions about abortion, the Senate Judiciary Committee divided 7–7, but the full Senate was expected to vote to confirm the nominee.

Outraged Americans

Early in October Americans learned that the Judiciary Committee had received an affidavit from Anita Hill, a law professor at the University of Oklahoma, charging Thomas with sexual harassment during the period 1981–83 while she was a member of his staff at the Equal Employment Opportunity Commission. Outraged by those charges, feminists demanded further hearings, which the Judiciary Committee held on national television. Hill's detailed testimony evoked Thomas's angry denial. They were both black Americans, but Thomas, suggesting that Democrats had leaked the news about the affidavit, denounced the hearings as a "high-tech lynching for uppity blacks." Only one of the two principals could have been telling the truth, but by a largely partisan vote of 52 to 48, the Senate confirmed Thomas. The obtrusive politics of the episode; the exposure it gave to the problem of sexual harassment, which Congress had slighted for so long; the charged feelings it provoked among women and black Americans alike—all those aspects of the affair drew national attention to civil rights and the Democratic bill on affirmative action.

At the same time, race had become a major issue in Louisiana, where David Duke, once a member of an American Nazi party, had won the Republican primary for governor by campaigning against foreigners, black Americans, and Jews. Those themes violated the sense of decency of most Americans. The president, who despised Duke, had to distance himself and his party from the rising nativism Duke was exploiting. Eager also to retrieve any loss of women's approval suffered during the Hill-Thomas affair, Bush now accepted a slightly modified version of the Democratic bill on affirmative action. The measure he signed was neither more nor less a "quota" bill than it had been. It significantly altered the bearing of the contravened Supreme Court decisions on affirmative action, it considerably eased suits brought by employees alleging racial or sexual discrimination against them, and it allowed employees who won those suits to collect large damages. Still, the interpretation of the application of the new act, like the interpretation of constitutional questions, would fall to a Supreme Court the conservatives controlled. The appointments made by Presidents Reagan and Bush would shape the law of the land for many years to come.

Education and Ecology Bush liked to call himself "the education president" and "the environment president." He talked about those issues, but in treating them he generally yielded to conservative opposition both to government spending and to federal regulation of business practices. The president appointed a national commission on educational goals. Its report recognized that American students were falling behind their contemporaries in Europe and Japan in their facility in science, mathematics, and language. They were failing to acquire the skills essential for gainful employment in a high-technology economy, and the paucity of adults with those skills retarded the national economic performance. To remedy those defects the commission set standards of achievement for both primary and secondary pupils. It urged state and local officials to meet those goals by improving teaching methods and facilities. But the states and localities had lost billions of dollars of annual federal support during the Reagan years, they lacked the funds to meet their existing obligations even though they were raising taxes, and Bush had no plan for providing new federal funds for local education. Federal support for financing loans to college students declined, and he approved only enough spending to adjust for inflation the budget for Head Start. At that level of financing, Head Start, a demonstrably successful educational program for disadvantaged young children, reached only a small percentage of those needing it. Bush did call for a controversial program of parental choice that would allow public money to follow children to private schools. Senator Edward Kennedy, speaking for the Democrats, rejected that "flawed proposal" to use tax dollars to support private education.

As "the environment president," Bush appointed informed and committed conservationists to the Environmental Protection Agency (EPA), which Reagan had gutted. The agency then issued new orders expensive for business interests but necessary and effective for preserving endangered species of fish, birds, and other wildlife. The EPA also urged the president to support tougher legislation for pure air and pure water. Public consciousness of the importance of that legislation grew when in 1989 the *Exxon Valdez,* an oil tanker, struck a reef and spilled thousands of gallons of oil into Alaskan waters, with devastating effects on national parks, the shoreline, and the local economy and fauna. Bush ordered the army and Coast Guard to assist in the cleanup, but neither he nor Congress acted to require oil companies to build tankers with double hulls that would prevent the kind of disaster the *Exxon Valdez* caused. The president yielded now to the ecologists, now to business pressures. In 1989 he signed a law to ease the effects of acid rain. It mandated a gradual 50 percent reduction in sulfur emissions from power plants burning coal. It also required the automobile industry to increase gradually the production of cars using fuels other than gasoline or diesel oil. But in 1991 Bush retreated. He put forward an energy plan to increase domestic production of oil by opening for exploration the Arctic Wildlife Refuge, some other Alaskan areas, and the continental shelf off the coasts of California and the Gulf of Mexico. He also opened vast areas of wetlands for development, and in 1992 his administration allowed logging in thousands of previously protected acres of forest in the Northwest. To the further dismay of environmentalists, he also recommended the development and use of nuclear power.

Bush liked to view himself as the foremost of world leaders, but when it came to preventing the warming of the earth, he stood near the rear of the pack. In 1989 the United States opposed an international declaration for banning by the year 2000 the production of chlorofluorocarbons (CFCs) that endangered the ozone layer. At the World Climate Conference of 1990, the United States, accompanied by the Soviet Union, prevented the establishment of firm targets for limiting emissions of carbon dioxide and other gases causing the "greenhouse effect." The United States did so again in 1992 at the United Nations Conference on Environment and Development. Bush then also paraded his priority interest in economic growth and jobs by refusing to sign an international biodiversity treaty—a treaty to protect existing species of flora and fauna—that he considered inhibiting for the American biotechnology industry. On ecological matters, the United States was not leading the world.

Political Economy The legacy of national debt that Reagan bequeathed to Bush, as well as Bush's own rash promise of "no new taxes," not only constrained federal spending but limited federal action on social problems and reduced the administration's flexibility in economic policy. During 1989 economic growth slowed. In the second half of 1990, with the decline continuing and unemployment edging up, most private economists considered the economy in recession. Bush and his advisers disagreed. They attributed the sluggishness to increased energy costs occasioned by the crisis in the Persian Gulf, and they acted only to persuade the Federal Reserve to reduce interest rates by half of 1 percent in order to induce more economic activity. In spite of the soaring expense of rescuing the savings and loan industry (see p. 925), the administration also urged Congress to accept a deflationary budget that would reduce the projected deficit of $250 billion. And Bush again proposed, as he had in 1989, lowering the capital gains tax, which he said would help the economy.

Congressional Democrats balked. Reducing the capital gains tax would benefit mostly the wealthy who owned stocks that had appreciated. They insisted therefore on offsetting such a change by raising the surtax on high incomes. But Bush had promised not to raise taxes. During talks with Democratic leaders to find some common ground, the White House backed down on capital gains and the two sides agreed on a budget package that included steep increases in excise taxes, a small increase in Medicare charges, and a cut in Medicare spending. Members of both parties in Congress rejected that solution, the Republicans holding that it would cost jobs, the Democrats that it bore too heavily on the middle class. Before negotiations resumed in October, Bush vetoed a stopgap spending bill. With talks again under way, he signed two others. He shifted back and forth about taxes. On October 29, 1991, the Congress at last approved a compromise acceptable to the president. It lifted the top surtax rate from 28 to 31 percent, gradually phased out income-tax exemptions for upper-income taxpayers, and raised the tax on gasoline, cigarettes, and beer. It also imposed a luxury tax on expensive automobiles, boats, furs, and jewelry, and raised Medicare premiums. In return for consenting to raise taxes, Bush obtained a budget agreement in which the Democrats committed Congress for five years to reduce expenditures in both of two categories, the military and the domestic, and to address each category separately. If it held, that arrangement would prevent the Democrats from trying to cut the military budget in order to increase social spending. But with the Cold War ending and the economy declining, budgetary rigidity could hamper federal attempts to devise corrective fiscal programs.

With victory in the Persian Gulf, the administration predicted a quick return of economic growth, but the gross national product did not pick up. During the summer and fall of 1991, unemployment reached a four-year high; housing construction fell off; bank failures increased, especially in New England; bankruptcies rose, especially in retailing; major industrial concerns, among them IBM and General Motors, announced plans for large layoffs of both managers and workers; and consumer confidence dropped. The

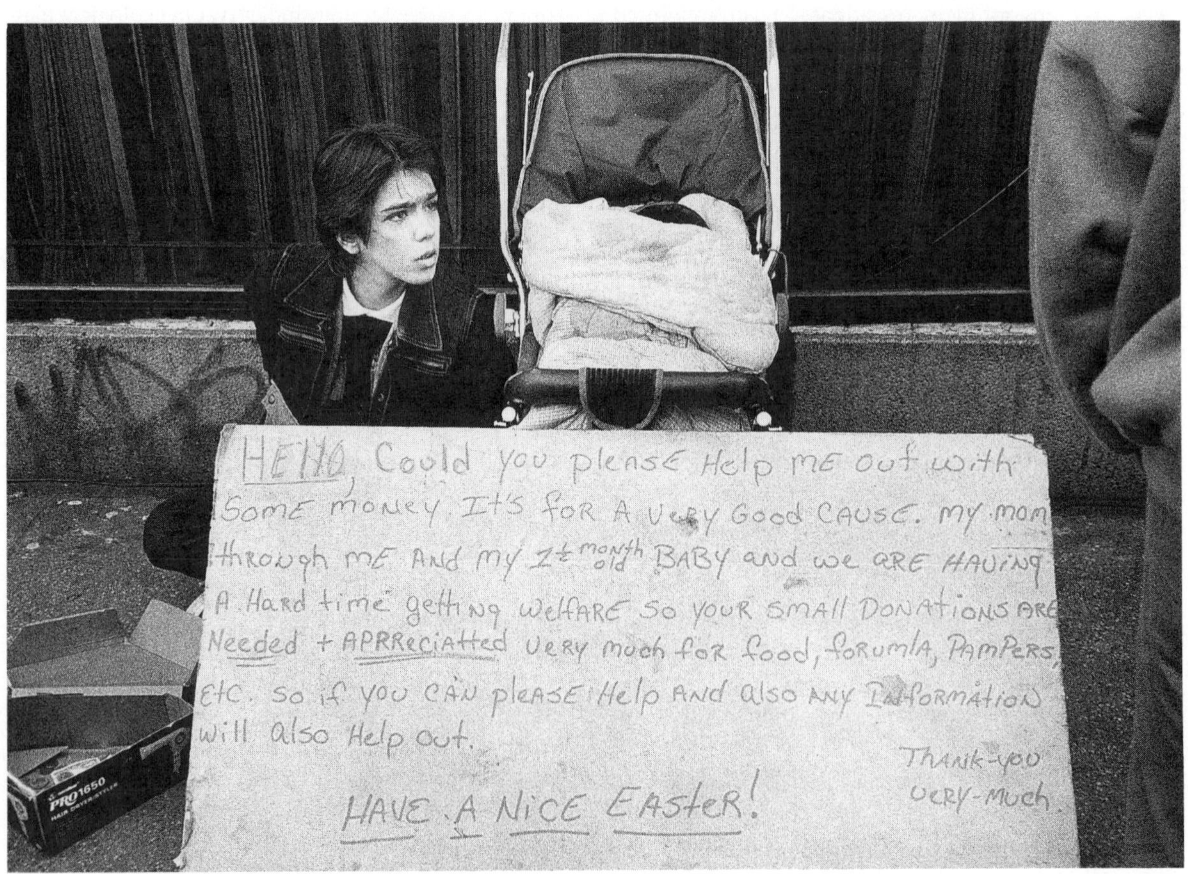

Unemployment was rising

Democrats had made small gains in the off-year elections of 1990. In 1991 in a special election, their senatorial candidate in Pennsylvania, Harris Wofford, a liberal veteran of the Kennedy administration, conducted a rousing campaign in which he attacked Republican economic policy. Wofford also stressed the need for a national medical policy to provide care for Americans without it, at least one-seventh of the population. Overcoming early odds against him, he defeated Bush's handpicked candidate, Richard Thornburgh, who had resigned as U.S. Attorney General in order to win what he believed to be a sure seat in the Senate. Wofford's victory exposed the vulnerability of the Republicans on economic and social issues. Heartened, Democrats for the first time since the Persian Gulf War began to think they might upset Bush in 1992.

The state of the economy also had other political ramifications. Economic stress, as it often had in the past, made Americans susceptible to nativist contentions that foreigners or members of minority groups were responsible for national woes. That scapegoating drew false plausibility from the heavy Hispanic and Asian immigration of the 1980s (see p. 934) and from the success of Japanese firms in gaining a growing share of the American market, particularly for automobiles. Many white males remained resentful about affirmative action. Playing to those biases, David Duke, after losing his race for governor in Louisiana, announced his candidacy for the Republican presidential nomination on an antiblack, anti-immigrant, anti-Semitic, and antiwelfare platform. A more serious challenge to the president came from journalist Patrick J. Buchanan, at one time a speech writer for Richard Nixon, when he also declared his candidacy. Buchanan, while less strident than Duke, had also sometimes seemed anti-Semitic. He appealed to the Republican right, castigating Bush for raising taxes and permitting the regulation of business. He had opposed the Gulf War and now criticized the president for neglecting domestic concerns. No one expected Buchanan to defeat Bush, but to counter his threat Bush had to lean further to the right. For Bush meant to win. "I'm certainly going into this as a dog-eat-dog fight," he told the press as the 1992 campaign got under way, "and I will do what I have to do to be reelected."

The polls showed his popularity falling, but he remained far ahead of any one of his rivals in either party. Bush ran hard. He reminded audiences of his leadership in the Gulf War. He berated "egghead liberals." He offered his own alternatives to Democratic plans for substantial cuts in military spending. In spite of the budget agreement of 1990, he proposed, as did the Democrats, using the "peace dividend" for domestic purpose. The crumbling national infrastructure needed an infusion of federal funds that would also spur the economy, but the White House and the Democrats alike saw greater political advantage in urging tax breaks for the middle class.

In December 1991 Bush postponed a diplomatic mission to Japan and other Asian countries in order to prove his concern about the recession, which he could no longer ignore. He had intended his trip to demonstrate the continuing commitment of the United States to the security of the Pacific area. Now he revised his travel plan, as he put it, for "jobs, jobs, jobs." To symbolize that purpose he expanded his entourage to include industrial leaders, among them the chief executives of General Motors, Ford, and Chrysler.

While talking free trade and open markets, Bush and his party asked Tokyo for help with American exports. He received only small concessions. But the president was trying to manage the market, just as the Japanese and the European Economic Community did. There had never been an entirely free market. There was no pure capitalism. Government had always operated to adjust the workings of capitalism to the perceived needs of the state. The countries emerging from communism were learning that lesson, and Americans had absorbed it, too. Some of them talked about the glory of a free market, but every economic group wanted government help for itself.

The excesses of the 1980s had left the United States with serious deficits in its social and economic capital, and many American industries had lost their competitive edge. Much of the responsibility for reconstruction belonged to the private sector. But as economists noted, government also had a role to play. Government could assist the development of new technologies in order to revive the economy and keep it competing internationally, could encourage business to apply more effective methods of management and of organizing work, could assure universal medical care and finance the education of the country's youth for useful employment. Only government could reverse the increasing polarization of rich and poor; only government could effectively promote justice, not the least for women and for people of color.

No presidential contender in 1992 chose to tell the American people just how he intended to meet national needs. As Bush maintained, domestic and international issues were inescapably related. But in the insular temper of the election year, neither the president nor his rivals explained how he would foster the nation's global interests in trade, immigration, human rights, the environment, the future of the former Soviet republics, or a nuclear-free world.

None of the Democratic candidates was a national figure, none said much about foreign policy, and no more than the president did any Democrat stand for a truly comprehensive domestic program based on a realistic budget. As the primary season rolled along, Governor Bill Clinton of Arkansas, a former Rhodes scholar, a political moderate with a strong record on civil rights, and the only Southerner in the field, moved into the lead. He called for a reduction in taxes on middle incomes to be offset by higher taxes on the rich. He also favored improved medical care, better schools, and an economic revival, but with few specific recommendations for reaching those goals and paying for them. Clinton showed strength among both black Americans and blue-collar Democrats. He denied charges of marital infidelity that hounded him, but he admitted that he had opposed the Vietnam War and resigned from the Reserve Officers' Training Corps in order to take his chances on the draft. He was not called up. He seemed vulnerable about those personal questions, because he did not answer them directly and completely when they were first asked. His critics called him "Slick Willie," but his supporters praised his stamina in the face of criticism and his record as governor.

Lagging Clinton in the Democratic primaries, former senator Paul Tsongas of Massachusetts, a candidate who played on his lack of glamour, talked about the need for economic discipline and sacrifice, opposed any tax cut, and won considerable support among college-educated and well-to-do voters. But Tsongas faded after a strong start and withdrew from the race. Former governor Jerry Brown of California, long a political maverick, attempted to reconstruct and expand the coalition that had supported Jesse Jackson in 1984 and 1988. Brown, who refused contributions in excess of $100, attacked the corruption he attributed to both parties, but his own record marked him as an insider rather than the rebel he tried to seem. Many observers considered him a spoiler rather than a potential nominee. By late April, Clinton had a commanding lead in delegates and was running evenly with Bush in public opinion polls.

For his part, the president, who now called his 1990 agreement to raise taxes an error, consistently defeated Pat Buchanan in Republican primaries, but some 20 to 30 percent of those voting regularly preferred either Buchanan or a slate of uncommitted delegates. That pattern suggested how much the weak economy had damaged the president's popularity.

L. A. Riots, May 1992

On April 29, rioting in central Los Angeles followed the verdict of a suburban jury that found Los Angeles policemen innocent of using undue force in beating a black motorist they had arrested. Television had repeatedly shown the brutality of that beating. Angered by the verdict and their own impoverished condition, gangs of youths, mostly black citizens, went on a two-day rampage of burning and looting, especially of local businesses owned by Korean merchants. The president was slow to criticize the verdict but quick to condemn the rioting. He recommended a $500 million federal grant to help restore the affected area but oppossed a larger appropriation that congressional Democrats favored. Bush's press secretary blamed the rioting on Great Society programs of the 1960s, and Vice President Quayle blamed them on a collapse of family values. Clinton, for his part, blamed 12 years of Republican neglect of the inner cities. But neither Bush nor Clinton made a positive impression on the electorate.

With polls showing pervasive disenchantment with all the candidates, H. Ross Perot, a Texas billionaire, began to organize to run as an independent. He had ample funds to do so, but no political experience and few known political beliefs. Utilizing television adroitly, Perot recruited hundreds of volunteers to circulate petitions to put his name on the ballot in all 50 states. He appealed to conservatives by speaking out against taxes, adultery, and homosexuality, but he was

Cycles of American Politics

History reminded Americans of an inherent cyclical rhythm in their politics, a continuing alteration between eras when private interests, private action, and private enterprise seem the best way of meeting problems and eras when the nation turns to public purposes and affirmative government.

Each of these eras runs its natural course. Public action, idealism and reform demand a high degree of popular participation. After a time people are worn out by the process and disenchanted by the results. They are ready to respond to leaders who tell them to stop worrying about public policy. . . . The pursuit of private interest is then seen as the means of social salvation. But that mood runs its course too. In time, rest recharges the national batteries; neglected problems become acute and threaten to become unmanageable . . . and the cycle turns again. . . . It is a 30-year cycle, as, in its progressive phase: Theodore Roosevelt in 1901, Franklin Roosevelt in 1933, John Kennedy in 1961.

Thirty years, after all, is the span of a generation. People tend to be formed politically by the ideals dominant in the years in which they attain political consciousness, roughly between 17 and 25. When their own generation's turn in power comes some thirty years later, they tend to carry forward ideas inbibed when young. . . . If the rhythm holds, the Kennedy generation's time was due to come in the 1990s, and Reagan's children would inaugurate a new conservative era about the year 2010.

From Arthur M. Schlesinger, Jr., in *The National Experience,* 7th ed., 1989

also pro-choice on the abortion issue. He remained evasive about his economic and social agenda, though he called for reduced spending and a tax on gasoline to balance the budget. In July, uncomfortable with the probings of the media, he announced his withdrawal from the campaign. The Democatic Party had "revitalized itself," Perot said, and he did not want to cause an electoral deadlock that would throw the election to Congress. But in October, returning to the race, he claimed he had withdrawn only to avoid Republican dirty tricks. By that time he had lost much of his following, many of whom remained disenchanted.

The Perot phenomenon, like the low turnout in primaries and caucuses for both parties, reflected the impatience of the electorate with politics as usual and the dissatisfaction of voters with the major parties and their presidential candidates. That mood worried incumbents at every level of government. An unprecedented number of members of Congress chose not to stand for reelection. Bush and Quayle, renominated by the Republicans, stressed "family values," a metaphor for the objectives of the religious right and for the attitudes of white ethnic groups and conservatives toward Americans of color and Americans on welfare. Emphasising, too, the importance of leadership, the president attacked Clinton as inexperienced and disingenuous. Bush also called for across-the-board tax cuts to be accompanied by unspecified reductions in federal spending.

The Democratic nominees, Governor Clinton and Senator Albert Gore of Tennessee, represented a new political generation, as they said, and expressed its eagerness for new policies, particularly those Clinton had been advocating. Gore stood for federal protection of the environment. Hilary Clinton, an accomplished lawyer and advocate of children's rights, as well as her husband's closest adviser, represented the successful professional woman in "The Year of the Woman." And Clinton, continuing to stress economic issues and the need for change, campaigned for federal initiatives to create new jobs, to improve the infrastructure, to assist public education, to expand and reform the delivery of health care, and to make American industry more competitive internationally.

The voters emphatically rejected Bush. He won only 38 percent of the popular vote and only 168 electoral votes. Perot, who carried only Maine but drew 19 percent of the popular vote, ran more strongly than any third-party candidate since Theodore Roosevelt in 1912. Clinton easily carried the electoral vote with 366 but attracted only 43 percent of the popular vote, too little to constitute a clear mandate. Still, the Democrats maintained large majorities in both houses of Congress, thereby ending twelve years of divided government, and voter turnout jumped more than 10 percent above that in 1988, an indication of renewed interest in politics.

Four women won their races for the Senate and twenty-four additional seats went to women in the House. Indeed, Clinton's victory reflected the decision of a majority of women, including a majority of white women, to vote Democratic, as did a majority of residents of suburbs. The Anita Hill hearings and the abortion issue obviously helped Clinton. Black Americans and Hispanic Americans also favored him. The president-elect promised that his cabinet would "look like America." He selected for the major positions in the executive branch an unprecedented proportion of women and minority appointees, as well as a large contingent of former members of Congress. Considered as a whole, Clinton's choices conformed to his commitments to youth, to social activism, and to sound economic policy. They were experienced men and women, educated for their responsibilities, politically adroit. The new administration seemed prepared to energize government to address the issues of the 1990s.

SUGGESTIONS FOR READING

THE STATE OF THE NATION

P. Kennedy, *The Rise and Fall of the Great Powers* (1987), advances the thesis of "imperial overstretch" with abundant historical illustration. For a contrary thesis, see J. S. Nye, Jr., *Bound to Lead* (1990), and H. R. Nau, *The Myth of America's Decline* (1990). For the "graying of America," see P. Longman, *Born to Pay: the New Politics of Aging in America* (1987). R. Fishman, *Bourgeois Utopias: the Rise and Fall of Suburbia* (1987), describes the vicissitudes of the suburban dream. R. H. K. Victor, *Energy Policy in America Since 1945* (1984), is a cogent study.

J. Crewdson, *The Tarnished Door* (1983), surveys immigration problems. E. D. Baltzell, *The Protestant Establishment* (1964), depicts the WASP at bay. S. Udall, *To the Inland Empire* (1987), is an engaging account of the Spanish contribution in American history; and P. S. J. Cafferty and W. McReady, eds., *Hispanics in the United States: A New Social Agenda* (1984), is a useful introduction. On black Americans, see W. J. Wilson, *The Declining Significance of Race* (1978), and for a conservative view, T. Sowell, *Civil Rights: Rhetoric or Reality?* (1984). Works on the American Indian include A. M. Josephy, ed., *Red Power: the American Indians' Fight for Freedom* (1985), and A. M. Josephy, *Now That the Buffalo's Gone: A Study of Today's American Indians* (1982). On some of the problems of pluralism, see A. M. Schlesinger, Jr., *The Disuniting of America* (1991).

Betty Friedan, *The Second Stage* (1981), points to new directions for liberated women. M. F. Berry, *Why ERA Failed* (1986), and J. Mansbridge, *Why We Lost the ERA* (1986), are scholarly discussions. J. D'Emilio, *Sexual Politics, Sexual Communities: The Making of a Homosexual Minority in the United States* (1983), describes the emergence of homosexuals. R. Shilts, *And the Band Played On: Politics, People and the AIDS Epidemic* (1987), is a pioneering study. Also illuminating are L. Gordon, *Woman's Body, Woman's Right: A Social History of Birth Control in America* (1976); J. C. Mohr, *Abortion in America* (1978); J. Reed, *The Birth Control Movement and American Society* (1983 ed.); C. N. Degler, *At Odds: Women and the Family in America* (1980); and J. D'Emilio and E. Freedman, *Intimate Matters: A History of Sexuality in America* (1988).

CULTURE

D. Ravaitch, *The Troubled Crusade: American Education, 1945–1980* (1983), is an intelligent critical account. D. Ravitch and C. Finn, Jr., *What Do Our 17-Year-Olds Know?* (1987), is a discouraging report; so, too, is E. D. Hirsch, *Cultural Literacy* (1987). A. Bloom, *The Closing of the American Mind* (1987), is a pretentious and murky polemic against relativism in the name of (unspecified) absolute values; its popular success was a symptom of the national anxiety over the quality of American education.

Marshall McLuhan's eccentric but suggestive ideas can be traced in *The Gutenberg Galaxy* (1962), *Understanding Media* (1964), and *The Medium Is the Message* (1967). D. J. Czitrom, *Media and the American Mind* (1982), and J. Meyrowitz, *No Sense of Place: The Impact of Electronic Media on Social Behavior* (1984), are stimulating analyses.

For the social history of movies, see R. Sklar, *Movie-Made America* (1975), and C. Jowett, *Film: the Democratic Art* (1976).

On literature, A. Kazin, *The Bright Book of Life* (1973), is a leading critic's rich discussion of novelists from Hemingway to Mailer. W. Berthoff, *A Literature without Qualities: American Writing Since 1945* (1979), is a sensitive account. F. Karl explains and defends literary modernism in *American Fictions: 1940–1980* (1984). J. N. Shurkin, *Engines of the Mind: A History of the Computer* (1984), recounts the evolution of the new technology; J. D. Bolter, *Turing's Man: Western Culture in the Computer Age* (1984), and S. Turkle, *The Second Self* (1984), attempt to assess the computer's impact on culture and society. T. Wolfe, *The Right Stuff* (1979), describes the first astronauts. G. O'Neill, *The High Frontier* (1977), considers the possibility of human colonies in space. The case for the existence of other beings in the universe is analyzed in P. Morrison et al., eds., *The Search for Extraterrestrial Intelligence* (1977); C. Sagan and I. S. Shklovsky, *Intelligent Life in the Universe* (1968), and Sagan, *The Cosmic Connection* (1973). J. Schell, *The Fate of the Earth* (1982), is an eloquent meditation on the possibility of human extinction.

On the Bush administration, K. Buckley, *Panama: the Whole Story* (1991), fulfills the promise of its title. Bob Woodward, *The Commanders* (1991), deals with both Panama and the Gulf War from the perspective of the Joint Chiefs of Staff. On the Gulf War, see also D. E. Decosse, ed., *But Was It Just?* (1992); J. E. Smith, *George Bush's War* (1992); and U.S. News and World Report, *Triumph without Victory* (1992). A. S. Blinder, *Growing Together: An Alternative Economic Strategy for the 1990s* (1991), discusses domestic policies that would produce a kinder, gentler America.

APPENDIX A

THE DECLARATION OF INDEPENDENCE

THE CONSTITUTION OF THE UNITED STATES OF AMERICA

ADMISSION OF STATES

POPULATION OF THE UNITED STATES

THE DECLARATION OF INDEPENDENCE

THE UNANIMOUS DECLARATION OF THE THIRTEEN UNITED STATES OF AMERICA,

WHEN in the Course of human events it becomes necessary for one people to dissolve the political bands which have connected them with another, and to assume among the Powers of the earth, the separate and equal station to which the Laws of Nature and of Nature's God entitle them, a decent respect to the opinions of mankind requires that they should declare the causes which impel them to the separation.

We hold these truths to be self-evident, that all men are created equal, that they are endowed by their Creator with certain unalienable Rights, that among these are Life, Liberty and the pursuit of Happiness. That to secure these rights, Governments are instituted among Men, deriving their just Powers from the consent of the governed. That whenever any Form of Government becomes destructive of these ends, it is the Right of the People to alter or to abolish it, and to institute new Government, laying its foundation on such principles and organizing its Powers in such form, as to them shall seem most likely to effect their Safety and Happiness. Prudence, indeed, will dictate that Governments long established should not be changed for light and transient causes; and accordingly all experience hath shewn, that mankind are more disposed to suffer, while evils are sufferable, than to right themselves by abolishing the forms to which they are accustomed. But when a long train of abuses and usurpations, pursuing invariably the same Object evinces a design to reduce them under absolute Despotism, it is their right, it is their duty, to throw off such Government, and to provide new Guards for their future security. Such has been the patient sufferance of these Colonies; and such is now the necessity which constrains them to alter their former Systems of Government. The history of the present King of Great Britain is a history of repeated injuries and usurpations, all having in direct object the establishment of an absolute Tyranny over these States. To prove this, let Facts be submitted to a candid world.

He has refused his Assent to Laws, the most wholesome and necessary for the public good.

He has forbidden his Governors to pass Laws of immediate and pressing importance, unless suspended in their operation till his Assent should be obtained; and when so suspended, he has utterly neglected to attend to them.

He has refused to pass other Laws for the accommodation of large districts of people, unless those people would relinquish the right of Representation in the Legislature, a right inestimable to them and formidable to tyrants only.

He has called together legislative bodies at places unusual, uncomfortable, and distant from the depository of their Public Records, for the sole Purpose of fatiguing them into compliance with his measures.

He has dissolved Representative Houses repeatedly, for opposing with manly firmness his invasions on the rights of the People.

He has refused for a long time, after such dissolutions, to cause others to be elected; whereby the Legislative Powers, incapable of Annihilation, have returned to the People at large for their exercise; the State remaining in the mean time exposed to all the dangers of invasion from without, and convulsions within.

He has endeavoured to prevent the Population of these States; for that purpose obstructing the Laws for Naturalization of Foreigners; refusing to pass others to encourage their migrations hither, and raising the conditions of new Appropriations of Lands.

He has obstructed the Administration of Justice, by refusing his Assent to Laws for establishing Judiciary Powers.

He has made Judges dependent on his Will alone, for the tenure of their offices, and the amount and payment of their salaries.

He has erected a multitude of New Offices, and sent hither swarms of Officers to harrass our People, and eat out their substance.

He has kept among us, in times of peace, Standing Armies without the Consent of our legislatures.

He has affected to render the Military independent of and superior to the Civil Power.

He has combined with others to subject us to a jurisdiction foreign to our constitution, and unacknowledged by our laws; giving his Assent to their Acts of pretended Legislation:

For Quartering large bodies of armed troops among us:

For protecting them, by a mock Trial, from Punishment for any Murders which they should commit on the Inhabitants of these States:

For cutting off our Trade with all parts of the world:

For imposing Taxes on us without our Consent:

For depriving us in many cases, of the benefits of Trial by Jury:

For transporting us beyond Seas to be tried for pretended offences:

For abolishing the free System of English Laws in a neighbouring Province, establishing therein an Arbitrary government, and enlarging its Boundaries so as to render

*Reprinted from the facsimile of the engrossed copy in the National Archives. The original spelling, capitalization, and punctuation have been retained. Paragraphing has been added.

it at once an example and fit instrument for introducing the same absolute rule into these Colonies:

For taking away our Charters, abolishing our most valuable Laws, and altering fundamentally the Forms of our Governments:

For suspending our own Legislatures, and declaring themselves invested with Power to legislate for us in all cases whatsoever.

He has abdicated Government here, by declaring us out of his Protection, and waging War against us.

He has plundered our seas, ravaged our Coasts, burnt our towns, and destroyed the lives of our people.

He is at this time transporting large Armies of foreign Mercenaries to compleat the works of death, desolation and tyranny, already begun with circumstances of Cruelty and perfidy scarcely paralleled in the most barbarous ages, and totally unworthy the Head of a civilized nation.

He has constrained our fellow Citizens taken Captive on the high Seas to bear Arms against their Country, to become the executioners of their friends and Brethren, or to fall themselves by their Hands.

He has excited domestic insurrections amongst us, and has endeavoured to bring on the inhabitants of our frontiers, the merciless Indian Savages, whose known rule of warfare, is an undistinguished destruction of all ages, sexes and conditions.

In every stage of these Oppressions We have Petitioned for Redress in the most humble terms: Our repeated Petitions have been answered only by repeated injury. A Prince, whose character is thus marked by every act which may define a Tyrant, is unfit to be the ruler of a free People.

Nor have We been wanting in attentions to our Brittish brethren. We have warned them from time to time of attempts by their legislature to extend an unwarrantable jurisdiction over us. We have reminded them of the circumstances of our emigration and settlement here. We have appealed to their native justice and magnanimity, and we have conjured them by the ties of our common kindred to disavow these usurpations, which, would inevitably interrupt our connections and correspondence. They too have been deaf to the voice of justice and of consanguinity. We must, therefore, acquiesce in the necessity, which denounces our Separation, and hold them, as we hold the rest of mankind, Enemies in War, in Peace Friends.

WE, THEREFORE, the Representatives of the UNITED STATES OF AMERICA, in General Congress, Assembled, appealing to the Supreme Judge of the world for the rectitude of our intentions, do, in the Name, and by Authority of the good People of these Colonies, solemnly publish and declare, That these United Colonies are, and of Right ought to be FREE AND INDEPENDENT STATES; that they are Absolved from all Allegiance to the British Crown, and that all political connection between them and the State of Great Britain, is and ought to be totally dissolved; and that, as Free and Independent States, they have full Power to levy War, conclude Peace, contract Alliances, establish Commerce, and to do all other Acts and Things which Independent States may of right do. And for the support of this Declaration, with a firm reliance on the protection of divine Providence, we mutually pledge to each other our Lives, our Fortunes and our sacred Honor.

THE CONSTITUTION OF THE UNITED STATES OF AMERICA

We the People of the United States, in Order to form a more perfect Union, establish Justice, insure domestic Tranquility, provide for the common defence, promote the general Welfare, and secure the Blessings of Liberty to ourselves and our Posterity, do ordain and establish this Constitution for the United States of America.

Article. I.

Section. 1. All legislative Powers herein granted shall be vested in a Congress of the United States, which shall consist of a Senate and House of Representatives.

Section. 2. The House of Representatives shall be composed of Members chosen every second Year by the People of the several States, and the Electors in each State shall have the Qualifications requisite for Electors of the most numerous Branch of the State Legislature.

No Person shall be a Representative who shall not have attained to the Age of twenty five Years, and been seven Years a Citizen of the United States, and who shall not, when elected, be an Inhabitant of that State in which he shall be chosen.

Representatives and direct Taxes† shall be apportioned among the several States which may be included within this Union, according to their respective Numbers, which shall be determined by adding to the whole Number of free Persons, including those bound to Service for a Term of Years, and excluding Indians not taxed, three fifths of all other Persons.‡ The actual Enumeration shall be made within three Years after the first Meeting of the Congress of the United States, and within every subsequent Term of ten Years, in such Manner as they shall by Law direct. The Number of Representatives shall not exceed one for every thirty Thousand, but each State shall have at Least one Representative; and until such enumeration shall be made, the State of New Hampshire shall be entitled to chuse three; Massachusetts eight; Rhode Island and Providence Plantations one; Connecticut five; New York six; New Jersey four; Pennsylvania eight; Delaware one; Maryland six; Virginia ten; North Carolina five; South Carolina five; and Georgia three.

When vacancies happen in the Representation from any State, the Executive Authority thereof shall issue Writs of Election to fill such Vacancies.

The House of Representatives shall chuse their Speaker and other Officers; and shall have the sole Power of Impeachment.

Section. 3. The Senate of the United States shall be composed of two Senators from each State, chosen by the Legislature thereof, for six Years; and each Senator shall have one Vote.*

Immediately after they shall be assembled in Consequence of the first Election, they shall be divided as equally as may be into three Classes. The Seats of the Senators of the first Class shall be vacated at the Expiration of the second Year, of the second Class at the Expiration of the fourth Year, and of the third Class at the Expiration of the sixth Year, so that one third may be chosen every second Year; and if Vacancies happen by Resignation, or otherwise, during the Recess of the Legislature of any State, the Executive thereof may make temporary Appointments until the next Meeting of the Legislature, which shall then fill such Vacancies.†

No Person shall be a Senator who shall not have attained to the Age of thirty Years, and been nine Years a Citizen of the United States, and who shall not, when elected, be an Inhabitant of that State for which he shall be chosen.

The Vice President of the United States shall be President of the Senate, but shall have no Vote, unless they be equally divided.

The Senate shall chuse their other Officers, and also a President pro tempore, in the Absence of the Vice President, or when he shall exercise the Office of President of the United States.

The Senate shall have the sole Power to try all Impeachments. When sitting for that Purpose, they shall be on Oath or Affirmation. When the President of the United States is tried, the Chief Justice shall preside: And no Person shall be convicted without the Concurrence of two thirds of the Members present.

Judgment in Cases of Impeachment shall not extend further than to removal from Office, and disqualification to hold and enjoy any Office of honor, Trust or Profit under the United States: but the Party convicted shall nevertheless be liable and subject to Indictment, Trial, Judgment and Punishment, according to Law.

Section. 4. The Times, Places and Manner of holding Elections for Senators and Representatives, shall be prescribed in each State by the Legislature thereof, but the Congress may at any time by Law make or alter such Regulation, except as to the Places of chusing Senators.

The Congress shall assemble at least once in every Year, and such Meeting shall be on the first Monday in December, **unless they shall by Law appoint a different Day.‡**

*From the engrossed copy in the National Archives. Original spelling, capitalization, and punctuation have been retained.
†Modified by the Sixteenth Amendment.
‡Replaced by the Fourteenth Amendment.

*Superseded by the Seventeenth Amendment.
†Modified by the Seventeenth Amendment.
‡ Superseded by the Twentieth Amendment.

Section. 5. Each House shall be the Judge of the Elections, Returns and Qualifications of its own Members, and a Majority of each shall constitute a Quorum to do Business; but a smaller Number may adjourn from day to day, and may be authorized to compel the Attendance of absent Members, in such Manner, and under such Penalties as each House may provide.

Each House may determine the Rules of its Proceedings, punish its Members for disorderly Behaviour, and, with the Concurrence of two thirds, expel a Member.

Each House shall keep a Journal of its Proceedings, and from time to time publish the same, excepting such Parts as may in their Judgment require Secrecy; and the Yeas and Nays of the Members of either House on any question shall, at the Desire of one fifth of those Present, be entered on the Journal.

Neither House, during the Session of Congress, shall, without the Consent of the other, adjourn for more than three days, nor to any other Place than that in which the two Houses shall be sitting.

Section. 6. The Senators and Representatives shall receive a Compensation for their Services, to be ascertained by Law, and paid out of the Treasury of the United States. They shall in all Cases, except Treason, Felony and Breach of the Peace, be privileged from Arrest during their Attendance at the Session of their respective Houses, and in going to and returning from the same; and for any Speech or Debate in either House, they shall not be questioned in any other Place.

No Senator or Representative shall, during the Time for which he was elected, be appointed to any civil Office under the Authority of the United States, which shall have been created, or the Emoluments whereof shall have been encreased during such time; and no Person holding any Office under the United States, shall be a Member of either House during his Continuance in Office.

Section. 7. All Bills for raising Revenue shall originate in the House of Representatives; but the Senate may propose or concur with Amendments as on other Bills.

Every Bill which shall have passed the House of Representatives and the Senate shall, before it become a Law, be presented to the President of the United States; If he approve he shall sign it, but if not he shall return it, with his Objections to that House in which it shall have originated, who shall enter the Objections at large on their Journal, and proceed to reconsider it. If after such Reconsideration two thirds of that House shall agree to pass the Bill, it shall be sent, together with the Objections, to the other House, by which it shall likewise be reconsidered, and if approved by two thirds of that House, it shall become a Law. But in all such Cases the Votes of both Houses shall be determined by yeas and Nays, and the Names of the Persons voting for and against the Bill shall be entered on the Journal of each House respectively. If any Bill shall not be returned by the President within ten Days (Sundays excepted) after it shall have been presented to him, the Same shall be a Law, in like Manner as if he had signed it, unless the Congress by their Adjournment prevent its Return, in which Case it shall not be a Law.

Every Order, Resolution, or Vote to which the Concurrence of the Senate and House of Representatives may be necessary (except on a question of Adjournment) shall be presented to the President of the United States; and before the Same shall take Effect, shall be approved by him, or being disapproved by him shall be repassed by two thirds of the Senate and House of Representatives, according to the Rules and Limitations prescribed in the Case of a Bill.

Section. 8. The Congress shall have Power To lay and collect Taxes, Duties, Imposts and Excises, to pay the Debts and provide for the common Defence and general Welfare of the United States; but all Duties, Imposts and Excises shall be uniform throughout the United States;

To borrow Money on the credit of the United States;

To regulate Commerce with foreign Nations, and among the several States, and with the Indian Tribes;

To establish an uniform Rule of Naturalization, and uniform Laws on the subject of Bankruptcies throughout the United States;

To coin Money, regulate the Value thereof, and of foreign Coin, and fix the Standard of Weights and Measures;

To provide for the Punishment of counterfeiting the Securities and current Coin of the United States;

To establish Post Offices and post Roads;

To promote the Progress of Science and useful Arts, by securing for limited Times to Authors and Inventors the exclusive Right to their respective Writings and Discoveries;

To constitute Tribunals inferior to the supreme Court;

To define and punish Piracies and Felonies committed on the high Seas, and Offences against the Law of Nations;

To declare War, grant Letters of Marque and Reprisal, and make Rules concerning Captures on Land and Water;

To raise and support Armies, but no Appropriation of Money to that Use shall be for a longer Term than two Years;

To provide and maintain a Navy;

To make Rules for the Government and Regulation of the land and naval Forces;

To provide for calling forth the Militia to execute the Laws of the Union, suppress Insurrections and repel Invasions;

To provide for organizing, arming, and disciplining, the Militia, and for governing such Part of them as may be employed in the Service of the United States, reserving to the States respectively, the Appointment of the Officers, and the Authority of training the Militia according to the discipline prescribed by Congress;

To exercise exclusive Legislation in all Cases whatsoever, over such District (not exceeding ten Miles square) as may, by Cession of particular States, and the Acceptance of

Congress, become the Seat of the Government of the United States, and to exercise like Authority over all Places purchased by the Consent of the Legislature of the State in which the Same shall be, for the Erection of Forts, Magazines, Arsenals, dock-Yards, and other needful Buildings;—And

To make all Laws which shall be necessary and proper for carrying into Execution the foregoing Powers, and all other Powers vested by this Constitution in the Government of the United States, or in any Department or Officer thereof.

Section. 9. The Migration or Importation of such Persons as any of the States now existing shall think proper to admit, shall not be prohibited by the Congress prior to the Year one thousand eight hundred and eight, but a Tax or duty may be imposed on such Importation, not exceeding ten dollars for each Person.

The Privilege of the Writ of Habeas Corpus shall not be suspended, unless when in Cases of Rebellion or Invasion the public Safety may require it.

No Bill of Attainder or ex post facto Law shall be passed.

No Capitation, or other direct, Tax shall be laid, unless in Proportion to the Census or Enumeration herein before directed to be taken.

No Tax or Duty shall be laid on Articles exported from any State.

No Preference shall be given by any Regulation of Commerce or Revenue to the Ports of one State over those of another: nor shall Vessels bound to, or from, one State, be obliged to enter, clear, or pay Duties in another.

No Money shall be drawn from the Treasury, but in Consequence of Appropriations made by Law, and a regular Statement and Account of the Receipts and Expenditures of all public Money shall be published from time to time.

No Title of Nobility shall be granted by the United States: And no Person holding any Office of Profit or Trust under them, shall, without the Consent of the Congress, accept of any present, Emolument, Office, or Title, of any kind whatever, from any King, Prince, or foreign State.

Section. 10. No State shall enter into any Treaty, Alliance, or Confederation; grant Letters of Marque and Reprisal; coin Money; emit Bills of Credit; make any Thing but gold and silver Coin a Tender in Payment of Debts; pass any Bill of Attainder, ex post facto Law, or Law impairing the Obligation of Contracts, or grant any Title of Nobility.

No State shall, without the Consent of the Congress, lay any Imposts or Duties on Imports or Exports, except what may be absolutely necessary for executing its inspection Laws: and the net Produce of all Duties and Imposts, laid by any State on Imports or Exports, shall be for the Use of the Treasury of the United States; and all such Laws shall be subject to the Revision and Controul of the Congress.

No State shall, without the Consent of Congress, lay any Duty of Tonnage, keep Troops, or Ships of War in time of Peace, enter into any Agreement or Compact with another State, or with a foreign Power, or engage in War, unless actually invaded, or in such imminent Danger as will not admit of delay.

Article. II.

Section. 1. The executive Power shall be vested in a President of the United States of America. He shall hold his Office during the Term of four Years, and, together with the Vice President, chosen for the same Term, be elected, as follows:

Each State shall appoint, in such Manner as the Legislature thereof may direct, a Number of Electors, equal to the whole Number of Senators and Representatives to which the State may be entitled in the Congress: but no Senator or Representative, or Person holding an Office of Trust or Profit under the United States, shall be appointed an Elector.

The Electors shall meet in their respective States, and vote by Ballot for two Persons, of whom one at least shall not be an Inhabitant of the same State with themselves. And they shall make a List of all the Persons voted for, and of the Number of Votes for each; which List they shall sign and certify, and transmit sealed to the Seat of the Government of the United States, directed to the President of the Senate. The President of the Senate shall, in the Presence of the Senate and House of Representatives, open all the Certificates, and the Votes shall then be counted. The Person having the greatest Number of Votes shall be the President, if such Number be a Majority of the whole Number of Electors appointed; and if there be more than one who have such Majority, and have an equal Number of Votes, then the House of Representatives shall immediately chuse by Ballot one of them for President; and if no Person have a Majority, then from the five highest on the List the said House shall in like Manner chuse the President. But in chusing the President, the Votes shall be taken by States, the Representation from each State having one Vote; A quorum for this Purpose shall consist of a Member or Members from two thirds of the States, and a Majority of all the States shall be necessary to a Choice. In every Case, after the Choice of the President, the Person having the greatest Number of Votes of the Electors shall be the Vice President. But if there should remain two or more who have equal Votes, the Senate shall chuse from them by Ballot the Vice President.*

The Congress may determine the Time of chusing the Electors, and the Day on which they shall give their Votes; which Day shall be the same throughout the United States.

*Superseded by the Twelfth Amendment.

No Person except a natural born Citizen, or a Citizen of the United States, at the time of the Adoption of this Constitution, shall be eligible to the Office of President, neither shall any Person be eligible to that Office who shall not have attained to the Age of thirty five Years, and been fourteen Years a Resident within the United States.

In Case of the Removal of the President from Office, or of his Death, Resignation, or Inability to discharge the Powers and Duties of the said Office, the Same shall devolve on the Vice President, and the Congress may by Law provide for the Case of Removal, Death, Resignation or Inability, both of the President and Vice President, declaring what Officer shall then act as President, and such Officer shall act accordingly, until the Disability be removed, or a President shall be elected.*

The President shall, at stated Times, receive for his Services, a Compensation, which shall neither be encreased nor diminished during the Period for which he shall have been elected, and he shall not receive within that Period any other Emolument from the United States, or any of them.

Before he enter on the Execution of his Office, he shall take the following Oath or Affirmation:—"I do solemnly swear (or affirm) that I will faithfully execute the Office of President of the United States, and will to the best of my Ability, preserve, protect and defend the Constitution of the United States."

Section. 2. The President shall be Commander in Chief of the Army and Navy of the United States, and of the Militia of the several States, when called into the actual Service of the United States; he may require the Opinion, in writing, of the principal Officer in each of the executive Departments, upon any Subject relating to the Duties of their respective Offices, and he shall have Power to grant Reprieves and Pardons for Offences against the United States, except in Cases of Impeachment.

He shall have Power, by and with the Advice and Consent of the Senate, to make Treaties, provided two thirds of the Senators present concur; and he shall nominate, and by and with the Advice and Consent of the Senate, shall appoint Ambassadors, other public Ministers and Consuls, Judges of the supreme Court, and all other Officers of the United States, whose Appointments are not herein otherwise provided for, and which shall be established by Law; but the Congress may by Law vest the Appointment of such inferior Officers, as they think proper, in the President alone, in the Courts of Law, or in the Heads of Departments.

The President shall have Power to fill up all Vacancies that may happen during the Recess of the Senate, by granting Commissions which shall expire at the End of their next Session.

Section. 3. He shall from time to time give to the Congress Information of the State of the Union, and recommend to their Consideration such Measures as he shall judge necessary and expedient; he may, on extraordinary Occasions, convene both Houses, or either of them, and in Case of Disagreement between them, with Respect to the Time of Adjournment, he may adjourn them to such Time as he shall think proper; he shall receive Ambassadors and other public Ministers; he shall take Care that the Laws be faithfully executed, and shall Commission all the Officers of the United States.

Section. 4. The President, Vice President and all civil Officers of the United States, shall be removed from Office on Impeachment for, and Conviction of, Treason, Bribery, or other high Crimes and Misdemeanors.

* Modified by the Twenty-fifth Amendment.

Article. III.

Section. 1. The judicial Power of the United States, shall be vested in one supreme Court, and in such inferior Courts as the Congress may from time to time ordain and establish. The Judges, both of the supreme and inferior Courts, shall hold their Offices during good Behaviour, and shall, at stated Times, receive for their Services, a Compensation, which shall not be diminished during their Continuance in Office.

Section. 2. The judicial Power shall extend to all Cases, in Law and Equity, arising under this Constitution, the Laws of the United States, and Treaties made, or which shall be made, under their Authority;—to all Cases affecting Ambassadors, other public Ministers and Consuls;—to all Cases of admiralty and maritime Jurisdiction;—to Controversies to which the United States shall be a Party;—to Controversies between two or more States;—between a State and Citizens of another State;*—between Citizens of different States,—between Citizens of the same State claiming Lands under Grants of different States, and between a State, or the Citizens thereof, and foreign States, Citizens or Subjects.

In all Cases affecting Ambassadors, other public Ministers and Consuls, and those in which a State shall be Party, the supreme Court shall have original Jurisdiction. In all the other Cases before mentioned, the supreme Court shall have appellate Jurisdiction, both as to Law and Fact, with such Exceptions, and under such Regulations as the Congress shall make.

The Trial of all Crimes, except in Cases of Impeachment, shall be by Jury; and such Trial shall be held in the State where the said Crimes shall have been committed; but when not committed within any State, the Trial shall be at such Place or Places as the Congress may by Law have directed.

Section. 3. Treason against the United States, shall consist only in levying War against them, or in adhering to their

*Modified by the Eleventh Amendment.

Enemies, giving them Aid and Comfort. No Person shall be convicted of Treason unless on the Testimony of two Witnesses to the same overt Act, or on Confession in open Court.

The Congress shall have Power to declare the Punishment of Treason, but no Attainder of Treason shall work Corruption of Blood, or Forfeiture except during the Life of the Person attainted.

Article. IV.

Section. 1. Full Faith and Credit shall be given in each State to the public Acts, Records, and judicial Proceedings of every other State. And the Congress may by general Laws prescribe the Manner in which such Acts, Records and Proceedings shall be proved, and the Effect thereof.
Section. 2. The Citizens of each State shall be entitled to all Privileges and Immunities of Citizens in the several States.

A Person charged in any State with Treason, Felony, or other Crime, who shall flee from Justice, and be found in another State, shall on Demand of the executive Authority of the State from which he fled, be delivered up, to be removed to the State having Jurisdiction of the Crime.

No Person held to Service or Labour in one State, under the Laws thereof, escaping into another, shall, in Consequence of any Law or Regulation therein, be discharged from such Service or Labour, but shall be delivered up on Claim of the Party to whom such Service or Labour may be due.
Section. 3. New States may be admitted by the Congress into this Union; but no new State shall be formed or erected within the Jurisdiction of any other State, nor any State be formed by the Junction of two or more States, or Parts of States, without the Consent of the Legislatures of the States concerned as well as of the Congress.

The Congress shall have Power to dispose of and make all needful Rules and Regulations respecting the Territory or other Property belonging to the United States; and nothing in this Constitution shall be so construed as to Prejudice any Claims of the United States, or of any particular State.
Section. 4. The United States shall guarantee to every State in this Union a Republican Form of Government, and shall protect each of them against Invasion; and on Application of the Legislature, or of the Executive (when the Legislature cannot be convened) against domestic Violence.

Article. V.

The Congress, whenever two thirds of both Houses shall deem it necessary, shall propose Amendments to this Constitution, or, on the Application of the Legislatures of two thirds of the several States, shall call a Convention for proposing Amendments, which, in either Case, shall be valid to all Intents and Purposes, as Part of this Constitution, when ratified by the Legislatures of three fourths of the several States, or by Conventions in three fourths thereof, as the one or the other Mode of Ratification may be proposed by the Congress; Provided that no Amendment which may be made prior to the Year One thousand eight hundred and eight shall in any Manner affect the first and fourth Clauses in the Ninth Section of the first Article; and that no State, without its Consent, shall be deprived of its equal Suffrage in the Senate.

Article. VI.

All Debts contracted and Engagements entered into, before the Adoption of this Constitution, shall be as valid against the United States under this Constitution, as under the Confederation.

This Constitution, and the Laws of the United States which shall be made in Pursuance thereof; and all Treaties made, or which shall be made, under the Authority of the United States, shall be the supreme Law of the Land; and the Judges in every State shall be bound thereby, any Thing in the Constitution or Laws of any State to the Contrary notwithstanding.

The Senators and Representatives before mentioned, and the Members of the several State Legislatures, and all executive and judicial Officers, both of the United States and of the several States, shall be bound by Oath or Affirmation, to support this Constitution; but no religious Test shall ever be required as a Qualification to any Office or public Trust under the United States.

Article. VII.

The Ratification of the Conventions of nine States, shall be sufficient for the Establishment of this Constitution between the States so ratifying the Same.

done in Convention by the Unanimous Consent of the States present the Seventeenth Day of September in the Year of our Lord one thousand seven hundred and Eighty seven and of the Independence of the United States of America the Twelfth. ***In witness*** whereof We have hereunto subscribed our Names,

Articles in Addition to, and Amendment of, the Constitution of the United States of America, Proposed by Congress, and Ratified by the Legislatures of the Several States, Pursuant to the Fifth Article of the Original Constitution.

Amendment I[*]

Congress shall make no law respecting an establishment of religion, or prohibiting the free exercise thereof; or abridging the freedom of speech, or of the press; or the right of the people peaceably to assemble, and to petition the Government for a redress of grievances.

Amendment II

A well regulated Militia, being necessary to the security of a free State, the right of the people to keep and bear Arms shall not be infringed.

Amendment III

No Soldier shall, in time of peace, be quartered in any house, without the consent of the Owner, nor in time of war, but in a manner to be prescribed by law.

Amendment IV

The right of the people to be secure in their persons, houses, papers, and effects, against unreasonable searches and seizures, shall not be violated, and no Warrants shall issue, but upon probable cause, supported by Oath or affirmation, and particularly describing the place to be searched, and the persons or things to be seized.

Amendment V

No person shall be held to answer for a capital or otherwise infamous crime, unless on a presentment or indictment of a Grand Jury, except in cases arising in the land or naval forces, or in the Militia, when in actual service in time of War or public danger; nor shall any person be subject for the same offence to be twice put in jeopardy of life or limb; nor shall be compelled in any criminal case to be a witness against himself, nor be deprived of life, liberty, or property, without due process of law; nor shall private property be taken for public use, without just compensation.

Amendment VI

In all criminal prosecutions, the accused shall enjoy the right to a speedy and public trial, by an impartial jury of the State and district wherein the crime shall have been committed, which district shall have been previously ascertained by law, and to be informed of the nature and cause of the accusation; to be confronted with the witnesses against him; to have compulsory process for obtaining witnesses in his favor, and to have the Assistance of Counsel for his defence.

*The first ten amendments were passed by Congress September 25, 1789. They were ratified by three-fourths of the states December 15, 1791.

Amendment VII

In suits at common law, where the value in controversy shall exceed twenty dollars, the right of trial by jury shall be preserved, and no fact tried by a jury, shall be otherwise reexamined in any Court of the United States, than according to the rules of the common law.

Amendment VIII

Excessive bail shall not be required, nor excessive fines imposed, nor cruel and unusual punishments inflicted.

Amendment IX

The enumeration in the Constitution, of certain rights, shall not be construed to deny or disparage others retained by the people.

Amendment X

The powers not delegated to the United States by the Constitution; nor prohibited by it to the States, are reserved to the States respectively, or to the people.

Amendment XI[*]

The Judicial power of the United States shall not be construed to extend to any suit in law or equity, commenced or prosecuted against one of the United States by Citizens of another State, or by Citizens or Subjects of any Foreign State.

Amendment XII[†]

The Electors shall meet in their respective States and vote by ballot for President and Vice-President, one of whom, at least, shall not be an inhabitant of the same State with themselves; they shall name in their ballots the person voted for as President, and in distinct ballots the person voted for as Vice-President, and they shall make distinct lists of all persons voted for as President, and of all persons voted for as Vice-President, and of the number of votes for each, which lists they shall sign and certify, and transmit sealed to the seat of the government of the United States, directed to the President of the Senate;—The President of the Senate shall, in the presence of the Senate and House of Representatives, open all the certificates and the votes shall then be counted;—The

*Passed March 4, 1794. Ratified January 23, 1795.
†Passed December 9, 1803. Ratified June 15, 1804.

person having the greatest number of votes for President, shall be the President, if such number be a majority of the whole number of Electors appointed; and if no person have such majority, then from the persons having the highest numbers not exceeding three on the list of those voted for as President, the House of Representatives shall choose immediately, by ballot, the President. But in choosing the President, the votes shall be taken by states, the representation from each state having one vote; a quorum for this purpose shall consist of a member or members from two-thirds of the states, and a majority of all the states shall be necessary to a choice. And if the House of Representatives shall not choose a President whenever the right of choice shall devolve upon them, before the fourth day of March next following, then the Vice-President shall act as President, as in the case of the death or other constitutional disability of the President.—The person having the greatest number of votes as Vice-President, shall be the Vice-President, if such number be a majority of the whole number of Electors appointed, and if no person have a majority, then from the two highest numbers on the list, the Senate shall choose the Vice-President; a quorum for the purpose shall consist of two-thirds of the whole number of Senators, and a majority of the whole number shall be necessary to a choice. But no person constitutionally ineligible to the office of President shall be eligible to that of Vice-President of the United States.

*Amendment XIII**

SECTION 1. Neither slavery nor involuntary servitude, except as a punishment for crime whereof the party shall have been duly convicted, shall exist within the United States, or any place subject to their jurisdiction.

SECTION 2. Congress shall have power to enforce this article by appropriate legislation.

Amendment XIV†

SECTION 1. All persons born or naturalized in the United States, and subject to the jurisdiction thereof, are citizens of the United States and of the State wherein they reside. No State shall make or enforce any law which shall abridge the privileges or immunities of citizens of the United States; nor shall any State deprive any person of life, liberty, or property, without due process of law; nor deny to any person within its jurisdiction the equal protection of the laws.

SECTION 2. Representatives shall be apportioned among the several States according to their respective numbers, counting the whole number of persons in each State, excluding Indians not taxed. But when the right to vote at any election for the choice of electors for President and Vice-President of the United States, Representatives in Congress, the Executive and Judicial officers of a State, or the members of the Legislature thereof, is denied to any of the male inhabitants of such State, being twenty-one years of age, and citizens of the United States, or in any way abridged, except for participation in rebellion, or other crime, the basis of representation therein shall be reduced in the proportion which the number of such male citizens shall bear to the whole number of male citizens twenty-one years of age in such State.

SECTION 3. No person shall be a Senator or Representative in Congress, or elector of President and Vice-President, or hold any office, civil or military, under the United States, or under any State, who, having previously taken an oath, as a member of Congress, or as an officer of the United States, or as a member of any State legislature, or as an executive or judicial officer of any State, to support the Constitution of the United States, shall have engaged in insurrection or rebellion against the same, or given aid or comfort to the enemies thereof. But Congress may by a vote of two-thirds of each House, remove such disability.

SECTION 4. The validity of the public debt of the United States, authorized by law, including debts incurred for payment of pensions and bounties for services in suppressing insurrection or rebellion, shall not be questioned. But neither the United States nor any State shall assume or pay any debt or obligation incurred in aid of insurrection or rebellion against the United States, or any claim for the loss or emancipation of any slave; but all such debts, obligations, and claims shall be held illegal and void.

SECTION 5. The Congress shall have the power to enforce, by appropriate legislation, the provisions of this article.

*Amendment XV**

SECTION 1. The right of citizens of the United States to vote shall not be denied or abridged by the United States or by any State on account of race, color, or previous condition of servitude—

SECTION 2. The Congress shall have power to enforce this article by appropriate legislation.

Amendment XVI

The Congress shall have power to lay and collect taxes on incomes, from whatever source derived, without apportionment among the several States, and without regard to any census or enumeration.

*Passed January 31, 1865. Ratified December 6, 1865.
†Passed June 13, 1866. Ratified July 9, 1868.

*Passed February 26, 1869. Ratified February 2, 1870.

*Amendment XVII**

The Senate of the United States shall be composed of two Senators from each State, elected by the people thereof, for six years; and each Senator shall have one vote. The electors in each State shall have the qualifications requisite for electors of the most numerous branch of the State legislatures.

When vacancies happen in the representation of any State in the Senate, the executive authority of such State shall issue writs of election to fill such vacancies: *Provided,* That the legislature of any State may empower the executive thereof to make temporary appointments until the people fill the vacancies by election as the legislature may direct.

This amendment shall not be so construed as to affect the election or term of any Senator chosen before it becomes valid as part of the Constitution.

Amendment XVIII†

SECTION 1. After one year from the ratification of this article the manufacture, sale, or transportation of intoxicating liquors within, the importation thereof into, or the exportation thereof from the United States and all territory subject to the jurisdiction thereof for beverage purposes is hereby prohibited.

SECTION 2. The Congress and the several States shall have concurrent power to enforce this article by appropriate legislation.

SECTION 3. This article shall be inoperative unless it shall have been ratified as an amendment to the Constitution by the legislatures of the several States, as provided in the Constitution, within seven years from the date of the submission hereof to the States by the Congress.

Amendment XIX‡

The right of citizens of the United States to vote shall not be denied or abridged by the United States or by any State on account of sex.

Congress shall have power to enforce this article by appropriate legislation.

Amendment XX§

SECTION 1. The terms of the President and Vice-President shall end at noon on the 20th day of January, and the terms of Senators and Representatives at noon on the 3d day of January, of the years in which such terms would have ended if this article had not been ratified; and the terms of their successors shall then begin.

SECTION 2. The Congress shall assemble at least once in every year, and such meeting shall begin at noon on the 3d day of January, unless they shall by law appoint a different day.

SECTION 3. If, at the time fixed for the beginning of the term of the President, the President elect shall have died, the Vice-President elect shall become President. If a President shall not have been chosen before the time fixed for the beginning of his term, or if the President elect shall have failed to qualify, then the Vice-President elect shall act as President until a President shall have qualified; and the Congress may by law provide for the case wherein neither a President elect nor a Vice-President elect shall have qualified, declaring who shall then act as President, or the manner in which one who is to act shall be selected, and such person shall act accordingly until a President or Vice-President shall have qualified.

SECTION 4. The Congress may by law provide for the case of the death of any of the persons from whom the House of Representatives may choose a President whenever the right of choice shall have devolved upon them, and for the case of the death of any of the persons from whom the Senate may choose a Vice-President whenever the right of choice shall have devolved upon them.

SECTION 5. Sections 1 and 2 shall take effect on the 15th day of October following the ratification of this article.

SECTION 6. This article shall be inoperative unless it shall have been ratified as an amendment to the Constitution by the legislatures of three-fourths of the several States within seven years from the date of its submission.

*Amendment XXI**

SECTION 1. The eighteenth article of amendment to the Constitution of the United States is hereby repealed.

SECTION 2. The transportation or importation into any State, Territory, or possession of the United States for delivery or use therein of intoxicating liquors, in violation of the laws thereof, is hereby prohibited.

SECTION 3. This article shall be inoperative unless it shall have been ratified as an amendment to the Constitution by conventions in the several States, as provided in the Constitution, within seven years from the date of the submission hereof to the States by the Congress.

Amendment XXII†

No person shall be elected to the office of the President more than twice, and no person who has held the office of President, or acted as President, for more than two

* Passed May 13, 1912. Ratified April 8, 1913.
† Passed December 18, 1917. Ratified January 16, 1919.
‡ Passed June 4, 1919. Ratified August 18, 1920.
§ Passed March 2, 1932. Ratified January 23, 1933.

* Passed February 20, 1933. Ratified December 5, 1933.
† Passed March 12, 1947. Ratified March 1, 1951.

years of a term to which some other person was elected President shall be elected to the office of the President more than once.

But this Article shall not apply to any person holding the office of President when this Article was proposed by the Congress, and shall not prevent any person who may be holding the office of President, or acting as President, during the term within which this Article becomes operative from holding the office of President or acting as President during the remainder of such term.

*Amendment XXIII**

SECTION 1. The District constituting the seat of Government of the United States shall appoint in such manner as the Congress may direct:

A number of electors of President and Vice President equal to the whole number of Senators and Representatives in Congress to which the District would be entitled if it were a State, but in no event more than the least populous State; they shall be in addition to those appointed by the States, but they shall be considered, for the purposes of the election of President and Vice President, to be electors appointed by the State; and they shall meet in the District and perform such duties as provided by the twelfth article of amendment.

SECTION 2. The Congress shall have power to enforce this article by appropriate legislation.

Amendment XXIV†

SECTION 1. The right of citizens of the United States to vote in any primary or other election for President or Vice President, or for Senator or Representative in Congress, shall not be denied or abridged by the United States or any State by reason of failure to pay any poll tax or other tax.

SECTION 2. The Congress shall have power to enforce this article by appropriate legislation.

Amendment XXV‡

SECTION 1. In case of the removal of the President from office or of his death or resignation, the Vice President shall become President.

SECTION 2. Whenever there is a vacancy in the office of the Vice President, the President shall nominate a Vice President who shall take office upon confirmation by a majority vote of both Houses of Congress.

SECTION 3. Whenever the President transmits to the President pro tempore of the Senate and the Speaker of the House of Representatives his written declaration that he is unable to discharge the powers and duties of his office, and until he transmits to them a written declaration to the contrary, such powers and duties shall be discharged by the Vice President as Acting President.

SECTION 4. Whenever the Vice President and a majority of either the principal officers of the executive department or of such other body as Congress may by law provide, transmit to the President pro tempore of the Senate and the Speaker of the House of Representatives their written declaration that the President is unable to discharge the powers and duties of his office, the Vice President shall immediately assume the powers and duties of the office of Acting President.

Thereafter, when the President transmits to the President pro tempore of the Senate and the Speaker of the House of Representatives his written declaration that no inability exists, he shall resume the powers and duties of his office unless the Vice President and a majority of either the principal officers of the executive department or of such other body as Congress may by law provide, transmit within four days to the President pro tempore of the Senate and the Speaker of the House of Representatives their written declaration that the President is unable to discharge the powers and duties of his office. Thereupon Congress shall decide the issue, assembling within forty-eight hours for that purpose if not in session. If the Congress, within twenty-one days after receipt of the latter written declaration, or, if Congress is not in session, within twenty-one days after Congress is required to assemble, determines by two-thirds vote of both Houses that the President is unable to discharge the powers and duties of his office, the Vice President shall continue to discharge the same as Acting President; otherwise, the President shall resume the powers and duties of his office.

*Amendment XXVI**

SECTION 1. The right of citizens of the United States, who are eighteen years of age or older, to vote shall not be denied or abridged by the United States or by any State on account of age.

SECTION 2. The Congress shall have power to enforce this article by appropriate legislation.

* Passed June 16, 1960. Ratified April 3, 1961.
† Passed August 27, 1962. Ratified January 23, 1964.
‡ Passed July 6, 1965. Ratified February 11, 1967.

*Passed March 23, 1971. Ratified July 5, 1971.

ADMISSION OF STATES

Order of admission	State	Date of admission	Order of admission	State	Date of admission
1	Delaware	December 7, 1787	26	Michigan	January 26, 1837
2	Pennsylvania	December 12, 1787	27	Florida	March 3, 1845
3	New Jersey	December 18, 1787	28	Texas	December 29, 1845
4	Georgia	January 2, 1788	29	Iowa	December 28, 1846
5	Connecticut	January 9, 1788	30	Wisconsin	May 29, 1848
6	Massachusetts	February 6, 1788	31	California	September 9, 1850
7	Maryland	April 28, 1788	32	Minnesota	May 11, 1858
8	South Carolina	May 23, 1788	33	Oregon	February 14, 1859
9	New Hampshire	June 21, 1788	34	Kansas	January 29, 1861
10	Virginia	June 25, 1788	35	West Virginia	June 20, 1863
11	New York	July 26, 1788	36	Nevada	October 31, 1864
12	North Carolina	November 21, 1789	37	Nebraska	March 1, 1867
13	Rhode Island	May 29, 1790	38	Colorado	August 1, 1876
14	Vermont	March 4, 1791	39	North Dakota	November 2, 1889
15	Kentucky	June 1, 1792	40	South Dakota	November 2, 1889
16	Tennessee	June 1, 1796	41	Montana	November 8, 1889
17	Ohio	March 1, 1803	42	Washington	November 11, 1889
18	Louisiana	April 30, 1812	43	Idaho	July 3, 1890
19	Indiana	December 11, 1816	44	Wyoming	July 10, 1890
20	Mississippi	December 10, 1817	45	Utah	January 4, 1896
21	Illinois	December 3, 1818	46	Oklahoma	November 16, 1907
22	Alabama	December 14, 1819	47	New Mexico	January 6, 1912
23	Maine	March 15, 1820	48	Arizona	February 14, 1912
24	Missouri	August 10, 1821	49	Alaska	January 3, 1959
25	Arkansas	June 15, 1836	50	Hawaii	August 21, 1959

POPULATION OF THE UNITED STATES (1790–1945)

Year	Total population (in thousands)	Number per square mile of land area (continental United States)	Year	Total population (in thousands)	Number per square mile of land area (continental United States)
1790	3,929	4.5	1829	12,565	
1791	4,056		1830	12,901	7.4
1792	4,194		1831	13,321	
1793	4,332		1832	13,742	
1794	4,469		1833	14,162	
1795	4,607		1834	14,582	
1796	4,745		1835	15,003	
1797	4,883		1836	15,423	
1798	5,021		1837	15,843	
1799	5,159		1838	16,264	
1800	5,297	6.1	1839	16,684	
1801	5,486		1840	17,120	9.8
1802	5,679		1841	17,733	
1803	5,872		1842	18,345	
1804	5,065		1843	18,957	
1805	6,258		1844	19,569	
1806	6,451		1845	20,182	
1807	6,644		1846	20,794	
1808	6,838		1847	21,406	
1809	7,031		1848	22,018	
1810	7,224	4.3	1849	22,631	
1811	7,460		1850	23,261	7.9
1812	7,700		1851	24,086	
1813	7,939		1852	24,911	
1814	8,179		1853	25,736	
1815	8,419		1854	26,561	
1816	8,659		1855	27,386	
1817	8,899		1856	28,212	
1818	9,139		1857	29,037	
1819	9,379		1858	29,862	
1820	9,618	5.6	1859	30,687	
1821	9,939		1860	31,513	10.6
1822	10,268		1861	32,351	
1823	10,596		1862	33,188	
1824	10,924		1863	34,026	
1825	11,252		1864	34,863	
1826	11,580		1865	35,701	
1827	11,909		1866	36,538	
1828	12,237		1867	37,376	

Figures are from *Historical Statistics of the United States, Colonial Times to 1957* (1961), pp. 7, 8; *Statistical Abstract of the United States: 1974,* p. 5; Census Bureau for 1974 and 1975; and *Statistical Abstract of the United States: 1988,* p. 7.

Year	Total population (in thousands)	Number per square mile of land area (continental United States)	Year	Total population (in thousands)*	Number per square mile of land area (continental United States)
1868	38,213		1907	87,000	
1869	39,051		1908	88,709	
1870	39,905	13.4	1909	90,492	
1871	40,938		1910	92,407	31.0
1872	41,972		1911	93,868	
1873	43,006		1912	95,331	
1874	44,040		1913	97,227	
1875	45,073		1914	99,118	
1876	46,107		1915	100,549	
1877	47,141		1916	101,966	
1878	48,174		1917	103,414	
1879	49,208		1918	104,550	
1880	50,262	16.9	1919	105,063	
1881	51,542		1920	106,466	35.6
1882	52,821		1921	108,541	
1883	54,100		1922	110,055	
1884	55,379		1923	111,950	
1885	56,658		1924	114,113	
1886	57,938		1925	115,832	
1887	59,217		1926	117,399	
1888	60,496		1927	119,038	
1889	61,775		1928	120,501	
1890	63,056	21.2	1929	121,770	
1891	64,361		1930	122,775	41.2
1892	65,666		1931	124,040	
1893	66,970		1932	124,840	
1894	68,275		1933	125,579	
1895	69,580		1934	126,374	
1896	70,885		1935	127,250	
1897	72,189		1936	128,053	
1898	73,494		1937	128,825	
1899	74,799		1938	129,825	
1900	76,094	25.6	1939	130,880	
1901	77,585		1940	131,669	44.2
1902	79,160		1941	133,894	
1903	80,632		1942	135,361	
1904	82,165		1943	137,250	
1905	83,820		1944	138,916	
1906	85,437		1945	140,468	

* Figure after 1940 represent total population including armed forces abroad, except in official census years.

POPULATION OF THE UNITED STATES (1946–1990)

Year	Total population (in thousands)*	Number per square mile of land area (continental United States)	Year	Total population (in thousands)*	Number per square mile of land area (continental United States)
1946	141,936		1969	202,599	
1947	144,698		1970	203,875	57.5†
1948	147,208		1971	207,045	
1949	149,767		1972	208,842	
1950	150,697	50.7	1973	210,396	
1951	154,878		1974	211,894	
1952	157,553		1975	213,631	
1953	160,184		1976	215,152	
1954	163,026		1977	216,880	
1955	165,931		1978	218,717	
1956	168,903		1979	220,584	
1957	171,984		1980	226,546	64.0
1958	174,882		1981	230,138	
1959	177,830		1982	232,520	
1960	178,464	60.1	1983	234,799	
1961	183,672		1984	237,001	
1962	186,504		1985	239,283	
1963	189,197		1986	241,596	
1964	191,833		1987	243,773	
1965	194,237		1988	245,051	
1966	196,485		1989	247,350	
1967	198,629		1990	250,122	
1968	200,619				

* Figures after 1940 represent total population including armed forces abroad, except in official census years.
† Figure includes Alaska and Hawaii.

APPENDIX B

PRESIDENTIAL ELECTIONS

PRESIDENTS, VICE PRESIDENTS, AND CABINET MEMBERS

JUSTICES OF THE U.S. SUPREME COURT

PRESIDENTIAL ELECTIONS (1789–1840)

Year	Number of states	Candidates	Parties	Popular vote	Electoral vote	Percentage of popular vote
1789	11	GEORGE WASHINGTON	No party designations		69	
		John Adams			34	
		Minor Candidates			35	
1792	15	GEORGE WASHINGTON	No party designations		132	
		John Adams			77	
		George Clinton			50	
		Minor Candidates			5	
1796	16	JOHN ADAMS	Federalist		71	
		Thomas Jefferson	Democratic-Republican		68	
		Thomas Pinckney	Federalist		59	
		Aaron Burr	Democratic-Republican		30	
		Minor Candidates			48	
1800	16	THOMAS JEFFERSON	Democratic-Republican		73	
		Aaron Burr	Democratic-Republican		73	
		John Adams	Federalist		65	
		Charles C. Pinckney	Federalist		64	
		John Jay	Federalist		1	
1804	17	THOMAS JEFFERSON	Democratic-Republican		162	
		Charles C. Pinckney	Federalist		14	
1808	17	JAMES MADISON	Democratic-Republican		122	
		Charles C. Pinckney	Federalist		47	
		George Clinton	Democratic-Republican		6	
1812	18	JAMES MADISON	Democratic-Republican		128	
		DeWitt Clinton	Federalist		89	
1816	19	JAMES MONROE	Democratic-Republican		183	
		Rufus King	Federalist		34	
1820	24	JAMES MONROE	Democratic-Republican		231	
		John Quincy Adams	Independent Republican		1	
1824	24	JOHN QUINCY ADAMS	Democratic-Republican	108,740	84	30.5
		Andrew Jackson	Democratic-Republican	153,544	99	43.1
		William H. Crawford	Democratic-Republican	46,618	41	13.1
		Henry Clay	Democratic-Republican	47,136	37	13.2
1828	24	ANDREW JACKSON	Democratic	647,286	178	56.0
		John Quincy Adams	National Republican	508,064	83	44.0
1832	24	ANDREW JACKSON	Democratic	687,502	219	55.0
		Henry Clay	National Republican	530,189	49	42.4
		William Wirt	Anti-Masonic	33,108	7	2.6
		John Floyd	National Republican		11	
1836	26	MARTIN VAN BUREN	Democratic	765,483	170	50.9
		William H. Harrison	Whig	739,795	73	49.1
		Hugh L. White	Whig		26	
		Daniel Webster	Whig		14	
		W. P. Mangum	Whig		11	
1840	26	WILLIAM H. HARRISON	Whig	1,274,624	234	53.1
		Martin Van Buren	Democratic	1,127,781	60	46.9

Candidates receiving less than 1 percent of the popular vote have been omitted. For that reason the percentage of popular vote given for any election year may not total 100 percent.

Before the passage of the Twelfth Amendment in 1804, the Electoral College voted for two presidential candidates; the runner-up became vice president.

Figures are from *Historical Statistics of the United States, Colonial Times to 1957* (1961), pp. 682–83; and the U.S. Department of Justice.

PRESIDENTIAL ELECTIONS (1844–1900)

Year	Number of states	Candidates	Parties	Popular vote	Electoral vote	Percentage of popular vote
1844	26	JAMES K. POLK	Democratic	1,338,464	170	49.6
		Henry Clay	Whig	1,300,097	105	48.1
		James G. Birney	Liberty	62,300		2.3
1848	30	ZACHARY TAYLOR	Whig	1,360,967	163	47.4
		Lewis Cass	Democratic	1,222,342	127	42.5
		Martin Van Buren	Free Soil	291,263		10.1
1852	31	FRANKLIN PIERCE	Democratic	1,601,117	254	50.9
		Winfield Scott	Whig	1,385,453	42	44.1
		John P. Hale	Free Soil	155,825		5.0
1856	31	JAMES BUCHANAN	Democratic	1,832,955	174	45.3
		John C. Frémont	Republican	1,339,932	114	33.1
		Millard Fillmore	American	871,731	8	21.6
1860	33	ABRAHAM LINCOLN	Republican	1,865,593	180	39.8
		Stephen A. Douglas	Democratic	1,382,713	12	29.5
		John C. Breckinridge	Democratic	848,356	72	18.1
		John Bell	Constitutional Union	592,906	39	12.6
1864	36	ABRAHAM LINCOLN	Republican	2,206,938	212	55.0
		George B. McClellan	Democratic	1,803,787	21	45.0
1868	37	ULYSSES S. GRANT	Republican	3,013,421	214	52.7
		Horatio Seymour	Democratic	2,706,829	80	47.3
1872	37	ULYSSES S. GRANT	Republican	3,596,745	286	55.6
		Horace Greeley	Democratic	2,843,446	*	43.9
1876	38	RUTHERFORD B. HAYES	Republican	4,036,572	185	48.0
		Samuel J. Tilden	Democratic	4,284,020	184	51.0
1880	38	JAMES A. GARFIELD	Republican	4,453,295	214	48.5
		Winfield S. Hancock	Democratic	4,414,082	155	48.1
		James B. Weaver	Greenback-Labor	308,578		3.4
1884	38	GROVER CLEVELAND	Democratic	4,879,507	219	48.5
		James G. Blaine	Republican	4,850,293	182	48.2
		Benjamin F. Butler	Greenback-Labor	175,370		1.8
		John P. St. John	Prohibition	150,369		1.5
1888	38	BENJAMIN HARRISON	Republican	5,477,129	233	47.9
		Grover Cleveland	Democratic	5,537,857	168	48.6
		Clinton B. Fisk	Prohibition	249,506		2.2
		Anson J. Streeter	Union Labor	146,935		1.3
1892	44	GROVER CLEVELAND	Democratic	5,555,426	277	46.1
		Benjamin Harrison	Republican	5,182,690	145	43.0
		James B. Weaver	People's	1,029,846	22	8.5
		John Bidwell	Prohibition	264,133		2.2
1896	45	WILLIAM McKINLEY	Republican	7,102,246	271	51.1
		William J. Bryan	Democratic	6,492,559	176	47.7
1900	45	WILLIAM McKINLEY	Republican	7,218,491	292	51.7
		William J. Bryan	Democratic; Populist	6,356,734	155	45.5
		John C. Wooley	Prohibition	208,914		1.5

*Greeley died shortly after the election; the electors supporting him then divided their votes among minor candidates.

Candidates receiving less than 1 percent of the popular vote have been omitted. For that reason the percentage of popular vote given for any election year may not total 100 percent.

PRESIDENTIAL ELECTIONS (1904–1932)

Year	Number of states	Candidates	Parties	Popular vote	Electoral vote	Percentage of popular vote*
1904	45	THEODORE ROOSEVELT	Republican	7,628,461	336	57.4
		Alton B. Parker	Democratic	5,084,223	140	37.6
		Eugene V. Debs	Socialist	402,283		3.0
		Silas C. Swallow	Prohibition	258,536		1.9
1908	46	WILLIAM H. TAFT	Republican	7,675,320	321	51.6
		William J. Bryan	Democratic	6,412,294	162	43.1
		Eugene V. Debs	Socialist	420,793		2.8
		Eugene W. Chafin	Prohibition	253,840		1.7
1912	48	WOODROW WILSON	Democratic	6,296,547	435	41.9
		Theodore Roosevelt	Progressive	4,118,571	88	27.4
		William H. Taft	Republican	3,486,720	8	23.2
		Eugene V. Debs	Socialist	900,672		6.0
		Eugene W. Chafin	Prohibition	206,275		1.4
1916	48	WOODROW WILSON	Democratic	9,127,695	277	49.4
		Charles E. Hughes	Republican	8,533,507	254	46.2
		A. L. Benson	Socialist	585,113		3.2
		J. Frank Hanly	Prohibition	220,506		1.2
1920	48	WARREN G. HARDING	Republican	16,143,407	404	60.4
		James N. Cox	Democratic	9,130,328	127	34.2
		Eugene V. Debs	Socialist	919,799		3.4
		P. P. Christensen	Farmer-Labor	265,411		1.0
1924	48	CALVIN COOLIDGE	Republican	15,718,211	382	54.0
		John W. Davis	Democratic	8,385,283	136	28.8
		Robert M. La Follette	Progressive	4,831,289	13	16.6
1928	48	HERBERT C. HOOVER	Republican	21,391,993	444	58.2
		Alfred E. Smith	Democratic	15,016,169	87	40.9
1932	48	FRANKLIN D. ROOSEVELT	Democratic	22,809,638	472	57.4
		Herbert C. Hoover	Republican	15,758,901	59	39.7
		Norman Thomas	Socialist	881,951		2.2

* Candidates receiving less than 1 percent of the popular vote have been omitted. For that reason the percentage of popular vote given for any election year may not total 100 percent.

PRESIDENTIAL ELECTIONS (1936–1992)

Year	Number of states	Candidates	Parties	Popular vote	Electoral vote	Percentage of popular vote*
1936	48	FRANKLIN D. ROOSEVELT	Democratic	27,752,869	523	60.8
		Alfred M. Landon	Republican	16,674,665	8	36.5
		William Lemke	Union	882,479		1.9
1940	48	FRANKLIN D. ROOSEVELT	Democratic	27,307,819	449	54.8
		Wendell L. Willkie	Republican	22,321,018	82	44.8
1944	48	FRANKLIN D. ROOSEVELT	Democratic	25,606,585	432	53.5
		Thomas E. Dewey	Republican	22,014,745	99	46.0
1948	48	HARRY S. TRUMAN	Democratic	24,105,812	303	49.5
		Thomas E. Dewey	Republican	21,970,065	189	45.1
		J. Strom Thurmond	States' Rights	1,169,063	39	2.4
		Henry A. Wallace	Progressive	1,157,172		2.4
1952	48	DWIGHT D. EISENHOWER	Republican	33,936,234	442	55.1
		Adlai E. Stevenson	Democratic	27,314,992	89	44.4
1956	48	DWIGHT D. EISENHOWER	Republican	35,590,472	457	57.6
		Adlai E. Stevenson	Democratic	26,022,752	73	42.1
1960	50	JOHN F. KENNEDY	Democratic	34,227,096	303	49.9
		Richard M. Nixon	Republican	34,108,546	219	49.6
1964	50	LYNDON B. JOHNSON	Democratic	43,126,506	486	61.1
		Barry M. Goldwater	Republican	27,176,799	52	38.5
1968	50	RICHARD M. NIXON	Republican	31,785,480	301	43.4
		Hubert H. Humphrey	Democratic	31,275,165	191	42.7
		George C. Wallace	American Independent	9,906,473	46	13.5
1972	50	RICHARD M. NIXON	Republican	47,169,911	520	60.7
		George S. McGovern	Democratic	29,170,383	17	37.5
1976	50	JIMMY CARTER	Democratic	40,827,394	297	50.0
		Gerald R. Ford	Republican	39,145,977	240	47.9
1980	50	RONALD W. REAGAN	Republican	43,899,248	489	50.8
		Jimmy Carter	Democratic	35,481,435	49	41.0
		John B. Anderson	Independent	5,719,437		6.6
		Ed Clark	Libertarian	920,859		1.0
1984	50	RONALD W. REAGAN	Republican	54,281,858	525	59.2
		Walter F. Mondale	Democratic	37,457,215	13	40.8
1988	50	GEORGE H. BUSH	Republican	47,917,341	426	54
		Michael Dukakis	Democratic	41,013,030	112	46
1992†	50	WILLIAM J. CLINTON	Democratic	43,727,625	366	43
		George H. Bush	Republican	38,165,180	168	38
		H. Ross Perot	Independent	19,236,411	8	19

* Candidates receiving less than 1 percent of the popular vote have been omitted. For that reason the percentage of popular vote given for any election year may not total 100 percent.

† Unofficial figures.

PRESIDENTS, VICE PRESIDENTS, AND CABINET MEMBERS (1789–1841)

President	Vice President	Secretary of State	Secretary of Treasury	Secretary of War
George Washington 1789–97	John Adams 1789–97	Thomas Jefferson 1789–94 Edmund Randolph 1794–95 Timothy Pickering 1795–97	Alexander Hamilton 1789–95 Oliver Wolcott 1795–97	Henry Knox 1789–95 Timothy Pickering 1795–96 James McHenry 1796–97
John Adams 1797–1801	Thomas Jefferson 1797–1801	Timothy Pickering 1797–1800 John Marshall 1800–01	Oliver Wolcott 1797–1801 Samuel Dexter 1801	James McHenry 1797–1800 Samuel Dexter 1800–01
Thomas Jefferson 1801–09	Aaron Burr 1801–05 George Clinton 1805–09	James Madison 1801–09	Samuel Dexter 1801 Albert Gallatin 1801–09	Henry Dearborn 1801–09
James Madison 1809–17	George Clinton 1809–13 Elbridge Gerry 1813–17	Robert Smith 1809–11 James Monroe 1811–17	Albert Gallatin 1809–14 George Campbell 1814 Alexander Dallas 1814–16 William Crawford 1816–17	William Eustis 1809–13 John Armstrong 1813–14 James Monroe 1814–15 William Crawford 1815–17
James Monroe 1817–25	Daniel D. Tompkins 1817–25	John Quincy Adams 1817–25	William Crawford 1817–25	George Graham 1817 John C. Calhoun 1817–25
John Quincy Adams 1825–29	John C. Calhoun 1825–29	Henry Clay 1825–29	Richard Rush 1825–29	James Barbour 1825–28 Peter B. Porter 1828–29
Andrew Jackson 1829–37	John C. Calhoun 1829–33 Martin Van Buren 1833–37	Martin Van Buren 1829–31 Edward Livingston 1831–33 Louis McLane 1833–34 John Forsyth 1834–37	Samuel Ingham 1829–31 Louis McLane 1831–33 William Duane 1833 Roger B. Taney 1833–34 Levi Woodbury 1834–37	John H. Eaton 1829–31 Lewis Cass 1831–37 Benjamin Butler 1837
Martin Van Buren 1837–41	Richard M. Johnson 1837–41	John Forsyth 1837–41	Levi Woodbury 1837–41	Joel R. Poinsett 1837–41

Secretary of Navy	Postmaster General	Attorney General
	Samuel Osgood 1789–91 Timothy Pickering 1791–95 Joseph Habersham 1795–97	Edmund Randolph 1789–94 William Bradford 1794–95 Charles Lee 1795–97
Benjamin Stoddert 1798–1801	Joseph Habersham 1797–1801	Charles Lee 1797–1801
Benjamin Stoddert 1801 Robert Smith 1801–09	Joseph Habersham 1801 Gideon Granger 1801–09	Levi Lincoln 1801–05 John Breckinridge 1805-07 Caesar Rodney 1807–09
Paul Hamilton 1809–13 William Jones 1813–14 Benjamin Crowninshield 1814–17	Gideon Granger 1809–14 Return Meigs 1814–17	Caesar Rodney 1809–11 William Pinkney 1811–14 Richard Rush 1814–17
Benjamin Crowninshield 1817–18 Smith Thompson 1818–23 Samuel Southard 1823–25	Return Meigs 1817–23 John McLean 1823–25	Richard Rush 1817 William Wirt 1817–25
Samuel Southard 1825–29	John McLean 1825–29	William Wirt 1825–29
John Branch 1829–31 Levi Woodbury 1831–34 Mahlon Dickerson 1834–37	William Barry 1829–35 Amos Kendall 1835–37	John M. Berrien 1829–31 Roger B. Taney 1831–33 Benjamin Butler 1833–37
Mahlon Dickerson 1837–38 James K. Paulding 1838–41	Amos Kendall 1837–40 John M. Niles 1840–41	Benjamin Butler 1837–38 Felix Grundy 1838–40 Henry D. Gilpin 1840–41

PRESIDENTS, VICE PRESIDENTS, AND CABINET MEMBERS (1841–1877)

President	Vice President	Secretary of State	Secretary of Treasury	Secretary of War
William H. Harrison 1841	John Tyler 1841	Daniel Webster 1841	Thomas Ewing 1841	John Bell 1841
John Tyler 1841–45		Daniel Webster 1841–43 Hugh S. Legaré 1843 Abel P. Upshur 1843–44 John C. Calhoun 1844–45	Thomas Ewing 1841 Walter Forward 1841–43 John C. Spencer 1843–44 George M. Bibb 1844–45	John Bell 1841 John C. Spencer 1841–43 James M. Porter 1843–44 William Wilkins 1844–45
James K. Polk 1845–49	George M. Dallas 1845–49	James Buchanan 1845–49	Robert J. Walker 1845–49	William L. Marcy 1845–49
Zachary Taylor 1849–50	Millard Fillmore 1849–50	John M. Clayton 1849–50	William M. Meredith 1849–50	George W. Crawford 1849–50
Millard Fillmore 1850–53		Daniel Webster 1850–52 Edward Everett 1852–53	Thomas Corwin 1850–53	Charles M. Conrad 1850–53
Franklin Pierce 1853–57	William R. King 1853–57	William L. Marcy 1853–57	James Guthrie 1853–57	Jefferson Davis 1853–57
James Buchanan 1857–61	John C. Breckinridge 1857–61	Lewis Cass 1857–60 Jeremiah S. Black 1860–61	Howell Cobb 1857–60 Philip F. Thomas 1860–61 John A. Dix 1861	John B. Floyd 1857–61 Joseph Holt 1861
Abraham Lincoln 1861–65	Hannibal Hamlin 1861–65 Andrew Johnson 1865	William H. Seward 1861–65	Salmon P. Chase 1861–64 William P. Fessenden 1864–65 Hugh McCulloch 1865	Simon Cameron 1861–62 Edwin M. Stanton 1862–65
Andrew Johnson 1865–69		William H. Seward 1865–69	Hugh McCulloch 1865–69	Edwin M. Stanton 1865–67 Ulysses S. Grant 1867–68 John M. Schofield 1868–69
Ulysses S. Grant 1869–77	Schuyler Colfax 1869–73 Henry Wilson 1873–77	Elihu B. Washburne 1869 Hamilton Fish 1869–77	George S. Boutwell 1869–73 William A. Richardson 1873–74 Benjamin H. Bristow 1874–76 Lot M. Morrill 1876–77	John A. Rawlins 1869 William T. Sherman 1869 William W. Belknap 1869–76 Alphonso Taft 1876 James D. Cameron 1876–77

Secretary of Navy	Postmaster General	Attorney General	Secretary of Interior
George E. Badger 1841	Francis Granger 1841	John J. Crittenden 1841	
George E. Badger 1841 Abel P. Upshur 1841–43 David Henshaw 1843–44 Thomas Gilmer 1844 John Y. Mason 1844–45	Francis Granger 1841 Charles A. Wickliffe 1841–45	John J. Crittenden 1841 Hugh S. Legaré 1841–43 John Nelson 1843–45	
George Bancroft 1845–46 John Y. Mason 1846–49	Cave Johnson 1845–49	John Y. Mason 1845–46 Nathan Clifford 1846–48 Isaac Toucey 1848–49	
William B. Preston 1849–50	Jacob Collamer 1849–50	Reverdy Johnson 1849–50	Thomas Ewing 1849–50
William A. Graham 1850–52 John P. Kennedy 1852–53	Nathan K. Hall 1850–52 Sam D. Hubbard 1852–53	John J. Crittenden 1850–53	Thomas McKennan 1850 A. H. H. Stuart 1850–53
James C. Dobbin 1853–57	James Campbell 1853–57	Caleb Cushing 1853–57	Robert McClelland 1853–57
Isaac Toucey 1857–61	Aaron V. Brown 1857–59 Joseph Holt 1859–61 Horatio King 1861	Jeremiah S. Black 1857–60 Edwin M. Stanton 1860–61	Jacob Thompson 1857–61
Gideon Welles 1861–65	Horatio King 1861 Montgomery Blair 1861–64 William Dennison 1864–65	Edward Bates 1861–64 James Speed 1864–65	Caleb B. Smith 1861–63 John P. Usher 1863–65
Gideon Welles 1865–69	William Dennison 1865–66 Alexander Randall 1866–69	James Speed 1865–66 Henry Stanbery 1866–68 William M. Evarts 1868–69	John P. Usher 1865 James Harlan 1865–66 O. H. Browning 1866–69
Adolph E. Borie 1869 George M. Robeson 1869–77	John A. J. Creswell 1869–74 James W. Marshall 1874 Marshall Jewell 1874–76 James N. Tyner 1876–77	Ebenezer R. Hoar 1869–70 Amos T. Akerman 1870–71 G. H. Williams 1871–75 Edwards Pierrepont 1875–76 Alphonso Taft 1876–77	Jacob D. Cox 1869–70 Columbus Delano 1870–75 Zachariah Chandler 1875–77

PRESIDENTS, VICE PRESIDENTS, AND CABINET MEMBERS (1877–1923)

President	Vice President	Secretary of State	Secretary of Treasury	Secretary of War	Secretary of Navy
Rutherford B. Hayes 1877–81	William A. Wheeler 1877–81	William M. Evarts 1877–81	John Sherman 1877–81	George W. McCrary 1877–79 Alexander Ramsey 1879–81	R. W. Thompson 1877–81 Nathan Goff, Jr. 1881
James A. Garfield 1881	Chester A. Arthur 1881	James G. Blaine 1881	William Windom 1881	Robert T. Lincoln 1881	William H. Hunt 1881
Chester A. Arthur 1881–85		F. T. Frelinghuysen 1881–85	Charles J. Folger 1881–84 Walter Q. Gresham 1884 Hugh McCulloch 1884–85	Robert T. Lincoln 1881–85	William E. Chandler 1881–85
Grover Cleveland 1885–89	T. A. Hendricks 1885	Thomas F. Bayard 1885–89	Daniel Manning 1885–87 Charles S. Fairchild 1887–89	William C. Endicott 1885–89	William C. Whitney 1885–89
Benjamin Harrison 1889–93	Levi P. Morton 1889–93	James G. Blaine 1889–92 John W. Foster 1892–93	William Windom 1889–91 Charles Foster 1891–93	Redfield Procter 1889–91 Stephen B. Elkins 1891–93	Benjamin F. Tracy 1889–93
Grover Cleveland 1893–97	Adlai E. Stevenson 1893–97	Walter Q. Gresham 1893–95 Richard Olney 1895–97	John G. Carlisle 1893–97	Daniel S. Lamont 1893–97	Hilary A. Herbert 1893–97
William McKinley 1897–1901	Garret A. Hobart 1897–99 Theodore Roosevelt 1901	John Sherman 1897–98 William R. Day 1898 John Hay 1898–1901	Lyman J. Gage 1897–1901	Russell A. Alger 1897–99 Elihu Root 1899–1901	John D. Long 1897–1901
Theodore Roosevelt 1901–09	Charles Fairbanks 1905–09	John Hay 1901–05 Elihu Root 1905–09 Robert Bacon 1909	Lyman J. Gage 1901–02 Leslie M. Shaw 1902–07 George B. Cortelyou 1907–09	Elihu Root 1901–04 William H. Taft 1904–08 Luke E. Wright 1908–09	John D. Long 1901–02 William H. Moody 1902–04 Paul Morton 1904–05 Charles J. Bonaparte 1905–06 Victor H. Metcalf 1906–08 T. H. Newberry 1908–09
William H. Taft 1909–13	James S. Sherman 1909–13	Philander C. Knox 1909–13	Franklin MacVeagh 1909–13	Jacob M. Dickinson 1909–11 Henry L. Stimson 1911–13	George von L. Meyer 1909–13
Woodrow Wilson 1913–21	Thomas R. Marshall 1913–21	William J. Bryan 1913–15 Robert Lansing 1915–20 Bainbridge Colby 1920–21	William G. McAdoo 1913–18 Carter Glass 1918–20 David F. Houston 1920–21	Lindley M. Garrison 1913–16 Newton D. Baker 1916–21	Josephus Daniels 1913–21
Warren G. Harding 1921–23	Calvin Coolidge 1921–23	Charles E. Hughes 1921–23	Andrew W. Mellon 1921–23	John W. Weeks 1921–23	Edwin Denby 1921–23

Postmaster General	Attorney General	Secretary of Interior	Secretary of Agriculture	Secretary of Commerce and Labor	
David M. Key 1877–80 Horace Maynard 1880–81	Charles Devens 1877–81	Carl Schurz 1877–81			
Thomas L. James 1881	Wayne MacVeagh 1881	S. J. Kirkwood 1881			
Thomas L. James 1881 Timothy O. Howe 1881–83 Walter Q. Gresham 1883–84 Frank Hatton 1884–85	B. H. Brewster 1881–85	Henry M. Teller 1881–85			
William F. Vilas 1885–88 Don M. Dickinson 1888–89	A. H. Garland 1885–89	L. Q. C. Lamar 1885–88 William F. Vilas 1888–89	Norman J. Colman 1889		
John Wanamaker 1889–93	W. H. H. Miller 1889–93	John W. Noble 1889–93	Jeremiah M. Rusk 1889–93		
Wilson S. Bissel 1893–95 William L. Wilson 1895–97	Richard Olney 1893–95 Judson Harmon 1895–97	Hoke Smith 1893–96 David R. Francis 1896–97	J. Sterling Morton 1893–97		
James A. Gary 1897–98 Charles E. Smith 1898–1901	Joseph McKenna 1897–98 John W. Griggs 1898–1901 Philander C. Knox 1901	Cornelius N. Bliss 1897–98 E. A. Hitchcock 1898–1901	James Wilson 1897–1901		
Charles E. Smith 1901–02 Henry C. Payne 1902–04 Robert J. Wynne 1904–05 George B. Cortelyou 1905–07 George von L. Meyer 1907–09	Philander C. Knox 1901–04 William H. Moody 1904–06 Charles J. Bonaparte 1906–09	E. A. Hitchcock 1901–07 James R. Garfield 1907–09	James Wilson 1901–09	George B. Cortelyou 1903–04 Victor H. Metcalf 1904–06 Oscar S. Straus 1906–09	
Frank H. Hitchcock 1909–13	G. W. Wickersham 1909–13	R. A. Ballinger 1909–11 Walter L. Fisher 1911–13	James Wilson 1909–13	Charles Nagel 1909–13	
				Secretary of Commerce	Secretary of Labor
Albert S. Burleson 1913–21	J. C. McReynolds 1913–14 T. W. Gregory 1914–19 A. Mitchell Palmer 1919–21	Franklin K. Lane 1913–20 John B. Payne 1920–21	David F. Houston 1913–20 E. T. Meredith 1920–21	W. C. Redfield 1913–19 J. W. Alexander 1919–21	William B. Wilson 1913–21
Will H. Hays 1921–22 Hubert Work 1922–23 Harry S. New 1923	H. M. Daugherty 1921–23	Albert B. Fall 1921–23 Hubert Work 1923	Henry C. Wallace 1921–23	Herbert C. Hoover 1921–23	James J. Davis 1921–23

PRESIDENTS, VICE PRESIDENTS, AND CABINET MEMBERS (1923–1963)

President	Vice President	Secretary of State	Secretary of Treasury	Secretary of War	Secretary of Navy
Calvin Coolidge 1923–29	Charles G. Dawes 1925–29	Charles E. Hughes 1923–25 Frank B. Kellogg 1925–29	Andrew W. Mellon 1923–29	John W. Weeks 1923–25 Dwight F. Davis 1925–29	Edwin Denby 1923–24 Curtis D. Wilbur 1924–29
Herbert C. Hoover 1929–33	Charles Curtis 1929–33	Henry L. Stimson 1929–33	Andrew W. Mellon 1929–32 Ogden L. Mills 1932–33	James W. Good 1929 Patrick J. Hurley 1929–33	Charles F. Adams 1929–33
Franklin Delano Roosevelt 1933–45	John Nance Garner 1933–41 Henry A. Wallace 1941–45 Harry S Truman 1945	Cordell Hull 1933–44 E. R. Stettinius, Jr. 1944–45	William H. Woodin 1933–34 Henry Morgenthau, Jr. 1934–45	George H. Dern 1933–36 Harry H. Woodring 1936–40 Henry L. Stimson 1940–45	Claude A. Swanson 1933–40 Charles Edison 1940 Frank Knox 1940–44 James V. Forrestal 1944–45
Harry S Truman 1945–53	Alben W. Barkley 1949–53	James F. Byrnes 1945–47 George C. Marshall 1947–49 Dean G. Acheson 1949–53	Fred M. Vinson 1945–46 John W. Snyder 1946–53	Robert P. Patterson 1945–47 Kenneth C. Royall 1947	James V. Forrestal 1945–47
				Secretary of Defense	
				James V. Forrestal 1947–49 Louis A. Johnson 1949–50 George C. Marshall 1950–51 Robert A. Lovett 1951–53	
Dwight D. Eisenhower 1953–61	Richard M. Nixon 1953–61	John Foster Dulles 1953–59 Christian A. Herter 1959–61	George M. Humphrey 1953–57 Robert B. Anderson 1957–61	Charles E. Wilson 1953–57 Neil H. McElroy 1957–61 Thomas S. Gates 1959–61	
John F. Kennedy 1961–63	Lyndon B. Johnson 1961–63	Dean Rusk 1961–63	C. Douglas Dillon 1961–63	Robert S. McNamara 1961–63	

Postmaster General	Attorney General	Secretary of Interior	Secretary of Agriculture	Secretary of Commerce	Secretary of Labor	Secretary of Health, Education and Welfare
Harry S. New 1923–29	H. M. Daugherty 1923–24 Harlan F. Stone 1924–25 John G. Sargent 1925–29	Hubert Work 1923–28 Roy O. West 1928–29	Henry C. Wallace 1923–24 Howard M. Gore 1924–25 W. M. Jardine 1925–29	Herbert C. Hoover 1923–28 William F. Whiting 1928–29	James J. Davis 1923–29	
Walter F. Brown 1929–33	J. D. Mitchell 1929–33	Ray L. Wilbur 1929–33	Arthur M. Hyde 1929–33	Robert P. Lamont 1929–32 Roy D. Chapin 1932–33	James J. Davis 1929–30 William N. Doak 1930–33	
James A. Farley 1933–40 Frank C. Walker 1940–45	H. S. Cummings 1933–39 Frank Murphy 1939–40 Robert Jackson 1940–41 Francis Biddle 1941–45	Harold L. Ickes 1933–45	Henry A. Wallace 1933–40 Claude R. Wickard 1940–45	Daniel C. Roper 1933–39 Harry L. Hopkins 1939–40 Jesse Jones 1940–45 Henry A. Wallace 1945	Frances Perkins 1933–45	
R. E. Hannegan 1945–47 Jesse M. Donaldson 1947–53	Tom C. Clark 1945–49 J. H. McGrath 1949–52 James P. McGranery 1952–53	Harold L. Ickes 1945–46 Julius A. Krug 1946–49 Oscar L. Chapman 1949–53	C. P. Anderson 1945–48 C. F. Brannan 1948–53	W. A. Harriman 1946–48 Charles Sawyer 1948–53	L. B. Schwellenbach 1945–48 Maurice J. Tobin 1948–53	
A. E. Summerfield 1953–61	H. Brownell, Jr. 1953–57 William P. Rogers 1957–61	Douglas McKay 1953–56 Fred Seaton 1956–61	Ezra T. Benson 1953–61	Sinclair Weeks 1953–58 Lewis L. Strauss 1958–61	Martin P. Durkin 1953 James P. Mitchell 1953–61	Oveta Culp Hobby 1953–55 Marion B. Folsom 1955–58 Arthur S. Flemming 1958–61
J. Edward Day 1961–63 John A. Gronouski 1963	Robert F. Kennedy 1961–63	Stewart L. Udall 1961–63	Orville L. Freeman 1961–63	Luther H. Hodges 1961–63	Arthur J. Goldberg 1961–62 W. Willard Wirtz 1962–63	A. H. Ribicoff 1961–62 Anthony J. Celebrezze 1962–63

PRESIDENTS, VICE PRESIDENTS, AND CABINET MEMBERS (1963–1977)

President	Vice President	Secretary of State	Secretary of Treasury	Secretary of Defense	Postmaster General*	Attorney General
Lyndon B. Johnson 1963–69	Hubert H. Humphrey 1965–69	Dean Rusk 1963–69	C. Douglas Dillon 1963–65 Henry H. Fowler 1965–68 Joseph W. Barr 1968–69	Robert S. McNamara 1963–68 Clark M. Clifford 1968–69	John A. Gronouski 1963–65 Lawrence F. O'Brien 1965–68 W. Marvin Watson 1968–69	Robert F. Kennedy 1963–65 N. deB. Katzenbach 1965–67 Ramsey Clark 1967–69
Richard M. Nixon 1969–74	Spiro T. Agnew 1969–73 Gerald R. Ford 1973–74	William P. Rogers 1969–73 Henry A. Kissinger 1973–74	David M. Kennedy 1969–70 John B. Connally 1970–72 George P. Shultz 1972–74 William E. Simon 1974	Melvin R. Laird 1969–73 Elliot L. Richardson 1973 James R. Schlesinger 1973–74	Winton M. Blount 1969–71	John M. Mitchell 1969–72 Richard G. Kleindienst 1972–73 Elliot L. Richardson 1973 William B. Saxbe 1974
Gerald R. Ford 1974–77	Nelson A. Rockefeller 1974–77	Henry A. Kissinger 1974–77	William E. Simon 1974–77	James R. Schlesinger 1974–75 Donald H. Rumsfeld 1975–77		William B. Saxbe 1974–75 Edward H. Levi 1975–77

*On July 1, 1971, the Post Office became an independent agency. After that date, the Postmaster General was no longer a member of the Cabinet.

Secretary of Interior	Secretary of Agriculture	Secretary of Commerce	Secretary of Labor	Secretary of Health, Education and Welfare	Secretary of Housing and Urban Development	Secretary of Transportation
Stewart L. Udall 1963–69	Orville L. Freeman 1963–69	Luther H. Hodges 1963–65 John T. Connor 1965–67 Alexander B. Trowbridge 1967–68 C. R. Smith 1968–69	W. Willard Wirtz 1963–69	Anthony J. Celebrezze 1963–65 John W. Gardner 1965–68 Wilbur J. Cohen 1968–69	Robert C. Weaver 1966–68 Robert C. Wood 1968–69	Alan S. Boyd 1966–69
Walter J. Hickel 1969–71 Rogers C. B. Morton 1971–74	Clifford M. Hardin 1969–71 Earl L. Butz 1971–74	Maurice H. Stans 1969–72 Peter G. Peterson 1972 Frederick B. Dent 1972–74	George P. Shultz 1969–70 James D. Hodgson 1970–73 Peter J. Brennan 1973–74	Robert H. Finch 1969–70 Elliot L. Richardson 1970–73 Caspar W. Weinberger 1973–74	George W. Romney 1969–73 James T. Lynn 1973–74	John A. Volpe 1969–73 Claude S. Brinegar 1973–74
Rogers C. B. Morton 1974–75 Stanley K. Hathaway 1975 Thomas D. Kleppe 1975–77	Earl L. Butz 1974–76	Frederick B. Dent 1974–75 Rogers C. B. Morton 1975 Elliot L. Richardson 1975–77	Peter J. Brennan 1974–75 John T. Dunlop 1975–76 W. J. Usery 1976–77	Caspar W. Weinberger 1974–75 Forrest D. Mathews 1975–77	James T. Lynn 1974–75 Carla A. Hills 1975–77	Claude S. Brinegar 1974–75 William T. Coleman 1975–77

PRESIDENTS, VICE PRESIDENTS, AND CABINET MEMBERS (1977–1992)

President	Vice President	Secretary of State	Secretary of Treasury	Secretary of Defense	Attorney General	Secretary of Interior
Jimmy Carter 1977–81	Walter F. Mondale 1977–81	Cyrus R. Vance 1977–80 Edmund S. Muskie 1980–81	W. Michael Blumenthal 1977–79 G. William Miller 1979–81	Harold Brown 1977–81	Griffin Bell 1977–79 Benjamin R. Civiletti 1979–81	Cecil D. Andrus 1977–81
Ronald W. Reagan 1981–89	George H. Bush 1981–89	Alexander M. Haig, Jr. 1981–82 George P. Shultz 1982–89	Donald T. Regan 1981–85 James A. Baker 1985–88 Nicholas F. Brady 1988–89	Caspar W. Weinberger 1981–87 Frank C. Carlucci 1987–89	William French Smith 1981–85 Edwin Meese 1985–88 Richard Thornburgh 1988–89	James G. Watt 1981–83 William P. Clark 1983–85 Donald P. Hodel 1985–89
George H. Bush 1989–	J. Danforth Quayle 1989–	James A. Baker 1989–	Nicholas Brady 1989–	Richard Cheney 1989–	Richard Thornburgh 1989–90 William Barr 1990–	Manuel Lujan 1989–

Secretary of Agriculture	Secretary of Commence	Secretary of Labor	Secretary of Health, Education and Welfare		Secretary of Housing and Urban Development	Secretary of Transportation	Secretary of Energy
Robert Bergland 1977–81	Juanita Kreps 1977–81	F. Ray Marshall 1977–81	Joseph Califano 1977–79 Patricia Roberts Harris 1979–80		Patricia Roberts Harris 1977–79 Moon Landrieu 1979–81	Brock Adams 1977–79 Neil E. Goldschmidt 1979–81	James R. Schlesinger 1977–79 Charles W. Duncan, Jr. 1979–81
			Secretary of Health and Human Services	**Secretary of Education**			
			Patricia Roberts Harris 1980–81	Shirley M. Hufstedler 1980–81			
John R. Block 1981–86 Richard E. Lyng 1986–89	Malcolm Baldrige 1981–87 C. William Verity, Jr. 1987–89	Raymond J. Donovan 1981–85 William E. Brock 1985–87 Ann Dore McLaughlin 1987–89	Richard S. Schweiker 1981–83 Margaret M. Heckler 1983–85 Otis R. Bowen 1985–89	Terrel H. Bell 1981–85 William J. Bennett 1985–88 Lauro Fred Cavazos 1988–89	Samuel R. Pierce, Jr. 1981–89	Drew Lewis 1981–83 Elizabeth H. Dole 1983–87 James H. Burnley 1987–89	James B. Edwards 1981–82 Donald P. Hodel 1982–85 John S. Harrington 1985–89
Clayton Yeutter 1989–90 Edward Madigan 1990–	Robert Mosbacher 1989–91 Barbara Franklin 1991–	Elizabeth Dole 1989– Lynn Martin	Louis Sullivan 1989–	Lamar Alexander 1990–	Jack Kemp 1989–	Samuel Skinner 1989–90 Andrew Card 1990–	James Watkins 1989–

JUSTICES OF THE U.S. SUPREME COURT

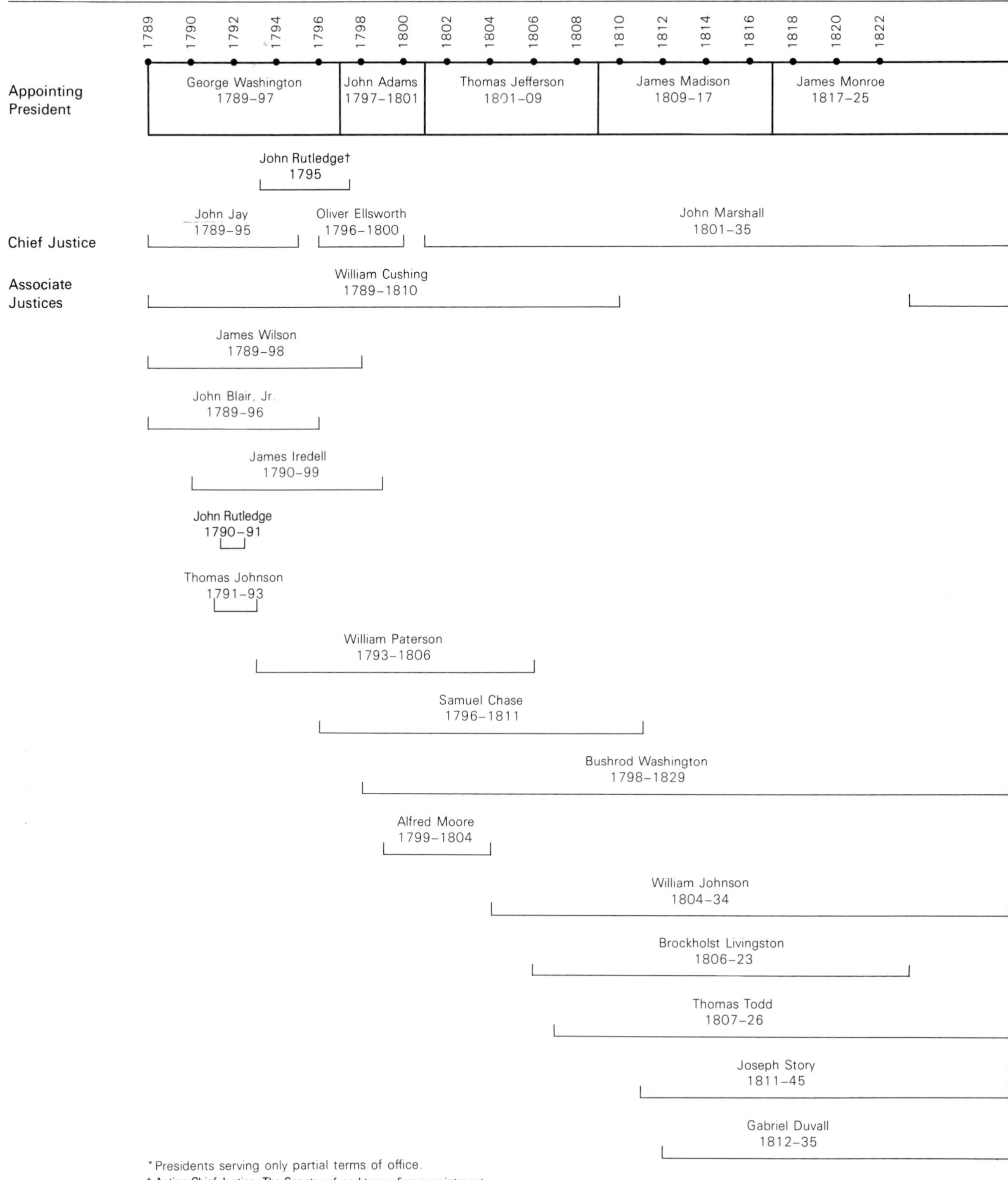

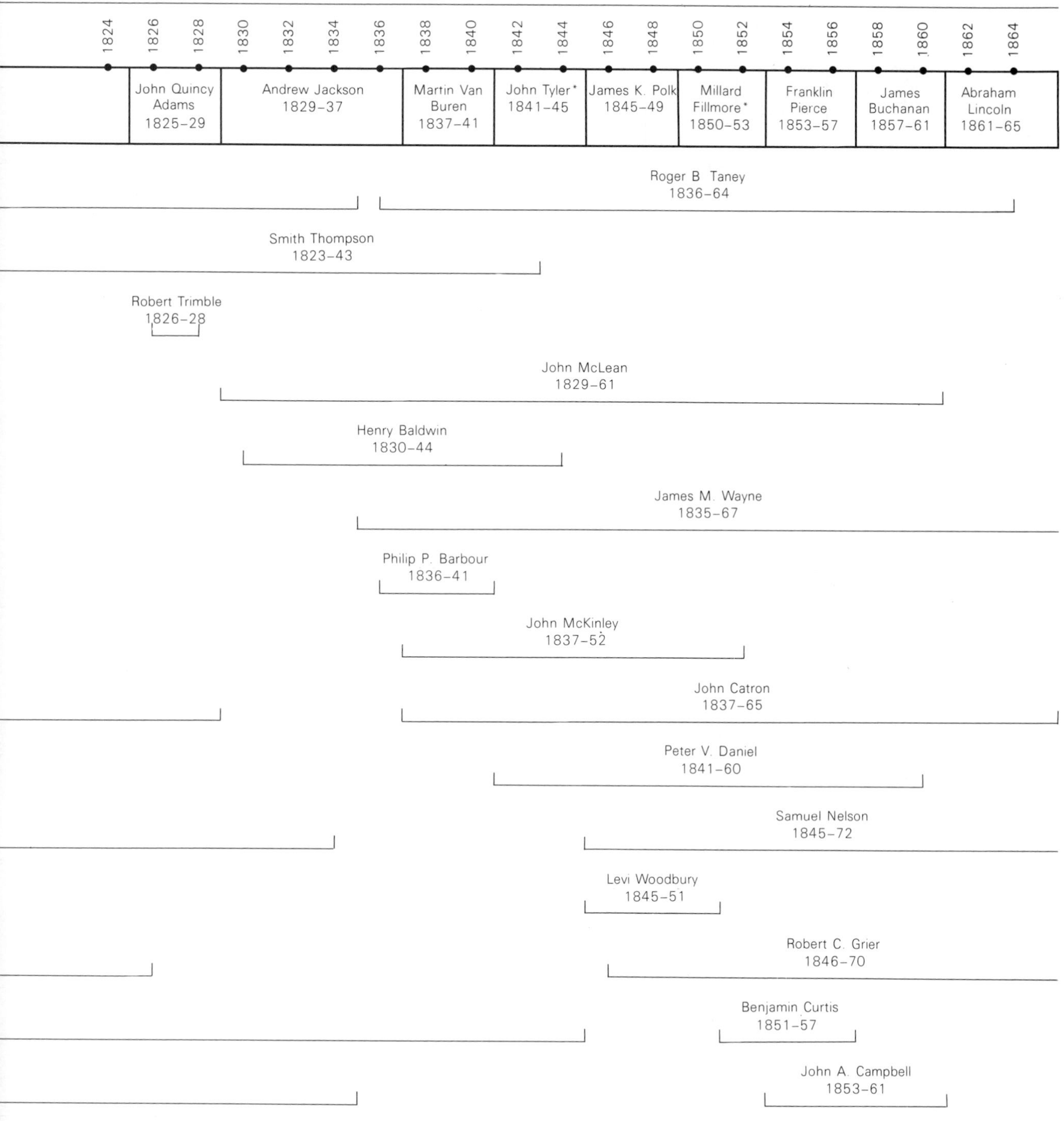
1824
1826
1828
1830
1832
1834
1836
1838
1840
1842
1844
1846
1848
1850
1852
1854
1856
1858
1860
1862
1864
John Quincy Adams 1825–29
Andrew Jackson 1829–37
Martin Van Buren 1837–41
John Tyler* 1841–45
James K. Polk 1845–49
Millard Fillmore* 1850–53
Franklin Pierce 1853–57
James Buchanan 1857–61
Abraham Lincoln 1861–65
Roger B. Taney 1836–64
Smith Thompson 1823–43
Robert Trimble 1826–28
John McLean 1829–61
Henry Baldwin 1830–44
James M. Wayne 1835–67
Philip P. Barbour 1836–41
John McKinley 1837–52
John Catron 1837–65
Peter V. Daniel 1841–60
Samuel Nelson 1845–72
Levi Woodbury 1845–51
Robert C. Grier 1846–70
Benjamin Curtis 1851–57
John A. Campbell 1853–61

JUSTICES OF THE U.S. SUPREME COURT (Cont.)

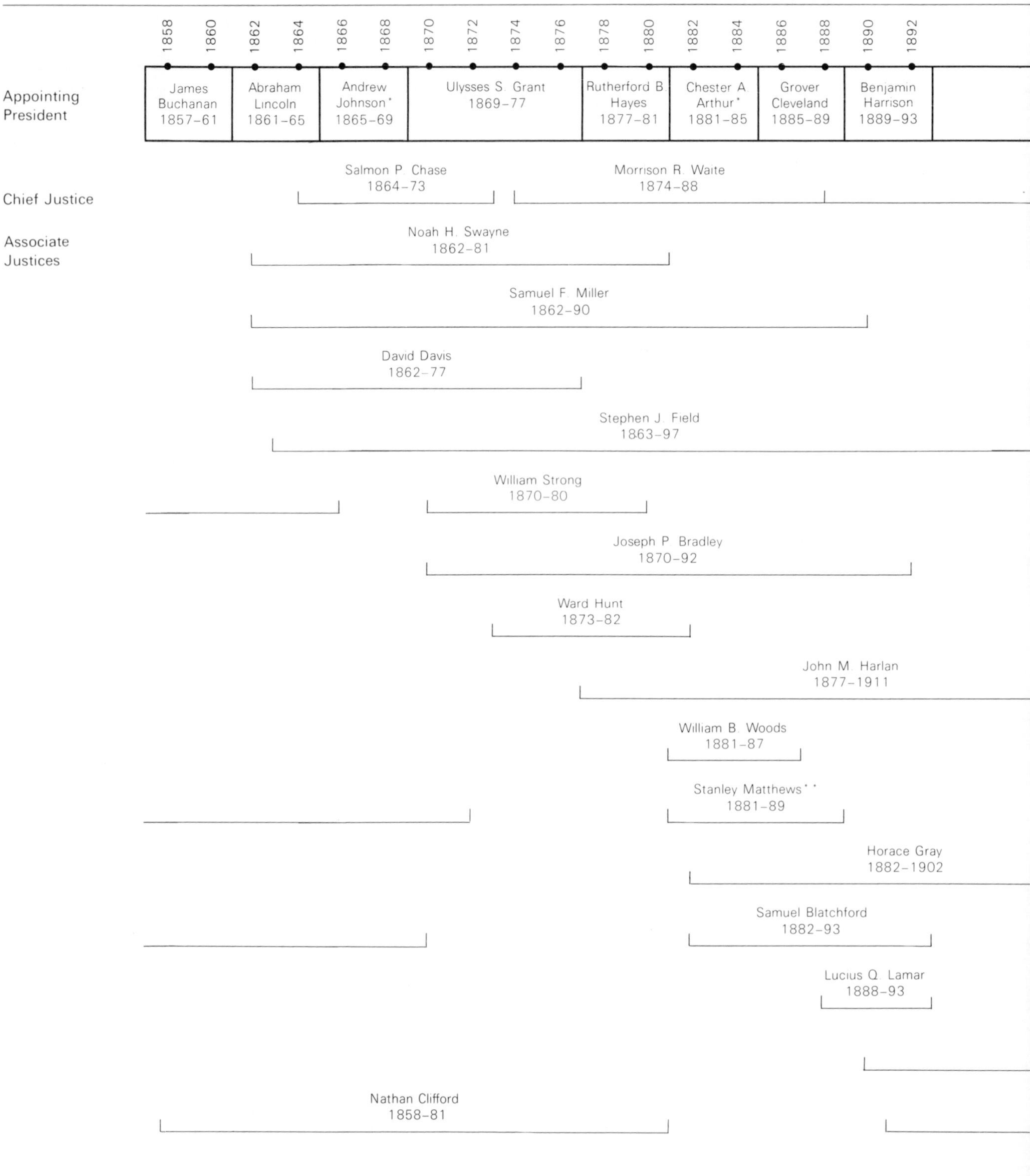

*Presidents serving only partial terms of office.

**Appointed by James A. Garfield.

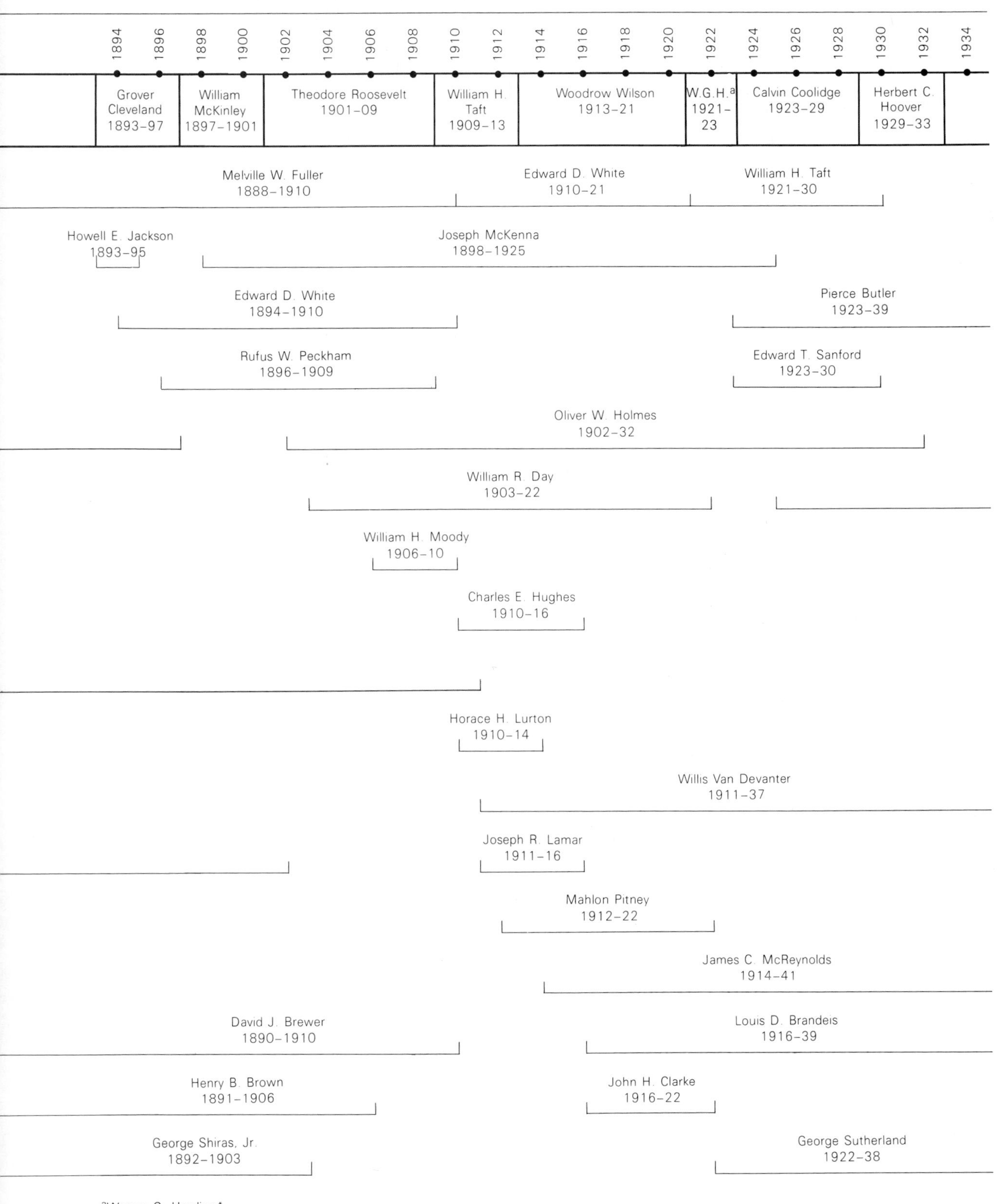

[a]Warren G. Harding*
1921-23

JUSTICES OF THE U.S. SUPREME COURT (Cont.)

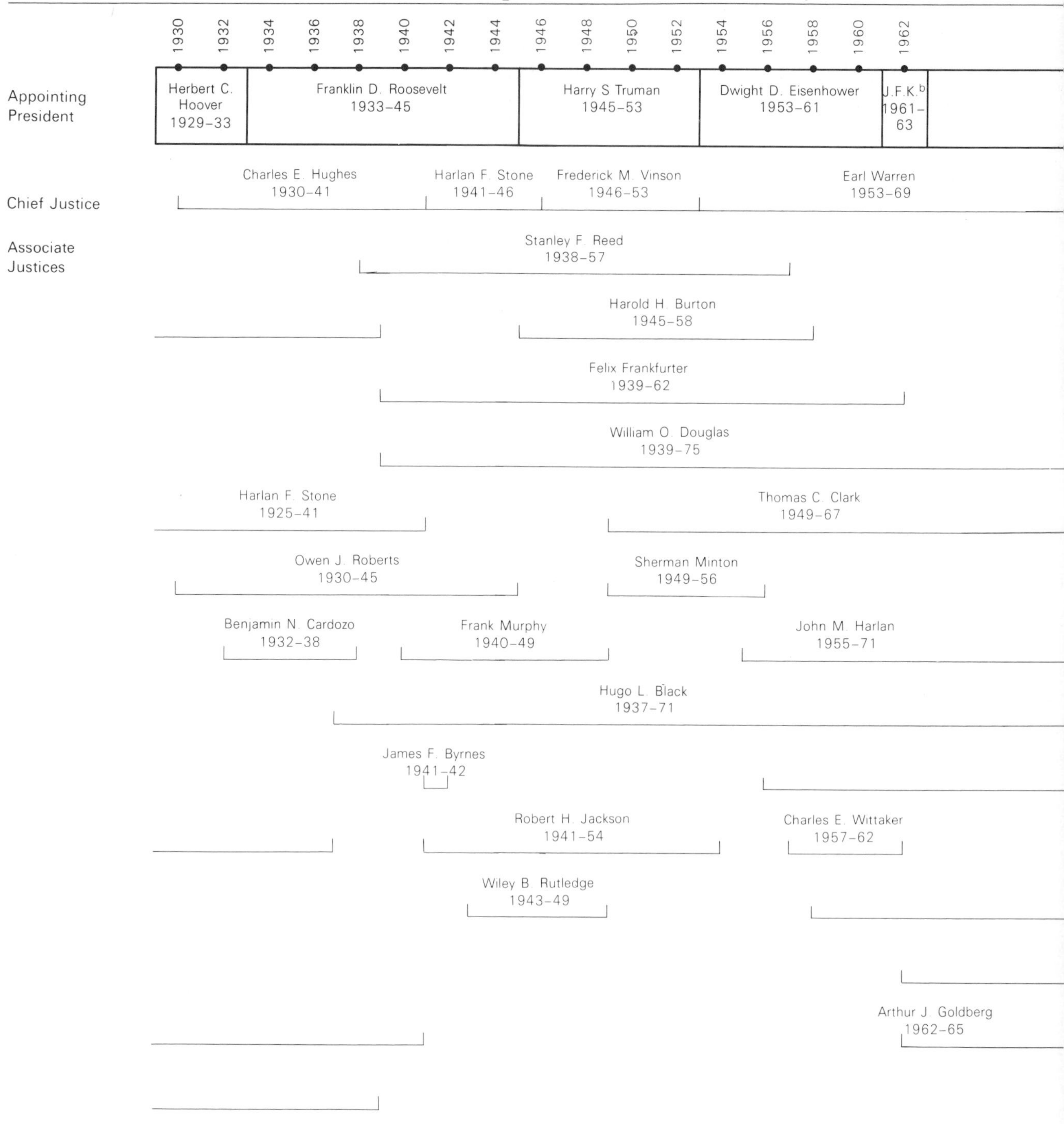

*Presidents serving only partial terms of office.

[b]John F. Kennedy*
1961–63

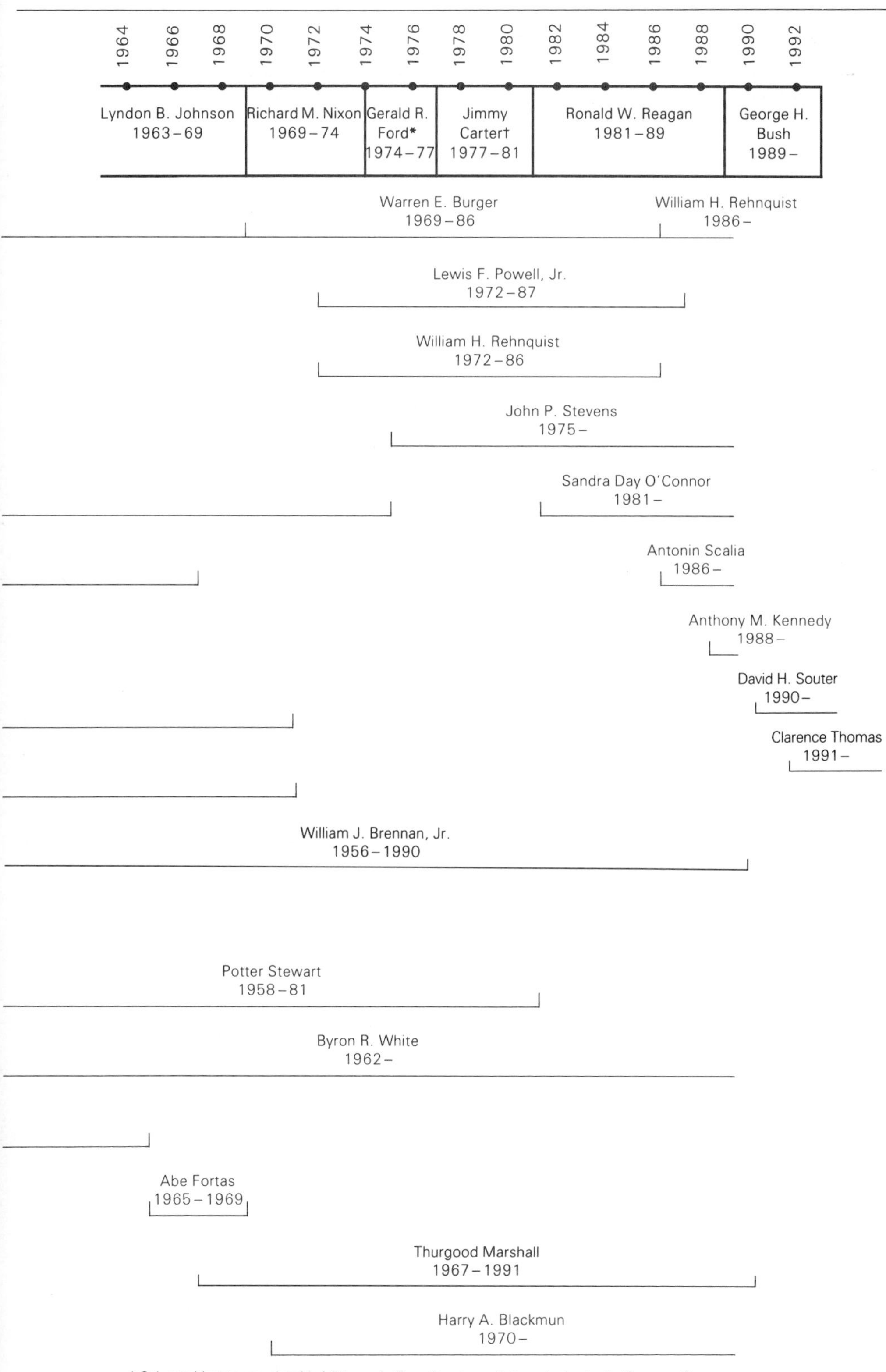

† Only president to complete his full term of office without appointing a justice to the Supreme Court.

PICTURE CREDITS

2 From *The Transformation of Virginia* 1740–1790, by Rhys Isaac. © 1982 The University of North Carolina Press. Published for the Institute of Early American History and Culture. Reprinted by permission.
4 The Mansell Collection
6 The Bettmann Archive, Inc.
7 (*t*) Musei Civici, Como, Italy
7 (*b*) Courtesy of the American Museum of National History
11 Courtesy of the New-York Historical Society, New York City
12 The British Museum, 1563, from the Huth Collection
15 Library of Congress
17 Pocahontas, detail. National Portrait Gallery, Smithsonian Institution, Washington, D.C.. Transfer from the National Gallery of Art. Gift of Andrew W. Mellon.
18 Courtesy of The Jamestown-Yorktown Foundation
20 Rare Book Division, The New York Public Library, Astor, Lenox and Tilden Foundations
22 Unknown American. *Mrs. Elizabeth Freake and Baby Mary, ca.* 1671–74. Worcester Art Museum, gift of Mr. and Mrs. Albert W. Rice.
24 Courtesy of the American Antiquarian Society
30 Edward Hicks, *Penn's Treaty with the Indians, ca.* 1840–45. Abby Aldrich Rockefeller Folk Art Center, Williamsburg, VA
32 HBJ Photo
37 Museum of the City of New York, J. Clarence Davies Collection 34.100.29
40 I. N. Phelps Stokes Collection, Miriam and Ira D. Wallach Division of Art, Prints & Photographs, The New York Public Library, Astor, Lenox and Tilden Foundations
42 Culver Pictures, Inc.
43 (*t*) Francis Place, detail, *William Penn*. The Historical Society of Pennsylvania.
43 (*b*) 64.456, *Quaker Meeting* (variant of a painting entitled "Grace Church Street Meeting, Society of Friends, London"), Anonymous, British, 4th quarter 18th c. or 1st quarter 19th c. Oil on canvas, $25\frac{1}{4} \times 30$ in. (64.0×76.2 cm.). Bequest of Maxim Karolik. Courtesy of the Museum of Fine Arts, Boston.
45 John Greenwood, *Sea Captains Carousing in Surinam,* 1758 (?). The Saint Louis Museum of Art. Museum purchase.
47 58.358, *Judge Samuel Sewell,* 1729. John Smibert, American, 1688–1751. Oil on canvas, painted oval, $30\frac{1}{4} \times 25\frac{1}{2}$ in. (76.8×64.8 cm.). Bequest of William L. Barnard, by exchange, and the Emily L. Ainsley Fund. Courtesy of the Museum of Fine Arts, Boston.
51 The Bettmann Archive
52 Courtesy of the John Carter Brown Library at Brown University
60 Edward Hicks, *The Residence of David Twining,* 1787. Abby Aldrich Rockefeller Folk Art Center, Williamsburg, VA.
62 Thomas Coram, *Mulberry Plantation*. Carolina Art Association, Gibbes Art Gallery.
65 Library of Congress
67 Unknown artist, *The Plantation, ca.* 1825. The Metropolitan Museum of Art. Gift of Edgar William and Bernice Chrysler Garbisch, 1963.
70 W. J. Bennett, after George Harvey, *Spring #2: Burning Fallen Trees in a Girdled Clearing—Western Scene*. Yale University Art Gallery. The Mabel Brady Gavan Collection.
73 Courtesy of The Bostonian Society, Old State House
74 Maryland Historical Society, Baltimore
76 Library of Congress
80 William Burgis, *A Prospect of the Colleges in Cambridge in New England,* 1726. Courtesy The Massachusetts Historical Society.
81 Joseph S. Dupplessis, *Benjamin Franklin*. The Metropolitan Museum of Art. Bequest of Michael Friedsam, 1931. The Friedsam Collection (32.100.32).
82 Frank B. Mayer, *My Lady's Visit—Annapolis*. Maryland Historical Society, deposited by the Peabody Institute.
83 Bowles & Carver, after Dighten, *Bowle Moral Pictures*. Yale University Art Gallery, The Mabel Brady Gavan Collection.
86 John Trumbull, *Battle of Bunker's Hill,* June 17, 1775. Copyright Yale University Art Gallery.
90 (*t*) After R. Brompton, *William Chatham, 1st Earl of Pitt*. National Portrait Gallery, London.
90 (*b*) J. Chapman, *General James Wolfe*. C 6296, Public Archives, Canada.
91 *Britain's Glory* or *The Reduction of Cape Breton,* 1758. The New Brunswick Museum, Saint John, New Brunswick/Le Musée du Nouveau-Brunswick, Saint John, Nouveau-Brunswick.
95 (*l*) Connecticut Historical Society; (*r*) Library of Congress
98 Library of Congress
99 Courtesy of the Essex Institute, Salem, MA
103 I. N. Phelps Stokes Collection, Miriam and Ira D. Wallach Division of Art, Prints & Photographs, The New York Public Library, Astor, Lenox and Tilden Foundations.
104 Print Collection, Miriam and Ira D. Wallach Division of Art, Prints & Photographs, The New York Public Library, Astor, Lenox and Tilden Foundations.
107 HBJ Collection
108 Edward Trumn, *Gov. Thomas Hutchinson*. Courtesy of the Massachusetts Historical Society.
110 The Historical Society of Pennsylvania.
114 John Trumbull, *Declaration of Independence*. Copyright Yale University Art Gallery.
118 Unknown artist, *The Spirit of '76*. The original painting hangs in the Selectmen's Meeting Room, Abbot Hall, Marblehead, Massachusetts.
121 Reproduced by courtesy of the Trustees of the British Museum
123 (*t*) James Peale, *The Battle of Princeton,* Princeton University Library

123 (*b*) British School, *The American Riflemen,* 1776. The Metropolitan Museum of Art. Bequest of Charles Allen Munn.

125 Library of Congress

128 Ann S. K. Brown Military Collection. Courtesy of the John Carter Brown Library at Brown University.

129 Benjamin West, detail, *American Commissioners of the Preliminary Peace Negotiations with Great Britain, ca.* 1783. Courtesy of The Henry Francis du Pont Winterthur Museum.

130 Library of Congress

135 Library of Congress

141 Charles Wilson Peale, detail, *George Washington.* The Metropolitan Museum of Art. Gift of Collis P. Huntington, 1896 (97.33).

142 Rembrandt Peale, detail, *Thomas Jefferson.* Independence National Historical Park Collection.

143 John Trumbull, detail, *Alexander Hamilton.* Copyright Yale University Art Gallery.

148 John Trumbull, *Washington at Verplanck's Point, York, 1782, Receiving the French Troops after the Victory at Yorktown.* Courtesy of The Henry Francis du Pont Winterthur Museum.

151 Library of Congress

154 W. Birch, *Bank of the United States in Third Street, Philadelphia.* Courtesy of the John Brown Carter Library of Brown University.

155 Commercial Exchange, Philadelphia

160 John Trumbull, *Thomas Pinckney.* Copyright Yale University Art Gallery.

163 (*t*) University of Hartford, Museum of American Political Life

163 (*b*) Charles Wilson Peale, *John Adams.* Independence National Historical Park Collection.

167 S. W. Fores, *Property Protected a la Francoise,* 1798. Courtesy of the Lilly Library, Indiana University, Bloomington, Indiana.

174 Library of Congress

176 Rembrandt Peale, detail, *Thomas Jefferson.* Courtesy of The New-York Historical Society, New York City.

182 Chicago Historical Society

184 Saint Mémin, *Aaron Burr.* Courtesy of The New-York Historical Society, New York City.

186 Michael P. Corne, *Bombardment of Tripoli,* 1804. Courtesy of the United States Naval Academy Museum.

187 (*t*) Pencil sketch of Thomas Jefferson formerly attributed to Benjamin Henry Latrobe. Maryland Historical Society, Baltimore.

187 (*b*) Gilbert Stuart (1755–1830). *Portrait of James Madison* (1751–1836). *ca.* 1821. Oil on canvas, 40 × 32 in., Mead Art Museum, Amherst College Bequest of Herbert L. Pratt, Class of 1895, 1945.82.

189 Unknown artist, *Tecumseh.* Courtesy, Field Museum of Natural History, Chicago, Neg. #93851.

190 Broadside, 1814. Courtesy of The New-York Historical Society, New York City.

192 Courtesy of The New-York Historical Society, New York City.

193 Library of Congress

195 Francis Alexander, detail, *Daniel Webster.* Hood Museum of Art, Dartmouth College, Hanover, NH. Gift of George C. Shattuck, Class of 1803.

200 J. H. Bufford, *View of the Upper Village of Lockport, Niagara County, New York,* 1836. Courtesy of The New-York Historical Society, New York City.

204 Thomas Birch, *Landscape with Covered Wagon,* 1821. Wadsworth Atheneum, Hartford. Bequest of Mrs. Clara Hinton Gould.

205 New York City Art Commission

207 Rembrandt Peale, detail, *John Marshall.* Supreme Court of the United States.

209 W. H. Lizars, *The Mississippi at New Orleans,* etching after drawing by Basil Hall. Courtesy of The New-York Historical Society, New York City.

212 (*t*) Courtesy of The New-York Historical Society, New York City

212 (*b*) Public Library of Cincinnati and Hamilton County

213 Photo, view from Court House Dome, 1858. Photo by Alexander Hesler. Chicago Historical Society.

214 United States Army Military History Institute

218 Courtesy of The Charleston Museum, Charleston, South Carolina

223 Museum of American Textile History

224 Museum of American Textile History

228 George Caleb Bingham, *Stump Speaking.* From the Art Collection of The Boatmen's National Bank of St. Louis.

230 1975.806, *Pat Lyon at the Forge.* John Neagle, American, 1796–1860. Oil on canvas, 93 × 68 in. Herman and Zoe Oliver Sherman Fund. Courtesy, Museum of Fine Arts, Boston.

232 The Metropolitan Museum of Art. Gift of I. N. Phelps Stokes, Edward S. Hawes, Alice Mary Hawes, Marion Augusta Hawes, 1937.

234 University of Hartford, Museum of American Political Life

235 Library of Congress

241 Rare Books and Manuscripts Division, The New York Public Library, Astor, Lenox and Tilden Foundations

243 Currier and Ives, detail, *Plantation of the Mississippi.* Yale University Art Gallery. The Mabel Brady Gavan Collection.

244 Brown Brothers

248 Courtesy of the American Antiquarian Society

250 Courtesy of The New-York Historical Society, New York City

251 Henry Inman, *Martin Van Buren.* The Metropolitan Museum of Art. Gift of Mrs. Jacob H. Lazarus, 1893 (93.19.2).

252 Indiana Historical Society

258 North Carolina Division of Archives and History

261 The Bettmann Archive, Inc.

262 E. W. Clay, *Methodist Camp Meeting.* Courtesy of The New-York Historical Society, New York City.

263 Sameul L. Waldo and William Jewett, detail, *Portrait of Charles Grandison Finney.* Allen Memorial Art Museum, Oberlin College. Gift of Lewis Tappan, 16.6.

264 97.65, *William Ellery Channing.* Washington Allston, American, 1779–1843. Oil on canvas, 31 × 27½ in. Gift of William Francis Channing. Courtesy of the Museum of Fine Arts, Boston.

266 Prints Division, The New York Public Library, Astor, Lenox and Tilden Foundations
268 Library of Congress
270 The Metropolitan Museum of Art. Gift of I. N. Phelps Stokes, Edward S. Hawes, Alice Mary Hawes, Marion Augusta Hawes, 1937.
271 The Bettmann Archive, Inc.
272 Smith College Archives, Smith College, (Warren photo)
273 Sophia Smith Collection, Smith College, photo by F. Gutekunst, Philadelphia
274 Sophia Smith Collection, Smith College, photo by F. Gutekunst, Philadelphia
276 Library of Congress
277 Library of Congress
278 Print Collection, Miriam and Ira D. Wallach Division of Art, Prints & Photographs, The New York Public Library, Astor, Lenox and Tilden Foundations.
282 Richard Woodville, *War News from Mexico,* 1848. National Academy of Design, New York City.
287 Alfred Jacob Miller, *Fort Laramie.* Walters Art Gallery, Baltimore.
289 HBJ Photo
290 Utah State Historical Society
295 Yale Collection of Western Americana, Beinecke Rare Book & Manuscript Library
297 The Metropolitan Museum of Art. Gift of I. N. Phelps Stokes, Edward S. Hawes, Alice Mary Hawes, Marion Augusta Hawes, 1937.
299 Library of Congress
300 The Bettmann Archive, Inc.
301 (*t*) Brown Brothers
301 (*b*) Brown Brothers
302 *(both)* The Metropolitan Museum of Art. Gift of I. N. Phelps Stokes, Edward S. Hawes, Alice Mary Hawes, Marion Augusta Hawes, 1937.
305 The Metropolitan Museum of Art. Gift of I. N. Phelps Stokes, Edward S. Hawes, Alice Mary Hawes, Marion Augusta Hawes, 1937.
308 Courtesy of The New-York Historical Society, New York City
310 (*t*) Library of Congress
310 (*b*) Joseph Oriel Eaton, *Portrait of Herman Melville.* Courtesy of the Harvard University Portrait Collection. Gift to the Houghton Library by Mrs. Henry K. Metcalf.
311 Library of Congress
314 The National Archives, 111-B-2325
315 The White House
316 Samuel B. Waugh, *The Battery, New York,* 1855. Museum of the City of New York.
318 University of Hartford, Museum of American Political Life
321 Nebraska State Historical Society Union Pacific Collection
322 Library of Congress
324 Chicago Historical Society. Lithograph, "Testing the First Reaping Machine near Steeles Tavern, VA, A. D. 1831," by Milwaukee Litho. and Engraving Company, Chicago.
325 The Bettmann Archive, Inc.
327 The National Archives, 86-G-1B-1
328 Courtesy, American Antiquarian Society
330 Library of Congress
333 Courtesy of The New-York Historical Society, New York City
336 Kansas State Historical Society
339 Library of Congress
340 (*t*) Courtesy of The New-York Historical Society, New York City
340 (*b*) Library of Congress
341 Library of Congress
342 From I. Garland Penn, *The Afro-American Press and Its Editors,* Springfield, MA, Wiley & Co., 1891, p. 5
344 Library of Congress
345 Library of Congress
347 Library of Congress
354 The Bettmann Archive, Inc
355 The National Archives
358 Chicago Historical Society
363 James E. Taylor Collection, The Huntington Library, San Marino, California
365 Florida State Archives
366 Chicago Historical Society
367 Louis A. Warren Lincoln Library and Museum, Fort Wayne, Indiana
368 The National Archives, 111-B-173
371 Courtesy of The Mariners' Museum Newport News, Virginia
372 American Heritage Picture Collection
374 (*t*) The Bettmann Archive, Inc.
374 (*b*) Courtesy of The New-York Historical Society, New York City
383 Library of Congress
384 Library of Congress
385 Association of American Railroads Washington, D.C.
387 Edouard Manet, *Alabama and Kearsarge, ca.* 1865. John C. Johnson Collection, Philadelphia Museum of Art.
389 HBJ Photo
390 Cook Collection, Valentine Museum, Richmond, Virginia
391 Library of Congress
394 Library of Congress
397 Winslow Homer, *Prisoners From the Front,* 1866. The Metropolitan Museum of Art. Gift of Mrs. Frank B. Porter, 1922.
398 Library of Congress
399 Winslow Homer. *A Visit From the Old Mistress,* 1876. National Museum of American Art, Smithsonian Institution, Gift of William T. Evans
400 Edgar Degas, *The Cotton Market in New Orleans.* Musée des Beaux-Arts, Pau
401 (*t*) Cook Collection, Valentine Museum, Richmond, Virginia
401 (*b*) Library of Congress
402 The Bettmann Archive, Inc.
405 Library of Congress
407 Moorland-Springarn Research Center, Howard University
409 The Granger Collection
415 Library of Congress
418 Sophia Smith Collection, Smith College, undated portrait of G. M. Cushing, photographer
420 Atlanta Historical Society
424 The Granger Collection
425 © Ewing Galloway

429 Library of Congress

430 Library of Congress

431 The Bettmann Archive, Inc.

432 Brown Brothers

433 Library of Congress

435 The Historic New Orleans Collection, Acq. no. 1972.5

437 Cook Collection, Valentine Museum, Richmond, Virginia

438 (*t*) Library of Congress

438 (*b*) Brown Brothers

440 National Anthropological Archives, Smithsonian Institution

443 Kansas State Historical Society, Topeka

445 The Bettmann Archive, Inc.

446 National Anthropological Archives Smithsonian Institution

448 Courtesy, Colorado Historical Society

450 Montana Historical Society, Helena MT

452 Nebraska State Historical Society

453 Baker Library, Harvard Business School

454 Archives and Manuscripts Division, Oklahoma Historical Society

459 (*t*) Solomon D. Butcher Collection, Nebraska State Historical Society

459 (*b*) Library of Congress

462 Keystone-Mast Collection California Museum of Photography, University of California, Riverside

464 Public Relations Department, Great Northern Railway, St. Paul, Minnesota

468 Steichen, Edward. *J. P. Morgan*. (1903) Silver bromide, $16\frac{3}{4} \times 13\frac{1}{2}''$. Collection, The Museum of Modern Art, New York. Gift of the photographer. Reprinted with the permission of Joanna T. Steichen.

470 Library of Congress

473 Brown Brothers

474 Brown Brothers

475 Brown Brothers

478 U.S. Department of Agriculture

479 Library of Congress

480 The Bettmann Archive, Inc.

484 W. Louis Sonntag, Jr., *The Bowery at Night,* 1895. Museum of the City of New York.

487 Courtesy of AT&T Archives

488 The Bettmann Archive, Inc.

489 Photo by Lewis W. Hine, George Eastman House Collection

491 Meseum of the City of New York

492 Library of Congress

493 Keystone-Mast Collection, California Museum of Photography, University of California, Riverside

497 The Salvation Army National Archives & Research Center

499 Brown Brothers

501 Museum of the City of New York

502 The Bettmann Archive, Inc.

503 Culver Pictures, Inc.

504 Mark Twain Memorial, Hartford, CT

505 The Bettmann Archive, Inc.

508 Library of Congress

512 Library of Congress

514 Library of Congress

515 (*t*) Library of Congress

515 (*b*) Brown Brothers

518 Library of Congress

520 Print Collection, Miriam and Ira D. Wallach Division of Art, Prints and Photographs, The New York Public Library, Astor, Lenox and Tilden Foundations

522 Library of Congress

524 Kansas State Historical Society

525 (*t*) Brown Brothers

525 (*b*) Kansas State Historical Society

528 Culver Pictures, Inc.

529 Culver Pictures, Inc.

530 Library of Congress

531 Library of Congress

534 Theodore Roosevelt Library

536 Print Collection, Miriam and Ira D. Wallach Division of Art, Prints and Photographs, The New York Public Library, Astor, Lenox and Tilden Foundations

538 Brown Brothers

539 The Bettmann Archive

540 The New York Public Library, Astor, Lenox and Tilden Foundations

543 Official United States Navy Photo

546 National Archives, 111-RB-1258

548 The Bettmann Archive, Inc.

549 The Bettmann Archive, Inc.

552 Museum of the City of New York

556 Photo by Lewis W. Hine Library of Congress LC-USZ62-12876

559 Library of Congress

560 HBJ Photo

561 Brown Brothers

562 HBJ Photo

563 Tamiment Institute Library, New York University

564 Library of Congress

568 Library of Congress

570 Brown Brothers

574 Brown Brothers

579 The Bettmann Archive, Inc.

584 Official United States Navy Photo

586 Brown Brothers

588 Library of Congress

589 General Research Division, The New York Public Library, Astor, Lenox and Tilden Foundations

590 The Bettmann Archive, Inc.

593 Culver Pictures, Inc.

594 Culver Pictures, Inc.

599 Library of Congress

601 The National Archives, 165-WW-165-1

603 Copyright © 1915 by The New York Times Co. Reproduced by permission.

606 The Bettmann Archive, Inc.

609 Culver Pictures, Inc.

610 U.S. Army Photograph

612 (*t*) Courtesy of The New-York Historical Society, New York City
612 (*b*) The National Archives, 111-SC-14591
613 The National Archives, SC-27427
614 The National Archives
617 The National Archives, 111-SC-3575
622 The National Archives, 111-SC-6297
625 UPI/Bettmann Newsphotos
631 The Bettmann Archive, Inc.
632 Courtesy Chicago Historical Society
633 VanderZee Institute
634 UPI/Bettmann Newsphotos
637 Brown Brothers
639 Culver Pictures, Inc.
641 The Bettmann Archive, Inc.
643 Library of Congress
646 Library of Congress
648 The National Archives, 306-NT-269G-5
650 (*t*) Courtesy of the Ford Archives, Henry Ford Museum & Greenfield Village
650 (*b*) Caufield & Shook Collection, Photographic Archives, University of Louisville
651 FPG International
654 Library of Congress
655 Speakeasy scene, interior. Mural project for Central Park Casino. Painting by Ben Shahn. Museum of the City of New York.
656 AP/Wide World Photos
657 State Historical Society of Wisconsin
658 AP/Wide World Photos
659 UPI/Bettmann Newsphotos
660 Brown Brothers
665 (*t*) Schomburg Center for Research in Black Culture, The New York Public Library, Astor, Lenox and Tilden Foundations
665 (*b*) Culver Pictures, Inc.
666 (*t*) The Bettmann Archive
666 (*b*) Brown Brothers
670 Museum of the City of New York
672 © Ewing Galloway
674 Copyright © 1929 by the New York Times Company, Reprinted by permission.
677 (*t*) UPI/Bettmann Newsphotos
677 (*b*) Reginald Marsh, *Bread Line—No One Has Starved,* 1932. Katherine Schmidt Schubert Bequest Collection of the Whitney Museum of American Art, New York.
678 Culver Pictures, Inc.
680 FSA Photo by Walker Evans
683 Library of Congress
685 UPI/Bettmann Newsphotos
689 The National Archives, 111-SC-97560
690 Franklin D. Roosevelt Library
691 AP/Wide World Photos
694 The National Archives, 69-N 24867
696 Brown Brothers
698 AP/Wide World Photos
700 Franklin D. Roosevelt Library
702 The National Archives, 35-G-3006
705 FPG International
706 The Bettmann Archive, Inc.
709 Library of Congress
709 Library of Congress
713 HBJ Photo
715 AP/Wide World Photos
716 Library of Congress
719 Brown Brothers
720 The New York Public Library, Collection of Romana Javitz
721 The National Archives, 69-N-23629-C
722 UPI/Bettmann Newsphotos
723 Museum of the City of New York
726 UPI/Bettmann Newsphotos
729 Camerique
730 The Bettmann Archive, Inc.
733 The Bettmann Archive, Inc.
736 AP/Wide World Photos
737 Bettmann Archive, Inc.
738 AP/Wide World Photos
741 McDonnell Douglas Corporation
742 Times Newspapers Ltd.
743 Imperial War Museum, London
745 AP/Wide World Photos
748 The National Archives, 80-A-57405
752 Library of Congress
753 AP/Wide World Photos
754 Margaret Bourke-White Life Magazine © 1943 Time Inc.
755 Culver Pictures, Inc.
756 AP/Wide World Photos
761 Signal Corp Photo, SC 192697
765 U.S. Army Photo
765 The Bettmann Archive, Inc.
767 UPI/Bettmann Newsphotos
769 The National Archives
773 AP/Wide World Photos
774 AP/Wide World Photos
776 U.S. Army Photo
778 U.S. Army Photo
779 HBJ Photo
782 UPI/Bettmann Newsphotos
785 UPI/Bettmann Newsphotos
786 UPI/Bettmann Newsphotos
788 UPI/Bettmann Newsphotos
789 AP/Wide World Photos
790 The Bettmann Archive, Inc.
791 Walter Sanders, *Life* Magazine, © 1948 Time Inc.
793 UPI/Bettmann Newsphotos
797 UPI/Bettmann
799 UPI/Bettmann
800 UPI/Bettmann Newsphotos
801 U.S. Army Photo
802 Carl Mydans, *Life* Magazine, © 1950 Time Inc.
804 UPI/Bettmann Newsphotos
806 UPI/Bettmann Newsphotos

807 UPI/Bettmann
810 Comstock/George Gerster
813 AP/Wide World Photos
814 © Cornell Capa/Magnum Photos, Inc.
816 AP/Wide World Photos
817 (*t*) AP/Wide World Photos
817 (*b*) AP/Wide World Photos
819 AP/Wide World Photos
820 United Nations/Photo by Saw Lwin
821 AP/Wide World Photos
823 UPI-Bettmann
825 UPI/Bettmann
826 UPI/Bettmann
828 Carl Byori & Associates
829 AP/Wide World Photos
831 Photo courtesy of The National Broadcasting Company, Inc.
832 © 1968 Burt Glinn/Magnum Photos Inc.
834 © Ollie Atkins
836 AP/Wide World Photos
837 UPI/Bettmann
841 UPI/Bettmann Newsphotos
842 AP/Wide World Photos
843 NASA
845 (*t*) UPI/Bettmann Newsphotos
845 (*b*) © Charles Harbutt/Archive Pictures, Inc.
846 UPI/Bettmann Newsphotos
849 © Philip Jones/Magnum Photos, Inc.
851 Photograph by Bernie Boston. Reprinted with permission of *The Washington Star* © *The Washington Star*
852 UPI/Bettmann Newsphotos
854 AP/Wide World Photos
855 (*t*) © Cary Wolinsky/Stock, Boston
855 (*b*) AP/Wide World Photos
856 Laurence Henry Collection Schomburg Center for Research in Black History, The New York Public Library, Astor, Lenox and Tilden Foundations
857 AP/Wide World Photos
858 (*t*) United Nations
858 (*b*) AP-Wide World Photos
859 © Burt Uzzle/Woodfin Camp & Associates
860 AP/Wide World Photos
861 AP/Wide World Photos
862 (*t*) White House Photo
862 (*b*) Photo by Burt Glinn © 1968 Magnum Photos
866 © Dennis Brack/Black Star
869 UPI/Bettmann Newsphotos
870 John Filo, Valley News Dispatch
871 AP/Wide World Photos
873 UPI/Bettmann
874 © A. Bernhaut/FPG
876 UPI/Bettmann Newsphotos
883 (*t*) AP/Wide World Photos
883 (*b*) AP/Wide World Photos
884 White House Photo
886 AP/Wide World Photos
887 © Owen Franken/Stock, Boston
889 UPI/Bettmann Newsphotos
890 UPI/Bettmann Newsphotos
891 UPI/Bettmann Newsphotos
892 UPI/Bettmann Newsphotos
893 (*t*) © Alex Webb/Magnum Photos, Inc.
893 (*b*) © David Burnett/Woodfin Camp & Associates
896 Bill Fitz-Patrick, White House Photo
899 UPI/Bettmann Newsphotos
900 UPI/Bettmann Newsphotos
901 UPI/Bettmann Newsphotos
902 AP/Wide World Photos
903 © 1983, Reprinted with permission. Auth/Universal Press Syndicate
906 UPI/Bettmann Newsphotos
907 UPI/Bettmann Newsphotos
908 © Peter Marlow/Magnum Photos
909 UPI/Bettmann Newsphotos
912 UPI/Bettmann Newsphotos
915 Reuters/Bettmann Newsphotos
917 © J. B. Diederich/Woodfin Camp & Associates
919 UPI/Bettmann Newsphotos
921 AP/Wide World Photos
924 UPI/Bettmann Newsphotos
925 UPI/Bettmann Newsphotos
927 UPI/Bettmann Newsphotos
927 AP/Wide World Photos
930 NASA
934 (*t*) AP/Wide World Photos
934 (*b*) © James Hanley/Photo Researchers
935 (*t*) © C. Vergara/Photo Researchers
935 (*b*) © Sara Krulwich/New York Times
936 AP/Wide World Photos
937 © Charles Kennard/Stock, Boston
938 © M. Courtney Clarke/Photo Researchers
939 AP/Wide World Photos
940 AP/Wide World Photos
941 © Joel Gordon 1990
942 UPI/Bettmann Newsphotos
944 Rick Kopstein/Monkmeyer Press Photo Service
945 AP/Wide World Photos
948 AP/Wide World Photos
950 AP/Wide World Photos
952 AP/Wide World Photos
956 AP/Wide World Photos
959 AP/Wide World Photos
962 © Larry Downing 1991/Woodfin Camp & Associates
964 © Bettye Lane, Photo Researchers
966 AP/Wide World Photos
968 AP/Wide World Photos

INDEX

Boldface numbers indicate a box or illustration.